D0083143

SHAKESPEARE
for Students

SHAKESPEARE
for Students

Critical Interpretations of *As You Like It, Hamlet, Julius Caesar, Macbeth, The Merchant of Venice, A Midsummer Night's Dream, Othello,* and *Romeo and Juliet*

Mark W. Scott
Editor

Joseph C. Tardiff
Associate Editor

Advisors

Kathy Lee Martin
Metropolitan School District
of Perry Township, Indiana

Gladys V. Veidemanis
Oshkosh Area Public Schools,
Wisconsin

Gale Research Inc. · DETROIT · WASHINGTON, D.C. · LONDON

SHAKESPEARE FOR STUDENTS STAFF

Mark W. Scott, *Editor*
Joseph C. Tardiff, *Associate Editor*

Zoran Minderović, Lawrence J. Trudeau, *Contributing Associate Editors*
Rogene M. Fisher, Janet Mullane, Eric Priehs, Debra A. Wells,
Contributing Assistant Editors

Jeanne A. Gough, *Permissions & Production Manager*

Linda M. Pugliese, *Production Supervisor*
Lorna Mabunda, Maureen Puhl, Jennifer VanSickle, *Editorial Associates*
Donna Craft, Brandy C. Johnson, Paul Lewon, Camille Robinson,
Sheila Walencewicz, *Editorial Assistants*

Maureen Richards, *Research Supervisor*
Mary Beth McElmeel, *Editorial Associate*
Kathleen Jozwiak, Amy Kaechele, Julie Karmazin, Tamara C. Nott,
Julie Synkonis *Editorial Assistants*

Sandra C. Davis, *Permissions Supervisor (Text)*
Maria L. Franklin, Josephine M. Keene, Denise M. Singleton,
Kimberly F. Smilay, *Permissions Associates*
Rebecca A. Hartford, Michele Lonoconus, Shelly Rakoczy (Co-op), Shalice Shah,
Nancy K. Sheridan, *Permissions Assistants*

Margaret A. Chamberlain, *Permissions Supervisor (Pictures)*
Pamela A. Hayes, *Permissions Associate*
Karla Kulkis, Nancy M. Rattenbury, Keith Reed, *Permissions Assistants*

Mary Beth Trimper, *Production Manager*
Mary Winterhalter, *Production Assistant*

Arthur Chartow, *Art Director*
C. J. Jonik, *Keyliner*
Kathleen A. Mouzakis, *Graphic Designer*

Because this page cannot legibly accommodate all copyright notices, the acknowledgments constitute an extension of the copyright notice.

While every effort has been made to ensure the reliability of the information presented in this publication, Gale Research Inc. neither guarantees the accuracy of the data contained herein nor assumes any responsibility for errors, omissions, or discrepancies. Gale accepts no payment for listing; and inclusion in the publication of any organization, agency, institution, publication, service, or individual does not imply endorsement of the editors or publisher. Errors brought to the attention of the publisher and verified to the satisfaction of the publisher will be corrected in future editions.

CIP 92-1148

This book is printed on acid-free paper that meets the minimum requirements of American National Standard for Information Sciences—Permanence Paper for Printed Library Materials, ANSI Z39.48-1984. ⊖™

ISBN 0-8103-8247-4

Printed in the United States of America

Published simultaneously in the United Kingdom
by Gale Research International Limited
(An affiliated company of Gale Research Inc.)

10 9 8 7 6 5 4 3

The trademark **ITP** is used under license.

Contents

How to Get the Most out of *Shakespeare for Students* vii

Acknowledgments ix

A Brief Chronology of Shakespeare's

Life and Major Works xiii

"Some Research Perspectives for Students of Shakespeare,"

a guest introduction

by Gladys V. Veidemanis xv

How to Get the Most out of *Shakespeare for Students*

Purpose of the Book

Shakespeare for Students is principally intended for beginning students of Shakespeare and for other interested readers, presenting information on some of Shakespeare's most popular and frequently taught plays. A further purpose of *Shakespeare for Students* is to acquaint the reader with the uses and function of literary criticism itself. Selected from an immense and often bewildering body of Shakespearean commentary, the essays and excerpts in *Shakespeare for Students* offer insights into Shakespeare's plays from the perspective of numerous twentieth-century critics. Readers will not need a wide background in literary studies to use this book. Students can benefit from *Shakespeare for Students* whether they seek information for class discussions and written assignments, new perspectives on traditional issues, or noteworthy and innovative analyses of Shakespeare's artistry.

About twenty percent of the essays and excerpts reprinted in *Shakespeare for Students* can also be found in Gale's companion literary series *Shakespearean Criticism,* a multi-volume set which provides a comprehensive collection of published criticism, spanning four centuries, on all of Shakespeare's plays and poems.

How an Entry Is Organized

Each play entry consists of the following elements: an introduction to the play, essays and excerpts of criticism prefaced by explanatory annotations, and an annotated bibliography of sources for further study.

- The **introduction** to each entry presents a descriptive list of the play's major characters, summarizes its plot, and outlines the principal thematic issues and character studies found in the criticism.

- The **literary criticism** is arranged by topics, such as significant thematic issues and studies of principal characters. In addition, all act, scene, and line references in the commentary have been changed to conform to *The Riverside Shakespeare,* published by Houghton Mifflin Company, which is a standard text used in many high school and college English classes.

- **Explanatory annotations** preface the critical essays and excerpts as an additional aid to students. These notes provide several types of useful information, including the scope and importance of the commentary that follows, as well as definitions of the literary terms and concepts found in the critical work. The names of characters who are the subject of substantial discussion in the commentary are identified by boldface type in the annotations. This feature simplifies the process of locating information on specific characters.

- A complete **bibliographic citation** follows each piece of criticism. This feature will help the interested reader locate the original essay or book from which the reprint is taken.

- The **sources for further study** list at the end of each entry comprises additional discussions of the play. The list is divided into two sections; the first offers suggestions for other literary commentary, the second recommends media adaptations of the play available on videocassette.

Other Features

- Throughout the book, **illustrations**—artistic renditions and performance photographs—add a visual dimension and enhance the reader's understanding of the critical discussions of each play.

- An alphabetical **index** to major themes and characters at the end of the book identifies the principal topics and character studies of each play, including issues and figures that, while significant, are not singled out for individual attention by entry sub-headings.

A Note to the Reader

When writing papers, students who quote directly from *Shakespeare for Students* may use the following general formats to footnote reprinted criticism. The first example pertains to material drawn from periodicals, the second to materials reprinted from books.

[1] Irving Ribner, " 'Macbeth': The Pattern of Idea and Action," *Shakespeare Quarterly* X, No. 2 (Spring 1959), 147-59; excerpted and reprinted in *Shakespeare for Students,* ed. Mark W. Scott (Detroit: Gale Research, 1992), pp. 245-51.

[2] Franklin M. Dickey, *Not Wisely but Too Well: Shakespeare's Love Tragedies* (The Huntington Library, 1957); excerpted and reprinted in *Shakespeare for Students,* ed. Mark W. Scott (Detroit: Gale Research, 1992), pp. 467-70.

Acknowledgments

The editors wish to thank the copyright holders of the excerpted criticism included in this volume, the permissions managers of many book and magazine publishing companies for assisting us in securing reprint rights, and Anthony Bogucki for assistance with copyright research. We are also grateful to the staffs of the Detroit Public Library, Wayne State University Purdy/Kresge Library Complex, and the University of Michigan Libraries for making their resources available to us. Following is a list of the copyright holders who have granted us permission to reprint material in this volume of *SFS.* Every effort has been made to trace copyright, but if omissions have been made, please let us know.

COPYRIGHTED EXCERPTS IN *SFS* WERE REPRINTED FROM THE FOLLOWING PERIODICALS:

The American Scholar, v. 42, Spring, 1973 for "As We Like it: How a Girl Can Be Smart and Still Popular" by Clara Claiborne Park. Copyright © 1973. Reprinted by permission of the author.—*CLA Journal,* v. XXVII, June, 1985. Copyright, 1985 by The College Language Association. Used by permission of The College Language Association.—*ELH,* v. 48, Spring, 1981. Copyright © 1981 by The Johns Hopkins University Press. All rights reserved. Reprinted by permission of the publisher.—*English Journal,* v. 74, February, 1985 for " 'Not Life, but Love in Death': Oxymoron at the Thematic Heart of 'Romeo and Juliet' " by C. Webster Wheelock. Copyright © 1985 by the National Council of Teachers of English. Reprinted by permission of the publisher and the author.—*Études Anglaises,* v. XVII, October-December, 1964. Reprinted by permission of the publisher.—*The Listener,* v. 100, December 21-28, 1978 for "As You Like Shakespeare" by Brigid Brophy. © British Broadcasting Corp. 1978. Reprinted by permission of the author.—*Neophilologus,* v. LVI, April, 1972 for "Shakespeare and the Green-Eyed Monster" by D. R. Godfrey. © 1972 by Wolters-Noordhoff. Reprinted by permission of the publisher and the Literary Estate of D. R. Godfrey.—*Papers on Language & Literature,* v. 2, Summer, 1966. Copyright © 1966 by the Board of Trustees, Southern Illinois University. Reprinted by permission of the publisher.—*Renaissance Drama,* n.s., v. XI, 1980. Copyright © 1980 by Northwestern University Press. All rights reserved. Reprinted by permission of the publisher.—*Shakespeare Quarterly,* v. XV, Autumn, 1964; v. XXI, Spring, 1970; v. XXIV, Winter, 1973. © The Folger Shakespeare Library 1964, 1970, 1973. All reprinted by permission of the publisher.—*Shakespeare Studies: An Annual Gathering of Research, Criticism, and Reviews,* v. 4, 1968; v. 9, 1976. Copyright © 1968, 1976, The Council for Research in the Renaissance. Both reprinted by permission of the publisher.—*Shakespeare Survey: An Annual Survey of Shakespearian Study and Production,* v. 19, 1966 for "Image and Symbol in 'Macbeth'," by Kenneth Muir; v. 32, 1979 for "Sexual Disguise in 'As You Like It' and 'Twelfth Night'," by Nancy K. Hayles. © Cambridge University Press, 1966, 1979. Both reprinted by permission of the respective authors.—*Stanford Literature Review,* v. 1, Fall, 1984. © 1984 by Anma Libri & Co. All rights reserved. Reprinted by permission of the publisher and Department of French and Italian, Stanford University.—*Studies in English Literature, 1500-1900,* v. II, 1962 for " 'No Clock in the Forest': Time in 'As You Like It' " by Jay L. Halio; v. XIII, Spring, 1973 for "The Perversion of Manliness in 'Macbeth' " by Jarold Ramsey. © 1962, 1973 William Marsh Rice University. Both reprinted by permission of the publisher and the respective authors.—*The Tulane Drama Review,* v. 9, Summer, 1965 for "Hamlet Nearly Absurd: The Dramaturgy of Delay" by Robert Hapgood. Copyright © 1965, *The Tulane Drama Review.* Reprinted by permission of the MIT Press and the author.—*Women's Studies: An Interdisciplinary Journal,* v. 9, 1981; v. 9, 1982. © Gordon and Breach Science Publishers. Both reprinted by permission of the publisher.—*The Yale Review,* v. XLI, June, 1952 for "The World of Hamlet" by Maynard Mack. Copyright 1952, renewed 1980 by Yale University. Reprinted by permission of the author./v. XXXII, Winter, 1943. Copyright 1942, renewed 1971 by Yale University. Reprinted by permission of the editors.

COPYRIGHTED EXCERPTS IN *SFS* WERE REPRINTED FROM THE FOLLOWING BOOKS:

Adelman, Janet. From " 'Born of Woman': Fantasies of Maternal Power in 'Macbeth'," in *Cannibals, Witches, and Divorce: Estranging the Renaissance.* Edited by Marjorie Gruber. The Johns Hopkins University Press, 1987. © 1987 The English Institute. All rights reserved. Reprinted by permission of the publisher.—Barnet, Sylvan. From "The Comedies," in *The Complete Signet Classic*

A Brief Chronology of Shakespeare's Life and Major Works

1564   Birth of William Shakespeare in Stratford-upon-avon. His notice of baptism is entered in the parish register at Holy Trinity Church on 26 April.

1571   Shakespeare probably enters grammar school, seven years being the usual age for admission.

1575   Queen Elizabeth visits Kenilworth Castle, near Stratford. Shakespeare may have witnessed the pageantry, which is possibly reflected in *A Midsummer Night's Dream.*

1582   Shakespeare marries Anne Hathaway.

1583   Birth of Susanna, the first child of William and Anne Shakespeare.

1585   Births of twins Hamnet and Judith Shakespeare.

1592   Robert Greene publishes a pamphlet entitled *Groats-worth of Wit;* it chides Shakespeare as an "upstart crow" on the theater scene.

1592-93   Shakespeare probably writes *Venus and Adonis.*

1593   Shakespeare probably begins composing his Sonnets.

1593-94   Shakespeare probably writes *The Rape of Lucrece.*

1594   Richard Burbage, William Kempe, and Shakespeare act with the Lord Chamberlain's Men at Greenwich Palace.

1595-96   Shakespeare probably writes *Romeo and Juliet* and *A Midsummer Night's Dream.*

1596   Henry Carey, Lord Hunsdon, lord chamberlain and patron of the Lord Chamberlain's Men, dies. Shakespeare's company comes under the patronage of George Carey, second Lord Hunsdon.

Hamnet Shakespeare dies at age eleven.

1596-97   Shakespeare probably writes *The Merchant of Venice.*

1597   Shakespeare purchases the New Place, a large Stratford mansion, and the surrounding grounds.

1598   Shakespeare is listed as a principal actor in a performance of Ben Jonson's *Every Man in His Humour.*

1599   Shakespeare probably composes *As You Like It* and *Julius Caesar.*

Land for the Globe Theatre is leased by Nicholas Brend to leading shareholders in the Lord Chamberlain's Men, including Shakespeare.

Thomas Platter, a German traveler, attends a production of *Julius Caesar* at the Globe Theatre, the earliest known performance of the play.

John Weever publishes the poem "Ad Guglielmum Shakespeare," praising Shakespeare's *Venus and Adonis, The Rape of Lucrece, Romeo and Juliet,* and other works.

1600-01   Shakespeare probably writes *Hamlet.*

1603   *A Midsummer Night's Dream* is performed at Hampton Court.

Queen Elizabeth dies. The new king, James I, arrives in London a month later.

King James grants a patent, or license, to the Lord Chamberlain's Men and renames them the King's

Men; Shakespeare's name is mentioned in the patent.

The King's Men enact a play, possibly *As You Like It,* before King James at Wilton.

Shakespeare appears in a performance of Ben Jonson's *Sejanus,* the last record of his acting career.

1604 Shakespeare probably writes *Othello,* which is first performed at Whitehall on 1 November.

1605 *The Merchant of Venice* is performed twice at court and commended by the king.

1606 Shakespeare probably writes *Macbeth,* which may have been performed at Hampton Court for the visiting King Christian IV of Denmark.

1607 *Hamlet* is performed aboard the British ship *Dragon* at Sierra Leone.

1608 Shakespeare, Richard and Cuthbert Burbage, Thomas Evans, John Hemminges, Henry Condell, and William Sly lease the Blackfriars Theatre for a period of twenty-one years.

1609 Shakespeare's Sonnets are published.

1612-13 Frederick V, the elector palatine and future king of Bohemia, arrives in England to marry Elizabeth, King James's daughter. The King's Men perform several plays, including *Othello* and *Julius Caesar,* during the wedding festivities.

1613 The Globe Theatre burns down during the first performance of *Henry VIII.*

1614 The Globe Theatre reopens.

1616 Shakespeare dies; his burial is recorded in the register of Holy Trinity Church on 25 April.

1619 *Hamlet* and several other Shakespearean plays are performed at court as part of the Christmas festivities.

1623 Anne Hathaway Shakespeare dies.

John Hemminges and Henry Condell, Shakespeare's fellow actors, compile and publish thirty-six of the dramatist's works in the First Folio, the earliest collected edition of Shakespeare's plays.

Some Research Perspectives for Students of Shakespeare

by Gladys V. Veidemanis, Oshkosh Area Public Schools

"The play's the thing . . . ," Hamlet concludes in Act II of *Hamlet* as he contemplates a strategy to entrap his murderous uncle, but his words apply as well to anyone endeavoring to be a student of Shakespeare's works. To write an essay, produce an oral report, or undertake an extensive research project on some aspect of a Shakespearean play—tasks you are likely to be assigned during your high school or college career—you must first begin with a close and careful reading of the text, view live or videotaped productions of the play, and listen to recordings of notable performances. Only after you have developed firm ideas of your own and formulated specific questions to be resolved are you truly ready to turn to critical studies of the play that will challenge, validate, or even revise your initial assumptions and interpretations.

Fortunately, this collection of criticism—the only work of its kind explicitly intended for use by high school students as well as other interested readers—has been designed to simplify the research process by providing a cross-section of critical commentary on the eight Shakespearean plays most commonly taught in America's high schools: *As You Like It, Hamlet, Julius Caesar, Macbeth, The Merchant of Venice, A Midsummer Night's Dream, Othello,* and *Romeo and Juliet.* For each play discussed in this volume you are given an introduction, which provides an overview of the play and discusses its historical importance; an annotated list of principal characters; an act-by-act plot synopsis; one or more overview essays which synthesize critical commentary on the play; and a selected group of critical essays that both survey the play as a whole and concentrate on its dominant themes, characters, imagery, and distinctive features.

To use this resource most efficiently, you will want to start by closely reading the introductory material provided on the play you are studying (and be sure to return for a rereading of this material after you have finished exploring the critical essays that follow). Next you should read the opening essays, so positioned in each entry as to provide an overview of the entire work and highlight major issues requiring scholarly consideration. Following this preliminary reading, you are ready to explore the principal topics that follow to help you locate the essays most applicable to your chosen research project. As a time-saver, each essay is preceded by a summary of content to alert you to whether or not the material that follows is pertinent to your subject. All of the critical essays in this collection have been carefully edited and abridged to enable you to focus more quickly and directly on specific themes, topics, or characters; however, you may occasionally wish to use the bibliographical citation at the end of each essay to locate a particular essay as originally published in order to read it in its entirety.

"Why consult the critics?" you well might ask. Shouldn't your own opinions and ideas be sufficient for the tasks you have been assigned? Of course your response to the text is what matters most, but reading literary criticism can help you in three important ways:

> (1) to clarify troublesome passages and problems in the text,

> (2) to stimulate thinking about aspects of the play you have overlooked or disregarded, and

> (3) to illuminate conflicting interpretations of characters and themes that need to be weighed in your analysis of the play.

Steeped in ambiguity, Shakespeare's plays always raise more questions than they answer, and every reading is likely to raise new questions and modify initial assumptions. For example, why does Hamlet delay his revenge—out of prudence, cowardice, or failure of will? In *Julius Caesar,* who are the villains—the conspirators Brutus and Cassius or the alleged tyrant Caesar himself? In *Romeo and Juliet,* are we meant to regard the doomed lovers as playthings of Fate or, instead, as victims of their intense infatuation and reckless impetuosity? In *Macbeth,* is Duncan truly as virtuous as Macbeth describes him or, as some readings suggest, is he power-hungry, personally weak, and possibly senile? And how do we explain our ambivalence about Shylock in *The Merchant of Venice,* our feelings of pity and sympathy in spite of his heartless greed, hypocrisy, and malicious behavior? To accentuate the diversity of critical opinion that abounds, occasionally in this volume essays that express opposing viewpoints have been juxtaposed, a reminder of how richly the plays lend themselves to divergent readings and conflicting interpretations.

Clearly, you don't have to agree with, or believe, everything you read. Literary criticism invites an engagement of intellects, a sharing of responses to the intensive study of a subtle and sophisticated literary text. For that matter, some essays may infuriate you or cause you to argue aloud to the corners of your room. Great! Then literary criticism will have served its central purpose: to make you defend your ideas about a given play and become better informed about your subject.

In reading literary criticism, you are best advised to read through the entire essay once (preferably twice), then go back and take selective notes. As much as possible, summarize important ideas and concepts in your own words, then judiciously identify and record quotations that will lend eloquence, authority, or textual proof to your written or oral presentation. And as you take notes, keep in mind that the primary skill required in literary research is the careful attribution of both borrowed opinion and direct citation. When you draw on other people's thinking, whether with a direct quote or a summary of ideas you have encountered, remember that you have a moral obligation to give credit to the person whose words or ideas you are borrowing. Phrases such as "According to . . ." or "As . . . asserts," should appear frequently in any oral or written report utilizing a wide range of supplemental critical research.

But never let yourself be dominated by the critics, however eloquent and authoritative they may seem. *You* are the writer, the reader, the researcher, the person in charge of the text you have read and the paper or speech you wish to create. Literary criticism, then, is essentially a tool to facilitate the tasks you have been assigned. But, happily, you will discover that reading what the critics have to say is also a pleasure in and of itself, an encounter with some of the best commentary that has been expressed about the greatest plays ever written. Make sure to enjoy the intellectual adventure this book enables!

AS YOU LIKE IT

INTRODUCTION

Commentators have described *As You Like It* as both a celebration of the spirit of pastoral romance and a satire of the pastoral ideal. Traditionally, a pastoral is a poem focusing on shepherds and rustic life; it first appeared as a literary form in the third century. The term itself is derived from the Latin word for shepherd, *pastor*. A pastoral consists of artificial and unnatural elements, for the shepherd characters often speak with courtly eloquence and appear in aristocratic dress. This poetic convention evolved over centuries until many of its features were incorporated into prose and drama. It was in these literary forms that pastoralism influenced English literature from about 1550 to 1750, most often as pastoral romance, a model featuring songs and characters with traditional pastoral names. Many of these elements manifest themselves in the commonly accepted source for Shakespeare's play, Thomas Lodge's popular pastoral novel *Rosalynde,* written in 1590. But by the time Shakespeare adapted Lodge's romance into *As You Like It* nearly a decade later, many pastoral themes were considered trite. As a result of these developments, Shakespeare treated pastoralism ambiguously in the comedy—it can be viewed as either an endorsement or a satire of the literary form—a method which is nowhere more evident than in the play's title.

PRINCIPAL CHARACTERS
(in order of appearance)

Orlando: The youngest son of Sir Rowland de Boys. He eventually marries Rosalind.

Adam: Oliver's aged servant who goes into exile with Orlando.

Oliver: The eldest son of Sir Rowland de Boys who governs his house like a tyrant. He is converted from villainy in Arden forest and marries Celia.

Charles: Duke Frederick's wrestler whom Orlando defeats.

Celia: Duke Frederick's daughter and Rosalind's cousin. She accompanies Rosalind in exile under the name Aliena and eventually marries the reformed Oliver.

Rosalind: The exiled Duke Senior's daughter and niece of Duke Frederick. She disguises herself as a youth named Ganymede when she goes into exile. She eventually marries Orlando.

Touchstone: A fool in Celia's service. He accompanies Celia and Rosalind into exile. He courts and marries Audrey.

Le Beau: One of Duke Frederick's courtiers.

Duke Frederick: Duke Senior's younger brother and usurper of his throne. He is also Celia's father and Rosalind's uncle.

Duke Senior: The exiled elder brother of Duke Frederick and father of Rosalind.

Amiens: A courtier attending Duke Senior in exile.

Corin: An old shepherd who befriends Rosalind, Celia, and Touchstone.

Silvius: A shepherd in love with the shepherdess Phebe. He eventually marries her.

Jaques: A melancholy lord attending Duke Senior in banishment.

Audrey: A country wench who marries Touchstone.

Sir Oliver Martext: A vicar whose marriage of Touchstone and Audrey is interrupted by Jaques.

Phebe: A shepherdess who falls in love with Ganymede. She eventually marries Silvius.

William: A country fellow who loves Audrey.

Hymen: The god of marriage who marries all the couples.

Jaques de Boys: The second son of Sir Rowland de Boys and Oliver and Orlando's brother.

PLOT SYNOPSIS

Act I: Orlando, who has been denied his inheritance and education by his brother Oliver, fights with him over his birthright. Envious of Orlando's virtues, Oliver schemes to have Charles the wrestler murder Orlando in an upcoming match. Rosalind and Celia attend the bout at Duke Frederick's court and watch Orlando defeat Charles. Rosalind gives him a necklace, and he falls in love with her. Later, Le Beau warns Orlando that the duke is threatened by his presence, and he advises the youth to flee the court. Meanwhile, Rosalind admits to Celia that she loves Orlando, but her happiness is interrupted when the duke banishes her.

She decides to journey to Arden forest disguised as a courtier named Ganymede, accompanied by Celia and Touchstone.

Act II: Upon reaching Arden, Rosalind, Celia, and Touchstone overhear Silvius professing his love of Phebe to Corin. Elsewhere, Orlando and Adam have also reached the forest in an exhausted and hungry state. In his search for food, Orlando discovers Duke Senior and his retainers. Orlando menacingly demands food, but is surprised when the duke kindly welcomes him to their table. While Orlando retrieves Adam, Jaques gives his "Seven Ages of Man" speech.

Act III: Smitten with the memory of Rosalind, Orlando wanders through the forest hanging love poems on trees. Eventually, the lovers meet, but he does not recognize her because she is still in disguise. She proposes to cure him of his love if he will pretend to court her as if she were Rosalind. Meanwhile, as Touchstone courts Audrey, Silvius attempts to woo Phebe. But Phebe falls in love with Ganymede, who castigates her for spurning Silvius's love.

Act IV: Jaques debates the nature of his melancholy with Rosalind, until Orlando appears. She admonishes him for his tardiness and the two lovers continue their wooing game, until Orlando departs, promising to return in an hour. Sometime after, Oliver—who has come to the forest seeking his brother—encounters Rosalind and Celia, who are waiting for Orlando to return. He explains that Orlando is late because he was wounded while saving Oliver from a hungry lioness. Presenting Rosalind with a bloody handkerchief, Oliver declares that the experience has reformed him. Shocked by the sight of Orlando's blood, Rosalind faints.

Act V: When Orlando learns that Oliver and Celia have fallen in love and are to be married the next day, he tires of his game with Rosalind. She then asserts that she knows a magician who can give him Rosalind as a bride. She also pledges to gratify both Silvius and Phebe. The next day, Rosalind reveals herself, and Phebe settles for Silvius, since Ganymede no longer exists. As the god of marriage Hymen begins the ceremony, Touchstone and Audrey appear, joining the couples to be married. The rite is again interrupted when Jaques de Boys suddenly arrives with the news that Duke Frederick has been reformed by an old religious man and that Duke Senior may reclaim his title. Everyone rejoices except Jaques, who declares that he will join Duke Frederick and the hermit in seclusion.

PRINCIPAL TOPICS

Numerous oppositions in *As You Like It* reveal Shakespeare's partiality toward the pastoral rustic life of Arden forest to life at court. At Duke Freder-ick's court, disorder holds sway. The deterioration of political authority is the most obvious form of disorder, for Duke Frederick has unlawfully seized Duke Senior's kingdom. This political degeneration is compounded by a more personal disorder, since the dukes are also brothers at odds with each other; this conflict is underscored by the antagonistic relationship of two other brothers at the court, Oliver and Orlando. Arden forest offers a sense of pure, spiritual order in contrast to the corrupt condition of Duke Frederick's court. The journey there is long and arduous; when the characters arrive they are physically exhausted and hungry. Moreover, such threatening elements as the "icy fang" and "churlish wind" portray life in Arden as anything but ideal. The harsh experience of nature acts as a purgative process, however, which lays bare the characters' virtuous natures calloused by court life. Some characters, like Orlando and Rosalind, need little improvement, yet find in Arden a liberation from the oppression they have endured at court. Others, such as Oliver and Duke Frederick, approach the forest with malicious intent only to undergo a complete spiritual reformation. Arden thus represents a morally pure realm whose special curative powers purge and renew the forest-dwellers, granting them a self-awareness which they will ultimately use to restore order at court. Closely allied with the opposition of court life and Arden forest is another dichotomy, that between fortune and nature. Here, "fortune" represents both material gain—which is achieved through power, birthright, or possession—and a force that unpredictably determines events. "Nature," on the other hand, reflects both the purifying force of Arden and humanity's fundamental condition stripped of the trappings of wealth, power, and material possessions. The opposition of these two entities provides another example of the overall theme of antithesis and conflict in *As You Like It.*

Time is another theme that is treated differently in the court scenes and those in Arden forest. At court, time is specific; it is marked by definite intervals which amplify the corrupt and violent nature of Duke Frederick's rule. In most cases, it is related to the duke's threats: he orders Rosalind to leave the court within ten days or she will be executed, and he gives Oliver one year to find Orlando or else his land and possessions will be confiscated. In Arden, however, the meaning of time is less precise. Some scholars argue that in the forest time is replaced by timelessness, enhancing Arden's mythical, otherworldly properties. Others interpret time not in the passage of hours and minutes, but in the progress of events, leading to self-awareness, that the characters experience in Arden. This view of time has a cause and effect aspect, determined by the characters' changes in attitude as events in the forest ultimately lead to the multiple marriages. Time is also explored in relation to the human being's aging process. Jaques's melancholy "Seven Ages of Man" speech (II. vii.

139ff.) pessimistically illustrates the individual's passage through life in distinct stages, ending with the image of man and woman as pathetically ineffectual and dependent creatures. Touchstone also offers a description of the aging process, but his concern is that as human beings age, they lose their ability to enjoy physical love. Rosalind presents a more optimistic opinion of aging, however, asserting that life is worth living when you can grow old with someone you love.

Sexual disguise and role-playing are two other closely related and important themes in *As You Like It*. These issues primarily focus on Rosalind, who disguises herself as a gentleman named Ganymede to insure her safe passage to Arden. Though she can discard her male costume when she reaches the forest, Rosalind does not do so until the end of the play. Critics generally agree that she continues to act as Ganymede because the disguise liberates her from her submissive role as a woman. She is therefore able to take more control of her own life, especially in her courtship with Orlando. In their play-acting scenes, Rosalind controls the tactics of courtship usually reserved for men, inverting the strategy to teach Orlando the meaning of real love rather than love based on his ideal vision of her. An added dimension to Rosalind's role-playing is evident if we consider the comedy in its Elizabethan context. In Shakespeare's age, it was common for boys to play the roles of women in dramas. The playwright takes advantage of this convention in *As You Like It* to accentuate the play's theatricality. If we consider that the boy actor who performs Rosalind must also play Ganymede, who in turn portrays Rosalind in the play-acting sessions with Orlando, we can appreciate that this subtle, yet complex, theatrical technique illustrates how disguise and role-playing often operate on several different levels in the play.

CHARACTER STUDIES

Of all the characters in *As You Like It,* Rosalind, Orlando, Touchstone, and Jaques have attracted the most critical commentary. Rosalind is perhaps the most important figure in the play, for it is through her influence that many of the play's conflicts and controversies are resolved. It is Rosalind's self-awareness, as well as her charming wit and individualism, that enables her to resist and correct the false definitions of love of those around her. It also allows her to assess other characters' motives and aspirations. Orlando—the primary focus of Rosalind's attention—has seemingly little appeal beyond his role as a stereotype of the romantic lover. Closer examination reveals, however, that for all of his passionate rhetoric and wretched verse-writing, Orlando is a character of nimble wit. This quality is perhaps most evident in his humor-

ous debate with Jaques in Act III, scene ii. Touchstone is all that his name implies: he acts as a touchstone or test of the qualities of the other characters both at Duke Frederick's court and in the forest. It is Touchstone's inherent skepticism of Arden that allows him to play the courtly observer and put the others to the comic test. By marrying Audrey, he parodies not only the shepherds' ideal pastoral life, but the pastoral romance convention as well. Jaques—Duke Senior's aloof and melancholy retainer—is commonly considered Touchstone's foil. He, too, provides commentary on the play's diverse issues, but from a completely different perspective. Jaques's misanthropy, or distaste for humanity, initially casts a dark shadow over the events in Arden forest, but as the other characters change for the better, his bitter pessimism appears stagnant and ineffectual. Jaques is a satire of another Elizabethan stereotype, the traveler who returns from abroad only to become discontented with domestic life. Shakespeare shows no sympathy for Jaques throughout the play: his cynical statements are rebuked time and again by such characters as Rosalind, Orlando, Touchstone, and Duke Senior. Ultimately, he is the only character who does not achieve some form of reformation and personal enlightenment from the Arden experience.

CONCLUSION

Although critics remain divided on whether or not *As You Like It* should be read as a satire or a celebration of the pastoral ideal, the reader cannot deny taking great pleasure in the play's festive atmosphere and its various love affairs. Perhaps it is just such an appeal that has made *As You Like It* one of Shakespeare's most popular and best loved comedies.

(See also *Shakespearean Criticism*, Vol. 5)

OVERVIEWS

Sylvan Barnet

[*Barnet presents a succinct overview of* As You Like It *in relation to* Much Ado about Nothing *and* Twelfth Night, *Shakespeare's other festive comedies. In this excerpt, the critic explores the contrasting elements of the court and Arden forest, relates the various implications that the courtships of* **Orlando** *and* **Rosalind, Oliver** *and* **Celia, Silvius** *and* **Phebe,** *and* **Touchstone** *and* **Audrey** *have on the whole play, and surveys the theme of redemption through* *the characters' gradual self-knowledge, especially the improbable conversions of **Oliver** and **Duke Frederick**. This essay has been reprinted in* Four Great Comedies *(1982) by Sylvan Barnet.*]

Near the turn of the [seventeenth] century—just after he had finished his second tetralogy of history plays and was nearing the great tragedies—Shakespeare wrote three comedies that for many readers and spectators are the essence of Shakespearean romantic comedy: *Much Ado About Nothing* (1598-1600), *As You Like It* (1599-1600), and *Twelfth Night* (1600-02). These plays, like *The Merchant of Venice* and to a lesser degree *A Midsummer Night's Dream* and *The Two Gentlemen of Verona,* are plays of courtship. The assumption behind them is that despite momentary absurdities and pains, love liberates, enriches, and fulfills the lovers. (p. 93)

Like *A Midsummer Night's Dream* and *The Merchant of Venice, As You Like It* presents two worlds. *A Midsummer Night's Dream* moves from Athens, with its harsh law and its harsh father, to the moonlit woods outside of Athens, where lovers are transformed into their better selves; *The Merchant of Venice* moves from the commercial world of Venice to the moonlit world of Portia's Belmont. In *As You Like It* the movement is from the court of the usurper, Duke Frederick, to the Forest of Arden, where lovers find what they seek and where the wicked are converted. Only Touchstone, the Clown, and Jaques, the melancholy man, remain unimproved by Arden, a sort of hint of man's recalcitrance or self-conceit.

The play is full of "holiday foolery," but the foolery is not devoid of meaning, for it embodies an enduring vision of love and of the triumph of the gifts of nature over those of fortune. Various kinds of lovers are juxtaposed: the romantic young lovers, Rosalind and Orlando and Celia and the reformed Oliver; the prettified artificial pastoral figures, hard-hearted Phebe and her mooning Silvius, who thinks no man has ever loved as he loves; the low pastoral figures, old Corin, who has forgotten the ridiculous actions that love moved him to in his youth, and the young bumpkins William and Audrey; and finally the clown Touchstone, who remembers that when he was in love he kissed "the cow's dugs that her pretty chopt [chapped] hands had milked" [II. iv. 49-50]. Love is wonderfully displayed in the "strange capers" of these figures, and it is treasured even when it is mocked—as when Rosalind realistically warns Phebe against scorning Silvius' offers, saying, "Sell when you can, you are not for all markets" [III. v. 60] or when Rosalind, concealing her love for Orlando, offers to cure him of the madness of loving Rosalind, and he replies, "I would not be cured" [III. ii. 425]. Nor, of course, would Rosalind or the audience want him cured. The love poems that Orlando writes are wretched (Touchstone drily offers to produce such

Susan Fleetwood as Rosalind and John Bowe as Orlando in a 1980 Royal Shakespeare Company staging of As You Like It. *Act V, scene ii.*

rhymes "eight years together, dinners and suppers and sleeping hours excepted" [III. ii. 96-7]), yet we would not have Orlando's rhymes improved; we value them for their delightful ineptitude. Rosalind herself is delightfully mocked, as in this bit of dialogue in which Celia (Aliena) prosaically reminds us that people in love can be very boring:

ROSALIND. I'll tell thee, Aliena, I cannot be out of the sight of Orlando. I'll go find a shadow, and sigh till he come.

CELIA. And I'll sleep.

[IV. i. 215-18]

In short everything in the play, including the folly, is in Celia's words "O wonderful, wonderful, and most wonderful wonderful, and yet again wonderful" [III. ii. 191-92]. Not least wonderful are the improbable conversions of Oliver and the wicked Duke Frederick; again we are grateful for these improbabilities because we would not deny to anyone the possibility of finding joy by shedding self-centeredness. These two men come late to self-knowledge and its concomitant generosity of spirit, but better late than never. The play ends with "a wedlock hymn" and other strong hints of a transfigured world—though Jaques' refusal to join in the dance suggests that the new joyous order is less than total. The return of the exiles to the court is not a bit of cynicism discrediting their experience in the forest; rather, it brings the vitality and harmony of the forest into the court, which earlier in the play is a place of tyranny. (pp. 95-7)

> Sylvan Barnet, "The Comedies," in his A Short Guide to Shakespeare, Harcourt Brace Jovanovich, 1974, pp. 73-112.

Alfred Harbage

[*Harbage provides a scene-by-scene summary of* As You Like It, *often accompanied by critical commentary. Each of the play's characters— particularly* **Rosalind, Orlando, Touchstone,** *and* **Jaques**—*are discussed as they appear in the text.*]

I, i

To Adam, an old family servant, Orlando de Boys complains that his elder brother Oliver is disregarding the will of their deceased father and is rearing him as an oaf. He repeats this complaint to Oliver and is rewarded with a blow, whereupon he lays hold of his surly guardian and demands the legacy due him so that he may make his own way in the world. Oliver half promises to meet the terms but has no intention of doing so. When Charles, the champion wrestler, comes with a warning that Orlando is apt to be injured if he persists in his plan to enter the matches about to be held at court, Oliver traduces the youth and incites Charles to do his worst. Secretly he hopes that the bouts will prove fatal to Orlando, whose natural graces have been putting his own merits in the shade. In the course of his conversation with the wrestler, we have learned of the situation at court. The rightful Duke has been forced to retreat to the Forest of Arden where he lives a Robinhood sort of life with some faithful comrades, while power at home resides in the hand of Duke Frederick, his usurping younger brother. The banished Duke's daughter Rosalind remains at court as companion to Frederick's daughter Celia.

1-22 This is a somber opening for a play with so beckoning a title. A recital of grievances can never be truly engaging, but the note of aspiration in Orlando's voice offsets the petulant tone. He craves the education, the *gentility,* proper to his birth. As he invokes the spirit of his honored father, he seems less concerned with personal status than with the honor of his line. The speech, evidently continuing a conversation with Adam (*as thou say'st*), but with something of the air of an expository soliloquy (*As I remember*) comes out as a compromise between the two. It has the virtue of indi-

cating at once the domestic situation and the nature of this ménage, a considerable manor, with home-farm, horse-trainers, *hinds;* the names *Oliver, Rowland, Jaques, Dennis* make it sufficiently 'French.' **23-78** The ethical basis of Orlando's rejoinders save them from seeming impudent. He gains greatly in contrast with his snarling brother, indeed seems the more mature and restrained of the two. His physical prowess is impressive: obviously he is able to subdue Oliver without much personal agitation or expenditure of energy. This physical conflict of brothers, one of whom stands in place of a parent, is an ominous sign of decay, as witness Adam's distress (58-59) and Orlando's own apologetic words at its conclusion. It is evidently no casual thing, but the first overt act of rebellion against long oppression. When Oliver's spleen is vented on Adam—*you old dog* (75)—the latter's remark makes clear which of these brothers is truly the family renegade. There is an iron-age atmosphere now; things were different in the days of the good Sir Rowland. **79-111** Charles's *old news* (92) is so obviously old that there is no reason why it should be conveyed except to post the audience. Shakespeare's expository devices are usually less flatfooted than this question-and-answer sequence, yet it contains the most memorable speech in the scene—on the merry men in the Forest of Arden who *fleet the time carelessly as they did in the golden world* (110-11). It is relieving to hear, in this gloomy establishment, that something *merry* and *golden* survives at least somewhere. (Charles, incidentally, is more articulate than most wrestlers we have known.) **112-49** And he is not ill-disposed. Actually he has come on a mission of good-will, and Oliver bends him to his purpose by deceiving him, in fact by appealing to his moral sense. Oliver's *brotherly* characterization of Orlando functions like a photographic negative: we deduce that the youth is the opposite of what he is here said to be. **150-59** The 'positive' of the portrait follows, furnished by the same villainous speaker but when no one is present to hear. This is one of many instances in Shakespeare where virtue receives tribute from vice. Oliver's rancor reminds us of Iago's remark about Cassio: 'He hath a daily beauty in his life That makes me ugly' [*Othello,* V. i. 19-20].

I, ii

Troubled by the absence of her banished father, Rosalind is rallied by her cousin Celia. The two amuse themselves with remarks about the vagaries of Dame Fortune and Lady Nature in bestowing their gifts upon women. With the appearance of the court-jester Touchstone, the conversation erratically swerves to the subjects of wisdom, folly, and empty oaths. The courtier Le Beau brings news that Charles the wrestler has just maimed three challengers and is about to take on a fourth. If they remain in this place, they will see the 'sport.' Touchstone is dubious about the appeal of bone-crushing as an entertainment for ladies, but Rosalind and Celia decide to stay when they see the young and handsome challenger. They add their pleas to Duke Frederick's to dissuade Orlando from the unequal match, but he is resolved to risk everything in this chance to distinguish himself. The girls lend him ardent support, and he easily defeats the champion, but Duke Frederick sourly withholds his favor upon learning that the young victor is a son of a former enemy. Celia deplores her father's ungraciousness, and Rosalind, who remembers old Sir Rowland as a supporter of her father, rewards Orlando with a guerdon. She gives him ample chance to improve the acquaintance, but he can only gaze at her in awe. Le Beau, who has departed with the Duke and his retinue, returns with a warning that Orlando stands in danger of the Duke's active displeasure, as does also the exile's daughter upon whom he has just been gazing. Orlando realizes that he is in worse plight than before, but consoles himself with thoughts of *heavenly Rosalind!* (270)

1-21 Our knowledge of the political situation is here reinforced, and we see the children of the enemy-brothers behaving as loving foster-sisters. Since Celia intends to right the wrong done by her usurping father, the future as well as the past is tinged with gold. **22-49** Rosalind's conversational gambit on *falling in love* (22) is dramatic 'foreshadowing.' Observe how swiftly the subject is switched off by Celia's moralistic reply. Shakespeare's heroines are not permitted to fall in love in the abstract; ripeness is not all in this area: there must be single and worthy objects. The logic-chopping about Nature and Fortune will do as a sample of small talk between lively and cultivated girls, but it seems to come from the top of their heads. **50-85** Touchstone will do better, too, when the occasion improves. The words *dullness of the fool* (51) promises no scintillating performance, indeed no more than the routine clowning we get. The 'demonstration' (about invalid oaths sworn on non-existent beards) is of the tried-and-true order of comic business such as would be part of any jester's repertory, but observe that aspersions are slyly cast upon the usurper, as his daughter notices (76-79): Touchstone's knight without honor is one whom Duke Frederick *loves.* **86-111** Le Beau is a tame courtier, in contrast with the *merry men* who have followed the elder Duke; he is a gossip and perhaps a fop, but his officiousness is good-natured, and there is nothing in his lines and actions to suggest the effeminacy that is often projected ad nauseam in modern productions; a slightly vapid timidity should do. The merriment of Rosalind and Celia is determinedly sophisticated. For the moment they appear as a pair of smart little minxes. **112-203** The impression does not endure. They grow tender when they hear of the injured wrestlers, more tender still when they see Orlando. Now they are sketched with swift contrasting strokes. They address the youth with a studied grown-up gravity, but when the match is on, show the delightfully uninhibited partisanship of children. Celia's impulses are especially fetching (193-94). Charles's boastfulness is just enough to set off the quiet modesty of Orlando, who is remarkably successful in concealing his uncouth rearing; in his plaintive and courtly address to the girls he proves quite the rhetorician. Again his physical prowess is impressive: he is Shakespeare's most muscular lover. **204-41** Duke Frederick has appeared anything but villainous thus far—trying to spare Orlando, limiting the bout to one fall, even making an inquiry (as the girls do not) about the condition of the loser. There is a hint of regret in his manner as he turns upon Orlando, so that the action seems prompted more by a bad conscience than by evil nature. Celia sides against her father in his churlishness (as does Jessica [in *The Merchant of Venice*]) without forfeiting our esteem. With the Duke's display of passion, the medium shifts to blank verse, and naturally remains so; it would not do for Orlando and Rosalind to fall in love in prose. As usual in these plays, it is the lady who makes the first practical overtures. Rosalind's four-line speech (233-36) illustrates the suppleness which the playwright required of his principal actors, as she lets a wish be father to a thought (*He calls me back*), speaks to herself in an aside (*My pride fell with my fortunes*), addresses a face-saving remark to Celia (*I'll ask him what he would*), and then almost proposes to Orlando. A fine bit of business is implied here, as she hovers invitingly before him while he stands too dumbfounded to speak. How he *should* have responded, of course he realizes later with chagrin. **242-70** Frederick's villainy is carefully kept within bounds. Le Beau speaks of his *condition,* his *manners,* his *humorous* state, rather than of inveterate malice. Perhaps he will not prove obdurate in evil, and this iron age will pass. Again the idea of a *better world than this* (265) is obtruded on our attention. To Frederick as to Oliver, it is someone's virtue (260-62) which seems to constitute a threat.

I, iii

Rosalind replies to Celia's questioning by confessing that she has a new reason to be pensive: she has fallen in love with Orlando. Duke Frederick breaks in on their council with an order that Rosalind leave the court within ten days on pain of death. Both she and Celia staunchly protest, but the Duke distrusts Rosalind as the daughter of his banished brother and the object of his subjects' love. Celia resolves to share Rosalind's exile; they will disguise themselves and seek out the elder Duke in the Forest of Arden. Rosalind will don male attire and swagger it out as 'Ganymede' while Celia will pose as 'Aliena.' Touchstone will be persuaded to go along.

1-35 The repartee of the girls has improved now that they have worthy matter to work on. Rosalind is no longer pensive about her father but about her *child's father* (11). How swiftly and implacably her thoughts have fixed upon ultimate objectives! **36-85** Again the shift is from prose to blank verse, with the shift from wit and whimsey to passion. Duke Frederick's anger seems a kind of seizure, like that of Leontes in *The Winter's Tale*. Rosalind and Celia are armed only with honesty, but their plain-speaking is so formidable that we almost pity the Duke. Twice he calls Celia a *fool* (76, 83) because, blinded by love, she fails to see that Rosalind's virtues make her a serious rival. The playwright loves these ironic collisions, where hatred and moral defect must, in self-defense, attack love and virtue as dangerous. The Duke is convinced that his appraisal of the situation is quite rational. **86-134** So resolute a moment before, Rosalind and Celia now sound defenseless and forlorn—but not for long. Cheerfulness seeps rapidly into their voices, so that by the end of the brief dialogue they sound less like refugees than like schoolgirls planning a Halloween junket. Especially captivating is Rosalind's eagerness to wear a *gallant curtle-axe* and to cloak her timidity in a *swashing and martial outside* (110-18). The two seem truly standing in half-water between childhood and womanhood. Of course Touchstone will go along; Shakespeare's fools all adhere to the right side.

II, i

In the Forest of Arden, Duke Senior extols the simple life and the sweet uses of adversity. His comrades share his content, if not his solicitude for the dappled deer whose dominion they have invaded. They tell of how one of their number, the melancholy Jaques, lies sighing by a brook, moralizing the fate of a wounded stag into an allegory of corrupt society. The Duke goes to seek Jaques out, since he loves to 'cope him' in his 'sullen fits.'

1 s.d. The direction *like Foresters* (later *like Outlaws*) indicates the Kendal green attire of the little band, in contrast with the courtly finery of Frederick and his retinue. We are in the Forest of Arden. After the somewhat asphyxiating atmosphere of Oliver's manor and Frederick's court, the air seems cleansed and cool. The effect is achieved by the relaxed words and conduct, as well as the Robinhood attire of the actors. **1-20** The rightful Duke is not even equipped with a proper name, but he has the composure and graciousness of the natural leader, like Theseus. Although his opening lines are filled with allusion to what is *painted* and *envious* in society, to what is *churlish* in nature, the tone is serene and the verse is limpid, in harmony with the theme of peace-of-mind. Amiens describes truly what the speaker does, *translate,* and the style in which he does it, *so quiet and so sweet* (20). The image of the ugly toad wearing in its head the precious jewel (13-14) lends just the touch of strangeness needed to set off the easy simplicity of the rest. His last two lines, with their artfully varied parallelism rising to a climax, *good in everything* (17), have a peculiar significance, as the first generalization we hear in the Forest of Arden spoken by its tutelary spirit. The Duke is not a Pangloss, since, in his pronouncement, that which is not *good* is absorbed and neutralized rather than ignored, and happiness is something earned. The Forest is not an earthly paradise, for here the *fang* of winter *bites* even though it bites to man's advantage; Arden seems to symbolize a process rather than a place. **21-69** The Duke's next brief speech contains the text of the two long speeches following. The suggestion of pathos in the fate of the hunted deer, and the idea of their being the *native burghers* (23) of this sylvan city, are imaginatively expanded. The picture of the brook which *brawls* past the gnarled oak-roots, the stag which stretches with groans its *leathern coat* (31-38), is painted from nature sharply observed, but the painting is stylized—decorative and consciously artificial rather than realistic, as is the treatment of the Forest as a whole, in harmony with the symbolic use to which it is being put. The 'moralization' of the picture attributed to Jaques is remarkable for its ingenuity and neat devices of condensation, but its excesses create the impression that the orator was enjoying himself, and we feel a little skeptical about his *weeping* (66). Perhaps he can weep at will.

II, ii

The absence of Celia and Touchstone as well as Rosalind leads Duke Frederick to suspect connivance on the part of Orlando. He orders the youth brought to court for questioning. If he is missing, his brother Oliver must answer for him.

1-21 The birds have flown as we knew they would, and Frederick scents treason as he was bound to do. However one new detail is introduced, the eavesdropping of *Hisperia,* which directs the Duke's attention to the de Boys household. Presumably this will have importance in the economy of the plot; at least we are pleased to hear that Oliver will have to answer for something.

II, iii

Old Adam warns Orlando that the praise he has won for his wrestling victory has inflamed his brother's rancor, so that if he tarries at home he is apt to be burned in his lodgings. Adam puts at Orlando's disposal his life's-savings of five hundred crowns, and the two set forth to seek in the world some 'settled low content.'

1-30 The virtues of Orlando and the danger to which they have exposed him are described in an excessively exclamatory style, but Adam is an octogenarian and we must give the aged leave to wail. **31-76** What follows, in addition to getting Orlando off on his journey, is a moral exemplum in its own right. First Orlando chooses, in exemplary fashion, the lesser evil, personal danger, to outlawry and vagrancy. Then Adam (surely the 'Adam before the fall') performs an act of charity in a spirit of Christian faith, explicitly expressed (43-45). Then comes an oblique lecture on good moral habits, with Adam's hale old age offered in evidence. All this is too well written to be dismissed as perfunctory padding. There is feeling in the reference to old and cashiered servants—*unregarded age in corners thrown* (42). Finally Orlando, using Adam for his text, reproves the world where men work only for *meed* and not for love and duty. The present is compared again to its disadvantage with a golden past. The weighty moral content of the scene suggests that regeneration is in order, and the direction the comedy will take. It would not have been surprising if it had been written throughout in couplets, such as appear in the last speech and sporadically just before it. There is pathos in Adam's rueful words about taking to the road at *fourscore,* and performers should defer to the playwright's obvious regard for this *good old man* (56). To portray him as ludicrously senile, on the principle that every play must have its Polonius, is a detestable piece of blotting. (A tradition, none too reliable, maintains that Shakespeare played this part himself.)

II, iv

Rosalind as 'Ganymede,' Celia as 'Aliena,' and Touchstone as himself arrive weary at Arden, where there appear to be pasturelands as well as trees. They overhear the young shepherd Silvius tell the old shepherd Corin of his love for disdainful Phebe; and Rosalind is put in mind of her own love-longings for Orlando. They ask Corin if he can supply them food and shelter, and learn that he is only the hireling of another man, whose cottage, flocks, and pastures are up for sale. When they offer to make the purchase themselves and retain Corin as their shepherd, they are led off to view the holding.

1-16 The runaways have made it, a little the worse for wear, so that Rosalind must look out for their morale. She speaks partly for herself, partly for 'Ganymede,' whose masculine courage she must emulate. Each of her companions is given a speech or two in character (and in prose) before natives step into view. **17-58** They step out of the literary pastoral-tradition, where shepherds are chronically in love, of exquisite sensibility, and speak a dialect as poetic as their names. Observe the patterned speech of Silvius, the three unrimed couplets, each followed by a half-line, *Thou hast not loved* (31-39), the last patly illustrated by his *passionate* exit. Rosalind and Touchstone, each after kind, is touched, so that *love* sounds a three-note chime. Touchstone's *Jane Smile,* with her chapped hands, is a less ethereal example of rural mistress than Silvius's Phebe, and there is more than a hint in the language that Touchstone's designs upon her were not ethereal either. Rosalind's love must be more in the ideal fashion of Silvius's, but it is odd, if the issue were clear, that she should

say so in a jingle (55-56). **59-65** There is something strange about this Forest of Arden. In the scenes back in 'civilization' there was a reasonably plausible consistency in the treatment of character and event. Here, experience has an amiably schizoid quality, with plausible and implausible consorting comfortably together. Touchstone's arrogant hail to one whom he deems even lower in the social scale than himself, and Rosalind's engaging embarrassment over his rude snobbery, are as natural as can be. But Corin, who a moment before was a conventional pastoral shepherd (whom love ere now had drawn into a *thousand* acts ridiculous) suddenly changes into an authentic old countryman, humble and kindly, who speaks with a lovely simplicity (70-95). Like the wood outside Athens, this one seems enchanted too, but the dreams are the dreams of daytime.

II, v

Amiens sings 'Under the greenwood tree' and, for reasons of his own, Jaques asks for more. As they spread for the Duke's evening banquet, Amiens sings again, with all joining in the chorus. Jaques produces a parody of the song, and Amiens sings this too, before going to summon the Duke.

1-7, 33-39 We are grateful to Jaques, whatever his motives, for persuading Amiens to give us the second *stanzo.* It is a festive song, just right for a woodland feast, and we are reminded of the line of light operas sired by this play. Fine solo and choral singing in a comradely atmosphere has its own undeniable appeal, and the scene would justify itself simply as a musical interlude. But it also adds a dimension to this forest world. Observe that the words of the song repeat, in their own way, the message of the Duke (II, i, 1-17), so that we have been twice greeted in Arden by the idea of triumphant contentment, but now the idea is challenged. **8-55** The Jaques we met 'in absentia,' sobbing over the fate of the stag and the inhumanity of man, struck us as a doleful sentimentalist. Either we were mistaken, or he himself has changed. Here he seems truculent and carping, a determined cynic—Diogenes with a parody up his sleeve. A moment ago we heard Touchstone say *now am I in Arden, the more fool I* (II, iv, 14). Now it is Jaques who says the same thing, in express opposition to the official sentiment of the place. The fool and the eccentric see eye to eye, and see what common sense tells us is true—that the efficacy of retreat into the great open spaces is a lot of sentimental nonsense. At least our common sense would tell us so if the issue came to debate. But there is no debating here. No one contradicted Touchstone, and no one contradicts Jaques. Instead, the same singer who sang of the joys of the forest-life happily sings the parody. This has the odd effect of keeping the issue open. Either the Duke and his followers are aware of some truth denied the dissenters, or they know the value of pretense. Perhaps this is the secret wisdom of Arden, a stronghold of passive resistance to disillusion.

II, vi

Adam, faint with hunger and fatigue, tells Orlando to go on alone. Orlando speaks words of cheer, and promises to find food somewhere in this forest to which they have wandered. He bears the old man to shelter before leaving for his search.

1-16 There is no condescension in Orlando's speech, but such eager assurances as are designed to put heart into the old and ill. Toward its end, the broken continuity indicates the pauses for action as he ministers to his servant. His actions must not be viewed casually. A young aristocrat carrying an old servitor to shelter is a symbol which would have had a strong ethical and emotional impact.

II, vii

At the woodland repast of the Duke and his following, Jaques describes with high glee his meeting with a fool in the forest, and he begs for a motley coat so that he may rail upon the times. When the Duke questions his motives, he defends the satiric mode. Orlando breaks in upon them with drawn sword, demanding a share of the food, but he relaxes his posture when the Duke addresses him kindly. He goes to bring Adam to the feast, and returns with the old man in his arms just as Jaques is concluding a survey of the seven ages of man. All sit to the repast, and Amiens sings another song. The scene ends with the Duke proffering permanent refuge to this young son and this former servant of his onetime friend, Sir Rowland de Boys.

1-11 For one alluded to in such terms—*nowhere . . . like a man* and *compact of jars* (2-5)—Jaques seems to have a strange fascination for the Duke. **12-43** The Touchstone whom Jaques describes bears small resemblance to the Touchstone we have met; he has undergone a Forest-change and gained a languid elegance as he poses for this brilliantly comic picture of utter boredom and futility. Jaques himself, now almost hysterically elated, keeps changing before our eyes. When we first heard of him, he was anguished, and when we first saw him, he was bitter. His moods are as motley as Touchstone's coat, and he has been virtually functioning as the Duke's jester before he requests the role. There is a chameleon quality about Jaques and Touchstone, their coloration exchangeable, so that it is hard to decide which if either is the 'touchstone' of what. The season in Arden appears to be a mixture of autumn, winter, spring, summer; and between them Touchstone and Jaques manage to mix up the spirit of the boxing days with the spirit of lent. **44-87** In two lengthy and nicely-turned speeches Jaques defends the integrity of satire. The burden of his discourses—'If the shoe fits, wear it'—is the standard apology of the satirists of the day. Between his speeches comes the Duke's 'ad hominem' charge that the satirist is a warped

and corrupted man, with an affinity for the vices he castigates. The issue is not resolved. The Duke is an important and incisive speaker, but Jaques is permitted to speak longest and last. **88-109** If the question is the relative powers of persuasion of vinegar and honey, the latter wins the palm in the action. As Orlando, always the tall-man-of-his-hands, bursts pugnaciously upon them, it is the Duke's mild courtesy which disarms him, not Jaques' witty sarcasms. **109-26** Orlando's inventory of those influences which account for humane action—gratitude for one's own well-being, religious teaching, good example—is repeated by the Duke so as to receive a ceremonial endorsement. The 'conventional' morality here has been used as a butt of Shavian wit, but there is nothing logically wrong with the liturgy. Orlando thinks that *all things had been savage here* (107), and he recognizes that things cease to be savage because of civilizing influences; he is mindful of the ultimate reasons why he will be eating instead of eaten. **127-66** The Duke's comment, as Orlando goes off to fetch Adam is cheerful in intent; he is telling the company that relatively they are not *unhappy* (unlucky). Jaques' extension of his metaphor of the theatre into *All the world's a stage . . .* (139-66) is different in spirit. It contains seven miniature portraits, sharp, animated, credible, the amount of detail increasing from one to the next, but all miracles of condensation. The data is highly selective: the babe is *mewling* and *puking* (not smiling), the child *creeping* to school (not running to play), and at no point is man seen to advantage. Although in the first five ages, he grows a little more imposing, in the last two, after the deft punctuating clause *And so he plays his part,* he suffers a devastating fall. Like the scorpion, Jaques' summation bears its sting in its tail: the crown of life is—senility! And yet generations of youngsters speaking their 'memory pieces' have cheerfully chirped out *Sans teeth, sans eyes, sans taste, sans everything;* and, in productions, the lines are often spoken like a benediction. How can we account for this oddity? In its substance the speech denigrates life, in spite of the few relieving touches, like the schoolboy's *shining* (fresh-scrubbed) *morning face,* but the tone of the speaker is not that of the malicious debunker; rather it is sympathetic, regretful, a little nostalgic. The words say one thing, the 'tune' something a trifle different, and as an act of faith we attend to the tune. The speech is a wonderful literary feat. **167-200** Although we should feel grateful for it, we should also feel grateful for the stage direction following: *Enter Orlando, with Adam.* Orlando will soon be composing sonnets to his mistress's eyebrow, and Adam is approaching Jaques' seventh age; indeed at the moment his life has come full cycle for he is resting in another's arms as at the beginning. But Orlando and Adam together are something different from Orlando and Adam apart, and different as individuals than as types. And which of Jaques' capsulated 'ages' fits this gentle and generous Duke? The tableau formed by these three is a silent commentary upon the preceding speech, for the nuances in Shakespearean drama are not confined to the words. For a moment we thought we were hearing something bravely definitive about the vanity of human life, but now we are less sure. There is ambiguity even in the concluding song—a wintry companion to the one sung before the banquet began. After Orlando, Adam, and the Duke have begun acting as if gratitude, friendship, and love are potent realities, the song voices serious doubts. Or does it? *Most friendship is fainting, most loving mere folly* (181); but 'Most' is not 'all,' as Celia would say, and little candles throw their lights far. Never have such melancholy verses been followed by such rollicking choruses.

III, i

Duke Frederick orders Oliver to set out and seek his brother while his house and lands are held in bail. If Orlando is not produced within a year, Oliver will lose everything.

1-18 We glimpse the court again, like a receding coastal point. The episode might easily have been included in II,ii, but it is split off for structural reasons: we are reminded that there is such a place as the court, that the exodus of characters has been noticed, and that something is being done about it. (This is anticipating, but observe that preparation is made for Oliver's appearance in Arden, but not for the Duke's warlike approach. Threat of invasion would not suit the atmosphere of the place.)

III, ii

Orlando adorns the trees with verses in praise of Rosalind. Touchstone and Corin debate the rival claims of court and country life. When Rosalind reads aloud a sample of the poetry, Touchstone extemporizes a parody. Celia reads another sample, and after impish delay, tells Rosalind that the poet is her Orlando. The two step back to witness an encounter between him and Jaques, demonstrating the antipathy of a person-in-love and a person-out-of-love. Rosalind, retaining her identity as 'Ganymede,' engages Orlando in conversation, and offers to cure him of love by posing as his loved-one and tormenting him with a woman's whims. He has no wish to be cured, but welcomes the chance to unburden his heart by addressing this youth as 'Rosalind.'

1-10 Orlando's speech is a sonnet lacking the first quatrain (no doubt spoken before his entrance) and a better lyric than any he is able to get on paper; perhaps he should dictate his poetry. He has seen so little of Rosalind that the second of the qualities he attributes to her, *The fair, the chaste, and unexpressive she* (10) must be known to him through pure intuition. We soon learn that he is now outfitted neatly as one of the Duke's foresters, so that we must visualize him as an amalgam of

Petrarchan love-lyricist and husky youth in Kendal green. At least one of the trees upon which he pins his verses is a palm (167), which here seems able to survive the *icy fang* of winter as readily as the *gnarled oak.* Since in Arden the glades of Arcadia are superimposed upon Sherwood Forest, and tropical flora and fauna (presently we shall hear of a *lioness*) flourish in France, Orlando can be two selves with perfect propriety. **11-82** There is an Alice-in-Wonderland inconclusiveness about this debate. After it is over, Corin might justly feel like a Kafka victim, wondering just what kind of guilt he has incurred, but luckily his nerves are sound. In one of his Sonnets [66] Shakespeare speaks sadly of 'simple truth miscalled simplicity,' but the miscalling proves a jolly business when done by a professional simpleton. Frivolousness is Touchstone's métier, and his air of tolerant superiority is as engaging as Corin's innocence. Although handicapped by his sincerity, as any *natural philosopher* (30) is bound to be in a skirmish with a wit and a punster, Corin manages to get his view of life on record, unforgettably so (69-73), and Touchstone's persiflage sounds no more damaging than the crackling of thorns under a pot. **83-117** Once having found his rime, Orlando has stuck to it, and to his jog-trot meter (*the right butterwomen's rank to market*). Touchstone is right in his critical judgment, but his parody, reducing love to lust and Rosalind to a trollop, turns Orlando's idealism inside out, and merits Rosalind's rebuke. But, as usual in this least cynical of all plays, the cynic is given the last word. **118-239** This second poem, achieving a quite respectable mediocrity, must have been composed after Orlando had acquired the knack of it. Perhaps Rosalind would like it better if she had not already been *berymed* like an *Irish rat* (169), or if she knew who the author was. When she is told, her first words are *Alas the day! What shall I do with my doublet and hose?* (208) What she does is keep them on, thus remaining incognito both to the lover she has been longing for and the father she has come to Arden to seek. Fortunately there is no attempt to rationalize this irrational behavior. To do so would be like trying to explain why palm trees are growing in this forest, or who is tending to Silvius's and Phebe's sheep. The clock has been stopped, the laws of logic suspended, and the dwellers in Arden freed from the obligation to do anything but what is enjoyable. Still, and this makes it unique, the play never labels itself 'fantasy,' thus apologizing for its devices, and its characters never become marionettes—but only pose as marionettes. One of the minor triumphs among them is Celia. In the constant presence of the witty, ardent, and magnetic Rosalind, she might have easily lost identity and dwindled to a cipher. Instead she remains quite distinct, alternately teasing and lecturing the friend in whose love-affair she is so whole-heartedly interested. Since there is no malice or envy in this interest, she can be as outspoken as she pleases. Her remark that she has found Orlando under a tree *like a dropped acorn* (224) is a sample of her piquant conversational style. **240-81** A moment ago Goodman Kersey-woolen encountered Sir Taffeta, and now *Signior Love* encounters *Monsieur Melancholy.* Orlando is the more hostile of the two, shying away as if he feared Jaques' malady to be catching. The dialogue lacks the 'articulated' style of real communication since the incompatibility of this pair is absolute; their speeches are pot-shots exchanged across a chasm. These interpolated encounters (Corin-Touchstone, Jaques-Orlando) provide time for Orlando's poems to be found, identified with their author, and serve as a means of bringing the lovers face to face, but they are rounded off as self-sufficient 'skits.' Through the remainder of the play similar encounters between substance and shadow (not always easily distinguishable) provide the true center of interest, with the plot-action slipped into the interstices. This fragmented dramatic technique resembles impressionistic painting, and renders commentary upon separate details somewhat irrelevant. The succession of impromptu charades, comic eclogues, musical interludes, wit-skirmishes, suggests an extemporal allegory, a parade of the seven-or-so-not-so-deadly-attitudes, a whimsical dance of love and life. Its proper lighting is dappled sunlight, and it could be set nowhere in the world but the Forest of Arden. **282-408** Rosalind's disguise as a *saucy lackey* (282) lets her express the misgivings about love and marriage which she is intelligent enough to have but healthy-spirited enough to disregard. Her mind says one thing, her heart another, and like the play as a whole, she is unromantically romantic. Orlando is reduced to the role of 'straight man' as he converses with this volatile youth who dwells on the skirts of Arden *like fringe upon a petticoat* (319), but he is passing a kind of test. His dogged refusal to escape the pangs of love—*I would not be cured, youth* (398)—although addressed to 'Ganymede' must sound sweet in the ears of Rosalind.

III, iii

Touchstone pays court to the country-maid Audrey while Jaques stands gloomily by. A forest wedding is about to take place, with Sir Oliver Mar-text officiating. Jaques steps forth to give the bride away, then persuades Touchstone to postpone the ceremony until it can be more properly performed.

1-94 The courtship of ideal lovers now in process casts this antic shadow—a travesty in action, like Touchstone's travesty of Orlando's love-lyric. Audrey is available and willing; and Touchstone, who *hath his desires* (70), is resigned. Any action involving Touchstone is bound to be subversive, and his remarks upon compatibility, poetry, chastity (*honesty*), fidelity, and the ultimate sanctions of marriage (69-71) are saturnalian in spirit. In contrast Jaques' spirit is saturnine; he here appears as primly censorious, and a stickler for propriety. Audrey, whose wit and beauty may leave something to be desired, lays stress on moral character: her question about poetry—*Is it honest in deed and word? Is it a true thing?* (14)—is as priceless as Touchstone's reply (16-17). Arden, we observe, is suddenly provided with a nearby village and *vicar.* Are his services rejected because of some Puritan taint? or because marriages in comedy should be reserved for the last scene? Poor proud Oliver Mar-text—we remember him always, although he is only given three speeches and then elbowed into oblivion.

III, iv

To Rosalind's distress, Orlando has failed to keep an appointment, and she and Celia discuss his truancy. Corin comes to invite them to witness a meeting between Silvius and the scornful Phebe.

1-54 In tantalizing Rosalind, Celia displays her usual deftness in the use of metaphor. The prose dialogue of this play sparkles with splintered poetry. Observe that Corin reverts to his 'pastoral' role whenever he is associated with Silvius and Phebe: his terms are not countrified as he invites the girls to see *the pageant truly played* (47).

III, v

As Silvius pleads for gentler treatment, Phebe makes mock of his devotion. Rosalind steps forth and indignantly upbraids her, giving short shrift to her alleged beauty and charm. The tirade succeeds only in arousing Phebe's interest in the one who utters it, and when Rosalind and Celia have left, she employs Silvius to convey a 'taunting' letter to the scolding 'Ganymede.'

1-138 Phebe's manner is wanton and irritating as she pecks away at Silvius's metaphors, ignoring the spirit in her literal interpretation (8-27). It is a small offense, but it will serve. Since Silvius is in love, and is the only eligible shepherd in view, Phebe seems to personify coy fastidiousness; and all male hearts respond as Rosalind pitches into her (8-27). A woman should indeed *thank heaven fasting for a good man's love;* it is a regular manifesto.

IV, i

Jaques defines the nature of his melancholy to Rosalind—who is unimpressed. She chides Orlando for coming late, then plays the part of skeptical mistress, subjecting his sentiments to stiff strokes of common sense. However, she acts out a marriage ceremony with him with Celia serving as 'priest,' and when he has left to attend upon the Duke, she admits how 'many fathom deep' she is in love.

1-201 Rosalind proves as hostile to Jaques as did Orlando—they are young growth resistant to frost. Our impression that Jaques alters in mood from scene to scene is confirmed by his own diagnosis:

his is an eclectic melancholy, *compounded of many simples, extracted from many objects* (15). What follows is a strange love-scene, with its haunting, *Men have died from time to time, and worms have eaten them, but not for love* (96-98). More critics have fallen in love with Rosalind than with any other of Shakespeare's heroines, and the reason is fairly clear. She is witty, warm, and presumably beautiful, but, further than that, she seems the perfect risk as a wife, since her capacity for love is so great that it has survived disillusionment in advance. In spite of the preposterous masquerade, Orlando and Rosalind remain convincing as lovers in the scenes where the masquerade is maintained—he a little subdued, hang-dog, put-upon, as young lovers are bound to be; she a little desperate, for all her high-larking spirits, as one who can only pretend that her soul remains her own.

IV, ii

The 'foresters' have killed a deer, and at Jaques' suggestion march off to present it to the Duke, singing a song of the 'lusty horn.'

1-18 We have not had foresters or a song for some time, and the scene needs no further justification. With horned beasts on the premises, and marriages in the making, a cuckoldry song was inevitable. It does not reflect upon the characters of Rosalind, Celia, Phebe, or even Audrey.

IV, iii

Apologetically, Silvius delivers Phebe's letter, supposing it to consist of insults. When it proves to be a protestation of love for 'Ganymede,' the receiver rebukes Silvius for his infatuation, and returns an answer to Phebe that her love will be reciprocated only when Silvius consents to act as her intercessor. Oliver now appears bearing a blood-stained handkerchief and a message from Orlando. The latter has been wounded by a lioness in rescuing Oliver from death, thus returning good for his brother's evil. Oliver is now penitent, and he and Celia minister to Rosalind, who has fainted upon hearing of Orlando's own narrow escape. They conduct her home, her jauntiness all wilted away.

1-181 Silvius has been too tame a lover. Phebe's emotions have been thawed by 'Ganymede's' fire, and need only the proper channeling. The idea of love-congealed, of frozen immobility awaiting a spring thaw, reminds us of Romeo and Rosaline, of Orsino and Olivia (*Twelfth Night*). (In all three plays the thawing agent is an ardent young girl.) An air of the miraculous attends Oliver's sudden appearance as a completely reformed man. His reformation borrows a semi-mystical character from the description of the circumstances (99-121, 128-33). He has been awakened from *miserable slumber* after Orlando has resisted the temptation to return evil for evil. The brightly-enameled image of the *green and gilded snake* which retreats at Or-

lando's approach, and of the *sucked and hungry lioness* which dies at Orlando's hands, suggest the allegorical illumination of ancient manuscripts. If anything were needed to endear Rosalind to us, it would be the collapse of her bravado when she sees Orlando's blood: *I would I were at home* (162).

V, i

Touchstone comforts Audrey, who sees no reason why their nuptials should have been interrupted. He then deals with William, her erstwhile suitor, treating the country swain to a display of courtly patronage and courtly swashbuckling.

1-60 William is an inoffensive youth although, like Silvius, a little wanting in fire. Still, better men than he might quail before Touchstone's invincible superciliousness. This jester, among other things, is a kind of 'fetch.' He is a living parody of the mannerisms which prevail in the effete courtly circles he loves to flout.

V, ii

Orlando learns that his brother Oliver has fallen in love with the shepherdess 'Aliena' (Celia), and the two wish to marry at once. Oliver will share her humble lot, and Orlando may take possession of the de Boys estates. Rosalind promises Orlando that he himself may marry on the morrow, not in another mock-ceremony but in a true one with his actual mistress, who will be brought hither by magical aids. Silvius and Phebe are also promised a resolution of their problem: 'Ganymede' will marry Phebe or never marry any woman, and yet Silvius will be satisfied. The principals in these crossed love-affairs chant out a litany of love, which Rosalind abruptly terminates with a repetition of assurances that all will be properly paired off.

1-117 *Is't possible . . . ?* asks Orlando. It must be, since it has happened. What would be *impossible* would be for the eminently marriageable Celia to finish the course unclaimed. The scene contains another and more elaborate passage of schematized repetition, this time a lovers' creed and testament, both poetic and absurd. It dissolves in Rosalind's laughter, so that the effect, like so much else in this play, is spicy-sweet, not cloying.

V, iii

Touchstone gives Audrey the joyous tidings that they, too, will be married on the morrow; then sits between two pages of the Duke and joins them in singing 'It was a lover and his lass.'

1-40 As the two little boys appear from nowhere, and perch on either side of this antic figure (who surely must be long and lean), and as the three voices join in this golden catch, we have a sense of the 'rightness' of the whole design—an unpremeditated rightness, as hard to describe as a peal of bells or the fragrance of a garden.

V, iv

Duke Senior will willingly accept Orlando as his son-in-law if 'Ganymede' is able to produce Rosalind as promised. Still posing as this masterful youth, Rosalind repeats her assurances, and makes certain that Phebe will accept Silvius if she decides not to wed 'Ganymede.' She and Celia retire, and Touchstone leads in Audrey to make up another couple in the impending nuptials. Prompted by Jaques, Touchstone expatiates upon the 'seventh cause' in the code of the duello. Rosalind and Celia return in their own proper forms, and to the sound of soft music, and an Epithalamion by Hymen, the four couples link hands, all mysteries resolved and all obstacles removed. Even Phebe seems contented—Silvius will do, now that 'Ganymede' is no more. At this juncture another brother of Orlando and Oliver appears on the scene, with news that Duke Frederick has abandoned plans to invade the Forest of Arden; instead he has been converted to the religious life and has abdicated the Dukedom in favor of its rightful ruler. All may now return to their inheritances. Jaques pronounces a benediction upon the fortunate ones, but withdraws from the celebration; he will join Duke Frederick and commune with the convertite. Duke Senior leads off the couples in a dance, and Rosalind speaks the Epilogue.

1-192 Despite the somewhat offhand methods used in the tying of it, a quite respectable knot is available for untying in this conclusion, and we have a comforting sense of accomplishment. Everyone is enlightened, united, reformed, reinstated, and, so far as possible, married. True to themselves, Touchstone, after pressing in with the *country copulatives* (53), gives a fine display of jesting virtuosity, and Jaques retires to enjoy his melancholy in peace. Hymen's hymn to that *blessed bond of board and bed* which *peoples every town* (135-40) is the properly decorous sequel to Touchstone's song of the *lover and his lass* in the vernal fields of rye (V, iii, 15-32). Thus ends a play which leaves the critical commentator always an awkward step in the rear. Its moods, sentiments, mockeries, perceptions form patterns as bright, translucent, shifting, and apparently accidental as those in a kaleidoscope. In the Epilogue Rosalind proceeds unscrupulously to coerce a display of audience approval with her charm. The play as a whole coerces us with its charm. What appears to be a medley, a structure of spontaneous improvisation, cannot be evaluated by objective standards, and we may well speak of the artistic level of this play as Orlando speaks of Rosalind's stature—*just as high as my heart* (III, ii, 258). One may say with Jaques that this is but a *pretty answer,* or, indeed, that *As You Like It* is but a pretty play. However, it does something which mere prettiness could never do. It makes the world seem young. It sweetens the imagination. (pp. 222-45)

Alfred Harbage, "Infinite Variety: 'As You Like It'," in his William Shakespeare: A Reader's Guide, *Farrar, Straus and Giroux, 1963, pp. 164-297.*

PASTORAL CONVENTIONS

Brigid Brophy

[*Brophy surveys the elements of pastoralism in* As You Like It *(pastoralism is a literary form that presents an ideal and virtuous vision of rustic life). In addition, the critic discusses the comedy in relation to its source, Thomas Lodge's novel* Rosalynde. *Brophy asserts that among the play's most moving aspects are Shakespeare's brilliant dramatization of the romantic love affair between* **Orlando** *and* **Rosalind** *and the bond of friendly love exhibited by* **Rosalind** *and* **Celia.**]

As You Like It is a play I have loved virtually all my life, but it was only recently that I realised that it is not what the Copyright Act would call 'an original work'. This is not a great feat of literary detection on my part. Almost all Shakespeare's plays have sources of some kind, and any school text will tell you that the source for *As You Like It* is a novel called *Rosalynde* by Shakespeare's contemporary, Thomas Lodge.

However, very few people bother to read Lodge's novel; and that is a pity, because it is a highly interesting novel in its own right—rather eccentric, deeply charming, very shrewd about psychology, very lively, very well written; and the moment you do read it you realise that it is very much more than just a source for *As You Like It. As You Like It* is, in fact, an absolutely straightforward, dramatised version of *Rosalynde.*

The novel was first published in 1590 and it evidently had a considerable success—it ran to three editions within the next decade. That, presumably, made it worthwhile for someone to cash in on it. It is notable that Shakespeare did not change the name of the heroine. He kept the name 'Rosalind', and it was towards the end of the decade, in 1598 or 1599—no one knows for sure which—that *As You Like It* appeared on the stage.

But, although Shakespeare changed the names of several of the characters, he did not change the characters themselves, or—which is more important—the relationships between them. He cut down the time spanned by the novel, because a novel has more room to sprawl than a play has. But he made fewer changes than a modern writer would if he were adapting a modern novel for the theatre or for television. Having stayed with Lodge in all the big things, relationships, characters, plot, sequence, Shakespeare often chose to stay with him right down to smallish detail.

The novel and the play are both set in France. One thread concerns a king of France who is driven out of his court by his usurping brother. Shakespeare demotes this pair of brothers from kings of France to dukes of an unnamed part of France. The exiled king or duke is eventually followed into exile by his daughter, Rosalind, but not before she has fallen in love with another ill-used brother, who has been driven out of his inheritance by his elder brother, and who also goes into voluntary exile. The place where all these exiles take refuge and where the threads of the story are woven is what Lodge and Shakespeare called the Forest of Arden—what we would call, now that it is no longer fashionable to Anglicise French names, the Ardennes.

The ups and downs of fortune which have turned these people into exiles give them all the opportunity to reflect on blind fortune, or random chance, as we would probably call it; and this gives the play its fashionable, philosophical tone. The fact that they have all taken refuge in the forest also puts the play slap in the middle of another high fashion of the Renaissance—which remained in fashion deep into the 18th century—the fashion for the pastoral.

Although a pastor is literally a shepherd who puts his sheep out to pasture, I can assure anyone who feels, as I do, that the countryside is highly overrated, that the pastoral fashion has remarkably little to do with real countryside or with real sheep-rearing. When they arrive in the forest, Rosalind and Celia do buy a sheep farm, but even in Lodge, who has more room, they are only moderately serious about working it. In Shakespeare, it obviously is left to run itself. The object of the pastoral was not to draw any morals from nature. It was to recreate the literature of the ancient world, in particular the pastoral poems—dialogues between shepherds, mainly—which Theocritus wrote in Greek in the third century BC, and Virgil's imitations of them in Latin.

If you bought a pastoral novel or went to see a pastoral play, you knew pretty much what you were going to get, just as nowadays if you go and see a thriller you know pretty much what you are going to get. You were going to get shepherds with Greek or Latinised names like Sylvius, Corin, Lycidas and Damon, and shepherdesses called things like Phoebe and Corinna. The point of the whole thing was going to be that people were going to fall desperately in love. You knew also that you would get large quantities of lyric verse. It may have begun—this idea that shepherds were poets—from the thought that shepherds piped to their flocks, and, perhaps, having piped a tune, they then set words to the tune.

In Shakespeare, only one of the characters, Orlan-

do, has the actual verse-writing mania—no doubt he picks it up from the pastoral setting like an infection when he arrives in the forest. His verses, incidentally, are all bad. But the entire play is punctuated by songs.

The shepherds in Theocritus and Virgil often fall passionately in love with shepherdesses and they also quite often fall passionately in love with shepherds. The same is probably true of the cowboys in the modern Western, which is a diluted descendant of the pastoral.

This tradition of the pastoral made it a particularly apt mode for Lodge, followed by Shakespeare, to set their story in. When the girl cousins and best friends, Rosalind and Celia, run away to the Forest of Arden, Rosalind—and it is Rosalind rather than Celia because, as she explains, she is the taller of the two—dresses up as a boy.

As you would expect, given that the novel is knee-deep in classical allusions and the play is at least ankle-deep, although some have been cut out to make it more easily assimilable in the theatre, the name which Rosalind chooses for herself while she is disguised as a boy is Ganymede, the name of the

Orlando and Adam. Act II, scene iii. By Robert Smirke (1798).

page whom Zeus, the father of the gods, fell in love with.

Lodge plays with grammar. He calls Rosalind, or Ganymede, 'he' and then 'she' within a single sentence. Shakespeare, of course, had an extra decorative dimension to play with, because women did not appear as actors on the English stage for another generation and therefore all the parts in *As You Like It* were taken by men. Rosalind was that old favourite of the English theatre, a drag act, from the word go, and when she disguises herself as a boy she goes into double drag, and, at the same time, a very delicate and charming air of sexual ambiguity comes over the story.

Phoebe falls in love with Ganymede; but, of course, Ganymede does not really exist. Is she, in fact, really in love with Rosalind? Orlando is in an even greater dilemma. He believes that if he pretends that Ganymede is his Rosalind and he woos him, he will be cured of his love for her, and so he does woo the boy and, in the process, falls deeper and deeper in love with the woman. Or *is* it with the woman? Is it, in fact, with the boy?

If I ask myself what makes *As You Like It* so moving, I locate the answer in two elements that Shakespeare dramatised quite brilliantly from Lodge's novel: the erotic love between Rosalind and Orlando, obviously; and, slightly less obviously, the non-erotic love between Rosalind and Celia. The dialogue that expresses these relationships may not be positively witty, in the sense that you could go through it taking out bits for an anthology of aphorisms, but it is witty in tone, witty in rhythm, and its tone is, of course, the tone of flirtation. Rosalind and Celia are limbering up their flirtatiousness on one another. If I go on to ask myself how Shakespeare achieved this technically, the answer is one that I think is rather surprising—or would be surprising if you knew only his other comedies. He does it in prose.

> CELIA: Trow you who hath done this?
>
> ROSALIND: Is it a man?
>
> CELIA: And a chain, that you once wore, about his neck. Change you colour?
>
> ROSALIND: I prithee, who?
>
> CELIA: O Lord, Lord! it is hard matter for friends to meet; but mountains may be remov'd with earthquakes, and so encounter.
>
> ROSALIND: Nay, but who is it?
>
> CELIA: Is it possible?
>
> ROSALIND: Nay, I prithee now, with most petitionary vehemence, tell me who it is.
>
> CELIA: O wonderful, wonderful, and most wonderful wonderful, and yet again wonderful, and after that, out of all whooping!

> ROSALIND: Good my complexion! dost thou think, though I am caparison'd like a man, I have a doublet and hose in my disposition? One inch of delay more is a South Sea of discovery. I prithee tell me who is it quickly, and speak apace . . . I prithee take the cork out of thy mouth that I may drink thy tidings.
>
> CELIA: So you may put a man in your belly.
> [III. ii. 179-204]

Even if you discount the superstitions about the innocence and simplicity of life in the country, there is a way in which shepherds can truly be said to be innocent. This does not apply to cowboys, incidentally. Shepherds are innocent of blood-guilt. Human beings do not always choose to do so, but it is possible to live on reasonably fair terms with a flock of sheep. You can deprive the sheep of their wool, which they are quite glad to get rid of, and not deprive them of their lives. One of the changes that Shakespeare did make in dramatising Lodge's novel was to shift the emphasis from sheep-minding to hunting. His exiled courtiers in the forest kill the deer. And in this way he darkens the sunny landscape he found in Lodge.

All the same, through that imperfect windy instrument Jaques, Shakespeare does allow the point of view of the deer to be stated. It is Jaques who has pointed out to his fellow courtiers in exile that wounded deer weep, which is a matter of fact, incidentally, not a matter of folklore as is usually thought. Jaques makes his entrance asking the telling question, 'Which is he that killed the deer?'—a question in which he is the detective hunting down a killer, as well as looking for someone to congratulate on his victory, and the song that follows—though it does congratulate the killer on his victory—also makes a mockery of him.

> What shall he have that kill'd the deer?
> His leather skin and horns to wear.
>   [*the rest shall hear this burden:*
>   Then sing him home.
> Take thou no scorn to wear the horn;
> It was a crest ere thou wast born.
>   Thy father's father wore it;
>   And thy father bore it.
> The horn, the horn, the lusty horn,
> Is not a thing to laugh to scorn.
> [IV. ii. 10-18]

The English-speaking theatre's other grand master of dramatic prose, Bernard Shaw, considered *As You Like It* a melodrama, on the grounds that the hero and heroine have no disagreeable qualities. Presumably he missed the distinct touch of sadism which I detect in Rosalind's personality. He considered that *As You Like It* gives unmixed delight, but he thought this was simply a bid for popularity. He said Shakespeare flung Rosalind at the public with a shout of 'As *you* like it'. Of course, it was a bid for popularity—a bid for popularity which Lodge's novel had already established with readers. My guess is that, when Shakespeare had finished making his adaptation, he riffled through the pages of Lodge's novel, casting about for a title, and finally he came back to the beginning and came upon Lodge's preface, which is addressed to the gentlemen readers. 'To be brief, gentlemen,' Lodge says, after relating how he wrote the book on a sea voyage when he was taking part in a military expedition, 'room for a soldier, and a sailor, that gives you the fruits of his labours that he wrought in the ocean, when every line was wet with a surge, and every humorous passion counterchecked with a storm. If you like it, so . . . ' By the time Shakespeare made his adaptation, the gentlemen readers had already proved that they did indeed like Lodge's novel. It was no longer a question of '*if* you like it', but '*as* you like it'. (pp. 837-38)

> *Brigid Brophy, "As You Like Shakespeare," in* The Listener, *Vol. 100, No. 2591, December 21-28, 1978, pp. 837-38.*

Kenneth Muir

[Muir contends that Shakespeare did not intend As You Like It *to be a traditional pastoral—a literary form which presents an ideal and virtuous vision of rustic life—but a work suited to his own dramatic purposes. The critic also emphasizes the irony throughout the play in the fact that* **Duke Senior** *and his entourage will return to the court at their first opportunity, and he warns against taking* **Jaques**'s *comments as Shakespeare's own point of view, for they are consistently undercut by the other characters. Additionally, Muir perceives Shakespeare exploiting other literary conventions besides the pastoral, including the notion of "love at first sight" and, in the cases of* **Oliver** *and* **Duke Frederick**, *the sudden conversion of a villain.]*

As *you* like it? Does the title suggest (as some critics have supposed) that Shakespeare was deploring the taste of his audience at the Globe, or was he happily proclaiming that their taste corresponded with his own? Most great writers begin by giving their public what it wants and end by making the public want what they choose to give. Before the end of the sixteenth century, Shakespeare was in this happy position, though he kept up the pretence in his titles and sub-titles—*As You Like It, Much Ado about Nothing, What You Will*—that the boot was on the other foot.

The same irony is apparent in his dramatisation of Thomas Lodge's *Rosalynde,* a euphuistic novel which, despite its charm and elegance, is entirely artificial and removed from reality. The characters never condescend to mere conversation: they orate to each other. Although Shakespeare follows Lodge's plot fairly closely, there are no verbal echoes of his dialogue. His aim, it soon becomes clear,

was different from that of Lodge: he was not trying to write a straight pastoral, but to use it for his own dramatic purposes.

The very first speech should alert us to what he is doing. Orlando is informing Adam, his old retainer, of facts which he already knows, and which Orlando knows that he knows:

> As I remember, Adam, it was upon this fashion bequeathed me by will but poor a thousand crowns, and, as thou say'st, charged my brother, on his blessing, to breed me well; and there begins my sadness.
>
> [I. i. 1-5]

This violates one of the most elementary rules of play-writing. There is no other exposition in all Shakespeare's works which is so unashamedly crude. As he had already written some seventeen competent plays, and as a writer of comedy was at the height of his powers, we are entitled to wonder why he should revert to such an unashamedly primitive technique—more primitive than that of his earliest experimental plays. The speech is, in fact, a way of preparing us for the tone of the rest of the play. Shakespeare is pretending that he is presenting a corny tale of a bad elder brother and a good younger brother, a tale which will end, as such tales do, with the good brother marrying a princess and living happily ever after. For good measure he introduces a usurping Duke and his exiled brother who lives in the greenwood like Robin Hood. On the face of it, the play is naïve in the extreme; but it is really as sophisticated as those of Marivaux.

Orlando, of course, defeats Charles the wrestler, who has been bribed to break his neck; but Shakespeare is careful to remind us that we are in a world of fiction by making Celia comment on Le Beau's account of Charles's prowess, 'I could match this beginning with an old tale' [I. ii. 120]. Rosalind, with the initiative expected of a fairy-tale princess, hints to Orlando that she has fallen in love at first sight:

> Sir, you have wrestled well, and over-
>   thrown
> More than your enemies.
>
> [I. ii. 253-54]

Before long, Rosalind and Celia (disguised as Ganymede and Aliena), go off with Touchstone to the forest of Arden and Orlando, to escape being murdered by his brother, makes the same journey with Adam. Meanwhile we have been introduced to the exiled Duke and his entourage, and they are depicted not without irony. However much they profess to believe in the superiority of the forest life to that of the court, however much Amiens extols the greenwood and the jolliness of its life, we know that they will hurry back to court as soon as they get the chance. The only one of their number who does not, Jaques, has mocked the insincerity of his fellow-exiles.

Yet we are prevented from accepting Jaques's comments as authorial by the fact they are undercut by the Duke, by Orlando and by Rosalind. The Duke accuses him of being a reformed libertine, satirising the vices he once enjoyed; when Orlando is invited to rail against mankind, he gently reproves Jaques; and when Rosalind hears his affected account of his particular brand of melancholy, she laughs at him:

> A traveller! By my faith you have great reason to be sad. I fear you have sold your own lands to see other men's; then to have nothing is to have rich eyes and poor hands . . . I had rather have a fool to make me merry than experience to make me sad—and to travel for it too!
>
> [IV. i. 21-9]

Even Jaques's set speech on the seven ages of man, suggested probably by the motto of the Globe theatre, cannot be taken as Shakespeare's considered opinion on human life; for its melancholy outlook is contradicted by the play as a whole, as well as by the situation which evokes it—for Orlando, courteously received by the outlaws, has gone out to fetch the exhausted Adam and courtesy, charity and fellow-feeling are apparently excluded from Jaques's philosophy of life.

The attitude we are forced to adopt to the outlaws is a complex one and the same complexity is apparent in the other versions of pastoral with which Shakespeare treats. The oldest matter of pastoral, dating back to Greek and Latin poetry, and still flourishing in Shakespeare's day in the eclogues of Spenser and Drayton, is that of a love-sick shepherd in love with a scornful shepherdess. The love of Silvius for Phebe is in this convention, and it is in the scenes in which they appear that Shakespeare comes nearest to the spirit of his source. Yet he provides a suitable antidote to the convention in the very scene in which the pastoral lovers are introduced when Rosalind intervenes:

> And why, I pray you? Who might be your mother,
> That you insult, exult, and all at once
> Over the wretched? What though you have no beauty—
> As, by my faith, I see no more in you
> Than without candle may go dark to bed—
> Must you be therefore proud and pitiless?
> Why, what means this? Why do you look on me?
> I see no more in you than in the ordinary
> Of nature's sale-work. 'Ods my little life,
> I think she means to tangle my eyes too!
> No, faith, proud mistress, hope not after it;
> 'Tis not your inky brows, your black silk hair,
> Your bugle eyeballs, nor your cheek of cream,

> That can entame my spirits to your worship.
> You foolish shepherd, wherefore do you follow her,
> Like foggy south, puffing with wind and rain?
> You are a thousand times a proper man
> Than she a woman. 'Tis such fools as you
> That makes the world full of ill-favour'd children.
> 'Tis not her glass, but you, that flatters her . . .
> But, mistress, know yourself. Down on your knees,
> And thank heaven, fasting, for a good man's love;
> For I must tell you friendly in your ear:
> Sell when you can; you are not for all markets.
>
> [III. v. 34-60]

Another form of pastoral convention is represented by Audrey and William, who are not real rustics but country bumpkins seen through urban eyes; they are illiterate, slow-witted and not very clean. Audrey does not know the meaning of 'poetical' and this provides Touchstone with the opportunity of telling her that 'the truest poetry is the most feigning' [III. iii. 19-20]—an ironical comment on the poetic conventions Shakespeare is exploiting in the play. Although Touchstone puts William to flight and goes through a form of marriage with Audrey, he does not intend it to be more than temporary. The simple-minded and 'foul' rustic is superior in some ways to the civilised fool. Indeed, when Touchstone attempts, by a series of quibbles, to prove that Corin is damned, that sensible and dignified shepherd gets the best of the argument.

The last kind of pastoral represented in the play is that of Rosalind and Celia, aristocrats who adopt the pastoral role. On the spur of the moment they decide to buy the farm belonging to Corin's master:

> *Ros.* I pray thee, if it stand with honesty
> Buy thou the cottage, pasture, and the flock,
> And thou shalt have to pay for it of us.
>
> *Cel.* And we will mend thy wages. I like this place,
> And willingly would waste my time in it.
>
> [II. iv. 91-5]

They buy the farm without even seeing it, much less calling in a surveyor or scrutinising the accounts. We hear nothing more about the farm. Presumably Corin continues to do all the work.

Shakespeare exploits other literary conventions. His lovers—Rosalind, Orlando, Celia, Oliver and Phebe—would all make answer to Marlowe's question 'Who ever loved that loved not a first sight?' with a chorus of 'No one'. Shakespeare goes out of his way to underline the absurdity, as when Rosalind tells Orlando of the match between Celia and Oliver:

Nay, 'tis true. There was never anything so sudden, but the fight of two rams and Caesar's thrasonical brag of 'I came, saw, and overcame'. For your brother and my sister, no sooner met but they look'd; no sooner look'd but they lov'd; no sooner lov'd but they sigh'd; no sooner sigh'd but they asked one another the reason; no sooner knew the reason but they sought the remedy—and in these degrees have they made a pair of stairs to marriage, which they will climb incontinent, or else be incontinent before marriage.

[V. ii. 29-39]

One other romantic convention may be mentioned—the sudden conversion of a villain. In the twinkling of an eye, Oliver is converted from being a murderous, avaricious scoundrel with no redeeming characteristics into a pleasant and acceptable husband for Celia. The usurping Duke is a cruel tyrant and in Act V is about to exterminate his brother and the other outlaws when he meets an old religious man, and, we are told,

After some question with him, was converted
Both from his enterprise and from the world.

[V. iv. 161-62]

Some actors of these parts, conscious of the improbability of the conversions, have attempted to prepare the audience by presenting Frederick and Oliver as psychological wrecks, on the verge of nervous breakdowns. This is surely wrong, for Shakespeare was merely rounding off his comedy with a happy ending, the improbability being part of the fun. To force *As You Like It* into a naturalistic mode is to maim it. In the last act there is a scene which becomes almost operatic in its mockery of naturalism, with a quartet of wailing lovers:

Pheb.   Good shepherd, tell this youth what 'tis to love.
Sil.   It is to be all made of sighs and tears;
     And so am I for Phebe.
Pheb.   And I for Ganymede.
Orl.   And I for Rosalind.
Ros.   And I for no woman. . . .
Sil.   It is to be all made of fantasy,
     All made of passion, and all made of wishes;
     All adoration, duty, and observance,
     All humbleness, all patience, and impatience,
     All purity, all trial, all obedience;
     And so am I for Phebe.
Pheb.   And so am I for Ganymede.
Orl.   And so am I for Rosalind.
Ros.   And so am I for no woman.
Pheb.   If this be so, why blame you me to love you?
Sil.   If this be so, why blame you me to love you?

Orl.   If this be so, why blame you me to love you?
Ros.   Why do you speak too 'Why blame you me to love you?'
Orl.   To her that is not here, nor doth not hear.

[V. ii. 83-108]

At this point Rosalind drops into prose and laughs at the artificiality of the scene:

Pray you, no more of this; 'tis like the howling of Irish wolves against the moon.

[V. ii. 109-10]

The finest scenes in the play are, of course, those in Arden between Orlando and Rosalind. Bernard Shaw [in his *Shaw on Shakespeare*] ascribed their success to the fact that they were written in prose and there is a grain of truth in this paradox since, as we have seen, Shakespeare at this time in his career found it easier to express individualities of character in prose than in verse. Not wholly true, however, for Shaw himself complained that if you wreck the beauty of Shakespeare's lines 'by a harsh, jarring utterance, you will make your audience wince, as if you were singing Mozart out of tune' and Dorothea Baird's 'dainty, pleading narrow-lipped, little torrent of gabble will not do for Shakespeare's Rosalind'. She resembled a 'canary trying to sing Handel'.

Shaw's explanation of Rosalind's popularity need not be taken seriously—that she speaks blank verse for only a few minutes, that she soon gets into doublet and hose, and that like Shaw's Ann Whitefield she takes the initiative and does not wait to be wooed. But Shaw was right to protest about the confusion of life and art by those critics who describe Rosalind as 'a perfect type of womanhood'. To him she was 'simply an extension into five acts of the most affectionate, fortunate, delightful five minutes in the life of a charming woman'. This is not quite true, however, because Rosalind is given misfortunes, as well as a wit that has never been excelled.

It is important to remember that the effect of these scenes in 1600 was rather different from that in the modern theatre: for Shakespeare did not have a Peggy Ashcroft or a Vanessa Redgrave to play his heroine. His original audience would have seen a boy impersonating a woman who was also a princess; they then saw this princess pretending to be Ganymede, and Ganymede pretending to be Rosalind, but in so doing guying the real Rosalind. It is sometimes said that the chief reason why Shakespeare's heroines so often disguised themselves as men was to simplify the task of the actors playing the parts. This may have been true with some of the early plays—the Induction to *The Taming of the Shrew*, Julia in *The Two Gentlemen of Verona*—but Rosalind is far too complex to be explained in this way. In Shakespeare's day there were a number of different images imposed one on the other. We have a boy pretending to be a woman, pretending to be a boy, pretending to be a woman, satirising feminine behaviour. Rosalind, moreover, though pretending to cure Orlando, is making certain she will fail; for she makes him love the pretended Rosalind, and love more the real one of which Ganymede is but the shadow.

In the scenes when Rosalind pretends to be Rosalind, Orlando is merely a feed to her brilliant improvisations. Luckily his character has been established early in the play. His name is that of a famous lover, Orlando Furioso, whose story had been dramatised by Greene; and like his namesake he carves his love's name on tree trunks. He shows both dignity and courage in his struggles with his brother and Charles the wrestler; he saves the lives of Adam and of Oliver; he answers Jaques's cynicism good-humouredly and sensibly; iconographically he has been compared with Hercules, and it is only as a lover that he is at a loss.

Most of Shakespeare's comedy is a critique of love; and in *As You Like It* different kinds of love are examined—the lust of Touchstone, the self-love of Jaques, the pride and vanity of Phebe, and the sentimental idealism of Orlando—are all found wanting. It would be a mistake, then, to regard the play as a mere pot-boiler, although it is obvious from the triumphant epilogue that it made the plot boil merrily: it is a highly sophisticated play that uses all the stalest devices of romantic fiction and popular drama so as to satisfy what Hamlet called 'the judicious' [*Hamlet*, III. ii. 26].

Perhaps the judicious of Shakespeare's day appreciated Touchstone more than we can. He never comes up to Jaques's description of him. Shaw, with pardonable exaggeration, asked, 'Who would endure such humour from anyone but Shakespeare?—an Eskimo would demand his money back if a modern author offered him such fare.' The wit of Rosalind is undimmed by time; but Touchstone is dimmed. Yet Armin, who played the part, must have given such a performance that he opened Shakespeare's eyes to his potentialities and encouraged the poet to write the parts of Feste [in *Twelfth Night*] and Lear's Fool. The name Touchstone alludes to the fact that Armin had been a goldsmith—a nice private joke which is superior to any he is given to speak. (pp. 84-91)

Kenneth Muir, " 'As You Like It'," in his Shakespeare's Comic Sequence, *Barnes & Noble Books, 1979, pp. 84-91.*

DUALITIES

George Ian Duthie

[*In the excerpt below, Duthie discusses* As You Like It *in light of the opposition of order and disorder generally found in Shakespeare's comedies. Although life is comfortable at* **Duke Frederick**'*s court and in* **Oliver**'*s house, the critic declares, moral order has been overthrown by the corrupting influence of materialism and envy. By contrast, the country setting of Arden is depicted as physically hard, but it offers an atmosphere of moral purity. Duthie insists, however, that this is not just a simple contrast between good and evil life.* **Jaques's** *and* **Touchstone's** *critical observations throughout the play establish that Arden is not the ideal alternative to court life. According to Duthie, Shakespeare never endorses escapism to Arden as an end; rather, it is a means by which those who come to the forest can discover the self-knowledge necessary to return to and purify the disordered outside world.*]

[We] find at the beginning of *As You Like It* a court environment in which order has been overthrown. The Duke Frederick has rebelled against his elder brother, the Duke Senior, has defeated him, driven him into exile, and usurped his domain. Here is a double attack on the principle of order—a subject has rebelled against his ruler, and a younger brother has behaved unnaturally towards an elder brother. In this court circle we have another opponent of order in the person of Oliver. He is treating his younger brother Orlando unnaturally. As Orlando says, Oliver keeps him "rustically at home, or, to speak more properly, stays me here at home unkept; for call you that keeping for a gentleman of my birth, that differs not from the stalling of an ox? His horses are bred better . . . He lets me feed with his hinds, bars me the place of a brother, and, as much as in him lies, mines my gentility with my education" [I. i. 7-21].

Oliver does not treat Orlando as a brother should treat a brother according to the divinely established order of things. Oliver is trying to degrade Orlando from his proper status of gentleman to a status far below it—to the status of a peasant ("you have trained me like a peasant, obscuring and hiding from me all gentleman-like qualities" [I. i. 68-70]), and even to the status of an animal. Orlando himself is not at all to blame. He willingly accords Oliver all the privileges of his seniority, and, despite the wrongs he suffers, will not harm Oliver physically. Oliver's animus against him is a result of envy. He says that he does not know why he hates Orlando, and then proceeds to give the reason. "My soul," he says, "yet I know not why, hates nothing more than he. Yet he's gentle, never schooled and yet learned, full of noble device, of all sorts enchantingly beloved, and indeed, so much in the heart of the world, and especially of my own people, who best know him, that I am altogether misprised" [I. i. 165-71]. Compare the Duke Frederick's reasons for driving Rosalind into exile. She was kept at court when her father, the Duke Senior, was banished, in order to be companion to Frederick's daughter Celia. Frederick now drives her out also. Le Beau says that of late the Duke Frederick

> Hath ta'en displeasure 'gainst his gentle
>   niece,
> Grounded upon no other argument
> But that the people praise her for her vir-
>   tues
> And pity her for her good father's sake.
> [I. ii. 278-81]

And Frederick himself says to Celia:

> her smoothness,
> Her very silence and her patience
> Speak to the people, and they pity her.
> Thou art a fool: she robs thee of thy name;
> And thou wilt show more bright and seem
>   more virtuous
> When she is gone.
> [I. iii. 77-82]

The Duke obviously thinks of Rosalind as a danger to his own usurped position (cf. I. iii. 58—"Thou art thy father's daughter"), but there is envy involved also, I think, as there certainly is in Oliver's case.

Shakespeare, then, gives us two parallel cases of opponents of order—Frederick who injures his elder brother, and Oliver who injures his younger brother. Shakespeare elsewhere makes use of such parallelism. In *King Lear,* both Lear and Gloucester err in trusting their elder offspring (two daughters in the one case, one son in the other) and distrusting their younger offspring. We may note also in passing that in Orlando we have a case of a youth who, though he has been denied the appropriate education and upbringing, shows the qualities of mind and character appropriate to his station ("never schooled and yet learned, full of noble device" [I. i. 167]). Shakespeare apparently believes that, no matter how unfavourable the environment, the qualities one inherits will inevitably assert themselves. Compare Guiderius and Arviragus in *Cymbeline*. Though they have been brought up from childhood in the Welsh mountains, unaware of their identity, living a life entirely different from that at court, the mettle appropriate in a King's offspring asserts itself in them by the force of nature.

The court milieu at the beginning of *As You Like It,* then, is one in which disorder flourishes. Life in the forest of Arden is contrasted with "that of painted pomp", with the perilous life in "the envious court" [II. i. 3-4]. This is the "court versus country" theme which recurs in Shakespeare in other plays. In *As You Like It* we have to deal with a very serious degree of disorder in the court life. The fidelity and conscientiousness of the old servant Adam are contrasted by Orlando with the general rule that obtains in this environment:

> O good old man, how well in thee appears
> The constant service of the antique world,
> When service sweat for duty, not for meed!

> Thou art not for the fashion of these times,
> Where none will sweat but for promotion,
> And having that, do choke their service up
> Even with the having: it is not so with
>   thee.
> [II. iii. 56-62]

And it is Adam himself who gives what is perhaps the most striking evidence of the disorder that is rampant. Speaking to Orlando he says:

> Know you not, master, to some kind of
>   men
> Their graces serve them but as enemies?
> No more do yours: your virtues, gentle
>   master,
> Are sanctified and holy traitors to you.
> O, what a world is this, when what is
>   comely
> Envenoms him that bears it!
> [II. iii. 10-15]

"Envenoms" means "kills by poison". In the true order of things a man's graces and virtues should assist him in his life, but here a man's virtues are a danger to him, exciting the envy of others. The true order of things is inverted. Compare again in *Macbeth* the Witches' cry of "Fair is foul, and foul is fair" [I. i. 11ff.]. A man's virtues are "sanctified and holy" things: but, since they here constitute a danger to him, they are spoken of in the passage as "sanctified and holy traitors". The oxymoron helps to emphasize the state of inversion with which we have to deal in the corrupt, disordered environment of the beginning of this play. (pp. 62-5)

[It] may be well to point out here that Shakespeare does not believe that court life must necessarily be corrupt and disordered. In fact he is concerned in *As You Like It* to point out by implication that escapism is no solution: at the end of the play we have most of the exiles returning from the forest of Arden, and we are clearly meant to understand that the court environment has been rid of its evil. Disorder has been set right. (p. 65)

In the comedies . . . Shakespeare concerns himself with exposing follies. In *As You Like It* he does this, too; but here he also concerns himself with vice, with evil. We have already seen that the court environment to which we are introduced at the beginning of the play is one in which disorder is rampant; a subject has dispossessed his ruler; in two cases a brother has behaved unnaturally towards a brother; men's virtues are their enemies; and so on. It is a disordered environment, and the disorder springs from evil. We have seen also that life in the forest of Arden is set in contrast with this corrupt court life. It is a case of a favourite Shakespearian theme—that of court *versus* country.

In the first scene of the play Oliver asks Charles the wrestler "Where will the old duke live?" And Charles replies:

> They say he is already in the forest of
> Arden, and a many merry men with him;

and there they live like the old Robin Hood of England: they say many young gentlemen flock to him every day, and fleet the time carelessly, as they did in the golden world.

[I. i. 114-19]

By "the golden world" is meant the Golden Age, the reign of Saturn on earth, when men lived in a state of ideal happiness and prosperity. There was no conflict, no war, no weapons. Man's food was brought forth from the earth without his having to labour to get it. "Perpetual spring reigned, flowers sprang up without seed, the rivers flowed with milk and wine, and yellow honey distilled from the oaks" [C. M. Gayley in *The Classic Myths in English Literature*].

Now many readers and critics speak as if life in Shakespeare's forest of Arden were, in fact, nothing but idyllic pleasure, happiness, ease, comfort, jollity. When we ourselves get into the forest, at the beginning of Act II, we quickly find that it is by no means altogether that. And when we look attentively at the passage in Act I which we have quoted, spoken by Charles the wrestler, we notice the twice repeated formula "they say". The account of life in the forest of Arden that Charles gives us is the account that is going round the court. It is based on rumour, hearsay. We are supposed to take it that the forest is a long way from the court. Sir Arthur Quiller-Couch points out [in The New Shakespeare: *As You Like It*] that "all the fugitives reach this Forest of Arden leg-weary and almost deadbeat. Sighs Rosalind, 'O Jupiter! how weary are my spirits!' invoking Jupiter as a Ganymede should. Touchstone retorts, 'I care not for my spirits, if my legs were not weary'; and Celia entreats, 'I pray you, bear with me, I cannot go no further' [II. iv. 1ff.]: as, later on, old Adam echoes, 'Dear master, I can go no further' [II. vi. 1]; and again, we remember, Oliver arrives footsore, in rags, and stretches himself to sleep, so dog-tired that even a snake, coiling about his throat, fails to awaken him. It is only the young athlete Orlando who bears the journey well."

Now Shakespeare may well have a symbolic purpose here: the forest of Arden is a place of spiritual refreshment—these people have come from an environment of disorder and evil—their need of spiritual refreshment is symbolized by their physical fatigue. But even if this is in Shakespeare's mind, we are entitled to interpret on a realistic plane as well. Admitting that Rosalind and Celia are girls and Adam almost an octogenarian, so that their fatigue need not be particularly significant, and admitting that Touchstone, the court fool, who, as we find in the play, likes physical comfort, may not be in the best of physical trim, there is the fact that even Oliver is exhausted when he gets to Arden. Arden is a long way from the court, and the journey is a hard one. When the idea of going to Arden is suggested to Rosalind in the first place she says:

Alas, what danger will it be to us,
Maids as we are, to travel forth so far!

[I. iii. 108-09]

Reverting to Charles's report of what life in the forest is like, we can be quite sure that whoever started the rumour had not trudged the long way there to see, and the long way back to report what he had seen. Charles's report is hearsay, and when we get into the forest ourselves we find that it is not in all respects accurate.

The first scene which takes place in the forest is II, i. At the beginning of this scene the exiled Duke speaks to his fellows:

Now, my co-mates and brothers in exile,
Hath not old custom made this life more sweet
Than that of painted pomp? Are not these woods
More free from peril than the envious court?
Here feel we not the penalty of Adam
The seasons' difference?—as the icy fang
And churlish chiding of the winter's wind,
Which, when it bites and blows upon my body,
Even till I shrink with cold, I smile and say
'This is no flattery: these are counsellors
That feelingly persuade me what I am.'

[II. i. 1-11]

What he asks in line 5 is—do we not here in Arden suffer those afflictions to which all men as such are subject, and only those afflictions, not the sort of man-made afflictions one has to suffer in the "envious court"? He contrasts the life in Arden and the life in the envious court very pointedly. At court there is "painted pomp", there is envy, flattery, and so on; it is a dangerous life (but, we may say, though it is only implied, not stated, in the passage, there are physical comforts at court). Here in Arden the moral atmosphere is pure—one does not have to put up with the evil that prevails at court: but there is little physical comfort here in Arden. The Duke uses words which are incisive—he means what he says: he speaks of "the icy fang" and the "churlish chiding" of the winter wind— "fang" is a very meaningful word; he speaks of the wind "biting" his body and of himself "shrinking" with cold, and we feel that the words themselves have bite. We have just got into the forest, and Shakespeare takes care to make us fully aware at the very start that this is a place where life is physically difficult, in contrast to life at court. Life in Arden is hard, physically uncomfortable, *but* the moral atmosphere is pure; life at court is physically comfortable, *but* the moral atmosphere is corrupt, evil.

If we do not realize the physical hardship of life in Arden, then we do not appreciate the distinction between Arden and the court in all its fullness: we blunt an essential point in the play. The Duke Senior speaks of Arden as "this desert city" [II. i. 23] and it is interesting to observe how often this word "desert" is used by those who come to Arden. It may be pointed out that in Shakespeare's day this word could be used to indicate simply an unfrequented place, as opposed to a town or city. But in *As You Like It* we observe that words such as "wild", "abandoned", "uncouth", and "savage" are used in connection with the forest. In II, vi, Orlando calls it "this uncouth forest" and a little later "this desert". In II, vii, he speaks of "this desert inaccessible", and he says: "I thought that all things had been savage here". In V, iv, Jaques de Boys speaks of "this wild wood" and the melancholy Jaques speaks of the Duke Senior's "abandon'd cave". "Uncouth", "savage", "wild", "abandoned"—the impression that such words are intended to convey is quite clear.

We have this fundamental antithesis, then, between Duke Frederick's court where there is physical comfort but moral corruption, and the forest of Arden where there is physical discomfort but moral purity. It is an antithesis between an evil life and a good life; but the matter is not just so simple as that.

The forest of Arden has its critics within the play. The melancholy Jaques is one of them. In II, v, Amiens sings the song "Under the greenwood tree", lyrically glorifying the life in Arden:

> Here shall he see
> No enemy
> But winter and rough weather.
>
> [II. v. 6-8]

And Jaques proceeds to parody the song:

> If it do come to pass
> That any man turn ass,
> Leaving his wealth and ease,
> A stubborn will to please,
> Ducdame, ducdame, ducdame:
> Here shall he see
> Gross fools as he,
> An if he will come to me.
>
> [II. v. 50-7]

According to Jaques, the Duke Senior and the others are gross fools to have left the wealth and ease of their former life at court and to have accepted instead the rigours of life in Arden. Now it is unquestionably true that Shakespeare satirizes Jaques in the play: but Touchstone also criticizes Arden. "Well", says Rosalind on their arrival, "this is the forest of Arden." "Ay," replies Touchstone, "now am I in Arden; the more fool I; when I was at home, I was in a better place: but travellers must be content" [II. iv. 15-18].

This is the attitude of the Fool in *King Lear* also. Having rejected the homes of his unnatural daughters, Lear is out on the heath, with the Fool. And the Fool's attitude is that "court holy-water in a dry house is better than this rain-water out o' door" (by "court holy-water" he means the well-sounding

but empty promises that people make to each other at court). According to the Fool in *Lear* "he that has a house to put's head in has a good headpiece" [III. ii. 10, 25]. That is Touchstone's view in *As You Like It*.

Now Touchstone and the Fool in *Lear* are both, like Feste in *Twelfth Night,* examples of the wise fool—the fool who can often see truth when supposedly wiser men deceive themselves. But in connection with Touchstone and the Fool in *Lear* we must be careful. The words they speak in the passages just quoted are not meant by Shakespeare as a full statement of the attitudes he wants us to take up. Shakespeare is not saying to us in either *As You Like It* or *King Lear* that a life of ease which involves corruption is actually better than a physically hard life which does not involve corruption. The truth which Shakespeare wants us to extract from those words of Touchstone and the Fool in *Lear* is simply that there is something to be said against fleeing to Arden, there is something to be said against going out into the storm. Touchstone and the Fool in *Lear* see that. We are meant to see it. Touchstone's criticism of Arden is valid to that extent. But we are not meant to accept as desirable the evil that the Duke Senior and his friends have escaped from.

As regards the antithesis between the corrupt court of Duke Frederick and the forest of Arden, we are, as we have said, expected to take Arden as morally a better place. But, having established that, Shakespeare very quickly lets us see that there are things to be said against Arden. When you are faced with a corrupt world, Shakespeare seems to say in this play, you should not just run away from it and stay away from it. At the end we have most of the courtier-inhabitants of Arden returning home, and we have the definite prospect of a purification of the court environment itself, the inspiration for the purification having been supplied by the moral atmosphere of Arden. Arden justifies itself by virtue of the fact that it does supply that purifying inspiration.

The villainous Oliver and Duke Frederick both come to Arden with hostile intentions, and both are there converted from their evil thoughts and ways. Oliver is saved by Orlando from dangers of the forest. Orlando has always behaved towards Oliver as a brother should behave towards a brother, but this had never had any salutary effect on Oliver until now in the forest of Arden. I think that Shakespeare means us to regard it as significant that this conversion of Oliver takes place in Arden—Arden is the morally pure place where such conversions naturally happen. Duke Frederick comes to Arden with a force of soldiers, intending to kill his brother: on the very skirts of the forest he meets with "an old religious man" and is converted from his enterprise. Again, I think that Shakespeare means us to take it as significant that this happens in this place, in Arden. The atmosphere of Arden, then, suggests purification. But that purification should, and must, be applied to the world outside it. Escapism is condemned in this play.

Now, while we are in the forest of Arden we hear a great deal about love, that so frequent theme of Shakespearian comedy. Arden is the place where Silvius and Phebe live, and in them we have reflections of the conventional figures of Arcadian love-literature. Silvius is the adoring shepherd, Phebe the disdainful shepherdess. And they are both satirized. Silvius is a self-deluder. Phebe herself reproves him for uttering love-conceits of the conventional kind. Silvius tells her such things as that her eyes will kill him—a conceit of old vintage (compare Chaucer's "Your yen two wol slee me sodenly"). Phebe herself brings the light of cold fact to bear on this, exposing it as a foolish fiction—"there is no force in eyes That can do hurt" [III. v. 26-7]. But Phebe too is a self-deluder. She affects disdainfulness, she puts on airs; but she has little call to do so—she is not by any means so beautiful as she (or Silvius) thinks, and Rosalind, speaking words of true wordly-wisdom, bids her accept a husband while she has a chance—"Sell when you can: you are not for all markets" [III. v. 60]—not everyone would have her. Rosalind chides them both for self-deception and tells them to face *facts*. To her Silvius is a "foolish shepherd":

> 'Tis not her glass, but you, that flatters
> her.
>
> [III. v. 54]

And to Phebe she recommends self-knowledge:

> But, mistress, know yourself: down on
> your knees,
> And thank heaven, fasting, for a good
> man's love.
>
> [III. v. 57-8]

Self-delusion is exposed to the light of down-to-earth common sense. And Touchstone is in agreement with Rosalind in this. The Jane Smile whom Touchstone professes in II, iv, to have loved once, and the Audrey whom he takes in marriage in the forest of Arden, may be crude and unlovely creatures, but they are at least *real*. The lover Orlando, too, is good-naturedly satirized in Arden—the lover who affixes rather poor love-verses to the barks of trees. In the forest of Arden, then, we have the pastoral love scene, and we have the extravagances and sentimentalities and illusions of conventional pastoral love exposed by having the standards of real-life common sense applied to them.

It must be pointed out that Shakespeare is not against romantic love as such, nor does he mean that all men should marry women like Jane Smile and Audrey. It is the extravagances and foolishnesses common amongst some romantic lovers that he satirizes. He attacks the unrealities in the minds of foolish romantic lovers. Jane Smile and Audrey are real. But they are not the only reality. Romantic love purged of extravagance and foolishness is to Shakespeare a fine thing. In this play, romantic love triumphs in the end. It may be pointed out that in the masque of Hymen we have something about as conventional as it might well be. But Shakespeare has made his point, and he can allow himself and his audiences the pleasure of a formal, artificial, but quite beautiful and amusing finish.

In *As You Like It,* then, we again have a Shakespearian comedy which is critical. Both vice and folly are exposed for what they are. And the tissue of criticism is quite complicated. Its complicated nature may be further exemplified by noting the fact that while, as we have seen, the moral atmosphere in Arden is pure, yet Arden is also the home of the shepherd Corin's master who is a man

> of churlish disposition
> And little recks to find the way to heaven
> By doing deeds of hospitality.
>
> [II. iv. 80-2]

And if Touchstone satirizes Arden, he also satirizes the court—

> I have trod a measure; I have flattered a
> lady; I have been politic with my friend,
> smooth with mine enemy; I have undone
> three tailors; I have had four quarrels, and
> like to have fought one.
>
> [V. iv. 44-7]

Again and again we find in dealing with Shakespeare's comedies that we are not dealing in simple blacks and whites. A person or a way of life may be criticized by a standard which is itself then found to be open to criticism. As regards *As You Like It,* it is, I think, fair to say that one way of life (the court life at the beginning) is criticized by a comparison with a second way of life (that in the forest of Arden): but that is in its turn criticized, and what emerges at the end as the dominant impression is a third way of life consisting of an amendment of the first (the purified court), the amendment being due to the influence of the second. (pp. 80-8)

George Ian Duthie, "Comedy," in his Shakespeare, *Hutchinson's University Library, 1951, pp. 57-88.*

John A. Hart

[Hart maintains that Shakespeare depicts two contrasting worlds in As You Like It: **Duke Frederick**'s *court, which is governed by Fortune, and Arden forest, which is dominated by Nature. Here, Fortune signifies not only power and material wealth, but the greed and envy that results from possessing them. By comparison, Nature reflects a more virtuous order that promotes humanity's higher qualities. According to Hart, the corrupt court gradually be-*

comes absorbed by the more harmonious world of Arden until it disappears from the play altogether. The critic ultimately asserts that those characters who have assimilated the lessons from both worlds—significantly, Rosalind, Orlando, and Duke Senior— emerge from the forest at the end of the play to redeem the degenerate court, replacing it with a more balanced and harmonious order.]

As You Like It presents an ideal world, just as *The Merchant of Venice* did. The Forest of Arden has as much romance, as many delightful lovers, more laughter and joy. Like *A Midsummer Night's Dream* and *The Merchant of Venice,* it is built by means of two worlds: the world ruled by Duke Frederick and the world of the Forest of Arden. The effect is not the "separate but equal" envelope structure of *A Midsummer Night's Dream,* nor the interlocking and necessary alternation of *The Merchant of Venice;* instead, Frederick's world first seems dominant and then dissolves and disappears into the world of Arden. Its life seems to be in the play not so much for itself as to help us understand and read its successor.

There is a set of contrasts between the two worlds of this play, but the contrasts are describable not in terms of opposition of power, as in *A Midsummer Night's Dream* and *The Merchant of Venice,* but in terms of attitudes of the dominant characters, as in *Much Ado About Nothing,* and in terms of differences in the settings and of changes in behavior for those characters who are part of both worlds. These contrasts are easy to describe because Shakespeare points the way clearly, making each world an extreme. Our approach will be to examine the qualities of Frederick's world, then to examine the qualities of Arden, and finally out of this contrast to see how the characters behave in each world.

1.

We have seen power presented in *A Midsummer Night's Dream* and *The Merchant of Venice.* In the former, Theseus rules according to judgment or reason; in the latter the Duke of Venice rules according to the laws of the city. Frederick's world is like neither of these. Frederick is in complete command of his court. He has taken his brother's place as Duke, exiled him with many of his followers, seized their lands for his own, and now rules. His high-handed behavior is illustrated by his usurpation of his brother's dukedom, his immediate displeasure at Orlando, the sudden dismissal of Rosalind, the quick seizure of Oliver's lands. What is most characteristic of his power is that it is arbitrary; neither reason nor law seems to control it.

When we look for his motives, we discover two kinds. His greed for power and possessions is obvious. But personal attitudes are just as strong. He treats Orlando rudely because he is the son of Sir Rowland de Boys, an old enemy of his. He comes to

hate Rosalind, giving as his reasons that he does not trust her, that she is her father's daughter, that his own daughter's prestige suffers by comparison; all these are half-hearted rationalizations rooted in jealousy and envy.

Frederick's behavior is echoed if not matched by Oliver's treatment of his brother Orlando and of his servant Adam. Oliver demeans and debases his younger brother; he plots his serious injury and later his death. He acts ignobly toward his faithful household servant Adam. Again, the motivations are mixed. He states explicitly that he wants Orlando's share of their father's bequest. But, beyond that, he wants to get rid of Orlando out of envy, out of fear of comparison made by others:

> . . . my soul (yet I know not why) hates nothing more than he. Yet he's gentle, never school'd and yet learned, full of noble device, of all sorts enchantingly belov'd, and indeed so much in the heart of the world, and especially of my own people, who best know him, that I am altogether mispris'd.
>
> [I. i. 165-71]

Thus, "tyrant Duke" and "tyrant brother" are described in tandem, public and private images of the same behavior. They have the power; they control their world; they do not fear disapproval or reprisal. Charles the wrestler, Lebeau and other lords surrounding Frederick, however many reservations they may have about the morality of their leaders, do not dare to question their authority. They have their own positions to protect.

Those chiefly harmed by the ruthless domination of these men are Orlando and Rosalind. They have committed no fault but they are hated. Their presence too gives definition to Frederick's world. Orlando has virtue, grace, beauty, and strength. Rosalind is beautiful, intelligent, virtuous, honest. Their actions, their reputations, the loyalty they command all testify to these wonders. Yet both of them are conscious of what they do not have—their proper place and heritage in this world. Orlando feels deeply his brother's injury in depriving him of his education and his place in the household. Rosalind is sad at her father's banishment and then indignant at her own dismissal. Both are too virtuous to think of revenge; but they are fully aware that they are being wronged. Having all the graces, they are nevertheless dispossessed of their rightful positions.

Yet, these two have their own power. When they leave Frederick's world, they draw after them others, too loyal, too loving to remain behind. Celia, meant to profit from her cousin's departure, follows Rosalind into banishment without question or remorse. She has already promised that what her father took from Rosalind's father by force, "I will render thee again in affection" [I. ii. 20-1]. And when the test occurs soon after, she meets it at

Marjorie Yates as Celia, Greg Hicks as Silvius, and Sara Kestelman as Rosalind in a 1979 National Theatre production of As You Like It.

once. In her, love triumphs hands down over possession and prestige.

Her example is followed by the Clown. Not only will he "go along o'er the wide world" [I. iii. 132] with Celia out of loyalty to her; he has also, in Frederick's world, lost place just as Rosalind has. There "fools may not speak wisely what wise men do foolishly" [I. ii. 86-7]. Since he has lost his usefulness as a fool, he may as well leave with Celia and Rosalind. And Adam is in comparable situation. To Oliver, he is an "old dog," to be thrust aside. But so strong is his loyalty to Orlando that he will give him his savings, serve him, accompany him wherever he goes.

These gifted models of humanity, Rosalind and Orlando, draw out of Frederick's world the loving, the truthful, the loyal. Frederick and Oliver, seeking to control and ultimately to crush their enemies, only succeed in driving away other worthwhile characters with them.

The world of Frederick is simple in structure. The powerful control, but they envy the virtuous; the

virtuous attract, but they want to have their rightful place. Those in authority triumph in their own terms, but things happen to them in the process. They turn against each other—Frederick would devour Oliver as he has so many others. Their world, as it grows more violent, diminishes in importance until it disappears altogether. The virtuous are undefeated though displaced.

2.

In contrast to the specific placing of Frederick's world, the Forest reaches beyond the bounds of any particular place, any specific time. Its setting is universalized nature. All seasons exist simultaneously. Duke Senior speaks of "the icy fang And churlish chiding of the winter's wind" [II. i. 6-7]; but Orlando pins verses to "a palm tree," "abuses our young plants with carving," and "hangs odes upon hawthorns, and elegies on brambles" [III. ii. 360-62]; and Rosalind and Celia live at the "tuft of olives." Again, Orlando does not wish to leave Adam "in the bleak air"; but in the next scene Jaques has met a fool who "bask'd him in the sun." The songs continue this mixture: "Here shall he see No enemy But winter and rough weather" [II. v. 6-8] alongside "the greenwood tree" and "the sweet bird's throat" [II. v. 1, 4] both in the same song, or the alternation between the "winter wind" [II. vii. 174] and the "spring time, the only pretty ring time" [V. iii. 19], dominant notes in two other songs. If the Forest is not to be defined in season, neither is it limited to any particular place. The variety of trees already indicates this; the variety of creatures supports it: sheep, deer, a green and gilded snake, a lioness. Meek and domestic creatures live with the untamed and fierce.

Yet the Forest is more than an outdoors universalized, which largely accommodates itself to the mood and attitude of its human inhabitants. It is a setting in which the thoughts and images of those who wander through it expand and reach out to the animate, as if the Forest were alive with spirits taken for granted by everyone. Even so mundane a pair as Touchstone and Audrey, discussing her attributes—unpoetical, honest, foul—assign these gifts to the gods. Orlando, who is able at first meeting Rosalind only to utter "Heavenly Rosalind," is suddenly released to write expansive verses in praise of her, some of which place her in a spiritual context:

> . . . heaven Nature charg'd
> That one body should be fill'd
> With all graces wide-enlarg'd. . . .
> Thus Rosalind of many parts
> By heavenly synod was devis'd. . . .
>   [III. ii. 141-43, 149-50]

Phoebe seconds his view by giving Rosalind qualities beyond the human:

> Art thou god to shepherd turn'd,
> That a maiden's heart hath burn'd? . . .
> Why, thy godhead laid apart,
> Warr'st thou with a woman's heart?
>   [IV. iii. 40-1, 44-5]

And Rosalind, replying to Celia's finding Orlando under a tree, "like a dropp'd acorn," says, "It may well be call'd Jove's tree, when it drops such fruit" [III. ii. 235-37]. Elsewhere he is "most gentle Jupiter." And she herself takes the name of Ganymed, cupbearer to Jupiter. Further, in her games with Orlando, she describes "an old religious uncle" who taught her (or him, for she is then playing Ganymed) how to speak well and who imparted knowledge of love, of women's faults, of the forlorn look of the true lover. To this fiction, she joins the later story of how, "since [she] was three year old, [she has] convers'd with a magician, most profound in his art, and yet not damnable" [V. ii. 60-1]. She improvises, but it fits the expansive attributes of the Forest.

But in addition to mind-expanding qualities, the Forest produces some real evidence of its extraordinary powers. Oliver, upon his first appearance in the Forest, is beset by the green and gilded snake

(of envy?) and by the lioness (of power?), but when these two are conquered, his whole behavior changes. And Frederick, intent on destroying his brother, meets an "old religious man" and

> After some question with him, was converted
> Both from his enterprise and from the world.
>   [V. iv. 161-62]

And these events harmonize with Rosalind's producing Hymen, the god of weddings, to perform the ceremony and bless the four pairs of lovers. The Forest is a world of all outdoors, of all dimensions of man's better nature, of contact with man's free imagination and magical happenings.

The Forest has still another quality in its setting. It is not timeless but it reflects the slow pace and the unmeasurable change of the earth. The newcomers notice the difference from the world outside. Orlando comments that "there's no clock in the forest" [III. ii. 300-01]; Rosalind tells us "who Time ambles withal, who Time trots withal, who Time gallops withal, and who he stands still withal" [III. ii. 309-11]. And Touchstone, as reported by Jaques, suggests the uselessness of measuring changes in the Forest by the clock:

> 'Tis but an hour ago since it was nine,
> And after one hour more 'twill be eleven,
> And so from hour to hour, we ripe and ripe,
> And then from hour to hour, we rot and rot;
> And thereby hangs a tale.
>   [II. vii. 24-8]

But he does notice, too, the withering away of man at the Forest's slow changes, a truism later elaborated by Jaques in his seven-ages-of-man speech.

But the qualities of the setting are only part of what goes into the definition of the Forest world. The natives to the Forest make their contributions as well. Corin and Silvius and Phoebe, Audrey and William and Sir Oliver Martext all appear, without seeming consequence or particular plot relevance, put there to show off different dimensions of the Forest, to strike their attitudes, to stand in contrast with the characters newly come from another world, and then, like the deer and the sheep and the snake and the lioness, to retire into the Forest again until or unless called upon by their visitors.

These characters have their separate occupations. Corin is an old shepherd, Silvius a young one, Phoebe—his beloved—a shepherdess, Audrey a goat girl, William a country bumpkin, Martext a clergyman. But these assignments are vaguely expressed. Martext, for instance, has professional status but mainly in his own eyes: "ne'er a fantastical knave of them all shall flout me out of my calling" [III. iii. 106-07]. But Jaques dismisses him as a phony and Touchstone wants him to officiate at his marriage to Audrey because he believes him to be a fake. They all seem satisfied to have the name of an occupation rather than the function itself.

But their thoughts are also dissociated from ownership, ambition, achievement. Corin, wanting to help Rosalind and Celia, says:

> [I] wish, for her sake more than for mine own,
> My fortunes were more able to relieve her;
> But I am shepherd to another man,
> And do not shear the fleeces that I graze.
> [II. iv. 76-9]

The man who owns the sheepcote is not hospitable, is not even there, and has his land up for sale. Silvius, who is supposed to be buying the flock and pasture, "little cares for buying any thing" [II. iv. 90]. Ownership is several steps removed from Corin, and until Rosalind offers to make the purchase he is uncertain who the landlord employing him is; nor does he particularly care.

Later, he generalizes his attitude toward life:

> I am a true laborer: I earn that I eat, get that I wear, owe no man hate, envy no man's happiness, glad of other men's good, content with my harm, and the greatest of my pride is to see my ewes graze and my lambs suck.
> [III. ii. 73-7]

The other natives share his view. William, Audrey's country lover, confesses to his name, to a certain unspecified amount of wealth, to having "a pretty wit," to loving Audrey, and to lack of learning; but when he is threatened by Touchstone and told to stay away from Audrey, he departs with "God rest you merry, sir" [V. i. 59], and we see no more of him or his love for Audrey. If it is love, it is love detached, without passion or claims.

Silvius dedicates himself entirely to love, Phoebe to being the scornful beloved and later the impassioned wooer of Ganymed. They do not express conflict or even action so much as attitude, as pose. "Loose now and then A scatt'red smile," Silvius says to Phoebe, "and that I'll live upon" [III. v. 103-04].

Audrey would be an honest woman, "a woman of the world," but she will not choose between lovers, she will not question Martext's legitimacy, she will be led by Touchstone wherever he wishes. Her future with Touchstone is not bright, as Jaques points out, but she doesn't question it.

In all these natives there is a non-critical quality, an innocence, a lack of competitiveness that suits well with the Forest world and helps to describe it. But Shakespeare gives us still other ways of distinguishing this world from Frederick's. Early in the play Celia and Rosalind engage in idle banter about the two goddesses, Fortune and Nature, who share equally in the lives of men. Fortune "reigns in gifts of the world," Rosalind says, "not in the lineaments of Nature" [I. ii. 41-2]. It is a shorthand way of distinguishing the Forest world from Frederick's. Frederick's world is a world of Fortune, from which the children of Nature are driven. Power, possession, lands, titles, authority over others characterize that world, and men to live there must advance their careers or maintain their positions in spite of everything. The Forest world is completely Nature's. In its natives the idleness, the lack of ambition and combativeness, the carelessness about ownership and possession, the interest in the present moment without plan for the future, all are signs of a Fortune-less world. Instead there is awareness of the gifts inherent from birth in the individual, no matter how untalented or unhandsome (Audrey's response to her foulness or William's self-satisfaction, for instance). These are "the lineaments of Nature," the basic materials of one's being. In the Forest, the natives neither can nor aspire to change them. And the qualities of the setting—universality, gradual rather than specific change, a linkage between the outdoors world and a projected though perhaps imaginary supernatural, these too are compatible with the world of Nature, Fortune having been removed. Both Fortune and Nature, then, are abbreviated terms to epitomize the kinds of worlds represented by Frederick's on the one hand and the Forest's on the other.

One further means of defining the Forest world emerges with the character of Jaques. He has been in the outside world, but he has chosen the Forest and he is its most eloquent spokesman. He is the personification of the speculative man. He will not react when Orlando threatens his life: "And you will not be answer'd with reason, I must die" [II. vii. 100-01]. He will not dance or rejoice in the final scene. He would prevent action in others if he could. He weeps that the Duke's men kill the deer, he would keep Orlando from marring the trees with his poems, he advises Touchstone not to "be married under a bush like a beggar" [III. iii. 84]. He is like the natives of the Forest, ambitionless, fortuneless, directionless.

Instead, he gives his attention to the long view and the abstract view. He is delighted when he overhears Touchstone philosophizing about time; he projects human neglect in the deer at the coming of death for one of their company; he argues the innocent indifference of the deer to corruption and inhumanity in man:

> Thus most invectively he pierceth through
> The body of the country, city, court,
> Yea, and of this our life, swearing that we
> Are mere usurpers, tyrants, and what's worse,
> To fright the animals and to kill them up
> In their assign'd and native dwelling-place.
> [II. i. 58-63]

When he would invoke the privilege of the fool to

"Cleanse the foul body of th' infected world" [II. vii. 60] the Duke replies that with his past experience of evil he would succeed only in doing "Most mischievous foul sin" [II. vii. 64]. In the abstract (in the Forest), his proposal sounds good; in the world of action it would be damaging.

But his greatest eloquence is saved for his seven-ages-of-man speech [II. vii. 139-66]. It is an official acknowledgement of Nature's supremacy over man and the insignificance of man's affairs on the stage of the world. The movement of the speech is circular, from Nature through the efforts to shape natural gifts in man, to Fortune's world, and back to Nature again. Thus, the helplessness of infancy gives way to "the whining schoolboy" which in turn is followed by "the lover, Sighing like furnace, with a woeful ballad Made to his mistress' eyebrow." In the first three, we find pleasantly humorous recognition of the supremacy of Nature and the attempts to shape and apply natural gifts in man. The fourth and fifth, the soldier and the justice, suggest the ascendancy of Fortune in man's life—the soldier seeking the "bubble reputation," the justice "Full of wise saws and modern instances." But these temporary achievements disappear as Nature reclaims her own, first in the "slipper'd pantaloon" whose "big manly voice" turns "again toward childish treble" and finally in frightening second childishness, "Sans teeth, sans eyes, sans taste, sans every thing." In such a view, and in the view most congenial to the Forest world, "All the world's a stage, And all the men and women merely players." There are no consequences that matter.

3.

Duke Senior, like Jaques, has had experience in both worlds. He too is being "philosophical." Their life in the Forest

> Finds tongues in trees, books in the running brooks,
> Sermons in stones, and good in every thing.
>
> [II. i. 16-17]

He and his men "fleet the time carelessly, as they did in the golden world" [I. i. 118-19]. But for the Duke and his men, it is only play-acting. They appear in one scene as Foresters, in another as outlaws. He himself has lost his name: he is Duke Senior, not specifically named like Frederick. More than that, he has nothing serious to do. While his brother is seizing Oliver's lands and organizing a search for his daughter and seeking to destroy him, he is contemplating a deer hunt or asking for Jaques to dispute with or feasting or asking someone to sing. Duke Senior has no function to perform; he cannot be a Duke except in title. All the philosophical consolations he may offer himself and his men cannot alleviate the loss he feels at being usurped and banished by his brother. When Orlando reminds him of the outside world, he confesses: "True is it that we have seen better days" [II. vii. 120] and reinforces this reminiscence of the past by commenting on his present condition:

> Thou seest we are not all alone unhappy:
> This wide and universal theatre
> Presents more woeful pageants than the scene
> Wherein we play in.
>
> [II. vii. 136-39]

He is remarking on shared misery; he is using the same imagery of playing used by Jaques. But for Jaques it is made speculative, objectified; for Duke Senior, he and his fellows are participating in a play. His longings are elsewhere. It is not surprising that at the end, he resumes leadership over everyone and plans to return to active rule of his dukedom.

What is true of him is true with more immediacy of others newly arrived in the Forest. The clown, who assumes the name Touchstone, undergoes the same ambivalence. His first reaction to the Forest is negative: "Ay, now am I in Arden, the more fool I. When I was at home, I was in a better place" [II. iv. 16-17]. He is no longer practicing his profession of fool, since he is in a fortuneless world: "Call me not fool till heaven hath sent me fortune" [II. vii. 19]. Instead, he assumes several other roles, a liberating exercise for him; the Forest allows him to become expansive, imaginative, to take on the personage of the courtier, of the philosopher, of the wit, of the lover, to condescend to others at random and without consequence. To be able to speak his mind, to express himself, is the Forest's gift to him.

On the other hand, in all these poses, he undercuts the natives of the Forest. He mocks the passionate outbursts of Silvius in praise of his mistress by making the extravagant claim but changing the imagery to mundane and sensual terms: "I remember the kissing of her batler and the cow's dugs that her pretty chopp'd hands had milk'd" [II. iv. 48-50]. He further shows off the silly self-absorption of Nature's pastoral lovers: he himself plays the lover in the Forest. The object of his love, Audrey the goat girl, has neither understanding nor beauty. He sees the disparity between his wit and her simplicity; he would have her poetical, "for the truest poetry is the most feigning" [III. iii. 19-20], he would not have her honest; he is glad she is foul. He strongly suspects that marriage to her would mean cuckoldry, yet he will have her at whatever cost: "man hath his desires; and as pigeons bill, so wedlock would be nibbling" [III. iii. 80-2]. He joins the others in the rush to be married at the end of the play:

> I press in here, sir, amongst the rest of the country copulatives, to swear and to forswear, according as marriage binds and blood breaks.
>
> [V. iv. 55-7]

At other times he has confrontations with Corin

and with William, the two natives seemingly most attuned to Nature's laws. Touchstone condescends to them, playing the courtier and the man of the world to men he treats as simpletons and inferiors. William, the rival for Audrey's hand, he questions as one would a child, and then threatens as one would an inferior being, and William, with no knowledge of position, with no wit, with no competitiveness, is easily routed. Touchstone challenges Corin too. Having never been in court, Corin is damned, says Touchstone. When Corin tries to defend life in the Forest, claiming that the manners of the court are not suitable to life in the country, Touchstone parries every explanation Corin gives with a witty rationalization. By measuring the life of the Forest against life at court, he brings together separate standards in the light of which either life by itself is preposterous. The Forest, which is the only way of life for all six of these natives, is by other values extremely limited. The importance of physical desire (the love affair with Audrey), of competitive relationships (the rivalry with William), of realistic appraisal (the reduction of Silvius's outbursts) is inherent in Touchstone's behavior; finally, the need for place, for function, for relationships with others runs throughout his criticism of Forest life:

> Corin. And how like you this shepherd's life, Master Touchstone?
> Touch. Truly, shepherd, in respect of itself, it is a good life; but in respect that it is a shepherd's life, it is naught.
>
> [III. ii. 11-15]

Touchstone's is the outsider's view of the Forest. His responses are the touchstones which set off the Forest natives most clearly. As Jaques is the "official" voice of the Forest, Touchstone is the "official" voice of the world outside.

The Forest is liberating for the newly arrived lovers, too. Oliver is freed from the burden of envy and absorption with power; and as a consequence he and Celia can fall immediately in love. So satisfying is it that Oliver would give up his possessions to Orlando and live a shepherd's life forever. Celia has assumed the name Aliena, left her father's court so completely that she never thinks of him again, and falls utterly in love when she meets the reformed Oliver. She has never been tied to the idea of possession or prestige and so she is easily open to the lures of the Forest.

Whereas Oliver's and Celia's love experience is muted, described rather than dramatized, Orlando's and Rosalind's is the heart of the play. Orlando, idle in the Forest and "love-shak'd," expresses his love for the lost Rosalind by writing passionate verses for her and hanging them on the trees; later he plays the game of wooing the young man Ganymed as if he were his Rosalind. He makes his protestations of love, he makes pretty speeches of admiration, he takes part in the mock-marriage ceremony, he promises to return to his wooing by a certain time. But his playing the game of courtship is as nothing compared to the game of deception and joyful play that Rosalind, safe in her disguise as Ganymed, engages in when she is with him. Her spirits soar and her imagination and wit expatiate freely and delightedly on the subject of men in love, on their looks, on their behavior, on the cure of their disease, and then specifically on Orlando's mad humor of love, on how he should woo, on how he can be cured through the lore she (he) acquired from the "old religious uncle." The Forest gives both of them an opportunity to play parts free of the restraints that might accompany acknowledged wooing.

But though their fanciful indulgence leads them to forget the rest of the world—Rosalind cries out, "But what talk we of fathers, when there is such a man as Orlando?" [III. iv. 38-9]—the play is only play and basically incompatible with their real natures.

Orlando's behavior outside and in the Forest suggests responsibility, suggests need for significant action. To him the Forest is a "desert inaccessible" and those in it "Lose and neglect the creeping hours of time" [II. vii. 110, 112]; he himself will keep appointments with Duke Senior, he will care for his loyal servant Adam, he will save his brother's endangered life. He has a general distaste for the company of the speculative Jaques, and he finally gives up the wooing game entirely: "I can live no longer by thinking" [V. ii. 50]. He is Nature's child, but he insists on living by Fortune's standards.

And Rosalind is even more emphatic in the attitudes founded in the outside world. Her first act in coming into the Forest is to buy a sheepcote; she uses the imagery of the market place when she is judging others: "Sell when you can, you are not for all markets" [III. v. 60], she says to Phoebe; "I fear you have sold your own lands to see other men's; then to have seen much, and to have nothing, is to have rich eyes and poor hands" [IV. i. 22-5], she says to Jaques. With Silvius and Phoebe, she has small patience. To him she says, "Wilt thou love such a woman? What, to make thee an instrument, and play false strains upon thee? . . . I see love hath made thee a tame snake" [IV. iii. 67-8, 69-70]. The natives receive short shrift from her, but she herself is in the depths of love for Orlando, and in her playing with Orlando partly mocks her own condition.

These two lovers, thoroughly based in the real world, are given the opportunity to exhibit, to spell out, a private love relationship thwarted or only implicit in earlier comedies. Portia and Bassanio, we pointed out, meet publicly and Bassanio has only begun to recognize the individuality of Portia at the end of the play; their public figures and their public relationships are the essential ones in *The*

Merchant of Venice. In *Much Ado About Nothing* Beatrice and Benedick meet as private individuals, but they do not know or at least acknowledge their love for one another until very late in the play, and their recognition coincides with a discovery of the empty world in which they must live. But Rosalind and Orlando have a chance to meet and to play in a world where public cares are temporarily set aside, where each can express love for the other without embarrassment, where each can feel the presence and the personality of the other, and especially where we can watch these most gifted of Nature's children completely free and private with one another. Though the world of Fortune is part of their consciousness and their future, this holiday of love is a complement to the all-public relationship of Portia and Bassanio and an equal complement to the ever-present social pressures on Beatrice and Benedick.

4.

Given the characteristics of the Forest world, given the attachments of Duke Senior, Touchstone, Orlando, and Rosalind to the outside world, the resolution of the play can be foreseen. Under the spell of the Forest, pretended marriage takes place between Orlando and Rosalind (as Ganymed) with Celia officiating. Marriage almost takes place between Touchstone and Audrey with Martext officiating. In the last scene, all four couples are married in the only way possible in the Forest, by the appearance of Hymen, god of marriage, to perform the ceremony: "Then is there mirth in heaven, When earthly things made even Atone together" [V. iv. 108-10]. Hymen joins the lovers and reintroduces the Duke to his daughter: "Good Duke, receive thy daughter, Hymen from heaven brought her . . . " [V. iv. 111-12]. He thus re-establishes the father-daughter relationship first devised through his means at Rosalind's birth. The hiatus caused by the Duke's exile and by the disguises in the Forest is broken and the societal structure of father and daughter is made clear once again.

With the appearance of Touchstone another relationship is given social standing. When he is introduced to Duke Senior by Jaques, Touchstone immediately resumes his professional position as fool. His comment on the life of the courtier, his long argument on "the quarrel on the seventh cause" is appreciated by the Duke: "I like him very well"; "By my faith, he is very swift and sententious"; "He uses his folly like a stalking-horse, and under the presentation of that he shoots his wit" [V. iv. 53, 62-3, 106-07]. A rapport is established between them which suggests that Duke will be Duke and master again and Fool will be Fool and servant. Adam, nearing Jaques' seventh age of man, has disappeared into the world of nature. But a new loyalty and interdependence is about to begin.

A final relationship is re-established among the sons of Rowland de Boys. Through its magic the Forest has brought Orlando and Oliver together. Now a third brother appears, carrier of the news of Frederick's resignation—"His crown bequeathing to his banish'd brother" [V. iv. 163]—and agent for restoring his own brothers to the outside world. His coming not only reunites all three but makes a necessary link to the outside world for them. It also sounds an echo: Charles the Wrestler sought advancement and distinction by breaking the ribs of three of his victims, all brothers. That was a symbol of the way power broke blood relationships in Frederick's world—Frederick with his niece and daughter, Oliver with his brother. Now separated families are reunited and friends.

That he is a young Jaques is also significant, arriving as the melancholy Jaques prepares to go off to another part of the forest. This young man prepares the way to future life in the world outside; the older is bound to the inactivity and the speculation of the Forest world.

But they have not yet left the Forest. Duke Senior's speech assuming his authority shows that he is in command of both the Forest world and his former Dukedom and that each of them is part of his experience and momentarily under his perfect control. Duke Senior's reference to the lands which will be given to the brothers is balanced and ambiguous:

> Welcome, young man;
> Thou offer'st fairly to thy brothers' wedding:
> To one his lands withheld, and to the other
> A land itself at large, a potent dukedom.
> [V. iv. 166-69]

To Oliver, the lands taken from him by Frederick are returned; to Orlando, his son-in-law, the heritage of his dukedom is given. Yet there is just a suspicion that the gifts might be directed the other way: to Orlando, whose lands have been taken from him by Oliver, will be returned his father's lands; to Oliver, the Forest world where he has determined to remain; for the Forest is without a ruler and without bounds, a place where he who does not have to own or possess anything may feel himself a powerful ruler.

This distinction between the brothers is followed by a statement of the Duke's own intention in regard to the Forest and the world outside it:

> First, in this forest let us do those ends
> That here were well begun and well begot;
> And after, every of this happy number,
> That have endur'd shrewd days and nights with us,
> Shall share the good of our returned fortune,
> According to the measure of their states.
> [V. iv. 170-75]

By "those ends," presumably, he means the marriages which have been the contribution and the fruit of the Forest world. Then his attention will be turned to the world outside the forest, where they will enjoy their "returned fortune, According to the measure of their states." Place and prestige are implied here, possession a necessary element. Both Forest and his Dukedom are in his mind and paired. And the retention of both worlds continues right to the end when he repeats the words *fall* and *measure* once to apply them to Nature's world and once to apply them to Fortune's:

> Mean time, forget this new-fall'n dignity,
> And fall into our rustic revelry.
> Play, music, and you brides and bride-
>   grooms all,
> With measure heap'd in joy, to th' mea-
>   sures fall.
>   [V. iv. 176-79]

"New-fall'n" applies to his returned Dukedom, "fall" applies to the current Forest life. "Measure heap'd in joy" could apply to both worlds, but it recalls for us "the measure of their states" and the assumption of rank and position looked upon as normal in Fortune's world; the final "measures" refers to the dance they will do in the Forest. We are left, after this balanced holding of both worlds at once, with the departure of Jaques and with the dance which is the sign of the harmony of the moment.

The Epilogue is all that marks the return to the workaday world, spoken by the boy who has played Rosalind. He has gone from the heights of role-playing—this boy playing Rosalind playing Ganymed playing Rosalind—step by step back down the ladder of fantasy to speak directly to the men and women in the audience before him. He speaks of attraction between the sexes, of possible kisses, of the need for appreciation and applause. It is not the Forest nor the Duke's realm. It is the theater, the living reality of the image used so extensively in the play.

What is left of the play? A dream of power and evil transmuted into a dream where power and evil have disappeared. The result has been joy, romance, and various dimensions of love. The lovers of the earlier plays are translated in *As You Like It* into a world which suggests they can combine completeness of personality with private expression of love; but the world is a dream, a play world. *As You Like It* is the closest Shakespeare gets to the realization of such a dream; *Twelfth Night* explores its comic failure. (pp. 81-97)

> *John A. Hart, "As You Like It: The Worlds of Fortune and Nature," in his* Dramatic Structure in Shakespeare's Romantic Comedies, *Carnegie-Mellon University Press, 1980, pp. 81-97.*

John Shaw

[*Shaw focuses on the meaning of* **Rosalind's** *and* **Celia's** *debate over Fortune and Nature (I.*

ii. 40ff.), determining that this is a philosophic controversy with which Shakespeare's Elizabethan audience would have been plainly familiar. In Renaissance tradition, the goddess Fortune is depicted as the symbol of inconstancy and change. She is illustrated as either blind or blind-folded, sitting on a spherical throne with one foot either on a slippery ball or a trap and one hand placed upon a wheel. The goddess Nature, on the other hand, represents beauty, strength, nobility, courage, and—most significantly—wisdom and virtue. With open eyes, she sits firmly on a four-square pedestal, holding the mirror of Prudence that represents self-knowledge. In the classical tradition, whenever a conflict arose between Fortune and Nature, the latter, through her superior wisdom and virtuousness, would prevail. In this essay, Shaw examines how the properties of both goddesses affect the plot and character development of As You Like It, *asserting that each of the major characters is in some way affected by the conflicts between them. In observance with the classical tradition, these conflicts are resolved at the end of the play when Nature overthrows Fortune and restores a more harmonious order for the characters.*]

When Rosalind draws a careful distinction between the gifts of Fortune and the gifts of Nature in the second scene of *As You Like It,* she is alluding to a familiar conception of the separate offices of the two goddesses. Few in Shakespeare's audience could have failed to recognize the Renaissance cliché that Fortune did indeed reign "in the gifts of the world", while Nature's bounties were to be found in the "lineaments" of the face and character [I. ii. 40ff.]. Moreover, Celia's reply that "Nature hath given us Wit to flout at Fortune" further refers to the philosophical tradition which considered the two goddesses as rivals, a conception current in Elizabethan times, and one reaching back to antiquity. A careful reading of the play will in fact show that behind the gay romancing of the characters throughout *As You Like It* there is a basic philosophic strife between Fortune and Nature that would be obvious to the Renaissance. Although it would be far from the point to be like Jaques and "moralize this spectacle" by insisting that Shakespeare's delightful comedy be read didactically, still the underlying philosophical strife between Fortune and Nature may be seen to form an important pattern throughout the play, affecting both character and plot.

Obviously, Shakespeare was well acquainted with the Renaissance tradition of Fortune and Nature. Fortune, the blind goddess who was so often depicted as sitting infirmly upon her throne—often a sphere—her foot upon a slippery ball or a treacherous trap, and her hand upon her wheel, was familiar to all, as Fluellen amply testifies:

> Fortune is painted blind, with a muffler
> afore her eyes, to signify to you that For-

tune is blind; and she is painted also with a wheel, to signify to you, which is the moral of it, that she is turning, and inconstant, and mutability, and variation; and her foot, look you, is fixt upon a spherical stone, which rolls, and rolls, and rolls:—in good truth, the poet makes a most excellent description of it: Fortune is an excellent moral.

[*Henry V,* III. vi. 30-8]

Fortune's rival, Nature, bestowed the gifts of body and mind upon her followers: beauty, strength, nobility, and courage, but especially wisdom and virtue, with which man could flout at Fortune. By a kind of extension Nature was often represented by the goddess Sapientia or Virtue, who might sit firmly on a four-square pedestal, eyes open, holding the mirror of Prudence, signifying self-knowledge. From classical times it was felt that when a conflict between Fortune and Nature occurred, wisdom or character, the gifts of Nature, would prevail. As Shakespeare put it in *Antony and Cleopatra,* "Wisdom and Fortune combatting together, if that the former dare but what it can, no chance may shake it" [III. xiii. 79-80]; or, as Machiavelli comments over some brave words of Camillus:

These words show that a truly great man is ever the same under all circumstances; and if his fortune varies, exalting him at one moment and oppressing him at another, he himself never varies, but always preserves a firm courage, which is so closely interwoven with his character that everyone can readily see that the fickleness of fortune has no power over him.

[*Discourses,* III, xxxi]

The motif of Fortune and Nature, or wit, "combatting together" is introduced early in the first act of *As You Like It,* during the witty repartee between Rosalind and Celia. "Let us sit and mock the good housewife Fortune from her wheel," cries Celia:

Rosalind. I would we could do so; for her benefits are mightily misplaced; and the bountiful blind woman doth most mistake in her gifts to women.

Celia. 'Tis true; for those that she makes fair, she scarce makes honest; and those that she makes honest, she makes very ill-favour'dly.

Rosalind. Nay, now thou goest from Fortune's office to Nature's: Fortune reigns in the gifts of the world, not in the lineaments of Nature.

Celia. No? when Nature hath made a fair creature, may not she by Fortune fall into the fire? Though Nature hath given us wit to flout at Fortune, hath not Fortune sent in this fool to cut off argument?

Rosalind. Indeed, there is Fortune too hard for Nature, when Fortune makes Na-

ture's natural the cutter off of Nature's wit.

Celia. Peradventure this is not Fortune's work neither, but Nature's: who perceiveth our natural wits too dull to reason of such goddesses, and hath sent this natural for our whetstone.

[I. ii. 31-54]

While this engaging banter need not be interpreted too seriously, on one level the passage may serve as the plot of *As You Like It* in epitome: when the play opens the good housewife Fortune has obviously "mightily misplaced" her benefits, the good Duke Senior having been banished by his "humorous" brother, and the naturally refined and popular Orlando having been cheated out of his patrimony by Oliver. Nor is it long before Rosalind is outrageously exiled by the usurping Duke Frederick. Then, during the course of the comedy, those worthy and contented followers of Duke Senior, who bear their injustices with wisdom, living cheerfully in the Forest of Arden, may be said to "flout at Fortune", until at the end she does indeed bestow her gifts on the deserving.

A close examination of the characters will reveal that generally speaking, Shakespeare has defined all of them—Rosalind, Orlando, Duke Senior, Duke Frederick, and Oliver—in terms of the conflict between Fortune and Nature. Rosalind, who speaks of herself as "one out of suits with Fortune" [I. ii. 246], accepts her misfortune gracefully, manifesting both wisdom and prudence. Moreover, when she is banished from the court to the forest, she and Celia go "in content / To liberty, and not to banishment" [I. iii. 137-38]. Orlando, besides his extraordinary strength and courage, has been endowed with natural wisdom and nobility:

he is gentle; never school'd, and yet learned: full of noble device; of all sorts enchantingly beloved; and, indeed . . . much in the heart of the world.

[I. i. 166-69]

It is noteworthy that he receives the news of his brother's treachery with equanimity, expressing his future plans in phrases similar to those of Rosalind and Celia: "We'll go along together, / And ere we have thy youthful wages spent, / We'll light upon some settled low content" [II. iii. 66-8]. Even old Adam, incidentally, scoffs at Fortune's gifts:

Yet Fortune cannot recompense me better Than to die well and not my master's debtor.

[II. iii. 75-6]

Finally, Duke Senior mocks Fortune by accepting his exile cheerfully, as seen in his speech in praise of adversity, beginning:

Now, my co-mates and brothers in exile, Hath not old custom made this life more sweet

Than that of painted pomp? Are not these
woods
More free from peril than the envious
court?

[II. i. 1-4]

This speech wins the admiration of Amiens:

Happy is your Grace
That can translate the stubbornness of
Fortune
Into so quiet and so sweet a style.

[I. ii. 18-20]

It has been pointed out that the goddess Sapientia was usually depicted with her mirror of Prudence in her hand, as an indication of the prime Socratic virtue of self-knowledge. In *As You Like It* each of the protagonists, as we might expect, clearly manifests an interest in self-knowledge. Orlando, for instance, rebukes Jaques with, "I will chide no breather in the world but myself, against whom I know most faults" [III. ii. 280-81], and Duke Senior, we remember, welcomes the "churlish chiding of winter's wind" as "counsellors / That feelingly persuade me what I am" [II. i. 7, 10-11]. Also, it is Rosalind who upbraids Silvius for his foolish servility to Phebe in terms definitely recalling Sapientia and her mirror:

'Tis not her glass, but you, that flatters her
And out of you she sees herself more
proper
Than any of her lineaments can show her.
But mistress, know yourself.

[III. v. 54]

The antagonists, Duke Frederick, the "humorous", capricious brother and usurper of Duke Senior's lands, and Oliver, Orlando's wicked brother, have benefited from the turn of the goddess Fortune's wheel. Lacking Nature's gifts of wisdom and self-knowledge, they have forfeited Nature's contentment in a perilous attempt to acquire Fortune's gifts of the world. But in order to win Fortune's gifts they must resort to policy and cunning and other indirect methods, some of which Oliver reveals to us when he speaks slanderously about Orlando to Charles:

he will practise against thee by poison, entrap thee by some treacherous device, and never leave thee till he hath ta'en thy life by some indirect means or other.

[I. i. 149-53]

And Touchstone's words, directed to simple William, describe equally well the practices of the man of Fortune:

I will kill thee, make thee away, translate thy life into death, thy liberty into bondage. I will deal in poison with thee, or in bastinado, or in steel. I will bandy thee in faction; I will o'errun thee with policy; I will kill thee a hundred and fifty ways.

[V. i. 52-7]

The fundamental plot conflict, then, between the forces of Duke Senior, Rosalind and Orlando in the forest and those of Duke Frederick and Oliver in the court may be described in terms of Nature "combatting against Fortune". Shakespeare has further emphasized this pattern in his setting. The court quickly becomes the habitat of the treacherous adherents of Fortune, while the magical forest shields the contented, worthy followers of Nature. We are told that all of the "men of great worth" [V. iv. 155] have poured from the court to join the contented exiles, and at court Orlando laments the passing of those days "when service sweat for duty, not for meed" [II. iii. 58ff.], for it is the "fashion of these times" to do nothing "but for promotion", that is, for the gifts of the world. LeBeau speaks of "hereafter, in a better world than this" [I. ii. 284], in reporting the unprovoked banishment of Rosalind, and Duke Frederick hopes that by dismissing Rosalind his own Celia will "show more bright and seem more virtuous" [I. iii. 81], another instance of the Duke's practice of policy at the court. Everywhere we hear of the peril, sham and corruption of the court, and the two songs, "Under the greenwood tree" [II. v. 1ff.], and "Blow, blow, thou winter wind" [II. vii. 174ff.], underline the contrast between court and forest.

It is in the setting, of course, that the conflict between Fortune and Nature joins with the familiar Elizabethan conflict between the court and pastoralism, between the ideals of the "aspiring mind" and those of the contented shepherd, who speaks the words of Corin:

Sir, I am a true labourer; I earn that I eat, get that I wear; owe no man hate, envy no man's happiness; glad of other men's good, content with my harm; and the greatest of my pride is to see my ewes graze and my lambs suck.

[III. ii. 73-7]

The court-pastoralism conflict, as well as the closely allied conflict between the modern world and the golden or "antique" world, are involved in the pattern of Nature and Fortune. This fact, however, does not lessen the importance of the strife between Nature and Fortune, exemplified in Corin's words by such phrases as "glad of other men's good, content with my harm," and "owe no man hate". It is interesting to note in this regard that while Shakespeare followed his source in establishing the setting of court and forest for his play, he especially pointed up the Nature-Fortune conflict by omitting certain motives in the treacherous actions of Oliver and Duke Frederick, thereby rendering their wickedness all the more capricious. Oliver, for instance, confessing that his "soul . . . hates nothing more than" Orlando, adds: "yet I know not why" [I. i. 65-6]. Nor can Orlando explain his brother's animosity, except in these words: "The something that Nature gave me his countenance seems to take from me." But in Lodge's *Rosalynde* it is quite clear that Oliver had been cheated out of most of his rightful patrimony as eldest son; there was thus motivation for his abusive treatment of Orlando. Similarly, when the Duke banishes Rosalind, who "never so much as in a thought unborn" [I. iii. 51] did offend her uncle, his explanation is little more than the undeserved retort, "Let it suffice thee that I trust thee not" [I. iii. 55]. Yet in Lodge Duke Frederick likewise had a reason for dismissing his daughter's beloved companion: one of the courtiers might marry her and thus lay claim (she being Duke Senior's daughter) to the dukedom. It would seem, then, that by not clarifying the basis for the conflict between Oliver and Orlando and between Frederick and Rosalind, which he might easily have done, Shakespeare has actually emphasized the Nature-Fortune motif.

Once the setting has shifted for good to the contentment and revelry of the Forest of Arden and the theme has turned to love, both Jaques and Touchstone (as his name implies) will occasionally remind us of the Nature and Fortune pattern. Jaques, who can "suck melancholy out of a song as a weasel sucks eggs" [II. v. 13], is anything but content with his lot, not so much because he desires worldly treasure, but more because he fails to know himself. Both Duke Senior and Rosalind tell him that his ridiculous pose is an outgrowth of his self-ignorance [II. vii. 65-69; IV. i. 1-29]. And Touchstone, whom we have already seen mocking poor William with threats of the usual devices of one following Fortune, is said by Jaques to have "rail'd on Lady Fortune in good terms / In good set terms" [II. vii. 16], as he lay basking in the sun.

The presence of the conflict is seen, finally, in the conversions of Oliver and Frederick. It is to be recalled that Nature or "Wisdom and Fortune combatting together, if that the former dare what it can, no chance may shake it," and we are not surprised, accordingly, to find such a conclusion to *As You Like It*. The "mighty power" led by Duke Frederick against the contented followers of Duke Senior in the forest is disbanded after an "old religious man" persuades Frederick and his followers to retire from the world. Oliver's conversion is yet more strange. Like Frederick, Oliver was converted away from his desire for the gifts of the world once he had gone into the Forest of Arden. The incident occurred after Orlando had come upon Oliver sleeping in the forest unaware of an approaching attack by a "suckt and hungry lioness" [IV. iii. 126]. Orlando, who had just cause to despise his depraved elder brother, might have let the lioness do her work:

> But Kindness, nobler ever than revenge,
> And Nature, stronger than his just occa-
> sion,
> Made him give battle to the lioness,
> Who quickly fell before him.
>
> [IV. iii. 128-31]

"Nature, stronger than his just occasion" quite precisely describes the moral traditionally taught by the allegoric strife between Nature and Fortune. Presumably, by accepting the gift of Fortune or Occasion, as Fortune was sometimes called, Orlando could quickly have assured himself of worldly wealth in the form of his brother's lands and possessions. But Nature, stronger than Fortune, intervened, and this act of nobility precipitated Oliver's conversion: Oliver had come to know himself, as he tells Rosalind and Celia:

> I do not shame
> To tell you what I was, since my conver-
> sion
> So sweetly tastes, being the thing I am.
>
> [IV. iii. 135-37]

Curiously enough, the two conversions are double-edged, for in one sense both are the direct result of Fortune. We may recall Celia's remark at the beginning of the play:

> When Nature hath made a fair creature,
> may she not by Fortune fall into the fire?
> Though Nature hath given us Wit to flout
> at Fortune, hath not Fortune sent in this
> fool to cut off argument?
>
> [I. ii. 43-7]

Perhaps it was Fortune that sent the "old religious man" to persuade Duke Frederick not to attack Duke Senior; perhaps it was Fortune who sent the "suckt and hungry lioness" to destroy Oliver. The lesson involved, if there is one, seems to concern the uses Nature allows one to make of Fortune: adversity can be sweet, if one's nature will but permit it to be, and Orlando's kindness, "nobler ever than revenge", was rewarded by the conversion of his brother. Above all is involved in this conclusion the Renaissance commonplace that for outstanding success the cooperation of both Fortune and Nature is required!

The quick conversions, it might be added, beyond their conventional use in romantic comedy to bring about the happy ending, may serve here as indications that neither Frederick nor Oliver was inherently evil: lacking self-knowledge, they both had simply allied themselves with the goddess Fortune, practiced her techniques, and, for a while, received her gifts of the world. But they were not to be at the summit of her wheel for long, especially Oliver, and when Fortune cast them down, they were readily enough brought to know themselves.

Throughout the course of the comedy, then, we have seen that the philosophical conflict between Fortune and Nature has influenced both the characterization and the plot. Accordingly, by the end of the play, it is only fitting that the worthies, who had wisely accepted their brief period of misfortune, could return to their court, and all would

> share the good of our returned Fortune
> According to the measure of their states.
>
> [V. iv. 174-75]

The "fickleness of fortune" had had no power over their good spirits, no chance could shake their contentment, because they had received the bounties of Nature. Even sour Jaques, not above wishing the group well, has to admit to Duke Senior:

> You to your former honour I bequeath;
> Your patience and your virtue well deserves it.
>
> [V. iv. 186-87]

The good housewife Fortune had indeed been delightfully mocked from her wheel, and her gifts of the world were once again bestowed on the deserving, "according to the measure of their states". (pp. 45-50)

> John Shaw, *"Fortune and Nature in 'As You Like It',"* in Shakespeare Quarterly, *Vol. VI, No. 1, Winter, 1955, pp. 45-50.*

DISGUISE AND ROLE-PLAYING

Nancy K. Hayles

[*In the excerpt below, Hayles discusses Shakespeare's use of sexual disguise in* As You Like It. *The critic argues that this device is developed in distinct stages: first,* **Rosalind** *assumes layers of disguise for the journey to Arden, then the layers are slowly removed as she gradually renounces the role of Ganymede, and finally they are eliminated altogether when the heroine abandons her disguise to marry* **Orlando**. *The layering-on movement, Hayles contends, suggests selfish control and creates conflict in the play, while the removal of layers fosters reconciliation. Moreover, the critic remarks, this unlayering allows* **Rosalind** *to convey her true personality to* **Orlando**, *which ultimately supplants his idealized notion of her. Hayles also explores how Shakespeare extended the pattern of sexual disguise and unlayering to the play's epilogue.*]

As You Like It opens with scenes that emphasize rivalry and competition. Orlando has been mistreated by his brother Oliver, and Oliver in turn feels that Orlando has caused him to be 'altogether misprised' and undervalued by his own people. The rivalry that Duke Frederick still feels with the rightful Duke is also apparent. Moreover, the chief event of the opening scenes, the wrestling match between Charles and Orlando, is a formalized and ritualistic expression of male rivalry. Against the backdrop of male rivalry, the female intimacy between Celia and Rosalind makes a striking contrast. It is an intimacy, however, maintained at some cost. When Duke Frederick peremptorily orders Rosalind into banishment, Celia's protest is countered by her father's attempt to transform intimacy into rivalry between the two girls, too:

> Thou art a fool; she robs thee of thy name,
> And thou wilt show more bright and seem
>   more virtuous
> When she is gone. Then open not thy lips.
>
> [I. iii. 80-2]

The opening scenes of the play, then, draw a society where intimacy among women is implicitly contrasted with the rivalry among men. When the scene changes to the forest, several incidents seem designed as signals that the forest is a world where co-operation rather than competition prevails. Orlando meets with civility instead of hostility when he seeks meat for the fainting Adam; Rosalind and Celia find the natives to be kind shepherds rather than would-be rapists; and the exiled Duke hails his followers as 'Co-mates and brothers'. But we soon discover that competition is not altogether absent from the Forest of Arden. Jaques accuses the Duke of himself usurping the forest from its rightful owners, the deer; Touchstone confronts and bests his country rival, William; and Silvius discovers that his beloved Phebe has fallen in love with a courtly newcomer. The situation is thus more complicated than a simple contrast between court competition and pastoral co-operation, or between female intimacy and male rivalry. The sexual disguise of Rosalind mirrors the complexities of these tensions.

We can consider the disguise as proceeding in two separate movements. First, the layers of disguise are added as Rosalind becomes Ganymede, and then as Ganymede pretends to be Orlando's Rosalind; second, the layers are removed as Ganymede abandons the play-acting of Rosalind, and then as Rosalind herself abandons the disguise of Ganymede. The layering-on movement creates conflict and the layering-off movement fosters reconciliation as the disguise confronts and then resolves the issue of competition versus co-operation.

In the most complex layering, Rosalind-as-Ganymede-as-Orlando's Rosalind, Rosalind presents Orlando with a version of his beloved very different from the one he imagines in his verses. When Rosalind-as-Ganymede insists that Orlando's Rosalind will have her own wit, her own will and her own way, implicit in the portrayal is Rosalind's insistence that Orlando recognize the discrepancy between his idealized version and the real Rosalind. In effect, Rosalind is claiming the right to be herself rather than to be Orlando's idealized version of her, as female reality is playfully set against male fantasy. In playing herself (which she can apparently do only if she first plays someone else) Rosalind is able to state her own needs in a way she could not if she were simply herself. It is because she is disguised as Ganymede that she can be so free in portraying a Rosalind who is a flesh and blood woman instead of a Petrarchan abstraction. Rosalind's three-fold disguise is therefore used to accentuate the disparity between the needs of the heroine and the expectations of the hero.

Even the simpler layering of Rosalind-as-Ganymede accentuates conflict, though this time the couple being affected is Phebe and Silvius. Rosalind's guise as Ganymede causes Phebe to fall in love with her. Rosalind's on-layering, which inadvertently makes her Silvius's rival, causes Phebe's desires to be even more at variance with Silvius's hopes than before. It takes Ganymede's transformation into Rosalind to trick Phebe into accepting her swain, as the off-layering of Rosalind's disguise reconciles these two Petrarchan lovers. The Silvius-Phebe plot thus shows in simplified form the correlation between on-layering and rivalry, and off-layering and co-operation. It also gives us a standard by which we can measure the more complicated situation between Orlando and Rosalind.

Phebe and Silvius are caricatures of courtly love, and through them we are shown female manipulation and male idealization in a way that emphasizes the less pleasant side of the courtly love tradition. But it is important to see that this rustic couple merely exaggerates tendencies also present in Rosalind and Orlando. Rosalind's disguise creates

Celia, Orlando, and Rosalind. Act I, scene ii. By Schwoerer. The Department of Rare Books and Special Collections, The University of Michigan Library.

an imbalance in her relationship with Orlando because it allows Rosalind to hear Orlando's love-confession without having to take any comparable risks herself. Rosalind's self-indulgence in demanding Orlando's devoted service without admitting anything in return could become a variation of the perversity that is anatomized for us in the relationship between Phebe and Silvius. Thus the expectations of Rosalind and the desires of Orlando are not only the responses of these two characters, but are also reflections of stereotypical male and female postures, familiar through the long tradition of courtly love. The layering of the disguise has served to accentuate the conflict between men and women; now the unlayering finally resolves that traditional tension between the needs of the female and the desires of the male.

The unlayering begins when Oliver appears to explain why Orlando is late. Oliver's tale reveals, in almost allegorical fashion, the struggle within Orlando when he sees his brother in peril, and the tale has as its point that Orlando put the needs of his brother before his own natural desire for revenge. More subtly, the tale with its depiction of the twin dangers of the snake and lioness hints at a symbolic nexus of male and female threats. The specificity of the imagery suggests that the details are important. The first beast is described as a lioness, not a lion; moreover, she is a lioness in suck, but now with teats sucked dry, her hunger presumably made more ferocious by her condition. The description thus links a specifically female animal, and a graphically specific female condition, with the threat of being eaten. The details, taken in sum, evoke the possibility of female engulfment. The snake about to enter the sleeping man's mouth, again a very specific image, suggests even to a non-Freudian the threat of phallic invasion. But perhaps most significant is simply the twinning of the threats itself, which suggests the presence of two different but related kinds of danger.

By overcoming the twin threats, Orlando conquers in symbolic form projections of both male and female fears. Rosalind responds to Oliver's account by swooning. Her faint is a literal relinquishing of conscious control; within the conventions of the play, it is also an involuntary revelation of female gender because fainting is a 'feminine' response. It is a subtle anticipation of Rosalind's eventual relinquishing of the disguise and the control that goes with it. The action surrounding the relation of the tale parallels its moral: Orlando performs a heroic and selfless act that hints at a triumph over threatening aspects of masculinity and femininity, and Rosalind responds to the dangers that Orlando faces with an unconscious gesture of sympathy that results, for a moment, in the loss of her conscious control over the disguise and with it, the loss of her manipulative control over Orlando. Rosalind's swoon thus provides a feminine counterpart to Orlando's selflessness.

Orlando's struggle and Rosalind's swoon mark a turning point. When they meet again, Rosalind tries at first to re-establish their old relationship, but when Orlando replies, 'I can live no longer by thinking' [V. ii. 50], she quickly capitulates and re-assumes control only in order to be able to relinquish it. From this point on, the removal of the disguise signals the consummation of all the relationships as all four couples are married. The play suggests that control is necessary to state the legitimate needs of the self, but also that it must eventually be relinquished to accommodate the needs of another. Consummation is paradoxically achieved through an act of renunciation.

The way that sexual disguise is used reflects the play's overall concern with the tension between rivalry and co-operation. The disguise is first used to crystallize rivalry between the woman's self-image and the man's desires; in this sense it recognizes male-female discord and implicitly validates it. But because the disguise can be removed, it prevents the discord from becoming perpetual frustration. The workings of the disguise suggest that what appears to be a generous surrendering of self-interest can in fact bring consummation both to man and woman, so that rivalry can be transcended as co-operation brings fulfillment. In As You Like It, fulfillment of desire, contentment and peace of mind come when the insistence on self-satisfaction ceases. Duke Senior's acceptance of his forest exile and the subsequent unlooked-for restoration of his dukedom; the reconciliation between the sons of Rowland de Boys, in which Oliver resigns his lands to Orlando and finds forgiveness and happiness in love; the miraculous conversion of Duke Frederick by the old hermit and the voluntary abdication of his dukedom—all express the same paradox of consummation through renunciation that is realized in specifically sexual terms by the disguise.

When the boy actor who plays Rosalind's part comes forward to speak the epilogue, the workings of the sexual disguise are linked with the art of the playwright. The epilogue continues the paradox of consummation through renunciation that has governed sexual disguise within the play, as the final unlayering of the disguise coincides with a plea for the audience to consummate the play by applauding [Epilogue, 11-23]. . . . At this moment the playwright relinquishes control of the audience. As with Rosalind and Orlando, his success is marked by a control that finally renounces itself, a control which admonishes only to release as the audience is asked to 'like as much . . . as please you' [Epilogue, 13-14]. Our applause is a gesture of acceptance which encompasses both the working of sexual disguise within the play, and the art whose operation parallels it as the play ends. At the same time, the boy actor alludes to the fact that he is not after all the woman he plays ('if I were a woman' [Epilogue, 18], and so relinquishes the last level of the sexual disguise. For the last time,

the unlayering of the disguise is linked with a reconciliation between the sexes as the boy actor speaking the epilogue appeals separately to the men and women in the audience. Within the play these two perspectives have been reconciled, and the joint applause of the men and women in the audience re-affirms that reconciliation and extends it to the audience.

The sexual disguise in As You Like It therefore succeeds in interweaving various motifs. Many of the problems considered in the play (Duke Frederick's tyranny, Oliver's unfair treatment of Orlando, Phebe's exultation over Silvius) stem from excessive control, and the heroine exercises extraordinary control over the disguise. The removal of the disguise signals a renunciation of control on her part, and this in turn is linked with a voluntary renunciation of control by others, so that the unlayering and the resolution of problems neatly correspond. Moreover, the sexual reversal inherent in the disguise, which itself implicitly promises a reconciliation of male and female perspectives, is used to reconcile the men and women in the play. Since the key to reconciliation has been the renunciation of control, the playwright uses his relinquishing of control over the play to signal a final reconciliation between the men and women in the audience. Because of the correspondence between Rosalind as controller of the disguise, and Shakespeare as controller of the disguised boy actor who plays Rosalind's part, Rosalind's control over her disguise is paradigmatic of the playwright's control over the play. Both use their control creatively and constructively, but for both the relinquishing of control corresponds with the consummation of their art.

The means by which resolution is achieved in As You Like It says a great deal about the kinds of problems the play considers. By having Rosalind as surrogate playmaker, the playwright must not pose problems that are beyond her power to solve. There are a few hints that Rosalind's control exceeds the merely human; she tells Orlando she possesses magical powers, and Hymen mysteriously appears to officiate at the wedding. The playwright likewise allows himself some hints of supernatural intervention—witness Duke Frederick's miraculous conversion. But positing a human problem-solver almost necessitates limiting the problems to human scale. Moreover, because the disguise is the key to Rosalind's ability to solve problems, the emphasis on male and female perspectives inherent in the sexual disguise places the problems in the context of the social roles of each sex. The disguise thus gives the play artistic unity, but it also imposes limitations on the play's thematic scope. The brilliance of As You Like It is that it so perfectly matches what the play attempts to the inherent limitations of its techniques that it makes us unaware there are limitations. (pp. 64-8)

Nancy K. Hayles, "Sexual Disguise in 'As You Like It' and 'Twelfth Night'," in Shakespeare Survey: An Annual Survey of Shakespearian Study and Production, *Vol. 32, 1979, pp. 63-72.*

Thomas F. Van Laan

[*Van Laan points out several instances where the characters in Arden either take part in or discuss role-playing sessions, proposing that the forest in a sense becomes the stage for these brief "playlets." Shakespeare composed variations of this theme, the critic continues, to explore the circumstances surrounding the way in which the play's four couples fall in love. Van Laan concludes that if being in love means assuming a role, then Shakespeare assures us in* As You Like It *that there is more than one way to play the lover.*]

The adherence of a character to one or more pre-formulated roles, his deriving his identity therefrom, by no means necessitates his being a lifeless stereotype, even if he is a character of type one and only a single role is involved. Some of the roles Shakespeare utilizes are themselves sufficiently fresh and new because they come into being, in effect, only through his work, through his supplying familiar social or literary categories (such as daughter, friend, fortune hunter) with gestures and moves so appropriate and convincing that they suggest the existence of a lengthy literary or dramatic tradition. Other roles achieve freshness and newness as well as a sense of living vitality through the richness of their execution. Dogberry [in *Much Ado About Nothing*] is more attractive and appealing than Shakespeare's two other versions of the malapropian constable, Dull and Elbow [in *Love's Labour's Lost*]—especially Dull, whose name is so apt—but the reason for his greater appeal has little to do with his possessing a larger percentage of genuinely felt life. It is a matter partly of Shakespeare's having given him more stage time and partly of his having a clearer and more consequential involvement with the action of his play, but mostly, it seems to me, it results from his having better material and being a more thoroughly rendered version of the role than the others. A more significant example of richness of execution can be found in Jaques, whose portrayal evokes the feeling that one is observing not simply the reworking of a familiar literary-dramatic stereotype but its perfection.

But perhaps the chief reason why Shakespeare's characters avoid flatness and repetitiveness is his highly flexible conception of individual roles: often enough a given character is recognizably fulfilling a specific role while nevertheless executing it in an unquestionably unique way. This flexibility can be glimpsed, for example, in the portrayal of the role of lover in the early comedies (from *Love's Labour's Lost* to *Much Ado About Nothing,* say), not only in the way that the various lovers differ one from another but also in the many shifts in Shakespeare's attitude towards the conventional literary version. The flexibility can also be glimpsed, just as clearly and more conveniently, in the unusual portrayal this role receives in the second half of *As You Like It.*

Time and time again, in the second half of *As You Like It,* the forest landscape becomes the stage for clearly defined momentary playlets, like those referred to by Rosalind when she tells Celia 'I will speak to [Orlando] like a saucy lackey, and under that habit play the knave with him' [III. ii. 295-97], and by both Rosalind and Corin when he, having found Silvius wooing Phebe, invites the others to 'see a pageant truly play'd' [III. iv. 52] and Rosalind promises to 'prove a busy actor in their play' [59]. In form, these playlets underscore the resemblance between the forest and a stage which is a central element in the play's contrast between forest and court. In content, however, the playlets utilize this stage as an arena for exploring one of the theatre's most familiar and popular roles, that of the lover. What takes place in the remarkably static second half of *As You Like It*—both in these playlets and elsewhere—is not action in the usual sense but, instead, an elaborate anatomy of the varieties of love.

The range of this anatomy is broad enough to include a 'Character' of the conventional stereotype (in Ganymede's account of its essential 'marks,' III. ii. 369ff.), several varieties of romantic love (Rosalind and Orlando, Celia and Oliver, Phebe and Silvius, Phebe and Ganymede), a parody of these relationships (in Touchstone's marrying the 'foul slut,' Audrey, in order to avoid living 'in bawdry,' III. iii. 36, 97), and the outright rejection of love (by Jaques, whose only 'mistress' is the world he loathes so much, III. ii. 278). Because of her dual role, Rosalind occupies a special position in the anatomy. In her own person she experiences and exhibits as intense a passion as anyone in the play. But as Ganymede, she is able to encompass as well the opposite extreme, to articulate for herself and the spectators the anti-love that Jaques for the most part can only enact.

Relationships like those linking Orlando and Adam and Rosalind and her father extend the range of the anatomy to include both friendship and familial love. But it is primarily the varieties of romantic love with which Shakespeare is concerned, and in the final act he underscores the importance of their portrayal for the meaning of the play through the three passages that juxtapose them rhetorically just as they have already been juxtaposed in the action [V. ii. 83ff., V. iv. 4ff., V. iv. 116ff.]. These three passages thus call attention to the dramatic design of the second half of *As You Like It.* Also suggesting this design is a passage that has little to do with love, Jaques' and Rosalind's anatomy of melancholy:

> JAQUES I have neither the scholar's melancholy, which is emulation; nor the musician's, which is fantastical; nor the courtier's, which is proud; nor the soldier's, which is ambitious; nor the lawyer's, which is politic; nor the lady's, which is nice; nor the lover's, which is all these; but it is a melancholy of mine own, compounded of many simples, extracted from many objects, and, indeed, the sundry contemplation of my travels; in which my often rumination wraps me in a most humorous sadness.
>
> . . .
>
> ROSALIND Farewell, Monsieur Traveller; look you lisp and wear strange suits, disable all the benefits of your own country, be out of love with your nativity, and almost chide God for making you that countenance you are; or I will scarce think you have swam in a gondola.
>
> [IV. i. 10-20, 33-8]

Rosalind corrects Jaques' attempt to claim uniqueness and originality for his melancholy by assuring him that it is as conventional a pose as any of those he mocks. She thus completes the partial awareness of the first half of his speech: there is not merely a single variety of melancholy, but several, and each of them is a role with specific dictates that its player must observe. Similarly, in the forest scenes as a whole, Shakespeare dramatizes an analogous awareness about the ceremony of love: that although falling in love means assuming a role, there is more than one way to 'play the lover.' (pp. 38-40)

> Thomas F. Van Laan, "Identity and Role," in his Role-playing in Shakespeare, University of Toronto Press, 1978, pp. 21-42.

TIME

Jay L. Halio

[Halio describes time's two functions in As You Like It: first, as a foil whose two extremes—timelessness and time-consciousness—favorably contrast virtuous rustic life in Arden with dissolute court life, and second, as timelessness alone, as a link between life in the present and life in an earlier, less corrupt, generally better time. The critic maintains that Shakespeare perceives the city and court to be ruthless and degenerate, threatening places from which Arden's timeless world is a refuge, a world where past and present merge and people flourish. Surveying the dramatic and thematic juxtapositions of these two worlds,

Halio especially focuses on **Rosalind**'s awareness of time; he notes how, unlike **Touchstone**'s fascination with time's power to ripen things and rot them, **Rosalind** is strongly influenced by time's regenerative power, particularly as it concerns lovers.]

In As You Like It Shakespeare exploits timelessness as a convention of the pastoral ideal along with other conventions taken from pastoralism, but unlike his treatment, say, of Silvius and Phebe, his treatment of time is not so thoroughly satirical. Though neither will quite do, timelessness in Arden (on the whole) contrasts favorably to the time-consciousness of court and city life which Touchstone, for example, brings to the forest. In addition, timelessness links life in Arden with the ideal of an older, more gracious way of life that helps regenerate a corrupt present.

I

Orlando's first speech immediately voices several aspects of the time theme. Speaking to Adam, he recalls his father's will and its provision that Oliver, the eldest son, should educate the younger brothers. This Oliver has failed to do, at least with respect to Sir Rowland's youngest son; but despite his enforced rusticity, Orlando reveals an innate gentility so wonderful that even his tyrannical brother is brought to remark: "Yet he's gentle, never schooled, and yet learned, full of noble device, of all sorts enchantingly beloved. . ." [I. i. 166-68]. These innate qualities derive directly from old Sir Rowland, for the identification between Orlando and his father, as we shall see, is repeatedly and pointedly made. Moreover, Orlando twice remarks in this scene that it is his father's spirit within him that prompts him to revolt against his present humiliation—a revelation which has more than ordinary implications later.

Unlike his counterpart Sir John of Bordeaux in Lodge's Rosalynde, Sir Rowland de Boys is dead before the play opens, but his memory is kept studiously alive. In the opening lines of Lodge's novel we can get some idea of what he stood for:

> There dwelled adjoining to the city of Bordeaux a knight of most honorable parentage, whom fortune had graced with many favors, and nature honored with sundry exquisite qualities, so beautified with the excellence of both, as it was a question whether fortune or nature were more prodigal in deciphering the riches of their bounties. Wise he was, as holding in his head a supreme conceit of policy, reaching with Nestor into the depth of all civil government; and to make his wisdom more gracious, he had that salem ingenii and pleasant eloquence that was so highly commended in Ulysses: his valor was no less than his wit, nor the stroke of his lance no less forcible than the sweetness of his tongue was persuasive; for he was

for his courage chosen the principal of all the Knights of Malta.

But we need not go outside the play to discover what Sir Rowland represents. Adam, the old retainer of the de Boys household and himself a living reminder of the former age, provides some important clues. When Oliver apparently consents to his brother's departure, he throws Adam out, too:

> *Oliver.* Get you with him, you old dog.
>
> *Adam.* Is "old dog" my reward? Most true,
> I have lost teeth in your service. God be
> with my old master! He would not have
> spoke such a word.
>
> [I. i. 81-4]

Later, when Adam warns Orlando to run from Oliver's treachery and even offers his life's savings—and his life—to assist in the escape, Orlando recognizes the gesture for what it is—the product of a gracious ideal:

> O good old man, how well in thee appears
> The constant service of the antique world,
> When service sweat for duty, not for meed!
> Thou art not for the fashion of these times,
> Where none will sweat but for promotion,
> And having that do choke their service up
> Even with the having. It is not so with
> thee.
>
> [II. iii. 56-62]

The two dukes also furnish evidence of the esteem in which Sir Rowland was universally held: Duke Frederick, villainously, found him an enemy, but Duke Senior (to Rosalind's evident gratification) "loved Sir Rowland as his soul" [I. ii. 235]. Orlando, who functions in the play partly to bear out the spirit of his father, naturally attracts similar feelings. It is not for nothing that he attaches to himself repeatedly the clumsy-naive epithet "old Sir Rowland's youngest son" [I. iii. 28]; besides, his name is both an anagram of Rowland and its Italian translation. The predicament in which the young man eventually discovers himself will test his true mettle and, more importantly, the worth of all that he and his name may symbolize. Adam awakens in him some sense of his plight when Orlando returns home after throwing Charles the wrestler:

> O you memory
> Of old Sir Rowland! Why, what make you
> here?
> Why are you so virtuous? Why do people
> love you?
> And wherefore are you gentle, strong, and
> valiant?
> Why would you be so fond to overcome
> The bonny prizer of the humorous Duke?
> Your praise is come too swiftly home before you.
> Know you not, master, to some kind of
> men
> Their graces serve them but as enemies?

> No more do yours. Your virtues, gentle
> master,
> Are sanctified and holy traitors to you.
> Oh, what a world is this when what is
> comely
> Envenoms him that bears it!
>
> [II. iii. 3-15]

Orlando's world of court and city is a far different world from his father's. It is a perverse world, where brother plots against brother and virtues become "sanctified and holy traitors" [II. iii. 13]. It is a world ruled over by the usurping Frederick (the "new" Duke), who banishes his elder brother (the "old" Duke) and keeps his niece only so long as convenience allows. When he fears Rosalind as a threat to the fame and popularity of his own daughter, he drives her out also—just as Oliver plans to kill the brother he fears he can no longer suppress. In short, it is a world based on expediency and the lust for power [III. i. 15-18], not a brave new world, but a degenerate new one. With no obligation to tradition—to the past—it is ruthless in its self-assertion. But while this "new" world may banish its principal threats, Rosalind and Orlando, it does not thus destroy them (we are, after all, in the realm of romantic comedy). In the timeless pastoral world of the Forest of Arden, where past and present merge, they find refuge and there flourish.

II

The first mention of the life led by Duke Senior and his fellows in the Forest of Arden occurs early in the play in the dialogue between Charles and Oliver. Oliver has decided to use the wrestler to rid himself of Orlando (thus perverting the intention of Charles's visit), but first he inquires into the "new news at the new Court" [I. i. 96-7]. Charles recounts what Oliver already knows: the new Duke has driven out the old Duke, and a number of lords have voluntarily accompanied him into exile. For no apparent reason, Oliver next inquires into Rosalind's position, and then asks where the old Duke will live. Charles replies:

> They say he is already in the Forest of
> Arden, and a many merry men with him;
> and there they live like the old Robin Hood
> of England. They say many young gentlemen flock to him every day, and fleet their
> time carelessly as they did in the golden
> world.
>
> [I. i. 114-19]

Here Oliver abruptly changes the subject to the next day's wrestling match. Now, merely as dramatic exposition this dialogue is at least ingenuous—if not downright clumsy. Obviously it must serve another function to justify itself; that is, by describing the conflict between the two dukes, it provides a parallel to the decisive quarrel between Orlando and Oliver which has just taken place. The inversion of roles played by the younger and older brothers is merely a superficial variation of the plot; the point is to suggest an alignment between Duke Senior and Sir Rowland de Boys, between the "golden world" and the "antique world," which coalesce in the fabulous Robin Hood life now led by the banished Duke. Should we require any further evidence of this significance, the change in Sir Rowland's name from its source is clear enough. The anagram *Rowland-Orlando* has already been explained, but the change from *de Bordeaux* is otherwise meaningful: *de Boys* is simply *de Bois,* "of the forest." Elizabethan spelling commonly substitutes *y* for *i,* as everyone knows, but the pronunciation is the same. While older editors, such as Malone and Dyce, modernize the spelling (without comment), more recent ones prefer the spelling of the Folios, a practice which tends to obscure the reference. And Dover Wilson's note [in his New Cambridge edition of the play], recording the fact that the de Boyses were an old Arden family, gives us more light than it perhaps suspects—or intends.

Lest there be any mistake about the kind of forest in which Duke Senior and (later) Orlando, Rosalind, and the others find themselves, we must listen carefully to the Duke's first speech [II. i. 1ff.]. Its theme is "Sweet are the uses of adversity"; only in this way can he and his followers discover "tongues in trees, books in the running brooks / . . . and good in everything." Here, unlike the conventional pastoral, others besides unrequited lovers may feel the shrewdness of the winter wind; shepherds will confess to smelling of sheep dip; and a Sir Oliver Martex is available for weddings as well as Hymen. The forest may be enchanted—the appearance of a god is only the least subtle indication that it is—but the enchantment is of an unusual kind; the forest still admits of other, qualifying realities. For the right apprehension of a natural, humane order of life, which emerges as Shakespeare's standard, takes account of both the ideal (what should or could be) and the actual (what is). By contrast, the standard of life in court and city is unnatural insofar as it stifles the ideal aspirations of the human imagination and sinks to the level of a crude, animal existence. If Duke Senior finally returns along with the others to his dukedom (despite his earlier assertion that he would not change his "life exempt from public haunt"), he returns not only because his dukedom is ready to receive him, but also (we must infer) because he is prepared to resume his proper role. Tempered by adversity, his virtue matures. To provide this temper, or balance, is the true function of the forest, its real "magic." Neither the Duke nor anyone else who comes to Arden emerges the same.

The trip to the forest is itself exhausting and fraught with danger. Rosalind and her little company are quite unable to take another step. Similarly, Adam is close to expiring when he arrives with Orlando. But on each occasion the forest at once works its charm. Corin and Silvius are at hand to entertain Rosalind and her friends and to provide them with a gentle welcome and a home. At the end of the scene even the fainting Celia quickens to remark, "I like this place, / And willingly could waste my time in it" [II. iv. 94-5]. Orlando, seeking food in what he calls an "uncouth" desert [II. vi. 6], comes upon the banquet of the banished Duke. Showing the valor of his heritage, he opposes single-handed the entire host of the Duke and his men. Under the conventions of this romance, this show of valor is not quixotic—it fits rather with Orlando's defeat of Charles. But, though hardly despised (except by Jaques), it is misdirected; and Orlando is made to recognize the code that here reigns:

> Speak you so gently? Pardon me, I pray
>   you.
> I thought that all things had been savage
>   here,
> And therefore put I on the countenance
> Of stern commandment. But whate'er you
>   are
> That in this desert inaccessible,
> Under the shade of melancholy boughs,
> Lose and neglect the creeping hours of
>   time,
> If ever you have looked on better days,
> If ever been where bells have knolled to
>   church,
> If ever sat at good man's feast,
> If ever from your eyelids wiped a tear
> And know what 'tis to pity and be pitied,
> Let gentleness my strong enforcement be.
> In the which hope I blush, and hide my
>   sword.
>   [II. vii. 106-19]

Gentleness joins with gentleness; golden world merges with antique world—at least through their modern representatives. If the parvenu at first mistakes the appearance of his surroundings, he is soon instructed: this is no ordinary forest. At the same time, he reminds us of what civilization *might* be like, or once was. Certainly he perceives another aspect of his new environment accurately, one he will quickly cultivate: the meaninglessness of time in the forest.

III

For unlike the life of the court and the city, "men fleet the time carelessly" in Arden, as Charles earlier remarked. Here are no power-seekers like Oliver and Duke Frederick, impatient to rid themselves of encumbrances [I. i. 124, I. iii. 52 ff.], but men who love to lie under the greenwood tree seeking—only the food they eat. Appropriately, this casualness is the theme of many of their songs. Touchstone's comment on the last—"I count it but lost time to hear such a foolish song" [V. iii. 39-40]—briefly expresses the opposing attitude brought from court into the forest. The attitude is shared by the malcontent Jaques, his fellow satirist, and in some respects by Rosalind. Touchstone is, in fact, the play's timekeeper, as Harold Jenkins has called him [in his *"As You Like It," Shakespeare Survey*

VII (1955): 40-51], and his most extended disquisition on time is fittingly recounted by Jaques:

> . . . he drew a dial from his poke,
> And looking on it with lack-lustre eye,
> Says very wisely, "It is ten o'clock.
> Thus we may see," quoth he, "how the
>   world wags.
> 'Tis but an hour ago since it was nine,
> And after one hour more 'twill be eleven;
> And so, from hour to hour, we ripe and
>   ripe,
> And then, from hour to hour, we rot and
>   rot;
> And thereby hangs a tale."
>
> [II. vii. 20-8]

Later in the same scene Jaques *in propria persona* also "morals on the time" in his speech on the Seven Ages of Man, calling our attention to the broader divisions of time's progress and pageant. Between these speeches, it should be noted, occur Orlando's entrance and his words, quoted above, on the neglect of time by the Duke and his foresters. Clearly, Shakespeare throughout the play contrasts the timelessness of the forest world with the time-ridden preoccupations of court and city life, but here the juxtaposition is both dramatically and thematically emphasized. For the court and city habitués, time is a measured progress to the grave—or worse! But for the foresters, time is merely "the stream we go a-fishing in" (to borrow the phrase of a later pastoralist [Henry David Thoreau in *Walden*]). Neither attitude, of course, will quite do in this sublunary world; hence, to present a more balanced view of time—as of love, pastoralism, and poetry—Shakespeare uses the dialectic characteristic of this play and centers it upon his hero and heroine.

For Rosalind's awareness of time, however related to the preoccupation imported from the "outside" world, is different from Touchstone's obsession with "riping and rotting." It is, partly, the awareness of a girl in love and impatient for the attentions of her lover, a healthy consciousness that recalls Juliet's except as it is undarkened by tragic fate. But her awareness has further implications. When she and Orlando first meet in the forest, their dialogue, appropriately enough, is itself about time. Rosalind's question, "I pray you, what is't o'clock?" [III. ii. 299], although banal, suits the occasion; for despite her boast that she will speak like a saucy lackey, she is momentarily confused by confronting Orlando and scarcely knows how to begin. What follows in her account of Time's "divers paces" [III. ii. 308-33], however, is something more than a verbal smokescreen to help her collect her wits, detain her lover, and make sure he keeps coming back: it is a development of Jaques' Seven Ages speech with important thematic variations. Jaques' speech describes a man in his time playing many parts and suggests that his speed, or "pace," will vary along with his role; the series of vignettes illustrates the movement of a person *in* time. Rosa-

lind not only adds appreciably to Jaques' gallery, but showing profounder insight, she shifts the emphasis from the movement *of a person,* to the movement *of time* as apprehended, for example, by the young maid "between the contract of her marriage and the day it is solemniz'd. If the interim be but a se'ennight, Time's pace is so hard that it seems the length of seven year" [III. ii. 314-17]. In this way, she more thoroughly accounts for *duration,* or the perception of time, which, unlike Jaques' portrait of our common destiny, is not the same for everyone.

IV

Naturally, Rosalind is most concerned with the perception of time by the lover, and here her behavior is in marked contrast to Orlando's. Quite literally—and like any fiancée, or wife—she is Orlando's timekeeper. When he fails to keep his appointments, she suffers both pain and embarrassment (III.iv) that are relieved only by the greater follies of Silvius and Phebe that immediately follow. When he finally does turn up an hour late—as if to dramatize his belief that "there's no clock in the forest" [III. ii. 300-01]—Rosalind rebukes him severely:

> *Rosalind.* Why, how now, Orlando? Where have you been all this while? You a lover? An you serve such another trick, never come in my sight more.
>
> *Orlando.* My fair Rosalind, I come within an hour of my promise.
>
> *Rosalind.* Break an hour's promise in love? He that will divide a minute into a thousand parts and break but a part of the thousand part of a minute in the affairs of love, it may be said of him that Cupid hath clapp'd him o' th' shoulder, but I'll warrant him heart-whole.
>
> *Orlando.* Pardon me, dear Rosalind.
>
> *Rosalind.* Nay, an you be so tardy, come no more in my sight. I had as lief be woo'd of a snail.
>
> [IV. i. 38-52]

Rosalind's time-consciousness goes beyond the mere moment: she knows the history of love—witness her speech on Troilus and Leander [IV. i. 94-108]—and she predicts its future, as she warns Orlando of love's seasons after marriage [IV. i. 143-149]. Her ardent impulse is thus in comic juxtaposition with her realistic insight, just as Orlando's "point-device" attire and time-unconsciousness comically contrast with his rimes and other protestations of love.

In this fashion we arrive at the theme's center, or balance. If Orlando, as we have seen, is an agent of regeneration, he appears through his forgetfulness of time to be in some danger of not realizing his function. He might like Silvius, were it not for Rosalind, linger through an eternity of unconsummated loving; certainly, like the Duke, he feels in the forest no urgency about his heritage—at least not until he comes upon his brother sleeping beneath an ancient oak tree and menaced by a starved lioness (the symbolism is obvious). Oliver's remarkable conversion after his rescue and his still more remarkable engagement to Celia pave the way for Rosalind's resolution of the action, for under the pressure of his brother's happiness, Orlando can play at games in love no longer. And despite the play's arbitrary finale—Duke Frederick's conversion and the end of exile, in all of which she has had no hand—nevertheless, it is again Rosalind who has had an important share in preparing the principals for this chance. Like her less attractive counterpart Helena in *All's Well That Ends Well*, she remains a primary agent for the synthesis of values that underlies regeneration in Shakespeare's comedy. At the very outset we see her, the daughter of Duke Senior at the court of Duke Frederick, as a link between two worlds, not unlike Orlando's representative linking of two generations. In love, she is realistic rather than cynical, but not without a paradoxical—and perfectly human—romantic bias. So, too, with regard to time she moves with Orlando to a proper balance of unharried awareness. For all of these functions—as for others—the timeless world of the forest, with its complement of aliens, serves as a haven; but more importantly, it serves as a school.

Neither the extremes of idealism nor those of materialism, as they are variously represented, emerge as "the good life" in *As You Like It*. That life is seen rather as a mean of natural human sympathy educated—since that is a major theme in the play—by the more acceptable refinements of civilization (II. vii) and the harsh realities of existence ("winter and rough weather" [II. v. 8]). The "antique world" stands for a timeless order of civilization still in touch with natural human sympathy that, under the "new" regime (while it lasted), had been forced underground. To the forest, the repository of natural life devoid of artificial time barriers, the champions of regeneration repair in order to derive new energy for the task before them. There they find refuge, gain strength, learn—and return. (pp. 197-207)

Jay L. Halio, " 'No Clock in the Forest': Time in 'As You Like It'," in Studies in English Literature, 1500-1900, *Vol. II, 1962, pp. 197-207.*

Frederick Turner

[*Turner maintains that the concept of measurable, social time prevalent at Duke Frederick's court is suspended by the holiday atmosphere of Arden. Time in the forest is a more natural time, governed by the seasons, not the clock. The critic then examines different characters' perspectives of time. In his "Seven Ages of Man" speech (II. vii. 138ff.),* **Jaques** *presents*

two notions of time: first, that human beings exist in time as they would in a play on stage, and second, that life is a history determined by distinct stages. Unlike **Jaques**'s *assumption that death is the ultimate realization of time,* **Touchstone** *perceives time in relation to physical love or sex in conjunction with the "natural order," in which Nature's purpose is to propagate itself. Time for* **Orlando** *and* **Rosalind,** *however, is more dynamic and personal. It represents their anticipation of love in which clock time drags and personal time is in a furious hurry. Turner concludes his essay with an examination of the idea of musical time in the play's final songs and dances.*]

As You Like It opens with two characters who, in terms of the hierarchy of social power, are weak and inferior: Orlando, the younger brother, and Adam, the old man. One is denied his place in society; the other is past his usefulness. Orlando tellingly distinguishes between the 'gentle condition of blood' and the 'courtesy of nations' [I. i. 44-6]; between what is owed him as a member of society, and what is due to his status as a human being. Adam has 'lost' his 'teeth' 'in service', and though his master's legal obligation to him has been fulfilled, Oliver refuses to honour his human obligations to look after the faithful servant in his old age.

Those who are weak in the power structure of society—children, old men, beggars, strangers, the insane—can possess the most potent moral power in the human community. But this moral power must be recognized, if it is to exist; Malvolio's crime [in *Twelfth Night*], we shall see, is to deny the moral power of the Fool. Orlando's description of his 'keeping' as no different from the 'stalling of an ox' [I. i. 10], and Oliver's characterizing Adam as an 'old dog', suggest that the socially strong in this play consider those who are socially weak to be no better than beasts, outside the community of man, and therefore ineligible for the basic human rights. But piety (or pité), insists that such figures are the true representatives of the human community, that we should treat them with the respect due to common humanity, whose dignity transcends the evanescent privileges of rank, wealth, or birth. There is only one thing that Orlando and Adam can do: leave the society which has rejected them.

Outcast also are the Duke Senior and his friends, and Rosalind, Celia, and Touchstone. Where can they go? What region of Shakespeare's poetic, philosophical, and moral world is appropriate to them?

If one escapes from the ordinary routine of society, one is on holiday. Rosalind can see nothing but 'briers' in this 'working-day' world; on 'holiday' they are but 'burs'. If, says Celia, 'we walk not in the trodden paths'—if we do not conform to the routines of society—'our very petticoats will catch them' [I. iii. 13-15]. The holiday that the outcasts must take is partly a holiday of the mind. 'Briers' become 'burs' when their attitude changes from 'working-day' to 'holiday'. Rosalind and Celia come to accept their existence with patience, but without paying the price of a vitiating and stoic detachment. On holiday life is only a game, even when it is a game of life and death. Rosalind and Celia are delightful partly because of their holiday attitude to the world—an attitude which combines levity with involvement, wisdom with feeling. Rosalind can satirize love and be in love at the same time.

Orlando, Rosalind, and the Duke Senior are all victims of injustice. They reject and are rejected by the power-structure of their society; and this structure includes its laws. The 'courtesy of nations' has become a tyranny for Orlando; for the Duke Senior it has been overturned. The accusation of treachery levelled by Duke Frederick at Rosalind is a legality divested of its sanctifying ritual of evidence, fair play, and impartiality. Thus the exiles become outlaws: they live 'like the old Robin Hood of England' [I. i. 116]. This brings to mind the connection of Robin Hood with the old holiday ritual of rural England, and the enormous popularity of his story among the common folk. He was the hero of the socially weak; the semi-pagan god of Holiday. The Puritans recognized this strain in his cult when they abolished it nearly fifty years later.

Time in the forest is not social time. The exiled nobles 'fleet the time carelessly, as they did in the golden world' [I. i. 118-19]. They 'lose and neglect the creeping hours of time' [II. vii. 112]; the human measurement of time has no meaning here. In Thomas Mann's *Magic Mountain,* holiday has a similar effect:

> Such is the purpose of our changes of air and scene, of all our sojourns at cures and bathing resorts; it is the secret of the healing power of change and incident. Our first days in a new place, time has a youthful, that is to say, a broad and sweeping flow, persisting for some six or eight days. Then, as one 'gets used to the place', a gradual shrinkage makes itself felt. He who clings or, better expressed, wishes to cling to life, will shudder to see how the days grow light and lighter, how they scurry by like dead leaves, until the last week, of some four, perhaps, is uncannily fugitive and fleet.

Here Mann is more interested in the subjective changes in the rate of time occasioned by circumstances than in the nature of holiday itself; but one interest tends to suggest the other, and we will find Shakespeare himself fascinated with subjective time in turn.

Helen Gardner discusses this subject illuminatingly in the context of the romantic comedies in general: 'In Shakespeare's comedies time . . . is not so much a movement onward as a space in which to work things out: a midsummer night, a space too short for us to feel time's movement, or the unmeasured time of *As You Like It* or *Twelfth Night* [in her "As You Like It" in *More Talking about Shakespeare,* ed. John Garrett]. Of *Much Ado About Nothing* she says: 'A sense of holiday, of *time off from the world's business,* reigns in Messina.'

Twice in *As You Like It* the absurdity of social, measurable time is suggested:

> And then he drew a dial from his poke,
> And, looking on it with lack-lustre eye,
> Says very wisely 'It is ten o'clock;
> Thus we may see' quoth he 'how the world wags;
> 'Tis but an hour ago since it was nine;
> And after one hour more 'twill be eleven; . . . '
>
>   . . . When I did hear
>
> The motley fool thus moral on the time,
> My lungs began to crow like chanticleer
> That fools should be so deep contemplative;
> And I did laugh sans intermission
> An hour by his dial.
>   [II. vii. 20-33]

Is it significant that Jaques compares his laughter to the sound of the chanticleer, the marker of natural time as opposed to the time of clocks?—

> *Ros:* I pray you, what is't o'clock?
> *Orl:* You should ask me what time o'day; there's no clock in the forest.
>   [III. ii. 299-301]

This last is reminiscent of Falstaff's first words in *I Henry IV,* and Hal's reply:

> *Fal:* Now, Hal, what time of day is it, lad? . . . etc.
>   [I. ii. 1]

The Boar's Head is similarly on holiday from ordinary time. It is interesting that what follows in each case is also similar. Rosalind asserts that

> Then there is no true lover in the forest, else sighing every minute and groaning every hour would detect the lazy foot of Time as well as a clock.
>   [III. ii. 302-05]

Hal says to Falstaff:

> What a devil hast thou to do with the time of the day? Unless hours were cups of sack, and minutes capons, and clocks the tongues of bawds . . . etc.
>   [I. ii. 6-8]

Time in each case is transmuted from the measurable, social time of clocks into the subjective time of experience. Falstaff now introduces another element:

> . . . we that take purses go by the moon and the seven stars, and not by Phoebus, he 'that wand'ring knight so fair'.
>   [I. ii. 14-16]

Falstaff operates, so he claims, according to the natural and mysterious time of the moon and the stars, rather than the tamed and social time of the sun—which he anthropomorphizes with impunity.

The Forest of Arden is a poetic region which contains, as well as holiday and outlawry, the forces of natural time, the time of the seasons, of the great rhythms of nature; 'time not our time', as T. S. Eliot puts it [in "The Dry Salvages"].

> Under the greenwood tree
> Who loves to lie with me,
> And turn his merry note
> Unto the sweet bird's throat . . .
> . . . Here shall he see
> No enemy
> But winter and rough weather.
>
> [II. v. 1-8]

> Here feel we but the penalty of Adam,
> The seasons' difference . . .
>
> [II. i. 5]

> Blow, blow, thou winter wind,
> Thou are not so unkind
> As man's ingratitude . . .
>
> [II. vii. 174ff.]

Shakespeare's Arden contains other seasons than a perpetual springtime. It can be 'melancholy', 'uncouth', a 'desert inaccessible'; it contains real, as well as conventional, shepherds. Most important of all, it works convincingly by natural time. It is a place one lives in, not an abstraction of the poet's mind; it has the obduracy and unconcern for human desires that we recognize as authentic in nature. People can get old here in the forest; time rules over man, but it is the time of the seasons and not the time of the clock.

The exiles carry with them into the forest many of their human attitudes and preconceptions. Jaques relentlessly anthropomorphizes the deer; the nobles are seen as 'usurpers' on the life of the forest, which is contrasted with the human domains of 'country, city, court'. For our purposes one of the most significant importations into the forest is Jaques' attitude to time in human existence:

> All the world's a stage,
> And all the men and women merely players;
> They have their exits and their entrances;
> And one man in his time plays many parts,
> His acts being seven ages . . .
>
> . . . Last scene of all,
> That ends this strange eventful history,
> Is second childishness and mere oblivion;
> Sans teeth, sans eyes, sans taste, sans everything.
>
> [II. vii. 139-66]

This passage resembles the conventional picture of the attitude of the philosopher. Jaques is above it all; he preserves a lofty detachment from the affairs of the common herd. But his detachment denies to him much of the truth about human existence. This celebrated passage is oddly hypermetropic: Jaques is longsighted, and cannot see the trees for the wood. The statistical studies of sociologists frequently give the same impression of selective blindness. The individual is devalued, exceptions are discounted, particulars yield to trends, freedom and significance are made to seem absurd or irrelevant.

Two elements of this speech are of particular interest: first, the life of man in time as a stage play; and, second, that life as a 'history', a succession of objectively observable characteristics of behaviour.

'All the world's a stage.' In a play, the actor is bound to the lines that the dramatist has written for him. He is not free to say or do what he likes; man, according to Jaques, is only reading off a preordained script. A play exists before it is performed; time is like a motion picture, every frame of which has already been prepared. Life is only the playing-out of a set sequence of events, the projection of a reel of scenes. Part of the irony of Jaques' speech is that it is, of course, delivered by an actor who is himself keeping to his part.

Walter Bagehot makes an interesting point about Jaques' speech in a passage which David Cecil quotes and discusses in his charming essay, 'Shakespearean Comedy', from *The Fine Art of Reading*. Bagehot's treatment deserves repetition:

> There seems an unalterable contradiction between the human mind and its employments. How can a soul be a merchant? What relation to an immortal being have the price of linseed, the fall of butter, the tare on tallow, or the brokerage on hemp? Can an undying creature debit 'petty expenses,' and charge for 'carriage paid'? All the world's a stage;—'the satchel, and the shining morning face'—the 'strange oaths';—'the bubble reputation'—the
>
> Eyes severe and beard of formal cut,
> Full of wise saws and modern instances.
>
> Can these things be real? Surely they are acting. What relation have they to the truth as we see it in theory? What connection with our certain hopes, 'in respect of itself, it is a good life; but in respect it is a Shepherd's life, it is nought'. The soul ties its shoes; the mind washes its hands in a basin. All is incongruous.

In a play the actors are not being themselves, but donning masks and acting a pretence. Jaques' vision of human life is essentially external. For him all there is is the pretence, the mask, the actor's part, the accidents. He describes behaviour, but not experience. Jaques is, perhaps, the first of those great satirical *personae* that Hugh Kenner discusses with such penetration and wit in his 'historical comedy', *The Counterfeiters.* Like Gulliver describing the Yahoos [in Jonathan Swift's *Gulliver's Travels*], like the extraordinary counterfeit sociologist who seems to have written *A Modest Proposal,* like the bad poet Pope invents to write the *Art of Sinking in Poetry,* Jaques is concerned not with the inner nature of a person, but with his surface, not with another 'I' but with an 'it'.

The reader, abetted by many critics, is often deceived in this passage by its breadth, inclusiveness, and metaphysical pathos into feeling that this is Shakespeare's viewpoint on the world, that here is some kind of ultimate wisdom about human life. On the contrary, Jaques' description of the schoolboy, lover, soldier, is only a series of brilliantly evoked stereotypes. If in some respects Shakespeare is *creating* or *originating* stereotypes (like Chaucer in the Prologue to the *Canterbury Tales*), this does not alter the fact that we are not being told the whole story about human existence; the sample of human information Jaques has chosen is not a fair one, and whole areas have been suppressed. Equally as important as what Jaques says is the insight we get into Jaques' point of view, and indeed into the flaws and virtues of a whole way of looking at existence.

Jaques' speech contains a certain cynicism, a mood alien, in some respects, to Shakespeare's own, as far as we can judge from his poems and sonnets, as well as from his plays. The other passages we should bear in mind when we read or hear 'All the world's a stage' include not only Prospero's 'our revels now are ended' [*The Tempest,* IV. i. 148], and 'as an unperfect actor on the stage' [Sonnet 23]; but also Macbeth's poor player, That struts and frets his hour upon the stage' [*Macbeth,* V. v. 24-5], and Lear's 'great stage of fools' [*King Lear,* IV. vi. 183]. Jaques' vision of human life ends as it began: with second childishness, sans everything; nothing has been gained, life is meaningless, it's all only a play. As soon as Jaques has finished his speech, Orlando, the young man and the lover, enters carrying Adam, the old man who is almost in his 'last scene'; the two are united and ennobled by a sense of love and care which somehow transcends and contradicts the stereotypical categories that would divide and degrade them.

The other theme of Jaques' speech that concerns us here is that of man's life as a history. 'History' can have two meanings, both of which are relevant in this context: 'story', and 'history' in the modern sense. The essential element in both is their dialectic: time in both is something expressed in terms of 'before' and 'after' rather than 'past', 'present', and 'future'. Time for 'history' is something static. The most obvious characteristic of Jacques' speech is the way for him human life seems to go in stages, each of which is changeless and restrict-

ingly self-consistent. We can all remember our sense of chagrin and frustration when we were told by our parents that we were 'just going through a stage'. Our individuality, the validity of our ideals and feelings, seemed threatened. When, we asked, would we be real people, when would we cease to be merely the result of a biological or social situation? Jaques would, it seems, reply 'never'.

'His acts being seven ages.' This ignores a fundamental characteristic of time—time as flux, time as dynamic process. Jaques' human actor develops in a curiously jerky fashion. We cannot for the life of us see how that particular kind of lover can become that particular kind of soldier or lawyer. How does the plump Justice become the 'lean and slipper'd pantaloon'? We have no sense of this man being one person. In our own lives we can look back and sometimes fail to recognize what we call 'I'; but usually beneath the affectations and obsessions, the attempts to be what we were not, we can see one person whom we greet with almost the delighted shock of meeting an old friend unexpectedly. There is none of this in Jaques' creed. Yet time is seamless. It has no stages. And it is in this intimate connection of each moment of time with the next that the possibility of being one person, not just an infinite sequence of stages, can exist. If one takes an individual out of his temporal context at various stages of his development, as Jaques does, one will inevitably falsify as well as omit much of what he is.

Jaques sees himself as an 'historian', chronicling the life of man. Now 'history' in this sense is concerned with events and states; it cannot afford to occupy itself with the subtle rhythms of gradual growth. The dialectic of 'historical' time, as I have pointed out . . . , is based on terms like 'before', 'after', 'earlier', and 'later', not on 'past', 'present', and 'future'. But the rhythm of growth is the rhythm of continuous, imperceptible change; and the growing-point of a human life is the present moment which carries with it the concepts of 'past' and 'future' as indications of the direction of growth. To take temporal cross-sections is to ignore the *process* of growth, concentrating only on its effects and results.

'History' in Jaques' sense, moreover, like philosophy, is a map; a map cannot reproduce the whole landscape in its minute detail. Yet we can only really know the landscape ('known' as *connaître,* not *savoir*), if we have all its details about us. A work of art can give us a sense of this but the pre-rational and personal principles of selection which are available to the artist are denied to Jaques' 'historian', who is in pursuit of impersonal truth, whose satire 'like a wild-goose flies, Unclaim'd of any man' [II. vii. 86-7], and who professes a disillusioned rationality.

Part of the force of Falstaff [in *1* and *2 Henry IV* and *The Merry Wives of Windsor*], perhaps, is that he is a dynamic character who changes and evolves in an environment of static, 'historical' time—the time of events and states. Falstaff is a work of art, and in fact develops from a wildly inaccurate selection and exaggeration by Shakespeare of meagre details in his sources.

Jaques' 'historical' viewpoint has other characteristics. One is that it is objective, rather than subjective. Jaques does not take into account what is almost the most important feature of time—the peculiar sensation, common to the human race, and therefore taken for granted, of living in time. What does it feel like to live in time? Everything that comes under that question is absent from Jaques' point of view. Since values and meaning exist only in the subjective sphere, Jaques is presenting a view of existence as valueless and meaningless. Since the sense of the living self exists only in the present moment (which is given no particular significance by Jaques), he is describing people who seem to have no self.

Jaques describes 'dead time'—time with no present moments. The advantage the dissector has when working with a dead body rather than a live one is that there is no change in the material being dissected: the body can get no deader. The vivisectionist, on the other hand, has always to beware of the fact that, like Heisenberg's electrons, his subject will be altered by the process of observation. Jaques is safe, working with dead time, and indeed his analytical method is appropriate to his subject. When we work with live time, however, we will find the present moment slipping away in an instant, and other methods of comprehension than Jaques' analytical and objective one must be found.

Finally, we may give attention to Jaques' use of generalization in this speech. 'In all cases, or at least in a good statistical majority, human beings will act in such and such a way' he seems to say. To generalize requires an initial comparison, or 'making equal', of those things about which one generalizes. If I use the generalizing word 'tree', I am assuming *a priori* that oaks, pines, elms, palms, etc., are all in some way basically the same. Indeed, generalization, like the historical dialectic, like objectivity, like the analytic method of thought itself, is essential in order to come at many kinds of truth. About human beings themselves we can and must generalize to a large extent in order to obtain the most primary understanding. But there seems to be something in every sane, undefeated human being that cries out for uniqueness, peerlessness, a sense of his own incomparability. Again, Jaques is not telling the whole story about human existence.

Both Jaques and Touchstone satirize the extravagant claims of love; but their points of view should not be confused. What Jaques says is 'see how absurd is the lover, with his sighs and ballads; for what is he, when his act is past? What a puny figure he cuts in the perspective of history! Does he not swiftly turn into something quite different? Surely his self-importance is misplaced. He is only a stage between schoolboy and soldier. His transports and agonies have no significance.' What Touchstone says is subtly different: 'What is love but Nature's mechanism for repeopling the earth? When it comes down to it, sex is what the whole thing amounts to after all. I myself, with all my wit, "press in" among the "country copulatives" [V. iv. 55-6], we are all part of the same natural rhythm, there is no qualitative difference between true lovers and the mating of beasts. The true significance of love is biological; the rest only icing on the cake.' Jaques sees the lover in the perspective of history; Touchstone, against the backdrop of brute nature; Jaques' ultimate reality is death, Touchstone's the natural cycle of reproduction; Jaques questions value, Touchstone's values are materialistic.

Posed against both viewpoints are the attitudes of the lovers. If Jaques in his great speech expresses the 'historical' view of time, Rosalind and Orlando are the representatives of 'personal' time. Time for them is dynamic:

> *Orl:* And why not the swift foot of Time? Had not that been as proper?
>
> *Ros:* By no means, sir. Time travels in divers paces with divers persons. I'll tell you who Time ambles withal, who Time trots withal, who Time gallops withal, and who he stands still withal.
>
> *Orl:* I prithee, who doth he trot withal?
>
> *Ros:* Marry, he trots hard with a young maid between the contract of her marriage and the day it is solemniz'd; if the interim be but a se'nnight, Time's pace is so hard that it seems the length of seven year.
>
> *Orl:* Who ambles Time withal?
>
> *Ros:* With a priest that lacks Latin and a rich man that hath not the gout; for the one sleeps easily because he cannot study, and the other lives merrily because he feels no pain; the one lacking the burden of lean and wasteful learning, the other knowing no burden of heavy tedious penury. These Time ambles withal.
>
> *Orl:* Who doth he gallop withal?
>
> *Ros:* With a thief to the gallows; for though he go as softly as foot can fall, he thinks himself too soon there.
>
> *Orl:* Who stays it still withal?
>
> *Ros:* With lawyers in the vacation; for they sleep between term and term, and they perceive not how Time moves.
>
> [III. ii. 306-33]

Here time is a pace or journey. At first glance this dialogue appears fairly simple: a witty expression of the commonplaces contained in such phrases as 'how time drags!' and 'time flies'. But in fact this passage is extravagantly difficult. Surely the conventional way of describing the young maid's suspense would be in terms of the slowness of time. Time 'crawls', we would imagine, for the waiting girl. But for Shakespeare it 'trots'. Why? Perhaps Shakespeare means that, for her, every moment is crowded with emotions, fancies, and anticipations. Clock time inches past; her own personal time is in a furious hurry. A week contains seven years' subjective events. The actual sense of motion is important here. When a horse trots, it throws one about a good deal more than when it gallops. One is not actually progressing as fast as at a gallop, but a half-hour's trot can leave as many unpleasant after-effects as a whole morning's gallop. Shakespeare is talking here as much about the *rhythm* of time as about anything else.

With the priest and the rich man the emphasis is different. Time 'ambles' for them because there is little in their lives of excitement, anticipation, or pain: but chiefly because an amble connotes indirection and a sense of 'let time take me where it will'. An ambling horse will stray off the path to munch at choice greenery; the rider does not care where he is going, or at any rate how soon he gets there.

The thief's progress again implies a different temporal epistemology; this time it is quite easily understood. Time 'flies' for the condemned man in its conventional way.

The lawyers present interesting problems. If they 'sleep between term and term', surely for them clock time flits by instantaneously: but according to Shakespeare it 'stands still'. What Shakespeare means, perhaps, is that subjective time is composed of changes and becomingness: if there is no change of becoming, time stands still. The lawyers 'perceive not how Time moves'.

It is clear that the operative words one would use to describe time in this passage would be 'past', 'present', and 'future'. Time here *is* movement, pace, change; man's life as the journey, not the road. Equally important here is the subjectivity of the temporal viewpoint. Rosalind sees her young maid, priest, rich man, thief, and lawyers not from the point of view of an impartial objective observer, but from their own point of view. Each has his own individual way of existing, his own perception of time. Rosalind is concerned not with what they appear to be externally, but what they feel themselves to be inside. Time is not something laid out inevitably before one, but is the motion of the present moment on which one rides into the unknown and non-existent world of the future, making it first exist and then part of the past. Man's life from this viewpoint can be full of meanings and direction: the young maid and the thief on his way to the gallows both see all their lives in relation to one hoped-for or feared event, some central fact that gives everything significance.

Rosalind, as we have seen earlier, is not 'above it all'; although her philosophy is more profound, perhaps, than Jaques', she is not 'philosophical'; she herself is in a plight not much different from that of her 'young maid'.

Elsewhere in the play the lovers' view of time is enlarged and elucidated for us. One of the most important aspects of it is the true lover's insistence on punctuality:

> *Orl:* My fair Rosalind, I come within an hour of my promise.
>
> *Ros:* Break an hour's promise in love! He that will divide a minute into a thousand parts, and break but a part of the thousand part of a minute in the affairs of love, it may be said of him that Cupid hath clapp'd him o' th' shoulder, but I'll warrant him heart-whole.
>
> [IV. i. 42-9]

The true lover is concerned not with measurable and divisible time, but with moments. The punctuality Rosalind insists on can be explained in terms of the etymology of the world. The Latin *punctus* means 'point'; for 'punctual' Webster gives '1. of or like point'. The lovers' time is a series of points; a temporal approximation is not good enough. The present moment is not an infinitesimal portion of the minute in which we are . . . ; it is like a point, it has no temporal thickness. (pp. 28-41)

The present is what is of importance to the Shakespearean lover:

> This carol they began that hour,
> With a hey, and a ho, and a hey nonino,
> How that a life was but a flower,
> In the spring time, etc.
>
> And therefore take the present time,
> With a hey, and a ho, and a hey nonino,
> For love is crowned with the prime,
> In the spring time, etc.
>
> [V. iii. 26-33]

This is living time, the only time we exist, the present moment.

The enemy and test of lovers' time is 'historical' time. 'Well,' says Rosalind, 'Time is the old justice that examines all such offenders, and let Time try [IV. i. 199-200]. Teasingly she assumes the attitudes of Jaques or Touchstone in order to wring denials out of Orlando: 'Say "a day" without the "ever". No, no, Orlando; men are April when they woo, December when they are wed: maids are May when they are maids, but the sky changes when they are wives' [IV. i. 146-49]. This echoes Jaques' view in its generalization and assumed 'philosophical' detachment; and Touchstone's in its subordination of love to the natural cycle. True love must ultimately deny both 'historical' and 'natural' time;

though it must also find some reconciliation or *modus vivendi* with them. (The tragedy of *Romeo and Juliet* is that the reconciliation is not made with 'historical' time, the time of the Montagues and Capulets; and it is snuffed out or smothered by it. The tragedy of *Troilus and Cressida* and *Othello*, on the other hand, is that there is a compromise with 'historical' and 'natural' time, and not a true reconciliation.

In *As You Like It* such a reconciliation can and does take place. In the 'lover and his lass' song, love is reconciled with the natural cycle:

> It was a lover and his lass,
> With a hey, and a ho, and a hey nonino,
> That o'er the green corn-field did pass
> In the spring time, the only pretty ring
> time
> When birds do sing, hey ding a ding, ding.
> Sweet lovers love the spring.
>   [V. iii. 16-21]

The great seasons allow a time for love: nature is not essentially opposed to the spiritual movements of man. This reconciliation is brought about thematically by the use of the idea of musical 'time': the rhythm and temporal order of a song can form a bridge between the great natural rhythms and the smaller human ones. The pages who sing the song indicate its significance: 'We kept time, we lost not our time' [V. iii. 37-8] Touchstone, who has consistently reduced human significances to sub-human natural drives, cannot accept the musical reconciliation: 'I count it but time lost to hear such a foolish song' [V. iii. 39-40]; applying the judgments of expediency to it. 'What use is it? It is only a waste of time.' The verdict of Jaques on Touchstone is that 'Time, the old justice that examines all such offenders', will find him wanting: ' . . . thy loving voyage Is but for two months victuall'd' [V. iv. 191-92]. It is significant that when Hymen characterizes the nature of Touchstone's alliance with Audrey, she uses a seasonal image: 'as the winter to foul weather' [V. iv. 136]. But Touchstone has served his purpose. He too is a test, an assay. His function, as his name implies, is to point out true love where it exists, to distinguish gold from base metal.

Touchstone rejects the song; Jaques rejects the dance. At the end of the play, we are shown another rhythmic reconciliation:

> . . . you brides and bridegrooms all,
> With measure heap'd in joy, to th' mea-
> sures fall.
>   [V. iv. 178-79]

Dancing is one of the ways we ritually reconcile the individual with society. The measures of the dance bring together moderation and joy; social, or 'historical' time is reconciled with individual or 'personal' time. Jaques cannot accept this. Though he recognizes Orlando's 'true faith,' he states that he is 'for other than for dancing measures'; 'to see no

pastime I' he insists—a sentiment almost identical to Touchstone's when he reacts to the 'spring time' song [V. iv. 188-96].

Obviously the most important thing about the last scene of *As You Like It* is its marriages. Helen Gardner, in a penetrating discussion of the difference between comedy and tragedy, declares: 'The great symbol of pure comedy is marriage by which the world is renewed, and its endings are always instinct with a sense of fresh beginnings. Its rhythm is the rhythm of the life of mankind, which goes on and renews itself as the life of nature does.' Marriage is the reconciliation of the subjective faith, love, and hope of the individual, the objectivity and commonsense of society, and the mighty forces of fertile nature:

> You to a love that your true faith doth
>   merit;
> You to your land, and love, and great allies;
> You to a long and well-deserved bed . . .
>   [V. iv. 188-90]

Marriage can contain love, a legal contract, and sex in an extraordinary harmony. 'Personal', 'historical', and 'natural' time are reconciled in its sacrament, its 'blessed bond':

> Then is there mirth in heaven,
> When earthly things made even
> Atone together.
>   [V. iv. 108-10]

What Jaques and Touchstone have to say is indeed valid, within limits. If their basilisk eye of satire and cynicism were not open in all of us, we should be very impractical creatures. More important, if their viewpoints were not represented in the play we should soon lose sympathy with the highfalutin' dialectics of romantic love. Jaques and Touchstone inoculate us: and they prepare us for the grand reconciliation that is to be performed by the other great comic character in the play, Rosalind herself. (pp. 42-4)

Frederick Turner, "As You Like It: 'Subjective', 'Objective', and 'Natural' Time," in his Shakespeare and the Nature of Time: Moral and Philosophical Themes in Some Plays and Poems of William Shakespeare, *Oxford at the Clarendon Press, 1971, pp. 28-44.*

ORLANDO

Thomas Kelly

*[Kelly provides an extensive analysis of **Orlando**'s character, asserting that he is distinct from Shakespeare's other romantic heroes who, as a rule, tend to be portrayed as inept and slightly ridiculous. The critic regards **Orlando** as generally self-possessed and capa-*

ble of controlling events in As You Like It; *according to Kelly, he also demonstrates a wisdom that sets him apart as a "romantic hero of a new stamp." For further commentary on **Orlando**'s character, see the excerpts by Alfred Harbage, Brigid Brophy, Kenneth Muir, John A. Hart, and Nancy K. Hayles.]*

As a rule . . . we are inclined to regard Shakespeare's romantic heroes as peculiarly inept and slightly ridiculous figures. The generalization seems warranted and may, in addition, offer a valuable insight into the deepest nature of Shakespearean comedy. Like all powerful generalizations, however, its very strength constitutes a danger. If our recognition of a pattern in many plays disposes us to discover less obvious but similar patterns in a few others, we can record a critical gain. But what if the general pattern prejudices our reading of apparently similar plays? What if it thereby threatens to subvert the special meaning a given work should develop?

I belabor what may be an obvious point because the abuse toward which it looks may well be responsible for the relative neglect of at least two of Shakespeare's romantic heroes. Both Florizel in *The Winter's Tale* and Orlando in *As You Like It* seem to me to deserve more credit than it is customary to give them. Florizel's is the simpler and the less crucial case. Like *The Tempest* (and unlike *Two Gentlemen of Verona*), *The Winter's Tale* is concerned with restoring, rather than rejuvenating, the old order. Thus, although Florizel may be more perceptive and more effective in shaping events than Perdita is, they are both clearly subordinate to Leontes and Hermione. Redressing an imbalance in favor of Florizel is therefore a marginal undertaking. The center of the play lies elsewhere.

This is patently not the case in *As You Like It*. Since the play is closer to the design of the earlier comedies, its primary interest is naturally the romance between Orlando and Rosalind. The values of the older generation are important, but they are subsumed under the various attributes of the two lovers. Consequently, to overlook Orlando or to see in him another Valentine [in *The Two Gentlemen of Verona*], Bassanio [in *The Merchant of Venice*], or Claudio [in *Much Ado about Nothing*] is, in a sense, to appreciate only half the play. To characterize him as the least conscious of Shakespeare's unconscious heroes . . . is certainly to misread the play. But even to patronize him, as is more often the case, is to obscure the fact that *As You Like It*, with its more "serious" and competent hero, is a nexus between the early and the late comedies— and perhaps between the early comedies and the tragedies as well. Orlando, in short, is a breed apart. Helen Gardner's observation that "Orlando has to prove that he truly is, as he seems at first sight, the right husband for Rosalind and show himself gentle, courteous, generous and brave, and a match for her in wit" is exceptionally perceptive

[in her "As You Like It." Reprinted in *Discussions of Shakespeare's Romantic Comedy*, ed. Herbert Weil (1966)]. Another way of putting it is that in Orlando, the romantic hero overcomes his earlier failings: he is, for the first time, a match for the heroine not only in wit but also in awareness and control.

Not everyone, of course, will agree. A fair measure of the general tendency to scant Orlando, for example, is the cursory analysis customarily accorded the events of the first act. The critical consensus seems to be that Shakespeare was in great haste to get his characters into the Forest of Arden. This, some would say, accounts for the confusion of the heights of Rosalind and Celia, of the ages of the two Dukes, and of the time since Frederick usurped the throne. Nothing could be further from the truth. The discrepancies can be discovered, but noticing them hardly strikes at the heart of Shakespeare's method in *As You Like It*. What should be noticed instead is the typical economy with which one scene in the first act is used to prefigure the rest of the play. The wrestling match may, as Bernard Shaw implied, have pleased the groundlings, but it requires only a little attention to detail to see how much more it does simultaneously.

In the broadest thematic terms, it is a graphic metaphor for the discord announced by the first lines of the play. "The spirit of my father, which I think is within me, begins to mutiny against this servitude," Orlando tells Adam [I. i. 22-4], and when Oliver enters Orlando is shortly at his throat. Discord at a higher level, in the state itself, is next disclosed by Charles, the professional wrestler. His reply to Oliver's request for news tells us of the overthrow of the old Duke and of his banishment. For the unruly, not to say chaotic, condition of public and private life in the world of the play, the wrestling match becomes a fitting visual symbol. Viewed from a distance, the movement of the play thus turns from the hurly-burly of the wrestling to the forester's informal march with the carcass of the slain deer, to the ritual harmony of the "dancing measures" with which the play ends.

Yet this only begins to disentangle the meanings worked into the "breaking of ribs" interlude. Because the match between Orlando and Charles occurs late in the act, they are each able to represent various aspects of the play's several themes when they finally meet. For example, by accepting Oliver's false report of Orlando's treachery, Charles becomes an agent, if not a surrogate, for Oliver. "This wrestler," Oliver says, "shall clear all," [I. i. 171-72].

Still more important is the alignment between Charles and the Court itself. Adam, at one point, speaks of Charles as "the bonny prizer of the humorous Duke" [II. iii. 8], and Charles himself admits to being as ambition-ridden and jealous of his position as any of the courtiers. Like them, he regards his footing atop Fortune's wheel as a precarious station, one which cannot be shared:

> To-morrow, sir, [he tells Oliver] I wrestle for my credit, and he that escapes me without some broken limb shall acquit him well. Your brother is but young and tender, and for your love I would be loath to foil him, as I must for my own honour if he come in.
>
> [I. i. 126-31]

Charles, it is true, speaks handsomely about the merry young gentlemen who have joined the exiled Duke in the golden world of the Forest, but his secondhand judgment of Arden is as impersonal as Oliver's unexpected praise of Orlando's gentleness, learning, and "noble device."

As Charles' opponent, Orlando rightly embodies the values of nature and of a less competitive but more peaceful past. Both literally and figuratively, he stands for the Forest of Arden itself. Translated from the French, his surname (de Bois in its original spelling) identifies Orlando as certainly as any morality figure with the pastoral ideal. Moreover, the frequent reminders that he is the youngest son

of Sir Rowland (Orlando is in fact an anagram for Rowland) make clear that the virtues of the antique world still live in Orlando. Adam's greeting after Orlando has bested Charles is especially pointed:

> O my sweet master! O you memory
> Of old Sir Rowland! Why, what make you here?
> Why are you virtuous? Why do people love you?
> And wherefore are you gentle, strong, and valiant?
> . . .
> O, what a world is this, when what is comely
> Envenoms him that bears it!
>
> [II. iii. 3-15]

A second but no less effective indication of Orlando's position is Adam's explicit assertion, however illogical and bumbling, that Oliver is *not* Sir Rowland's son:

> Within this roof
> The enemy of all your graces lives.
> Your brother (no, no brother! yet the son—
> Yet not the son—I will not call him son

Charles, Duke Frederick, Celia, Rosalind, Touchstone, Orlando, and others. Act I, scene ii. By Daniel Maclise.

Of him I was about to call his father.)
[II. iii. 17-21]

The awkwardness of the lines may even be informative. May it not typify the disjointed times over which Oliver and Duke Frederick preside?

The more purely natural aspect of Orlando's character is established by his account of his training at his brother's charge. "He keeps me rustically at home" [I. i. 7], Orlando tells Adam. And to Oliver himself he complains, "You have trained me like a peasant, obscuring and hiding from me all gentlemanlike qualities" [I. i. 68-70]. That Orlando goes on to demand "such exercises as may become a gentleman" [I. i. 74] need discomfort no one. Touchstone, it is true, makes memorable sport of such gentlemanly exercises as poison, bastinado, faction, and policy, just as Oliver shows them in practice. But the irony of Orlando's demanding membership in such a class, like the irony of his competing with Charles, has been carefully measured. Because of it, Orlando is saved from becoming either a stereotyped prig or a sentimental cartoon.

Still, for those who prefer to take their heroes straight, the play permits the feeling that Orlando is neither corrupted nor corruptible. There is nothing to suggest and much to deny that, as a member of the Court, Orlando would also succumb to its code of expediency and lust for power and privilege. Hence, when the wrestlers meet, we are prepared to take one, Charles, as the hireling of the Court and Fortune, and the other, Orlando, as the champion of Nature and the pastoral ideal.

The Wrestling Scene is instructive, furthermore, in confirming that comic time governs *As You Like It*. The news that the old Duke and the many young gentlemen who surround him "fleet the time carelessly" [I. i. 118] merely posits an alternative to the brawling present. Somewhat more hopeful is the early speech by Celia, the immediate purpose of which is to declare the deep regard in which she holds Rosalind:

> You know my father hath no child but I,
> nor none is like to have; and truly, when
> he dies, thou shalt be his heir; for what he
> hath taken away from thy father perforce,
> I will render thee again in affection.
> [I. ii. 17-21]

The secondary effect of such a promise, it seems to me, is to commit time to a redemptive role, rather than a destructive one. It remains, however, for Orlando to dramatize, in the wrestling match, the full vigor of comic time, to demonstrate that our normal causative expectations can be upset. Life, in Susanne Langer's terms, triumphs over Fate when Orlando throws Charles, the man who, by all odds, ought to have won. Other "accidents" abound in the play and finally crown it, but most of them are only actions which had no reason to happen. Orlando's success is in another class altogether—it

has a reason not to happen. For once, not even Rosalind is able to see beyond appearance. "Pray heaven I be deceived in you," she says to Orlando [I. ii. 197-98]. And, of course, she is—a fact commonly disregarded by critics who want Orlando always to play the dupe to Rosalind's Ganymede.

Rosalind's other remarks at the wrestling also deserve attention. As surely as Charles is leagued with Oliver, Rosalind leagues herself with Orlando. "The little strength I have, I would it were with you" [I. ii. 194-95], she says. But Oliver and Rosalind are clearly passive participants. For the moment, the stage is the wrestlers' and, after Charles is borne away speechless, Orlando's alone. Later, in a thinly disguised rehearsal for the wedding to come, Rosalind claims her share of the victory by placing a lightly ironic chain around Orlando's neck. "Wear this for me, one out of suits with Fortune" [I. ii. 246], are her words as she links Nature with Nature's own. How Shakespeare could have done more in one act to give Orlando a place equal in every respect to Rosalind's I find hard to imagine.

A single scene, however, especially a symbolic one, does not constitute a play. The sense that Orlando determines the final shape of the comedy may be conveyed in the Wrestling Scene, but his ability to recognize more of reality than its conventional surface must be proved in Arden. This is not to say that he must possess either perfect vision or complete knowledge. Probably no one does: each of the likely contenders for such perfection in *As You Like It* fails one or more times to comprehend fully the experience in which he is involved. Thus, though the old Duke can find "tongues in trees, books in the running brooks, sermons in stones, and good in everything" [II. i. 16-17], he does not recognize his daughter; Rosalind, as we have already seen, is deceived in Orlando's power; and Touchstone, the play's great realist, mistakes among other things the author of the verses which Rosalind enters reading. (He is also blind to parody of any but the most gross kind—that is, his own.)

A more reasonable criterion of Orlando's perception therefore is whether he sees as much or as deeply as the best of the others. His understanding, to be estimable, must rival Rosalind's, not ours. Consequently, it is worth noting several passages which show that his perceptions and hers are admirably alike. Consider, for example, their initial responses to the "green world" of the Forest of Arden. Despite Duke Frederick's imperious threats, the departure of Celia and Rosalind for Arden retains the character of a prank. One is reminded most perhaps of *The Merchant of Venice*. The distinction between a daughter's manners and her father's, the gathering of jewels, and the masquerade all echo the elopement of Lorenzo and Jessica. But Arden, like Prospero's island [in *The Tempest*], is a more subjective paradise than Belmont, a lesson that both Rosalind and Orlando quickly learn from appropriate "counselors."

The notable lack of enthusiasm in Rosalind's lines when she, Celia, and Touchstone arrive at Arden has often been remarked:

> O Jupiter, how weary are my spirits!
>
> . . .
>
> I could find it in my heart to disgrace my man's apparel
> and to cry like a woman.
>
> . . .
>
> Well, this is the Forest of Arden.
>
> [II. iv. 1-15]

To quicken her spirits she has to observe and to talk to Corin, the old shepherd who has so thoroughly assimilated Nature's lessons that he cannot utter an unsound word or do an ungenerous deed. His advice to Silvius is compassionate, humble, and wise. Within Rosalind's hearing Corin admits to having been drawn by his fancy into a thousand actions "most ridiculous." (One thinks, without disapproving, of Orlando's dashing from tree to tree, carving Rosalind's name.) Moreover, when Rosalind asks help for the fainting Celia, Corin's instinctive response pointedly affirms the true and permanent value of the pastoral ideal:

> Corin. Fair sir, I pity her
> And wish, for her sake more than for mine own,
> My fortunes were more able to relieve her;
> But I am shepherd to another man
> And do not shear the fleeces that I graze.
> My master is of churlish disposition
> And little recks to find the way to heaven
> By doing deeds of hospitality.
>
> . . .
>
> By reason of his absence, there is nothing
> That you will feed on; but what is, come see,
> And in my voice most welcome shall you be.
>
> [II. iv. 75-87]

Were Touchstone allowed to intrude, he would doubtless observe that one can make but a poor meal of words. It is Celia, however, surely speaking for Rosalind as well as herself, who responds "I like this place and willingly could waste my time in it" [II. iv. 86-7].

Orlando's initiation to the forest is strikingly similar. When Adam, like Celia, "can go no further" and calls a temporary halt, Orlando sees around him an "uncouth forest," a "desert." The air, he says, is "bleak." He discovers the genius of the place, however, when, searching for food for Adam, he comes upon the banquet spread for the old Duke and finds his rude demands answered by gracious, natural hospitality:

> Duke Senior. What would you have? Your gentleness shall force
> More than your force move us to gentleness.

> . . .
>
> Sit down and feed, and welcome to our table.
>
> [II. vii. 102-05]

But Orlando, much like Rosalind, had been playing a part to protect himself:

> Speak you so gently? Pardon me, I pray you.
> I thought that all things had been savage here,
> And therefore put I on the countenance
> Of stern commandment.
>
> [II. vii. 106-09]

Moreover, in his response to the Duke's assurance of "what help we can," Orlando quietly discloses a revised view of Arden:

> Then but forebear your food a little while,
> Whiles, like a doe, I go to find my fawn
> And give it food.
>
> [II. vii. 127-29]

The ease and clarity with which Rosalind and Celia on the one hand and Orlando on the other perceive the moral climate of Arden is in pointed contrast to the hypercritical vision of Jaques and to the sharp, but essentially superficial, vision of Touchstone. Although Jaques' moralizing on the deer "that from the hunter's aim had ta'ken a hurt" shows "a mind full of matter," it is a mind unable to conceive solutions for the discords it sees everywhere. He can pierce through "the body of the country, city, court; Yea, and of this our life" [II. i. 34, 59-60], but he cannot ascend to the irrational world of love and grace.

As a cynic, Jaques is one of two real aliens in Arden's green world. The other, of course, is Touchstone. Jaques dissolves the distinctions between Court and country by regarding them through the prism of his pessimism; Touchstone dissolves them through his unrefracted realism. When he arrives at Arden, not his spirits but his legs are tired. Given the opportunity to make sport of Orlando's parody of romantic verse, Touchstone is careful to exempt time for "dinners, and suppers and sleeping hours" [III. ii. 97]. His offer of marriage to Audrey, the goatgirl, is the fitting expression of a frank, physical need. How close, yet how far, Touchstone stations himself from Corin's natural perspective can be seen by the fine line that separates the focus of two of their juxtaposed speeches:

> Corin. Sir, I am a true labourer; I earn that I eat, get that I wear; owe no man hate, envy no man's happiness; glad of other men's good, content with my harm; and the greatest of my pride is to see my ewes graze and my *lambs suck.*

> Touchstone. That is another simple sin in you: to bring the ewes and the rams together and to offer to get your living by the *copulation of cattle*; to be bawd to a bell-

wether, and to betray a she-lamb of a twelve-month [Audrey] to a crooked-pated old cuckoldy ram [himself] out of all reasonable match.

[III. ii. 73-83, italics added]

The relative awareness of Orlando, Rosalind, Touchstone, and Jaques can also be plotted by analyzing their respective perceptions of another of Arden's defining parameters—time. Touchstone's attitude toward time has been accurately understood when we see him as Fortune's timepiece. He does not, however, hold that office alone. Because his famous "And so from hour to hour we ripe and ripe and then from hour to hour we rot and rot" [II. vii. 26-7], is related with approval by Jaques, and because he (Jaques) has his own set speech on time, the moribund Seven Ages, the honor should be shared between them. Touchstone's time, moreover, strongly resembles the Court's time. Like Touchstone, Duke Frederick rules, in a sense, by the clock. When he exiles Rosalind, for example, he leans heavily on temporal terms for force:

Duke Frederick. Mistress, dispatch you
  with your safest haste
And get you from our court!

Rosalind. Me, uncle?

Duke Frederick. You, cousin.
Within these ten days if that thou beest
  found
So near our public court as twenty miles,
Thou diest for it.

[I. iii. 41-4]

Moreover, lest the point be missed, the threat is repeated fifty lines later. "If you outstay the time," Frederick tells his niece, "you die" [I. iii. 88-9]. Again, after learning that Celia has fled with Rosalind, he commands that Orlando or Oliver be brought before him "suddenly." And when Oliver appears, he is told to produce his brother

Within this twelvemonth, or turn thou no
  more
To seek a living in our territory.

[III. i. 7-8]

Time therefore is inflexible and threatening for the Court, as for the realist and the cynic. Like Fortune's wheel, its movement is inexorable and destructive. It is a primary source of limitation. In another context, it would be tragic: it leads forth death.

The natural time of Arden, on the other hand, is comic: it leads forth life. As Jaques concludes his "strange eventful history" of man in

Second childishness and mere oblivion,
Sans teeth, sans eyes, sans taste, sans everything

[II. vii. 165-66]

Orlando enters with the fawn-like Adam. It is Orlando, moreover, who comments most often and

most explicitly on this special quality of Arden's time scheme. His comments come, furthermore, in those two encounters with the disguised Rosalind which have always been regarded as the great comic heart of the play. The first is unusual inasmuch as Orlando is allowed to exploit one of Rosalind's few failures of poise. Having learned from Celia that the verse hung "upon hawthornes" is Orlando's work, Rosalind is distracted with nervous anticipation:

Alas the day! what shall I do with my doublet and hose? What did he when thou
saw'st him? What said he? How looked
he? Wherein went he? What makes he
here? Did he ask for me? Where remains
he? How parted he with thee? and when
shalt thou see him again? Answer me in
one word.

[III. ii. 219-24]

Orlando's entrance a moment later unquestionably increases her girlish excitement. His parody of courtly manners as he takes his leave of Jaques ("I do desire we may be better strangers" [III. ii. 258]) and his defense of Rosalind ("There was no thought of pleasing you when she was christened" [III. ii. 266-67]) prompt even the cynic to grant Orlando's "nimble wit." And when Jaques invites him to join in railing against the world, Orlando answers, "I will chide no breather in the world but myself, against whom I know most faults" [III. ii. 280-81]. It is an answer steeped in the humility of self-knowledge. If it is also obtruded somewhat heavyhandedly into a satiric scene, it is nonetheless irrefutable evidence that Orlando is, indeed, an exceptional romantic hero.

From Rosalind's point of view, however, the next exchange may be more precious still:

Jaques. The worst fault you have is to be
  in love.
Orlando. 'Tis a fault I will not change for
  your best virtue.

[III. ii. 282-84]

Love wedded to wit and humility! Is it any wonder, then, that as Rosalind steps forward to "speak to him like a saucy lackey," she blunders and asks lamely, "I pray you, what is it o'clock?" [III. ii. 295-96, 299] Orlando's reply, fortunately, gives unexpected point to the question. "You should ask me, what time o' day," he says. "There is no clock in the forest" [III. ii. 300-01]. Rosalind's rejoinder that time is relative, traveling in "divers paces with divers persons" [III. ii. 308-09], is a brilliant recovery but does not erase Orlando's equally shrewd insight.

Because so much more than a statement of Arden's comic time is accomplished in the second encounter between Orlando and "Ganymede," it would perhaps be wise to approach the scene more broadly, noting Orlando's superiority within the context of his and Rosalind's total achievement.

That achievement, one might begin by noticing, is partly the product of the action which surrounds it. The first encounter takes place at the end of the longest scene in the play and gains, as I have intimated, from what precedes it. Following it is a scene between Audrey and Touchstone. The scene between Silvius and Phoebe, which follows next, precedes in turn the second and principal encounter between Rosalind and Orlando. The principle of juxtaposition is important, of course, throughout *As You Like It.* Once the action has moved to the Forest of Arden, however, the ideas which are juxtaposed are not always the narrow dichotomies of Court versus country, Fortune versus Nature. The hierarchy represented by the three pairs of lovers, for example, can hardly continue the contrast between Court and country since only one of the number, Touchstone, can be taken in any sense as a courtier.

Yet there *is* a thematic element common to them all. One ambitious suggestion is that the second and deeper theme is "the relation of love and wisdom" [Harold C. Goddard, *The Meaning of Shakespeare*]. A less abstract, and perhaps more defensible, way of putting it might be that the second theme is the definition of wisdom as comic flexibility. Rigidity, like limitation and Fate, denies life. In Arden, where perception is the index of character, the ability to recognize multiple levels of experience is salutary. It is superseded, in fact, only by the ability to move at will between various levels, to realize in practice several modes of experience without being locked in the iron embrace of any one. This, I submit, is the profound truth which determines our preference for Rosalind and Orlando. The flesh-bound life of a Touchstone and Audrey, we see, is as much a dead end as the fossilized conventional ideal of a Silvius and Phoebe. By achieving a fluid synthesis between these frozen poles, Orlando and Rosalind infuse life with a comic warmth in which we can bask with profit.

That Rosalind possesses the requisite imagination for such a synthesis is, as I understand it, the thematic import of Ganymede's proposing to cure Orlando's love if he would but come every day to the sheep cote and woo a make-believe lover. The dazzling circumstance of a child actor playing Shakespeare's Rosalind playing Rosalind's Ganymede playing Ganymede's Rosalind is, by general agreement, the finest moment in the play. Since we must simultaneously cope with a choice of speaker—Rosalind, Ganymede, or "Rosalind"—and with the possibility that two or more of these speakers may share some speeches, the multiple layers of character create seemingly inexhaustible layers of irony. Between Shakespeare's Rosalind and Ganymede's Rosalind we sense a variable field of force which often holds the figures apart but which sometimes collapses to let them overlap and occasionally merge.

Unfortunately, the delight we take in Rosalind's marvelous virtuosity seems to have obscured the fact that Orlando is her imaginative equal. Rosalind, we have already seen, is not the only one to enter Arden disguised: Orlando's countenance of stern commandment at the forester's feast was also "put on." Armed with the memory of that charade, we may suspect that the Silvius side of Orlando:

> I would not have my right Rosalind of this
> mind, for I protest her frown might kill me
> [IV. i. 109-10]

is no more "real" and no more limiting than the Touchstone side of Rosalind:

> Maids are May when they are maids, but the sky changes when they are wives. I will be more jealous of thee than a Barbary cock-pigeon over his hen [*sic*], more clamorous than a parrot against rain, more newfangled than an ape, more giddy in my desires than a monkey.
> [IV. i. 148-53]

The body of external evidence which supports the feeling that while Ganymede is playing "Rosalind" Orlando is playing "Orlando," is not inconsiderable. Perhaps the clearest sign of the distance which separates the two Orlando's is his pointed failure to dress as becomes his assumed part. The marks of the conventional prisoner of love are "a lean cheek . . . a beard neglected . . . sleeve unbuttoned . . . shoe untied, and everything . . . demonstrating a careless desolation." But, says Rosalind to Orlando, "You are no such man: you are rather point-device in your accoutrements, as loving yourself, than seeming the lover of any other" [III. ii. 373-84].

Additional indications that Orlando has adopted a role for the nonce frame the Wooing Scene. Orlando's greeting to Rosalind ("Good day and happiness, dear Rosalind" [IV. i. 30]) is jeered at by Jaques as "blank verse"—as language, in other words, appropriate to artificial discourse, if not explicitly to the stage. Moreover, Orlando proves as shamelessly tardy a lover as earlier he had proved point-device. "I come within an hour of my promise," he says [IV. i. 42-3], provoking from Rosalind both some courtly railings about lovers being prompt to the thousandth part of a minute and a Touchstonesque quip about horned snails and cuckoldry.

The importance of the exchange is confirmed, I think, when Rosalind returns to the question in her last full speech in the scene:

> *Rosalind.* . . . if you break one jot of your promise or come one minute behind your hour, I will think you the most pathetical break-promise, and the most hollow lover. . . . Therefore beware my censure and keep your promise.
> [IV. i. 190-96]

Orlando's rejoinder, "With no less religion than if thou wert indeed my Rosalind" [IV. i. 197-98], is as steeped in irony as any line spoken by Rosalind. On the level of the private play in which Orlando and Rosalind have been engaged, the vow is securely within the courtly convention. (We may remember Silvius protesting, "So holy and so perfect is my love, and I in such a poverty of grace. . . . " [III. v. 99-100]) The ironic coloring—the strength of the vow depends on a fact which Orlando does not know to be true—complicates, but does not subvert, the convention. If, on the other hand, the speaker is the Orlando who overthrew Charles and who fed Adam, the vow is a useful means of demonstrating where Orlando's values lie. Since, in effect, Orlando fails to keep his hour when he elects to save Oliver from the "sucked and hungry lioness" [IV. iii. 126], we must either applaud his breach of romantic faith or, much better, see that conventional romanticism as a momentary role.

A final sign that Orlando has consciously adopted a momentary role deserves special attention. The decision to bring down the curtain on the masquerade within Arden is, not without reason, given to Orlando. His "I can live no longer by thinking" [V. ii. 50] is the cue for Ganymede's metamorphosis, but it is also a reminder of Orlando's initiative. Moreover, it shows that Orlando knows what Shakespeare never forgets, namely, that Arden, like the theater itself, is only a means to an end. It is misleading, therefore, to think of *As You Like It* as a test of Orlando. From the moment he triumphs over Charles, Orlando establishes himself as a romantic hero of a new stamp. The succeeding scenes may fill in the outline and deepen the colors, but there should never be the least doubt of Orlando's unique stature. Unlike his peers among Shakespeare's romantic heroes, Orlando is self-possessed and possessed of exceptional self-knowledge. (pp. 13-24)

Thomas Kelly, "Shakespeare's Romantic Heroes: Orlando Reconsidered," in Shakespeare Quarterly, *Vol. XXIV, No. 1, Winter, 1973, pp. 12-24.*

ROSALIND

Lorentz Eckhoff

[*In the following excerpt, Eckhoff examines* **Rosalind**'s *character, particularly the "sparkling gaiety and wit" she maintains even in the face of adversity. It is the heroine's "proud and benevolent nature," according to the critic, that makes her not only a stable person, but a source of encouragement for other characters in the play. For further commentary on* **Rosalind**'s *character, see the excerpts by Alfred Harbage, Brigid Brophy, Kenneth Muir, John*

A. Hart, Nancy K. Hayles, Thomas F. Van Laan, Thomas Kelly, and Clara Claiborne Park.]

Let us consider Rosalind in *As you like it*. It goes without saying that she is closely related to many others of Shakespeare's favourite daughters, such as Viola [in *Twelfth Night*], Imogen [in *Cymbeline*] and Marina [in *Pericles*]. She has their wisdom, their firmness of character, and at the same time their pliancy, their indomitable courage in the face of adversity. On the other side of the family tree she is related to Portia from *The Merchant of Venice*, and has in common with her a precious gift, which is invaluable if one is to play the part of heroine in a comedy: sparkling gaiety and wit.

When the duke banishes her, she has to all appearances no complaint to make, no bitterness to vent. Her conduct is as impeccable and sensible as that of the lamb in the fable faced with the provocations of the wolf. She only asks what wrong she has done, and thereby brings into full relief the duke's cowardice and brutality.

> I do beseech your Grace,
> Let me the knowledge of my fault bear
> with me.
>
> [I. iii. 45-6]

She is told that she is her father's daughter, and replies:

> So was I when your highness took his
> dukedom;
> So was I when your highness banish'd
> him.
> Treason is not inherited, my lord;
> Or, if we did derive it from our friends,
> What's that to me? My father was no trai-
> tor:
> Then, good my liege, mistake me not so
> much
> To think my poverty is treacherous.
>
> [I. iii. 59-65]

Life is not easy for her at court, her father has been exiled, and she senses no doubt that the fate which overtook her father is hanging over her own head. When Celia, rather exacting, bids her be merry, Rosalind can with justice reply:

> Dear Celia, I show more mirth than I am
> mistress of, and would you yet I were mer-
> rier? Unless you could teach me to forget
> a banished father, you must not learn me
> how to remember any extraordinary plea-
> sure.
>
> [I. ii. 3-7]

But since Celia bids her, she is at once ready with a merry thought: what think you of falling in love?—little knowing that before the hour is past her jest will be reality. Later they reach the forest, Celia and Touchstone are fainting with weariness, and Rosalind herself is on the point of disgracing her man's apparel and weeping like a woman. But she must comfort the weaker vessels, "as doublet and hose ought to show itself courageous to petticoat: therefore, courage, good Aliena!" [II. iv. 6-8].

She meets the peasant Corin, buys his farmstead, and thus procures a solid foundation for her bodily comforts; and soon after she gets as sure a foundation for her merriment, namely the poems which Orlando has hung up in the trees, and which in bad verse declare his love for Rosalind. At first she is terrified, what can she do now in her doublet and hose? But he comes in person, and fails to recognise her, and Rosalind is bursting with suppressed gaiety; what a wonderful chance she has to act! And at the same time to hear him in person, every hour of the day, re-assure her of his great love for Rosalind! And without having to blush at his declarations! And she finds a delightful pretext for keeping the game up. Love, she declares,—or rather *he,* Ganymede, declares, is sheer madness, and should be cured, and if only the patient will submit to his treatment, he Ganymede will cure him. He has been successful in his treatment before, and knows the remedy. The only thing required is for Orlando to pretend that Ganymede is his beloved, his beloved mistress, and woo him each day; and Ganymede guarantees "he" will be able to "wash his liver as clean as a sound sheep's heart, that there be not one spot of love in't" [III. ii. 422-23]. Orlando is not exactly keen to be cured of his passion, but he would like to come each day and call Ganymede Rosalind, and woo her each day. He, Ganymede, is however not quite convinced that Orlando is a prisoner in love's "cage of rushes" [III. ii. 371], for he can find none of the marks of that madness on him, which she enumerates:

> A lean cheek, which you have not; a blue eye and sunken, which you have not; an unquestionable spirit, which you have not; a beard neglected, which you have not; but I pardon you for that, for, simply, your having in beard is a younger brother's revenue. Then, your hose should be ungartered, your bonnet unbanded, your sleeve unbuttoned, your shoe untied, and everything about you demonstrating a careless desolation. But you are no such man: you are rather point-device in your accoutrements; as loving yourself than seeming the lover of any other.
>
> [III. ii. 373-84]

Such is the nature of Rosalind's wit and merriment. It springs first and foremost from a proud and benevolent nature, jealous of its own honour, which demands of itself the ability to gladden other people and give them courage, and not burden them with its own sorrows. It springs also from the abounding joy of living which fills a resolute and courageous woman, who is sure of her own youth and beauty, knows that she is beloved, and is determined to make the best out of life. And may be more than that, she has imagination, and understanding of human nature, and a loving tolerance toward its weaknesses and foibles. Let us look at

another sample. Orlando is unable to tell her what the time is, as there is no clock in the forest.

Rosalind:

Then there is no true lover in the forest; else sighing every minute and groaning every hour would detect the lazy foot of Time as well as a clock.

Orlando:

And why not swift foot of Time? had not that been as proper?

Rosalind:

By no means, sir. Time travels in divers paces with divers persons. I'll tell you who Time ambles withal, who Time trots withal, who Time gallops withal, and who he stands still withal.

Orlando:

I prithee, who doth he trot withal?

Rosalind:

Marry, he trots hard with a young maid between the contract of her marriage and the day it is solemnized; if the interim be but a se'nnight, Time's pace is so hard that it seems the length of seven years.

Orlando:

Who ambles Time withal?

Rosalind:

With a priest that lacks Latin, and a rich man that hath not the gout; for the one sleeps easily because he cannot study, and the other lives merrily because he feels no pain; the one lacking the burden of lean and wasteful learning, the other knowing no burden of heavy tedious penury. These Time ambles withal.

Orlando:

Who doth he gallop withal?

Rosalind:

With a thief to the gallows; for though he go as softly as foot can fall he thinks himself too soon there.

Orlando:

Who stays it still withal?

Rosalind:

With lawyers in the vacation; for they sleep between term and term, and then they perceive not how Time moves.

[III. ii. 302-33]

So she keeps the fun going until one day she is quite put out when he comes a few minutes late for their rendez-vous, and Oliver frightens her out of her wits, and she swoons at the sight of a handkerchief red with Orlando's blood. Then she finds it difficult to play her part and in a sudden spirit of "let's get it done with" she exclaims:

> Come, woo me, woo me; for now I am in a holiday humour, and like enough to consent.

> [IV. i. 68-9]
> (pp. 163-68)

Lorentz Eckhoff, "The Merry Ones," in his Shakespeare: Spokesman of the Third Estate, *translated by R. I. Christophersen, Basil Blackwell, 1954, pp. 163-82.*

Clara Claiborne Park

[*In the excerpt below, Park maintains that Shakespeare belongs to a small minority of authors in the history of western literature who created influential woman characters in his works.* **Rosalind**'s actions control the progression of events in As You Like It, *the critic remarks, and it is through her machinations that the four couples assemble for the multiple marriages at the end of the play. According to Park, Shakespeare is careful, however, to make sure that* **Rosalind**'s wit in no way oversteps the feminine domain of "love-matters." Ultimately, the critic points out, **Rosalind** willingly and unregrettably relinquishes her male disguise in favor of her more traditional female role. For further commentary on* **Rosalind**'s character, see the excerpts by Alfred Harbage, Brigid Brophy, Kenneth Muir, John A. Hart, Nancy K. Hayles, Thomas F. Van Laan, Thomas Kelly, and Lorentz Eckhoff. This essay was recently reprinted in Clara Claiborne Park,* Rejoining the Common Reader: Essays, 1962-1990 *(Northwestern University Press, 1991).*]

In the major literature there are no useful Bildungsromans [novels about the moral and psychological growth of the main character] for girls. A boy's development into manhood through testing experience is one of the oldest themes in literature; Homer's Telemachus presents the first model of how to grow into the kind of man one's society approves and has need of. From the [Homer's] *Odyssey* to [William Faulkner's] "The Bear," literature affords a long procession of raw youths; almost all manage to become men. Girls, however, had to wait out a twenty-five-hundred-year literary history before anyone made fiction of their growth. When Evelina and Emma did at length appear on the scene, a capable girl—let us imagine, for example, the young Florence Nightingale—might have been pardoned for feeling that whatever else they did, these characters scarcely enlarged her sense of possibility. The scope of their activities was even more restricted than that of the ladies who created them—who did, at least, write books. Only the dearth of images of the possibilities open to a developing girl can explain the immense influence of a

novel that most males never read—Louisa May Alcott's *Little Women*.

Yet young females, like young males, create themselves according to the models their society provides for them; and like young males, those who read look in literature for images of what they could be and what they ought to be. Stories of female trial and initiation are by their nature difficult for male writers to provide, and we should remember that from Sappho—*floruit* 600 B.C.—to Jane Austen, there were hardly any writers who were not male. Male writers, of course, can and do provide models for females, but not very many. A cursory check of the dramatis personae of any Elizabethan play will demonstrate what is still true of modern fictions: female characters are greatly outnumbered. (A London director estimated last year that there are five times as many parts for actors as for actresses.) Still, quantity is not everything. Literate girls could find without difficulty images which, although they lacked the dimension of development, still provided a warm variety of ways of being female. They could—like everybody else— read Shakespeare.

As classics go, Shakespeare isn't bad reading for a girl. The conventions of tragedy and romance offer horizons considerably wider than those available in Fanny Burney and Jane Austen; the courts of Europe and the seacoasts of Bohemia provide backgrounds in which a girl can imagine herself doing far more interesting things than she could at home. It is true that, unlike those paradoxical dramatists of male-chauvinist Athens, Shakespeare never allows a woman a play of her own. He provides neither *Antigones* nor *Medeas*; no feminine name appears in his titles except as the second member of a male-female pair. Yet a girl can read Shakespeare without calling upon the defenses necessary for [John] Milton or [Ernest] Hemingway, or [D. H.] Lawrence or [Norman] Mailer—writers she must read calloused for survival, a black in Mr. Charlie's land. Shakespeare liked women and respected them; not everybody does. We do not find him, like Milton, luxuriating in the amoebic submissiveness of an Eve in Paradise, and we can surmise that he would have found little interest in the dim Marias and complaisant Catherines whom Hemingway found nonthreatening. He is not afraid of the kind of assertiveness and insistence on her own judgment that Eve displays when she gets busy bringing death into the world and all our woe; the evidence of the plays is that he positively enjoyed it.

From Mrs. Jameson [the nineteenth-century literary critic] on, critics, male and female, have praised Shakespeare's women. "The dignity of Portia [in *The Merchant of Venice*], the energy of Beatrice [in *Much Ado About Nothing*], the radiant high spirits of Rosalind [in *As You Like It*], the sweetness of Viola [in *Twelfth Night*]"—William Allan Neilson's encomia can stand for thousands of others. Juliet, Cordelia [in *King Lear*], Rosalind, Beatrice; Cleopatra, Hermione [in *The Winter's Tale*], Emilia [in *Othello*], Paulina [in *The Winter's Tale*]—Shakespeare's girls and mature women are individualized, realized, fully enjoyed as human beings. His respect for women is evident in all the plays, but it is in the middle comedies that the most dazzling image recurs. It is an image significant for what it can tell us about the extent—and the limits—of acceptable feminine activity in the Shakespearean world, a world which in this as in other things remains, over time and change, disconcertingly like our own. (pp. 262-64)

Neilson [an early twentieth-century scholar and educator] describes [Rosalind] as having "the wit of Portia and Beatrice softened by the gentleness of Viola"—exactly as we like it. In *As You Like It,* however, Shakespeare does not hesitate to tip the equal balance that affords the fun of *Much Ado* in favor of the lady; in wit and energy, Rosalind has no male rival. Insofar as any other character is able to match her repartee, it is Celia, who although she is usually remembered as the gentle foil, the "other kind" of girl, turns out to have a surprising number of the snappy lines. Orlando, however, is merely a nice young man; as is true at Radcliffe and Harvard, the girls come out with noticeably higher College Entrance Examination Board verbals.

Rosalind, however, is more than witty. *As You Like It* is her play. This is, of course, unusual in Shakespeare. Heroes act, but heroines commonly do not, which is why, unlike Antigone and Lysistrata, none of them gets a Shakespearean title to herself. Neither does Rosalind—although Thomas Lodge had accorded her one [in *Rosalynde*]—but nevertheless it is she who moves the play. She is energetic, effective, successful. She has the courage to accept exile; she decides to assume male dress, and, playing brother, she guides her friend to the Forest of Arden. The late comedies no longer present these forceful young women, and the faithful Imogen of *Cymbeline* retroactively exposes the extent of Rosalind's autonomy. It is not Imogen but her husband's servant who originates the idea of male disguise; the necessity for her journey originates not in her own position but in her relation to her husband, and as soon as she lacks a man to guide her, she gets lost. Her complaint at this point measures her distance from Rosalind: "I see a man's life is a tedious one" [*Cymbeline,* III. vi. 1]. (Her previous remark to Cloten also bears thinking about: "You put me to forget a lady's manners / By being so verbal" [II. iii. 105-06].) Through Imogen we can appreciate the unique position of Rosalind in her play. Rosalind's decisions control the progress of *As You Like It,* and it is by her agency that the four couples assemble in the concluding nuptial dance which, as in *The Boke of the Governor,* "betokeneth concord" and embodies for the audience the

harmony restored that is the essence of Shakespearean comedy.

Yet Shakespeare arranges for her to do all this without making the ladies censorious or the gentlemen nervous. He has various methods of rendering her wit painless and her initiatives acceptable. The most obvious way is to confine them to love matters, a proper feminine sphere. Rosalind is a political exile, but she shows no disposition to meddle in politics; it is not through her agency that her father is restored to his rightful place. Her wit is not, like Portia's, exercised in the service of sensible men engaged in the serious business of the world, nor are her jokes made at their expense. Her satire is, in fact, narrowly directed at two classes of beings—sighing lovers, and women. In the course of the fun she works her way through most of the accusations already traditional in a large anti-feminist literature (inconstancy, contrariness, jealousy, unfaithfulness, et cetera) to the point where Celia tells her, "We must have your doublet and hose plucked over your head, and show the world what the bird has done to her own nest." [IV. i. 202-04]. Add that we know all along that she herself is the butt of her own jokes, being herself both lovesick and female, and it would be a fragile Benedick indeed who could feel himself stabbed by her poniard.

The most useful dramatic device for mediating the initiatives of the female, however, is the male disguise. Male garments immensely broaden the sphere in which female energy can manifest itself. Dressed as a man, a nubile woman can go places and do things she couldn't do otherwise, thus getting the play out of the court and the closet and into interesting places like forests or Welsh mountains. Once Rosalind is disguised as a man, she can be as saucy and self-assertive as she likes. (We can observe a similar change come over sweet Viola of *Twelfth Night* as soon as she begins to play the clever page.) The male characters will accept her behavior because it does not offend their sense of propriety, the female characters because (like the audience) they know she's playing a role. With male dress we feel secure. In its absence, feminine assertiveness is viewed with hostility, as with Kate the Shrew, or at best, as with Beatrice, as less than totally positive. Male dress transforms what otherwise could be experienced as aggression into simple high spirits.

The temporary nature of the male disguise is of course essential, since the very nature of Shakespearean comedy is to affirm that disruption is temporary, that what has turned topsy-turvy will be restored. It is evident that Rosalind has enjoyed the flexibility and freedom that come with the assumption of the masculine role, but it is also evident that she will gladly and voluntarily relinquish it. "Down on your knees," she tells the proud shepherdess who scorns her faithful swain, "and thank

Heaven, fasting, for a good man's love" [III. v. 57-8]. Rosalind, clearly, is thankful for Orlando's, and although she is twice the person he is, we are willing to believe that they live happily ever after, since that's obviously what she wants. (pp. 269-71)

> Clara Claiborne Park, "As We Like It: How a Girl Can Be Smart and Still Popular," in The American Scholar, Vol. 42, No. 2, Spring, 1973, pp. 262-78.

TOUCHSTONE

John Palmer

[*In the following excerpt, Palmer discusses* **Touchstone**'*s character in* As You Like It. *According to the critic,* **Touchstone** *is a wise fool who acts as a kind of guide or point of reference throughout the play, putting everyone, including himself, to the comic test. This function is apparent in* **Touchstone**'*s parodic exchanges with* **Corin, Silvius, Audrey,** *and— especially—***Jaques,** *with whom the fool acts as a foil throughout the play. For further commentary on* **Touchstone**'*s character, see the excerpts by Alfred Harbage, Kenneth Muir, John A. Hart, and Enid Welsford.*]

In most of Shakespeare's comedies there is a character who stands, as it were, at the centre. To get a clear view of the composition as a whole we must take up our position as near as possible beside him.

In 'Love's Labour's Lost' we found our point of reference for the comic values of the play in Berowne. In 'A Midsummer Night's Dream' it may be said concerning Bottom that 'if he comes not, the play is marred'. For 'As You Like It' the author has named his own Touchstone. It is as though Shakespeare, setting out for Arden, where so many excellent poets have lost themselves in affected sentiment, mislaid their common sense in refining upon their sensibility and, in their self-conscious pursuit of nature, found themselves grasping a pale misfeatured shadow, had determined in advance to take with him a guide who should keep him in the path of sanity. Touchstone puts all things and every person in the play, including himself, to the comic test. Entering Arden with Touchstone you cannot go astray or mistake the wood for the trees.

It is his function to 'speak wisely what wise men do foolishly' [I. ii. 86-7] and he loses no time about it. We are to accept him at once as no respecter of false persons:

> TOUCHSTONE: Mistress, you must come away to your father.
> CELIA: Were you made the messenger?

> TOUCHSTONE: No, by mine honour, but I was bid to come for you.
> ROSALIND: Where learned you that oath, fool?
> TOUCHSTONE: Of a certain knight, that swore by his honour they were good pancakes, and swore by his honour the mustard was naught: now I'll stand to it, the pancakes were naught and the mustard was good, and yet was not the knight forsworn.
> CELIA: How prove you that, in the great heap of your knowledge?
> ROSALIND: Ay, marry, now unmuzzle your wisdom.
> TOUCHSTONE: Stand you both forth now: stroke your chins, and swear by your beards that I am a knave.
> CELIA: By our beards (if we had them) thou art.
> TOUCHSTONE: By my knavery (if I had it) then I were: but if you swear by that that is not, you are not forsworn:
>
> [I. ii. 57-77]

We are next to observe that this Touchstone has a lively sense of the fitness of things. Le Beau enters to tell the ladies of much good sport—how Charles, the wrestler, has broken the ribs of three proper young men, of excellent growth and presence:

> TOUCHSTONE: But what is the sport, monsieur, that the ladies have lost?
> LE BEAU: Why, this that I speak of.
> TOUCHSTONE: Thus men may grow wiser every day. It is the first time that ever I heard breaking of ribs was sport for ladies.
>
> [I. ii. 134-39]

We are to esteem him also as a loyal servant who, without any illusions as to the sequel, is ready at a word to 'go along o'er the wide world' [I. iii. 132] with his mistress. This is no merely incidental touch. That Touchstone should set out in sturdy devotion, with an agreeably romantic expectation, is a fact essential to our appreciation of his quality. *His* part in the comedy is to shed the light of reality and common sense upon its fanciful figures and diversions. To play such a part he must be either a true cynic or one that affects his cynicism to mask a fundamentally genial spirit. Now a true cynic would be out of place in the forest of Arden. So Touchstone must be a thoroughly good fellow at heart. His brain may be as dry as the remainder biscuit after a voyage but he must be essentially a genial spirit. His acidity must be no more than skin-deep. He will see things as they are but without malice. He will have a keen flair for absurdity in people and things—not least for his own infirmities. He will, moreover, bring all things to the test of action, and the climax of *his* comedy will be to marry a slut so that he may embrace in reality the simple life which for his companions is no more than a holiday affectation.

How characteristic is his entry into the pastoral pleasaunce:

> ROSALIND: O Jupiter! How weary are my spirits!
> TOUCHSTONE: I care not for my spirits, if my legs were not weary.
>
> ROSALIND: Well, this is the forest of Arden.
> TOUCHSTONE: Ay, now am I in Arden, the more fool I. When I was at home, I was in a better place, but travellers must be content.
>
> [II. iv. 1-3, 15-18]

This is wholesome correction and it comes most aptly between a touching scene in which Adam displays 'the constant service of the antique world' [II. iii. 57], and our first encounter with Silvius and Corin—a young man and an old in solemn talk. Note, too, how he pricks the bladder of sentiment, not by rejecting its appeal, but by claiming a share in its manifestations. The love of Silvius for Phebe and of Rosalind for Orlando prompts him to declare: 'We that are true lovers run into strange capers; but as all is mortal in nature, so is all nature in love mortal in folly' [II. iv. 54-6]; and he is driven to remember—nor do we doubt the fidelity of the reminiscence—his own love for Jane Smile and the kissing of her batler and the cow's dugs that her pretty chopt hands had milked. All Touchstone is in that little speech—his quaint pretension to philosophy and a capacity for romance, rooted in nature but aware of its own excess. Jane Smile's hands were pretty but the eye of the realist could not avoid noticing that they were chopt.

Touchstone, coming to terms with the simple life, cannot forget that he has been, and remains, a courtier. He cannot refrain from airing his graces and indulging his gentility. But there is no conceit nor any hint of unkindness in his teasing of a country bumpkin. It is a fault in him to show off in this way and he knows it for one:

> It is meat and drink to me to see a clown. By my troth, we that have good wits have much to answer for; we shall be flouting; we cannot hold.
>
> [V. i. 10-12]

But even his flouting has about it a quality which distinguishes him from all the rest. Touchstone, 'above all things', is *interested* in people and places and ways of life. He must get to the bottom of a subject and take its measure. Of Corin he asks, as much in an honest desire to know as in a spirit of mockery: 'Hast any philosophy in thee, shepherd?' [III. ii. 21-2] And when Corin expounds—

> No more, but that I know the more one sickens, the worse at ease he is; and that he that wants money, means and content is without three good friends; that the property of rain is to wet and fire to burn; that good pasture makes fat sheep; and

that a great cause of the night is lack of the sun—

> [III. ii. 23-8]

Touchstone's rejoinder ('Such a one is a natural philosopher' [III. ii. 32]) is a shrewd companionable comment and no sneer. He must, as he confesses, be flouting. He takes an impish pleasure in maintaining that Corin, never having been at court or seen good manners, is damned; but Corin takes it all—as Touchstone intends it—in good part and serenely states his simple faith in the knowledge that, though it may be amiably mocked, it will nevertheless be respected:

> Sir, I am a true labourer. I earn that I eat, get that I wear, owe no man hate, envy no man's happiness, glad of other men's good, content with my harm; and the greatest of my pride is to see my ewes graze and my lambs suck.
>
> [III. ii. 73-7]

The whole thing is an epitome of Shakespeare's management of the pastoral theme. He presents the simple life with a most convincing innocence, but Touchstone is there to relate it justly to the scheme of things entire:

> CORIN: And how like you this shepherd's life, Master Touchstone?
> TOUCHSTONE: Truly, shepherd, in respect of itself, it is a good life; but in respect that it is a shepherd's life, it is naught. In respect that it is solitary, I like it very well; but in respect that it is private, it is a very vile life. Now in respect it is in the fields, it pleaseth me well; but in respect it is not in the court, it is tedious. As it is a spare life, look you, it fits my humour well; but as there is no more plenty in it, it goes much against my stomach.
>
> [III. ii. 11-21]

Even the incomparable Rosalind, whose tide of wit and flush of love set her above any need of correction by the comic spirit, must be brought to the test if only to show how triumphantly she survives it. Orlando's rhymes are redeemed by the sincerity of his passion. But some of them have more feet than the verses will bear and the feet are lame. Indeed they are very tedious homilies of love, and all this she merrily declares. And Touchstone must also have his say. It is he who, on his author's behalf, must intimate very clearly that poetasters of the pastoral school are more deserving of mockery than imitation:

> ROSALIND: 'From the east to western Ind,
> No jewel is like Rosalind.
> Her worth being mounted on the wind,
> Through all the world bears Rosalind.
> All the pictures fairest lined
> Are but black to Rosalind.

Let no face be kept in mind
But the fair of Rosalind.'

TOUCHSTONE: I'll rhyme you so eight
years together, dinners,
and suppers, and sleep-
ing-hours excepted: it is
the right butter-women's
rank to market.

ROSALIND: Out, fool!
TOUCHSTONE: For a taste. . . .
If a hart do lack a hind,
Let him seek out Rosa-
lind:
If the cat will after kind,
So be sure will Rosalind:
Wintered garments must
be lined,
So must slender Rosa-
lind.
They that reap must
sheaf and bind,
Then to cart with Rosa-
lind.
Sweetest nut hath sour-
est rind,
Such a nut is Rosalind.
He that sweetest rose will
find,
Must find love's prick and
Rosalind.

This is the very false gallop of verses. Why
do you infect yourself with them?

ROSALIND: Peace, you dull fool! I found
them on a tree.
TOUCHSTONE: Truly, the tree yields bad
fruit.

[III. ii. 88-116]

Orlando's poem is itself a parody. Touchstone's is
a parody twice over. Again he plays for us the author's trick. The pastoral exercise is pleasant in itself but still more pleasant for being so easily
mocked. (pp. 35-9)

The supreme test for Touchstone is his encounter
with Jaques. But it is well, before we examine an
incident which will determine our outlook on the
entire comedy, to become more intimately acquainted with the man himself. Shakespeare affords us an opportunity in the episode of Touchstone's courting of Audrey. Here we behold the
man who has no illusions concerning nature
frankly responding to her call. The others merely
trifle with her; Touchstone sees, hears and obeys:

As the ox hath his bow, sir, the horse his
curb, and the falcon her bells, so man hath
his desires; and as pigeons bill, so wedlock
would be nibbling.

[III. iii. 79-82]

He has found rich honesty, dwelling like a miser in
a poor house, 'as your pearl in your foul oyster' [V.
iv. 61], and, having found it, has the courage of his
convictions and will not let it go. His wooing of Au-

*Rachel Roberts as Audrey and Paul Rogers as Touch-
stone in a 1955 production of* As You Like It. *Act III,
scene iii.*

drey is at the same time a burlesque and a true reflection in nature of the three romantic courtships
among which it intrudes. There is conscious irony
in his claim to be pressing in 'among the rest of the
country copulatives, to swear and to forswear, according as marriage binds and blood breaks' [V. iv.
55-7], for none knows better than Touchstone
himself that he alone is paying a genuine tribute
to the ancient gods of the forest. His surrender to
the great god, Pan, is the more complete, and certainly the more entirely comic, for his being clearly
aware of what he is doing. He is still the courtier
and he must still be flouting—even at the 'poor virgin, sir, an ill-favoured thing, sir, but mine own' [V.
iv. 57-8]. He will go so far as to suggest that 'not
being well-married, it will be a good excuse hereafter to leave my wife' [III. iii. 92-4]. But all these
floutings are superficial. Touchstone's comedy, in
fact, shows all the rest of the comedy in reverse. His
wooing of Audrey is irony in action. Orlando, Rosalind, Silvius, Phebe and the rest affect their pastoral simplicity but remain entirely civilised. Touchstone affects his urbanity but is at heart a truly
natural philosopher. None knows better than he

what he is doing, for it is of the essence of his character to see himself as he sees everyone else in the play in detachment:

> A man may, if he were of a fearful heart,
> stagger in this attempt; for here we have
> no temple but the wood, no assembly but
> horn-beasts. But what though? Courage!
>   [III. iii. 48-51]

He begins his courtship with a double pun and a sidelong mockery of the whole pastoral outfit:

> I am here with thee and thy goats, as the
> most capricious poet, honest Ovid, was
> among the Goths—
>   [III. iii. 7-9]

but his deeds in plain English speak louder than the word-play in Latin.

Now that we begin to know our Touchstone we can have no doubt of what really happened upon his first encounter with Jaques. It is Jaques himself who describes the meeting:

> A fool, a fool! I met a fool i' th' forest,
> A motley fool—a miserable world!—
> As I do live by food, I met a fool,
> Who laid him down and basked him in the
>   sun,
> And railed on Lady Fortune in good terms,
> In good set terms, and yet a motley fool.
> 'Good morrow, fool,' quoth I: 'No, sir,'
>   quoth he,
> 'Call me not fool till heaven hath sent me
>   fortune.'
> And then he drew a dial from his poke,
> And looking on it with lack-lustre eye,
> Says very wisely, 'It is ten o'clock:
> Thus we may see', quoth he, 'how the
>   world wags:
> 'Tis but an hour ago since it was nine,
> And after one hour more 'twill be eleven,
> And so from hour to hour, we ripe, and
>   ripe,
> And then from hour to hour, we rot, and
>   rot—
> And thereby hangs a tale.' . . . When I did
>   hear
> The motley fool thus moral on the time,
> My lungs began to crow like chanticleer,
> That   fools   should   be   so   deep-
>   contemplative;
> And I did laugh, sans intermission,
> An hour by his dial. . . . O noble fool!
> O worthy fool! Motley's the only wear.
>   [II. vii. 12-34]

Jaques relates how he has been amusing himself with a fool, but Touchstone, we perceive, has been amusing himself—and more to the purpose—with a philosopher. While Jaques was laughing at the fool, the fool was taking his measure and pulling his leg. Here Touchstone saw at once was a fashionable cynic, venting a shallow disappointment with men and things in well-turned homilies upon the way of the world. Playing up to his man the fool rails on Lady Fortune in good set terms. The phi-

losopher is hooked and the fool lands his fish with a solemn descant upon the passage of time. Jaques, completely taken in, marvels that a fool should be so *deep-contemplative*. (pp. 43-6)

The relations between the pair are unobtrusively maintained throughout the play. When Jaques, in search of someone from whom to suck melancholy as a weasel sucks eggs, follows Touchstone and Audrey through the forest and overhears their conference, Touchstone, though Jaques has laughed sans intermission an hour by his dial, does not even remember his name—or affects not to remember it. 'Good-even, good Master What-ye-call 't' is his greeting [III. iii. 73]. Touchstone, in fact, is as indifferent in his dealings with Jaques as Jaques is eager to improve the acquaintance. For Jaques, Touchstone is a collector's piece—*un objet d'art et de vertu*. He introduces him to the Duke with a 'Good my lord, give him welcome: this is the motley-minded gentleman that I have so often met in the forest; he hath been a courtier, he swears' [V. iv. 40-2]. Touchstone plays up to Jaques in their last as in their first encounter. He gives the Duke, as we have noted, a taste of his quality. Jaques plays the part of a delighted *compère,* showing off the paces of the fool like a circus master, prompting him to perform worthily before company and not to let his sponsor down. *'Good my lord, like this fellow. . . . Is not this a rare fellow, my lord? He's as good at anything and yet a fool'* [V. iv. 51-2, 104-05]. And the cream of the jest is that Jaques casting himself for the part of exhibitor is really the exhibitionist. Touchstone is only too willing to give the Duke a run for his money but pays not the slightest attention to Monsieur Melancholy.

But what of the seven ages of man? They too serve the double purpose. The speech is good hearing. It holds the stage and lingers in the memory. It is the most successful example of sententious commonplace declamation in English literature. At the same time it exposes the speaker for what he is and puts a final touch to his character. It is a good summary of life lived on the average. It has no depth, not a touch of magic, no suggestion of anything beyond its narrow limits; and it is coloured throughout by the bilious disposition of the orator. The infant mewls, the schoolboy whines, the lover sighs, the soldier swears, the judge proses, the pantaloon shrinks and the old man loses his teeth. Nor is there any indication anywhere that anyone has truly striven, aspired, suffered, meditated or seen beyond the end of his nose.

'As You Like It' has been the least fortunate in its critics of all the plays of Shakespeare. It has often been injudiciously praised—or scandalously dispraised—for its obvious merits to the neglect of its finer qualities. Shakespeare in this play brought off two achievements on two different lines of appreciation. The first was to present his native

Arden, to show us true love running happily to a foregone conclusion (no easy matter), to convey in his own sweet idiom the pastoral pleasures of woodland and sheep-cote, to moralise agreeably on the changes of fortune and the simple life—in a word to give us a sample of the pastoral-comical stripped of its more elaborate affectations. This part of his task he performed so well that it has been praised with eloquence and propriety by many critics who are content to look no further.

Shakespeare's second achievement has been obscured by the success of his first. The charming, life-like, conversible comic figures of the story have been too easily accepted at their own valuation. The gentle irony that plays about them and their relationships, the constant reference of character, conduct and environment to the test of nature, the poise maintained in every scene between permitted romance and prohibitive reality—these often tend to be partly misconceived or wholly ignored. (pp. 50-2)

> *John Palmer, "Touchstone," in his* Comic Characters of Shakespeare, *Macmillan and Co., Limited, 1946, pp. 28-52.*

Enid Welsford

[In the following excerpt, Welsford regards **Touchstone** *as a kind of intermediary between the playwright and the audience, and is literally what his name implies: a "test of the quality of men and manners." The critic considers both* **Touchstone** *and* **Jaques** *social commentators in* As You Like It, *but while* **Touchstone** *is sympathetic and truly partial,* **Jaques** *is a superficial critic whose chief interest is with his own, not society's, reactions. For further commentary on* **Touchstone's** *character, see the excerpts by Alfred Harbage, Kenneth Muir, John A. Hart, and John Palmer.]*

In *As You Like It* the fool's name indicates his dramatic rôle: he serves as a touchstone or test of the quality of men and manners, and so helps to poise an otherwise somewhat kaleidoscopic play. For here, as elsewhere, Shakespeare expresses a complex point of view, making the most of the comic as well as of the romantic possibilities of his theme, and even at times burlesquing the pastoral convention in which his play is written. In such a play as this, where so much depends on a skilful use of allusion, contrast, and a variety produced by constant shift of focus, the rôle of the court-jester can be turned to very useful account. As privileged truth-teller, he can both serve as a mouthpiece for his author's criticism of prevailing literary fashions, and also by an occasional tartness preserve the play from the insipidity which so often mars pastoral literature. As an onlooker by profession he can supply us with that *punctum indifferens,*

or point of rest, which . . . is particularly necessary for the enjoyment of a complicated work of art.

The plan of *As You Like It* is indeed unexpectedly subtle. Touchstone is, as it were, the authorized commentator, but he has a rival in the person of that self-constituted critic of society, the melancholy Jaques. It is as though, the curtain which veils Arcadia having been drawn aside, two of the inhabitants separate themselves from the rest, and step forward to the front of the stage offering themselves as guides to the spectators in the auditorium. Both of them are equally ready to act as showmen, but in every other respect they are sharply contrasted: the one a sophisticated traveller, professedly intellectual, melancholy and dressed in black, the other a natural court-jester, professionally mad, merry and dressed in motley. This contrast of colour is not unimportant in a play which derives much of its charm from its picturesque qualities, and has many affinities with masque and ballet. But the contrast of outward appearances corresponds to a contrast of critical attitudes, which is still more significant. In spite of his varied experiences, Jaques is a superficial critic of life, because his apparent curiosity as to the doings of other people is really only an intense interest in his own reactions. He is essentially a poseur. Touchstone, on the other hand, exposes affectation; but he is capable of sympathy as well as of criticism, and his judgments are really impartial because his mental peculiarities and his degraded social position prevent him from having any private axe to grind. So, although Jaques and Touchstone stand side by side as showmen, their points of view are not equally valid; and it is the fool, not the cynic, who is the touchstone of the play. But although, like the shepherd whom he twits, 'such an one is a natural philosopher' [III. ii. 32], he is not to be taken over-sadly; for, after all, he jests in an evanescent world of romantic freedom where the only touchstones are beauty and delight. For all his protests the fool is at home in Arden, as he was long ago in the fairy-haunted town of Arras, and it is only the over-clever, introverted victim of ennui who excludes himself from the jovial harmony and hymeneal mirth 'when earthly things made even, atone together' [V. iv. 109-10].

The use made of the fool in the play is a striking illustration of Shakespeare's successful craftsmanship. Ben Jonson's verdict that 'Shakespeare wanted arte' becomes amusing when we compare the subtly conceived rôle of Touchstone with the repulsive clowns of *Volpone,* who may well be life-like portraits of the more unpleasant inmates of an Italian palace, but contribute practically nothing to the meaning of the comedy. In fact, although Shakespeare's fecundity was too great to allow him to be over-meticulous, he excelled his fellow-playwrights not only as a poet and student of human nature, but also as a thinker and as an artist. He was the only dramatist of the time to make use of the technical peculiarities of the dramatic tradition which he inherited, and in the creation of Touchstone he did very nearly, though not quite, succeed in making the fool's rôle as potent a theatrical device as the Greek chorus. (pp. 249-51)

> *Enid Welsford, "The Court-Fool in Elizabethan Drama," in his* The Fool: His Social and Literary History, *1935. Reprint by Farrar & Rinehart, 1936, pp. 243-72.*

JAQUES

Oscar James Campbell

[*Campbell interprets* **Jaques** *from a historical perspective, noting events in Shakespeare's own lifetime that strongly influenced his dramatization of the character. According to the critic,* **Jaques** *reflects the stock Elizabethan literary figure of the malcontent traveler who, upon returning home from his sojourn to other countries, is corrupt, bitter, and bored with life.* **Jaques**'s *melancholy, like that of the character-type in Elizabethan literature, is thus both real and exaggerated, Campbell states. The critic further maintains, however, that* **Jaques** *is also "something much more significant," namely Shakespeare's "amusing representative of the English satirists whose works streamed from the press during the years from 1592 to 1599 inclusive." Importantly, Campbell argues that* **Jaques**'s *pessimistic tirades against humanity—even his famous soliloquy on the seven ages of man in Act II, scene vii— are never accepted by Shakespeare as complete "truths," but are always shown to be "ridiculously false" and "blind to the realities of the world." For further commentary on* **Jaques**'s *character, see the excerpts by Alfred Harbage, Kenneth Muir, John A. Hart, Frederick Turner, John Palmer, and Harold C. Goddard.*]

In *As You Like It* (1600) and *Twelfth Night* (1601), we enter a brave new world of comedy. These plays reveal a larger poetic reach and an ampler view of human absurdity than Shakespeare's earlier comedies. In them, too, the dramatist seasons romance with a liberal admixture of satire. Two events in the world of letters at the turn of the century suggested to Shakespeare ways of making pungent his satiric spice.

The first was the order of 1 June 1599 . . . , which suppressed the formal satires of a number of authors mentioned by name and prohibited the further printing of any satires or epigrams [short satirical poems or paradoxical sayings]. Despite these vigorous efforts at suppression, the ecclesiastical censors [church authorities] did not succeed in forcing into duress the satiric spirit then abroad

in English literature. Almost immediately dramatists, led by Ben Jonson, devised a form of comedy which preserved the subject matter, the salutary purpose, and the methods of the proscribed literary form. Shakespeare was perfectly familiar with this contest between ecclesiastical authorities and rebellious artists. He observed the struggle with the detachment of a great artist and transformed into high comedy some of the issues of the quarrel. He went even further, and adapted to his own uses the devices which Jonson invented to circumvent the angry suppression of the bishops.

While Shakespeare was composing *As You Like It*, a change took place in the personnel of his company which exerted almost as much influence upon his methods of writing comedy as did the progress of the satiric movement. In 1599 Will Kemp left the Lord Chamberlain's Men [Shakespeare's acting company] to be succeeded by Robert Armin. . . . Shakespeare had provided Kemp with parts filled with more and more amusing ridicule of folly. Beginning as the conventional type figure of the stupid lout, the talented comedian had gradually been promoted to parts like the Bastard and Falstaff, in which he could give rein to a keen spirit of joyous satire. Kemp's successor, Robert Armin, by the time he entered the company had developed a different clownish line. Hence Kemp's departure forced Shakespeare to abandon one of his most successful forms of comic invention in order to create parts better suited to Armin's peculiar talents.

For these reasons the satire in *As You Like It* is quite different from that which Shakespeare had introduced into his earlier comedies. An informed reader of the play soon realizes that the dramatist was thoroughly familiar with the temper and achievements of the satiric movement in poetry which came to an abrupt end in 1599. (pp. 44-5)

Though disturbed social conditions in England gave the initial impulse to the satiric movement, once launched, it slavishly imitated Latin satire. . . . Some members of this English school—Sir John Davies, Sir John Harington, Thomas Bastard, and John Weaver—wrote only epigrams. Though their master [the Roman epigrammatist] Martial composed epigrams of many sorts, they seem to have been aware only of his satiric vein. Hence an epigram to them was merely a short satire, less severe in tone. It attacked social absurdity rather than sin. (p. 45)

The members of [the] English school repeatedly asserted that their satires were always impersonal, that they attacked not individuals but general faults. Therefore only those guilty of the follies assailed were justified in taking umbrage at any particular charge. [Thomas] Lodge, in a preface to *A Fig for Momus*, thus explains the significance of the poems in the volume: 'In them (under the names of certain Romaines) where I reprehend vice, I purposely wrong no man, but observe the lawes of that kind of poeme [that is, a satire]. If any repine thereat, I am sure he is guiltie, because he bewrayeth himself.' Such a pronouncement was intended to close the mouths of everyone who objected to any expression of the wrathful spirit then abroad. Jaques, we shall see, represents Shakespeare's idea of one of these satirists of the old school. In characterizing him the dramatist expresses his opinion of the entire group. But Jaques' temper is quite unlike that which establishes the tone of *As You Like It*. It is just because his sour comments on life are discordant with the spirit of Arden that they are so arresting.

The comedy, as everyone knows, is the dramatization of a very popular pastoral romance, Thomas Lodge's *Rosalynde,* first published in 1590. It should be, therefore, completely romantic in key. To be sure, heroic adventures told at length in the novel do not appear in the comedy. Such incidents as the capture of the heroine by a band of robbers and her subsequent rescue by the hero and her brother were obviously too violent for the atmosphere of a pastoral play. But Orlando is the typical love-shaken, sonneteering lover of romance. Rosalind and Celia are the perfect friends of idealistic fiction. That they are women is a late Renaissance variation of the conventional theme. Adam is the extravagantly loyal retainer of medieval tale, representing 'the constant service of the antique world.' The play is also filled with surprising adventures and strange incidents, and it ends, as all romantic comedies should, with marriages galore.

Yet as a reader explores more deeply the meaning of the play, he finds in it much besides the high spirits and thoughtless gaiety of pure romance. Externally the setting is that of a conventional pastoral play. The forest is full of shepherds, foresters, and other creatures who could live together only in an Elysium of escape from the real world. But the Forest of Arden is no mirage of wish-fulfilment. It is not like the world of Italian pastoral romance, not a country in which the longings of those bored with city life were realized. It is an actual English woodland through which real winds blow, a region near the haunts of Robin Hood and his merry men.

This is the place to which Orlando and Rosalind flee when driven away from society by injustice and tyranny. They hope to find in the Forest of Arden that life in accord with nature which they had read about in some Italian pastoral. . . . The authors of these works celebrate a natural habitat of dreamy indolence and idyllic freedom, where none of the restraints and artifices of society prevail. Erasmus in his *Praise of Folly,* taking the side of nature as against art, writes, 'Nature hates all false coloring and is ever best where she is least adulterated with art.'

It is the Nature imagined by such writers that Orlando and Rosalind seek in the Forest of Arden.

And what creatures do they find there? They meet characters who belong to the most artificial of all worlds of fiction, the pastoral romance. Silvius, the sighing love-sick swain, is there, and Phebe, the obstinately chaste shepherdess. So are William and Audrey, neither of whom has ever been washed by the romantic imagination or any other known cleansing agent. They are the shepherd and his lass as they really are, ignorant dirty louts—simple folk who know nothing but what Nature has taught them. 'Here,' says Shakespeare, 'are two authentic children of Nature.' This is the heterogeneous company to which Rosalind and Orlando must belong if they prefer Arcadia to the artifices of civilized life. The play thus ridicules the belief that life close to Nature is best. (pp. 46-8)

In this utopian pastoral world the fugitives also come upon the melancholy Jaques. He has no counterpart in Lodge's novel; he is entirely Shakespeare's invention. Because his only part in the comedy is to stand aloof from the action and make satiric comment upon all that happens, critics have been tempted to regard him as Shakespeare's mouthpiece. Many readers have therefore mistaken the famous soliloquy beginning 'All the world's a stage' [II. vii. 139ff.] for a succinct revelation of the pessimism which captured Shakespeare's mind about 1600. Life to him, they say, had then become just the pageant of futility of the melancholy Jaques' vision.

This is a naïve view of a highly effective dramatic figure—one that had become a popular stage type. Jaques is Shakespeare's representative of the traveller recently returned from a sojourn on the continent, laden with boredom and histrionic pessimism. His melancholy is artificial and his disgust with everything at home is a pose. (pp. 48-9)

It is true that in Shakespeare's day melancholy was thought often to be an affectation, an imitation of a foreign fashion. Shakespeare makes Prince Arthur in *King John* say:

> Yet I remember, when I was in France,
> Young gentlemen would be as sad as night
> Only for wantonness.
>
> [IV. i. 14-16]

But the travellers' melancholy was sometimes clearly a mental disorder produced by the diseases they had contracted while abroad. It was an unnatural melancholy caused by what the Elizabethans called adustion, but what we should diagnose as a persistent fever. The doctors believed that a melancholy disposition heated by high temperature produced that mixture of understanding and imagination which made its possessor prone to figurative and sententious utterance.

Jaques exhibits all the characteristics of the type, except the foppery. His licentious life abroad has fired his naturally phlegmatic nature to a point at which he can make pithy comment upon the ridiculous spectacle of life even as it is lived in the Forest of Arden. Being by temperament averse to action, he has plenty of leisure for meditation upon the ways of mankind. And his pathological melancholy renders him incapable of taking delight in anything he sees or hears. Life, so he believes, is nothing but folly and futility. In brief, Jaques is a malcontent traveller anatomized according to the approved psychology of Shakespeare's day.

Jaques' utterances resemble those of the typical returned traveller, except that they are directed not so much against the corrupted age as against all human life. Moreover Shakespeare's superior eloquence gives Jaques' tirades a poetic sincerity which is easily mistaken for the author's passionate convictions. This has been particularly true of his most famous soliloquy [II. vii. 139-66], a speech which expresses more than the disillusionment of an old roué. Its pessimism, though profound, is relieved by flashes of humor. The whining schoolboy creeping like snail unwillingly to school; the lover sighing like furnace; the justice full of wise saws and modern instances; the futility of each of these human creatures is drawn with broad ludicrous strokes. The satire levelled against them is seasoned with laughter.

It should now be clear that, like all of his fellow malcontent travellers, Jaques is usually the object of his author's ridicule, but on occasions he is just as clearly the mouthpiece of Shakespeare's own satiric comment. In playing this dual role he combines the functions of two characters who had appeared in some plays written just before *As You Like It* was produced, notably Labesha and Dowsecer in [George] Chapman's *An Humorous Day's Mirth*. The first was a social would-be who affected melancholy because the pose was fashionable. The second was a man of strong native intelligence whose mind had nevertheless been invaded by melancholy. As a result, his intellect had been put into the service of a misanthropic spirit. His insight enabled him to ferret out hidden abuses in society and absurdities in human beings. But his persistent low spirits filled his just comments with so much bitterness that they seemed ludicrously exaggerated. Jaques is an amalgam of the two types. He is both affected malcontent and true melancholiac.

In the first role Jaques is self-conscious about his melancholy and proud of its singularity. He warms to self-analysis when he explains his humor to Rosalind:

> I have neither the scholar's melancholy, which is emulation; nor the musician's, which is fantastical; nor the courtier's, which is proud; . . . but it is a melancholy of mine own, compounded of many simples, extracted from many objects; and indeed the sundry contemplation of my travels, in which my often rumination wraps me in a most humorous sadness.
>
> [IV. i. 10-20]

It is his travels on the continent, of this he is sure, that have reduced him to habitual gloom and melancholy reflection. Rosalind immediately recognizes him as a disillusioned traveller:

> 'Farewell, Monsieur Traveller,' she cries. 'Look, you lisp and wear strange suits, disable all the benefits of your own country, be out of love with your nativity, and almost chide God for making you that countenance you are; or I will scarce think you have swam in a gondola.'
>
> [IV. i. 33-8]
> (pp. 50-2)

Jaques, then, is for the most part Shakespeare's portrait of a familiar satiric type. But on occasions he becomes something much more significant. He stands forth as an amusing representative of the English satirists whose works streamed from the press during the years from 1592 to 1599 inclusive. Jaques enunciates the critical doctrines of these writers in a form only a little exaggerated.

The satirists took great pains to justify the critical freedom which they assumed by insisting that their satire was all impersonal. They attacked the vice, not the individual. Sir John Davies in one of his epigrams states this principle with becoming terseness:

> But if thou find any so grosse and dull,
> That think I do to private taxing leane,
> Bid him go hang, for he is but a gull
> And knowes not what an epigramme doth meane:
> Which taxeth under a particular name,
> A general vice that merits publike blame.
>
> (p. 53)

Jaques in one of his soliloquies expands and illustrates this tenet of the satiric school with his characteristic imaginative reach.

> Why, who cries out on pride
> That can therein tax any private party?
> Doth it not flow as hugely as the sea
> Till that the wearer's very means do ebb?
> What woman in the city do I name
> When that I say the city woman bears
> The cost of princes on unworthy shoulders?
> Who can come in and say that I mean her,
> When such a one as she, such is her neighbour?
> Or what is he of basest function
> That says his bravery is not on my cost,
> Thinking that I mean him, but therein suits
> His folly to the mettle of my speech?
> There then! how then? what then? Let me see wherein
> My tongue hath wrong'd him. If it do him right,
> Then he hath wrong'd himself. If he be free,

Why, then my taxing like a wild goose
   flies,
Unclaim'd of any man.

                [II. vii. 70-87]

The formal satirists also filled their work with expressions of fierce zeal to purge the world of its foulness. Asper's threat in [John Marston's] *Every Man Out of his Humor* is a succinct expression of the mood:

I'll strip the ragged follies of the time,
Naked, as at our birth.

                (pp. 53-4)

All of the satirists at frequent intervals echo these expressions of moral fervor. And Jaques joins their chorus, crying:

   . . . Give me leave
To speak my mind, and I will through and
   through
Cleanse the foul body of the infected
   world,
If they will patiently receive my medicine.

                [II. vii. 58-61]

These resemblances between Jaques and the English satirists have led some critics to believe that he is portrait of Sir John Harington, Ben Jonson, or some other author famous at the moment. But Jaques is not a caricature of any one satirist. He is merely a character through whom Shakespeare expresses his unfavorable opinion of the entire group.

The dramatist manipulates his dramatic action in such a way that Jaques' sour generalities are immediately shown to be ridiculously false. The wretched malcontent urges Orlando 'to rail against our mistress the world and all our misery' [III. ii. 278-79] just before the lover meets his Rosalind for a joyous antiphonal. The poet also places the famous soliloquy of the seven ages of man in a context which neutralizes its tone and contradicts all its assumptions. Adam's hunger and Orlando's desperation stimulate Jaques' cynical review of the seven futile stages of man's life. But the Duke's sympathy and benevolence turn the woeful pageant into a scene of contentment and joy. Amien's song which follows undergoes the same transformation. He begins with a lyric variation on Jaques' eternal theme.

Blow, blow, thou winter wind,
Thou art not so unkind
As man's ingratitude.

                [II. vii. 174-76]

But this mood artfully reminiscent of court life cannot survive in the sunlight of Arden. It cannot persist to the end of any of the stanzas ostensibly dedicated to lamentation. They all close with:

Then, heigh ho, the holly!
This life is most jolly.

                [II. vii. 182-83]

In such indirect ways the play at every turn is made to contradict the skillfully turned phrases of the pessimist. Events reveal him as blind to the realities of the world into which he has intruded. Shakespeare's ridicule of Jaques is in this way much more significant than derision of a roué's scorn of life in England. It is amused disapproval of the headlong moral ardor which the satirists in both poem and play felt or pretended to feel. Such a temper, Shakespeare says, is ridiculous and utterly destructive to the comic spirit. (pp. 54-6)

Oscar James Campbell, " 'As You Like It'," in his Shakespeare's Satire, Oxford University Press, *1943, pp. 44-64.*

Harold C. Goddard

[*In the following excerpt, Goddard maintains that* **Jaques** *cannot completely withdraw from the society he hates because he needs an audience for his tirades against humanity. In his philosophical debates with both* **Rosalind** *and* **Orlando**, *the critic declares,* **Jaques** *is upstaged by the lovers because their lives are not governed by self-pity as is his.* **Jaques's** *"Seven Ages of Man" speech (II. vii. 139ff.), Goddard continues, does not deserve to be called a lesson in wisdom, for Shakespeare invalidates the character's reasoning at the end of his speech by presenting* **Adam**—*an old man who has just completed an arduous journey—in refutation of* **Jaques** *observation that old age leaves human beings "Sans teeth, sans eyes, sans taste, sans every thing." For further commentary on* **Jaques's** *character, see the excerpts by Alfred Harbage, Kenneth Muir, John A. Hart, Frederick Turner, John Palmer and Oscar James Campbell.*]

One way of taking Jaques is to think of him as a picture, duly attenuated, of what Shakespeare himself might have become if he had let experience sour or embitter him, let his critical powers get the better of his imagination, "philosophy" of poetry. As traveler-libertine Jaques has had his day. Now he would turn spectator-cynic and revenge himself on a world that can no longer afford him pleasure, by proving it foul and infected. The more his vision is darkened the blacker, naturally, what he sees becomes in his eyes. He would withdraw from society entirely if he were not so dependent on it for audience. That is his dilemma. So he alternately retreats and darts forth from his retreat to buttonhole anyone who will listen to his railing. But when he tries to rationalize his misanthropy and pass it off as medicine for a sick world, the Duke Senior administers a deserved rebuke. Your very chiding of sin, he tells him, is "mischievous foul sin" itself [II. vii. 64].

Jaques prides himself on his wit and wisdom. But he succeeds only in proving how little wit and even "wisdom" amount to when indulged in for their own sakes and at the expense of life. His jests and "philosophy" give the effect of having been long pondered in solitude. But the moment he crosses swords with Orlando and Rosalind, the professional is hopelessly outclassed by the amateurs. Extemporaneously they beat him at his own carefully rehearsed game. Being out of love with life, Jaques thinks of nothing but himself. Being in love with Rosalind, Orlando thinks of himself last and has both the humility and the insight that love bequeaths. When the two men encounter, Jaques' questions and answers sound studied and affected, Orlando's spontaneous and sincere.

> JAQ.: Rosalind is your love's name?
> ORL.: Yes, just.
> JAQ.: I do not like her name.
> ORL.: There was no thought of pleasing you when she was christened.
> JAQ.: What stature is she of?
> ORL.: Just as high as my heart.
> JAQ.: You are full of pretty answers. Have you not been acquainted with goldsmiths' wives, and conn'd them out of rings?
> ORL.: Not so; but I answer you right painted cloth, from whence you have studied your questions.
> JAQ.: You have a nimble wit: I think 'twas made of Atalanta's heels. Will you sit down with me? and we two will rail against our mistress the world, and all our misery.
> ORL.: I will chide no breather in the world but myself, against whom I know most faults.
> [III. ii. 263-81]

There is not a trace of any false note in that answer. It has the ring of the true modesty and true wisdom that only true love imparts. Jaques, of course, misses the point diametrically:

> JAQ.: The worst fault you have is to be in love.
> ORL.: 'Tis a fault I will not change for your best virtue. I am weary of you.
> [III. ii. 282-84]

(To tell the truth we are a bit weary of him too.)

And Rosalind outphilosophizes Jaques as utterly as Orlando has outjested him.

> JAQ.: I prithee, pretty youth, let me be better acquainted with thee.
> ROS.: They say you are a melancholy fellow.
> JAQ.: I am so; I do love it better than laughing.
> ROS.: Those that are in extremity of either are abominable fellows, and betray themselves to every modern censure worse than drunkards.
> JAQ.: Why, 'tis good to be sad and say nothing.
> ROS.: Why, then, 'tis good to be a post.

> JAQ.: I have neither the scholar's melancholy, which is emulation; nor the musician's . . .
> [IV. i. 1-11]

and after enumerating seven different types of melancholy, he concludes,

> . . . but it is a melancholy of mine own, compounded of many simples, extracted from many objects; and indeed the sundry contemplation of my travels, in which my often rumination wraps me in a most humorous sadness—
> ROS.: A traveller! By my faith, you have great reason to be sad. I fear you have sold your own lands to see other men's; then, to have seen much, and to have nothing, is to have rich eyes and poor hands.
> JAQ.: Yes, I have gained my experience.
> ROS.: And your experience makes you sad. I had rather have a fool to make me merry than experience to make me sad; and to travel for it too!
> [IV. i. 15-29]

Love bestows on those who embrace it the experience and wisdom of the race, compared with which the knowledge schools and foreign lands can offer is at the worst a mere counterfeit and at the best a mere beginning. What wonder that Jaques, after being so thoroughly trounced by the pretty youth whose acquaintance he was seeking a moment before, is glad to sneak away as Orlando enters (what would they have done to him together?), or that Rosalind, after a "Farewell, Monsieur Traveller," turns with relief to her lover.

Even Jaques' most famous speech, his "Seven Ages of Man" as it has come to be called [II. vii. 139ff.], which he must have rehearsed more times than the modern schoolboy who declaims it, does not deserve its reputation for wisdom. It sometimes seems as if Shakespeare had invented Adam (that grand reconciliation of servant and man) as Jaques' perfect opposite and let him enter this scene, pat, at the exact moment when Jaques is done describing the "last scene of all," as a living refutation of his picture of old age. How Shakespeare loved to let life obliterate language in this way! And he does it here prospectively as well as retrospectively, for the Senior Duke a second later, by his hospitable welcome of Adam and Orlando, obliterates or at least mitigates Amiens' song of man's ingratitude ("Blow, blow, thou winter wind" [II. vii. 174-90]) that immediately follows. (pp. 283-85)

Harold C. Goddard, "As You Like It," in his The Meaning of Shakespeare, *The University of Chicago Press, 1951, pp. 281-93.*

SOURCES FOR FURTHER STUDY

LITERARY COMMENTARY:

Brown, John Russell. *"As You Like It."* In his *Shakespeare's Dramatic Style,* pp. 72-103. New York: Barnes & Noble, 1971.

> Overview of several scenes in *As You Like It.* The critic suggests that the play's consistent dramatic development depends on its diverse thematic elements. Brown supports this thesis by reviewing the language, entrances, exits, character groupings, and movements at I. ii. 216-89, IV. i. 123-218, and V. iv. 108-50.

Craig, Hardin. *"As You Like It."* In his *An Interpretation of Shakespeare,* pp. 122-24. New York: The Citadel Press, 1949.

> Analyzes the function and influence of Touchstone and Jaques in *As You Like It.*

Fergusson, Francis. "As You Like It." In his *Shakespeare: The Pattern in his Carpet,* pp. 148-55. New York: Delacorte Press, 1958.

> Examines how Shakespeare uses pastoralism in the play. Act I serves as a prologue to the Arden experience, the critic declares, and it is in the forest that the characters test notions of Love, Fortune, and Nature.

Fink, Z. S. "Jaques and the Malcontent Traveler." *Philological Quarterly* XIV, No. 2 (April 1935): 237-52.

> Maintains that Jaques's melancholy is partly derived from that of the typical foreign traveler depicted in sixteenth-century literature. Unlike the usual traveler of the time, the critic continues, Jaques's sadness is more than a melodramatic pose.

Goldsmith, Robert Hillis. "Shakespeare's Wise Fools." In his *Wise Fools in Shakespeare,* pp. 47-67. East Lansing: Michigan State University Press, 1955.

> Claims that the discrepancy between Touchstone's portrayal as a simple fool in Act I and as a wise fool in Act V stems from the fact that Shakespeare wrote the part for a particular actor. Another possibility, the critic suggests, is that Touchstone may have disguised his wit in Act I for fear that Duke Frederick might punish him.

Grice, Maureen. "As You Like It." In *The Reader's Encyclopedia of Shakespeare,* edited by Oscar James Campbell and Edward G. Quinn, pp. 41-8. New York: Thomas Y. Crowell Co., 1966.

> Provides date and source information, a plot synopsis, commentary, stage history, and critical extracts about the play.

Hunter, G. K. *"As You Like It."* In his *The Later Comedies: "A Midsummer Night's Dream," "Much Ado About Nothing," "As You Like It," "Twelfth Night,"* pp. 32-43. London: The British Council, 1962.

> Discusses the importance in *As You Like It* of "humanely poised and socially accepted love" and relates this concern to the themes of self-knowledge and self-discipline that affect each of the play's characters.

Jenkins, Harold. *"As You Like It." Shakespeare Survey* 8 (1955): 40-51.

> Examines Shakespeare's comic juxtaposition of themes in the play as well as his subtle criticism of Arden's ideal elements. While the characters offer various perspectives on the play's major themes, the critic contends, the sum of their observations is ultimately more gratifying than their individual viewpoints.

Palmer, D. J. " 'As You Like It' and the Idea of Play." *Critical Quarterly* 13, No. 3 (Autumn 1971): 234-45.

> Studies *As You Like It* as a demonstration of humanity's natural propensity for play. The critic notes that Arden is an apparently timeless realm where the mating game is the principal concern of most of the characters.

Sen Gupta, S. C. "Pastoral Romance and Romantic Comedy: 'Rosalynde' and 'As You Like It'." In his *A Shakespeare Manual,* pp. 69-84. Calcutta: Oxford University Press, 1977.

> Examines how Shakespeare adapted *As You Like It* from Thomas Lodge's novel *Rosalynde.* Although Shakespeare borrowed much material from Lodge's book, the critic asserts, his literary genius is evident in his extensive exploration of pastoralism through the interaction of the play's major characters.

Stauffer, Donald A. "The Garden of Eden." In his *Shakespeare's World of Images: The Development of Moral Ideas,* pp. 67-109. New York: W. W. Norton & Co., 1949.

> Proposes that love is natural in *As You Like It* and therefore it flourishes in Arden forest. Shakespeare accentuates the comic spirit of love in this play through the use of romantic and pastoral love conventions, the critic declares. Stauffer then explores how the major characters respond to these conventions in a way that contributes to the play's balance.

Van Doren, Mark. "As You Like It." In his *Shakespeare,* pp. 151-60. New York: Henry Holt and Co., 1939.

> Argues that Shakespeare intended *As You Like It* to be a criticism of pastoral romance, but denies that it is a satire, since it examines the subject without prejudice.

Wain, John. "Laughter and Judgement." In his *The Living World of Shakespeare: A Playgoer's Guide,* pp. 73-103. New York: St Martin's Press, 1964.

> Places *As You Like It* in the tradition of pastoralism and romantic comedy. Asserts that Arden forest is a place of healing where self-knowledge is gained through meditation and renewal of essential human qualities, such as love and moral order.

MEDIA ADAPTATIONS:

As You Like It. International Allied, 1936.

> Motion picture version of Shakespeare's comedy, featuring Laurence Olivier and Elisabeth Bergner. Distributed by Video Yesteryear, Blackhawk Films, Prism Entertainment, Cable Films,

Video Connection, Hollywood Home Theatre, Western Film Video, Inc., and Discount Video Tapes, Inc. 96 minutes.

As You Like It: An Introduction. BHE Education Ltd.; Seabourne Enterprises, Ltd., 1969.
Educational video which offers performances of key scenes from the comedy, accompanied by brief instructional narratives. Distributed by Phoenix/BFA Films. 24 minutes.

As You Like It. BBC, Time Life Television, 1979.
Television adaptation of Shakespeare's play and part of the series "The Shakespeare Plays." Distributed by Time-Life Video. 150 minutes.

HAMLET

INTRODUCTION

Hamlet is without question the most famous play in the English language. Probably written in 1601 or 1602, the tragedy is a milestone in Shakespeare's dramatic development; according to most critics, the playwright achieved artistic maturity in this work through his brilliant depiction of the hero's struggle with two opposing forces: moral integrity and the need to avenge his father's murder. Shakespeare's focus on this conflict was a revolutionary departure from contemporary revenge tragedies which tended to graphically dramatize violent acts on stage in that it emphasized the hero's dilemma rather than the depiction of bloody deeds. The dramatist's genius is also evident in his transformation of the play's literary sources—especially the contemporaneous *Ur-Hamlet*—into an exceptional tragedy. The *Ur-Hamlet*, or "original *Hamlet*," is a lost play that scholars believe was written mere decades before Shakespeare's *Hamlet*, providing much of the dramatic context for the later tragedy. Numerous sixteenth-century records attest to the existence of the *Ur-Hamlet*, with some references linking its composition to Thomas Kyd, the author of *The Spanish Tragedy*. Other principal sources available to Shakespeare were Saxo Grammaticus's *Historiae Danicae* (circa 1200), which features a popular legend with a plot similar to *Hamlet*, and François de Belleforest's *Histoires Tragiques, Extraicts des Oeuvres Italiennes de Bandel* (7 Vols.; 1559-80), which provides an expanded account of the story recorded in the *Historiae Danicae*. From these sources Shakespeare created *Hamlet*, a supremely rich and complex literary work that continues to delight both readers and audiences with its myriad meanings and interpretations.

PRINCIPAL CHARACTERS
(in order of appearance)

Barnardo and *Marcellus:* Two guards at Elsinore. They witness the Ghost of King Hamlet and report the event to Horatio, who joins them on the night watch during the spirit's third visit.

Horatio: Hamlet's friend. He informs the prince of the Ghost's appearance during the night watch. As Hamlet plots to avenge his father's murder, Horatio becomes the Dane's sole confidant.

Ghost: King Hamlet's spirit. He instructs his son to avenge his murder and rid Denmark of his killer, Claudius.

Claudius: Hamlet's uncle. After he succeeds in murdering his brother without raising suspicions, Claudius replaces King Hamlet as ruler of Denmark and marries the widowed queen, Gertrude. When Claudius realizes that Hamlet has discovered the murder, he plots to kill the prince.

Laertes: Polonius's son and a student. He wrathfully returns from his studies in Paris after Hamlet kills his father. Claudius persuades him to take part in a plot in which he will fatally poison the prince during a fencing match.

Polonius: Claudius's chief counselor and Laertes and Ophelia's father. He is accidentally killed by Hamlet while he eavesdrops behind a curtain in Gertrude's chamber.

Hamlet: Prince of Denmark. He is King Hamlet's son and Claudius's nephew. Through his meeting with the Ghost, Hamlet learns of his father's murder and Claudius's villainy, which he vows to avenge. He is mortally wounded during the fencing match, but not before he kills Laertes with the poison sword and Claudius with both the sword and the chalice of tainted wine.

Gertrude: Queen of Denmark. King Hamlet's widow and Hamlet's mother who marries Claudius two months after her husband's death. She dies during the fencing match when she mistakenly drinks from the poisoned chalice intended for Hamlet.

Ophelia: Polonius's daughter. She obeys her father's instructions and ends her relationship with Hamlet. After Hamlet kills Polonius, Ophelia goes insane and eventually drowns in a stream.

Rosencrantz and *Guildenstern:* Two of Hamlet's school friends. They are enlisted by Claudius and Gertrude to discover the source of the prince's madness. They attempt to escort the prince to England where he is to be executed, but he turns the tables on them and escapes.

Fortinbras: Prince of Norway. His father was killed by King Hamlet in combat years before and he demands certain territories as recompense. When Claudius achieves a diplomatic resolution to the issue, Fortinbras leads the army he initially directed at Denmark to war in Poland. At the end of the play, Hamlet names Fortinbras king of Denmark.

The Gravediggers: Two clowns (country peasants)

who dig Ophelia's grave. One of these workers engages Hamlet in a conversation about corpses.

PLOT SYNOPSIS

Act I: For two nights, the Ghost of King Hamlet has haunted the soldiers guarding Elsinore castle. On the third night, Horatio joins the watch; when the Ghost appears, however, it does not speak. Horatio surmises that the spirit represents a bad omen of Denmark's future. The next day, Claudius addresses the assembled aristocrats at court; he thanks them for helping him to succeed to the throne of Denmark and for permitting his hasty marriage to Gertrude. The king then directs two ambassadors to travel to Norway and resolve the conflict with Fortinbras, who threatens Denmark with war. Claudius next turns his attention to Hamlet, whom he and Gertrude chide for expressing excessive melancholy over his father's death. Once alone, Hamlet describes the depth of his grief and his disgust at Gertrude's marriage to Claudius so soon after her husband's death. After the prince's speech, Horatio enters and tells him about the Ghost; Hamlet decides to stand watch with the guards that night. Elsewhere, Laertes, who has secured the king's permission to return to his studies in Paris, warns Ophelia to beware Hamlet's romantic advances. When Polonius enters, he gives Laertes some parting advice and upon learning of his daughter's budding relationship with Hamlet, forbids her to see him again. That night the Ghost appears to Hamlet, demanding revenge for his murder at the hands of Claudius. The prince promises to undertake the task, swearing that he will concentrate on nothing else until it is accomplished.

Act II: Though several weeks have passed since Hamlet's meeting with the Ghost, he cannot bring himself to act. He not only dislikes the bloody deed he must perform, but, in a deep depression, begins to suspect that the Ghost is an evil spirit trying to trick him. While the prince bides his time, he assumes an "antic disposition" and at one point frightens Ophelia with his madness. Because the girl has ended their relationship, Polonius concludes that Hamlet's insanity reflects lovesickness. He reports his observations to Claudius, and the two men plot a meeting between the prince and Ophelia to further determine the nature of Hamlet's madness. Meanwhile, Claudius enlists Rosencrantz and Guildenstern to discern the cause of the prince's insanity. A troupe of actors arrives at Elsinore after Hamlet's school friends, and the prince resolves to have them perform before Claudius that evening a reenactment of King Hamlet's murder. Hamlet concludes that any demonstration of guilt by his uncle during the performance will confirm the Ghost's story and justify his revenge.

Act III: The next day Polonius and Claudius eavesdrop on Hamlet and Ophelia as the prince abuses the girl with violent denunciations of women and marriage. After Hamlet storms away, Polonius recommends that they attempt a similar interview between Hamlet and Gertrude; Claudius agrees, but concerned with the prince's increasingly dangerous behavior, decides to send him to England. Later, the players follow Hamlet's instructions and re-enact Claudius's crime before the royal court. After witnessing the performance, the king flees the hall in a state of distress. Alone in his chambers, Claudius tries to pray. Hamlet discovers his uncle knelt in prayer and, though the moment is ideal, restrains himself from taking revenge, reasoning that if the king is killed in an act of repentance his soul will immediately go to heaven. Instead, the prince proceeds to Gertrude's chamber, where he denounces her so violently that Polonius—who is concealed behind a curtain—becomes alarmed and cries for help. In a rage, Hamlet thrusts his sword through the curtain and fatally stabs the counselor. The prince resumes berating his mother until the Ghost reappears to remind him of his mission; Hamlet implores her to repent of her sins before leaving with Polonius's body.

Act IV: After Hamlet leaves his mother, Gertrude informs Claudius that the prince has killed Polonius. Following a face-to-face encounter, the king orders Hamlet to leave immediately for England and gives Rosencrantz and Guildenstern a sealed letter authorizing the prince's execution. As he prepares to board ship, Hamlet observes Fortinbras's army encamped nearby. In a long soliloquy he compares his own dilemma to the impending slaughter that Fortinbras's forces will surely face over a worthless plot of land. He ultimately resolves that from now on he will show no mercy in his quest for revenge. Meanwhile, Laertes returns from France, furiously demanding an explanation for his father's murder. The youth's grief and anger mounts when he discovers that Ophelia has gone insane. While Claudius attempts to placate the incensed youth, sailors arrive at Elsinore bearing letters from Hamlet. Horatio receives the first note, which describes how the prince was taken prisoner by pirates who attacked his ship on the high seas and thereafter returned him to Denmark. Hamlet's note to Claudius announces his imminent return to Elsinore, prompting the king and Laertes to devise a plot to murder him during a fencing match in which Laertes will fight with a poison-tipped foil. Gertrude then enters in a distraught state and informs the two men that Ophelia has drowned.

Act V: Hamlet and Horatio meet in a graveyard near Elsinore where the prince and a gravedigger have a candid discussion about corpses. As Ophelia's funeral procession approaches, the two men conceal themselves to watch the ceremony. When Hamlet realizes that the funeral is Ophelia's, he reveals himself and protests that his love for the girl was greater than Laertes's, whereupon the two men scuffle over the grave. Later, Hamlet tells Horatio about Claudius's plot to have him killed in England and about switching the king's letter with one ordering the execution of Rosencrantz and Guildenstern instead. When a courtier enters with Laertes's invitation to a fencing match, Horatio warns Hamlet of a trap. The prince accepts the challenge, however, maintaining that he must yield his fate to divine will. During the match, Claudius drops a poisoned pearl in a cup of wine intended for the prince. When Hamlet refuses the proffered drink, Gertrude unwittingly drinks it herself. As they continue the match, Laertes cuts the prince with his tainted sword; Hamlet furiously retaliates, the two switch foils, and the prince in turn wounds Laertes with the poisoned weapon. When Gertrude collapses, Laertes realizes Claudius's treachery; he begs Hamlet's forgiveness and blames the king before he dies. Hamlet attacks Claudius, stabbing him first with his sword and then forcing him to drink from the venomous cup before he, too, succumbs to the effects of the poison. Distressed at the sight of his dying friend, Horatio tries to drink some tainted wine, but Hamlet prevents him, telling him that he must explain to the world how such a catastrophe happened. The prince then names Fortinbras king of Denmark. After Hamlet dies, the prince of Norway enters, having victoriously returned from the war with Poland, and orders some of his soldiers to bury Hamlet with full military honors.

PRINCIPAL TOPICS

The most fundamental issue in *Hamlet,* one which opens the door to countless readings of the play, can be stated in one simple question: Why does Hamlet delay taking revenge on Claudius? While critics offer various answers to this question, their theories generally differ in two distinct ways: one group focuses on the inner workings of Hamlet's mind as the primary cause of his procrastination; the other stresses the external obstacles that prohibit the prince from carrying out his task. Critics who find the cause of Hamlet's delay in his internal meditations typically view the prince as a man of great moral integrity who is forced to commit an act that goes against his deepest principles. On numerous occasions, the prince tries to make sense of his moral dilemma through personal meditations, which Shakespeare presents as soliloquies (a soliloquy is a speech delivered while the speaker is alone and devised to inform the reader what the character is thinking, or to provide essential information concerning other participants in the action). Another perspective of Hamlet's internal

struggle suggests that the prince has become so disenchanted with life since his father's death that he has neither the desire nor the will to exact revenge. In addition, Hamlet has been shocked and appalled that, in the midst of his grief, Gertrude has yielded to Claudius's affections, marrying him only two months after her husband's funeral. To the prince, these events have degraded the Danish court to nothing more than "an unweeded garden / That grows to seed, things rank and gross in nature / Possess it merely" (I. ii. 135-37). Hamlet's strongest impulse is to kill himself to avoid further debasement, and yet he fears the damning consequences of suicide. With such heavy matters weighing on his mind, the Ghost's call for revenge only complicates Hamlet's ability to make decisions, leading to many other interludes of self-questioning and prolonged inaction.

Critics who view Hamlet's hesitation as a result of external rather than internal obstacles often emphasize one point: the prince's difficulty in determining the difference between appearance and reality as a primary barrier that restricts him from taking action. For example, Hamlet questions whether the Ghost is really a benevolent spirit or a devil who tries to trick him into killing Claudius. In addition, the Ghost's accusations pose a very practical problem for Hamlet because Claudius does not at first seem to be a villainous murderer, but rather a competent and responsible monarch. As far as Hamlet is concerned, the king's only transgression is his hasty and incestuous marriage to Gertrude. Other impediments prohibit Hamlet from killing Claudius once he has convinced himself that the king is indeed guilty. The most obvious is that the monarch is almost always surrounded by guards. The one instance in which he is not protected occurs during the prayer scene (Act III, scene iii), where Hamlet hesitates killing Claudius for fear of sending his soul to heaven. The prince's inaction here is perhaps the most controversial aspect of his delay: critics who see Hamlet's procrastination as the result of an internal struggle maintain that this episode clearly demonstrates his inability to exact revenge; on the other hand, commentators who support the theory of external influences assert that the prince delays killing Claudius not only because he fears sending the king's soul to heaven, but—more importantly— because he has not proven to anyone (except possibly Horatio) that his uncle is a murderer. If Hamlet is thus viewed as a victim of external influences, his internal meditations on his hesitation do not necessarily demonstrate his inability to act; rather, they reflect his need to vent his frustration through self-reproaches at the fact that he cannot find an adequate opportunity to avenge his father's murder.

Closely related to Hamlet's delay is the theme of revenge. The prince is not the only character preoccupied with revenge in *Hamlet:* Fortinbras bears a grudge against Denmark because King Hamlet killed his father, and Laertes—infuriated by Polonius's murder—threatens to overthrow the Danish government before joining Claudius in a plot to murder the prince. Further, *Hamlet* belongs to the genre of the Revenge Tragedy. Revenge Tragedy is a dramatic form made popular on the English stage by Thomas Kyd, whose *Spanish Tragedy* is an early example of the type. Such plays call for the revenge of a father's death by a son, or vice versa; this act is usually directed by the ghost of the murdered man. Other devices found in Revenge Tragedies include hesitation by the hero, real or feigned madness, suicide, intrigue, and murders on stage. Some critics theorize that Shakespeare despised the Revenge Tragedy as a form whose conventions had become trite. Yet because revenge theater was immensely popular with Elizabethan audiences, the playwright had to follow certain guidelines to produce a financially successful play. As a result, Shakespeare modified the theatrical type by creating a *double entendre* (double meaning) in which he subtly denounced the banality of the Revenge Tragedy without denying his audience many of its popular components. Hamlet's distaste for revenge throughout the play therefore reflects Shakespeare's disgust with revenge theater, and yet the dramatist fulfilled the audience's expectations for a tragic conclusion.

Many different patterns of imagery give a visual dimension to the dramatic action of *Hamlet.* Perhaps the most striking imagery is that of bodily corruption and disease. Throughout the play, Hamlet is preoccupied with the degeneration of the Danish court and the foul implications of Claudius and Gertrude's incestuous relationship. Although images of corruption and disease run throughout the play, they are never associated with Hamlet himself; however, a sense of infection underscores Claudius's crime and Gertrude's sin. Further, the description of disease and corruption exceeds the visual dimension and operates on an olfactory level (relating to the sense of smell). Shakespeare offers a vivid depiction of decay and stench by employing imagery of cancerous infection, rotting flesh, and the sun as an agent of corruption. These rank odors highlight the cunning and lecherousness of Claudius's evil crime, which has poisoned the whole kingdom of Denmark. War imagery is another important visual pattern that frequently occurs in *Hamlet.* In fact, images of war occur more frequently than those of corruption and decay; their dramatic function is to underscore the notion that Hamlet and Claudius are in a duel to the death.

CHARACTER STUDIES

The reasons for Hamlet's delay have led to various critical interpretations of his character. One critical perspective treats the prince as a tragic hero having three prominent characteristics: a will-power that surpasses average human beings, an extraordinarily intense power of feeling, and an unusually high level of intelligence. Each of these traits can be found in Hamlet, but the ambiguity surrounding his tragic flaw, or the defect in his character that leads to his downfall, remains the subject of critical debate. One argument is that the prince's fatal error which causes him to delay killing Claudius is his preoccupation with moral beauty and, with its loss in Denmark, his desire to die. Hamlet's obsession with death and suicide thus demonstrates that even before he encounters the Ghost, he has lost the will to involve himself in worldly affairs. This notion corresponds to another important reading of the prince as a victim of excessive melancholy, or of an abnormal state of depression. Hamlet's melancholy is initially attributed to his father's death and his uncle's hasty marriage to his mother. The appearance of the Ghost, however, intensifies his grief, and the spirit's demand that his son remember him arrests the natural progression of Hamlet's mourning and recovery. Further, the prince is grieved by a mounting sense of loss—not only does he lose his father, but he is betrayed by his mother, he loses Ophelia's affections, and he is confronted with deception by his two friends Rosencrantz and Guildenstern. Hamlet dwells on these problems in periods of brooding inaction that reveal the full extent of his pain and suffering. Another, more controversial, reading of the hero's character is that he suffers from an Oedipus Complex. This psychological disorder reflects the unconscious desire of a son to kill his father and replace him as the object of the mother's love. Viewed in this light, Hamlet delays killing Claudius because he subconsciously identifies with his uncle's crime and shares his guilt. According to some critics, Hamlet's Oedipal impulse also explains why he speaks to Gertrude like a jealous lover, why he dwells on his mother's sexual relations with Claudius, and why he treats his uncle as a rival throughout the play.

Of the other major characters in *Hamlet,* the Ghost is important because his demand for revenge sets the plot into motion. The apparition's ambiguous role in the drama reflects the general confusion about spirits in Shakespeare's day. Throughout the tragedy, the Ghost is alternately viewed as an illusion, a portent foreshadowing danger to Denmark, a spirit returning from the grave because of a task left undone, a spirit from purgatory sent with divine permission, and a devil who assumes the form of a dead person to lure mortals to doom. While Hamlet is chiefly concerned with this last possibility, each of these perspectives are put to the test at some point in the play. Claudius's character provides perhaps the best illustration of the theme of appearance versus reality in *Hamlet*. Initially, Shakespeare depicts Hamlet's uncle as the consummate monarch who justifies his ascent to the throne and his marriage to Gertrude with confident eloquence and who competently handles Fortinbras's threat to Denmark. But as the play progresses, Claudius's villainy becomes more apparent, revealing that he is little more than an evil hypocrite. In addition, critics generally regard Gertrude as highly dependent on and easily manipulated by Claudius; her chief contribution to the drama is the anger and disillusionment she arouses in Hamlet by marrying his uncle. Some critics have risen to the queen's defense, however, arguing that she often offers concise and pithy remarks in the play which reflect her ability to grasp the magnitude of various situations. Moreover, she demonstrates strong character in the closet scene (Act III, scene iv) by accepting Hamlet's accusation of lust and admitting her sin. Ophelia's character represents the ideals of youth and innocence that are ultimately corrupted by the Danish court in *Hamlet*. Her descent into madness begins as the result of the "nunnery scene" (Act III, scene i), where she is manipulated by her father and cruelly abused by Hamlet. At the outset, Ophelia trusts both Hamlet's nobility and Polonius's wisdom, but by the end of the episode her emotions are damaged and she loses faith in both men. Ophelia's insanity and tragic drowning thus illustrate how the Danish court has degenerated to the point that it poisons even the purest form of beauty and innocence.

CONCLUSION

In the words of Ernest Johnson, "the dilemma of Hamlet the Prince and Man" is "to disentangle himself from the temptation to wreak justice for the wrong reasons and in evil passion, and to do what he must do at last for the pure sake of justice. . . . From that dilemma of wrong feelings and right actions he ultimately emerges, solving the problem by attaining a proper state of mind." Hamlet endures as the object of universal identification because his central moral dilemma transcends the Elizabethan period, making him a man for all ages. In his difficult struggle to somehow act within a corrupt world and yet maintain his moral integrity, Hamlet ultimately reflects the fate of all human beings.

(See also *Shakespearean Criticism*, Vol. 1)

OVERVIEWS

David Bevington

[Bevington presents an in-depth survey of the dramatic action and major themes of Hamlet. *The critic initially focuses on* Hamlet's *role in the play, examining his interactions with the other characters as well as his several soliloquies in an attempt to determine his "tragic flaw," the defect in a tragic hero which leads to his downfall. (A soliloquy is a speech delivered while the speaker is alone, devised to inform the reader of what the character is thinking or to provide essential information concerning other participants in the action.) Bevington also comments on the dramatic structure of* Hamlet, *especially Shakespeare's balancing the tragedy with many foils. (A foil refers to any literary character that through strong contrast accentuates the distinctive characteristics of another.) Perhaps the most obvious foil to* Hamlet *is* Laertes, *who acts in haste upon hearing of his father's murder, while* Hamlet *himself delays his revenge. The critic also assesses the play's language, describing various instances of punning (a kind of wordplay which manipulates two words with different meanings based on their similarity of sound) which occur throughout the text. Finally, Bevington discusses metaphors such as clothing, acting, and disease, which all contribute to the predominant image patterns in the play.]*

It is appropriate that for modern critics *Hamlet* should be Shakespeare's greatest dramatic enigma, for misunderstanding is the unavoidable condition of Hamlet's quest for certainties. Not only is he baffled by riddling visions and by commands seemingly incapable of fulfillment, but he is the victim of misinterpretation by those around him. Well may the dying Hamlet urge his friend Horatio to "report me and my cause aright To the unsatisfied" [V. ii. 340], for no one save Horatio has caught more than a glimpse of Hamlet's true situation. We as omniscient audience, hearing the inner thoughts of Claudius as well as of Hamlet and learning of Polonius' or Laertes' secret plottings with the king, should remember that we know vastly more than the play's characters, and that this discrepancy between our viewpoint and theirs is one of Shakespeare's richest sources of dramatic irony.

The basis of misunderstanding, and hence of Hamlet's estrangement, is the secret murder. Claudius, before the opening of the play, has slain his brother by such cunning means that no mortal suspects him—not even at first the sorrowing Hamlet, until the ghost's horrid news awakens the unstated imaginings of Hamlet's "prophetic soul." Ever the masterly politician, Claudius has engineered his own succession to the throne in place of his nephew Hamlet not by usurpation, but by full consent of the Danish court. Claudius is to outward appearances an apt choice. Polonius and other reputedly sage counselors welcome the rule of one so fit for soothing public utterance and for pragmatic foreign diplomacy. Claudius, to his credit, disarms the threat of invasion by young Fortinbras of Norway that hangs so ominously over the beginning of the play. The king's instructions to the ambassadors, Voltemand and Cornelius, are seasoned by years of hard political calculation. His marriage with the dead king's widow, even if technically incestuous, gives an aura of continuity to the new reign. It is without conscious irony that Rosencrantz and Guildenstern, appointed guardians of the unpredictable Hamlet, echo great Elizabethan commonplaces in their defense of legitimate monarchical authority. The life of their king is threatened, and they know that majesty "Dies not alone, but like a gulf doth draw What's near it with it" [III. iii. 16-17]. Ophelia, ignorant of the murder, cannot fathom the sudden and vindictive hostility of one who had professed love to her "In honorable fashion" [I. iii. 111]. Passively becoming part of a scheme designed, as far as she can tell, to help Hamlet recover his wits, Ophelia instead loses her own. Her brother Laertes' rashness is similarly made plausible, even if it cannot be condoned, by his total unawareness of Hamlet's reasons for opposing the king and Polonius. Only in the final scene does Laertes perceive too late that he is caught like "a woodcock to mine own springe" [V. ii. 306], and is "justly killed with mine own treachery" [V. ii. 307].

Hamlet by contrast is from the first a stranger in the court of Denmark, despite his position as son of the dead king and as "most immediate to our throne" after Claudius [I. ii. 109]. An outsider, he returns from years of advanced study at Wittenberg to a society he considers too worldly and corrupted. It is "as a stranger" [I. v. 165] that he shares with Horatio a secret knowledge of there being "more things in heaven and earth" [I. v. 166] than are dreamt of in mere philosophy. He upbraids the Danish for their heavy drinking, a custom better broken than observed. Well before he learns of the murder, he spurns the hypocrisy of meats baked for a funeral coldly furnishing forth the wedding festivities of his uncle-father and aunt-mother. He knows not "seems." Hamlet's innate antipathy to false appearances, exacerbated by his mother's overhasty wedding, helps explain both his suspicion of others' motives and their bafflement at his seeming caprice. Claudius is sincere in his attempts to make a reconciliation with a young prince who is cherished by his mother and beloved by the common people. Gertrude can only suppose that her son is offended by her infidelity to the memory of her dead husband—for she like the others apparently knows nothing of the actual murder—and so she fondly hopes that Hamlet will marry Ophelia and settle down into tranquil domesticity. Polonius, whose routine it is to make in-

telligence reports on potential troublemakers, finds an easy clue to Hamlet's "madness" in Ophelia's rejection of him. Rosencrantz and Guildenstern are equally convinced that Hamlet's malady is political—his lack of "advancement" to the throne.

These answers formulated by the Danish court to explain Hamlet's mystery are not unusually obtuse. They are the guesswork of shrewd observers who merely lack knowledge of Hamlet's awful truth. The answers are in fact all valid in their limited ways. Gertrude may well fear that Hamlet's distemper needs no other explanation than "His father's death and our o'erhasty marriage" [II. ii. 57]. Hamlet becomes a mirror reflecting the conscience of each observer, and the guilty marriage is what Gertrude sees in herself. "You go not till I set you up a glass," he exhorts his mother, "Where you may see the inmost part of you" [III. iv. 20]. Claudius, having reason to surmise more than most, has most to fear. Polonius creates a fantasy of love based on his own stratagems in matchmaking, but his fiction only exaggerates Hamlet's real obsession with feminine frailty. When Rosencrantz and Guildenstern speak of ambition, they are talking mostly about themselves; yet Hamlet does belatedly admit, at least to Horatio, that Claudius has "Popped in between th' election and my hopes" [V. ii. 65]. All these explorations of motive have meaning to us who know the prime cause.

What Hamlet objects to is the oversimplification and the prying that destroys the integrity of his whole and complex being. "If circumstances lead me, I will find Where truth is hid, though it were hid indeed Within the center," opines Polonius, irritating us as well as Hamlet with his officious claims to omniscience. Similarly, Hamlet is incensed at Rosencrantz and Guildenstern for supposing they can sound his inner nature more easily than one might play a recorder. "You would play upon me, you would seem to know my stops, you would pluck out the heart of my mystery," he accuses them, adding with a pun, "though you can fret me, you cannot play upon me" [III. ii. 364-66, 371-72]. Hamlet here expresses one of the most profound bases of our identification with his loneliness. Every human being is unique and believes that others can never fully understand or appreciate him. And every human being experiences some perverse delight in this proof of the world's callousness.

If, in his turn, Hamlet also indulges in amateur motive-hunting and so alienates those who would seek an accommodation with him, he merely typifies in dramatically heightened form a human tendency to prefer estrangement. His is, after all, an extraordinary situation. It is plausible that a young man so suddenly deprived of his father and confronted with evidence of his mother's fleshly weakness should generalize upon the depravity of the human condition, even in himself. Moreover Hamlet is intellectually inclined to searching out hidden meanings in events. The cold watch on the tower at midnight, the appearance of the ghost, and the cruel contrast between the ugly truth here revealed and the empty glitter of the court, impel him to the conclusion that "All is not well" [I. ii. 254]. Humanity itself, so potentially noble in reason and godlike in its infinite faculties, dissolves in his imaginative vision into a quintessence of dust. The goodly frame of nature becomes a "foul and pestilent congregation of vapors" [II. ii. 302-03]. Man's very being, infected by some "vicious mole [blemish] of nature" [I. iv. 24] inherited involuntarily at birth, overthrows "the pales and forts of reason" [I. iv. 28] and thereby corrupts the whole. Men are prisoners of their appetites, helpless to achieve the goodness so mockingly revealed by their philosophic quest for the ideal.

Overwhelmed by this negation, Hamlet can only suspect others of inconstancy. He need not overhear Polonius' scheme of using Ophelia to bait a trap, for Hamlet is predisposed to expect collusion. He has tested womankind by the behavior of his mother and knows them all to be false. "Frailty, thy name is woman" [I. ii. 146], he concludes in his first soliloquy. If Hamlet senses something amiss in Ophelia's suddenly returning his love letters to him, he only guesses intuitively what in fact Polonius has said to his daughter. She must learn to play a wary game to treat Hamlet's advances as "springes to catch woodcocks" [I. iii. 115], and to regard his holy vows as devices to undo her virginity. Princes are expected to claim their rights as libertines, in Polonius' complacent vision of the universal lewdness in human nature. However cruel in its treatment of Ophelia, Hamlet's response is in kind. He becomes afflicted by the ruthless mores prevailing in Denmark, because he has a distasteful business to accomplish. Only too late can he publicly acknowledge that he loved the fair Ophelia, stressing the tragedy of misunderstanding that has obliged him to destroy what he most cherished. Similarly he acknowledges too late his real respect for Laertes and his regret at their fatal enmity. These two men might in better times have loved one another. A chief source of the melancholic mood in *Hamlet* derives from this sense of lost opportunity.

Hamlet does grow harsh and cynical like his opponents. Yet he never ceases to tax himself as severely as he does the others. He is indeed much like them. Polonius, his seeming opposite in so many ways, is, like Hamlet, an inveterate punster. To whom else but Polonius should Hamlet direct the taunt of "Words, words, words"? [II. ii. 192]. The aged counselor recalls that in his youth he "suffered much extremity for love, very near this" [II. ii. 189-90], and he has been an actor at the university. Polonius too has advice for the players: "Seneca cannot be too heavy, nor Plautus too light" [II.

ii. 400-01], When Hamlet jibes at "so capital a calf " [III. ii. 105-06] enacting Julius Caesar, killed in the Capitol, he reinforces the parallel to his own play-acting and anticipates the slaying of Polonius behind the arras. If Hamlet is a mirror to the others, the reflection works both ways.

Perhaps the central reflection of this sort is between Hamlet and Claudius. Not only has Claudius taken Hamlet's mother and his crown, but Claudius is a prisoner of circumstance, burdened with a guilty responsibility, unable to rid himself of his enemy by forthright action. Hamlet is a constant danger to the king, and yet no plausible grounds can at first be discovered for proceeding against Hamlet. Only after the "mousetrap" play do both of them know that action is imperative; and yet both of them find their subsequent moves thwarted by unforeseen circumstances and deceptive appearances. Claudius is the only character other than Hamlet whom we overhear in soliloquy, and we learn on this occasion that Claudius too cannot resolve seemingly impossible alternatives. How is he to retain the queen, whom he has won by sinful lust, and at the same time free his tortured soul of guilt? It is ironically appropriate that Claudius' prayer should offer Hamlet his sole opportunity for successful revenge, an opportunity lost because Claudius gives the semblance of being in a state of contrition. Ultimately Hamlet and Claudius slay one another in a finale that neither could have anticipated.

Sharing the weaknesses of those he reviles, Hamlet turns his most unsparing criticisms upon himself. The appalling contrast between his uncle and father reminds him of the contrast between himself and Hercules—although when the fit of action is upon him he is as hardy as "The Nemean lion's nerve" [I. iv. 83]. "We are arrant knaves all," he warns Ophelia, "believe none of us" [III. i. 128]. Although more honest than most, Hamlet accounts himself unworthy to have been born: "I am very proud, revengeful, ambitious, with more offenses at my beck than I have thoughts to put them in, imagination to give them shape, or time to act them in" [III. i. 123-25]. His self-remonstrances repeatedly sound the note of generalization. He is like other men in being "a breeder of sinners" [III. i. 121], and he includes all mankind in his dilemma of action: "conscience doth make cowards of us all" [III. i. 82]. Paradoxically, although he characterizes himself as a vengeful man too full of sinful deeds, he reproaches himself most often for his failure to take arms against his sea of troubles. "O, what a rogue and peasant slave am I!" [II. ii. 550]. The son of a dear father murdered, he can only unpack his heart with words. Is this the result, he ponders, of "Bestial oblivion, or some craven scruple Of thinking too precisely on th' event" [IV. iv. 40-1]. Is he allowing himself to be paralyzed into inaction by his introspection, obscuring "the native hue of resolution" and "the pale cast of thought?" [III. i. 83-4]? If Hamlet asks this question and has no clear answer, we need not be surprised that it has tantalized modern criticism.

Several limits can be placed upon the search for an explanation of Hamlet's apparent hesitation to avenge. He is not ineffectual under ordinary circumstances. Elizabethan theories of melancholy did not suppose the sufferer to be made necessarily inactive. Hamlet has a deserved reputation in Denmark for manliness and princely demeanor. He keeps up his fencing practice and will "win at the odds" [V. ii. 212] against Laertes. He threatens with death those who would restrain him from speaking with the ghost—even his friend Horatio—and stabs the concealed Polonius unflinchingly. On the sea voyage to England he boards a pirate ship singlehanded in the grapple, after having arranged without remorse for the deaths of Rosencrantz and Guildenstern. In light of these deeds, Hamlet's self-accusations are signs of burning impatience in one who would surely act if he could. His contemplations of suicide follow similarly upon his frustrated perceptions of an impasse; suicide is a logical alternative when action appears meaningless, even if suicide must be rejected on grounds of Christian faith.

Such considerations turn our attention from Hamlet's supposed "fault" or "tragic flaw" to the context of his world and its philosophical absurdities. Wherein can he find trust and certitude? "Say, why is this?" he begs his father's ghost. "Wherefore? what should we do?" [I. iv. 57]. According to popular Elizabethan belief, both Catholic and Protestant, spirits from the dead could indeed "assume a pleasing shape" [II. ii. 599-600], in order to abuse a person in Hamlet's vulnerable frame of mind and so lead him to damnation. If Hamlet's plan to test the ghost's message by the "mousetrap" play causes him to wonder about his own cowardice and inconstancy, the accusations are directed against the impotent and self-contradictory nature of his situation.

Even after the clear revelation of Claudius' guilt at Hamlet's play, the exact plan of action remains anything but clear. Hamlet must face the ghost once again to explain why he "lets go by Th' important acting of your dread command" [III. iv. 107-08]; yet his purpose in confronting Gertrude with her weakness is the laudable one of returning her to at least an outward custom of virtue. Having earlier been uncertain of appearances in the apparition of his father, Hamlet now is deceived and hence delayed in his resolve by the semblance of Claudius' praying. Hamlet has always believed that heavenly justice will prevail among men: "Foul deeds will rise, Though all the earth o'erwhelm them, to men's eyes" [I. ii. 256-57]. Murder, though it have no tongue, "will speak With most miraculous organ" [II. ii. 593-94]. Nevertheless, man's perception of that divine revelation, and his role in

aiding the course of justice, are obscured by man's own corruption and blindness. Whenever Hamlet moves violently, he moves in error. Horatio, in summing up the play, speaks tellingly of "accidental judgments, casual slaughters" [V. ii. 382], and of "purposes mistook Fall'n on th' inventors' heads" [V. ii. 384-85]. The judgment applies to Hamlet as to Laertes and Claudius. Hamlet has already realized that he must pay the price of heaven's displeasure for killing Polonius, just as Polonius himself has paid the price for his own meddling. "Heaven hath pleased it so, To punish me with this, and this with me." Such fitting reciprocity can be brought about only by the far-reaching arm of providence. The engineer must be "Hoist with his own petar" [III. iv. 207].

Hamlet quests for clear action, but it mockingly eludes him. He yearns to be like Fortinbras, proceeding resolutely in a military action against Poland, but perceives at the same time that Fortinbras, in his absurd campaign for a patch of barren ground, for "this straw," for "an eggshell," must risk two thousand souls and a kingly fortune. The tomb in which these vast numbers will be laid to rest for no purpose anticipates the graveyard of Yorick and Ophelia, reaching back in its universal history to King Alexander and to Adam, the first gravemaker. The magnificent Alexander and imperious Caesar, renowned for exploits greater than those of Fortinbras, are now turned to clay and can serve only to stop a bunghole. This generalized vision of earthly vanity is no mere excuse for Hamlet's irresolution, for it shows the benign intention of providence in achieving a coherence beyond the grasp of human comprehension. Fortinbras of course succeeds politically where Hamlet must fail, and is chosen by Hamlet to restore Denmark to political health; but to acknowledge this discrepancy is merely to confirm the distance between order on earth and the higher perfection which Hamlet conceives.

It is only when Hamlet has come to terms with the absurdity of human action, and has resigned himself to the will of heaven, that a way is opened for him at last. Fittingly, he achieves this detachment in the company of Horatio. However much Horatio's philosophic skepticism may limit his own ability to perceive those "things in heaven and earth" [I. v. 116] that Hamlet would have him observe, Horatio remains the companion from whom Hamlet has most to learn. Hamlet can trust his friend not to angle for advancement, or to reveal the terrible secret of royal murder. Best of all, Horatio is "As one in suff'ring all that suffers nothing, A man that Fortune's buffets and rewards Hast ta'en with equal thanks" [III. ii. 66-8]. The true stoic, choosing to "suffer The slings and arrows of outrageous fortune" [III. i. 57] rather than futilely oppose them, is proof against the insidious temptation of worldly success as well as against disappointment. While other courtiers gravitate to Claudius with his seemingly magical formula for prospering, and so lose themselves in worldliness, Horatio sides with one who is sacrificed and so receives his commission as guardian of the truth. (pp. 1-7)

Structurally, the play of *Hamlet* is dominated by the pairing of various characters to reveal one as the "foil" of another. "I'll be your foil, Laertes" [V. ii. 255], says Hamlet, punning on the resemblance that elsewhere he seriously acknowledges: "by the image of my cause I see The portraiture of his" [V. ii. 77-8]. Laertes has returned from abroad to help celebrate the royal wedding; he loses a father by violent means and seeks vengeance. The common people, usually loyal to young Hamlet, are roused to a new hero-worship upon the occasion of Laertes' second return to Denmark. "Choose we! Laertes shall be king!" [IV. v. 107]. Ophelia too has been deprived of a father; so has Fortinbras. Hamlet stands at the center of these comparisons, the proper focus of the play. He is the composite man, graced as Ophelia observes with "The courtier's, soldier's, scholar's, eye, tongue, sword" [III. i. 151]. From each comparison we see another facet of his complex being, and another danger from extremes which he must learn to avoid.

We have already seen the similarities of Claudius and Polonius to Hamlet. Laertes, burdened with a responsibility like Hamlet's, moves to expedient action without scruple. He turns at first on Claudius, who is technically innocent of Polonius' death. The popular insurrection will simultaneously feed Laertes' revenge and his ambition. Presented with untested and partial evidence concerning Hamlet's part in Polonius' murder, Laertes would "cut his throat i' th' church" [IV. vii. 126]. He does in fact grapple with Hamlet in the graveyard, striking the first blow and prompting Hamlet to assure his rival that he is not "splenitive and rash" [V. i. 261]. More than that, Laertes connives with the king in underhanded murder; it is Laertes who thinks of poisoning the sword's point with an unction already bought of a mountebank. This poison recalls the murder of King Hamlet and the murder of Gonzago. Purposes of this sort can only return to plague the inventor.

Ophelia's response to her father's death is quite opposite to her brother's, but no less a reflection on Hamlet's dilemma. Her mind is not equal to the buffets of fortune, and she will not draw her breath in pain. She wanders from her mad sexual fantasies to muddy death. If the gravediggers and the priest are to be believed, her dreams, once she has "shuffled off this mortal coil" [III. i. 66], must give us pause. Fortinbras is a more positive figure, since he withholds his hand against the Danes in vengeance of his father, choosing to inherit the Danish throne by diplomatic patience and canny timing rather than by battle; but at best his counsel is "greatly to find quarrel in a straw When

honor's at the stake" [IV. iv. 55-6]. Horatio's philosophy of stoical indifference to fortune offers the greatest consolation to Hamlet, and yet it cannot predict the important outcome by which divinity will reveal itself in the fall of a sparrow.

Characters also serve as foils to one another as well as to Hamlet. Gertrude wishfully sees in Ophelia the blushing bride of Hamlet, innocently free from the compromises and surrenders which Gertrude has never mastered the strength to escape. Yet to Hamlet, Ophelia is no better than another Gertrude: both are tender of heart but submissive to the will of importunate men, and so are forced into uncharacteristic vices. Both would be other than what they are, and both receive Hamlet's exhortations to begin repentance by abstaining from pleasure. "Get thee to a nunnery"; "Assume a virtue if you have it not" [III. i. 120; III. iv. 160].

Hamlet's language puts much stress on the pun and other forms of wordplay. This habit of speech, so often a lapse in taste, is here appropriate to the portrayal of a keen mind tortured by alternatives. In his first appearance, Hamlet offers a double meaning in each of his answers to the king and queen. Because he is now both Claudius' cousin and son, Hamlet is "A little more than kin, and less than kind" [I. ii. 65]—too incestuously close, and yet neither kindly disposed nor bound by the legitimate ties of nature ("kind") as is a son to his true father. Denying that the clouds of sorrow still hang on him, Hamlet protests he is "too much in the sun" [I. ii. 67]—basking more than he wishes in the king's unctuous favor, and so, more a "son" than he thinks right. To his mother, who must cling to her worldly belief that the death of husbands and fathers is "common" or commonplace and hence to be taken in one's stride, Hamlet wryly counters: "Ay, madam, it is common" [I. ii. 74]. It is low, coarse, revolting.

In each double meaning Hamlet pierces to the heart of seeming. Mere forms, moods, or shapes of grief cannot denote him truly; he must discover the "absolute" in meaning and so quibbles with words and their deceptive masks. When his friend Horatio says to Hamlet "There's no offense" [I. ii. 74], meaning conventionally that Horatio is not affronted by Hamlet's wild and whirling words on the battlements, Hamlet is quick to remember the larger issue of morality in Denmark: "Yes, by Saint Patrick, but there is, Horatio, And much offense too" [I. v. 136-37]. When Polonius, merely to encourage small talk, asks Hamlet "What is the matter" [II. ii. 193] that he reads, Hamlet will have no chitchat. What is the matter "Between who?" Small wonder that Hamlet exults in the gravedigger's playing upon the idiotic and profound question of the ownership of a grave: this one belongs to one that is not a woman, but who *was* a woman. "How absolute the knave is!" [V. i. 137]. This digger is the same natural philosopher who has explicated the three branches of acting—"to act, to do, and to perform" [V. i. 12].

In patterns of images, *Hamlet* employs metaphors of clothes, of acting, and of disease. Again, like the wordplay, these images aim at the discrepancy between a handsome exterior and corrupted inner being. Hamlet decries inky cloaks, "windy suspiration of forced breath" [I. ii. 79], and other appurtenances of mourning, even though he himself is still dressed in black and so is visibly separated from the wedding party at court. Polonius reveals his trust in the game of preserving appearances by his worldly advice to his son: "the apparel oft proclaims the man" [I. iii. 72]. This maxim loses its irony when quoted out of context. Osric's sterile infatuation with clothes and mannerisms serves as one last reminder of the world's hypocrisy that Hamlet can now regard with almost comic detachment. Hamlet as actor is a master of many styles, frighting Ophelia in his fouled stockings, ungartered "As if he had been loosed out of hell" [II. i. 80], or composing jingling love doggerel to be read solemnly in open court, or declaiming in an outmoded and stilted tragical rhetoric on the massacre of Troy. He is critical of the professional players' fondness for exaggerated gestures, interpolated bawdry, and overblown rhetoric, because they must aid him in a subtle resemblance of truth designed to lay bare a human conscience. They must hold "the mirror up to nature, to show virtue her own feature, scorn her own image, and the very age and body of the time his form and pressure" [III. ii. 22-4]. Acting becomes a process of reality in uncovering the veneer of court life.

At the center of this revelation is the figure of the dead King Hamlet, whose magnificent person has been "barked about Most lazar-like with vile and loathsome crust" [I. v. 71-2]. Denmark, and the world itself, is "an unweeded garden That grows to seed. Things rank and gross in nature Possess it merely" [I. ii. 135-37]. Hamlet's role is that of a physician who must lance the ulcerous sore or corruption, by putting Claudius "to his purgation" [III. ii. 306] or speaking "daggers" to his mother in order to cure her soul. He must reveal Claudius to Gertrude for what her husband truly is, "a mildewed ear Blasting his wholesome brother" [III. iv. 64-5]. Without such exposure, Gertrude's complacency "will but skin and film the ulcerous place Whiles rank corruption, mining all within, Infects unseen" [III. iv. 147-49]. The poison that precipitates the action of the play, both a metaphor of disease and an actual evil, must be transformed into a providential weapon ending the lives of Claudius, Gertrude, and Laertes, as well as Hamlet. (pp. 8-10)

David Bevington, in an introduction to Twentieth Century Interpretations of Hamlet: A Collection of Critical Essays, *edited by David Bevington, Prentice-Hall, Inc., 1968, pp. 1-12.*

Maynard Mack

[*In this general analysis of* Hamlet, *Mack discusses three aspects of the play: its mysteriousness, the relationship between appearance and reality, and a concept the critic terms "mortality." The element of mysteriousness is not only created by the play's various ambiguities and uncertainties, the critic contends, but also by the numerous questions, especially* **Hamlet**'s, *that pervade the dramatic action. Further, the difficulty in distinguishing appearance from reality poses a crucial dilemma for* **Hamlet** *early in the play, Mack asserts, for although the* **Ghost** *seems to be a benevolent spirit, it may in fact be a devil who assumes the form of the prince's father. This concern with appearance and reality recurs time and again in* Hamlet, *especially in such issues as* **Claudius**'s *true nature and the manipulation of* **Rosencrantz** *and* **Guildenstern** *and* **Ophelia** *to spy on* **Hamlet**. *In addition, the critic continues, the sense of "mortality" in the tragedy is developed in three ways: through the play's emphasis on human weakness, the instability of human purpose, and humankind's submission to fortune, all of which point to the realization of the inevitability of human mortality. Mack concludes that* **Hamlet** *ultimately transcends these obstacles by accepting the world as it is and not as he would like it to be.*]

My subject is the world of *Hamlet*. I do not of course mean Denmark, except as Denmark is given a body by the play; and I do not mean Elizabethan England, though this is necessarily close behind the scenes. I mean simply the imaginative environment that the play asks us to enter when we read it or go to see it. (p. 502)

[Of] all the tragic worlds that Shakespeare made, [Hamlet's is] easily the most various and brilliant, the most elusive. It is with no thought of doing justice to it that I have singled out three of its attributes for comment. I know too well . . . that no one is likely to accept another man's reading of *Hamlet*, that anyone who tries to throw light on one part of the play usually throws the rest into deeper shadow, and that what I have to say leaves out many problems—to mention only one, the knotty problem of the text. All I would say in defense of the materials I have chosen is that they seem to me interesting, close to the root of the matter even if we continue to differ about what the root of the matter is, and explanatory, in a modest way, of this play's peculiar hold on everyone's imagination, its almost mythic status, one might say, as a paradigm of the life of man.

The first attribute that impresses us, I think, is mysteriousness. We often hear it said, perhaps with truth, that every great work of art has a mystery at the heart; but the mystery of *Hamlet* is something else. We feel its presence in the numberless explanations that have been brought forward for Hamlet's delay, his madness, his ghost, his treatment of Polonius, or Ophelia, or his mother; and in the controversies that still go on about whether the play is "undoubtedly a failure" ([T. S.] Eliot's phrase) or one of the greatest artistic triumphs; whether, if it is a triumph, it belongs to the highest order of tragedy; whether, if it is such a tragedy, its hero is to be taken as a man of exquisite moral sensibility ([A. C.] Bradley's view) or an egomaniac ([Salvador de] Madariaga's view).

Doubtless there have been more of these controversies and explanations than the play requires; for in Hamlet, to paraphrase a remark of Falstaff's, we have a character who is not only mad in himself but a cause that madness is in the rest of us. Still, the very existence of so many theories and counter-theories, many of them formulated by sober heads, gives food for thought. *Hamlet* seems to lie closer to the illogical logic of life than Shakespeare's other tragedies. And while the causes of this situation may be sought by saying that Shakespeare revised the play so often that eventually the motivations were smudged over, or that the original old play has been here or there imperfectly digested, or that the problems of Hamlet lay so close to Shakespeare's heart that he could not quite distance them in the formal terms of art, we have still as critics to deal with effects, not causes. If I may quote . . . from Mr. [E. M. W.] Tillyard, the play's very lack of a rigorous type of causal logic seems to be a part of its point.

Moreover, the matter goes deeper than this. Hamlet's world is preëminently in the interrogative mood. It reverberates with questions, anguished, meditative, alarmed. There are questions that in this play, to an extent I think unparalleled in any other, mark the phases and even the nuances of the action, helping to establish its peculiar baffled tone. There are other questions whose interrogations, innocent at first glance, are subsequently seen to have reached beyond their contexts and to point towards some pervasive inscrutability in Hamlet's world as a whole. Such is that tense series of challenges with which the tragedy begins: Bernardo's of Francisco, "Who's there?" [I. i. 1] Francisco's of Horatio and Marcellus, "Who is there?" [l. 13] Horatio's of the ghost, "What art thou . . . ?" [l. 46]. And then there are the famous questions. In them the interrogations seem to point not only beyond the context but beyond the play, out of Hamlet's predicaments into everyone's: "What a piece of work is a man! . . . And yet to me what is this quintessence of dust?" [II. ii. 303-04, 308]. "To be, or not to be, that is the question" [III. i. 55]. "Get thee to a nunnery. Why wouldst thou be a breeder of sinners?" [III. i. 120-21]. "I am very proud, revengeful, ambitious, with more offences at my beck than I have thoughts to put them in, imagination to give them shape, or time to act them in. What should such fellows as I do crawling between earth and heaven?" [III. i. 123-28]. "Dost

thou think Alexander look'd o' this fashion i' th' earth? . . . And smelt so?" [V. i. 197, 200].

Further, Hamlet's world is a world of riddles. The hero's own language is often riddling, as the critics have pointed out. When he puns, his puns have receding depths in them, like the one which constitutes his first speech: "A little more than kin, and less than kind" [I. ii. 65]. His utterances in madness, even if wild and whirling, are simultaneously, as Polonius discovers, pregnant: "Do you know me, my lord?" "Excellent well. You are a fishmonger" [II. ii. 173-74]. Even the madness itself is riddling: How much is real? How much is feigned? What does it mean? Sane or mad, Hamlet's mind plays restlessly about his world, turning up one riddle upon another. The riddle of character, for example, and how it is that in a man whose virtues else are "pure as grace" [I. iv. 33], some vicious mole of nature, some "dram of eale" [I. iv. 36], can "all the noble substance oft adulter" [I. iv. 37]. Or the riddle of the player's art, and how a man can so project himself into a fiction, a dream of passion, that he can weep for Hecuba. Or the riddle of action: how we may think too little—"What to ourselves in passion we propose," says the player-king, "The passion ending, doth the purpose lose" [III. ii. 194-95]; and again, how we may think too much: "Thus conscience does make cowards of us all, And thus the native hue of resolution Is sicklied o'er with the pale cast of thought" [III. i. 82-5].

There are also more immediate riddles. His mother—how could she "on this fair mountain leave to feed, And batten on this moor?" [III. iv. 66-7]. The ghost—which may be a devil, for "the de'il hath power T' assume a pleasing shape" [II. ii. 599-600]. Ophelia—what does her behavior to him mean? Surprising her in her closet, he falls to such perusal of her face as he would draw it. Even the king at his prayers is a riddle. Will a revenge that takes him in the purging of his soul be vengeance, or hire and salary? As for himself, Hamlet realizes, he is the greatest riddle of all—a mystery, he warns Rosencrantz and Guildenstern, from which he will not have the heart plucked out. He cannot tell why he has of late lost all his mirth, forgone all custom of exercises. Still less can he tell why he delays: "I do not know Why yet I live to say, 'This thing's to do,' Sith I have cause and will and strength and means To do 't" [IV. iv. 43-6].

Thus the mysteriousness of Hamlet's world is of a piece. It is not simply a matter of missing motivations, to be expunged if only we could find the perfect clue. It is built in. It is evidently an important part of what the play wishes to say to us. And it is certainly an element that the play thrusts upon us from the opening word. Everyone, I think, recalls the mysteriousness of that first scene. The cold middle of the night on the castle platform, the muffled sentries, the uneasy atmosphere of apprehension, the challenges leaping out of the dark, the questions that follow the challenges, feeling out the darkness, searching for identities, for relations, for assurance. (pp. 503-06)

Meantime, such is Shakespeare's economy, a second attribute of Hamlet's world has been put before us. This is the problematic nature of reality and the relation of reality to appearance. The play begins with an appearance, an "apparition," to use Marcellus's term—the ghost. And the ghost is somehow real, indeed the vehicle of realities. Through its revelation, the glittering surface of Claudius's court is pierced, and Hamlet comes to know, and we do, that the king is not only hateful to him but the murderer of his father, that his mother is guilty of adultery as well as incest. Yet there is a dilemma in the revelation. For possibly the apparition *is* an apparition, a devil who has assumed his father's shape.

This dilemma, once established, recurs on every hand. From the court's point of view, there is Hamlet's madness. Polonius investigates and gets some strange advice about his daughter: "Conception is a blessing, but as your daughter may conceive, friend, look to 't" [II. ii. 184-86]. Rosencrantz and Guildenstern investigate and get the strange confidence that "Man delights not me; no, nor woman neither" [II. ii. 309]. Ophelia is "loosed" to Hamlet (Polonius's vulgar word), while Polonius and the king hide behind the arras; and what they hear is a strange indictment of human nature, and a riddling threat: "Those that are married already, all but one, shall live" [III. i. 148-49].

On the other hand, from Hamlet's point of view, there is Ophelia. Kneeling here at her prayers, she seems the image of innocence and devotion. Yet she is of the sex for whom he has already found the name Frailty, and she is also, as he seems either madly or sanely to divine, a decoy in a trick. The famous cry—"Get thee to a nunnery" [III. i. 120]—shows the anguish of his uncertainty. If Ophelia is what she seems, this dirty-minded world of murder, incest, lust, adultery, is no place for her. Were she "as chaste as ice, as pure as snow" [III. i. 135], she could not escape its calumny. And if she is not what she seems, then a nunnery in its other sense of brothel is relevant to her. In the scene that follows he treats her as if she were indeed an inmate of a brothel.

Likewise, from Hamlet's point of view, there is the enigma of the king. If the ghost is *only* an appearance, then possibly the king's appearance is reality. He must try it further. By means of a second and different kind of "apparition," the play within the play, he does so. But then, immediately after, he stumbles on the king at prayer. This appearance has a relish of salvation in it. If the king dies now, his soul may yet be saved. Yet actually, as we know, the king's efforts to come to terms with heaven have been unavailing; his words fly up, his thoughts remain below. If Hamlet means the con-

ventional revenger's reasons that he gives for sparing Claudius, it was the perfect moment not to spare him—when the sinner was acknowledging his guilt, yet unrepentant. The perfect moment, but it was hidden, like so much else in the play, behind an arras.

There are two arrases in his mother's room. Hamlet thrusts his sword through one of them. Now at last he has got to the heart of the evil, or so he thinks. But now it is the wrong man; now he himself is a murderer. The other arras he stabs through with his words—like daggers, says the queen. He makes her shrink under the contrast he points between her present husband and his father. But as the play now stands (matters are somewhat clearer in the bad Quarto), it is hard to be sure how far the queen grasps the fact that her second husband is the murderer of her first. And it is hard to say what may be signified by her inability to see the ghost, who now for the last time appears. In one sense at least, the ghost is the supreme reality, representative of the hidden ultimate power, in Bradley's terms—witnessing from beyond the grave against this hollow world. Yet the man who is capable of seeing through to this reality, the queen thinks is mad. "To whom do you speak this?" she cries to her son. "Do you see nothing there?" he asks, incredulous. And she replies: "Nothing at all; yet all that is I see" [III. iv. 131-33]. Here certainly we have the imperturbable self-confidence of the worldly world, its layers on layers of habituation, so that when the reality is before its very eyes it cannot detect its presence.

Like mystery, this problem of reality is central to the play and written deep into its idiom. Shakespeare's favorite terms in *Hamlet* are words of ordinary usage that pose the question of appearances in a fundamental form. "Apparition" I have already mentioned. Another term is "seems." When we say, as Ophelia says of Hamlet leaving her closet, "He seem'd to find his way without his eyes" [II. i. 95], we mean one thing. When we say, as Hamlet says to his mother in the first court-scene, "Seems, Madam! . . . I know not 'seems'" [I. ii. 76], we mean another. And when we say, as Hamlet says to Horatio before the play within the play, "And after, we will both our judgments join In censure of his seeming" [III. ii. 86-7], we mean both at once. The ambiguities of "seem" coil and uncoil throughout this play, and over against them is set the idea of "seeing." So Hamlet challenges the king in his triumphant letter announcing his return to Denmark: "Tomorrow shall I beg leave to see your kingly eyes" [IV. vii. 44-5]. Yet "seeing" itself can be ambiguous, as we recognize from Hamlet's uncertainty about the ghost; or from that statement of his mother's already quoted: "Nothing at all; yet all that is I see."

Another term of like importance is "assume." What we assume may be what we are not: "The de'il hath power T' assume a pleasing shape" [II. ii. 599-600]. But it may be what we are: "If it assume my noble father's person, I'll speak to it" [I. ii. 243-44]. And it may be what we are not yet, but would become; thus Hamlet advises his mother, "Assume a virtue, if you have it not" [III. iv. 160]. The perplexity in the word points to a real perplexity in Hamlet's and our own experience. We assume our habits—and habits are like costumes, as the word implies: "My father in his habit as he liv'd!" [III. iv. 135]. Yet these habits become ourselves in time: "That monster, custom, who all sense doth eat Of habits evil, is angel yet in this, That to the use of actions fair and good He likewise gives a frock or livery That aptly is put on" [III. iv. 161-65].

Two other terms I wish to instance are "put on" and "shape." The shape of something is the form under which we are accustomed to apprehend it: "Do you see yonder cloud that's almost in shape of a camel?" [III. ii. 376]. But a shape may also be a disguise—even, in Shakespeare's time, an actor's costume or an actor's role. This is the meaning when the king says to Laertes as they lay the plot against Hamlet's life: "Weigh what convenience both of time and means May fit us to our shape" [IV. vii. 149-50]. "Put on" supplies an analogous ambiguity. Shakespeare's mind seems to worry this phrase in the play much as Hamlet's mind worries the problem of acting in a world of surfaces, or the king's mind worries the meaning of Hamlet's transformation. Hamlet has put an antic disposition on, that the king knows. But what does "put on" mean? A mask, or a frock or livery—our "habit"? The king is left guessing, and so are we. (pp. 507-10)

The mysteriousness of Hamlet's world, while it pervades the tragedy, finds its point of greatest dramatic concentration in the first act, and its symbol in the first scene. The problems of appearance and reality also pervade the play as a whole, but come to a climax in Acts II and III, and possibly their best symbol is the play within the play. Our third attribute, though again it is one that crops out everywhere, reaches its full development in Acts IV and V. It is not easy to find an appropriate name for this attribute, but perhaps "mortality" will serve, if we remember to mean by mortality the heartache and the thousand natural shocks that flesh is heir to, not simply death.

The powerful sense of mortality in *Hamlet* is conveyed to us, I think, in three ways. First, there is the play's emphasis on human weakness, the instability of human purpose, the subjection of humanity to fortune—all that we might call the aspect of failure in man. Hamlet opens this theme in Act I, when he describes how from that single blemish, perhaps not even the victim's fault, a man's whole character may take corruption. Claudius dwells on it again, to an extent that goes far beyond the needs

of the occasion, while engaged in seducing Laertes to step behind the arras of a seemer's world and dispose of Hamlet by a trick. Time qualifies everything, Claudius says, including love, including purpose. As for love—it has a "plurisy" in it and dies of its own too much. As for purpose—"That we would do, We should do when we would, for this 'would' changes, And hath abatements and delays as many As there are tongues, are hands, are accidents; And then this 'should' is like a spendthrift's sigh, That hurts by easing" [IV. vii. 118-23]. The player-king, in his long speeches to his queen in the play within the play, sets the matter in a still darker light. She means these protestations of undying love, he knows, but our purposes depend on our memory, and our memory fades fast. Or else, he suggests, we propose something to ourselves in a condition of strong feeling, but then the feeling goes, and with it the resolve. Or else our fortunes change, he adds, and with these our loves: "The great man down, you mark his favorite flies" [III. ii. 204]. The subjection of human aims to fortune is a reiterated theme in *Hamlet,* as subsequently in *Lear.* Fortune is the harlot goddess in whose secret parts men like Rosencrantz and Guildenstern live and thrive; the strumpet who threw down Troy and Hecuba and Priam; the outrageous foe whose slings and arrows a man of principle must suffer or seek release in suicide. Horatio suffers them with composure: he is one of the blessed few "Whose blood and judgment are so well co-mingled That they are not a pipe for fortune's finger To sound what stop she please" [III. ii. 69-71]. For Hamlet the task is of a greater difficulty.

Next, and intimately related to this matter of infirmity, is the emphasis on infection—the ulcer, the hidden abscess, "th' imposthume of much wealth and peace That inward breaks and shows no cause without Why the man dies" [IV. iv. 27-9]. Miss [Caroline F. E.] Spurgeon, who was the first to call attention to this aspect of the play [in her *Shakespeare's Imagery*], has well remarked that so far as Shakespeare's pictorial imagination is concerned, the problem in *Hamlet* is not a problem of the will and reason, "of a mind too philosophical or a nature temperamentally unfitted to act quickly," nor even a problem of an individual at all. Rather, it is a condition—"a condition for which the individual himself is apparently not responsible, any more than the sick man is to blame for the infection which strikes and devours him, but which, nevertheless, in its course and development, impartially and relentlessly, annihilates him and others, innocent and guilty alike." "That," she adds, "is the tragedy of *Hamlet,* as it is perhaps the chief tragic mystery of life." This is a perceptive comment, for it reminds us that Hamlet's situation is mainly not of his own manufacture, as are the situations of Shakespeare's other tragic heroes. He has inherited it; he is "born to set it right." [I. v. 189].

We must not, however, neglect to add to this what

another student of Shakespeare's imagery has noticed—that the infection in Denmark is presented alternatively as poison. Here, of course, responsibility is implied, for the poisoner of the play is Claudius. The juice he pours into the ear of the elder Hamlet is a combined poison and disease, a "leperous distilment" that curds "the thin and wholesome blood" [I. v. 70]. From this fatal center, unwholesomeness spreads out till there is something rotten in all Denmark. Hamlet tells us that his "wit's diseased," the queen speaks of her "sick soul," the king is troubled by "the hectic" in his blood, Laertes meditates revenge to warm "the sickness in my heart" [IV. vii. 55], the people of the kingdom grow "muddied, Thick and unwholesome in their thoughts" [IV. v. 81-2]; and even Ophelia's madness is said to be "the poison of deep grief" [IV. v. 75]. In the end, all save Ophelia die of that poison in a literal as well as figurative sense.

But the chief form in which the theme of mortality reaches us, it seems to me, is as a profound consciousness of loss. Hamlet's father expresses something of the kind when he tells Hamlet how his "most seeming-virtuous queen" [I. v. 46], betraying a love which "was of that dignity That it went hand in hand even with the vow I made to her in marriage" [I. v. 48-50], had chosen to "decline Upon a wretch whose natural gifts were poor To those of mine" [ll. 50-2]. "O Hamlet, what a falling off was there!" [I. v. 47]. Ophelia expresses it again, on hearing Hamlet's denunciation of love and woman in the nunnery scene, which she takes to be the product of a disordered brain:

> O what a noble mind is here o'erthrown!
> The courtier's, soldier's, scholar's, eye,
>   tongue, sword;
> Th' expectancy and rose of the fair state,
> The glass of fashion and the mould of
>   form,
> Th' observ'd of all observers, quite, quite
>   down!
>
> [III. i. 150-54]

The passage invites us to remember that we have never actually seen such a Hamlet—that his mother's marriage has brought a falling off in him before we meet him. And then there is that further falling off, if I may call it so, when Ophelia too goes mad—"Divided from herself and her fair judgment, Without the which we are pictures, or mere beasts" [IV. v. 85-6].

Marcellus, Horatio, Hamlet, and the Ghost. Act I, scene iv. By Henry Fuseli (1803).

Time was, the play keeps reminding us, when Denmark was a different place. That was before Hamlet's mother took off "the rose From the fair forehead of an innocent love" [III. iv. 42-3] and set a blister there. Hamlet then was still "th' expectancy and rose of the fair state" [III. i. 152]; Ophelia, the "rose of May" [IV. v. 158]. For Denmark was a garden then, when his father ruled. There had been something heroic about his father—a king who met the threats to Denmark in open battle, fought with Norway, smote the sledded Polacks on the ice, slew the elder Fortinbras in an honorable trial of strength. There had been something godlike about his father too: "Hyperion's curls, the front of Jove himself, An eye like Mars . . . , A station like the herald Mercury" [III. iv. 56-8]. But, the ghost reveals, a serpent was in the garden, and "the serpent that did sting thy father's life Now wears his crown" [I. v. 39-40]. The martial virtues are put by now. The threats to Denmark are attended to by policy, by agents working deviously for and through an uncle. The moral virtues are put by too. Hyperion's throne is occupied by "a vice of kings" [III. iv. 98], "a king of shreds and patches" [III. iv. 102]; Hyperion's bed, by a satyr, a paddock, a bat, a gib, a bloat king with reechy kisses. The garden is unweeded now, and "grows to seed; things rank and gross in nature Possess it merely" [I. ii. 136-37]. Even in himself he feels the taint, the taint of being his mother's son; and that other taint, from an earlier garden, of which he admonishes Ophelia: "Our virtue cannot so inoculate our old stock but we shall relish of it" [III. i. 116-17]. "Why wouldst thou be a breeder of sinners?" [III. i. 120-21]. "What should such fellows as I do crawling between earth and heaven?" [III. i. 126-27].

"Hamlet is painfully aware," says Professor Tillyard [in his *Shakespeare's Problem Plays*], "of the baffling human predicament between the angels and the beasts, between the glory of having been made in God's image and the incrimination of being descended from fallen Adam." To this we may add, I think, that Hamlet is more than aware of it; he exemplifies it; and it is for this reason that his problem appeals to us so powerfully as an image of our own.

Hamlet's problem, in its crudest form, is simply the problem of the avenger: he must carry out the injunction of the ghost and kill the king. But this problem, as I ventured to suggest at the outset, is presented in terms of a certain kind of world. The ghost's injunction to act becomes so inextricably bound up for Hamlet with the character of the world in which the action must be taken—its mysteriousness, its baffling appearances, its deep consciousness of infection, frailty, and loss—that he cannot come to terms with either without coming to terms with both.

When we first see him in the play, he is clearly a very young man, sensitive and idealistic, suffering the first shock of growing up. He has taken the garden at face value, we might say, supposing mankind to be only a little lower than the angels. Now in his mother's hasty and incestuous marriage, he discovers evidence of something else, something bestial—though even a beast, he thinks, would have mourned longer. Then comes the revelation of the ghost, bringing a second shock. Not so much because he now knows that his serpent-uncle killed his father; his prophetic soul had almost suspected this. Not entirely, even, because he knows now how far below the angels humanity has fallen in his mother, and how lust—these were the ghost's words—"though to a radiant angel link'd Will sate itself in a celestial bed, And prey on garbage" [I. v. 55-7]. Rather, because he now sees everywhere, but especially in his own nature, the general taint, taking from life its meaning, from woman her integrity, from the will its strength, turning reason into madness. "Why wouldst thou be a breeder of sinners?" "What should such fellows as I do crawling between earth and heaven?" [III. i. 120-21, 126-27]. Hamlet is not the first young man to have felt the heavy and the weary weight of all this unintelligible world; and, like the others, he must come to terms with it.

The ghost's injunction to revenge unfolds a different facet of his problem. The young man growing up is not to be allowed simply to endure a rotten world, he must also act in it. Yet how to begin, among so many enigmatic surfaces? Even Claudius, whom he now knows to be the core of the ulcer, has a plausible exterior. And around Claudius, swathing the evil out of sight, he encounters all those other exteriors, as we have seen. Some of them already deeply infected beneath, like his mother. Some noble, but marked for infection, like Laertes. Some not particularly corrupt but infinitely corruptible, like Rosencrantz and Guildenstern; some mostly weak and foolish like Polonius and Osric. Some, like Ophelia, innocent, yet in their innocence still serving to "skin and film the ulcerous place" [III. iv. 147].

And this is not all. The act required of him, though retributive justice, is one that necessarily involves the doer in the general guilt. Not only because it involves a killing; but because to get at the world of seeming one sometimes has to use its weapons. He himself, before he finishes, has become a player, has put an antic disposition on, has killed a man—the wrong man—has helped drive Ophelia mad, and has sent two friends of his youth to death, mining below their mines, and hoisting the engineer with his own petard. He had never meant to dirty himself with these things, but from the moment of the ghost's challenge to act, this dirtying was inevitable. It is the condition of living at all in such a world. To quote Polonius, who knew that world so well, men become "a little soil'd i' th' working" [II. i. 40]. Here is another matter with which Hamlet has to come to terms.

Human infirmity—all that I have discussed with reference to instability, infection, loss—supplies the problem with its third phase. Hamlet has not only to accept the mystery of man's condition between the angels and the brutes, and not only to act in a perplexing and soiling world. He has also to act within the human limits—"with shabby equipment always deteriorating," if I may adapt some phrases from Eliot's "East Coker," "In the general mess of imprecision of feeling, Undisciplined squads of emotion." Hamlet is aware of that fine poise of body and mind, feeling and thought, that suits the action to the word, the word to the action; that acquires and begets a temperance in the very torrent, tempest, and whirlwind of passion; but he cannot at first achieve it in himself. He vacillates between undisciplined squads of emotion and thinking too precisely on the event. He learns to his cost how easily action can be lost in "acting," and loses it there for a time himself. But these again are only the terms of every man's life. As Anatole France reminds us in a now famous apostrophe to Hamlet: "What one of us thinks without contradiction and acts without incoherence? What one of us is not mad? What one of us does not say with a mixture of pity, comradeship, admiration, and horror, Goodnight, sweet Prince!"

In the last act of the play (or so it seems to me, for I know there can be differences on this point), Hamlet accepts his world and we discover a different man. Shakespeare does not outline for us the process of acceptance any more than he had done with Romeo or was to do with Othello. But he leads us strongly to expect an altered Hamlet, and then, in my opinion, provides him. We must recall that at this point Hamlet has been absent from the stage during several scenes, and that such absences in Shakespearean tragedy usually warn us to be on the watch for a new phase in the development of the character. . . . Furthermore, and this is an important matter in the theatre—especially important in a play in which the symbolism of clothing has figured largely—Hamlet now looks different. He is wearing a different dress—probably, as [Harley] Granville-Barker thinks [in his *Preface to "Hamlet"*], his "seagown scarf'd" about him, but in any case no longer the disordered costume of his antic disposition. The effect is not entirely dissimilar to that in *Lear*, when the old king wakes out of his madness to find fresh garments on him.

Still more important, Hamlet displays a considerable change of mood. This is not a matter of the way we take the passage about defying augury, as Mr. Tillyard among others seems to think. It is a matter of Hamlet's whole deportment, in which I feel we may legitimately see the deportment of a man who has been "illuminated" in the tragic sense. Bradley's term for it is fatalism, but if this is what we wish to call it, we must at least acknowledge that it is fatalism of a very distinctive kind—a

kind that Shakespeare has been willing to touch with the associations of the saying in St. Matthew about the fall of a sparrow, and with Hamlet's recognition that a divinity shapes our ends. The point is not that Hamlet has suddenly become religious; he has been religious all through the play. The point is that he has now learned, and accepted, the boundaries in which human action, human judgment, are enclosed.

Till his return from the voyage he had been trying to act beyond these, had been encroaching on the role of providence, if I may exaggerate to make a vital point. He had been too quick to take the burden of the whole world and its condition upon his limited and finite self. Faced with a task of sufficient difficulty in its own right, he had dilated it into a cosmic problem—as indeed every task is, but if we think about this too precisely we cannot act at all. The whole time is out of joint, he feels, and in his young man's egocentricity, he will set it right. Hence he misjudges Ophelia, seeing in her only a breeder of sinners. Hence he misjudges himself, seeing himself a vermin crawling between earth and heaven. Hence he takes it upon himself to be his mother's conscience, though the ghost has warned that this is no fit task for him, and returns to repeat the warning: "Leave her to heaven, And to those thorns that in her bosom lodge" [I. v. 86-7]. Even with the king, Hamlet has sought to play at God. *He* it must be who decides the issue of Claudius's salvation, saving him for a more damnable occasion. Now, he has learned that there are limits to the before and after that human reason can comprehend. Rashness, even, is sometimes good. Through rashness he has saved his life from the commission for his death, "and prais'd be rashness for it" [V. ii. 7]. This happy circumstance and the unexpected arrival of the pirate ship make it plain that the roles of life are not entirely self-assigned. "There is a divinity that shapes our ends, Roughhew them how we will" [V. ii. 10-11]. Hamlet is ready now for what may happen, seeking neither to foreknow it nor avoid it. "If it be now, 'tis not to come; if it be not to come, it will be now; if it be not now, yet it will come: the readiness is all" [V. ii. 220-22].

The crucial evidence of Hamlet's new frame of mind, as I understand it, is the graveyard scene. Here, in its ultimate symbol, he confronts, recognizes, and accepts the condition of being man. It is not simply that he now accepts death, though Shakespeare shows him accepting it in ever more poignant forms: first, in the imagined persons of the politician, the courtier, and the lawyer, who laid their little schemes "to circumvent God" [V. i. 79], as Hamlet puts it, but now lie here; then in Yorick, whom he knew and played with as a child; and then in Ophelia. This last death tears from him a final cry of passion, but the striking contrast between his behavior and Laertes's reveals how deeply he has changed.

Still, it is not the fact of death that invests this scene with its peculiar power. It is instead the haunting mystery of life itself that Hamlet's speeches point to, holding in its inscrutable folds those other mysteries that he has wrestled with so long. These he now knows for what they are, and lays them by. The mystery of evil is present here— for this is after all the universal graveyard, where, as the clown says humorously, he holds up Adam's profession; where the scheming politician, the hollow courtier, the tricky lawyer, the emperor and the clown and the beautiful young maiden, all come together in an emblem of the world; where even, Hamlet murmurs, one might expect to stumble on "Cain's jawbone, that did the first murther" [V. i. 77]. The mystery of reality is here too—for death puts the question, "What is real?" in its irreducible form, and in the end uncovers all appearances: "Is this the fine of his fines and the recovery of his recoveries, to have his fine pate full of fine dirt?" [V. i. 106-07]. "Now get you to my lady's chamber, and tell her, let her paint an inch thick, to this favor she must come" [V. i. 192-94]. Or if we need more evidence of this mystery, there is the anger of Laertes at the lack of ceremonial trappings, and the ambiguous character of Ophelia's own death. "Is she to be buried in Christian burial when she wilfully seeks her own salvation?" [V. i. 1-2] asks the gravedigger. And last of all, but most pervasive of all, there is the mystery of human limitation. The grotesque nature of man's little joys, his big ambitions. The fact that the man who used to bear us on his back is now a skull that smells; that the noble dust of Alexander somewhere plugs a bunghole; that "Imperious Caesar, dead and turn'd to clay, Might stop a hole to keep the wind away" [V. i. 213-14]. Above all, the fact that a pit of clay is "meet" for such a guest as man, as the gravedigger tells us in his song, and yet that, despite all frailties and limitations, "That skull had a tongue in it and could sing once" [V. i. 75].

After the graveyard and what it indicates has come to pass in him, we know that Hamlet is ready for the final contest of mighty opposites. He accepts the world as it is, the world as a duel, in which, whether we know it or not, evil holds the poisoned rapier and the poisoned chalice waits; and in which, if we win at all, it costs not less than everything. I think we understand by the close of Shakespeare's *Hamlet* why it is that unlike the other tragic heroes he is given a soldier's rites upon the stage. For as William Butler Yeats once said, "Why should we honor those who die on the field of battle? A man may show as reckless a courage in entering into the abyss of himself." (pp. 514-23)

Maynard Mack, "The World of Hamlet," in The Yale Review, *Vol. XLI, No. 4, June, 1952, pp. 502-23.*

DELAY

Robert Hapgood

[*Hapgood examines the dramaturgy, or the dramatic representation, of "delay" in* Hamlet, *pointing out that while* **Hamlet** *is the primary focus of this issue, other characters—most notably* **Claudius, Laertes,** *and* **Fortinbras**— *often delay or are hindered during the course of events. The critic explores how action begins and ends at various moments in the play in a sequence of events that often culminates in a standstill in which a character experiences a direct contradiction to his or her purposes. Hapgood defines* **Hamlet's** *particular form of delay as "inertia" because he experiences difficulty both in getting started and in coming to a stop. For instance, although it takes the prince nearly the whole play to exact his revenge on* **Claudius,** *when he finally kills the king he does so first with his sword and second with the poisoned wine. The critic also asserts that the dramaturgy of delay occurs in the play's dialogue. Although* **Hamlet's** *soliloquies represent a form of dramatic action and move the plot forward, ironically the character himself is physically inactive. (A soliloquy is a speech delivered while the speaker is alone and devised to inform the reader what the character is thinking or to provide essential information concerning other participants in the action.) According to Hapgood, Shakespeare's dramatic representation of delay ultimately "interpenetrates with the theme of death." The catastrophe in the play's finale puts an end to delay, for it resolves the tragedy's three most compelling revenge motives:* **King Hamlet's** *murder,* **Claudius's** *marriage to* **Gertrude,** *and* **Polonius's** *murder.*]

I

The actions of *Hamlet* are all beginning and end, with no middle. The play takes place in the shadow of three events—the murder of King Hamlet, the marriage of Claudius and Gertrude, and the death of Polonius. The consequences of these events— the suffering of the wronged, the remorse of the wrongers, the extensive repercussions in subsequent events—are fully and inexorably worked out. Within this atmosphere of prolonged aftermath, numerous actions are begun, stopped, started again, stopped, and not generally brought to completion until the finale. It is these arrested actions which set the main rhythm of the play. Of course, any powerful conflict is likely to involve strong purposes which are somehow frustrated before their decisive fulfillment. What is distinctive about *Hamlet* is that the purposes are extraordinarily strong, even vowed; the frustrations reach the point of utter deadlock and standstill; and the completions, when they finally come, are sudden, violent, and unexpected.

This is pre-eminently the rhythm of Hamlet's own actions. The central instance comes when he is about to stab Claudius at prayer yet halts his blow. This interrupted gesture, deflected to Polonius, remains suspended in our minds until it is carried through in the finale. The same rhythm is there, in little, when he determines to follow the ghost, is detained by Horatio and Marcellus, and then breaks loose: "Unhand me, gentlemen. / By heaven, I'll make a ghost of him that lets me!" [I. iv. 84-5]. In the large it is there in his progression from high resolution ("the play's the thing" [II. ii. 604]) to relapsing doubts in the "to be or not to be" soliloquy (fifty-five lines later) to the substitute-fulfillment of the play-within-a-play.

But Hamlet is by no means the only character in the play who delays, or is delayed from, accomplishing what he sets out to do. Laertes is often taken as a contrast to Hamlet, the son who moves immediately and directly to the revenge of his father's death; and so he seems when he first storms in to see the king. But his momentum is soon halted, first—physically—by the queen ("Let him go, Gertrude," Claudius twice directs [IV. v. 123, 127]) and then, as Claudius puts it, by the divinity that doth hedge a king. Spent in his own rodomontade [ranting], his rage is soon calmed, and he willingly becomes the king's "organ." Again, his attack on Hamlet in the graveyard is halted and deferred. Fortinbras, the man of military action, is also held back from his purposes. As Claudius' ambassadors report, the Norwegian king

> . . . sends out arrests
> On Fortinbras; which he in brief obeys,
> Receives rebuke from Norway, and in fine
> Makes vow before his uncle never more
> To give th' assay of arms against your majesty.
>
> [II. ii. 67-71]

Does Claudius delay? In *Scourge and Minister*, G. R. Elliott puts it too strongly when he says, "It is true that Hamlet dies because he postpones too long the killing of the king. But it is equally significant that Claudius dies because he postpones too long the killing of Hamlet." As Elliott admits, Claudius' delay is never given direct comment; nor as the play unfolds is it as clear as it is in hindsight that Claudius must kill Hamlet. Yet Claudius seems to be speaking from experience, as well as influencing Laertes, when he says:

> . . .That we would do
> We should do when we would, for this "would" changes,
> And hath abatements and delays as many
> As there are tongues, are hands, are accidents . . .
>
> [IV. vii. 118-21]

And he does make certain slight—but very important—delays. Although he has made up his mind to send Hamlet to England, he follows Polonius' advice to postpone action until after the play and a conference between Hamlet and his mother. Even after he has broken off the play and directed Rosencrantz and Guildenstern to prepare for the voyage, he delays in confining Hamlet, a nearly fatal pause which receives its visual symbol as he kneels attempting to pray during Hamlet's long deliberations. His first plot on Hamlet's life is utterly frustrated, and his final one comes close to it, as Laertes repeatedly fails to score a "hit" in the fencing match. Even the slightest delay for Claudius can be disastrous. It takes only a second's hesitation for it to be "too late" for him to stop Gertrude from drinking the poisoned wine. (pp. 132-34)

Arrested movement is especially striking in the play's many delayed exits. Shakespeare's characters often begin to part and then pause to add an afterthought. But in *Hamlet* the name of action is again and again thus sicklied o'er with the pale cast of thought. For a small instance, when Hamlet has broken loose and followed the ghost, Horatio declares, "Have after"; but then pauses to reflect:

> . . . To what issue will this come?
> **Marcellus.** Something is rotten in the state of Denmark.
> **Horatio.** Heaven will direct it.
>
> [I. iv. 89-91]

Only then does Marcellus return to the demands of the situation: "Nay, let's follow him." So the ghost, after scenting the morning air, declares "Brief let me be" [I. v. 59]; yet continues for thirty lines, and lingers after his "adieu, adieu, adieu" [I. v. 91] to cry "swear" again and again from the cellarage. So Laertes bids Ophelia farewell, only to add forty lines of admonition. So while Laertes' servants tend and the wind sits in the shoulder of his sail, Polonius chooses to deliver his few precepts and multiple blessings. So, after he says farewell to Reynaldo, Polonius amusingly keeps adding further directions. So, after Ophelia tells him of Hamlet's visit to her, Polonius immediately determines: "Come, go with me. I will go seek the king" [II. i. 98]; yet it takes twenty lines and two more repetitions of "Come" before they do so.

Claudius is a study in haste and pause. At first he is full of dispatch, sending off the ambassadors to Norway with "Farewell, and let your haste commend your duty" [I. ii. 39]. He seems less assured but still fully in control in his "hasty sending" for Rosencrantz and Guildenstern and in his "quick determination" to send Hamlet "with speed to England" [III. i. 168-69]. Yet his resolution can be brought up short by his conscience. When he and Polonius are about to withdraw to spy on Hamlet, they pause to reflect in turn on their guilts, until Polonius breaks in with "I hear him coming" [III. i. 54]. And of course the king's abrupt exit after the mousetrap is followed by his main moment of pause as he tries to pray. This is not only a delay in his plot against Hamlet; it also represents a moment of deadlock in his inner life. As he says:

Pray can I not,
Though inclination be as sharp as will.
My stronger guilt defeats my strong intent,
And like a man to double business bound
I stand in pause where I shall first begin,
And both neglect.

[III. iii. 38-43]

After Polonius' death, there is something truly hectic about Claudius' haste in sending Rosencrantz and Guildenstern to catch Hamlet, while delaying their departure three times with afterthoughts. At this same point, he repeatedly tells Gertrude to "Come"—each time interrupting their exit, however, by his further reflections. And while he knows that he should pretend "to bear all smooth and even, / This sudden sending him away must seem / Deliberate pause" [IV. iii. 7-9], he plainly cannot wait for the party bound for England to be off with "fiery quickness." After that, he is all calm and patience, even after Hamlet returns. He is masterful in restraining Laertes, persuading him to "keep close within your chamber" [IV. vii. 129] and controlling his outburst at Ophelia's grave. The funeral scene closes with the most sinisterly dynamic pause in the play; Claudius promises Laertes:

This grave shall have a living monument.
An hour of quiet shortly shall we see;
Till then in patience our proceeding be.

[V. i. 297-99]

Hamlet makes many delayed exits. While others leave, he often remains on stage at the end of a scene, for a full soliloquy or a brief comment. After the ghost episode, he shakes hands and parts from Horatio and Marcellus to "go pray," only to return to swear them repeatedly to secrecy. He ends the scene characteristically, starting off ("Let us go in together" [I. v. 186]), but pausing for

And still your fingers on your lips, I pray.
The time is out of joint. O cursed spite
That ever I was born to set it right!

[I. v. 187-89]

before concluding: "Nay, come, let's go together." In the "get thee to a nunnery" episode [III. i. 87ff.], he again and again tells Ophelia "farewell." . . . In the bedroom scene, Hamlet over and over bids his mother "goodnight." His most notable "delayed exit" comes at his death, marked as it is by his "I am dead, Horatio . . . Horatio, I am dead . . . I die, Horatio! . . . the rest is silence" [V. ii. 332-58].

There is an inertia about Hamlet. He has difficulty both in getting under way and in coming to a stop. He puts off killing Claudius but then kills him twice. Both kinds of inertia are involved in his penchant for dallying speculatively on the verge of important events. . . . In the last act, this is intensified. For then, when every moment before the ambassadors arrive should count, Hamlet is delighted to spend his "interim" matching wits with a gravedigger and having some fun with a fop. Because of

his new-found willingness to "let be," these moments of prolonged distraction from his task do not seem as outrageously frivolous as they otherwise would. Yet neither Hamlet's graveyard musings nor his toyings with Osric are as fascinating as his reflections on the dram of eal or his theory of drama; and I suspect that we are meant, toward the end of this long play, to grow weary of Hamlet's dallyings and wish that he would get on with it.

At long last, of course, he does so; but, like the other dominant characters, in an unexpected and sudden way. His great opportunity comes about not through is own planning but through Claudius' machinations and the accidents of the moment. At the last minute, he regains the initiative he lost in the prayer scene and ends his prolonged conflict with Claudius in reckless haste. Oddly, much the same can be said of his conflict with himself. For his unhesitating decision to enter a fencing match with the man whose father he has killed, sponsored by the man who has killed his father and ordered his own death, comes close to the self-slaughter he earlier longed for but gave pause to.

Claudius succeeds in killing Hamlet by proxy, as planned, but in a fashion which proves suddenly to be self-incriminating and self-destructive. Laertes, though it is almost against his conscience, completes his interrupted attack on Hamlet; yet its outcome is not, finally, the satisfaction of revenge but an exchange of forgiveness. Curiously, Laertes' earlier threat to Claudius gets carried through in his cry, "The king, the king's to blame" [V. ii. 320]. Fortinbras' frustrated drive toward conquest is more than fulfilled, without battle, when at the end he walks into the whole kingdom of Denmark.

Thus in some sixty lines, the play's main actions reach abrupt completion. Only among themselves do the strongest characters (Hamlet, Claudius, Laertes, Fortinbras) work out the whole cadence from resolution through frustration and standstill to odd fulfillment. Hamlet's conflict with his mother suggests certain phases of this pattern. On the way to her bedroom, he checks his impulse to use daggers, resolving to speak them instead. (Even so, however, Gertrude thinks that he intends to murder her and calls for help.) But her death when it comes, though sudden and unexpected, is her husband's doing, not her son's. Polonius and Rosencrantz and Guildenstern all die in bizarre ways and in an atmosphere of haste, no shriving time allowed; yet their preceding conflicts with Hamlet were no more than a series of verbal skirmishes, in which Hamlet successfully frustrated their attempts to pluck out the heart of his mystery. Amid all these sudden deaths, Ophelia's is notably gradual; indeed, in no way does her career follow the main rhythm of arrested action.

II

The same kind of overarching irony that applies to

the action applies to the dialogue. In the same sense that *Hamlet*—for all that happens in it—is about not acting, *Hamlet*—for all its more than 3700 lines—is also about not talking. Like Laertes, many of the characters have in them a "speech of fire" [IV. vii. 190]. Yet at first they cannot, will not, or dare not communicate it. Sometimes they are literally silent; sometimes they say everything *but* what they really have to say; sometimes they lie; sometimes they speak darkly, or to the wrong person, or to someone who chooses not to listen. With some, this speech of fire remains uncommunicated. With others, especially Hamlet, it finally blazes forth in an outburst all the more intense, and often extended, for its previous frustration. Of course, not all of the impulses to speak in the play are arrested. Far from it. No one in literature is quicker of tongue than Hamlet himself, and many of the other characters are notably articulate, in fact, loquacious. Only the most important things are held back.

Every step in transmitting the truth about King Hamlet's death is marked by delay. The ghost must appear twice to the guards, silent himself and distilling them to speechless fear, before they go to Horatio, whose ears are fortified against their story. Again, the ghost is dumb (and dumbfounding to Horatio, who has to be urged to speak) but seemingly about to speak when the cock crows. When it appears to Hamlet, speech is again arrested on both sides. Hamlet vows to speak to the ghost "though hell itself should gape / And bid me hold my peace" [I. ii. 244-45]. . . . Still the ghost does not speak until Hamlet declares: "Speak. I'll go no further" [I. v. 1].

The ghost is forbid to tell the secrets of its prison house, and thus holds back the eternal blazon "whose lightest word / Would harrow up thy soul, freeze thy young blood, / Make thy two eyes like stars start from their spheres" [I. v. 15-17]. But the tale it does tell is almost as harrowing. For fifty lines after learning the name of the murderer, Hamlet says nothing. Not until after the ghost's exit does he break his silence with an extended and extravagant protestation that his father's "commandment all alone shall live / Within the book and volume of my brain" [I. v. 102-03]. Yet communication of the ghost's message to Hamlet is still not complete. The ghost was well advised to insist that Hamlet "lend thy serious hearing" and "List, list, O, list!" [I. v. 5, 22]. For he does not finally take the ghost's word until he has grounds more relative.

The central instance of arrested speech is that of Hamlet toward Claudius. At his first appearance, after his enigmatic "I am too much in the sun" [I. ii. 67], Hamlet has nothing whatever to say to his uncle; every subsequent speech in this scene is pointedly addressed to his mother. In his first soliloquy, he expresses to himself his contempt for

Claudius, calling him a satyr, "no more like my father / Than I to Hercules" [I. ii. 152-53]. After the ghost reveals that Claudius is a murderer, Hamlet denounces to himself and his tables that "smiling, damned villain!" [I. v. 106] and seems on the verge of telling Horatio and Marcellus his "news" immediately. It may be that he is about to say it when he begins "There's never a villain dwelling in all Denmark," only then to catch himself short and add, "But he's an arrant knave" [I. v. 123-24]. (pp. 135-40)

Claudius meanwhile has built a court of concealment and lies, founded on the forged process of King Hamlet's death. "Give thy thoughts no tongue" [I. iii. 59], Polonius advises Laertes, and perfectly hits off the atmosphere at Elsinore. There is a progression in falsity, as the king's secret contaminates his own life and that of his court. At first, the one key lie having already been told, it is a matter of tacit concealment and smiling hypocrisy. As Hamlet takes malicious delight in demonstrating, Claudius has surrounded himself with yes-men. Then in his service his subjects (even Ophelia) begin to engage in small deceptions. His own out-and-out lies do not come until late in the play, when he deceives Laertes about Hamlet's guilt, misleads Gertrude about calming Laertes' rage, and at the end, with truly extraordinary presence of mind, declares that Gertrude merely "sounds to see them bleed" [V. ii. 308] and—his last words—"I am but hurt" [V. ii. 324]. Although he suffers keenly from the gap between his deed and his most painted word, his cry for "light" is as far as he ever goes toward the kind of public confession of his guilt which, with its consequences, would allow him to pray for forgiveness. For all his easy public address, Claudius in the speech which most concerns him remains in effect mute:

> My words fly up. My thoughts remain below.
> Words without thoughts never to heaven go.
>
> [III. iii. 97-8]
> (p. 141)

Hamlet's one-line denunciation of dying Claudius is necessarily brief, but it is for that reason all the more powerful. In contrast to his earlier, private mouth-curse ("Bloody, bawdy villain! / Remorseless, treacherous, lecherous, kindless villain!" [II. ii. 580-81]), his final, public one is tersely comprehensive: "thou incestuous, murd'rous, damned Dane" [V. ii. 325]. Each word adds a further area of villainy: familial, social, religious, and political. Though still sibilant and assonant, these sound effects are no longer excessive, and the dentals at the end add bite.

Unlike Amleth in the legend, Hamlet is not allowed to deliver a final, explanatory public oration. To the end, his communication of what he most wants to say is arrested:

You that look pale and tremble at this
    chance,
That are but mutes or audience to this act,
Had I but time—as this fell sergeant,
    Death,
Is strict in his arrest—O, I could tell
    you . . .

                                      [V. ii. 334-37]

And it is left to Horatio to report him and his cause
aright. It is fully in the rhythm of arrested speech
that Horatio's own report to the yet unknowing
world should be promised and adumbrated but deferred.

III

For too long, too much critical attention was given
to Hamlet's delay and its causes. One of the healthi-
est tendencies of recent *Hamlet* criticism has been
a widening of interest from Hamlet to the whole
work, from Hamlet's delay to other important
themes. Along with this, however, has come a tendency to minimize the importance of delay. . . .
For the rhythms of arrested action and speech in-
terwork endlessly with other major elements: the
play's images of hidden disease jibe with the prevailing sense of fatally suppressed deeds and
words; its revelations of evil petrify not only Hamlet
but Claudius and Laertes; its constant questionings result from the atmosphere of secrecy created
by arrested speech. Above all, the dramaturgy of
delay interpenetrates with the theme of death.
Hamlet is acutely aware both of the fixity and the
silence of death: dead Polonius will "stay" for the
guards and that prating knave "Is now most still,
most secret, and most grave" [III. iv. 214]; Yorick's
smile is fixed on his grinning skull and his gibes
will no longer set the table on a roar. It is at the end,
where that fell sergeant is most strict in his arrest,
that death is most in the rhythm of the play, ending at last the reverberations of the three original
sins (the murder of King Hamlet, the marriage, and
the killing of Polonius) and fulfilling, in ironically
mutual destruction, the vows of Hamlet, Claudius,
and Laertes which followed in their wake.

The rhythms of delay also re-enforce one another.
The moments of silence and inaction tend to be
one, and the same loquaciousness that postpones
what really needs saying, postpones what really
needs doing. There is a sense in which everything
Hamlet says and does is a substitute for the delayed
act of killing the king. Above all, the dramaturgy of
delay contributes to our sense of a world in which
direct action and speech are extremely difficult, almost impossible. Actions are not to be carried
through without the utmost persistence, the most
desperate measures, and the most extraordinary
luck—and even then they may well miscarry. Communication is at best minimal and dubious. For
Hamlet lives in a world of "bad dreams." The battlements of Elsinore are haunted, its corridors are
dark and circuitous, its rooms prisonlike, its halls
filled with elaborately disguised figures. Its inhabi-

tants are subject to attacks of paralysis at crucial
moments, followed by fits of wild activity and
speech. In this nightmare world, Hamlet's difficulties in acting and speaking are nothing unusual.
He delays because he suffers in their most acute
form from maladies endemic in human life as it is
lived in Elsinore.

It is true that Hamlet has his distinctive susceptibilities to this prevailing condition, one of which is
his own awareness of it. But that is another
essay—and of a different sort from this one, where
I have resisted making still another analysis of
Hamlet's delay in itself in order to study the virtually unnoticed instances of delay in other characters
and in other aspects of Shakespeare's dramaturgy.
(pp. 142-44)

Robert Hapgood, "Hamlet Nearly Ab-
surd: The Dramaturgy of Delay," in
The Tulane Drama Review, *Vol. 9, No. 4,*
Summer, 1965, pp. 132-45.

Robert R. Reed, Jr.

[*Reed analyzes not only* **Hamlet's** *internal*
meditations on his hesitation to exact revenge
on **Claudius,** *but also various external obsta-*
cles which prevent him from killing the king.
According to the critic, **Hamlet 's** *misgivings*
about the **Ghost** *are perhaps the chief impedi-*
ment to his taking revenge, noting that the
prince almost immediately questions its identi-
ty and motives. **Hamlet** *is therefore reluctant to*
act upon its demands. Furthermore, once **Clau-**
dius's *guilt is established,* **Hamlet** *refrains*
from killing him at prayer because the king is
in an act of repentance and his soul might go
to heaven. Because such external obstacles
hinder **Hamlet** *from taking his revenge, Reed*
asserts, he vents his frustration in furious self-
reproaches throughout the play. The critic pro-
vides a psychoanalytic analysis of **Hamlet 's**
self-castigation, deducing that the prince relies
on self-incrimination to soothe his irrational
mood swings. Unconsciously, **Hamlet 's** *mind*
becomes so irrational due to its inability to
evaluate these external obstacles that it mag-
nifies his frustration by imposing unreason-
able guilt on his consciousness.]

In view of the countless "solutions" to the paradox
of Hamlet's conduct, the reader may understandably suspect me of cross boldness in adding a further comment. I take heart, however, from my conviction that even the most thoughtful of recent criticisms have not departed completely from the nineteenth-century tradition which condones expedient evasions of one or more of the major facts. My
purpose is to correlate these facts into an intelligible pattern of conduct. Neither the external problems that render close to impossible Hamlet's execution of vengeance upon Claudius nor the
prince's bitter self-accusations blaming the delay

wholly upon himself need be side-stepped or mini-mized; but the evasion or, at best, the distortion of one or the other has traditionally been the custom of the critics, since from the viewpoint of logic the two phenomena are strikingly incompatible. Dr. Ernest Jones, employing a tenet of modern psycho-analysis, goes so far as to argue that Hamlet pro-crastinates because of an Oedipus complex. In-deed, from the time of [Johann Wolfgang von] Goe-the, the majority of critics have ascribed Hamlet's delay in avenging his murdered father to a weak-ness of character. But those more familiar with Elizabethan traditions have insisted that the delay is motivated by manifest external obstacles; they have stressed two main difficulties: Hamlet's ortho-dox doubt as to the veracity of the Ghost and, sec-ond, the complications of executing vengeance upon a heavily guarded monarch, against whom there is no tangible evidence of his crime. With the latter critics I concur in full, except for one thing—their custom of side-stepping or, at best, awkward-ly explaining Hamlet's self-accusations of delay. The psychotic factors, I agree, are in no way re-sponsible for Hamlet's delay in avenging his father; on the contrary, a not uncommon neurosis results from Hamlet's enforced inactivity and is the cause of his self-recriminations, which, in view of the ex-ternal obstacles to vengeance, are clearly unwar-ranted. Yet, as I shall hope to prove, they are per-fectly intelligible—in fact, so intelligible that Ham-let's conduct would appear obtuse and unnatural without them.

The two traditional schools of thought concerning the character of Hamlet are both unsound for the reason that each bases its interpretation on only a part of the important facts. The school that ad-heres to the principle that Hamlet's delay is inter-nally motivated may be divided into three groups: the critics led by Goethe with his theory that Ham-let is weak-willed; those led by [August Wihelm von] Schlegel and [Samuel Taylor] Coleridge, who maintained that the habit of meditation paralyzes the capacity for action; and those who have fol-lowed Hermann Ulrici's doctrine that Christian ethics, or moral scruples, are a deterrent to blood revenge. Whatever their basic differences of opin-ion, these critics have pursued a similar method of argument: they have ignored or minimized the ex-ternal obstacles to vengeance and, citing those pas-sages in which Hamlet upbraids himself for pro-crastinating, have concluded that the prince is by nature incapable of executing a ruthless deed. The opposing critics, following the lead of the Germans J. L. Klein and Karl Werder, have correctly pointed out the external obstacles to Hamlet's motive of re-venge, but are embarrassed by his self-accusations of delay, and—Werder in part excepted—explain them oddly or ignore them. A third, more modern group, including Ernest Jones and Oscar J. Camp-bell, has attempted to compromise these view-points; these men recognize Hamlet as a youth ca-pable of decisive action, but ascribe his failure in

the particular motive of revenge to psychotic short-comings. Professor Campbell's theory [see excerpt in section on Melancholy] has aroused the fewest objections. He regards Hamlet as a manic-depressive, who vacillates between violent action and brooding inaction: "Adverse fate so times the rhythm of Hamlet's malady that at any given mo-ment he is in the grip of the emotions which fit him least to deal with the situation confronting him." One objection to Campbell's theory is that, in ex-plaining Hamlet's failure to act at the proper mo-ment, it depends too strongly on coincidence—as Campbell suggests, on "adverse fate". More impor-tant, although it recognizes that Hamlet is at times a man of action, it fails to consider in full the exter-nal obstacles confronting the motive of vengeance, a consideration which a complete account of the facts cannot evade.

Ernest Jones's argument that Hamlet suffers an Oedipus complex is the most ingenious attempt to solve the Hamlet problem [see excerpt in section on Hamlet's character]. Like the arguments of his pre-decessors who have insisted that Hamlet's delay in exacting vengeance is internally motivated, it ade-quately explains those speeches, three in number, in which the prince reproaches himself for pro-crastination; but it also recognizes Hamlet as a man of action—a fact that the adherents of the "pa-ralysis of doubt" theory have been obliged to over-look—and concludes that only in the matter of re-venge is the prince incapable of action. This is ex-plained by the fact that Hamlet, having inade-quately repressed a desire to possess his mother, identifies himself with his intended victim, now es-poused to his mother, and thus cannot, in clear conscience, bring himself to act against him. To ac-cept the principle that an Oedipus complex deters Hamlet in his motive, we are asked to give credence to two hypotheses: first, that Shakespeare (who knew nothing of Freudian psychology) suffered from a marked Oedipus complex and, thus, depict-ed Hamlet in his own likeness as powerless to act against a man who had done away with his father and married his mother; second, that Hamlet's delay in the motive of vengeance cannot be ade-quately explained by external obstacles. The first hypothesis neither can nor need be refuted; Dr. Jones has convinced himself and a sizable minori-ty of his readers that Shakespeare was the victim of an Oedipus complex in spite of the fact that Jones and his professional confrères [colleagues] are the first to emphasize the months of laborious probing and examination essential to the psycho-analysis of a patient. Shakespeare's "Oedipus com-plex" must, I think, remain a dubious hypothesis from now until Doomsday. The second hypothesis is simply a contradiction of the truth. Along with other critics, John Ashworth (*Atlantic Monthly*, April 1949) has emphatically pointed out that we cannot expect an avenger to strike down his royal victim in full sight of a gathering of courtiers and bodyguards, by whom he is customarily attended.

Such actions may result from desperation or mania, but not from calculated vengeance. Jones argues that the prince has an excellent opportunity to kill his uncle at the close of the play-within-the-play and points to only one reason for his failure to do so: namely, his so-called "Oedipus complex". But, one unavoidably asks, what would have been the outcome of such a public attempt at vengeance? Whether he succeeded or failed, Hamlet would almost assuredly have lost his own life. Even more distressing to a man of cherished honor, he—and not Claudius—would have been recorded by history as the blackguard; the reason for this is evident, even to the blind: of the large and influential assemblage of persons who are present, only Hamlet and indirectly Horatio have knowledge that Claudius is a murderer. To the others, the King's implied confession of guilt is meaningless. One marvels at the assumption—made by so intelligent a man as Dr. Jones—that the testimony of a ghost, delivered *in absentia,* is sufficient evidence to convict a king of fratricide.

Moreover, unlike many of my predecessors, some of them clearly ignorant of Elizabethan traditions, I cannot dismiss Hamlet's expressed doubts as to the veracity of the Ghost as mere talk and babble. The Protestant and consequently the Elizabethan belief, in contrast to the Roman Catholic creed, was that the souls of the dead went directly to Heaven or Hell, not to Purgatory, and could not return to this world. The Swiss Protestant Ludwig Lavater in *De Spectris* (1570) and King James I in *Daemonologie* (1597) upheld this viewpoint, maintaining that the Devil could assume either the shape or the dead body of a newly deceased person and thus give the illusion of a ghost; but the reality of ghosts was positively denied by both men. James argued that an intelligent Christian knows that "neither can the spirite of the defunct return to his friend, or yet an Angel use such formes." Lavater . . . wrote: "Evil spirits do use this kind of deceyt, to fayne themselves to be soules of such as are deceased." This attitude, both Protestant and Elizabethan, is expressed not only by Horatio and Marcellus but also by Hamlet as they gaze upon the apparition of the dead king. Horatio fears that it "may assume some other horrible form" [I. iv. 72]; Marcellus, like Horatio, begs Hamlet not to follow it; and Hamlet supposes that it may be "a goblin damned" [I. iv. 40]. Nevertheless, he is undecided because of its "questionable shape" and consequently agrees to "call [it] Hamlet, / King, father" [I. iv. 44-5]. When alone with the Ghost, Hamlet has neither the will nor the rational power nor the courage to doubt its authenticity; for the moment, "the pales and forts of reason" [I. iv. 28] are inundated completely under emotional predilection. Later, in a mood governed by reason rather than emotion, Hamlet expresses serious doubt concerning the authenticity of the Ghost: "The spirit that I have seen / May be the devil [who] . . . / Abuses me to damn me" [II. ii. 598-603]. It seems odd, of

course, that he should not announce this renewed doubt as to the Ghost until after he has arranged with the itinerant actors the play-within-the-play, the intent of which is to elicit some sort of confession from Claudius and thus prove, or disprove, the reliability of the Ghost. But only one day after this doubt is expressed, Hamlet makes it apparent that he had discussed his misgivings about the Ghost with Horatio at a time precedent to the Players' coming to Elsinore; careful to inform his friend that a play will shortly be staged "before the king", he explains:

> One scene of it comes near the circumstance
> Which I have told thee of my father's death . . .
>   If his [Claudius'] occulted guilt
> Do not itself unkennel in one speech,
> It is a damnèd ghost that we have seen,
> And my imaginations are as foul
> As Vulcan's stithy [forge].
> [III. ii. 76-84]

How long Hamlet has entertained a renewed doubt concerning the Ghost's identity, we are not told by the text of the play. It is, however, logical to believe that as soon as the emotional stimuli of coming face to face with the Ghost had worn off, the Protestant attitude, which denied the reality of ghosts, began to re-assert itself in Hamlet's mind. There can, furthermore, be little doubt that Hamlet's misgivings about the veracity of the Ghost are honest ones and not a "cogent" excuse, as Jones has insisted, for his failure to carry out promptly his motive of vengeance. Upon the very first opportunity of determining whether his informant is an honest ghost or a deceitful devil intent on his damnation, Hamlet acts with remarkable despatch and precision: only a single day elapses between his meeting with the Players and the performance of the play-scene; moreover, the speech which he has prepared to be inserted in the "Murder of Gonzago" is so deadly in its pointedness that the first six of its "dozen or sixteen" lines [II. ii. 541] are sufficient to bring a tacit confession from Claudius. Thus, having fashioned an unexpected opportunity to his own purposes, Hamlet removes the paramount obstacle to his motive of vengeance, and consequently his most cogent reason *not* to slay Claudius, without an iota of evasion.

Once the uncertainty about the Ghost's identity has been removed—once Claudius, witnessing the satanic murder featured in the play-within-the-play, has cried, "Give me some light: away!" [III. ii. 269]—Hamlet finds the King alone at prayers. Again, we must not forget the viewpoint of the Elizabethan; to him, repentance of past sins, however heinous, was tantamount to the soul's salvation. To do away with Claudius while he is in the act of repentance would have been, as Hamlet says, mere "hire and salary, not revenge" [III. iii. 79]. His father had been slain, to quote the Ghost, "with all my imperfections on my head: O horrible! O horrible! most horrible!" [I. v. 79-80] In Fletcher's *The Pilgrim,* revenge is put aside for the reason that the intended victim, a man who prays hourly, is too well prepared for Heaven. To the extent that the Elizabethan accepted the fact that King Hamlet (slain without benefit of repentance) was "confin'd to fast in fires" [I. v. 11], he was bound to understand that the prince could not slay Claudius "in the purging of his soul" [III. iii. 85] without, in all likelihood, securing the salvation of his victim.

It is manifest, I think, that Hamlet was thwarted in the motive of vengeance by external obstacles. But the critics who have promulgated this theory have, with unfailing regularity, weakly interpreted or side-stepped his self-accusations of delay, the very passages on which the opposing school has built its thesis that the delay was internally motivated. In consequence, even the best criticisms of Hamlet's conduct have been unduly one-sided. Before I turn to an explanation of Hamlet's "admissions" of delay—his pseudo-procrastination—I wish to add one thought in support of the evidence that Hamlet's obstacles were external. In the saga of Amleth, as recorded by Saxo Grammaticus, the hero awaits, as he informs his mother, the "fitting hour" to avenge his slain father against Feng. This principle of the avenger's biding his time, of awaiting the appropriate opportunity, was later to be the almost invariable technique of Elizabethan tragedy. Hamlet as an avenger was the product of this and no other tradition. He is confronted by the normal number of external problems; what distinguishes him from his fellow avengers of the stage is his hypersensitive response to the delay imposed by these obstacles.

We come now to the apparent paradox of Hamlet's self-accusations of delay, which are clearly unwarranted. This paradox can in part be clarified by Elizabethan tenets that explain the functions of conscience and especially its morbid preoccupation with past sins and omissions. But, in so far as Shakespeare's insight into character went far beyond the scope of Elizabethan psychology, a more complete explanation of Hamlet's conduct must depend upon a modernization of these concepts. In the respect that the present-day concepts which best explain Hamlet's paradoxical conduct are basically identical to the Elizabethan tenets available to Shakespeare, they have a validity that is not shared by the Oedipus complex theory.

Tenets of Elizabethan psychology fully support the hypothesis that Hamlet's unwarranted self-reproaches are the outgrowth of a conscience that is preoccupied with some past sin or omission; but they do not contain an adequate explanation of the psychic origins of his guilt complex, a task that must depend on the help of those modern principles which explain the relation of the superego, or the conscience, to abnormal behavior. The Elizabe-

than physician Timothy Bright in his once-famous *Treatise of Melancholie* (1586) recognized "a molestation [that] riseth from conscience, condemning the guilty soul of those ingraven laws of nature, which no man is voide of. . . . Neither is the guiltiness brought to us by foreine report, but the knowledge riseth from the conscience of the offender." Thirty-five years later, Robert Burton, restating the established Elizabethan causes of melancholy [in his *The Anatomy of Melancholy*], wrote: "The last and greatest cause of this malady is our conscience. . . . Our conscience . . . grinds our souls with remembrance of some precedent sins, makes us reflect upon, accuse and condemn our own selves. . . . This scrupulous conscience . . . tortures so many, [who] . . . accuse themselves and aggravate every small offence." In fine, Bright and Burton have told us that a disquieting sense of guilt arises from the dictates of conscience when they are violated; second, that victims of conscience deal in self-accusations and, as Burton states, "out of a deep apprehension of their unworthiness . . . aggravate" every trivial sin or personal failure. That Shakespeare was keenly aware of the distempers that a violated conscience could evoke is frequently evident in his plays; Richard III, after the dream in which the ghosts of his victims appear, cries:

> O coward conscience, how dost thou afflict me! . . .
> My conscience hath a thousand several tongues,
> And every tongue brings in a several tale,
> And every tale condemns me for a villain.
>   [*Richard III,* V. iii. 179, 193-95]

The principles of Bright and Burton provide us with a broad formula outlining Hamlet's abnormal tendency to abase himself. His over-developed conscience is violated by something that he has done or, equally possible, by something that he has failed to do, which is—as is clear from the context of the play—his failure to avenge his father; in consequence, informed by his conscience of his "guiltiness", he falls into excessive and, in his case, unwarranted self-accusations.

A second important aspect that I believe underlies Hamlet's conduct is hinted at, but not clarified, by Elizabethan mental science. To counteract melancholy imposed by conscience, Burton advised "repentance", which he termed "a remedy . . . of our miseries." Burton meant "repentance to God"; but this does not preclude the probability that Shakespeare considered self-rebuke, certainly a major aspect of repentance, to be a potent means of inactivating the "molestation" which, as Bright maintained, "riseth from conscience". (pp. 177-82)

Two facts are clear: for external reasons Hamlet is unable to carry out his motive of vengeance; on the other hand, he violently upbraids himself for not doing so. So far, in relying on Elizabethan principles of conscience, I have made only a tenuous explanation of this enigma. The psychic origin and the ultimate structure of the dictate that tyrannizes over Hamlet's mind are not yet clear, nor has it been adequately shown *why* a conscience-stricken person has need to resort to self-accusation. Freud has argued that the superego, or conscience, takes its beginning from a threat of castration essential to suppress the infantile Oedipus complex. But this hypothesis, right or wrong, is hardly material to the actual existence of the superego, which, as psychoanalysts and many psychologists agree, is comprised of dictates acquired through moral discipline in childhood and, remaining thereafter "wholly or very largely unconscious" [Edmund S. Conklin, in his *Principles of Abnormal Psychology*], has the duty of censorship over the conscious mind. Freud points out that the earliest and strongest of these dictates evolve from the child's relation with his parents, both from self-identification with them and their ideals and from their precepts; he also recognizes that a principal dictate acquired in childhood is that of filial obedience, which is expressed in a high regard by the child for his parents and without which the inculcation of further discipline would be all but impossible. Furthermore, the stronger has been a child's moral discipline, the more tyrannical, according to Freud, tend to be the dictates of the superego, which, in his interpretation, "the ego [consciousness] forms . . . out of the id" [*The Ego and the Id*]. That Hamlet, a prince and only child, has been subjected to the strictest kind of discipline, especially in regard for his parents, is not merely a logical hypothesis; it is a truth manifest throughout the play. His filial obedience is hinted at in his attitude toward his mother at the outset: "I shall in all my best obey you, madam" [I. ii. 120]. But far stronger are Hamlet's devotion and feeling of duty toward his dead father. This attitude, even before the Ghost has appeared to him, underscores his first soliloquy: "So excellent a king; that was, to this, / Hyperion to a satyr" [I. ii. 139-40]. When seconds later—having severely censured the queen's hasty remarriage—he sobs, "But break, my heart, for I must hold my tongue" [I. ii. 159], he is not stifling a jealousy for his mother and her "incestuous sheets", as the adherents of the Oedipus complex theory have insisted. On the contrary, so strong has been his moral training, so strong at present are the dictates of his offended conscience, that he is horrified at her infidelity to his father; his despair is made complete, and he is stunned into silence, by the knowledge that his words and actions are powerless to atone for his mother's immense sacrilege, which, as he describes it, "cannot come to good" [I. ii. 158]. His accustomed esteem for his mother—and with it much of his moral outlook on life—has crashed about him, in irreparable fragments.

Shortly, Hamlet learns from the Ghost that his paramount responsibility is to avenge his father's murder. In a passion of filial obedience, he vows to "sweep to . . . revenge" on "wings as swift as meditation" [I. v. 30]; later, just after the Ghost has departed, he pledges: "Thy commandment all alone shall live / Within the book and volume of my brain" [I. v. 102-03]. Once his conscious mind has reasserted itself, Hamlet is fully aware that he is confronted by hazardous external obstacles, and hence plans to put on "an antic disposition" [I. v. 172] in order to conceal his motive. But his conscience, the "precipitate" of childhood years of strictest moral discipline, is not able to take account of such practical matters. Since it had been activated, while his reason was largely suppressed, during the encounter with the Ghost—a matter confirmed by his unqualified expressions of filial duty at that time—it has dedicated itself to an immediate course of vengeance which, although consistent with Hamlet's deep sense of loyalty, is independent of the commitments later resolved upon by his rational mind. That part of it, moreover, which is unconscious . . . is completely isolated from the faculty of reason and has not the power even to comprehend Hamlet's rationally developed doubt as to the veracity of the Ghost. Hamlet's self is divided by two injunctions, one resulting from the precautions of reason, the other from the unconscious and insistent dictates of the superego. Consider, for example, the soliloquy ending Act II: it is sharply contradictory in substance for the reason that Hamlet's mind is at first engaged in response to the dictates of his conscience. This response, confirming the superego's unqualified acceptance of the duty imposed by the Ghost, takes the form of violent self-accusations for his failure to have avenged his father; then, with an obvious effort, he cries, "Fie upon 't, foh! About, my brain" [II. ii. 587-88], and turns his mind to the world of reality and the practical consideration with which he is faced: the fact that the Ghost may be the Devil, and that therefore he has arranged the play-within-the-play, hopeful of proving to himself his *right* to slay Claudius. The phrase, "About, my brain", is clear indication of Hamlet's realization that he is confronted by two diametrically opposite criteria of values, the one unreasonable in its demands and quite mystifying, the other realistic and understandable, and each completely isolated from the other.

Both the compelling nature of Hamlet's inner conscience and the fact that it has no information of the external obstacles that have deterred the motive of vengeance are irrefutably testified by the final appearance of Hamlet senior's ghost. Unseen and unheard by his mother, who is present, it speaks to him from the realm of the inner mind: "This visitation / Is but to whet thy almost blunted purpose" [III. iv. 110-11]. The embodiment of Hamlet's conscience is ultimate proof of what has been tormenting him from the time of his first encounter with the Ghost—then a ghost of revenge—when he was intrusted with its "dread command". The longer Hamlet must delay in carrying out his pledge—first, for absolute proof of Claudius's guilt, later for the "fitting hour"—the more forcible are the demands of the superego that its dictate of prompt vengeance in obedience to his father be fulfilled. "The tension", wrote Freud [in his *An Outline of Psychoanalysis*], "between the demands of the conscience and the actual attainments of the ego [whether misdeeds or 'unexecuted intentions'] is experienced as a sense of guilt", which, as he stresses elsewhere, is "contributed by a superego that has grown peculiarly severe and cruel". It is inevitable, therefore, that Hamlet, whose conscience is unable to comprehend the problems imposed on him by the real world, falls victim to a marked guilt complex. Freud and other psychoanalysts have pointed out that only through abasement and self-injury can the neurotic's sense of guilt (described by them as basically unconscious) be relieved: "Self-torments of melancholiacs . . . are without doubt pleasurable" [*Collected Papers*]. Dr. Martin W. Peck is more explicit [in his *The Meaning of Psychoanalysis*]: The neurotic finds "relief from guilt by abasement and self-punishment"—and, as he later states, "by self-depreciation". As Hamlet's guilt complex becomes unbearably strong, he relies instinctively on the only available remedy—abasement and self-torment. By undeservedly reproaching himself for weakness of character, in particular by transposing the causes that obstruct his vengeance from external obstacles to himself, Hamlet can temporarily assuage the painful sense of guilt and gain relief from it. He undergoes what Dr. A. A. Brill has termed [in his *Freud's Contribution to Psychiatry*] an "emotional catharsis" that follows the fulfillment of the "need for punishment". His self-reproaches for not having avenged his father suggest that he becomes at times conscious of the precise nature of the superego's dictate; according to Freud and Brill, an awareness of this sort, though not found in most neurotic disorders, is not uncommon among melancholiacs: "In melancholia, the ego humbly submits to the criticism and tyrannical oppression of the superego and admits its guilt." Hamlet's other methods of abasement—for example, his ludicrous appearance in "doublet all unbrac'd" before Ophelia [II. i. 75]—are less directly related to the demands of the conscience; but, like his self-accusations, they are means of satisfying a need for punishment and attest to a potent sense of guilt.

Hamlet's procrastination, consequently, is apparent, not real. Since circumstances—prior to his ruthless betrayal of the King's henchmen, Rosencrantz and Guildenstern—have rendered impossible the performance of a well-planned act of aggression against his father's murderer, he is forced to rely on self-incrimination to calm the storms of the superego, which, lying largely in the unconscious mind, is unable to evaluate the external problems and hence imposes an unreasonable dictate upon the ego, or consciousness. In this re-

spect, it is noteworthy that Hamlet's most tempestuous self-accusation, climaxed by "Or ere this / I should have fatted all the region kites / With this slave's offal" [II. ii. 578-80], precedes his outburst against his mother, which is an indirect aggression against Claudius. During and after the scene with his mother, he again reproaches himself for the failure to avenge his father, but less tempestuously: the demands of the superego, having found partial satisfaction in Hamlet's aggressive conduct, are now less strong and, therefore, less a threat to his sanity.

My purpose in this essay has not been to establish a new interpretation of Hamlet's character. I accept the thesis, first emphatically stated by Werder, that Hamlet is a man of action and that he is deterred in his motive of vengeance solely by the external obstacles, among which is the orthodox doubt as to the identity of the Ghost. My purpose has been to explain only the reasons behind Hamlet's self-accusations of delay. These self-reproaches are undoubtedly the factor chiefly responsible for the school which insists that Hamlet's failure in the revenge motive is the result of an innate weakness; on the other hand, the upholders of what has been termed the "external difficulty" theory have been compelled to ignore or to explain them awkwardly. The result, in almost every instance, has been a marked disproportion of criticism. In view of the apparent incompatibility between Hamlet's self-accusations of delay and the manifest external obstacles to his motive of vengeance, evasions or distortions of one or more of the major facts relating to his conduct have been inevitable. As I see it, only the tenets of "conscience"—those of the Elizabethans abetted by those of modern times—can adequately resolve this particular problem. Moreover, these tenets, although they stamp Hamlet as a neurotic, do not contravene the theory that he is a man capable of ruthless action. His failure to execute prompt vengeance upon Claudius does not stem from his neurosis; on the contrary, his neurosis—a potent but temporary guilt complex—is the effect of the inaction which is prolonged by the external problems, and for which he is brought to task by the predetermined and altogether illogical dictates of his conscience. (pp. 183-86)

Robert R. Reed, Jr., "Hamlet, the Pseudo-Procrastinator," in Shakespeare Quarterly, *Vol. IX, No. 2, Spring, 1958, pp. 177-86.*

REVENGE

René Girard

[Girard maintains that Hamlet *belongs to the Revenge Tragedy genre. Revenge Tragedy is a dramatic form made popular on the English*

stage by Thomas Kyd, a contemporary of Shakespeare, whose Spanish Tragedy *is an early example of the type. Such a play calls for the revenge of a father by a son or vice versa, an act which is initiated by the murdered man's ghost. Other devices found in Revenge Tragedies include hesitation by the hero, real or feigned madness, suicide, intrigue, and murders on stage. In the critic's opinion, Shakespeare despised the Revenge Tragedy genre as a form whose conventions had become trite. Yet, because revenge theater was highly popular among Elizabethan audiences, the dramatist had to conform to certain guidelines of the genre to produce a financially successful tragedy. As a result, Shakespeare innovated the theatrical type by creating a* double entendre *(double meaning) in which he subtly denounced the banality of revenge theater without denying the audience its* katharsis *(a purification of emotions stirred by tragic conflict). Shakespeare expressed his disgust for revenge theater through* **Hamlet** *'s deploring revenge throughout the play, yet fulfilled his audience's expectations for a tragic conclusion. Girard also discusses* **Hamlet** *'s use of "mimetic models," by which he attempts to put himself in the necessary frame of mind to murder* **Claudius** *by mimicking other characters' actions. According to the critic,* **Hamlet** *projects his desire for revenge first through the actor who enacts the Hecuba speech, and then through* **Gertrude,** *but it is* **Laertes,** *who acts without thinking, who serves as the "mimetic model" which finally motivates* **Hamlet** *to kill the king. Girard concludes his discussion by drawing an analogy between* Hamlet *and modern society.* **Hamlet** *'s dilemma essentially represents the modern day evolution of society to a "no man's land," the critic argues, where revenge remains a force upon which we often dwell, but seldom act.]*

Hamlet belongs to the genre of the revenge tragedy, as hackneyed and yet inescapable in Shakespeare's days as the "thriller" in ours to a television writer. . . . The weariness with revenge and *katharsis* [a purification of emotions stirred by tragic conflict] which can be read, I believe, in the margins of the earlier plays must really exist because, in *Hamlet,* it moves to the center of the stage and becomes fully articulated.

Some writers who were not necessarily the most unimaginative found it difficult, we are told, to postpone for the whole duration of the lengthy Elizabethan play an action which had never been in doubt in the first place and which is always the same anyway. Shakespeare can turn this tedious chore into the most brilliant feat of theatrical *double entendre* [double meaning] because the tedium of revenge is really what he wants to talk about, and he wants to talk about it in the usual Shakespearean fashion; he will denounce the revenge theater and all its works with the utmost daring

without denying his mass audience the *katharsis* it demands, without depriving himself of the dramatic success which is necessary to his own career as a dramatist.

If we assume that Shakespeare really had this double goal in mind, we will find that some unexplained details in the play become intelligible and that the function of many obscure scenes becomes obvious.

In order to perform revenge with conviction, you must believe in the justice of your own cause. . . . [The] revenge seeker will not believe in his own cause unless he believes in the guilt of his intended victim. And the guilt of that intended victim entails in turn the innocence of that victim's victim. If the victim's victim is already a killer and if the revenge seeker reflects a little too much on the circularity of revenge, his faith in vengeance must collapse.

This is exactly what we have in *Hamlet.* It cannot be without a purpose that Shakespeare suggests the old Hamlet, the murdered king, was a murderer himself. In the various sources of the play there may be indications to that effect, but Shakespeare would have omitted them if he had wanted to strengthen the case for revenge. However nasty Claudius may look, he cannot look nasty enough if he appears in a context of previous revenge; he cannot generate, as a villain, the absolute passion and dedication which is demanded of Hamlet. The problem with Hamlet is that he cannot forget the context. As a result, the crime by Claudius looks to him like one more link in an already long chain, and his own revenge will look like still another link, perfectly identical to all the other links.

In a world where every ghost, dead or alive, can only perform the same action, revenge, or clamor for more of the same from beyond the grave, all voices are interchangeable. You can never know with certainty which ghost is addressing whom. It is one and the same thing for Hamlet to question his own identity and to question the ghost's identity, and his authority.

To seek singularity in revenge is a vain enterprise but to shrink from revenge, in a world which looks upon it as a "sacred duty" is to exclude oneself from society, to become a nonentity once more. There is no way out for Hamlet and he shifts endlessly from one impasse to the other, unable to make up his mind because neither choice makes sense.

If all characters are caught in a cycle of revenge that extends in all directions beyond the limits of its action, *Hamlet* has no beginning and no end. The play collapses. The trouble with the hero is that he does not believe in his play half as much as the critics do. He understands revenge and the theater too well to assume willingly a role chosen for him by others. His sentiments are those, in other words, which we have surmised in Shakespeare himself. What the hero feels in regard to the act of revenge, the creator feels in regard to revenge as theater.

The public wants vicarious victims and the playwright must oblige. Tragedy is revenge. Shakespeare is tired of revenge, and yet he cannot give it up, or he gives up his audience and his identity as a playwright. Shakespeare turns a typical revenge topic, *Hamlet,* into a meditation on his predicament as a playwright. (pp. 173-75)

There would be no Hamlet "problem" if the hero really believed what he says. It is also himself, therefore, that he is trying to convince. The anger in his voice and the exaggeration of his language with its coldly contrived metaphors suggest that he labors in vain:

> Look here upon this picture, and on this
> The counterfeit presentment of two broth-
> ers.
> See what a grace was seated on this brow.
> Hyperion's curls, the front of Jove himself,
> An eye like Mars, to threaten and
> command . . .
> A combination and a form indeed
> Where every god did seem to set his seal
> To give the world assurance of a man.
> This was your husband. Look you now
> what follows.
> Here is your husband, like a mildewed ear,
> Blasting his wholesome brother. Have you
> eyes?
>
> [III. iv. 53-65]

The gentleman doth protest too much. The symmetry of the whole presentation, and of Hamlet's own expressions tend to reassert the resemblance he denies: "This was your husband . . . / Here is your husband, . . ."

Hamlet begs his mother to give up her conjugal relationship with Claudius. The tons of Freud which have been poured over the passage have obscured its significance. Hamlet does not feel indignant enough to rush out and kill the villain. As a result he feels uncomfortable about himself and he blames his mother because she obviously feels even more indifferent to the whole affair than he does. He would like his mother to initiate the revenge process for him. He tries to arouse in her the indignation he himself cannot feel, in order to catch it secondhand from her, perhaps, out of some kind of mimetic sympathy. Between Gertrude and Claudius he would like to see a dramatic break that would force him to side resolutely with his mother.

It is a generally accepted view nowadays that Gertrude must have felt a tremendous attachment to Claudius. Far from confirming that view, the following lines suggest exactly the opposite:

> Nor sense to ecstasy was ever so thralled
> But it reserved some quantity of choice
> To serve in such a difference
>
> [III. iv. 74-6]

Hamlet does not say that his mother is madly in love with Claudius; he says that even if she were, she should still be able to preceive some difference between her two husbands. Hamlet assumes, therefore, that his mother like himself, perceives *no difference whatever.* This assumption is obviously correct. Gertrude remains silent during her son's tirade because she has nothing to say. The reason she could marry the two brothers in rapid succession is that they are so much alike and she feels the same indifference to the one as to the other. It is this overwhelming indifference that Hamlet perceives and he resents it because he is trying to fight it in himself. Like so many other queens of Shakespeare, like the queens of *Richard III,* for instance, Gertrude moves in a world where prestige and power count more than passion. (pp. 176-77)

What Hamlet needs, in order to stir up his vengeful spirit, is a revenge theater more convincing than his own, something less half-hearted than the play Shakespeare is actually writing. Fortunately for the hero and for the spectators who are eagerly awaiting their final bloodbath, Hamlet has many opportunities to watch rousing spectacles during his play and he tries to generate even more, in a conscientious effort to put himself in the right mood for the murder of Claudius. Hamlet must receive from someone else, a mimetic model, the impulse which he does not find in himself. This is what he tried to achieve with his mother, we found, and he did not succeed. He is much more successful with the actor who impersonates for him the role of Hecuba. It becomes obvious, at this point, that the only hope for Hamlet to accomplish what his society—or the spectators—require, is to become as "sincere" a showman as the actor who can shed real tears when he pretends to be the queen of Troy!

> Is it not monstrous that this player here,
> But in a fiction, in a dream of passion,
> Could force his soul so to his own conceit
> That from her working all his visage
> wanned,
> Tears in his eyes, distraction in's aspect,
> A broken voice, and his whole function
> suiting
> With forms to his conceit? And all for
> nothing!
> For Hecuba!
> What's Hecuba to him or he to Hecuba,
> That he should weep for her? What would
> he do
> Had he the motive and the cue for passion
> That I have?
>
> [II. ii. 551-62]

Another catchy example for Hamlet comes from the army of Fortinbras on its way to Poland. The object of the war is a worthless speck of land. Thousands of people must risk their lives:

Even for an eggshell. Rightly to be great
Is not to stir without great argument,
But greatly to find quarrel in a straw
When Honor's at the stake.
[IV. iv. 53-6]

The scene is as ridiculous as it is sinister. It would
not impress Hamlet so much if the hero truly believed in the superiority and urgency of his cause.
His words constantly betray him, here as in the
scene with his mother. As a cue for passion, his revenge motif is no more compelling, really, than the
cue of an actor on the stage. He too must
greatly . . . find quarrel in a straw, he too must
stake everything *even for an eggshell.*

The effect of the army scene obviously stems, at
least in part, from the large number of people involved, from the almost infinite multiplication of
the example which cannot fail to increase its mimetic attraction enormously. Shakespeare is too
much a master of mob effects not to remember at
this point the cumulative effect of mimetic models.
In order to whip up enthusiasm for the war against
Claudius, the same irrational contagion is needed
as in the war against Poland. The type of mimetic
incitement from which Hamlet "benefits" at this
point resembles very much the kind of spectacle
which governments never fail to organize for their
citizenry when they have decided it is time to go to
war: a rousing military parade.

But it is not the actor, ultimately, or the army of
Fortinbras; it is Laertes, I believe, who determines
Hamlet to act. Laertes provides the most persuasive spectacle not because he provides the "best"
example but because his situation parallels that of
Hamlet. Being Hamlet's peer, at least up to a point,
his passionate stance constitutes the most powerful challenge imaginable. In such circumstances,
even the most apathetic man's sense of emulation
must rise to such a pitch that the sort of disaster
that the fulfillment of the revenge demands can finally be achieved.

The simple and unreflective Laertes can shout to
Claudius "give me my father" [IV. v. 117] and then
leap into his sister's grave in a wild demonstration
of grief. Like a well-adjusted gentleman or a consummate actor, he can perform with the utmost
sincerity all the actions his social milieu demands,
even if they contradict each other. He can mourn
the useless death of a human being at one minute
and the next he can uselessly kill a dozen more if
he is told that his honor is at stake. The death of
his father and sister are almost less shocking to
him than the lack of pomp and circumstance at
their burial. At the rites of Ophelia, Laertes keeps
asking the priest for "more ceremony." Laertes is
a formalist and he reads the tragedy of which he is
a part very much like the formalists of all stripes.
He does not question the validity of revenge. He
does not question the literary *genre.* He does not
question the relationship between revenge and

*John Gielgud as Hamlet and Jessica Tandy as Ophelia
in Gielgud's 1934 staging of* Hamlet *at the New Theatre, London.*

mourning. These are not valid critical questions to
him; they never enter his mind, just as it never occurs to most critics that Shakespeare himself
could question the validity of revenge.

Hamlet watches Laertes leap into Ophelia's grave
and the effect on him is electrifying. The reflective
mood of the conversation with Horatio gives way to
a wild imitation of the rival's theatrical mourning.
At this point, he has obviously decided that he, too,
would act according to the demands of society, that
he would become another Laertes in other words.
He, too, as a result, must leap into the grave of one
who has already died, even as he prepares other
graves for those still alive:

'Swounds, show me what thou'lt do.
Woo't weep? Woo't fight? Woo't fast?
  Woo't tear thyself?
Woo't drink up eisel? Eat a crocodile?
I'll do't. Dost thou come here to whine?
To outface me with leaping in her grave?
Be buried quick with her, and so will
  I. . . .
I'll rant as well as thou.
[V. i. 274-79, 284]

In order to embrace the goal of revenge, Hamlet
must enter the circle of mimetic desire and rivalry;

this is what he has been unable to achieve so far but here he finally reaches a hysterical pitch of that "pale and bloodless emulation". . . . (pp. 177-80)

Shakespeare can place these incredible lines in the mouth of Hamlet without undermining the dramatic credibility of what follows. Following the lead of Gertrude, the spectators will ascribe the outburst to "madness."

> This is mere madness.
> And thus awhile the fit will work on him.
> Anon, as patient as the female dove
> When that her golden couplets are dis-
>   closed,
> His silence will sit drooping.
>
> [V. i. 284-88]

A little later Hamlet himself, now calmly determined to kill Claudius, will recall the recent outburst in most significant words:

> I am very sorry, good Horatio,
> That to Laertes I forgot myself,
> For by the image of my cause I see
> The portraiture of his. I'll court his favors.
> But, sure, the bravery of his grief did put
>   me
> Into a towering passion.
>
> [V. ii. 75-80]

Like all victims of mimetic suggestion, Hamlet reverses the true hierarchy between the other and himself. He should say: "by the image of *his* cause I see the portraiture of *mine.*" This is the correct formula, obviously, for all the spectacles that have influenced Hamlet. The actor's tears and the military display of Fortinbras were already presented as mimetic models. In order to realize that Laertes, too, functions as a model, the last two lines are essential. The cool determination of Hamlet, at this point, is the transmutation of the "towering passion" which he had vainly tried to build up before and which Laertes has finally communicated to him through the "bravery of his grief." This transmutation is unwittingly predicted by Gertrude when she compares Hamlet to the dove who becomes quiet after she has laid her eggs. Gertrude only thinks of Hamlet's previous changes of mood, as sterile as they were sudden, but her metaphor suggests a more tangible accomplishment, the birth of something portentous:

> Anon, as patient as the female dove
> When that her golden couplets are dis-
>   closed,
> His silence will sit drooping.
>
> [V. i. 286-88]
>
> (pp. 180-81)

. . . . .

In *Hamlet,* the very absence of a case against revenge becomes a powerful intimation of what the modern world is really about. Even at those later stages in our culture when physical revenge and blood feuds completely disappeared or were limited to such marginal milieux as the underworld, it would seem that no revenge play, not even a play of reluctant revenge, could strike a really deep chord in the modern psyche. In reality the question is never entirely settled and the strange void at the center of *Hamlet* becomes a symbolic expression of the Western and modern malaise, no less powerful than the most brilliant attempts to define the problem, such as Dostoevsky's underground revenge. Our "symptoms" always resemble that unnamable paralysis of the will, that ineffable corruption of the spirit that affect not only Hamlet, but the other characters as well. The devious ways of these characters, the bizarre plots they hatch, their passion for watching without being watched, their propensity to voyeurism and spying, the general disease of human relations make a good deal of sense as a description of an undifferentiated no man's land between revenge and no revenge in which we ourselves are still living.

Claudius resembles Hamlet in his inability to take a prompt and healthy revenge on his enemies. The king should react more explicitly and decisively to the murder of Polonius who was, after all, his private councillor; the crime was a personal offense to him. His reasons for hesitating, then acting only in secret, may be different from Hamlet's but the final result is the same. When Laertes asks Claudius why he failed to punish a murderer, the reply betrays embarrassment.

Even Claudius presents Hamlet-like symptoms. Not Hamlet alone but the time is out of joint. And when Hamlet describes his revenge as "sick," or "dull," he speaks for the whole community. In order to appreciate the nature and the extent of the disease, we must realize that all behavior we tend to read as strategic or conspiratorial, in that play, can also be read as symptomatic of "sick revenge." (pp. 192-93)

Everybody must conceive the same strategic tricks at the same time and the reciprocity which everybody tries to sidestep simultaneously and through the same means must still win in the long run. Strategic thinking, as a result, demands ever increasing subtlety; it involves less and less action, more and more calculation. In the end, it becomes difficult to distinguish strategy from procrastination. The very notion of strategy may be strategic in regard to the self-defeating nature of revenge which no one wants to face, not yet at least, so that the possibility of revenge is not entirely removed from the scene. Thanks to the notion of strategy, men can postpone revenge indefinitely without ever giving it up. They are equally terrified by both radical solutions and they go on living as long as possible, if not forever, in the no man's land of sick revenge.

In that no man's land it becomes impossible to define anything. All actions and motivations are their own opposites as well as themselves. When Hamlet does not seize the opportunity to kill Claudius during his prayer, it could be a failure of the will or a supreme calculation; it could be instinctive humaneness or a refinement of cruelty. Hamlet himself does not know. The crisis of Degree has reached the most intimate recesses of the individual consciousness. Human sentiments have become as mixed up as the seasons of the year in *A Midsummer Night's Dream.* Even he who experiences them can no longer say which is which, and the critic's search for neat differentiations misses the point entirely. Most interpreters cling to the illusion that differences alone must be real behind deceptive similarities, whereas the opposite is true. Similarities alone are real. We must not be misled by Ophelia's blond hair and pitiable death. Or rather, we must realize that Shakespeare consciously misleads his less attentive spectators with these gross theatrical signs of what a pure heroine should be. Just like Rosenkrans and Guildenstern, Ophelia allows herself to become an instrument in the hands of her father and of the king. She, too, is affected by the disease of the time. Another sign of her contamination is her language and behavior which are both contaminated with the erotic strategy of a Cressida and the other least savory Shakespearean heroines. What Hamlet resents in Ophelia is what any human being always resents in another human being, the visible signs of his own sickness. It is the same sickness, therefore, that corrupts Ophelia's love for Hamlet and debases Hamlet's love for the theater. (pp. 193-94)

. . . . .

To read *Hamlet* against revenge is anachronistic, some people say, because it goes against the conventions of the revenge genre. No doubt, but could Shakespeare be playing according to the rules of the game at one level and undermine these same rules at another? Has not this ambiguous practice become a commonplace of modern criticism? Is Shakespeare too slow-witted for such a device? Indications abound that in many other plays, he is doing precisely that, still providing the crowd with the spectacle they demand while simultaneously writing between the lines, for all those who can read, a devastating critique of that same spectacle?

If we fear that *Hamlet,* in the present perspective, becomes a pretext, once more, for comments on the contemporary situation, let us look at the alternative. The traditional perspectives on *Hamlet* are far from neutral; their first consequence is that the ethics of revenge are taken for granted. The most debatable question of the play cannot be reached; we exclude it *a priori* [from prior knowledge].

Hamlet's problem thus shifts from revenge itself to hesitation in the face of revenge. Why should a well-educated young man have second thoughts when it comes to killing a close relative who also happens to be the king of the land and the husband of his own mother? This is some enigma indeed and the problem is not that a satisfactory answer has never been found but that we should expect to find one after our *a priori* exclusion of the one sensible and obvious answer.

Should our enormous critical literature on *Hamlet* fall some day into the hands of people otherwise ignorant of our mores, they could not fail to conclude that our academic tribe must have been a savage breed, indeed. After four centuries of controversies, Hamlet's temporary reluctance to commit murder still looks so outlandish to us that more and more books are being written in an unsuccessful effort to solve that mystery. The only way to account for this curious body of literature is to suppose that, back in the twentieth century no more was needed than some ghost to ask for it, and the average professor of literature would massacre his entire household without batting an eyelash.

Contrary to the official doctrine among us, the insertion of Hamlet into our contemporary situation, and in particular the reference to something as apparently alien to literature as our nuclear predicament, cannot lead the critic further astray than he already is; it cannot distract him from his proper function which is to read the text. Amazingly enough, the effect is just the opposite. The nuclear reference can shock us back into a sense of reality. It is symptomatic of our condition, no doubt, that we avoid more and more the real issues, and we empty great literary texts of all affective and even intellectual content as we really intend to do the opposite, as we try to concentrate exclusively upon these same texts by excluding only what is extraneous to them.

Let us imagine a contemporary Hamlet with his finger on a nuclear button. After forty years of procrastination he has not yet found the courage to push that button. The critics around him are becoming impatient. The psychiatrists have volunteered their services and come up with their usual answer. Hamlet is a sick man. (pp. 196-97)

Almost all critics today stick to the ethics of revenge. The psychiatrist sees the very thought of its abandonment as an illness he must cure, and the traditional critic sees revenge as a literary rule he must respect. Others still try to read *Hamlet* through one of the popular ideologies of our time, like political rebellion, the absurd, the individual's right to an aggressive personality, etc. It is no accident if the sanctity of revenge provides a perfect vehicle for all the masks of modern *ressentiment* [resentment]. The remarkable consensus in favor of revenge verifies, I believe, the conception of the play as that no man's land between total revenge and no revenge at all, that specifically modern space where everything becomes suffused with sick revenge.

It is fashionable nowadays to claim that we inhabit an entirely new world in which even our greatest masterpieces have become irrelevant. I would be the last one to deny that there is something unique about our world, but there is something unique also about *Hamlet,* and we may well be deceiving ourselves in order not to face a type of relevance we do not want to welcome.

We must declare irrelevant not *Hamlet* but the wall of conventions and ritualism with which we surround the play, in the name of innovation almost as often as in the name of tradition. As more events, objects, and attitudes around us proclaim the same message ever more loudly, in order not to hear that message, we must condemn more of our experience to insignificance and absurdity. With our most fashionable critics today we have reached the point when history must make no sense, art must make no sense, language and sense itself must make no sense. (p. 198)

Hamlet is no mere word game. We can make sense out of *Hamlet* just as we can make sense out of our world, by reading both against revenge. This is the way Shakespeare wanted *Hamlet* to be read and the way it should have been read long ago. If now, at such a time in our history, we still cannot read *Hamlet* against revenge, who ever will? (p. 200)

René Girard, "Hamlet's Dull Revenge," in Stanford Literature Review, *Vol. 1, No. 2, Fall, 1984, pp. 159-200.*

MELANCHOLY AND GRIEF

Oscar James Campbell

[*Campbell contends that the nature of **Hamlet**'s melancholy, or state of depression, was more easily perceived by an Elizabethan audience than by a modern one. Further, the critic asserts that while **Hamlet** is indeed emotionally unstable, he is not insane. Shakespeare dramatizes the prince's changeability by altering the mood of the play's structure from periods of meditative pauses to bursts of action. Since **Hamlet** is usually at the center of these pauses and surges, his character conveys a manic-depressive quality. In essence, his depressed phase is marked by brooding inaction, whereas his manic phase includes abrupt lunges toward action. Campbell asserts that **Hamlet** is more than a "creature of psychotic impulse," however, for Shakespeare generates sympathy for him by "enabling his melancholy to express itself in some of the most profound philosophical lyrics ever written in the English language." Because of his emotional state, the critic continues, **Hamlet** in some ways represents an Elizabethan stock character known as a "malcontent." A malcontent is a figure whose perspective of life is so pessimistic that he holds nothing but contempt for the world and humanity. In Act V, **Hamlet** reaches his highest point of excitement through his*

"hysterical" struggle with **Laertes** during the sword fight, and this emotion enables him to take revenge in the final catastrophe. Thus, Campbell concludes, **Hamlet** 's revenge "ironically appears, not as an act of solemn retribution, but as an uncalculated result of the frantic brandishing of a murderous sword."]

Something very serious is the matter with Hamlet. And the full meaning of the great tragedy will never be clear until critics discover in the drama a conscious artistic design pertinent both to Hamlet the tortured man and to the events in the play.

We must, then, make an honest effort to discover just what ails Hamlet. Everyone knows that he is melancholy, but few realize that to Shakespeare's audiences the precise nature of his emotional disturbance was much more easily recognizable than to an audience today. Melancholy was a malady described at length in all their household medical handbooks. Elizabethan doctors, like the practitioners of our own day, were making careful attempts to analyze its symptoms. The fact that their analyses completed three centuries ago were naïve and inexact need not concern us. In any case, Shakespeare, a busy dramatist, was perhaps only imperfectly acquainted with their diagnoses. But he was certainly far from ignorant of them. Moreover, in everyday conversation in Shakespeare's time, "melancholy" was probably as often referred to as the "inferiority complex" is today—and there can be no doubt that any dramatic character who described himself as suffering from an inferiority complex would explain himself to a modern audience immediately.

Besides, Shakespeare may well have had many chances to observe victims of the disease that his contemporaries referred to as "melancholy." In Elizabeth's day, persons with nervous afflictions were confined only for actual dementia. And Hamlet is in no sense irrational. His mind is unimpaired. Circumstances which have put an irresistible strain upon his self-control have rendered him emotionally unstable, but certainly not mad.

Persons in such a mental state as his were not imprisoned or even given systematic medical treatment in Elizabethan times. Hence many cases of "melancholy" were at large in society and easily recognizable. Anyone who has an opportunity to watch a victim of this sort of emotional disturbance cannot fail to identify its symptoms. And Shakespeare, the keenest of observers, would see at once that in many men whom he called "melancholy" the moods of uncontrolled excitement alternated with periods of deep depression. He would also notice that these two pathological states succeeded each other with a kind of mechanical regularity.

It is here, I think, that the key to Hamlet's character must be sought. That alternation of mood Shakespeare seized upon to form the inner structure of his play. One of Shakespeare's favorite dramatic practices was to force the current of his play to fluctuate between meditative pauses and bursts of action. All of his tragic heroes in the very fever of the dramatic action stand aside from the rush of events long enough to soliloquize reflectively upon themselves and the plots in which they are involved. The rhythmic vacillation in Hamlet's emotions is thus but a subtle variant of one of the favorite devices of Shakespeare's stagecraft. Moreover, adverse fate so times the rhythm of Hamlet's malady that at any given moment he is in the grip of the emotions which fit him least to deal with the situation confronting him. When the circumstances demand action, he finds himself so deeply depressed that he can do nothing but brood. When he needs his finest poise to wield the weapon of his reason, he is beaten by gusts of uncontrollable excitement. With each new revelation of this irrepressible conflict Hamlet's inner tension mounts until at the final catastrophe his tortured will explodes in a wild frenzy of unconsidered action.

A brief review of the dramatic movement of the tragedy will show how regular is the beat of its pulse. When Hamlet first appears, he is already profoundly depressed. He has been overwhelmed by grief at his father's death and his mother's "o'erhasty marriage" [II. ii. 57] to his uncle. Life has lost its meaning. It is vile and empty. He longs for death—for the moral right to kill himself. Such is the depth of his dejection even before the ghost of his father lays upon him the supremely difficult task.

From this depression Hamlet is briefly rescued by the appearance of his old friend Horatio. Shakespeare takes advantage of the moment to show his audience what Hamlet was like before grief had overwhelmed him. Here and on various other occasions in the play, the hero's natural charm and graciousness shine forth. Those short intervals of emotional equilibrium occur, as in the present case, during his transition from depression to mad elation. They come with the reappearance of friends out of his untroubled past—of Horatio or of the actors in whom he had always taken delight. Such brief glimpses of the normal Hamlet add poignancy to the abnormal seizures that follow as the night the day.

After the ghost has described the circumstances of his murder and has laid upon his son the duty of revenge, Hamlet for the first time becomes frenzied. Then he wildly beseeches aid from the spirits of earth, of heaven, even of hell. He shouts to the skies his execrations of Claudius, "O villain, villain, smiling, damned villain" [I. v. 106]. He answers Horatio's solicitous questions with "wild and whirling words" [I. v. 133]. His uncontrolled tumult is presently intensified by the strange actions of the ghost, who gives Hamlet orders from the cellarage, as though he were one of the demons

who dwelt underground, a familiar of the Devil. In order to shut Marcellus's mouth, Hamlet cooperates in the deception. He rushes from one part of the stage to another as the ghost moves under him. Consequently, the spirit's effort to protect a secret which only the avenger must know, ironically compels Hamlet to dance about in what seems to be a wild paroxysm of excitement.

It is during this seizure that Hamlet decides to feign madness. Every critic knows that, as an aid to his revenge, the pretense is a mistake. Hamlet's reason for donning emotional motley may well have been subjective, an instinctive impulse towards self-protection. He realizes that his emotions are often going to rush beyond his control. The fiction that he is mad will not only cloak his designs against the King, but will also free him from any necessity to control the uncontrollable. During the rest of the play, Hamlet's feigned madness is merely his acquiescence in the two-fold intensities of his melancholy.

By the end of the first act, the audience has been given a full view of both phases of Hamlet's emotional disturbance. But only the most discerning would catch so soon its inner rhythm. His malady must continue to fall to its ebb and mount to its crest before its regular configuration becomes unmistakable. The next time that Hamlet appears to any characters in the play, he is obviously under the spell of his depression. He visits Ophelia in the complete disarray that literary tradition had made the inevitable symptom of the melancholy of a rejected lover. An irresistible impulse had driven him for sympathy to the woman he still loved even though she seemed no longer to return his affection. Hamlet's carefully prepared deshabille shows that he had given his impulse full rein. Yet his inability to utter a word in Ophelia's presence is proof of the tragic depth of his depression.

When Hamlet next appears on the stage, his clothes should be in the disorder which Ophelia has described. His mind, too, is pervaded by the same gloom. His ridicule of Polonius is not lighthearted. The figures of speech in which he clothes his abhorrence are all drawn from the low and physically disgusting—maggots, carrion, wrinkled faces, weak hams, and thick discharge oozing from the eyes. Through such symbols as these Shakespeare translates intellectual pessimism into poetic feeling.

From this new "low" in his depression Hamlet is rescued by the actors who come to play at Elsinore. They carry him out of the dreary present into the happy days when the theatre moved and delighted him as it did many cultivated gentlemen of the Renaissance. Once his emotions are swept clean by the breath from his healthful past, he is able to plan and to act. But just as soon as the players leave him alone, he again becomes the slave of his malady, and his mood mounts quickly to emotional tumult. He unpacks his heart again with wild and whirling words, which he shouts to the unresponsive air. He has again swept from gloom to uncontrolled excitement.

At this point in the play, the intelligent members of Shakespeare's audience should sense the rhythm of Hamlet's melancholy. They should also realize what are to be the characteristic dramatic expressions of each of its phases. The depressed phase is to be marked by brooding inaction, by the utterance of pessimistic ideas clothed in poetic images borrowed from physical dissolution and from low and disgusting forms of life. The heightened phase will be characterized by violent lunges towards action, by expressions in which excitement exaggerates and obscures the sense, and even by exclamations that resemble the inarticulate cries of a wounded animal. But most important for the comprehension of the play, the audience will now understand that Hamlet's mood of sluggish depression is to be followed by a seizure of feverish excitement; and that, though the length of the intervals between the two states may vary, they will succeed each other with clock-like regularity. When these characteristics of the play are clearly understood, clarity takes the place of perplexity. Hamlet's actions no longer form a puzzle. By understanding the cause of even his wildest emotional seizures, we can look forward, not with bewilderment, but with tense expectancy, to the forms which his tragic melancholy must inevitably assume.

This clue to the aesthetic movement of the action makes Hamlet's conduct clear at many crises in the play. It explains, for example, why he could not kill the King when he came upon him at prayer. At that moment, a mood of depression darkened Hamlet's mind—the inevitable reaction to the excitement he had just felt at the success of his play in catching the conscience of the King. His will is paralyzed. Resolute action of any sort is beyond his power. So he cannot make use of the heaven-sent opportunity to revenge his father's murder. No other scene in the play is so fully charged with tragic irony.

When we next see Hamlet, he is in his mother's chamber beseeching her to break off all sexual relations with King Claudius. Only thus can she save her soul. Now if ever Hamlet should be undisputed master of all his faculties. Only calm severity can make the solemn impression upon his mother which the situation demands. Yet we see at once that he has again become a slave to his recurrent excitement, and we anticipate only the wildest goings-on. Our worst fears are realized; for he kills Polonius in a frantic lunge through the arras, he scolds his mother in a frenzy of excitement, he talks to the vacant air, and finally, he rushes off the stage, dragging Polonius's body by the heels. None of these acts really surprises us. They fill us with

pity and terror, for we realize that Hamlet's emotional tumult has rendered worse than futile his visit to the Queen. Its sole result has been to convince his mother that he is mad indeed. This conflict between the clock of Hamlet's malady and the situations which face him persists to the end of the drama. It defeats all his impulses towards action and increasingly paralyzes his will.

But Hamlet is more than this creature of psychotic impulse dancing between gloom and febrile agitation. Otherwise he would never have been universally acclaimed as the greatest character in dramatic fiction. His mind seems to have a reach and a depth greater in both degree and kind than any other tragic hero in all literature. Shakespeare establishes this transcendence of Hamlet largely by enabling his melancholy to express itself in some of the most profound philosophical lyrics ever written in the English language. When Hamlet falls into the depressed phase of his malady, his mind is corroded by skepticism and pessimism. Then he feels that human life is meaningless and that the universe is a foul and pestilent congregation of vapors. In expressing his despair he is not giving voice to Shakespeare's personal dejection. He is rather invoking a mood congenial to many men of his age. For even while Elizabethan audiences were charmed by the verbal harmonies which rang through Hamlet's melancholy utterances, they must frequently have detected in them commonplaces of late Renaissance pessimism. (pp. 311-17)

On occasions Hamlet also conforms to another current dramatic conception of the melancholy man. He allows his disgust with life to turn to derision of the world and of all human life. That is, he takes on the color of a conventional stage character called "the malcontent." Jaques in *As You Like It* is cast for this role. His greatest delight is to sit at his ease and "rail against our mistress the world, and all our misery" [*As You Like It*, III. ii. 278-79]. The humorously bleak view of life which he expresses in the soliloquy beginning "All the world's a stage" [*As You Like It*, II. vii. 139ff.] is evidence not of Shakespeare's descent into the depths but of the malcontent's habit of mind.

When Hamlet betrays the satiric impulses of a malcontent, his remarks give edge both to his depression and to his burst of hysterical playfulness. When he strikes out against women's use of cosmetics, he is at once a tortured lover and a satirist practising his art on one of the timeworn subjects of the craft. He cries to Ophelia, "I have heard of your paintings, too, well enough. God has given you one face, and you make yourselves another; you jog, you amble, you lisp, and nickname God's creatures." [III. i. 142-45]. When he is making a fool of Polonius, he flings at him the remarks about old men which had been stock ridicule since the dawn of satire. "The satirical rogue," begins Hamlet, referring to the author of the book he has been reading, "says here that old men have grey beards, that their faces are wrinkled, their eyes purging thick amber and plum-tree gum, and that they have a plentiful lack of wit together with most weak hams" [II. ii. 196-200].

Once having understood the nature of Hamlet's pessimistic ideas, the spectator feels the melancholy to be enriched and deepened by the philosophical terms in which it is expressed. And once having sensed the rhythmic beat of Hamlet's inner life, an audience is borne through the exciting events of the plot on the irresistible tide of the character's fluctuating emotion to the final catastrophe. It thus becomes the supreme dramatic utterance of Hamlet's psychological essence.

Critics who think of Hamlet as a purely contemplative man have assumed that Shakespeare made him too introspective a person to do the final deeds demanded by the plot. In the last act, so they say, Shakespeare's Hamlet disappears to make way for an automaton better able to bring to a climax the old tale of revenge. But there is no such artistic hiatus in the drama. The pendulum of Hamlet's melancholy continues to swing during the fifth act just as it has done throughout the play. Only now, as we near the catastrophe, its beat becomes more and more agitated.

The last act carries Hamlet from his despairing and macabre mood in the churchyard through his hysterical struggle with Laertes at the edge of Ophelia's grave and on to the final catastrophe. There the hot excitement of the duel, intensified by his discovery of Laertes's treachery, drives Hamlet to the highest point of his excitement. Now at last, instead of abandoning himself to extravagant speech, he plunges into extravagant action. So his revenge ironically appears, not as an act of solemn retribution, but as an uncalculated result of the frantic brandishing of a murderous sword. In acting thus Hamlet has not become a puppet of the plot. He is merely giving us a culminating exhibition of his melancholy and lending final emphasis to the tragic irony of his career.

The fatal wound in Hamlet's breast re-establishes his emotional equilibrium, as physical shocks often do in cases of this kind. With his mental restoration reappears the sweetness and the charm of his uncontaminated personality. Then he finds words to capture and retain for all time the qualities of the man who, in his happy youth, was the ideal prince and gentleman of the Renaissance.

It may be objected that this analysis destroys all the richness of Hamlet's personality, that it reduces him to a mere automaton, driven willy-nilly from one emotional extravagance to another. But the discovery of a simple aesthetic pattern in the tragedy need have no such result. It makes Hamlet's inner nature an integral part of his tragic story. It also banishes much perplexity from the spectators' minds. Hamlet ceases to be an utterly incalculable creature. Holding the clue to the precise nature of his melancholy, we come to a full and sympathetic understanding of his fate. (pp. 319-22)

To the Elizabethan audience familiar with the multifarious ways of melancholy, Hamlet's uncontrollable grief was a complete explanation of his emotional disaster. To us his anguish represents the destructive emotion which lies at the root of every disintegration of the will. For Hamlet is not insane. His reason functions normally, his mind is subtle and acute. His tragedy is inevitable because his emotions become an intricate tangle whenever life confronts him with a demand for action. Every normal man has on occasion been similarly at the mercy of tyrannical feelings. Understanding the life cycle of Hamlet's melancholy, we are able to focus our attention upon the universal meanings implicit in his situation. With emancipated imagination, we are free to feel all the irony, the pathos, and the terror in the most famous of tragedies. (p. 322)

Oscar James Campbell, "What Is the Matter with Hamlet?" in The Yale Review, *Vol. XXXII, No. 2, Winter, 1943, pp. 309-22.*

Arthur Kirsch

[Kirsch considers Hamlet *a play which generates great intellectual energy, but perhaps more importantly reflects an experience of profound pain and suffering for the protagonist. According to the critic, grief is* **Hamlet** *'s predominant emotion and thus acts as a controlling force in the play: the prince needs sympathy for his grief, but he does not receive it from the court, his uncle, or, most significantly, his mother. Kirsch then examines how* **Hamlet** *'s intense anger at his mother has come to be interpreted by some scholars as indicating that he suffers from an Oedipus Complex, a repressed desire to kill his father and marry his mother. Followers of this theory maintain that this psychological disorder is the source of* **Hamlet** *'s hesitation, for* **Claudius** *has carried out the deed which the prince himself had unconsciously wanted to perform. (See the excerpt by Ernest Jones in the section on Hamlet's character.) Questioning the validity of this interpretation, the critic asserts that Shakespeare's purpose in raising the Oedipal question was not "to call* **Hamlet** *'s character into judgment, but to expand our understanding of the nature and intensity of his suffering." In addition to* **Gertrude** *'s actions, the* **Ghost** *also intensifies* **Hamlet** *'s grief by repeatedly demanding that he remember him, thus arresting the natural process of mourning and recovery. Another emotional catalyst for the prince is a mounting sense of loss—not only does* **Hamlet**

lose his father to death, but he also feels betrayed by his mother, loses the affections of **Ophelia,** *and* **Rosencrantz** *and* **Guildenstern,** *two school friends, serve the king as spies. The critic contends that Act V represents a turning point in* **Hamlet** *'s character, for, paradoxically, the termination of his grief comes at the same time as his realization that he faces his own death.*]

Hamlet is a tragedy perhaps most often, and justly, admired for its intellectual energy. Hamlet's mind comprehends a universe of ideas, and he astonishes us with the copiousness and eloquence and luminousness of his thoughts. But I think we should remember, as Hamlet is compelled to remember, that behind these thoughts, and usually their occasion, is a continuous and tremendous experience of pain and suffering. We are accustomed to thinking of the other major tragedies, *Lear* and *Othello* especially, as plays whose greatest genius lies in the depiction of the deepest movements of human feeling. I think we should attend to such movements in *Hamlet* as well. As Hamlet himself tells us, it is his heart which he unpacks with words, it is against what he calls the "heart-ache" [III. i. 61] of human existence that he protests in his most famous soliloquy (and this is the first use of the term in that sense the *OED* [*Oxford English Dictionary*] records), and there are few plays in the canon in which the word "heart" itself is more prominent. (p. 17)

In Shakespeare's play . . . [Hamlet] talks explicitly of sorrow and blood, relating them directly to the ghost as well as each other in the scene in his mother's bedchamber in which the ghost appears for the last time. "Look you," he tells his mother, who characteristically cannot see the ghost,

> how pale he glares.
> His form and cause conjoin'd, preaching
>   to stones,
> Would make them capable.—Do not look
>   upon me
> Lest with this piteous action you convert
> My stern effects; then what I have to do
> Will want true colour—tears perchance
>   for blood.
>
> [III. iv. 125-30]

These lines suggest synapses between grief and vengeance which help make the whole relation between the plot and emotional content of *Hamlet* intelligible, but of more immediate importance to an understanding of the play is Hamlet's own emphasis in this speech, his focus on his grief and the profound impact which the ghost has upon it.

The note of grief is sounded by Hamlet in his first words in the play, before he ever sees the ghost, in his opening dialogue with the King and his mother. The Queen says to him:

> Good Hamlet, cast thy nighted colour off,

> And let thine eye look like a friend on Denmark.
> Do not for ever with thy vailed lids
> Seek for thy noble father in the dust.
> Thou know'st 'tis common—all that lives
>   must die,
> Passing through nature to eternity.
>
> [I. ii. 68-73]

Hamlet answers, "Ay, madam, it is common." "If it be, / Why seems it so particular with thee?" [I. ii. 74-5] she says; and he responds,

> Seems, madam! Nay, it is; I know not
>   seems.
> 'Tis not alone my inky cloak, good mother,
> Nor customary suits of solemn black,
> Nor windy suspiration of forc'd breath,
> No, nor the fruitful river in the eye,
> Nor the dejected haviour of the visage,
> Together with all forms, moods, shapes of
>   grief,
> That can denote me truly. These, indeed,
>   seem;
> For they are actions that a man might
>   play;
> But I have that within which passes
>   show—
> These but the trappings and the suits of
>   woe.
>
> [I. ii. 76-86]

Though Hamlet's use of the conventional Elizabethan forms of mourning expresses his hostility to an unfeeling court, he is at the same time speaking deeply of an experience which everyone who has lost someone close to him must recognize. He is speaking of the early stages of grief, of its shock, of its inner and still hidden sense of loss, and trying to describe what is not fully describable—the literally inexpressible wound whose immediate consequence is the dislocation, if not transvaluation, of our customary perceptions and feelings and attachments to life. It is no accident that this speech sets in motion Hamlet's preoccupation with seeming and being, including the whole train of images of acting which is crystallized in the play within the play. The peculiar centripetal pull of anger and sorrow which the speech depicts remains as the central undercurrent of that preoccupation, most notably in Hamlet's later soliloquy about the player's imitation of Hecuba's grief:

> Is it not monstrous that this player here,
> But in a fiction, in a dream of passion,
> Could force his soul so to his own conceit
> That from her working all his visage
>   wann'd;
> Tears in his eyes, distraction in's aspect,
> A broken voice, and his whole function
>   suiting
> With forms to his conceit? And all for
>   nothing!
> For Hecuba!
> What's Hecuba to him or he to Hecuba,
> That he should weep for her? What would
>   he do,
> Had he the motive and the cue for passion

    That I have?

          [II. ii. 551-62]

Hamlet then goes on to rebuke himself for his own inaction, but the player's imitation of grief nonetheless moves him internally, as nothing else can, in fact to take action, as he conceives of the idea of staging a play to test both the ghost and the conscience of the King.

After Hamlet finishes answering his mother in the earlier court scene, the King offers his own consolation for Hamlet's grief:

> 'Tis sweet and commendable in your nature, Hamlet,
> To give these mourning duties to your father;
> But you must know your father lost a father;
> That father lost lost his; and the survivor bound,
> In filial obligation, for some term
> To do obsequious sorrow. But to persever
> In obstinate condolement is a course
> Of impious stubbornness; 'tis unmanly grief;
> It shows a will most incorrect to heaven,
> A heart unfortified, a mind impatient,
> An understanding simple and unschool'd;
> For what we know must be, and is as common
> As any the most vulgar thing to sense,
> Why should we in our peevish opposition
> Take it to heart? Fie! 'tis a fault to heaven,
> A fault against the dead, a fault to nature,
> To reason most absurd; whose common theme
> Is death of fathers, and who still hath cried,
> From the first corse till he that died to-day,
> 'This must be so'.

         [I. ii. 87-106]

There is much in this consolation of philosophy which is spiritually and psychologically sound, and to which every human being must eventually accommodate himself, but it comes at the wrong time, from the wrong person, and in its essential belittlement of the heartache of grief, it comes with the wrong inflection. It is a dispiriting irony of scholarship on this play that so many psychoanalytic and theological critics should essentially take such words, from such a King, as a text for their own indictments of Hamlet's behavior. What a person who is grieving needs, of course, is not the consolation of words, even words which are true, but sympathy—and this Hamlet does not receive, not from the court, not from his uncle, and more important, not from his own mother, to whom his grief over his father's death is alien and unwelcome.

After the King and Queen leave the stage, it is to his mother's lack of sympathy not only for him but for her dead husband that Hamlet turns in particular pain [in I. ii. 129ff.]. . . . This is an exceptionally suggestive speech and the first of many which seem to invite Oedipal interpretations of the play. About these I do not propose to speak directly, except to remark that the source of Hamlet's so-called Oedipal anxiety is real and present, it is not an archaic and repressed fantasy. Hamlet does perhaps protest too much, in this soliloquy and elsewhere, about his father's superiority to his uncle (and to himself), and throughout the play he is clearly preoccupied with his mother's sexual appetite; but these ambivalences and preoccupations, whatever their unconscious roots, are elicited by a situation, palpable and external to him, in which they are acted out. The Oedipal configurations of Hamlet's predicament, in other words, inhabit the whole world of the play, they are not simply a function of his characterization, even though they resonate with it profoundly. There is every reason, in reality, for a son to be troubled and decomposed by the appetite of a mother who betrays his father's memory by her incestuous marriage, within a month, to his brother, and murderer, and there is surely more than reason for a son to be obsessed for a time with a father who literally returns from the grave to haunt him. But in any case, I think that at least early in the play, if not also later, such Oedipal echoes cannot be disentangled from Hamlet's grief, and Shakespeare's purpose in arousing them is not to call Hamlet's character to judgment, but to expand our understanding of the nature and intensity of his suffering. For all of these resonant events come upon Hamlet while he has still not even begun to assimilate the loss of a living father, while he is still freshly mourning, seemingly alone in Denmark, for the death of a King, and their major psychic impact and importance, I think, is that they protract and vastly dilate the process of his grief. (pp. 18-22)

As I have already suggested, in his first speech to his mother, "Seems, madam! Nay, it is; I know not seems" [I. ii. 76], Hamlet speaks from the very heart of grief of the supervening reality of his loss and of its inward wound, and I think the accent of normal, if intense, grief remains dominant in his subsequent soliloquy as well. It is true that in that soliloquy his mind turns to thoughts of "self-slaughter," but those thoughts notwithstanding, the emphasis of the speech is not one of self-reproach. It is not himself, but the uses of the world which Hamlet finds "weary, stale, flat, and unprofitable" [I. ii. 133], and his mother's frailty suggests a rankness and grossness in nature itself. The "plaints" against his mother which occupy the majority of this speech are conscious and both his anger and ambivalence towards her fully justified. Even on the face of it, her hasty remarriage makes a mockery of his father's memory that intensifies the real pain and loneliness of his loss; and if he also feels his own ego threatened, and if there is a deeper cadence of grief in his words, it is because he is already beginning to sense that the shadow of a crime "with the primal eldest curse upon't" [III. iii. 37] has fallen upon him, a crime which is not delusional and not his, and which eventually inflicts a punishment upon him which tries his spirit and destroys his life. The last lines of Hamlet's soliloquy are:

> It is not, nor it cannot come to good.
> But break, my heart, for I must hold my
> tongue.
>
> [I. ii. 158-59]

These lines show Hamlet's prescience, not his disease, and the instant he completes them, Horatio, Marcellus and Barnardo enter to tell him of the apparition of his dead father, the ghost which is haunting the kingdom and which has been a part of our own consciousness from the very outset of the play.

Hamlet's subsequent meeting with the ghost of his father is, it seems to me, both the structural and psychic nexus of the play. The scene is so familiar to us that the extraordinary nature of its impact on Hamlet can be overlooked, even in the theater. The whole scene deserves quotation, but I will concentrate upon only the last part of it. The scene begins with Hamlet expressing pity for the ghost and the ghost insisting that he attend to a more "serious" purpose:

> *Ghost.*   List, list, O,
> list!
> If thou didst ever thy dear father
> love—
>
> *Ham.*   O God!
> *Ghost.*   Revenge his foul and most unnat-
> ural murder.
>
> [I. v. 22-5]

The ghost then confirms to Hamlet's prophetic soul that "The serpent that did sting thy father's life / Now wears his crown" [I. v. 39], and he proceeds to describe both Gertrude's remarriage and his own murder in his orchard in terms that seem deliberately to evoke echoes of the serpent in the garden of Eden. The ghost ends his recital saying:

> O, horrible! O, horrible! most horrible!
> If thou hast nature in thee, bear it not;
> Let not the royal bed of Denmark be
> A couch for luxury and damned incest.
> But, howsomever thou pursuest this act,
> Taint not thy mind, nor let thy soul con-
> trive
> Against thy mother aught; leave her to
> heaven,
> And to those thorns that in her bosom
> lodge
> To prick and sting her. Fare thee well at
> once.
> The glowworm shows the matin to be
> near,
> And gins to pale his uneffectual fire.
> Adieu, adieu, adieu! Remember me. [*Exit.*]
>
> [I. v. 80-91]

Hamlet's answering speech, as the ghost exits, is profound, and it predicates the state of his mind and feeling until the beginning of the last act of the play:

> O all you host of heaven! O earth! What
> else?
> And shall I couple hell? O, fie! Hold, hold,
> my heart;
> And you, my sinews, grow not instant old,
> But bear me stiffly up. Remember thee!
> Ay, thou poor ghost, whiles memory holds
> a seat
> In this distracted globe. Remember thee!
> Yea, from the table of my memory
> I'll wipe away all trivial fond records,
> All saws of books, all forms, all pressures
> past,
> That youth and observation copied there,
> And thy commandment all alone shall live
> Within the book and volume of my brain,
> Unmix'd with baser matter. Yes, by heav-
> en!
> O most pernicious woman!
> O villain, villain, smiling, damned villain!
> My tables—meet it is I set it down
> That one may smile, and smile, and be a
> villain;
> At least I am sure it may be so in Denmark.
> [*Writing.*]
> So, uncle, there you are. Now to my word:
> It is 'Adieu, adieu! Remember me'.
> I have sworn't.
>
> [I. v. 92-112]

This is a crucial and dreadful vow for many reasons, but the most important . . . is that the ghost's injunction to remember him, an injunction which Shakespeare's commitment to the whole force of the revenge genre never really permits either us or Hamlet to question, brutally intensifies Hamlet's mourning and makes him incorporate in its work what we would normally regard as the pathology of depression. For . . . the essence of the work of mourning is the internal process by which the ego [the organized conscious self] heals its wound, differentiates itself from the object, and slowly, bit by bit, cuts its libidinal [emotional energy tied to primitive biological urges] ties with the one who has died. Yet this is precisely what the ghost forbids, and forbids, moreover, with a lack of sympathy for Hamlet's grief which is even more pronounced than the Queen's. He instead tells Hamlet that if ever he loved his father, he should remember him; he tells Hamlet of Gertrude's incestuous remarriage in a way which makes her desire, if not the libido itself, seem inseparable from murder and death; and finally he tells Hamlet to kill. Drawing upon and crystallizing the deepest energies of the revenge play genre, the ghost thus enjoins Hamlet to identify with him in his sorrow and to give murderous purpose to his anger. He consciously compels in Hamlet, in other words, the regressive movement towards identification and sadism which together usually constitute the unconscious dynamics of depression. It is only after this scene that Hamlet feels punished with what he later calls "a sore distraction" [V. ii. 230] and that he begins to reproach himself for his own nature and to meditate on suicide. The ghost, moreover, not only compels this process in Hamlet, like much of the world of the play, he incarnates it. The effect of his appearance and behest to Hamlet is to literalize Hamlet's subsequent movement toward the realm of death which he inhabits, and away from all of the libidinal ties which nourish life and make it desirable, away from "all trivial fond records, / All saws of books, all forms, all pressures past" [I. v. 99-100] As C. S. Lewis insisted long ago [in his "Hamlet: The Prince or the Poem," *Proceedings of the British Academy,* 28 (1942)], the ghost leads Hamlet into a spiritual and psychic region which seems poised between the living and the dead. It is significant that Hamlet is subsequently described in images that suggest the ghost's countenance and significant too, as we shall see later, that Hamlet's own appearance and state of mind change, at the beginning of Act V, at the moment when it is possible to say that he has finally come to terms with the ghost and with his father's death and has completed the work of mourning.

I think Shakespeare intends us always to retain a sense of intensified mourning rather than of disease in Hamlet, partly because Hamlet is always conscious of the manic roles he plays and is always lucid with Horatio, but also because his thoughts and feelings turn outward as well as inward and his behavior is finally a symbiotic response to the actually diseased world of the play. And though that diseased world, poisoned at the root by a truly guilty King, eventually represents an overwhelming tangle of guilt, its main emphasis, both for Hamlet and for us, is the experience of grief. The essential focus of the action as well as the source of its consistent pulsations of feeling, the pulsations which continuously charge both Hamlet's sorrow and his anger (and in which the whole issue of delay is subsumed) is the actuality of conscious, not unconscious loss. For in addition to the death of his father in this play, Hamlet suffers the loss amounting to death of all those persons, except Horatio, whom he has most loved and who have most animated and given meaning to his life. He loses his mother, he loses Ophelia, and he loses his friends; and we can have no question that these losses are real and inescapable.

The loss of his mother is the most intense and the hardest to discuss. One should perhaps leave her to heaven as the ghost says, but even he cannot follow that advice. As I have already suggested, Hamlet is genuinely betrayed by her. She betrays him most directly, I think, by her lack of sympathy for him. She is clearly sexually drawn and loyal to her new husband, and she is said to live almost by Hamlet's looks, but she is essentially inert, oblivious to the whole realm of human experience through which her son travels. She seems not to care, and seems particularly not to care about his

grief. Early in the play, when Claudius and others are in hectic search of the reason for Hamlet's melancholy, she says with bovine imperturbability, "I doubt it is no other but the main, / His father's death and our o'erhasty marriage" [II. ii. 56-7]. That o'erhasty and incestuous marriage, of course, creates a reservoir of literally grievous anger in Hamlet. It suggests to him the impermanence upon which the Player King later insists, the impermanence of human affection as well as of life, and it also, less obviously, compels him to think of the violation of the union which gave him his own life and being. It is very difficult, in any circumstance, to think precisely upon our parents and their relationship without causing deep tremors in our selves, and for Hamlet the circumstances are extraordinary. In addition marriage itself has a sacramental meaning to him which has been largely lost to modern sensibility. Like the ghost, Hamlet always speaks reverently of the sanctity of marital vows, and the one occasion on which he mocks marriage is in fact an attack upon Claudius's presumption to have replaced his father. As he is leaving for England, Hamlet addresses Claudius and says, "Farewell, dear Mother." Claudius says, "Thy loving father, Hamlet," and Hamlet answers, "My mother: father and mother is man and wife; man and wife is one flesh; and so, my mother" [IV. iii. 51-2]. Behind the Scriptural image in this ferocious attack upon Claudius, it seems to me, is both Hamlet's memory of his father's true marriage with his mother, a memory which has an almost pre-lapsarian resonance, and a visualization of the concupiscence through which his mother has defiled that sacrament and made Claudius's guilt a part of her own being. This same adulterated image of matrimony, I think, lies behind his intense reproaches both against himself and Ophelia in the speech in which he urges Ophelia to go to a nunnery:

> Get thee to a nunnery. Why wouldst thou be a breeder of sinners? I am myself indifferent honest, but yet I could accuse me of such things that it were better my mother had not borne me: I am very proud, revengeful, ambitious; with more offences at my beck than I have thoughts to put them in, imagination to give them shape, or time to act them in. What should such fellows as I do crawling between earth and heaven?
>
> [III. i. 120-28]

Some of Hamlet's anger against Ophelia spills over, as it does in this speech, from his rage against his mother, but Ophelia herself gives him cause. I don't think there is any reason to doubt her own word, at the beginning of the play, that Hamlet has importuned her "with love / In honourable fashion . . . And hath given countenance to his speech . . . With almost all the holy vows of heaven" [I. iii. 110-14]; and there is certainly no reason to question his own passionate declaration at the end of the play, over her grave, that he loved her deeply.

> I loved Ophelia: forty thousand brothers
> Could not, with all their quantity of love,
> Make up my sum.
>
> [V. i. 269-71]

Both Hamlet's grief and his task constrain him from realizing this love, but Ophelia's own behavior clearly intensifies his frustration and anguish. By keeping the worldly and disbelieving advice of her brother and father as "watchman" to her "heart" [I. iii. 46], she denies the heart's affection not only in Hamlet but in herself; and both denials add immeasurably to Hamlet's sense of loneliness and loss—and anger. Her rejection of him echoes his mother's inconstancy and denies him the possibility even of imagining the experience of loving and being loved by a woman at a time when he obviously needs such love most profoundly; and her rejection of her own heart reminds him of the evil court whose shadow, he accurately senses, has fallen upon her and directly threatens him. Most of Hamlet's speeches to Ophelia condense all of these feelings. They are spoken from a sense of suppressed as well as rejected love, for the ligaments between him and Ophelia are very deep in the play. It is she who first reports on his melancholy transformation, "with a look so piteous in purport / As if he had been loosed out of hell / To speak of horrors" [II. i. 79-81]; it is she who remains most acutely conscious of the nobility of mind and form which has, she says, been "blasted with ecstasy" [III. i. 160]; and it is she, after Hamlet has gone to England, who most painfully takes up his role and absorbs his grief to the point of real madness and suicide.

Rosencrantz and Guildenstern are less close to Hamlet's heart, and because they are such unequivocal sponges of the King, he can release his anger against them without any ambivalence, but at least initially they too amplify both his and our sense of the increasing emptiness of his world. We are so accustomed to treating Rosencrantz and Guildenstern as vaguely comic twins that we can forget the great warmth with which Hamlet first welcomes them to Denmark and the urgency and openness of his plea for the continuation of their friendship. "I will not sort you with the rest of my servants," he tells them,

> for, to speak to you like an honest man, I am most dreadfully attended. But, in the beaten way of friendship, what make you at Elsinore?
>
> Ros. To visit you, my lord; no other occasion.
>
> Ham. Beggar that I am, I am even poor in thanks; but I thank you; and sure, dear friends, my thanks are too dear a half-penny. Were you not sent for? Is it your own inclining? Is it a free visitation? Come, come,

> deal justly with me. Come, come; nay, speak.
>
> Guil. What should we say, my lord?
>
> Ham. Why any thing. But to th' purpose: you were sent for; and there is a kind of confession in your looks, which your modesties have not craft enough to colour; I know the good King and Queen have sent for you.
>
> Ros. To what end, my lord?
>
> Ham. That you must teach me. But let me conjure you by the rights of our fellowship, by the consonancy of our youth, by the obligation of our ever-preserved love, and by what more dear a better proposer can charge you withal, be even and direct with me, whether you were sent for or no?
>
> [II. ii. 267-88]

Rosencrantz and Guildenstern, of course, cannot be direct with him, and Hamlet cuts his losses with them quite quickly and eventually quite savagely. But it is perhaps no accident that immediately following this exchange, when he must be fully realizing the extent to which, except for Horatio, he is now utterly alone in Denmark with his grief and his task, he gives that grief a voice which includes in its deep sadness and its sympathetic imagination a conspectus of Renaissance thought about the human condition. (pp. 24-31)

At the beginning of Act V, when Hamlet returns from England, that world seems to change, and Hamlet with it. Neither the countenance of the ghost nor his tormented and tormenting spirit seem any longer to be present in the play, and Hamlet begins to alter in state of mind as he already has in his dress. He stands in the graveyard which visually epitomizes the play's preoccupation with death, a scene which the clowns insistently associate with Adam's sin and Hamlet himself with Cain's, and he contemplates the "chap-fall'n" skull of the man who carried him on his back when he was a small child. His mood, like the scene, is essentially sombre, but though there is a suggestion by Horatio that he is still considering death "too curiously" [V. i. 205], there is no longer the sense that he and his world are conflated in the convulsive activity of grief. That activity seems to be drawing to a close, and his own sense of differentiation is decisively crystallized when, in a scene reminiscent of the one in which he reacts to the imitation of Hecuba's grief, he responds to Laertes's enactment of a grief which seems a parody of his own:

> What is he whose grief
> Bears such an emphasis, whose phrase of sorrow
> Conjures the wand'ring stars, and makes them stand
> Like wonder-wounded hearers. This is I, Hamlet the Dane.
>
> [V. i. 254-58]

It is an especially painful but inescapable paradox of Hamlet's tragedy that the final ending of his grief and the liberation of his self would be co-extensive with the apprehension of his own death. After agreeing to the duel with Laertes that he is confident of winning, he nevertheless tells Horatio, "But thou wouldst not think how ill all's here about my heart; but it is no matter" [V. ii. 212-13]; and when Horatio urges him to postpone the duel, he says, in the famous speech which signifies, if it does not explain, the decisive change of his spirit:

> Not a whit, we defy augury: there is a special providence in the fall of a sparrow. If it be now, 'tis not to come; if it be not to come, it will be now; if it be not now, yet it will come—the readiness is all. Since no man owes of aught he leaves, what is't to leave betimes? Let be.
>
> [V. ii. 219-24]

The theological import of these lines, with their luminous reference to Matthew, has long been recognized, but the particular emphasis upon death also suggests a psychological coordinate. For it seems to me that what makes Hamlet's acceptance of Providence finally intelligible and credible to us emotionally, what confirms the truth of it to our own experience, is our sense, as well as his, that the great anguish and struggle of his grief is over, and that he has completed the work of mourning. He speaks to Horatio quietly, almost serenely, with the unexultant calm which characterizes the end of the long, inner struggle of grief. He has looked at the face of death in his father's ghost, he has endured death and loss in all the human beings he has loved, and he now accepts those losses as an inevitable part of his own condition. He recognizes and accepts his own death. "The readiness is all" suggests the crystallization of his awareness of the larger dimension of time which has enveloped his tragedy from the start, including the revenge drama of Fortinbras's grievances on the outskirts of the action and that of the appalling griefs of Polonius's family deep inside it, but the line also most specifically states what is perhaps the last and most difficult task of mourning, his own readiness to die. (pp. 31-3)

Hamlet is an immensely complicated tragedy, and anything one says about it leaves one haunted by what has not been said. But precisely in a play whose suggestiveness has no end, it seems to me especially important to remember what actually happens. Hamlet himself is sometimes most preoccupied with delay, and with the whole attendant metaphysical issue of the relation between thought and action, but as his own experience shows, there is finally no action that can be commensurate with his grief, not even the killing of a guilty King, and it is Hamlet's experience of grief, and his recovery from it, to which we ourselves respond most deeply. He is a young man who comes home from his university to find his father dead and his mother remarried to his father's murderer. Subsequently the woman he loves rejects him, he is betrayed by his friends, and finally and most painfully, he is betrayed by a mother whose mutability seems to strike at the heart of human affection. In the midst of these waves of losses, which seem themselves to correspond to the spasms of grief, he is visited by the ghost of his father, who places upon him a proof of love and a task of vengeance which he cannot refuse without denying his own being. The ghost draws upon the emotional taproot of the revenge play genre and dilates the natural sorrow and anger of Hamlet's multiple griefs until they include all human frailty in their protest and sympathy and touch upon the deepest synapses of grief in our own lives, not only for those who have died, but for those, like ourselves, who are still alive. (p. 35)

Arthur Kirsch, "Hamlet's Grief," in ELH, *Vol. 48, No. 1, Spring, 1981, pp. 17-36.*

IMAGERY

Richard D. Altick

[*Altick argues that Shakespeare not only emphasized the theme of bodily corruption in* Hamlet, *but also the "revolting odors that accompany the process." The critic then provides an analysis of various elements of the play, focusing on such images of decay as the sun as an agent of corruption, cancerous infection, and the stench which accompanies rotting. This stench, Altick observes, represents the cunning and lecherousness of* **Claudius**'s *evil which has corrupted the whole kingdom of Denmark. According to the critic, these and other image patterns demonstrate that "the text reeks with terms symbolic of the loathsomeness of moral disintegration." Altick also discusses the olfactory (relating to the sense of smell) connotations of such key words as "foul," "rank," and "offence," and examines instances of punning (a kind of wordplay which manipulates the use of two words with different meanings based on their similarity of sound) between the terms "offence" and "offend."*]

In writing *Hamlet,* Shakespeare was preoccupied with the corruption of mortal flesh. From the famous first statement of the idea in Marcellus' "Something is rotten in the state of Denmark" [I. iv. 90] to Hamlet's discourse with the Gravediggers on the lamentable condition of the bodies they disinter, the reader of the play may never long forget that after death the human body putrifies. To Shakespeare's contemporaries, of course, the idea was the most familiar of commonplaces, the center of a cluster of time-worn platitudes which, by making pious capital of a universal biological process, reminded man that flesh was foul and that even a king could go a progress through the guts of a beggar. It was a commonplace, but much more. Every Elizabethan citizen knew from personal observation the reek of a gangrenous wound or a cancerous sore. Thus the fact that human flesh may well begin to rot even before death, and that the process is accelerated and even more loathsome afterwards—witness the stench of unburied "pocky corses" in plague time and of bones being transferred to the charnel house after their sojourn in hallowed ground—was removed from the abstract realm of folk-say and sermon, and made immediate and unforgettable by the nauseating testimony of the nostrils.

The ancient moral therefore was constantly and repellently illustrated in the everyday life of Shakespeare's time. In his plays generally, Shakespeare habitually uses allusions to the rotting of flesh as a vivid way of symbolizing repugnant ideas. In *Hamlet,* however, he not only lays heavier emphasis than in any other play upon bodily corruption, but stresses, to a degree found nowhere else, the revolting odors that accompany the process. The play indeed may justly be said to be enveloped in an atmosphere of stench. The stink that rises from dead flesh emblematizes the sheer loathsomeness of the sort of evil, cunning and lecherous, with which Claudius has corrupted the whole kingdom; the fact that once begun, the process of rotting gains inexorable headway and the odor it generates spreads far and wide, suggests the dynamic and infectious quality of sin; and the further fact that the process transforms the beautiful human body into a horrid, malodorous mass of corruption is symbolic of the dread effect of sin upon the human soul. It is not only to Hamlet that, as G. Wilson Knight has remarked, "the universe smells of mortality"; all the leading characters manifest, through their choice of language, their awareness of the odor, originating in the foul soul of Claudius, that permeates the kingdom.

Since the detailed work of Caroline Spurgeon and Wolfgang Clemen especially, no student of *Hamlet* has been unaware of the way in which images of corrupting disease dominate the poetic fabric of the play. But the importance of the accompanying suggestion of nauseating smell has not, I think, been generally appreciated. It is not a matter of images alone—images represent simply the points at which the hovering theme is made explicit by embodiment in a metaphor—but also of the many single related words scattered through the text whose sensory suggestion, dormant now as it was not in Shakespeare's time, is overlooked unless the chief image-motif is constantly recalled.

The opening scene has long been admired as a masterpiece of atmospheric writing. Francisco's line in the first minute of the play, " 'Tis bitter cold, / And I am sick at heart" [I. i. 8-9], not only defines the foreboding, uneasy atmosphere of the setting, but, by associating the idea of sickness with an as yet unknown evil, initiates the use of a word which from time to time will reinforce the play's dominant image. Before the end of the scene *sick* appears in a new context:

> the moist star
> Upon whose influence Neptune's empire
> stands
> Was sick almost to doomsday with eclipse
> [I. i. 118-20]

—and by the recurrence of the word in such an image we are led to feel that the disturbance in the common soldier's heart is simply a reflection, in microcosm, of the vast upset which is visiting Elsinore now as it did the state of Rome a little ere the mightiest Julius fell. (Brutus, it will be recalled, had "some sick offence" [*Julius Caesar,* II. i. 268] within his mind the very night that the ominous portents visited Rome.) The association between sickness and night, thus formed, is further defined when Marcellus, in one of the few lyrical passages of the play, speaks of the happy Christmas season when "the nights are wholesome" [I. i. 162], and thus makes clear that in Elsinore, at the present moment, the nights are *not* wholesome. The Elizabethans, of course, feared the night air as the carrier of contagion, especially from the putrescent matter in marshes and churchyards. Thus this early allusion to the unwholesomeness of the Elsinore nights begins the process, to be continued throughout the play, of appealing to the medical, the epidemiological lore of the contemporary playgoer.

This heretofore general sense of sickness is localized and given specific connection with physical decay in the second line Hamlet utters. In response to the King's question, "How is it that the clouds still hang on you?" Hamlet says, "Not so, my lord. I am too much i' th' sun" [I. ii. 66-7]. The usual interpretation of the line (a quibble on *son* and *sun*—I am too conscious of my character as son, and I am uncomfortable in the presence of the King, the sun) does not convey the entire meaning. Claudius *is* the sun, of course; but what is often overlooked is that the sun is a powerful agent of corruption. Since Hamlet does not yet recognize the King's vast influence for evil, the line is ironical; only looking back, especially from the point where Hamlet envisions the sun breeding maggots in a dead dog, do we realize that he is characterizing the King more truly than he can, at this point, know. Like the sun, particularly in time of plague, the King can spread corruption wherever his influence falls, and Hamlet is exposed to the full glare of that malign power. The idea contained in the line is resumed in "O that this too too solid flesh would melt, / Thaw, and resolve itself into a dew!" [I. ii. 129-30]. Hamlet wishes that the physical disintegration which the sun promotes would be his own immediate fortune. (A simpler, and equally plausible, explanation which still connects the two separate passages would be in terms of the sun as the melter, not of flesh, but of snow. But the "god kissing carrion" image later on [II. ii. 182], which picks up the "too much i' th' sun" notion again, inclines me to the former interpretation.) The rest of Hamlet's speech, contrasting with the high sentences of the King's address to him, is flecked with base images of decay (the world is overgrown by "things rank and gross in nature" [I. ii. 136]—*rank* in two senses) and of parasitism, which is often linked with decay (the Queen had clung to the elder Hamlet "As if increase of appetite had grown / By what it fed on" [I. ii. 144-45]). There may even be a double pun in "How weary, stale, flat, and unprofitable / Seem to me all the uses of this world!" [I. ii. 133-34]. To an Elizabethan auditor, the obvious meaning of the word *stale* in context, "musty," would have chimed with a second meaning, "prostitute"—appropriate enough in the light of what Hamlet proceeds to say about his mother—and even with a third, "horse's urine," which would add a certain measure to the malodorousness of the whole text and detract nothing from the auditor's appreciation of the hopelessness of Hamlet's outlook.

The concluding lines of the scene,

> I doubt some foul play. Would the night were come!
> Till then sit still, my soul. Foul deeds will rise,
> Though all the earth o'erwhelm them, to men's eyes
>
> [I. ii. 255-57]

carry on the association begun in the first scene between night and apparitions, and relate it to the image-pattern. The allusion is to the way in which decaying animal (or vegetable) matter, though deeply buried, seems to rise again at night in miasmatic mists or phosphorescent glows, or in phantasmic shapes which old superstition identified as ghosts. Evil, Hamlet's image says, may be put out of sight, but it will return, in some new manifestation which will affront not only the eyes but—the force of *foul* is clear—the nose. It may be no accident that in the first minute of the next scene, which followed without pause on the Elizabethan stage, Shakespeare has Laertes speak of violets and perfume; an effective contrast to the repeated *foul* of Hamlet's last lines.

At this point, there enters a second corruption image, which shifts attention from the putrescence of a dead organism to that in a still living one. Laertes' image, "The canker galls the infants of the spring / Too oft before their buttons be disclos'd" [I. iii. 39-40], is usually, and rightly, read as referring to the action of a caterpillar in young buds. But the other, equally common, meaning of *canker*—cancer—is likely to have occurred as well to the hearers of the lines. In the next scene the idea of cancerous decay in a living organism recurs, although still only by implication. In his rambling, time-filling discourse to Horatio and Marcellus as they await the Ghost, Hamlet dwells upon the "vicious mole of nature" (some particular shortcoming) in certain men which leads them "in the general censure [to] take corruption" [I. iv. 24-35]—i.e., to be condemned for that single fault. The image, although interrupted and blurred by Hamlet's nervous loquacity, is plainly suggestive of a spreading cancer (the "vicious" makes it plain that he is not thinking of an ordinary mole or skin blemish), which leads to total infection. The cancerous nature of evil is about to be illustrated by the Ghost's narrative. "Something is rotten in the state of Denmark" [I. iv. 90], says Marcellus as he watches the Ghost lead Hamlet off.

The Ghost tells his story to Hamlet in language dominated by a sense of rottenness, disease, and stench. He is "confin'd to fast in fires," he says, "Til the *foul* crimes done in my days of nature / Are burnt and purg'd away" [I. v. 11-13]. The word *foul*, given no less prominence than the key-word *murther*, reverberates in his solemn lines, which are among the most dramatic in all the play:

> *Ghost.*   Revenge his *foul* and most unnatural murther.
> *Hamlet.* Murther?
> *Ghost.*   Murther most *foul*, as in the best it is;
> But this most *foul*, strange, and unnatural.
>
> [I. v. 25-8]

"The fat weed / That rots itself in ease on Lethe wharf," spoken of in the lines just following [I. v. 32-3], continue the idea of foulness; as [George Lyman] Kittredge notes, "the very existence of a slimy water-weed seems to be decay; it thrives in corruption and 'rots itself' through its lazy, stagnant life." The ear of Denmark is "*rankly* abused." Lust, says the Ghost, now for the first time applying the idea of repulsive odor to the sexual sin of Claudius and Gertrude,

> though to a radiant angel link'd,
> Will sate itself in a celestial bed
> And prey on *garbage*
>
> [I. v. 55-7]

—the olfactory suggestion of which is made explicit by the contrast provided by the very next line: "But soft! Methinks I scent the morning air" [I. v. 58]. Rather ironically, considering the state of his own mind, as manifested in his language, the Ghost commands Hamlet, "*Taint* not thy mind" [I. v. 85]. But by this time evil has as vile a smell to Hamlet as it does to his father; and, being Hamlet, he reveals it by the wild and whirling play on *offend/offence*, to which we shall return presently.

Even in the succeeding scene, involving Polonius, Reynaldo, and Ophelia, though the subject-matter

The Ghost, Hamlet, Horatio, and Marcellus. Act I, scene iv. From the Art Collection of the Folger Shakespeare Library.

has no relation to what has just preceded, the suggestion of vile smell is not entirely absent. Polonius directs Reynaldo to take care not to set afloat any rumors about Laertes that are "so *rank* / As may dishonour him" but rather to "breathe his faults so quaintly / That they may seem the *taints* of liberty" [II. i. 20-1, 31-2]. But it is only when Hamlet is seen again that the evil-smell theme is signally resumed. Hamlet identifies Polonius as a fishmonger, a term which, in addition to other appropriate aspects that have been pointed out by the commentators, has its own odorous value. And then he reads in his book: "For if the sun breed maggots in a dead dog, being a god kissing carrion—Have you a daughter?" he suddenly asks. "Let her not walk i' th' sun. Conception is a blessing, but not as your daughter may conceive" [II. ii. 181-85]. And here we have a recurrence of the image already noted in the second scene of the play: Claudius as the sun, and the sun as an agent of noisome corruption, which, according to the pseudo-science of the time, resulted in turn in the breeding of new life. Hamlet is now fully conscious of the evil influence of the King, and he warns that Ophelia too is endangered by the same corruptive force which he had, albeit unconsciously, identified in his "I am too much i'

th' sun"—though Ophelia, as a woman, is imperilled in a different way. Hamlet, his father, Gertrude, and now (Hamlet fears) Ophelia: the roll of the King's victims is increasing; the evil generated by Claudius' sick soul is spreading insidiously through the court. No wonder, then, that to Hamlet the air "appeareth no other thing . . . than a foul and pestilent congregation of vapours" [II. ii. 302-03]: vapors spreading the evil of a dead crime far and wide. "What a piece of work is a man" [II. ii. 303] indeed—a man whose sin has the power so to infect a whole kingdom. A far cry, this Hamlet whose "imaginations are as foul / As Vulcan's stithy" [III. ii. 83-4]—any Elizabethan's nostrils would have quivered, as ours may not, to the suggestion of thick smoke and the reek of seared horses' hoofs—from the young man who once was accustomed to utter to Ophelia "words of so sweet breath compos'd" [III. i. 97]. Where now is the perfume of his former discourse?

The hovering suggestions of physical contagion in the night air, which had been lost since the Ghost scene, are brought to a new focus in Lucianus' concluding incantation in the play-within-a-play:

Thou mixture rank, of midnight weeds
    collected,
With Hecate's ban thrice blasted, thrice in-
    fected,
Thy natural magic and dire property
On wholesome life usurp immediately.
                              [III. ii. 257-60]

Rank, midnight, blasted, infected have powerful connotations of physical evil, especially as contrasted with *wholesome*. And the connection of these midnight horrors with the stench of putrifying flesh is made specific in Hamlet's speech at the close of the scene:

'Tis now the very witching time of night,
When churchyards yawn, and hell itself
    breathes out
Contagion to this world.
                              [III. ii. 388-90]

The following scenes (III. iii-iv) have the highest incidence of corruption-smell images and puns in the play, which is but natural when we recall that these scenes are the direct, if delayed, sequel to the odor-laden interview with the Ghost. The King's speech beginning "O, my offence is rank, it smells to heaven" [III. iii. 36], with its repeated use of words like *offence, strong, foul,* and *corrupted,* sets the tone of all that follows. Hamlet refers to Claudius as "a mildew'd ear / Blasting his wholesome brother" [III. iv. 64-5], *mildew'd* providing a clear image of bad-smelling fungi communicating infection to a hitherto healthy organism. The Queen envisions her soul as full of "such black and grained spots / As will not leave their tinct" [III. iv. 90-1], a phrase suggestive of cancerous or other corruptive growth. And, resuming the very imagery which the Ghost had used to describe the incest, Hamlet bursts out:

Nay, but to live
In the *rank* sweat of an enseamed bed,
Stew'd in *corruption,* honeying and mak-
    ing love
Over the nasty sty!
                              [III. iv. 91-4]

"Mother, for love of grace," he continues after the reappearance of the Ghost,

Lay not that flattering unction to your
    soul,
That not your trespass but my madness
    speaks.
It will but skin and film the ulcerous place,
Whiles *rank corruption,* mining all with-
    in,
Infects unseen
                              [III. iv. 144-49]

—a deservedly admired image of the insidious action of a cancer in or near the skin, the stench of which is made unmistakably vivid by "rank corruption." Finally, Hamlet begs the Queen henceforth to avoid the "reechy kisses" of her lecherous husband. In Hamlet's mind the evil of the Queen's incest is firmly symbolized by a noisome smell; the marriage bed is associated with garbage and the nasty sty; and her sense of guilt is a cancerous sore whose spread cannot be arrested by any rationalization.

In the following scene (IV.i), by a nice stroke of irony, Claudius picks up the same image of cancer and applies it, in the presence of the Queen, to Hamlet's affliction:

so much was our love
We would not understand what was most
    fit,
But, like the owner of a *foul* disease,
To keep it from divulging, let it feed
Even on the pith of life.
                              [IV. i. 19-23]

"Diseases desperate grown," he decides after an interval—anticipating Hamlet's own conclusion following his return from England—"By desperate appliance are reliev'd, / Or not at all" [IV. iii. 9-11]. Hamlet does nothing to alleviate the morbidity of Claudius' mind when he proceeds to lecture him on the manner in which we mortal men "fat ourselves for maggots," and to assure him that, if Polonius' corpse is not meanwhile discovered, "you shall nose him as you go up the stairs into the lobby" [IV. iii. 22-3, 36-7].

Except for small reminders in the scene between Claudius and Laertes (allusions to *plague, sickness, pleurisy* [excess], *the quick o' the ulcer,* and a gangrenous sore arising from the scratch of a poisoned sword), the corruption-smell theme lapses until the graveyard scene, when, in a sense, it reaches its climax. The significance of this scene in terms of the motif we have been tracing lies not so much in the actual lines—although the Gravedigger's instructive remarks on the number of years required for a corpse to rot after the laying-in, and Hamlet's subsequent exclamation of disgust upon smelling Yorick's skull are parts of the pattern—as in the abundant suggestions which the very setting would have for the Elizabethan playgoer. Here *is* the yawning churchyard, the symbol of man's mortality, the place where flesh, whose corruption may have begun in life, was laid in earth—and where flesh continued to rot after death, its fetid exhalations assaulting men's noses and not merely making their gorges rise but warning them of the danger of fatal contagion. All the preceding imagery and word-play dealing with the odor of mortality have pointed toward this scene; and after the scene is ended, the motif is heard but once more, in Hamlet's simple query to Horatio:

And is't not to be damn'd
To let this canker of our nature come
In further evil?
                              [V. ii. 68-70]

In this tracing of the various forms which imagery suggestive of corruption and evil odor takes in *Hamlet,* we have not noticed the occurrence of dozens of detached words which support the dominant motif. Read in their immediate context, they usually seem colorless, with little metaphorical force; but read against the whole atmospheric pattern as we have just outlined it, they are revealed to have an indispensable relation to it. The text reeks with terms symbolic of the loathsomeness of moral disintegration.

The pervasiveness of the idea of the odor of disease in the play is due no more to the formal metaphors which incorporate it than to the simple recurrence of the words *sick* (*sickly, sicklied*) and *disease,* even when these do not in their context refer to physical illness. (Indeed, there is no actual bodily sickness in the play, unless it is the rather ambiguous malady of the Player King.) To the Elizabethans, in days long before asepsis had robbed illness of some of its malodorousness, *sick* and *diseased* probably had a specific sensory association which is now largely lost. The often-noted emphasis on these words in the play is not designed to convey the idea of an unhealthy state of mind, of moral degeneration, alone; the words contribute their share to the general effect of physical smell which in the images is so strongly associated with disease.

In our time, *foul* has lost most of its power of sensory suggestion. It had begun to do so in Shakespeare's time, and we may doubt whether, on most of the scores of occasions upon which the word is used in his plays, it evoked any sensory reaction in his audience. Normally it was a rather neutral adjective of censure. But at the same time the word did continue to designate the odor generated by decaying flesh, and in appropriate contexts it did retain an unmistakable connotative power, roughly equivalent perhaps to our epithet *stinking.* In *Hamlet* this specific connotation is predominant, as it is nowhere else in the canon, because the word *foul* occurs frequently in conjunction with other words which serve to develop its definite, but normally latent, olfactory reference. Because of this, and because of the presence in the text of so many other passages suggestive of smell, the word, no matter how casually used, has a special significance. It is noteworthy that in two separate passages, both of them quoted above, Shakespeare uses *foul* in rhetorical repetition, as if to make sure that its full connotative value is not lost upon the audience.

The repulsive sensory connotation of *rank* ("corrupt, foul, festering") in some contexts is obscured by another meaning. But by neglecting the possibility of a pun, we fail to realize how this word too supports the prevailing theme. Actually, in several instances, in which the primary meaning is "luxuriant, overgrown," the pun is double: *rank* in the sense of "stinking" and also in the more specialized sense of "in lecherous heat," as in Hamlet's description of Denmark as

> an unweeded garden

> That grows to seed; things *rank* and gross in nature
> Possess it merely

[I. ii. 135-37]

and his admonition to his mother, "Do not spread the compost on the weeds / To make them *ranker*" [III. iv. 151-52].

Possibly we are on less certain ground when we include *offence* with *foul* and *rank* as a word which recurrently supports the sickness-foul odor theme in *Hamlet.* Yet there is evidence that in Elizabethan times the word was frequently related to olfactory affront; for example, a passage cited in the *New English Dictionary* from Sir John Harington's *Metamorphosis of Ajax* (1596) runs: "They quickly found not only offence but infection to grow out of great concourss of people"—*offence* referring most explicitly to the effect upon the nostrils of the sweaty, unwashed, and disease-ridden populace. In Shakespeare's mind there was an unmistakable, though of course not constant, association between *offence/offend* and bad odors. In the plays one can find some fifteen or twenty passages in which one or the other of these words occurs in intimate proximity to words or images of smell or disease (*infected, sick, taint, foul, strong, rank, nose, breathe, corruption, rotten*). I am persuaded that the repeated occurrence of *offend* and *offence* in *Hamlet* is part of the pattern of submerged punning. That the words embodied for Shakespeare not only the abstract concept (sin, crime) but also the symbolic sensory manifestation (something disagreeable, disgusting: specifically, a foul odor) seems clear, above all in Claudius' speech in the prayer scene, in the first line of which the connection is made between *offence* and smell, and in the remainder of which *offence,* despite the shift in image, is interlaced with other terms suggestive of smell:

> O, my *offence* is *rank,* it *smells* to heaven;
> It hath the primal eldest curse upon't,
> A brother's murther! Pray can I not,
> Though inclination be as sharp as will.
> My *stronger* guilt defeats my *strong* intent,
> And, like a man to double business bound,
> I stand in pause where I shall first begin,
> And both neglect. What if this cursed hand
> Were thicker than itself with brother's blood,
> Is there not rain enough in the sweet heavens
> To wash it white as snow? Whereto serves mercy
> But to confront the visage of *offence?*
> And what's in prayer but this twofold force,
> To be forestalled ere we come to fall,
> Or pardon'd being down? Then I'll look up;
> My fault is past. But, O, what form of prayer

Can serve my turn? "Forgive me my *foul*
  murther"?
That cannot be; since I am still possess'd
Of those effects for which I did the mur-
  ther—
My crown, mine own ambition, and my
  queen.
May one be pardon'd and retain th' *of-*
  fence?
In the *corrupted* currents of this world
Offence's gilded hand may shove by jus-
  tice,
And oft 'tis seen the wicked prize itself
Buys out the law; but 'tis not so above.

                    [III. iii. 36-59]

It is remarkable that this speech, as printed in the first quarto, does not contain a single one of the recurrent quibbling allusions to foul smell; such odorless words as *trespass, fault,* and *sin* are used instead. Although most scholarly opinion today holds that the first quarto text is a debased and garbled version of that of the second quarto, and that Shakespeare did not, as was formerly thought, write two separate versions of *Hamlet,* it is tempting to think that Shakespeare rewrote the speech with the conscious purpose of intensifying the prevalent aura of corruption in the play. (Why, if the text known to the abridger who made the first quarto was substantially that which is printed above, did he systematically omit every *offence* and every other word suggestive of smell?) Noteworthy too is the fact that, as is twice the case with *foul,* Shakespeare employs *offence* recurrently within other brief passages, as if to emphasize its specific connotative significance. As early as the first act, when Marcellus' remark that something is rotten in Denmark and the Ghost's bitter reference to lust preying on garbage are still fresh in our ears, we hear Hamlet apologizing to Horatio for his wild words:

Hamlet. I am sorry they *offend* you,
        heartily . . .

Horatio. There's no *offence,* my lord.
Hamlet. Yes, by Saint Patrick, but there
        is, Horatio,
        And much *offence* too
                  [I. v. 134-37]

—a passage which amounts to a three-way, or progressive, pun, *offence* having not only the obvious meanings of "irritation" or "affront" (which alone is what Hamlet first intended) and "crime" (which is what he includes in the meaning after Horatio has converted the verb into a noun), but, thirdly, that of "foul odor," the physical emblem of evil. Hamlet gives the same double twist to the word in the mousetrap scene:

King.   Have you heard the argument?
        Is there no *offence* in't?
Hamlet. No, no! They do but jest, poison
        in jest; no *offence* i' th' world.
               [III. ii. 232-35]

And two scenes later (the prayer scene, with its own quadruple use of the word, has intervened) Shakespeare gives fresh rhetorical emphasis to the verb:

Queen. Hamlet, thou hast thy father
        much *offended.*
Hamlet. Mother, you have my father
        much *offended.*

                  [III. iv. 9-10]

—an exchange which sets the tone of the ensuing interview with the Queen, in which Hamlet's utterance abounds with allusions to smell. In no other play does Shakespeare dwell so insistently upon *offend/offence* by having the characters thrust the words back and forth within the compass of a few lines. To me this unusual, conspicuous dwelling upon the words suggests that Shakespeare must have found a significance in them over and above their abstract suggestion of "sin" or "crime." They act as hovering puns, which, once we have recognized them as such, remind us repeatedly of the play's preoccupation with foul smell. Interestingly enough, *offend* appears last of all in the play by virtue of a slip of the Gravedigger's tongue [V. i. 9]. "It must be *se defendendo*," he should say, referring to the coroner's verdict on Ophelia's drowning; but, by having him blunder into "*se offendendo*," Shakespeare ekes out one more occasion for the pun.

The degree to which Shakespeare was conscious (if he was conscious at all) of his making repulsive odors as a symbol of moral corruption permeate the text of *Hamlet* can never, of course, be determined. Whatever his mental processes may have been, the fact remains that, in addition to the series of metaphors in which fleshly corruption so often is associated with stench, the play contains dozens of occurrences of words which intensify the dominant scent of foulness—which make the moral evil of Elsinore a stink in our nostrils. To miss them, as Dover Wilson says of Shakespeare's punning habit in general, a "often to miss the interwoven thread which connects together a whole train of images; for imagery and double meaning are generally inseparable."

The sense of evil which permeates the play, therefore, is not created merely, as critics have generally assumed, by the iterated allusions to corruption. It is deepened and made more repulsive by being constantly associated with one of the most unpleasant of man's sensory experiences. Above all, the suggestion of noisome odors reminds us of that aspect of evil which Shakespeare seems most concerned to emphasize in *Hamlet:* the evil residing in the soul of one man cannot be contained there, nor can a single sin be without far-reaching consequences. Insidiously, irresistibly, it spreads into a whole society, just as the reek generated by a mass of putrid flesh bears infection to many who breathe it. In an age when everyday experience made men nauseatingly conscious of the way in which the odor arising from bodily decay cannot be localized, Shakespeare's use of the language of smell must have provided an extraordinarily vivid lesson in the continuous, contagious quality of sin. (pp. 167-76)

> *Richard D. Altick, " 'Hamlet' and the Odor of Mortality," in* Shakespeare Quarterly, *Vol. V, No. 2, Spring, 1954, pp. 167-76.*

Kenneth Muir

[*Muir discusses imagery and symbolism in* Hamlet, *beginning with an examination of what he considers the most apparent image pattern in the play—disease. The critic suggests that images of disease are not associated with* **Hamlet** *himself, but a sense of infection surrounds both* **Claudius's** *crime and guilt and* **Gertrude's** *sin. Muir attributes* **Hamlet's** *disorder to his melancholic grief over his father's death and his mother's frailty. In addition, the critic includes images of decay, flowers, and prostitution, with those of disease in the larger patterns of corruption and appearance versus reality. Finally, Muir explores war imagery in* Hamlet, *noting that it frequently recurs in the text and that its dramatic function is to underscore the fact that* **Hamlet** *and* **Claudius** *are engaged in a duel to the death.*]

A good many of the sickness images are merely designed to lend atmosphere [in *Hamlet*], as when Francisco on the battlements remarks that he is "sick at heart" [I. i. 9] or when Hamlet speaks of the way the courtier's chilblain is galled by the peasant's. Other images . . . are connected with the murder of Hamlet's father or with the corresponding murder of Gonzago. Several of the images refer to the sickness of the state, which some think to be due to the threat of war, but which the audience soon comes to realize is caused by Claudius' unpunished crime. Horatio believes that the appearance of the Ghost "bodes some strange eruption to our state" [I. i. 69] and Marcellus concludes that

> Something is rotten in the state of Denmark.
>
> [I. iv. 90]

Hamlet himself uses disease imagery again and again in reference to the King's guilt. He thinks of himself as a surgeon probing a wound: "I'll tent him to the quick" [II. ii. 597]. He tells Guildenstern that Claudius should have sent for a physician rather than himself, and when he refrains from assassinating him he remarks:

> This physic but prolongs thy sickly days.
>
> [III. iii. 96]

He compares Claudius to "a mildewed ear Blasting his wholesome brother" [III. iv. 64-5] and in the last scene of the play he compares him to a cancer:

> Is't not to be damn'd
> To let this canker of our nature come
> In further evil.
>
> [V. ii. 68-70]

It is true that Claudius reciprocates by using disease images in reference to Hamlet. He compares his leniency to his nephew to the behaviour of one suffering from a foul disease who conceals it and lets it feed "Even on the pith of life" [IV. i. 23]. He supports his stratagem of sending Hamlet to England with the proverbial maxim:

> Diseases desperate grown
> By desperate appliance are reliev'd,
> Or not at all.
>
> [IV. iii. 9-11]

In hatching his plot with Laertes, he calls Hamlet's return "the quick of th'ulcer" [IV. vii. 123]. It is surely obvious that these images cannot be used to reflect on Hamlet's character: they exhibit rather the King's guilty fear of his nephew.

Some of the disease images are used by Hamlet in reference to the Queen's adultery at which, he tells her, "Heaven's face . . . Is thought-sick" [III. iv. 48-51]. He urges her not to lay to her soul the "flattering unction" that he is mad:

> It will but skin and film the ulcerous place,
> Whiles rank corruption, mining all within,
> Infects unseen.
>
> [III. iv. 147-49]

Gertrude herself, suffering from pangs of remorse, speaks of her "sick soul".

Laertes uses three disease images, two in his warnings to Ophelia not to allow herself to be seduced by Hamlet since in youth

> Contagious blastments are most imminent.
>
> [I. iii. 42]

In the third he tells Claudius that the prospect of avenging himself "warms the very sickness" [IV. vii. 55] in his heart.

Hamlet uses one image to describe the cause of the war between Norway and Poland—

> the imposthume of much wealth and peace
> That inward breaks, and shows no cause without
> Why the man dies.
>
> [IV. iv. 27-9]

We have now examined nearly all the disease imagery without finding any evidence to support the view that Hamlet himself is diseased—the thing that is rotten in the state of Denmark. It is rather Claudius' crime and his guilty fears of Hamlet, and Gertrude's sin to which the imagery mainly refers; and in so far as it relates to the state of Denmark it emphasizes that what is wrong with the country is the unpunished fratricide committed by its ruler. But four disease images remain to be considered.

While Hamlet is waiting for his interview with his father's ghost he meditates on the drunkenness of the Court and of the way a single small defect in a man's character destroys his reputation and nullifies his virtues in the eyes of the world—"the general censure" [I. iv. 35]. The dram of evil,—some bad habit, an inherited characteristic, or "some vicious mole of nature"—

> Doth all the noble substance of a doubt.
>
>   [I. iv. 24-5]

The line is textually corrupt, but the general meaning of the passage is plain. Some critics, and Sir Laurence Olivier in his film of the play [see Sources for Further Study], have assumed that Hamlet, consciously or unconsciously, was thinking of the tragic flaw in his own character. But there is no reason to think that at this point in the play Hamlet suffers from some vicious mole of nature—he has not yet been tested. In any case he is not arguing that a single defect outweighs infinite virtues, but merely that it spoils a man's reputation. The lines cannot properly be applied to Hamlet himself.

Two more disease images occur in the speech in which Claudius is trying to persuade Laertes to murder Hamlet. He tells him that love is apt to fade,

> For goodness, growing to a plurisy
> Dies in his own too much : that we would
>   do
> We should do when we would.
>
>   [IV. vii. 117-19]

If we put it off,

>   this 'should' is like a spendthrift's
>   sigh
> That hurts by easing.
>
>   [IV. vii. 122-23]

The speech is designed to persuade Laertes to avenge his father's death without delay. But as Hamlet and Laertes are characters placed in a similar position, and as by this time Hamlet's vengeance has suffered abatements and delays, many critics have suggested that Shakespeare is commenting through the mouth of Claudius on Hamlet's failure to carry out his duty. It is not inherently impossible; but we should surely apply these lines to Hamlet's case only if we find by the use of more direct evidence that Shakespeare so conceived Hamlet's failure to carry out his duty.

Only one sickness image remains to be discussed, but this is the most famous one. In his soliloquy in Act III scene 1 (which begins "To be or not to be" [III. i. 55ff.]) Hamlet shows that thinking about the possible results of action is apt to inhibit it. People refrain from committing suicide (in spite of the miseries of this life) because they fear that death will be worse than life. They may, for example, be punished in hell for violating the canon against self-slaughter. Hamlet continues:

> Thus conscience does make cowards of us
>   all,
> And thus the native hue of resolution
> Is sicklied o'er with the pale cast of
>   thought,
> And enterprises of great pitch and mo-
>   ment
> With this regard their currents turn awry
> And lose the name of action.
>
>   [III. i. 82-7]

Obviously these lines are an important clue to the interpretation of the play. I used to think that conscience meant both "thinking too precisely on the event" and also the "craven scruple" of which Hamlet speaks in his last soliloquy—*conscience* as well as conscience, in fact. I now think the word is used (as in the words "the conscience of the King" [II. ii. 605]) only in its modern sense. Since Hamlet foresees that in taking vengeance on Claudius he may himself be killed, he hesitates—not because he is afraid of dying, but because he is afraid of being punished for his sins in hell or purgatory. But, as G. R. Elliott has pointed out [in his *Scourge and Minister*], Hamlet is speaking not merely of himself but of every man:

> Thus conscience does make cowards of us
>   all.
>
>   [III. i. 82]

It is apparent from this analysis of the sickness imagery in the play that it throws light on Elsinore rather than on Hamlet himself. He is not the diseased figure depicted by a long line of critics—or, at least, the imagery cannot justifiably be used in support of such an interpretation. On the other hand, the parallels which have been pointed out with Timothy Bright's *Treatise of Melancholy* do suggest that Shakespeare conceived his hero as suffering from melancholy. As depicted in the course of the play, he is not the paragon described by Ophelia, the observer of all observers, the glass of fashion,

> The expectancy and rose of the fair state.
>
>   [III. i. 152]

But it is necessary to emphasize that his melancholy has objective causes in the frailty of his mother and the death of his father.

Closely connected with the sickness imagery is what may loosely be called symbolism concerned with the odour of corruption. . . . Hamlet, like Webster in Eliot's poem, is much possessed by death. He speaks of the way the sun breeds maggots in a dead dog, he refers to the corpse of Polonius as "the guts"; he tells Claudius that the dead man is at supper at the diet of worms and he proceeds to show how a king may go a progress through the guts of a beggar. The Graveyard scene is designed not merely to provide a last expression of Hamlet's love for Ophelia, and an opportunity for screwing up Laertes' hatred of Hamlet to the sticking-point. This could have been done without the conversation between the gravediggers, and that between the gravedigger and Hamlet. The scene is clearly used to underline the death-theme. Hamlet's meditation on the various skulls serves as a *memento mori* [a reminder of mortality]. We are reminded of Cain, who did the first murder, of Lady Worms, "chapless and knocked about the mazard with a sexton's spade" [V. i. 89-90], of Yorick's stinking skull, and of the noble dust of Alexander which may be stopping a bung-hole. Hamlet is thinking of the base uses to which we may return; but his meditations in the graveyard, though somewhat morbid, are calmer and less bitter than his thoughts earlier in the play.

All through the play there are words and images which reinforce the idea of corruption. Hamlet, feeling himself to be contaminated by the frailty of his mother wishes that his sullied flesh would melt. He suspects "foul play" when he hears of the appearance of the ghost. The intemperance of the Danes makes foreigners *soil* their addition with swinish phrase. Denmark's ear is "rankly abused" by the false account of the death of Hamlet's father; and later Claudius, at his prayers confesses that his "offence is rank" [III. iii. 36]. The Ghost tells Hamlet that Lust

> Will sate itself in a celestial bed
> And prey on garbage.
>
> [I. v. 56-7]

Polonius speaks of his son's youthful vices as "the taints of liberty" [II. i. 32]. The air seems to Hamlet "a foul and pestilent congregation of vapours" [II. ii. 302-03] and he declares that if his uncle's guilt is not revealed, his

> imaginations are as foul
> As Vulcan's stithy.
>
> [III. ii. 83-4]

In the scene with his mother, Hamlet speaks of "the rank sweat of an enseamed bed"; he urges her not to "spread the compost on the weeds To make them ranker"; and he speaks of "rank corruption mining all within". The smell of sin blends with the odour of corruption. [III. iv. 92, 151-52, 148]

The only alleviation to this atmosphere is provided by the flowers associated with the "rose of May" [IV. v. 158], Ophelia. Laertes compares Hamlet's love for her to a violet; Ophelia warns her brother not to tread "the primrose path of dalliance" [I. ii. 50], and later she laments that the perfume of Hamlet's love is lost. In her madness she distributes flowers and the last picture we have of her alive is wearing "fantastic garlands". Laertes prays that violets may spring from her unpolluted flesh and the Queen scatters flowers in the grave with the words "Sweets to the sweet" [V. i. 243]. Hamlet, probably referring to his love for Ophelia, tells Gertrude that her adultery

> takes off the rose
> From the fair forehead of an innocent love
> And sets a blister there.
>
> [III. iv. 42-4]

The rose colour again reminds us of the flower. But the flowers and perfumes associated with Ophelia do not seriously counterbalance the odour of corruption.

A smaller group of images concerned with the harlot has several ramifications. In its simplest form, the harlot's cheek, "beautied with plastering art" [III. i. 50], is a symbol of hypocrisy, of the contrast between appearance and reality—the contrast between the King's deed and his "most painted word" [III. i. 52]. In the same scene Hamlet takes up the theme. He implies that, since harlots paint, women who paint, including the "beautified" Ophelia, are harlots. "God hath given you one face, and you make yourselves another" [III. i. 143]. Beauty is itself a snare because

> the power of beauty will sooner transform
> honesty from what it is to a bawd than the
> force of honesty can translate beauty into
> his likeness.
>
> [III. i. 110-13]

Hamlet tells his mother that "reason panders will" [III. iv. 88]; and he instructs Yorick's skull to get him "to my lady's chamber, and tell her, let her paint an inch thick, to this favour she must come" [V. i. 193-94]. Earlier in the play he treats Polonius as a pander, and Polonius speaks of "loosing" Ophelia to Hamlet, as though she were an animal to be mated. Both Laertes and his father assume that Hamlet will try to seduce Ophelia.

Hamlet himself is troubled by the contrast between appearance and reality, between seeming and sincerity and these harlot images reinforce the point. But the same imagery is used for a different purpose: a witty exchange between Hamlet and Rosencrantz and Guildenstern ends with the statement that Fortune is a strumpet. Later in the same scene, in the extract from the Dido play [II. ii. 493], Aeneas cries: "Out, out, thou strumpet, Fortune!" Hamlet tells Horatio that he admires him as one who is not passion's slave, one who has accepted "Fortune's buffets and rewards" [III. ii. 67], one who is

> not a pipe for Fortune's finger
> To sound what stop she please.
>
> [III. ii. 70-1]

In the same scene Hamlet asks Guildenstern:

> Do you think I am easier to be play'd on
> than a pipe?
>
> [III. ii. 369-70]

The Fortune theme is brought out in other ways—the Player King declares that it is not strange "That even our Loves should with our fortunes change" [III. ii. 201] and he gives as an example the desertion of a fallen great man by his favourites; Hamlet comments on the way courtiers who used to mock Claudius now wear his portrait round their necks and on the way the adult actors have lost their popularity; and Rosencrantz, in describing how the lives of subjects depend on the life of the King, uses the image of the wheel of Fortune.

I tried to show in my book on *Hamlet* [*Shakespeare: "Hamlet"*] that before the end of the play the fortune theme is modified. Instead of the strumpet fortune, the blind fate which directs our lives, we have the idea of a providence which directs our lives. Hamlet declares:

> There's a divinity that shapes our ends
> Rough-hew them how we will.
> [V. ii. 10-11]

This newly-found conviction enables him to face what he thinks may be his death, with the confidence that an opportunity will be provided for him to execute justice on his father's murderer: "We defy augury : there is a special providence in the fall of a sparrow" [V. ii. 219-20]. (pp. 353-58)

I have left to the end what by my reckoning is the largest group of images. This is derived not from sickness, but from war. Many of these war images may have been suggested by the elder Hamlet's campaigns and by the activities of Fortinbras; but we should remember that Prince Hamlet himself is not without martial qualities, and this fact is underlined by the rites of war ordered for his obsequies and by Fortinbras' final tribute. But the dramatic function of the imagery is no doubt to emphasise that Claudius and Hamlet are engaged in a duel to the death, a duel which does ultimately lead to both their deaths.

Hamlet speaks of himself and his uncle as mighty opposites, between whose "pass and fell incensed points" [V. ii. 61] Rosencrantz and Guildenstern had come. All through the play the war imagery reminds us of the struggle. Bernardo proposes to "assail" Horatio's ears which are "fortified against" his story. Claudius in his first speech tells of discretion fighting with nature and of the defeated joy of his wedding. Later in the scene he complains that Hamlet has a heart unfortified. Laertes urges his sister to "keep in the rear" of her affection,

> Out of the shot and danger of desire;
> [I. iii. 34-5]

and he speaks of the "calumnious strokes" sustained by virtue and of the danger of youth's rebellion. Ophelia promises to take Laertes' advice as a "watchman" to her heart. Polonius in the same scene carries on the same imagery : he urges her to set her "entreatments at a higher rate Than a command to parley" [I. iii. 122-23]. In the next scene Hamlet speaks of the way "the o'ergrowth of some complexion" breaks down "the pales and forts of reason" [I. iv. 27-8]. Polonius compares the

temptations of the flesh to a "general assault". The noise of Ilium's fall "takes prisoner Pyrrhus' ear" [II. ii. 477], and Pyrrhus' sword is "rebellious to his arm" [II. ii. 470]. Hamlet thinks the actor would "cleave the general ear with horrid speech", and says that "the clown shall make those laugh whose lungs are tickle o'th'sere" (*i.e.* easily set off) [II. ii. 563, 323-24]. He speaks of "the slings and arrows of outrageous fortune" and derides the King for being "frighted with false fire" [III. i. 57; III. ii. 266]. Rosencrantz talks of the "armour of the mind" [III. iii. 12] and Claudius admits that his "guilt defeats" his "strong intent" [III. iii. 40].

Hamlet fears that Gertrude's heart is so brazed by custom that it is "proof and bulwark against sense", and he speaks of the way "compulsive ardour" (sexual appetite) "gives the charge" [III. iv. 86]. He tells his mother that he will outwit Rosencrantz and Guildenstern:

> For 'tis the sport to have the engineer
> Hoist with his own petar; and it shall go
> hard
> But I will delve one yard below their mines
> And blow them at the moon.
> [III. iv. 206-09]

The Ghost speaks of Gertrude's 'fighting soul'. Claudius says that slander's whisper

> As level as the cannon to his blank
> Transports his pois'ned shot.
> [IV. i. 42-3]

He tells Gertrude that when sorrows come,

> They come not single spies
> But in battalions!
> [IV. v. 78-9]

and that Laertes' rebellion,

> Like to a murd'ring piece, in many places
> Gives me superfluous death.
> [IV. v. 95-6]

In explaining to Laertes why he could not openly proceed against Hamlet because of his popularity with the people, he says that his arrows,

> Too slightly timber'd for so loud a wind,
> Would have reverted to my bow again,
> But not where I have aim'd them.
> [IV. vii. 22-4]

Hamlet, in apologising to Laertes, says that his killing of Polonius was accidental:

> I have shot my arrow o'er the
> house
> And hurt my brother.
> [V. ii. 243-44]

(These last two images are presumably taken from archery rather than from battle.) Gertrude compares Hamlet's hairs to "sleeping soldiers in the alarm".

Six of the images are taken from naval warfare. Polonius tells Ophelia he thought Hamlet meant to *wreck* her [II. i. 110] and he advises Laertes to *grappe* his friends to his 'heart with hoops of steel' [I. iii. 63] and, in a later scene, he proposes to *board* the Prince [II. ii. 170]. Hamlet, quibbling on "crafts", tells his mother:

> O, 'tis most sweet
> When in one line two crafts directly meet.
> [III. iv. 209-10]

In the same scene he speaks of hell that *mutines* in a matron's bones; and, in describing his voyage to England, he tells Horatio:

> Methought I lay
> Worse than the mutines in the bilboes.
> [V. ii. 5-6]

In addition to the war images there are a large number of others that suggest violence. There are four images about knives, as when the Ghost tells Hamlet that his visitation is "to whet" his "almost blunted purpose" [III. iv. 111].

The images of war and violence should have the effect of counteracting some interpretations of the play, in which the psychology of the hero is regarded as the centre of interest. Equally important is the struggle between Hamlet and his uncle. Hamlet has to prove that the Ghost is not a devil in disguise, luring him to damnation, by obtaining objective evidence of Claudius' guilt. Claudius, for his part, is trying to pierce the secret of Hamlet's madness, using Rosencrantz and Guildenstern, Ophelia, and finally Gertrude as his instruments. Hamlet succeeds in his purpose, but in the very moment of success he enables Claudius to pierce the secret of his madness. Realising that his own secret murder has come to light, Claudius is bound to arrange for Hamlet's murder; and Hamlet, knowing that the truth of his antic disposition is now revealed to his enemy, realises that if he does not kill Claudius, Claudius will certainly kill him.

We have considered most of the patterns of imagery in the play—there are a few others which do not seem to throw much light on the meaning of the play—and I think it will be agreed that . . . the various image-patterns we have traced in *Hamlet* show that to concentrate on the sickness imagery, especially if it is divorced from its context, unduly simplifies the play. I do not pretend that a study of all the imagery will necessarily provide us with one—and only one—interpretation; but it will at least prevent us from assuming that the play is wholly concerned with the psychology of the hero. And that, I hope you will agree, is a step in the right direction. It may also prevent us from adopting the view of several modern critics—Wilson Knight, Rebecca West, Madariaga, L. C. Knights—who all seem to me to debase Hamlet's character to the extent of depriving him of the status of a tragic hero. It may also prevent us from assuming that the complexities of the play are due to Shakespeare's

failure to transform the melodrama he inherited, and to the survival of primitive traits in his otherwise sophisticated hero. (pp. 361-63)

> *Kenneth Muir, "Imagery and Symbolism in 'Hamlet'," in* Études Anglaises, *Vol. XVII, No. 4, October-December, 1964, pp. 352-63.*

HAMLET

George Detmold

[*Detmold addresses the question of why* **Hamlet** *delays taking revenge on* **Claudius** *by assessing his status as a tragic hero. According to the critic, a tragic hero has three prominent characteristics: (1) a will-power which surpasses that of average people, (2) an exceptionally intense power of feeling, and (3) an unusually high level of intelligence. From this definition of a tragic hero, Detmold especially focuses on* **Hamlet**'s *unorthodox demonstration of will-power in the play, arguing that the protagonist's preoccupation with moral integrity is what ultimately delays him from killing* **Claudius**. *Further, the critic asserts that Hamlet is distinct from other tragedies in that its action commences in the soliloquy of Act I, scene ii where most other tragedies end: "with the discovery by the tragic hero that his supreme good is forever lost to him." Perhaps the most significant reason why* **Hamlet** *hesitates, the critic concludes, is that although he is tempted by love, kingship, and even revenge, he is long past the point where he desires to do anything about them. None of these objectives gives him a new incentive for living. For further commentary on* **Hamlet**'s *character, see the excerpts by David Bevington, Maynard Mack, Robert Hapgood, Robert R. Reed, Jr., René Girard, Oscar James Campbell, Arthur Kirsch, Kenneth Muir, Edgar Johnson, Ernest Jones, Theodore Lidz and J. Dover Wilson.*]

Hamlet is surely the most perplexing character in English drama. Who has not sympathized with the Court of Denmark in their bewilderment at his mercurial conduct? Theatre-goers, to be sure, are seldom baffled by him; perhaps the spectacle and melodrama of his undoing are powerful enough to stifle any mere doubts about his motives. But the more dispassionate audience of scholars and critics—if one may judge from the quantity of their published remarks—are often baffled. Seeking an intellectual satisfaction which will correspond to the pleasant purging of pity and terror in the spectator, they are only perplexed by Hamlet's behavior. They fail to understand his motives. How can a man so dilatory, who misses every opportunity to achieve what apparently he desires, who requires nearly three months to accomplish a simple and well-justified killing—how can such a man be classed a tragic hero? Is he not merely weak and contemptible? How can he be ranked with such forceful men as Lear, Macbeth, Othello, or even Romeo? And yet he is a great tragic hero, as the playgoers will testify. The spectacle of his doings and undoing is profoundly stirring; it rouses the most intense emotions of awe and admiration; it never moves us to scorn or contempt.

In order to understand Hamlet, we must be able to answer the old question about him: "Why does he delay?" Granting—as he does—that he has sufficient "cause, and will, and strength, and means" [IV. iv. 45] to avenge his father, why should he require approximately three months to do so, and then succeed almost purely by accident or afterthought? There is only one possible reason why a strong, vigorous, intelligent man does not kill another when he feels no revulsion against the deed, when his duty requires that he do it, when he is not afraid, when the man to be killed is not invulnerable, and when the consequences of the act are either inconsiderable or are not considered at all. Hamlet delays to kill his uncle only because he has little interest in doing so. His thoughts are elsewhere. Most of the time he forgets about it, as we forget about a letter that should be answered—and only occasionally does he remember it and ponder his reluctance to perform this simple duty. Rightly or wrongly, he is preoccupied with other things.

Yet revenge, especially when it entails murder, is a tremendously important affair; how can any man overlook it? What kind of man can consider what kind of thing more important? Is Hamlet in any way unique, beyond or above or apart from our experience of human nature? Let us examine him as a man and—more important—as a tragic hero.

We must realize that there is nothing curious or abnormal about him. He is recognizably human; he is not diseased or insane. If this were not so he would rouse no admiration in an audience, for it will never accord to a sick or crazy man the allegiance it usually gives to the tragic hero. The normal attitude toward abnormality is one of aversion. We worship strength and health and power, and will identify ourselves with the hero who displays these qualities. We may even identify ourselves with a Lear during his temporary insanity, but only because we have known him sane and can appreciate the magnitude of his disaster. For the Fool who is his companion we can feel only a detached and tender compassion. Hamlet rouses stronger emotions than these, and only because we can recognize ourselves in him, because he is in the finest sense a universal man: Homo sapiens, man thinking—and man feeling, man acting. The proper habitat of the freak is the side-show or museum, not the stage.

But within this humanity and universality we may distinguish three characteristics which are usually found in the tragic hero. The first of these is a will-power surpassing in its intensity anything displayed by average men; the hero admits of no obstacle and accepts no compromise; he drives forward with all his strength to his desired goal. The second is a power of feeling likewise more intense than that possessed by average men; he rises to heights of happiness forever unattainable to the majority of us, and correspondingly sinks to depths of misery. The third is an unusually high intelligence, displayed in his actions and in his power of language. Aristotle sums up these characteristics in the term *hamartia:* the tragic flaw, the failure of judgment, the refusal to compromise. Passionately pursuing the thing he desires, the hero is incapable of compromise, of the calm exercise of judgment.

It will be seen that Hamlet possesses these three characteristics. His power of feeling surpasses that of all other characters in the play, expresses itself in the impassioned poetic diction peculiar to great tragedy. His intelligence is subtle and all-embracing, displaying itself not only in his behavior but also in word-plays beyond the comprehension of the others in the drama, and in metaphors beyond their attainment. But what can be said of his will-power, the one pre-eminently heroic characteristic? He is apparently a model of hesitation, indecision, procrastination; we seem to be witnessing an examination of the failure of his will. And yet demonstrably it has not failed, and does at odd moments stir itself violently. In no other way can we account for the timidity of his enemies, the respect of his friends, and his own frank acknowledgement that he has "cause, and will, and strength, and means" to avenge his father. And though he is a long time in killing Claudius, he does kill him at last, and he is capable of other actions which argue the rash and impulsive nature of a man with strong will. He will "make a ghost" [I. iv. 85] of any man who tries to prevent him from following his father's spirit. He murders Polonius. He engineers the murder of Rosencrantz and Guildenstern. He boards the pirate ship single-handed. He takes so long to kill Claudius only because he has little interest in revenge—not because he lacks will, but because it is inactive. Will-power does not spread itself in a circle around the possessor, but lies in a straight line toward the thing he desires.

Hamlet, then, has the heroic traits of Lear, Othello, Tamburlaine, Macbeth, and Oedipus: high intelligence, deep sensitivity, and strong will. There is another characteristic of the tragic hero without which the former ones would never be perceived: his delusion that there is some one thing in the world supremely good or desirable, the possession of which will make him supremely happy. And to the acquisition of the thing he desires he devotes all his will, all his intelligence, all his power of feeling. Thus Romeo dedicates himself to the pursuit of love, Macbeth to power, Lear to filial gratitude—and Hamlet to moral beauty.

Hamlet's dedication to moral beauty is not difficult to perceive; and once understood, it explains his every action in the play. It is probably an unusual subject for devotion: love, honor, power, wealth, intellectual supremacy are the more customary idols of the tragic hero. Yet Hamlet seems a more normal character than Coriolanus or Barabas [in Christopher Marlowe's *The Jew of Malta*], and a more sympathetic one than Macbeth or Othello. There should be nothing unusual in a preoccupation with morality, since man is a moral animal as well as a greedy, a passionate, or an intelligent one. And there is nothing harsh or unlovely in Hamlet's conception of the good. He is no Puritan. What he seeks among men is not mere compliance with religious and ethical standards, but a moral loveliness in their thoughts and actions. Men, in his conception, are godlike; they should not conduct themselves like beasts. "What a piece of work is a man! how noble in reason! how infinite in faculties! in form and moving how express and admirable! in action how like an angel, in apprehension how like a god!" [II. ii. 303-07]—whether the words are spoken in seriousness or in irony they argue a deepseated idealism in their author.

It is clear that, at some point before the opening of the play, Hamlet has been completely disillusioned. He has failed to discover moral beauty in the world; indeed, by the intensity of his search he has roused instead his supreme evil: moral ugliness. The majority of us, the non-heroes, might disapprove of the sudden remarriage of a mother after the death of her husband—but we would probably not be nauseated. Hamlet, supremely sensitive to the godliness and beastliness in men, was overwhelmed by what he could interpret as nothing but lust. To be sure, the marriage of his mother and uncle was technically incestuous. But his objection to it lies much deeper than surface technicalities. He has worshipped his father, adored his mother (his love for her is everywhere apparent beneath his bitterness). Gertrude has mourned at the funeral "like Niobe, all tears" [I. ii. 149]. And then within a month she has married his uncle—a vulgar, contemptible, scheming drunkard—exposing without shame her essentially shallow, thoughtless, amoral, animal nature.

The blow has been too much for Hamlet, sensitive as he is to moral beauty.

> O, most wicked speed, to post
> With such dexterity to incestuous sheets!
> It is not, nor it cannot come to good.
> [I. ii. 156-58]

That is, it cannot come to his conception of the good, whatever may be said for Gertrude's. He is unable to offer her understanding or sympathy, since to do so would mean compromising with his ideal of her. He fails to realize that no amount of scolding will ever improve her. Instead of accepting her conduct as inevitable or even endurable, he fights it, exaggerates it into a disgusting and an intolerable sin against everything he holds dear. And because the sin may not be undone, and since it has destroyed his pleasure and purpose in living, he wishes to die. The only thing that restrains him from suicide is the moral injunction against it:

> O that this too too sullied flesh would melt,
> Thaw and resolve itself into a dew,
> Or that the Everlasting had not fix'd
> His canon 'gainst self-slaughter.
> [I. ii. 129-32]

The longing for death, once the supreme good has been destroyed, is entirely normal and usual in the tragic hero. Romeo, hearing that Juliet is dead, goes immediately to her tomb in order to kill himself:

> O, here
> Will I set up my everlasting rest
> And shake the yoke of inauspicious stars
> From this world-wearied flesh. . . .
> Thou desperate pilot, now at once run on
> The dashing rocks thy sea-sick weary
> bark.
> [*Romeo and Juliet*, V. iii. 110-14]

Othello, when he realizes that in seeking to preserve his honor he has ruined it, prepares to die in much the same state of mind:

> Here is my journey's end, here is my butt
> And very sea-mark of my utmost sail.
> [*Othello*, V. ii. 267-68]

Macbeth, discovering at last that his frantic efforts to maintain and increase his power have only destroyed it, finds life a tale told by an idiot—and he too longs for death:

> I 'gin to be a-weary of the sun,
> And wish the estate of the world were now
> undone.
> Ring the alarum bell. Blow wind, come
> wrack,
> At least we'll die with harness on our back.
> [*Macbeth*, V. v. 48-51]

Lear, instead of dying, is driven mad. His counterpart, Gloucester, who also has lived for the love of his children, tries to throw himself from the cliff at Dover. Oedipus [in Sophocles's *Oedipus Rex*], too, when he discovers that he has ruined the city he tried to save, finds life worthless—blinds himself, and begs to be cast out of Thebes. As a general rule, whenever the tragic hero discovers that in his efforts to attain his supreme good he has only aroused his supreme evil, he kills himself, or goes mad, or otherwise sinks into a state that is death compared to his former state. Once he has lost all hope of gaining what he desires, he quite naturally finds no reason for continuing to live. Life in itself is always meaningless to him; he lives only for the good that he can find in it.

The curious thing about *Hamlet* is that it begins at the point where most other tragedies end: with the discovery by the tragic hero that his supreme good is forever lost to him. The play is surely unique among great tragedies. Elizabethan drama usually presents a double reversal of fortune—the rise and fall in the hero's prosperity and happiness—or sometimes, as in *King Lear,* the fall and rise. Greek tragedy, limited to a single curtainless stage and thus to a late point of attack in the plot, could show only a single reversal—usually the fall in fortune from prosperity to misery, as is observed by Aristotle. But certainly nowhere else is there a tragedy like *Hamlet,* with no reversal at all, which begins after the rise and fall of the hero have taken place, in which the action does not coincide with his pursuit of the good, and which presents him throughout in despair and in bad fortune. We never see Hamlet striving for or possessing his good. Rather, he knows only the evil which is its counterpart; and in this unhappy condition he finds nothing further desirable except death. The kingship does not interest him; love does not interest him; revenge never interests him for long. He can think only about the foulness of mankind, of the beastly conduct of those people from whom he has expected the most godly—and in his despair he is intensely unhappy. Death, he knows, will be his only release. We find him longing for death at the outset of the play, in his first speech to us. Death is continually on his mind until he finally attains it at the end, the only "felicity" of which life is capable.

We are now in a position to understand why Hamlet takes so long to effect his revenge. Everyone in the play, including himself, recognizes that he is potentially dangerous, that he has the necessary courage and will to accomplish anything he desires. But the demand upon these qualities has come at a time when he has forever lost interest in exercising them. Upholding the divinity of man, he is betrayed by the one he thought most divine, exposed to her rank shameless adultery, bitterly disillusioned in all mankind, and desperate of any further good in existence. The revelation by the Ghost that murder has cleared a way for the new husband shocks Hamlet to the base of his nature, but it gives him no new incentive for living; it merely adds to his misfortune and confirms him in his despair. The further information that his mother has committed adultery provides a final shock. All evidence establishes him immovably in his disillusion. The Ghost's appeal to him for revenge is, remotely, an appeal to his good: if he may not reestablish the moral beauty of the world he may at least punish those who have violated it. But it is a distant appeal. The damage already done is irreparable. After giving passionate promises to "remember" his father, he regrets them:

> The time is out of joint; O cursed spite,
> That ever I was born to set it right.
>
> [I. v. 188-89]

Within ten minutes after his first meeting with the Ghost he has succumbed again to his anguish, which is now so intense after the discovery of his mother's adultery and the murder of his father that his mind threatens to crack under the strain. His conversation with his friends is so strange that Horatio comments upon it:

> These are but wild and whirling words,
>   my lord.
>
> [I. v. 133]

A few minutes later Hamlet announces his intention to feign madness, to assume an "antic disposition"—presumably as a means of relieving his surcharged feelings and possibly forestalling true madness, but certainly not as a means of deceiving Claudius and thus accomplishing his revenge. At the moment there is no point in deceiving Claudius, who knows of no witnesses to the murder and who is more vulnerable to attack now than he will be at any point later in the play.

Two months later the antic disposition has succeeded only in arousing the King's suspicions. Hamlet has not effected his revenge; there is no sign that he has even thought about it. All we know is that he is badly upset—as Ophelia reports to her father:

> My lord, as I was sewing in my closet,
> Lord Hamlet, with his doublet all un-
>   brac'd,
> No hat upon his head, his stockings foul'd,
> Ungartered and down-gyved to his ancle,
> Pale as his shirt, his knees knocking each
>   other,
> And with a look so piteous in purport
> As if he had been loosed out of hell
> To speak of horrors, he comes before me,
>
> [II. i. 74-81]

It is doubtful that he wishes to deceive the court into thinking that he is mad with unrequited love—only the fool Polonius is so deceived. Most probably he goes to Ophelia because he loves her as he loves his mother, and fears to discover in her the same corruption that has poisoned his mind towards Gertrude. He suspects that her love for him is insincere; his suspicions are later reinforced when he catches her acting as the decoy of Claudius and Polonius. But the one significant thing here is that his mind is still upon his old sorrow and not upon his father.

He does not recall his father until the First Player, in reciting the woes of Troy, speaks of the "mobled queen" who

>   saw Pyrrhus make malicious
>   sport
> In mincing with his sword her husband's
>   limbs.
>
> [II. ii. 513-14]

Shortly afterwards Hamlet asks him to "play the

Murder of Gonzago" and to "study a speech of some dozen lines, which I would set down and insert in 't" [II. ii. 541-42]. This, as we learn in the following soliloquy, is to be a trap for the conscience of Claudius. And why is a trap necessary? Because perhaps the Ghost was not a true ghost, but a devil trying to lure him to damnation. Most likely Hamlet is here rationalizing, trying to find an excuse for his dilatoriness, for forgetting the injunction of his father—yet the excuse is a poor one, for never before has he questioned the authenticity of the Ghost. Furthermore, he does not wait for the trap to be sprung; throughout the performance of "The Mousetrap" he seems convinced of the guilt of Claudius, he taunts him with it. But for a while he has stilled his own conscience and found a refuge from the flood of self-incrimination.

Before "The Murder of Gonzago" is enacted we see Hamlet alone once more. What is on his mind? His uncle? His father? Revenge? Not at all. "To be, or not to be, that is the question" [III. i. 55ff.]. He is back where he started, and where he has been all along, with

> The heart-ache, and the thousand natural
>   shocks
> That flesh is heir to.
>   [III. i. 61-2]

He is still preoccupied with death.

"The Mousetrap" convicts Claudius beyond any doubt; he bolts from the room, unable to endure for a second time the poisoning of a sleeping king. And yet Hamlet, fifteen minutes later, with an admirable opportunity to kill his uncle, fails to do so—for reasons that are evidently obscure even to himself. He wishes, he says, not only to kill the man, but to damn his soul as well, and thus will wait to kill him unconfessed. At this, apparently, the Ghost itself loses patience, for it returns once more to Hamlet in the next scene and exhorts him:

> Do not forget: this visitation
> Is but to whet thy almost blunted purpose.
>   [III. iv. 110-11]

The exhortation is wasted. On the same night, Hamlet allows the King to send him to England. Possibly he has no recourse but obedience; probably he knows what is in store for him; quite likely he does not care, may even welcome a legitimate form of dying; certainly he cannot, in England, arrange to kill his uncle. The next day, on his way to exile and death, he meets the army of Fortinbras, whose courage and purposefulness stimulate him to reflect upon his own conduct:

> How all occasions do inform against me,
> And spur my dull revenge!
>   [IV. iv. 32-3]

He considers how low he has sunk in his despair:

> What is a man,
> If his chief good and market of his time

Be but to sleep and feed? A beast, no more.
>   [IV. iv. 33-4]

Lamenting nothing in men so much as their beastliness, he has become little better than a beast himself. Why has he not performed the simple act of vengeance required by his dead father? He does not know:

> Now, whether it be
> Bestial oblivion, or some craven scruple
> Of thinking too precisely on the event,—
> A thought which, quartered, hath but one
>   part wisdom
> And ever three parts coward,—I do not
>   know
> Why yet I live to say 'This thing's to do,'
> Sith I have cause, and will, and strength,
>   and means
> To do 't.
>   [IV. iv. 39-46]

He is ashamed to have forgotten his duty:

> How stand I then,
> That have a father kill'd, a mother stain'd,
> Excitements of my reason and my blood,
> And let all sleep . . . ?
>   [IV. iv. 56-9]

And with the resolve:

> O, from this time forth,
> My thoughts be bloody, or be nothing
>   worth!
>   [IV. iv. 65-6]

he is off for England, where even the bloodiest thoughts will be utterly of no avail.

When he returns he is unchanged, still preoccupied with death. He haunts the graveyard with Horatio, reflects upon the democratizing influence of corruption. Overcome with disgust at the "rant" at Ophelia's funeral (he has seen too much insincerity at funerals), he wrestles with Laertes. He acquaints Horatio with the crimes of Claudius and resolves to revenge himself—and then accepts the invitation to the fencing match, aware that it is probably a trap, but resigned to whatever fate is in store for him. And with the discovery of his uncle's final perfidy, he stabs him with the envenomed foil and forces the poisoned wine down his throat. But there is still no thought of his father or of the accomplishment of an old purpose. He is stirred to action principally by anger at his mother's death:

> Here, thou incestuous, murderous,
>   damned Dane,
> Drink off this potion: is thy union here?
> Follow my mother.
>   [V. ii. 325-27]

The murder of Claudius is simply accomplished. We see how easily it could have been managed at any time in the past by a man like Hamlet, with whatever tools might have come to his hand. Even though the King is fully awake to his peril he is powerless to avert it. The only thing necessary is that Hamlet should at some time choose to kill him.

That Hamlet finally does so choose is the result of accident and afterthought. The envenomed foil, the poisoned wine, Laertes and Gertrude and himself betrayed to their deaths—these things finally arouse him and he strikes out at the King. But he has no sense of achievement at the end, no final triumph over unimaginable obstacles. His uncle, alive or dead, is a side-issue. His dying thoughts are of the blessedness of death and of the sanctity of his reputation—he would clear it of any suggestion of moral evil but realizes that he has no time left to do so himself. Accordingly he charges Horatio to stay alive a little while longer:

> Absent thee from felicity a while,
> And in this harsh world draw thy breath
>   in pain,
> To tell my story.
>
>   [V. ii. 347-49]

Then, after willing the kingdom to Fortinbras, he sinks into the oblivion which he has courted so long, and which now comes to him honorably and gives him rest. (pp. 23-34)

> *George Detmold, "Hamlet's 'All but Blunted Purpose'," in* The Shakespeare Association Bulletin, *Vol. XXIV, No. 1, January, 1949, pp. 23-36.*

Ernest Jones

[Jones applies Sigmund Freud's techniques of psychoanalysis to **Hamlet***'s character, asserting that the prince is afflicted with an Oedipus Complex. This psychological disorder involves the unconscious desire of a son to kill his father and take his place as the object of the mother's love. According to the critic,* **Hamlet** *delays taking revenge on* **Claudius** *because he identifies with his uncle and shares his guilt. Thus* **Hamlet***'s inaction stems from a "tortured conscience," and his affliction is caused by "repressed" feelings. Furthermore, this theory accounts for* **Hamlet***'s speaking to* **Gertrude** *like a jealous lover, dwelling on his mother's sexual relations with* **Claudius,** *and treating his uncle like a rival. Significantly, the critic also claims that while his father's murder evokes "indignation" in* **Hamlet,** **Gertrude***'s perceived "incest" awakes his "intensest horror." In addition, Jones maintains that the prince suffers from "psychoneurosis," or "a state of mind where the person is unduly, often painfully, driven or thwarted by the 'unconscious' part of his mind." This internal mental conflict reflects* **Hamlet***'s condition throughout much of the play. For further commentary on* **Hamlet***'s character, see the excerpts by David Bevington, Maynard Mack, Robert Hapgood, Robert R. Reed, Jr., René Girard, Oscar James Campbell, Arthur Kirsch, Kenneth Muir, George Detmold,*

Edgar Johnson, Theodore Lidz and J. Dover Wilson.]

[The] whole picture presented by Hamlet, his deep depression, the hopeless note in his attitude towards the world and towards the value of life, his dread of death, his repeated reference to bad dreams, his self-accusations, his desperate efforts to get away from the thoughts of his duty, and his vain attempts to find an excuse for his procrastination; all this unequivocally points to a *tortured conscience,* to some hidden ground for shirking his task, a ground which he dare not or cannot avow to himself. We have, therefore, . . . to seek for some evidence that may serve to bring to light the hidden counter-motive.

The extensive experience of the psycho-analytic researches carried out by Freud and his school during the past half-century has amply demonstrated that certain kinds of mental process show a greater tendency to be inaccessible to consciousness (put technically, to be "repressed") than others. In other words, it is harder for a person to realize the existence in his mind of some mental trends than it is of others. In order therefore to gain a proper perspective it is necessary briefly to inquire into the relative frequency with which various sets of mental processes are "repressed." Experience shows that this can be correlated with the degree of compatibility of these various sets with the ideals and standards accepted by the conscious ego; the less compatible they are with these the more likely are they to be "repressed." As the standards acceptable to consciousness are in considerable measure derived from the immediate environment, one may formulate the following generalization: those processes are most likely to be "repressed" by the individual which are most disapproved of by the particular circle of society to whose influence he has chiefly been subjected during the period when his character was being formed. Biologically stated, this law would run: "That which is unacceptable to the herd becomes unacceptable to the individual member," it being understood that the term herd is intended here in the sense of the particular circle defined above, which is by no means necessarily the community at large. It is for this reason that moral, social, ethical, or religious tendencies are seldom "repressed," for, since the individual originally received them from his herd, they can hardly ever come into conflict with the dicta of the latter. This merely says that a man cannot be ashamed of that which he respects; the apparent exceptions to this rule need not be here explained.

The language used in the previous paragraph will have indicated that by the term "repression" we denote an active dynamic process. Thoughts that are "repressed" are actively kept from consciousness by a definite force and with the expenditure of more or less mental effort, though the person

John Gielgud as Hamlet and Frank Vosper as Claudius in Gielgud's 1934 New Theatre production of Hamlet. *Act III, scene iii.*

concerned is rarely aware of this. Further, what is thus kept from consciousness typically possesses an energy of its own; hence our frequent use of such expressions as "trend," "tendency," etc. A little consideration of the genetic aspects of the matter will make it comprehensible that the trends most likely to be "repressed" are those belonging to what are called the innate impulses, as contrasted with secondarily acquired ones. . . . It only remains to add the obvious corollary that, as the herd unquestionably selects from the "natural" instincts the sexual one on which to lay its heaviest ban, so it is the various psycho-sexual trends that are most often "repressed" by the individual. We have here the explanation of the clinical experience that the more intense and the more obscure is a given case of deep mental conflict the more certainly will it be found on adequate analysis to centre about a sexual problem. On the surface, of course, this does not appear so, for, by means of various psychological defensive mechanisms, the depression, doubt, despair, and other manifestations of the conflict are transferred on to more tolerable and permissible topics, such as anxiety about worldly success or failure, about immortality and the salvation of the soul, philosophical con-

siderations about the value of life, the future of the world, and so on.

Bearing these considerations in mind, let us return to Hamlet. . . . We . . . realize—as his words so often indicate—that the positive striving for vengeance, the pious task laid on him by his father, was to him the moral and social one, the one approved of by his consciousness, and that the "repressed" inhibiting striving against the act of vengeance arose in some hidden source connected with his more personal, natural instincts. The former striving . . . indeed is manifest in every speech in which Hamlet debates the matter: the second is, from its nature, more obscure and has next to be investigated.

This is perhaps most easily done by inquiring more intently into Hamlet's precise attitude towards the object of his vengeance, Claudius, and towards the crimes that have to be avenged. These are two: Claudius' incest with the Queen, and his murder of his brother. Now it is of great importance to note the profound difference in Hamlet's attitude towards these two crimes. Intellectually of course he abhors both, but there can be no question as to which arouses in him the deeper loathing. Whereas the murder of his father evokes in him indignation and a plain recognition of his obvious duty to avenge it, his mother's guilty conduct awakes in him the intensest horror. (pp. 64-8)

Now, in trying to define Hamlet's attitude towards his uncle we have to guard against assuming offhand that this is a simple one of mere execration, for there is a possibility of complexity arising in the following way: The uncle has not merely committed *each* crime, he has committed *both* crimes, a distinction of considerable importance, since the *combination* of crimes allows the admittance of a new factor, produced by the possible inter-relation of the two, which may prevent the result from being simply one of summation. In addition, it has to be borne in mind that the perpetrator of the crimes is a relative, and an exceedingly near relative. The possible inter-relationship of the crimes, and the fact that the author of them is an actual member of the family, give scope for a confusion in their influence on Hamlet's mind which may be the cause of the very obscurity we are seeking to clarify.

Let us first pursue further the effect on Hamlet of his mother's misconduct. Before he even knows with any certitude, however much he may suspect it, that his father has been murdered he is in the deepest depression, and evidently on account of this misconduct. (p. 69)

According to [A. C.] Bradley, [in his *Shakespearean Tragedy*], Hamlet's melancholic disgust at life was the cause of his aversion from "any kind of decided action." His explanation of the whole problem of Hamlet is "the moral shock of the sudden ghastly disclosure of his mother's true nature," and he regards the effect of this shock, as depicted in the play, as fully comprehensible. He says:

> Is it possible to conceive an experience more desolating to a man such as we have seen Hamlet to be; and is its result anything but perfectly natural? It brings bewildered horror, then loathing, then despair of human nature. His whole mind is poisoned . . . A nature morally blunter would have felt even so dreadful a revelation less keenly. A slower and more limited and positive mind might not have extended so widely through the world the disgust and disbelief that have entered it.

But we can rest satisfied with this seemingly adequate explanation of Hamlet's weariness of life only if we accept unquestioningly the conventional standards of the causes of deep emotion. Many years ago [John] Connolly, a well-known psychiatrist, pointed out [in his *A Study of Hamlet*] the disproportion here existing between cause and effect, and gave as his opinion that Hamlet's reaction to his mother's marriage indicated in itself a mental instability, "a predisposition to actual unsoundness"; he writes: "The circumstances are not such as would at once turn a healthy mind to the contemplation of suicide, the last resource of those whose reason has been overwhelmed by calamity and despair." In T. S. Eliot's opinion, also, Hamlet's emotion is in excess of the facts as they appear, and he specially contrasts it with Gertrude's negative and insignificant personality [in his *The Sacred Wood*] . . . We have unveiled only the exciting cause, not the predisposing cause. The very fact that Hamlet is apparently content with the explanation arouses our misgiving, for, as will presently be expounded, from the very nature of the emotion he cannot be aware of the true cause of it. If we ask, not what ought to produce such soul-paralysing grief and distaste for life, but what in actual fact does produce it, we are compelled to go beyond this explanation and seek for some deeper cause. In real life speedy second marriages occur commonly enough without leading to any such result as is here depicted, and when we see them followed by this result we invariably find, if the opportunity for an analysis of the subject's mind presents itself, that there is some other and more hidden reason why the event is followed by this inordinately great effect. The reason always is that the event has awakened to increased activity mental processes that have been "repressed" from the subject's consciousness. His mind has been specially prepared for the catastrophe by previous mental processes with which those directly resulting from the event have entered into association. . . . In short, the special nature of the reaction presupposes some special feature in the mental predisposition. Bradley himself has to qualify his hypothesis by inserting the words "to a man such as we have seen Hamlet to be."

We come at this point to the vexed question of Hamlet's sanity, about which so many controversies have raged. Dover Wilson authoritatively writes [in his *What Happens in Hamlet*]: "I agree with Loening, Bradley and others that Shakespeare meant us to imagine Hamlet as suffering from some kind of mental disorder throughout the play." The question is what kind of mental disorder and what is its significance dramatically and psychologically. The matter is complicated by Hamlet's frequently displaying simulation (the Antic Disposition), and it has been asked whether this is to conceal his real mental disturbance or cunningly to conceal his purposes in coping with the practical problems of this task? (pp. 70-3)

What we are essentially concerned with is the psychological understanding of the dramatic effect produced by Hamlet's personality and behaviour. That effect would be quite other were the central figure in the play to represent merely a "case of insanity." When that happens, as with Ophelia, such a person passes beyond our ken, is in a sense no more human, whereas Hamlet successfully claims our interest and sympathy to the very end. Shakespeare certainly never intended us to regard Hamlet as insane, so that the "mind o'erthrown" must have some other meaning than its literal one. Robert Bridges has described the matter with exquisite delicacy [in his *The Testament of Beauty*, I]:

> Hamlet himself would never have been aught to us, or we
> To Hamlet, wer't not for the artful balance whereby
> Shakespeare so gingerly put his sanity in doubt
> Without the while confounding his Reason.

I would suggest that in this Shakespeare's extraordinary powers of observation and penetration granted him a degree of insight that it has taken the world three subsequent centuries to reach. Until our generation (and even now in the juristic sphere) a dividing line separated the sane and responsible from the irresponsible insane. It is now becoming more and more widely recognized that much of mankind lives in an intermediate and unhappy state charged with what Dover Wilson well calls "that sense of frustration, futility and human inadequacy which is the burden of the whole symphony" and of which Hamlet is the supreme example in literature. This intermediate plight, in the toils of which perhaps the greater part of mankind struggles and suffers, is given the name of psychoneurosis, and long ago the genius of Shakespeare depicted it for us with faultless insight.

Extensive studies of the past half century, inspired by Freud, have taught us that a psychoneurosis means a state of mind where the person is unduly, and often painfully, driven or thwarted by the "unconscious" part of his mind, that buried part that was once the infant's mind and still lives on side by side with the adult mentality that has developed out of it and should have taken its place. It signifies *internal* mental conflict. We have here the reason why it is impossible to discuss intelligently the state of mind of anyone suffering from a psychoneurosis, whether the description is of a living person or an imagined one, without correlating the manifestations with what must have operated in his infancy and is *still operating*. That is what I propose to attempt here.

For some deep-seated reason, which is to him unacceptable, Hamlet is plunged into anguish at the thought of his father being replaced in his mother's affections by someone else. It is as if his devotion to his mother had made him so jealous for her affection that he had found it hard enough to share this even with his father and could not endure to share it with still another man. Against this thought, however, suggestive as it is, may be urged three objections. First, if it were in itself a full statement of the matter, Hamlet would have been aware of the jealousy, whereas we have concluded that the mental process we are seeking is hidden from him. Secondly, we see in it no evidence of the arousing of an old and forgotten memory. And,

thirdly, Hamlet is being deprived by Claudius of no greater share in the Queen's affection than he had been by his own father, for the two brothers made exactly similar claims in this respect—namely, those of a loved husband. The last-named objection, however, leads us to the heart of the situation. How if, in fact, Hamlet had in years gone by, as a child, bitterly resented having had to share his mother's affection even with his own father, had regarded him as a rival, and had secretly wished him out of the way so that he might enjoy undisputed and undisturbed the monopoly of that affection? If such thoughts had been present in his mind in childhood days they evidently would have been "repressed," and all traces of them obliterated, by filial piety and other educative influences. The actual realization of his early wish in the death of his father at the hands of a jealous rival would then have stimulated into activity these "repressed" memories, which would have produced, in the form of depression and other suffering, an obscure aftermath of his childhood's conflict. This is at all events the mechanism that is actually found in the real Hamlets who are investigated psychologically.

The explanation, therefore, of the delay and self-frustration exhibited in the endeavour to fulfil his father's demand for vengeance is that to Hamlet the thought of incest and parricide combined is too intolerable to be borne. One part of him tries to carry out the task, the other flinches inexorably from the thought of it. How fain would he blot it out in that "bestial oblivion" which unfortunately for him his conscience contemns. He is torn and tortured in an insoluble inner conflict. (pp. 76-9)

> *Ernest Jones, "The Psycho-Analytical Solution," in his* Hamlet and Oedipus, *1949. Reprint by Doubleday & Company, Inc., 1954, pp. 51-79.*

Edgar Johnson

[*Johnson discusses the major interpretations of* **Hamlet**'s *character that have evolved over the past two centuries, concluding with Ernest Jones's Freudian reading of the role (see excerpt above). The critic takes particular exception to Jones's view of* **Hamlet,** *asserting that if such a perspective were true, there would be no moral dilemma in the tragedy. Johnson then details his own interpretation of the protagonist as a hero whose complex dilemma is "to disentangle himself from the temptation to wreak justice for the wrong reasons and in an evil passion, and to do what he must do at last for the pure sake of justice, for the welfare of the State, to weed the unweeded garden of Denmark and set right the time that is out of joint." The critic also focuses on the concept of appearance versus reality in* Hamlet, *applying this issue to the characters of* **Hamlet, Claudius, Polonius,** *and* **Laertes.** *For further com-*

*mentary on **Hamlet**'s character, see the excerpts by David Bevington, Maynard Mack, Robert Hapgood, Robert R. Reed, Jr., René Girard, Oscar James Campbell, Arthur Kirsch, Kenneth Muir, George Detmold, Theodore Lidz and J. Dover Wilson.]*

I

Hamlet is a play and Hamlet is a character in that play. In exploring our topic, "The Dilemma of Hamlet," although the problem of the play and the problem of the man are tightly interknit, it is important for us to keep clearly in mind when we are talking about the one and when about the other.

My thesis about the play is that its leading theme is the relationship of appearance and reality—that its dilemma, or the series of dilemmas it poses for us, so to speak, is the difficulty of distinguishing between the actuality and the plausible appearance of wisdom or virtue or right action. This note is struck almost at the beginning, with Hamlet's acid, "I know not 'seems'" [I. ii. 76], and his hatred of hypocrisy and deception, coming hard upon his own distrustful and evasive answers to Horatius and Marcellus after speaking with his father's ghost, and followed immediately by his assumption of an "antic disposition" apparently designed to deceive Claudius and the Court into believing him insane, but leaving the spectator as well sometimes uncertain whether Hamlet's madness is assumed or whether his reason is breaking down under inward emotional strain. Madness and sanity, true wisdom and corruptly shrewd worldliness, real kingly leadership and tricky opportunism, genuine heroism and its showy counterfeit; these are some of the distinctions the play challenges us to make. But they lead us to Hamlet the man, about whom my thesis—partly paralleling that of G. R. Elliott [in his *Scourge and Minister: A Study of "Hamlet" As Tragedy of Revengefulness and Justice*]—is that his dilemma is not only to bring about justice but to do so in a right frame of mind and feeling, acting as the scourge and minister of heavenly justice, not poisoned in soul by vengefulness and hatred.

In order to test these two theses and explore the dilemmas they deal with, we must glance at what Hamlet himself is like and what happens in the drama that bears his name. It might seem at first that this is simply done, merely by reading the play or seeing it performed. But history shows an extraordinary chaos of voices offering confused and contradictory explanations of both.

First, there is what may almost be called the orthodox version of the past one hundred and fifty years, the romantic interpretation that sees the young Prince Hamlet as an introvert entangled in hesitating thought to the point where he is frustrated to follow any course of action. This is the view of Hamlet's character most early and most eloquently voiced by [Johann Wolfgang von] Goethe and [Samuel Taylor] Coleridge. "A lonely, pure, noble and most moral character, without the strength of nerve that forms the hero," Goethe says of Hamlet, "sinks beneath the burden which it cannot bear and must not cast away. Impossibilities are required of him; not in themselves impossibilities, but such for him. He winds, and turns, and torments himself; he advances and recoils; is ever put in mind, ever puts himself in mind; at last does all but lose his purpose from his thoughts; yet still without recovering his peace of mind."

This description seems to imply that Shakespeare's hero was a fusion of Goethe's own Werther and Wilhelm Meister [in *The Sorrows of Young Werther* and *Wilhelm Meister's Travels*]; Coleridge paid Hamlet the compliment of assuming that Shakespeare had been painting a sixteenth century version of the nineteenth century Coleridge. "He intended," wrote Coleridge, "to portray a person in whose view the external world and all its incidents and objects, were comparatively dim and of no interest in themselves, and which began to interest only when they were reflected in the mirror of his mind. . . . [Hamlet indulges in] endless reasoning and hesitating—constant urgency and solicitation of the mind to act, and as constant an escape from action; ceaseless reproaches of himself for sloth and negligence, while the whole energy of his resolution evaporates in these reproaches. This, too, not from cowardice, for he is drawn as one of the bravest of his time—not from want of forethought or slowness of apprehension, for he sees through the very souls of those who surround him; but merely from that aversion to action which prevails among such as have a world in themselves."

Such a view of Hamlet is on the whole accepted by [A. C.] Bradley and E. K. Chambers, and is essentially that of Laurence Olivier's film version of the play [see Sources for Further Study], where, in the beginning, while ghostly mists swirl around the battlements and cold vaulted interiors of Elsinore, a disembodied voice intones, "This is the tragedy of a man who could not make up his mind."

Opposed to this judgment is the approach of those like [George Lyman] Kittredge, who see Hamlet as a man of action moving to avenge his father's death with no essential hesitation and all practicable dispatch, his self-reproaches caused only by chafing at the slowness imposed upon him by circumstances. This Hamlet demands, in conscience, to be sure, reasonable certitude that he has not been deceived by a lying phantom. When he has that assurance, in the King's guilty reaction to the play-within-the-play, he is still delayed by the difficulty of producing objective proof, convincing to the world, that he has not simply invented an accusation to justify regicide and a merely ambitious desire to seize the throne. This view argues, furthermore, that as a King, Claudius—except on the one accidental occasion when Hamlet comes on him at his prayers—is constantly surrounded by armed courtiers and attendants and even a corps of Swiss mercenaries; and after Hamlet has put him on his guard by showing that his crime is known, he not only takes steps for his own safety by sending Hamlet off to what he hopes will be the nephew's death in England, but would not be likely to let Hamlet approach him thenceforth without being surrounded by protection. In the culminating duel scene, it is only the conspiracy between Claudius and Laertes to kill Hamlet that allows him to be in the King's presence armed—and even then only in consequence of seizing Laertes's foil, the single one with an unbated point.

J. Dover Wilson, in turn, takes issue with a part of this argument by insisting that Hamlet never wanted to prove to the *world* that Claudius was his father's murderer. Such a view would always leave at least a stain of suspicion that Queen Gertrude was implicated, and, indeed, until after the play scene, in the interview in his mother's closet, Hamlet himself is by no means certain that she has not been privy to his father's death. But the ghost has bade Hamlet leave her to heaven, and therefore Hamlet has with great ingenuity, Wilson argues, devised the play to show *Claudius* that his guilt is known, but at the same time to make it appear to the scandalized court that it embodies his own threat to murder the present King. (Hamlet himself, you will recall, identifies the murderer in the play as *nephew* to the King.)

W. W. Greg has devised a still more radical overturn of previous themes. For him, the reason Claudius fails to be alarmed by the dumbshow of the murder, but breaks up the performance of the play, is that he is in fact innocent. He has not recognized the dumbshow as directed against himself, but does, with the court, take the subsequent action of the play as prefiguring an attempt on his own life. The ghost's accusations, heard by no one but Hamlet, are simply a hallucinating projection of his own deluded suspicions and have no basis in fact. Hamlet is in truth even madder than he has been pretending to be.

T. S. Eliot concludes that none of these explanations will really do. More, Hamlet's self-disgust and his revulsion at his mother's adultery and what Hamlet calls her incest, the nauseated loathing with which his imagination dwells in revolted detail upon "The bloat King" "honeying and making love" to his mother "in the rank sweat of an enseamed bed" "over the nasty stye" [III. iv. 182, 92-4], seem to Eliot emotions so excessive for the facts that he regards them as insufficiently motivated in the drama, and drawn from some hidden source in Shakespeare himself. *"Hamlet,"* he says, ". . . is full of some stuff that the writer could not drag to light, contemplate, or manipulate into art."

Consequently, "So far from being Shakespeare's masterpiece, the play is certainly a failure."

At this point, generations of theatergoers who have regarded Hamlet with absorbed sympathy and no conscious puzzlement whatever might well feel tempted to exclaim in the witty words of one Shakespearean commentator, "Are the critics of *Hamlet* mad or only pretending to be?" We seem to be in [Edmund] Spenser's wandering wood in which the thousands of paths lead only to Error's Den [in *The Faerie Queene*]. But there is one more, with which I shall bring this survey of the critics to a conclusion, the psychoanalytic theory originally propounded by Freud and elaborated by Ernest Jones.

According to this, Hamlet is suffering from what he cannot possibly recognize himself, the Oedipal desire of a son to kill his father and supplant him in his mother's love. Only so, Jones claims, can we explain Hamlet speaking to her like a jealous lover, torturing himself with hideous images of her lovemaking, and hating the King with all the hysterical loathing of a rival. But because Claudius has done only what Hamlet himself desired to do, killed the father and mated with the mother, Hamlet partly identifies himself with his uncle, shares his guilt, and cannot bring himself to execute vengeance on one who has put into action what he himself dreamed in childhood fantasy. He consequently oscillates, between his conscious and acquired adult devotion to his father and his infantile hatred and aggression, and is inhibited from acting upon either. He would never be able to act effectively on either of his divided motives, and only accident brings the play to a catastrophic ending as fatal to himself as to Claudius.

II

The refutation of the argument is essential in my position, for if Jones is right, there *is* no moral dilemma in the drama. By definition Hamlet *cannot* understand his difficulty; only if—what is impossible—we could bring a twentieth century psychoanalyst to the imaginary twelfth century court of Elsinore as described by the sixteenth century dramatist, could Hamlet be taught to resolve his own confusions and solve his problems. Such an objection, of course, does not dispose of Jones's theory, nor does any mere skepticism about Shakespeare having thus foreshadowed a Freudian case history. Only if there are within the play itself and its effect upon a fit audience elements that do not square with this explanation, may we set aside it or the Goethe-Coleridge interpretation of which it is a more scientific sounding variant. And in the same way, to deal with any of the interpretations we have surveyed, we must look to the play and the impression it must produce on an audience that responds to it in the way molded by the dramatist.

But there are such elements to negate many of

these interpretations. It is a minor caveat, no doubt, to object that the interview between mother and son in the Queen's closet, with Polonius hiding behind the arras, does not take place in her bedroom, as Freud and Jones say, with Hamlet violently flinging her upon the bed in the way Olivier does in the film. In Shakespeare's day, a closet was a small private room or study; Queen Gertrude would no more receive Polonius in her bedroom than Queen Elizabeth II would Winston Churchill. But (what is more fatal for the entire Jones-Freud-Coleridge-Goethe theory) Hamlet has not, before the opening of the play, been at all a frustrated introvert entangled in morbid thought and incapable of action, nor, as I shall show, does he really—except in certain very limited respects—show himself inactive in the course of the play.

It is true that with his father's death he has been plunged into the deepest grief and melancholy and that his mother's hasty marriage has filled him with horror and revulsion. Hamlet does indeed bear within him a misery "that passes show" [I. ii. 85], and feels that the earth is "a sterile promontory" [II. ii. 299], the heavens "a pestilent congregation of vapors" [II. ii. 303], man a "quintessence of the dust" [II. ii. 308]. But it is important to note that the world *had not* been so for him; it had been a "goodly frame," the heavens a "majestical roof fretted with golden fire" [II. ii. 301], and man "the beauty of the world" [II. ii. 307], "the paragon of animals" [II. ii. 307]. In saying he has lost his mirth and foregone all customary exercise, he reveals that melancholy and inactivity had not been his habits when his father lived (of whom, according to Jones, he was no less secretly jealous than he now is of his uncle). But even now, throughout his present distresses, he *does* exercise, and has even moments of highspirited jesting. Before he becomes suspicious that Rosencrantz and Guildenstern are spying emissaries of the King, his greeting of them is gay rather than gloomy; and we learn later that he has been practising fencing daily all the while Laertes has been in France, and see Hamlet easily outmatch that skilled swordsman.

Others in the play testify not only to his multitudinous and shining accomplishments, but to his ease, grace, and charm. "The courtier's, soldier's, scholar's, eye, tongue, sword; The expectancy and rose of the fair state; The glass of fashion and the mold of form, the observed of all observers," Ophelia says of him [III. i. 151-54]. These are not the words in which one would describe a melancholy moper, who could not take the place of brilliant leadership at court to which his rank entitled him. When he is dead, Fortinbras, decreeing him a soldier's burial, summarizes general report in the valediction that "he was likely to have proved most royally" [V. ii. 397-98]. Are these the things others would say of an ineffectual dreamer?

Hamlet's behavior during the course of the play,

furthermore, reveals none of the inwardturned embarrassment in social relations that characterize the introvert. He talks readily and cordially with soldiers, actors, gravediggers, gets along well with pirates, and is so beloved by the common people that Claudius dares not openly harm him, the last a popularity that introverts have seldom enjoyed with the populace. He easily takes command of any conversation in which he participates, usually with unassuming courtesy; and in the play scene he dominates the whole court. He is *not* hesitant or inhibited in action, even against Claudius; he plans the play to test the King's conscience in a flash, and carries it out flawlessly; he stabs Polonius through the arras more than half suspecting it to be the King (what of the notion that he *cannot* act against Claudius?); he sends the traitorous Rosencrantz and Guildenstern to their deaths instantly and without a qualm; he leaps on board the pirate ship before any can follow him; he accepts Laertes's challenge without a moment's pause; he sends Claudius a letter announcing himself landed naked in his Kingdom, as it were warning Claudius of his intentions; and he calmly plans to use the period before news can arrive from England to finish his task.

Jones argues that Hamlet's "mother fixation" stands between him and his courtship of Ophelia, but it does nothing of the kind. He has written her letters so ardent that Laertes warns her not to be moved by them, and won her with "words of so sweet breath composed," she herself says, "as made [his gifts] more rich" [III. i. 97-8]. He has not drawn back from her; it is she, obedient to her father's command, not of her own will, who has repulsed him. Where in all this is the self-frustrated lover?

Given Hamlet's intense but not at all abnormal devotion to his father, is there anything excessive in his disgust at his mother's conduct? In any society except that of second century Rome, Hollywood, or the fast set of a modern cosmopolitan city, a son might well be shocked at his mother's adultery. And for an Elizabethan audience there was no question that her marriage to Claudius was incest as well. When Henry VIII married his elder brother's widow, Catherine of Aragon, in 1509, it was necessary to support a dispensation permitting it by bringing forward testimony that her previous marriage had never been consummated, and the feeling of horror that such a wedding violated biblical law endured long past Shakespeare's day. Hamlet only gives eloquent voice to an emotion all sixteenth century audiences understood.

Finally, there is the allegation that Hamlet delays unconscionably, unintelligibly, and fatally in executing justice upon Claudius. One might ask why it is no sign of Claudius's having some Freudian complex that he delays, no less fatally for himself, to kill Hamlet, long after he has realized that his nephew is dangerous. But the truth is that neither is dilatory except for quite intelligible reasons. It was entirely clear to an Elizabethan audience that a ghost might be a lying spirit and that a Prince intent on acting justly must prove its accusations, however strongly he felt impelled to believe them. The events of Acts II and III, and the first half of Act IV, all take place in a single day and night, and that day is so short a time after Polonius has forbidden Ophelia to see Hamlet, that only then has Hamlet become aware that her avoidance of him is deliberate and made his way into her chamber. The very next day the players come to Elsinore, Hamlet forms his plan, and puts it into effect. After he has lost his one chance to kill the King at prayer, he is packed off to England under guard. The intervening time is only long enough to bring Laertes back from Paris and permit Hamlet to land from the pirate ship. Hamlet can hardly slay Claudius during Ophelia's burial, on sacred ground, but he knows he has until messages arrive from England, coolly plans to use that interim, and, when he finds himself poisoned, kills the King an instant later. What an indecisive, will-less jack-o'-dreams!

In thus analyzing the Freudian interpretation, I have also dealt implicitly with most of the others I outlined in the first third of this paper, but I should still say a few words about Greg's theory that Claudius is innocent and Hamlet suffering from delusions. Dover Wilson's suggestion that during the dumbshow Claudius is discussing with Polonius the renewed display Hamlet has just given them of love-madness, and consequently has not observed the pantomime, in my opinion, partly answers Greg, but he is fully refuted by Claudius's own soliloquy in the prayer scene where the King explicitly admits "the primal curse" of "a brother's murder" [III. iii. 37-8]. This is unanswerable and we need say no more of it.

III

There remains only to sketch in such aspects of my own position as have not been anticipated in the previous part of the discussion. The theme of the play, I have said, is the relationship of appearance and reality, the gradual classification of moral identities deliberately portrayed ambiguously in the beginning. "Something is rotten in the State of Denmark" [I. iv. 90], says Marcellus, and Hamlet cries out that it is "an unweeded garden" [I. ii. 135], lamenting "the time is out of joint: Oh cursed sprite, that ever I was born to set it right" [I. v. 188-89]. But we do not know at this point lest perhaps it is Hamlet himself who is the canker in the State, proud, revengeful, consumed with frustrated ambition to ascend the throne himself and rationalizing his fury at having been passed over in the election. (We might note that, like Hamlet, Fortinbras has failed to secure *his* father's throne, which is likewise now occupied by an uncle, but that unlike Hamlet he seems to feel no sense of injustice in

this; he is more concerned to win back the half of Norway his father lost to the elder Hamlet.)

During the opening scenes of the play, I must re-emphasize the point, we do not *know* whether Hamlet or Claudius is in the right. Let us try to imagine seeing or reading it for the first time, without having heard anything about it. Can we tell with certainty that Hamlet's jealousies and suspicions are true in fact? The original Hamlet story in *Saxo Grammaticus* was a pure revenge drama, with small moral cause to prefer the murdered King to his fratricide brother; and Hamlet's motives are entirely those of filial partisanship demanding an eye for an eye, a tooth for a tooth, not those of horror at a noble and virtuous King done to death by an evil one. Not, of course, that the Elizabethan audience before whom Shakespeare's play was first acted was likely to have known anything about *Saxo Grammaticus,* but the earlier Hamlet play of the 1590's, from which Shakespeare probably derived his own, also seems in turn to have been derived from *Saxo Grammaticus* and possibly Belleforest, and to have been straight melodrama, with a ghost crying "Hamlet, revenge!" Elizabethan playgoers may well have been surprised by the turn Shakespeare gave the old materials. From neither the opening of *Hamlet* nor its title have we any more assurance that Hamlet will be justified in its sequel than we have of Julius Caesar being the hero or Macbeth the villain of the Shakespearean plays that bear their names.

In the same way, we have in the pseudo-kingly Claudius, at first, a deceptively persuasive imitation of genuine kingliness: dignity, courtesy, affability, vigorous and effective diplomatic and military action against external danger, an eloquent and seemingly sincere statement of sound principles, both of feeling and of conduct. It is possible, for all we know at the moment, that Hamlet may indeed be giving way to a too protracted, unmanly, and self-indulgent grief in which he evades his duty to himself and to others. There is even a real regard for Hamlet in Claudius at first, a genuine kindness and good feeling, and there is no question of his affection for his Queen. Even when by degrees we pierce beneath his smiling mask, we find that he still struggles with conscience, that his slowness to act against his dangerous nephew is not all policy, and that only after his situation has grown desperate is conscience strangled.

With the old councillor Polonius, we have an impressive appearance of wise understanding and justice of judgment gradually yielding to vanity, worldliness, and senility. When he bids Laertes be faithful in friendship, and tells him "To thine own self be true" [I. iii. 78], his morality sounds like that of Socrates, but the rest of his maxims are all prudential and concerned with the figure a man cuts in the world, rather than with essence—like his advice on money and on dress, a mere cautiousness of conduct or of taste. As the action proceeds, he sinks lower, and we see him willing to dispatch spies and informers upon his own son, eavesdropping and spying himself, flattering and hypocritical, obstinately determined to prove his own theories, a conceited busybody foolishly self-deceived.

Laertes is the pseudo-heroic as Claudius is the pseudo-kingly. How gallant a figure he seems at first, how earnest is his concern for his sister, how admirable his promptness of action in demanding an explanation of his father's death (strikingly contrasted with Hamlet's seeming—though only seeming—slowness). But then, in more significant contrast to Hamlet's insistence on having proof and acting in right conscience, see Laertes storming into the King's presence, shouting before he knows the facts, "Conscience and grace to the profoundest pit" [IV. v. 133], "To hell allegiance" [IV. v. 132], and follow how easily the smooth King not merely deludes him but works him to a weak participation in villainy. Laertes, like his father, is concerned with appearance, not reality; he wants "formal ostentation" of funeral rites for Polonius and is concerned lest the world think he has not done enough. "What ceremony else?" [V. i. 223], he demands at Ophelia's grave, and his showy sorrow revolts Hamlet's inward grief "which passes show" [I. ii. 85].

But Hamlet, the hero, too, is not all heroic, or only gradually becomes so. His wit is fiercely intolerant of stupidity and sycophancy; he is mockingly contemptuous of the affected Osric. He is consistently and publicly rude to Claudius, even before he knows the ghost's accusations; he is indecently discourteous, almost invariably, in deriding Polonius, whose daughter he loves; he is brutally harsh to his mother. Until well on in his plans, he is mistrustful of the sane and truehearted Horatio, refusing to confide in him, seeking neither the comfort nor the good counsel of a faithful friend, but bottling all his feelings and his purposes up within his breast, in a proud and suspicious secrecy. He is insultingly suspicious of Ophelia, leaping from the realization that her pathetic attempt to return his gifts means that their encounter is no accident, as it was meant to seem, to the raging conviction that she is her father's willing tool conniving to betray him. With furious bitterness he all but calls her a whore, and, despite the likelihood that spies are listening, recklessly shouts, "We'll have no more marriages. Those that are married already, all but one, shall live" [III. i. 147-48]. Worst of all, for more than half the play, his determination to avenge his father's murder is a ferocious, hysterical, vindictive, bloody hatred that he can hardly keep within bounds. It is revenge with hardly a trace of concern for any nobler concept of justice.

This is the dilemma of Hamlet the Prince and Man—to disentangle himself from the temptation to wreak justice for the wrong reasons and in evil passion, and to do what he must do at last for the pure sake of justice, for the welfare of the State, to weed the unweeded garden of Denmark and set right the time that is out of joint. From that dilemma of wrong feelings and right actions he ultimately emerges, solving the problem by attaining a proper state of mind. At the end of the play scene, it is true, he refuses to kill Claudius at prayer, and excuses that evasion to himself by arguing that he wants to damn his uncle's soul more deep in hell by taking him at some time that has no relish of grace or salvation in it. But there is no improbability in suggesting that Hamlet is trying here to excuse a reluctance he does not yet understand but that springs from a revolt of his own conscience against acting with such poisonous feeling. He is acting—or rather refraining—on right motives, but giving himself mistaken reasons. (It is a dramatic irony of course, that Claudius has been unable to pray with sincerity, and is *not* in a state of grace.)

Slowly, however, in the course of the last two acts, Hamlet subdues his violence of feeling. Even by the end of the interview in his mother's closet, he sorrows for his impetuous murder of Polonius: "For this same Lord," he says, "I do repent" [III. iv. 173]; and he gently bids his mother good night, telling her, "When you are desirous to be blest, I'll blessing beg of you" [III. iv. 171-72]. He prays Laertes's pardon for the wrong he has done him, and throughout all the ending moderates even those wild and whirling words of hatred he has previously spoken against Claudius. Instead he asks, calmly, "Is't not perfect conscience to quit him with this arm?" and prevent "This canker of our nature" from proliferating "further evil" [V. ii. 67-70]. He has resolved the moral dilemma of vengeance *versus* justice. (Although it is true that when he has transfixed the King with Laertes's "envenomed point" he has a last spasm of hatred for the "incestuous, murderous, damned Dane" [V. ii. 325].) At the end, Hamlet is even able to think of providing for a peaceful succession to the crown by giving his dying voice to Fortinbras. He expires with noble serenity, "The rest is silence" [V. ii. 358]. He has purged his nature of its fierce passions and become the great and heroic figure we always felt struggling in him to be born. As restoring peace descends over troubled Denmark, we can echo Horatio:

Good night, sweet prince,
And flights of angels sing thee to thy rest!
[V. ii. 359-60]
(pp. 99-111)

Edgar Johnson, "The Dilemma of Hamlet (William Shakespeare: 'Hamlet')," in Great Moral Dilemmas in Literature, Past and Present, *edited by R. M. MacIver, 1956. Reprint by Cooper Square Publishers, Inc., 1964, pp. 99-111.*

THE GHOST

Kenneth Muir

[*Muir analyzes the* **Ghost** *in* Hamlet *in several ways, first by proposing several attitudes an Elizabethan audience may have held regarding its nature. The apparition may have been viewed as an illusion, a portent foreshadowing danger to Denmark, a spirit returning from the grave because a task was left undone, a spirit come from purgatory with divine permission, or a devil who assumes the form of a dead person to lure mortals to their doom. According to the critic,* **Hamlet** *tests each of these perspectives during the play's course of events, most notably in his production of "The Mousetrap." Muir also discusses the* **Ghost's** *two warnings to* **Hamlet,** *namely not to taint his mind and to leave* **Gertrude** *"to heaven." In addition, the critic explores* **Hamlet's** *reaction to his meeting with the* **Ghost** *by studying the nature of the prince's depression and his assumption of an "antic disposition." For further commentary on the* **Ghost's** *charcter see the excerpts by Maynard Mack, Robert R. Reed, Jr., and Arthur Kirsch.*]

The first act of *Hamlet,* except for the third scene, is concerned with the revelation by the Ghost that Claudius is a murderer and Gertrude an adultress. This revelation is carefully prepared. The Ghost appears twice in the first scene without speaking; and before his appearance, Shakespeare, without the aid of scenery or artificial lighting, creates in the course of the dialogue a vivid impression of time, place, coldness, and expectancy, and after the Ghost has vanished an equally vivid impression of dawn, four or five hours having passed in ten minutes of playing-time. We also hear in the first scene of preparations for war, and Bernardo thinks that the Ghost has come to warn them of the threat to the state. The scholar, Horatio, at first believes that the Ghost will not appear, and later addresses it as 'illusion'. According to the various beliefs current in Shakespeare's day, a ghost could be either an illusion, 'a phantom seen as a portent of danger to the state', a spirit come from the grave because of something left undone, a spirit come from purgatory by divine permission, or a devil disguised as a dead person in order to lure the living into mortal sin. All these theories are tested in the course of the play. Horatio, abandoning the idea that the Ghost is an illusion, assumes first that it has come as a portent and then that it can be laid if they carry out its wishes. When the Ghost appears to Hamlet himself in the fourth scene, both Marcellus and Horatio are afraid that it is a goblin damned rather than a spirit of health, and that it will drive the Prince into madness and suicide; and, although Hamlet, after he has listened to the Ghost's message, is fully convinced that it is indeed his father's spirit, later on he has moments of doubt when he

thinks it may be the devil. He has, in any case, to obtain confirmation of the truth of the Ghost's story.

Hamlet appears for the first time in the second scene of the play, dressed in black, which is an implied criticism of the royal marriage which has just been celebrated. Claudius, although Hamlet dislikes him and regards him as a usurper, appears to be a competent and even an amiable ruler. After referring diplomatically to his marriage, dispatching ambassadors to Norway, and giving Laertes permission to return to France, he urges Hamlet to stop his excessive mourning, and not to return to Wittenberg. The audience, having already seen the Ghost, is aware that something is rotten in the state of Denmark, and will sympathise with Hamlet's feelings about his mother's hasty re-marriage, especially as marriage with a deceased husband's brother was not permitted without a special dispensation.

Hamlet's first soliloquy is designed to show his state of mind before his interview with the Ghost. He is profoundly shocked by Gertrude's marriage to his uncle in less than two months after her first husband's death, although he has no conscious suspicion that his father has been murdered or that his mother had committed adultery. He wishes suicide were permissible, he compares the world to Eden after the Fall, he contrasts Gertrude's two husbands, the godlike and the bestial, and, with a tendency to generalise characteristic of him, he assumes that all women are like his mother: 'Frailty, thy name is woman!' [I. ii. 146]. We learn later that the melancholy and disillusionment apparent in this soliloquy are not part of his normal state of mind. It is necessary to emphasise this, because those critics who form a low opinion of his character tend to forget that his behaviour in the play is partly explicable by the successive shocks he receives.

His depression and his tears are underlined by his initial failure to recognise Horatio; but he rouses himself sufficiently to make the bitter witticism about the funeral baked meats, and his cross-examination of the three men who have seen the Ghost reveals that his intelligence has not been blunted by his grief. It is apparent from the four-line soliloquy at the end of the scene, in which he speaks of 'foul play' and 'foul deeds', that he now suspects that his father has been murdered.

In the fourth scene, before the appearance of the Ghost, Hamlet is given a speech on the drunkenness of the court, which leads him to generalise on the way 'some vicious mole of nature' [I. iv. 24] or some bad habit outweighs a man's good qualities and destroys his reputation in the eyes of the world. Hamlet had already referred in the second scene to the drinking habits of the new court, and one function of this speech is to show the deterioration of Elsinore in the reign of Claudius. Another function, equally important from the theatrical point of view, is to distract the attention of the audience so that they are surprised by the reappearance of the Ghost, and this function is aided by the extreme complexity of the syntax, which would require the undivided attention of the audience.

Bernard Shaw spoke of the Ghost's part as

> one of the wonders of the play. . . . The weird music of that long speech . . . should be the spectral wail of a soul's bitter wrong crying from one world to another in the extremity of its torment.

He is, apparently, released from purgatory, although Shakespeare makes use of some of the characteristics of the classical Hades. He speaks of his 'foul crimes', which suggests that Hamlet has idealised his character; and it is stressed that he has been sent to his account 'Unhous'led, disappointed, unanel'd' [I. v. 77]—without having taken the sacrament, unprepared, and without having received extreme unction. Hamlet promises to sweep to his revenge, and the Ghost leaves him with two cautions:

> Taint not thy mind, nor let thy soul contrive
> Against thy mother aught.
>
> [I. v. 85-6]

Gertrude is to be left to the prickings of conscience; but the meaning of the first four words of this sentence is ambiguous. They could refer to Hamlet's attitude to his mother, or they may have a more general application: he is to execute justice on Claudius, without allowing his own mind to become tainted with evil. It is important to realise that Hamlet's task is almost impossible. How can he kill Claudius in such a way that justice appears to be done, without at the same time exposing the guilt of his mother? It is apparent from the speech Hamlet utters immediately after the Ghost's disappearance that he is more concerned with his mother's guilt than with his uncle's blacker crime: he speaks first of her. It is also clear from this soliloquy and from the scene which follows that Hamlet's mind is reeling in the distracted globe of his skull. Knowing that he will be unable to behave normally till his vengeance is accomplished, he decides to 'put an antic disposition on', as Hieronimo (in *The Spanish Tragedy*) had done, or—to use a comparison made in *The Historie of Hamblet*—as the Brutus who had driven out the Tarquins had done. How near to breaking-point Hamlet is after the revelation by the Ghost is made apparent by his inability to stand, by his 'wild and whirling words' [I. v. 133] to his friends, and by the hysterical remarks about the 'fellow in the cellarage' [I. v. 151], which are not a sign of his egotism and callousness as Rebecca West assumes, but which may well make his friends suspect that the Ghost is the devil in disguise. The antic disposition is not merely a defence mechanism. It also enables Ham-

let to play the rôle of Fool and so make remarks which will appear mad to everyone except the guilty King, and which are a means of undermining his self-control, so that his conscience will be caught by the performance of 'The Murder of Gonzago'.

Hamlet nearly reveals the Ghost's secret twice: first, when he breaks off to inform Horatio and Marcellus that

> There's never a villain dwelling in all Denmark
> But he's an arrant knave;
>
> [I. v. 123-24]

and, secondly, when he begins:

> It is an honest ghost, that let me tell you . . .
>
> [I. v. 138]

and then finishes:

> For your desire to know what is between us,
> O'ermaster it as you may.
>
> [I. v. 139-40]

Later on, off-stage, he makes Horatio his confidant; but he keeps the secret from Marcellus because he realises that his own safety depends on secrecy. The scene ends with a significant couplet:

> The time is out of joint. O cursed spite,
> That ever I was born to set it right!
>
> [I. v. 188-89]

These lines, in which Hamlet both accepts and revolts against his mission, contrast with his earlier promise to 'sweep to his revenge' [I. v. 31], and with his determination to confront the Ghost, when his fate cries out: they prepare the way for the long months of inaction. (pp. 20-3)

Kenneth Muir, in his Shakespeare: Hamlet, *Barron's Educational Series, Inc., 1963, 61 p.*

CLAUDIUS

Bertram Joseph

*[Joseph examines the concept of appearance versus reality with regard to **Claudius**'s character in* Hamlet. *When the play begins, the critic asserts, there is no indication that **Claudius** is a villain; rather, he appears to be the consummate monarch, who effectively transacts private and public business. As the play progresses, however, the quality of his villainy is gradually revealed to the audience. Joseph also defines the term "hypocrisy" in relation to **Claudius**, maintaining that Elizabethans viewed it as a particularly serious character flaw. The king's hypocrisy is perhaps most evi-*

*dent in his eloquent speech in Act I, scene ii in which he openly discusses his hasty marriage to **Gertrude** and downplays its awkwardness by providing sound reasons for establishing the union. As a result, the grief-stricken **Hamlet**—with whom we are supposed to identify— seems to be the only abnormal character at the court. The critic explores several Renaissance perspectives on **Claudius's** character which might not be apparent to a modern audience. For instance, Joseph maintains that an Elizabethan audience would not likely sympathize with the monarch as he tries to pray in Act III, scene iii, for his admission of sinning coupled with his inability to repent only makes his wickedness more pronounced. Further, the critic shows how Elizabethan audiences would understand that images of sickness and disease in the play relate to **Claudius's** hypocrisy. Finally, Joseph notes that the king's duplicity reflects a truly evil devilishness, and discusses the concept of "white devil"—a term given to hypocrites by Martin Luther—in relation to this observation. For further commentary on **Claudius's** character, see the excerpts by Robert Hapgood, Robert R. Reed, Jr., Richard D. Altick, Kenneth Muir, Edgar Johnson, Ernest Jones, Carolyn Heilbrun, and Baldwin Maxwell.]*

The last minutes of the play are taken up with preparations for the dead to be placed "high on a stage . . . to the view," as silent witnesses when Horatio comes to tell the

> yet unknowing world
> How these things came about.
>
> [V. ii. 379-80]

What is there to be told? No more than we, the audience or the readers, have just lived through in our imagination with the poet. And yet we have not imagined the whole of the story as it was present in its author's mind unless we remember, unless we are acutely conscious of, the fact that it is concerned with a country still completely unaware of what has been taking place since the murder of the elder Hamlet.

Horatio has now to speak of that murder, telling how it was committed by Claudius, the brother who seized the throne and lived incestuously with the murdered king's widow. There will be mention of the Ghost, the Mousetrap, the unintentional killing of Claudius and its results. Denmark must learn of the plot to kill the Prince in England, of the foul details of the second plot after his sudden return home. It is a story of rebounding treachery and multiple slaughter, with the wiping out not of Hamlet alone, but of Gertrude, Laertes, and finally of Claudius himself. At this moment, if we imagine Horatio about to tell all this to the Danes, with the grim procession forming, we know for certain that the truth in the dying words of Laertes can be ap-

plied not merely to one episode, but to all the crime and horror of the story—

> —the King, the King's to blame.
>
> [V. ii. 320]

But when the play opens it is by no means certain that Claudius is a villain. Even when the Prince swears vengeance there is still a strong possibility that the Ghost's word ought not to be taken. What we have seen of Claudius suggests a clear conscience: we have been present whilst a very gracious and most noble-looking renaissance monarch transacted private and public business with an admiring court around him. With competence and regal assurance he disposes of the problem of young Fortinbras, sending a statesmanlike embassy to the old king. Claudius never appears to better advantage than in this scene: with what sincere interest in the affairs of a trusted adviser does he assure the young Laertes:

> You cannot speak of reason to the Dane
> And lose your voice. What wouldst thou
>   beg, Laertes,
> That shall not be my offer, not thy asking?
> The head is not more native to the heart,
> The hand more instrumental to the
>   mouth,
> Than is the throne of Denmark to thy father.
>
> [I. ii. 44-9]

When Claudius turns to "my cousin Hamlet, and my son" [I. ii. 64], there is the same healthy assurance, tempered now with a sympathetic restraint which suggests immeasurable reserves of strength and kindliness. He seems to be justified in everything that he says to cajole or persuade Hamlet to take more interest in the incidents of everyday life.

In the face of his nephew's inability to reconcile himself to that "common theme," the "death of fathers" [I. ii. 104], Claudius seems sincere. When the Prince has promised his mother to remain, the gloriousness of Claudius is even more pronounced: now the court departs in a magnificent procession, joyfully expectant of great splendour and felicities to come, with their king proclaiming to the world a liberality and magnanimity of soul which renaissance minds found fitting to a monarch. The scene moves inevitably to his final speech; and this sets the seal on the picture which Shakespeare wants us to have of a personage whose grandeur swells more and more until at last he holds the stage, dominating the whole company with a radiant splendour:

> No jocund health that Denmark drinks today
> But the great cannon to the clouds shall
>   tell,
> And the King's rouse the heaven shall
>   bruit again,
> Re-speaking earthly thunder.
>
> [I. ii. 125-28]

For Claudius, this is the moment of greatest triumph: in his appearance, in the attitude of others towards him, there is no suggestion that he is anything but an ideal king, with all the superb qualities which that implies. To look at him no one would imagine the foul crimes of which he is guilty, the murder of a brother, the filthy, animal sin of incest. Not the mark of Cain, but a clear conscience seems to show itself on Claudius' brow; he seems to emanate health and brightness of soul, and a gracious spirit of nobility. And yet as he wrote the play, Shakespeare, even as he imagined Claudius seeming so splendid, had also imagined him guilty at this very moment of two horrid, ugly crimes. A few scenes later, in the heat of his first reaction to the Ghost's tale, Hamlet cries bitterly:

> O villain, villain, smiling, damned villain!
> My tables—meet it is I set it down
> That one may smile, and smile, and be a
>   villain;
> At least I am sure it may be so in Denmark.
>   [I. v. 106-09]

Yet even Hamlet begins to wonder if what the Ghost says is true, and no ordinary mortal looking at Claudius and his loving queen, surrounded with a joyful court, a picture of all that is healthily vital in human beings, could be expected to peer beneath the smile and find the villain. We would rather be disposed to think that of the world in general it is true that "one may smile, and smile, and be a villain," but if ever there were a sure exception to that rule it is to be found in this particular case of Denmark, and of Claudius, its magnificent king.

From one point of view, then, the progress of the play is a revelation of the quality of Claudius' villainy; only gradually do we come to a true experience of his real nature. How successfully he imposes on Denmark, and how difficult it is to prevent oneself from being deceived by this kind of person, is exemplified excellently by his very first speech. The peculiar quality of this hypocrite lies in his ability not merely to hide evil, but to present it openly when he chooses, in a manner which leads ordinary people not to recognize it emotionally for what it is, but to respond to it as good. Claudius reminds his listeners that his behaviour could indeed be regarded as not in accordance with what is normally held as the best of taste:

> Though yet of Hamlet our dear brother's
>   death
> The memory be green; and that it us befitted
> To bear our hearts in grief, and our whole
>   kingdom
> To be contracted in one brow of woe;
> Yet so far hath discretion fought with nature
> That we with wisest sorrow think on him,
> Together with remembrance of ourselves.
>   [I. ii. 1-7]

As this scene develops, with an obviously admiring court and a loving queen, from none of whom comes any hint of shame or disapproval, it is easy to accept Claudius' words as perfectly reasonable, and to forget that he is guilty of at the least a gross breach of etiquette in marrying so soon, and in putting an end to court mourning within two months of the last king's death. In a sense which Claudius did not intend his words, "so far hath discretion fought with nature" that he has managed to marry his brother's widow without stimulating in his courtiers their normal reaction to incest; and yet in this case, too, he does not attempt to hide what he has done, he merely contrives to make the world mistake the real quality of his actions:

> Therefore our sometime sister, now our
>   queen, . . .
> Have we, as 'twere with a defeated joy, . . .
> Taken to wife; nor have we herein barr'd
> Your better wisdoms, which have freely
>   gone
> With this affair along.
>   [I. ii. 8-16]

It is the measure of his uncle's success that Hamlet, the only person to react normally to an abnormal situation, is himself made to seem abnormal. The sight of Claudius, to hear him speak, is enough to dispel disapproval; and in the behaviour of Gertrude is so much love and radiance that we can be forgiven for not realizing that this is a woman who buried a beloved husband in frenzied grief a few short weeks ago. Shakespeare has presented the facts in such a way that our own normal reactions are dulled, and if we recognize later how strange it was that we had no comprehension of the true facts at this moment, we become more aware of the evil emanating from Claudius as a part of the poet's fundamental conception of his play.

Claudius' nature, then, adds to the difficulties of Hamlet's task. After the King has betrayed himself, when the Mouse-trap has been sprung, the position is rectified to a certain extent: the Prince and his only friend are now sure that the appearance of a murderer who does not look guilty is not to be weighed against the word of a Ghost which might have been false. But we, the audience, do not react correctly to *The Murder of Gonzago*, unless we are conscious of the kind of problem which it solves, and this means an awareness of Claudius as a hypocrite in the renaissance understanding of that term.

According to the *Oxford English Dictionary*, hypocrisy may be defined as:

> The assuming of a false appearance of virtue or goodness, with dissimulation of real character or inclinations, esp. in respect of religious life or beliefs; hence in general sense, dissimulation, pretence, sham.

We tend to interpret "the assuming of a false appearance" metaphorically; but the renaissance looked literally at the face and actions which in a hypocrite were by definition considered to express the opposite of the real nature within; for instance, Robert Cawdrey's *Table Alphabetical* (1604) states: "such a one as in his outward apparel, countenance and behaviour, pretendeth to be other than he is indeed, or a deceiver." (pp. 50-5)

It is because men are only human that hypocrites like Claudius are able to pass themselves off successfully. Only God and the evil-doer's own conscience, says the renaissance, know him as he is with certainty. "Our inward disposition is the life of our actions," [Bishop] Hall declares [in his *Works,* I], "according to that doth the God of Spirits judge us, while men censure according to our external motions." It is for this reason that the disguise of the hypocrite makes him so dangerous: "wicked hypocrites care not to play with God, that they may mock men." And we are assured that: "An open wicked man doth much hurt, with notorious sins; but an hypocrite doth at last more shame goodness, by seeming good" [*Works,* VIII]. (pp. 60-1)

Claudius dares to be both a villain and a hypocrite; his heart does not smile with his face; he is guilty of murder and incest, the smile on his face hides guilt and the planning of yet more villainy in his heart. *Pericles* treats a situation resembling that in *Hamlet*: like Claudius, Antiochus is guilty of incest and plans fresh murder; and like Claudius he dissembles: where Hamlet cries that "one may smile and smile and be a villain" [I. v. 108], Pericles comments:

> How courtesy would seem to cover sin,
> When what is done is like an hypocrite,
> The which is good in nothing but in sight!
> [*Pericles,* I. i. 121-23]

As Hall says: "Hypocrisy gains this of men, that it may do evil unsuspected" [*Works,* I].

After the moment when Claudius has shown his guilt fleetingly in his face and gesture, "upon the talk of the poisoning" [III. ii. 289], there is no more doubt for Hamlet and Horatio, and for audience and reader. And up to this moment Shakespeare does not show Claudius in such a way that we know him for what he is: but once murder has spoken with miraculous organ we can see him without the disguise. Denmark, however, is still deluded; his subjects cannot peer through the smile to the guilty heart. And as a result he is able to send Hamlet away to a treacherously planned death: and even when the Prince returns, Claudius still appears to be the splendid monarch striving hard to reconcile his nephew and Laertes in a fair and generous manner.

Claudius shows himself to us as hypocrite in the use he makes of Laertes:

> Laertes, was your father dear to you?
> Or are you like the painting of a sorrow,

A face without a heart?
> [IV. vii. 107-09]

These words are spoken by the very man who turned to chide another sorrowing son; to Hamlet, Claudius declared at the beginning of the play:

> to persever
> In obstinate condolement is . . .
> . . . unmanly grief;
> . . . Fie! 'tis a fault to heaven,
> A fault against the dead, a fault to nature,
> To reason most absurd; whose common theme
> Is death of fathers.
> [I. ii. 92-104]

Shakespeare put these sentiments into the mouth of the character whom he had imagined guilty of the murder of the man for whom such grief was being shown. The same hypocritical murderer, as he incites Laertes to yet more killing, asks:

> what would you undertake
> To show yourself in deed your father's son
> More than in words?
> [IV. vii. 124-26]

And when the answer comes: "to cut his throat i' th' church" [IV. vii. 126], Claudius approves with every show of honest sympathy and indignation, using words which are unwittingly a sentence passed on himself:

> No place, indeed, should murder sanctuarize;
> Revenge should have no bounds.
> [IV. vii. 127-28]

Shakespeare makes Claudius a hypocrite in what he says and does as the action progresses, and when the last scene has arrived we have been able to understand the kind of villainy that lurks beneath his fair and smooth appearance. It is obvious then that he has been created by the playwright as this particular kind of dangerous person, the hypocrite, who by virtue of his position and of his seeming splendour can pervert not merely his queen, but the very land which he has stolen from his victim. Claudius is not a mixture of good and bad, he is an evil man who seems good.

But it might well be objected that the King tries to pray, that he shows remorse, especially when admitting to himself the justice of the remark made by Polonius:

> 'Tis too much prov'd, that with devotion's visage
> And pious action we do sugar o'er
> The devil himself.
> [III. i. 46-8]

Then Claudius admits to himself:

> O, 'tis too true!
> How smart a lash that speech doth give my conscience!
> The harlot's cheek, beautied with plast'ring art,

Is not more ugly to the thing that helps it
Than is my deed to my most painted word.
O heavy burden!

>   [III. i. 48-53]

At this point the audience cannot be certain that the King's guilt involves murder of a brother, but incest and usurpation are burdens enough. Yet the trouble with Claudius from the renaissance point of view is that however smart a lash his conscience may receive, it is powerless to make him really contrite. For Elizabethans there was no more to be seen in his behaviour, especially when he tries to pray (III. iii.); nothing more than horror at the realization of the consequences of his wrongdoing. As Bishop Hall puts it: "Consciences that are without remorse, are not without horror: wickedness makes men desperate." He says this in his commentary on the story of Cain and Abel: and Claudius, who has also slain his brother, is another example of despairing wickedness.

When Claudius tries to pray he fails, because, like Faustus [in Christopher Marlowe's *Dr. Faustus*], he cannot bear to part with the fruits of his sinning; and as a result, in another more deadly sense, he learns to feel the full quality of those fruits as a burden round his neck, pressing him down into the swamp of hell:

> "Forgive me my foul murder"!
> That cannot be; since I am still possess'd
> Of those effects for which I did the murder—
> My crown, mine own ambition, and my queen.
> May one be pardon'd and retain th' offence?
>
>   [III. iii. 52-6]

And the answer which he gives himself is in tune with what we have heard in other renaissance comments on hypocrisy:

> In the corrupted currents of this world
> Offence's gilded hand may shove by justice; . . .
>   . . . But 'tis not so above:
> There is no shuffling; there the action lies
> In his true nature.
>
>   [III. iii. 57-62]

But Claudius has reduced himself to a state of such depravity that in the corruption of his will his soul is limed:

> that, struggling to be free,
> Art more engag'd.
>
>   [III. iii. 68-9]

As he rises from his knees, having given every outward sign of penitent devotion, he seems to the sentimental modern mind to be pathetic and not all unworthy. But the Elizabethan would not necessarily have had this view: he would more likely have given a verdict more in keeping with John Bulwer's denunciation of hypocrites [in his *Chirologia*]:

Idolators and hypocrites, in lifting up their hands in prayer, are but apes, who while they by the outward symbol profess to have their minds erected upwards, the first of them stick in the wood and stone, as if God were enclosed there: the second sort, entangled in vain cares, or wicked cogitations, lie grovelling on the earth, and by a contradiction of gesture, bear witness against themselves.

Even so does Claudius grieve, that "above," malefactors are

> compell'd,
> Even to the teeth and forehead of our faults,
> To give in evidence.
>
>   [III. iii. 62-4]

Thus for Elizabethans the enormous extent of his guilt became more visible with his own despairing recognition:

> My words fly up, my thoughts remain below.
> Words without thoughts never to heaven go.
>
>   [III. iii. 97-8]

When William Lathum, in *Phyala Lachrymarum* (1633), gives a list of the flowers fit to be thrown upon the bier of his friend, Nathaniel Weld, tulips are rejected:

> No gaudy tulips here admitted be,
> (Emblems of false (fair-fained) sanctity),
> Whose worth all outward is in show alone,
> But inward scent hath not, ne virtue none.

From one point of view, Claudius is like the "gaudy tulips," but fundamentally they are inadequate as symbols for what Shakespeare has imagined of him. The dramatist is thinking of Claudius in terms of Cain, who is associated in the Bible, not only with the murder of a brother, but with a hypocritical sacrifice which was literally a foul stench. For that reason we are reminded of Cain when Claudius exclaims in horror:

> O, my offence is rank, it smells to heaven;
> It hath the primal eldest curse upon 't—
> A brother's murder!
>
>   [III. iii. 36-8]

This is his second reference to his biblical prototype: the first occurs in the early hypocritical reproof to Hamlet for mourning his dead father:

> a fault to nature,
> To reason most absurd; whose common theme
> Is death of fathers, and who still hath cried
> From the first corse till he that died to-day,
> "This must be so."
>
>   [I. ii. 102-06]

The "first corse," Abel, was killed by his brother, Cain, in fulfilment of the primal curse; but while this is an appropriate example, I do not think its appearance here should be taken as anything more than contributory evidence of the way in which Shakespeare himself was reacting to his story; for there is direct evidence enough later when Claudius refers openly to the nature of his own offence. It is, however, important not to neglect the association of Claudius with Cain, for here we have an essential element in Shakespeare's conception of the Hamlet story.

In *Shakespeare's Imagery* (1935), Professor [Carolyn F. E.] Spurgeon calls attention to the number of images in *Hamlet* in which disease is involved:

> In *Hamlet* there hovers all through the play in both words and word pictures the conception of disease, especially of a hidden corruption infecting and destroying a wholesome body.

Professor Spurgeon suggests that the reason for this lies in the author's having imagined Hamlet as infected and killed by disease of the spirit: she believes that the imagery of this play suggests that Hamlet's tragedy is the result of

Norman Wooland as Horatio, Laurence Olivier as Hamlet, and Stanley Holloway as the Gravedigger in Olivier's 1948 film adaptation of Hamlet. *Act V, scene i.*

a *condition* for which the individual himself is apparently not responsible any more than the sick man is to blame for the infection which strikes and devours him.

But the Elizabethans knew of a form of sickness for which there was no doubt that the sick man was himself to blame, and that was hypocrisy. Where Professor Spurgeon has assumed that the imagery of disease expresses Shakespeare's attitude to Hamlet, there are stronger grounds for suggesting that the hidden corruption which hovers all through the play emanates from the central conception of Claudius and the part which he occupies in the story as a whole. It is here that we perceive the importance of the association with Cain; for not only did Cain slay his brother, like Claudius, and is known for the foulness of his sacrifice, but Cain like Claudius was a hypocrite. Moreover, the renaissance, with the authority of Holy Writ, often speaks of hypocrisy itself as an inner corruption, a conception which we have retained with the term "whited sepulchre." Claudius' mention of his "rank" offence, just before his useless show of prayer, should be imagined in the light of the distinction made by Hall between sin and penitence:

> There is no sense, that gives so lively a refreshing to the spirits, as that of smelling: no smell can yield so true and feeling delight to the sense, as the offerings of our penitence, obedience, praise, send up into the nostrils of the Almighty. [*Works,* V]

But sins, he adds, are unsavoury: "no carrion is so noisome." (pp. 62-8)

It is not strange that the world in which Claudius flourishes should be seen by Hamlet in its true light as

> an unweeded garden
> That grows to seed; things rank and gross
>   in nature
> Possess it merely.
>
> [I. ii. 135-37]

And "rank" is the word which Claudius himself uses of his offence.

When Hamlet breaks away and follows the Ghost, Horatio asks: "To what issue will this come?" And Marcellus gives the right answer: "Something is rotten in the state of Denmark" [I. iv. 89-90]. But what neither of them can yet realize is that the rottenness lies at the heart of the country, its king. We cannot understand fully what Hamlet has to fight unless we realize that the triumph of Claudius means spiritual death for Denmark. No wonder that he himself describes his subjects as:

> muddied,
> Thick and unwholesome in their thoughts
>   and whispers.
>
> [IV. v. 81-2]

And so it must be until the foul deed, never hidden from the sight of God, has risen to the eyes of men, and the cause, the core of corruption, the seemingly fine king, has been removed.

This view of Claudius becomes even more justified if we consider yet another aspect of the hypocrite as conceived of in the renaissance: he is not only rotten, he is devilish. Hall describes how when a hypocrite meets a friend in the street, "the other thinks he reads his heart in his face," and rejoices at receiving a vague invitation which will never materialize into hospitality: and in his heart all the time the hypocrite mocks:

> In brief, he is the stranger's saint; the neighbour's disease; the blot of goodness; a rotten stick, in a dark night; a poppy, in a cornfield; an ill tempered candle, with a great snuff, that in going out smells ill; an angel abroad, a devil at home; and worse when an angel than when a devil.

Another devil of this kind to whom Shakespeare gave a central part is Angelo in *Measure for Measure.* In each play the situation is similar: a hypocrite rules in each. Isabella finds that it would be useless to

> tell the world
> Aloud what man thou art.
> [*Measure for Measure,* II. iv. 153-54]

Angelo sneers triumphantly:

> Say what you can: my false o'erweighs your true.
> [II. iv. 170]

And the Duke sums up as he moralizes in a string of couplets at the end of the Third Act:

> O, what may man within him hide,
> Though Angel on the outward side!
> [III. ii. 271-72]

In *Measure for Measure* the audience can appreciate the truth of this at once: from what has been shown of Angelo we recognize that Isabella is not mistaken in her words to her brother:

> This outward-sainted deputy,
> . . . is yet a devil;
> His filth within being cast, he would appear
> A pond as deep as hell.
> [III. i. 88-93]

The ordinary kind of devil is black within and black without: that is why Thomas Adams followed Martin Luther in applying the term "White Devil" to a hypocrite: "A devil he was," writes Adams of Judas, "black within and full of rancour, but white without, and skinned over with hypocrisy; therefore to use *Luther's* word, we will call him the *white devil"* [*The White Devil, or the Hypocrite Uncased*].

Claudius shows so white that it takes half a play before we know him for what he is, and a second half before anyone is in a position to unmask him in public. Much of the horror of the situation with which Hamlet is confronted lies in the certainty that in virtue of his "seeming," Claudius can continue to impose on the world. In *Measure for Measure,* the Duke has retired, but only temporarily: in *Hamlet* the king has been murdered, and everything lies at the murderer's feet. Isabella can cry in public to her legitimate ruler:

> do not banish reason
> For inequality; but let your reason serve
> To make the truth appear where it seems hid,
> And hide the false seems true.
> [V. i. 64-7]

But there is no one to whom Hamlet can make this appeal; even his own friends and well-wishers are, without knowing it, at the usurper's disposal. Again, when Isabella is at first unsuccessful in her supplication to the Duke, she comforts herself with the apostrophe:

> O, you blessed ministers above,
> Keep me in patience; and, with ripened time,
> Unfold the evil which is here wrapt up
> In countenance!
> [V. i. 115-18]

But Hamlet must not delay, he cannot afford to wait for time to "unfold the evil" which is here "wrapt up" in Claudius' countenance.

In Isabella's speech, Shakespeare has used the image of wrapping and unfolding in association with a countenance: in *Hamlet* he concentrates on the smile into which a face folds when it covers villainy: but in *Titus Andronicus,* that early play, he combines the two. There the word "fold" means not only "wrap," but "cover," "protect," "conceal," with the suggestion of "crease," ending in the concrete "smile." Tamora is made to wonder greatly

> that man's face can fold
> In pleasing smiles such murderous tyranny.
> [*Titus Andronicus,* II. iii. 266-67]

And crude as *Titus Andronicus* undoubtedly is, the situation there is nevertheless not so different from what we have in *Hamlet.* In each play deceit seems to triumph, the normal ways in which murder may be denounced are frustrated. Where Hamlet must say nothing, the opponents of evil in the Roman play lose tongues and hands, the symbols and "adjuncts" of expression. In each play a smile hides villainy, and in each, murder speaks at last with most miraculous organ.

To read *Pericles, Measure for Measure, The Merchant of Venice* and *Titus Andronicus* is to find that whenever Shakespeare deals with the elements which for him are present in the story of *Hamlet,* he reacts in the same way, stressing the contrast between inside and outside, linking apparent health with hidden corruption, the seeming angelic with the actual diabolic. Centuries earlier, *The Proverbs of Alfred* had observed:

> Mony appel is bryht with-ute
> And Bitter with-inne.

The early Middle English Lambeth Homily declares that the hypocrite is 'al swa is an eppel iheoweth. he bith with-uten feire and frakel with-innen"— "like a rosy apple, fair without and rotten within." And the tradition went on into Shakespeare's own day.

In this tradition Claudius can be viewed in the right perspective, not as an unfortunate mixture of good and bad qualities, but as an example of how utter corruption can pass itself off as good, an example who makes the words of Antonio in *Twelfth Night* ring true:

> Virtue is beauty; but the beauteous evil
> Are empty trunks o'erflourish'd by the
>   devil.
>   [*Twelfth Night*, III. iv. 369-70]

If anyone object today that to take Claudius thus is to reduce him from a credible human being, a mixture of good and bad in tragedy, to an impossible puppet, a villain who fits nothing but melodrama, only one reply can be given. Shakespeare's age believed that people of this sort actually existed, and that tragedy was often the outcome of their success in deception. And if it be objected further that this is thrusting Shakespeare back into his age, the reply is that he wrote for that age, and that his plays could have succeeded in the theatre only if they had been intelligible to his contemporaries, offering them situations and ideas which were familiar to the early seventeenth century. For Shakespeare's contemporaries, Claudius as a hypocrite in their sense of the word was no caricature. To say that one could smile and be a villain was to express a deep truth which goes right into the nature of things in a world which has suffered a fall; and for the renaissance that was the world of all who came after Adam. To read into Hamlet's words nothing more than a picturesque statement that Claudius is not to be trusted would be to blind ourselves to a great part of Shakespeare's vision of this particular battle between good and evil as involved in the continual struggle of Satan to assert himself. Only when we are prepared to consider Claudius as an overwhelmingly evil person, whose seeming is the opposite of his being, are we able to appreciate how his creator has organized the elements of the story of the Prince of Denmark into a shape which awakens an understanding of what was to the renaissance mind a true comment on the place of evil in the world. (pp. 68-73)

> Bertram Joseph, " '—The King, the King's to Blame'," in his Conscience and the King: A Study of "Hamlet," Chatto and Windus, 1953, pp. 50-73.

GERTRUDE

Carolyn Heilbrun

*[Heilbrun contends that, contrary to the predominant critical opinion, **Gertrude** is not a weak character who lacks "depth and vigorous intelligence." The critic then evaluates **Gertrude**'s lines in* Hamlet *to demonstrate that while the queen is not "profound," she is certainly never "silly." The character's actions in fact reveal her to be clear-headed and courageous, especially during the closet scene in Act III, scene iv when, after **Hamlet** accuses her of lust, she accepts his judgment and admits her sin. Heilbrun also provides an Elizabethan definition of the term "adultery," asserting that the word does not necessarily imply that **Claudius** and **Gertrude** had an affair while **King Hamlet** was alive, rather it suggests that their marriage reflects an unchaste sexual relationship. The critic concludes that while **Gertrude** is indeed lustful, she is also "intelligent, penetrating, and gifted with a remarkable talent for concise and pithy speech." For a critical reaction to Heilbrun's interpretation of the queen, see the excerpt below by Baldwin Maxwell. For further commentary on **Gertrude**'s character, see the excerpts by Arthur Kirsch, Kenneth Muir, Edgar Johnson, and Ernest Jones.]*

The character of Hamlet's mother has not received the specific critical attention it deserves. Moreover, the traditional account of her personality as rendered by the critics will not stand up under close scrutiny of Shakespeare's play.

None of the critics of course has failed to see Gertrude as vital to the action of the play; not only is she the mother of the hero, the widow of the Ghost, and the wife of the current King of Denmark, but the fact of her hasty and, to the Elizabethans, incestuous marriage, the whole question of her "falling off", occupies a position of barely secondary importance in the mind of her son, and of the Ghost. Indeed, Freud and Jones see her [see excerpt in section on Hamlet's character], the object of Hamlet's Oedipus complex, as central to the motivation of the play. But the critics, with no exception that I have been able to find, have accepted Hamlet's word "frailty" as applying to her whole personality, and have seen in her not one weakness, or passion in the Elizabethan sense, but a character of which weakness and lack of depth and vigorous intelligence are the entire explanation. Of her can it truly be said that carrying the "stamp of one defect", she did "in the general censure take corruption from that particular fault" [I. iv. 35-6].

The critics are agreed that Gertrude was not a party to the late King's murder and indeed knew nothing of it; a point which on the clear evidence of the play, is indisputable. They have also discussed whether or not Gertrude, guilty of more than an "o'er-hasty marriage" [II. ii. 57], had committed adultery with Claudius before her husband's death. I will return to this point later on. Beyond discussing these two points, those critics who have dealt specifically with the Queen have traditionally seen her as well-meaning but shallow and feminine, in the pejorative sense of the word: incapable of any sustained rational process, superficial and flighty. It is this tradition which a closer reading of the play will show to be erroneous.

Professor [A.C.] Bradley describes the traditional Gertrude thus [in his *Shakespearean Tragedy*]:

> The Queen was not a bad-hearted woman, not at all the woman to think little of murder. But she had a soft animal nature and was very dull and very shallow. She loved to be happy, like a sheep in the sun, and to do her justice, it pleased her to see others happy, like more sheep in the sun. . . . It was pleasant to sit upon her throne and see smiling faces around her, and foolish and unkind in Hamlet to persist in grieving for his father instead of marrying Ophelia and making everything comfortable. . . . The belief at the bottom of her heart was that the world is a place constructed simply that people may be happy in it in a good-humored sensual fashion.

Later on, Bradley says of her that when affliction comes to her "the good in her nature struggles to the surface through the heavy mass of sloth."

[Harley] Granville-Barker is not quite so extreme. Shakespeare, he says [in his *Prefaces to Shakespeare*],

> gives us in Gertrude the woman who does not mature, who clings to her youth and all that belongs to it, whose charm will not change but at last fade and wither; a pretty creature, as we see her, desperately refusing to grow old. . . . She is drawn for us with unemphatic strokes, and she has but a passive part in the play's action. She moves throughout in Claudius' shadow; he holds her as he won her, by the witchcraft of his wit.

Elsewhere Granville-Barker says "Gertrude who will certainly never see forty-five again, might better be 'old'. (That is, portrayed by an older, mature actress.) But that would make her relations with Claudius—and *their* likelihood is vital to the play—quite incredible." Granville-Barker is saying here that a woman about forty-five years of age cannot feel any sexual passion nor arouse it. This is one of the mistakes which lie at the heart of the misunderstanding about Gertrude.

Professor [John] Dover Wilson sees Gertrude as more forceful than either of these two critics will admit, but even he finds the Ghost's unwillingness to shock her with knowledge of his murder to be one of the basic motivations of the play, and he says of her "Gertrude is always hoping for the best" [*What Happens in Hamlet*].

Now whether Claudius won Gertrude before or after her husband's death, it was certainly not, as Granville-Barker implies, with "the witchcraft of his wit" alone. Granville-Barker would have us believe that Claudius won her simply by the force of his persuasive tongue. "It is plain", he writes, that the Queen "does little except echo his [Claudius'] wishes; sometimes—as in the welcome to Rosencrantz and Guildenstern—she repeats his very words," though Wilson must admit later that Gertrude does not tell Claudius everything. Without dwelling here on the psychology of the Ghost, or the greater burden borne by the Elizabethan words "witchcraft" and "wit", we can plainly see, for the Ghost tells us, how Claudius won the Queen: the Ghost considers his brother to be garbage, and "lust", the Ghost says, "will sate itself in a celestial bed and prey on garbage" [I. v. 55-7]. "Lust"—in a woman of forty-five or more—is the key word here. Bradley, Granville-Barker, and to a lesser extent Professor Dover Wilson, misunderstand Gertrude largely because they are unable to see lust, the desire for sexual relations, as the passion, in the Elizabethan sense of the word, the flaw, the weakness which drives Gertrude to an incestuous marriage, appals her son, and keeps him from the throne. Unable to explain her marriage to Claudius as the act of any but a weak-minded vacillating woman, they fail to see Gertrude for the strong-minded, intelligent, succinct, and, apart from this passion, sensible woman that she is.

To understand Gertrude properly, it is only necessary to examine the lines Shakespeare has chosen for her to say. She is, except for her description of Ophelia's death, concise and pithy in speech, with a talent for seeing the essence of every situation presented before her eyes. If she is not profound, she is certainly never silly. We first hear her asking Hamlet to stop wearing black, to stop walking about with his eyes downcast, and to realize that death is an inevitable part of life. She is, in short, asking him not to give way to the passion of grief, a passion of whose force and dangers the Elizabethans were aware. . . . Claudius echoes her with a well-reasoned argument against grief which was, in its philosophy if not in its language, a piece of commonplace Elizabethan lore. After Claudius' speech, Gertrude asks Hamlet to remain in Denmark, where he is rightly loved. Her speeches have been short, however warm and loving, and conciseness of statement is not the mark of a dull and shallow woman.

We next hear her, as Queen and gracious hostess, welcoming Rosencrantz and Guildenstern to the court, hoping, with the King, that they may cheer Hamlet and discover what is depressing him. Claudius then tells Gertrude, when they are alone, that

Polonius believes he knows what is upsetting Hamlet. The Queen answers:

> I doubt it is no other than the main,
> His father's death and our o'er-hasty mar-
>   riage.
>
> [II. ii. 56-7]

This statement is concise, remarkably to the point, and not a little courageous. It is not the statement of a dull, slothful woman who can only echo her husband's words. Next, Polonius enters with his most unbrief apotheosis to brevity. The Queen interrupts him with five words: "More matter with less art" [II. ii. 95]. It would be difficult to find a phrase more applicable to Polonius. When this gentleman, in no way deterred from his loquacity, after purveying the startling news that he has a daughter, begins to read a letter, the Queen asks pointedly "Came this from Hamlet to her?" [II. ii. 114].

We see Gertrude next in Act III, asking Rosencrantz and Guildenstern, with her usual directness, if Hamlet received them well, and if they were able to tempt him to any pastime. But before leaving the room, she stops for a word of kindness to Ophelia. It is a humane gesture, for she is unwilling to leave Ophelia, the unhappy tool of the King and Polonius, without some kindly and intelligent appreciation of her help:

> And for your part, Ophelia, I do wish
> That your good beauties be the happy
>   cause
> Of Hamlet's wildness. So shall I hope your
>   virtues
> Will bring him to his wonted way again,
> To both your honors.
>
> [III. i. 37-41]

It is difficult to see in this speech, as Bradley apparently does, the gushing shallow wish of a sentimental woman that class distinctions shall not stand in the way of true love.

At the play, the Queen asks Hamlet to sit near her. She is clearly trying to make him feel he has a place in the court of Denmark. She does not speak again until Hamlet asks her how she likes the play. "The lady doth protest too much, methinks" [III. ii. 230] is her immortal comment on the player queen. The scene gives her four more words: when Claudius leaps to his feet, she asks "How fares my Lord?" [III. ii. 267].

I will for the moment pass over the scene in the Queen's closet, to follow her quickly through the remainder of the play. After the closet scene, the Queen comes to speak to Claudius. She tells him, as Hamlet has asked her to, that he, Hamlet, is mad, and has killed Polonius. She adds, however, that he now weeps for what he has done. She does not wish Claudius to know what she now knows, how wild and fearsome Hamlet has become. Later, she does not wish to see Ophelia, but hearing how distracted she is, consents. When Laertes bursts in ready to attack Claudius, she immediately steps between Claudius and Laertes to protect the King, and tells Laertes it is not Claudius who has killed his father. Laertes will of course soon learn this, but it is Gertrude who manages to tell him before he can do any meaningless damage. She leaves Laertes and the King together, and then returns to tell Laertes that his sister is drowned. She gives her news directly, realizing that suspense will increase the pain of it, but this is the one time in the play when her usual pointed conciseness would be the mark neither of intelligence nor kindness, and so, gently, and at some length, she tells Laertes of his sister's death, giving him time to recover from the shock of grief, and to absorb the meaning of her words. At Ophelia's funeral the Queen scatters flowers over the grave:

> Sweets to the sweet; farewell!
> I hop'd thou shouldst have been my Ham-
>   let's wife.
> I thought thy bride-bed to have deck'd,
>   sweet maid,
> And not t' have strew'd thy grave.
>
> [V. i. 243-46]

She is the only one present decently mourning the death of someone young, and not heated in the fire of some personal passion.

At the match between Hamlet and Laertes, the Queen believes that Hamlet is out of training, but glad to see him at some sport, she gives him her handkerchief to wipe his brow, and drinks to his success. The drink is poisoned and she dies. But before she dies she does not waste time on vituperation; she warns Hamlet that the drink is poisoned to prevent his drinking it. They are her last words. Those critics who have thought her stupid admire her death; they call it uncharacteristic.

In Act III, when Hamlet goes to his mother in her closet his nerves are pitched at the very height of tension; he is on the edge of hysteria. The possibility of murdering his mother has in fact entered his mind, and he has just met and refused an opportunity to kill Claudius. His mother, meanwhile, waiting for him, has told Polonius not to fear for her, but she knows when she sees Hamlet that he may be violently mad. Hamlet quips with her, insults her, tells her he wishes she were not his mother, and when she, still retaining dignity, attempts to end the interview, Hamlet seizes her and she cries for help. The important thing to note is that the Queen's cry "Thou wilt not murder me" [III. iv. 21] is not foolish. She has seen from Hamlet's demeanor that he is capable of murder, as indeed in the next instant he proves himself to be.

We next learn from the Queen's startled "As kill a king" [III. iv. 30] that she has no knowledge of the murder, though of course this is only confirmation here of what we already know. Then the Queen asks Hamlet why he is so hysterical:

What have I done, that thou dar'st wag thy
  tongue
In noise so rude against me?
                                                    [III. iv. 39-40]

Hamlet tells her: it is her lust, the need of sexual
passion, which has driven her from the arms and
memory of her husband to the incomparably
cruder charms of his brother. He cries out that she
has not even the excuse of youth for her lust:

> O Shame! where is thy blush? Rebellious
>   hell,
> If thou canst mutine in a matron's bones,
> To flaming youth let virtue be as wax
> And melt in her own fire. Proclaim no
>   shame
> When the compulsive ardor gives the
>   charge,
> Since frost itself as actively doth burn,
> And reason panders will.
>   [III. iv. 81-8]

This is not only a lust, but a lust which throws out
of joint all the structure of human morality and relationships. And the Queen admits it. If there is one
quality that has characterized, and will characterize, every speech of Gertrude's in the play, it is the
ability to see reality clearly, and to express it. This
talent is not lost when turned upon herself:

> O Hamlet, speak no more!
> Thou turn'st mine eyes into my very soul,
> And there I see such black and grained
>   spots
> As will not leave their tinct.
>   [III. iv. 88-91]

She knows that lust has driven her, that this is her
sin, and she admits it. Not that she wishes to linger
in the contemplation of her sin. No more, she cries,
no more. And then the Ghost appears to Hamlet.
The Queen thinks him mad again—as well she
might—but she promises Hamlet that she will not
betray him—and she does not.

Where, in all that we have seen of Gertrude, is there
the picture of "a soft animal nature, very dull and
very shallow?" She may indeed be "animal" in the
sense of "lustful". But it does not follow that because she wishes to continue a life of sexual experience, her brain is soft or her wit unperceptive.

Some critics, having accepted Gertrude as a weak
and vacillating woman, see no reason to suppose
that she did not fall victim to Claudius' charms before the death of her husband and commit adultery
with him. These critics, Professor Bradley among
them, claim that the elder Hamlet clearly tells his
son that Gertrude has committed adultery with
Claudius in the speech beginning "Ay that incestuous, that adulterate beast" [I. v. 41ff.] Professor
Dover Wilson presents the argument:

> Is the Ghost speaking here of the o'er-
> hasty marriage of Claudius and Gertrude?
> Assuredly not. His "certain term" is draw-
> ing rapidly to an end, and he is already be-

ginning to "scent the morning air." Hamlet knew of the marriage, and his whole
soul was filled with nausea at the thought
of the speedy hasting to "incestuous
sheets." Why then should the Ghost waste
precious moments in telling Hamlet what
he was fully cognisant of before? . . .
Moreover, though the word "incestuous"
was applicable to the marriage, the rest of
the passage is entirely inapplicable to it.
Expressions like "witchcraft", "traitorous
gifts", "seduce", "shameful lust", and
"seeming virtuous" may be noted in passing. But the rest of the quotation leaves no
doubt upon the matter. . . .

Professor Dover Wilson and other critics have accepted the Ghost's word "adulterate" in its modern
meaning. The Elizabethan word "adultery", however, was not restricted to its modern meaning, but
was used to define any sexual relationship which
could be called unchaste, including of course an incestuous one. Certainly the elder Hamlet considered the marriage of Claudius and Gertrude to be
unchaste and unseemly, and while his use of the
word "adulterate" indicates his very strong feelings about the marriage, it would not to an Elizabethan audience necessarily mean that he believed
Gertrude to have been false to him before his death.
It is important to notice, too, that the Ghost does
not apply the term "adulterate" to Gertrude, and
he may well have considered the term a just description of Claudius' entire sexual life.

But even if the Ghost used the word "adulterate"
in full awareness of its modern restricted meaning,
it is not necessary to assume on the basis of this
single speech (and it is the only shadow of evidence
we have for such a conclusion) that Gertrude was
unfaithful to him while he lived. It is quite probable that the elder Hamlet still considered himself
married to Gertrude, and he is moreover revolted
that her lust for him ("why she would hang on him
as if increase of appetite had grown by what it fed
on" [I. ii. 143-44]) should have so easily transferred
itself to another. This is why he uses the expressions "seduce", "shameful lust", and others. Professor Dover Wilson has himself said "Hamlet
knew of the marriage, and his whole soul was filled
with nausea at the thought of the speedy hasting
to incestuous sheets"; the soul of the elder Hamlet
was undoubtedly filled with nausea too, and this
could well explain his using such strong language,
as well as his taking the time to mention the matter
at all. It is not necessary to consider Gertrude an
adulteress to account for the speech of the Ghost.

Gertrude's lust was, of course, more important to
the plot than we may at first perceive. Charlton
Lewis, among others, has shown how Shakespeare
kept many of the facts of the plots from which he
borrowed without maintaining the structures
which explained them. In the original Belleforest
story, Gertrude (substituting Shakespeare's more
familiar names) was daughter of the king; to be-

come king, it was necessary to marry her. The elder Hamlet, in marrying Gertrude, ousted Claudius from the throne. Shakespeare retained the shell of this in his play. When she no longer has a husband, the form of election would be followed to declare the next king, in this case undoubtedly her son Hamlet. By marrying Gertrude, Claudius "popp'd in between th' election and my hopes" [V. ii. 65], that is, kept young Hamlet from the throne. Gertrude's flaw of lust made Claudius' ambition possible, for without taking advantage of the Queen's desire still to be married, he could not have been king.

But Gertrude, if she is lustful, is also intelligent, penetrating, and gifted with a remarkable talent for concise and pithy speech. In all the play, the person whose language hers most closely resembles is Horatio. "Sweets to the sweet," she has said at Ophelia's grave [V. i. 243]. "Good night sweet prince", Horatio says at the end [V. ii. 359]. They are neither of them dull, or shallow, or slothful, though one of them is passion's slave. (pp. 201-06)

Carolyn Heilbrun, "The Character of Hamlet's Mother," in Shakespeare Quarterly, *Vol. VII, No. 2, Spring, 1957, pp. 201-06.*

Baldwin Maxwell

[Maxwell takes exception to Carolyn Heilbrun's reading of Gertrude *as a strong and intelligent character (see excerpt above) and provides a scene-by-scene analysis of the queen to prove that she is highly dependent on, and manipulated by,* Claudius. *The critic maintains that because Gertrude has generally fewer lines than the other characters with whom she interacts, principally* Claudius *and* Hamlet, *she is at best a minor force in the play. Maxwell also compares the queen to her counterpart in the Belleforest version of Hamlet, one of the chief sources for Shakespeare's tragedy. Unlike Shakespeare's queen, the critic observes, the* Gertrude *of the Belleforest account is "neither weak nor neutral." Maxwell then presents examples of the queen's ineffectuality; when* Gertrude *describes her marriage as merely "o'er-hasty," she does not recognize the union as adulterous or incestuous because she has been duped by* Claudius's *charm to accept it as normal; and, during the closet scene when she asks* Hamlet *"What shall I do?" (III. iv. 180), she further demonstrates her lack of initiative because she needs to depend on others for guidance. Perhaps the most startling evidence of* Gertrude's *pronounced dependence, the critic continues, is that she submissively remains with* Claudius *after* Hamlet *has told her of the king's crimes. Maxwell further contends that* Gertrude's *first independent act occurs when she defies* Claudius *and drinks from the poisoned cup, but "her crossing him*

means her death." For further commentary of Gertrude's *character, see the excerpts by Arthur Kirsch, Kenneth Muir, Edgar Johnson, and Ernest Jones.]*

In an article entitled "The Character of Hamlet's Mother" [see excerpt above], Miss Carolyn Heilbrun expressed strong disagreement with what had been the generally accepted estimate of Queen Gertrude. Seemingly unaware of the essay by Professor [John W.] Draper [in his *The Hamlet of Shakespeare's Audience*], the Queen's most ardent defender, Miss Heilbrun wrote that "critics, with no exception that I have been able to find, have accepted Hamlet's word 'frailty' as applying to [Gertrude's] whole personality, and have seen in her . . . a character of which weakness and lack of depth and rigorous intelligence are the entire explanation." She, as had Professor Draper, rejected almost *in toto* the views of such critics as A. C. Bradley, Miss Agnes Mackenzie, H. Granville-Barker, and others who had declared the Queen "weak", "neutral", or "little more than a puppet".

Professor Draper, who thought Gertrude innocent of adultery prior to King Hamlet's death, not only denied her weakness but excused her hasty and incestuous marriage as politically necessary because of a national crisis, "a marriage more of convenience than of love." To him the Queen appeared "dignified, gracious, and resourceful", one who "as a wife, as a mother, as a queen . . . seems to approximate, if not the Elizabethan ideal, at least the Elizabethan norm". She is, he insisted, "no slave to lust." It is only on this last point that Miss Heilbrun and Professor Draper markedly disagreed. Although persuaded that Gertrude was innocent of adultery prior to the elder Hamlet's death, Miss Heilbrun argued that her marriage to Claudius was brought about not by a need to settle a national crisis, not by the witchcraft of Claudius' wit, but by lust alone, "the need of sexual passion" in her widowhood. Apart from this passion, the Queen is, Miss Heilbrun believed, a "strongminded, intelligent, succinct, and . . . sensible woman", who is, except for her description of Ophelia's death, "concise and pithy in speech, with a talent for seeing the essence of every situation presented before her eyes."

This view of the Queen's character is at such variance with that previously current that one may wish to reexamine her appearances in the play, scene by scene, for light upon the impression Shakespeare sought to create. Little time is needed to do so, for however important the part of the Queen in *the story* of Hamlet, her role in *the play* is definitely subordinate. She appears in ten of the play's twenty scenes, but in those ten scenes she speaks fewer lines than does Ophelia, who appears in only five; and, unlike Ophelia, the Queen is never the central or dominant figure on the stage. She speaks but one brief aside and never the concluding line of a scene. To be sure, a gifted actress may, by clever stage business and a gracious manner, provide for the role an illusion of importance; but this importance is not supported by the lines she speaks and presumably was not purposed by Shakespeare.

Practically all recent critics have agreed that Gertrude was not only innocent of complicity in the murder of her first husband but wholly unaware of it. That she was, however, guilty of an "o'erhasty [second] marriage" [II. ii. 57], she herself testifies. Nor is it permissible to see that marriage as other than incestuous. The one sin of which the Queen has been accused but of which her guilt may be debatable is that she had been Claudius' mistress while the elder Hamlet was alive.

When in I. ii, the Queen appears on stage for the first time, the audience has heard nothing whatsoever about her. It is prejudiced neither in her favor nor against her. She doubtless enters on the arm of King Claudius, who directs his ingratiating smile towards her during part of the remarkable speech with which the scene opens and from which we learn that he, having shortly before lost a brother, has recently taken to wife his brother's widow. Incest, to be sure—a horrible sin in the eyes of both church and state. But with such consummate skill has the King's speech been phrased that all on the crowded stage—or at least all but one—show neither shock nor disapproval. As a result the audience may naturally assume that the general satisfaction should outweigh the displeasure of one individual, and, in the absence of other details, accept the unusual marriage—at least for the time being—as an act which may well be shown to be both wise and—under the circumstances—permissible.

After the King has explained the present situation and expressed "For all, our thanks" [I. ii. 16], the Queen, apart perhaps from a smile, offers no word of thanks for herself. She remains silent as the King instructs the departing ambassadors and questions Laertes and Polonius on the former's desire to return to France. Gertrude is the last to speak. Upon Hamlet's bitter punning reply to the King,

> Not so, my lord. I am too much in the sun,
> [I. ii. 67]

the Queen makes her first speech—six lines, one of the three longest she speaks in the entire play. She urges Hamlet to "look like a friend on Denmark", to cease mourning for his father since

> Thou know'st 'tis common. All that lives
>   must die,
> Passing through nature to eternity.
> [I. ii. 69, 72-3]

That she misunderstands Hamlet's reply to her cliché, "Ay madam, it is common", is shown by her then asking

> If it be,
> Why seems it so particular with thee?—
> [I. ii. 74-5]

indicative not only that she has herself ceased to mourn her late husband's death but as well that she completely fails to understand her son. After Hamlet's answer, the King, his composure recovered, quickly speaks thirty-one lines, ending with the wish that Hamlet remain at Elsinore. This wish the Queen now seconds in her third and last speech of the scene:

> Let not thy mother lose her prayers, Hamlet.
> I pray thee stay with us, go not to Wittenberg.
>
> [I. ii. 118-19]

Nine lines later all exeunt save Hamlet.

Such is the Queen's part on her first appearance. She speaks slightly over nine lines in her three speeches—nine lines to the King's ninety-four. Her speeches are short but hardly seem more "concise and pithy" than speech in dramatic verse normally is. Nor do they, composed as they are of a cliché, a misunderstanding, and an echo, encourage the view that she is a "resourceful", "strong-minded" woman, "with a talent for seeing the essence of every situation presented before her eyes". Perhaps, too, her obedient rising at the King's "Madam, come", suggests her domination by him. Such a suggestion is supported by her leaving the stage in three later scenes upon similar words from the King ("Come, Gertrude", IV. i; "Let's follow, Gertrude", IV. vii; "Sweet Gertrude, leave us", III. i) and by her only once speaking as she makes her exit.

Such is our introduction to Queen Gertrude. So much do we know about her when Hamlet later in the scene, in his first soliloquy, expresses his disgust that his mother

> A little month, or ere those shoes were old
> With which she followed my poor father's
>   body
> Like Niobe, all tears, why she, even she—
> O God, a beast that wants discourse of reason
> Would have mourned longer—married
>   with mine uncle,
> My father's brother. . . .
>   O, most wicked speed, to post
> With such dexterity to incestuous sheets!
> [I. ii. 147-57]

That unusual marriage, upon which we had earlier in the scene passed no verdict, we now begin to question. But Hamlet is only one; the court as a whole had seemed neither to disapprove of the marriage nor to condemn its haste. Yet Hamlet's view, as we are soon to learn, is not peculiar to him, does not spring from thwarted ambition or from an excess of filial affection for his mother. Before we again see Queen Gertrude we are to hear another witness, one eminently qualified to judge her. Three scenes later the Ghost of the dead king is to inform Hamlet that his uncle,

> . . . that incestuous, that adulterate
> beast,
> With witchcraft of his wit, with traitorous
> gifts—
> O wicked wit and gifts, that have the
> power
> So to seduce!—won to his shameful lust
> The will of my most seeming-virtuous
> queen. . . .
> But virtue, as it never will be moved,
> Though lewdness court it in the shape of
> heaven,
> So lust, though to a radiant angel linked,
> Will sate itself in a celestial bed
> And prey on garbage.
>
> [I. v. 41-57]

Surely we are not now likely to attribute Gertrude's quietness during her earlier appearance either to remorse for her o'erhasty marriage or to an awareness that her former husband was to her present as "Hyperion to a satyr" [I. ii. 140].

But, one may ask, is the Ghost a wholly disinterested witness? Are we to accept everything he relates? Does he really know whereof he speaks? To the accuracy of his knowledge of the present and the future, I must return later, but I think it can hardly be contested that we are to assume that he has, from his vantage point beyond the grave, learned specifically all that concerned his murder. He was asleep when the poison was poured into his ear, and the dumb-show of the play-within-the-play—though that at best is only Hamlet's interpretation of what the Ghost had revealed—does not show him as awakening before he died. Yet, be it noted, the Ghost reveals not only the identity of the murderer and the instant effect which the poison had upon him but, even more remarkable, the very poison used—the "juice of cursed hebona" [I. v. 62]. Further, the King's reaction to the play-within-the-play confirms the Ghost's account of the murder in every detail. Must we not assume, therefore, that every other revelation of the past which the Ghost gives is equally accurate: that Claudius,

> With witchcraft of his wit, with traitorous
> gifts
> . . . won to his shameful lust
> The will of [the] most seeming-virtuous
> queen.
>
> [I. v. 42-6]

Miss Heilbrun, who thinks Gertrude had not been Claudius' mistress, denies that Claudius had won her by the witchcraft of his wit. The real reason Gertrude had entered upon her hasty second marriage, Miss Heilbrun claimed, was given by the Ghost later in the same speech:

> But virtue, as it never will be moved,
> Though lewdness court it in the shape of
> heaven,

> So lust, though to a radiant angel linked,
> Will sate itself in a celestial bed
> And prey on garbage.
>
> [I. v. 53-7]

But if we accept as true one part of the Ghost's speech, must we not accept the other also? And do not the last three lines quoted above suggest a violation of the marriage vows? That they were intended to do so is evidenced by the Ghost's having protested in the same speech, in lines immediately preceding, that his

> . . . love was of that dignity
> That it went hand in hand even with the
> vow
> I made to her in marriage;
>
> [I. v. 48-50]

and that Hamlet understood the Ghost's words as indicating Gertrude's adultery is shown by his charging her in the Closet Scene with

> Such an act
> That blurs the grace and blush of modes-
> ty,
> . . . makes marriage vows
> As false as dicers' oaths.
>
> [III. iv. 40-5]

So much, then, do we learn of Gertrude in Act I. On these lines must be based the original impression Shakespeare wished to give us. It is interesting and, I suspect, significant that a very large part of what we have so far learned of Gertrude and Claudius represents modification or elaboration by Shakespeare of what is found in Belleforest's account. There, of course, Gertrude is neither weak nor neutral. Although she is not said to have participated in planning the murder of her husband, she was an accomplice after the murder, for she did not deny her lover's claim that it was in defence of her that he had slain his brother. Where, asked Belleforest, would one find "a more wicked and bold woman?" Such a question would never be asked by one writing of the Gertrude of the play. Her character Shakespeare has decidedly softened, even though in the play she appears guilty on every count cited by Belleforest except that of giving support to a false account of her husband's slaying. Shakespeare has softened her character not only by making her ignorant of the murder of her husband but by elaborating, in a way most effective upon the stage, that artful craft of Claudius as reported in Belleforest's account. There the murderer "covered his boldnesse and wicked practise with so great subtiltie and policie, and under the vaile of meere simplicitie . . . that his sinne found excuse among the common people, and of the nobilitie was esteemed for justice". Claudius' persuasive cunning is further suggested by Belleforest's observing that Gertrude, "as soone as she once gave eare to [her husband's brother], forgot both the ranke she helde . . . and the dutie of an honest wife". To portray this smooth persuasiveness and subtle craft the dramatist introduced a brilliant dramatic touch for which there is no suggestion in Belleforest—the ingratiating smiling which leads Hamlet to declare Claudius a "smiling damned villain", and to cry out:

> My tables—meet it is I set it down
> That one may smile, and smile, and be a
> villain.
> At least I am sure it may be so in Denmark.
>
> [I. v. 106-09]

So much for Act I. The Queen next appears in II. ii. Rosencrantz and Guildenstern have been summoned to spy upon Hamlet, and Gertrude's first two speeches merely echo in fewer words the welcome given them by the King. With one exception her five remaining speeches in this scene are of one line or less, most of them designed to break and give a semblance of dialogue to Polonius' artful narration. The one exception is a speech of two lines in reply to the King's reporting to her that Polonius claims to have found

> The head and source of all your son's dis-
> temper.
>
> [II. ii. 55]

The Queen replies:

> I doubt it is no other but the main,
> His father's death, and our o'erhasty mar-
> riage.
>
> [II. ii. 56-7]

This speech, which some critics (mistakenly, I think) have seen as evidence that the Queen's conscience is already troubled, Miss Heilbrun pronounced "concise, remarkably to the point, and not a little courageous." One could the more readily agree with her had Gertrude omitted the word "o'erhasty". When the King first announced his marriage to his brother's widow, he passed quickly on to important affairs of state, but since then we have heard the incestuous nature of that marriage emphasized by both Hamlet and the Ghost. Are we to assume from her mentioning only the hastiness of their marriage—a censurable indiscretion perhaps but no mortal sin—that Gertrude failed to realize that her marriage to Claudius, no matter when performed, must bear the graver stain of incest? As she is at the time alone with the King, I think we must so assume. She hardly reveals here "a talent for seeing the essence of every situation presented before her eyes". But how can she have been so blind to the true nature of her marriage? The only explanation would seem to be that she is blinded by the traitorous gifts of Claudius, by the witchcraft of his wit. She thinks as he directs, acts as he wishes.

The next scene in which the Queen appears is III. ii—the play scene. Here she is on stage for 187 lines and speaks a total of two and one half lines. When to her first speech, "Come hither, my dear Hamlet, sit by me" [III. ii. 108], Hamlet replies that he prefers to sit by Ophelia, the Queen is silent

until 127 lines later, when, to emphasize the purport of such lines as "None wed the second but who killed the first", Hamlet asks, "Madam, how like you this play?" She answers simply, "The lady doth protest too much, methinks" [III. ii. 180; 229-30]—a speech which need not suggest stupidity, for she, unlike us, has not heard the ghost and knows not what is in Hamlet's mind; but unless we are to think of her as an artful villainess indeed, the simplicity of her reply is enough to urge her complete innocence of any participation in the murder. She now follows the play intently, saying nothing more until, when the frightened King rises, she anxiously enquires "How fares my lord?" [III. ii. 267] In this scene then, aside from the first clear indication that Gertrude has been no accomplice in the murder, we see in her just what we see in her in other scenes—her love for her son, her devoted concern for Claudius, and her remarkable quietness, with long periods of silence.

It is when she next appears, in III. iv—the so-called Closet Scene—that the Queen has her biggest part. The scene opens with Polonius' hiding himself behind the arras that he may overhear the interview between mother and son—an interview in which the Queen has promised to "be round with him" [III. iv. 5] in the hope of discovering the cause of Hamlet's strange behavior. The scheme had been conceived by Polonius and suggested to Claudius in II. ii, when Gertrude was not on stage. We do not witness the King's persuading the Queen to assist in this eavesdropping upon her son, but that she had received specific instructions on how the interview should be conducted is brought out in her conversation with Polonius before Hamlet enters:

> *Polonius:* 'A will come straight. Look you
> lay home to him.
> Tell him his pranks have been too broad
> to bear with,
> And that your grace hath screened and
> stood between
> Much heat and him. I'll silence me even
> here.
> Pray you be round with him. . . .
> *Queen:* I'll warrant you; fear me not.
>
> [III. iv. 1-6]

The Queen had consented to these "lawful espials", as she had consented earlier when Ophelia had been used as a decoy, probably both because she is hopeful that such a scheme may indeed unearth the secret of Hamlet's strange behavior and because the stronger Claudius is able always to dominate her will and persuade her to serve his purpose. That this second explanation is sound is, I believe, shown by a departure which Shakespeare here makes from the account of the Closet Scene as related by Belleforest. In Belleforest the King and his councillor, without taking the Queen into their confidence, arrange for the councillor to secrete himself where he may overhear mother and son; the Queen not only has no part in planning the interview, but does not suspect the presence of the eavesdropper until he is discovered by the crafty and suspicious Hamlet's beating his arms upon the hangings. By this change in the Queen's part from that of an unwitting participant to that of an active accomplice Shakespeare seems to emphasize the extent to which Claudius dominates her and uses her as his tool.

The Queen begins the closet interview with bluster and some confidence. She has apparently been well briefed as to what she shall say. But when Hamlet proves recalcitrant, when in an ugly mood he assumes the offensive and by so doing throws her out of the part she has been coached to play, she is for a brief moment bold and stubborn. "What have I done?" she cries:

> What have I done, that thou dar'st wag thy
> tongue
> In noise so rude against me?
> [III. iv. 39-40]

But as Hamlet becomes more specific in his charges, Gertrude has neither the strength nor the inclination to bluster it further. She appears, indeed, stricken in conscience:

> O Hamlet, speak no more,
> Thou turn'st mine eyes into my very soul,
> And there I see such black and grainèd
> spots
> As will not leave their tinct.
> [III. iv. 88-91]

And again,

> O Hamlet, thou hast cleft my heart in
> twain.
> [III. iv. 156]

Although in this scene the Queen has more speeches and more lines than she has in any other scene, she is throughout overshadowed by Hamlet. In the same number of speeches he speaks four times as many lines as does she. Of her twenty-four speeches, thirteen—more than half—are one line or less, and four others are less than two lines.

Some of her speeches invite comment. Miss Mackenzie has noted that Gertrude sees her penitence not as the consequence of her own actions but rather as a result of Hamlet's harsh words to her:

> O Hamlet, thou hast cleft my heart in
> twain.
> [III. iv. 156]

Second, it is important to note that the question which she, contrite, puzzled, and helpless, addresses to Hamlet as he prepares to leave, "What shall I do?" [III. iv. 180], illustrates the lack of initiative and independence which mark her throughout. Too weak to determine any procedure for herself, she must rely upon others for guidance in every action.

More puzzling is the Queen's last speech in the scene—a reply to Hamlet's

> I must to England, you know that?
> *Ger.* Alack,
> I had forgot. 'Tis so concluded on.
> [III. iv. 200-01]

No one has ever questioned Gertrude's devotion to her son, although in urging him earlier to "stay with us, go not to Wittenberg" [I. ii. 119], she may have spoken the instructions of Claudius as well as her motherly affection. It is impossible that by "I had forgot" she could have meant other than that the many unhappy events of the evening had crowded out of her mind the realization that Hamlet was to be sent to England. But the King's decision that he be sent away she had apparently accepted without protest as one accustomed to accepting without question what others decide for her.

In Belleforest's account the Queen, although she never appears after the Closet Scene, is definitely and actively an ally of her son, working in his absence to facilitate his revenge. In Shakespeare, although she protests to Hamlet:

> Be thou assured, if words be made of
> breath,
> And breath of life, I have no life to breathe
> What thou hast said to me,
> [III. iv. 197-99]

and although she keeps her promise, the Queen utters not one word in condemnation of the crimes of Claudius which Hamlet has revealed to her, and indeed in the very next scene greets him as "mine own lord" [IV. i. 5]. Never is there an indication in the later scenes that her attitude toward Claudius or her relations with him have been altered by what Hamlet has told her. True it is that immediately following the Closet Scene she apparently lies to the King in an effort to protect her son. Although Hamlet has confessed to her that he is "not in madness, But mad in craft", she assures the King that Hamlet is

> Mad as the sea and wind when both con-
> tend
> Which is the mightier. In his lawless fit,
> Behind the arras hearing something stir,
> Whips out his rapier, cries 'A rat, a rat!'
> And in this brainish apprehension kills
> The unseen good old man.
> [IV. i. 7-12]

And she reports that Hamlet has gone

> To draw apart the body he hath killed;
> O'er whom his very madness, like some
> ore
> Among a mineral of metals base,
> Shows itself pure. 'A weeps for what is
> done.
> [IV. i. 24-7]

One need have little hesitation in concluding that

Gertrude is here lying in an effort to render Hamlet's act less responsible and therefore more pardonable. The Queen has not seen Hamlet since the audience witnessed their parting, and Hamlet was surely not weeping then. But though the Queen lies to help her son, it is important to add in any assay of her character that it was not upon her own initiative that she does so. Here no more than earlier is she acting independently. Incapable of herself determining any course of action, she is merely following the course which Hamlet had suggested to her. To her helpless "What shall I do?" Hamlet had replied:

> Not this, by no means, that I bid you do:
> Let the bloat King . . .
> Make you to ravel all this matter out,
> That I essentially am not in madness,
> But mad in craft. 'Twere good you let him
>   know,
> For who that's but a queen, fair, sober,
>   wise,
> Would from a paddock, from a bat, a gib,
> Such dear concernings hide? Who would
>   do so?
> No, in despite of sense and secrecy,
> Unpeg the basket on the house's top,
> Let the birds fly, and like the famous ape,
> To try conclusions, in the basket creep
> And break your own neck down.
> *[III. iv. 180-96]*

Such is Hamlet's sarcastic direction in answer to the Queen's uncertain "What shall I do?" She must decide upon some course immediately, for the King is impatiently awaiting a report of the interview. Accordingly she follows Hamlet's direction; she lies to keep his secret, perhaps because maternal love demands that she protect him, but also because, accustomed to having others make all important decisions for her, she is incapable of substituting for Hamlet's direction any procedure of her own.

In Belleforest, as has been said, the Queen never appears after the account of the interview in her closet. Although we learn later that she had kept her promise to assist her son in his revenge upon her second husband by fashioning, during her son's absence in England, the means of his revenge, we are told nothing of her later life—how she conducted herself in her relations with the King or how she died. In Shakespeare's play, however, she figures in five later scenes—exactly half of the total number in which she appears. Her part in these scenes, having no basis in the older accounts, must have been added either by Shakespeare or by the author of an earlier lost play. The first of these scenes is that just mentioned—that in which she reports to the King. In only one of them, IV. v, her next appearance, does she reveal any remorse or any sense of guilt; and before the end of that scene her sense of guilt seems completely erased by a determination to follow the easier way,

to accept the *status quo,* to continue a way of life she had found pleasant.

IV. v opens with her refusal to admit the mad Ophelia to her presence—a refusal due perhaps to a characteristic desire to escape any distressing situation, or perhaps to her already being burdened with grief and remorse. When Ophelia enters, Gertrude is sympathetic but quite inarticulate. Her three speeches to Ophelia are—in full:

> 1. How now, Ophelia?
> 2. Alas, sweet lady, what imports this
>   song?
> 3. Nay, but Ophelia—
> *[IV. v. 22, 27, 34]*

Then, upon the King's welcome entry, with "Alas, look here, my lord" [IV. v. 37], the Queen turns the unpleasant situation over to him and retires into silence until after Ophelia has departed. Her unwillingness to see Ophelia and her inability to express any words of comfort or sympathy may, as I have said, be due in part to her being, at the moment, too heavily oppressed by her own griefs and her own sense of guilt. As Ophelia enters, Gertrude offers in an aside the only admission of guilt she makes after the Closet Scene:

> To my sick soul (as sin's true nature is)
> Each toy seems prologue to some great
>   amiss.
> So full of artless jealousy is guilt,
> It spills itself in fearing to be split.
> *[IV. v. 17-20]*

Before the end of the scene, however, the Queen is to cry out upon Laertes' mob threatening the King:

> How cheerfully on the false trail they cry!
> O, this is counter, you false Danish dogs!
> *[IV. v. 110-11]*

and, in order to save Claudius, is first to seize Laertes' arm and then to assure him that it was not Claudius who had caused the death of his father. Having, perhaps unconsciously, directed Laertes' hatred towards Hamlet, she offers no fuller explanation and is silent for the remaining ninety lines of the scene. Her extended silence here is certainly not indicative of remorse for her earlier acts; it has been characteristic of her throughout the play. In this scene she reveals perhaps, as she reveals nowhere else in the play, the sensual side of her love for Claudius. Before the scene is half over her sense of guilt has been crowded out of her mind. She shows no repentance. Unlike the Queen in Belleforest or the Queen in the pirated first quarto, she has not aligned herself on the side of her son. Now that he has gone, she finds it easier simply to continue the life she had led before he had made his dreadful revelation. Had Hamlet remained in Denmark, had he been at hand to remind her of her weakness and to answer whenever necessary her question "What shall I do?" it is possible that her sense of guilt might have persisted, that she might even have repented and changed her way of life. But without initiative and independence, she can in Hamlet's absence only drift with the current.

Only twice, then, does Gertrude reveal the least remorse—in the latter part of the Closet Scene and in the single aside as she awaits the entrance of the mad Ophelia. From that time on, as earlier in the play, her actions and speeches evince no prick of conscience although the Ghost, in his instructions to Hamlet in I. v, had implied that she was to suffer the consequence of her sins. " . . . Howsomever thou pursues this act", the Ghost had told his son,

> Taint not thy mind, nor let thy soul con-
>   trive
> Against thy mother aught. Leave her to
>   heaven
> And to those thorns that in her bosom
>   lodge
> To prick and sting her. . . .
>
> [I. v. 85-8]

The Ghost is, as I have noted, most accurately informed of the past. That ghosts were often well informed of the future is indicated by Horatio's beseeching the Ghost to speak

> If thou art privy to thy country's fate,
> Which happily foreknowing may avoid.
>
> [I. i. 133-34]

But that ghosts might be ignorant of the future and even uncomprehending of the present is shown in *The Spanish Tragedy* by the repeated questioning by the Ghost of Andrea as he watches the play unfold. The Ghost of King Hamlet clearly expects his son to sweep to a swift revenge; he does not understand the delay; nor surely did he expect such complete catastrophe to engulf the entire royal family. In spite of his exact knowledge of the past, therefore, it would appear that the Ghost's knowledge of the immediate present and of the future was far too limited to warrant our acceptance as testimony of Gertrude's remorse his mention of

> . . . those thorns that in her bosom lodge
> To prick and sting her. . . .
>
> [I. v. 87-8]

Indeed, if one may, without confusing life and art, delve into the past of characters in a drama, it may be said that King Hamlet had ever but slenderly known his wife. Created in an heroic mould, he understood not the mortal frailties which might lead his "most seeming-virtuous queen"

> to decline
> Upon a wretch whose natural gifts were
>   poor
> To those of [his].
>
> [I. v. 46, 50-2]

Just as he had, before learning of her transgressions, been deceived by his wife's seeming-virtue, so, after learning of them, he expected her to be tortured by the stings of conscience. He was apparently twice deceived.

But to continue tracing the Queen's part in the play. She appears, of course, in all of the last three scenes. She enters late in IV. vii, after the King and Laertes have completed their plans for bringing about Hamlet's death, and in her longest speech in the play announces Ophelia's drowning. Her purpose here, however, is that of a messenger; her speech throws little light on her character—and certainly reveals no awareness of her own responsibility for the young girl's death.

In V. i, the scene in the graveyard, the Queen first mentions in a single speech her thwarted hope that Ophelia might have been Hamlet's bride, and then, as Hamlet and Laertes struggle in the grave, she, in her remaining speeches, follows the lead of Claudius:

> *King:* Pluck them asunder.
> *Queen:* Hamlet, Hamlet!
> *King:* O, he is mad, Laertes.
> *Queen:* For love of God, forbear him.
>
> [V. i. 264, 272-73]

Then:

> This is mere madness;
> And thus a while the fit will work on him.
> Anon as patient as the female dove . . .
> His silence will sit drooping,
>
> [V. i. 284-88]

The Queen, of course, does not know of the treachery plotted by Claudius and Laertes. She must by these speeches have sought to end the struggle in the grave and to lessen Laertes' resentment at Hamlet's behavior, but it is noticeable—and I think characteristic—that in each of her speeches she echoes or enlarges upon ideas just expressed by Claudius.

In V. ii, the concluding scene of the play, the Queen for the first time, I believe, acts with initiative and speaks for herself. Just before the court enters to watch the fencing match, an unnamed lord brings a message to Hamlet: "The Queen desires you to use some gentle entertainment to Laertes before you fall to play" [V. ii. 206-07]. As the effect of this message would be to lessen any suspicions of foul play, to encourage Hamlet's acceptance of the match as a "brother's wager frankly play[ed]" [V. ii. 253], one is tempted to suggest that the Queen's message may have originated with the King, that here as earlier the Queen is being used to further the plan of another. (It will be remembered that immediately after the play-within-the-play Polonius brought Hamlet word that "the Queen would speak with you, and presently" [III. ii. 375], but, as previously noted, the idea of the interview was not the Queen's. It had originated with Polonius, and the King, to whom he suggested it [III. i. 182ff.], had off-stage persuaded the Queen to cooperate.) However, in the absence of any statement to the contrary, I presume we must accept the message as the lord delivers it, as the Queen's own suggestion. And in some respects it is a thoroughly characteristic suggestion, revealing as it does her recurring hope that in spite of all that had gone before, she and others, without being required to pay the price of penitence, may go on enjoying the present by simply refusing to remember the past.

During the closing scene the Queen is silent for the first sixty-one lines she is on stage. She then within a space of twenty-four lines has four speeches, totaling six pentameter lines. She refers to Hamlet's scantness of breath and offers her napkin to mop his brow. Then, for the first time in the play escaping the dominance of Claudius, she acts independently and counter to his expressed wish—and her crossing him means her death.

> Queen: . . . The queen carouses to thy for-
>   tune, Hamlet.
> King: Gertrude, do not drink.
> Queen: I will, my lord; I pray you pardon
>   me.
>
> [V. ii. 289-91]

And so she drinks from the poisoned cup. I can see no justification whatsoever for the view of a critic who sought to defend the Queen's character by suggesting that she, suspecting the wine to be poisoned, drank it to protect Hamlet and to atone for the wrongs and sins of her past. Others, like the author of the *New Exegesis of Shakespeare* (1859), have remarked that her death was "as exquisitely negative as possible—that is, by poison, from *her own hand,* in a VINOUS BEVERIDGE [sic], and THROUGH MISTAKE." But however negative her death, it was, ironically, the result of her one act of independence. And her final speech, in answer to the King's hasty explanation, "She swounds to see them bleed":

> No, no, the drink, the drink! O my dear
>   Hamlet!
> The drink, the drink! I am poisoned—
>   [V. ii. 309-10]

Here for the first time the Queen seems to understand the essence of the situation. Only in this last speech does she recognize or admit to herself the villainy of her second husband. Only here—long after her counterpart in Belleforest had done so— does she take her position beside her son and against the King. (pp. 235-46)

> *Baldwin Maxwell "Hamlet's Mother,"
> in* Shakespeare 400: Essays by Ameri-
> can Scholars on the Anniversary of the
> Poet's Birth, *edited by James G. Mc-
> Manaway, Holt, Rinehart and Wins-
> ton, Inc., 1964, pp. 235-46.*

OPHELIA

Theodore Lidz

[*Lidz argues that Shakespeare dramatized*

*Ophelia's madness to provide a countertheme to action surrounding **Hamlet's** own insanity. But whereas the playwright remains ambiguous about the reality of the prince's madness, the critic continues, he portrays Ophelia as classically insane. According to Lidz, **Ophelia's** descent into madness does not merely the result from her father's murder, but rather his murder by **Hamlet,** whom she loves. As a result, **Ophelia** is placed in "the intolerable predicament of having to turn away from the person she loves and idealizes because that person is responsible for her father's murder." For further commentary on **Ophelia's** character, see the excerpts by Arthur Kirsch and J. Dover Wilson.*]

Shakespeare carefully places Ophelia's madness in apposition to Hamlet's, illuminating the causes of each by making Ophelia's plight the female counterpart of Hamlet's dilemma. The action around Ophelia's insanity forms the countertheme to the action surrounding Hamlet's madness, balancing the plot and leading to Hamlet's death as well as to Ophelia's. Each dies more or less because there is nothing left for them but to desire death as an escape from an existence that has become intolerable.

Whereas Shakespeare is ambiguous about the reality of Hamlet's insanity and depicts him as on the border, fluctuating between sanity and madness, he portrays Ophelia as definitely, one might even say classically, insane. Even before she comes on stage, a gentleman gives us an excellent description of her condition. Would that psychiatric texts could describe as clearly!

> She speaks much of her father; says she
>   hears
> There's tricks i' the world; and hems and
>   beats her heart;
> Spurns enviously at straws; speaks things
>   in doubt,
> That carry but half sense; her speech is
>   nothing,
> Yet the unshaped use of it doth move
> The hearers to collection; they aim at it,
> And botch the words up fit to their own
>   thoughts;
> Which, as her winks and nods and ges-
>   tures yield them,
> Indeed would make one think there might
>   be thought,
> Though nothing sure, yet much unhappi-
>   ly.
>
> [IV. v. 4-13]

She does not storm, or "take arms against a sea of troubles" [III. i. 58]; but rather, as a passive, obedient and very feminine person she is simply

> poor Ophelia,
> Divided from herself and her fair judge-
>   ment,
> Without the which we are pictures, or
>   mere beasts.
>
> [IV. v. 84-6]

156

She sings one ditty about her love who is dead and gone, as if referring to her father, then another about a girl abandoned because she let her valentine tumble her before being wed—a bawdy bit that has led some critics to consider that the sweet Ophelia might have been distraught because she had given in to Hamlet's "unmaster'd importunity" [I. iii. 32] and was now pregnant, with marriage to Hamlet no longer possible. However, to most, including those in the play, who knew her best, the cause of Ophelia's madness seems apparent. Claudius says:

> Oh, this' the poison of deep grief; it springs
> All from her father's death.
> [IV. v. 75-6]

And Laertes muses about his mad sister:

> O heavens! is't possible a young maid's
>   wits
> Should be as mortal as an old man's life?
> Nature is fine in love, and where 'tis fine
> It sends some precious instance of itself
> After the thing it loves.
> [IV. v. 160-64]

The comment is accentuated by Ophelia's chant:

> *They bore him barefaced on the bier;*
> *Hey non nonny, nonny, hey nonny;*
> *And on his grave rain'd many a tear.—*
> [IV. v. 165-67]

The gentle Ophelia, it seems, cannot absorb her father's murder. However, it is not her father's murder that has driven her mad but, rather, his murder by Hamlet, the person she loves and upon whose love she has placed her hopes. Now, she can never marry him, and worse still, she has an obligation to hate him; indeed she must feel hatred toward him for depriving her of her beloved father, her original love. Shakespeare, then, has not only placed Ophelia's insanity in apposition to Hamlet's but has emphasized the same crucial human frailty as the cause of the emotional disturbance in both the hero and heroine.

As we have seen, Hamlet mourns for his father, but his melancholy is induced by his bitterness against his mother because of her hasty marriage to his uncle; and his anguish and rage against his mother become intolerable when he learns that she has been untrue to his father. Hamlet is tormented by his desire to take vengeance against his mother, the person who had once been closest and most dear to him. He manages to control his matricidal impulses, but his mother is lost to him as a love object. He struggles to regain her by imploring her to renounce her sexual life with Claudius and return to him and become faithful to his father's memory. At the very moment when Hamlet believes he may have succeeded, he inadvertently kills Polonius bringing new woes on himself and sealing Ophelia's fate.

Ophelia, like Hamlet, mourns for her father, but his death is not a sufficient reason for her to lose her sanity. She, too, is in the intolerable predicament of having to turn away from the person she loves and idealizes because that person is responsible for her father's murder. Her father is dead, and Hamlet, as his slayer, is barred to her affections. She can no longer transfer her attachment from her father to Hamlet. Her entire orientation to the future has suddenly been destroyed.

Both Hamlet and Ophelia, then, are faced by the sudden and irretrievable loss of a love object because of that person's unforgivable behavior in killing, actually or symbolically, a beloved parent whose death requires vengeance. Shakespeare clearly saw how such situations could engender a violently confused emotional state and lead a person to feel that the world was empty and worthless and those who inhabit it perfidious and deceitful. Life becomes intolerable; the sufferer escapes the dilemma by abandoning rationality and when that fails, by abandoning life itself.

Now, the reader might not think that Polonius, a man already in his dotage, a spying busybody whom Hamlet considered a tedious old fool, could be so important to Ophelia. Indeed, one might similarly wonder why Hamlet should be so concerned about the deceitful and wanton Gertrude. Oedipal attachments do not, as we know from countless patients, involve a rational evaluation of the parent. If raised with reasonable parental care, the boy has a deep attachment to his mother, and the girl to her father. Ophelia's attachment to Polonius is accentuated by her motherless state. As a widower, Polonius may have been overly protective of his daughter and especially affectionate to her; and Ophelia, as commonly happens in such situations, may have felt free to fantasy that she could become a replacement for her mother in her father's life, and thus form a particularly intense attachment to him. Similarly, Hamlet is fatherless, but his situation differed from Ophelia's as he had lost his father much more recently. Nevertheless, as we have noted, his father's death could lead to a recrudescence of Hamlet's old attachment to his mother as well as a heightening of his identification with his father. He could then feel that his mother's infidelity to his father was also an infidelity to him.

Ophelia, we should note, is already under considerable emotional stress at the time her father is killed. The vacillations in Hamlet's attitude and behavior toward her could not but be extremely unsettling to the very young woman who idolized and idealized him. She is, one day, his most beloved, who must never doubt his love [II. ii. 116-24]; shortly thereafter, she is the object of his venom and the recipient of his malignant curse; and then, on the same day, she finds him bantering salaciously with her. She cannot know that Hamlet's attitude toward her reflects his disillusionment in

Hamlet (Alec Guinness) duels with Laertes (Michael Gough) in the climatic final scene of Hamlet. *The 1951 New Theatre staging of the Tragedy.*

his mother. To her, Hamlet's inconstancy can only mean deceitfulness or madness. Ophelia finds him mad, and, hopefully, mad because she has been forced to reject him. Hamlet slays Polonius by mistake; he had not, like Claudius, committed a premeditated murder for his own advancement. We must even consider that were Hamlet not so out of control, he might still beg Ophelia's forgiveness for his error. However, that is not the way the play was written, or could have been written. (pp. 88-92)

> Theodore Lidz, in his Hamlet's Enemy: Madness and Myth in "Hamlet," *1975. Reprint by International Universities Press, Inc., 1990, 258 p.*

J. Dover Wilson

[Wilson provides a detailed interpretation of the "nunnery scene" between **Hamlet** *and* **Ophelia** *in Act III, scene i. The critic discusses* **Ophelia's** *role as a decoy, describing how she makes the prince suspicious of a plot by overplaying her part when returning his love letters.* **Hamlet** *is disgusted by her role as a decoy, Dover Wilson maintains, for it mirrors his own mother's betrayal when she married* **Claudius.** *According to the critic,* **Hamlet** *tests*

Ophelia *by asking where her father is, but when she lies, she provokes the frenzy with which the prince concludes the scene. Wilson also emphasizes* **Hamlet's** *repetition of the word "nunnery," maintaining that for Elizabethans the word not only meant a convent, but also carried the bawdy connotation of a brothel. For a defense of* **Ophelia's** *character and motives in the "nunnery scene," see the essay by Harold Jenkins cited in the Sources for Further Study. For other commentary on* **Ophelia's** *character, see the excerpts by Arthur Kirsch and Theodore Lidz.]*

[In Act III, scene i, the] King bids the Queen leave him with Polonius and Ophelia; and tells her of their purpose. He insists, and she accepts the point without question, that they are "lawful espials". The innocent little scheme is justified in the interests of Denmark, and of Hamlet himself; and she expresses the hope that the outcome will bring happiness for them all, Ophelia included. Gertrude is always hoping for the best. The King's words,

> For we have closely sent for Hamlet hither,
> That he, as 'twere by accident, may here
> Affront Ophelia,
>
> [III. i. 29-31]

should be carefully noted in passing, if we wish to understand exactly what follows. Hamlet is not coming to the lobby of his own motion; he has been sent for. Not, of course, ostensibly by Claudius, but "closely", that is privately or without his knowledge of the real sender of the message. Nevertheless some kind of pretext has been given; and, when he arrives, he will find, not what he expects, but Ophelia. There would be no flaw in this expedient, if the object of it had not happened to overhear the whole plot the day before.

The snare is now laid; the decoy made to appear at once innocent and tempting; and the fowlers take cover. Polonius gives Ophelia a prayer-book, and says "walk you here" [III. i. 42]; "here" being, of course, the lobby at the back of the stage. There is, however, a theatrical tradition that she should be kneeling when Hamlet enters, which is I think a sound one; for, if she is only walking up and down with a book in her hands, how does he know that she is at her "orisons"? I presume, therefore, that some kind of prie-dieu stood in the lobby. Finally, before actually "bestowing" himself behind the arras, Claudius utters an aside, which it is also important not to miss. "Read on this book", says the moralising father to his daughter,

> That show of such an exercise may colour
> Your loneliness; we are oft to blame in
>   this,
> 'Tis too much proved, that with devotion's
>   visage
> And pious action we do sugar o'er
> The devil himself;
>
>   [III. i. 43-8]

upon which the King comments to himself:

>   O, 'tis too true,
> How smart a lash that speech doth give my
>   conscience.
> The harlot's check, beautied with
>   plast'ring art,
> Is not more ugly to the thing that helps it,
> Than is my deed to my most painted word:
> O heavy burden!
>
>   [III. i. 48-53]

It is the first indication in the play that Claudius possesses a conscience; and it leads up to the "blenching" in the play scene and to the prayer that follows. But there is more in it than this. The reference, after "devotion's visage", to

> The harlot's cheek, beautied with
>   plast'ring art

is leitmotiv on Shakespeare's part. The linked images hark back to the "fishmonger" and his "good kissing carrion" [II. ii. 174, 182]; and reopen a theme which Hamlet will presently elaborate.

Hamlet walks into the trap in complete unconsciousness. As he enters, his mind is not on the plot, his uncle or Ophelia. If he remembers the Ghost at all, it is to write it off as a snare of the evil one. He is back again where he was when we first had sight of his inner self; back in the mood of the soliloquy which begins

> O that this too too sullied flesh would melt,
> Thaw and resolve itself into a dew,
> Or that the Everlasting had not fixed
> His canon 'gainst self-slaughter.
>
>   [I. ii. 129-32]

But he is no longer thinking of his own "sullied flesh", still less of the divine command. By constantly turning it over he has worn the problem to the bone:

> To be, or not to be, that is the question.
>
>   [III. i. 55]

A like expression of utter weariness is not to be found in the rest of human literature. Sleep, death, annihilation, his whole mind is concentrated upon these; and the only thing that holds his arm from striking home with "the bare bodkin" [III. i. 75] is the thought of "what dreams may come", "the dread of something after death" [III. i. 65, 77]. . . . He believes in immortality, which means that by death he may exchange one nightmare for a worse. Eternity has him in a trap, which dwarfs the little traps of Claudius and Polonius to nothingness. No one but Shakespeare could have interrupted an exciting dramatic intrigue with a passage like this. The surprise and the audacity of it take our breath away, and render the pity of it the more overwhelming.

As the meditation finishes, Hamlet sees Ophelia behind him upon her knees. The sight reminds him of nothing except "the pangs of disprized love", and those have long been drowned in "a sea of troubles" [III. i. 71, 53]. "The fair Ophelia!" [III. i. 88] he exclaims; the words have no warmth in them. And, when he addresses her, he speaks in irony:

>   Nymph, in thy orisons
> Be all my sins remembered.
>
>   [III. i. 88-9]

Romantic actors interpret this as gushing tenderness; and even [Samuel] Johnson calls it "an address grave and solemn, such as the foregoing meditation excited in his thoughts". [Edward] Dowden, however, sees "estrangement in the word 'nymph' "; and I find deliberate affectation in that word and in "orisons". They are both pretentious expressions, while the reference to "all my sins", the sins for which she has jilted him, the sins he will enlarge upon later in the scene, surely indicates a sardonic tone. In any event, it is certain that most critics have completely misunderstood the dialogue that follows, because in their sympathy with Ophelia they have forgotten that it is not Hamlet who has "repelled" her, but she him. She had refused to see him and had returned his letters; she could not even speak a word of comfort when in deep trouble he forced his way into her room with mute pitiable appeal.

After that he had done with her; and the Ophelia he now meets is a stranger. Stranger indeed! For listen:

> Good my lord,
> How does your honour for this many a
>   day?
>
> [III. i. 89-90]

Is she implying that *he* has neglected *her?* It was only yesterday he had been with her despite her denial of his access. But at first he takes small note of her words and answers with polite aloofness:

> I humbly thank you, well, well, well.
>
> [III. i. 91]

It is a form of address he employs later with people like the Norwegian Captain and Osric, while the repeated "well" sounds bored. Nevertheless, she continues:

> My lord, I have remembrances of yours,
> That I have longed long to re-deliver.
> I pray you now receive them.
>
> [III. i. 92-4]

What should that mean? Once again, however, he brushes it aside: "I never gave *you* aught" [III. i. 95],—the woman to whom I once gave gifts is dead. Yet still she persists:

> My honoured lord, you know right well
>   you did,
> And with them words of so sweet breath
>   composed
> As made the things more rich. Their per-
>   fume lost,
> Take these again, for to the noble mind
> Rich gifts wax poor when givers prove un-
>   kind.
> There, my lord.
>
> [III. i. 96-101]

And here she draws the trinkets from her bosom and places them on the table before him.

The unhappy girl has sadly overplayed her part. Her little speech, ending with a sententious couplet, as Dowden notes, "has an air of being prepared". Worse than that, she, the jilt, is accusing him of coldness towards her. Worst of all, Hamlet who has been "sent for", who meets her in the lobby "by accident", finds her prepared not only with a speech but with the gifts also. She means no harm; she has romantically arranged a little play scene, in the hope no doubt of provoking a passionate declaration of affection, which perhaps

> Will bring him to his wonted way again,
>
> [III. i. 40]

as the Queen had remarked just before Hamlet's entrance, and will at any rate prove to the King that she and her father are right in their diagnosis of the distemper. But the effect upon Hamlet is disas-

trous. Until that moment he had forgotten the plot; it is a far cry from thoughts of "the undiscovered country" [III. i. 78] to this discovery. But he is now thoroughly awake, and sees it all. Here is the lobby and the decoy, playing a part, only too unblushingly; and there at the back is the arras, behind which lurk the Fishmonger and Uncle Claudius. His wild "Ha, ha!" the fierce question "are you honest?" [III. i. 102] that is to say "are you not a whore?" together with a significant glance round the room, are enough to show the audience that he realises at last, and warn them to expect "antic disposition". Everything he says for the rest of the scene is intended for the ears of the eavesdroppers. As for the daughter who has been "loosed" to him, she will only get what she deserves. For play-acting has completed her downfall in his eyes. First the abrupt breaking-off of all intercourse between them, without any reason given, then the failure to meet his last appeal, then the overhearing of the plot in which she was to take a leading part, and last this willing and all too facile participation: is it surprising that to an imagination "as foul as Vulcan's stithy" [III. ii. 83-4] such things should appear in the worst possible light, or that he should treat her from henceforth as the creature he believes her to be? He puts her to one final test before the scene is over; but the dice are loaded against her. Thus, through a chain of misconceptions, due to nothing worse than narrowness of vision and over-readiness to comply with her father's commands, Ophelia blackens her own character in her lover's eyes. The process has been obscured hitherto owing to the absence of one important link in the chain; but the link now in place makes all clear, explains Hamlet's attitude, and shows her fate as even more pathetic than we had supposed.

Everything he says, I repeat, for the rest of the scene is intended for the ears of Claudius and Polonius, whom he knows to be behind the arras. The restored entry at [II. ii. 167] happily rids us of the traditional stage-business of Polonius exposing himself to the eye of Hamlet and the audience, which has hitherto been the only way open to stage-managers of putting any meaning at all into the scene. It is a trick at once crude and inadequate: crude, because the chief councillor of Denmark is neither stupid nor clumsy, and to represent him so, as producers are apt to do, is to degrade intrigue to buffoonery; inadequate, because it only tells Hamlet of one, whereas his words clearly lose a great deal of force if he is not known to be conscious of the presence of two. He speaks at both; but he speaks, of course, to Ophelia, while as he speaks he has yet a fourth person constantly in mind, his mother. If this be remembered, and if we also keep in view Hamlet's habitual lack of self-control once he becomes excited, the dialogue is easy to follow.

I return to it:

Hamlet. Ha, ha! are you honest?
Ophelia. My lord?
Hamlet. Are you fair?
Ophelia. What means your lordship?
Hamlet. That if you be honest and fair,
your honesty should admit no
discourse to your beauty.
[III. i. 102-07]

If, that is, you were the chaste maiden you pretend to be, you would not allow your beauty to be used as a bait in this fashion. Ophelia, of course, misunderstands and, supposing him to mean that her beauty and his honesty ought not to discourse together, wonderingly enquires: "Could beauty, my lord, have better commerce than with honesty?" [III. i. 108-09] To which he, twisting her words back to his own meaning, replies:

Ay truly, for the power of beauty will sooner transform honesty from what it is to a bawd, than the force of honesty can translate beauty into his likeness. This was sometime a paradox, but now the time gives it proof.
[III. i. 110-14]

To paraphrase again: "physical Beauty is stronger than virtue, and will make use of Virtue herself as her procuress. People used to think this incredible, but your conduct proves its truth." He refers to "devotion's visage" and the "pious action" with which Ophelia had tried to "sugar o'er" her designs upon him. But he is probably also thinking of his mother's conduct, as is suggested by the talk of "our old stock" that follows [III. i. 117]. Indeed, from this point onwards Ophelia becomes identified in his mind with the Frailty whose name is Woman, and that in turn leads to thoughts of his own "sullied flesh". He goes on: "I did love you once" [III. i. 114], that is, before my mother took off the rose

From the fair forehead of an innocent love.
[III. iv. 43]

But a son of Gertrude is "rank and gross in nature" [I. ii. 136] and capable of nothing except lust; so that I did not really love you. "Conception is a blessing" [II. ii. 184], but what children could a man like me and a woman like you hope for save a brood of sinners? Better a nunnery!

So far Hamlet's talk has been in fishmonger-vein, and is meant for the Jephthah [cf. II. ii. 403ff.] behind the arras. But now is the turn for Uncle Claudius. The mention of corrupt stock leads by natural transition to an elaborate confession of criminal propensities on Hamlet's part which *we* know to be ridiculous, but which is intended to make the King's blood run cold. "I am very proud, revengeful, ambitious" [III. i. 123-24] is the gist of it. Could any other three epithets be found less appropriate to Hamlet? But Claudius says he is ambitious; and Claudius is a reasonable man. The following, too, sounds terrible:

with more offences at my beck, than I have thoughts to put them in, imagination to give them shape, or time to act them in:
[III. i. 124-25]

—until we scan it and find that it amounts to nothing at all, since the same might be said of any mortal.

At this point Hamlet gives Ophelia her last chance with his sudden "Where's your father?" [III. i. 129]. She answers with a lie, as it would seem to him, though of course she is observing the most ordinary precautions and, as she thinks, humouring a madman. But it is this crowning proof of her treachery, I suggest, that provokes the frenzy with which the episode closes. He goes out, perhaps in the hope that the rats may emerge from their hole and that he may catch them in the act of so doing. Twice he rushes from the room and with each return his manner grows more excited. His two final speeches are mainly food for fishmongers, and he concludes by coming very near to calling Ophelia a prostitute to her face. The repeated injunction "to a nunnery go" [III. i. 120, 129, 136, 139, 149] is significant in this connection, since "nunnery" was in common Elizabethan use a cant term for a house of ill-fame. And that this was the traditional interpretation of Hamlet's meaning on the seventeenth-century stage is shown by the *Der bestrafte Brudermord* which makes him say "go to a nunnery, but not to a nunnery where two pairs of slippers lie at the bed side".

As he leaves for the last time he throws his uncle one more morsel to chew: "I say we will have no mo marriage—those that are married already, *all but one,* shall live, the rest shall keep as they are" [III. i. 147-49]. Why, it may be asked, does Hamlet deliberately and recklessly threaten the King in this way? Partly, as I have already suggested, because Hamlet always acts as if he were just on the point of killing his uncle, and partly for reasons which will become clear later. In any event, these threats show that the Prince has thoroughly grasped the hints about ambition dropped by Rosencrantz and Guildenstern; and is now posing as the discontented heir thirsting for revenge, a rôle he will play to remarkable purpose in the next scene.

After Hamlet's final departure, Ophelia is given twelve lines of lamentation over his fallen state, before the espials steal warily from their hiding place, a circumspection natural after his repeated exits, but surely enough to warn us that Polonius, with whom caution is almost a disease, could never have revealed his presence to Hamlet, as the traditional stage practice makes him do. The discussion of what they have heard shows that their points of view have in no way converged. Claudius scornfully dismisses the forlorn love theory; nor does he think that melancholy has yet developed into utter madness. But Hamlet has said enough to prove himself to be in a very dangerous frame of mind;

too dangerous to remain any longer near the royal person:

> He shall with speed to England,
> For the demand of our neglected tribute.
> Haply the seas, and countries different,
> With variable objects, shall expel
> This something-settled matter in his heart,
> Whereon his brains still beating puts him thus
> From fashion of himself.
>
> [III. i. 169-75]

At present Claudius thinks of England as a health-resort; it is only after the play scene that he sees it as a grave. Polonius agrees with the scheme but cannot subscribe to his royal master's diagnosis of the disease. "But yet I do believe", he mutters while assenting to the projected voyage,

> The origin and commencement of his grief
> Sprung from neglected love;
>
> [III. i. 176-78]

and he urges that the theory shall be put to one more test before the voyage takes place. (pp. 125-36)

> *J. Dover Wilson, in his* What Happens in Hamlet, *third edition, Cambridge at the University Press, 1962, 357 p.*

SOURCES FOR FURTHER STUDY

LITERARY COMMENTARY:

Bonjour, Adrien. "The Question of Hamlet's Grief." *English Studies: A Journal of English Letters and Philology* 43 (1962): 336-43.

Refutes the notion that Hamlet suffers from excessive grief over his father's death by studying the critical perspective which treats him as a "slave of passion."

Brown, John Russell and Harris, Bernard, eds. *Hamlet,* Stratford-Upon-Avon Studies 5. London: Edward Arnold (Publishers), 1963.

Contains ten essays discussing a wide range of topics in *Hamlet* by such noted scholars as G. K. Hunter, R. A. Foakes, John Russell Brown, and Stanley Wells.

Burge, Barbara. " 'Hamlet': The Search for Identity." *A Review of English Literature* 5, No. 2 (April 1964): 58-71.

Maintains that Hamlet's search for identity focuses on the merging of two different perspectives: external observations by Hamlet himself and others and the internal workings of his mind.

Calderwood, James L. "Hamlet: The Name of Action."

Modern Language Quarterly 39, No. 4 (December 1978): 331-62.

Explores the significance of proper names and titles, examining how they reflect the various roles the characters play in *Hamlet.*

Camden, Carroll. "On Ophelia's Madness." In *Shakespeare 400,* edited by James G. McManaway, pp. 247-55. New York: Holt, Rinehart, and Winston, Inc., 1964.

Argues that Ophelia's ruined relationship with Hamlet, rather than her father's death, is the overriding cause of her madness.

Campbell, Lily B. "*Hamlet:* A Tragedy of Grief." In her *Shakespeare's Tragic Heroes: Slaves of Passion,* pp. 109-47. 1930. Reprint. New York: Barnes & Noble, Inc., 1960.

Contends that since Hamlet's passion is not moderated by reason, his grief becomes so excessive that it "will not yield to the consolations of philosophy." This intense grief, the critic declares, causes the protagonist's reason to "fail in directing the will" to carry out his revenge.

———. "Polonius: The Tyrant's Ears." In *Joseph Quincy Adams Memorial Studies,* edited by James G. McManaway, Giles E. Dawson, and Edwin E. Willoughby, pp. 295-313. Washington D. C.: The Folger Shakespeare Library, 1948.

Claims that Polonius is "a well-rounded and consistent character" even though Shakespeare portrays him as a meddling buffoon. Polonius is integral to the play's plot, the critic asserts, for his death precipitates its tragic conclusion.

Charney, Maurice. "Claudius: 'Break not your sleep for that'." In his *Style in* Hamlet, pp. 221-41. Princeton: Princeton University Press, 1969.

Analyzes Claudius's language in *Hamlet,* noting that he alternates between two styles: an eloquent rhetorical style for generally formal occasions and a simple, more direct style to discuss his personal affairs.

Craig, Hardin. "Hamlet as a Man of Action." *The Huntington Library Quarterly* XXVII, No. 3 (May 1964): 229-37.

Examines the nature of Hamlet's procrastination, focusing on the protagonist as he appeared in the literary sources of *Hamlet* and on major critical interpretations of his character.

Dessen, Alan C. "Hamlet's Poisoned Sword: A Study in Dramatic Imagery." *Shakespeare Studies* V (1969): 53-69.

Discusses the symbolic role of Hamlet's sword in the play.

Elliott, G. R. "Introduction: On Pride, Justice, and the Gentleman-Prince." In his *Scourge and Minister: A Study of* Hamlet *as Tragedy of Revengefulness and Justice,* pp. xv-xxxv. 1951. Reprint. New York: AMS Press, Inc., 1965.

Maintains that both Hamlet's and Claudius's delay are dramatically inseparable elements of the tragedy. The critic also notes that Renaissance audiences would have considered Hamlet the "Complete Gentleman"—a role model for the whole social structure—which would be reason enough for his hesitation.

Goodman, Paul. "Novelistic Plots." In his *The Structure of Literature*, pp. 127-83. Chicago: The University of Chicago Press, 1954.
  Brief overview of the structure of *Hamlet*, focusing on such issues as the characterization of Fortinbras, Hamlet's disposition, the king's plot, and the soliloquies.

Halio, Jay L. "Hamlet's Alternatives." *Texas Studies in Literature and Language* 8, No. 2 (Summer 1966): 169-88.
  Proposes alternatives to revenge for Hamlet based on various elements in the text, as well as the options dramatized in Shakespeare's sources and by contemporary playwrights.

Hartwig, Joan. "Parodic Polonius." *Texas Studies in Literature and Language* XII, No. 2 (Summer 1971): 215-25.
  Examines Polonius as a parody of the other more serious characters in *Hamlet*.

Jenkins, Harold. "Hamlet and Ophelia." *Proceedings of the British Academy* 49 (1964): 135-51.
  Offers a close examination of the "nunnery scene" between Hamlet and Ophelia (Act III, scene i), defending Ophelia's character from critics who have considered her a weak, easily manipulated decoy.

Kirschbaum, Leo. "Hamlet and Ophelia." *Philological Quarterly* XXXV, No. 4 (October 1956): 376-93.
  Provides a scene-by-scene analysis of the relationship between Hamlet and Ophelia.

Lawlor, J. J. "The Tragic Conflict in *Hamlet*." *The Review of English Studies* I, No. 2 (April 1950): 97-113.
  Places the issue of Hamlet's delay in its Elizabethan context and relates it to the genre of the Revenge Tragedy—a popular dramatic form in Shakespeare's day.

Reno, Raymond H. "Hamlet's Quintessence of Dust." *Shakespeare Quarterly* XII, No. 2 (Spring 1961): 107-13.
  Discusses Hamlet's perplexing change of attitude from the time he is sent to England in Act IV until his return to Denmark in Act V.

Smith, Rebecca. "A Heart Cleft in Twain: The Dilemma of Shakespeare's Gertrude." In *The Woman's Part: Feminist Criticism of Shakespeare*, edited by Carolyn Ruth Swift Lenz, Gayle Green, and Carol Thomas Neely, pp. 194-210. Urbana: University of Illinois Press, 1980.
  Interprets Gertrude as not a "deceitful, highly sexual" woman as depicted in Shakespeare's sources, but a "nuturant and loving one" endowed with great complexity of character.

Van Doren, Mark. "Hamlet." In his *Shakespeare*, pp. 190-201. New York: Henry Holt and Company, 1939.
  General overview of *Hamlet*.

MEDIA ADAPTATIONS:

Hamlet. Universal, J. Arthur Rank, 1948.
  Film adaptation of *Hamlet* by Laurence Olivier, who directed and starred in the production. The motion picture also features Eileen Herlie, Basil Sydney, Jean Simmons, and Anthony Quayle. Distributed by RCA VideoDiscs. 155 minutes.

Hamlet. Neil Hartley and Martin Rashonoff, 1969.
  Motion picture version of Shakespeare's tragedy, featuring Nicol Williamson, Anthony Hopkins, and Marianne Faithful. Directed by Tony Richardson. Distributed by RCA/Columbia Home Video. 114 minutes.

Hamlet. BBC, Time Life Television, 1979.
  Television adaptation of Shakespeare's tragedy and part of the series "The Shakespeare Plays." Features Derek Jacobi as Hamlet. Distributed by Time-Life Video. 150 minutes.

Hamlet. Warner Brothers, 1990.
  Film version of Shakespeare's tragedy directed by Franco Zeffirelli and starring Mel Gibson, Glenn Close, Alan Bates, Ian Holm, Helena Bonham-Carter, and Paul Scofield. Distributed by Warner Brothers Home Video, Inc. 135 minutes.

JULIUS CAESAR

INTRODUCTION

Scholars generally agree that *Julius Caesar* was first written and performed in 1599. The drama was apparently quite popular among Elizabethan audiences, most of whom were familiar with Caesar's assassination from numerous other literary sources. For the dramatic events of the play, Shakespeare chiefly drew on the biographies of Brutus, Caesar, and Antony in Plutarch's *Parallel Lives,* translated by Thomas North as *The Lives of the Noble Grecianes and Romans* in 1579. Plutarch was a Greek biographer and essayist whose work constitutes a faithful record of the historical tradition, moral views, and ethical judgments of second century A. D. Greek and Roman cultures. While the action of *Julius Caesar* closely follows the events described by Plutarch, Shakespeare greatly modifies their significance. By Elizabethan times two sharply contrasting views of this period in Roman history had emerged. One held that Brutus and the other conspirators were ruthless murderers who unjustly killed their would-be emperor; the other interpreted their actions as the rightful deposing of a tyrant. Shakespeare carefully designed his play in such a way that it seems to support both views. As a result, critics have long debated whether Brutus or Caesar is the chief protagonist of *Julius Caesar* and whether either qualifies as a tragic hero. (In drama, a tragedy recounts the significant events or actions in a protagonist's life which, taken together, bring about the catastrophe.) This fundamental ambiguity in the play is further complicated by the different political motivations of the characters: Cassius assassinates Caesar ostensibly because the leader is an alleged tyrant, but also out of personal envy; Brutus joins the conspiracy because he wants to preserve the Roman republic; Mark Antony rouses the Roman populace against the traitors out of loyalty to Caesar, but later benefits from the leader's death when he becomes a co-ruler of the empire. The circumstances surrounding Caesar's assassination reveal that although the major characters strive to attain different political ends, the means by which they achieve their aims are often quite similar. Furthermore, despite the supposed good intentions of all these men, they all become corrupted in some way and their actions lead only to violence and civil strife.

PRINCIPAL CHARACTERS
(in order of appearance)

Flavius and *Murellus:* Roman tribunes. They want to protect the commoners from Caesar's tyranny and are later "put to silence" for removing decorations from Caesar's statues.

Julius Caesar: Roman general, consul, and would-be emperor. He is assassinated by Brutus, Cassius, and others for his ambition. His spirit later haunts Brutus at Sardis and Philippi.

Casca: Tribune and member of Caesar's entourage. He joins Cassius's plot and is the first conspirator to stab Caesar.

Calphurnia: Caesar's wife. After having nightmares about his murder, she urges her husband not to go to the Capitol on the day he is killed.

Mark Antony: Roman general and Caesar's friend. His funeral oration rouses the Roman populace against the conspirators. He and Octavius defeat Brutus and Cassius at Philippi and, with M. Aemilius Lepidus, form the triumvirate ruling Rome.

Soothsayer: A mystic. He unsuccessfully attempts to warn Caesar twice about the leader's assassination.

Marcus Brutus: A Roman senator. He joins the conspiracy for fear that Caesar's tyranny will destroy the Roman republic. After losing the second battle of Philippi, he commits suicide.

Cassius: Roman politician. He organizes the conspiracy against Caesar and recruits Brutus to his cause. He is defeated by Antony at the first battle of Philippi and commits suicide when he mistakenly believes Brutus too has been defeated.

Cinna: Tribune and conspirator. He urges Cassius to recruit Brutus for their cause.

Decius Brutus: Roman general and conspirator. He persuades Caesar to come to the Senate on the day he is assassinated.

Portia: Brutus's wife. She attempts to persuade Brutus to confide in her the secret of the conspiracy. She later commits suicide when his plot fails.

Artemidorus: Teacher of rhetoric. He gives Caesar a letter revealing the plot to assassinate him, but Caesar does not read it.

Cinna the poet: He is mistaken for Cinna the conspirator by the mob. He explains the error, but the crowd kills him anyway for his "bad verses."

Octavius Caesar: Julius Caesar's heir. He and Antony defeat Brutus and Cassius at Philippi and, with M. Aemilius Lepidus, form the triumvirate ruling Rome.

M. Aemilius Lepidus: Roman politician. He joins Antony and Octavius to rule the Roman Empire after Caesar's assassination. Antony takes advantage of his weak nature, essentially ordering him to run errands.

Titinius: An officer of Cassius. Pindarus mistakenly reports that he has been captured by Antony's army, which causes Cassius to commit suicide.

Pindarus: A servant of Cassius. He mistakenly informs Cassius that Antony's forces have captured Titinius and are about to overtake the camp, which precipitates Cassius's decision to kill himself.

PLOT SYNOPSIS

Act I: Caesar triumphantly returns to Rome after defeating the forces of Pompey, but not all the Romans are pleased with his victory. Cassius is particularly envious of the ruler's newly-won power and hatches a plot to assassinate him. He discusses Caesar's political gains with Brutus, who fears that the leader may become a tyrant and thus jeopardize the Roman republic. While they talk, they hear cheers from the area where Caesar is celebrating the feast of the Lupercal. They learn from Casca that Mark Antony has offered Caesar the crown three times, and each time he has reluctantly refused it, finally collapsing with an attack of falling-sickness (epilepsy). Cassius and Brutus's conversation ends without a resolution, but Cassius decides to further entice Brutus by sending him forged letters from citizens who fear Caesar's ambition. Later during a violent storm that he interprets as a heavenly warning against Caesar's rise to power, Cassius meets and persuades Casca to join the conspiracy. The two then go to Brutus's house to further urge his participation.

Act II: Brutus is in his orchard contemplating his friendship with Caesar and his fear that the leader will become a tyrant if crowned king. He concludes that since the ruler could become a despot, he should be killed. During his meditation, he is interrupted by Cassius and his fellow-conspirators and agrees to join them in their plot against Caesar. Cassius proposes that they all swear to their resolution, but Brutus disagrees, arguing that their honorable motives require no such oath. Cassius also suggests that Mark Antony should be murdered along with Caesar, but again Brutus intercedes, maintaining that Antony will not be a threat once Caesar is dead. After the meeting, Portia begs

Brutus to explain the cause of his strange behavior, and he promises to tell her his secret. Meanwhile, Calphurnia has had nightmares of Caesar's death and implores him not to go to the senate that day. Caesar resists her pleas, but her warning is confirmed by the augurers. Caesar relents and agrees to stay home. However, Decius Brutus, who arrives to escort him to the Capitol, offers a favorable interpretation of Calphurnia's nightmares and tells Caesar that the senators will ridicule him if he does not appear. Caesar changes his mind again and departs for the Capitol. As he is leaving, he is joined by Brutus and several of the conspirators as well as by Antony.

Act III: On his way to the Capitol, Caesar receives two more warnings, one from the soothsayer and one from Artemidorus in the form of a letter, which he does not read. Once in the senate house, Trebonius lures Mark Antony away while the other conspirators ask Caesar to allow the banished Metellus Cimber to return to Rome. The senators use this diversion to encircle the leader, whereupon they stab him one by one. After Caesar is dead, the traitors bathe their hands in his blood. Initially shocked, Mark Antony nevertheless apparently pledges himself to the conspirators' cause; he asks, however, to speak at Caesar's funeral. Against Cassius's recommendation, Brutus grants Antony his wish. Left alone with Caesar's body, Antony vows revenge on the murderers. At the funeral, Brutus speaks to the Roman populace first, explaining that Caesar was killed because of his ambition. After winning the crowd's approval, Brutus steps aside to allow Antony to speak. Once he obtains the crowd's attention, Antony defends Caesar's virtuousness and sways the crowd's opinion against the traitors. The angry mob then goes on a rampage through the streets of Rome searching for conspirators. Coming upon Cinna the poet, they kill him simply because he bears the same name as one of Caesar's murderers. Meanwhile, Brutus and Cassius flee the city.

Act IV: Antony forms an alliance with Octavius and Lepidus to prepare for the impending war with the conspirators. During the meeting, the three men discuss which Romans should live and die under the new government. Once Lepidus leaves, Antony tells Octavius that he believes their partner is unfit to help rule the empire. Meanwhile, near Sardis, Cassius meets Brutus and expresses his anger over Brutus's decision to condemn one of his men for taking bribes. The two men have a tremendous argument in which Brutus accuses Cassius of also taking bribes. The fight continues to escalate until Cassius, deeply offended, bares his breast and offers Brutus his dagger. Brutus's overcomes his anger and the two are reconciled. The senator then reveals to his friend that Portia has committed suicide. Turning to the discussion of battle plans, Brutus resists Cassius's strategy of making the enemy seek them and decides to engage Octavius and Antony at Philippi. Later, when he is alone, Brutus sees the ghost of Caesar, who tells him they will meet again at Philippi.

Act V: Brutus and Cassius meet Antony and Octavius at Philippi to confer; instead, the two sides exchange insults and agree to face each other on the battlefield. During the battle, Cassius's troops become vulnerable to an attack by Antony. Fearing that some approaching soldiers are the enemy, Cassius sends Titinius to find out who they are and orders Pindarus to observe what happens. While the troops are really members of Brutus's army who welcome Titinius into their ranks, Pindarus mistakenly reports that the scout has been captured. Cassius despairs the hopelessness of his cause and orders Pindarus to stab him. After learning of Cassius's death, Brutus prepares to engage the enemy again. Brutus's forces are defeated in this second battle and he commits suicide to avoid being displayed as a prisoner in Rome. Upon finding Brutus's body, Antony delivers a brief oration proclaiming him the noblest Roman. In addition, Octavius declares that Brutus will be buried with full honors.

PRINCIPAL TOPICS

The depiction of Roman politics is a major issue in *Julius Caesar.* The nature of this concern lies in the question of whether Caesar's assassination should be considered murder or a justifiable action. One argument maintains that Shakespeare portrayed Caesar as a contemptible despot with a seemingly limitless appetite for conquest. Brutus joins the conspirators because he fears that the Roman republic will be destroyed if Caesar becomes king. From this perspective, *Julius Caesar* can be interpreted as a conflict between liberty and tyranny in which the conspirators' assassination of the would-be dictator is noble and just. A contrary reading asserts that Shakespeare created a benevolent, if somewhat vain, leader in Caesar, who is brutally murdered by envious traitors who manipulate Brutus's republican ideals to give their cause some credibility. This interpretation is manifested in the character of Antony, who remains loyal to Caesar and avenges his murder by rousing the Roman populace against the conspirators. Antony's and Brutus's use of rhetoric, or persuasive language, has a decided effect on the dramatic action in *Julius Caesar.* Particularly in their opposing funeral speeches in Act III, scene ii, the two men present different verbal strategies, though their goals are in some ways similar. In his oration, Brutus's principal technique is to imply that the commoners must choose between mutually exclusive alternatives—dying as slaves under Caesar's tyrannical rule or living as freemen in the republic—without proving that these are the only alter-

natives. Antony's eulogy, however, is characterized by its extensive use of irony and repetition, as well as by action words, exciting the commoners' emotions rather than appealing to their sensibilities. Neither Brutus nor Antony offer rational proofs of their arguments regarding Caesar, and consequently the more eloquent rhetorician, not the truth, sways public opinion. The fickle crowd, too, plays an important role in *Julius Caesar;* its willingness to summarily exchange rulers and to be easily led, first by the arguments of Brutus, then by the rhetoric of Antony, demonstrates its instability and lack of purpose. Shakespeare's depiction of the populace in *Julius Caesar,* in fact, has often been viewed as his condemnation of class rule, or democracy, in favor of monarchy.

Another principal topic concerns the private and public values of Brutus and Caesar and the relationship between human endeavors and history. While the private Brutus is a sensitive man who loves Caesar and abhors violence, the public figure is a noble idealist who puts his personal feelings aside to protect the Roman state from his leader's ambition. The private Caesar is a superstitious man plagued by illness, but the public figure is a demigod or a superman who, in the words of Cassius, "doth bestride the narrow world / Like a Colossus" (I. ii. 136-37). The private world represents the characters' interior motives, but the public world depicts their actions which, once performed, become independent of them and a part of history. More broadly speaking, this process in the play reflects the larger issue of humanity's inability to control the results of its deeds because history ultimately neglects one's private intentions and records only one's public actions.

Ritual also plays a key role in the interpretation of *Julius Caesar.* This aspect of the play is structured around one central ceremonial rite—Brutus's attempted exalting of Caesar's assassination to the level of a formal sacrifice. Brutus almost literally states this intent when he declares: "Let's kill [Caesar] boldly, but not wrathfully; / Let's carve him as a dish fit for the gods, / Not hew him as a carcass fit for hounds" (II. i. 172-74). Shakespeare provides added theatrical effect to the ritual motif when, after the conspirators stab Caesar to death, Brutus orders them to wash their hands in his blood. This episode emphasizes Brutus's chief character flaw, self-deception, for he truly believes that he can purify Caesar's assassination by regarding it as a ceremonial sacrifice. In addition, the treatment of blood establishes one of three major image patterns in *Julius Caesar,* along with the patterns of storm and fire. Each of these groups of images serves a dual purpose, thus heightening the thematic ambiguity of the play. The blood can symbolize either the injustice of Caesar's murder and the conspirators' guilt or a ritual blood-letting that restores the Roman political state to new health. The storm can represent the evil of Caesar's tyranny or the evil of the traitors' plot to assassinate him. Finally, fire can signify a purifying force that eliminates political treachery or the destructive power of civil strife.

CHARACTER STUDIES

The character of Caesar is perhaps the most difficult to interpret, since reading it one way or another can alter one's perspective on the entire play. If the ruler is viewed as an overly ambitious, vain, and pompous tyrant, then his assassination can be seen as a noble and necessary act to purge Rome of a potentially corrupt dictatorship. On the other hand, if Caesar is regarded as a wise and benevolent leader, then the conspiracy appears to be an attempt to overthrow the government by a group of envious and power-hungry politicians. Perhaps the most effective way to resolve the issue of Caesar's character is to consider that Shakespeare intentionally presented an enigmatic figure to emphasize the contradictory nature of the assassination itself and to leave undecided the question of whether the conspirators' actions were justified. Brutus, the other protagonist of *Julius Caesar,* is often regarded as the tragic hero of the play. He is a character of seemingly irreproachable honor and virtue, who believes that he is a descendent of Lucius Junius Brutus, who centuries before had expelled the autocratic Tarquin dynasty from Rome and established the republic. But Brutus also possesses the tragic characteristic known as *hubris*—excessive pride that leads to misfortune—which derives from his arrogance, self-righteousness, and lack of self-knowledge. His involvement in the conspiracy is grounded in his earnest belief that Caesar's death will benefit Rome, but he is blind to the potential repercussions of the assassination and to his accomplices' lack of moral principles. Ultimately, Brutus's tragic flaw is his inability to realize the consequences of his actions, and this lack of self-awareness leads to his downfall at the end of the play.

Two other characters have a significant influence over events in *Julius Caesar:* Cassius and Mark Antony. Cassius has traditionally been described as a villainous, self-seeking politician who helps murder Caesar out of envy and spitefulness. While acknowledging these traits in Cassius's character, some critics have also emphasized his Machiavellianism. Machiavellianism is a precept that considers politics amoral and claims that any means, however unscrupulous, are justified in achieving and holding onto power. Recently, Cassius has been credited with having more dimension than that of the Machiavellian villain. Support for this perspective can be found in his leadership and keen powers of judgment, his apparent enthusiasm for Brutus's ideal of republicanism, and his

great respect and friendship for his co-conspirator. Mark Antony shares some of Cassius's characteristics. Antony's loyalty to Caesar—similar to Cassius's friendship with Brutus—motivates him to give his funeral oration in Act III, scene ii and to avenge Caesar's death. Antony also displays a high level of cunning in the way he uses the funeral oration to manipulate the crowd's emotions; such techniques include his repeated ironic references to the conspirators as "honorable men," his displaying of Caesar's cloak and corpse, and finally his reading of the ruler's will. But there is also an undercurrent of Machiavellian opportunism in Antony's character as well, for after he rouses the crowd with his speech he meets with Octavius to plot how they can take advantage of the turmoil. Much like those of Cassius and Brutus, Antony's actions, while initially admirable, reveal a pragmatic political motivation which has a significant bearing on the dramatic events of *Julius Caesar.* These characters are ultimately linked by the common bond of ambition which precipitates, and in some cases is thwarted by, the central crisis of the play—Caesar's assassination.

CONCLUSION

Scholars have increasingly come to regard *Julius Caesar* as a work of rich complexity. Whereas earlier commentators attempted to provide definitive analyses of Brutus and Caesar, more recent ones have concluded that Shakespeare's portraits are not necessarily explicit; rather, they feature ironic, even ambiguous elements. Today, critics generally agree that the uncertainties surrounding the protagonists and the political issues raised by the drama are intentional. The ambiguities in *Julius Caesar,* they maintain, serve to intensify Shakespeare's depiction of the limitations on human understanding and the difficulty of defining absolute "truths" regarding individuals and historical events.

(See also *Shakespearean Criticism,* Vol. 7)

OVERVIEWS

Lawrence Danson

[*Danson presents an in-depth overview of Julius Caesar, focusing on how the linguistic strategies in the play's major scenes contribute to the overall tragic progression of the play. The critic also assesses whether* **Caesar** *or* **Brutus** *is the tragic hero of the drama and examines the circumstances surrounding Caesar's assassination and* **Mark Antony**'s *subsequent funeral speech (III. ii. 73ff.). Danson con-*

*cludes the essay by briefly contrasting the themes developed in Shakespeare's tragedy with the known historical facts of **Brutus**'s conspiracy and **Caesar**'s murder, ultimately arguing that the two points of view cannot necessarily be reconciled.*]

In *Julius Caesar* we find . . . those problems of communication and expression, those confusions linguistic and ritualistic, which mark the world of the tragedies. The play opens with the sort of apparently expository scene in which Shakespeare actually gives us the major action of the play in miniature. Flavius and Marullus, the tribunes, can barely understand the punning language of the commoners . . . It is ostensibly broad daylight in Rome, but the situation is dreamlike; for although the language which the two classes speak is phonetically identical, it is, semantically, two separate languages. The cobbler's language, though it sounds like the tribunes', is (to the tribunes) a sort of inexplicable dumb show.

And as with words, so with gestures; the certainties of ceremonial order are as lacking in Rome, as are the certainties of the verbal language. The commoners present an anomaly to the tribunes simply by walking "Upon a labouring day without the sign / Of [their] profession" [I. i. 4-5]. To the commoners it is a "holiday," to the tribunes (although in fact it is the Feast of Lupercal), a "labouring day." The commoners have planned an observance of Caesar's triumph—itself, to the tribunes, no triumph but rather a perversion of Roman order—but the tribunes send the "idle creatures" off to perform a quite different ceremony:

> Go, go, good countrymen, and for this fault
> Assemble all the poor men of our sort;
> Draw them to Tiber banks, and weep your
>   tears
> Into the channel, till the lowest stream
> Do kiss the most exalted shores of all.
> > [I. i. 56-60]

Thus, in a Rome where each man's language is foreign to the next, ritual gestures are converted into their opposites; confusion in the state's symbolic system makes every action perilously ambiguous. The tribunes, having turned the commoners' planned ritual into its opposite, go off bravely to make their own gesture, to "Disrobe the images" of Caesar [I. i. 64]: but shortly we learn that they have actually been made to play parts in a bloodier ritual (one which, as we shall see, becomes increasingly common in the play). And when, in a later scene, we find Brutus deciding upon *his* proper gesture, the confusions of this first scene should recur to us.

The second scene again opens with mention of specifically ritual observance, as Caesar bids Calphurnia stand in Antony's way to receive the touch which will "Shake off [her] sterile curse" [I. ii. 9]. Perhaps Shakespeare intends to satirize Caesar's

superstitiousness; at least we can say that Calphurnia's sterility and the fructifying touch introduce the question, what sort of ritual can assure (political) succession in Rome? Directly, the Soothsayer steps forth, warning Caesar, "Beware the ides of March." But this communication is not understood: "He is a dreamer; Let us leave him. Pass" [I. ii. 24].

What follows, when Caesar and his train have passed off the stage leaving Brutus and Cassius behind, is an enactment—virtually an iconic presentation—of the linguistic problem. More clearly even than the first scene, this scene gives us the picture of Rome as a place where words and rituals have dangerously lost their conventional meanings. As Cassius begins to feel out Brutus about the conspiracy—telling him of Rome's danger and wishes, of Caesar's pitiful mortality, of Brutus's republican heritage—their conversation is punctuated by shouts from offstage, shouts at whose meaning they can only guess. (pp. 52-3)

Casca, an eyewitness to the ritual in the marketplace, finally arrives to be their interpreter; but even he has understood imperfectly. Caesar (he says) has been offered the crown, but

> I can as well be hang'd as tell the manner
> of it: it was mere foolery; I did not mark it.
> I saw Mark Antony offer him a crown—yet
> 'twas not a crown neither, 'twas one of
> these coronets. . . .
> > [I. ii. 235-38]

Caesar refused the crown, but Casca suspects "he would fain have had it." "The rabblement hooted," and Caesar "swooned and fell down at" the stench [I. ii. 244, 248]. As for the rest, Cicero spoke, but again the language problem intervened: "He spoke Greek" [I. ii. 279]. There is other news: "Marullus and Flavius, for pulling scarfs off Caesar's images, are put to silence" [I. ii. 285-86]. And, "There was more foolery yet, if I could remember it" [I. ii. 287].

The dramatic point of it all lies not so much in the conflict between republican and monarchical principles, as in the sheer confusion of the reported and overheard scene. It is all hooting and clapping and uttering of bad breath, swooning, foaming at the mouth, and speaking Greek. Casca's cynical tone is well suited to the occasion, for the farcical charade of the crown-ritual, with Caesar's refusal and Antony's urging, is itself a cynical manipulation. The crowd clapped and hissed "as they use to do the players in the theatre" [I. ii. 260]—and rightly so.

These two opening scenes give us the world in which Brutus is to undertake his great gesture. When we next see Brutus, his decision is made: "It must be by his death" [II. i. 10]. Behind Brutus's decision is that linguistic and ceremonial confusion which is comic in the case of the commoners and sinister in the case of Caesar's crown-ritual.

The innovations in Rome's ceremonial order give evidence to Brutus for the necessity of his gesture. But those same innovations, attesting to a failure in Rome's basic linguistic situation, also make it most probable that his gesture will fail. Brutus is not unlike Hamlet: he is a man called upon to make an expressive gesture in a world where the commensurate values necessary to expression are lacking. The killing of Caesar, despite the honorable intentions that are within Brutus and passing show, will thus be only one more ambiguous, misunderstood action in a world where no action can have an assured value. Brutus's grand expression might as well be Greek in this Roman world.

Brutus's position is not unlike Hamlet's, but he does not see what Hamlet sees. Indeed, he does not even see as much as his fellow conspirators do. To Cassius, the dreadful and unnatural storm over Rome reflects "the work we have in hand" [I. iii. 129]; to the thoughtful Cassius, the confusion in the heavens is an aspect of the confusion in Rome. But Brutus is, typically, unmoved by the storm, and calmly makes use of its strange light to view the situation: "The exhalations, whizzing in the air, / Give so much light that I may read by them" [II. i. 44-5]. And what he reads by this deceptive light is as ambiguous as the shouts of the crowd at the crown-ritual: the paper bears temptations slipped into his study by the conspirators, words that mislead and may betray. On the basis of this mysterious communication, revealed by a taper's dim light and the unnatural "exhalations" above, Brutus determines to "speak and strike" [II. i. 55]. Every sign is misinterpreted by Brutus; and the world that seems to him to make a clear demand for words and gestures is in fact a world where words are equivocal and where gestures quickly wither into their opposites.

The situation, as I have so far described it, forces upon us the question critics of the play have most frequently debated: who is the play's hero? A simple enough question, it would seem: the title tells us that this is *The Tragedy of Julius Caesar.* But that answer only serves to show the actual complexity of the question, for if Caesar (who is, after all, dead by the middle of the play) is to this play what, say, Hamlet is to his, then *Julius Caesar* is, structurally at least, a most peculiar tragedy. The question of the hero—and a glance at the critical literature shows that the position is indeed questionable—bears upon fundamental matters of meaning and structure.

Now it is a curious fact about Shakespeare's plays (and, to an extent, about all drama) that the questions the critics ask have a way of duplicating the questions the characters ask, as though the playwright had done his best to make all criticism redundant. As if the play were not enough, nor the characters sufficient unto their conflicts, the critical audience continues to fight the same fights and

ask the same questions the characters in the play do. Of *Julius Caesar,* as I have said, the question we most often ask concerns the play's hero: Caesar or Brutus? I have not bothered to tally the choices; for our purposes it is more interesting to notice the mode of critical procedure and the way in which it tends to imitate the actions of the characters in the play. Both critics and characters tend to choose sides in their respective conflicts on the bases of political prejudice and evaluations of moral rectitude. Since the moral and political issues in *Julius Caesar* are themselves eternally moot, it is not surprising that the critical debate continues unresolved.

About Caesar, for instance: if we try to make our determination of herohood on the basis of Caesar's moral stature, we are doing precisely what the characters do; and we find, I think, that he becomes for us what he is for Shakespeare's Romans, less a man than the object of men's speculations. Caesar is the Colossus whose legs we may peep about but whom we can never know; characters and audience alike peep assiduously, each giving us a partial view which simply will not accord with any other. Within the play, Caesar is virtually constituted of the guesses made about him: Casca's rude mockery, Cassius's sneers, Brutus's composite portrait of the present Caesar (against whom he knows no wrong) and the dangerous serpent of the future, Antony's passionate defense, the mob's fickle love and hate: these are the guesses, and contradictory as they are, they give us the Caesar of the play—and of the play's critics.

Of Caesar's, or for that matter of Brutus's, moral status we can have little more certain knowledge than the characters themselves have. What we are in a privileged position to know is the *structure* of the play: the characters' prison, the play's encompassing form, is our revelation. What I propose to do, therefore, is to look at the implicit answer Brutus gives (through his actions) to the question, who is the play's tragic hero?, and compare that answer to the answer revealed by the play's unfolding structure.

Everything Brutus does (until the collapse of the conspiracy) is calculated to justify the title of the play, to make it indeed *The Tragedy of Julius Caesar.* As we watch Brutus directing the conspiracy, we watch a man plotting a typical Shakespearean tragedy; and it is crucial to the success of his plot that Caesar indeed be its hero-victim. The assassination, as Brutus conceives it, must have all the solemnity and finality of a tragic play. The wonder of the spectacle must, as in tragedy, join the audience (both within and without the play) into a community of assent to the deed. For his part, Brutus is content with a necessary secondary role, the mere agent of the hero's downfall. . . . (pp. 54-7)

But of course Brutus's plot (in both senses of the word) is a failure. The withholding of assent by the audience (again, both within and without the play) proves his failure more conclusively than do moral or political considerations. Brutus misunderstands the language of Rome; he misinterprets all the signs both cosmic and earthly; and the furthest reach of his failure is his failure to grasp, until the very end, the destined shape of his play. Brutus's plot is a failure, but by attending to the direction he tries to give it we can find, ironically, a clear anatomy of the typical tragic action.

Brutus makes his decision and in Act II, scene i he meets with the conspirators. Decius puts the question, "Shall no man else be touch'd but only Caesar?" [II. i. 154]. Cassius, whose concerns are wholly practical, urges Antony's death. But Brutus demurs: the assassination as he conceives it has a symbolic dimension as important as its practical dimension; and although Brutus is not able to keep the two clearly separated (he opposes Antony's death partly out of concern for the deed's appearance "to the common eyes" [II. i. 179]) he is clear about the need for a single sacrificial victim. His emphasis on sacrifice indicates the ritual shape Brutus hopes to give the assassination:

> Let's be sacrificers, but not butchers, Caius.
> We all stand up against the spirit of Caesar,
> And in the spirit of men there is no blood.
> O that we then could come by Caesar's spirit,
> And not dismember Caesar! But, alas,
> Caesar must bleed for it! And, gentle friends,
> Let's kill him boldly, but not wrathfully;
> Let's carve him as a dish fit for the gods,
> Not hew him as a carcass fit for hounds. . . .
> We shall be call'd purgers, but not murderers.
>
> [II. i. 166-74, 180]

The "sacrifice" must not be confused with murder, with mere butchery. The name of the deed becomes all important, indicating the distance between a gratuitous, essentially meaningless gesture, and a sanctioned, efficacious, unambiguous ritual.

But Brutus's speech, with a fine irony, betrays his own fatal confusion. "In the spirit of men there is no blood," but in this spirit—this symbol, this embodiment of Caesarism [dictatorship]—there is, "alas," as much blood as Lady Macbeth will find in Duncan. Whatever we may feel about Brutus's political intentions, we must acknowledge a failure which has, it seems to me, as much to do with logic and language as with politics: Brutus is simply unclear about the difference between symbols and men. And his confusion, which leads to the semantic confusion between "murder" and "sacrifice," and between meaningless gestures and sanctioned ritual, is the central case of something we see at

every social level in Rome. The assassination Brutus plans as a means of purging Rome dwindles to just more of the old ambiguous words and empty gestures. The assassination loses its intended meaning as surely as the commoners' celebration did in scene i.

The assassination is surrounded by Brutus with all the rhetoric and actions of a sacrificial rite. It becomes ritually and literally a bloodbath, as Brutus bids,

> Stoop, Romans, stoop,
> And let us bathe our hands in Caesar's blood
> Up to the elbows, and besmear our swords.
>
> [III. i. 105-07]

Even the disastrous decision to allow Antony to address the mob arises from Brutus's concern that "Caesar shall / Have all true rites and lawful ceremonies" [III. i. 240-41]. In Brutus's plot, where Caesar is the hero-victim whose death brings tragedy's "calm of mind, all passion spent," no one, not even Antony, should be left out of the ceremonious finale. With the conspirators' ritualized bloodbath, indeed, the implied metaphor of the assassination-as-drama becomes explicit—if also horribly ironic:

> *Cas.* Stoop then, and wash. How many ages hence
> Shall this our lofty scene be acted over
> In states unborn and accents yet unknown!
> *Bru.* How many times shall Caesar bleed in sport. . . .
>
> [III. i. 111-14]

Trapped in their bloody pageant, these histrionic conspirators cannot see what, in the terms they themselves suggest, is the most important point of all: this lofty scene occurs, not at the end, but in the middle of a tragic play.

Brutus's plot is not Shakespeare's; and immediately after the conspirators have acted out what should be the denouement of their tragic play, the actual shape of the play (the one they cannot see as such) begins to make itself clear. Antony, pointedly recalling Brutus's distinction between "sacrificers" and "butchers," says to the slaughtered symbol of tyranny, "O, pardon me, thou bleeding piece of earth, / That I am meek and gentle with these butchers!" [III. i. 254-55], and announces the further course of the action:

> And Caesar's spirit, ranging for revenge,
> With Ate by his side come hot from hell,
> Shall in these confines with a monarch's voice
> Cry 'Havoc!' and let slip the dogs of war,
> That this foul deed shall smell above the earth
> With carrion men, groaning for burial.
>
> [III. i. 270-75]

Brutus's revolutionary gesture, which was intended to bring to birth a stabler order, has been (in an esthetic as well as a political sense) premature. His ritual has failed, and now, as Caesar's spirit ranges for revenge (for there *is* blood in the spirits of men), it still remains for the proper ritual to be found. Now Brutus will at last assume his proper role: Brutus must be our tragic hero.

Of course he does his best to deny that role. His stoicism—the coolness, for instance, with which he dismisses Caesar's ghost: "Why, I will see thee at Philippi, then" [IV. iii. 286]—is hardly what we expect of the grandly suffering tragic hero. Still, it is to Brutus that we owe one of the finest descriptions of the peculiar moment in time occupied by a Shakespearean tragedy:

> Since Cassius first did whet me against
>   Caesar,
> I have not slept.
> Between the acting of a dreadful thing
> And the first motion, all the interim is
> Like a phantasma or a hideous dream.
> The Genius and the mortal instruments
> Are then in council; and the state of man,
> Like to a little kingdom, suffers then
> The nature of an insurrection.
>
>   [II. i. 61-9]

The moment is suspended, irresolute, but charged with the energy to complete itself. The separation of "acting" from "first motion," of "Genius" from "mortal instruments," is an intolerable state—the measure of it is the insomnia—which demands resolution. . . . [It] is the tragic moment, and Brutus, for all his Roman calm, must pass through it to its necessary completion.

The acting of the "dreadful thing"—or, rather, what Brutus thinks is the dreadful thing, Caesar's death—does not bring the promised end; that is made immediately clear. Antony's funeral oration shows that Brutus's grand gesture has changed little. Antony easily converts Brutus's sacrifice into murder. In Rome . . . men's actions merely "seem," and Antony can shift the intended meaning of Brutus's action as easily as the tribunes had changed the intended meaning of the commoner's actions in Act I, scene i. Antony can use virtually the same words as the conspirators—he can still call Brutus an "honourable man" and Caesar "ambitious"—and yet make condemnation of approval and approval of condemnation. Even after the revolutionary moment of Caesar's death, this Rome is all of a piece: a volatile mob, empty ceremonies, and a language as problematic as the reality it describes.

Even names are problematic here. It was with names that Cassius first went to work on Brutus:

> 'Brutus' and 'Caesar'. What should be in
>   that 'Caesar'?
> Why should that name be sounded more
>   than yours?

> Write them together: yours is as fair a
>   name.
> Sound them: it doth become the mouth as
>   well.
> Weigh them: it is as heavy. Conjure with
>   'em:
> 'Brutus' will start a spirit as soon as 'Caesar'.
>
>   [I. ii. 142-47]

Cassius's contemptuous nominalism reminds one of Edmund in *King Lear,* who also thinks that one name—that of "bastard," for instance—is as good as any other. Names, to Cassius and Edmund, are conventional signs having reference to no absolute value, and they may be manipulated at will.

In his funeral oration, Antony also plays freely with names; and with the repetition of those two names "Brutus" and "Caesar" he does indeed conjure a spirit. It is the spirit of riot, of random violence, and its first victim (with a grotesque appropriateness) is a poet and a name:

> *3 Pleb.* Your name sir, truly.
> *Cin.* Truly, my name is Cinna.
> *1 Pleb.* Tear him to pieces; he's a conspirator!
> *Cin.* I am Cinna the poet, I am Cinna the poet.
> *4 Pleb.* Tear him for his bad verses, tear him for his bad verses!
> *Cin.* I am not Cinna the conspirator.
> *4 Pleb.* It is no matter, his name's Cinna; pluck but his name out of his heart, and turn him going.
> *3 Pleb.* Tear him, tear him!
>
>   [III. iii. 26-35]

"Pluck but his name out of his heart, and turn him going": it is like Brutus's impossible, "And in the spirit of men there is no blood" [II. i. 168]. Again, it is the confusion between symbol and reality, between the abstract name and the blood-filled man who bears it. Poets, whose genius it is to mediate symbol and reality and to find the appropriate name to match all things, generally have rough going in *Julius Caesar.* Brutus the liberator shows how he has insensibly aged into a figure indistinguishable from the tyrant when he dismisses a peace-making poet with a curt, "What should the wars do with these jigging fools?" [IV. iii. 137]. And Caesar, too, had rebuffed a poetical soothsayer.

The gratuitous murder of Cinna the poet reflects ironically upon the murder of Caesar. The poet's rending at the hands of the mob is unreasonable, based solely on a confusion of identities (of names, words), and while it bears some resemblance to the sacrifice of a scapegoat figure, it is really no sacrifice at all but unsanctioned murder. Caesar's death, similarly, was undertaken as a sacrificial gesture, but quickly became identified with plain butchery. In the mirror of the Cinna episode the assassination is seen as only one case in a series of perverted rituals—a series that runs with increasing frequency now, until the proper victim and the proper form are at last found.

Immediately following the murder of Cinna we see the new triumvirate pricking the names of its victims. The death of Caesar has released the motive force behind the tragedy, and that force runs unchecked now until the final sacrifice at Philippi. From the very first scene of the play we have witnessed ritual gestures that wither into meaninglessness; with the conspiracy and Caesar's death, we become aware of sacrifice as the particular ritual toward which the world of the play is struggling: the series of mistaken rituals becomes a series of mistaken sacrifices, culminating at Philippi.

The wrong sacrifice, the wrong victim: the play offers an astonishing gallery of them. It has been noticed that all of the major characters implicate themselves in this central action:

> each character in the political quartet in turn makes a similar kind of theatrical gesture implying the sacrifice of his own life: to top his refusal of the crown, Caesar offers the Roman mob his throat to cut; Brutus shows the same people that he has a dagger ready for himself, in case Rome should need his death; with half-hidden irony, Antony begs his death of the conspirators; and in the quarrel scene, Cassius gives his "naked breast" for Brutus to strike. [Adrien Bonjour, in his *The Structure of "Julius Caesar"*]

The idea of sacrifice is imagistically linked to the idea of hunters and the hunted. Caesar, says Antony, lies "like a deer strucken by many princes" [III. i. 209]. The ruthless Octavius feels, improbably enough, that he is "at the stake, / And bay'd about with many enemies" [IV. i. 48-9]. But it was the conspirators themselves who first suggested the analogy between sacrifice and hunting: their blood-bathing ceremony suggests (as Antony makes explicit) the actions of a hunter with his first kill. And finally, appropriately, the sacrifice-hunting imagery fastens on Brutus: "Our enemies have beat us to the pit" [V. v. 23].

From a slightly different perspective, the final scenes at Philippi might be a comedy of errors. Military bungles and mistaken identities follow quickly on each other's heels; the number of suicides, especially, seems excessive. Of the suicide of Titinius, a relatively minor character, [Harley] Granville-Barker asks [in his *Prefaces to Shakespeare*], "why, with two suicides to provide for, Shakespeare burdened himself with this third?" The answer to his question, and the explanation for the apparent excesses generally, must be found, I believe, in the context of false sacrifice throughout the play. Caesar's death was one such false sacrifice; Cinna the poet's a horrible mistake; the political murders by the triumvirate continued the chain; and now Cassius sacrifices himself on the basis of a mistake, while Titinius follows out of loyalty to the dead Cassius. Brutus embarked on the conspiracy because he misinterpreted the confused signs in, and above, Rome; the intended meaning of his own gesture was in turn subverted by Antony and the mob. And now Cassius has misinterpreted the signs: friendly troops are mistaken for hostile, their shouts of joy are not understood; thus "Caesar, thou art reveng'd," as Cassius dies, in error, "Even with the sword that kill'd thee" [V. iii. 45-6]. And, because Cassius has "misconstrued every thing" (as Titinius puts it [V. iii. 84]), Titinius now dies, bidding, "Brutus, come apace" [V. iii. 87].

Titinius places a garland on the dead Cassius before he dies himself; and Brutus, entering when both are dead, pronounces a solemn epitaph:

> Are yet two Romans living such as these?
> The last of all the Romans, fare thee well!
> It is impossible that ever Rome
> Should breed thy fellow. Friends, I owe
>   moe tears
> To this dead man than you shall see me
>   pay.
> I shall find time, Cassius, I shall find time.
>   [V. iii. 98-103]

The words and the actions form an appropriate tragic device of wonder—but this is no more the end than it was when Brutus spoke an epitaph for Caesar. The death of Cassius is still not the proper sacrifice, and the play has still to reach its culminating ritual.

At Philippi, Brutus at last accepts his role. Against the wishes of Cassius, Brutus insists upon meeting the enemy even before (as the enemy puts it), "we do demand of them" [V. i. 6]. The ghost of Caesar has appeared and Brutus has accepted its portent: "I know my hour is come" [V. v. 20]. Most significant in Brutus's final speeches is their tone of acceptance:

>   Countrymen,
> My heart doth joy that yet in all my life
> I found no man but he was true to me.
> I shall have glory by this losing day,
> More than Octavius and Mark Antony
> By this vile conquest shall attain unto.
> So fare you well at once; for Brutus'
>   tongue
> Hath almost ended his life's history.
> Night hangs upon mine eyes; my bones
>   would rest,
> That have but labour'd to attain this hour.
>   [V. v. 33-42]

The expressed idea of the glorious defeat is an authentic sign of Shakespearean tragedy. . . . Brutus recognizes here the necessary end of "his life's history" [V. v. 40]: all, from the very start, has tended to this gesture. (pp. 57-66)

And this gesture receives, as the assassination of Caesar did not, the requisite assent. Brutus "hath honour by his death" [V. v. 57], says Strato; and

Lucilius, "So Brutus should be found" [V. v. 58]. The opposing parties join together now in Octavius's service, and it is Antony himself who can pronounce the epitaph, "This was the noblest Roman of them all" [V. v. 68]. His words and the gestures are universally accepted.

But what of Rome and its future? . . . [It] is the close involvement of *Julius Caesar* with widely known historical facts which forces upon us the recognition of . . . truth's limitations. Indeed, the play contains hints—the bloody, divisive course of the triumvirate has been made plain, for instance—which, even without prior historical knowledge, might make us temper our optimism over the play's conclusion. With Brutus's death the play has revealed its tragic entelechy [scheme]; the destined shape has been found, and the discovery brings its esthetic satisfactions. That the price of our pleasure is the hero's death is not (as in *King Lear* it will so terribly be) a source of discomfort. But what we cannot dismiss is our knowledge that every end is also a beginning. History will have its way; "fate" will defeat men's "wills"; and the "glory" of this "losing day" will tarnish and become, in the movement of time, as ambiguous as the glorious loss on the ides of March.

Thus we must entertain two apparently opposite points of view. With Brutus's sacrificial gesture the ritual has been found which can satisfy the dramatic expectations created by the play. The final words are spoken, the language is understood; and thus the play has given us what Robert Frost demanded of all poetry, "a momentary stay against confusion." But if we stress in Frost's definition his modifying word *momentary*, we find ourselves cast back upon history; and once out of the timeless world of the play, "confusion" predominates. (pp. 66-7)

Lawrence Danson, "Julius Caesar," in his Tragic Alphabet: Shakespeare's Drama of Language, *Yale University Press, 1974, pp. 50-67.*

Robert E. Knoll

[*Knoll presents a comprehensive overview of* Julius Caesar, *arguing that the play lends itself remarkably well to the five-act dramatic structure. Each of the major characters occupies a significant place in one of the five acts, the critic maintains, for their actions generally overshadow and shape the events of those acts which they dominate. Knoll attributes Act I to* **Cassius,** *who determines the course of events in the play by persuading* **Brutus** *to join the conspiracy. Act II belongs to* **Brutus,** *for his soliloquies and conversations establish the idealistic context by which he legitimates* **Caesar's** *assassination.* **Antony** *is the protagonist of Act III, for it is his rousing funeral oration that turns the tables on the conspirators and*

ultimately leads to their failure. **Caesar** *is the focus of Act IV, not only because his spirit haunts the guilt-ridden* **Brutus,** *but also because his murder creates a chaotic political vacuum in Rome. Finally,* **Octavius** *dominates Act V because his confident assumption of leadership over the other major characters promises future political stability in the Roman Empire.*]

Though Shakespeare did not divide all his plays uniformly into scenes and acts—these conventional divisions were regularized by editors long after his death—he seems to have conceived *Julius Caesar* in a five-act structure. If we look at it an act at a time, we may see how it combines to create a unified dramatic whole. The play is "brilliantly constructed," as the editors say. Each act is dominated by a single personage who commands our attention by controlling the direction of its action. By the end of the fifth act a series of archetypical Romans have paraded across the stage and caused us to think of fundamental political and human issues. In Act I, though we learn important facts about the Roman plebians, Caesar, and others, Cassius dominates the stage. In Act II, Brutus is in the center. We follow him in his moment of highest decision. Act III belongs to Antony, who steals the scene from the conspirators and enflames the Roman populace. Act IV belongs to Caesar, whose ghost haunts the quarrel between Cassius and Brutus. Act V is Octavius's and the play ends with his words. Let us consider the play in some detail, act by act.

Cassius is the protagonist in Act I. That is, he determines the course of events. The decisive action in this act is his conversation with Brutus, and it is through this exchange that we come to understand his nature and the political situation in Rome.

When the play begins, we perceive that Rome has reached a turning point in its history. The "Establishment," represented by Flavius and Marullus, is clearly out of touch with the people. The plebians may be mercurial in their loyalties, but they are hardly insensitive or stupid; they are certainly not the blocks and stones and worse than senseless things Marullus says they are. They are witty and full of life. Notice how the cobbler delights in punning and playing with language [I. i. 21ff.]. The Tribunes, however, fail to understand the temper of contemporary events and want to "disrobe the images" [I. i. 64] that have been decorated for this day of Caesar's celebrations without sympathy for their significance in the popular Feast of Lupercal. (pp. 6-7)

The second scene gives us Caesar, over whose nature and position the controversy turns. Though the episode in which he first appears is brief, we have an early impression of his authoritative manner. He is one of those rare men who command whatever group they appear in: Wherever this man sits is the "head of the table." "Charisma," that rather silly fashionable word, is much too small for what Caesar has. Everyone accedes to his wishes, whether they want to or not, so much authority has he in his manner. Nearly every line he speaks has a command in it. In this and other scenes, as we will see, he seems aware of this remarkable magnetism and in a sense stands aside from it, observing himself. He seems as fascinated by his power over others as we are.

But in these first lines, we are only given a hint of what we will see later; in Act I the emphasis is not on Caesar's personality. If he were given more lines, he would so overbalance the play that we would neglect to follow the fortunes of Cassius, Brutus, and the others, and the play as Shakespeare has conceived it is not so much about Caesar as it is about the reactions of those persons to his magnificence.

After only twenty-five lines, the scene directs our attention to Cassius, as he persuades Brutus to join in a rebellion against Julius Caesar [I. ii. 25ff.]. We will see as the play proceeds that Cassius, though an intellectual, is a passionate man, a man of feeling. He is filled from top to toe with envy; and from this envy, rebellion grows. Caesar's magnificence diminishes him (see I. ii. 116-17; 135-8; 209-10). As second in command to Brutus, Cassius can be large, for Brutus is not a demi-god, not a superman, not larger than life. As second or third to Caesar, Cassius would disappear and Caesar, of course, does not even give him this chance. Cassius rationalizes his envy by merging it into what he takes to be a passion for republican freedom, but we fear that he is as much concerned with his own place as with the public good. Personal goals and public values are combined inextricably in his mind.

Cassius does have very considerable gifts, and we can admire them. A great observer, "he looks quite through the deeds of men" [I. ii. 202-03] and senses the emotions of persons he talks to. He easily matches his words to their feelings. Watching Brutus, he perceives Brutus's innermost thoughts, and his long speeches of persuasion follow the movements of Brutus's mind, playing first on Brutus's pride in himself and then on what he asserts is Caesar's dangerous ambition. Cassius is genuinely fond of Brutus. Indeed, his ability to love is the other side of his envy; an emotional man, he loves as readily as he hates. His is a restless, not a passive, nature (see I. ii. 139-41). He loves no plays, as Caesar says of him; and he listens to no music. His mind is too active, too full of observations and schemes to be diverted by gaming and play-acting [I. ii. 192-214].

For all his imaginative perception, Cassius allows envy to warp his judgments. He complains that Caesar is not the athlete that he himself is, that Caesar is aging, that his body is less vigorous than it once was. His observations are correct. Caesar speaks of his own deafness [I. ii. 213], and we learn later that he is given to "the falling sickness" [I. ii. 254]; but Cassius should know that it is the spirit of Caesar that rules, not his arm; that leaders may be crippled (like Roosevelt) or small (like Napoleon) or physically weak (like Joan of Arc) and still be strong.

Cassius's judgments of other persons are fairer. He has a fundamental contempt for Casca, but he sees the danger in Casca's malice. Casca is "sour" as the grapes are "sour" in Aesop's fable. Notice how Casca begins each reply to Brutus with a disparaging "Why" [I. ii. 219; 221; 225; 227; 233]. Cassius's judgment of Brutus is not warped either. He knows that Brutus is large-minded; he also knows that he and Brutus are not made of the same stuff [I. ii. 308-15]. The difference neither intimidates him nor puts him off, for Cassius knows how to deal with people. He turns Casca's superstitious fear of the night storm to his own purposes, even while he rationally remains unmoved. As he spoke of honor to the honorable Brutus, he speaks of violence to the violent Casca [I. iii. 89-115], and he does not waste his rhetoric on Cinna, who has already been won to the conspiracy. Coolly, he simply directs Cinna to manipulate the vain Brutus [I. iii. 142-47]. Cassius is clearly the ringleader of the faction.

Act I is dominated by Cassius, and by the end we are confident that he will win Brutus over, he is so clever, so determined, so affectionate, and so clear-eyed. He knows what he is doing, and Caesar has reason to be afraid of him. He is a man to have on your team. He is too perceptive, by half, to be left with an enemy, unchecked. But Cassius is also one of those thinkers who prefer people to ideas. The proposed rebellion against Caesar is not ideological for him. It is personal. He rejects the authority of Julius Caesar, but he only incidentally defends republicanism.

The first act of this play is Cassius's. The second belongs to Brutus, and he dominates all its scenes, even those in which he does not appear. The act begins with what amounts to an eighty-five line soliloquy in which Brutus speaks of the decision he has made to kill Caesar [II. i. 10ff.]. The soliloquy is dramatically interrupted four times by the serving boy, Lucius, who briefly turns Brutus's attention to the everyday world. Three of these interruptions are not necessary to the action of the play but serve to intensify our sense of Brutus's purpose. The cumulative strength of this soliloquy is such that Brutus does not need to speak to us directly ever again.

In the first act, we have seen that Brutus's central emotion is a consistent concern for his "honor," an honor that is his by right of both birth and attainment. He is an aristocrat, and this fact is the key to his conduct and his temper. Because he is descended from the founders of the Roman Republic, he holds himself to the highest standards on its defense (II. i. 53ff., for example). He cannot be bought, for he feels himself judged by his ancestors. His personal affection for Julius Caesar and his private relationship to his wife must submit to the high ideals he has had set for him by his forebears. Kind to his servants, he is filled with *noblesse oblige* [obligations of rank]. Patronizing of his peers insofar as he recognizes any peers—Cassius, his only confidant, does not appear to be a member of the aristocratic party by virtue of ancient birth—he is confident of his judgment as young men brought up in privileged circles are confident of themselves. When Cassius, Decius, and others fear to leave Antony alive, Brutus overrules them without hesitation. [II. i. 155-70]. But Brutus is not young, and by this time he should have learned to respect the judgments of men of the world. Instead, he is ignorant of general human nature, so secluded by his class has he been from the general run of men. He assumes naively that all the conspirators are as disinterested as he is [II. i. 118-40]; and it never occurs to him that the populace might judge his actions as less noble than he claims them to be. He thinks (like Macbeth) that he can commit murder without becoming a murderer and that an assassination is a state ritual, because he says it is [II. i. 166-80].

Right here the trouble lies: Brutus is so high-minded that his vision is distorted. He is not very bright; and worse, by far, he does not know it. He is the only figure in the play whom we see in the agony of decision (II. i. 61-9; 78-85, for example), and we therefore know him considerably better than we know the others. We know him better than he knows himself. He doesn't explore issues but passes hastily over first principles, though he prides himself on his philosophical nature. "A fastidious contempt of the shameful means necessary to achieve his ends is the constant mark of the political idealist," one shrewd critic, John Palmer, has noted. When Brutus finds that he must choose between loyalty to his friend, whom he loves, and loyalty to his country, which he venerates, we see that his patriotic ideals are more important to him than people. Dostoevsky observes that men of philosophic mind are necessarily cruel, and this seems true of Brutus.

Fancying himself a philosopher, Brutus deals in abstract values in a political situation that calls for the practicality of a precinct politician. Brutus is the kind of "idealist" who wants to shape public events rather than that kind of practical man who makes the most of a situation, accepting the "given" and building on that. He is insufficiently humble before facts, before events, before political reality. One might say, rather paradoxically, that he is an intellectual—one who deals in concepts and ideas—who is not very intelligent.

Brutus knows, as all the conspirators know, that without him the rebellion against Julius Caesar will fail. One might say that Brutus "legitimatizes" the operation (see I. iii. 158-60), for everybody knows that his hands are clean. But clean hands are only one requirement of statesmanship, and perhaps not the most important. A little touch of humanity might help, but we see in the scene with his wife that even in his bedroom he is a public figure [II. i. 234-309]. He never forgets that he is a Roman, with Roman duties.

Portia is his counterpart, the very model of one kind of Roman matron. Notice how she repeatedly speaks to Brutus in the third person [II. i. 258; 261; 263; 287]. But like Brutus she is a republican aristocrat, making herself morally tall by standing on tiptoe. Perhaps she is playing over her head; her wounding of herself to prove her constancy [II. i. 299-301] and her shocking death suggest that her moral grandeur has more than a touch of neuroticism in it. In her scene with Lucius and the soothsayer [II. iv] she lacks the self control that Stoics like Brutus and Cato admire [A Stoic is a member of the school of philosophy founded by the Greek thinker Zeno about 300 B. C. This discipline holds that wise men should be free from passion, unmoved by joy or grief, and submissive to natural law]. In her relationship with Brutus, we see that both have a greater sense of duty than of love; both of them aspire to live by principle.

Caesar, whom we next see in II. ii, is not less an aristocrat than Brutus, but for Caesar, being an aristocrat is not an important fact. He and Calpurnia do not act like aristocrats. Calpurnia "never stood on ceremonies" [II. ii. 13] or strove to be highminded. She is the wife of a successful politician, superstitious and ordinary. Caesar, like Brutus, has considerable vanity—he refers to himself in the third person even when talking to his wife!—but he has all the confidence necessary to the truly great. He does seem to be infected with what has come to be called Caesarism, that passion for unlimited power, and like Brutus, he can be manipulated by lesser men. Decius knows how to touch his vanity, although it is not flattery that changes Caesar's mind about going to the Forum. It is ambition [II. ii. 92-105]. His eagerness for power overcomes his respect for his wife's premonitions. But for all his awareness of his high place, Caesar the politician, unlike Brutus the philosopher, never forgets that he deals with men who respond to hospitality and who cherish their own pride of place. Caesar speaks by name to each person who comes to him, and he offers them wine.

Brutus wins our reluctant admiration because of his fidelity to his ideals, his sincerity; but Caesar fascinates us by his complex response to fact. Just as Act I belongs to Cassius only because Caesar is kept in the wings, so Act II belongs to Brutus only because Caesar is kept off center stage.

The climax of *Julius Caesar* is reached with the assassination in the Forum [III. i. 77]. All the action has been leading to this event, and the first part of Act III increases the rising suspense.

In what transpires before the killing, we learn nothing new about the conspirators or of Caesar himself. All act well within their established natures. Caesar shows not only that he is a kind of superman but that he knows it. He plays a part. "In his two short speeches in the Capitol [III. i. 35-48; 58-73]," Ernest Schanzer has written, "Shakespeare gives us a compendium of Caesar's most unamicable qualities: the cold, glittering hardness, the supreme arrogance, and again the dissociation of himself from the rest of mankind." Brutus's continued self-deception is also exhibited. His political naivete shows itself in his lack of planning for what is to happen after the ceremonial blood bath. "Let us bathe our hands in Caesar's blood," he says [III. i. 106]. He seems to feel, as many revolutionists feel, that once the power they identify as evil is removed, good will automatically rise; though a philosopher, Brutus has not thought through the political problem that will face Rome once its leader is removed. Cassius exhibits his continuing emotional and personal dependence on Brutus, but he also shows his understanding of individuals and crowds in urging that Antony not be given the pulpit from which to preach a funeral sermon [III. i. 227-43]. Cassius, like Antony, as we will see, is an enthusiast, one who feels his way to conclusions as often as he thinks his way to them; and he understands Antony's fidelity to Caesar. He has a similar fidelity to Brutus.

The act belongs, however, not to Brutus, Cassius, or even to Caesar, it is Antony who seizes the initiative from the conspirators and determines the future. The conspirators may have set the stage for a new order of things, but it is Antony who acts on it, instinctively and quickly. Hardly is Caesar dead than, without time to plan, he seizes the opportunity that comes to him. Sending a servant to announce his arrival [III. i. 123-37], he quickly appears himself [III. i. 147]. His leader being gone, he has pulled himself together (as we might say) and in his celebrated address to "Friends, Romans, countrymen" [III. ii. 73ff.] instigates civil war in Rome, presumably as vengeance for the assassination. The rhetorical fervor of his address is in marvelous contrast to the rational remarks by Brutus a moment before [III. ii. 12ff.]. Antony plays on the prejudices of his Roman audience like an organist at his console. He is one of that frightening kind of rabblerouser who is moved by his own words, taken in by his own half-truths. As Granville-Barker says, "Antony . . . is more than an actor; for one thing he writes his own part as he goes along. But he gathers the ideas for it as he goes too, with no greater care for their worth than the actors need have so long as they are effective at the moment."

When his speech is finished, Antony is half drunk with the delight of the occasion. He exults [III. ii. 266-67]. The fact that the plebians can be so quickly taken in suggests that the days of Republican individualism are already past, that Caesar or someone like him is necessary to keep Roman order. Certainly after Antony's address all chaos breaks loose, and murder and rampage fill the streets. The plebians who in Act I seemed so witty, so lively, have now become Nazi bully-boys, urged on by Antony (see III. iii). It is significant that Antony does not set out to seize the power of the state exclusively for himself but that he automatically looks for an alliance with Octavius [III. i. 287-97; IV. i]. Younger, less experienced in peace and battle both, on the face of it Octavius should offer Antony little competition for Caesar's position, but Antony, rather like Cassius, is a perpetual number-two man. In the end he is incapable of bearing full authority on his own. In his dealings with Lepidus and the young, cool Octavius [IV. i], Antony talks the most, but Octavius has the veto. Had he observed this conference, Cassius would have seen this in a minute—but then though similar in passion to Antony, Cassius is brighter. "He reads much, / He is a great observer" [I. ii. 201-02]. Antony reaches the peak of his achievement in the Forum immediately after the assassination. Never again does he come so close to final power. His moment of ultimate glory is brief.

The principal scene of Act IV contains a bitter quarrel between Brutus and Cassius. In the previous two scenes, the one with the plebians attacking Cinna the poet [III. iii] and the other with the counterconspiracy of Lepidus, Octavius, and Antony [IV. i], we have seen what happens when the linchpin of an axletree is drawn. Communities become mobs and generals become bandits. In this complementary scene [IV. ii] and the next one [IV. iii] we see what happens to the political idealist and his colleague when central authority has been dissolved. The memory of Caesar and then (a bit later) his ghost preside throughout. In this act we are not allowed to forget Julius Caesar.

The quarrel tells us of Rome and the two conspirators. We see [IV. ii] that they have fallen out even before Cassius and Brutus retire to Brutus's tent. Cassius does not deal "with such free and friendly conference / As he hath used of old" [IV. ii. 17-18], and Brutus has to quiet him: "Speak your grief softly" [IV. ii. 41], he says. Cassius in anger protests that his orders have been countermanded by Brutus, whose authority he says is no greater than his own. With the power of Rome dispersed, this raises a central question: Where does authority lie? Brutus feels that his financial needs have not been met, that Cassius has failed his contractual obligations. Too fine to soil his own hands at collecting revenue from reluctant peasants, Brutus still requires gold from Cassius. Both men act within their natures as we have come to know them, yet

John Gielgud as Cassius, Harry Andrews as Brutus, and other conspirators in a 1950 Shakespeare Memorial Theatre production of Julius Caesar. *Act II, scene i.*

we perceive that the stated cause of their anger and the real cause of it are different.

Cassius suffers from a bone fatigue; he is "aweary of the world" [IV. iii. 95] because he can see no possibility of real success. The conspiracy has failed both to bring him unqualified place and to bring freedom to Rome. In his emotional way, he compensates for his disappointment by turning to Brutus for love [IV. iii. 85-7]. If Rome is not his, at least Brutus may be: "I, that denied thee gold, will give my heart" [IV. iii. 104], he says. He is almost childish in his appeal for sympathy, almost uxorious in his dependence.

Brutus is no less frustrated. All his hopes for Republican Rome have come to nothing, and the conspiracy that was to return the state to individual responsibility and to insure it peace and harmony has delivered it, rather, into civil war. We know that without Brutus the conspiracy might have succeeded. Without him Antony as well as Caesar would have been assassinated in the Forum, and more knowing generals than Brutus would have conducted the battles against Octavius. It is ironical that the conspirators needed Brutus and that he is also the cause of their failure. Brutus's dream-revolution has collapsed.

But there is more than this. Brutus suffers from a troubled spirit. He has killed his dearest friend and is attacked by what G. Wilson Knight calls "his own trammelling and hindering conscience." Brutus does not confront all this, of course; his aristocratic pride combined with his philosophical obtuseness refuse to allow him to see his actions objectively, let alone his spiritual state accurately. Having chosen his way, he will brave it out, stoically holding to his solitary course, giving way to no remorse or grief, though his wife kill herself in sorrow and in loneliness. Even when Caesar's ghost appears to tell him of impending disaster at Philippi, he clings to his masculine dignity. By the end of the act, Brutus is overwrought beyond endurance; and yet he endures; and however mistaken his individual choices turn out to have been, we come to admire his Roman tenacity. He is as fatigued as Cassius ("If I do live . . ." [IV. iii. 265], he says), and like Cassius half longs for an end to the course he must run. But where Cassius gives way, Brutus resists, and his opponent is Caesar. Long before the ghost of Caesar appears on stage, Caesar's spirit has brooded over these proceedings. Caesar is inescapable. His shadow lies across this act as it lies across the Mediterranean world.

Act V is dominated by Octavius, however brief his

lines may be. Antony shows himself the enthusiast we have seen before, and Octavius overrules him. "I do not cross you," Octavius says to him, "but I will do so" [V. i. 20]. In the subsequent exchange with Cassius and Brutus, before the approaching battle, Octavius is confident. But even when Octavius is not on stage, he dominates the action. Cassius and Brutus say farewell to each other with a kind of half yearning that the end may quickly come. As in the previous act, Cassius solicits Brutus's love, leaning on it as on a value that no battle can take from him. Perhaps he is even sentimental. Brutus returns his love, insofar as he is capable of considering any person other than himself; and he assures us that his honor will not allow him to be led in Octavius's triumphant procession through the streets of Rome. Cassius thinks of human relationships whereas Brutus thinks of public responsibility; and both are dominated by their awareness of Octavius.

In the next scene Cassius kills himself, thinking his forces defeated because "Brutus gave the word too early" [V. iii. 5]. "My life is run its compass" [V. iii. 25], he says. But it is Octavius who determines Cassius's ultimate fate, though he remains in another part of the battlefield, off stage. When Brutus discovers Cassius dead, like Macbeth whose wife also kills herself, Brutus can only promise that there will be time in another place for thought of him [V. iii. 103]. Octavius's forces command his energies.

If the spirit of Julius Caesar "walks abroad and turns our swords / In our own proper entrails" [V. iii. 95], as Brutus tells us, it is in part to bequeath Octavius Caesar his legacy. Cassius has died impetuously, before his necessary time; Brutus now dies deliberately, unable to see that he has been used, that his life has been a failure because he has been the instrument of other men's aspirations. With nearly his last words, "I found no man but he was true to me" [V. v. 35], he shows that he is unable to understand that all who knew him have used him, the conspirators for their devious political ends, Antony for his. Even in his death Brutus lacks self-knowledge; and though he says that he will have more glory in losing than Octavius and Mark Antony in conquering [V. v. 36ff.], we are not so sure. Indeed we may wonder if there is glory for any of them, in this confused world of politics. Brutus may have been "the noblest Roman of them all" [V. v. 68], because he strove to be disinterested; but he hardly possessed the spirit that calls up the awe due heroic figures—Hamlet, say, Othello, the magnificent Lear. "This was a man!" [V. v. 75]—but he was only a man. Octavius can safely lay his bones ceremonially on the battlefield of Philippi; for Brutus's ghost unlike Caesar's will not walk. His spirit has been exhausted in life. The story of Brutus ends with the end of the play, whereas the story of Julius Caesar continues into the life of Rome. Even if we knew no Roman history, we would know that the last scene of the play is not the last Roman scene. Octavius, Caesar's heir, commands the future as he has dominated this act. (pp. 7-17)

> *Robert E. Knoll, "The Organization of the Play," in* The Shakespeare Plays: A Study Guide, *The University of California, 1978, pp. 4-19.*

ROMAN POLITICS

Alice Shalvi

[*Shalvi seeks to determine whether Shakespeare condemns or condones* **Caesar**'s *assassination. The critic argues that while Shakespeare makes it evident that* **Brutus**'s *fears of* **Caesar**'s *tyranny are justified, he nonetheless presents the murder as an immoral act that must be avenged. In Shalvi's opinion,* **Brutus**'s *sole motive for participating in the plot against* **Caesar** *is to safeguard the liberty of the Roman citizens; ironically, however, it is this noble purpose that causes his political ineptitude and contributes to the failure of the conspiracy. Despite the play's insistence on the idea that "blood will have blood," the critic argues,* Julius Caesar *is more than a revenge tragedy, for it dramatizes the effect of* **Caesar**'s *assassination not just on the murderers, but also on the Roman populace, who, in another example of irony, will suffer greater injustice under the rule of* **Octavius** *and* **Antony** *than under* **Caesar**. *Although* Julius Caesar *ends tragically, Shalvi concludes, it affirms humankind's essential goodness by showing how* **Brutus** *and* **Cassius** *are ennobled through suffering and eventually become aware of the relation between their acts and their destinies.*]

The mature comedies which Shakespeare wrote at the turn of the century posited an ideal of nobility, goodness, generosity and moderation—an ideal, based both on chivalry and on Christian-Humanist teaching, which was the guide of the Elizabethan gentleman in his every action. The earliest of Shakespeare's mature tragedies, *Julius Caesar* and *Hamlet*, both present a similar ideal in the characters of their heroes, but they serve to illustrate what happens to the noble man when he is placed in a situation which tests his nobility to the uttermost and they show the tragic limitations of nobility when it is confronted by really evil forces such as did not exist in the golden landscapes of Arden [in *As You Like It*] and Illyria [in *Twelfth Night*].

Despite the title of the play, it is Brutus who is the tragic hero of *Julius Caesar;* it is his fate which is the central concern of the play. Brutus's prime characteristic is his honour. Descended of valiant ancestors who 'did from the streets of Rome / The Tarquin drive when he was called a king' [II. i. 53-4], derived from that Brutus who 'would have brooked / The eternal Devil to keep his state in Rome / As easily as a king' [I. ii. 159-61], Marcus Brutus fears the threat to Rome's liberty which is implied in Caesar's desire for kingship and autocratic rule. Unlike Cassius, whose prime motivation is clearly a personal envy of Caesar, Brutus is wholly unselfish in his devotion to the welfare of the Roman Republic and prepared to face even death if this is required for his country's good. 'What is it that you would impart to me?' [I. ii. 84] he asks Cassius, when the latter first broaches the subject of Caesar's ambition:

> If it be aught toward the general good,
> Set honour in one eye and death i' the
>   other,
> And I will look on both indifferently,
> For let the gods so speed me as I love
> The name of honour more than I fear
>   death.
>   [I. ii. 85-9]

Brutus is the only one of the conspirators who is portrayed as inwardly debating the justification for committing the 'dreadful thing' which Cassius proposes, and once again Shakespeare stresses that it is no personal animosity towards Caesar that motivates Brutus, but only a regard for the 'general good'. The ultimate factor in persuading Brutus to join the conspiracy is his belief that his countrymen wish him to act on their behalf, a belief based on the letters cast in at his window or conspicuously left for him in public places. These letters we, however, know to come from the wily Cassius, who realises that there is no other way to win over an honourable man to commit an act of violence and evil than by making him believe the act to be honourable. The conspirators need Brutus precisely because he is known to be honourable and will therefore lend colour to their conspiracy when the time comes to justify their action to the people of Rome. As Casca says:

> . . . he sits high in all the people's hearts:
> And that which would appear offence in
>   us,
> His countenance, like richest alchemy,
> Will change to virtue and to worthiness.
>   [I. iii. 157-60]

So we are shown how the man of virtue, with none but the best of motives, may become the tool of men less noble than himself. Cassius himself draws the correct conclusion:

> Well, Brutus, thou art noble; yet, I see,
> Thy honourable metal may be wrought
> From that it is disposed: therefore it is
>   meet
> That noble minds keep ever with their
>   likes;
> For who so firm that cannot be seduced?
>   [I. ii. 308-12]

Yet, ironically, it is Brutus's nobility which in fact unfits him for the conspiracy and brings about the reversal of his noble aims. Inevitably, because of his greatness, Brutus becomes the leader of the conspirators and his essential goodness and moderation overrule the subtler perceptions of the wily Cassius. He refuses to permit Antony to be killed together with Caesar and, despite Cassius's arguments to the contrary, he permits Antony to make the funeral-oration over Caesar's body which rouses the populace against the conspirators. Secure in the knowledge that he has acted in all sincerity and for the good of his country, Brutus fails to take into account both Antony's Machiavellian wiles (which the equally Machiavellian Cassius *does* suspect) and the fickleness of the masses, who are like 'blocks and stones and worse than senseless things' [I. i. 35; Machiavellianism represents the view that politics is amoral and that any means, however unscrupulous, can justifiably be used in achieving political power]. He makes the tactical errors of allowing Antony to have the last word, of leaving him alone with the crowd and of letting him produce the dead body of Caesar. The great difference between Brutus and Antony is excellently conveyed by the contrast between the monotonous rhythms of Brutus's prose and the impassioned, oratorical art of Antony, who skilfully uses the device of repetition with the recurrent phrase, 'honourable men'. There is no doubt which of them better understands the mentality of Rome's masses. It is Brutus's political ineptitude after the assassination and his military ineptitude in insisting on meeting the enemy at Philippi that bring about his own downfall and that of Cassius, and the ineptitude stems primarily from essential innocence, naïveté and goodness. As in the case of Henry VI, Shakespeare here stresses that goodness is not sufficient qualification for the dirty business of politics, indeed that it virtually disables a man from fulfilling the tasks of leadership.

But it is not alone Brutus's ineptitude that brings about the reversal of the conspirators' hopes and plans. The real cause of the defeat of Brutus lies in the fact that the murder of Caesar is an act of evil, an act of horror, that has to be expiated. Politically, the overthrow of Caesar may be necessary for the welfare of Rome. This is brought out by the way in which Caesar is portrayed. He is a great warrior, who, in the past, has done good service for his country but he returns to Rome now having triumphed over no alien power but over Pompey, the great Roman general. Caesar is vain and conceited. Infirm in body, deaf in one ear and subject to epileptic fits, fearful of attack from men such as Cassius who 'think too much' [I. ii. 195], Caesar nevertheless believes himself 'immortal' and aspires to be king of Rome. He grows angry when the crowd cheer his repeated rejection of the coronet offered him by Mark Antony instead of urging him to accept it. The people's tribunes are put to death for 'pulling scarves off Caesar's images' [I. ii. 285-86] and, when Calpurnia's prophetic dreams and the augurers' warnings dissuade him from venturing forth on the Ides of March, Caesar camouflages his fears with an imperious message to the senators, whom he contemptuously dismisses as 'grey-beards':

> Decius, go tell them Caesar will not come. . . .
> The cause is in my will: I will not come;
> That is enough to satisfy the senate.
>
> [II. ii. 68, 71-2]

Like most conceited men, Caesar is susceptible to flattery and yet prides himself on being immune to it. As Decius says: 'When I tell him he hates flatterers, / He says he does, being then most flattered' [II. i. 207-08]. It is by appealing to Caesar's vanity and ambition that Decius persuades him to reject the counsels of Calpurnia and the soothsayers, for he tells Caesar that this is the day on which the senators mean to offer him the crown and that they may well change their minds if he fails to appear. Arrived at the Senate, Caesar further reveals his weaknesses of character. Once again he prides himself on immunity to flattery as he rejects the supplications of Metellus Cimber:

> . . . Be not fond,
> To think that Caesar bears such rebel blood
> That will be thaw'd from the true quality
> With that which melteth fools; I mean, sweet words,
> Low-crooked court'sies and base spaniel-fawning.
> Thy brother by decree is banished:
> If thou dost bend and pray and fawn for him,
> I spurn thee like a cur out of my way.
> Know, Caesar doth not wrong, nor without cause
> Will he be satisfied.
>
> [III. i. 39-48]

As supplicant after supplicant kneels before him to urge the repeal of Publius Cimber's banishment, Caesar remains firm in his sentence, and speaks of himself in terms which indicate clearly that he thinks of himself as a demi-god:

> . . . I am constant as the northern star,
> Of whose true-fix'd and resting quality
> There is no fellow in the firmament.
> The skies are painted with unnumber'd sparks,
> They are all fire and every one doth shine,
> But there's but one in all doth hold his place:
> So in the world; 'tis furnish'd well with men,
> And men are flesh and blood, and apprehensive;
> Yet in the number I do know but one
> That unassailable holds on his rank,
> Unshaked of motion: and that I am he.
>
> [III. i. 60-70]

How ironic these assertions of steadfastness are in the light of the previous scene in which we saw him vacillating between the conflicting advice of Calpurnia and Decius. What Caesar is being so adamant about is in refusing pardon and mercy, the truly god-like qualities in man. It is the moment of his downfall: his unyielding pride and vanity lead to his death.

Thus Shakespeare makes it clear that Brutus's fears are justified. It is apparent that Caesar in power would bring servitude to Rome, and, if the only way to prevent Caesar from attaining power is by murdering him, the murder is presumably justified. Nevertheless, the murder is never wholly condoned by Shakespeare. Brutus speaks of it beforehand as a 'dreadful thing' [II. i. 63] and it is important to note his uncertainty as to Caesar's tyranny; the outcome of crowning Caesar is left deliberately uncertain: 'So Caesar *may:* / Then lest he may, prevent' [II. i. 27-8]. The murder itself is shown onstage in its full brutality and violence, with the out-numbered Caesar helplessly overwhelmed by his enemies, and almost immediately after the murder our feelings are swayed in favour of Caesar by Antony's genuine mourning and the terms of praise in which he refers to the dead man: 'Thou art the ruins of the noblest man / That ever lived in the tide of times' [III. i. 256-57]. Brutus's treachery in participating in the murder is particularly stressed, since it is his presence among the assassins which so appals Caesar as to make him cry out the famous 'Et tu, Brute? Then fall, Caesar!' [III. i. 77]. And after the murder we have the strange appeal of Brutus to his colleagues to stoop and bathe their hands in Caesar's blood and then proceed with their blood-besmeared swords to cry 'Peace, freedom and liberty' [III. i. 110] in the market-place. This serves as an ironic counter to his earlier remonstrances:

> Let's kill him boldly, but not wrathfully;
> Let's carve him as a dish fit for the gods,
> Not hew him as a carcass fit for hounds:
> And let our hearts, as subtle masters do,
> Stir up their servants to an act of rage,
> And after seem to chide 'em . . .
>
> [II. i. 172-77]

Indeed, the corruption in Brutus has, inevitably, set in earlier, since it was essential for him, together with the other conspirators, to pretend a friendliness towards Caesar which none of them really felt. Brutus is aware of this terrible hypocrisy, for his reaction on seeing the masked conspirators arriving at his house in the night is:

> . . . O conspiracy,
> Shamest thou to show thy dangerous brow by night,
> When evils are most free? O, then by day
> Where wilt thou find a cavern dark enough
> To mask thy monstrous visage? Seek none, conspiracy;

Hide it in smiles and affability:
For if thou path, thy native semblance on,
Not Erebus itself were dim enough
To hide thee from prevention.

                              [II. i. 77-85]

Yet he himself later bids them

. . . look fresh and merrily;
Let not our looks put on our purposes,
But bear it as our Roman actors do,
With untired spirits and formal constan-
    cy.

                              [II. i. 224-27]

Shakespeare implicitly condemns the conspiracy, then, on two scores: firstly, because it inevitably involves moral corruption even in the best and noblest of men and, secondly, because murder is always, no matter in what circumstances or however it may be justified, bloody and cruel. 'Blood' is the word that echoes and re-echoes throughout the scenes which follow the assassination—and blood will have blood. Murder must be avenged and Caesar does indeed achieve vengeance. Though his ghost appears physically only once, in visitation upon Brutus before the battle of Philippi, Caesar's presence broods over the action after his murder just as much, if not more, than it did during his life-time. 'He doth bestride the narrow world like a Colossus' [I. ii. 135-36] and his influence does not end with his death. Antony, at the close of Act III, sc. i, utters a terrible prophecy which ends with what is, in effect, an invocation of Caesar's ghost:

Woe to the hand that shed this costly
    blood!
Over thy wounds now do I prophesy,—
Which, like dumb mouths, do ope their
    ruby lips,
To beg the voice and utterance of my
    tongue—
A curse shall light upon the limbs of men;
Domestic fury and fierce civil strife
Shall cumber all the parts of Italy;
Blood and destruction shall be so in use
And dreadful objects so familiar
That mothers shall but smile when they
    behold
Their infants quarter'd with the hands of
    war;
All pity choked with custom of fell deeds:
And Caesar's spirit, ranging for revenge,
With Ate by his side come hot from hell,
Shall in these confines with a monarch's
    voice
Cry 'Havoc,' and let slip the dogs of war;
That this foul deed shall smell above the
    earth
With carrion men, groaning for burial.

                              [III. i. 258-75]

The prophecy is most horribly fulfilled and Caesar has his revenge on the men who murdered him.

The revenge takes various forms. Firstly, we learn of Brutus and Cassius's desperate flight from the vengeful mob, a flight from the very city they had

sought to free from tyranny and for which Brutus, at least, had been prepared to lay down his life. Then we see the dissension which develops between these two men, leading to insult, accusation and open quarrel in IV, iii. We may note the way in which the assassination is referred to here, when Brutus warns Cassius of the consequences of corruption:

Remember March, the ides of March re-
    member:
Did not great Julius bleed for justice'
    sake?
What villain touch'd his body, that did
    stab,
And not for justice? . . .

                              [IV. iii. 18-21]

There is irony here in the fact that Brutus still believes that the murder was commited for wholly noble ends and has still not seen through the essentially corrupt and self-centred motives of the other conspirators.

Later in the same scene we learn of the death of Portia, Brutus's wife, and this, too, is indirectly the outcome of the assassination, for, Brutus says,

Impatient of my absence,
And grief that young Octavius with Mark
    Antony
Have made themselves so strong: . . .
. . . with this she fell distract,
And, her attendants absent, swallow'd
    fire.

                              [IV. iii. 152-56]

The ghost of Caesar calls himself Brutus's 'evil spirit' [IV. iii. 282]; he is unseen by any of the other people present and may, like the ghost of Banquo [in Macbeth], be interpreted as an emanation of the murderer's guilty conscience. He warns Brutus that he will see him at Philippi and although the ghost never reappears it is indeed the assassination which is once again the central theme referred to by the leaders on both sides during the parley that precedes the battle. Octavius warns his opponents that the battle will not end 'till Caesar's three and thirty wounds / Be well avenged; or till another Caesar / Have added slaughter to the sword of traitors' [V. i. 53-5]. The two sides join battle, Cassius's tents are set on fire and he sends his good friend Titinius to ascertain whether the nearby troops are friends or enemies. By a tragic error, he is deceived into believing them enemies, into believing himself responsible for his friend's death and into thinking capture imminent. He takes the truly noble way out: he kills himself—with the same sword as he had used in killing Caesar. His last words are significant: 'Caesar, thou art revenged, Even with the sword that killed thee' [V. ii. 44-5]. . . . And equally significant is [Brutus's] comment on Cassius's death: 'O Julius Caesar, thou art mighty yet! / Thy spirit walks abroad, and turns our swords / In our own proper entrails' [V. iii. 94-6]. The same point is made again at the close of the play, when Brutus's dying words as he kills himself are 'Caesar, now be still, / I killed not thee with half so good a will' [V. v. 50-1]. With the death of Brutus the crime is finally expiated and Caesar's ghost may rest at ease. Vengeance has been achieved.

But to show that blood will have blood and that murder will be avenged is not Shakespeare's main purpose in this play. It is not simply a revenge tragedy in the Senecan tradition so popular in Elizabethan England [Seneca, a Roman statesman, author, and philosopher of the first century A. D., is famous for nine melodramas which had a great influence on tragic drama in Elizabethan England]. The consequences of the murder of Caesar are not confined to his murderers, for perhaps the most tragic result of the assassination lies in Brutus's failure to achieve by this act of violence the original, noble goal for which he had committed the crime. He had, as we have seen, one sole justification for killing his friend: Caesar's death was demanded by the 'common good', the general welfare and prosperity and freedom of the Roman people and the Roman Republic. What we are shown is that an act may lead to the very reverse of what the committer of the act intended and bring about precisely what it aimed at preventing. The immediate result of the assassination is Mark Antony's successful oratorical exploitation of the assassination and the hacked body to arouse the ignorant, fickle Roman mob against the conspirators. Antony cares nothing for the 'common good'. He seeks vengeance for his friend's death and power for himself. This is clear from the coldly callous comment as the mob goes off in fury: 'Mischief, thou art afoot, / Take thou what course thou wilt' [III. iii. 260-61]. The course it takes is the most terrible one of irrational, bloodthirsty violence. In the very next scene we witness the lynching of Cinna the poet, torn to pieces despite his desperate avowals that he is not Cinna the conspirator: 'Tear him to pieces for his bad verses . . . Pluck but his name out of his heart, and turn him going . . . Tear him, tear him' [III. iii. 30, 33-5]. This wild, unrestrained, bloodthirsty mob-rule finds an icy counter-point in Act IV, sc. i, the scene that immediately follows it. What has been the outcome for Roman government of Caesar's assassination? Who is in power *now?* Three dictators instead of one. The opening words of the first scene in which we witness the new triumvirate at work are ominous: 'These many then shall die, their names are prick'd' [IV. i. 1]. The cold-bloodedness is stressed by the equanimity with which Lepidus and Antony barter a brother's death for that of a nephew:

ANTONY: These many, then, shall die; their names are prick'd.
OCTAVIUS: Your brother too must die; consent you, Lepidus?
LEPIDUS: I do consent,—
OCTAVIUS: Prick him down, Antony.
LEPIDUS: Upon condition Publius shall not live,

Who is your sister's son, Mark Antony.
ANTONY: He shall not live; look, with a spot I damn him.
[IV. i. 1-6]

And Antony's cold, calculating hypocrisy is proved by the contempt with which he speaks of 'old Lepidus' and plots to get rid of him once Lepidus has served his own and Octavius's purpose.

It is to this, then, that Brutus's act of salvation has brought Rome and it is now that we can appreciate the full irony of that cry of 'Liberty, Freedom and Justice' [cf. III. i. 81] which succeeded the assassination. The country is divided in civil war, its government in the hands of men as ruthless as Caesar and probably far less honest and valiant than he was—men who, in injustice, will not fall short of what Caesar would have been even had he become king. Brutus's aims are, therefore, tragically reversed; it is for this that he has betrayed friendship and committed a crime.

Nevertheless, despite the tragic reversal of Brutus's aims and the vision of Rome governed by ruthlessly cruel men, the play concludes with a re-affirmation of the dignity of man and the worthwhileness of human life and this re-affirmation is to be found in the essential nobility of Brutus, which is re-asserted and confirmed in the final scenes of the play that show his suffering and defeat. Similarly, Cassius is now displayed as possessing a nobility of character which had not been revealed earlier in the play. Both men accept their fate with truly noble Roman stoicism [A stoic is a member of the school of philosophy founded by the Greek thinker Zeno about 300 B. C. This discipline holds that wise men should be free from passion, unmoved by joy or grief, and submissive to natural law]. 'No man bears sorrow better' we are told of Brutus's response to Portia's death [IV. iii. 147], and the same noble acceptance of fate is typical of him and of Cassius before and during the final battle at Philippi.

Acceptance of fate's decrees does not, however, mean passivity and inaction on the part of the individual. Brutus is no Romeo, bemoaning the way in which Fate overrules his plans and hopes. The key words in this play, spoken by Brutus and indicating what is now Shakespeare's view of the respective rôles of Destiny and Free Will, are:

There is a tide in the affairs of men,
Which, taken at the flood, leads on to fortune;
Omitted, all the voyage of their life
Is bound in shallows and in miseries.
On such a full sea are we now afloat; ·
And we must take the current when it serves,
Or lose our ventures.
[IV. iii. 218-24]

This is an echo of Cassius's earlier words: 'The

fault, dear Brutus, is not in our stars, / But in our-selves that we are underlings' [I. ii. 140-41]. Our destiny lies in ourselves, is dependent on the way we seize the opportunities given to us by chance or fate or destiny or whatever name we choose to give to the superior force which exists in the universe.

Thus both Brutus and Cassius, enlightened as to the cause of their downfall, aware of their guilt in murdering Caesar, take the painful, courageous way of suicide rather than allowing themselves to be led as captives through the streets of Rome. As in the case of Richard II, we feel the truth of Bru-tus's dying assertion:

> I shall have glory by this losing day
> More than Octavius and Mark Antony
> By this vile conquest shall attain unto.
> [V. v. 36-8]

The important thing here, as in all tragedy, is not physical triumph and survival, but self-conquest, the exorcism of all that is weak, ignoble and vilely human in the hero's nature, so that he goes to his death purified and spiritually triumphant over the forces that oppose him.

Courage and endurance are the two important qualities which Brutus proves himself to possess. His plans may have gone tragically awry and, what is more, the very act which he committed may have been shown by Shakespeare to have been evil. Nev-ertheless his crime is counterbalanced by the mag-nificent way in which he expiates it, by the suffer-ing which it causes him. This suffering ennobles Brutus, it ennobles his fellow-conspirator, Cassi-us, its spectacle ennobles the audience and, most significantly, it impresses his enemies. It is Mark Antony who delivers the valedictory oration and correctly describes Brutus as 'the noblest Roman of them all' [V. v. 68]. Antony is aware that:

> All the conspirators save only he
> Did that they did in envy of great Caesar;
> He only in a general honest thought
> And common good to all, made one of
>   them.
> His life was gentle, and the elements
> So mix'd in him that Nature might stand
>   up
> And say to all the world 'This was a man!'
> [V. v. 69-75]

This is a fitting summary of the way in which Bru-tus has been portrayed throughout the play: a truly gentle, noble, man, kind to his servants, loving to his wife, slow to anger and speedily pacified, hon-est and generous. He makes one tragic error: he be-lieves a crime to be justified when the aim is a noble one. This is fiercely negated by Shakespeare who here, as in the history-plays, shows that noth-ing justifies murder. But Shakespeare presents no satisfactory alternative solution to the problem of the just, honourable man living in a time of vice and corruption, other than to imply that if one en-gages in political combat one must be utterly ruth-less and discard all thoughts of mercy and modera-tion. Had Brutus heeded Cassius and slain Antony all might have been well—except that Brutus would have shown himself even more corrupt and evil. Shakespeare here shows us the tragic dilem-ma of the good man called upon to combat evil and stresses that it is impossible to fight evil without becoming corrupted oneself. The tragic dilemma of Brutus is also the tragic dilemma of Hamlet. In this, the earlier of the two plays, no solution is of-fered to the dilemma. However firm a reassertion Shakespeare here makes, through the character of Brutus, of man's essential nobility and his capacity for spiritual greatness in the face of physical de-feat, politically the play ends on a note of pessimis-tic query. (pp. 169-78)

> *Alice Shalvi, "Shakespeare's 'High Roman Fashion': Julius Caesar," in* The World & Art of Shakespeare *by A. A. Mendilow and Alice Shalvi, Israel University Press, 1967, pp. 169-78.*

Brents Stirling

[*Stirling examines the extent to which Shake-speare relied upon his source material in his presentation of the Roman populace in* Julius Caesar. *The critic notes that although Shake-speare's portrait of the commoners as fickle, unreasonable, and opportunistic generally echoes Plutarch's lives of* **Caesar** *and* **Brutus**, *the dramatist also elaborated upon Plutarch's account, notably in Act III, scene ii, when* **Bru-tus** *and* **Antony** *deliver their funeral orations for* **Caesar**, *and in Act III, scene iii, when the citizens interrogate the poet* **Cinna**. *While the effect of the changes in the first of these scenes is to accentuate the instability of the mob, Stir-ling maintains, Shakespeare did not deliber-ately alter his source to further denigrate the populace; rather, the changes were made for dramatic effect and, moreover, were warrant-ed by Plutarch's descriptions of the mob in other episodes of his narratives. The critic states that the second of these scenes, not re-corded by Plutarch, reveals an Elizabethan understanding of mob behavior in its empha-sis on the hostility and irrationality of class conflict; similarly,* **Brutus** *and* **Antony**'s *funer-al orations, only briefly outlined by Plutarch, lend political realism to the tragedy.*]

In *Julius Caesar* the self-interest and sorry insta-bility of the Roman populace turn the tide against Brutus and the other conspirators. Although their ill fortune materializes at Philippi, the climactic change from good to ill for the conspirators occurs in Act III with the shift against them of mob senti-ment. Accordingly, it will not surprise those famil-iar with Shakespeare's methods of exposition that the note of plebeian stupidity and mutability is struck powerfully in the opening scene of the play. There the disorderly citizens, who have decked themselves in their best "to make holiday, to see Caesar and to rejoice in his triumph" [I. i. 30-1], are denounced by their own tribunes for ingratitude and change of heart. After the cynical speech by Marullus on the crowd's erstwhile devotion to Caesar's adversary, Flavius pronounces chorally upon its exit:

> See, whether their basest metal be not
>   moved;
> They vanish tongue-tied in their guilti-
>   ness.
>
> [I. i. 61-2]

The next we hear of the Roman mob is from Casca who, in the well-known lines of Scene 2, reports its reception of Caesar's refusal of the crown.

> . . . and still as he refus'd it, the rabble-
> ment hooted and clapp'd their chapp'd
> hands and threw up their sweaty night-
> caps and uttered such a deal of stinking
> breath because Caesar refus'd the crown,
> that it had almost choked Caesar, for he
> swounded and fell down at it; and for mine
> own part, I durst not laugh, for fear of
> opening my lips and receiving the bad air.
>
> [I. ii. 243-50]

Casca ends his splenetic account of the populace with the "three or four wenches, where I stood" who cried "Alas, good soul!" [I. ii. 271-72] and one is reminded of Richard II on Bolingbroke's court-ship of the people: "Off goes his bonnet to an oyster wench" [*Richard II*, I. iv. 31]. Both Richard and Casca are jaundiced personalities, and their allu-sions to humanity in the mass are doubtless in character and part of the characterization process. . . . [it] will be observed that Shakespeare generally uses characters of a cynically patrician humor for comment upon the populace and that a dramatist's calculation of audience response may be largely revealed by such consistent choice of commentators. Moreover, when the "slanting" is not done by aristocrats, when it is done by the tri-bunes in the present play, and by Cade's own fol-lowers or indeed by Cade himself in *2 Henry VI*, the picture drawn of popular assemblage is altogether as scurrilous.

The next appearance of the citizenry is in the sec-ond scene of Act III. After the killing of Caesar in the previous scene, Brutus and Cassius enter with a throng of citizens who are given the first line, "We will be satisfied; let us be satisfied" [III. ii. 1]. The citizens divide, some to hear Cassius, others to hear Brutus. The honest and highly epigrammatic speech of Brutus quickly converts the suspicious crowd, and they clamor, "Let him be Caesar"; "Cae-sar's better parts shall be crown'd in Brutus" [III. ii. 51-2]. The uproar of impulsive approval is so loud that Brutus must implore silence so that An-tony may speak, and as Antony goes into the pulpit there are cries, "'Twere best he speak no harm of Brutus here" and "This Caesar was a tyrant" [III. ii. 68-9]. (pp. 25-7)

In complete contrast with Brutus, Antony is no ex-pounder but rather an evoker who pulls, one by one and each at the strategic moment, all the stops of the organ. Some forty lines following a self-effacing start, his nostalgic reminiscences of Cae-sar and his apparent emotional breakdown have the citizens murmuring in his favor. His mention of Caesar's will and quick disavowal of intent to read it increase the murmur to a clamor, in the midst of which he produces Caesar's bloody man-tle; the clamor then becomes a frenzy as the citi-zenry cry, "About! Seek! Burn! Fire! Kill! Slay!" [III. ii. 205]. Caesar's wounds, "poor dumb mouths" [III. ii. 225] are given tongues as the mob is tensed to the critical pitch. In their upheaval the common-ers forget the will, and Antony, with what seems cold-blooded cynicism, calls them back to hear Caesar's bequests in their favor. After that there is no check which can be put on them as they rush through the city with firebrands; significantly enough, they accomplish only irrelevant violence in killing Cinna the poet who, for want of a better reason, is torn for his bad verses.

In his chapter on the source of *Julius Caesar,* [in *Shakespeare's Roman Plays and Their Back-ground*], M. W. MacCallum is not specifically con-cerned with Shakespeare's presentation of Rome's unreasonable populace. At the outset, however, he does discuss the peculiar shiftiness of the mob's bullying questions addressed to the poet Cinna. MacCallum observes that none of this is in Plu-tarch and that it is Shakespeare's realistic contri-bution based upon intuitive understanding of the behavior of bravoes who have run down a victim. This is valuable. As a short scene in which the bland sadistic stare and the irrelevant retort are thrust upon an innocent who tries to explain him-self, the episode deserves more space than MacCal-lum devotes to it. In its forty lines are packed such an awareness of the hostility and cogent unreason found in class conflict that the scene could be called modern in all senses, sober and ironical, of the term. For in Shakespeare's conception there is surely none of the wistful expectation that aroused masses will act objectively; the scene rests upon a knowledge of such behavior in crisis which is hard to explain other than by the dramatist's intuitive observation.

While he comments briefly upon this bit of realism as a factor not found in Shakespeare's source, Mac-Callum is silent upon a similar and far more elabo-rate transmutation of source material. It is well known that the speeches of Brutus and Antony in the funeral scene are Shakespeare's own, but no discussion of altered sources would be adequate which failed to note the political realism which un-derlies these additions. From Plutarch Shake-speare certainly derived Brutus's high-minded-ness and his tactical error in allowing Antony to speak, but there is no implication, in the source, of the kind of speech Brutus made. It has the laconic and functional sparseness of the Gettysburg Address. Tragically, however, it is not delivered as a tribute to men who died in battle, but as justification of a political *coup* and as an appeal for mass support. Shakespeare conceives of Brutus as an idealist who believes that facts honestly and simply explained are politically adequate. Because of his concern not to sully himself and his pains to represent his opposition fairly, Brutus wins support only until Antony begins to explore crowd responses. And although Shakespeare may not have intended it, Brutus's speech exhibits perfectly the egocentrism of those who make a religion of objectivity. The scorn of emotionality suggested by it, the conviction implied in it that orderly analysis is pre-eminent, and the perfectionistic compactness of it as a composition, all suggest a self-regard by the inward eye which may be the bliss of solitude, but which is fatal in an emergency requiring audience response.

Antony's famous rejoinder is a *tour de force* which completes Shakespeare's picture of the kind of persuasion most effective with the citizenry. Plutarch does give the prescription for this speech, but only in formula. "When [Antony] saw that the people were very glad and desirous also to hear Caesar spoken of, and his praises uttered, he mingled his oration with lamentable words, and by amplifying of matters did greatly move their hearts and affections."

The gist of this is the essence of Antony's oration. Antony, above all, is an analyst of audience temper; he first finds what his listeners want to hear and then wanders among the bypaths of their "hearts and affections." Shakespeare's grasp of crowd psychology has been the subject of study [see Frederick Tupper, "The Shakespearean Mob," *PMLA* XXVII (1912): 486-523], but there remains a need to examine Antony's speech for its surprising arsenal of cynical devices. There is the vivid and platitudinous beginning:

> The evil that men do lives after them;
> The good is oft interred with their bones.
> [III. ii. 75-6]

Next comes the apparent admission against interest: "If it [Caesar's ambition] were so, it was a grievous fault" [III. ii. 79]. Now occurs a hint of the common touch, "When that the poor have cried, Caesar hath wept" [III. ii. 91]. Then, just as Antony is beginning to warm to his subject, comes his first exploratory halt; apparently inarticulate with emotion, he must pause till his heart, "in the coffin there with Caesar," [III. ii. 106], comes back to him. The commoners begin to mutter and Antony, sensing it, advances to the next strategic point: he mentions Caesar's will but disclaims all intention of capitalizing upon material interest. Another exploratory pause, and as the citizens clamor for the will Antony knows that he can throw caution away. His subsequent move is to produce the con-

crete object, the evocative thing which men can touch and see, Caesar's gown with the bloody rents in it. But first he recalls old times and old campaigns.

> I remember
> The first time ever Caesar put it on;
> 'Twas on a summer's evening, in his tent
> That day he overcame the Nervii.
> [III. ii. 170-73]

And now, in a climax of mingled sentiment and abuse, he holds the grisly thing up for the crowd to see. Next, and in clinching employment of the concrete objective device, he drives the crowd's attention directly to the hacked body of Caesar, and there is no holding them. They even forget the will which Antony, who has saved material interest as the most telling and final point, must call them back to hear.

This is not a pretty example of how to manipulate the electorate, and it is even less so when we perceive two ingredients which do not occur at any one point, but are pervasive. In contrast with the understatement of Brutus, who tells the crowd briefly why he killed his best friend, Antony's irony, with its six-fold repetition of the "honorable men" phrase, evolves steadily into the most blatant kind of sarcasm. He knows the inadequacy of quiet irony; he also knows the value of repetition and how to use it climactically. The second pervasive factor in Antony's speech is that the crowd really makes it for him. He could have learned nothing from a Dale Carnegie [the author of *How to Win Friends and Influence People*], for he knows with sure insight that he cannot really convince people unless they think they are convincing themselves or, better yet, that they are convincing him. He is "no orator, as Brutus is," but "just a plain blunt man" [III. ii. 217-18] who is trying to think this thing out with the rest of them.

Shakespeare's penetration into this darker side of political behavior rivals two modern fictional efforts in that direction, both of them based in a non-literal way upon the career of Huey Long [the controversial Louisiana governor; see *Number One*, by John Dos Passos, and *All the King's Men*, by Robert Penn Warren]. Whether his cynical picture of mass persuasion is based upon intuition or observation or both, it is impossible to say. One thing is certain, however: the contributions of Plutarch to Shakespeare's conception of how the popular mind may be translated into action are limited to a skeletal formula with bare details concerning the will, the bloody gown, and Caesar's body.

In evaluating Shakespeare's use of Plutarch in this episode, we have not only the demagoguery of Antony's speech to consider but also a portrait of the populace itself. Concerning the latter, the evidence is conflicting. As the account in Plutarch is followed, it would seem at first that Shakespeare had made a gratuitous and major change in order to emphasize the instability of crowd responses. All readers of Shakespeare know that in his play the citizenry plumps solidly for Brutus, only to change over suddenly at Antony's provocation. Plutarch's account of Marcus Brutus, however, runs entirely counter to this.

> When the people saw him [Brutus] in the pulpit, although they were a multitude of rakehells of all sorts, and had a good will to make some stir: yet being ashamed to do it for the reverence they bare unto Brutus, they kept silence to hear what he would say. When Brutus began to speak, they gave him quiet audience: *howbeit immediately after, they showed that they were not at all contented with the murder.* For when another called Cinna [the conspirator] would have spoken, and began to accuse Caesar, they fell into a great uproar among them and marvelously reviled him.

The account of the same event in Plutarch's life of Caesar depicts the citizenry as being moved by Brutus neither one way nor the other.

There are two reasons, however, why this change taken by itself cannot be relied upon to show a transmutation by Shakespeare with intention of casting discredit upon the populace. The first of these is that there is dramatic reason for the change: it is simply more effective to show a populace swayed first one way and then the other, and the story would be flat without it. Perhaps this principle, if extended, would also account, upon a purely dramatic basis, for the cynical virtuosity exhibited in Antony's speech. . . . A second reason why little can be made of Shakespeare's change in this episode is that although Plutarch does not exhibit a fickle citizenry first in agreement with Brutus and immediately afterward with Antony, he does elsewhere and generally give clear hints of its instability. In the life of Marcus Brutus, and but a few pages beyond the excerpt just quoted, occurs this description of the populace just after Antony's winning of their favor: "The people growing weary now of Antonius' pride and insolency, who ruled all things in manner with absolute power: they desired that Brutus might return again."

Beyond the specific data described in the last few pages, there are some general notions in Plutarch which bear upon the problem and find their way into Shakespeare's adaptation of the episode. There is material throughout which establishes the opportunistic allegiance of the populace to Caesar. Cato, for example, feared "insurrection of the poor needy persons, which were they that put all their hope in Caesar." Caesar, moreover, "began to put forth laws meeter for a seditious Tribune than for a Consul: because by them he preferred the division of lands, and the distributing of corn to every citizen, *gratis,* to please them withal." The people are described, however, as antagonistic to the idea

of Caesar as emperor, and as making outcries of joy when he refused the crown. And in direct line with Shakespeare's conception of a Rome plagued with popular insurrection, we learn from Plutarch that

> Rome itself also was immediately filled with the flowing repair of all the people their neighbors thereabouts, which came hither from all parties like droves of cattle, that there was neither officer nor magistrate that could any more command them by authority, neither by any persuasion of reason bridle such a confused and disorderly multitude: so that Rome had in manner destroyed itself for lack of rule and order.

Plutarch, in fact, declares that "men of deep judgment and learning" were so concerned with the "fury and madness" of the people that they "thought themselves happy if the commonwealth were no worse troubled than with the absolute state of a monarchy and sovereign lord to govern them." Unlike his story of Coriolanus, Plutarch's account of Caesar, and to some extent his story of Brutus, provided Shakespeare with a ready-made aversion to the populace which amounts to contempt. Apparently unnoticed by source studies, which have been more concerned with story and characterization than with social bias, is a brief passage in the life of Marcus Brutus which probably furnished the cue for Shakespeare's opening scene. This scene is begun by Flavius with a denunciation of the commoners, containing the line, "What! know you not, being mechanical . . . "[I. i. 2-3]. In the scene, moreover, six of the seven responses from the citizenry are made by a cobbler. The suggestion for this may well have been words in Plutarch addressed by Cassius to Brutus: "*What! knowest thou not* that thou art Brutus? Thinkest thou that they be *cobblers,* tapsters, or suchlike base *mechanical* people, that write these bills and scrolls . . . ?" Whether the passage suggested part of Shakespeare's opening scene or not, it is typical of the social point of view toward commoners which was available to Shakespeare in his source data.

Finally, in a source-play comparison involving *Julius Caesar* it should be made plain that Plutarch supplied Shakespeare with the flagrant and literally inflammatory action of the mob which follows Antony's oration.

> But when they had opened Caesar's testament and found a liberal legacy of money bequeathed unto every citizen of Rome, and that they saw his body (which was brought into the market place) all bemangled with gashes of swords: then there was no order to keep the multitude and common people quiet. . . . Then . . . they took the firebrands, and went unto their houses that had slain Caesar, to set them afire. Others also ran up and down the city to

see if they could meet with any of them, to cut them in pieces.

Directly after this comes Plutarch's description of the mobbing of Cinna the poet. (pp. 27-35)

> Brents Stirling, "The Plays: Julius Caesar," in his The Populace in Shakespeare, *Columbia University Press*, *1949, pp. 25-35.*

Virgil K. Whitaker

[*Whitaker discusses the political and moral implications of Shakespeare's characterization of* **Brutus** *and* **Caesar**. *The critic describes in detail how Shakespeare altered Plutarch's narratives to represent* **Caesar** *as a great ruler and* **Brutus** *as a virtuous but self-righteous and muddle-headed man. Shakespeare's purpose in deviating from his source, the critic argues, was to portray* **Brutus** *as the tragic hero of the drama—"the first of Shakespeare's superb tragic figures who fail through false moral choice."* **Brutus's** *tragic error is presented in his soliloquy at II.i.10-34, in which he assumes that* **Caesar** *will become a tyrant if he is crowned emperor and that his death is in the best interests of the Roman people. According to Whitaker,* **Brutus's** *wrong moral choice reflects Shakespeare's belief in the superiority of monarchy to democracy; it also underscores his conviction that immoral conduct results from faulty reasoning.*]

Julius Caesar, the first of Shakespeare's mature tragedies, can be very confidently dated in 1599, just after *Henry V* and alongside *As You Like It* and *Twelfth Night.* It is a landmark in the development of Shakespeare's thought. Its very structure results from applying to the sources in Plutarch two postulates . . . encountered in the earlier plays—namely, that monarchy is necessary to social order and that wrong conduct results from a failure of reason. (p. 224)

When Shakespeare first read Plutarch, presumably while he was writing the Henry VI plays, he obviously did not approach the life of Caesar without preconceptions. He had doubtless already encountered two contrasting views of the man. The first was that exemplified by Dante, who placed Brutus and Cassius along with Judas Iscariot in the lowest circle of hell. For him the murder of Caesar by his friends was the second greatest crime recorded in history. The other interpretation was derived from Plutarch himself and from later Roman writers. It portrayed Caesar as a commanding genius but fundamentally an evil man. In later tradition he had become vainglorious as well. (p. 226)

Let us now turn to Shakespeare's handling of his source material in *Julius Caesar.* . . . [Contradictory] indications appear; but the preponderant evidence indicates that Shakespeare, while in the main accepting Plutarch's account, attempted to reconcile it with his notion of a great man and ruler.

In Plutarch's "Caesar" Shakespeare found a portrait that emphasized the man's courage, his ambition, his vanity, and his superstition but did scant justice to his greatness as a statesman. Beginning his play in the last days of Caesar's life further emphasized this bias of his source. The conquests were past, and Plutarch gives no adequate indication of the statesmanlike schemes for the government of Rome that we know Caesar to have formulated during his last months. Shakespeare found only one element in his source that he recognized as commensurate with the greatness of Caesar's influence—namely, the omens which marked his approaching death. To these he gave maximum emphasis. There is no reason to doubt that Shakespeare, like his contemporaries, accepted these details in classical writers as historically accurate. The achievement of pagan gods and of oracles Christian theory explained by assuming that the fallen angels had masqueraded as gods to work the further damnation of man. But Shakespeare perhaps had no need to rely upon such an explanation of these omens, for subsequent history amply demonstrated Caesar's place in the divine scheme of things; Providence might be expected to intervene directly to foretell his death. As Calphurnia tells him: "The heavens themselves blaze forth the death of princes" [II. ii. 31]. Shakespeare therefore seized upon these details and emphasized them as properly indicating Caesar's surpassing greatness. (p. 228)

In finding a second means of squaring his source with his own notion of Caesar's greatness, Shakespeare was perhaps guided by a passage in the life of Caesar . . . :

> But his [Caesar's] great prosperity and good fortune, that favoured him all his lifetime, did continue afterwards in the revenge of his death, pursuing the murtherers both by sea and land, till they had not left a man more to be executed, of all them that were actors or counsellors in the conspiracy of his death.

This sentence, which has a marginal gloss "The revenge of Caesar's death," is followed by the information that Cassius "slew himself with the same sword, with the which he strake Caesar" and an account of various prodigies of nature. Plutarch then continues:

> But, above all, the ghost that appeared unto Brutus showed plainly that the gods were offended with the murther of Caesar. . . . looking towards the light of the lamp that waxed very dim, he saw a horrible vision of a man, of a wonderful greatness, and dreadful look, which at the first made him marvellously afraid. But, when he saw that it did him no hurt, but

stood by his bedside and said nothing, at length he asked him what he was. The image answered him: "I am thy ill angel, Brutus, and thou shalt see me by the city of Philippi."

Shakespeare had only to convert Plutarch's evil genius into the ghost of Caesar to achieve not only a perfect dramatic revenge ghost but also a personification of the greatness of the man, whose influence Brutus himself confesses on the battlefield:

> O Julius Caesar, thou art mighty yet!
> Thy spirit walks abroad, and turns our
>   swords
> In our own proper entrails.
>
>   [V. iii. 94-6]

In addition to selecting his material carefully, Shakespeare attempted by changing various details to alter the impression created by the source. (pp. 229-30)

In Plutarch Caesar, who is himself superstitious, is frightened by the prodigies of nature and by Calphurnia's dream, whereas she "until that time was never given to any fear or superstition." He has to be shamed out of his decision to stay home by Decius Brutus. Shakespeare presents him as without superstition and gives him bravery. In the play Caesar at first refuses to heed warnings that he stay home, and the fears are Calphurnia's. His words during this episode have been taken as boasting, vacillating, and rationalizing; but they are more likely to be simple statements of fact, such as Shakespeare gives to his great men even though in lesser men they might seem immodest. They are further justified in that they involve a clever reinterpretation of the omens taken by the augurers to be unfavorable:

> Caesar should be a heart without a heart,
> If he should stay at home today for
>   fear. . . .
> We are two lions litter'd in one day:
> And I the elder and more terrible:
>
>   [II. ii. 42-3, 46-7]
>   (p. 231)

Events on the way to the Senate have also been changed to ennoble Caesar. In Plutarch he "many times attempted" to read the crucial message from Artemidorus warning of the conspiracy, but he could not because of the people who pressed about him. Shakespeare gives the soothsayer significant motives:

> My heart laments that virtue cannot live
> Out of the teeh of emulation.
>
>   [II. iii. 13-14]

Caesar refuses to read the paper because Artemidorus urges that it touches him personally: "What touches us ourself shall be last serv'd" [III. i. 8]. (Notice, incidentally, that in a public pronouncement he uses the royal "us.")

Most meaningful of all, perhaps, is Shakespeare's handling of Brutus' crucial soliloquy [II. i. 10-34]. This will need to be discussed at length in connection with the structure of the play. But we may note here that it is apparently based in part upon Plutarch's introductory summary of Caesar's character:

> His enemies, judging that this favour of the common people would soon quail, when he could no longer hold out that charge and expense, suffered him to run on, till by little and little he was grown to be of great strength and power. But in fine, when they had thus given him the bridle to grow to this greatness, and that they could not then pull him back, though indeed in sight it would turn one day to the destruction of the whole state and commonwealth of Rome: "too late they found, that there is not so little a beginning of anything, but continuance of time will soon make it strong, when through contempt there is no impediment to hinder the greatness. Thereupon Cicero, like a wise shipmaster that feareth the calmness of the sea, was the first man that, mistrusting his manner of dealing in the commonwealth, found out his craft and malice, which he cunningly cloked under the habit of outward courtesy and familiarity.

What the source states as fact, the play develops as a hypothesis, and Brutus says explicitly that it is a hypothesis unsupported by past conduct.

How is one to reconcile these contrary changes from the source, which make Caesar more subject to physical infirmities but also more careful and unselfish as a ruler? In part, probably, Shakespeare is actually trying to contrast human weakness and royal power. But the obvious explanation is to be found, I think, in Plutarch. Shakespeare took Caesar as one who "yielded not to the disease of his body," but triumphed by the strength of his will and intellect as well as by his bravery:

>   What can be avoided
> Whose end is purpos'd by the mighty
>   Gods? . . . .
> Cowards die many times before their
>   death;
> The valiant never taste of death but once.
>
>   [II. ii. 26-7, 32-3]

To magnify Caesar's achievements, Shakespeare presented him as weaker of body than in the source, and therefore stronger of will. No one ever regarded Franklin D. Roosevelt's paralysis as detracting from his greatness. Quite the contrary. His triumph over it was part of his hold upon men. Shakespeare expected those who were without Cassius' envy to take the same view of Caesar. He was a great and good ruler. To kill him was regicide. (pp. 232-34)

There may be question as to what Shakespeare was trying to accomplish by the changes he made in portraying Caesar. There can be no doubt whatever as to what he was trying to do to Brutus. To Plutarch Brutus was an almost perfect example of the antique and heroic republican mould. To Shakespeare he was a very great man, but, because of fundamental defects in his own mind and character, he made a horrible and tragic error—in short, he was a tragic hero.

Shakespeare therefore emphasized both Brutus' self-righteousness and his impractical and muddled head. His deviations from his source indicate that such was his intention. In the meeting of the conspirators that occupies the latter half of Act II, Scene i, Brutus overrules three suggestions by Cassius. The first is an outright invention, and the other two involve significant divergences from the account of Brutus' reasoning in the source. Cassius first proposes an oath, which Brutus rejects on the grounds that it would "stain the even virtue of our enterprise" [II. i. 132-33]. Cassius then suggests that they invite Cicero to join them. Plutarch implies that the conspirators agreed to omit Cicero "for they were afraid that he being a coward by nature, and age also having increased his fear, he would quite turn and alter all their purpose, and quench the heat of their enterprise, the which especially required hot and earnest execution, seeking by persuasion to bring all things to such safety, as there should be no peril." For this general distrust of a born politician Shakespeare substituted a rejection by Brutus alone on grounds more indicative of his own vanity than of Cicero's incompetence:

> O, name him not; let us not break with him.
> For he will never follow anything
> That other men begin.
>
> [II. i. 150-52]

In Plutarch Brutus' reasons for refusing to kill Antonius, as Cassius wishes, at least show genuine idealism:

> But Brutus would not agree to it. First, for that he said it was not honest; secondly, because he told them there was hope of change in him. For he did not mistrust, but that Antonius, being a noble-minded and courageous man, (when he should know that Caesar was dead) would willingly help his country to recover her liberty, having them an example unto him, to follow their courage and virtue.

Shakespeare makes his motives reflect both self-righteousness and a lack of worldly experience. He argues that, because Antony is given to wild living, he is not dangerous:

> If he love Caesar, all that he can do
> Is to himself—take thought and die for Caesar;
> And that were much he should, for he is given
> To sports, to wildness, and much company.

[II. i. 186-89]

Later, when Antony asks to deliver a funeral oration over Caesar's body, Shakespeare attributes to Brutus himself the very arguments for granting the request which Plutarch makes Antony advance. Coming from Antony they were crafty; coming from Brutus they are fatuous. Brutus also demands the impossible in the following proviso: praise Caesar without dispraising us!

> You shall not in your funeral speech blame us,
> But speak all good you can devise of Caesar.
>
> [III. i. 245-46]

Shakespeare tried so obviously to accentuate Brutus' self-righteousness in the quarrel between Brutus and Cassius just before Philippi that his writing is actually clumsy. In Plutarch Brutus gets money from Cassius while they are at Smyrna. Some time later, during the quarrel upon which Shakespeare's scene is based, he reproves Cassius for his way of exacting money. But Shakespeare so arranges matters that Brutus first reproves Cassius for his methods of getting money . . . and then, all the while protesting his own superior virtue, upbraids Cassius for not sending him some of the ill-gotten wealth:

> I did send to you
> For certain sums of gold, which you deni'd me;
> For I can raise no money by vile means.—
> By heaven, I had rather coin my heart
> And drop my blood for drachmas than to wring
> From the hard hands of peasants their vile trash
> By any indirection.—I did send
> To you for gold to pay my legions,
> Which you deni'd me.
>
> [IV. iii. 69-77]

These lines suggest that Shakespeare took more pains to emphasize Brutus' self-righteous inconsistency than to construct a credible speech.

Finally, Shakespeare made Brutus alone responsible for the disaster at Philippi by attributing to his order [V. iii. 5] the fatal premature charge which lost the battle. Plutarch says that it was caused by the impatience of the troops. Brutus' failure is further emphasized by Cassius' speech protesting that he fights against his will [V. i. 70-88]. The protest is taken from the source; but this speech, being much the longest in the entire act, focuses attention upon what Plutarch mentions in passing.

Brutus therefore emerges from Shakespeare's hand considerably shorn of the perfection which Plutarch gave him. The importance that one attaches to this shift of emphasis depends, of course, upon the view that one takes of the structure of the play. I must therefore confess my conviction that

David Waller as Caesar in a 1987 Royal Shakespeare Theatre staging of the tragedy. Act III, scene i.

Julius Caesar is a well-constructed tragedy of which Brutus is the hero. The name is obviously irrelevant; for the respect due kingly rank made Shakespeare name a serious play after the reigning monarch as inevitably as his first printers placed a king's name at the head of the *dramatis personae,* no matter how slight his part in the action of the play, and we have noted that Shakespeare thought of Caesar as a ruler. (pp. 234-37)

If it be granted that Brutus is the real hero, the changes in characterization fit into an orderly pattern, and the play proves to be worked out in terms of two sets of ideas. . . . : Shakespeare's political theory and his concept of moral choice.

The very first scene develops the political background for the play. In Plutarch the images were decked by Caesar's flatterers "to allure the common people to call him king, instead of dictator." The tribunes, "meeting with them that first saluted Caesar as king . . . committed them to prison." The people rejoiced at this defence of Roman liberty. For Shakespeare all this simply had no meaning. The images are decked for Caesar's triumph over Pompey, and the tribunes are moved by loyalty to the fallen leader. The people are a fickle rabble, as in so many of the plays. As Sir Mark Hunter

observed in a stimulating essay on "Politics and Character in Shakespeare's *Julius Caesar*" [in *Essays by Diverse Hands,* Vol. X, edited by Sir Francis Youngblood], "Liberty" as an end in itself had no meaning for Shakespeare, obedience being the chief virtue in his political philosophy. Brutus' reliance upon liberty as the basis of his own thinking and in his appeal to the people is simply self-deception. This the people themselves make clear when they respond to his oration by saying, "Let him be Caesar" [III. ii. 51], and Antony's oration depends for its effect upon the contrast between his appeal to Caesar's good deeds and Brutus' nebulous charge that Caesar was ambitious.

As the play progresses, we are introduced to a Roman state organized in the hierarchical fashion that Tudor theory prescribed. . . .

> The throng that follows Caesar at the
>   heels,
> Of senators, of praetors, common suitors.
>   [II. iv. 34-5]

Here we have the degrees of society that should wait upon a monarch, arranged in proper order. Caesar is still, in fact though not in name, what Margaret called him in *3 Henry VI* [III. i. 18]—a king. And he has for Shakespeare the sanctity that surrounds a king. (pp. 238-39)

The conspirators also add their testimony that Shakespeare regarded Caesar as a monarch. They do not justify their attack, as in Plutarch, only on the grounds that he wanted to be king. They repeat the word "king," it is true; but, like all Shakespeare's regicides, they add "tyrant" and "tyranny." "And why should Caesar be a tyrant then?" asks Cassius [I. iii. 103]. "Liberty! Freedom! Tyranny is dead!" proclaims Cinna as Caesar is stabbed [III. i. 78]. The first plebian concedes, "This Caesar was a tyrant" [III. ii. 69]. And young Cato boasts three distinctions: he is "the son of Marcus Cato, ho! a foe to tyrants, and my country's friend" [V. iv. 4-5].

Shakespeare's Tudor absolutism was therefore at complete odds with Plutarch's idealization of Brutus as the epitome of the old republican virtues. That Shakespeare approached his source with the presuppositions of his own times is not surprising. What does mark his intellectual development is the fact that he was able to read Plutarch with such sympathetic understanding and to portray Brutus, not as a villain, but as a tragic hero, whose sin was the error of judgment of a great and virtuous man. Brutus is the first of Shakespeare's superb tragic figures who fail through false moral choice. (p. 240)

Shakespeare presents Brutus' false choice in a famous soliloquy [II. i. 10-34] that has been a puzzle to scholars. (p. 242)

As numerous writers upon Shakespeare and poetic drama have reminded us, quite rightly, his technique is one of suggestion rather than of complete representation. There was no need for him to portray the entire mental struggle leading up to a crucial choice, but he did have to imply how it came about convincingly enough to stimulate the imagination of his audience. He might attempt to parallel all stages of the inner conflict. That he did in *Othello,* with somewhat doubtful success. Or he might present the climax of the struggle, giving only a hint of what had gone before. This is his method in *Julius Caesar,* as it is in *Macbeth* and, with variations, in *King Lear.* The first line of Brutus' soliloquy resumes an interrupted process of cogitation. "It must be by his death" [II. i. 10]. Two assumptions are implicit in this remark. Caesar can be prevented from being king only by killing him, and killing a ruler is justified only if he is a tyrant. The former was axiomatic to anyone with a knowledge either of English history or of Machiavelli, and it is explicit in Brutus' first words [Machiavellianism represents the view that politics is amoral and that any means, however unscrupulous, can justifiably be used in achieving political power]. The latter should have been clear to the audience, since Cassius had just harped throughout the preceding scene on the weakness of those who submit to tyrants. It is clearly implied by the reasoning throughout the soliloquy. Having established his premises, Brutus continues:

> It must be by his death; and for my part,
> I know no personal cause to spurn at him
> But for the general. He would be crown'd:
> How that might change his nature, there's the question.
> It is the bright day that brings forth the adder,
> And that craves wary walking. . . .
>   So Caesar may;
> Then, lest he may, prevent. And, since the quarrel
> Will bear no colour for the thing he is,
> Fashion it thus: that what he is, augmented,
> Would run to these and these extremities;
> And therefore think him as a serpent's egg
> Which, hatch'd, would, as his kind, grow mischievous,
> And kill him in the shell.
>   [II. i. 10-15, 27-34]

His meaning is somewhat as follows. I have no personal grievance; so, if I act, it must be for the Roman people. The question that I must answer is whether crowning Caesar might change his nature. If we crown him, we give him the power to do great harm. But he will do harm and abuse his greatness only if he uses power without remorse (that is, without a moral sense). But, to speak truthfully, Caesar has never let his affections win control over his reason (in other words, he has never shown any inclination to irrational and immoral conduct). But it is common experience that humility is merely the ladder to ambition (ambition was for the Elizabethans a vice). Once the climber has achieved his ambition, he scorns the humility by which he ascended. Caesar may do so; therefore anticipate him. And, *since his present conduct gives no warrant whatever* for concluding that he will be a tyrant and therefore for killing him, assume that, once he gains absolute power, he will proceed to extremities; and kill him to prevent what he may become, as one would destroy a serpent's egg because a serpent is, by nature, dangerous.

Shakespeare has done his best to make the fallacies in the reasoning obvious. Brutus says explicitly that he has no evidence to support the conclusion that Caesar will become immoral and that he must kill on an assumption without basis; he ends by remarking that one destroys a serpent's egg because it is the "kind" (nature) of a serpent to be poisonous, but he has opened by observing that Caesar will be a tyrant only if crowning him changes his nature. His error in assuming that he is acting for the Roman people is proved by later events.

I take it that Brutus' doubling back upon his previous reasoning, as he does in the last seven lines, is intended by Shakespeare to suggest that his mind is still not made up at the end of the soliloquy. But there follows an appeal to his fatal weakness. Lucius reenters with another letter. Logic yields to pride, and reason becomes the tool of appetite. Brutus resolves upon action, and Caesar's doom is sealed. (pp. 243-45)

From Brutus' decision followed action. As a result of the killing of Caesar chaos engulfed all Rome, and discord and then death overwhelmed Brutus and Cassius themselves.

This kind of scene was new to Shakespeare and indeed, so far as I know, to all drama except for [Christopher Marlowe's] *Faustus*. A choice that involves moral issues is, of course, fundamental to most serious action. It underlies Antigone's defiance of Creon [in Sophocles' *Antigone*] or Bolingbroke's deposition of Richard II. What was new was the attempt to make the act of choice an important part of the play and to work it out in detail according to accepted psychological theory. Shakespeare motivates his action by a formal scene of moral choice.

In comparison with the chronicle plays just preceding it and even with the comedies contemporary with it, *Julius Caesar* is remarkable as being the first Shakespearean play in which the motivation is really adequate and in which we become acquainted with the characters through their mental processes as well as through their actions. (p. 246)

> *Virgil K. Whitaker, "'Julius Caesar' and Tragedy of Moral Choice," in his* Shakespeare's Use of Learning: An Inquiry into the Growth of His Mind & Art, *The Huntington Library, 1953, pp. 224-50.*

John Dover Wilson

[*Wilson maintains that the sole theme of* Julius Caesar *is the conflict between liberty and tyranny. The critic demonstrates how Shakespeare manipulated his source, Plutarch's* Lives of the Noble Grecianes and Romans, *to portray* **Caesar** *as a contemptible despot by emphasizing his physical and moral weaknesses, his haughtiness, and his seemingly limitless appetite for conquest. Shakespeare clearly supports* **Brutus** *and the other conspirators in their defense of liberty, Dover Wilson asserts, and their failure to prevail in the struggle against tyranny is our tragedy as well as theirs, for "Caesarism," or dictatorship, remains a threat to modern society.*]

Written in our day [*Julius Cæsar*] might have been called *Cæsar and Cæarism;* but abstract words were not then in vogue, and this particular one was not invented till 1857. Yet Shakespeare's title was adequate enough in view of what the name of Julius stood for in 1599. For the play's theme is the single one, Liberty *versus* Tyranny, which implies on the one hand a diagnosis of the situation confirmed by modern historians, viz. the necessity of absolutism for the Rome of Cicero; and on the other a sense of the greatness of Rome and the Empire, never more powerfully realized than in Shakespeare's day. That greatness is symbolized by one aspect of the character of Shakespeare's Cæsar, who stands not only for the man who died in March 44 B.C., but also for the semi-mythical Colossus who 'doth bestride the narrow world' [I. ii. 135] both of Cassius and of Shakespeare, and whose spirit still, from time to time, as we know to our cost, 'walks abroad' and 'turns our swords In our own proper entrails' [V. iii. 95-6]. When Brutus exclaims

> We all stand up against the spirit of Cæsar,
> [II. i. 167]

he sums up the play in one line. For the spirit of Cæsar, which was the destiny of Rome, is the fate against which Brutus struggles in vain. And his failure to do so is his tragedy (and ours), inasmuch as Cæsarism is a secular threat to the human spirit, and the living 'Julius', as Shakespeare shows him, is the mouthpiece of that threat. Some think Shakespeare's Cæsar adumbrates Mommsen's, a being 'of mighty creative power and . . . most penetrating judgment' [in *History of Rome*], a historical superman. . . . But Shakespeare, who had read neither Mommsen nor Nietzsche, had before him a different kind of myth altogether, the classico-medieval image, seen through renaissance eyes, of an almost supernatural conqueror who out of lust for power ruined the Roman republic. In other words the paradox of Shakespeare's Cæsar is a paradox of renaissance thought, which combined a well-nigh religious awe for Rome and Cæsar with sympathy for Brutus and his fellows as Rome's liberators from a tyrant. (pp. xxi-xxiii)

Yet when all is said, Shakespeare's Cæsar is his own portrait and more 'caustic' than any other of the age. The word is Herford's [in his introduction to the *Eversley Shakespeare* edition of *Julius Cæsar*], who has well brought out the exhibition of Cæsar's physical and moral weaknesses, his superstition, his 'vacillation' on the fatal morning, and 'above all' the profession of immovable constancy which that vacillation so ironically refutes. Shakespeare adds to the infirmities in Plutarch a deafness in one ear; and makes 'the falling sickness' [I. ii. 254], which Plutarch does mention, seize him at the most awkward and humiliating moment— when being offered a crown. Worse still, he substitutes for the pluck, resolution, and endurance often praised by Plutarch, a 'feeble temper'; and derives the three examples of this from passages in [Thomas North's translation of Plutarch] which show the exact opposite. Cassius is here, indeed, the speaker, and the points illustrate his malice; but Brutus does not reply to the charge, and it is fully borne out by stroke after stroke later. Cassius begins by hinting at the great man's sensitiveness to 'the winter's cold' [I. ii. 99], whereas Plutarch, while admitting a delicate constitution, gives instances of his hardiness in ignoring it. Cassius tells a story of a swimming match in which Cæsar has to cry to him for help; Plutarch on the contrary stresses his strength and skill in swimming and tells of a wonderful aquatic feat. Lastly, of Cæsar's 'fever in Spain', when according to Cassius his 'coward lips' cried out for water 'as a sick girl' [I. ii. 128], Plutarch writes:

> Yet therefore [he] yielded not to the disease of his body, to make it a cloak to cherish him withal, but contrarily took the pains of war as a medicine to cure his sick body, fighting always with his disease, travelling continually, living soberly, and commonly lying abroad in the field.

Or take our impressions as Shakespeare brings him first on to the stage. . . . Picture a great concourse of people; a ceremonial procession, consisting of priests and other persons bound for the Lupercalia, among them Antony and a number of young men stripped for the chase; then, from the distance and drawing ever nearer, the sound of music such as Elizabethans were wont to associate with royalty; and lastly, the great man himself, surrounded with all the pomp of an oriental monarch, and borne in, as I think, upon a litter: a figure haughty, ageing, infirm. And, if this be set down as in part the creation of editorial fancy, it cannot be denied that Shakespeare makes Cæsar ride or walk alone, so that when he desires to lay his commands upon Calphurnia, she has to hurry up from the rear; or that those commands at once express his anxiety for an heir and publicly brand her as the barren party responsible for his childlessness, words upon which Elizabethans would be quick to set their own interpretation. Thus in stroke after stroke . . . Shakespeare builds up a portrait of the man for his spectators; and all this, the contemptible side of the character, is solely of his own making.

What then? Are we not left to conclude that, faced with the problem of Julius, Shakespeare made up his own mind about him? Long before, when called upon to depict a very different sort of dictatorship, he had shown that he knew how the system worked. 'When I am king,' declares Jack Cade, 'all shall eat and drink on my score, and I will apparel them all in one livery, that they may agree like brothers and worship me their lord' [*2 Henry VI,* IV. ii. 69, 73-5]. Such is Cæsarism, including 'panem' [bread] if not 'circenses' [circuses], with the equality of all in one classless mob, united in reverence before a semi-divine being, whether Napoleon, Führer, or general secretary of the communist party. But Cade was a comic figure; and 'Julius' must be taken seriously; for Shakespeare has now to exhibit on the stage the effects of Cæsarism on the soul of Cæsar himself. Having written, or taken a large share in, eight history plays before 1599, he had been contemplating, almost continu-

ously for eight years or more, men struggling for power by fair means or foul, and exercising it fairly or foully. [E. K. Chambers, in his *Shakespeare: A Survey*] points out that *Julius Cæsar,* written just after *Henry V,* shows 'the same preoccupation with a political problem in the relations of leader and mob'. I agree, while wholly dissenting from his further deduction that both leaders are 'supermen'. Rather, as it seems to me, having written of a hero who, singing 'Non nobis' [not ours] in the hour of victory, preserves his integrity, Shakespeare turns to consider the sort of conqueror whose appetite grows by what it feeds on, who, having become the 'foremost man of all this world' [IV. iii. 22], begins to think and speak of himself as more than mortal; in a word, the Man of Success, as the Elizabethans understood him.

For what he thought of such a man we have in evidence not only the portrait in the first three Acts, but the soliloquy of Brutus at the beginning of the second, which has puzzled all the critics. . . . Brutus's theme is the effect of power upon character, and his conclusion is that to crown Cæsar would endow him with that absolute power which, as Acton notes, corrupts absolutely. So far, Brutus admits, Cæsar had not shown himself the tyrant; but then he has not yet attained 'the upmost round' [II. i. 24] of the ladder. Once thus high he will scorn 'the base degrees by which he did ascend' [II. i. 26-7]. Once crowned, all barriers will be down; and, human nature being what it is, 'the bright day will bring forth the adder' [II. i. 14], since absolute rulers have no use for mercy ('remorse'). . . . Shakespeare does all he can to show us that the reading of Cæsar's character in the soliloquy is correct. Had he represented Cæsar as 'the perfect statesman' of Mommsen, or the clear-eyed realistic opportunist of a living historian [Ronald Syme, in his *The Roman Revolution*], or the magnaminous, genial and wise, if over-ambitious, dictator whom Plutarch draws, he would have given us a very different play, at once far less tragic and less profound. And we who have come to know what dictators look like when the façade of their synthetic magnificence is down and their myth exploded, can feel nothing but astonishment at a genius which lacking our experience could so penetrate to their secret.

But this, I shall be told, was an accident. Shakespeare, Bernard Shaw declares [in his preface to *Caesar and Cleopatra* published in *Three Plays for Puritans*], wrote 'Cæsar down for the merely technical purpose of writing Brutus up'. He might have added that he wrote Brutus down for a like purpose in the Forum scene, and Antony down in the Proscription scene immediately after, and then wrote Brutus and Cassius up again more and more from that moment until the catastrophe. Shakespeare is always busy adjusting his dramatic scales, making bids for the sympathies of the audience on behalf, now of this character, then of that;

now of this side, then of the other. These things are of the essence of his craft, and by such means he creates that final impression of dramatic justice which all allow to be one of his chief claims to greatness. Moreover, he had a technical reason of special weight for disparaging Cæsar while still alive, namely, that his assassination scene was an extraordinarily difficult corner for an Elizabethan playwright to turn. Cæsar was not a crowned head, nor the anointed of the Lord. . . . But he was 'the first emperor', and to the Elizabethans . . . a being of almost superhuman stature, so that the spectacle of his being hacked to pieces by assassins would inevitably strike them as something appalling, if not sacrilegious.

But what is dramatically convenient, is not necessarily false. On the contrary, at any rate in Shakespearian tragedy, it is likely to be truer than history itself. For 'poetry is a more philosophic and a finer thing than history, since poetry speaks of universals and history only of particulars' [Aristotle, in his *Poetics*]. The Gaius Julius who fell in the Curia Pompeiana on the Ides of March, 44 B.C. was a 'particular' man over whose character and schemes historians will continue to dispute; the Cæsar who falls on Shakespeare's Capitol is the universal Dictator. (pp. xxvii-xxxiii)

> *John Dover Wilson, in an introduction to* Julius Caesar, *by William Shakespeare, edited by John Dover Wilson, 1949. Reprint by Cambridge University Press, 1968, pp. vii-xxxiii.*

PUBLIC AND PRIVATE VALUES

Maynard Mack

[*Mack discusses the public and private values of* **Brutus** *and* **Caesar** *in terms of what he views as the primary theme of the play: "the always ambiguous impact between man and history." The private* **Brutus,** *the critic asserts, is a gentle, sensitive, and studious man who loves* **Caesar** *and deplores violence, while the public figure is a noble idealist who participates in the conspiracy because he believes he must act on behalf of the state. Mack contends that in the first half of the drama Shakespeare focuses on "human will as a force in history" by portraying individuals, such as* **Brutus,** *choosing courses of action and controlling events; in contrast, the second half of* Julius Caesar *demonstrates the inadequacies of noble intentions, rationalism, and human will, once they are displayed in action, in influencing history.* **Caesar**'s *dual nature, the critic continues, similarly dramatizes Shakespeare's thesis that history is only partially responsive to human will. The private* **Caesar,** *an ordinary man plagued by physical weak-*nesses and susceptible to superstition, cannot escape being assassinated. However, the public* **Caesar** *is the "marble superman of state," the "everlasting Big Brother—the Napoleon, Mussolini, Hitler, Franco, Peron, Stalin, Kruschev, to mention only a handful of his more recent incarnations . . . who must repeatedly be killed but never dies."*]

I am one of those who believe that Shakespeare can be taught to almost any sort of audience. I am perfectly aware, of course, of the language problem that Shakespeare presents for today's students . . . ; and I am perfectly willing to admit that there are classes to whom it would be preposterous to offer his plays. I would only argue that to any group to whom literature in any form may be offered with a prospect of success, Shakespeare may be offered with equal and usually with greater success. After all, it was not mainly the verbalizers and the "brighties" of Elizabethan London who showed up with their penny at the Globe to stand for two and a half hours in the pit. It was the odoriferous and stupid, the groundlings, capable, as Shakespeare himself said, of little but "inexplicable dumb shows and noise" [*Hamlet*, III. ii. 12]. Yet he had something to say to these people: he *held* them. In the hands of a patient teacher, who will make the most of student participation, he still does—as no other reading but the comics will. And when he does not, I suggest it is almost invariably for one of two reasons. On the one hand, the teacher is a bardolater and holds the play aloft for distant veneration as if it were a thing too refined for human nature's daily food. I had a teacher like this myself. Whenever we came to any of the great speeches in the plays, he would lean back in his chair, close his eyes, and murmur, in a voice you could pour on a waffle, "ah, the magic of it, the magic!" That same magic took me a whole year to get over and almost sent me into chemical engineering.

Then there is the other alternative: the teacher is not actually interested in the play except as a scratching post of the student's memory. In *this* teacher's class, the interminable question is "What next? What after that? What then?" as though the play were a timetable to a destination that will never be reached. I get a good many of that teacher's pupils in my classes. . . . They know exactly what follows what in the first act of *Macbeth*, say, but nobody has ever asked them any questions beginning with "Why?" Why does the play *open* with the witch scene? Why is the number of the witches *three?* Is there any significance in the fact that there are also three banquets, three murders, three apparitions, and even three murderers at Banquo's death? And what does the second witch mean by saying "When the battle's lost *and* won"? What battle? and how can it be won and lost at the same time?

Questions like these, I feel, suggest the approach that most of us who are neither bardolaters nor mnemonicists will wish to take to Shakespeare, and if we are taking it with *Julius Caesar,* I think the place we may want to begin is with I. ii; for here, as in the first witch scene in *Macbeth,* most of the play to come is already implicit. We have just learned from scene i of Caesar's return in triumph from warring on Pompey's sons, we have seen the warm though fickle adulation of the crowd and the apprehension of the tribunes; now we are to see the great man himself. The procession enters to triumphal music; with hubbub of a great press of people; with young men stripped for the ceremonial races, among them Antony; with statesmen in their togas: Decius, Cicero, Brutus, Cassius, Casca; with the two wives Calpurnia and Portia; and, in the lead, for not even Calpurnia is permitted at his side, the great man. As he starts to speak, an expectant hush settles over the gathering: what does the great man have on his mind?

CAES. Calpurnia.
CASCA   Peace, ho! Caesar speaks.
CAES.   Calpurnia.
CAL. Here, my lord.
CAES. Stand you directly in Antonius' way
    When he does run his course. Antonius.
ANT. Caesar, my lord?
CAES. Forget not, in your speed, Antonius,
    To touch Calpurnia; for our elders say,
    The barren, touched in this holy chase,
    Shake off their sterile curse.
ANT.   I shall remember:
    When Caesar says, "Do this," it is perform'd.

                         [I. ii. 1-10]

What the great man had on his mind, it appears, was to remind his wife, in this public place, that she is sterile; that there is an old tradition about how sterility can be removed; and that while of course he is much too sophisticated to accept such a superstition himself—it is "our elders" who say it—still, Calpurnia had jolly well better get out there and get tagged, or else!

Then the procession takes up again. The hubbub is resumed, but once more the expectant silence settles as a voice is heard.

SOOTH. Caesar!
CAES. Ha! Who calls?
CASCA Bid every noise be still; peace yet again!
CAES. Who is it in the press that calls on me?
    I hear a tongue shriller than all the music
    Cry "Caesar!" Speak. Caesar is turn'd to hear.
SOOTH. Beware the ides of March.

CAES.   What man is that?
BRU. A soothsayer bids you beware the ides of March.
CAES. Set him before me; let me see his face.
CAS. Fellow, come from the throng; look upon Caesar.
CAES. What say'st thou to me now? Speak once again.
SOOTH. Beware the ides of March.
CAES. He is a dreamer. Let us leave him. Pass.

                        [I. ii. 11-24]

It is easy to see from even these small instances, I think, how a first-rate dramatic imagination works. There is no hint of any procession in Plutarch, Shakespeare's source. "Caesar," says Plutarch, "*sat* to behold." There is no mention of Calpurnia in Plutarch's account of the Lupercalian race, and there is no mention anywhere of her sterility. Shakespeare, in nine lines, has given us an unforgettable picture of a man who would like to be emperor pathetically concerned that he lacks an heir, and determined, even at the cost of making his wife a public spectacle, to establish that this is owing to no lack of virility in him. The first episode thus dramatizes instantaneously the oncoming theme of the play: that a man's will is not enough; that there are other matters to be reckoned with, like the infertility of one's wife, or one's own affliction of the falling sickness which spoils everything one hoped for just at the instant when one had it almost in one's hand. Brutus will be obliged to learn this lesson too.

In the second episode the theme develops. We see again the uneasy rationalism that everybody in this play affects; we hear it reverberate in the faint contempt—almost a challenge—of Brutus' words as he turns to Caesar: "A soothsayer bids you beware the ides of March." Yet underneath, in the soothsayer's presence and his sober warning, Shakespeare allows us to catch a hint of something else, something far more primitive and mysterious, from which rationalism in this play keeps trying vainly to cut itself away: "He is a dreamer. Let us leave him. Pass." Only we in the audience are in a position to see that the dreamer has foretold the path down which all these reasoners will go to that fatal encounter at the Capitol.

Meantime, in these same two episodes, we have learned something about the character of Caesar. In the first, it was the Caesar of human frailties who spoke to us, the husband with his hopeful superstition. In the second, it was the marble superman of state, impassive, impervious, speaking of himself in the third person: "Speak! Caesar is turn'd to hear." He even has the soothsayer brought before his face to repeat the message, as if he thought that somehow, in awe of the marble presence, the message would falter and dissolve: how can a superman need to beware the ides of March?

We hardly have time to do more than glimpse here a man of divided selves, when he is gone. But in his absence, the words of Cassius confirm our glimpse. Cassius' description of him exhibits the same duality that we had noticed earlier. On the one hand, an extremely ordinary man whose stamina in the swimming match was soon exhausted, who, when he had a fever once in Spain, shook and groaned like a sick girl, who even now, as we soon learn, is falling down with epilepsy in the market place. On the other hand, a being who has somehow become a god, who "bears the palm alone," who "bestrides the narrow world like a colossus" [I. ii. 131, 135-36]. When the procession returns, no longer festive now, but angry, tense, there is the same effect once more. Our one Caesar shows a normal man's suspicion of his enemies, voices some shrewd human observations about Cassius, says to Antony, "Come on my right hand, for this ear is deaf" [I. ii. 213]. Our other Caesar says, as if he were suddenly reminded of something he had forgotten, "I rather tell thee what is to be fear'd / Than what I fear, for always I am Caesar" [I. ii. 211-12].

Whenever Caesar appears hereafter, we shall find this singular division in him, and nowhere more so than in the scene in which he receives the conspirators at his house. Some aspects of this scene seem calculated for nothing else than to fix upon our minds the superman conception, the Big Brother of Orwell's *1984,* the great resonant name echoing down the halls of time. Thus at the beginning of the scene:

> the things that threatened me
> Ne'er look'd but on my back; when they shall see
> The face of Caesar, they are vanished.
>
> [II. ii. 10-12]

And again later:

> danger knows full well
> That Caesar is more dangerous than he:
> We are two lions litter'd in one day,
> And I the elder and more terrible.
>
> [II. ii. 44-7]

And again still later: "Shall Caesar send a lie?" [II. ii. 65]. And again: "The cause is in my will: I will not come" [II. ii. 71]. Other aspects, including his concern about Calpurnia's dream, his vacillation about going to the senate house, his anxiety about the portents of the night, plainly mark out his human weaknesses. Finally, as is the habit in this Rome, he puts the irrational from him that his wife's intuitions and her dream embody; he accepts the rationalization of the irrational that Decius skillfully manufactures, and, as earlier at the Lupercalia, hides from himself his own vivid sense of forces that lie beyond the will's control by attributing it to her:

> How foolish do your fears seem now, Calpurnia!

> I am ashamed I did yield to them.
> Give me my robe, for I will go.
>
> [II. ii. 105-07]

So far in our consideration of the implications of I. ii. we have been looking only at Caesar, the title personage of the play, and its historical center. It is time now to turn to Brutus, the play's tragic center, whom we also find to be a divided man—"poor Brutus," to use his own phrase, "with himself at war" [I. ii. 46]. The war, we realize as the scene progresses, is a conflict between a quiet essentially domestic and loving nature, and a powerful integrity expressing itself in a sense of honorable duty to the commonweal. This duality in Brutus seems to be what Cassius is probing at in his long disquisition about the mirror. The Brutus looking into the glass that Cassius figuratively holds up to him, the Brutus of this moment, now, in Rome, is a grave studious private man, of a wonderfully gentle temper, as we shall see again and again later on, very slow to passion, as Cassius' ill-concealed disappointment in having failed to kindle him to immediate response reveals, a man whose sensitive nature recoils at the hint of violence lurking in some of Cassius' speeches, just as he has already recoiled at going on with Caesar to the market place, to witness the mass hysteria of clapping hands, sweaty nightcaps, and stinking breath. This is the present self that looks into Cassius' mirror.

The image that looks back out, that Cassius wants him to see, the potential Brutus, is the man of public spirit, worried already by the question of Caesar's intentions, the lineal descendant of an earlier Brutus who drove a would-be monarch from the city, a man whose body is visibly stiffening in our sight at each huzza from the Forum, and whose anxiety, though he makes no reply to Cassius' inflammatory language, keeps bursting to the surface: "What means this shouting? I do fear the people / Choose Caesar for their king" [I. ii. 79-80]. The problem at the tragic center of the play, we begin to sense, is to be the tug of private versus public, the individual versus a world he never made, any citizen anywhere versus the selective service greetings that history is always mailing out to each of us. And this problem is to be traversed by that other tug this scene presents, of the irrational versus the rational, the destiny we think we can control versus the destiny that sweeps all before it.

Through I. ii, Brutus' public self, the self that responds to these selective service greetings, is no more than a reflection in a mirror, a mere anxiety in his own brain, about which he refuses to confide, even to Cassius. In II. i, we see the public self making further headway. First, there is Brutus' argument with himself about the threat of Caesar, and in his conclusion that Caesar must be killed we note how far his private self—he is, after all, one of Caesar's closest friends—has been invaded by the self of public spirit. From here on, the course of the invasion accelerates. The letter comes, tossed from the public world into the private world, into Brutus' garden, and addressing, as Cassius had, that public image reflected in the mirror: "Brutus, thou sleep'st: awake and see thyself " [II. i. 46]. Then follows the well-known brief soliloquy . . . , showing us that Brutus' mind has moved on now from the phase of decision to the inquietudes that follow decision:

> Between the acting of a dreadful thing
> And the first motion, all the interim is
> Like a phantasma, or a hideous dream.
> [II. i. 63-5]

What is important to observe is that these lines stress once again the gulf that separates motive from action, that which is interior in man and controllable by his will from that which, once acted, becomes independent of him and moves with a life of its own. This gulf is a no man's land, a phantasma, a hideous dream.

Finally, there arrives in such a form that no audience can miss it the actual visible invasion itself, as this peaceful garden quiet is broken in on by knocking, like the knocking of fate in Beethoven's fifth symphony, and by men with faces hidden in their cloaks. Following this, a lovely interlude with Portia serves to emphasize how much the private self, the private world has been shattered. We have something close to discord here—as much of a discord as these very gentle people are capable of—and though there is a reconciliation at the end and Brutus' promise to confide in her soon, this division in the family is an omen. So is that knock of the latecomer, Caius Ligarius, which reminds us once again of the intrusions of the public life. And when Ligarius throws off his sick man's kerchief on learning that there is an honorable exploit afoot, we may see in it an epitome of the whole scene, a graphic visual renunciation, like Brutus', of the private good to the public; and we may see this also in Brutus' own exit a few lines later, not into the inner house where Portia waits for him, but out into the thunder and lightning of the public life of Rome. It is perhaps significant that at our final view of Portia, two scenes later, she too stands outside the privacy of the house, her mind wholly occupied with thoughts of what is happening at the Capitol, and trying to put on a public self for Brutus' sake: "Run, Lucius, and commend me to my Lord / Say I am merry . . . " [II. iv. 44-5].

Meantime, up there by the Capitol, the tragic center and the historical center meet. The suspense is very great as Caesar, seeing the Soothsayer in the throng, reminds him that the ides of March are come, and receives in answer, "Ay, Caesar, but not gone" [III. i. 2]. More suspense as Artemidorus presses forward with the paper that we know contains a full discovery of the plot. Decius, apprehensive, steps quickly into the breach with another

paper, a petition from Trebonius. More suspense still as Popilius sidles past Cassius with the whisper, "I wish your enterprise today may thrive" [III. i. 13], and then moves on to Caesar's side, where he engages him in animated talk. But they detect no telltale change in Caesar's countenance; Trebonius steps into his assignment and takes Antony aside; Metellus Cimber throws himself at Caesar's feet; Brutus gives the signal to "press near and second him," and Caesar's "Are we all ready?" draws every eye to Caesar's chair [III. i. 29, 31]. One by one they all kneel before this demigod—an effective tableau which gives a coloring of priest-like ritual to what they are about to do. Caesar is to bleed, but, as Brutus has said, they will sublimate the act into a sacrifice:

> Let's kill him boldly but not wrathfully;
> Let's carve him as a dish fit for the gods,
> Not hew him as a carcass fit for hounds.
> [II. i. 172-74]

Everything in the scene must underscore this ceremonial attitude, in order to bring out the almost fatuous cleavage between the spirit of this enterprise and its bloody purpose.

The Caesar that we are permitted to see while all this ceremony is preparing is almost entirely the superman, for obvious reasons. To give a color of justice to Brutus' act and so to preserve our sense of his nobility even if we happen to think the assassination a mistake, as an Elizabethan audience emphatically would, Caesar has to appear in a mood of superhumanity at least as fatuous as the conspirators' mood of sacrifice. Hence Shakespeare makes him first of all insult Metellus Cimber: "If thou dost bend and pray and fawn for him, / I spurn thee like a cur" [III. i. 45-6]; then comment with intolerable pomposity, and, in fact, blasphemy, on his own iron resolution, for he affects to be immovable even by prayer and hence superior to the very gods. Finally, Shakespeare puts into his mouth one of those supreme arrogances that will remind us of the destroying *hubris* which makes men mad in order to ruin them. "Hence!" Caesar cries, "Wilt thou lift up Olympus?" [III. i. 74]. It is at just this point, when the colossus Caesar drunk with self-love is before us, that Casca strikes. Then they all strike, with a last blow that brings out for the final time the other, human side of this double Caesar: "Et tu, Brute?" [III. i. 77].

And now this little group of men has altered history. The representative of the evil direction it was taking toward autocratic power lies dead before them. The direction to which it must be restored becomes emphatic in Cassius' cry of "Liberty, freedom, and enfranchisement" [III. i. 81]. Solemnly, and again like priests who have just sacrificed a victim, they kneel together and bathe their hands and swords in Caesar's blood. Brutus exclaims:

> Then walk we forth, even to the market
>   place;

And waving our red weapons o'er our
  heads,
Let's all cry, "Peace, freedom, and liberty!"
                              [III. i. 108-10]

If the conjunction of those red hands and weapons
with this slogan is not enough to bring an audience up with a start, the next passage will be, for
now the conspirators explicitly invoke the judgment of history on their deed. On the stages of theatres the world over, so they anticipate, this lofty
incident will be re-enacted, and

So oft as that shall be.
So often shall the knot of us be call'd
The men that gave their country liberty.
                              [III. i. 16-18]

We, the audience, recalling what actually did result
in Rome—the civil wars, the long line of despotic
emperors—cannot miss the irony of their prediction, an irony that insists on our recognizing that
this effort to control history is going to fail. Why
does it fail?

One reason why is shown us in the next few moments. The leader of this assault on history is, like
many another reformer, a man of high idealism,
who devoutly believes that the rest of the world is
like himself. It was just to kill Caesar—so he persuades himself—because he was a great threat to
freedom. It would not have been just to kill Antony,
and he vetoed the idea. Even now, when the consequence of that decision has come back to face him
in the shape of Antony's servant, kneeling before
him, he sees no reason to reconsider it. There are
good grounds for what they have done, he says; Antony will hear them, and be satisfied. With Antony,
who shortly arrives in person, he takes this line
again:

Our reasons are so full of good regard
That were you, Antony, the son of Caesar
You should be satisfied.

                              [III. i. 224-26]

With equal confidence in the rationality of man, he
puts by Cassius' fears of what Antony will do if allowed to address the people: "By your pardon; I will
myself into the pulpit first / And show the reason
of our Caesar's death" [III. i. 235-37]. Here is a man
so much a friend of Caesar's that he is still speaking of him as "our Caesar," so capable of rising to
what he takes to be his duty that he has taken on
the leadership of those who intend to kill him, so
trusting of common decency that he expects the
populace will respond to reason, and Antony to the
obligation laid on him by their permitting him to
speak. At such a man, one hardly knows whether
to laugh or cry.

The same mixture of feelings is likely to be stirring
in us as Brutus speaks to the people in III. ii. As everybody knows, this is a speech in what used to be
called the great liberal tradition, the tradition that
assumed, as our American founding fathers did,

that men in the mass are reasonable. It has therefore been made a prose oration, spare and terse in
diction, tightly patterned in syntax so that it requires close attention, and founded, with respect to
its argument, on three elements: the abstract sentiment of duty to the state (because he endangered
Rome, Caesar had to be slain); the abstract sentiment of political justice (because he was ambitious, Caesar deserved his fall); and the moral authority of the man Brutus. As long as that moral
authority is concretely before them in Brutus'
presence, the populace is impressed. But since
they are not trained minds, and only trained minds
respond accurately to abstractions, they do not understand the content of his argument at all, as one
of them indicates by shouting, "Let him be Caesar!" [III. ii. 51]. What moves them is the obvious
sincerity and the known integrity of the speaker;
and when he finishes, they are ready to carry him
off on their shoulders on that account alone, leaving Antony a vacant Forum. The fair-mindedness
of Brutus is thrilling but painful to behold as he
calms this triumphal surge in his favor, urges
them to stay and hear Antony, and then, in a moment very impressive dramatically as well as symbolically, walks off the stage, alone. We see then, if
we have not seen before, the first answer to the
question why the attack on history failed. It was
blinded, as it so often has been, by the very idealism that impelled it.

When Antony takes the rostrum, we begin to get a
second answer. It has been said by somebody that
in a school for demagogues this speech should be
the whole curriculum. Antony himself describes
its method when he observes in the preceding
scene, apropos of the effect of Caesar's dead body
on the messenger from Octavius, "Passion, I see, is
catching" [III. i. 283]. This is a statement that cannot be made about reason, as many a school teacher learns to his cost. I have not time at my disposal
to do anything like justice to Antony's speech, but
I should like to make the following summary
points.

First, Brutus formulates from the outset positive
propositions about Caesar and about his own motives, on no other authority than his own. Because
of his known integrity, Brutus can do this. Antony
takes the safer alternative of concealing propositions in questions, by which the audience's mind
is then guided to conclusions which seem its own:

He hath brought many captives to Rome,
Whose ransoms did the general coffers fill:
Did this in Caesar seem ambitious? . . .
You all did see that on the Lupercal
I thrice presented him a kingly crown,
Which he did thrice refuse: was this ambi-
  tion?

                           [III. ii. 88-90, 95-7]

How well Shakespeare knew his crowds can be
seen in the replies to Antony. Brutus, appealing to
their reason, was greeted with wild outbursts of

uncomprehending emotion: "Let him be Caesar!" [III. ii. 51]. Antony appeals only to their emotions and their pockets, but now they say, "Methinks there is much reason in his sayings" [III. ii. 108], and chew upon it seriously.

Second, Antony stirs up impulses and then thwarts them. He appeals to their curiosity and their greed in the matter of the will, but then he doesn't come clean on it. In the same manner, he stirs up their rage against the conspirators, yet always pretends to hold them back: "I fear I wrong the honorable men / Whose daggers have stabb'd Caesar; I do fear it" [III. ii. 151-52]. Third, and this is largely the technical means by which he accomplishes the stirring up, his speech is baited with irony. The passage just quoted is a typical specimen. So is the famous refrain, "For Brutus is an honorable man" [III. ii. 82, 87, 94]. Now the rhetorical value of irony is that it stimulates the mind to formulate the contrary, that is, the intended meaning. It stimulates what the psychologists of propaganda nowadays call the assertive factor. "Are you the one man in seven who shaves daily?" "Did your husband forget to kiss you this morning?" The advertiser's technique is not, of course, ironical, but it illustrates the effect.

Finally, Antony rests his case, not, like Brutus, on abstractions centering in the state and political justice, but on emotions centering in the individual listener. The first great crescendo of the speech, which culminates in the passage on Caesar's wounds, appeals first to pity and then to indignation. The second one, culminating in the reading of Caesar's will, appeals first to curiosity and greed and then to gratitude. The management of the will is particularly cunning: it is an item more concrete than any words could be, an actual tantalizing document that can be flashed before the eye. . . . It is described, at first vaguely, as being of such a sort that they would honor Caesar for it. Then, closer home, as something which would show "how Caesar lov'd you" [III. ii. 141]. Then, with an undisguised appeal to self-interest, as a testament that will make them his "heirs." The emotions aroused by this news enable Antony to make a final test of his ironical refrain about the "honorable men," and finding the results all that he had hoped, he can come down now among the crowd as one of them, and appeal directly to their feelings by appealing to his own: "If you have tears to shed, prepare to shed them now" [III. ii. 169].

The success of this direct appeal to passion can be seen at its close. Where formerly we had a populace, now we have a mob. Since it is a mob, its mind can be sealed against any later seepage of rationality back into it by the insinuation that reasoning is always false anyway—simply a surface covering up private grudges, like the "reason" they have heard from Brutus; whereas from Antony himself, the plain blunt friend of Caesar, they are getting the plain blunt truth and (a favorite trick of politicians) only what they already know to be the truth.

But also, since it is a mob and therefore will eventually cool off, it must be called back one final time to hear the will. Antony no longer needs this as an incentive to riot; the mingled rage and pity he has aroused will take care of that. But when the hangover comes, and you are remembering how that fellow looked swaying a little on the rope's end, with his eyes bugging out and the veins knotted at his temples, then it is good to have something really reasonable to cling to, like seventy-five drachmas (or even thirty pieces of silver) and some orchards along a river.

At about this point, it becomes impossible not to see that a second reason for the failure of the attack on history is what it left out of account—what all these Romans from the beginning, except Antony, have been trying to leave out of account: the phenomenon of feeling, the nonrational factor in men, in the world, in history itself—of which this blind infuriated mob is one kind of exemplification. Too secure in his own fancied suppression of the subrational, Brutus has failed altogether to reckon with its power. Thus he could seriously say to Antony in the passage I quoted earlier: Antony, even if you were "the son of Caesar / You should be satisfied," as if the feeling of a son for a murdered father could ever be "satisfied" by reasons. And thus, too, he could walk off the stage alone, urging the crowd to hear Antony, the very figure of embodied "reason," unaware that only the irrational is catching.

Meantime, the scene of the mob tearing Cinna the Poet to pieces simply for having the same name as one of the conspirators (III. iii) gives us our first taste of the chaos invoked by Antony when he stood alone over Caesar's corpse. And as we consider that prediction and this mob, we are bound to realize that there is a third reason why the attack on history failed. As we have seen already, history is only partly responsive to noble motives, only partly responsive to rationality. Now we see—what Shakespeare hinted in the beginning with those two episodes of Calpurnia and the soothsayer—that it is only partly responsive to human influence of any sort. With all their reasons, the conspirators and Caesar only carried out what the soothsayer foreknew. There is, in short, a determination in history, whether we call it natural or providential, which at least *helps* to shape our ends, "rough hew them how we will" [*Hamlet*, V. ii. 11]. One of the names of that factor in this play is Caesarism. Brutus put the point, all unconsciously, in that scene when the conspirators were gathered at his house. He said:

> We all stand up against the spirit of Caesar:
> And in the spirit of men there is no blood:

O that we then could come by Caesar's
　　spirit,
And not dismember Caesar! But, alas,
Caesar must bleed for it.
[II. i. 167-71]

Then Caesar did bleed for it; but his spirit, as Brutus' own remark should have told him, proved to be invulnerable. It was only set free by his assassination, and now, as Antony says, "ranging for revenge, . . . Shall in these confines with a monarch's voice / Cry 'Havoc' and let slip the dogs of war" [III. i. 272-73].

The rest of the play, I think, is self-explanatory. It is clear all through Acts IV and V that Brutus and Cassius are defeated before they begin to fight. Antony knows it and says so at V. i. Cassius knows it too. Cassius, an Epicurean in philosophy, and therefore one who has never heretofore believed in omens, now mistrusts his former rationalism: he suspects there may be something after all in those ravens, crows, and kites that wheel overhead. Brutus too mistrusts *his* rationalism. As a Stoic, his philosophy requires him to repudiate suicide, but he admits to Cassius that if the need comes he will repudiate philosophy instead. This, like Cassius' statement, is an unconscious admission of the force of unreason in human affairs, an unreason that makes its presence felt again and again during the great battle. Cassius, for instance, fails to realize that Octavius "Is overthrown by noble Brutus' power" [V. iii. 52], becomes the victim of a mistaken report of Titinius' death, runs on his sword crying, "Caesar, thou are reveng'd" [V. iii. 45], and is greeted, dead, by Brutus, in words that make still clearer their defeat by history: "O Julius Caesar, thou art mighty yet! / Thy spirit walks abroad, and turns our swords / In our own proper entrails" [V. iii. 94-6]. In the same vein, when it is Brutus' turn to die, we learn that the ghost of Caesar has reappeared, and he thrusts the sword home, saying, "Caesar, now be still" [V. v. 50].

To come then to a brief summary. Though I shouldn't care to be dogmatic about it, it seems clear to me that Shakespeare's primary theme in *Julius Caesar* has to do with the always ambiguous impact between man and history. During the first half of the play, what we are chiefly conscious of is the human will as a force in history—men making choices, controlling events. Our typical scenes are I. ii, where a man is trying to make up his mind; or II. i, where a man first reaches a decision and then, with his fellows, lays plans to implement it; or II. ii, where we have Decius Brutus persuading Caesar to decide to go to the senate house; or III. i and ii, where up through the assassination, and even up through Antony's speech, men are still, so to speak, impinging on history, moulding it to their conscious will.

But then comes a change. Though we still have men in action trying to mould their world (or else we would have no play at all), one senses a real shift in the direction of the impact. We begin to feel the insufficiency of noble aims, for history is also consequences; the insufficiency of reason and rational expectation, for the ultimate consequences of an act in history are unpredictable, and usually, by all human standards, illogical as well; and finally, the insufficiency of the human will itself, for there is always something to be reckoned with that is non-human and inscrutable. . . . Accordingly, in the second half of the play, our typical scenes are those like III. iii, where Antony has raised something that is no longer under his control; or like IV. i, where we see men acting as if, under the control of expediency or necessity or call it what you will, they no longer had wills of their own but prick down the names of nephews and brothers indiscriminately for slaughter; or like IV. iii and all the scenes thereafter, where we are constantly made to feel that Cassius and Brutus are in the hands of something bigger than they know.

In this light, we can see readily enough why it is that Shakespeare gave Julius Caesar that double character. The human Caesar who has human ailments and is a human friend is the Caesar that can be killed. The marmoreal Caesar, the everlasting Big Brother—the Napoleon, Mussolini, Hitler, Franco, Peron, Stalin, Kruschev, to mention only a handful of his more recent incarnations—that Caesar is the one who must repeatedly be killed but never dies, because he is in you, and you, and you, and me. Every classroom is a Rome, and there is no reason for any pupil, when he studies *Julius Caesar,* to imagine that this is ancient history. (pp. 322-36)

Maynard Mack, "Teaching Drama: 'Julius Caesar'," in Essays on the Teaching of English: Reports of the Yale Conferences on the Teaching of English, *edited by Edward J. Gordon and Edward S. Noyes, Appleton-Century-Crofts, Inc., 1960, pp. 320-36.*

RITUAL

Brents Stirling

[*Stirling discusses the significance of ritual and ceremony to the thematic design of* Julius Caesar. *According to the critic, the play is structured around a central ceremonial rite—* **Brutus***'s attempt to raise* **Caesar***'s assassination to the level of formal sacrifice. Nearly every scene prior to* **Caesar***'s murder, Stirling asserts, features a ceremony, which is then followed by a counter-ritual mocking it. The effect of these satirical scenes, the critic argues, is to reveal* **Brutus***'s self-deception in thinking he can purify* **Caesar***'s assassination through ceremony. After* **Caesar***'s death, Stirling con-*

*tinues, the hollowness of the ritual surrounding the murder and the savagery of the conspirators' act are further underscored by **Antony** in another series of counter-rituals. Stirling also notes that Shakespeare's portrait of **Brutus** is consistent with the sixteenth-century view of Roman history, for most Elizabethans acknowledged the figure's honorable intentions but questioned the validity of both his political goals and his efforts to justify **Caesar's** assassination.*]

Modern readers are prone to find the tragedy of Brutus in his rigid devotion to justice and fair play. Many members of the Globe audience, however, believed that his virtues were complicated by self-deception and doubtful principle. In sixteenth-century views of history the conspiracy against Caesar often represented a flouting of unitary sovereignty . . . and exemplified the anarchy thought to accompany "democratic" or constitutional checks upon authority. Certain judgments of Elizabethan political writers who refer to Brutus are quite clear upon this point. Although naturally aware of his disinterested honor and liberality, contemporary audiences could thus perceive in him a conflict between questionable goals and honorable action, a contradiction lying in his attempt to redeem morally confused ends by morally clarified means. The Elizabethan tragedy of Brutus, like that of Othello, is marked by an integrity of conduct which leads the protagonist into evil and measures him in his error.

The distinction between modern and Elizabethan views of *Julius Caesar* is not the point of our inquiry, but it is a necessary beginning, for the older view of Brutus determines both the symbolic quality and the structure of the play. I hope to show that a sixteenth-century idea of Brutus is as thoroughly related to Shakespeare's art as it is to his meaning.

When a dramatist wishes to present an idea, his traditional method, of course, is to settle upon an episode in which the idea arises naturally but vividly from action and situation. Such an episode in *Julius Caesar* is the one in which Brutus resolves to exalt not only the mission but the tactics of conspiracy: having accepted republicanism as an honorable end, he sets out to dignify assassination, the means, by lifting it to a level of rite and ceremony. In II. i, as Cassius urges the killing of Antony as a necessary accompaniment to the death of Caesar, Brutus declares that "such a course will seem too bloody . . . / To cut the head off and then hack the limbs" [II. i. 162-63]. With this thought a sense of purpose comes over him: "Let's be sacrificers, but not butchers, Caius" [II. i. 166]. Here his conflict seems to be resolved, and for the first time he is more than a reluctant presence among the conspirators as he expands the theme which ends his hesitation and frees his moral imagination:

> We all stand up against the spirit of Caesar,

> And in the spirit of men there is no blood;
> Oh, that we then could come by Caesar's spirit,
> And not dismember Caesar! But, alas,
> Caesar must bleed for it! And, gentle friends,
> Let's kill him boldly, but not wrathfully;
> Let's carve him as a dish fit for the gods,
> Not hew him as a carcass fit for hounds.
> [II. i. 167-74]

This proposed conversion of bloodshed to ritual is the manner in which an abstract Brutus will be presented in terms of concrete art. From the suggestion of Plutarch that Brutus' first error lay in sparing Antony, Shakespeare moves to the image of Antony as a limb of Caesar, a limb not to be hacked because hacking is no part of ceremonial sacrifice. From Plutarch's description of Brutus as high-minded, gentle and disinterested, Shakespeare proceeds to the Brutus of symbolic action. Gentleness and disinterestedness become embodied in the act of "unwrathful" blood sacrifice. High-mindedness becomes objectified in ceremonial observance.

A skeptical reader may ask why the episode just described is any more significant than a number of others such as Brutus' scene with Portia or his quarrel with Cassius. If more significant, it is so only because of its relation to a thematic design. I agree, moreover, that Shakespeare gains his effects by variety; as a recognition, in fact, of his complexity I hope to show that the structure of *Julius Caesar* is marked by reference both varied and apt to Brutus' sacrificial rite, and that this process includes expository preparation in earlier scenes, emphasis upon "mock-ceremony" in both earlier and later scenes, and repeated comment by Antony upon butchery under the guise of sacrifice— ironical comment which takes final form in the parley before Philippi.

Derived in large measure from Plutarch, but never mechanically or unselectively, the theme of incantation and ritual is thus prominent throughout *Julius Caesar,* and this is no less true at the beginning than during the crucial episodes of Acts II and III. In the opening scene of the play we are confronted with a Roman populace rebuked by Marullus for ceremonial idolatry of Caesar:

> And do you now put on your best attire?
> And do you now cull out a holiday?
> And do you now strew flowers in his way
> That comes in triumph over Pompey's blood?
> [I. i. 48-51]

For this transgression Marullus prescribes a counter-observance by the citizens in immediate expiation of their folly:

> Run to your houses, fall upon your knees,
> Pray to the gods to intermit this plague
> That needs must light on this ingratitude.
> [I. i. 53-5]

Mark Antony and the body of Caesar. Act III, scene i. By Bernard Partridge.

based upon Plutarch's description of the "feast Lupercalia" in which the rite of touching or striking barren women by runners of the course is made prominent. Caesar, moreover, after ordering Calpurnia to be so touched by Antony, commands: "Set on; and leave no ceremony out" [I. ii. 11]. It can be said, in fact, that the whole of this scene is written with ceremonial observance as a background. Its beginning, already described, is followed by a touch of solemnity in the soothsayer's words; next comes its main expository function, the sounding of Brutus by Cassius, and throughout this interchange come at intervals the shouts and flourishes of a symbolic spectacle. When the scene is again varied by a formal reentry and exit of Caesar's train, Casca remains behind to make a mockery of the rite which has loomed so large from off-stage. Significantly, in Casca's travesty of the ceremonial crown-offering and of the token offering by Caesar of his throat for cutting, Shakespeare has added a satirical note which does not appear in Plutarch.

The process, then, in each of the two opening episodes has been the bringing of serious ritual into great prominence, and of subjecting it to satirical treatment. In the first scene the tribunes denounce the punctilio planned for Caesar's entry, send the idolatrous crowd to rites of purification, and set off themselves to desecrate the devotional images. In the second scene a multiple emphasis of ceremony is capped by Casca's satire which twists the crown ritual into imbecile mummery. At this point, and in conformity with the mood set by Casca, occurs Cassius' mockery in soliloquy of Brutus:

> Well, Brutus, thou art noble; yet I see
> Thy honorable mettle may be wrought
> From that it is dispos'd; therefore it is meet
> That noble minds keep ever with their
>   likes;
> For who is so firm that cannot be seduc'd?
>   [I. ii. 308-12]

The next scene [I. iii] is packed with omens and supernatural portents, a note which is carried directly into II. i where Brutus, on receiving the mysterious papers which have been left to prompt his action, remarks,

> The exhalations whizzing in the air
> Give so much light that I may read by
>   them.
>   [II. i. 44-5]

Appropriately, the letters read under this weird glow evoke his first real commitment to the "cause":

> O Rome, I make thee promise
> If the redress will follow, thou receivest
> Thy full petition at the hand of Brutus!
>   [II. i. 56-8]

Now appear his lines on the interim "between the acting of a dreadful thing / And the first motion" in which "the state of man / Like to a little kingdom, suffers then / The nature of a insurrection"

To which Flavius adds:

> Go, go, good countrymen, and for this
>   fault,
> Assemble all the poor men of your sort;
> Draw them to Tiber banks, and weep your
>   tears
> Into the channel, till the lowest stream
> Do kiss the most exalted shores of all.
>   [I. i. 56-60]

And after committing the populace to these rites of atonement for their festal celebration of Caesar, the two tribunes themselves leave to remove the devotional symbols set up for his welcoming. "Go you . . . towards the Capitol; / This way will I. Disrobe the images / If you do find them decked with ceremonies. / . . . let no images / Be hung with Caesar's trophies" [I. i. 63-5, 68-9]. It is the hope of Flavius that these disenchantments will make Caesar "fly an ordinary pitch, / Who else would soar above the view of men" [I. i. 73-4].

Act I, scene ii is equally unusual in carrying the theme of ritual. It is apparent that Shakespeare had a wide choice of means for staging the entry of Caesar and his retinue; yet he selects an entry

[II. i. 63-4, 67-9]. This conventional symbolizing of political convulsion by inward insurrection is followed by the soliloquy on conspiracy:

> O, then by day
> Where wilt thou find a cavern dark
>   enough
> To mask thy monstrous visage? Seek
>   none, Conspiracy!
> Hide it in smiles and affability.
>   [II. i. 79-82]

The conflict within Brutus thus becomes clear in this scene. First, the participant in revolution suffers revolution within himself; then the hater of conspiracy and lover of plain dealing must call upon Conspiracy to hide in smiling courtesy.

We have now reached the critical point [II. i. 154ff.] to which attention was first called, an outward presentation of Brutus' crisis through his acceptance of an assassin's role upon condition that the assassins become sacrificers. Already a theme well established in preceding scenes, the idea of ritual is again made prominent. As the soliloquy on conspiracy closes, the plotters gather, and the issue becomes the taking of an oath. Brutus rejects this as an idle ceremony unsuited to men joined in the honesty of a cause and turns now to the prospect of Caesar's death. This time, however, honorable men do need ceremony, ceremony which will purify the violent act of all taint of butchery and raise it to the level of sacrifice. But although Brutus has steadied himself with a formula his conflict is still unresolved, for as he sets his course he "unconsciously" reveals the evasion which Antony later will amplify: to transmute political killing into ritual is to cloak it with appearances. We began with Brutus' passage on carving Caesar as a dish for the gods; these are the lines which complete it:

> And let our hearts, as subtle masters do,
> Stir up their servants to an act of rage,
> And after seem to chide 'em. This shall
>   make
> Our purpose necessary and not envious;
> Which so appearing to the common eyes,
> We shall be called purgers, not murderers.
>   [II. i. 175-80]

The contradiction is interesting. In an anticlimax, Brutus has ended his great invocation to ritual with a note on practical politics: our hearts shall stir us and afterward seem to chide us; we shall thus "appear" to the citizenry as purgers, not murderers.

Shakespeare never presents Brutus as a demagogue, but there are ironical traces of the politician in him. . . . It is curious, in fact, that although Brutus is commonly thought to be unconcerned over public favor, he expresses clear concern for it in the passage just quoted and in III. i. 244-51, where he sanctions Antony's funeral speech only if Antony agrees to tell the crowd that he speaks by generous permission, and only if he agrees to utter

no evil of the conspiracy. Nor is Brutus' speech in the Forum wholly the nonpolitical performance it is supposed to be; certainly Shakespeare's Roman citizens are the best judges of it, and they react tempestuously. Although compressed, it scarcely discloses aloofness or an avoidance of popular emotive themes.

Act II, scene ii now shifts to the house of Caesar, but the emphasis on ritual continues as before. With dramatic irony, in view of Brutus' recent lines on sacrificial murder, Caesar commands, "Go bid the priests do present sacrifice" [II. ii. 5]. Calpurnia who has "never stood on ceremonies" (omens) is now terrified by them [II. ii. 13]. News comes that the augurers, plucking the entrails of an offering, have failed to find a heart. Calpurnia has dreamed that smiling Romans have laved their hands in blood running from Caesar's statue, and Decius Brutus gives this its favorable interpretation which sends Caesar to his death.

The vivid assassination scene carries out Brutus' ritual prescription in dramatic detail, for the killing is staged with a formalized approach, ending in kneeling, by one conspirator after another until the victim is surrounded. This is met by a series of retorts from Caesar ending in "Hence! Wilt thou lift up Olympus," and the "sacrifice" is climaxed with his "Et tu Brute!" [III. i. 74, 77]. The conspirators ceremonially bathe their hands in Caesar's blood, and Brutus pronounces upon "this our lofty scene" with the prophecy that it "shall be acted over / In states unborn and accents yet unknown!" [III. i. 112-13].

The mockery in counterritual now begins as a servant of Antony enters and confronts Brutus:

> Thus, Brutus, did my master bid me
>   kneel,
> Thus did Mark Antony bid me fall down;
> And being prostrate, thus he bade me say:
> Brutus is noble, wise, valiant, and honest.
>   [III. i. 123-26]

Here a threefold repetition, "kneel," "fall down," and "being prostrate," brings the ceremonial irony close to satire. Following this worship of the new idol by his messenger, Antony appears in person and with dramatic timing offers himself as a victim. In one speech he evokes both the holy scene which the conspirators so desired and the savagery which underlay it:

> Now, whilst your purpled hands do reek
>   and smoke,
> Fulfill your pleasure. Live a thousand
>   years,
> I shall not find myself so apt to die;
> No place will please me so, no mean of
>   death,
> As here by Caesar, and by you cut off.
>   [III. i. 158-62]

The murder scene is thus hallowed by Antony in a manner which quite reverses its sanctification by the conspirators. Brutus, forbearing, attempts to mollify Antony with his cherished theme of purgation:

> Our hearts you see not. They are pitiful,
> And pity to the general wrong of Rome—
> As fire drives out fire, so pity pity—
> Hath done this deed on Caesar.
>
> [III. i. 169-72]

Antony's response is again one of counterceremony, the shaking of hands in formal sequence which serves to make each conspirator stand alone and unprotected by the rite of blood which had united him with the others. The assassins had agreed as a token of solidarity that each of them should stab Caesar. Antony seems to allude to this:

> Let each man render me his bloody hand.
> First, Marcus Brutus, will I shake with you;
> Now, Caius Cassius, do I take your hand;
> Now, Decius Brutus, yours; now yours, Mettellus;
> Yours, Cinna; and, my valiant Casca, yours;
> Though last, not least in love yours, good Trebonius.
> Gentlemen all—alas what shall I say?
>
> [III. i. 184-90]

It is then that Antony, addressing the body of Caesar, suddenly delivers his first profanation of the ritual sacrifice:

> Here wast thou bay'd brave hart;
> Here didst thou fall; and here thy hunters stand,
> Sign'd in thy spoil, and crimson'd in thy lethe.
>
> [III. i. 204-06]

And lest the allusion escape, Shakespeare continues Antony's inversion of Brutus' ceremonial formula: the dish carved for the gods is doubly transformed into the carcass hewn for hounds with further hunting metaphors of Caesar as a hart in the forest and as "a deer strucken by many princes" [III. i. 209]. Brutus agrees to give reasons why Caesar was dangerous, "or else were this a savage spectacle" [III. i. 223], and the stage is set for what may be called the play's chief counterritual. Only Brutus, who planned the rite of sacrifice, could with such apt irony arrange the "true rites" and "ceremonies" which are to doom the conspiracy.

> I will myself into the pulpit first
> And show the reason of our Caesar's death.
> What Antony shall speak, I will protest
> He speaks by leave and by permission,
> And that we are contented Caesar shall
> Have all true rites and lawful ceremonies.
>
> [III. i. 236-41]

But exactly after the manner of his speech announcing the ritual sacrifice [II. i] Brutus concludes again on a note of policy: "It shall advantage more than do us wrong" [III. i. 242].

Next follows Antony *solus* [alone] rendering his prophecy of "domestic fury and fierce civil strife" [III. i. 263] symbolized in Caesar's ghost which will

> Cry "Havoc," and let slip the dogs of war,
> That this foul deed shall smell above the earth.
>
> [III. i. 273-74]

The passage is similar in utterance, function, and dramatic placement to Carlisle's prophecy on the deposition of Richard II, and for that reason it is to be taken seriously as a choric interpretation of Caesar's death. Significantly, the beginning lines again deride Brutus' erstwhile phrase, "sacrificers but not butchers":

> O, pardon me, thou bleeding piece of earth,
> That I am meek and gentle with these butchers!
>
> [III. i. 254-55]

It is unnecessary to elaborate upon the Forum scene; Antony's oration follows the speech of Brutus with consequences familiar to all readers. But there is an element in Antony's turning of the tables which is just as remarkable as the well-known irony of his references to "honorable men." If we remember that Shakespeare has emphasized ritual at various planes of seriousness and of derision, the conclusion of Antony's speech to the populace will link itself with the previous theme. For here Antony reenacts the death of Caesar in a ritual of his own, one intended to show that the original "lofty scene" presented a base carnage. Holding Caesar's bloody mantle as a talisman, he reproduces *seriatim* [in a series] the sacrificial strokes, but he does so in terms of the "rent" Casca made and the "cursed steel" that Brutus plucked away with the blood of Caesar following it. Again, each conspirator had struck individually at Caesar and had symbolically involved himself with the others; for the second time Antony reminds us of this ritual bond by recounting each stroke, and his recreation of the rite becomes a mockery of it. Brutus' transformation of blood into the heady wine of sacrifice is reversed both in substance and in ceremony.

For the "realists" among the conspirators what has occurred can be summed up in the bare action of the play: the killing of Caesar has been accomplished, but the fruits of it have been spoiled by Brutus' insistence that Antony live and that he speak at Caesar's funeral. "The which," as [Thomas North's translation of] Plutarch has it, "marred all." With reference to Brutus, however, something much more significant has been enacted; the "insurrection," the contradiction, within him has taken outward form in his attempt to purify assassination through ceremony. This act, not to be found in Plutarch, symbolizes the "Elizabethan"

Brutus compelled by honor to join with conspirators but required by conscience to reject Conspiracy.

We have followed the ritual theme in *Julius Caesar* from early scenes to the point of Antony's oration, at which it is completely defined. There remains, however, a terminal appearance of the theme in the first scene of Act V. The ultimate clash between the idealism of Brutus and Antony's contempt for it comes during the parley on the eve of Phillippi, at which Antony again drives home the old issue of ceremonial imposture. Brutus has observed that his enemy wisely threats before he stings; the reply is Antony's last disposition of the sacrificial rite:

> Villains, you did not so when your vile daggers
> Hack'd one another in the sides of Caesar,
> You show'd your teeth like apes, and fawn'd like hounds,
> And bow'd like bondmen, kissing Caesar's feet;
> Whilst damned Casca, like a cur, behind
> Struck Caesar on the neck.
>
> [V. i. 39-44]

Antony invokes the "hacking" which Brutus earlier foreswore, and he again inverts the cherished formula of sacrifice: once more the dish carved for gods becomes the carcass hewn for hounds. Over the body of Caesar he had previously employed the hunting-hound figure ("Here wast thou bay'd, brave hart."); the apes, the hounds, and the cur of these lines complete his vengeful irony of metaphor.

What, finally, is to be inferred from Antony's concluding passage on "the noblest Roman of them all" [V. v. 68]? Commonly found there is a broad vindication of Brutus which would deny an ironical interpretation. When Antony's elegiac speech is read plainly, however, its meaning is quite limited: it declares simply that Brutus was the only conspirator untouched by envy, and that, in intention, he acted "in a general honest thought / And common good to all" [V. v. 71-2]. The Elizabethan view of Brutus as tragically misguided is thus consistent with Anthony's pronouncement that he was the only disinterested member of the conspiracy. But Brutus is not to be summed up in an epitaph; as the impersonal member of a conspiracy motivated largely by personal ends, he sought in a complex way to resolve his contradiction by depersonalizing, ritualizing, the means.

Shakespeare's achievement, however, is not confined to the characterization of a major figure, for we have seen that the ceremonial motive extends beyond the personality of Brutus into the structure of the play. Exposition stressing the idea of ritual observance leads to the episode in which Brutus formulates the "sacrifice," and clear resolution of the idea follows in event and commentary. Struc-

tural craftsmanship thus supplements characterization and the two combine, as in *Richard II,* to state the political philosophy implicit in the play. (pp. 34-43)

Brents Stirling, " 'Or Else Were This a Savage Spectacle' [*Ritual in 'Julius Caesar'*]," *in* Shakespeare, The Tragedies: A Collection of Critical Essays, *edited by Alfred Harbage, Prentice-Hall, Inc., 1964, pp. 34-43.*

IMAGERY AND LANGUAGE

Maurice Charney

[*Charney provides a detailed analysis of the principal image patterns in* Julius Caesar—*the storm and its supernatural elements, blood, and fire—and demonstrates how each set of images connotes two contradictory meanings that contribute to the thematic ambiguity of the play. According to the critic, the violent storm in Act I, scene iii can be interpreted as evidence of either the evil of* **Caesar's** *tyranny or the evil of the conspirators who plot to assassinate him. Charney also suggests that blood imagery in the play may, on the one hand, be viewed as a symbol of the injustice of* **Caesar's** *murder and the conspirators' guilt or, on the other, as a ritual blood-letting that restores the Roman political state to new health. Similarly, fire may be regarded as a purifying force that eliminates political treachery (either* **Caesar's** *tyranny or the evil of the conspiracy) or as a destructive force symbolizing civil strife. Additionally, the critic points out, fire imagery is used to signify passion and its power to enkindle emotion. Charney also stresses that regardless of the way the storm, blood, and fire imagery are interpreted in* Julius Caesar, *the action of the play progresses from chaos to restoration of order.*]

1

. . . The chief image themes in *Julius Caesar* are the storm and its portents, blood, and fire. All of these have two opposed meanings, depending upon one's point of view. With reference to the conspirators, the storm and its portents indicate the evil of Caesar's tyranny in the body politic of Rome, while blood and fire are the means of purging and purifying this evil. But with reference to Caesar and his party, the storm and its portents indicate the evil of conspiracy that is shaking the body politic of Rome, while blood and fire are the signs of assassination and civil strife this evil brings in its wake. From either point of view, however, the action of the play moves from disorder (Caesar's tyranny or the conspiracy) to an uneasy restoration of order at the end (murder of Caesar or destruction of the conspiracy). These issues are never clearly resolved in the play. Although the defeat and death of the conspirators seem to be a comment on the futility of their enterprise, the rise of Antony and Octavius is by no means an affirmation of justice, truth, and human values.

The imagery of the storm and its portents allows Shakespeare to range freely among the correspondences of man, the state, and the cosmos. The tempest in nature reflects disturbances in man and the state, or, conversely, these disturbances are projected or externalized in the tempest. (pp. 42-3)

The final couplet of Cassius' soliloquy in I. ii serves as a prologue to the storm theme:

> And after this let Caesar seat him sure,
> For we will shake him, or worse days endure.
>
> [I. ii. 321-22]

The thunder and lightning of I. iii follow immediately as a comment of the heavens on Cassius' words; this is the beginning of "worse days" for Rome. After the thunder and lightning, Casca enters "breathless" and staring [I. iii. 2], with his sword drawn [I. iii. 19], and in great anxiety. This disordered entrance conveys an immediate visual impression of the storm's awesome power, for the present Casca is entirely different from the blunt and somewhat cynical figure of I. ii. He asks Cicero with obvious agitation: "Are not you mov'd when all the sway of earth / Shakes like a thing unfirm?" [I. iii. 3-4]. There has never been such a storm as this, so terrible and so full of unnatural prodigies, for

> never till to-night, never till now,
> Did I go through a tempest dropping fire.
> Either there is a civil strife in heaven,
> Or else the world, too saucy with the gods,
> Incenses them to send destruction.
>
> [I. iii. 9-13]

Casca seeks the meaning of the storm in the relations between the "gods" and the "world," and the "civil strife in heaven" will soon serve as a pattern for the conflict on earth.

Casca goes on to enumerate wonders—the slave with the burning hand, the lion near the Capitol, the men in fire seen by women, the screech-owl at noon in the market place—they are all impossible things that the gods have sent as signs and warnings to men:

> When these prodigies
> Do so conjointly meet, let not men say
> 'These are their reasons—they are natural,'
> For I believe they are portentous things
> Unto the climate that they point upon.
>
> [I. iii. 28-32]

These prodigies serve as a choric comment on the evil that is taking place (growing conspiracy) and on the evil that is about to occur (murder of Caesar and consequent civil war).

The entrance of Cassius marks a movement from description of the storm to an application of its meaning. Since it signifies so much, this is indeed "A very pleasing night" [I. iii. 43] to Cassius, who has walked about the streets

> And, thus unbraced, Casca, as you see,
> Have bar'd my bosom to the thunder-stone;
> And when the cross blue lightning seem'd to open
> The breast of heaven, I did present myself
> Even in the aim and very flash of it.
>
> [I. iii. 48-52]

Cassius does not remain in fear and trembling like Casca, because the "true cause" [I. iii. 62] of this "strange impatience of the heavens" [I. iii. 61] is at once apparent:

> Why all these fires, why all these gliding ghosts,
> Why birds and beasts, from quality and kind;
> Why old men, fools, and children calculate;
> Why all these things change from their ordinance,
> Their natures, and preformed faculties,
> To monstrous quality—why, you shall find
> That heaven hath infus'd them with these spirits
> To make them instruments of fear and warning
> Unto some monstrous state.
>
> [I. iii. 63-71]

This is a key passage for understanding the effect of the storm, and unnaturalness and disorder are emphasized in every line. These prodigies represent a twisting of things from their natural course ("ordinance") and essential being ("preformed faculties") into a "monstrous" sort. The word "monstrous" specifically links the condition of the state with what is occurring in external nature, and it is a strong indication of disorder. Remember that conspiracy wears a "monstrous visage" [II. i. 81], and that the Ghost of Caesar is to Brutus a "monstrous apparition" [IV. iii. 277]. Cassius proceeds to identify the storm and its portents with Caesar, the ruler of the "monstrous state":

> Now could I, Casca, name to thee a man
> Most like this dreadful night
> That thunders, lightens, opens graves, and roars
> As doth the lion in the Capitol;
> A man no mightier than thyself or me
> In personal action, yet prodigious grown
> And fearful, as these strange eruptions are.
>
> [I. iii. 72-8]

The analogy is very close, and Cassius' identification is driven home by the naïve question of Casca: " 'Tis Caesar that you mean. Is it not, Cassius?" [I. iii. 79].

The sense of storm is maintained in II. i by several references, although it remains a minor motif. Brutus comments that "The exhalations, whizzing in the air, / Give so much light that I may read by them" [II. i. 44-5]. Further, Cassius wonders whether Caesar will stay away from the Capitol because of

> these apparent prodigies,
> The unaccustom'd terror of this night,
> And the persuasion of his augurers.
> [II. i. 198-200]

Cassius fears that Caesar may be interpreting the signs of the storm as he himself has done in I. iii. In the dialogue between Brutus and Portia atmospheric detail is added to our feeling of the storm by references to the "raw cold morning" [II. i. 236], the "dank morning" [II. i. 263], and the "rheumy and unpurged air" [II. i. 266].

At the very end of the scene there is a stage direction, *"Thunder,"* and the next scene opens with *"Thunder and lightning."* Julius Caesar appears in his dressing gown ("nightgown") and comments on what is occurring:

> Nor heaven nor earth have been at peace
>   to-night.
> Thrice hath Calphurnia in her sleep cried
>   out
> 'Help, ho! They murther Caesar!'
> [II. ii. 1-3]

To Calphurnia the storm and its portents point to the murder of Caesar, and we should remember that this is the same storm in which Casca and Cassius have actually plotted his death, and in which Brutus has been won to the conspiracy. Calphurnia tries to dissuade Caesar from going forth by an account of unnatural prodigies: "O Caesar, these things are beyond all use, / And I do fear them!" [II. ii. 25-6]. "Use" is a word for what is to be expected, what is natural, the proper "ordinance" [II. iii. 66] of things. Calphurnia fears that the portents by their very magnitude cry out the death of Caesar; there is a proportion in these things, and portents are not the same for all men:

> When beggars die there are no comets
>   seen;
> The heavens themselves blaze forth the
>   death of princes.
> [II. ii. 30-1]

Finally, we have Calphurnia's dream of Caesar's statue running pure blood, which she interprets as "warnings and portents / And evils imminent" [II. ii. 80-1].

2

The central issue about the meaning of *Julius Caesar* is raised most forcefully and vividly by the imagery of blood. If the murder of Caesar is indeed a "savage spectacle" [III. i. 223], then the blood with which the conspirators are smeared "Up to

the elbows" [III. i. 107] is the sign of their guilt. But if the murder of Caesar is a ritual blood-letting of the body politic of Rome, then blood is the sign of purification and new life. The latter point of view marks the tragedy of Brutus, for he cannot foresee that his high-minded but specious motives will be drowned in the bloodiness of murder and civil strife. He is tragically unable to bridge the gap between reasons and acts.

The blood theme begins in II. i, where it becomes a powerful symbol for the conspiracy. The question of what to do with Antony after the murder of Caesar is a crucial one. The shrewd and practical Cassius wants to kill him, but Brutus objects and makes . . . the first great tactical error of his career. This decision also indicates the rift between the other conspirators and Brutus, who argues his position from the analogy between the bodies human and politic:

> Our course will seem too bloody, Caius
>   Cassius,
> To cut the head off and then hack the
>   limbs,
> Like wrath in death and envy afterwards;
> For Antony is but a limb of Caesar.
> [II. i. 162-65]

He thinks of blood as the symbol of common murder, and he fears the stain of its guilt. The slaying of Caesar is a necessary and beneficial act, but Brutus wishes that there were no blood:

> Let's be sacrificers, but not butchers,
>   Caius.
> We all stand up against the spirit of Cae-
>   sar,
> And in the spirit of men there is no blood.
> O that we then could come by Caesar's
>   spirit
> And not dismember Caesar! But, alas,
> Caesar must bleed for it!
> [II. i. 166-71]

This is one of the most important passages in the play for showing the tragic wrongness of Brutus. The murder of Caesar proves to be not a loving sacrifice, but only a fruitless act of butchery, and its bloodiness is stressed as significantly as the murder of Duncan in *Macbeth*. When all is done, only the body of Caesar has been killed, not the spirit, which stays very much alive in Antony and Octavius and wins vengeance in civil strife. The meaning of the play can almost be formulated by taking the negative of all these statements of Brutus. (pp. 44-9)

Blood imagery is of greatest importance in III. i, where it is not only a repeated verbal theme, but also enters into the stage action. Animal blood from concealed bladders or sponges was probably used to represent Caesar's murder on the Elizabethan stage, and, from all indications, there was a frank emphasis on the spectacular effects of murder scenes. (p. 51)

A number of blood images in III. i show Caesar in the height of pride just before his fall. He thrusts aside Metellus Cimber, who "might fire the blood of ordinary men" [III. i. 37], but not Caesar's. He does not bear "such rebel blood" [III. i. 40] that can be melted by emotional persuasion, and the chief connotation of "blood" is the passion that Caesar forswears. The world is full of men who are "flesh and blood, and apprehensive" [III. i. 67], but only Caesar remains in cold, unchanging constancy. Yet ten lines later he is stabbed to death as readily as any mortal, and the blood that would not be fired or thawed now flows freely from the dagger wounds of the conspirators.

From this point until the end of the play the fact of Caesar's assassination is kept constantly before the audience, and this is done to a large extent by blood imagery. Of course, Caesar's bloody and rent body is on stage through all of this scene, and at a number of important moments [III. i. 148-50, 194-210, 254-75] Antony addresses it as if it were a living presence; Octavius' Servant does the same [III. i. 281]. In the next scene it is absent only for the short time of Brutus' oration. At line 41 Antony and others enter with the body, which remains on stage until removed by the plebeians for the funeral pyre [s.d., III. ii. 259]. Thus Caesar's body dominates the scene for almost 450 lines after his death. The body plays a conspicuous role during Antony's funeral oration, but throughout the time it is on stage it serves as a visible indictment of the conspirators. Its commanding presence on stage, possibly on the elevated platform or dais on which the "throne" usually stood, keeps the audience aware of the crime of assassination.

Shortly after the murder, Brutus directs the conspirators in a fearful blood ritual:

> Stoop, Romans, stoop,
> And let us bathe our hands in Caesar's
>   blood
> Up to the elbows and besmear our swords.
> Then walk we forth, even to the market
>   place,
> And waving our red weapons o'er our
>   heads,
> Let's all cry 'Peace, freedom, and liberty!'
>   [III. i. 105-10]

This action fulfills the prophecy of Calphurnia's dream [II. ii. 76-9], and we may assume that stage blood was liberally used for these effects, since the conspirators' hands and swords need to remain very vividly bloody for about 150 lines (until the exit at III. i. 253). The blood ritual that Brutus began at II. i. 166 seems now a sacrilege rather than a consecration. It is continued as Cassius takes up Brutus' invocation:

> Stoop then and wash. How many ages
>   hence
> Shall this our lofty scene be acted over
> In states unborn and accents yet un-
>   known!

[III. i. 111-13]

And Brutus answers antiphonally in the same spirit of uncontrolled exaltation:

> How many times shall Caesar bleed in
>   sport,
> That now on Pompey's basis lies along
> No worthier than the dust!
>   [III. i. 114-16]

The eyes of the conspirators are on posterity, which they are sure will approve their present acts. These speeches represent the highest point in the development of the conspirators; with the entrance of Antony's Servant their downward course begins.

Antony's speeches in this scene reiterate "blood" both as the symbol of the murdered Caesar and as the sign of the conspirators' guilt. The double emphasis is made almost in his first words:

> I know not, gentlemen, what you intend,
> Who else must be let blood, who else is
>   rank.
> If I myself, there is no hour so fit
> As Caesar's death's hour; nor no instru-
>   ment
> Of half that worth as those your swords,
>   made rich
> With the most noble blood of all this
>   world.
> I do beseech ye, if you bear me hard,
> Now, whilst your purpled hands do reek
>   and smoke,
> Fulfil your pleasure.
>   [III. i. 151-59]

Antony's thoughts run on blood as he boldly dares the conspirators to kill him, too. Their hands and swords have been bathed in Caesar's blood, whose visual signs they now flaunt to all Rome as justification of their deed. Throughout this scene Antony provides a bitter, sarcastic commentary on these "purpled hands" and swords, for they bear the stain of guilt upon them just as surely as Macbeth's hands and dagger do. (pp. 51-4)

[It] is the bloody hands of the conspirators that Antony is insisting on as the outward badge of their guilt. In a supremely ironic ceremony Antony shakes each of their hands:

> Let each man render me his bloody hand.
> First, Marcus Brutus, will I shake with
>   you;
> Next, Caius Cassius, do I take your hand;
> Now, Decius Brutus, yours; now yours,
>   Metellus;
> Yours, Cinna; and, my valiant Casca,
>   yours.
> Though last, not least in love, yours, good
>   Trebonius.
>   [III. i. 184-89]

This ceremony parallels the one by which Brutus entered the conspiracy: "Give me your hands all over, one by one" [II. i. 112]. We need to supply the all-important expression and attitude of Antony here, the mingling of intense loathing and feigned reconciliation. From this handshaking Antony acquires "bloody fingers" [III. i. 198] . . . , and he speaks as if to undo the guilty ritual in which he has participated:

> Pardon me, Julius! Here wast thou bay'd,
>   brave hart;
> Here didst thou fall; and here thy hunters
>   stand,
> Sign'd in thy spoil, and crimson'd in they
>   lethe.
> O world, thou wast the forest to this hart;
> And this indeed, O world, the heart of thee!
> How like a deer, stroken by many princes,
> Dost thou here lie!
>
> [III. i. 204-10]

He has almost gone too far, and Cassius says menacingly "Mark Antony—" [III. i. 211], but Brutus, who himself loved Caesar, will now shield Antony. The hunting imagery of this speech stresses butchery rather than the sacrifice Brutus hoped for in [II. i. 166ff.]. A grotesque pun demonstrates that the "heart" of the world can be killed bloodily like a "hart." Perhaps "lethe," too, is a part of this imagery and refers to the marking of hunters with the blood of a slain deer. When Cassius asks Antony if he will be a friend, Antony answers ironically: "Therefore I took your hands . . . " [III. i. 218]. By sharing in Caesar's blood he has seemed to condone the murder, but behind this mask vengeance for Caesar is being prepared. (pp. 54-5)

Antony's soliloquy after the conspirators leave says directly and forcefully what has already been said ironically.. . . . Antony apologizes to the dead Caesar for his conciliatory role with "these butchers" [III. i. 255], and he prophesies the vengeance of blood for blood that must follow:

> Woe to the hand that shed this costly
>   blood!
> Over thy wounds now do I prophesy
> (Which, like dumb mouths, do ope their
>   ruby lips
> To beg the voice and utterance of my
>   tongue),
> A curse shall light upon the limbs of men;
> Domestic fury and fierce civil strife
> Shall cumber all the parts of Italy;
> Blood and destruction shall be so in use
> And dreadful objects so familiar
> That mothers shall but smile when they
>   behold
> Their infants quartered with the hands of
>   war,
> All pity chok'd with custom of fell
>   deeds. . . .
>
> [III. i. 258-69]

Antony's vision of civil war is like the Bishop of Carlisle's in *Richard II* [IV. i. 136-49], and both serve as turning points in the action. The conspirators have shed Caesar's "costly" (precious) blood,

which will indeed prove "costly" (dear, expensive) to them.

In III. i we learn that Antony will use his funeral oration to see "how the people take / The cruel issue of these bloody men . . . " [III. i. 293-94], and the oration never allows us to forget the blood of Caesar. If Antony read Caesar's will, the commons would "go and kiss dead Caesar's wounds / And dip their napkins in his sacred blood . . . " [III. ii. 133-34]. This blood has now become that of a martyr or a saint. Brutus' "most unkindest cut of all" [III. ii. 183] burst Caesar's heart, and

> Even at the base of Pompey's statuë
> (Which all the while ran blood) great Cae-
>   sar fell.
>
> [III. ii. 188-89]

We recall Caesar's triumphing "over Pompey's blood" [I. i. 51] at the beginning of the play; now Pompey triumphs over Caesar's blood. Antony very artfully disclaims any power as an orator "To stir men's blood" [III. ii. 223]. The "most bloody sight" [III. ii. 202] of Caesar's body and "sweet Caesar's wounds, poor poor dumb mouths" [III. ii. 225] speak for themselves and act as a powerful persuasion to vengeance.

There is a general slackening of the blood imagery in Acts IV and V. After Brutus' "bloody spur" [IV. ii. 25] image for the civil war, the next significant use of "blood" is in the quarrel scene. Brutus counters Cassius' waspish indignation with the fact of Caesar's murder:

> Remember March; the ides of March re-
>   member.
> Did not great Julius bleed for justice sake?
> What villain touch'd his body that did stab
> And not for justice?
>
> [IV. iii. 18-21]

If the purpose of the assassination were not justice, then Caesar's blood is the mark of butchery and murder. By the time of this scene the first flush of idealism has gone out of the conspiracy. It is seen here on the defensive, and Cassius' venality is a sign of disillusion. Only Brutus persists in his original uprightness, which is repeatedly expressed with all the insolent frankness of the morally sure. There is also a suggestion here that Brutus is beginning to be aware of the tragic betrayal of the original ideals of the conspiracy. This awareness creates a sense of doom and fatality in the scene, which is climaxed by the appearance of Caesar's Ghost.

The blood imagery of V. i sets the tone for the battle of Philippi in V. ii. A Messenger reports the enemy's "bloody sign of battle" [V. i. 14] to Antony and Octavius. Further on, Octavius cuts off the ingenious conceits of the battle parley with the words of a practical man:

> Come, come, the cause! If arguing make us
>   sweat,

The proof of it will turn to redder drops.
Look,
I draw a sword against conspirators.
When think you that the sword goes up
　again?
Never, till Caesar's three-and-thirty
　wounds
Be well aveng'd, or till another Caesar
Have added slaughter to the sword of trai-
　tors.

　　　　　　　　　　　　　[V. i. 48-55]

This is the case against Brutus, Cassius, and their party: they are "conspirators" and "traitors" who must answer for it in battle; the arbitration of the issue will be in blood, not words. The final blood image is used by Titinius for the dead Cassius:

　　　O setting sun,
As in thy red rays thou dost sink to night,
So in his red blood Cassius' day is set!
The sun of Rome is set.

　　　　　　　　　　　　　[V. iii. 60-3]

So Cassius ends in his own "red blood," slain by the same hand and with the same sword that stabbed Caesar. This is the reciprocity of blood for blood.

3

The fire imagery of *Julius Caesar* follows the basic conflicts in the play in a manner similar to the themes of storm and blood. Here, too, the interpretation of the images depends on our attitude toward Caesar and the conspirators.

Does fire refer to Caesar's tyranny or to the evils of conspiracy? It is the conspirators' tragic error to think of the destructive power of fire as also being purgative and purifying. Brutus, for example, justifies the murder by a proverb: "As fire drives out fire, so pity pity" [III. i. 171]—the fire of conspiracy will destroy the fire of Caesar's tyranny. But the conspirators are themselves consumed in the fire of civil war that avenges Caesar. These comments may serve as a schematic and simplified pattern of the fire imagery, in which there are also two distinct lines of development. First, "fire" is used in the sense of passion, emotional power, the ability to inflame or enkindle, as Antony's oration inflames the mob. Second, "fire" is considered as a destructive and purifying force. This is the literal sense of fire, and it is carried into the stage action when the mob which Antony has inflamed lights firebrands to burn the conspirators' houses. In this scene the two meanings of fire merge.

The theme of fire as passion and its kindling power begins in the dialogue of Brutus and Cassius in I. ii. Brutus is aware of the fact that Cassius is "working" him to conspiracy [I. ii. 163], so that there is a certain sense of triumph in Cassius' remark:

　　　I am glad
That my weak words have struck but thus
　much show
Of fire from Brutus.

　　　　　　　　　　　　　[I. ii. 176-77]

Brutus is the flint that the passionate Cassius strikes against in his effort of persuasion. The flint image is used again more explicitly in the quarrel scene, where Brutus confesses his weakness:

O Cassius, you are yoked with a lamb
That carries anger as the flint bears fire;
Who, much enforced, shows a hasty
　spark,
And straight is cold again.

　　　　　　　　　　　　　[IV. iii. 110-13]

This imagery points the contrast between the hot Cassius and the cold Brutus (compare the hot-cold contrast between Cleopatra and Octavia in *Antony and Cleopatra*).

The fire of conspiracy that Cassius ignited in Brutus is thoroughly confirmed in the fire imagery of II. i. Brutus shrinks from a formal oath, since the motives for conspiracy themselves should

　　　bear fire enough
To kindle cowards and to steel with valour
The melting spirits of women. . . .

　　　　　　　　　　　　　[II. i. 120-22]

The noble Brutus thinks of himself as kindled to conspiracy by justice alone. "Enkindled" [II. i. 249] is indeed the word which Portia uses for her husband later in the scene (it is significant how often Portia uses Brutus' words—it strengthens the bond between them and attests to Portia's dependence on her husband). At the end of the scene Brutus is able to persuade Caius Ligarius to abandon his sickness for an "exploit worthy the name of honour" [II. i. 317]. Caius needs only the example of Brutus,

And with a heart new-fir'd I follow you,
To do I know not what; but it sufficeth
That Brutus leads me on.

　　　　　　　　　　　　　[II. i. 332-34]

Brutus, fired to conspiracy by Cassius, is now able to fire others, and Caius Ligarius is a good example of Brutus' power to win an unquestioning assent. This passage suggests one obvious reason why Cassius was so anxious to gain the support of Brutus.

These images of fire as passion and its kindling power are strongly associated with the conspiracy. It is interesting to note that shortly before his murder in III. i Caesar renounces this sense of fire by asserting his cold constancy. Metellus Cimber's suit "Might fire the blood of ordinary men . . ." [III. i. 37], but not Caesar's. He is "constant as the Northern Star" [III. i. 60], and fire to him implies inconstancy:

The skies are painted with unnumb'red
　sparks,
They are all fire, and every one doth shine;
But there's but one in all doth hold his
　place.

　　　　　　　　　　　　　[III. i. 63-5]

Caesar's murder follows soon after these declarations of starry stability.

The second sense of fire, as a destructive and purifying force, is developed in the theme of the storm and its portents. Casca has never until this night been through "a tempest dropping fire" [I. iii. 10], nor seen a sight like this:

> A common slave (you know him well by
>   sight)
> Held up his left hand, which did flame and
>   burn
> Like twenty torches join'd; and yet his
>   hand,
> Not sensible of fire, remain'd unscorch'd.
> [I. iii. 15-18]

Shakespeare dramatizes Plutarch here with a personal touch: the anonymous "common slave" becomes a figure whom Cicero knows "well by sight." Among the prodigies are also the "Men, all in fire," who "walk up and down the streets" [I. iii. 25]. In II. ii, Calphurnia warns Caesar that "Fierce fiery warriors fight upon the clouds . . ." [II. ii. 19], and the fiery comet portent of this scene [II. ii. 30-1] is a heavenly emblem of Caesar's murder. To Cassius fire is a symbol of the base passivity of Rome, which lets itself be used as kindling matter for Caesar's tyranny:

> Those that with haste will make a mighty
>   fire
> Begin it with weak straws. What trash is
>   Rome,
> What rubbish and what offal, when it
>   serves
> For the base matter to illuminate
> So vile a thing as Caesar!
> [I. iii. 107-11]

This "monstrous state" [I. iii. 71] of Rome can only be righted by deeds "Most bloody, fiery, and most terrible" [I. iii. 130].

Both senses of fire—as passion and its kindling power, and as a destructive and purifying force—are brought together in the scene of Antony's funeral oration. At the end of this scene the fire imagery emerges into the dramatic action, which marks the culmination of the theme in the play. Antony's oration, by its persuasive rhetoric, enkindles and inflames the mob. When he pauses for tears, the Second Plebeian remarks: "Poor soul! his eyes are red as fire with weeping" [III. ii. 115]. Antony's success depends on his ability to communicate the "fire" of his own emotions, and he has soon gained such hypnotic power over the mob that he is able to control their reactions. At line 169, for example, he says: "If you have tears, prepare to shed them now"; this achieves its effect some twenty-five lines further: "O, now you weep, and I perceive you feel / The dint of pity" [III. ii. 193-94].

It is just this technique of suggestion that Antony uses in connection with Caesar's will:

> You are not wood, you are not stones, but
>   men;
> And being men, hearing the will of Caesar,
> It will inflame you, it will make you mad.
> [III. ii. 142-44]

With masterful rhetoric Antony suggests the effect if only he provide the cause, and he seems to take pleasure in playing with effects. In this respect both he and Cassius (compare his soliloquy at the end of I. ii) have qualities of the Machiavel [one who views politics as amoral and that any means, however unscrupulous, can justafiably be used in achieving political power]. Antony is able to withhold the will for almost a hundred lines while he himself stirs up the mob to cry for vengeance: "Revenge! About! Seek! Burn! Fire! Kill! Slay! / Let not a traitor live!" [III. ii. 204-05]. Fire now becomes the instrument of destruction as Antony's own insinuation of mutiny is taken up by the plebeians:

> *1. Pleb.*   We'll burn the house of Bru-
>   tus.
> *3. Pleb.* Away then! Come, seek the con-
>   spirators.
> [III. ii. 231-32]

When Antony reads the will, the incensed mob seeks fire to wreak havoc on its enemies:

> *1. Pleb.*   Come, away, away!
> We'll burn his body in the holy place
> And with the brands fire the traitors'
>   houses.
> Take up the body.
> *2. Pleb.* Go fetch fire!
> *3. Pleb.* Pluck down benches!
> *4. Pleb.* Pluck down forms, windows, any-
>   thing!
> [III. ii. 253-58]

We recall that this same violent, enthusiastic mob was the hostile group of citizens before whom Antony began his oration. Antony observes his effect with all the aloofness of the successful plotter: "Now let it work. Mischief, thou art afoot, / Take thou what course thou wilt" [III. ii. 259-60]. He has finished with his inflammatory rhetoric, and he now speaks in the cold, political tone of the proscription scene (IV. i) some fifty lines further.

After the concentrated verbal imagery of fire in Antony's oration, we have the image of actual fire as the mob goes to burn Caesar's body and the houses of the conspirators. This stage imagery of fire is the logical climax of the theme. The Second Plebeian's cry, "Go fetch fire!" suggests that firebrands are brought in from off-stage, but the mob could also ignite the firebrands right there in front of the audience. Actual fire at this hectic moment is a powerful image of the citizens' passionate and destructive temper, and there is a sense of poetic justice in the use of brands from Caesar's funeral pyre to burn the conspirators' houses. It shows the double aspect of fire: consecration and destruction. In an over-all view, fire, which was first identified with the conspiracy as a symbol of destruction, has now, after the murder of Caesar, become an instrument of vengeance. It thus takes on a purgative, consecrating role. (pp. 56-65)

There is not much further use of fire imagery in Acts IV and V. In IV. iii Brutus tells Cassius of Portia's death by swallowing fire [IV. iii. 156]; the political events in their personal turn have been too much for her. The only reference to fire in the battle of Philippi is made when Cassius asks Titinius: "Are those my tents where I perceive the fire?" [V. iii. 13]. This is a further indication of the destruction of the conspirators by fire, a point emphasized in III. ii and III. iii. The final fire image provides a significant conclusion to the theme. Strato, who held the sword for Brutus, affirms the honor of his master:

> The conquerors can but make a fire of
>   him;
> For Brutus only overcame himself,
> And no man else hath honour by his
>   death.
>   [V. v. 55-7]

The fire of conspiracy, having been turned as an instrument of vengeance against the conspirators, now ends with the dead body of Brutus ready for the pyre. This is the final requiting of Caesar. (p. 66)

> Maurice Charney, "The Imagery of 'Julius Caesar'," in his Shakespeare's Roman Plays: The Function of Imagery in the Drama, *Cambridge, Mass.: Harvard University Press, 1961, pp. 41-78.*

Gayle Greene

[*Greene examines the use of rhetoric and persuasive language in four crucial passages of* Julius Caesar. *In the first of these scenes, the critic claims,* **Cassius** *attempts to convince* **Brutus** *to join the conspiracy against* **Caesar** *(Act I, scene ii) by making vague, unspecified charges of* **Caesar**'s *tyranny and by subtly suggesting that* **Brutus** *is the "ideal of Roman manhood." Greene then demonstrates that although* **Brutus** *appears to be offering rational arguments for the necessity of killing* **Caesar** *in his soliloquy in Act II, scene i, his use of analogy and metaphor lead him to numerous lapses in logic. For example, he likens* **Caesar** *to a dangerous "serpent's egg" though he has no solid reason for doing so; nevertheless, he pursues the image and concludes that, like a serpent,* **Caesar** *should be killed before he can do harm. The critic then examines the rhetorical strategies of* **Brutus**'s *and* **Antony**'s *speeches in Act III, scene ii.* **Brutus**'s *principal technique, she notes, is to imply that his listeners must choose between mutually exclusive*

alternatives—dying as slaves under **Caesar**'s *tyrannical rule or killing him and living as freemen in the republic, for example—without proving that these are the actual alternatives.* **Antony**'s *oration is, Greene states, characterized by its extensive use of irony and repetition, as well as by action words, and therefore excites the commoners' emotions rather than appealing to their sensibilities. Significantly, since neither* **Brutus** *nor* **Antony** *present rational proofs of their arguments regarding* **Caesar** *but rely solely on verbal strategies, we are left "at the mercy of rhetoric" and cannot determine what is true. The play thus reveals that "if a point of view is persuasively stated, it passes for truth."*]

When Antony concludes his funeral oration by modestly disclaiming the powers of rhetoric he has so abundantly displayed—

> I am no orator, as Brutus is;
> But (as you know me all) a plain blunt
>   man. . . .
> For I have neither wit, nor words, nor
>   worth,
>   . . . nor the power of speech
> To stir men's blood; I only speak right on.
>   [III. ii. 217-18, 221, 222-23]

—he draws attention to the very arts of oratory which have enabled him to seize triumphant control of his world. Indeed, his rhetorical tour de force turns the course not only of the action of the play, but of the tide of times. Effecting the shift of power from Brutus to Antony, it marks the end of the Republic and the beginning of events which will issue in the Empire; and, as his words "inflame" [III. ii. 144] his audience, their "fire" [III. ii. 15] becomes more than metaphorical, to spark the actual blaze that burns Rome. Nor is the oration an isolated instance: it is but one of a series of persuasion scenes on which the play as a whole is structured, wherein language is used to "work," "fashion," "move," "fire," it listeners. (pp. 67-8)

The markedly rhetorical style has often been noted, and Dr. [Samuel] Johnson's opinion [in his *Notes on Shakespeare's Plays: "Julius Caesar"*] that "Shakespeare's adherence to . . . Roman manners [was] cold and unaffecting" has been echoed by critics such as Mark Van Doren, who characterizes the play as "more rhetoric than poetry" and its characters as "more orators than men" [see Sources for Further Study]. But rhetoric in this play is a theme as well as a style: according prominence by structure and imagery, it is integral to characterization, culture, and to the central political and epistemological concerns [Epistemology is the study of what knowledge is and how it is acquired]. In Shakespeare's depiction of Rome as a society of skilled speakers whose rhetorical expertise masks moral and political truth is implied a criticism of rhetoric and of language itself which is central to the play's tragic vision. (p. 69)

An analysis of four crucial "persuasion" scenes will demonstrate how language functions to "work," "fashion," "move," "fire" its listeners, leaving the central political questions veiled in obscurity. Brutus is, as we hear repeatedly from him and from others, an honorable man and a man of reason, a stoic who prides himself on reason and is forever urging "reasons" to others; this leads us to expect that his participation in the conspiracy will be undertaken with deliberation and cause [A stoic is a member of the school of philosophy founded by the Greek thinker Zeno about 300 B.C. This discipline holds that wise men should be free from passion, unmoved by joy or grief, and submissive to natural law]. But if we look to the scenes where we most expect to find cause for Caesar's assassination—the scene in which Cassius "seduces" [I. ii. 312] Brutus to come into the conspiracy; the soliloquy in which Brutus "fashions" [II. i. 30] an argument for himself to join the conspiracy; the forum scene, where first Brutus, then Antony, "move" [III. ii. 229] the crowd, Antony "working" [III. ii. 271] and "inflaming" [III. ii. 144] them to riot and mutiny—we find no reasons, only a rhetoric that obscures questions of Caesar's ambition and the justice of his death.

The "seduction scene" [I. ii. 31-175], in which "Cassius first did whet [Brutus] against Caesar" [II. i. 61], is the first place where we would expect to hear the case against Caesar, or at least some specific grievance. Yet, as [Ernest] Schanzer observes, "in this crucial scene . . . Cassius . . . does not mention any specific acts of tyrannical behaviour" [see excerpt in section on Julius Caesar's character]. Schanzer concludes that Cassius is not well suited to his role of guileful seducer. His case against Caesar is made in terms like "this age's yoke" [I. ii. 61], "these hard conditions as this time / Is like to lay upon us" [I. ii. 174-75]—hardly convincing enough to warrant murder. In fact, on the surface, Cassius and Brutus seem barely to hear or to speak to one another. In the first part of the scene (to [I. ii. 88]), they essay one another, Cassius trying both to ascertain Brutus's feelings and to persuade him of his own point of view, without actually stating that point of view, while Brutus, partly defensive, partly enticed, simultaneously backs off and beckons him on. Twice, Brutus asks directly what Cassius wants of him ("Into what dangers would you lead me, Cassius?" [I. ii. 63]; "wherefore do you hold me here so long?" [I. ii. 83], and twice, Brutus's attention is deflected so that Cassius does not have to reply. On neither occasion does Brutus seem to notice or object. The first time, Cassius merely continues his line of thought, without any indication that he has even heard Brutus's question [I. ii. 66]; and the second time, rather than waiting for a reply to his question, Brutus continues his own line of thought [I. ii. 85-9]. Twice, Cassius declares intentions to speak of subjects he never again refers to: Brutus's hidden worthiness" [I. ii. 57] and "honor." Though he announces

"honor is the subject of my story" (in the first of the two long speeches [I. ii. 92-131] which comprise the second movement of the scene), honor is not his subject; it is, rather, his outrage at Caesar's physical infirmities.

Yet by the end of the exchange, they have communicated, and Brutus indicates, in veiled, vague terms, that he assents:

> What you would work me to, I have some
>   aim:
> How I have thought of this, and of these
>   times,
> I shall recount hereafter. . . .
>   What you have said
> I will consider; what you have to say
> I will with patience hear, and find a time
> Both meet to hear and answer such high
>   things.
>   [I. ii. 163-65, 167-70]

In measured, balanced phrases (as though a control of language could assure a control of reality), he refers the whole matter to another time.

Though Brutus nowhere, here or later, insists on clearer definition of Cassius's suggestions, he is persuaded because something else is going on in the exchange. Cassius's real appeal is made in veiled, allusive terms which communicate, not through what they state but through what they suggest: "thoughts of great value, worthy cogitations" [I. ii. 50], noncommittal terms with enticing innuendoes which Brutus is echoing by the end of the scene—"such high things" [I. ii. 170]. The real argument is made through indirection and insinuation because the actual grounds of Cassius's appeal are not the sort he can state: they are to Brutus's vanity and image of himself as a noble Roman, and are inarticulated because inadmissible.

Cassius reveals these terms in solioquy at the end of the scene, when he describes the petitions he plans to throw in at Brutus's window:

> . . . all tending to the great opinion
> That Rome holds of his name; wherein ob-
>   scurely
> Caesar's ambition shall be glanced at.
>   [I. ii. 318-20]

"Opinion," "Rome," the "name"—and only then is Caesar's ambition "obscurely glanced at." Indeed, these terms are implicit throughout the "seduction," and are the power of an otherwise nonexistent argument. When Cassius offers to be Brutus's "glass" [I. ii. 68] to show him an image of his "hidden worthiness" [I. ii. 57], Brutus's acknowledgment that "the eye sees not itself / But by reflection, by some other things" [I. ii. 52-3] is an admission of his dependence on the opinions of others for knowledge of himself. A few lines later, Cassius again evokes the imaginary audience he knows is so essential to Brutus's self-esteem, mirrors without which he cannot see and does not know himself: "many of the best respect in Rome / . . . Have wish'd that noble Brutus had his eyes" [I. ii. 59, 62]. A similar appeal is contained in his second long speech ("Why, man, he doth bestride the narrow world" [I. ii. 135ff.], where he weaves the words "Rome," "man," "Brutus," "Caesar," "name," "fame," and "shame" into a pattern that creates an ideal of Roman manhood: an ideal represented by the name ("yours is as fair a name" [I. ii. 144]), by opinion ("When could they say, till now, that talk'd of Rome . . . " [I. ii. 154]), by "our fathers" and the first Brutus [I. ii. 158, 159]). According to this ideal, Cassius urges Brutus to define himself, and this "works" [I. ii. 163, 308] more strongly than logical argument.

"Rome," "honor," "name" are words which are loaded with affective connotations that make them capable of kindling powerful responses. Though for the moment Brutus says nothing, their effect on him is obvious later when, again asked to "see thyself!" [II. i. 46], he responds with an outburst about Rome and his ancestors [II. i. 53-5]. These words are powerful because they enshrine the dominant cultural values, the thought and belief of the past—libertarian ideals of republican Rome passed down through what "our fathers say" [I. ii. 158]. . . . These words and notions are bound up with Brutus's conception of himself, determining the way he experiences himself and reality.

The most important of these is "honor." Honor words are used so frequently by Brutus or with reference to him that they become, as [Maurice] Charney notes, "almost an identifying tag for his character" [in *Shakespeare's Roman Plays: The Function of Imagery in Drama*]. Brutus's susceptibility to what touches his honor is indicated by his outburst in this scene:

> Set honour in one eye, and death i' th'
>   other,
> And I will look on both indifferently;
> For let the gods so speed me as I love
> The name of honour more than I fear
>   death.
>
> [I. ii. 86-9]

Though his general intention is clear, his language is not, and this is typical of Brutus's confusions when his imagination has been kindled and of his real confusions concerning honor: it is, as he says, "the name of honor" he loves. This conception of honor—as "name" or "reputation"—was associated, by the Renaissance, with classical antiquity, and is an aspect of Shakespeare's depiction of Rome. But the idea of honor as a social attribute conferred by the "opinion" of the community is a notion of which Shakespeare is elsewhere critical, one which he associates elsewhere, as here, with confusion in language. (pp. 73-7)

Brutus's uncritical acceptance of the Roman ideal both results from and reinforces the confusions in

language which make him obtuse to the real terms of Cassius's appeal.

The real strengths of Cassius's argument are thus weaknesses in Brutus's character—his concern with reputation and appearance, his subtle vanity and pride—and it is on these grounds that the noble Brutus is seduced. Depending on the opinions of others for his image of himself, Brutus does not know himself, and is vulnerable to whoever provides the desired "reflection." Indeed, the entire exchange begins with Cassius's assurance that he loves Brutus, and ends with Brutus's "That you do love me, I am nothing jealous" [I. ii. 162], as though its entire purport had been to assure Brutus only of this—which, in a way, it has. It is Brutus's confusion of real and professed motives that accounts for Cassius's verbal obliquity: Cassius "palters with him in a double sense" [*Macbeth*, V. viii. 20], with different meanings for the heart and ear, seeming to appeal to "honor" and concern for "the general good" [I. ii. 85], while actually appealing to vanity. He is, contrary to what Schanzer says of him, an extremely guileful seducer, who looks quite through the words of men to their real concerns and appeals to the one while seeming to appeal to the other.

But Brutus's fatal confusions are most apparent when, in soliloquy [II. i. 10-34], he defends his decision to take part in the murder of a man he protests he loves. He is, as Antony says, the only conspirator not motivated by "envy of great Caesar" [V. v. 70], so we look to these lines when he is alone with himself—the only time in the play—for a cause why Caesar should be killed. Yet the issue disturbingly blurs, disappearing into a tangle of strange and disconnected images of uncertain relevance to one another or to their supposed subject, Caesar. Brutus's language, always more metaphorical than the other characters', is even more metaphorical than usual in this speech. Attempts to make sense of the soliloquy—like John Dover Wilson's "Brutus' theme is the effect of power upon character" [see excerpt in section on Roman Politics]—probably represent something like what Brutus would have like to have said, but nothing this coherent emerges until we have supplied certain missing logical links, and in making this much sense of it, we are ignoring what the language is communicating. Its broken rhythms, uncompleted thoughts, and associational movement present a glimpse into the mind of a man who has not slept for weeks and who has never, in his clearest moments, defined the issues that are tearing him. The sequence of thought and statement is not logical, the conscious, active intellect is not in control, and what emerges is a sense of exhaustion, a linguistic image of the "phantasma" [II. i. 65] Brutus describes a few lines later.

Brutus begins with "It must be by his death" [II. i. 10]—words which have more clarity and conviction than any in the soliloquy, until, perhaps, the final "kill him in the shell" [II. i. 34]. Finding "no personal cause to spurn at him [II. i. 11], he looks to "the general" [II. i. 12], but finding no "general" cause either, by the third line, he has shifted to the conditional: "He would be crown'd: / How that might change his nature, there's the question" [II. i. 12-13]. Now, instead of evidence from Caesar's past or present conduct to answer the "question" he has posed about a hypothetical future, Brutus reaches for a metaphor:

> It is the bright day that brings forth the
>   adder,
> And that craves wary walking.
> > [II. i. 14-15]

Again he returns to the question of Caesar's potential—"Crown him?—That;—" [II. i. 15]. The broken thought creates the sense of groping, but what Brutus is groping for is not, as we might expect, reasons for supposing that Caesar is like an adder; rather, he develops the metaphor: "And then I grant we put a sting in him" [II. i. 16].

Brutus's next statement is a generalization, somewhat confusingly worded, about the misuse of power: "Th' abuse of greatness is when it disjoins / Remorse from power" [II. i. 18-19]. But he has difficulty applying this generalization specifically to Caesar, since he can find nothing in Caesar's conduct to warrant it:

> . . . and, to speak truth of Caesar,
> I have not known when his affections
>   sway'd
> More than his reason.
> > [II. i. 19-21]

So he makes another generalization—"But 'tis a common proof" [II. i. 21]—which he supports with a metaphor: " . . . That lowliness is young ambition's ladder" [II. i. 22]. Though he has admitted difficulty in applying his general principle to Caesar, finding an appropriate metaphor seems to suffice and relieve him of having to justify its applicability. The relevance of this image to Caesar is even less obvious than that of the "adder"; perhaps, in view of the associational movement of the lines, it is there because it rhymes. It is startling, as Schanzer points out, "to find Brutus . . . speak of Caesar as if he were still at the beginning of his career." But it seems to satisfy Brutus because he develops it for the next seven lines, until the "climber-upward" attains "the upmost round" and,

> . . . then unto the ladder turns his back,
> Looks in the clouds, scorning the base de-
>   grees
> By which he did ascend.
> > [II. i. 23, 24, 25-7]

Though strangely ineffectual for the weight it carries in the argument, the figure seems to serve Brutus's need, demonstrating his general principle about the effect of power upon purpose, while still

not specifying its relevance to Caesar. What follows weakens the argument even further: "So Caesar may; / Then lest he may, prevent" [II. i. 27-8]. The only possible application of "vehicle" to "tenor" puts the whole case back in the conditional. Since "the thing he is" [II. i. 29] will not warrant killing him, Brutus states his intention to "fashion," "color," "And therefore think him," and thus takes the leap that clinches the argument—once more, reaching for metaphor:

> And since the quarrel
> Will bear no colour for the thing he is,
> Fashion it thus: that what he is, augment-
>   ed,
> Would run to these and these extremities;
> And therefore think him as a serpent's
>   egg,
> Which, hatch'd, would as his kind, grow
>   mischievous,
> And kill him in the shell.
> > [II. i. 28-34]

There is the same incongruity about this metaphor as the last: Caesar is not "in the shell"; he is, as Brutus himself calls him, "the foremost man of all this world" [IV. iii. 22].

What Brutus has said in this soliloquy is that there is no complaint about Caesar as he is or has been, but, on the basis of what often happens to people when they get power. Caesar might, given power, change. Brutus cites no "reasons," no cause, for supposing that he would change: images of "adder," "ladder," and "serpent's egg" develop his argument, carrying it to the conclusion to which he is committed. His thought moves back and forth between general observations about human behavior and metaphors that illustrate them, and nowhere does he look outside this self-referential linguistic construct to the supposed subject, Caesar himself. Brutus could "think him" anything on the basis of metaphors enlisted to support "common proofs," and his interpretation need bear no more, or less, relation to his subject than "a serpent's egg"; but the progression of tenses in the soliloquy, from the tentative "might" [II. i. 13] to "may" [II. i. 17], to the final "would" [II. i. 33], indicates that he has blurred the distinction between the hypothetical or metaphorical and the actual. The tentativeness of the subordinate clauses and appositions of the last five lines are overriden by the inexorable rhythms of "And since . . .

And therefore . . . And kill," with their strong sense of causal necessity; the uncertain, choppy rhythms find release in the smooth, clinching "kill him in the shell." With his conscious mind relaxed, the conceptual controls dulled by exhaustion, the mechanism of Brutus's fatal construing is obvious: his willingness to let words do his thinking for him. (pp. 77-81)

The strategies of deception that work privately, between a man and his friend, and, more insidiously, between a man and himself, are merely subtler, less obvious versions of the rhetorical tactics used publicly in the funeral orations. Brutus's oration [III. ii. 13-47], his prose, "attic" statement of "public reasons" [III. ii. 7], is traditionally contrasted to Antony's impassioned "asiatic" style, and is usually read as an appeal to the intellect rendered powerless by Antony's more effective appeal to the emotions. These misreadings of Brutus's lines are extremely revealing, since they are based on effects which Brutus himself carefully creates. Brutus explicitly, in the first lines, establishes his authority as a man of reason addressing the reason of others—

> Romans, countrymen, and lovers, hear me for my cause, and be silent, that you may hear. Believe me for mine honour, and have respect to mine honour, that you may believe. Censure me in your wisdom, and awake your senses, that you may the better judge.
>
> [III. ii. 13-17]

—associating himself, by the repetition of key words, with honor, wisdom, and judgment. The technique is *ethos,* establishing the personal character of the speaker, on the basis of the principle—stated by Aristotle—that we are likely to accept the argument of a good man. And despite the confusions Brutus has manifested, critics seem simply to have taken him at his word, interpreting the oration, nearly unanimously, as an appeal to the reason—a "straightforward statement" of "real reasons" "logically delivered." Yet when we look more closely, no reasons appear, no argument that could appeal to logic. The one accusation of Caesar—"he was ambitious" [II. i. 26-7]—is slipped in among protestations of Brutus's love for him and is nowhere supported or even referred to again. Caesar's ambition is again, in Cassius's phrase, "obscurely . . . glanced at" [I. ii. 319-20], in a linguistic construction which makes use of formal patterning, abstract terminology, and brevity to gloss over issue and event. Yet critics who have read the oration as an appeal to the reason are taking their cues from actual elements in it, from rhetorical and syntactical effects carefully contrived to create the illusion Brutus desires.

Brutus's most effective device is to present the issue as though it were a choice between two alternatives which leave no choice but to assassinate Caesar, but which rest on unexamined assumptions concerning Caesar: so that, again, the argument is a self-referential construct that makes sense in its own terms but casts no light outside itself to its supposed subject. He is aided in this by rhetorical figures that are related to logical processes and enable him to suggest logical distinctions and relationships, while actually falsifying the distinctions they imply. The first three sentences (quoted above) make use of one such figure, "antimetabole," a figure which "repeats words in

converse order, often thereby sharpening their sense" [Miriam Joseph, in her *Shakespeare's Use of the Arts of Language*]. But, while seeming to "sharpen the sense," its function in Brutus's speech is simply tautology [a redundant or self-defining statement]: "Believe me for mine honor and for mine honor believe." The necessity of choice between two mutually exclusive alternatives, love of Caesar and love of Rome, is asserted in the line, "Not that I lov'd Caesar less, but that I lov'd Rome more" [III. ii. 21-2], but nowhere does Brutus substantiate that these were the alternatives, or that they excluded one another. The question he then springs ("Had you rather Caesar were living, and die all slaves, than that Caesar were dead, to live all freemen?" [III. ii. 22-4]) again implies logical distinction and the necessity of choice between alternatives suggested to be mutually exclusive—living in freedom or dying in bondage—but again, without evidence that these were the real alternatives. Both these distortions involve "enthymeme," an abridged syllogism, in which the omission of one premise results in "a strong tendency to accept the conclusion without scrutinizing the missing premise on which the argument rests" [Joseph]. The implicit premise on which all these claims depend is an assumption about Caesar: that Caesar's nature was such that it was necessary to choose between love of him and love of Rome, that Caesar living would have necessitated their "dying all slaves." This is the missing premise, nowhere confronted or supported, on which Brutus bases his entire case. The rhetorical questions which conclude his oration again present a choice between alternatives that again rest on an unexamined assumption regarding Caesar: "Who is here so base that he would be a bondman? If any, speak, for him have I offended" [III. ii. 29-30]. Brutus creates a context wherein any objection would be an admission of rudeness, baseness, or vileness—so that, within this circular construct, it is indeed true, "Then none have I offended" [III. ii. 36].

There are, moreover, close-knit causal relationships implied within nearly every line that further this illusion of logic. The first three sentences make use of a construction that twice implies causality—"for" (on account of) and "that" (in order that). The next two lines are conditional clauses setting up "if . . . then" relationships. Brutus uses the figure "taxis" to mete reward and penalty in a syntactical arrangement implying distribution of effect according to cause: the cumulative effect of "as Caesar was . . . so I," repeated three times, lends finality to the concluding "but, as he was ambitious, I slew him" [III. ii. 26-7]. Of the sixteen sentences in the oration, six begin with "if," lending the final "Then none have I offended" a weight that clinches the argument. Even his last lines, which are not part of the argument but merely refer his audience to the records in the Capitol, use a construction that metes out reward and punishment

Mark Antony, the body of Caesar, and Roman citizens. Act III, scene ii. By Heinrich Spiess. The Department of Rare Books and Special Collections, The University of Michigan Library.

in logical distribution: "his glory . . . wherein he was worthy . . . his offences . . . for which he suffer'd death" [III. ii. 38-40]. Such syntactical arrangements occur from beginning to end of his speech, creating an illusion of irrefutable logic, causing the mind to fill out the pattern suggested by the syntax and to perceive reasons where there are none.

The oration is far from an appeal to the intellect with "real reasons"; nor is it an ineffective piece of oratory showing the intellectual's inability to communicate with the masses, as it has also been interpreted. It is a brilliant piece of oratory, brilliantly suited to manipulating a difficult crowd, while resorting to none of the obviously cheap tricks so conspicuous in Antony's performance. Thus it enables Brutus to preserve his conception of himself in his own eyes and others' as a rational man reasonably motivated—an effect he accomplishes with spectacular success, judging from critics' misreadings. (pp. 82-5)

All Antony does in the opening speech of his remarkable oration—"Friends, Romans, countrymen" [III. ii. 73-107]—is to pretend to accept Brutus's claim, Caesar "was ambitious," and then set about undermining it, by twisting a few crucial

words. Merely by repeating, at regular and strategic intervals within a subtly changing context, "Brutus says he was ambitious and Brutus is an honorable man" [III. ii. 86-7, 93-4, 98-9], he causes the words "honor" and "ambition" to assume opposite and ironic meanings, and Brutus's claim to redound on itself; the repetition is "antiphrases, or the broad flout . . . irony of one word" [Joseph]. Thus twenty-one lines into the speech, "Brutus says he was ambitious, / And Brutus is an honorable man" actually means, "Caesar was not ambitious, nor is Brutus honorable," and by [III. ii. 153], the crowd itself can draw the conclusion which Antony nowhere has to state: "They were traitors; honorable men!" Master of irony, Antony is a master of language who has power to make words mean what he wills.

His power derives from his understanding of irony, his skill in adapting language to audience, and his superior insight into the value of *pathos* in persuasion. The oration is a lurid and dramatic appeal to a whole range of feelings, from grief for the loss of a leader and friend, desire to honor the dead, to curiosity, greed, fury, and revenge. At the end of this first long section, Antony pauses, ostensibly to compose himself, actually to calculate his effect on the crowd, and from this point on, he makes use of techniques and props to supplement the verbal: the will, the bloody mantle, and the body. In the next long speech [III. ii. 169-97], he "comes down," has the crowd make a ring around the corpse, and, holding up the bloody mantle, reenacts the murder. Antony's language and action are all concentrated on evoking the deed, with effects quite opposite to Brutus's distancing, obfuscating techniques. Injunctions occur at the beginnings of four lines—"Look" [III. ii. 174], "See" [III. ii. 175], "Mark" [III. ii. 178], "Judge" [iii. ii. 184]—building to the final moment when he reveals the body itself: "Look you here" [III. ii. 196]. His language is characterized by a quality R. W. Zandvoort describes as "animation," the ascription of life to lifeless objects, somewhat in the manner of the pathetic fallacy ["Brutus's Forum Speech in *Julius Caesar*," *Review of English Studies* XVI, No. 61 (January 1940): 62-6]: Caesar's wounds are "poor, dumb mouths" which "speak for me" [III. ii. 225-26]; the "blood of Caesar" followed Brutus's sword "As rushing out of doors to be resolv'd / If Brutus so unkindly knock'd or no" [III. ii. 179-80]; while Pompey's statue "all the while ran blood" [III. ii. 189]. This is the key to the vitality of his language, the energy that enables him to seize hold of his world. Finally, sweeping aside the garment to reveal the body, he releases forces of chaos and destruction: "Revenge! About! Seek! Burn! Fire! Slay!" [III. ii. 204-05].

Having worked them to this pitch, Antony is now so confident that he can afford to play, so audacious that he can disavow the very arts of oratory he has so lavishly displayed—"wit," "words," "power of speech" [III. ii. 222]—in a triumphant flourish of his own showmanship. This gesture is an appropriate conclusion to a performance which is pervaded with irony, for irony is the essence of his oration, from his persona of "a plain blunt man / That . . . speak[s] right on" [III. ii. 218-19, 223], to the more specific rhetorical forms of "antiphrases" and "paralipsis." "Paralipsis," a mode of irony which works by disclaiming the very things the speaker wishes to emphasize, is one of his most effective techniques. Repeating the word "wrong" six times within four lines [III. ii. 123, 125, 126, 127], he insinuates that wrong has been done in the very process of denying that it has. Pretending to try to quiet the crowd, to dissuade them from "mutiny and rage" [III. ii. 122], he achieves his ends even as he disclaims them. His handling of the will, "which, pardon me, I do not mean to read" [III. ii. 131], similarly makes use of "paralipsis": in enumerating all his reasons for withholding the will, he describes exactly the ways it will "inflame" [III. ii. 144] them.

Not the least of his ironies is his claim to appeal to the reason: "O judgment! thou art fled to brutish beasts, / And men have lost their reason" [III. ii. 104-05]. Yet in a sense, for all his histrionics, Antony does offer more information about Caesar than Brutus did, offering at least the assertions, "He was my friend" [III. ii. 85], he brought captives home to Rome [III. ii. 88], he wept for the poor [III. ii. 91], he thrice refused the crown [III. ii. 97]. But at least two of these statements have been contradicted by other characters. With reference to the second, we have Marullus's words, "What conquest brings he home? / What tributaries . . . " [I. i. 32-3]. And to Caesar's refusal of the crown, we have Casca's wry commentary, "but, to my thinking, he was very loath to lay his fingers off it" [I. ii. 241-42]—even without which, we would be a little more judicious than to leap to the crowd's conclusion, "Therefore 'tis certain he was not ambitious" [III. ii. 113]. Thus nothing Antony says of Caesar leaves us more enlightened than we were as to his character, and though his language evokes the murder visually and dramatically, questions of Caesar's ambition and the justice of his death are, again, "obscurely glanced at." (pp. 85-7)

Thus each oration creates its own Caesar, or its own illusion of Caesar. Both cannot be true, yet nothing we have seen of Caesar enables us to know which to accept. The Roman mob first applauds Brutus, then, under the influence of Antony's oratory, shifts its allegiance to Antony. . . . The crowd reflects its rulers, and their behavior is consistent: in the forum, as with Cinna the poet, they care only for the word, not the reality, and do not bother with fine distinctions between the two—"It is no matter, his name's Cinna. Pluck but his name out of his heart" [III. iii. 33-4]. Casca's identification of the mob with an audience, "clap[ping]" and "hiss[ing]" as they "do the players in the theatre" [I. ii.

260-61], implies, as well, an identification of the audience with the mob. We have, finally, no better basis than they to judge the truth of Brutus's or Antony's claims, and are left as much at the mercy of rhetoric—"led by the ears" rather than the "force of reason." It is this which accounts for the play's central ambiguities: if a point of view is persuasively stated, it passes for truth. (pp. 88-9)

Julius Caesar follows a pattern familiar in Shakespeare's tragedies: the protagonist's error, his misjudgment of external reality, is related to lack of self-knowledge and to self-deception, and his confusions are facilitated by language. But . . . the protagonist's disillusionment, his discovery of evil and deception from within and without, usually involves a discovery about language: that words do not necessitate the existence of the things they name. . . . But Brutus dies deluded, consoling himself that no man was ever false to him; and because he does not awaken to his own self-deception, he never awakens to the deceptions involved in language to express a disenchantment like that of the others. His confusions are too deeply sanctioned by a society that assumes honor is a name and rhetoric is reality. In fact, as the consequences of his deeds unravel before him, Brutus shows even less ability to confront the meanings of things, and there is, in these last scenes, a sense of strain and self-righteousness about him that makes him resemble, increasingly, the man he has murdered. And when "Brutus' tongue / Hath . . . ended his life's history" [V. v. 39-40], Antony's epigraph preserves the fiction of "the noblest Roman of them all" [V. v. 68].

But there is another kind of "actor" in the play who does not confuse the self with the role. Whereas Brutus and Caesar are lost in their own language and posturing and beguiled by the rhetoric and role playing of others, Antony and Cassius keep private selves separate from public personae and understand distinctions between words and realities. The pairings are familiar from *Richard II* and *Othello*, where self-deluded word spinners are similarly destroyed by undeluded, unprincipled nominalists. Victors are differentiated from victims in these plays by their understanding of words. (pp. 89-91)

In *Julius Caesar*, it is the negative potentials of language that are most strongly emphasized. Rhetoric is an instrument of appearance which can make, as Plato says, the worse appear the better. Stimulating passion and imagination, it disrupts the proper workings of the mind, perpetuating psychological and social disorder which, in Christian terms, repeats the error of the Fall. Its strength is in human weakness, the corrupt will and unreason: pandering vanity in Brutus and Caesar, it kindles worse passions in the mob. Though language is supposedly man's medium for "coming to terms with the objective world" (as Cassirer calls it [in his

An Essay on Man]), it can be enlisted in the service of subjectivity, of seeming rather than significance, to facilitate the perception of "things that are not" [V. iii. 69]—to "misconstrue every thing" [V. iii. 84]. (p. 92)

> *Gayle Greene, " 'The Power of Speech / To Stir Men's Blood': The Language of Tragedy in Shakespeare's 'Julius Caesar',"* in Renaissance Drama, *n.s. Vol. XI, 1980, pp. 67-93.*

JULIUS CAESAR

Ernest Schanzer

[*Schanzer suggests that Shakespeare intentionally presented an enigmatic, or contradictory, portrait of* **Caesar** *to satisfy the different views of him held by Elizabethan audiences. By the close of Act III, the critic declares, various characters offer evaluations of* **Caesar's** *nature that bear little resemblance to one another. Shakespeare calls into question the validity of each of these estimates, at the same time presenting* **Caesar** *as a figure who is alternately pompous, shrewd, and benevolent. The dramatist thus provides no direct response to the question of who is the real* **Caesar**. *Noting that our view of* **Caesar** *depends to a large extent on our estimate of the justifiability of the assassination, Schanzer asserts that although Shakespeare points up the futility of the murder through his emphasis on* **Caesar's** *spirit in the last two acts of the play, he offers no conclusive judgment of the morality of the conspiracy. For further commentary on* **Caesar's** *character, see the excerpts by Lawrence Danson, Robert E. Knoll, Alice Shalvi, Virgil K. Whitaker, John Dover Wilson, Maynard Mack, and Brents Stirling.*]

Julius Caesar is one of Shakespeare's most controversial plays. Commentators have been quite unable to agree on who is its principal character or whether it has one; on whether it is a tragedy and, if so, of what kind; on whether Shakespeare wants us to consider the assassination as damnable or praiseworthy; while of all the chief characters in the play contradictory interpretations have been given. To illustrate this polarity of views it will be enough to quote two of its editors. Professor Dover Wilson tells us that in this play Shakespeare adopted what he claims to be the traditional Renaissance view of Caesar, derived from Lucan, which regarded him as 'a Roman Tamburlaine of illimitable ambition and ruthless irresistible genius; a monstrous tyrant who destroyed his country and ruined "the mightiest and most flourishing commonwealth that the world will ever see" '. The play's theme 'is the single one, liberty *versus* Tyranny' [see excerpt in section on Roman Politics].

The assassination is depicted as wholly laudable, the conspirators as unselfish champions of freedom, while Brutus's tragedy consists in his vain struggle against the destiny of Rome which lies in the establishment of Caesarism.

When we turn to Sir Mark Hunter's interpretation of the play, we find that 'there can be no doubt that to Shakespeare's way of thinking, however much he extends sympathy to the perpetrators of the deed, the murder of Julius was the foulest crime in secular history'. Of Caesar we learn, 'when put to the test of the stage the personality of Julius "moves before us as something right royal", a character sufficiently great to render the impassioned eulogy of Antony and the calm tribute of Brutus not inconsistent with what we have actually heard and seen of the object of their praise'. Of the conspirators we are told, 'Brutus excepted, there is no sign anywhere that the enemies of the Dictator, though they have all the political catchwords at command—Liberty, Enfranchisement, etc.—care one jot for the welfare of any one outside their own order'. And of Brutus, 'Noble-hearted and sincere beyond question, Brutus is intellectually dishonest', he is self-righteous, pathetically inconsistent, a 'befogged and wholly mischievous politician' [*Transactions of the Royal Society of Literature* 10 (1931): 136ff.]. Thus, while Dover Wilson roots the play in the republican tradition of the Renaissance, which is overwhelmingly hostile to Caesar, Hunter, with equal confidence, places it in the popular medieval and Renaissance tradition, which is wholly eulogistic.

The reader of Shakespeare's play is consequently faced with a difficult choice. Is he to throw in his lot with Dover Wilson and Cassius, and regard Shakespeare's Caesar as a boastful tyrant, strutting blindly to his well-merited doom, and the assassination as a glorious act of liberation? Or is he to follow Mark Hunter and Mark Antony, and look at him as 'the noblest man / That ever lived in the tide of times' [III. i. 256-57], and at the assassination as a hideous crime? Fortunately for the irresolute there is a third way in which the play may be viewed and a third tradition in which it may be placed.

Perhaps more than any other figure in history, Julius Caesar has evoked a divided response in the minds of those who have written about him. Indeed, it would not be an exaggeration to say that such a response, made up of attraction and repulsion, admiration and hostility, was the prevailing one among informed and educated men throughout Antiquity, the Middle Ages, and the Renaissance, so that we can speak of it as forming a tradition extending from Caesar's own day down to that of Shakespeare. (pp. 10-11)

[This] tradition of a complex and divided response to the Caesar story [makes] clear that in all ages well-informed men have belonged to it and that it . . . includes, with very few exceptions, all writers on Caesar whom Shakespeare is known or suspected to have read. A simple, undivided response, like that claimed by Dover Wilson, or, conversely, by Sir Mark Hunter, would thus constitute a surprising deviation by Shakespeare from almost all his known reading. But I do not wish to argue that the complex and divided attitude to the Caesar story found in Shakespeare's play is merely an accidental inheritance from his 'sources'. On the contrary, I believe, and hope to show, that, however much it may also be a reflection of what he had read and felt about the matter, it is used by him as a deliberate dramatic device. (pp. 22-3)

[Let us look at Shakespeare's] presentation of Caesar in this play. Its true nature will be most clearly perceived if we follow it rapidly, scene by scene, from the play's opening until Antony's funeral oration.

In Flavius and Marullus we get our first glimpse of the Republican opposition to Caesar's rule. The metaphor which Flavius uses to justify their 'disrobing' of Caesar's images strikes an ominous note.

> These growing feathers pluck'd from Caesar's wing
> Will make him fly an ordinary pitch,
> Who else would soar above the view of men,
> And keep us all in servile fearfulness.
>
> [I. i. 72-5]

It points forward to the image of the serpent's egg applied to Caesar in Brutus's soliloquy. There a more drastic operation is advocated, but in both cases the action is thought of as preventive, directed not against what Caesar is but what he may become if not checked in time. (pp. 24-5)

Immediately upon Flavius's words Caesar makes his first appearance, and the imaginative impact of this short scene tends to bear out rather than to discredit Flavius's fears. With the utmost economy Shakespeare creates the atmosphere of an oriental court, with its cringing attendants and fawning favourites. 'Peace, ho! Caesar speaks' [I. ii. 1]. 'When Caesar says "Do this", it is perform'd' [I. ii. 10]. And into this atmosphere intrudes the first of many warnings that come ever thicker as the moment of the murder approaches, and like all the others it is contemptuously brushed aside by Caesar. 'He is a dreamer; let us leave him. Pass' [I. ii. 24].

From this slow-moving and portentous scene we pass at once to the rapid, feverish, and impassioned utterances of Cassius in his great seduction-scene. The contrast which he draws between Caesar's physical defects, which make him succumb in a swimming-match and shake when suffering from a fever-fit, and the greatness of the position he has come to occupy, is part of a general contrast, pervading the whole play, between Caesar's frailties of body and the strength of his spirit, which has enabled him to become 'the foremost man of all the world' [IV. iii. 22]. Cassius is genuinely perplexed by this contrast. He is like a schoolboy who is puzzled and angry that someone whom he has always beaten at games should have become perfect and exact obedience from his physical equals and superiors.

> Now, in the names of all the gods at once,
> Upon what meat doth this our Caesar feed,
> That he is grown so great?
>
> [I. ii. 148-50]

Contrary to his intention, he does not throw doubt on Caesar's courage but unwittingly testifies to it. It is the fever-fit that makes him shake, not the prospect of jumping into 'the troubled Tiber chafing with her shores' [I. ii. 101]. The story of the swimming-match epitomizes the triumph of Caesar's 'spirit' over his physical frailties.

It is significant that in this crucial scene, where Cassius can be relied upon to make the most of the opposition's case against Caesar, he does not mention any specific acts of tyrannical behaviour. There is only the general assertion that Rome is 'groaning underneath this age's yoke' [I. ii. 61]. But the yoke to Cassius lies in one man's usurpation of the honours and powers that previously belonged to many. To him it is therefore very much an existing reality, whereas to Brutus the threat lies not in present but in impending conditions.

> Brutus had rather be a villager
> Than to repute himself a son of Rome
> Under these hard conditions as this time
> Is like to lay upon us,
>
> [I. ii. 172-75]

he tells Cassius. And in his soliloquy it is again not what Caesar *is* but what he may *become* that causes his fears.

What, then, is the effect of this scene upon our mental picture of Caesar? It heightens, rather than alters, our previous impression of him as an oriental monarch, a Colossus with clay feet, and begins the process, continuing through much of the play, of disjoining and contrasting the human and the super-human Caesar, the man with his physical and moral frailties and the God who is beyond all frailties. Caesar, by constantly putting himself outside the pale of humanity, collaborating, as John Palmer so well puts it [in his *Political Characters of Shakespeare*], in his own deification, yet reminding us of his weaknesses on each of his appearances, underlines this dissociation. In the very next episode we find him angry at the mob's opposition to his acceptance of the crown, afraid of Cassius, yet assuring Antony,

> I rather tell thee what is to be fear'd
> Than what I fear; for always I am Caesar.
>
> [I. ii. 211-12]

And at once follows the body-spirit contrast:

> Come on my right hand, for this ear is
>   deaf,
> And tell me truly what thou think's of
>   him.
>
> [I. ii. 213-14]

As Dover Wilson remarks, the atmosphere is again that of an oriental court. When Caesar is angry, 'all the rest look like a chidden train' [I. ii. 184]. In his remarks about Cassius we get our chief glimpse of the Caesar we know from Plutarch, the shrewd politician, the keen observer of men, the writer of the Commentaries.

In Casca's narration of the day's events a new Caesar is revealed to us, again with Plutarchian traits; Caesar the play-actor, skilfully exploiting the passions of the common people. While his fall in the market-place is a kind of preview of his later fall in the Capitol, his adroit play upon the feelings of the *plebs* [commoners] adumbrates Antony's manipulation of them in his funeral oration. Casca's report ends on an ominous note, which for the moment makes the worst fears of the enemies of Caesar seem justified: 'Marullus and Flavius, for pulling scarfs off Caesars' images, are put to silence' [I. ii. 285-86]. Not deprived of their tribuneship, as in Plutarch. Just the sinister 'put to silence'.

Up to this point Shakespeare has tipped the balance in favour of the conspirators' views of Caesar and has made us share Brutus's apprehensions. Now, by making Cassius, in his soliloquy, so frankly impugn the integrity of his own motives and show so clearly the personal nature of his opposition, Shakespeare brings us to question the truth of our impressions of Caesar, so many of which we have received through Cassius. And our doubts are strengthened by the play's next image of him, again drawn by Cassius, this time for the terror-stricken Casca. For Cassius's picture of Caesar and his explanation of the portents are clearly part of an *argumentum ad hominem* [evasive argument]. Cassius himself is an Epicurean and does not, at least not yet, 'credit things that do presage' [V. i. 78]. But to convince Casca, who *does* credit them, of the monstrosity of Caesar's rule, he is quite ready to put them to use to prop up his arguments. Against Cassius's explanation of the omens we have been indirectly warned just before by Cicero:

> But men may construe things after their
>   fashion,
> Clean from the purpose of the things
>   themselves.
>
> [I. iii. 34-5]

The groundwork of Cassius's indictment of Caesar here is much the same as in his scene with Brutus. There is again the contrast between what Caesar really is and what he has become, but what he has become is something rather different, fitting the altered circumstances. It is no longer a God or a Colossus who dwarfs his fellow-men and blocks the road to glory. This image of Caesar had seemed appropriate for Brutus, in whom Cassius is trying to awaken a feeling of thwarted ambition. But upon the terrified Casca it is above all a sense of the fearfulness of Caesar that he is trying to impress.

> Now could I, Casca, name to thee a man
> Most like this dreadful night;
> That thunders, lightens, opens graves,
>   and roars
> As doth the lion in the Capitol;
> A man no mightier than thyself or me
> In personal action, yet prodigious grown,
> And fearful, as these strange eruptions
>   are. . . .
>
> [I. iii. 72-8]

But while the picture of Caesar as a God and Colossus bore some resemblance to the reality of which we have been allowed a few glimpses, the Caesar that 'thunders, lightens, opens graves, and roars' is too obviously a fabrication of the moment to affect our conceptions of him. (The ironic fact that Caesar later seems to bear out this description by referring to himself as a lion, and Danger's elder twin-brother, does not alter this impression. For it is Caesar's most ludicrous utterance, and no more affrights us than Snug the joiner's impersonation of that 'fearful wildfowl' [in *A Midsummer Night's Dream*].)

Our image of Caesar receives its next modification in Brutus's soliloquy. His Caesar bears no resemblance either to Cassius's God and Colossus or to his roaring lion. He appears to Brutus in the image of a serpent's egg, someone yet harmless, but potentially mischievous. At the very moment when it is most in his interest to incriminate Caesar, his honesty forces him to declare,

> and to speak truth of Caesar,
> I have not known when his affections
>   sway'd
> More than his reason.
>
> [II. i. 19-21]

But are we to take this as a valid view of Caesar? Or is it as mistaken as Brutus's view of Antony? His reference to Caesar's 'lowliness' suggests this, for it is absurdly out of accord with what we see of him in this play. Thus Shakespeare calls in doubt the validity of Brutus's image of Caesar, just as he calls in doubt that of Cassius's and Antony's image, so that the nature of the real Caesar remains an enigma.

Nor is this enigma dispelled by what we see of Caesar in the following scenes. Even in the privacy of his home he is strenuously engaged in the creation of the legendary figure. There is never any real intimacy in his scene with Calpurnia, no momentary lifting of the mask in soliloquy or aside. Here and in the Capitol Shakespeare gives us above all the thrasonical [boastful] Caesar, who sees himself as outside and above humanity. Only upon the arrival of the conspirators does he unbend a little, for the

Brutus and the Ghost of Caesar. Act IV, scene iii. By William Blake. The Department of Rare Books and Special Collections, The University of Michigan Library.

first and last time in the play. For his bearing here Shakespeare was, no doubt, drawing on Plutarch's description of the youthful Caesar. 'And the people loved him marvellously also, because of the courteous manner he had to speak to every man, and to use them gently, being more ceremonious therein than was looked for in one of his years. Furthermore, he ever kept a good board, and fared well at his table, and was very liberal besides.' Plutarch's coupling of Caesar's hospitality with his courtesy probably suggested to Shakespeare his

> Good friends, go in and taste some wine with me;
> And we, like friends, will straightway go together.
>
> [II. ii. 126-27]

But these lines also call up memories of the ceremonial sharing of wine before another betrayal, memories which are strengthened by the kiss which Brutus gives to Caesar in the Capitol ('I kiss thy hand, but not in flattery, Caesar [III. i. 52]), and later by Antony's reproach of Brutus at Philippi:

> In your bad strokes, Brutus, you give good words;
> Witness the hole you made in Caesar's heart,
> Crying 'Long live! Hail, Caesar!'
>
> [V. i. 30-2]

('And forthwith he came to Jesus, and said, Hail master; and kissed him.' *Matthew* xxvi, 49.)

We are next given another view of Caesar and the conspiracy in Artemidorus's

> My heart laments that virtue cannot live
> Out of the teeth of emulation.
> If thou read this, O Ceasar, thou mayest live;
> If not, the fates with traitors do contrive.
>
> [II. iii. 13-16]

Having engaged our sympathies for Caesar more fully than at any previous point in the play, Shakespeare loses little time to alienate them again, so that by the moment of the assassination our antipathies are more strongly aroused than ever before. In his two short speeches in the Capitol Shakespeare gives us a compendium of his Caesar's most unamiable traits. He here speaks with the voice of the Angelo of *Measure for Measure*, rejecting, like him, a plea for the pardon of a brother by insisting on the rigour of the law and on his own separateness from common humanity.

> I must prevent thee, Cimber.
> These couchings and these lowly courtesies
> Might fire the blood of ordinary men,
> And turn pre-ordinance and first decree
> Into the law of children . . .
> Thy brother by decree is banished;
> If thou dost bend, and pray, and fawn for him,
> I spurn thee like a cur out of my way.
>
> [III. i. 35-9, 44-6]

His next speech, like Othello's comparison of himself to the Pontic sea, is full of irony, both in view of the vacillation we have witnessed in his scene with Calpurnia, and of his impending fall.

> I could be well mov'd, if I were as you;
> If I could pray to move, prayers would move me;
> But I am constant as the northern star,
> Of whose true-fix'd and resting quality
> There is no fellow in the firmament.
>
> [III. i. 58-62]

A final ironic touch is added in his 'Hence! Wilt thou lift up Olympus?' [III. i. 74], which, juxtaposed with the immediately succeeding spectacle of his lifeless body lying at the foot of Pompey's statue, crystallizes the contrast between the corporeal and spiritual Caesar, which is summed up a little later by Antony's

> O mighty Caesar! dost thou lie so low?
> Are all thy conquests, glories, triumphs, spoils,

Shrunk to this little measure?

[III. i. 148-50]

From Antony we now receive our last image of Caesar. His is the Caesar of popular tradition, the mighty conqueror, the Mirror of Knighthood, the noble Emperor. There is Caesar's nobility,

Thou art the ruins of the noblest man
That ever lived in the tide of times;

[III. i. 256-57]

his fidelity,

He was my friend, faithful and just to me;

[III. ii. 85]

his largesse,

To every Roman citizen he gives,
To every several man, seventy-five drachmas;

[III. ii. 241-42]

his military prowess,

He hath brought many captives home to
Rome;

[III. ii. 88]

his compassion,

When that the poor have cried, Caesar
hath wept.

[III. ii. 91]

Yet though we are not made to doubt the sincerity of Antony's tribute to Caesar in his soliloquy, the image of him created in the funeral oration is called into question by its forming part of his carefully contrived play upon the emotions of the *plebs*. Nor are we encouraged to put much trust in the judgement of the man who assures Caesar that Cassius is not dangerous but 'a noble Roman, and well given' [I. ii. 19].

Throughout the first half of the play, then, we are given a series of images of Caesar, none of which bear much mutual resemblance, though some of them are not irreconcilable. But doubt is thrown in one way or another on the validity of most of them. And to these Shakespeare adds his own presentation of Caesar, a presentation so enigmatic and unrevealing that none of the other images are really dispelled by it. It is a dramatic treatment of Caesar in the manner of [Luigi] Pirandello. 'Which of all these is the real Caesar?', Shakespeare seems to ask. And he takes care not to provide an answer. But does not Shakespeare further anticipate Pirandello by making us feel that perhaps there *is* no real Caesar, that he merely exists as a set of images in other men's minds and his own? For his Caesar is continuously engaged in what Pirandello calls *costruirsi*, 'building himself up', creating his own image of himself, until we are left to wonder whether a lifting of the mask would reveal any face at all. (pp. 25-32)

Shakespeare seems to me to be playing on his au-

dience's varied and divided views of Caesar, encouraging and discouraging in turn each man's preconceptions. And since on our view of Caesar depends, very largely, our judgement of the justifiability of the entire conspiracy, the whole drama is thus kept within the area of the problem play. For though, as it seems to me, Shakespeare makes abundantly clear the folly and the catastrophic consequences of the murder, he does not, I think, make clear its moral indefensibility. His enigmatic presentation of Caesar's character and motives allows responses like that of Dover Wilson to be formed. And I see no reason to doubt that there were people who shared these responses in Shakespeare's audience. In fact, the diversity of critical opinion on the main characters and on Shakespeare's attitude to the conspiracy bears witness to his success in making *Julius Caesar* a problem play. It is a problem play in much the same way as [Henrik] Ibsen's *Wild Duck*, which has a very similar theme: the tragic mischief created by the actions of a young idealist in fulfilment of the highest principles, partly through his utter blindness to what people really are like. In both cases the question is put to the audience: 'Was he morally justified in doing what he did?' And in both cases the dramatist's answer seems to me to be an insistent but not a compulsive 'No'.

The main purpose of Shakespeare's persistent dissociation of Caesar's body and spirit is, no doubt, to show up the foolishness and futility of the assassination. The whole second part of the play is an ironic comment on Brutus's

We all stand up against the spirit of Caesar,
And in the spirit of men there is no blood.
O that we then could come by Caesar's
spirit,
And not dismember Caesar!

[II. i. 167-70]

What is involved in the last two acts is something more than a grim pun, which makes the conspirators find that, while they have dismembered Caesar's body, his spirit, i.e. his ghost, still walks abroad, and exacts his revenge. For the spirit of Caesar is also that legendary figure, that God and Colossus, whom Cassius deplores, and whom Caesar seeks to impose upon the imagination of his countrymen. In this he is handicapped by frailties of body and character from which the murder frees him and allows the legendary Caesar to come into his own, assisted by Antony's rhetoric, just as Antony's military skill later assists that other 'spirit' of Caesar, his ghost, in executing his revenge.

That the spirit of Caesar in the sense of 'Caesarism', the absolute rule of a single man, informs the second part of the play, as many critics maintain, seems to me unsupported by anything in the text. Dover Wilson, for instance, writes: 'When Brutus exclaims

We all stand up against the spirit of Caesar,

[II. i. 167]

he sums up the play in one line. For the spirit of Caesar, which was the destiny of Rome, is the fate against which Brutus struggles in vain.' And Mac-Callum [in his *Shakespeare's Roman Plays*] from a rather different standpoint, tells us that 'Shakespeare makes it abundantly clear that the rule of the single master-mind is the only admissible solution for the problems of the time.' Both these critics seem to me to be reading Plutarch's view into Shakespeare's play. Nothing there suggests to me that Caesar is to be thought of as the Man of Destiny, or that the establishment of one man's rule is the inevitable outcome of the Civil Wars. As in Plutarch, who declares that the people 'could not abide the name of a king, detesting it as the utter destruction of their liberty', they are shown to be strongly opposed to Caesar's acceptance of the crown [I. ii. 241ff.]. Against this can only be set the people's shouts after Brutus's oration, 'Let him be Caesar', 'Caesar's better parts shall be crown'd in Brutus' [III. ii. 51-2], but to take this as evidence of strong monarchic feelings in the *plebs* seems rather naïve. At Philippi it is not Caesarism or the providential scheme of Plutarch and Dante which defeats Brutus and Cassius, but their human flaws, which make Brutus give the word for attack too early, and make Cassius slay himself rashly, in premature despair. As far as the supernatural interferes in the affairs of men, it is Caesar's ghost rather than Destiny or the hand of God that contributes to the defeat of the conspirators. Nor are we made to feel anywhere . . . that the Roman Republic has sunk into a state of disorder and corruption which only the establishment of one man's rule can cure. (pp. 33-6)

> *Ernest Schanzer, "Julius Caesar," in his* The Problem Plays of Shakespeare: A Study of "Julius Caesar," "Measure for Measure," "Antony and Cleopatra," *Routledge & Kegan Paul, 1963, pp. 10-70.*

BRUTUS

T. S. Dorsch

[*Dorsch argues that critics have generally viewed* **Brutus** *as a more admirable person than Shakespeare intended him to be. While acknowledging* **Brutus's** *honor and virtue, Dorsch contends that he is arrogant, self-righteous, and opinionated. According to the critic,* **Brutus** *honestly believes that* **Caesar's** *death will benefit Rome, but he is blind to the consequences of the assassination and to his fellow conspirators' lack of moral principles. Dorsch does note, however, that* **Brutus** *is ca-*

pable of expressing love and tenderness, as shown by his relationships with his wife **Portia** *and his servant* **Lucius**. *For further commentary on* **Brutus's** *character, see the excerpts from Lawrence Danson, Robert E. Knoll, Alice Shalvi, Brents Stirling, Virgil K. Whitaker, John Dover Wilson, Maynard Mack, and Gayle Greene.*]

Brutus is the dramatic hero of *Julius Caesar.* He is the most prominent figure, and at almost every stage our interest is focused on his deliberations and decisions. Obviously Shakespeare was greatly interested by the mind of Brutus. As presented by Plutarch, he was a man of great probity and integrity, and of sound judgement backed by a philosophical training, and he was loved and esteemed by his compatriots. Yet he slew the one undoubted genius of his age, partly, we gather from Plutarch, because he was ambitious of succeeding him as leader of the state, partly because of some not clearly specified private quarrel, and partly because he was incensed against him by Cassius. His hatred of tyranny, which is mentioned almost in passing, made him the readier to listen to Cassius's promptings. We may suppose that Shakespeare found it difficult to reconcile the conspicuous wisdom and virtue of Plutarch's Brutus with the motives he was given for desiring Caesar's death. At any rate, he modified his character in several ways, making him at the same time more obviously consistent in the purity of his intentions, and less amiable and less intelligent.

I cannot help feeling that the majority of past critics have been misled by Brutus's estimate of himself into regarding him as a more wholly admirable person than Shakespeare intended him to be. The dramatist, says MacCallum [in his *Shakespeare's Roman Plays*], "reserves his chief enthusiasm for Brutus"; and "throughout the piece, it is the personality of Brutus that attracts our chief sympathy and concern." The terms in which almost all other commentators discuss the character of Brutus are similarly those of admiration and approval.

In *Julius Caesar* the virtue and nobility of Plutarch's Brutus are brought out, but beside them are set a number of faults for which there is little or no warrant in Plutarch. Shakespeare's Brutus is, with all his estimable qualities, pompous, opinionated and self-righteous. His judgement is not to be trusted. He is led by the nose by Cassius and gulled by Antony. At almost every crisis in his fortunes he makes decisions, against the advice of experienced men of the world, that contribute materially to the failure of his cause. He seems completely blind to reality, an ineffectual idealist whose idealism cannot prevent him from committing a senseless and terrible crime. We may respect the motives for which he spares Antony's life, and later allows him to speak in Caesar's funeral—if not the reasoning by which he led himself to think Caesar's death necessary; but on both occasions his decisions are foolish blunders as far as the success of the conspiracy is concerned.

The character of Caesar is established by incidental phrases and by implication rather than by statement or description. Of Brutus we hear much more, both from other people and from himself. We soon learn that he is greatly respected by all who know him. Cassius declares that he is noble [I. ii. 308], and adds that he is one of those honourable men who, themselves innocent of guile, may easily be "seduced" by less honourable but cleverer men. At the end of the next scene Casca pays him a high tribute:

> O, he sits high in all the people's hearts:
> And that which would appear offence in
>   us,
> His countenance, like richest alchemy,
> Will change to virtue and to worthiness.
>   [I. iii. 157-60]

All the conspirators, even Cassius, defer to his opinions at their first meeting. Caius Ligarius calls him "Soul of Rome" [II. i. 321], and pledges himself to an unknown enterprise simply because Brutus leads him on. Caesar, too, loves Brutus dearly.

For the modern play-goer admiration is somewhat tempered by the manner in which Brutus himself frequently stresses his sense of his own disinterestedness and honour. In one of his very first speeches he says:

> What is it that you would impart to me?
> If it be aught toward the general good,
> Set honour in one eye, and death i' th'
>   other,
> And I will look on both indifferently;
> For let the gods so speed me as I love
> The name of honour more than I fear
>   death.
>   [I. ii. 84-9]

It should be remembered, however, that one of Shakespeare's simplest—and habitual—methods of telling us what a person is really like is to let that person himself tell us. We must be on our guard against judging Brutus's estimate of himself according to modern notions of how people should speak about themselves, and saying that in this and similar utterances he is merely "talking big". Nevertheless, his manner at various points in the play does not give us as favourable an impression of him as his friends entertain.

Although he has been drawn into the conspiracy by Cassius, he assumes the rôle of leader as his natural due, though it must be admitted that no one questions his right to the position. However, he takes advantage of it to veto every proposal put forward by any one else. Cassius wants the conspirators to bind themselves by an oath. No, says Brutus, conscious of his own integrity, the word of a Roman is inviolable; and he delivers a pompous little homily on the virtue of their enterprise and the sacredness of a Roman promise. Then Cassius,

seconded by Casca, Cinna, and Metellus, suggests that Cicero be sounded about joining them, but Brutus firmly rejects the suggestion. Cassius points out the potential danger in sparing Antony's life, and urges that he should fall with Caesar. And again Brutus knows better: Antony, he says, "can do no more than Caesar's arm when Caesar's head is off" [II. i. 182-83]. It is not the moral rightness of his decision here that we question, but the immediate grounds on which he bases it, and his inability to see that, once committed to the monstrous conspiracy, he would be defeating its ends if he did not ensure its success by whatever means. Surely it is with deliberate irony that Shakespeare in the middle of this discussion makes Brutus say of another man,

> For he will never follow any thing
> That other men begin.
>   [II. i. 151-52]

In much the same tone Brutus, after the death of Caesar, overrides Cassius's prudent objection to letting Antony speak in Caesar's funeral. Antony will be speaking with his gracious permission, and after he himself has given the people unanswerable reasons for Caesar's death; and in any case he sees no cause to distrust Antony's professions. Throughout this episode he shows an almost ludicrous naïveté, yet at the end his self-esteem is probably higher than at any other time in the play—as of course Antony intended it should be.

It is during his quarrel with Cassius that Brutus shows to least advantage. No one who reads with care the first hundred lines of Act IV, Scene iii, could feel that Shakespeare meant us to have any sympathy with Brutus during this exchange. It is otherwise in later parts of the scene; but while the altercation is at its height, though we may grant that Brutus has right on his side in the main points at issue, his demeanour is intolerable. He adopts the tone of an Olympian god chiding an erring mortal, and at the same time lapses into the language of a squabbling schoolboy. Caesar himself is no more arrogant than Brutus when he says, for example:

> There is no terror, Cassius, in your
>   threats;
> For I am arm'd so strong in honesty
> That they pass by me as the idle wind,
> Which I respect not.
>   [IV. iii. 66-9]

This aspect of Brutus is brought into prominence several times in later scenes. For instance, when Octavius says, "I was not born to die on Brutus' sword," Brutus replies,

> O, if thou wert the noblest of thy strain,
> Young man, thou could'st not die more
>   honourable.
>   [V. i. 58-60]

Later in the same scene he declares to Cassius:

> Think not, thou noble Roman,
> That ever Brutus will go bound to Rome;
> He bears too great a mind.
>
> 　　　　　　　　　　　　[V. i. 110-12]

And finally, a few moments before he abjures his Stoic principles and takes his life, when the battle to which he has illadvisedly committed the republican armies is lost, and all that he stands for is in ruins, he says:

> I shall have glory by this losing day
> More than Octavius and Mark Antony
> By this vile conquest shall attain unto.
>
> 　　　　　　　　　　　　[V. v. 36-8]

However, as I have said, we must beware of hasty judgements. "All that he stands for is in ruins"; "this vile conquest": if we bear these words in mind we shall not put too harsh a construction on Brutus's speeches. Some of his "thrasonical" utterances must be put down to Shakespeare's technique of making his characters reveal their own qualities by direct reference to them; some, in the later scenes, to a species of unconscious compensation in Brutus for the defeat of all the high principles by which he had been governed in joining the conspiracy and in his subsequent actions. In Brutus Shakespeare gives us a very subtle portrait of a man divided against himself—"with himself at war" [I. ii. 46], to use Brutus's own phrase. Even before his first encounter with Cassius he has been torn by conflicting passions: his admiration for Caesar's high gifts and noble qualities and his fears of his ambition, his love for Caesar as a personal friend and his sense of duty to the republic. Throughout the play he is to some degree accompanied by this internal conflict. It is this that leads him to justify and assert himself so positively, this that stands behind much of his demeanour to Cassius during the quarrel, this that causes him to kill himself with a better will than that with which he slew Caesar. He is an entirely honourable man engaged in what he does not realize is a dishonourable cause, and associated with unscrupulous men whose lack of principle he does not see and would not understand. The sense of conflict in him is best seen in his soliloquy in his garden. . . . [This] soliloquy is a wonderful exposition of the state of mind of a man who, with reasons that are very nearly right, reaches a conclusion that is entirely wrong.

It is impossible not to sympathize with Brutus in his agonizing dilemma; but it is even more impossible to sympathize with its outcome. For, having reached the wrong conclusion, Brutus goes no further. The other conspirators "did that they did in envy of great Caesar" [V. v. 70]; all that mattered to them was that Caesar should be got out of the way. Brutus thinks that he is acting from the purest patriotic motives; it does not occur to him that he is doing the state no service by robbing it of its head and making no provision for its safety thereafter— for so it appears in the play. When Caesar has fall-

en the conspirators, including Brutus, are at a loss. Until Antony imposes on them a course of action for the following day, all they can think of doing, apart from bathing their hands in the murdered man's blood, is to walk about in a transport of republican enthusiasm, waving their bloody swords and shouting, "Peace, freedom, and liberty!" [III. i. 110]. Within twenty-four hours of Caesar's death, Antony is in charge of the city, not Brutus; he and Cassius have fled for their lives.

Caesar grows in stature as the play proceeds; Brutus deteriorates. In his quarrel with Cassius he is irritable, undignified, and unjust; he is more intolerant of the meddlesome poet than Cassius; and though he vehemently disputes Cassius's claim to be the abler soldier, his reasons for engaging the enemy at Philippi are less convincing than those of Cassius for deferring the battle. It is impossible to reconcile Shakespeare's presentation of Brutus with the common Renaissance view of him as the great liberator and patriot, the second of his name to free the Romans from the tyrant's yoke.

He is shown at his most sympathetic in his intimate personal relationships. Hard upon the meeting of the conspirators comes the beautiful episode in which Portia insists on sharing his anxieties. Here he is seen as the tender and loving, and dearly loved, husband. The prelude to this encounter brings out his affectionate consideration for his serving-lad Lucius, and this is seen again at the end of the quarrel scene.

The loyal friendship that Brutus can inspire is well illustrated in the last scene of the play, when he and the poor remains of his supporters are resting from the battle which they now know to be lost. He asks them in turn to hold his sword while he runs upon it, and they shrink back from the request in horror. In this moment of defeat and humiliation their sorrow is all for him, not for themselves; and conscious of their love, Brutus is moved to say,

> My heart doth joy that yet in all my life
> I found no man but he was true to me.
>
> 　　　　　　　　　　　　[V. v. 34-5]

If I seem to have emphasized Brutus's less admirable qualities at the expense of the many fine qualities with which Shakespeare endows him, it is not that I underrate the latter, but because the majority of commentators have brought out what is sympathetic in him to the virtual exclusion of the faults that Shakespeare must equally want us to see in him. Brutus seems to me to be a man whom we must respect, but for whom it is difficult to feel love. Shakespeare accentuates any weaknesses or errors for which there is the slightest warrant in Plutarch, and gives him what is in many respects a disagreeable personality—such a personality, indeed, as is not uncommon in perfectly upright men who cannot see beyond their own strict code of conduct. On the other hand, he makes him act from an entirely sincere belief that he is serving his country by killing Caesar. He shows him struggling with a problem beyond his capacity to resolve, and in his perplexity coming to the wrong decision. A man who committed Brutus's crime could not be portrayed as a wholly sympathetic character; but Shakespeare shows him as blind, not evil. And finally he buries Brutus's crime in his virtues, and ends the play with Antony's tribute:

> This was the noblest Roman of them all.
> All the conspirators save only he
> Did that they did in envy of great Caesar;
> He only, in a general honest thought
> And common good to all, made one of
>   them.
> His life was gentle, and the elements
> So mix'd in him, that Nature might stand
>   up
> And say to all the world, "This was a
>   man!"
>   [V. v. 68-75]

This is the impression of Brutus that Shakespeare leaves with us. He leaves us with the feeling, too, that the play, though it rightly bears Caesar's name, is rather "The Death and Revenge of Julius Caesar" than "The Tragedy of Julius Caesar", for its tragedy is the tragedy of Marcus Brutus. (pp. xxxix-xliv)

> *T. S. Dorsch, in an introduction to Ju-*
> *lius Caesar by William Shakespeare,*
> *edited by T. S. Dorsch, revised edition,*
> *Cambridge, Mass.: Harvard University*
> *Press, 1955, pp. xxvi-lxi.*

CASSIUS

M. W. MacCallum

*[Focusing on **Cassius**'s intellectual preoccupations, self-sufficiency, championship of liberty and equality, and rejection of the supernatural, MacCallum contends that the character's behavior is guided by his belief in the philosophy of Epicureanism. Epicurus was a Greek philosopher who asserted that pleasure was the highest good in life. For Epicurus, the greatest joy derived from emotional calm and serenity; he therefore considered intellectual activities superior to all others. The philosopher also extolled the virtues of freedom and denied that gods had any control over human affairs. MacCallum also discusses **Cassius**'s strengths and weaknesses of character, faulting his spitefulness, jealousy, and lack of fortitude, but praising his enthusiasm for the cause of republicanism and his keen powers of judgment. For further commentary on **Cassius**'s character, see the excerpts by Lawrence Danson, Robert E. Knoll, and Gayle Greene.]*

The main lines of [Cassius's] character are given in Caesar's masterly delineation, which follows Plu-

tarch in regard to his spareness, but in the other particulars freely elaborates the impression that Plutarch's whole narrative produces.

> Yond Cassius has a lean and hungry look:
> He thinks too much: such men are
>   dangerous . . .
>   He reads much;
> He is a great observer, and he looks
> Quite through the deeds of men; he loves
>   no plays,
> As thou dost, Antony; he hears no music;
> Seldom he smiles, and smiles in such a
>   sort
> As if he mock'd himself and scorn'd his
>   spirit
> That could be moved to smile at anything.
> Such men as he be never at heart's ease
> Whiles they behold a greater than them-
>   selves,
> And therefore are they very dangerous.
>   [I. ii. 194-95, 201-10]

Lean, gaunt, hungry, disinclined to sports and revelry, spending his time in reading, observation, and reflection—these are the first traits that we notice in him. He too, like Brutus, has learned the lessons of philosophy, and he finds in it the rule of life. He chides his friend for seeming to fail in the practice of it:

> Of your philosophy you make no use,
> If you give place to accidental evils.
>   [IV. iii. 145-46]

And even when he admits and admires Brutus' self-mastery, he attibutes it to nature, and claims as good a philosophic discipline for himself. There is, however, a difference between them even in this point. Brutus is a Platonist with a Stoic tinge; Cassius is an Epicurean [Platonists held that the highest reality is intellectual rather than based on sensory perception. Stoics believed that wise men should be free from passion, unmoved by joy or grief, and submissive to natural law. Epicureans considered emotional calm the highest good, held intellectual pleasures superior to others, and advocated the renunciation of momentary in favor of more permanent pleasures]. That strikes us at first as strange, that the theory which identified pleasure with virtue should be the creed of this splenetic solitary: but it is quite in character. Epicureanism appealed to some of the noblest minds of Rome, not as a cult of enjoyment, but as a doctrine that freed them from the bonds of superstition and the degrading fear of death. . . . And these are the reasons that Cassius is an Epicurean. At the end, when his philosophy breaks down, he says:

> You know that I held Epicurus strong
> And his opinion: now I change my mind,
> And partly credit things that do presage.
>   [V. i. 76-8]

He has hitherto discredited them. . . .

> Nor stony tower, nor walls of beaten brass,

> Nor airless dungeon, nor strong links of
>   iron,
> Can be retentive to the strength of spirit:
> But life, being weary of these worldly bars,
> Never lacks power to dismiss itself.
>   [I. iii. 93-7]

Free from all superstitious scruples and all thought of superhuman interference in the affairs of men, he stands out bold and self-reliant, confiding in his own powers, his own will, his own management:

> Men at some time are masters of their
>   fates:
> The fault, dear Brutus, is not in our stars
> But in ourselves, that we are underlings.
>   [I. ii. 139-41]

And the same attitude of mind implies that he is rid of all illusions. He is not deceived by shows. He looks quite through the deeds of men. He is not taken in by Casca's affectation of rudeness. He is not misled by Antony's apparent frivolity. He is not even dazzled by the glamour of Brutus' virtue, but notes its weak side and does not hesitate to play on it. Still less does Caesar's prestige subdue his criticism. On the contrary, with malicious contempt he recalls his want of endurance in swimming and the complaints of his sick-bed, and he keenly notes his superstitious lapses. He seldom smiles and when he does it is in scorn. We only once hear of his laughing. It is at the interposition of the poet, which rouses Brutus to indignation; but the presumptuous absurdity of it tickles Cassius' sardonic humour [IV. iii. 124-38].

For there is no doubt that he takes pleasure in detecting the weaknesses of his fellows. He has obvious relish in the thought that if he were Brutus he would not be thus cajoled, and he finds food for satisfaction in Caesar's merely physical defects. Yet there is as little of self-complacency as of hero-worship in the man. He turns his remorseless scrutiny on his own nature and his own cause, and neither maintains that the one is noble or the other honourable, nor denies the personal alloy in his motives. This is the purport of that strange soliloquy that at first sight seems to place Cassius in the ranks of Shakespeare's villains along with his Iagos and Richards, rather than of the mixed characters, compact of good and evil, to whom nevertheless we feel that he is akin.

> Well, Brutus, thou art noble: yet, I see,
> Thy honourable metal may be wrought
> From that it is disposed: therefore it is
>   meet
> That noble minds keep ever with their
>   likes:
> For who so firm that cannot be seduced?
> Caesar doth bear me hard: but he loves
>   Brutus:
> If I were Brutus now and he were Cassius,
> He should not humour me.
>   [I. ii. 308-15]

It frequently happens that cynics view themselves as well as others in their meaner aspects. Probably Cassius is making the worst of his own case and is indulging that vein of self-mockery and scorn that Caesar observed in him. But at any rate the lurking sense of unworthiness in himself and his purpose will be apt to increase in such a man his natural impatience of alleged superiority in his fellows. He is jealous of excellence, seeks to minimise it and will not tolerate it. It is on this characteristic that Shakespeare lays stress. Plutarch reports the saying "that Brutus could evill away with the tyrannie and that Cassius hated the tyranne, making many complayntes for the injuries he had done him"; and instances Caesar's appropriation of some lions that Cassius had intended for the sports, as well as the affair of the city praetorship. But in the play these specific grievances are almost effaced in the vague statement, "Caesar doth bear me hard"; which implies little more than general ill-will. It is now resentment of pre-eminence that makes Cassius a malcontent. Caesar finds him "very dangerous" just because of his grudge at greatness; and his own avowal that he "would as lief not be as live to be in awe" [I. ii. 95-6] of a thing like himself, merely puts a fairer colour on the same unamiable trait. He may represent republican liberty and equality, at least in the aristocratic acceptation, but it is on their less admirable side. His disposition is to level down, by repudiating the leader, not to level up, by learning from him. In the final results this would mean the triumph of the second best, a dull and uniform mediocrity in art, thought and politics, unbroken by the predominance of the man of genius and king of men. And it may be feared that this ideal, translated into the terms of democracy, is too frequent in our modern communities. But true freedom is not incompatible with the most loyal acknowledgment of the master-mind. . . . (pp. 275-79)

Yet notwithstanding this taint of enviousness and spite, Cassius is far from being a despicable or even an unattractive character. He may play the Devil's Advocate in regard to individuals, but he is capable of a high enthusiasm for his cause, such as it is. We must share his calenture of excitement, as he strides about the streets in the tempest that fills Casca with superstitious dread and Cicero with discomfort at the nasty weather. His republicanism may be a narrow creed, but at least he is willing to be a martyr to it; when he hears that Caesar is to wear the crown, his resolution is prompt and Roman-like:

> I know where I will wear this dagger then:
> Cassius from bondage will deliver Cassius.
>   [I. iii. 89-90]

And surely at the moment of achievement, whatever was mean and sordid in the man is consumed in his prophetic rapture that fires the soul of Brutus and prolongs itself in his response.

The armies of Brutus and Octavius Caesar meet at Philippi in a 1950 Shakespeare Memorial Theatre presentation of Julius Caesar. *Act V, scene i.*

Cassius.   How many ages hence
Shall this our lofty scene be acted over
In states unborn and accents yet un-
   known!
Brutus. How many times shall Caesar
bleed in sport
That now on Pompey's basis lies along
No worthier than the dust!

                              [III. i. 111-16]

And even to individuals if they stand the test of his mordant criticism, he can pay homage and admiration. The perception that Brutus may be worked upon is the toll he pays to his self-love, but, that settled, he can feel deep reverence and affection for Brutus' more ideal virtue. Perhaps the best instance of it is the scene of their dispute. Brutus . . . is practically, if not theoretically, in the wrong, and certainly he is much the more violent and bitter; but Cassius submits to receive his forgiveness and to welcome his assurance that he will bear with him in future. This implies no little deference and magnanimity in one who so ill brooks a secondary role. But he does give the lead to Brutus, and in all things, even against his better judgment, yields him the primacy.

And then it is impossible not to respect his thorough efficiency. In whatsoever concerns the management of affairs and of men, he knows the right thing to do, and, when left to himself, he does it. He sees how needful Brutus is to the cause and gains him—gains him, in part by a trickery, which Shakespeare without historical warrant ascribes to him; but the trickery succeeds because he has gauged Brutus' nature aright. He takes the correct measure of the danger from Antony, of his love for Caesar and his talents, which Brutus so contemptuously underrates. So, too, after the assassination, when Brutus says,

I know that we shall have him well to
   friend;

                              [III. i. 143]

he answers,

I wish we may: but yet I have a mind
That fear him much; and my misgiving
   still
Falls shrewdly to the purpose.

                              [III. i. 144-46]

Brutus seeks to win Antony with general considerations of right and justice, Cassius employs a more effective argument:

Your voice shall be as strong as any man's
In the disposing of new dignities.

                              [III. i. 177-78]

He altogether disapproves of the permission granted to Antony to pronounce the funeral oration. He grasps the situation when the civil war breaks out much better than Brutus:

> In such a time as this it is not meet
> That every nice offence should bear his
> comment.
>
> [IV. iii. 7-8]

His plans of the campaign are better, and he has a much better notion of conducting the battle.

All such shrewd sagacity is entitled to our respect. Yet even in this department Cassius is outdone by the unpractical Brutus, so soon as higher moral qualities are required, and the wisdom of the fox yields to the wisdom of the man. . . . [however] passionate and wrong-headed Brutus may be in their contention, he has too much sense of the becoming to wrangle in public, as Cassius begins to do. Another more conspicuous example is furnished by the way in which they bear anxiety. (pp. 279-82)

[When Popilius Lena speaks with Caesar at the Capitol at the beginning of Act III, scene i,] Cassius believes the worst, loses his head, now hurries on Casca, now prepares for suicide. But Brutus, the disinterested man, is less swayed by personal hopes and fears, keeps his composure, urges his friend to be constant, and can calmly judge of the situation. It is the same defect of endurance that brings about Cassius' death. Really things are shaping well for them, but he misconstrues the signs just as he has misconstrued the words of Lena, and kills himself owing to a mistake; as Messala points out:

> Mistrust of good success hath done this
> deed.
>
> [V. iii. 65]

This want of inward strength explains the ascendancy which Brutus with his more dutiful and therefore more steadfast nature exercises over him, though Cassius is in many ways the more capable man of the two. They both have schooled themselves in the discipline of fortitude, Brutus in Stoic renunciation, Cassius in Epicurean independence; but in the great crises where nature asserts herself, Brutus is strong and Cassius is weak. And as often happens with men, in the supreme trial their professed creeds no longer satisfy them, and they consciously abandon them. But while Cassius in his evil fortune falls back on the superstitions which he had ridiculed Caesar for adopting on his good fortune, Brutus falls back on his feeling of moral dignity, and gives himself the death which theoretically he disapproves.

Yet, when all is said and done, what a fine figure Cassius is, and how much both of love and respect he can inspire. (pp. 282-83)

> M. W. MacCallum, "Julius Caesar: The
> Remaining Characters," in his Shake-

speare's Roman Plays and Their Background, *1910. Reprint by Russell & Russell, 1967, pp. 275-99.*

MARK ANTONY

Harley Granville-Barker

*[Granville-Barker maintains that on the surface **Antony** appears to be a "good sort," initially supporting the conspirators after they have assassinated **Caesar**; but underneath he is really an instinctive politician, the critic declares, who demonstrates his opportunism by manipulating the crowd to avenge **Caesar's** death. Granville-Barker further contends that **Antony's** rousing the Roman populace is not altogether mischievous; rather, it also reflects his empathy for them because he considers himself a common man whose sensibilities are outraged at the injustice of **Caesar's** murder. For further commentary on **Antony's** character, see the excerpts by Lawrence Danson, Robert E. Knoll, Brents Stirling, and Gayle Greene.]*

> There is a tide in the affairs of men
> Which, taken at the flood, leads on to
> fortune. . . .
>
> [IV. iii. 218-19]

Mark Antony cannot always talk so wisely, but he takes the tide that Brutus loses. He is a born opportunist, and we see him best in the light of his great opportunity. He stands contrasted with both Cassius and Brutus, with the man whom his fellows respect the more for his aloofness, and with such a rasping colleague as Cassius must be. Antony is, above all things, a good sort.

Shakespeare keeps him in ambush throughout the first part of the play. Up to the time when he faces the triumphant conspirators he speaks just thirty-three words. But there have already been no less than seven separate references to him, all significant. And this careful preparation culminates as significantly in the pregnant message he sends by his servant from the house to which it seems he has fled, bewildered by the catastrophe of Caesar's death. Yet, as we listen, it is not the message of a very bewildered man. Antony, so far, is certainly—in what we might fancy would be his own lingo—a dark horse. And, though we may father him on Plutarch, to English eyes there can be no more typically English figure than the sportsman turned statesman, but a sportsman still. Such men range up and down our history. Antony is something besides, however, that we used to flatter ourselves was not quite so English. He can be, when occasion serves, the perfect demagogue. Nor has Shakespeare any illusions as to what the harsher needs of politics may convert your sportsman once he is out to kill. The conspirators are fair game doubtless. But Lepidus, a little later, will be the carted stag.

> A barren-spirited fellow; one that feeds
> On abject orts and imitations,
> Which, out of use and staled by other men,
> Begin his fashion: do not talk of him
> But as a property . . .
>
> [IV. i. 36-40]

to serve the jovial Antony's turn! This is your good sort, your sportsman, your popular orator, stripped very bare.

The servant's entrance with Antony's message, checking the conspirators' triumph, significant in its insignificance, is the turning point of the play. But Shakespeare plucks further advantage from it. It allows him to bring Antony out of ambush completely effective and in double guise; the message foreshadows him as politician, a minute later we see him grieving deeply for his friend's death. There is, of course, nothing incompatible in the two aspects of the man, but the double impression is all-important. He must impress us as uncalculatingly abandoned to his feelings, risking his very life to vent them. For a part of his strength lies in impulse; he can abandon himself to his feelings, as Brutus the philosopher cannot. Moreover, this bold simplicity is his safe-conduct now. Were the conspirators not impressed by it, did it not seem to obliterate his politic side, they might well and wisely take him at his word and finish with him then and there. And at the back of his mind Antony has this registered clearly enough. It must be with something of the sportsman's—and the artist's—happy recklessness that he flings the temptation at them:

> Live a thousand years,
> I shall not find myself so apt to die:
> No place will please me so, no mean of
>   death,
> As here by Cæsar, and by you cut off,
> The choice and master spirits of this age.
>
> [III. i. 159-63]

He means it; but he knows, as he says it, that there is no better way of turning the sword of a so flattered choice and master spirit aside. It is this politic, shadowed aspect of Antony that is to be their undoing; so Shakespeare is concerned to keep it clear at the back of our minds too. Therefore he impresses it on us first by the servant's speech, and Antony himself is free a little later to win us and the conspirators both.

Not that the politician does not begin to peep pretty soon. He tactfully ignores the cynicism of Cassius,

> Your voice shall be as strong as any man's
> In the disposing of new dignities.
>
> [III. i. 177]

But by Brutus' reiterated protest that Cæsar was killed in wise kindness what realist, what ironist—and Antony is both—would not be tempted?

> I doubt not of your wisdom.
> Let each man render me his bloody
>   hand. . . .
>
> [III. i. 183-84]

And, in bitter irony, he caps their ritual with his own. It is the ritual of friendship, but of such a friendship as the blood of Cæsar, murdered by his friends, may best cement. To Brutus the place of honor in the compact; to each red-handed devotee his due; and last, but by no means least, in Antony's love shall be Trebonius who drew him away while the deed was done. And so to the final, most fitting apostrophe:

> Gentlemen all!
>
> [III. i. 190]

Emotion subsided, the politician plays a good game. They shall never be able to say he approved their deed; but he is waiting, please, for those convincing reasons that Cæsar was dangerous. He even lets slip a friendly warning to Cassius that the prospect is not quite clear. Then, with yet more disarming frankness, comes the challenging request to Brutus to let him speak in the market place. As he makes it, a well-calculated request! For how can Brutus refuse, how admit a doubt that the Roman people will not approve this hard service done them? Still, that there may be no doubt at all, Brutus will first explain everything to his fellow-citizens himself, lucidly and calmly. When reason has made sure of her sway, the emotional, the "gamesome," Antony may do homage to his friend.

> Be it so;
> I do desire no more.
>
> [III. i. 251-52]

responds Antony, all docility and humility, all gravity—though if ever a smile could sharpen words, it could give a grim edge to these. So they leave him with dead Cæsar.

In this contest thus opened between the man of high argument and the instinctive politician, between principle (mistaken or not) and opportunism, we must remember that Antony can be by no means confident of success. He foresees chaos. He knows, if these bemused patriots do not, that it takes more than correct republican doctrines to replace a great man. But as to this Roman mob—this citizenry, save the mark!—whoever knows which way it will turn? The odds are on the whole against him. Still he'll try his luck; Octavius, though, had better keep safely out of the way meanwhile. All his senses are sharpened by emergency. Before ever Octavius' servant can speak he has recognized the fellow and guessed the errand. Shakespeare shows us his mind at its swift work, its purposes shaping.

> Passion, I see, is catching, for mine eyes,
> Seeing those beads of sorrow stand in
>   thine,
> Began to water.
>
> [III. i. 283-85]

—from which it follows that if the sight of Cæsar's body can so move the man and the man's tears so move him, why, his own passion may move his hearers in the market place presently to some purpose! His imagination, once it takes fire, flashes its way along, not by reason's slow process though in reason's terms.

To what he is to move his hearers we know: and it will be worth while later to analyze the famous speech, that triumph of histrionics. For though the actor of Antony must move us with it also—and he can scarcely fail to—Shakespeare has set him the further, harder and far more important task of showing us an Antony the mob never see, of making him clear to us, moreover, even while we are stirred by his eloquence, of making clear to us just by what it is we are stirred. It would, after all, be pretty poor playwriting and acting which could achieve no more than a plain piece of mob oratory, however gorgeous; a pretty poor compliment to an audience to ask of it no subtler response than the mob's. But to show us, and never for a moment to let slip from our sight, the complete and complex Antony, impulsive and calculating, warm-hearted and callous, aristocrat, sportsman and demagogue, that will be for the actor an achievement indeed; and the playwright has given him all the material for it.

Shakespeare himself knows, no one better, what mere historionics may amount to. He has been accused of showing in a later play [*Coriolanus*] (but unjustly, I hold) his too great contempt for the mob; he might then have felt something deeper than contempt for the man who could move the mob by such means; he may even have thought Brutus made the better speech. Antony, to be sure, is more than an actor; for one thing he writes his own part as he goes along. But he gathers the ideas for it as he goes too, with no greater care for their worth than the actor need have so long as they are effective at the moment. He lives abundantly in the present, his response to its call is unerring. He risks the future. How does the great oration end?

> Mischief, thou are afoot;
> Take thou what course thou wilt!
> [III. ii. 260-61]

A wicked child, one would say, that has whipped up his fellow-children to a riot of folly and violence. That is one side of him. But the moment after he is off, brisk, cool and businesslike, to play the next move in the game with that very cool customer, Octavius.

He has had no tiresome principles to consult or to expound.

> I only speak right on. . . .
> [III. ii. 223]

he boasts;

> I tell you that which you yourselves do know. . . .
> [III. ii. 224]

An admirable maxim for popular orators and popular writers too! There is nothing aloof, nothing superior about Antony. He may show a savage contempt for this man or that; he has a sort of liking for men in the mass. He is, in fact, the common man made perfect in his commonness; yet he is perceptive of himself as of his fellows, and, even so, content.

What follows upon his eloquent mourning for Cæsar? When the chaos in Rome has subsided he ropes his "merry fortune" into harness. It is not a very pleasant colloquy with which the fourth act opens.

> *Antony.* These many then shall die; their names are pricked.
> *Octavius.* Your brother too must die; consent you, Lepidus?
> *Lepidus.* I do consent.
> *Octavius.* 　　　Prick him down, Antony.
> *Lepidus.* Upon condition Publius shall not live,
> Who is your sister's son, Mark Antony.
> *Antony.* He shall not live; look, with a spot I damn him.
> [IV. i. 1-6]

The conspirators have, of course, little right to complain. But four lines later we learn that Lepidus himself, when his two friends have had their use of him, is to fare not much better than his brother—than the brother he has himself just given so callously to death! Can he complain either, then? This is the sort of beneficence the benevolent Brutus has let loose on the world.

But Antony finishes the play in fine form; victorious in battle, politically magnanimous to a prisoner or two, and ready with a resounding tribute to Brutus, now that he lies dead. Not in quite such fine form, though; for the shadow of that most unsportsmanlike young man Octavius is already moving visibly to his eclipse. (pp. 21-6)

> *Harley Granville-Barker, "Antony," in* Twentieth Century Interpretations of Julius Caesar: A Collection of Critical Essays, *edited by Leonard F. Dean, Prentice-Hall, Inc., 1968, pp. 21-6.*

SOURCES FOR FURTHER STUDY

LITERARY COMMENTARY:

Bonjour, Adrien. *The Structure of "Julius Caesar."* Liverpool: Liverpool University Press, 1958, 81 p.

Analyzes the structure, themes, and imagery of *Julius Caesar.* Bonjour identifies the play's central issue as the "twofold theme" of political and personal crisis. He also maintains that the drama has two heroes, Caesar and Brutus, who alternately evoke our praise and blame until, at the end, our sympathies are divided.

Coursen, Herbert R., Jr. "The Fall and Decline of *Julius Caesar.*" *Texas Studies in Literature and Language* IV, No. 2 (Summer 1962): 241-51.
Contends that the structure of *Julius Caesar* is closely linked to Shakespeare's use of "height and lowness" imagery. According to Coursen, this imagery is successfully employed in the first three acts of the play, where it serves to contrast Caesar's greatness with the conspirators' lesser status. This structural design disintegrates with Caesar's death, however, and lowness imagery predominates the rest of the play.

Dean, Leonard F., ed. *Twentieth Century Interpretations of Julius Caesar.* Englewood Cliffs, N.J.: Prentice-Hall, 1968, 120 p.
Eighteen essays on *Julius Caesar* by noted critics.

Foakes, R. A. "An Approach to *Julius Caesar.*" *Shakespeare Quarterly* V, No. 3 (Summer 1954): 259-70.
Argues that the structural unity of *Julius Caesar* is directly related to the conspiracy and shows how language and imagery contribute to this dramatic framework. Foakes also discusses the imagery of blood, fire, dreams, and omens, Brutus and Caesar's habit of referring to themselves in the third person, and the symbolic implications of various characters' names.

Frye, Roland Mushat. "Rhetoric and Poetry in *Julius Caesar.*" *The Quarterly Journal of Speech* 37, No. 1 (February 1951): 41-8.
Examines Antony's funeral oration, outlining why it is effective both as poetry and rhetoric. Frye also explores the continuing appeal of the speech.

Goddard, Harold C. *"Julius Caesar."* In his *The Meaning of Shakespeare*, pp. 307-30. Chicago: University of Chicago Press, 1951.
Asserts that the central political theme of *Julius Caesar*—that violent opposition to imperialism only breeds further tyranny—is dramatized through the character of Brutus. Goddard distinguishes between the "true" Brutus, whose innocence and wisdom are symbolized by his relationships with Lucius and Portia, and that the "false" Brutus, who, in convincing himself of his own moral infallibility, demonstrates his kinship with the imperious Caesar.

Humphreys, Arthur. Introduction to *Julius Caesar,* by William Shakespeare, edited by Arthur Humphreys, pp. 1-83. Oxford: Clarendon Press, 1984.
A broad overview of several issues associated with *Julius Caesar.* Humphreys provides sections on the play's composition date, stage history, language, and imagery, as well as on Shakespeare's sources, political attitudes, and treatment of Rome and its values.

Kirschbaum, Leo. "Shakespeare's Stage Blood and Its Critical Significance." *PMLA* LXIV, No. 3 (June 1949): 517-49.
Speculates on the specific dramatic effect Shakespeare sought to achieve by having the conspirators bathe their hands and swords in the blood of Caesar's corpse.

Kittredge, George Lyman. Introduction to *The Tragedy of "Julius Caesar,"* by William Shakespeare, edited by George Lyman Kittredge, pp. vii-xix. Boston: Ginn and Co., 1939.
Discusses Shakespeare's characterizations of Caesar, Brutus, and Cassius and dismisses the objection frequently raised by critics that the drama lacks structural and thematic unity. Kittredge also comments on how Shakespeare's presentation of Roman history diverges from actual historical events.

Knights, L. C. "Shakespeare and Political Wisdom: A Note on the Personalism of *Julius Caesar* and *Coriolanus.*" *The Sewanee Review* LXI, No. 1 (Winter 1953): 43-55.
Examines how the characters' public conduct in *Julius Caesar* is influenced by their private emotions.

Levin, Richard A. "Brutus: 'Noblest Roman of Them All.'" *Ball State University Forum* 23, No. 2 (Spring 1982): 15-25.
Maintains that our judgment of Brutus must be based on the notion of friendship and loyalty in *Julius Caesar.* Levin questions whether Brutus is capable of true friendship, distinguishing him from the other conspirators through his willingness to betray a man for whom he has expressed deep affection. Brutus's lack of knowledge about friendship is his undoing, Levin concludes, for it causes him to underestimate the depth of Antony's loyalty to Caesar.

Matthews, Brander. "The Plays from Plutarch." In his *Shakespeare as a Playwright,* pp. 254-63. New York: Charles Scribner's Sons, 1913.
Contrasts the funeral orations of Brutus and Antony, analyzing what the speeches reveal about the two men's personalities.

Platt, Michael. "Rome, Empire and Aftermath: *Julius Caesar.*" In his *Rome and Romans According to Shakespeare,* rev. ed., pp. 185-257. Lantham, Md.: University Press of America, 1983.
Focuses on a wide range of political issues associated with *Julius Caesar,* including the influence of Caesar's rise to power on his Roman friends and followers, the justifiability of Caesar's assassination, and Brutus's motivation for leading the conspiracy against Caesar.

Rabkin, Norman. "Structure, Convention, and Meaning in *Julius Caesar.*" *The Journal of English and Germanic Philology* LXIII, No. 2 (April 1964): 240-54.
Maintains that with Antony's soliloquy at the

close of Act III, scene i, the play shifts from a historical drama to a revenge tragedy in which each bloody act must be answered by another. Rabkin also argues that the similarities between Caesar and Brutus suggested by the many parallels between Act II, scene i and Act II, scene ii indicate that Caesar's assassination was not justified.

Smith, Gordon Ross. "Brutus, Virtue, and Will." *Shakespeare Quarterly* X, No. 3 (Summer 1959): 367-79.

Asserts that Brutus's chief character trait is his "egotistical willfulness" and discusses fourteen separate occasions in the play where the politician demonstrates his need to dominate others.

Taylor, Myron. "Shakespeare's *Julius Caesar* and the Irony of History." *Shakespeare Quarterly* XXIV, No. 3 (Summer 1973): 301-08.

Contrasts Cassius's and Caesar's philosophical points of view and argues that Shakespeare's purpose in the play was to show that humankind is incapable of controlling its own destiny.

Van Doren, Mark. *"Julius Caesar."* In his *Shakespeare,* pp. 180-89. New York: Henry Holt and Co., 1939.

Argues that *Julius Caesar* is "more rhetoric than poetry" because the language of the play is stylized and formulaic.

Velz, John W. "Cassius as a 'Great Observer.'" *The Modern Language Review* 68, No. 2 (April 1973): 256-59.

Discusses Cassius's shrewd powers of observation in relation to his pessimism and his ability to distinguish appearance from reality.

Wall, Annie Russell. "Is Shakespeare's Caesar Ignoble?" *Poet-Lore* 4, No. 4 (15 April 1892): 191-99.

Maintains that although Shakespeare portrays Caesar's weaknesses, readers are left with a final impression of him as a wise and benevolent man who restored order and prosperity to Rome. Wall describes Brutus and Cassius as "base and vulgar murderers" and condemns Brutus for betraying a friend who loved and trusted him.

Wilson, Harold S. "Thesis: *Julius Caesar* and *Coriolanus.*" In his *On the Design of Shakespearian Tragedy,* pp. 85-114. University of Toronto Department of English, Studies and Texts, No. 5, Toronto: University of Toronto Press, 1958.

Contends that the justifiability of Caesar's assassination is the central theme of *Julius Caesar.* Wilson concentrates on the moral downfalls of Caesar and Brutus and also emphasizes the impartiality of Shakespeare's account of the two men.

MEDIA ADAPTATIONS:

Julius Caesar. Metro-Goldwyn-Mayer, Inc., 1953.

Critically acclaimed motion picture version of the tragedy, featuring Marlon Brando, James Mason, and John Gielgud. The film was directed by Joseph L. Mankiewicz and produced by John Houseman. 120 minutes.

Julius Caesar. BHE Education Ltd.; Seaborne Enterprises Ltd., 1969.

Educational video offering performances of key scenes in the play. Distributed by Phoenix/BFA Films. 28 minutes.

Julius Caesar. Peter Snell; Commonwealth United, 1970.

Film version of the drama starring Charlton Heston, John Gielgud, Jason Robards, Richard Chamberlain, Robert Vaughn, and Diana Rigg. Distributed by Republic Pictures Home Video. 116 minutes.

Julius Caesar. BBC, Time-Life Television, 1979.

Televised performance of the tragedy, part of the "Shakespeare Plays" series. Distributed by Time-Life Video. 161 minutes.

MACBETH

INTRODUCTION

At about 2100 lines, *Macbeth* is Shakespeare's shortest tragedy and among the briefest of his plays. Scholars generally agree that the drama was written around 1606 because various references in the play correspond to events which occurred in that year. Many also believe that it was composed for a performance before King James I, who had a deep interest in witchcraft. Quite possibly the play was one of the court entertainments offered to King Christian IV of Denmark during his visit to London in 1606. In addition, researchers suggest that Shakespeare may have written *Macbeth* to glorify King James's ancestry by associating him, through the historical Banquo, to the first Scottish king, Kenneth MacAlpin. The principal literary source for *Macbeth* is Raphael Holinshed's *Chronicles of England, Scotlande, and Irelande* (1577). However, Shakespeare took great liberties with this source, adapting various historical events to increase the dramatic effect of his tragedy. Considerable debate exists regarding the tragic context of Macbeth's downfall. In drama, a tragedy traditionally recounts the significant events or actions in a protagonist's life which, taken together, bring about the catastrophe. Classical rules of tragedy also require that the hero's ruin evokes pity and fear in the audience. Some critics assert that since Macbeth's actions throughout the play are inherently evil, he gets what he deserves in the end and therefore his downfall is not catastrophic in a tragic sense. Other commentators, however, argue that although Macbeth embraces evil, his feelings of guilt, combined with the coercion of the witches and his wife, generate pity and fear among readers and spectators at his ruin, a feeling identified in classical tragedy as catharsis.

PRINCIPAL CHARACTERS
(in order of appearance)

The Witches, or *The Weird Sisters:* Three hags who practice black magic. Their prophecies to Macbeth and Banquo suggest that Macbeth will rule Scotland and that Banquo's descendants will be kings. Later, the witches conjure up three apparitions who warn Macbeth against Macduff, assure him that no man born of woman will harm him, and declare that he will not be conquered until Birnam wood comes to Dunsinane.

Duncan: The king of Scotland. While a guest at Macbeth's castle, Duncan is murdered by his host. His assassination sets into motion a series of evil actions and unnatural disturbances that are not corrected until Malcolm and Macduff restore order at the end of the play.

Malcolm: Duncan's son, Donalbain's brother, and heir to the Scottish throne. After his father's murder, Malcolm flees to England in fear of his life. There, he recruits an army to invade Scotland and conquers Macbeth's forces at Dunsinane.

Donalbain: Duncan's son and Malcolm's brother. After the king's murder, he flees to Ireland in fear of his life.

Macbeth: The Thane of Glamis and a general in Duncan's army. He encounters three witches who predict that he will become king of Scotland. Influenced by his ambition and Lady Macbeth's urgings, Macbeth plots to murder Duncan and take the throne. His evil deed introduces corruption and unnatural disturbances into the kingdom. Macbeth is ultimately conquered by Malcolm and Macduff.

Banquo: A nobleman and a general in Duncan's army. With Macbeth, he encounters the Weird Sisters, and from their prophecies he learns that his descendants will be kings. Macbeth later arranges the murder of Banquo and his son Fleance to thwart the witches' prediction. Banquo's ghost later haunts Macbeth at a banquet.

Lady Macbeth: Macbeth's wife. She coerces her husband into murdering Duncan. When Macbeth becomes unnerved during the murder, she covers up the assassination by placing the knives belonging to the king's attendants near his corpse. After the murder, Lady Macbeth is driven insane with guilt and commits suicide.

Macduff: The Thane of Fife. After Duncan's murder, he becomes suspicious of Macbeth and flees to England to join forces with Malcolm. When Macduff returns to Scotland with Malcolm's invading army, he meets Macbeth on the battlefield. He kills his enemy after informing him that he was "untimely ripp'd" from his mother's womb, thus fulfilling the witches' prophesy that no man born of woman can harm Macbeth.

Fleance: Banquo's son. Macbeth attempts to assassinate him along with his father in order to thwart the witches' prophecy that Banquo's descendants will become kings. Fleance escapes, however, and assures the survival of the family line.

Lady Macduff: Macduff's wife. Macbeth sends assassins to murder Lady Macduff and her family when he learns that her husband has fled to England.

PLOT SYNOPSIS

Act I: After crushing Macdonwald's rebellion against Duncan, Macbeth and Banquo are journeying to the king's castle when they are surprised by the sudden appearance of three witches. The hags predict that Macbeth, who holds the title of Thane of Glamis, will also become Thane of Cawdor and then king of Scotland and that although Banquo will never rule, his descendants will be monarchs. After the witches vanish, Macbeth learns that Duncan has condemned the Thane of Cawdor for treason and that the king will bestow the title on Macbeth. As a result of this development, Macbeth contemplates fulfilling the rest of the witches' prophecy himself by assassinating the king. After receiving a letter from Macbeth detailing the Weird Sisters' revelations, Lady Macbeth also resolves to murder Duncan, who plans to stay the night at their castle in Inverness. When her husband arrives at the castle, Lady Macbeth scoffs at his fear and lack of determination and finally persuades him to assassinate the king that very night.

Act II: To conceal his treachery, Macbeth stabs the sleeping Duncan with knives belonging to the king's attendants. He becomes so unnerved by the deed, however, that he forgets to leave the daggers in Duncan's chamber, and Lady Macbeth must finish the task. Despite his wife's confidence that the murder was a success, Macbeth continues to fear that their treachery will lead to further trouble. When Duncan's corpse is discovered, Malcolm and Donalbain fear for their own lives and flee Scotland. As a result, they are suspected of murdering their father, and Macbeth is crowned king.

Act III: Although Macbeth has fulfilled the witches' prophecy that he will become king, he still feels threatened by the prediction that Banquo's heirs will one day rule Scotland. He therefore invites Banquo and Fleance to a banquet and hires assassins to murder them on the way to the castle. The murderers succeed in killing Banquo, but Fleance escapes. At the banquet, Macbeth expresses his regret at the absence of his friend; but as he approaches his seat at the table, he is horrified to find Banquo's bloody ghost sitting in his chair. Macbeth's fearful cries startle the other guests, who cannot see the spirit, and Lady Macbeth sends them away. Once Macbeth calms down, he decides to seek out the witches to receive their assurance about his future as king of Scotland.

Act IV: The Weird Sisters meet with Macbeth and conjure up three apparitions who warn him to beware Macduff, assure him that no man born of woman can harm him, and tell him that he will not be conquered until Birnam wood comes to his castle at Dunsinane. He is disturbed, however, by the apparition of a succession of eight kings followed by Banquo's ghost—an indication that Banquo's heirs will indeed rule Scotland. Later, when Macbeth learns that Macduff has fled Scotland to join forces with Malcolm, he sends assassins to murder Lady Macduff and her children. Meanwhile in England, Malcolm tests Macduff's loyalty by pretending to be a lascivious and immoral man incapable of ruling a kingdom. When Macduff expresses his indignation at Malcolm's supposed exploits, the prince is satisfied that he is honest and invites the fugitive to join his army. During his interview with Malcolm, Macduff receives word that Macbeth has slaughtered his family and vows to avenge their deaths.

Act V: Driven insane by fear and guilt over Duncan's murder, Lady Macbeth walks in her sleep and tries to rub out imaginary blood stains on her hands. Meanwhile, Macbeth desperately clings to the witches' assurances that he is invulnerable as he prepares to engage Malcolm's army at Dunsinane castle. He experiences an increasingly overwhelming fear and nervousness as a result of his past actions, but when he learns that his wife has committed suicide, his reaction is impassive. Macbeth is initially disconcerted when he hears reports that his enemies approach Dunsinane camouflaged by trees from Birnam wood, but reassures himself that no man born of woman can harm him. When he encounters Macduff on the battlefield, however, Macbeth learns that his opponent was "untimely ripp'd" from his mother's womb. Realizing that his fate is sealed, Macbeth nevertheless battles on until he is killed by Macduff. Upon defeating his enemy, Macduff triumphantly holds Macbeth's severed head aloft to Malcolm, who is proclaimed king of Scotland.

PRINCIPAL TOPICS

Macbeth is a complex study of evil and its corrupting influence on humanity. Some critics argue that Shakespeare adapted historical accounts of Macbeth to illustrate his larger view of evil's operation in the world. The particular evil that the protagonist commits has wide-spread consequences, causing a series of further evils. As a result, the tragedy is not fully resolved through the fallen hero's death, but through the forces of good that ultimately correct all the evil Macbeth has unleashed. The witches, through their ambiguous prophecies, represent a supernatural power that introduces evil into *Macbeth*. Their equivocations—the intentional stating of half-truths—conceal the sinister nature of their predictions, and Macbeth does not consider the possibility that they are trying to deceive him. In fact, the Weird Sisters' attempts at misinformation succeed not only because they favorably interpret the hero's future, but also because their revelations seem to come true almost immediately. Although inherently malevolent, the witches' prophecies do not necessarily signify the actual existence of evil, but suggest instead the potential for evil in the world. The Weird Sisters themselves do not have the power to enact a diabolic course of events such as that which ensues in *Macbeth;* rather, their power lies in tempting humans like Macbeth to sin. When Macbeth succumbs to the temptation to commit murder, he himself is the active catalyst that unleashes evil upon the world. The evil which initially manifests itself in Duncan's murder not only disintegrates Macbeth's personal world, but also expands until it corrupts all levels of creation, contaminating the family, the state, and the physical universe. For example, Macduff's family is murdered, Scotland is embroiled in a civil war, and during Duncan's assassination "the earth was feverous, and did shake" (II. iii. 60).

Shakespeare's depiction of time is another central concern in *Macbeth.* Macbeth dislocates the passage of time—a process fundamental to humankind's existence—when he succumbs to evil and murders Duncan. Shakespeare uses this displacement as a key symbol in dramatizing the steady disintegration of the hero's world. Macbeth's evil actions initially interrupt the normal flow of time, but order gradually regains its proper shape and overpowers the new king, as demonstrated by his increasing guilt and sleeplessness. Ironically, the Weird Sisters can be seen as an element that contributes to the restoration of order. Although Macbeth disrupts the natural course of events by acting on the witches' early prophecies, their later predictions suggest that his power will shortly end. This premonition is apparent in the Birnam wood revelation; while Macbeth believes that the prediction insures his invulnerability, it really implies that his rule will soon expire. Some critics observe that different kinds of time interact in *Macbeth.* The most apparent form of time can be described as chronological. Chronological time establishes the sense of physical passage in the play, focusing on the succession of events that can be measured by clock, calendar, and the movement of the sun, moon, and stars. Another aspect of time, identified as providential, overarches the action of the entire play. Providential time is the divine ordering of events that is initially displaced by Macbeth's evil actions, but which gradually overpowers him and re-establishes harmony in the world. Macbeth conceives of another kind of time that seems to defy cause and effect when he unsuccessfully attempts to reconcile his anticipation of the future with the memory of his ignoble actions. This dilemma initiates a period of inaction in the protagonist's life

that culminates in his resigned acceptance of death as the inexorable passage of time. This confused displacement of time pervades the action of *Macbeth* until Malcolm and Macduff restore a proper sense of order at the end of the play.

Another important issue in *Macbeth* is Shakespeare's ambiguous treatment of gender and sex roles. In many instances, the playwright either inverts a character's conventional gender characteristics or divests the figure of them altogether. Lady Macbeth is perhaps the most obvious example of this dispossession. In Act I, scene v, she prepares to confront her husband by resolving to "unsex" herself, to suppress any supposed weakness associated with her feminine nature, so that she can give Macbeth the strength and determination to carry out Duncan's murder. After the king is killed, however, her feelings of guilt gradually erode her resolve and she goes insane. Macbeth is perhaps the character most affected by the question of gender in the tragedy. From the beginning of the play, he is plagued by feelings of doubt and insecurity which his wife attributes to "effeminate" weakness. Fearing that her husband does not have the resolve to murder Duncan, Lady Macbeth cruelly manipulates his lack of self-confidence by questioning his manhood. Some critics maintain that as a result of his wife's machinations, Macbeth develops a warped perspective of manliness, equating it with the less humanistic attribute of self-seeking aggression. The more the protagonist pursues his ideal understanding of manliness—first by murdering Duncan, then Banquo, and finally Macduff's family—the less humane he becomes. Commentators who subscribe to this reading of Macbeth's character argue that the ruthlessness with which he strives to obtain this perverted version of manhood ultimately separates him from the rest of humankind. Through his diminishing humaneness, the protagonist essentially forfeits all claims on humanity itself—a degeneration, he ultimately realizes, that renders meaningless his ideal of manliness.

Various image patterns support the sense of corruption and deterioration that pervades the dramatic action of *Macbeth.* Perhaps one of the most dominant groups is that of babies and breast-feeding. Infants symbolize pity throughout the play, and breast-milk represents humanity, tenderness, sympathy, and natural human feelings, all of which have been debased by Macbeth and Lady Macbeth's evil actions. Another set of images focuses on sickness and medicine, all of which occur, significantly, in the last three acts of the play, after Macbeth has ascended the Scottish throne. These patterns are given greater depth through Shakespeare's graphic depiction of blood in the tragedy. The numerous references to blood not only provide Macbeth's ruthless actions with a visual dimension, they also underscore Scotland's degeneration after Macbeth murders Duncan and usurps the crown. Ironically, blood also symbolizes the purifying process by which Malcolm and Macduff—the restorers of goodness—purge the weakened country of Macbeth's villainy. Other major image patterns include sleep and sleeplessness, order versus disorder, and the contrast between light and darkness.

CHARACTER STUDIES

One of the most significant reasons for the enduring critical interest in Macbeth's character is that he represents humankind's universal propensity to temptation and sin. Macbeth's excessive ambition motivates him to murder Duncan, and once the evil act is accomplished, he sets into motion a series of sinister events that ultimately lead to his downfall. But Macbeth is not merely a cold-blooded, calculating murderer; even before he kills the king, he is greatly troubled by his conscience. While plotting Duncan's murder, his better nature warns him that the act is wrong; he nearly persuades himself to reject the plan, but his wife forces him to reaffirm his determination. In addition, Macbeth possesses a powerful imagination—demonstrated by his excessive philosophizing over his condition—that sways his actions. In fact, the hero's imagination contributes greatly to his decision to murder Duncan: after his first meeting with the Weird Sisters, Macbeth acknowledges that he can wait to see if their prediction of his imminent kingship will come true, but his imagination persuades him to fulfill the prophecy with his own hands. Later, Macbeth's overworked imagination produces feelings of guilt and betrayal that throw his mind into disorder, gradually eroding his bravery and replacing it with inexplicable fear and paranoia. Several critics remark that although Macbeth fully embraces evil, his philosophizing over the hopelessness of his situation results in some of the greatest poetry ever written on the human condition. Others argue, however, that the hero's rhetoric becomes less sincere as his actions become more ruthless.

Most critics contend that Lady Macbeth's principal dramatic function in *Macbeth* is to persuade her husband to commit evil. Some critics further suggest that Lady Macbeth embodies a feminine malevolence in the play that corresponds to a masculine fear of domination by women. This antagonism is particularly evident in the unusual level of control Lady Macbeth exerts over her husband. Further, she serves much the same role as the witches do in manipulating Macbeth to murder Duncan, but her influence is of a more frightening nature. As supernatural beings, the Weird Sisters represent a remote, abstract evil, and their mode of exploitation exists only on a cosmic level. Lady Macbeth's coercion of her husband is more terrify-

ing because she brings the full magnitude of the witches' evil influence to the domestic level by calling on demonic forces to suppress her femininity and give her the power to make Macbeth murder Duncan. This unholy contract does not endure, for, after she actively participates in covering up Duncan's murder, Lady Macbeth's feminine nature reasserts itself, and she is driven insane. Many commentators assert that Lady Macbeth's mental breakdown manifests itself in the sleepwalking episode (Act V, scene i), in which she is not so much distracted by the guilt over her role in Duncan's murder as she is by the inability to escape the memory of it.

While much of the action of *Macbeth* revolves around the protagonist and his wife, Banquo is also an important figure. One critical perspective views Banquo's function as essentially symbolic: he is portrayed as a man who, like Macbeth, has the capacity for both God's grace and sin; but unlike the protagonist, he puts little stock in the Weird Sisters' prophecies and does not succumb to their temptations. Banquo's reluctance to dwell on the witches' predictions therefore underscores, by contrast, the nature of Macbeth's descent into evil. Another critical viewpoint, however, suggests that Banquo is just as guilty as Macbeth of succumbing to the witches' temptations. By complying with Macbeth's accession to the throne and not raising suspicions about the protagonist's role in Duncan's murder, Banquo reveals a secret hope that the Weird Sisters' prophecy for him will also come true. Shakespeare also contrasts Duncan and Macbeth. Through his benevolence, graciousness, and almost naive trust, Duncan embodies a sense of harmony which generally inspires loyalty among his followers. These attributes become inverted in Macbeth, who introduces tumult and disorder into the kingdom when he murders the king and assumes his place on the throne. The sense of order inherent in Duncan's reign is thus displaced until the end of the play when Malcolm and Macduff, who signify purification in *Macbeth*, restore a proper sense of "measure, time, and place" (V. ix. 39) to a world devastated by Macbeth's evil actions.

CONCLUSION

Frank Kermode asserts that "*Macbeth* is a play about the eclipse of civility and manhood, the temporary triumph of evil; when it ends, virtue and justice are restored." Shakespeare displays a remarkable perception of the human condition by dramatizing not only the way in which evil enters Macbeth's world, but also the devastating effect it has on those who yield to temptation and sin. Shakespeare concludes the tragedy on a hopeful note, however, for as awesome and corruptive as the evil is that pervades *Macbeth*, it is only temporary. Ultimately, time and order are restored through the actions of the defenders of goodness.

(See also *Shakespearean Criticism,* Vol. 3)

OVERVIEW

Mark Van Doren

[Van Doren presents a broad survey of Macbeth, asserting that Shakespeare's triumph lies in his construction of a strange, dark, and shapeless world which from the outset pits itself against the protagonist. Ironically, **Macbeth** *himself represents the ever-changing form and shape of this bizarre world, the critic notes, for his own wavering over whether or not to kill* **Duncan** *is a predominant trait of his character. Van Doren also discusses the figure of* **Lady Macbeth,** *arguing that because she is less imaginative than her husband, her mind cannot withstand the torture of guilt as long as* **Macbeth's** *does. The critic also briefly examines some important symbols in* Macbeth— *including fear, blood, and sleep—but focuses chiefly on the representation of time and death. According to Van Doren, time—an element fundamental to human experience—goes awry and disintegrates* **Macbeth's** *world. Consequently, the hero develops a pessimistic view of death as merely an extension of the inexorable and eternal passage of time. The critic also discusses* **Duncan's** *dramatic function in Mac-*beth, *observing that many of his characteristics directly contradict those of* **Macbeth.** *In addition,* **Malcolm** *and* **Macduff** *bring order and healing to* **Macbeth's** *strange and shapeless world, and with their return "blood will cease to flow, movement will recommence, fear will be forgotten, sleep will season every life, and the seeds of time will blossom in due order."]*

The brevity of *Macbeth* is so much a function of its brilliance that we might lose rather than gain by turning up the lost scenes of legend. This brilliance gives us in the end somewhat less than the utmost that tragedy can give. The hero, for instance, is less valuable as a person than Hamlet, Othello, or Lear; or Antony, or Coriolanus, or Timon. We may not rejoice in his fall as Dr. [Samuel] Johnson says we must, yet we have known too little about him and have found too little virtue in him to experience at his death the sense of an unutterable and tragic loss made necessary by ironies beyond our understanding. He commits murder in violation of a nature which we can assume to have been noble, but we can only assume this. Macbeth has surrendered his soul before the play begins.

When we first see him he is already invaded by those fears which are to render him vicious and which are finally to make him abominable. They will also reveal him as a great poet. But his poetry, like the poetry of the play, is to be concerned wholly with sensation and catastrophe. *Macbeth* like *Lear* is all end; the difference appearing in the speed with which doom rushes down, so that this rapidest of tragedies suggests whirlwinds rather than glaciers, and in the fact that terror rather than pity is the mode of the accompanying music. *Macbeth,* then, is not in the fullest known sense a tragedy. But we do not need to suppose that this is because important parts of it have been lost. More of it would have had to be more of the same. And the truth is that no significant scene seems to be missing. *Macbeth* is incomparably brilliant as it stands, and within its limits perfect. What it does it does with flawless force. It hurls a universe against a man, and if the universe that strikes is more impressive than the man who is stricken, great as his size and gaunt as his soul may be, there is no good reason for doubting that this is what Shakespeare intended. The triumph of *Macbeth* is the construction of a world, and nothing like it has ever been constructed in twenty-one hundred lines.

This world, which is at once without and within Macbeth, can be most easily described as strange. The word, like the witches, is always somewhere doing its work. Even in the battle which precedes the play the thane of Glamis has made "strange images of death" [I. iii. 97], and when he comes home to his lady his face is "as a book where men may read strange matters" [I. v. 62-3]. Duncan's horses after his murder turn wild in nature and devour each other—"a thing most strange and certain" [II. iv. 14]. Nothing is as it should be in such a world. "Who would have thought the old man to have had so much blood in him?" [V. i. 39-40]. There is a drift of disorder in all events, and the air is murky with unwelcome miracles.

It is a dark world too, inhabited from the beginning by witches who meet on a blasted heath in thunder and lightning, and who hover through fog and filthy air as they leave on unspeakable errands. It is a world wherein "men must not walk too late" [III. vi. 7], for the night that was so pretty in *Romeo and Juliet, A Midsummer Night's Dream,* and *The Merchant of Venice* has grown terrible with ill-smelling mists and the stench of blood. The time that was once a playground for free and loving spirits has closed like a trap, or yawned like a bottomless pit. The "dark hour" that Banquo borrows from the night is his last hour on an earth which has lost the distinction between sun and gloom.

> Darkness does the face of earth entomb,
> When living light should kiss it.
> [II. iv. 9-10]

The second of these lines makes a sound that is notable in the play for its rarity: the sound of life in its normal ease and lightness. Darkness prevails because the witches, whom Banquo calls its instruments, have willed to produce it. But Macbeth is its instrument too, as well as its victim. And the weird sisters no less than he are expressions of an evil that employs them both and has roots running farther into darkness than the mind can guess.

It is furthermore a world in which nothing is certain to keep its shape. Forms shift and consistencies alter, so that what was solid may flow and what was fluid may congeal to stone.

> The earth hath bubbles, as the water has,
> And these are of them,
>
> [I. iii. 79-80]

says Banquo of the vanished witches. Macbeth addresses the "sure and firm set earth" [II. i. 56], but nothing could be less firm than the whole marble and the founded rock he has fancied his life to be. At the very moment he speaks he has seen a dagger which is not there, and the "strange infirmity" he confesses at the banquet will consist of seeing things that cannot be. His first apostrophe to the witches had been to creatures

> That look not like the inhabitants o' the
> earth,
> And yet are on 't.
>
> [I. iii. 41-2]

So now a dead man lives; Banquo's brains are out but he rises again, and "this is more strange than such a murder is" [III. iv. 81-2].

> Take any shape but that, and my firm
> nerves
> Shall never tremble.
>
> [III. iv. 101-02]

But the shape of everything is wrong, and the nerves of Macbeth are never proof against trembling. The cardinal instance of transformation is himself. Bellona's bridegroom has been turned to jelly.

The current of change pouring forever through this universe has, as a last effect, dissolved it. And the dissolution of so much that was solid has liberated deadly fumes, has thickened the air until it suffocates all breathers. If the footing under men is less substantial than it was, the atmosphere they must push through is almost too heavy for life. It is confining, swarming, swelling; it is viscous, it is sticky; and it threatens strangulation. All of the speakers in the play conspire to create the impression that this is so. Not only do the witches in their opening scene wail "Fair is foul, and foul is fair" [I. i. 11], but the military men who enter after them anticipate in their talk of recent battle the imagery of entanglement to come.

> Doubtful it stood,
> As two spent swimmers that do cling to-
> gether

And choke their art. . . .
> The multiplying villainies of nature
> Do swarm upon him. . . .
> So from that spring whence comfort
> seem'd to come
> Discomfort swells.
>
> [I. ii. 7-9; 11-12; 27-8]

Macbeth's sword is reported to have "smok'd with bloody execution" [I. ii. 18], and he and Banquo were "as cannons overcharg'd with double cracks" [I. ii. 37]; they

> Doubly redoubled strokes upon the foe.
>
> [I. ii. 38]

The hyperbole is ominous, the excess is sinister. In the third scene, after what seemed corporal in the witches has melted into the wind, Ross and Angus join Banquo and Macbeth to report the praises of Macbeth that had poured in on Duncan "as thick as hail" [I. iii. 97], and to salute the new thane of Cawdor. The witches then have been right in two respects, and Macbeth says in an aside:

> Two truths are told,
> As happy prologues to the swelling act
> Of the imperial theme.
>
> [I. iii. 127-29]

But the imagined act of murder swells in his mind until it is too big for its place, and his heart beats as if it were choking in its chamber.

> Why do I yield to that suggestion
> Whose horrid image doth unfix my hair
> And make my seated heart knock at my
> ribs,
> Against the use of nature? Present fears
> Are less than horrible imaginings.
> My thought, whose murder yet is but fan-
> tastical,
> Shakes so my single state of man that
> function
> Is smother'd in surmise, and nothing is
> But what is not.
>
> [I. iii. 134-42]

Meanwhile Lady Macbeth at home is visited by no such fears. When the crisis comes she will break sooner than her husband does, but her brittleness then will mean the same thing that her melodrama means now: she is a slighter person than Macbeth, has a poorer imagination, and holds in her mind less of that power which enables it to stand up under torture. The news that Duncan is coming to her house inspires her to pray that her blood be made thick; for the theme of thickness is so far not terrible in her thought.

> Come, thick night,
> And pall thee in the dunnest smoke of hell,
> That my keen knife see not the wound it
> makes,
> Nor heaven peep through the blanket of
> the dark
> To cry, "Hold, hold!"
>
> [I. v. 50-4]

The blanket of the dark—it seems to her an agreeable image, and by no means suggests an element that can enwrap or smother. With Macbeth it is different; his soliloquy in the seventh scene shows him occupied with images of nets and tangles: the consequences of Duncan's death may coil about him like an endless rope.

> If it were done when 't is done, then 't were
>   well
> It were done quickly. If the assassination
> Could trammel up the consequence, and
>   catch
> With his surcease success; that but this
>   blow
> Might be the be-all and the end-all here,
> But here, upon this bank and shoal of
>   time,
> We'd jump the life to come. But in these
>   cases
> We still have judgement here, that we but
>   teach
> Bloody instructions, which, being taught,
>   return
> To plague the inventor.
>
> > [I. vii. 1-10]

And his voice rises to shrillness as he broods in terror upon the endless echo which such a death may make in the world.

>   His virtues
> Will plead like angels, trumpet-tongu'd,
>   against
> The deep damnation of his taking-off;
> And pity, like a naked new-born babe
> Striding the blast, or heaven's cherubin
>   hors'd
> Upon the sightless couriers of the air,
> Shall blow the horrid deed in every eye,
> That tears shall drown the wind.
>
> > [I. vii. 18-25]

It is terror such as this that Lady Macbeth must endeavor to allay in what is after all a great mind. Her scolding cannot do so. She has commanded him to screw his courage to the sticking-point, but what is the question that haunts him when he comes from Duncan's bloody bed, with hands that can never be washed white again?

>   Wherefore could not I pronounce
> "Amen"?
> I had most need of blessing, and "Amen"

Paul Rogers as Macbeth and Eric Porter as Banquo face the three witches in a 1954 production of Macbeth at the Old Vic Theatre. Act I, scene iii.

> Stuck in my throat.
>
> [II. ii. 28-30]

He must not consider such things so deeply, his lady warns him. But he does, and in good time she will follow suit. That same night the Scottish earth, shaking in a convincing sympathy as the Roman earth in *Julius Caesar* never shook, considers the grievous state of a universe that suffocates in the breath of its own history. Lamentings are heard in the air, strange screams of death, and prophecies of dire combustion and confused events [II. iii. 56-8]. And the next morning, says Ross to an old man he meets,

> By the clock 't is day,
> And yet dark night strangles the travelling
>   lamp.
>
> [II. iv. 6-7]

Macbeth is now king, but his fears "stick deep" in Banquo [III. i. 49]. The thought of one more murder that will give him perhaps the "clearness" he requires [III. i. 132] seems for a moment to free his mind from its old obsessive horror of dusk and thickness, and he can actually invoke these conditions—in the only verse he ever uses with conscious literary intention.

> Come, seeling night,
> Scarf up the tender eye of pitiful day,
> And with thy bloody and invisible hand
> Cancel and tear to pieces that great bond
> Which keeps me pale! Light thickens, and
>   the crow
> Makes wing to the rooky wood;
> Good things of day begin to droop and
>   drowse,
> While night's black agents to their preys
>   do rouse.
>
> [III. ii. 46-53]

The melodrama of this, and its inferiority of effect, may warn us that Macbeth is only pretending to hope. The news of Fleance's escape brings him at any rate his fit again, and he never more ceases to be "cabin'd, cribb'd, confin'd" [III. iv. 23]. He is caught in the net for good, his feet have sunk into quicksands from which they cannot be freed, his bosom like Lady Macbeth's is "stuff'd" with "perilous stuff which weighs upon the heart" [V. iii. 44-5]—the figure varies, but the theme does not. A strange world not wholly of his own making has closed around him and rendered him motionless. His gestures are spasmodic at the end, like those of one who knows he is hopelessly engulfed. And every metaphor he uses betrays his belief that the universal congestion is past cure:

> What rhubarb, senna, or what purgative
>   drug,
> Would scour these English hence?
>
> [V. iii. 55-6]

The answer is none.

The theme never varies, however rich the range of symbols employed to suggest it. One of these symbols is of course the fear that shakes Macbeth as if he were an object not human; that makes him start when the witches call him "King hereafter," that sets his heart knocking at his ribs, that wrings from him unsafe extremities of rhetoric, that reduces him to a maniac when Banquo walks again, that spreads from him to all of Scotland until its inhabitants "float upon a wild and violent sea" of terror [IV. ii. 21], and that in the end, when he has lost the capacity to feel anything any longer, drains from him so that he almost forgets its taste [V. v. 9]. Another symbol, and one that presents itself to several of our senses at once, is blood. Never in a play has there been so much of this substance, and never has it been so sickening. "What bloody man is that?" [I. ii. 1]. The second scene opens with a messenger running in to Duncan red with wounds. And blood darkens every scene thereafter. It is not bright red, nor does it run freely and wash away. Nor is it a metaphor as it was in *Julius Caesar*. It is so real that we see, feel, and smell it on everything. And it sticks. "This is a sorry sight," says Macbeth as he comes from Duncan's murder, staring at his hands [II. ii. 17]. He had not thought there would be so much blood on them, or that it would stay there like that. Lady Macbeth is for washing the "filthy witness" off, but Macbeth knows that all great Neptune's ocean will not make him clean; rather his hand, plunged into the green, will make it all one red. The blood of the play is everywhere physical in its looks and gross in its quantity. Lady Macbeth "smears" the grooms with it, so that when they are found they seem "badg'd" and "unmannerly breech'd" with gore, and "steep'd" in the colors of their trade. The murderer who comes to report Banquo's death has blood on his face, and the "blood-bolter'd Banquo" when he appears shakes "gory locks" at Macbeth [IV. i. 123], who in deciding upon the assassination has reflected that

> I am in blood
> Stepp'd in so far that, should I wade no
>   more,
> Returning were as tedious as go o'er.
>
> [III. iv. 135-37]

Richard III had said a similar thing, but he suggested no veritable pool or swamp of blood as this man does; and his victims, wailing over their calamities, did not mean the concrete thing Macduff means when he cries, "Bleed, bleed, poor country!" [IV. iii. 31]. The world of the play quite literally bleeds. And Lady Macbeth, walking in her sleep, has definite stains upon the palms she rubs and rubs. "Yet here's a spot. . . . What, will these hands ne'er be clean? . . . Here's the smell of the blood still; all the perfumes of Arabia will not sweeten this little hand" [V. i. 31; 43; 50-1].

A third symbol, of greater potency than either fear or blood, is sleeplessness. Just as there are more terrors in the night than day has ever taught us, and more blood in a man than there should be, so there is less sleep in this disordered world than the minimum which once had been required for health and life. One of the final signs of that disorder is indeed the death of sleep.

> Methought I heard a voice cry, "Sleep no
>   more!
> Macbeth does murder sleep. . . .
> Glamis hath murder'd sleep, and therefore
>   Cawdor
> Shall sleep no more; Macbeth shall sleep
>   no more."
>
> [II. ii. 32-3; 39-40]

Nothing that Macbeth says is more terrible than this, and no dissolution suffered by his world is more ominous. For sleep in Shakespeare is ever the privilege of the good and the reward of the innocent. If it has been put to death there is no goodness left. One of the witches knows how to torture sailors by keeping sleep from their pent-house lids [I. iii. 19-20], but only Macbeth can murder sleep itself. The result in the play is an ultimate weariness. The "restless ecstasy" with which Macbeth's bed is made miserable, and

> the affliction of these terrible dreams
> That shake us nightly
>
> [III. ii. 18-19]

—such things are dreadful, but his final fatigue is more dreadful still, for it is the fatigue of a soul that has worn itself out with watching fears, wading in blood, and waking to the necessity of new murders for which the hand has no relish. Macbeth's hope that when Macduff is dead he can "sleep in spite of thunder" [IV. i. 86] is after all no hope. For there is no sleep in Scotland [III. vi. 34], and least of all in a man whose lids have lost the art of closing. And whose heart has lost the power of trembling like a guilty thing.

> The time has been, my senses would have
>   cool'd
> To hear a night-shriek, and my fell of hair
> Would at a dismal treatise rouse and stir
> As life were in 't. I have supp'd full with
>   horrors;
> Direness, familiar to my slaughterous
>   thoughts,
> Cannot once start me.
>
> [V. v. 10-15]

Terror has degenerated into tedium, and only death can follow, either for Macbeth who lacks the season of all natures or for his lady who not only walks but talks when she should sleep, and who will not die holily in her bed.

Meanwhile, however, another element has gone awry, and it is one so fundamental to man's experience that Shakespeare has given it a central position among those symbols which express the disintegration of the hero's world. Time is out of joint, inoperative, dissolved. "The time has been," says Macbeth, when he could fear; and "the time has been" that when the brains were out a man would

die, and there an end [III. iv. 77-9]. The repetition reveals that Macbeth is haunted by a sense that time has slipped its grooves; it flows wild and formless through his world, and is the deep cause of all the anomalies that terrify him. Certain of these anomalies are local or specific: the bell that rings on the night of the murder, the knocking at the gate, the flight of Macduff into England at the very moment Macbeth plans his death, and the disclosure that Macduff was from his mother's womb untimely ripp'd. Many things happen too soon, so that tidings are like serpents that strike without warning. "The King comes here tonight," says a messenger, and Lady Macbeth is startled out of all composure: "Thou 'rt mad to say it!" [I. v. 31]. But other anomalies are general, and these are the worst. The words of Banquo to the witches:

> If you can look into the seeds of time,
> And say which grain will grow and which
>   will not,
>
> [I. iii. 58-9]

plant early in the play a conception of time as something which fulfills itself by growing—and which, the season being wrong, can swell to monstrous shape. Or it can find crannies in the mold and extend secret, sinister roots into dark soil that never has known them. Or it can have no growth at all; it can rot and fester in its place, and die. The conception wavers, like the courage of Macbeth, but it will not away. Duncan welcomes Macbeth to Forres with the words:

> I have begun to plant thee, and will labour
> To make thee full of growing.
>
> [I. iv. 28-9]

But Macbeth, like time itself, will burgeon beyond bounds. "Nature's germens" will

> tumble all together,
> Even till destruction sicken.
>
> [IV. i. 59-60]

When Lady Macbeth, greeting her husband, says with excited assurance:

> Thy letters have transported me beyond
> This ignorant present, and I feel now
> The future in the instant,
>
> [I. v. 56-8]

she cannot suspect, nor can he, how sadly the relation between present and future will maintain itself. If the present is the womb or seed-bed of the future, if time is a succession of growths each one of which lives cleanly and freely after the death of the one before it, then what is to prevail will scarcely be recognizable as time. The seed will not grow; the future will not be born out of the present; the plant will not disentangle itself from its bed, but will stick there in still birth.

> Thou sure and firm set earth,
> Hear not my steps, which way they walk,
>   for fear
> Thy very stones prate of my whereabout,

And take the present horror from the time,
Which now suits with it,

[II. i. 56-60]

prays Macbeth on the eve of Duncan's death. But time and horror will not suit so neatly through the nights to come; the present moment will look like all eternity, and horror will be smeared on every hour. Macbeth's speech when he comes back from viewing Duncan's body may have been rehearsed and is certainly delivered for effect; yet he best knows what the terms signify:

Had I but died an hour before this chance,
I had liv'd a blessed time; for, from this in-
stant,
There's nothing serious in mortality.

[II. iii. 91-3]

He has a premonition even now of time's disorders; of his own premature descent into the sear, the yellow leaf [V. iii. 23]; of his failure like any other man to

pay his breath
To time and mortal custom.

[IV. i. 99-100]

"What, will the line stretch out to the crack of doom?" he cries when Banquo's eight sons appear to him in the witches' cavern [IV. i. 117]. Time makes sense no longer; its proportions are strange, its content meaningless. For Lady Macbeth in her mind's disease the minutes have ceased to march in their true file and order; her sleep-walking soliloquy [V. i] recapitulates the play, but there is no temporal design among the fragments of the past—the blood, the body of Duncan, the fears of her husband, the ghost of Banquo, the slaughter of Lady Macduff, the ringing of the bell, and again the blood—which float detached from one another in her memory. And for Macbeth time has become

a tale
Told by an idiot, full of sound and fury,
Signifying nothing.

[V. v. 26-8]

Death is dusty, and the future is a limitless desert of tomorrows. His reception of the news that Lady Macbeth has died is like nothing else of a similar sort in Shakespeare. When Northumberland was told of Hotspur's death he asked his grief to wait upon his revenge:

For this I shall have time enough to
mourn.

[2 Henry IV, I. i. 136]

And when Brutus was told of Portia's death he knew how to play the stoic:

With meditating that she must die once,
I have the patience to endure it now.

[Julius Caesar, IV. iii. 191-92]

But Macbeth, drugged beyond feeling, supped full with horrors, and tired of nothing so much as of co-

incidence in calamity, can only say in a voice devoid of tone:

She should have died hereafter;
There would have been a time for such a
word.

[V. v. 17-18]

There would, that is, if there were such a thing as time. Then such words as "died" and "hereafter" would have their meaning. Not now, however, for time itself has died.

Duncan was everything that Macbeth is not. We saw him briefly, but the brilliance of his contrast with the thane he trusted has kept his memory beautiful throughout a play whose every other feature has been hideous. He was "meek" and "clear" [I. vii. 17-18], and his mind was incapable of suspicion. The treachery of Cawdor bewildered him:

There's no art
To find the mind's construction in the
face.
He was a gentleman on whom I built
An absolute trust

[I. iv. 11-14]

—this at the very moment when Macbeth was being brought in for showers of praise and tears of plenteous joy! For Duncan was a free spirit and could weep, a thing impossible to his murderer's stopped heart. The word "love" was native to his tongue; he used it four times within the twenty lines of his conversation with Lady Macbeth, and its clear beauty as he spoke it was reflected that night in the diamond he sent her by Banquo [II. i. 15]. As he approached Macbeth's castle in the late afternoon the building had known its only moment of serenity and fairness. It was because Duncan could look at it and say:

This castle hath a pleasant seat; the air
Nimbly and sweetly recommends itself
Unto our gentle senses.

[I. vi. 1-3]

The speech itself was nimble, sweet, and gentle; and Banquo's explanation was in tone:

This guest of summer,
The temple-haunting martlet, does ap-
prove,
By his loved masonry, that the heaven's
breath
Smells wooingly here; no jutty, frieze,
Buttress, nor coign of vantage, but this
bird
Hath made his pendent bed and procreant
cradle.
Where they most breed and haunt, I have
observ'd
The air is delicate.

[I. vi. 3-10]

Summer, heaven, wooing, and procreation in the delicate air—such words suited the presence of a king who when later on he was found stabbed in his bed would actually offer a fair sight to guilty eyes. His blood was not like the other blood in the play, thick and fearfully discolored. It was bright and beautiful, as no one better than Macbeth could appreciate:

> Here lay Duncan,
> His silver skin lac'd with his golden blood
> [II. iii. 109-10]

—the silver and the gold went with the diamond, and with Duncan's gentle senses that could smell no treachery though a whole house reeked with it. And Duncan of course could sleep. After life's fitful fever he had been laid where nothing could touch him further [III. ii. 22-6]. No terrible dreams to shake him nightly, and no fears of things lest they come stalking through the world before their time in borrowed shapes.

Our memory of this contrast, much as the doings of the middle play work to muffle it, is what gives power to Malcolm and Macduff at the end.

> Angels are bright still, though the brightest fell.
>
> [IV. iii. 22]

Scotland may seem to have become the grave of men and not their mother [IV. iii. 166]; death and danger may claim the whole of that bleeding country; but there is another country to the south where a good king works miracles with his touch. The rest of the world is what it always was; time goes on; events stretch out through space in their proper forms. Shakespeare again has enclosed his evil within a universe of good, his storm center within wide areas of peace. And from this outer world Malcolm and Macduff will return to heal Scotland of its ills. Their conversation in London before the pious Edward's palace [IV. iii] is not an interruption of the play; it is one of its essential parts, glancing forward as it does to a conclusion wherein Macduff can say, "The time is free" [V. ix. 21], and wherein Malcolm can promise that deeds of justice, "planted newly with the time," will be performed "in measure, time, and place" [V. ix. 31, 39]. Malcolm speaks the language of the play, but he has recovered its lost idiom. Blood will cease to flow, movement will recommence, fear will be forgotten, sleep will season every life, and the seeds of time will blossom in due order. The circle of safety which Shakespeare has drawn around his central horror is thinly drawn, but it is finely drawn and it holds. (pp. 252-66)

> *Mark Van Doren, "Macbeth," in his* Shakespeare, *Henry Holt and Company, 1939, pp. 252-66.*

EVIL

Irving Ribner

[*Ribner maintains that* **Macbeth** *symbolizes Shakespeare's larger view of evil's operation in the world. Therefore, the tragedy is not resolved through the fallen hero's redemption, but through good correcting the evil that* **Macbeth** *has unleashed. The critic further contends that the play provides comparisons between* **Macbeth** *and Satan: both are always conscious of the evil they embrace; both have excessive ambition and pride; and both openly defy the natural law of God, the devil by rebelling against his maker and* **Macbeth** *by calling on satanic forces in order to gain the kingship. This "voluntary choice of evil," Ribner notes, "closes the way of redemption to [***Macbeth**], *for in denying nature he cuts off his source of redemption, and he must end in total destruction and despair." According to the critic, the other major characters serve similar symbolic functions in* Macbeth: *the witches represent evil, tempting man's sinful nature by means of prophecy;* **Banquo**, *in contrast to* **Macbeth**, *stands as a kind of morality figure who is able to resist the witches' temptation because the grace of God inherent in his nature is stronger than his propensity to sin;* **Lady Macbeth**, *who supports her husband in his wrong moral choice and quells the forces in him opposed to evil, signifies an unnatural reversal of the common symbol of woman as the giver of life and nourishment. Ribner then examines* **Duncan's** *murder, arguing that this specific act of evil corrupts all levels of creation, contaminating the family, the state, and the physical universe. Shakespeare chiefly focuses on the disintegration of* **Macbeth** *himself, the critic asserts, initially portraying him as a great man and savior of his country, but one who ultimately becomes the symbol of unnatural man, "cut off from his fellow men and from God." Macbeth's spiritual ruin must be reflected in ignoble physical destruction, Ribner concludes, and "thus the play ends with the gruesome spectacle of the murderer's head held aloft in triumph."*]

I

Macbeth is in many ways Shakespeare's maturest and most daring experiment in tragedy, for in this play he set himself to describe the operation of evil in all its manifestations: to define its very nature, to depict its seduction of man, and to show its effect upon all of the planes of creation once it has been unleashed by one man's sinful moral choice. It is this final aspect which here receives Shakespeare's primary attention and which conditions the sombre mood of the play. Shakespeare anatomizes evil both in intellectual and emotional terms, using all of the devices of poetry, and most notably the images of blood and darkness which so many commentators have described. For his final end of reconciliation, he relied not upon audience identification with his hero, but rather upon an intellectual perception of the total play. In this lay his most original departure.

Macbeth is a closely knit, unified construction, every element of which is designed to support an intellectual statement, to which action, character, and poetry all contribute. The idea which governs the plays is primarily explicit in the action of the central character, Macbeth himself; his role is cast into a symbolic pattern which is a reflection of Shakespeare's view of evil's operation in the world. The other characters serve dramatic functions designed to set off the particular intellectual problems implicit in the action of the central figure. The basic pattern of the play is a simple one, for which Shakespeare returned to an earlier formula he had used in *Richard III.* The hero accepts evil in the third scene of the play. In the second act he commits the deed to which his choice of evil must inevitably lead him, and for the final three acts, as he rises higher in worldly power he sinks deeper and deeper into evil, until at the end of the play he is utterly and finally destroyed.

There is here no pattern of redemption or regeneration for the fallen hero as in *King Lear.* Shakespeare's final statement, however, is not one of despair, for out of the play comes a feeling of reconciliation which does affirm the kind of meaning in the world with which great tragedy must end. In the earlier tragedies this feeling had been created largely through the regeneration of an essentially sympathetic hero. In *Macbeth,* however, there can be little doubt of the final damnation of "this dead butcher and his fiend-like queen" [V. ix. 35]. The audience is made to see, however, that Macbeth is destroyed by counterforces which he himself sets in motion. We may thus, viewing the play in its totality, see good, through divine grace, inevitably emerging from evil and triumphant at the play's end with a promise of rebirth. (pp. 147-48)

The action of *Macbeth* falls into two distinct parts, each carefully shaped as part of the greater whole. There is first a choice of evil by the hero, in which Shakespeare defines the nature of evil and explains the process by which man is led to choose it. This occupies roughly the first two acts, although Shakespeare by recurrent image and symbol keeps these dominant ideas before his audience throughout the rest of the play. The last three acts exhibit the manner of evil's operation simultaneously on four levels: that of fallen man himself, that of the family, the state, and the physical universe. As evil operates on each of these planes, however, it generates at the same time forces of good, until at the end of the play we see evil destroyed on each of the four planes of creation and the harmonious order of God restored. The play is an ordered and controlled exploration of evil, in

which Shakespeare fulfills the function of the philosophical poet as surely as did Dante in the *Divine Comedy.*

II

It has been pointed out that Othello and Lear in their falls parallel the fall of Adam, and like Adam they are able to learn in their disasters the nature of evil and thus attain a kind of victory in defeat. The destruction of Macbeth, on the contrary, is cast in the pattern of the fall of Satan himself, and the play is full of analogies between Satan and Macbeth. Like Satan, Macbeth is from the first entirely aware of the evil he embraces, and like Satan he can never renounce his free-willed moral choice, once it has been made. It is thus appropriate that the force of evil in *Macbeth* be symbolized by Satan's own sin of ambition. This sin for Shakespeare, as it had been for Aquinas, was an aspect of pride, the worst of the medieval seven deadly sins. In the neatly ordered and harmonious universe of which Renaissance man conceived, it stood for a rebellion against the will of God and thus against the order of nature. . . . Macbeth, through love of self, sets his own will against that of God, chooses a lesser finite good—kingship and power—rather than a greater infinite one. Shakespeare in Macbeth's moral choice is offering a definition of evil in fairly traditional terms.

The ambitious man will strive to rise higher on the great chain of being than the place which God has ordained for him. To do so he must break the bond which ties him on the one hand to God and on the other to humanity. Immediately before the murder of Banquo, Macbeth utters lines which often have been misinterpreted by commentators:

> Come seeling night,
> Scarf up the tender eye of pitiful day;
> And with thy bloody and invisible hand
> Cancel and tear to pieces the great bond
> Which keeps me pale!
>
> [III. ii. 46-50]

The "great bond" has usually been glossed either as the prophecy of the witches or as Banquo's lease on life, neither of which is very meaningful within the context of the passage. The bond . . . can only refer to the link which ties Macbeth to humanity and enjoins him to obey the natural law of God. Macbeth is calling upon the Satanic forces of darkness to break this bond of nature and thus enable him again to defy the laws of man and God, to murder his friend and guest. (pp. 148-50)

Macbeth's sin, like that of Satan before him, is thus a deliberate repudiation of nature, a defiance of God. All of the natural forces which mitigate against the deed are evoked by Macbeth himself:

> He's here in double trust,
> First, as I am his kinsman and his subject,
> Strong both against the deed; then, as his
> host,

Who should against his murderer shut the
　　door,
Not bear the knife himself. Besides, this
　　Duncan
Hath borne his faculties so meek, hath
　　been
So clear in his great office, that his virtues
Will plead like angels, trumpet-tongued,
　　against
The deep damnation of his taking-off.
　　　　　　　　　　　　　　　　[I. vii. 12-20]

His realization of the unnaturalness of the act he
contemplates is in his reply to his wife's reflection
on his courage:

I dare do all that may become a man,
Who dares do more is none.
　　　　　　　　　　　　　　　[I. vii. 46-7]

It is Macbeth's knowing and deliberate denial of
God and his rejection of the law of nature which set
him apart from the heroes of *Hamlet, Othello* and
Lear. His voluntary choice of evil, moreover, closes
the way of redemption to him, for in denying nature he cuts off the source of redemption, and he
must end in total destruction and despair. He is
like [Christopher] Marlowe's Faustus in this. Once
he has given his "eternal jewel" to the "common
enemy of man", he must abide by the contract he
has made. (p. 150)

III

The characters of *Macbeth* are not shaped primarily to conform to a psychological verisimilitude, but
to make explicit the intellectual statements with
which the play is concerned. They have choral and
symbolic functions. The illusion of reality with
which Shakespeare endows them serves merely to
embody their symbolic functions in specific emotional terms. Successful as the illusion may be,
Lady Macbeth, Banquo, the witches are not whole
figures about whom we can ask such questions as
[A. C.] Bradley asked [in his *Shakespearean Tragedy*] and could only answer by divorcing them
from the context of the play. All that we need know
about the witches is that they are as [John] Dover
Wilson has well put it [in the Cambridge edition of
Macbeth], "the incarnation of evil in the universe,
all the more effective dramatically that their nature
is never defined". They are no more than convenient dramatic symbols for evil. To question closely
the motives of Banquo or Lady Macbeth, with their
many and obvious inconsistencies, is equally fruitless, for they function primarily as dramatic vehi-
cles whose action is governed by the demands not
of fact or psychology, but of intellectual design.

As symbols of evil, the witches are made contrary
to nature. They are women with the beards of men;
their incantation is a Black Mass, and the hell
broth they stir consists of the disunified parts of
men and animals, creation in chaos. They deliberately wait for Macbeth and Banquo, as they wait for
all men. They do not, however, suggest evil to

man . . . , for the impulse to evil must come from
within man himself. They simply suggest an object
which may incite the inclination to evil which is always within man because of original sin, and they
do this by means of prophecy. Thus the good man,
like Banquo, can resist their appeal, for man
shares in the grace of God as well as in original sin.

The witches hold forth the promise of worldly
good, as all evil must, for if it were not attractive it
would offer no temptation to man. What Shakespeare wishes to stress is that its promises are
false ones, that seeming truths are half truths, and
that, in general, evil works through deception, by
posing as the friend of man. Thus Eve had been seduced by Satan, and thus Othello had been seduced by "Honest" Iago. Banquo recognizes the Satanic origin of the witches: "What, can the devil
speak true?" [I. iii. 107], and he perceives the manner in which they work:

And oftentimes, to win us to our harm,
The instruments of darkness tell us
　　truths,
Win us with honest trifles, to betray's
In deepest consequence.
　　　　　　　　　　　　　　[I. iii. 123-26]

To make this statement about the deceptive nature
of evil, Shakespeare works into the texture of his
play the theme of appearance versus reality which
so many critics have noticed. There is always confusion and uncertainty in the appearance of evil,
darkness rather than light, never the clear, rational certainty which is in the natural order of the
good. This theme is in Macbeth's opening remark:
"So foul and fair a day I have not seen" [I. iii. 38].
"There's no art / To find the mind's construction
in the face" [I. iv. 11-12] says Duncan, and Lady
Macbeth cautions her husband to "look like the innocent flower, / But be the serpent under't" [I. v.
65-6]. Macbeth himself acknowledges that "False
face must hide what the false heart doth know" [I.
vii. 82].

Not until the very end of the play does Macbeth
learn how evil works. It offers to him, it seems, the
finite good, kingship and power, which his perverted will causes him to place above the infinite good
of God's order; thus evil becomes his good. He relies
upon this promise, trusting the prophecy of the
witches to the very last, and thus unknowingly
bringing about his own destruction and the restitution of natural order. Only when Birnam wood
has in fact come to Dunsinane and he faces a foe
not born of woman, does the deception in the
witches' promises become apparent to him:

And be these juggling fiends no more be-
　　lieved,
That palter with us in a double sense;
That keep the word of promise to our ear,
And break it to our hope.
　　　　　　　　　　　　　　[V. viii. 19-22]

Banquo, as [Leo] Kirchbaum has indicated, stands

opposed to Macbeth as a kind of morality figure [see excerpt in section on Banquo]. The witches offer him temptation not unlike what they offer Macbeth, and Banquo is sorely tempted, as any man must be. This is best revealed in a short speech which both for Bradley and [G.] Wilson Knight [in his *Shakespearean Tragedy*] was evidence that Banquo too had been corrupted by evil:

> yet it was said
> It should not stand in thy posterity,
> But that myself should be the root and father
> Of many kings. If there come truth from them—
> As upon thee, Macbeth, their speeches shine—
> Why, by the verities on thee made good,
> May they not be my oracles as well,
> And set me up in hope? But hush! no more.
>
> [III. i. 3-10]

The difference between the two men is that Banquo is able to resist the temptation to which Macbeth succumbs. Banquo is ordinary man, with his mixture of good and evil, open to evil's soliciting, but able to resist it. It is in such a man, Shakespeare is saying, that the hope for the future lies. This hope is embodied in Fleance, and thus, in terms of the play's total conceptual pattern, it is impossible for Macbeth to kill him. Evil can never destroy the ultimate promise of good.

Banquo, humanly weak and subject to temptation, stands nevertheless, "in the great hand of God" [III. iii. 130]. Symbolically he represents one aspect of Macbeth, the side of ordinary humanity which Macbeth must destroy within himself before he can give his soul entirely to the forces of darkness. For this reason he must murder Banquo, and it is why the dead Banquo returns to him as a reminder that, as a man, he cannot easily extinguish the human force within himself, that the torment of fear, the "terrible dreams / that shake us nightly" [III. ii. 18-19], the scorpions in his mind [III. ii. 36], will continue until his own final destruction. Banquo and his ghost are used to illuminate the basic conflict within the mind of Macbeth.

Macduff and Malcolm serve similar symbolic functions. Macduff, in particular, is a force of nemesis generated by Macbeth's own course of evil. Malcolm . . . is Shakespeare's portrait of the ideal king, and his function chiefly is to represent a restitution of order in the state. (pp. 151-53)

Just as Banquo symbolizes that side of Macbeth which would accept nature and reject evil, Lady Macbeth stands for the contrary side. Her function is to second Macbeth in the moral choice which is his alone, to mitigate against those forces within him which are in opposition to evil. Macbeth is thus much in the position of the traditional morality play hero placed between good and evil angels.

The side of his wife seduces him, and that of Banquo must be destroyed.

It is for this reason, as has so often been pointed out, that the imagery of her speeches draws upon corruptions of nature and reversal of the normal life impulses. She calls upon the forces of darkness to support her in her purposes:

> Come you spirits
> That tend on mortal thoughts, unsex me here,
> And fill me from the crown to the toe topfull
> Of direst cruelty! make thick my blood;
> Stop up the access and passage to remorse,
> That no compunctious visiting of nature
> Shake my fell purpose, nor keep peace between
> The effect and it! Come to my women's breasts,
> And take my milk for gall, you murdering ministers,
> Wherever in your sightless substances
> You wait on nature's mischief! Come, thick night,
> And pall me in the dunnest smoke of hell,
> That my keen knife see not the wound it makes,
> Nor heaven peep through the blanket of the dark,
> To cry 'Hold, hold.'
>
> [I. v. 40-54]

It is fitting that Shakespeare should use a woman for this purpose, for woman is the normal symbol of life and nourishment, and thus the dramatist can emphasize the strangeness and unnaturalness of the very contraries to which Lady Macbeth appeals and for which she stands. She must become unsexed, and her milk must convert to gall. Her very need, moreover, to put aside her feminine nature informs the illusion of reality in her characterization and gives to her emotional appeal as well as intellectual meaning.

The motif of the unnatural is evoked again in her savage cry:

> I have given suck, and know
> How tender 'tis to love the babe that milks me:
> I would, while it was smiling in my face,
> Have pluck'd my nipple from his boneless gums
> And dash'd the brains out.
>
> [I. vii. 54-8]

We cannot say whether she actually has children or not, for this speech is not designed to convey fact. It is a ritual statement in which Shakespeare seizes upon a strikingly unnatural image to emphasize that she is urging Macbeth on the basis of all which is opposed to nature and the order of God. If Shakespeare, later in the play, in Macduff's "He has no children" [IV. iii. 216] seems to indicate that Macbeth is childless, it is not that he has forgotten

*Ann Todd as Lady Macbeth in Act I, scene v of a 1954
Old Vic Theatre staging of* Macbeth.

the earlier speech. There he wishes merely to emphasize the intensity of Macduff's feeling in the same ritual manner.

Throughout the play Lady Macbeth's femininity is held in constant juxtaposition to the unnatural forces she would call into play. In the murder scene her unnatural aspect is dominant, but her femininity comes through in her inability to kill the king herself. When the body is discovered, she is the first to collapse. This careful juxtaposition of contraries comes to a head when she walks in her sleep in the fifth act. Here the images of blood are mingled with her feminine desire for the "perfumes of Arabia" to "sweeten this little hand" [V. i. 51]. No more than Macbeth can lightly break his bond with humanity, can his wife escape the woman in her which mitigates against the unnatural force of evil which in the thematic structure of the play she represents. In her death by suicide, moreover, there is further emphasis upon the theme which dominates the play; that evil inevitably must breed its own destruction. (pp. 153-54)

IV

The specific act of evil occurs on two planes, that of the state and that of Macbeth's "single state of man" [I. iii. 140]; the crime is both ethical and political, for Macbeth murders not only his kinsman and guest, but his king as well. Once evil is unleashed, however, it corrupts all of the planes of creation, not only those of man and the state, but those of the family and the physical universe as well. Action, character, symbolic ritual and the powerful emotional impact of poetic imagery all combine to further a specific intellectual concept: the all-embracing destructive force of evil which touches every area of God's creation.

That the physical universe itself is thrown out of harmony is made clear in the speech of Lennox immediately following the murder:

> The night has been unruly: where we lay,
> Our chimneys were blown down; and, as they say,
> Lamentings heard i' the air; strange screams of death,
> And prophesying with accents terrible
> Of dire combustion and confused events
> New hatched to the woeful time: the obscure bird
> Clamour'd the livelong night: some say, the earth
> Was feverous and did shake.
>
> [II. iii. 54-61]

This theme is even more strongly emphasized in a short scene in which Ross speaks to a nameless old man. The strange phenomena here described are all perversions of physical nature which indicate that one man's crime has thrown the entire universe out of harmony:

> Thou seest, the heavens, as troubled with man's act,
> Threaten his bloody stage: by the clock 'tis day,
> And yet dark night strangles the travelling lamp:
> Is't night's predominance, or the day's shame,
> That darkness does the face of earth entomb,
> When living light should kiss it?
>
> [II. iv. 5-10]

The order of nature is reversed, the sun blotted out. On the animal level, a falcon is killed by a mousing owl, and most horrible of all:

> Duncan's horses—a thing most strange and certain—
> Beauteous and swift, the minions of their race,
> Turn'd wild in nature, broke their stalls, flung out,
> Contending 'gainst obedience, as they would make
> War against mankind.
>
> [II. iv. 14-18]

Man by his sin has forfeited his dominion over nature: horses turn against their natural master, and, as the old man affirms, "they eat each other" [II. iv. 18].

This perversion of nature, however, contains within itself the means of restoring harmony, for Shakespeare uses the very perversion itself, a moving forest and a child unborn of mother to herald the downfall of the tyrant and thus to restore the physical universe to its natural state of perfection. That the forest does not really move, and that Macduff was only technically so born is of no significance, for Shakespeare is giving us here not scientific fact, but dramatic symbol to emphasize the theme of the play that in the working out of evil is implicit a rebirth of good.

On the level of the state Macbeth unleashes the greatest evils of which Shakespeare's audience could conceive, tyranny, civil war, and an invading foreign army. The tyranny of Macbeth's reign, moreover is set off by the initial description of the gentility and justice of Duncan's previous rule. Shakespeare here deliberately alters his source, for Holinshed had stressed Duncan's feeble and slothful administration, and he had, by way of contrast, praised Macbeth for his striving after justice and for the excellence of at least the first ten years of his reign.

The disorder in the state as it works out its course is also the source of its own extinction and the restoration of political harmony. The very tyranny of Macbeth arouses Macduff against him, causes Malcolm to assert the justice of his title, and causes the saint-like English King, Edward the Confessor, to take arms against Macbeth. King Edward's curing of the scrofula [IV. iii. 146-49], an episode which Dover Wilson like so many other critics has regarded as "of slight dramatic relevance", is Shakespeare's means of underscoring that Edward is an instrument of supernatural grace, designed to cleanse the unnatural evil in the state, just as he may remove evil from individual man. It is Macbeth's very tyranny which has made him "ripe for shaking, and the powers above / Put on their instruments" [IV. iii. 238-39].

On the level of the family, the relationship between Macbeth and his wife steadily deteriorates. At the beginning of the play their relationship is one of the closest and most intimate in all literature. She is "my dearest partner in greatness" [I. v. 11], and much as it harrows him himself to think of its implications, he sends her immediate word of the witches' prophecy, so that she may not "lose the dues of rejoicing" [I. v. 12]. The very terror of the murder scene only further emphasizes the closeness of the murderers. But as the force of evil severs Macbeth from the rest of humanity, it breaks also the bond which ties him to his wife. He lives more and more closely with his own fears into which she cannot intrude, as the banquet scene well illustrates. She cannot see the ghost which torments her husband.

The gradual separation of man and wife first becomes apparent just before the murder of Banquo. No longer does he confide in her. At the play's beginning they plan the future together; at the end each dies alone, and when the news of her death comes to Macbeth, he shows little concern:

> She should have died hereafter;
> There would have been a time for such a
> word.
>
> [V. v. 17-18]

This theme of family disintegration is echoed, moreover, in Macduff's desertion of his wife and children to be destroyed by the tyrant whom the father flees.

It is upon the disintegration of Macbeth himself, however, that Shakespeare lavishes his principal attention. He is careful to paint his hero in the opening scenes as a man of great stature, the savior of his country, full of the "milk of human kindness" [I. v. 17], with an infinite potentiality for good. He has natural feelings which link him to his fellow men and make him view with revulsion the crime to which ambition prompts him. Once the crime is committed, however, these feelings are gradually destroyed, until at the end of the play he is a symbol of unnatural man, cut off from his fellow men and from God. As his link with humanity weakens, moreover, so also does his desire to live, until finally he sinks into a total despair, the medieval sin of *acedia* [apathy], which is the surest evidence of his damnation.

Macbeth's extraordinary powers of imagination have been amply commented upon. Imagination itself, however, cannot be viewed as a cause of man's destruction within any meaningful moral system. Shakespeare endows Macbeth with this ability to see all of the implications of his act in their most frightening forms even before the act itself is committed as an indication of Macbeth's initial strong moral feelings. Bradley wisely recognized the "principle of morality which takes place in his imaginative fears". Imagination enables Macbeth emotionally to grasp the moral implications of his crime, to participate imaginatively, as does the audience, in the full horror of the deed. Macbeth is entirely aware of God's moral system with its "even-handed justice", which "commends the ingredients of our poison'd chalice / To our own lips" [I. vii. 10-12]. His great soliloquy in contemplation of Duncan's murder [I. vii. 1-28] is designed to underscore Macbeth's initial feelings of kinship with the natural order.

As he prepares to commit the act he dreads, he calls for the suppression of these feelings within him. In a kind of devilish incantation he calls for darkness and the extinction of nature, conjuring the earth itself to look aside while he violates the harmonious order of which he and it are closely related parts:

> Now o'er the one half world
> Nature seems dead, and wicked dreams
>   abuse
> The curtain'd sleep, witchcraft celebrates
> Pale Hecate's offerings, and wither'd mur-
>   der,
> Alarum'd by his sentinel, the wolf,
> Whose howl's his watch, thus with his
>   stealthy pace,
> With Tarquin's ravishing strides, towards
>   his design
> Moves like a ghost. Thou sure and firm-set
>   earth,
> Hear not my steps, which way they walk,
>   for fear
> Thy very stones prate of my whereabouts,
> And take the present horror from the time,
> Which now suits with it.
>   [II. i. 49-60]

The figure of the wolf is an appropriate one, for here Macbeth allies himself with the destroyer of the innocent lamb, symbolic of God, just as he allies himself with the ravisher Tarquin, the destroyer of chastity, symbolic in the Renaissance of the perfection of God.

That Macbeth cannot say "amen" immediately after the murder is the first clear sign of his alienation from God. He will sleep no more, for sleep is an aspect of divine mercy. Steadily Macbeth moves farther and farther from God and his fellow men, and his bond with nature is weakened. He becomes committed entirely to an unnatural course from which he cannot retreat:

> For mine own good,
> All causes shall give way: I am in blood
> Stepp'd in so far that, should I wade no
>   more,
> Returning were as tedious as go o'er.
>   [III. iv. 134-37]

He has become the center of his own little alien world, for which "all causes shall give way". Now Macbeth is ready to seek the witches out, a commitment to evil as total as that of Marlowe's Faustus in his summoning of Mephistopheles. And the words of the weird sisters lead him to the most horrible excess of all, the wanton murder of the family of Macduff. At the beginning of the play, evil had come to Macbeth unsought, as it does to all men; he had followed its promptings in order to attain definite ends, and not without strong misgivings. Now he seeks evil himself; he embraces it willingly and without fear, for no other end than the evil act itself.

The divided mind and the fear felt by the early Macbeth were not weakness; they were . . . signs of his kinship with man and God. But, by the fifth act:

> I have almost forgot the taste of
>   fears:
> The time has been, my senses would have
>   cool'd
> To hear a night-shriek; and my fell of hair
> Would at a dismal treatise rouse and stir

> As life were in't: I have supped full with
>   horrors;
> Direness, familiar to my slaughterous
>   thoughts,
> Cannot once start me.
>   [V. v. 9-15]

With the loss of human fear, Macbeth must forfeit also those human attributes which make life livable: "that which should accompany old age, / As honour, love, obedience, troops of friends" [V. iii. 24-5]. There is nothing left for him but the utter despair of his "To-morrow and to-morrow" speech [V. v. 19-28]. Even with this unwillingness to live, which is in itself a denial of the mercy of God (as the medieval mind conceived of *acedia*), Shakespeare will not allow to Macbeth the heroic gesture of suicide which he grants to Brutus [in *Julius Caesar*] and Othello. Macbeth will not "play the Roman fool" [V. viii. 1]. His spiritual destruction must be reflected in an ignominious physical destruction, and thus the play ends with the gruesome spectacle of the murderer's head held aloft in triumph. (pp. 155-59)

If we are to isolate a dominant theme in the play, it must be one of idea: that through the working out of evil in a harmonious world order good must emerge. This idea is embodied in specific action and specific character, and thus by imaginative exploration the dramatist is able to illuminate it more fully than any prose statement ever could. Great tragedy involves a tension between emotion and intellect. The horrors of the action move our emotions as the play progresses, but when the last curtain has fallen and we can reflect upon *Macbeth* in its totality, we see that although one man has been damned, there is an order and meaning in the universe, that good may be reborn out of evil. We may thus experience that feeling of reconciliation which is the ultimate test of tragedy. (p. 159)

> *Irving Ribner, " 'Macbeth': The Pattern of Idea and Action," in* Shakespeare Quarterly, *Vol. X, No. 2, Spring, 1959, pp. 147-59.*

J. Lyndon Shanley

[*Shanley considers the tragic context of **Macbeth**'s evil actions in an attempt to determine whether or not his downfall warrants sympathy or arouses fear at the end of the play. The critic maintains that **Macbeth** has a fundamentally different experience from Shakespeare's other great tragic heroes: he does not achieve a great recovery in the end because his actions throughout the play were ignoble. Shanley suggests, however, that **Macbeth**'s end is perhaps more tragic than that of the other heroes because he ultimately loses himself to a degree that none of them does. According to the critic, our pity for **Macbeth** might therefore lie in the fact that by declaring that* *life signifies nothing, he acknowledges "the almost complete destruction of the human spirit." Shanley also observes that our ability to pass judgment on the hero's ruin is further complicated by several factors. While it is true that* **Macbeth** *sins, his actions rouse our pity and fear not only because he succumbs, as we might, to temptation, but also because he feels tremendous guilt for his actions. Further, the critic contends,* **Macbeth** *is a victim of external circumstances; he falls into a trap set by the witches, who tempt him with prophecies that stimulate his excessive pride and ambition. The hero may have resisted this temptation had he been left to himself, Shanley continues, but* **Lady Macbeth** *uses her superior willpower to overrule his "moderately good" nature and coaxes him into murdering* **Duncan.** *After* **Macbeth** *performs the evil deed, our sympathy for him increases as he tries to extricate himself from evil, only to be pulled deeper into its depths. In the critic's opinion, "we are deeply moved by* **Macbeth's** *suffering and ruin because we are acutely aware of the dangerous forces before which he falls, and because we recognize their power over one like ourselves. . . . Of such suffering and loss is tragedy made."]*

Nowhere can we see the essential humanity of Shakespeare more clearly than in *Macbeth,* as he shows that the darkest evil may well be human, and so, though horrible, understandable in terms of our own lives and therefore pitiable and terrible. Yet nowhere apparently are we so likely to miss the center of Shakespeare's view of the action; for *Macbeth,* while less complex than Shakespeare's other major tragedies, frequently raises the crucial question: Is Macbeth's fall really tragic?

Many who are deeply moved by the action of the play cannot satisfactorily explain their feelings. The doctrine of *Tout comprendre, c'est tout pardonner* [if all is understood then all is pardoned] leads them to think (most of the time) that there is no guilt, that there should be no punishment. When faced with unpardonable evil and inescapable punishment for the guilty, and when moved at the same time to pity and fear by the suffering of the evil-doer, they are confused. Since they confound the understanding of an act with the excusing of it, they are prevented from understanding acts (and their reactions to them) for which excuse is impossible. Some, of course, find an excuse for Macbeth in the witches. But those who do not see him as the victim of agents of destiny appear to wonder if they have not been tricked into sympathy by Shakespeare's art. How, they ask, in view of Macbeth's monstrous career and sorry end, so different from those of Hamlet, Lear, or Othello, how can his fortunes win our pity and arouse our fear?

I

Macbeth is defeated as is no other of Shakespeare's

great tragic figures. No pity and reverent awe attend his death. Dying off-stage, he is, as it were, shuffled off, in keeping with his dreadful state and the desire of all in his world to be rid of him. The sight of his "cursed head" is the signal for glad hailing of Malcolm as king; all thought of him is dismissed with "this dead butcher and his fiend-like queen" [V. ix. 35]. The phrase is dramatically fitting, but it does not express the whole truth that Shakespeare shows us of Macbeth's story. Seldom do we feel so strongly both the justice of the judgment and the retribution and at the same time pity for him on whom they fall; for behind this last scene lies the revelation of Macbeth's almost total destruction.

Hamlet, Lear, and Othello lose much that is wonderful in human life; their fortunes are sad and terrible. So near, their stories seem to say, is man's enjoyment of the world's best gifts—and yet so far, because his own errors and weakness leave him unable to control his world. To lose Hamlet's delight in man and his powers, and the glory of life; to have Cordelia's love and tender care snatched away, after such suffering as Lear's; or to have thrown away the jewel of one's life as did Othello—this is painful. But their fortunes might have been worse. At one time they were: when the losers thought that what they had served and believed in were mere shows that made a mockery of their noblest love; when life and all their efforts seemed to have been utterly without meaning.

But before the end they learned that their love had value and that life had meaning. On this knowledge depends the twofold effect of the heroes' deaths: death at once seals, without hope of restitution, the loss of the world and its gifts, but at the same time it brings relief from the pain of loss. Furthermore, this knowledge restores the courage and nobility of soul that raise them far above their enemies and the ruins of their world. Without this knowledge, Hamlet and Lear and Othello were far less than themselves, and life but a fevered madness. With it, there is tragedy but not defeat, for the value of what is best in them is confirmed beyond question.

But in the end of Macbeth we have something fundamentally different. Macbeth's spirit, as well as his world, is all but destroyed; no great recovery is possible for him. He does not, for he cannot, see that what he sought and valued most was good and worthy of his efforts. He is aware that he has missed much; shortly before Lady Macbeth dies, he broods over the "honour, love, obedience, troops of friends" [V. iii. 25] he has lost and cannot hope to regain. But this knowledge wins no ease for his heart. It does not raise him above the conditions that have ruined him. Macbeth, it is true, is no longer tortured as he once was, but freedom from torture has led only to the peace of despair in which he looks at life and denounces it as "a tale told by an idiot" [V. v. 26-7].

Bitter as life was for Hamlet, Lear, and Othello, it was not empty. But all Macbeth's efforts, all his hopes and dreams were in vain, because of the way he went; and when he discovers that they were, he concludes that nothing can be realized in life. Hence his terrible indictment of life—terrible because it reveals him to be all but hopelessly lost in the world of Shakespearean tragedy, as he desperately and ironically blasphemes against a basic tenet of that world, to the truth of which his own state bears overwhelming evidence: that man's life signifies everything.

It is the despair and irony in this blasphemy that makes Macbeth's lot so awful and pitiful. We see the paralyzing, the almost complete destruction of a human spirit. The threat of hostile action galvanizes Macbeth into action to protect himself, but the action is little more than an instinctive move toward self-preservation and the last gesture of despair. "At least," he cries, "we'll die with harness on our back" [V. v. 51]. There is no sense of effective power and will to give life meaning, such as there is in [Gerard Manley] Hopkins' lines:

> Not, I'll not, carrion comfort, Despair, not
>   feast on thee;
> Not untwist—slack they may be—these
>   last strands of man
> In me or, most weary, cry *I can no more.*
>   I can;
> Can something, hope, wish day come, not
>   choose not to be.
>   [*Carrion Comfort*]

Here the speaker knows despair for what it is, and knows that something else is both possible and worth any effort. But not so Macbeth; he can see only the circumstances from which his despair arises; he can imagine no condition of life other than that he is in.

He has not even the bitter satisfaction of rebelling and saying, "As flies to wanton boys, are we to the gods" [*King Lear,* IV. i. 36]. Only sheer animal courage remains to flash out and remind us of a Macbeth once courageous in an honorable cause. This reminder is pitiful, for Macbeth has not even the slim hope of a trapped animal which, if it fights loose, has something to escape to. All Macbeth did resulted in nothing; whatever he does now will result in nothing but the anguish of meaningless action. It is hard enough to realize that one has been on the wrong track for part of life; to be convinced that there is no right track to get on because there is no place for any track to go—this is to be lost with no hope at all.

At the very end we see some saving touches of humanity in Macbeth: he has not lost all human virtue; he would have no more of Macduff's blood on his soul; and even with the collapse of his last security, his bravery does not falter. These touches show him a man still, and not a fiend, but they by no means reestablish him in his former self. There is no greatness in death for him. Rather than the human spirit's capacity for greatness in adversity, we see its possible ruin in evil. Because we never see Macbeth enjoying the possession of the great prize he sought, and because from the beginning of his temptation we have no hope that he will be able to enjoy it, his loss of the world's gifts is not so poignant as that of Hamlet, Lear, or Othello. But to a degree that none of them does, Macbeth loses himself, and this is most tragic of all.

II

It may be objected, however, that Macbeth alone of Shakespeare's great tragic figures is fully aware of the evil of the act by which he sets in motion the train of events leading to his ruin. His culpability seriously weakens the sympathy of many. In the face of this difficulty, some interpreters justify sympathy for Macbeth by seeing him as the victim of the witches, the agents of destiny. This point of view, however, seems to cut through the complex knot of human life as Shakespeare saw it, instead of following the various strands which make it up. We cannot dodge Macbeth's responsibility and guilt—he never does.

His ruin is caused by the fact that he sins: he wilfully commits an act which he knows to be wrong. This ruin and sin are seen to be tragic, as Shakespeare, like Dante, reveals the pity and fear in a man's succumbing to grievous temptation, and in the effects of sin on his subsequent thoughts and deeds. Macbeth's guilt and the circumstances upon which it depends do not decrease our pity and fear; they produce it; for Shakespeare presents Macbeth as one who had hardly any chance to escape guilt.

The concatenation of circumstances which make Macbeth's temptation is such as to seem a trap. At the very moment when he is returning victorious from a battle in which he has played a chief part in saving his country from disaster, there comes to him a suggestion—touching old dreams and desires—that he may be king. Shakespeare uses the witches to convey the danger of the suggestion. The witches and their prophecies are poetic symbols of the bafflingly indeterminate character of the events that surround men. The witches force nothing; they advise nothing; they simply present facts. But they confound fair and foul; just so, events may be good or ill. The witches will not stay to explain their greetings any more than events will interpret themselves. The witches' prophecies and the events that forever surround men are dangerous because they may appear simple and are not, because they may be so alluring as to stultify prudence, and because their true significance may be very hard to come at. Depending on conditions, they may be harmless, or they may be delusive, insidious, and all but impossible to read correctly.

Macbeth is in no condition to read them aright. He had restrained his desire for greatness in the past since he would not do the wrong which was needed to win greatness. The hunger of his ambitious mind had not died, however; it had only been denied satisfaction. Now, when the sense of his own power and his taste of it are high indeed, the old hunger is more than reawakened; it is nourished with hope, as immediate events seem to establish the soundness of the suggestion. Enough hope to lead him to ponder the suggestion seriously, and then, in spite of an attempt to put it out of his mind since he recognizes the evil of his thoughts, to retail the wonderful news of possible greatness to his wife.

There follow immediately two events which press the matter on most hastily. The king proclaims his eldest son as his heir, and in the next breath announces his visit to Macbeth's castle. Thus, while desire and hope are fresh, Macbeth sees put before him, first, an obstacle which time will only make greater, and then an opportunity for him to prevent time from working against him. "If it were done when 'tis done, then 'twere well it were done quickly" [I. vii. 1-2]. In fact, it must be done quickly if it is to be done at all.

Desire, apparent promise of fulfillment, need for speedy action, and immediate opportunity fall together so rapidly as to create an all but inescapable force.

Yet Macbeth would have resisted temptation had he been left to himself. Great though his hunger for power and glory, especially when whetted by such circumstances, it would not have completely overcome his fears and scruples. Even if he were to jump the life to come, he knew that if he could and would kill Duncan, another might well do the same for him. On a higher plane, the double loyalty he owed to the king held him back. Finally, a point that reveals the virtue that was in him, he felt the goodness of Duncan so strongly that killing him seemed too terrible a thing to do. Worldly prudence, loyalty, reverence for what is good—these turned Macbeth back. Lady Macbeth's fears were well founded; his nature was not such as to let him "catch the nearest way."

But that nature could, as she felt, be worked. It was good, but not firm in its goodness. Macbeth is a moderately good man, no better, but also no worse, than the next one. The point is (and it is a grim one) that the virtue of the ordinarily good man is not enough to keep him from disaster under all possible circumstances—especially when some of them are such as may be for good or evil.

This was the nature of Lady Macbeth's influence on Macbeth. She could sway him because she understood him and loved him, and because he loved her and depended on her love and good thoughts of him. She could and would have urged him to

noble deeds had occasion arisen. To prevent her from urging him on to evil ones, he needed more than the ordinary firmness to act as he saw right. But to cut clear of such a source of strength and comfort is difficult; too difficult for Macbeth. It is the old story of the perversion of the potentially good, and of the problem of getting only the good from the baffling mixture of good and evil in all things.

Just after Macbeth has decided to give up his murderous plot, but before intention can harden to resolve, Lady Macbeth adds the force of her appeals to that of Macbeth's desires and the press of circumstance. She sees his chance to win the prize of life; she knows he wants it, as she does not know in their full strength his reasons for renouncing it. She beats down, at least long enough for her immediate purpose, the fears and scruples which would otherwise have kept him from the crown, and murder and ruin. She does not answer Macbeth's scruples; her attack is personal. Whether she knows or simply feels his need of her admiration and support, she strikes at the right point. The spur of ambition did not drive Macbeth too hard toward his great opportunity, but her goading taunts he could not withstand, though they drove him on to horrors.

All this does not excuse Macbeth; no excuse is possible for one who, with full knowledge of the nature of the act, murders a good man to whom he owes hospitality, loyalty, and gratitude. Shakespeare makes us realize, however, how dangerous the battle, how practically irresistible may be the forces arrayed against a man. Some men are saved from evil because they marry a Cordelia or a Viola [in *Twelfth Night*]; others because opportunity never favors their desires; and still others because the stakes do not justify the risk of being caught in evil doing. For Macbeth, the stakes are the highest, the opportunity golden, and the encouragement to evil from a wife whom he loves and needs.

Macbeth is terrified by the warnings of his conscience, but he cannot surrender. That he acts with full knowledge of the evil only increases the pity and fear aroused by his deed. For this knowledge causes much of his suffering; it makes his condition far worse than it would have been had he acted with less than complete knowledge; and, finally, it emphasizes the power of the trickery, the lure, and the urging to which he was subjected. We pity his suffering even as he does evil because we understand why he could not hold on to the chance which he ought to have taken to save himself; and we are moved to fear when we see his suffering and understand how slight may be the chance to escape it.

III

Once that chance is lost greater suffering and evil follow inescapably. The bloody career on which

Macbeth now embarks can no more be excused than could his first crime, but it increases rather than detracts from our pity and fear. The trap of temptation having been sprung, there is no escape for Macbeth, and his struggles to escape the consequences of his sin serve only to ensnare him more deeply. As we witness that struggle, our pity and fear increase because we feel how incompetent he is to do anything but struggle as he does.

Evil brings its own suffering with it, but Macbeth cannot learn from it. The unknown fifteenth-century author of *The Book of the Poor in Spirit* wrote of evil and suffering: "One's own proper suffering comes from one's own sins and he suffers quite rightly who lives in sins, and each sin fosters a special spiritual suffering. . . . This kind of suffering is similar to the suffering in hell, for the more one suffers there the worse one becomes. This happens to sinners; the more they suffer through sin the more wicked they become and they fall more and more into sufferings in their effort to escape." Just so did Shakespeare conceive of Macbeth's state.

Macbeth has no enemy he can see, such as Iago or one of Lear's savage daughters; he is within himself. In first overriding the warnings of his conscience, he brings on the blindness which makes it impossible for him to perceive his own state and things outside him as they really are, and which therefore sends him in pursuit of a wholly illusory safety. When he puts away all thought of going back on his first evil deed, he deals the last blow to his conscience which once urged him to the right, and he blinds himself entirely.

No sooner does he gain what he wanted than he is beset by fears worse than those he overrode in murdering Duncan. But having overridden the proper fears, he cannot deal rightly with the new ones. His horror of murder is lost in the fear of discovery and revenge, and the fear of losing what he has sacrificed so much to gain. Briefly at least he wishes the murder undone and Duncan waking to the knocking at the gate. But just as earlier he thought, but failed, to put the witches' prophecies and his evil thoughts out of mind, so now his better thoughts die. By the time he appears in answer to the knocking at the gate, he is firmly set on a course to make good the murder of Duncan and to keep himself safe.

All is terrible irony from this point on. With a new decisiveness Macbeth kills the grooms in Duncan's chamber; alive, they were potential witnesses; dead, they can serve as plausible criminals. Then he plays brilliantly the part of a grief-stricken host and loyal subject:

> Had I but died an hour before this chance,
> I had liv'd a blessed time; for from this instant
> There's nothing serious in mortality;
> All is but toys; renown and grace is dead;

> The wine of life is drawn, and the mere lees
> Is left this vault to brag of.
>
> [II. iii. 91-6]

Irony could not be sharper. At the very moment when he seems to himself to be complete master of the situation, Macbeth, all unknowingly, utters the bitter truth about his state. He is still to be troubled by thoughts of evil, but the drive of his desire for peace from fear is greater; and to win security he is hurrying on the way in which he thinks it lies, but it is the way to the utter, empty loneliness he describes for us here.

Macbeth finds that the death of the grooms was not enough; Banquo and Fleance must go if he is to be free from torment. Through Macbeth's conversation first with Banquo about his journey, then with the murderers, and finally with Lady Macbeth, we comprehend to its full extent the disastrous change in him; he now contemplates murder with hope rather than horror. He still sees it as something to be hidden: "Come, seeling night, scarf up the tender eye of pitiful day" [III. ii. 46-7]. But he is willing to do more evil since he believes it will insure his safety: "Things bad begun make good themselves by ill" [III. ii. 55]. With the appearance of Banquo's ghost comes the last flicker of conscience, but also an increasing terror of discovery and revenge which drives Macbeth further than ever: "For mine own good all causes shall give way" [III. iv. 134-35].

The only thing he can gain in his blinded state is the very worst for him. He now seeks out the witches to get that reassurance in his course which he cannot find in himself. Although they will not stay for all his questions, he unhesitatingly accepts their equivocations; since they do reassure him, his doubts of them are gone. With their answers, and having lost "the initiate fear that wants hard use" and being no longer "young in deed" [III. iv. 142-43]. Macbeth enjoys the sense of security of any gangster or tyrant who has the unshrinking will to crush any possible opponents, and who thinks he has power to do so with impunity. All that he has gained, however, is the freedom to commit "every sin that has a name to it" [IV. iii. 59-60].

His delusion is complete; his ruin inevitable. Not until he experiences the bitter fruition of his earthly crown does he discover what has happened to him. Even then, however, he sees only in part; the blindness he suffered when he succumbed to temptation was never to be lightened; and hence the final irony of

>   a tale
> Told by an idiot, full of sound and fury,
> Signifying nothing.
>
> [V. v. 26-8]

In [Nathaniel Hawthorne's] *The Scarlet Letter* when Hester Prynne seeks mercy for Dimmesdale from Roger Chillingworth, the old physician replies: "It is not granted me to pardon. I have no such power as thou tellest me of. My old faith, long forgotten, comes back to me, and explains all that we do, and all we suffer. By thy first step awry thou didst plant the germ of evil; but since that moment, it has all been a dark necessity." So we feel, in part, about Macbeth, since we see him, not as a victim of destiny, but as one responsible for the misery and deaths of others as well as for his own suffering. But in spite of his responsibility we cannot withhold our sympathy from him.

The action of *Macbeth* evokes a somber "there but for the grace of God." We understand but we do not therefore pardon all. Rather we acknowledge the evil and the guilt and so acquiesce in the inevitable retribution, but at the same time we are deeply moved by Macbeth's suffering and ruin because we are acutely aware of the dangerous forces before which he falls, and because we recognize their power over one like ourselves—a moderately good man who succumbs to temptation and who, having succumbed, is led to more evil to make good the first misstep, until there is no chance of withdrawal or escape. As we watch him, we know that he should not have fallen; he might have resisted; but Shakespeare's vision here is of a world in which men can hardly do better amid the forces of circumstance; and in which, if men do no better, they must suffer, and lose not only the world but themselves as well. Of such suffering and loss is tragedy made. (pp. 305-11)

J. Lyndon Shanley, " 'Macbeth': The Tragedy of Evil," in College English, *Vol. 22, No. 5, February, 1961, pp. 305-11.*

SUPERNATURAL ELEMENTS

Walter Clyde Curry

[Curry examines the **Weird Sisters** *and the precise nature of the evil they embody in Macbeth. The critic argues that Shakespeare's witches are consistent with how Elizabethans envisioned demonic spirits, not as mere hallucinations, but as representatives of an actual evil. Curry also explores the nature of the witches' prophecies in* Macbeth, *asserting that while their predictions are inherently sinister, only* **Macbeth** *can introduce evil into the world by yielding to the temptation of their assertions. The* **Weird Sisters**, *the critic continues, represent only one element of the demonic forces which pervade* Macbeth; *the natural disturbances,* **Macbeth**'s *visionary dagger,* **Banquo**'s *ghost, and* **Lady Macbeth**'s *"demoniacal somnambulism," or sleepwalking episode, are also manifestations of these evil powers. Taken together, Curry declares, these supernatural phenomena in* Macbeth *represent the*

Christian perspective of a world full of objective evil.]

That the Weird Sisters possess . . . perennial and astounding vitality is attested by the whole sweep of Shakespearean criticism. All hands seem to be convinced that they symbolize or represent evil in its most malignant form, though there is to be found little unanimity of opinion regarding the precise nature of that evil, whether it is subjective or objective or both, whether mental or metaphysical. (pp. 55-6)

The single purpose of this study is to examine, as thoroughly as possible, the nature of that evil which the Weird Sisters are said to symbolize or represent, and to reproduce one aspect at least of the metaphysical groundwork of the drama. It presupposes that in Shakespeare's time evil was considered to be both subjective and, so far as the human mind is concerned, a nonsubjective reality; that is to say, evil manifested itself subjectively in the spirits of men and objectively in a metaphysical world whose existence depended in no degree upon the activities of the human mind. This objective realm of evil was not governed by mere vague and irrational forces; it was peopled and controlled by the malignant wills of intelligences—evil spirits, devils, demons, Satan—who had the ability to project their power into the workings of nature and to influence the human spirit. Such a system of evil was raised to the dignity of a science and a theology. (p. 58)

Since . . . this belief was so universal at the time, we may reasonably suppose that Shakespeare's Weird Sisters are intended to symbolize or represent the metaphysical world of evil spirits. Whether one considers them as human witches in league with the powers of darkness, or as actual demons in the form of witches, or as merely inanimate symbols, the power which they wield or represent or symbolize is ultimately demonic. Let us, therefore, exercise wisdom in the contemplation of the nature, power, and illusions of unclean spirits.

In the meantime, we may conveniently assume that in essence the Weird Sisters are demons or devils in the form of witches. At least their control over the primary elements of nature . . . would seem to indicate as much. Why, then, should Shakespeare have chosen to present upon his stage these witch-likenesses rather than devils in devil-forms? Two equally valid reasons may be suggested. In the first place, the rather sublime devil and his angels of the earlier drama, opponents of God in the cosmic order and destroyers of men, had degenerated in the hands of later dramatists into mere comic figures; by Shakespeare's time folk conception had apparently so dominated dramatic practice and tradition that cloven hoof, horns, and tail became associated in the popular imagination only with the ludicrous. . . . In the second place, witches had acquired no such comic

Laurence Olivier as Macbeth and Vivien Leigh as Lady Macbeth in a 1955 Shakespeare Memorial Theatre production of the tragedy.

associations. They were essentially tragic beings who, for the sake of certain abnormal powers, had sold themselves to the devil. As we have seen, everybody believed in them as channels through which the malignity of evil spirits might be visited upon human beings. Here, then, were terrifying figures, created by a contemporary public at the most intense moment of witchcraft delusion, which Shakespeare found ready to his hand. Accordingly he appropriately employed witch-figures as dramatic symbols, but the Weird Sisters are in reality demons, actual representatives of the world of darkness opposed to good. (pp. 59-61)

[The] Weird Sisters take on a dignity, a dark grandeur, and a terror-inspiring aspect which is in no way native to the witch-symbol as such. In the first place, they are clairvoyant in the sense that whatever happens outwardly among men is immediately known to them. In the thunder and lightning of a desert place they look upon the distant battle, in which Macbeth overcomes the King's enemies, and conjecture that it will be lost and won before the day ends. They do not travel to the camp near Forres where Duncan receives news of the battle, but when Macbeth is created Thane of Cawdor they seem to know it instantly. They must be aware that it is Macbeth who murders Duncan, because Hecate berates them for having trafficked with him in affairs of death without her help. All the events of

the drama—the murder of Banquo and the escape of Fleance, the striking down of Lady Macduff and her children, Macbeth's accumulating sins and tragic death—must, as they unfold in time, be immediately perceived by these creatures in whom the species of these things are connatural. Moreover, by virtue of their spiritual substance they are acquainted with the causes of things, and, through the application of wisdom gained by long experience, are able to prognosticate future events in relation to Macbeth and Banquo: Macbeth shall be king, none of woman born shall harm him, he shall never be overcome until Birnam wood shall come against him to Dunsinane; Banquo shall be no king, but he shall beget kings. The external causes upon which these predictions are based may to a certain extent be manipulated by these demonic forces: but the internal causes, *i.e.,* the forces which move the will of Macbeth to action, are imperfectly known and only indirectly subject to their influence. They cannot read his inmost thoughts—only God can do that—but from observation of facial expression and other bodily manifestations, they surmise with comparative accuracy what passions drive him and what dark desires of his await their fostering. Realizing that he desires the kingdom, they prophesy that he shall be king, thus arousing his passions and inflaming his imagination to the extent that nothing is but what is not. This influence gained over him is later augmented when they cause to appear before him evil spirits, who condense the air about them into the shapes of an armed Head, a bloody Child, and a crowned Child. These demonic presences materialize to the sound of thunder and seem to speak to him with human voices, suggesting evil and urging him toward destruction with the pronouncement of half-truths. These are illusions created by demonic powers, objective appearances with a sensible content sufficient to arouse his ocular and auditory senses.

Indeed, the Weird Sisters are always illusions when they appear as such upon the stage; that is to say, their forms clothe the demonic powers which inform them. This is suggested by the facility with which they materialize to human sight and disappear. King James suspects that the Devil is able to render witches invisible when he pleases, but these Weird Sisters seem of their own motion to melt into thin air and vanish like a dream. Instead of disappearing with the swift movement which characterizes demonic transportation of bodies, they simply fade into nothingness. This suggests that their movements from place to place are not continuous necessarily. Though one of them plans to sail to Aleppo in a sieve, we feel that for the most part they appear in one place at one instant and at another place the next instant, or at whatever time pleases them, without being subject to the laws of time and place. I would not, however, force this point. At any rate, all their really important actions in the drama suggest that they are demons in the guise of witches.

But the witch-appearances constitute only a comparatively small part of the demonic manifestations in *Macbeth*. Many of the natural occurrences and all of the supernatural phenomena may be attributed to the activities of the metaphysical world of evil spirits. Whether visible or invisible these malignant substances insinuate themselves into the essence of the natural world and hover about the souls of men and women; they influence and in a measure direct human thought and action by means of illusions, hallucinations, and inward persuasion. For example, since they are able to manipulate nature's germens and control the winds, we may reasonably suppose that the storm which rages over Macbeth's castle and environs in Act II is no ordinary tempest caused by the regular movements of the heavenly bodies, but rather a manifestation of demonic power over the elements of nature. Indeed, natural forces seem to be partly in abeyance; o'er the one half-world nature seems dead. A strange, mephitic atmosphere hangs over and pervades the castle and adjacent country-side; an unnatural darkness, for ages the milieu of evil forces, blots out the stars and in the morning strangles the rising sun. Where Lennox lies—evidently not far distant—the night is so unruly that chimneys are blown down, lamentings and strange screams of death are heard in the air; and the firm-set earth is so sensitized by the all-pervading demonic energy that it is feverous and shakes. Macbeth senses this magnetization, and fears that the very stones will prate of his whereabouts. As the drunken Porter feels, Macbeth's castle is literally the mouth of hell through which evil spirits emerge in this darkness to cause upheavals in nature. Within the span of his seventy years the Old Man has experienced many strange and dreadful things, but they are as trifles in comparison with the occurrences of this rough night. Demonic powers are rampant in nature. (pp. 77-81)

Macbeth's vision of a dagger is an hallucination caused immediately, indeed, by disturbed bodily humours and spirits but ultimately by demonic powers, who have so controlled and manipulated these bodily forces as to produce the effect they desire. And a like explanation may be offered of the mysterious voice which Macbeth seems to hear after the murder, crying exultantly to all the house, 'Sleep no more! Macbeth does murder sleep' [II. ii. 32-3]. (p. 84)

Banquo's ghost is an infernal illusion, created out of air by demonic forces and presented to Macbeth's sight at the banquet in order that the murderer may be confused and utterly confounded. The second appearance of Banquo's ghost, together with the show of eight kings [IV. i. 112], is undoubtedly the result of demonic machinations. Having persuaded and otherwise incited Macbeth

to sin and crime, the Devil and his angels now employ illusions which lead to his betrayal and final destruction.

And finally, certain aspects of Lady Macbeth's experience indicate that she is possessed of demons. At least, in preparation for the coming of Duncan under her battlements, she calls upon precisely those metaphysical forces which have seemed to crown Macbeth. The murdering ministers whom she invokes for aid are described as being sightless substances, *i.e.*, not evil thoughts and 'grim imaginings' but objective substantial forms, invisible bad angels, to whose activities may be attributed all the unnatural occurrences of nature. Whatever in the phenomenal world becomes beautiful in the exercise of its normal function is to them foul, and *vice versa;* they wait upon nature's mischief. She recognizes that they infest the filthy atmosphere of this world and the blackness of the lower regions; therefore she welcomes a night palled in the dunnest smoke of hell, so dense that not even heaven may pierce the blanket of the dark and behold her projected deed. Her prayer is apparently answered; with the coming of night her castle is, as we have seen, shrouded in just such a blackness as she desires. (pp. 85-6)

What happens to Lady Macbeth in the course of Act IV is not immediately clear. Apparently there is a steady deterioration of her demon-possessed body until, at the beginning of Act V, the organs of her spirit are impaired to the point of imminent dissolution. Such a great perturbation of nature has seized upon her that she walks night after night in slumbery agitation, with eyes wide open but with the senses shut. There appears a definite cleavage in her personality. Her will, which in conscious moments guards against any revelation of her guilty experiences, is submerged; and her infected mind is forced to discharge its secrets in the presence of alien ears. Her symptoms in these circumstances resemble those of the ordinary somnambulist, but the violence of her reactions indicates that her state is what may be called 'somnambuliform possession' or 'demoniacal somnambulism.' . . . The most outstanding characteristic of this demoniacal somnambulism, which in the course of history has been more common than any other form of possession, is that the normal individuality disappears and seems to be replaced by a second personality, which speaks through the patient's mouth. This strange individuality always confesses wrong-doing, and sometimes relates a sort of life-history consisting frequently of the patient's reminiscences or memories. Now the physician to Lady Macbeth recognizes these symptoms in his patient. Sometimes, to be sure, he has known those who have walked in their sleep who have died holily in their beds. But this disease is beyond his practice; this heart sorely charged with perilous stuff needs the divine more than the physician. The demonic substances she welcomed into her body now employ her bodily functions to disclose her criminal experiences. (pp. 89-90)

Shakespeare's age would undoubtedly have pronounced Lady Macbeth's sleep-walking an instance of demoniacal somnambulism. Practically everybody, so far as may be determined, accepted demonic possession as an established fact. The New Testament affirmed it; the Church Fathers had elaborated and illustrated it; the Catholic Church made of it a firm article of faith and proceeded to exorcise demons by means of recognized rituals involving holy-water and cross, bell, book, and candle; and Protestants could not consistently deny it, or if some of them did, peremptory experience forced them to take a doubtful refuge in the conception of obsession, which produced the effects of possession. . . . Fortunately Shakespeare has spared us, in the case of Lady Macbeth, a representation of the more disgusting physical symptoms of the diabolically possessed, such as astounding contortions of the body and fantastic creations of the delirious mind. He merely suggests these horrors in the report of the Doctor that the Lady is troubled with thick-coming fancies and in the expressed opinion of some that she took her own life by self and violent hands. He is interested primarily in presenting not so much the physical as the spiritual disintegration of this soul-weary creature possessed of devils.

In this manner, it seems to me, Shakespeare has informed *Macbeth* with the Christian conception of a metaphysical world of objective evil. The whole drama is saturated with the malignant presences of demonic forces; they animate nature and ensnare human souls by means of diabolical persuasion, by hallucination, infernal illusion, and possession. They are, in the strictest sense, one element in that Fate which God in his providence has ordained to rule over the bodies and, it is possible, over the spirits of men. And the essence of this whole metaphysical world of evil intelligences is distilled by Shakespeare's imagination and concentrated in those marvellous dramatic symbols, the Weird Sisters. (pp. 91-3)

> *Walter Clyde Curry, "The Demonic Metaphysics of Macbeth," in his* Shakespeare's Philosophical Patterns, *Louisiana State University Press, 1937, pp. 53-93.*

TIME

Tom F. Driver

[*Driver proposes that* Macbeth *contains three kinds of time: chronological time, providential time, and* Macbeth's *time. The critic notes that at a literal level, frequent references to chrono-*

logical time serve to establish the concrete reality of time in the play. Driver describes providential time as "an expression of social and universal righteousness," a natural order which is initially displaced by Macbeth's *evil actions, but which gradually overwhelms the protagonist and re-establishes its position in the universe. Opposed to providential time, the critic contends, is* Macbeth's *view of time, in which he futilely attempts to control the future by separating it from the past.* Macbeth *ultimately acknowledges his inability to reconcile these two elements of time, the critic concludes, by realizing in his soliloquy in Act V, scene v, that "the mortality of time is followed by . . . man's mortality."*]

In *Macbeth* there are three kinds of time: (1) time measured by clock, calendar, and the movement of sun, moon, and stars, which for the sake of convenience we may call "chronological time"; (2) an order of time which overarches the action of the entire play and which may be called "providential time"; and (3) a time scheme, or an understanding of time, belonging to Macbeth, which may be called "Macbeth's time." (pp. 143-44)

The play contains a very large number of references to chronological time; that is, to the day, the night, or the hour. There is no point in citing all of them, but one example may serve to show the deliberateness with which the hour is sometimes established. Act I, scene vii, in which the resolution to commit the murder of Duncan is made firm, takes place at supper time.

The next scene (II. i) must establish that the hour has come for all to be retired, a matter accomplished in four lines:

> BAN. How goest the night, boy?
> FLE.   The moon is down; I have not heard
>   the clock.
> BAN. And she goes down at twelve.
> FLE.   I take 't, 'tis later,
>   sir.
> BAN. Hold, take my sword. There's hus-
>   bandry in heaven:
>   Their candles are all out.
>
> > [II. i. 1-5]
> > (p. 145)

In addition to such specific references to time (of which there are many) the play contains a very great number of lines which give merely a sense of time, inducing in the spectator a kind of temporal anxiety. For instance, there is such a large number of speeches employing the words "when," "yet," and "until" that the effect is striking. As an example, the opening lines of the play:

> 1. WITCH. When shall we three meet
>   again
>   In thunder, lightning, or in
>   rain?
> 2. WITCH. When the hurlyburly's done,
>   When the battle's lost and won.
>
> > [I. i. 1-4]

Throughout the play, adverbs of time are important because the weird sisters, at the beginning, put the future into our minds. In scene iv, Macbeth, having learned that two of the prophecies are true, talks with himself about the third:

> Present fears
> Are less than horrible imaginings.
> My thought, whose murder yet is but fantastical,
> Shakes so my single state of man that function
> Is smother'd in surmise. . . .
>
> [I. iii. 137-41]

At the end of the scene he invites Banquo to speak with him "at more time" regarding what has transpired, and arouses our expectations with the concluding phrase, "Till then, enough" [I. iii. 153, 156]. (p. 146)

In *Macbeth,* Shakespeare, as usual, is careful in his "imitation" of chronological time. He is not slavish to detail, but he strives for an effect in which the feeling of being in a real world of time is extremely important. Shakespeare's adroit compression of time, his use of a fast and slow scheme of double-time, his concrete references to passing time, and the temporal note diffused throughout the speeches, all locate the audience in a temporal world and prepare it to accept time as a meaningful reality upon which rests much of the imaginative structure of the play.

Connected with chronological time in *Macbeth,* but not equated with it, is providential time, which is to say, time as an expression of social and universal righteousness. (p. 148)

How does Shakespeare communicate the idea of a providential time? In the first place, he assumes an objective, temporal order, distinguished on the one hand from mere chronology and on the other hand from anyone's subjectivity. Early in the play, Duncan sets the order of historical succession:

> Sons, kinsmen, thanes,
> And you whose places are the nearest, know
> We will establish our estate upon
> Our eldest, Malcolm, whom we name hereafter
> The Prince of Cumberland; which honor must
> Not unaccompanied invest him only.
> But signs of nobleness, like stars, shall shine
> On all deservers.
>
> [I. iv. 35-42]

Here is the proper relationship of past and future, the historical succession guaranteeing order a passage through the present into what comes "hereafter." To such historical order, Macbeth is immediately thrown into opposition:

> MACB. (*Aside*) The Prince of Cumberland! That is a step
> On which I must fall down, or else o'erleap,
> For in my way it lies.
>
> [I. iv. 48-50]

The prophecies of the weird sisters also contribute to an idea of objective time. They provide a sense of destiny, or an order in future events already set. The objectivity of the time they represent would, of course, evaporate if it were admitted that the weird sisters are primarily a symbol of Macbeth's imagination. That they are not. They appear to the audience before they are seen by Macbeth, so that the spectator naturally takes them to have an existence apart from Macbeth. The sisters therefore stand for a knowledge of the future, and the accuracy of their knowledge is confirmed in the unfolding events of the play. After seeing them, the audience harbors a conception of what is *supposed* to happen, which it continually plays off against what it sees taking place.

The weird sisters' first speeches to Macbeth (I. iii) imply a fulfillment of time. "Glamis," "Cawdor," and "King" are not only names designating rank in the Scottish hierarchy, they are also, in this case, expressions of past, present, and future; Macbeth has been thane of Glamis, he this day becomes thane of Cawdor, and he shall "be King hereafter" [I. iii. 50]. (pp. 149-51)

In Macbeth's second meeting with the weird sisters the temporal note is struck yet more distinctly. Macbeth is given assurance of victory until a certain event ("until / Great Birnam wood to high Dunsinane hill / Shall come against him"—[IV. i. 92-4]. Although he does not know it, the moment of his defeat is set. It is noteworthy that he is not given a certain number of days, but rather he is vouchsafed power until certain things shall come to pass. He is actually given a lease which will expire very shortly, while he confidently interprets it to be "the lease of nature" [IV. i. 99]. In this scene also there is a return to the theme of historical continuity. The time which the weird sisters proclaim is partner to the time which Duncan had represented in establishing the historical succession upon his son. The show of eight kings, which is set before Macbeth upon his own insistence to know the future of Banquo's line, implies a continuation of the historical succession through Banquo's descendants as far as the mind can reach:

> What, will the line stretch out to th' crack of doom?
> Another yet! A seventh! I'll see no more.
> And yet the eighth appears, who bears a glass
> Which shows me many more.
>
> [IV. i. 117-20]

This vision of the ordering of the future, bringing the constituted authority in a straight line to Shakespeare's new monarch, James I, and on to the rim of time, is a step which Macbeth cannot o'erleap. It is a "horrible sight" [IV. i. 122] and because of it Macbeth damns the time in which he stands: "Let this pernicious hour / Stand aye accursed in the calendar!" [IV. i. 133-34].

It is possible to see the full reality of providential time only when Macbeth's time is thrown into relief against it. More than one critic has noticed that a change takes place in Macbeth's understanding and experience of time. (pp. 151-52)

Macbeth opposes a more ultimate time than his own. He would "let the frame of things disjoint" [III. ii. 16]; he would "jump the life to come" [I. vii. 7]; he murders sleep, that daily symbol of man's finitude in time; he destroys the meaning of tomorrow and tomorrow, the ironic consequence of his attempt to control the future.

In his attempt to gain control over the future . . . , Macbeth reveals that his experience of time is compounded of memory and anticipation. In order to gain control of the future, to o'erleap the steps which lie in his way, he must create memories. Memories, the past haunting the present as guilt, reduce Lady Macbeth to her pitiful end. Her "What's done is done" of Act III [III. ii. 12] later becomes, "What's done cannot be undone" [V. i. 68]. It is as a bulwark against memories that Macbeth erects his doctrine of the meaninglessness of life.

Much as he would like, Macbeth cannot separate the present from the past and the future. By the act of murder he has made his own history, and the rest of the play is the account of the fulfillment of that history, ultimately self-defeating. His sin (skillfully portrayed by Shakespeare as a combination of will and temptation) blinds him to the meaning of providential time, while it does not remove him from subordination to it, nor does it remove him from his own inner historical experience. He therefore continues . . . to make use of biblical images of history and human finitude, although entirely without the biblical awareness of grace. The petty pace creeps in "To the last syllable of recorded time" [V. v. 21], a phrase which not only recalls Macbeth's earlier vision of the line which stretches out "to the crack of doom" [IV. i. 117], but which also reflects biblical eschatology. This picture of the mortality of time is followed by that of man's mortality, sketched in four images: the brief candle, the walking shadow, the strutting and fretting upon the stage, and the tale which is told, each of which has biblical parallels. Even in his final despair, therefore, Macbeth is made to speak of an order of time which he has not been able to destroy, although that had been his hope when he and his Lady stood in what proved to be a completely decisive moment upon the "bank and shoal of time" [I. vii. 6]. (pp. 153-54)

> *Tom F. Driver, "The Uses of Time: The 'Oedipus Tyrannus' and 'Macbeth',"* in *his* The Sense of History in Greek and Shakespearian Drama, *Columbia University Press, 1960, pp. 143-67.*

Stephen Spender

[*Spender discusses the unsuccessful efforts of* **Macbeth** *and* **Lady Macbeth** *to separate the past, present, and future aspects of time. In the critic's opinion, the couples' happiness depends on their ability to prevent both the anticipated and, later, the remembered murder of* **Duncan** *from affecting their present situation. In addition, the critic observes, the "chaos of time" initiated by* **Duncan**'s *murder pervades* Macbeth *until* **Malcolm** *restores a proper sense of order at the end of the play. Spender concludes his discussion by paralleling the "loss of the sense of time and measure and place" in* Macbeth *with a similar loss in the modern world.*]

I do not know whether any Shakespearean critic has ever pointed out the significant part played by ideas of time in *Macbeth*.

One often hears quoted:

> Come what may
> Time and the hour runs through the
>   roughest day.
>   [I. iii. 146-47]

Actually the tragedy of Macbeth is his discovery that this is untrue.

Macbeth and Lady Macbeth are . . . haunted . . . by the sense of time. After she has received his letter describing the meeting with the witches, Lady Macbeth's first words to her husband are:

> Thy letters have transported me beyond
> The ignorant present, and I feel now
> The future in the instant.
>   [I. v. 56-8]

Their trouble is though that the future does not exist in the instant. There is another very unpleasant instant preceding it which has to be acted on— the murder of Duncan.

In the minds of Macbeth and Lady Macbeth there are, after the prophetic meeting with the weird sisters, three kinds of time: the time before the murder, the time of the murder of Duncan, and the enjoyable time afterwards when they reap the fruits of the murder. Their problem is to keep these three times separate and not to allow them to affect each other. If they can prevent their minds showing the sense of the future before the murder, and of the past, after it, they will have achieved happiness. As soon as the murder has been decided on, Lady Macbeth scents the danger:

> Your face, my thane, is as a book where
>   men
> May read strange matters: to beguile the
>   time,
> Look like the time.
>   [I. v. 62-4]

How little Macbeth succeeds in this, we gather from his soliloquy before the murder:

> If it were done—when 'tis done—then
>   'twere well
> If it were done quickly: if the assassination
> Could trammel up the consequence, and
>   catch
> With his surcease, success: that but this
>   blow
> Might be the be-all and the end-all here,
> But here upon this bank and shoal of
>   time,
> We'ld jump the life to come. But in these
>   cases
> We still have judgement here; that we but
>   teach
> Bloody instructions, which, being taught,
>   return
> To plague th' inventor.
>
>   [I. vii. 1-10]

Macbeth certainly has good reason to fear 'even-handed justice' [I. vii. 10]. But, I think, the second part of this speech is only a rationalization of his real fear, as unconvincing in its way as Hamlet's reasons against self-murder. The real fear is far more terrible: it is a fear of the extension into infinity of the instant in which he commits the murder. 'The bank and shoal of time' is time that has stood still; beyond it lies the abyss of a timeless moment.

He loses his nerve, but Lady Macbeth rallies him:

> When you durst do it, then you were a
>   man;
> And, to be more than what you were you
>   would
> Be so much more the man. Nor time nor
>   place
> Did then adhere, and yet you would make
>   both:
> They have made themselves, and that
>   their fitness now
> Does unmake you.
>
>   [I. vii. 49-54]

She forces his mind upon the conjunction of time and place which may never occur again. They never do, indeed, recur. The murder of Banquo is ill-timed, Malcolm escapes, everything is botched, and Macbeth swears that after this he will carry out those crimes which are the 'firstlings of his heart' [IV. i. 147].

The soliloquy in which Macbeth sees the dagger before him is the first of his hallucinations. Yet the delusion is not complete. He is able to dismiss it from his mind, and he does so by fixing down the time and place, in order to restore his mind to sanity.

>   There's no such thing:
> It is the bloody season which informs
> Thus to mine eyes. Now o'er the one half
>   world
> Nature seems dead.
>
>   [II. i. 47-50]

He reminds himself of the exact time of night, and this calms him. He invokes the hour, and he invokes the place, with a reason: to relegate this moment preceding the murder to the past from which it cannot ever escape into a future. As some people say, 'I will remember this moment for the rest of my life,' Macbeth tries to say, 'I will uproot this moment from my memory.'

>   Thou sure and firm-set earth,
> Hear not my steps, which way they walk,
>   for fear
> Thy very stones prate of my whereabout,
> And take the present horror from the time
> Which now suits with it.
>
>   [II. i. 56-60]

He is more afraid of the associations of the stones than any evidence they may actually reveal to living witnesses.

Immediately after the murder we are left in no doubt that Macbeth and Lady Macbeth have failed in their main purpose of killing in memory the moment of the murder itself.

Macbeth tells his wife how he could not say 'Amen' to the prayer of the man in his sleep. 'Amen' is the conclusion of prayer, which is inconcludable. 'Methought I heard a voice cry, "Sleep no more! Macbeth does murder sleep" ' [II. ii. 32-3].

There is no 'Amen' nor night of sleep which will ever end that moment which opens wider and wider as the play proceeds. Macbeth's speech in the next scene is a naif deception, which happens also to be the truth wrung from his heart:

> Had I but [died] an hour before this
>   chance,
> I had lived a blessed time.
>
>   [II. iii. 91-2]

With this he tries to fob off his followers. Meanwhile, one is left in some doubt as to Lady Macbeth's state of mind. The Sleepwalking scene is a shocking revelation which shows that the moment when she smeared the faces of the grooms has died no more for her than has the murder for Macbeth. 'Here's the smell of blood still' [V. i. 50]. The ailment of indestructible time is revealed by Macbeth to the doctor:

> Canst thou not minister to a mind dis-
>   eased;
> Pluck from the memory a rooted sorrow;
> Raze out the written troubles of the brain;
> And with some sweet oblivious antidote
> Cleanse the stuft bosom of the perilous
>   stuff
> Which weighs upon the heart?
>
>   [V. iii. 40-5]

Thus, after the murder the past comes to life again and asserts itself amid the general disintegration. An old man appears on the stage to compare the horrors of the past with the monstrosities of the present. Ross says:

> By the clock 'tis day,
> And yet dark night strangles the travelling lamp.
>
> [II. iv. 6-7]

The present disgorges the past. The horror of not being able to live down his deeds is symbolized by the appearance of Banquo's ghost. Macbeth looks back on a time when the past was really past and the present present:

> The time has been
> That, when the brains were out, the man would die,
> And there an end.
>
> [III. iv. 77-9]

There is no end within the control of Macbeth. In the fourth act, we even have a feeling that everything has stopped. The play seems to spread out, burning up and destroying a wider and wider area, without moving forward.

'To-morrow, and to-morrow and to-morrow' [V. v. 19-28] is not merely the speech of a disillusioned tyrant destroyed by the horror which he has himself created; it has a profound irony, coming from Macbeth's mouth, because he of all people ought to have been able to make to-morrow different from to-day and yesterday. But all his violence has done is to create a deathly sameness.

This view of *Macbeth* struck me as I was reading it recently. The only doubt in my mind was whether the last speech in the play would bear out my theory that it was time which, even more than in *Hamlet,* had got out of joint in *Macbeth.* This is what Malcolm says to the lords who have rebelled against the tyrant:

> We shall not spend a large expense of time
> Before we reckon with your several loves
> And make us even with you. . . .
>
> What's more to do,
> Which would be planted newly with the time . . .
> We will perform in measure, time, and place.
>
> [V. ix. 26-39]

The emphasis of Malcolm is on time and measure and place, which he is restoring.

Macbeth is naturally the play of Shakespeare's to which we are most likely to turn if we look for parallels with the present. It is impossible to read the lines beginning 'Our country sinks beneath the yoke; It weeps, it bleeds' [IV. iii. 38-9], without thinking of half a dozen countries under the yoke of a tyrant. It is impossible not to wonder whether modern tyrants are haunted by their Banquos, and surrounded by a sense of gloomy waking nightmare. But the instruments of justice are weaker than in Shakespeare's time; the consciences of men, brought up on an inverted philosophy of materialism, are not so tender, or so superstitious perhaps. The loss of the sense of time and measure and place, the past rising in solemn visions and portents in the midst of the present, the sense of endless waiting and of time standing still in the midst of the most violent happenings; these provide deeper parallels.

In his book *Pain, Time and Sex,* Gerald Heard claims that man has reached a stage in his evolution in which he has to take a great and decisive step forward which would involve revising not only his social institutions but also his whole conception of the meaning of life. A tyranny, a murder, and a great decision at the end, are the plot of *Macbeth.* The chaos of time, the sense of being haunted by past examples, is connected not only with the tyranny, but also with the decision. The strange scene between Malcolm and Macduff in which Malcolm recites all the vices of past kings and declares that he embodies them; and then contradicts himself and stands forth in his virginity; this is a ranking of all the forces of evil against the forces of the good; and the decision is for the good.

But Malcolm is a restorer, not a revolutionary or an innovator. He takes it for granted that the strange confusion of time that has opened out in *Macbeth* is wrong. It is here that the parallel of our own day with Shakespeare fades. It is even possible that in a sense the stage which we have reached is an advance on Shakespeare. We are living in an age of chaos and confusion, but we cannot go back, we have to go forward. It may be then that the very disorder may show us the way out of our confusion. Our loss of the sense of the continuity of time may give us an entirely new idea of time within which it will be possible to establish a new kind of order. We cannot dismiss the dreams and hallucinations of art in our time as a sign of decadence and of an end. They may be an end; on the other hand, they may be the beginning of something. We only know that we do not exist to restore a past, but to create a future which embodies the greatness of the past. (pp. 120-26)

Stephen Spender, "Books and the War—II," in The Penguin New Writing, *No. 3, February, 1941, pp. 115-26.*

GENDER AND SEX ROLES

Jarold Ramsey

[*Ramsey argues that one of the organizing themes of* Macbeth *is that of manliness. Furthermore, the critic maintains, the more **Macbeth** pursues his ideal of manliness, the less humane he becomes, until he at last forfeits*

The Three Witches, Macbeth, Hecat, and Apparitions. Act IV, scene i. By Sir Joshua Reynolds.

humanity, only to realize that his concept of manhood is worthless. Ramsey then explores Lady Macbeth's repudiation of gender and her cruel questioning of Macbeth's manhood in an attempt to turn his wavering over Duncan's murder into determination. According to the critic, the upshot of this "incredible mixture of insinuation and bullying is that Macbeth is forced to accept a concept of manliness that consists wholly in rampant self-seeking aggression." Even after Macbeth murders Duncan, the critic contends, he continues to distance himself from humaneness by ruthlessly pursuing this vision of manliness. Ramsey also examines the interview between Malcolm and Macduff in Act IV, scene iii, noting that their emphasis on manhood reflects Shakespeare's notion that to "purge Scotland of Macbeth's diseased 'manliness,' the forces of right and order must to some extent embrace that inhuman code." Ramsey concludes his analysis by observing that the swift recovery of the audience's pity for the hero represents one of Shakespeare's greatest manipulations of tone. Unlike the Scottish soldiers who celebrate Macbeth's execution at the end of the play, the critic maintains, we who have been privy to his

inner turmoil as he heads toward his ruin sympathize with his tragic downfall.]

One of the organizing themes of *Macbeth* is the theme of manliness: the word (with its cognates) echoes and re-echoes through the scenes, and the play is unique for the persistence and subtlety with which Shakespeare dramatizes the paradoxes of self-conscious "manhood." In recoiling from Macbeth's outrageous kind of manliness, we are prompted to reconsider what we really mean when we use the word in praising someone. Macbeth's career may be described in terms of a terrible progressive disjunction between the manly and the humane. In any civilized culture—even among the samurai, Macbeth's counterparts in feudal Japan—it would be assumed that the first set of values is complementary to and subsumed in the second. But, as he so often does, Shakespeare exposes with memorable clarity the dangers of such a comfortable assumption: the more Macbeth is driven to pursue what he and Lady Macbeth call manliness—the more he perverts that code into a rationale for reflexive aggression—the less *humane* he becomes, until at last he forfeits nearly all claims on the race itself, and his vaunted man-hood, as he finally realizes, becomes meaningless.

After the play begins with the three witches promising a general season of inversion—"Fair is foul, and foul is fair" [l. 11]—in I. i., the human action commences with the arrival of a wounded sergeant at Duncan's camp: "What bloody man is that?" [I. ii. 1]. The sergeant's gore, of course, is emblematic of his valor and hardihood and authorizes his praise of Macbeth himself, "valor's minion"—and it also betokens his vulnerable humanity, his mortal consanguinity with the King and the rest of his nation, which he like Macbeth is loyally risking to preserve. These are traditional usages, of course, and they are invoked here at the beginning as norms which Macbeth will subsequently disjoin from each other and pervert.

That process of disjunction begins in Scene v when Lady Macbeth contemplates her husband's heretofore humane character against what the coming-on of time might bring:

> It is too full o' the milk of human kindness
> To catch the nearest way. Thou wouldst be
>   great,
> Art not without ambition, but without
> The illness should attend it. What thou
>   wouldst highly,
> That wouldst thou holily—wouldst not
>   play false
> And yet wouldst wrongly win.
>   [I. v. 17-22]

Greatness must be divorced from goodness, highness of estate from holiness, "the nearest way" from "human kindness"—with, as usual, a serious Shakespearian play on *kind*ness: charity, and fellowship in the race. And then, carrying the process to its logical end, Lady Macbeth ritually prepares herself for the deed her husband must commit by calling on the spirits of murder first to divest her of all vestiges of womanliness—"unsex me here' [I. v. 41]—with the implication that she will be left with male virtues only; and then to nullify her "kind-ness" itself: "Make thick my blood, / Stop up the access and passage to remorse, / That no compunctious visitings of nature / Shake my fell purpose" [I. v. 43-6].

In his great agonized soliloquy while Duncan is at dinner, the object of this dire rehearsal sternly reminds himself that he owes the King a "double trust," as subject to his monarch, and, on the basis of kindness again, simply as host to his guest. He then clinches the argument by conjuring up that strange image of "pity, like a naked newborn babe / Striding the blast" [I. vii. 21-2]—strange indeed for the battle hero, so recently ruthless in his king's behalf, to embrace this vision of an ultimate object of human pity. The sexless naked babe is the antithesis of himself, of course, as the manly military cynosure: and Macbeth's failure to identify with his own cautionary emblem is foretold, per-

haps, in the incongruously strenuous postures of the babe: *"striding* the blast," *"horsed* / Upon the sightless couriers of the air" [I. vii. 22-3].

At any rate, Lady Macbeth enters and makes short work of her husband's virtuous resolution. The curious thing about her exhortation is that its rhetorical force is almost wholly negative. Dwelling hardly at all on the desirability of Duncan's throne, she instead cunningly premises her arguments on doubts about Macbeth's manly virtue. All of his previous military conquests and honors in the service of Duncan will be meaningless unless he now seizes the chance to crown that career by killing the king. And, striking more ruthlessly at him, she scornfully implies that his very sexuality will be called into question in her eyes if he refuses the regicide—"From this time / Such I account thy love" [I. vii. 38-9]. When Macbeth sullenly retorts, "I dare do all that may become a man, / Who dares do more is none" [I. vii. 46-7], he gives Lady Macbeth the cue she needs to begin the radical transvaluation of his code of manliness that will lead to his ruin. As Robert Heilman has observed about this and other plays [in "Manliness in the Tragedies: Dramatic Variations," in *Shakespeare 1564-1964,* ed. Edward A. Bloom], the psychic forces concentrated in that code are all the more potent for being ill-defined; and in the scene at hand, Lady Macbeth's onslaught against Macbeth—coming from a woman, after all, his sexual partner—is virtually unanswerable:

> What beast was it then
> That made you break this enterprise to
>   me?
> When you durst do it, then you were a
>   man,
> And to be more than what you were, you
>   would
> Be so much more the man. . . .
>   [I. vii. 47-51]

Against Macbeth's stern but theoretical retort that he will perform only that which becomes a man, and no more, she replies that, on the contrary, by his own manly standards he will be a dull-spirited beast, no man, if he withdraws from the plot.

Then, with a truly fiendish cunning she goes on to tie up all the strands of her argument in a single violent image, the murder of her own nursing infant. In this, of course, she re-enacts for Macbeth her earlier appeal for a strategic reversal of sex—the humiliating implication being that she would be more truly masculine in her symbolic act than he can ever be. And in offering to dash out the brains of "the babe that milks me" [I. vii. 55], in effect she ritually murders the naked babe of pity that Macbeth has just summoned up as a tutelary spirit. The upshoot of this incredible mixture of insinuation and bullying is that Macbeth is forced to accept a concept of manliness that consists wholly in rampant self-seeking aggression. True masculinity has nothing to do with those more gentle virtues men are supposed to share with women as members of their kind; these are for women alone, as Lady Macbeth's violent rejections of her own femaleness prove. When she has finished the exhortation, Macbeth can only respond with a kind of over-mastered tribute to her ferocity, which would be more proper in him—"Bring forth men children only, / For thy undaunted mettle should compose / Nothing but males" [I. vii. 72-4].

When the murder of Duncan is discovered, Macbeth betters his wife's instructions to "make our griefs and clamors roar / Upon his death" [I. vii. 78-9], and slays the grooms outright, before they can talk. Even in his state of grief and shock, the humane Macduff is astonished at this new burst of violence—"Wherefore did you so?" [II. iii. 107]—and, in a speech that verges steadily towards hysteria, Macbeth explains that he slew the grooms in a reflex of outraged allegiance and love for his murdered king. It is the praiseworthy savage and ruthless Macbeth of recent military fame who is supposed to be talking: his appeal is to a code of manly virtue he has already perverted. "Who can be wise, amazed, temperate, and furious, / Loyal and neutral, in a moment? *No man*" [II. iii. 108-09]. The speech runs away with itself, but after Lady Macbeth's timely collapse, Macbeth collects his wits and calls for an inquest: "Let's briefly put on manly readiness, / And meet in the hall together" [II. iii. 133-34]. "Manly" here, of course, means one thing—vengeful self-control—to the others, and something else—the ability to be crafty and dissemble—to Macbeth.

In Act III, confirming Hecate's later observation that "security / Is mortals' chiefest enemy" [III. v. 32-3]—or in this case the vexing lack of it—King Macbeth seeks to be "safely thus" by killing Banquo and cutting off his claims on the future in Fleance. Macbeth's exhortation to the three murderers is an instance of the general principle of repetition and re-enactment that governs the entire drama and helps give it its characteristic quality of compulsive and helpless action. Macbeth begins his subornation by identifying for the murderers the very same grievance against Banquo he has just named for himself—

> Do you find
> Your patience so predominant in your nature
> That you can let this go? Are you so gospeled,
> To pray for this good man and for his issue,
> Whose heavy hand hath bowed you to the grave
> And beggared yours forever?
>   [III. i. 85-90]

When the First Murderer retorts ambiguously, just as Macbeth has earlier to Lady Macbeth, "We are men, my liege" [III. i. 90], the King twists this appeal from an undefined code of manliness exactly as his wife taught him to do in I. vii—

> Aye, in the catalogue ye go for men,
> As hounds and greyhounds, mongrels, spaniels, curs,
> Shoughs, water rugs, and demiwolves are clept
> All by the name of dogs.
>   [III. i. 91-4]

In protesting that he and his fellows are *men*, the First Murderer means that they are as capable of moral indignation and of violent response to wrongs "as the next man." But Macbeth, like his wife before him, undermines this position by declaring that this hardly qualifies them as men or even as humans, except in the merely zoological sense. There is simply no intrinsic distinction, no fundamental basis of identity to be had in declaring one's male gender and beyond this one's membership in the human race. What Macbeth in the next scene refers to as "that great bond / Which keeps me pale" [III. ii. 49-50], that shared humanity deeper than sex or class denoted in the cry "Man overboard," is here pronounced to be a mere figment, valid neither as a source of positive virtue nor as the ultimate basis of moral restraint. "*Real* men" (the argument is old and has its trivial as well as its tragic motives) will prove their manhood in violently self-assertive action: Macbeth is, in a sense, talking here to himself, still answering his wife's aspersions.

Those aspersions return to haunt him—along with Banquo's ghost—in the banquet scene. As he recoils from the bloody apparition, Lady Macbeth hisses, predictably, "Are you a man?" and his shaky reply, "Aye, and a bold one, that dare look upon that / Which might appall the Devil" [III. iv. 57-9], she mocks with another insinuation that under duress he is womanish. One thinks of Goneril's sneer at Albany, "Marry, your manhood! Mew!" [*King Lear,* IV. ii. 68], but Lady Macbeth's humiliating slur is a continuation of her strategy of negative exhortation—

> Oh, these flaws and starts,
> Imposters to true fear, would well become
> A woman's story at a winter's fire
> Authorized by her grandam. Shame itself!
>   [III. iv. 62-5]

When the ghost reappears, Macbeth in a frenzy "quite unmanned" recapitulates as if by rote everything he has heard against his manliness. Once more there is the dubious appeal to a perverted code—"What man dare, I dare" [III. iv. 98]. And then follows the references to beasts, here prefiguring Macbeth's own fall from humaneness to bestiality—the beasts he names *would be* fitting adversaries:

> Approach thou like the rugged Russian bear,
> The armed rhinoceros, or the Hyrcan tiger,

> Take any shape but that and my firm
>   nerves
> Shall never tremble.
>
> [III. iv. 99-102]

and then an almost pathetic desire to prove himself in single combat, like the old Macbeth: "Or to be alive again, / And dare me to the desert with thy sword" [III. iv. 102-03], and finally a humiliating comparison, worthy of his wife, to the antithesis of manliness: "If trembling I inhabit then, protest me / The baby of a girl" [III. iv. 104-05].

This harrowing scene concludes with Macbeth—now isolated not just in his crimes from his peers but in his hallucination from Lady Macbeth—brooding on the emblematic meanings of blood: the gore of regicide and homicide, of retribution in the name of human blood-ties he had denied. The "bloody man" of the first scenes, whose wounds, like Macbeth's, were public tokens of his manly courage and valor, is now succeeded wholly in the play's imagery by "the secret'st man of blood" [III. iv. 125].

The final step in the degeneration of Macbeth's manliness comes in Act IV when he appears before the witches demanding to know his manifest future more certainly. The first of the prophetic apparitions, an "Armed Head," is suggestive both of the traitor Macdonwald's fate and of Macbeth's own gruesome final appearance; the second apparition, a bloody child, points backward to the "naked newborn babe" of pity and to Lady Macbeth's hypothetically murdered child, and ahead to the slaughter of Macduff's children, as well as to Macduff himself, Macbeth's nemesis, who was from his mother's side "untimely ripped." With a fearsome irony, the prophecy of the second apparition, an object of pity, serves to release Macbeth from all basic humane obligations to his fellows. If "none of woman born / Shall harm Macbeth" [IV. i. 80-1], then he need recognize no common denominators either of origin or of mortal vulnerability with his kind, and nothing in the name of "kind-ness" can interfere, it seems, with the perfection of his monstrous "manliness." "Be bloody, bold, and resolute, laugh to scorn / The power of man" [IV. i. 79-80].

The pageant of Banquo's lineage and the bad news of Macduff's flight to England, which follow immediately according to the breakneck pace of this play, only serve to confirm Macbeth in his new freedom from all kindness: henceforth, beginning with the slaughter of Macduff's family, he will act unconstrained either by moral compunction or by reason. "From this moment / The very firstlings of my heart shall be / The firstlings of my hand" [IV. i. 146-47]. So, having earlier remarked, ominously, that "Returning were as *tedious* as go o'er" [III. iv. 137], and having just witnessed a seemingly endless procession of Scottish kings in Banquo's line, he now enters fully into what can be termed the doom of reflex and repetition, in which Lady Macbeth, with her hellish somnambulism, shares.

At this point in the play, as he so often does in the histories and tragedies, Shakespeare widens our attention beyond the fortunes of the principals; we are shown the cruel effects of such villainous causes, and much of the action on this wider stage parallels and ironically comments on the central scenes. The evils of Macbeth's epoch are dramatized in a peculiarly poignant way, for example, in IV. ii., when Lady Macduff denounces her virtuous husband to their son for what seems to her to be Macduff's unmanly, even inhuman abandonment of his family. It is a strange twisted version of Lady Macbeth's harangue and her husband's responses earlier; there is the inevitable appeal to an assumed human nature, and even the by-now-familiar comparison of man and beast—

> He loves us not,
> He wants the natural touch. For the poor
>   wren,
> The most diminutive of birds, will fight,
> Her young ones in her nest, against the
>   owl.
>
> [IV. ii. 8-11]

And this poor woman, who fears her husband lacks that milk of human kindness that Lady Macbeth deplores in *her* spouse, ends her life with a terrible commentary on the badness of the times, in which to protest one's innocence is accounted mere womanish folly. Macbeth's reign of "manliness" prevails: "Why, then, alas, / Do I put up that womanly defense, / To say I have done no harm?" [IV. ii. 77-9]. This lament assumes a really dreadful irony in the next scene when Ross assures Malcolm in Macduff's presence that "your eye in Scotland / Would create soldiers, make our women fight / To doff their dire distress" [IV. iii. 186-88].

In this next scene, before Macduff learns of the sacrifice he has made to his patriotism, he labors to persuade young Malcolm to lead an army of "good men" in the liberation of Scotland. For the first time since the opening scenes, a concept of manly virtue that is alternative to Macbeth's is broached; it is, of course, the code that Macbeth himself once served so valorously. Malcolm shrewdly responds to the invitation with a remarkable double test of Macduff as the emissary of the Scottish loyalists—first and directly of his honesty and allegiance (is he really only another assassin sent by Macbeth?), and second and indirectly of the depth and quality of that allegiance. By representing himself vice by vice as a monster even more depraved than Macbeth, by forcing a disjunction of patriotism from morality, the politic Malcolm can determine the exact limits of Macduff's offered support. As King he could not, presumably, accept an allegiance so desperate and indiscriminant that it would ignore the total viciousness he paints himself with. (pp. 286-94)

Given Macduff's straightforward soldierly goodness, his fervent hopes for his country, and his growing apprehensions (which Malcolm plays on) about the family he has left at the mercy of the tyrant, it is a deeply cruel if necessary test, one that the unhappy patriot must painfully "fail" in order to pass. In its tone and in the logic of its placement, the entire scene in London is analogous to that remarkable sequence of scenes in [*2 Henry IV*]—Hal's oblique denunciation of Poins and other small beer [II. ii], Lady Percy's denunciation of Northumberland [II. iii], and Hal and Poin's spying on and rather brutal exposure of Falstaff [II. iv]. There, as here, a persistent cruelty between allies seems to signal the beginnings of a drastic homeopathic cure of the whole diseased nation.

In *Macbeth,* this homeopathy takes a predictable form: in order to purge Scotland of Macbeth's diseased "manliness," the forces of right and order must to some extent embrace that inhuman code. As Macduff collapses under the news of his family's slaughter, Malcolm exhorts him to convert his grief and guilt without delay into "manly" vengeful rage: "Be comforted. Let's make us medicines of our great revenge / To cure this deadly grief. . . . Dispute it like a man." To which advice Macduff cries back, "I shall do so, But I must feel it like a man" [IV. iii. 214-15; 220-21]. Nowhere in the play is there a more cruel disjunction of the moral claims on "Man", between a narrow code of manliness, and a general "natural" humaneness. Soon Macduff is driven into that familiar harsh polarization according to sex of human feelings that should belong to the race as a whole: "Oh I could play the woman with mine eyes" [IV. iii. 230]. In other circumstances, Macduff would be profoundly unworthy of his manhood if he could not feel and show his losses, and Malcolm's impatient urgings would simply be intolerable. As it is, if his strategy is cruelly necessary, there is an unpleasant note of politic satisfaction in his endorsement of Macduff's wrenching of private grief into public wrath, the wrath, after all, that will place Malcolm on the throne: he says, briskly, "This tune goes manly" [IV. iii. 235]. As Edmund says to the murderer of Cordelia in a very different context, "men / Are as the times is" [*King Lear*, V. iii. 30-1]: the reformers, it seems, to a considerable degree, as well as the evildoers. Whatever his kingly virtues otherwise, it seems clear that Malcolm will never rule Scotland with the simple graciousness and humane trust of a Duncan. The times forbid it; Macbeth's savage reign requires that he be succeeded by a king of cold blood and clear mind who stands with that Shakespearean company distinguished by "little love but much policy" [cf. *Richard II,* V. i. 84]. . . .

In the concluding scenes, while Macbeth betrays his special preoccupations by referring to "the *boy* Malcolm" and abusing his servant as "lily-livered *boy*", [V. iii. 2, 15] Malcolm has, we are told, enlisted the support of a whole generation of untried "boys" whose valorous service in his great cause will "Protest their first of manhood" [V. ii. 11]. Young Siward is their leader, and his subsequent brave, fatal encounter with Macbeth is recognized by all as evidence of a resurgent true manliness in Scotland, based (as Macbeth's conduct was at the beginning!) on selflessness and heroic violence in the cause of right and justice. Old Siward refuses to allow Malcolm to lionize his dead son beyond the simple terms of Ross's eulogy:

> He only lived but till he was a man,
> The which no sooner had his prowess con-
> firmed
> In the unshrinking station where he
> fought
> But like a man he died.
>
> [V. ix. 6-9]

The larger questions in this familiar declaration of praise—"What *is* a man? What should he be? What standards of manhood?" are begged, as they were in the beginning of Macbeth's story: indeed, there is again the existentialistic implication that man's nature is not an *a priori* [presumptive] constant but rather an evolving and unstable set of possibilities. But if young Siward's kind of manliness is seen in the context of the story as being ambiguous, volatile, capable of hideous perversions as well as of glories, it is nonetheless offered to us dramatically as the only moral alternative in the play. In the familiar Shakespearan manner, a hypothetical code has been realistically *tested* in action for us as viewers—not merely nullified and replaced with another set of unexamined verities. No one would deny that young Siward has indeed achieved a form of manhood—but the structure of the play allows us to cherish no illusions about that kind of achievement.

The swift resurgence of a measure of sympathy for Macbeth in the last scenes has always been recognized as one of Shakespeare's most brilliant manipulations of tone. As Wayne Booth [see excerpt in section on Macbeth's character] and others have demonstrated, it is based upon our almost insupportable intimacy with Macbeth—we know him as no one in his own world does—and upon the terrible imaginative fullness of his knowledge of his crimes, if not of the effects of those crimes on himself. What triggers an access of sympathy in the final scenes is chiefly his return to a semblance of direct, uncomplex action, "we'll die with harness on our back," [V. v. 51] so painfully suggestive of the old Macbeth. But now he is champion of nothing human or humane; he must "try the last" [V. viii. 32] in utter alienation from the community of men, which in some other life would have granted him, as to any man, "that which should accompany old age, / As honor, love, obedience, troops of friends" [V. iii. 24-5]. At the last, all the invidious comparisons of earlier scenes between men and beasts come due as he feels himself reduced to the state of a solitary animal in a bear-baiting: "bear-like I must fight the course" [V. vii. 1-2].

Nowhere is Macbeth's alien condition more starkly revealed than at the moment of his wife's death in Scene v. As he and his followers doubtfully parade on stage with banners and prepare for the siege of Dunsinane, there comes a "cry of women" offstage [s.d., V. v. 7]. It is a hair-raising stroke of theater, worthy of the Greeks: at the death of the ambitious wife who would have unsexed herself to provoke her husband into forgetting his ties with humanity, the women of Dunsinane raise the immemorial voice of their sex in grief and sympathy, so long banished from Scotland. It is as if a spell is broken; all the deaths in the play are bewailed, those of the victims as well as that of the murderess—but so barren is Macbeth now of humane feeling that it takes Seyton to tell him that what he has heard is "the cry of women" [V. v. 8], and when he learns it is his own wife who has died, he can only shrug wearily over what he cannot feel, and then lament a life devoid of all human meaning: "Tomorrow, and tomorrow, and tomorrow" [V. v. 19]. After a brutal career of striving "manfully" to impose his own consequentiality upon the future, Macbeth now foresees a future of mere repetitive subsequence—"time and the hour" do *not* "run through the roughest day" but are stuck fast in it [I. iii. 148]. The First Witch's curse against the Master of the *Tiger,* "I shall drain him dry as hay" [I. iii. 18], has come true in Macbeth's soul.

Yet it is still a human soul, and in the last scene Shakespeare seems to take pains to enforce our unwilling rediscovery of that fact. Confronted at last by Macduff, Macbeth recoils momentarily with an unwonted remorse: "get thee back, my soul is too much charged / With blood of thine already" [V. viii. 5-6]. And when he perceives that Macduff is the object of the witches' equivocation, the mortal man Fate has chosen to be its instrument against him, Macbeth gains the last and fullest fragment of tragic knowledge the dramatist grants him in this tragedy of limited and helpless knowledge. Though he confesses that Macduff's revelation "hath cowed my better part of man" [V. viii. 18]—meaning the reckless, savage manhood he has embraced—the insight itself suggests a step back towards the common human condition and its "great bond."

> be these juggling fiends no more believed
> That palter with us in a double sense,
> That keep the word of promise to our ear
> And break it to our hope. I'll not fight with thee.
>
> [V. viii. 19-22]

The plurality of these pronouns is more than royal: having already extrapolated from his own ruin to a nihilistic view of all human life in the "tomorrow" speech, Macbeth here generalizes validly for the human race at large. Fate is enigmatic to us all;

it is, he realizes too late, one of the immutable common denominators of our condition; no career of rampant "manly" self-assertion can hope to circumvent or control it.

In this frame of mind, then, at least tenuously re-awakened to the circumstances binding him to his race, Macbeth is roused by Macduff's threat that he will be exhibited "as our rarer monsters are" if captured alive [V. viii. 25], and hurls himself into single combat for the first time since he was "valor's minion." There is no more question of redemption than of escape, of course, as Macbeth himself knows: but who would deny a stirring of fellow-feeling at this spectacle of a single mortal man actively facing his mortality, "trying the last" [cf. V. viii. 32]? When Macduff reappears bearing Macbeth's severed head, and Malcolm triumphantly announces his succession to "this dead butcher and his fiendlike queen" [V. ix. 35], it seems impossible to deny the sense of a dramatic imbalance between the claims of justice and those of humaneness. We know Macbeth far better than do any of the Scottish worthies who celebrate his gruesome death; we have been privy to all the steps of his ruin: the tragic paradox in his nature is that the medium of his degeneration—his extraordinary imaginative susceptability—is also the medium of our never wholly suspended empathy with him. Such is the main thrust of these concluding scenes: they reveal Macbeth to us as a monster of degenerate "manliness"—but as a human monster for all that. The circle of human sympathy and *kind*ness, broken by Macbeth's career of regicide and slaughter, is re-formed: narrowly and vengefully, on-stage; broadly and with a heavy sense of man's undefinable limits and capabilities, in the audience. (pp. 295-99)

Jarold Ramsey, "The Perversion of Manliness in 'Macbeth'," in Studies in English Literature, 1500-1900, *Vol. XIII, No. 2, Spring, 1973, pp. 285-300.*

IMAGERY

Kenneth Muir

[Muir analyzes various image patterns in Mac-beth. The first pattern the critic examines is that of babies and breast-feeding. According to Muir, infants symbolize pity throughout the play, and breast-milk represents "humanity, tenderness, sympathy, natural human feelings, [and] the sense of kinship, all of which have been outraged by the murderers." Another group of images focuses on sickness and medicine, all of which occur, significantly, in the last three acts of the play, after Macbeth has ascended the throne. Images of sickness, the critic contends, signify the "disease of tyr-

anny" which has infected Scotland, and which can only be cured by "bleeding or purgation." Muir also observes a contrast between the powers of light and darkness in Macbeth. *Darkness pervades all the action in* **Macbeth's** *world, whereas light manifests itself in the scenes in England and those in which* **Malcolm** *and* **Macduff** *restore order at the end of the play. Other dualities related to the light/dark motif include contrasts between angel and devil, heaven and hell, and truth and falsehood. Muir briefly discusses several other image patterns in* Macbeth, *focusing especially on blood, sleep and sleeplessness, and order versus disorder.*]

The total meaning of [*Macbeth*] depends on a complex of interwoven patterns and the imagery must be considered in relation to character and structure.

One group of images to which Cleanth Brooks called attention [in his *The Well-Wrought Urn*] was that concerned with babes. It has been suggested by Muriel C. Bradbrook that Shakespeare may have noticed in the general description of the manners of Scotland included in Holinshed's *Chronicles* that every Scotswoman 'would take intolerable pains to bring up and nourish her own children' [*Shakespeare Survey* 4 (1951)]; and H. N. Paul pointed out that one of the topics selected for debate before James I, during his visit to Oxford in the summer of 1605, was whether a man's character was influenced by his nurse's milk [*The Royal Play of 'Macbeth'*]. Whatever the origin of the images in *Macbeth* relating to breast-feeding, Shakespeare uses them for a very dramatic purpose. Their first appearance is in Lady Macbeth's invocation of the evil spirits to take possession of her:

> Come to my woman's breasts,
> And take my milk for gall, you murd'ring
>   ministers,
> Wherever in your sightless substances
> You wait on nature's mischief.
>
> > [I. v. 47-50]

They next appear in the scene where she incites Macbeth to the murder of Duncan:

> I have given suck, and know
> How tender 'tis to love the babe that milks
>   me—
> I would, while it was smiling in my face,
> Have pluck'd my nipple from his boneless
>   gums,
> And dash'd the brains out, had I so sworn
>   as you
> Have done to this.
>
> > [I. vii. 54-9]

In between these two passages, Macbeth himself, debating whether to do the deed, admits that

> Pity, like a naked new-born babe
> Striding the blast,
>
> > [I. vii. 21-2]

would plead against it; and Lady Macbeth, when she first considers whether she can persuade her husband to kill Duncan, admits that she fears his nature:

> It is too full o' th' milk of human kindness
> To catch the nearest way.
>
> > [I. v. 17-18]

Later in the play, Malcolm, when he is pretending to be worse even than Macbeth, says that he loves crime:

> Nay, had I pow'r, I should
> Pour the sweet milk of concord into hell,
> Uproar the universal peace, confound
> All unity on earth.
>
> > [IV. iii. 97-100]

In these passages the babe symbolizes pity, and the necessity for pity, and milk symbolizes humanity, tenderness, sympathy, natural human feelings, the sense of kinship, all of which have been outraged by the murderers. Lady Macbeth can nerve herself to the deed only by denying her real nature; and she can overcome Macbeth's scruples only by making him ignore his feelings of human-kindness—his kinship with his fellow-men.

Cleanth Brooks suggests therefore that it is appropriate that one of the three apparitions should be a bloody child, since Macduff is converted into an avenger by the murder of his wife and babes. On one level, the bloody child stands for Macduff; on another level, it is the naked new-born babe whose pleadings Macbeth has ignored. Helen Gardner took Cleanth Brooks to task for considering these images in relation to one another. She argued that in his comments on 'Pity, like a naked new-born babe' [I. vii. 21] he had sacrificed

> a Shakespearian depth of human feeling . . . by attempting to interpret an image by the aid of what associations it happens to arouse in him, and by being more interested in making symbols of babes fit each other than in listening to what Macbeth is saying. *Macbeth* is a tragedy and not a melodrama or a symbolic drama of retribution. The reappearance of 'the babe symbol' in the apparition scene and in Macduff's revelation of his birth has distracted the critic's attention from what deeply moves the imagination and the conscience in this vision of a whole world weeping at the inhumanity of helplessness betrayed and innocence and beauty destroyed. It is the judgment of the human heart that Macbeth fears here, and the punishment which the speech foreshadows is not that he will be cut down by Macduff, but that having murdered his own humanity he will enter a world of appalling loneliness, of meaningless activity, unloved himself, and unable to love. [*The Business of Criticism*]

Lady Macbeth, Macbeth, Banquo's Ghost, Lennox, and Rosse. Act III, scene iv. By Max Adamo.

Although this is both eloquent and true, it does not quite dispose of Brooks's interpretation of the imagery. Miss Gardner shows that, elsewhere in Shakespeare, 'a cherub is thought of as not only young, beautiful, and innocent, but as associated with the virtue of patience'; and that in the *Macbeth* passage the helpless babe and the innocent and beautiful cherub 'call out the pity and love by which Macbeth is judged. It is not terror of heaven's vengeance which makes him pause, but the terror of moral isolation.' Yet, earlier in the same speech Macbeth expresses fear of retribution in this life—fear that he himself will have to drink the ingredients of his own poisoned chalice—and his comparison of Duncan's virtues to 'angels, trumpet-tongued' [I. vii. 19] implies a fear of judgment in the life to come, notwithstanding his boast that he would 'jump' it. We may assume, perhaps, that the discrepancy between the argument of the speech and the imagery employed is deliberate. On the surface Macbeth appears to be giving merely prudential reasons for not murdering Duncan; but Shakespeare makes him reveal by the imagery he employs that he, or his unconscious mind, is horrified by the thought of the deed to which he is being driven.

Miss Gardner does not refer to the breast-feeding images—even Cleanth Brooks does not mention one of the most significant—yet all these images are impressive in their contexts and, taken together, they coalesce into a symbol of humanity, kinship and tenderness violated by Macbeth's crimes. Miss Gardner is right in demanding that the precise meaning and context of each image should be considered, but wrong, I believe, in refusing to see any significance in the group as a whole. *Macbeth,* of course, is a tragedy; but I know of no valid definition of tragedy which would prevent the play from being at the same time a symbolic drama of retribution.

Another important group of images is concerned with sickness and medicine, and it is significant that they all appear in the last three acts of the play after Macbeth has ascended the throne; for Scotland is suffering from the disease of tyranny, which can be cured, as fever was thought to be cured, only by bleeding or purgation. The tyrant, indeed, uses sickness imagery of himself. He tells the First Murderer that so long as Banquo is alive he wears his health but sickly; when he hears of Fleance's escape he exclaims 'Then comes my fit again' [III. iv. 20]; and he envies Duncan in the grave, sleeping after life's fitful fever, since life itself is one long illness. In the last act of the play a doctor, called in to diagnose Lady Macbeth's illness, confesses that he cannot

> minister to a mind diseas'd,
> Pluck from the memory a rooted sorrow,
> Raze out the written troubles of the brain,
> And with some sweet oblivious antidote
> Cleanse the stuff 'd bosom of that perilous
>   stuff
> Which weighs upon the heart.
> [V. iii. 40-5]

Macbeth then professes to believe that what is amiss with Scotland is not his own evil tyranny but the English army of liberation:

> What rhubarb, cyme, or what purgative
>   drug
> Would scour these English hence?
> [V. iii. 55-6]

On the other side, the victims of tyranny look forward to wholesome days when Scotland will be freed. Malcolm says that Macbeth's very name blisters their tongues and he laments that 'each new day a gash' [IV. iii. 40] is added to Scotland's wounds. In the last act Caithness refers to Malcolm as 'the medicine of the sickly weal',

> And with him pour we in our country's
>   purge
> Each drop of us.

Lennox adds:

> Or so much as it needs
> To dew the sovereign flower and drown
>   the weeds.
> [V. ii. 27-30]

Macbeth is the disease from which Scotland is suffering; Malcolm, the rightful king, is the *sovereign* flower, both royal and curative. Macbeth, it is said,

> Cannot buckle his distemper'd cause
> Within the belt of rule.
> [V. ii. 15-16]

James I, in *A Counter-blast to Tobacco,* referred to himself as 'the proper Phisician of his Politicke-bodie', whose duty it was 'to purge it of all those diseases, by Medicines meet for the same'. It is possible that Shakespeare had read this pamphlet, although, of course, disease-imagery is to be found in most of the plays written about this time. In *Hamlet* and *Coriolanus* it is applied to the body politic, as indeed it was by many writers on political theory. Shakespeare may have introduced the King's Evil as an allusion to James I's reluctant use of his supposed healing powers; but even without this topical reference, the incident provides a con-

trast to the evil supernatural represented by the Weird Sisters and is therefore dramatically relevant.

The contrast between good and evil is brought out in a variety of ways. There is not merely the contrast between the good and bad kings, which becomes explicit in the scene where Malcolm falsely accuses himself of avarice, lechery, cruelty and all of Macbeth's vices, and disclaims the possession of the king-becoming graces:

> Justice, verity, temperance, stableness,
> Bounty, perseverance, mercy, lowliness,
> Devotion, patience, courage, fortitude.
> [IV. iii. 92-4]

There is also a contrast throughout the play between the powers of light and darkness. It has often been observed that many scenes are set in darkness. Duncan arrives at Inverness as night falls; he is murdered during the night; Banquo returns from his last ride as night is again falling; Lady Macbeth has light by her continually; and even the daylight scenes during the first part of the play are mostly gloomy in their setting—a blasted heath, wrapped in mist, a dark cavern. The murder of Duncan is followed by darkness at noon—'dark night strangles the travelling lamp' [II. iv. 7]. Before the murder Macbeth prays to the stars to hide their fires and Lady Macbeth invokes the night to conceal their crime:

> Come, thick night,
> And pall thee in the dunnest smoke of hell,
> That my keen knife see not the wound it
>   makes,
> Nor heaven peep through the blanket of
>   the dark
> To cry 'Hold, hold'.
> [I. v. 50-4]

Macbeth, as he goes towards the chamber of the sleeping Duncan, describes how

> o'er the one half-world
> Nature seems dead, and wicked dreams
>   abuse
> The curtain'd sleep.
> [II. i. 49-51]

The word 'night' echoes through the first two scenes of the third act; and Macbeth invokes night to conceal the murder of Banquo:

> Come, seeling night,
> Scarf up the tender eye of pitiful day . . .
>   Light thickens, and the crow
> Makes wing to th' rooky wood;
> Good things of day begin to droop and
>   drowse,
> Whiles night's black agents to their preys
>   do rouse.
> [III. ii. 46-53]

In the scene in England and in the last act of the play—except for the sleep-walking scene—the darkness is replaced by light.

The symbolism is obvious. In many of these contexts night and darkness are associated with evil, and day and light are linked with good. The 'good things of day' [III. ii. 52] are contrasted with 'night's black agents' [III. ii. 53]; and, in the last act, day stands for the victory of the forces of liberation [V. iv. 1; V. vii. 27; V. ix. 3]. The 'midnight hags' are 'the instruments of darkness' [I. iii. 124]; and some editors believe that when Malcolm (at the end of Act iv) says that 'The Powers above / Put on their instruments' [IV. iii. 238-39] he is referring to their human instruments—Malcolm, Macduff and their soldiers.

The opposition between the good and evil supernatural is paralleled by similar contrasts between angel and devil, heaven and hell, truth and falsehood—and the opposites are frequently juxtaposed:

> This supernatural soliciting
> Cannot be ill; cannot be good.
> [I. iii. 130-31]

> Merciful powers
> Restrain in me the cursed thoughts that
>   nature
> Gives way to in repose!
> [II. i. 7-9]

> It is a knell
> That summons thee to heaven or to hell.
> [II. i. 63-4]

Several critics have pointed out the opposition in the play between night and day, life and death, grace and evil, a contrast which is reiterated more than four hundred times.

The evidence for this has gone beyond imagery proper and most modern imagistic critics have extended their field to cover not merely metaphor and simile, but the visual symbols implied by the dialogue, which would be visible in performance, and even the iteration of key words. . . . *Macbeth* is about blood; and from the appearance of the bloody sergeant in the second scene of the play to the last scene of all, we have a continual vision of blood. Macbeth's sword in the battle 'smok'd with bloody execution' [I. ii. 18]; he and Banquo seemed to 'bathe in reeking wounds' [I. ii. 39]; the Sergeant's 'gashes cry for help' [I. ii. 42]. The Second Witch comes from the bloody task of killing swine. The visionary dagger is stained with 'gouts of blood' [II. i. 46]. Macbeth, after the murder, declares that not all great Neptune's ocean will cleanse his hands:

> this my hand will rather
> The multitudinous seas incarnadine,
> Making the green one red.
> [II. ii. 58-60]

Duncan is spoken of as the fountain of his sons' blood; his wounds

> look'd like a breach in nature
> For ruin's wasteful entrance.
> [II. iii. 113-14]

The world had become a 'bloody stage'. Macbeth, before the murder of Banquo, invokes the 'bloody and invisible hand' of night [III. ii. 48]. We are told of the twenty trenched gashes on Banquo's body and his ghost shakes his 'gory locks' at Macbeth, who is convinced that 'blood will have blood' [III. iv. 121]. At the end of the banquet scene, he confesses wearily that he is 'stepp'd so far' in blood, that

> should I wade no more,
> Returning were as tedious as go o'er.
> [III. iv. 136-37]

The Second Apparition, a bloody child, advises Macbeth to be 'bloody, bold, and resolute' [IV. i. 79]. Malcolm declares that Scotland bleeds,

> and each new day a gash
> Is added to her wounds.
> [IV. iii. 40-1]

Lady Macbeth, sleep-walking, tries in vain to remove the 'damned spot' from her hands:

> Here's the smell of the blood still. All the
> perfumes of Arabia will not sweeten this
> little hand.
> [V. i. 50-1]

In the final scene, Macbeth's severed head is displayed on a pole. As [Jan] Kott has recently reminded us, the subject of the play is murder, and the prevalence of blood ensures that we shall never forget the physical realities in metaphysical overtones.

Equally important is the iteration of sleep. The first statement of the theme is when the First Witch curses the Master of the *Tiger:*

> Sleep shall neither night nor day
> Hang upon his penthouse lid.
> [I. iii. 19-20]

After the murder of Duncan, Macbeth and his wife

> sleep
> In the affliction of these terrible dreams
> That shake us nightly;
> [III. ii. 17-19]

while Duncan, 'after life's fitful fever . . . sleeps well' [III. ii. 23]. Anonymous lord looks forward to the overthrow of the tyrant, when they will be able to sleep in peace. Because of 'a great perturbation in nature', Lady Macbeth

> is troubled with thick coming
>   fancies
> That keep her from her rest.
> [V. iii. 38-9]

The key passage in the theme of sleeplessness . . . occurs just after the murder of Duncan, when Macbeth hears a voice which cries 'Sleep no more!' [II. ii. 38]. It is really the echo of his own conscience. As [A. C.] Bradley noted, the voice 'denounced on him, as if his three names [Glamis, Cawdor, Macbeth] gave him three personalities to suffer in, the doom of sleeplessness' [*Shakespearean Tragedy*]; and, as [J. M.] Murry puts it:

> He has murdered Sleep, that is 'the death of each day's life'—that daily death of Time which makes Time human. [*Shakespeare*]

The murder of a sleeping guest, the murder of a sleeping king, the murder of a saintly old man, the murder, as it were, of sleep itself, carries with it the appropriate retribution of insomnia.

As Murry's comment suggests, the theme of sleep is linked with that of time. Macbeth is promised by the Weird Sisters that he will be king 'hereafter' and Banquo wonders if they 'can look into the seeds of time' [I. iii. 58]. Macbeth, tempted by the thought of murder, declares that 'Present fears / Are less than horrible imaginings' [I. iii. 137-38] and decides that 'Time and the hour runs through the roughest day' [I. iii. 147]. Lady Macbeth says she feels 'The future in the instant' [I. v. 58]. In his soliloquy in the last scene of Act I, Macbeth speaks of himself as 'here upon this bank and shoal of time' [I. vii. 6], time being contrasted with the sea of eternity. He pretends that he would not worry about the future, or about the life to come, if he could be sure of success in the present; and his wife implies that the conjunction of time and place for the murder will never recur. Just before the murder, Macbeth reminds himself of the exact time and place, so that he can relegate (as Stephen Spender suggests) 'the moment to the past from which it will never escape into the future' [see excerpt in section on Time]. Macbeth is troubled by his inability to say amen, because he dimly realizes he has forfeited the possibility of blessing and because he knows that he has become 'the deed's creature'. The nightmares of the guilty pair and the return of Banquo from the grave symbolize the haunting of the present by the past. When Macbeth is informed of his wife's death, he describes how life has become for him a succession of meaningless days, the futility he has brought upon himself by his crimes:

> To-morrow, and to-morrow, and to-
> morrow,
> Creeps in this petty pace from day to day
> To the last syllable of recorded time,
> And all our yesterdays have lighted fools
> The way to dusty death.
>   [V. v. 19-23]

At the very end of the play, Macduff announces that with the death of the tyrant 'The time is free' [V. ix. 21] and Malcolm promises, without 'a large expense of time' [V. ix. 26] to do what is necessary ('which would be planted newly with the time' [V. ix. 31]) and to bring back order from chaos 'in measure, time, and place' [V. ix. 39].

From one point of view *Macbeth* can be regarded as a play about the disruption of order through evil, and its final restoration. The play begins with

what the witches call a hurly-burly and ends with the restoration of order by Malcolm. Order is represented throughout by the bonds of loyalty; and chaos is represented by the powers of darkness with their upsetting of moral values ('Fair is foul and foul is fair' [I. i. 11]). The witches can raise winds to fight against the churches, to sink ships and destroy buildings: they are the enemies both of religion and of civilization. Lady Macbeth invokes the evil spirits to take possession of her; and, after the murder of Duncan, Macbeth's mind begins to dwell on universal destruction. He is willing to 'let the frame of things disjoint, both the worlds suffer' [III. ii. 16] merely to be freed from his nightmares. Again, in his conjuration of the witches in the cauldron scene, he is prepared to risk absolute chaos, 'even till destruction sicken' through surfeit [IV. i. 60], rather than not obtain an answer. In his last days, Macbeth is 'aweary of the sun' and he wishes 'the estate of the world' were undone [V. v. 48-9]. Order in Scotland, even the moral order in the universe, can be restored only by his death. (pp. 45-51)

All through the play ideas of order and chaos are juxtaposed. When Macbeth is first visited by temptation his 'single state of man' is shaken and 'nothing is but what is not' [I. iii. 140-42]. In the next scene [I. iv] Shakespeare presents ideas of loyalty, duty, and the reward of faithful service, in contrast both to the treachery of the dead Thane of Cawdor and to the treacherous thoughts of the new thane. Lady Macbeth prays to be spared 'compunctious visitings of nature' [I. v. 45] and in the next scene, after the description of the 'pleasant seat' of the castle with its images of natural beauty, she expresses her gratitude and loyalty to the king. Before the murder, Macbeth reminds himself of the threefold tie of loyalty which binds him to Duncan, as kinsman, subject and host. He is afraid that the very stones will cry out against the unnaturalness of the murder, which is, in fact, accompanied by strange portents:

> Lamentings heard i' th' air, strange
>   screams of death,
> And prophesying, with accents terrible,
> Of dire combustion and confus'd events
> New hatch'd to th' woeful time.
>   [II. iii. 56-9]

The frequent iteration of the word 'strange' is one of the ways by which Shakespeare underlines the disruption of the natural order. (pp. 51-2)

Reference must be made to two other groups of images . . . , those relating to equivocation and those which are concerned with with the contrast between what the Porter calls desire and performance. The theme of equivocation runs all through the play. . . . [It] links up with 'the equivocation of the fiend / That lies like truth' [V. v. 42-3], the juggling fiends 'That keep the word of promise to our ear / And break it to our hope' [V.

viii. 21-2], and Macbeth's own equivocation after the murder of Duncan:

> Had I but died an hour before this chance,
> I had liv'd a blessed time; for, from this in-
>   stant,
> There's nothing serious in mortality—
> All is but toys; renown and grace is dead;
> The wine of life is drawn, and the mere
>   lees
> Is left this vault to brag of.
>
>   [II. iii. 91-6]

Macbeth's intention is to avert suspicion from himself by following his wife's advice to make their 'griefs and clamour roar upon' Duncan's death [I. vii. 78]. But, as he speaks the words, the audience knows that he has unwittingly spoken the truth. Instead of lying like truth, he has told the truth while intending to deceive. As he expresses it later, when full realization has come to him, life has become meaningless, a succession of empty tomorrows, 'a tale told by an idiot' [V. v. 26-7].

The gap between desire and performance, enunciated by the Porter, is expressed over and over again by Macbeth and his wife. It takes the form, most strikingly, in the numerous passages contrasting eye and hand, culminating in Macbeth's cry—

> What hands are here? Ha! They pluck out
>   mine eyes—
>
>   [II. ii. 56]

and in the scene before the murder of Banquo when the bloodstained hand is no longer Macbeth's, but Night's:

> Come, seeling night,
> Scarf up the tender eye of pitiful day,
> And with thy bloody and invisible hand
> Cancel and tear to pieces that great bond
> Which keeps me pale.
>
>   [III. ii. 46-50]

In the sleep-walking scene, Lady Macbeth's unavailing efforts to wash the smell of the blood from her hand symbolize the indelibility of guilt; and Angus in the next scene declares that Macbeth feels

> His secret murders sticking on his hands.
>   [V. ii. 17]

The soul is damned for the deeds committed by the hand. (pp. 52-3)

A study of the imagery and symbolism in *Macbeth* does not radically alter one's interpretation of the play. It would, indeed, be suspect if it did. In reading some modern criticisms of Shakespeare one has the feeling that the critic is reading between the lines and creating from the interstices a play rather different from the one which Shakespeare wrote and similar to a play the critic himself might have written. Such interpretations lead us away from Shakespeare; they drop a veil between us and the plays; and they substitute a formula for the liv-

ing reality, a philosophy or a theology instead of a dramatic presentation of life. I have not attempted to reshape *Macbeth* to a particular ideological image, nor selected parts of the play to prove a thesis. Some selection had to be made for reasons of space, but I have tried to make the selection representative of the whole.

We must not imagine, of course, that *Macbeth* is merely an elaborate pattern of imagery. It is a play; and in the theatre we ought to recover, as best we may, a state of critical innocence. We should certainly not attempt to notice the images of clothing or breast-feeding or count the allusions to blood or sleep. But, just as Shakespeare conveys to us the unconscious minds of the characters by means of the imagery, so, in watching the play, we may be totally unconscious of the patterns of imagery and yet absorb them unconsciously by means of our imaginative response to the poetry. In this way they will be subsumed under the total experience of the play. (p. 53)

> *Kenneth Muir, "Image and Symbol in 'Macbeth,'" in* Shakespeare Survey: An Annual Survey of Shakespearian Study and Production, *Vol. 19, 1966, pp. 45-54.*

MACBETH

Wayne C. Booth

[*Booth discusses the dramatic technique Shakespeare used to portray* **Macbeth** *as a sympathetic tragic hero. The critic argues that the testimony of the other characters as well as* **Macbeth**'s *own moral vacillations early in the play suggest that the protagonist "is not a naturally evil man but a man who has every potentiality for goodness." Booth also points out the effect that* **Macbeth**'s *limited role in the onstage murders has on his sensitive portrayal.* **Duncan**'s *death, the critic observes, is neither explicitly shown nor described, and the murders of* **Banquo** *and* **Macduff**'s *family are committed by accomplices. Thus the hero is never seen as an active participant in any act of violence. In addition, Booth contends, the protagonist's eloquent poetic language seemingly contradicts the evil of his actions and, instead, helps establish him as a sympathetic tragic figure. The critic concludes that the spectator "can feel great pity that a man with so much potentiality for greatness should have fallen so low." For further commentary on* **Macbeth**'s *character, see the excerpts by Mark Van Doren, Irving Ribner, J. Lyndon Shanley, Walter Clyde Curry, Tom F. Driver, Stephen Spender, Jarold Ramsey, Kenneth Muir, Mary McCarthy, and Leo Kirschbaum.*]

Put even in its simplest terms, the problem Shakespeare gave himself in *Macbeth* was a tremendous one. Take a good man, a noble man, a man admired by all who know him—and destroy him, not only physically and emotionally, as the Greeks destroyed their heroes, but also morally and intellectually. As if this were not difficult enough as a dramatic hurdle, while transforming him into one of the most despicable mortals conceivable, maintain him as a tragic hero—that is, keep him so sympathetic that, when he comes to his death, the audience will pity rather than detest him and will be relieved to see him out of his misery rather than pleased to see him destroyed. Put in Shakespeare's own terms: take a "noble" man, full of "conscience" and "the milk of human kindness" [I. v. 17], and make of him a "dead butcher" [V. ix. 35], yet keep him an object of pity rather than hatred. If we thus artificially reconstruct the problem as it might have existed before the play was written, we see that, in choosing these "terminal points" and these terminal intentions, Shakespeare makes almost impossible demands on his dramatic skill, although at the same time he insures that, if he succeeds at all, he will succeed magnificently. If the trick can be turned, it will inevitably be a great one. (p. 17)

I

The first step in convincing us that Macbeth's fall is a genuinely tragic occurrence is to convince us that there was, in reality, a fall: we must believe that Macbeth was once a man whom we could admire, a man with great potentialities. One way to convince us would have been to show him . . . in action as an admirable man. But, although this is possible in a leisurely novel, it would, in a play, have wasted time needed for the important events, which begin only with Macbeth's great temptation at the conclusion of the opening battle. Thus the superior choice in this case (although it would not necessarily always be so) is to begin your representation of the action with the first real temptation to the fall and to use testimony by other characters to establish your protagonist's prior goodness. We are thus given, from the beginning, sign after sign that Macbeth's greatest nobility was reached at a point just prior to the opening of the play. When the play begins, he has already coveted the crown, as is shown by his excessively nervous reaction to the witches' prophecy; it is indeed likely that he has already considered foul means of obtaining it. But, in spite of this wickedness already present to his mind as a possibility, we have ample reason to think Macbeth a man worthy of our admiration. He is "brave" and "valiant," a "worthy gentleman"; Duncan calls him "noble Macbeth." These epithets have an ironic quality only in retrospect; when they are first applied, one has no reason to doubt them. Indeed, they are true epithets, or they would have been true if applied, say, only a few days or months earlier.

Of course, this testimony to his prior virtue given by his friends in the midst of other business would not carry the spectators for long with any sympathy for Macbeth if it were not continued in several other forms. We have the testimony of Lady Macbeth (the unimpeachable testimony of a "bad" person castigating the goodness of a "good" person):

> Yet do I fear thy nature;
> It is too full o' the milk of human kindness
> To catch the nearest way. Thou wouldst be
>   great,
> Art not without ambition, but without
> The illness should attend it. What thou
>   wouldst highly,
> That wouldst thou holily; wouldst not play
>   false,
> And yet wouldst wrongly win.
>   [I. v. 16-22]

No verbal evidence would be enough, however, if we did not see in Macbeth himself signs of its validity, since we have already seen many signs that he is *not* the good man that the witnesses seem to believe. Thus the best evidence we have of his essential goodness is his vacillation before the murder. Just as Raskolnikov is tormented [in Dostoevski's *Crime and Punishment*] and just as we ourselves—virtuous theater viewers—would be tormented, so Macbeth is tormented before the prospect of his own crime. Indeed, much as he wants the kingship, he decides in Scene iii against the murder:

> If chance will have me King, why, chance
>   may crown me,
> Without my stir. . . .
>
>   [I. iii. 143-44]

And when he first meets Lady Macbeth he is resolved not to murder Duncan. In fact, as powerful a rhetorician as she is, she has all she can do to get him back on the course of murder.

In addition, Macbeth's ensuing soliloquy not only weighs the possible bad practical consequences of his act but shows him perfectly aware, in a way an evil man would not be, of the moral values involved:

> He's here in double trust:
> First, as I am his kinsman and his subject,
> Strong both against the deed; then, as his
>   host,
> Who should against his murderer shut the
>   door,
> Not bear the knife myself. Besides, this
>   Duncan
> Hath borne his faculties so meek, hath
>   been
> So clear in his great office, that his virtues
> Will plead like angels, trumpet-tongued,
>   against
> The deep damnation of his taking-off. . . .
>   [I. vii. 12-16]

In this speech we see again, as we saw in the opening of the play, Shakespeare's wonderful economy:

the very speech which shows Macbeth to best advantage is the one which shows the audience how very bad his contemplated act is, since Duncan is blameless. One need only think of the same speech if it were dealing with a king who *deserves* to be assassinated or if it were given by another character commenting on Macbeth's action, to see how right it is as it stands.

After this soliloquy Macbeth announces again to Lady Macbeth that he will not go on ("We will proceed no further in this business" [I. vii. 31]), but her eloquence is too much for him. Under her jibes at his "unmanliness," he progresses from a kind of petulant, but still honorable, boasting ("I dare do all that may become a man; / Who dares do more is none" [I. vii. 46-7]), through a state of amoral consideration of mere expediency ("If I should fail?" [I. vii. 59]), to complete resolution, but still with a full understanding of the wickedness of his act ("I am settled . . . this terrible feat" [I. vii. 80]). There is never any doubt, first, that he is bludgeoned into the deed by Lady Macbeth's superior rhetoric and force of character and by the pressure of unfamiliar circumstances (including the witches) and, second, that even in the final decision to go through with it he is extremely troubled by a guilty conscience ("*False* face must hide what the *false* heart doth know" [I. vii. 82]). In the entire dagger soliloquy he is clearly suffering from the realization of the horror of the "bloody business" ahead. He sees fully and painfully the wickedness of the course he has chosen, but not until after the deed, when the knocking has commenced, do we realize how terrifyingly alive his conscience is: "To know my deed, 't were best not know myself. / Wake Duncan with thy knocking! I would thou couldst!" [II. ii. 70-1]. This is the wish of a "good" man who, though he has become a "bad" man, still thinks and feels as a good man would.

To cite one last example of Shakespeare's pains in this matter, we have the testimony to Macbeth's character offered by Hecate:

> And which is worse, all you have done
> Hath been but for a wayward son,
> Spiteful and wrathful, who, as others do,
> Loves for his own ends, not for you.
> [III. v. 10-14]

This reaffirmation that Macbeth is not a true son of evil comes, interestingly enough, immediately after the murder of Banquo, at a time when the audience needs a reminder of Macbeth's fundamental nobility.

The evil of his acts is thus built upon the knowledge that he is not a naturally evil man but a man who has every potentiality for goodness. This potentiality and its frustration are the chief ingredients of the tragedy of Macbeth. Macbeth is a man whose progressive external misfortunes seem to produce, and at the same time seem to be produced by, his parallel progression from great goodness to great wickedness. Our emotional involvement (which perhaps should not be simplified under the term "pity" or "pity and fear") is thus a combination of two kinds of regret: (1) We regret that any potentially good man should come to such a bad end: "What a pity that things should have gone this way, that things should *be* this way!" (2) We regret even more the destruction of this particular man, a man who is not only morally sympathetic but also intellectually and emotionally interesting. In eliciting both these kinds of regret to such a high degree, Shakespeare goes beyond his predecessors and establishes trends which are still working themselves out in literature. The first kind—never used at all by classical dramatists, who never employed a genuinely degenerative plot—has been attempted again and again by modern novelists. Their difficulty has usually been that they have relied too completely on a general humane response in the reader and too little on a realized prior height or potentiality from which to fall. The protagonists are shown succumbing to their environment—or, as in so many "sociological" novels, already succumbed—and the reader is left to himself to infer that something worth bothering about has gone to waste, that things might have been otherwise, that there is any real reason to react emotionally to the final destruction. The second kind—almost unknown to classical dramatists, whose characters are never "original" or "fresh" in the modern sense—has been attempted in ever greater extremes since Shakespeare, until one finds many works in which mere *interest* in particular characteristics completely supplants emotional response to *events* involving men with interesting characteristics. The pathos of Bloom [in James Joyce's *Ulysses*], for example, is an attenuated pathos, just as the comedy of Bloom is an attenuated comedy; one is not primarily moved to laughter or tears by events involving great characters, as in *Macbeth*, but rather one is primarily interested in details about characters. It can be argued whether this is a gain or a loss to literature, when considered in general. Certainly, one would rather read a modern novel like *Ulysses*, with all its faults on its head, than many of the older dramas or epics involving "great" characters in "great" events. But it can hardly be denied that one of Shakespeare's triumphs is his success in doing many things at once which lesser writers have since done only one at a time. He has all the generalized effect of classical tragedy. We lament the "bad fortune" of a great man who has known good fortune. To this he adds the much more poignant (at least to us) pity one feels in observing the moral destruction of a great man who has once known goodness. And yet with all this he combines the pity one feels when one observes a highly characterized individual—whom one knows intimately, as it were, in whom one is *interested*—going to destruction. One difference between watching Macbeth go to destruction and watching the typical modern hero, whether in the drama (say, Willy Loman [in Arthur Miller's *Death of a Salesman*]) or in the novel (say, Jake [in *The Sun Also Rises*] or any other of Hemingway's heroes), is that in *Macbeth* there is some "going." Willy Loman doesn't have very far to fall; he begins the play on the verge of suicide, and at the end of the play he has committed suicide. Even if we assume that the "beginning" is the time covered in the earliest of the flashbacks, we have not "far to go" from there to Willy's destruction. It is true that our contemporary willingness to exalt the potentialities of the average man makes Willy's fall seem to *us* a greater one than it really is, dramatically. But the reliance on convention will, of course, sooner or later dictate a decline in the play's effectiveness. *Macbeth* continues to be effective at least in part because everything necessary for a complete response to a complete action is given to us. A highly individualized, noble man is sent to complete moral, intellectual, and physical destruction.

II

But no matter how carefully the terminal points of the drama are selected and impressed on the spectator's mind, the major problem of how to represent such a "plot" still remains. Shakespeare has the tremendous task of trying to keep two contradictory dynamic streams moving simultaneously: the stream of events showing Macbeth's growing wickedness and the stream of circumstances producing and maintaining our sympathy for him. In effect, each succeeding atrocity, marking another step toward complete depravity, must be so surrounded by contradictory circumstances as to make us feel that, in spite of the evidence before our eyes, Macbeth is still somehow admirable.

The first instance of this is the method of treating Duncan's murder. The chief point here is Shakespeare's care in avoiding any "rendering" or representation of the murder itself. It is, in fact, not even narrated. We *hear* only the details of how the guards reacted and how Macbeth reacted to their cries. We *see* nothing. There is nothing about the actual dagger strokes; there is no report of the dying cries of the good old king. We have only Macbeth's conscience-stricken lament for having committed the deed. Thus what would be an intolerable act if depicted with any vividness becomes relatively bearable when seen only afterward in the light of Macbeth's suffering and remorse. This may seem ordinary enough; it is always convenient to have murders take place offstage. But if one compares the handling of this scene, where the perpetrator must remain sympathetic, with the handling of the blinding of Gloucester [in *King Lear*], where the perpetrators must be hated, one can see how important such a detail can be. The blinding of Gloucester is not so wicked an act, in itself, as murder. If we had seen, say, a properly motivated Goneril come in from offstage wringing her hands and crying, "Methought I heard a voice cry, 'Sleep

no more' [cf. *Macbeth*, II. ii. 32]. Goneril does put out the eyes of sleep . . . I am afraid to think what I have done," and on thus for nearly a full scene, our reaction to the whole episode would, needless to say, be exactly contrary to what it now is.

A second precaution is the highly general portrayal of Duncan before his murder. It is necessary only that he be known as a "good king," the murder of whom will be a wicked act. He must be the *type* of benevolent monarch. But more particular characteristics are carefully kept from him. There is nothing for us to love, nothing for us to "want further existence for," within the play. We hear of his goodness; we do not see it. We know practically no details about him, and we have little, if any, personal interest in him at the time of his death. All the personal interest is reserved for Macbeth and Lady Macbeth. So, again, the wickedness is played up in the narration but played down in the representation. We must identify Macbeth with the murder of a blameless king, but only intellectually; emotionally we should be concerned as far as is possible only with the *effects on Macbeth.* We *know* that he has done the deed, but we *feel* primarily only his own suffering.

Banquo is considerably more "particularized" than was Duncan. Not only is he also a good man, but we have seen him acting as a good man, and we know quite a lot about him. We saw his reaction to the witches, and we know that he has resisted temptations similar to those of Macbeth. We have seen him in conversation with Macbeth. We have heard him in soliloquy. We know him to be very much like Macbeth, both in valor and in being the subject of prophecy. He thus has our lively sympathy; his death is a personal, rather than a general, loss. Perhaps more important, his murder is actually shown on the stage. His dying words are spoken in our presence, and they are unselfishly directed to saving his son. We are forced to the proper, though illogical, inference: it is more wicked to kill Banquo than to have killed Duncan.

But we must still not lose our sympathy for Macbeth. This is partially provided for by the fact that the deed is much more necessary than the previous murder; Banquo is a real political danger. But the important thing is again the choice of what is represented. The murder is done by accomplices, so that Macbeth is never *shown* in any real act of wickedness. When we see him, he is suffering the torments of the banquet table. Our incorrect emotional inference: the self-torture has already expiated the guilt of the crime.

The same devices work in the murder of Lady Macduff and her children, the third and last atrocity explicitly shown in the play (except for the killing of young Siward, which, being military, is hardly an atrocity in this sense). Lady Macduff is more vividly portrayed even than Banquo, although she appears on the stage for a much briefer time. Her complaints against the absence of her husband, her loving banter with her son, and her stand against the murderers make her as admirable as the little boy himself, who dies in defense of his father's name. The murder of women and children of such quality is wicked indeed, the audience is made to feel. And when we move to England and see the effect of the atrocity on Macduff, our active pity for Macbeth's victims is at the high point of the play. For the first time, perhaps, pity for Macbeth's victims really wars with pity for him, and our desire for his downfall, to protect others and to protect himself from his own further misdeeds, begins to mount in consequence.

Yet even here Macbeth is kept as little "to blame" as possible. He does not do the deed himself, and we can believe that he would have been unable to, had he seen the wife and child as we have seen them. . . . He is much further removed from them than from his other victims; as far as we know, he has never seen them. They are as remote and impersonal to him as they are immediate and personal to the audience, and personal blame against him is thus attenuated. More important, however, immediately after Macduff's tears we shift to Lady Macbeth's scene—the effect being again to impress on us the fact that the punishment for these crimes is always as great as, or greater than, the crimes themselves. Thus all three crimes are followed immediately by scenes of suffering and self-torture. Shakespeare works almost as if he were

Lady Macbeth, Doctor, and Gentlewoman. Act V, scene i. By William Kaulbach. The Department of Rare Books and Special Collections, The University of Michigan Library.

following a master-rulebook: By your choice of what to represent from the materials provided in your story, insure that each step in your protagonist's degeneration will be counteracted by mounting pity for him.

All this would certainly suffice to keep Macbeth at the center of our interest and sympathy, even with all our mounting concern for his victims. But it is reinforced by qualities in his character separate and distinct from his moral qualities. Perhaps the most important of these is his gift . . . of expressing himself in great poetry. We naturally tend to feel with the character who speaks the best poetry of the play, no matter what his deeds (Iago would never be misplayed as protagonist if his poetry did not rival, and sometimes surpass, Othello's). When we add to this poetic gift an extremely rich and concrete set of characteristics, over and above his moral qualities, we have a character which is in its own way more sympathetic than any character portrayed in only moral colors could be. Even the powers of virtue gathering about his castle to destroy him seem petty compared with his mammoth sensitivity, his rich despair. When he says:

> my way of life
> Is fall'n into the sere, the yellow leaf;
> And that which should accompany old age,
> As honour, love, obedience, troops of friends,
> I must not look to have.
>
> [V. iii. 22-6]

we feel that he wants these things quite as honestly and a good deal more passionately than even the most virtuous man could want them. And we regret deeply the truth of his conclusion that he "must not look to have" them.

III

If Macbeth's initial nobility, the manner of representation of his atrocities, and his rich poetic gift are all calculated to create and sustain our sympathy for him throughout his movement toward destruction, the kind of mistake he makes in initiating his own destruction is equally well calculated to heighten our willingness to forgive while deploring. On one level it could, of course, be said that he errs simply in being overambitious and underscrupulous. But this is only partly true. What allows him to sacrifice his moral beliefs to his ambition is a mistake of another kind—of a kind which is, at least to modern spectators, more probable or credible than any conventional tragic flaw or any traditional tragic error such as mistaking the identity of a brother or not knowing that one's wife is one's mother. Macbeth knows what he is doing, yet he does not know. He knows the immorality of the act, but he has no conception of the effects of the act on himself or on his surroundings. Accustomed to murder of a "moral" sort, in battle, and having valorously and successfully "carv'd out his passage" with "bloody execution" [I. ii. 18-19] many times previously, he misunderstands completely what will be the devastating effect on his own character if he tries to carve out his passage in civil life. The murder of Duncan on one level resembles closely the kind of thing Macbeth has done professionally, and he lacks the insight to see the great difference between the two kinds of murder. He cannot foresee that success in the first murder will only lead to the speech "to be thus is nothing; But to be safely thus" [III. i. 47-8], and to ever increasing degradation and suffering for himself and for those around him. Even though he has a kind of double premonition of the effects of the deed both on his own conscience and on Duncan's subjects ("If it were done when 't is done, then 't were well . . ." [I. vii. 1ff.]), he does not really understand. If he did understand, he could not do the deed.

This ignorance is made more convincing by being extended to a misunderstanding of the forces leading him to the murder. Macbeth does not really understand that he has two spurs "to prick the sides" of his intent [I. vii. 26], besides his own vaulting ambition. The first of these is, of course, the witches and their prophecy. A good deal of nonsense has been written about these witches, some in the direction of making them totally responsible for the action of Macbeth and some making them merely a fantastical representation of Macbeth's mental state. Yet they are quite clearly real and objective, since they say and do things which Macbeth could know nothing about—such as their presentation of the ambiguous facts of Macduff's birth and the Birnam wood trick. And equally they are not "fate," alone responsible for what happens to Macbeth. He deliberately chooses from what they have to say only those things which he wishes to hear; and he has already felt the ambition to be king and even possibly to become king through regicide. Dramatically they seem to be here both as a needed additional goad to his ambition and as a concrete instance of Macbeth's tragic misunderstanding. His deliberate and consistent mistaking of what they have to say objectifies for us his misunderstanding of everything about his situation. He should realize that, if they are true oracles, *both* parts of their prophecy *must* be fulfilled. He makes the mistake of acting criminally to bring about the first part of the prophecy, and then acting criminally to prevent the fulfilment of the second part, concerning Banquo. But only if they were not true oracles would the slaying of Duncan be necessary or the slaying of Banquo be of any use. Macbeth tries to pick and choose from their promises, and they thus aid him in his self-destruction.

The second force which Macbeth does not understand, and without which he would find himself incapable of the murder, is Lady Macbeth. She, of course, fills several functions in the play, besides her inherent interest as a character, which is great indeed. But her chief function, as the textbook

commonplace quite rightly has it, is to incite Macbeth to the murder of Duncan. Shakespeare has realized the best possible form for this incitation. She does not urge Macbeth with pictures of the pleasures of rewarded ambition; she does not allow his thoughts to remain on the moral aspects of the problem, as they would if he were left to himself. Rather, she shifts the whole ground of the consideration to questions of Macbeth's valor. She twits him for cowardice, plays upon the word "man," making it seem that he becomes more a man by doing the manly deed. She exaggerates her own courage (although significantly she does not offer to do the murder herself), to make him fear to seem cowardly by comparison. Macbeth's whole reputation for bravery seems at last to be at stake, and even questions of success and failure are made to hang on his courage: "But screw your courage to the sticking-place / And we'll not fail" [I. vii. 60-1]. So that the whole of his past achievement seems to depend for its meaning on his capacity to go ahead with the contemplated act. He performs the act, and from that point his final destruction is certain.

His tragic error, then, is at least three-fold: he does not understand the forces working upon him to make him commit the deed, neither his wife nor the weird sisters; he does not understand the differences between "bloody execution" in civilian life and in his past military life; and he does not understand his own character—he does not know what will be the effects of the evil act on his own future happiness. Only one of these—the misunderstanding of the witches' prophecy—can be considered similar to, say, Iphigenia's ignorance of her brother's identity [in Euripides's *Iphigenia in Tauris*]. Shakespeare has realized that simple ignorance of that sort will not do for the richly complex degenerative plot. The hero here must be really aware of the wickedness of his act, in advance. The more aware he can be—and still commit the act convincingly—the greater the regret felt by the reader or spectator. Being thus aware, he must act under a special kind of misunderstanding: it must be a misunderstanding caused by such powerful forces that even a good man might credibly be deceived by them into "knowingly" performing an atrocious deed.

All these points are illustrated powerfully in the contrast between the final words of Malcolm concerning Macbeth—"This dead butcher and his fiendlike queen" [V. ix. 35]—and the spectator's own feelings toward Macbeth at the same point. One judges Macbeth, as Shakespeare intends, not merely for his wicked acts but in the light of the total impression of all the incidents of the play. Malcolm and Macduff do not know Macbeth and the forces that have worked on him; the spectator does know him and, knowing him, can feel great pity that a man with so much potentiality for greatness should have fallen so low. The pity is that everything was not otherwise, since it so easily could have been otherwise. Macbeth's whole life, from the time of the first visitation of the witches, is felt to be itself a tragic error, one big pitiful mistake. And the conclusion brings a flood of relief that the awful blunder has played itself out, that Macbeth has at last been able to die, still valiant, and is forced no longer to go on enduring the knowledge of the consequences of his own misdeeds. (pp. 18-25)

> *Wayne C. Booth, "Macbeth as Tragic Hero," in* The Journal of General Education, *Vol. VI, No. 1, October, 1951, pp. 17-25.*

Mary McCarthy

[*McCarthy provides a detailed analysis of* **Macbeth**'s *character, asserting that he is an average man with common thoughts and little imagination, who is manipulated into performing evil deeds by both the witches and his wife. In the critic's opinion,* **Macbeth**'s *response to the witches's predictions is too literal; it never occurs to him to test their assertions, which were commonly known to be "ambiguous and tricky." McCarthy further declares that* **Macbeth** *is dominated by his wife, noting that while he is "old Iron Pants in the field," at home "she has to wear the pants; she has to unsex herself." Among the protagonist's other traits, the critic asserts, is a lack of feeling for others, excessive envy, and absence of conscience. Each of these traits not only contributes to the hero's deliberate choice to murder* **Duncan,** *but also to his subsequent isolation as the play unfolds. McCarthy also addresses the claim that* **Macbeth** *speaks some of Shakespeare's finest poetry throughout the tragedy, arguing that since the verses come from his mouth, they are merely empty words difficult to take seriously. According to the critic,* **Macbeth**'s *soliloquies "are not poetry but rhetoric. They are tirades. . . . Like so many unfeeling men, he has a facile emotionalism, which he turns on and off." Ultimately, McCarthy observes that it is not just the hero who rants in* Macbeth, *but also Nature, whose stormy disorder turns the world upside down and unleashes numerous physical disturbances in Scotland. For further commentary on* **Macbeth**'s *character, see the excerpts by Mark Van Doren, Irving Ribner, J. Lyndon Shanley, Walter Clyde Curry, Tom F. Driver, Stephen Spender, Jarold Ramsey, Kenneth Muir, Wayne C. Booth, and Leo Kirschbaum.*]

He is a general and has just won a battle; he enters the scene making a remark about the weather. "So foul and fair a day I have not seen" [I. iii. 38]. On this flat note Macbeth's character tone is set. "Terrible weather we're having." "The sun can't seem to make up its mind." "Is it hot/cold/wet enough for you?" A commonplace man who talks in com-

monplaces, a golfer, one might guess, on the Scottish fairways, Macbeth is the only Shakespeare hero who corresponds to a bourgeois type: a murderous Babbitt [in Sinclair Lewis's *Babbitt*], let us say.

You might argue just the opposite, that Macbeth is over-imaginative, the prey of visions. It is true that he is impressionable. Banquo, when they come upon the witches, amuses himself at their expense, like a man of parts idly chaffing a fortune-teller. Macbeth, though, is deeply impressed. "Thane of Cawdor and King." He thinks this over aloud. "How can I be Thane of Cawdor when the Thane of Cawdor is alive?" [cf. I. iii. 72-5] When this mental stumbling-block has been cleared away for him (the Thane of Cawdor has received a death sentence), he turns his thoughts *sotto voce* [under his breath] to the next question. "How can I be King when Duncan is alive?" The answer comes back, "Kill him" [cf. I. iii. 137-42]. It does fleetingly occur to Macbeth, as it would to most people, to leave matters alone and let destiny work it out. "If chance will have me King, why, chance may crown me, Without my stir" [I. iii. 143-44]. But this goes against his grain. A reflective man might wonder how fate would spin her plot, as the Virgin Mary must have wondered after the Angel Gabriel's visit. But Macbeth does not trust to fate, that is, to the unknown, the mystery of things; he trusts only to a known quantity—himself—to put the prophecy into action. In short, he has no faith, which requires imagination. He is literal-minded; that, in a word, is his tragedy.

It was not *his* idea, he could plead in self-defense, but the witches', that he should have the throne. *They* said it first. But the witches only voiced a thought that was already in his mind; after all, he was Duncan's cousin and close to the crown. And once the thought has been put into *words,* he is in a scrambling hurry. He cannot wait to get home to tell his wife about the promise; in his excitement, he puts it in a letter, which he sends on ahead, like a businessman briefing an associate on a piece of good news for the firm.

Lady Macbeth takes very little stock in the witches. She never pesters her husband, as most wives would, with questions about the Weird Sisters: "What did they say, exactly?" "How did they look?" "Are you sure?" She is less interested in "fate and metaphysical aid" [I. v. 29] than in the business at hand—how to nerve her husband to do what he wants to do. And later, when Macbeth announces that he is going out to consult the Weird Sisters again, she refrains from comment. As though she were keeping her opinion—"O proper stuff!" [III. iv. 59]—to herself. Lady Macbeth is not superstitious. Macbeth is. This makes her repeatedly impatient with him, for Macbeth, like many men of his sort, is an old story to his wife. A tale full of sound and fury signifying nothing. Her contempt for him perhaps extends even to his ambition. "Wouldst not play false, And yet wouldst wrongly win" [I. v. 21-2]. As though to say, "All right, if that's what you want, have the courage to get it." Lady Macbeth does not so much give the impression of coveting the crown herself as of being weary of watching Macbeth covet it. Macbeth, by the way, is her second husband, and either her first husband was a better man than he, which galls her, or he was just another general, another superstitious golfer, which would gall her too.

Superstition here is the opposite of reason on the one hand and of imagination on the other. Macbeth is credulous, in contrast to Lady Macbeth, to Banquo, and, later, to Malcolm, who sets the audience an example of the right way by mistrusting Macduff until he has submitted him to an empirical test. Believing and knowing are paired in Malcolm's mind; what he *knows* he believes. Macbeth's eagerness to believe is the companion of his lack of faith. If all works out right for him in this world, Macbeth says, he can take a chance on the next ("We'd jump the life to come" [I. vii. 7]). Superstition whispers when true religion has been silenced, and Macbeth becomes a ready client for the patent medicines brewed by the jeering witches on the heath.

As in his first interview with them he is too quick to act literally on a dark saying, in the second he is too easily reassured. He will not be conquered till "great Birnam Wood to high Dunsinane Hill shall come against him." "Why, that can never happen!" [cf. IV. i. 92-4] he cries out in immediate relief, his brow clearing.

It never enters his mind to examine the saying more closely, test it, so to speak, for a double bottom, as was common in those days (Banquo even points this out to him) with prophetic utterances, which were known to be ambiguous and tricky. Any child knew that a prophecy often meant the reverse of what it seemed to say, and any man of imagination would ask himself how Birnam Wood *might* come to Dunsinane and take measures to prevent it, as King Laius took measures to prevent his own death by arranging to have the baby Oedipus killed [in Sophocles's *Oedipus Rex*]. If Macbeth had thought it out, he could have had Birnam Wood chopped down and burned on the spot and the ashes dumped into the sea. True, the prophecy might still have turned against him . . . , but that would have been another story, another tragedy, the tragedy of a clever man not clever enough to circumvent fate. Macbeth is not clever; he is taken in by surfaces, by appearance. He cannot think beyond the usual course of things. "None of woman born" [IV. i. 80]. All men, he says to himself, sagely, are born of women; Malcolm and Macduff are men; therefore I am safe. This logic leaves out of account the extraordinary: the man brought into the world by Caesarean section. In the same way, it leaves out

of account the supernatural—the very forces he is trafficking with. He might be overcome by an angel or a demon, as well as by Macduff.

Yet this pedestrian general sees ghosts and imaginary daggers in the air. Lady Macbeth does not, and the tendency in her husband grates on her nerves; she is sick of his terrors and fancies. A practical woman, Lady Macbeth, more a partner than a wife, though Macbeth treats her with a trite domestic fondness—"Love," "Dearest love," "Dearest chuck," "Sweet remembrancer." These middle-aged, middle-class endearments, as though he called her "Honeybunch" or "Sweetheart," as well as the obligatory "Dear," are a master stroke of Shakespeare's and perfectly in keeping with the prosing about the weather, the heavy credulousness.

Naturally Macbeth is dominated by his wife. He is old Iron Pants in the field (as she bitterly reminds him), but at home *she* has to wear the pants; she has to unsex herself. No "chucks" or "dearests" escape her tightened lips, and yet she is more feeling, more human finally than Macbeth. She thinks of her father when she sees the old King asleep, and this natural thought will not let her kill him. Macbeth has to do it, just as the quailing husband of any modern virago is sent down to the basement to kill a rat or drown a set of kittens. An image of her father, irrelevant to her purpose, softens this monster woman; sleepwalking, she thinks of Lady Macduff. "The Thane of Fife had a wife. Where is she now?" [cf. IV. i. 150-53]. Stronger than Macbeth, less suggestible, she is nevertheless imaginative, where he is not. She does not see ghosts and daggers; when she sleepwalks, it is simple reality that haunts her—the crime relived. "Yet, who would have thought the old man to have had so much blood in him?" [V. i. 39-40]. Over and over, the epiphenomena of the crime present themselves to her dormant consciousness. This nightly reliving is not penitence but more terrible—remorse, the agenbite of the restless deed. Lady Macbeth's uncontrollable imagination drives her to put herself in the place of others—the wife of the Thane of Fife—and to recognize a kinship between all human kind: the pathos of old age in Duncan has made her think, "Why, he might be my father!" This sense of a natural bond between men opens her to contrition—sorrowing with. To ask whether, waking, she is "sorry" for what she has done is impertinent. She lives with it and it kills her.

Macbeth has no feeling for others, except envy, a common middle-class trait. He *envies* the murdered Duncan his rest, which is a strange way of looking at your victim. What he suffers on his own account after the crimes is simple panic. He is never contrite or remorseful; it is not the deed but a shadow of it, Banquo's spook, that appears to him. The "scruples" that agitate him before Duncan's murder are mere echoes of conventional opinion, of what might be *said* about his deed: that Duncan was his king, his cousin, and a guest under his roof. "I have bought golden opinions," he says to himself (note the verb), "from all sorts of people" [I. vii. 32-3]; now these people may ask for their opinions back—a refund—if they suspect him of the murder. It is like a business firm's being reluctant to part with its "good will." The fact that Duncan was such a good king bothers him, and why? Because there will be universal grief at his death. But his chief "scruple" is even simpler. "If we should fail?" he says timidly to Lady Macbeth [I. vii. 59]. Sweet chuck tells him that they will not. Yet once she has ceased to be effectual as a partner, Dearest love is an embarrassment. He has no time for her vapors. "Cure her of that" [V. iii. 39], he orders the doctor on hearing that she is troubled by "fancies." Again the general is speaking.

The idea of Macbeth as a conscience-tormented man is a platitude as false as Macbeth himself. Macbeth has no conscience. His main concern throughout the play is that most selfish of all concerns: to get a good night's sleep. His invocation to sleep, while heartfelt, is perfectly conventional; sleep builds you up, enables you to start the day fresh. Thus the virtue of having a good conscience is seen by him in terms of bodily hygiene. Lady Macbeth shares these preoccupations. When he tells her he is going to see the witches, she remarks that he needs sleep.

Her wifely concern is mechanical and far from real solicitude. She is aware of Macbeth; she *knows* him (he does not know her at all, apparently), but she regards him coldly as a thing, a tool that must be oiled and polished. His soul-states do not interest her; her attention is narrowed on his morale, his public conduct, the shifting expressions of his face. But in a sense she is right, for there is nothing to Macbeth but fear and ambition, both of which he tries to hide, except from her. This naturally gives her a poor opinion of the inner man.

Why is it, though, that Lady Macbeth seems to us a monster while Macbeth does not? Partly because she is a woman and has "unsexed" herself, which makes her a monster by definition. Also because the very prospect of murder quickens an hysterical excitement in her, like the discovery of some object in a shop—a set of emeralds or a sable stole—which Macbeth can give her and which will be an "outlet" for all the repressed desires he cannot satisfy. She behaves as though Macbeth, through his weakness, will deprive her of self-realization; the unimpeded exercise of her will is the voluptuous end she seeks. That is why she makes naught of scruples, as inner brakes on her throbbing engines. Unlike Macbeth, she does not pretend to harbor a conscience, though this, on her part, by a curious turn, *is* a pretense, as the sleepwalking scene reveals. After the first crime, her will sub-

sides, spent; the devil has brought her to climax and left her.

Macbeth is not a monster, like Richard III or Iago or Iachimo [in *Cymbeline*], though in the catalogue he might go for one because of the blackness of his deeds. But at the outset his deeds are only the wishes and fears of the average, undistinguished man translated into halfhearted action. Pure evil is a kind of transcendence that he does not aspire to. He only wants to be king and sleep the sleep of the just, undisturbed. He could never have been a good man, even if he had not met the witches; hence we cannot see him as a devil incarnate, for the devil is a fallen angel. Macbeth does not fall; if anything, he somewhat improves as the result of his career of crime. He throws off his dependency and thus achieves the "greatness" he mistakenly sought in the crown and scepter. He swells to vast proportions, having supped full with horrors.

The isolation of Macbeth, which is at once a punishment and a tragic dignity or honor, takes place by stages and by deliberate choice; it begins when he does not tell Lady Macbeth that he has decided to kill Banquo and reaches its peak at Dunsinane, in the final action. Up to this time, though he has cut himself off from all human contacts, he is counting on the witches as allies. When he first hears the news that Macduff is not "of woman born" [V. viii. 12-15], he is unmanned; everything he trusted (the literal word) has betrayed him, and he screams in terror, "I'll not fight with thee!" [V. viii. 22]. But Macduff's taunts make a hero of him; he cannot die like this, shamed. His death is his first true act of courage, though even here he has had to be pricked to it by mockery, Lady Macbeth's old spur. Nevertheless, weaned by his very crimes from a need for reassurance, nursed in a tyrant's solitude, he meets death on his own, without metaphysical aid. "Lay on, Macduff" [V. viii. 33].

What is modern and bourgeois in Macbeth's character is his wholly *social* outlook. He has no feeling for others, and yet until the end he is a vicarious creature, existing in his own eyes through what others may say of him, through what they tell him or promise him. This paradox is typical of the social being—at once a wolf out for himself and a sheep. Macbeth, moreover, is an expert buck-passer; he sees how others can be used. It is he, not Lady Macbeth, who thinks of smearing the drunken chamberlains with blood (though it is she, in the end, who carries it out), so that they shall be caught "red-handed" the next morning when Duncan's murder is discovered. At this idea he brightens; suddenly, he sees his way clear. It is the moment when at last he decides. The eternal executive, ready to fix responsibility on a subordinate, has seen the deed finally take a *recognizable* form. Now he can do it. And the crackerjack thought of killing the grooms afterward (dead men tell no tales—old adage) is again purely his own on-the-spot inspiration; no credit to Lady Macbeth.

It is the sort of thought that would have come to Hamlet's Uncle Claudius, another trepidant executive. Indeed, Macbeth is more like Claudius than like any other character in Shakespeare. Both are doting husbands; both rose to power by betraying their superior's trust; both are easily frightened and have difficulty saying their prayers. Macbeth's "Amen" sticks in his throat, he complains, and Claudius, on his knees, sighs that he cannot make what priests call a "good act of contrition." The desire to say his prayers like any pew-holder, quite regardless of his horrible crime, is merely a longing for respectability. Macbeth "repents" killing the grooms, but this is for public consumption. "O, yet I do repent me of my fury, That I did kill them" [II. iii. 106-07]. In fact, it is the one deed he does *not* repent (*i.e.*, doubt the wisdom of) either before or after. This hypocritical self-accusation, which is his sidelong way of announcing the embarrassing fact that he has just done away with the grooms, and his simulated grief at Duncan's murder ("All is but toys. Renown and grace is dead, The wine of life is drawn" [II. iii. 94-5], etc.) are his basest moments in the play, as well as his boldest; here is nearly a magnificent monster.

The dramatic effect too is one of great boldness on Shakespeare's part. Macbeth is speaking pure Shakespearean poetry, but in his mouth, since we know he is lying, it turns into facile verse, Shakespearean poetry buskined. The same with "Here lay Duncan, His silver skin lac'd with his golden blood . . ." [II. iii. 111-12]. If the image were to Macduff, it would be uncontaminated poetry; from Macbeth it is "proper stuff"—fustian. This opens the perilous question of sincerity in the arts: is a line of verse altered for us by the sincerity of the one who speaks it? In short, is poetry relative to the circumstances or absolute? Or, more particularly, are Macbeth's soliloquies poetry, which they sound like, or something else? Did Shakespeare intend to make Macbeth a poet, like Hamlet, Lear, and Othello? In that case, how can Macbeth be an unimaginative mediocrity? My opinion is that Macbeth's soliloquies are not poetry but rhetoric. They are tirades. That is, they do not trace any pensive motion of the soul or heart but are a volley of words discharged. Macbeth is neither thinking nor feeling aloud; he is declaiming. Like so many unfeeling men, he has a facile emotionalism, which he turns on and off. Not that his fear is insincere, but his loss of control provides him with an excuse for histrionics.

These gibberings exasperate Lady Macbeth. "What do you mean?" [II. ii. 37] she says coldly after she has listened to a short harangue on "Methought I heard a voice cry 'Sleep no more!'" [II. ii. 32]. It is an allowable question—what *does* he mean? And his funeral oration on *her,* if she could have heard

it, would have brought her back to life to protest. "She should have died hereafter" [V. v. 17]—fine, that was the real Macbeth. But then, as if conscious of the proprieties, he at once begins on a series of bromides ("Tomorrow, and tomorrow . . ." [V. v. 19ff.]) that he seems to have had ready to hand for the occasion like a black mourning suit. All Macbeth's soliloquies have that ready-to-hand, if not hand-me-down, air, which is perhaps why they are given to school children to memorize, often with the result of making them hate Shakespeare. What children resent in these soliloquies is precisely their sententiousness—the sound they have of being already memorized from a copybook. (pp. 3-12)

The play between poetry and rhetoric, the *conversion* of poetry to declamation, is subtle and horrible in *Macbeth.* The sincere pent-up poet in Macbeth flashes out not in the soliloquies but when he howls at a servant. "The Devil damn thee black, thou cream-faced loon! Where got'st thou that goose look?" [V. iii. 11]. Elsewhere, the general's tropes are the gold braid of his dress uniform or the chasing of his armor. If an explanation is needed, you might say he learned to *use* words through long practice in haranguing his troops, whipping them and himself into battle frenzy. Up to recent times a fighting general, like a football coach, was an orator.

But it must be noted that it is not only Macbeth who rants. Nor is it only Macbeth who talks about the weather. The play is stormy with atmosphere—the screaming and shrieking of owls, the howling of winds. Nature herself is ranting, like the witches, and Night, black Hecate, is queen of the scene. Bats are flitting about; ravens and crows are hoarse; the house-martins' nests on the battlements of Macbeth's castle give a misleading promise of peace and gentle domesticity. "It will be rain tonight," says Banquo simply, looking at the sky (note the difference between this and Macbeth's pompous generality), and the First Murderer growls at him, striking, "Let it come down" [III. iii. 16]. The disorder of Nature, as so often in Shakespeare, presages and reflects the disorder of the body politic. Guilty Macbeth cannot sleep, but the night of Duncan's murder, the whole house, as if guilty too, is restless; Malcolm and Donalbain talk and laugh in their sleep; the drunken porter, roused, plays that he is gatekeeper of hell.

Indeed, the whole action takes place in a kind of hell and is pitched to the demons' shriek of hyperbole. This would appear to be a peculiar setting for a study of the commonplace. But only at first sight. The fact that an ordinary philistine like Macbeth goes on the rampage and commits a series of murders is a sign that human nature, like Nature, is capable of any mischief if left to its "natural" self. The witches, unnatural beings, are Nature spirits, stirring their snake-filet and owl's wing, newt's eye and frog toe in a camp stew: earthy ingredients boil down to an unearthly broth. It is the same with the man Macbeth. Ordinary ambition, fear, and a kind of stupidity make a deadly combination. Macbeth, a self-made king, is not kingly, but just another Adam or Fall guy, with Eve at his elbow.

There is no play of Shakespeare's (I think) that contains the words "Nature" and "natural" so many times, and the "Nature" within the same speech can mean first something good and then something evil, as though it were a pun. Nature is two-sided, double-talking, like the witches. "Fair is foul and foul is fair," they cry [I. i. 11], and Macbeth enters the play unconsciously echoing them, for he is never original but chock-full of the "milk of human kindness" [I. v. 17], which does not mean kindness in the modern sense but simply human "nature," human kind. The play is about Nature, and its blind echo, human nature.

Macbeth, in short, shows life in the cave. Without religion, animism rules the outer world, and without faith, the human soul is beset by hobgoblins. This at any rate was Shakespeare's opinion, to which modern history, with the return of the irrational in the Fascist nightmare and its fear of new specters in the form of Communism, Socialism, etc., lends support. It is a troubling thought that bloodstained Macbeth, of all Shakespeare's characters, should seem the most "modern," the only one you could transpose into contemporary battle dress or a sport shirt and slacks. (pp. 12-14)

> *Mary McCarthy, "General Macbeth," in her* The Writing on the Wall and Other Literary Essays, *Harcourt Brace Jovanovich, 1970, pp. 3-14.*

LADY MACBETH

Janet Adelman

*[Adelman discusses **Lady Macbeth's** character based on her reading of* Macbeth *as a play that illustrates both a fantasy of absolute and destructive maternal power and a fantasy of escape from this power. According to the critic, maternal power in* Macbeth *is not evoked in the figure of a particular mother; rather, it is projected through both the witches and **Lady Macbeth's** manipulation of the protagonist. Adelman argues that Shakespeare initially associates **Lady Macbeth** with the **Weird Sisters** by showing how she attempts to mirror their disturbance of gender in psychological terms by desiring to unsex herself. Despite the witches' supernatural status, the critic continues, **Lady Macbeth** ultimately appears to be the more frightening figure. For all of their eeriness, the **Weird Sisters** exist on a cosmic level apart from **Macbeth's** physical world; but, by embracing evil herself, **Lady Macbeth** brings the psychic force of their power home. **Lady Macbeth** exercises the full potential of this maternal malevolence over her husband by attacking his virility, the critic asserts, and she acquires this strength "partly because she can make him imagine himself as an infant vulnerable to her." For further commentary on **Lady Macbeth's** character, see the excerpts by Mark Van Doren, Irving Ribner, J. Lyndon Shanley, Walter Clyde Curry, Stephen Spender, Jarold Ramsey, and Mary McCarthy.]*

Maternal power in *Macbeth* is not embodied in the figure of a particular mother (as it is, for example, in *Coriolanus*); it is instead diffused throughout the play, evoked primarily by the figures of the witches and Lady Macbeth. Largely through Macbeth's relationship to them, the play becomes (like *Coriolanus*) a representation of primitive fears about male identity and autonomy itself, about those looming female presences who threaten to control one's actions and one's mind, to constitute one's very self, even at a distance. (p. 90)

The witches constitute our introduction to the realm of maternal malevolence unleashed by the loss of paternal protection; as soon as Macbeth meets them, he becomes . . . their "wayward son" [III. v. 11]. This maternal malevolence is given its most horrifying expression in Shakespeare in the image through which Lady Macbeth secures her control over Macbeth:

> I have given suck, and know
> How tender 'tis to love the babe that milks me:
> I would, while it was smiling in my face,
> Have pluck'd my nipple from his boneless gums,
> And dash'd the brains out, had I so sworn
> As you have done to this.
>
> [I. vii. 54-9]

This image of murderously disrupted nurturance is the psychic equivalence of the witches' poisonous cauldron; both function to subject Macbeth's will to female forces. For the play strikingly constructs the fantasy of subjection to maternal malevolence in two parts, in the witches and in Lady Macbeth, and then persistently identifies the two parts as one. Through this identification, Shakespeare in effect locates the source of his culture's fear of witchcraft in individual human history, in the infant's long dependence on female figures felt as all-powerful: what the witches suggest about the vulnerability of men to female power on the cosmic plane, Lady Macbeth doubles on the psychological plane.

Lady Macbeth's power as a female temptress allies her in a general way with the witches as soon as we see her. The specifics of that implied alliance begin to emerge as she attempts to harden herself in preparation for hardening her husband: the disturbance of gender that Banquo registers when he

first meets the witches is played out in psychological terms in Lady Macbeth's attempt to unsex herself. Calling on spirits ambiguously allied with the
witches themselves, she phrases this unsexing as
the undoing of her own bodily maternal function:

> Come, you Spirits
> That tend on mortal thoughts, unsex me
>   here,
> And fill me, from the crown to the toe, top-
>   full
> Of direst cruelty! make thick my blood,
> Stop up th'access and passage to remorse;
> That no compunctious visitings of Nature
> Shake my fell purpose, nor keep peace be-
>   tween
> Th'effect and it! Come to my woman's
>   breasts,
> And take my milk for gall, you murth'ring
>   ministers.
>
>   [I. v. 40-8]

In the play's context of unnatural births, the thick-
ening of the blood and the stopping up of access
and passage to remorse begin to sound like attempts to undo reproductive functioning and perhaps to stop the menstrual blood that is the sign
of its potential. The metaphors in which Lady Macbeth frames the stopping up of remorse, that is,
suggest that she imagines an attack on the reproductive passages of her own body, on what makes
her specifically female. And as she invites the spirits to her breasts, she reiterates the centrality of the
attack specifically on maternal function: needing
to undo the "milk of human kindness" [I. v. 17] in
Macbeth, she imagines an attack on her own literal
milk, its transformation into gall. This imagery locates the horror of the scene in Lady Macbeth's unnatural abrogation of her maternal function. But
latent within this image of unsexing is the horror
of the maternal function itself. Most modern editors follow [Samuel] Johnson in glossing "take my
milk for gall" as "take my milk in exchange for
gall," imagining in effect that the spirits empty out
the natural maternal fluid and replace it with the
unnatural and poisonous one. But perhaps Lady
Macbeth is asking the spirits to take her milk *as*
gall, to nurse from her breast and find in her milk
their sustaining poison. Here the milk itself is the
gall; no transformation is necessary. In these lines
Lady Macbeth focuses the culture's fear of maternal nursery—a fear reflected, for example, in the
common worries about the various ills (including
female blood itself) that could be transmitted
through nursing and in the sometime identification of colostrum as witch's milk. Insofar as her
milk itself nurtures the evil spirits, Lady Macbeth
localizes the image of maternal danger, inviting the
identification of her maternal function itself with
that of the witch. For she here invites precisely that
nursing of devil-imps so central to the current understanding of witchcraft that the presence of supernumerary teats alone was often taken as sufficient evidence that one was a witch. Lady Macbeth

and the witches fuse at this moment, and they fuse
through the image of perverse nursery.

It is characteristic of the play's division of labor between Lady Macbeth and the witches that she;
rather than they, is given the imagery of perverse
nursery traditionally attributed to the witches. The
often noted alliance between Lady Macbeth and the
witches constructs malignant female power both
in the cosmos and in the family; it in effect adds the
whole weight of the spiritual order to the condemnation of Lady Macbeth's insurrection. But despite
the superior cosmic status of the witches, Lady
Macbeth seems to me finally the more frightening
figure. For Shakespeare's witches are an odd mixture of the terrifying and the near comic. Even
without consideration of the Hecate scene [III. v]
with its distinct lightening of tone and its incipient
comedy of discord among the witches, we may
begin to feel a shift toward the comic in the presentation of the witches: the specificity and predict-
ability of the ingredients in their dire recipe pass
over toward grotesque comedy even while they
create a (partly pleasurable) shiver of horror. There
is a distinct weakening of their power after their
first appearances: only halfway through the play,
in [IV. i], do we hear that they themselves have
masters [IV. i. 63]. The more Macbeth claims for
them, the less their actual power seems: by the
time Macbeth evokes the cosmic damage they can
wreak [IV. i. 50-61], we have already felt the presence of such damage, and felt it moreover not as issuing from the witches but as a divinely sanctioned nature's expressions of outrage at the disruption of patriarchal order. The witches' displays
of thunder and lightning, like their apparitions,
are mere theatrics compared to what we have already heard; and the serious disruptions of natural
order—the storm that toppled the chimneys and
made the earth shake [II. iii. 54-61], the unnatural
darkness in day [II. iv. 5-10], the cannibalism of
Duncan's horses [II. iv. 14-18]—seem the horrifying but reassuringly familiar signs of God's displeasure, firmly under His—not their—control.
Partly because their power is thus circumscribed,
nothing the witches say or do conveys the presence
of awesome and unexplained malevolence in the
way that Lear's storm does. Even the process of
dramatic representation itself may diminish their
power: embodied, perhaps, they lack full power to
terrify: "Present fears"—even of witches—"are less
than horrible imaginings" [I. iii. 137-38]. They
tend thus to become as much containers for as expressions of nightmare; to a certain extent, they
help to exorcise the terror of female malevolence by
localizing it. (pp. 96-9)

Lady Macbeth brings the witches' power home:
they get the cosmic apparatus, she gets the psychic
force. That Lady Macbeth is the more frightening
figure—and was so, I suspect, even before belief in
witchcraft had declined—suggests the firmly do-

Paul Rogers as Macbeth in Act V, scene v of a 1954 Old Vic Theatre production of the tragedy.

mestic and psychological basis of Shakespeare's imagination.

The fears of female coercion, female definition of the male, that are initially located cosmically in the witches thus find their ultimate locus in the figure of Lady Macbeth, whose attack on Macbeth's virility is the source of her strength over him and who acquires that strength, I shall argue, partly because she can make him imagine himself as an infant vulnerable to her. In the figure of Lady Macbeth, that is, Shakespeare rephrases the power of the witches as the wife/mother's power to poison human relatedness at its source; in her, their power of cosmic coercion is rewritten as the power of the mother to misshape or destroy the child. The attack on infants and on the genitals characteristic of Continental witchcraft belief is thus in her returned to its psychological source: in the play these beliefs are localized not in the witches but in the great central scene in which Lady Macbeth persuades Macbeth to the murder of Duncan. In this scene, Lady Macbeth notoriously makes the murder of Duncan the test of Macbeth's virility; if he cannot perform the murder, he is in effect reduced to the helplessness of an infant subject to her rage. She begins by attacking his manhood, making her love for him contingent on the murder that she identifies as equivalent to his male potency: "From this time / Such I account thy love" [I. vii. 38-9]; "When you durst do it, then you were a man" [I. vii. 49]. Insofar as his drunk hope is now "green and pale" [I. vii. 37], he is identified as emasculated, exhibiting the symptoms not only of hangover, but also of the green-sickness, the typical disease of timid young virgin women. Lady Macbeth's argument is, in effect, that any signs of the "milk of human kindness" [I. v. 17] mark him as more womanly than she; she proceeds to enforce his masculinity by demonstrating her willingness to dry up that milk in herself, specifically by destroying her nursing infant in fantasy: "I would, while it was smiling in my face, / Have pluck'd my nipple from his boneless gums, / And dash'd the brains out" [I. vii. 56-8]. That this image has no place in the plot, where the Macbeths are strikingly childless, gives some indication of the inner necessity through which it appears. For Lady Macbeth expresses here not only the hardness she imagines to be male, not only her willingness to unmake the most essential maternal relationship; she expresses also a deep fantasy of Macbeth's utter vulnerability to her. As she progresses from questioning Macbeth's masculinity to imagining herself dashing out the brains of her infant son, she articulates a fantasy in which to be less than a man is to become interchangeably a woman or a baby, terribly subject to the wife/mother's destructive rage.

By evoking this vulnerability, Lady Macbeth acquires a power over Macbeth more absolute than any the witches can achieve. The play's central fantasy of escape from woman seems to me to unfold from this moment; we can see its beginnings in Macbeth's response to Lady Macbeth's evocation of absolute maternal power. Macbeth first responds by questioning the possibility of failure ("If we should fail?" [I. vii. 59]). Lady Macbeth counters this fear by inviting Macbeth to share in her fantasy of omnipotent malevolence: "What cannot you and I perform upon / Th'unguarded Duncan?" [I. vii. 69-70]. The satiated and sleeping Duncan takes on the vulnerability that Lady Macbeth has just invoked in the image of the feeding, trusting infant; Macbeth releases himself from the image of this vulnerability by sharing in the murder of this innocent. In his elation at this transfer of vulnerability from himself to Duncan, Macbeth imagines Lady Macbeth the mother to infants sharing her hardness, born in effect without vulnerability; in effect, he imagines her as male and then reconstitutes himself as the invulnerable male child of such a mother:

> Bring forth men-children only!
> For thy undaunted mettle should compose
> Nothing but males.
>
> [I. vii. 72-4]

Through the double pun on *mettle/metal* and *male/mail*, Lady Macbeth herself becomes virtually male, composed of the hard metal of which the armored male is made. Her children would necessarily be men, composed of her male mettle, armored by her mettle, lacking the female inheritance from the mother that would make them vulnerable. The man-child thus brought forth would be no trusting infant; the very phrase *men-children* suggests the presence of the adult man even at birth, hence the undoing of childish vulnerability. The mobility of the imagery—from male infant with his brains dashed out to Macbeth and Lady Macbeth triumphing over the sleeping, trusting Duncan, to the all-male invulnerable man-child, suggests the logic of the fantasy: only the child of an all-male mother is safe. We see here the creation of a defensive fantasy of exemption from the woman's part: as infantile vulnerability is shifted to Duncan, Macbeth creates in himself the image of Lady Macbeth's hardened all-male man-child; in committing the murder, he thus becomes like Richard III, using the bloody axe to free himself in fantasy from the dominion of women, even while apparently carrying out their will. (pp. 100-03)

Janet Adelman, " 'Born of Woman': Fantasies of Maternal Power in 'Macbeth'," in Cannibals, Witches, and Divorce: Estranging the Renaissance, *edited by Marjorie Gruber, The Johns Hopkins University Press, 1987, pp. 90-121.*

BANQUO

A. C. Bradley

[*Bradley asserts that* **Banquo** *is influenced by the* **Weird Sisters** *"much more truly than* **Macbeth.**" *According to the critic,* **Banquo** *essentially loses his innocence when he acquiesces to* **Macbeth**'s *method of accession, even though he suspects* **Macbeth** *of committing* **Duncan**'s *murder. When* **Banquo** *willingly complies with* **Macbeth**'s *rise to power, Bradley argues, he reveals his own secret hope that the witches' prediction concerning his descendants will also come true. For a reaction to this reading of* **Banquo**, *see the excerpt below by Leo Kirschbaum. For other commentary on the character, see the excerpts by Irving Ribner and Walter Clyde Curry.*]

The main interest of the character of Banquo arises from the changes that take place in him, and from the influence of the Witches upon him. And it is curious that Shakespeare's intention here is so frequently missed. Banquo being at first strong-ly contrasted with Macbeth, as an innocent man with a guilty, it seems to be supposed that this contrast must be continued to his death; while, in reality, though it is never removed, it is gradually diminished. Banquo in fact may be described much more truly than Macbeth as the victim of the Witches. If we follow this story this will be evident.

He bore a part only less distinguished than Macbeth's in the battles against Sweno and Macdonwald. He and Macbeth are called 'our captains,' and when they meet the Witches they are traversing the 'blasted heath' alone together. Banquo accosts the strange shapes without the slightest fear. They lay their fingers on their lips, as if to signify that they will not, or must not, speak to *him*. To Macbeth's brief appeal, 'Speak, if you can: what are you?' [I. iii. 47] they at once reply, not by saying what they are, but by hailing him Thane of Glamis, Thane of Cawdor, and King hereafter. Banquo is greatly surprised that his partner should start as if in fear, and observes that he is at once 'rapt'; and he bids the Witches, if they know the future, to prophesy to *him*, who neither begs their favour nor fears their hate. Macbeth, looking back at a later time, remembers Banquo's daring, and how

> he chid the sisters,
> When first they put the name of king upon me,
> And bade them speak to him.
>
> [III. i. 56-8]

'Chid' is an exaggeration; but Banquo is evidently a bold man, probably an ambitious one, and certainly has no lurking guilt in his ambition. On hearing the predictions concerning himself and his descendants he makes no answer, and when the Witches are about to vanish he shows none of Macbeth's feverish anxiety to know more. On their vanishing he is simply amazed, wonders if they were anything but hallucinations, makes no reference to the predictions till Macbeth mentions them, and then answers lightly.

When Ross and Angus, entering, announce to Macbeth that he has been made Thane of Cawdor, Banquo exclaims, aside, to himself or Macbeth, 'What! can the devil speak true?' [I. iii. 107]. He now believes that the Witches were real beings and the 'instruments of darkness.' When Macbeth, turning to him, whispers,

> Do you not hope your children shall be kings,
> When those that gave the Thane of Cawdor to me
> Promised no less to them?
>
> [I. iii. 118-20]

he draws with the boldness of innocence the inference which is really occupying Macbeth, and answers,

> That, trusted home,
> Might yet enkindle you unto the crown

Besides the thane of Cawdor.

[I. iii. 120-22]

Here he still speaks, I think, in a free, off-hand, even jesting, manner ('enkindle' meaning merely 'excite you to *hope* for'). But then, possibly from noticing something in Macbeth's face, he becomes graver, and goes on, with a significant 'but,'

> But 'tis strange:
> And oftentimes, to win us to our harm,
> The instruments of darkness tell us truths,
> Win us with honest trifles, to betray's
> In deepest consequence.
>
> [I. iii. 122-26]

He afterwards observes for the second time that his partner is 'rapt'; but he explains his abstraction naturally and sincerely by referring to the surprise of his new honours; and at the close of the scene, when Macbeth proposes that they shall discuss the predictions together at some later time, he answers in the cheerful, rather bluff manner, which he has used almost throughout, 'Very gladly.' Nor was there any reason why Macbeth's rejoinder, 'Till then, enough' [I. iii. 156], should excite misgivings in him, though it implied a request for silence, and though the whole behaviour of his partner during the scene must have looked very suspicious to him when the prediction of the crown was made good through the murder of Duncan.

In the next scene Macbeth and Banquo join the King, who welcomes them both with the kindest expressions of gratitude and with promises of favours to come. Macbeth has indeed already received a noble reward. Banquo, who is said by the King to have 'no less deserved' [I. iv. 30], receives as yet mere thanks. His brief and frank acknowledgment is contrasted with Macbeth's laboured rhetoric; and, as Macbeth goes out, Banquo turns with hearty praises of him to the King.

And when next we see him, approaching Macbeth's castle in company with Duncan, there is still no sign of change. Indeed he gains on us. It is he who speaks the beautiful lines,

> This guest of summer,
> The temple-haunting martlet, does approve,
> By his loved mansionry, that the heaven's breath
> Smells wooingly here: no jutty, frieze,
> Buttress, nor coign of vantage, but this bird
> Hath made his pendent bed and procreant cradle:
> Where they most breed and haunt, I have observed,
> The air is delicate;
>
> [I. vi. 3-10]

—lines which tell of that freedom of heart, and that sympathetic sense of peace and beauty, which the Macbeth of the tragedy could never feel.

But now Banquo's sky begins to darken. At the opening of the Second Act we see him with Fleance crossing the court of the castle on his way to bed. The blackness of the moonless, starless night seems to oppress him. And he is oppressed by something else.

> A heavy summons lies like lead upon me,
> And yet I would not sleep: merciful powers,
> Restrain in me the cursed thoughts that nature
> Gives way to in repose!
>
> [II. i. 6-9]

On Macbeth's entrance we know what Banquo means: he says to Macbeth—and it is the first time he refers to the subject unprovoked,

> I dreamt last night of the three weird sisters.
>
> [II. i. 20]

His will is still untouched: he would repel the 'cursed thoughts'; and they are mere thoughts, not intentions. But still they are 'thoughts,' something more, probably, than mere recollections; and they bring with them an undefined sense of guilt. The poison has begun to work.

The passage that follows Banquo's words to Macbeth is difficult to interpret:

> I dreamt last night of the three weird sisters:
> To you they have show'd some truth.
> *Macb.*   I think not of them:
> Yet, when we can entreat an hour to serve,
> We would spend it in some words upon that business,
> If you would grant the time.
> *Ban.*   At your kind'st leisure.
> *Macb.* If you shall cleave to my consent, when 'tis,
> It shall make honour for you.
> *Ban.*   So I lose none
> In seeking to augment it, but still keep
> My bosom franchised and allegiance clear,
> I shall be counsell'd.
> *Macb.*   Good repose the while!
> *Ban.* Thanks, sir: the like to you!
>
> [II. i. 20-30]

Macbeth's first idea is, apparently, simply to free himself from any suspicion which the discovery of the murder might suggest, by showing himself, just before it, quite indifferent to the predictions, and merely looking forward to a conversation about them at some future time. But why does he go on, 'If you shall cleave,' etc.? Perhaps he foresees that, on the discovery, Banquo cannot fail to suspect him, and thinks it safest to prepare the way at once for an understanding with him (in the original story he makes Banquo his accomplice *before* the murder). Banquo's answer shows three things,—that he fears a treasonable proposal, that he has no idea of accepting it, and that he has no fear of Macbeth to restrain him from showing what is in his mind.

Duncan is murdered. In the scene of discovery Banquo of course appears, and his behaviour is significant. When he enters, and Macduff cries out to him,

> O Banquo, Banquo,
> Our royal master's murdered,

and Lady Macbeth, who has entered a moment before, exclaims,

> Woe, alas!
> What, in our house?

his answer,

> Too cruel anywhere,
> > [II. iii. 86-8]

shows, as I have pointed out, repulsion, and we may be pretty sure that he suspects the truth at once. After a few words to Macduff he remains absolutely silent while the scene is continued for nearly forty lines. He is watching Macbeth and listening as he tells how he put the chamberlains to death in a frenzy of loyal rage. At last Banquo appears to have made up his mind. On Lady Macbeth's fainting he proposes that they shall all retire, and that they shall afterwards meet,

> And question this most bloody piece of work
> To know it further. Fears and scruples shake us:
> In the great hand of God I stand, and thence
> Against the undivulged pretence I fight
> Of treasonous malice.
> > [II. iii. 128-32]

His solemn language here reminds us of his grave words about 'the instruments of darkness' [I. iii. 124], and of his later prayer to the 'merciful powers.' He is profoundly shocked, full of indignation, and determined to play the part of a brave and honest man.

But he plays no such part. When next we see him, on the last day of his life, we find that he has yielded to evil. The Witches and his own ambition have conquered him. He alone of the lords knew of the prophecies, but he has said nothing of them. He has acquiesced in Macbeth's accession, and in the official theory that Duncan's sons had suborned the chamberlains to murder him. Doubtless, unlike Macduff, he was present at Scone to see the new king invested. He has, not formally but in effect, 'cloven to' Macbeth's 'consent'; he is knit to him by 'a most indissoluble tie' [III. i. 17]; his advice in council has been 'most grave and prosperous' [III. i. 21]; he is to be the 'chief guest' at that night's supper. And his soliloquy tells us why:

> Thou hast it now: king, Cawdor, Glamis, all,
> As the weird women promised, and, I fear,

Thou play'dst most foully for't: yet it was said
It should not stand in thy posterity,
But that myself should be the root and father
Of many kings. If there come truth from them—
As upon thee, Macbeth, their speeches shine—
Why, by the verities on thee made good,
May they not be my oracles as well,
And set me up in hope? But hush! no more.
> > [III. i. 1-10]

This 'hush! no more' is not the dismissal of 'cursed thoughts': it only means that he hears the trumpets announcing the entrance of the King and Queen.

His punishment comes swiftly, much more swiftly than Macbeth's, and saves him from any further fall. He is a very fearless man, and still so far honourable that he has no thought of *acting* to bring about the fulfilment of the prophecy which has beguiled him. And therefore he has no fear of Macbeth. But he little understands him. To Macbeth's tormented mind Banquo's conduct appears highly suspicious. *Why* has this bold and circumspect man kept his secret and become his chief adviser? In order to make good *his* part of the predictions after Macbeth's own precedent. Banquo, he is sure, will suddenly and secretly attack him. It is not the far-off accession of Banquo's descendants that he fears; it is (so he tells himself) swift murder; not that the 'barren sceptre' will some day droop from his dying hand, but that it will be 'wrenched' away now [III. i. 62]. So he kills Banquo. But the Banquo he kills is not the innocent soldier who met the Witches and daffed their prophecies aside, nor the man who prayed to be delivered from the temptation of his dreams. (pp. 379-86)

> *A. C. Bradley, "Lecture X: Macbeth," in his* Shakespearean Tragedy: Lectures on 'Hamlet,' 'Othello,' 'King Lear,' 'Macbeth,' *1904. Reprint by Macmillan and Co., 1905, pp. 366-400.*

Leo Kirschbaum

*[Kirschbaum challenges the position taken by A. C. Bradley that **Banquo**, as well as **Macbeth**, is influenced by the witches' prophecies (see excerpt above). Bradley, the critic charges, misinterprets **Banquo** as a "psychologically valid being" whose motives contribute to the advancement of the dramatic action of Macbeth rather than as a symbolic contrast to **Macbeth**'s evil. Kirschbaum argues that **Banquo** represents innocence, and thus he is less a fully developed character than an "instrument" that "must be maintained as contrast" to **Macbeth**. The critic concludes that **Macbeth**'s murder of **Banquo** essentially reflects*

*his efforts to "destroy his own better humanity" because he "is jealous of **Banquo**'s virtues, wants them but cannot have them, feels belittled by them, fears them, and hence must destroy them." For further commentary on **Banquo**'s character, see the excerpts by Irving Ribner and Walter Clyde Curry.]*

If we consider Banquo as a dramatic function rather than as a character in the usual sense, we shall be able to avoid [A.C.] Bradley's erroneous and confusing misreading of him as another whom the witches' influence finally debases [*Shakespearean Tragedy*]. Bradley, with his customary approach, tended to consider Banquo as a whole man, a psychologically valid being; he did not see that the playwright has so depicted the character that he will always be a dramaturgic foil to Macbeth.

As Banquo and Macbeth meet the witches in [I. iii], Banquo notes that Macbeth 'start[s]' and 'seem[s] to fear' the witches' [I. iii. 51] prophecies, that he 'seems rapt withal'; but by his bold words to them, Banquo indicates that *he* has a free soul, 'who neither beg nor fear / Your favors nor your hate' [II. iii. 60-1]. Again, when Ross calls Macbeth Thane of Cawdor, it is Banquo who once and for all clearly indicates to the audience the true nature of the witches: 'What, can the devil speak true?' [III. iii. 107]. Although Banquo suspects nothing of Macbeth's intentions, he does know the nature of man and of Satan:

> And oftentimes to win us to our harm,
> The instruments of darkness tell us
>   truths,
> Win us with honest trifles, to betray's
> In deepest consequence.
>
> [III. iii. 123-26]

Hence, he already knows what Macbeth does not learn completely until the very end: he has immediately recognized the witches as cunning emissaries of the enemy of mankind. And it is significant that Macbeth immediately wants to win Banquo to his side: 'let us speak / Our free hearts each to other' [III. iii. 154-55]. *Free* means *open* as well as *innocent*. Banquo replies, 'Very gladly.' The ease of the answer indicates once more a truly free heart. So, already, Shakespeare's pattern is emerging; Macbeth, tempted by evil, feels a strong desire to negate the difference which Banquo stands for.

In [I. v], Lady Macbeth prays (I mean this word literally) the 'murth'ring ministers' to unsex her. Begging the devil to deprive her of the ordinary human qualities of pity and remorse, she requests the 'dunnest smoke of hell' [I. v. 51] in which to commit the crime. It is meaningfully to Banquo in [I. vi] that Shakespeare gives the lines describing Inverness castle in semi-religious terms—'temple-haunting martlet', 'heaven's breath', 'pendent bed and procreant cradle' [I. vi. 4-8]. We are meant to feel deeply here the contrast between Banquo's vision and the devil-haunted castle of actuality. The

next scene, [I. vii] shows us a Macbeth who almost seems to have felt the implications of those words of Banquo:

> [Duncan's] virtues
> Will plead like angels, trumpet-tongu'd,
>   against
> The deep damnation of his taking off;
> And pity, like a naked new-born babe,
> Striding the blast, or heaven's cherubin,
>   hors'd
> Upon the sightless couriers of the air,
> Shall blow the horrid deed in every eye,
> That tears shall drown the wind.
>
> [I. vii. 18-25]

But his devil-possessed lady wins him over. And note how tightly Shakespeare has woven his pattern of contrasts: In [I. v] Lady Macbeth prayed to Satan to turn her 'milk' into 'gall'. In [I. vi] Banquo referred to the evidence of a godly home, the 'procreant cradle'. In [I. vii] Macbeth speaks of 'pity, like a naked new-born babe' [I. vii. 21]. Later in [I. vii] Lady Macbeth says that she could snatch the smiling babe from her breast and dash its brains out!

At the beginning of Act II, just before the entrance of Macbeth, who will leave the stage to murder Duncan, Shakespeare once more presents Banquo. In his customary manner, he is aware of the supernatural powers above and below. It is a dark night: 'There's husbandry in heaven; / Their candles are all out' [II. i. 4-5]. ('Stars, hide your fires!' 'Nor heaven peep through the blanket of the dark' [I. iv. 50, I. v. 53]. Apparently, the demonic prayers of Macbeth and his lady have been answered.) But though the night is indeed dark, Banquo's words have, beyond his awareness, a prophetic undertone: if *husbandry* means thrift, it also means wise management. Hence, through Banquo, obliquely, the irresistible justice and omniscience of heaven is being urged. Banquo continues to Fleance, 'A heavy summons lies like lead upon me, / And yet I would not sleep' [II. i. 6-7]. The first line might suggest that the dark powers are working upon him to get him out of the way of the criminals; at any rate, his soul apprehends evil. So, being the kind of man he is, he prays to the instruments of light to fight against the instruments of darkness:

> Merciful powers,
> Restrain in me the cursed thoughts that
>   nature
> Gives way to in repose.
>
> [II. i. 7-9]

To Bradley, 'the poison [of the witches] has begun to work' but that is not at all the purport of these lines; they are there for comparison. Everyman is constantly being tempted by evil: during waking hours, he is free to expel it from his mind; but while he and his will are asleep, the demons can invade his dreams. (Macbeth a few lines later puts the matter clearly: 'wicked dreams abuse / The curtain'd sleep' [I. ii. 50-1].) Therefore, Banquo prays for grace, for holy power outside himself to repel the demons. In contrast Macbeth and Lady Macbeth have prayed far otherwise.

After Macbeth's entrance, Banquo declares: 'I dreamt last night of the three weird sisters. / To you they have showed some truth' [I. ii. 20-1]. These are the 'cursed thoughts' that Banquo wishes to expunge—and it is as though Banquo, as instrument rather than as character, unwittingly, is testing Macbeth. Macbeth feels this, he wants to get Banquo on his side, he wants to talk to Banquo about the witches.

> *Ban.* At your kind'st leisure.
> *Mac.* If you shall cleave to my consent, when 'tis,
> It shall make honor for you.
> *Ban.*   So I lose none
> In seeking to augment it but still keep
> My bosom franchis'd and allegiance clear,
> I shall be counsel'd.
>   [I. ii. 24-9]

Bradley found this Banquo-Macbeth colloquy 'difficult to interpret'. So it is, inspected as realism, but if one regards the two speakers here not so much as people but as morality play figures who have chosen different sides in the struggle between Heaven and Hell, there is little difficulty. Macbeth is the representative of the Tempter, and Banquo refuses the bait, not with polite evasiveness but with formal rejection. For there is a dichotomy both in Macbeth and in Macbeth's world as long as Banquo represents the good; from Macbeth's viewpoint, Banquo must either be absorbed or destroyed if Macbeth is to gain ease.

In [II. iii], when Macduff tells Banquo that their king has been murdered, Lady Macbeth cries, 'Woe, alas! / What, in our house?' [II. iii. 87-8]. Banquo's reply is a semi-rebuke that comes automatically to his lips, 'Too cruel anywhere' [II. iii. 88]. He is not hiding anything: there is such correspondence between his mind and his mouth that his three words dismiss his hostess' apparently limited morality and express a universal reaction. But Banquo is not suspicious of any single person, yet; he does not know who or what the enemy is, yet. All he knows is that he is innocent and that a great crime has been committed:

> In the great hand of God I stand, and thence
> Against the undivulg'd pretense I fight
> Of treasonous malice.
>   [II. iii. 130-32]

Note how the combatants in the action have been depersonalized by Banquo's words; the war between Good and Evil is larger than people. (pp. 2-5)

Act III begins with Macbeth king, and Banquo suspecting he played most foully for it. It is not allowable, dramatically speaking, to conjecture any-thing about Banquo between his last appearance and his present appearance. Furthermore, the 'indissoluble tie' is that between a king and his subject, and there is nothing evil in it. The 'grave and prosperous' advice [III. i. 21] is not criminal aid to the murderer but political counsel to his sovereign. As to Banquo's character and motives in regard to the crown, all the soliloquy tells us is that he anticipates great honour as a founder of a royal line. There is not a hint that he will play 'most foully' to make the prophecy come true. Primarily, the soliloquy is meant to remind the audience of what the witches told Banquo two full acts back, for that promise may be said to guide the action of the play until the blood-boltered Banquo points at the show of the eight kings—and even then Macbeth's horror at this truth motivates his slaughter of Lady Macduff. As usual Shakespeare's purpose with Banquo here is not similarity but dissimilarity. Dramaturgically, Banquo *must* be maintained as contrast.

That it is not Banquo so much as person but what he still epitomizes which prompts Macbeth to kill his one-time companion is brought out, I believe, in Macbeth's famous soliloquy:

> To be thus is nothing
> But to be safely thus. Our fears in Banquo
> Stick deep, and in his royalty of nature
> Reigns that which would be fear'd. . . .
>   [III. i. 48-51]

What is it that Macbeth fears? Is it really Banquo the man? Or is it the latter's still unsullied qualities—his natural royalty, his dauntless temper, his wise valour? Banquo represents what a part of Macbeth wants and, also, what a part of Macbeth hates. He is truly, as the witches declared, both happier and greater than the regicide. Let us put it this way: Macbeth is jealous of Banquo's virtues, wants them but cannot have them, feels belittled by them, fears them, and hence must destroy them. The killing of Banquo may be interpreted as a futile effort on Macbeth's part to destroy his own better humanity; it is a ghastly effort to unify Macbeth's inner and outer world, for Banquo has a daily beauty in his life that makes Macbeth ugly. The fear of an 'unlineal hand', the belief that Banquo's issue will immediately succeed him are rationalizations, the false coinage of an agonized man who has sold his soul to the devil, who has exchanged his 'eternal jewel' for a poisoned, tortured mind. It is not really Banquo the person whom Macbeth fears: it is Banquo as symbol, he who stood 'In the great hand of God'. (pp. 6-8)

Leo Kirschbaum, "Banquo and Edgar: Character or Function?" in Essays in Criticism, *Vol. VII, No. 1, January, 1957, pp. 1-21.*

SOURCES FOR FURTHER STUDY

LITERARY COMMENTARY:

Asp, Caroline. " 'Be bloody, bold and resolute': Tragic Action and Sexual Stereotyping in *Macbeth*." *Studies in Philology* LXXVIII, No. 2 (Spring 1981): 153-69.

Discusses the effect that stereotyping sexual roles has on the major characters in *Macbeth*.

Biggins, Dennis. "Sexuality, Witchcraft, and Violence in *Macbeth*." *Shakespeare Studies* VIII (1975): 255-77.

Contends that there are structural and thematic links between sexuality and various forms of violence in *Macbeth*. Biggins notes that these issues are also associated with the depiction of witchcraft in the play.

Boyer, Clarence Valentine. "Macbeth." In his *The Villain as Tragic Hero in Elizabethan Tragedy*, pp. 187-219. 1914. Reprint. New York: Russell & Russell, 1964.

Presents a detailed examination of Macbeth's character, tracing the development of his thought throughout the play's action.

Brown, John Russell, ed. *Focus on "Macbeth"*. London: Routledge & Kegan Paul, 1982, 258 p.

Contains eleven essays on *Macbeth* by prominent critics. The subjects of these essays range from thematic concerns and language to theatrical considerations of the play.

Foakes, R. A. "Macbeth." In *Stratford Papers on Shakespeare*, edited by B. W. Jackson, pp. 150-74. Toronto: W. J. Gage Limited, 1963.

Comments on the overall intensity of *Macbeth*, which is chiefly apparent in its language and imagery. Foakes argues that the drama's simplicity of action and character belies the fact that Shakespeare was attempting to develop a new kind of tragedy distinct from *Hamlet*, *King Lear*, and *Othello*.

Fosse, Jean. "The Lord's Anointed Temple: A Study of Some Symbolic Patterns in *Macbeth*." *Cahiers Élisabéthains*, No. 6 (October 1974): 15-22.

Studies a group of images in *Macbeth* concerned with the human body to demonstrate that they are closely related and that they form an important symbolic pattern.

Heilman, Robert B. "The Criminal as Tragic Hero: Dramatic Methods." *Shakespeare Survey* 19 (1966): 12-24.

Focuses on Shakespeare's attempts to evoke sympathy for Macbeth despite the character's increasing villainy. Heilman asserts that the playwright "so manages the situation that we become Macbeth or at least assent to complicity with him."

Jaarsma, Richard J. "The Tragedy of Banquo." *Literature and Psychology* XVII, Nos. 2-3 (1967): 87-94.

Maintains that Banquo undergoes a radical change as a result of the witches' prophesies and becomes Macbeth's "silent accomplice" to Duncan's murder. Jaarsma argues that by illustrating how evil affects a man "who is more realistic and less susceptible to it than Macbeth," Shakespeare generalizes the tragedy of yielding to temptation.

Kimbrough, Robert. "Macbeth: The Prisoner of Gender." *Shakespeare Studies* XVI (1983): 175-90.

Examines the role of gender in *Macbeth*, asserting that the protagonist's "failure to allow the tender aspects of his character to check those tough characteristics which are celebrated by the chauvinistic war ethic of his culture [and] championed by his wife" results first in his emotional, then his physical death.

Knights, L. C. " 'Macbeth.' " In his *Some Shakespearean Themes*, pp. 120-42. London: Chatto and Windus, Ltd., 1959.

Provides a general overview of the play's major themes and images, noting that "the essential structure of *Macbeth* . . . is to be sought in the poetry."

Lawlor, John. "Natural and Supernatural." In his *The Tragic Sense in Shakespeare*, pp. 107-46. London: Chatto & Windus, 1966.

Presents a broad discussion of *Macbeth*, touching on the subjects of free will, Shakespeare's wordplay, and imagery.

Leary, William G. "The World of *Macbeth*." In *How to Read Shakespearean Tragedy*, edited by Edwin Quinn, pp. 234-49. New York: Harper & Row, 1978.

Analyzes the "world" of Macbeth, dividing it into four parts: the physical, the psychological, the political, and the moral. Leary considers each of these aspects separately, but maintains that they are "all parts of a unified whole."

Moorthy, P. Rama. "Fear in *Macbeth*." *Essays in Criticism* XXIII, No. 2 (April 1973): 154-66.

Asserts that fear is a unifying theme in *Macbeth*. Moorthy examines how fear affects Macbeth in particular, noting that it is his peculiar fate to be continually exposed to its horrifying consequences.

Rackin, Phyllis. "*Macbeth*." In her *Shakespeare's Tragedies*, pp. 107-22. New York: Frederick Ungar Publishing Co., 1978.

Offers a general discussion of *Macbeth*. Rackin's book, which she states is "written for amateurs," includes photographs from numerous theatrical productions.

Sadler, Lynn Veach. "The Three Guises of Lady Macbeth." *CLA Journal* XIX, No. 1 (September 1975): 10-19.

Declares that Lady Macbeth is more imaginative than her husband and that she projects three guises in the play: the public Lady Macbeth, the woman who plays to the audience of her husband only, and the private Lady Macbeth.

Smidt, Kristian. "Two Aspects of Ambition in Elizabethan Tragedy: *Doctor Faustus* and *Macbeth*." *English Studies* 50, Nos. 1-6 (1969): 235-48.

Discusses how Elizabethan attitudes toward ambition are represented in the protagonists of both Christopher Marlowe's *Doctor Faustus* and Shakespeare's *Macbeth.* Smidt notes that Macbeth's primary character fault is that "he mistakes the honours received and promised for his natural right and greatness for a thing he may seize into his own hands."

Speaight, Robert. "Macbeth." In his *Nature in Shakespearian Tragedy,* pp. 44-68. London: Hollis and Carter Limited, 1955.

Examines Shakespeare's depiction of nature in *Macbeth,* arguing that it maintains an adversarial relationship with Macbeth and Lady Macbeth, whose unnatural actions force it "to [take] up arms in self-defence."

Stirling, Brents. "The Unity of Macbeth." *Shakespeare Quarterly* IV, No. 4 (October 1953): 385-94.

Proposes that the poetic and dramatic structures of *Macbeth* are unified in four traditionally Elizabethan themes: darkness, sleep, raptness, and contradiction.

Walton, J. K. "*Macbeth.*" In *Shakespeare in a Changing World,* edited by Arnold Kettle, pp. 102-22. London: Lawrence & Wisehart, 1964.

Analyzes Macbeth's individualism and associates it with the play's imagery of isolation and sterility. Walton also notes that opposed to this individualism is a combination of forces that challenge Macbeth, stating that the play's optimism is partly suggested by "the fact that a unified people overcome the tyrant."

West, Robert H. "Night's Black Agents in *Macbeth.*" *Renaissance Papers* (1956): 17-24.

Contends that the witches are agents of supernatural evil in *Macbeth.* West asserts that such an interpretation is necessary to apprehend the "wholeness of the dramatic effect."

MEDIA ADAPTATIONS:

Macbeth. Republic, 1948.

Motion picture version of Shakespeare's tragedy, featuring Orson Welles, Jeanette Nolan, Dan O'Herlihy, and Roddy McDowall. Directed by Orson Welles. Distributed by Republic Pictures Home Video. 111 minutes.

Macbeth. Andrew Draunsberg and Hugh Hefner, 1971.

Roman Polanski's controversial film adaptation of the tragedy, which features realistic design, graphic violence, and a fatalistic atmosphere. The cast includes Jon Finch, Nicholas Selby, and Martin Shaw. Distributed by RCA/Columbia Pictures Home Video. 139 minutes.

Macbeth. BBC, Time Life Television, 1976.

Television adaptation of *Macbeth* and part of the series "The Shakespeare Plays." Features Eric Porter and Janet Suzman. Distributed by Time-Life Video. 137 minutes.

Macbeth. Miami Dade Community College, BBC, 1978.

Presents key scenes from Shakespeare's tragedy. Narrated by José Ferrer. Distributed by Films, Inc. 60 minutes.

THE MERCHANT OF VENICE

INTRODUCTION

The Merchant of Venice ranks with *Hamlet* as one of Shakespeare's most frequently performed dramas. Written sometime between 1594 and 1598, the play is primarily based on a story in *Il Pecorone,* a collection of tales and anecdotes by the fourteenth-century Italian writer Giovanni Fiorentino. There is considerable debate concerning the dramatist's intent in *The Merchant of Venice* because, although it conforms to the structure of a comedy, the play contains many tragic elements. One school of critics maintains that the drama is fundamentally allegorical, addressing such themes as the triumph of mercy over justice, New Testament forgiveness over Old Testament law, and love over material wealth. Another group of commentators, observing several ambiguities in the play's apparent endorsement of Christian values, contends that Shakespeare actually censures Antonio and the Venetians who oppose Shylock. In essence, these critics assert that the Christians' discrimination against Shylock, which ultimately results in his forced conversion from Judaism, contradicts the New Testament precepts of love and mercy. Other commentators suggest that Shakespeare intentionally provided for both interpretations of the drama; although the playwright does not entirely support Shylock, they contend, neither does he endorse the actions of Antonio and the other Venetians in their punishment of the Jew.

PRINCIPAL CHARACTERS
(in order of appearance)

Antonio: A Venetian merchant. He signs a bond authorizing Bassanio to borrow 3,000 ducats from Shylock. His life is later threatened when the moneylender demands a pound of his flesh as payment for the overdue loan.

Bassanio: A Venetian gentleman and Antonio's close friend. He solves the riddle of the caskets by choosing the lead box and wins Portia for his bride.

Lorenzo: A Venetian gentleman and Antonio and Bassanio's friend. He elopes with Jessica.

Gratiano: A Venetian gentleman and Bassanio's companion. He marries Nerissa in a double wedding with Bassanio and Portia.

Portia: A rich heiress in Belmont. She marries Bas-

sanio, who successfully passes the casket test. Determined to help her husband save Antonio from Shylock's bond, Portia travels to Venice disguised as a lawyer named Balthazar to represent the merchant at the trial.

Nerissa: Portia's lady-in-waiting. She marries Gratiano and later accompanies Portia to Venice disguised as a law clerk.

Shylock: A Jewish moneylender and Jessica's father. He loans Bassanio 3,000 ducats on Antonio's behalf, stipulating that he will take a pound of Antonio's flesh if the sum is not repaid on time. During Antonio's trial, Portia turns the tables on Shylock, rescuing the merchant on a legal technicality and leaving the Jew himself to face the punishment of Venetian law.

The Prince of Morocco: A suitor to Portia. He incorrectly chooses the golden box during the casket test.

Launcelot Gobbo: Shylock's comic servant. He convinces Bassanio to employ him because Shylock does not treat him well.

Jessica: Shylock's daughter. She elopes with Lorenzo, stealing a portion of her father's wealth for her dowry.

The Prince of Arragon: A suitor to Portia. He incorrectly selects the silver box during the casket test.

PLOT SYNOPSIS

Act I: In Venice, Antonio is describing his mysterious state of melancholy to his companions Solanio and Salerio when Bassanio approaches him for a loan. Bassanio is already in debt to the merchant, but he asks for an additional sum so that he can woo the wealthy and beautiful Portia in Belmont. Because most of his money is invested in three merchant vessels that have not returned from abroad, Antonio is unable to comply with his friend's request. Nevertheless, he authorizes Bassanio to borrow money using his name. Bassanio turns to Shylock, who hates Antonio because he is a Christian and because he lends money without interest. Shylock agrees to lend Antonio 3,000 ducats for three months; if the loan is not repaid in time, he will demand a pound of the merchant's flesh. Bassanio objects, but Antonio signs the bond, confident that his ships will return before the term expires. Meanwhile in Belmont, Portia laments the provision of her father's will that states she must wed the suitor who, from three caskets—one of gold, one of silver, and one of lead—chooses the one containing her picture. She expresses her relief to Nerissa that all the previous suitors have failed the test, and then confesses her admiration for Bassanio.

Act II: On a Venetian street, Launcelot Gobbo meets his nearly blind father and convinces the old man of his identity with considerable difficulty. The two men then encounter Bassanio and his friends. Launcelot relates the unhappy circumstances of his service to Shylock, ultimately convincing Bassanio to employ him instead. Meanwhile, Jessica steals a sizable portion of Shylock's wealth and elopes with Lorenzo while the Jew dines with Antonio. It is later reported that when Shylock discovers Jessica has run away, he laments the loss of his money as much as that of his daughter. In Belmont, Portia contends with two suitors: the Princes of Arragon and Morocco. Morocco boldly chooses the gold casket, but it contains a death's-head and a scroll that reads "All that glisters is not gold" (II. vii. 65). Arragon selects the silver casket, which bears the motto "Who chooseth me shall get as much as he deserves" (II. vii. 7). Inside he finds a fool's-head.

Act III: Amid rumors that Antonio's ships have been lost, Shylock maintains that he will demand payment of his bond in return for enduring Venetian slurs against his race and faith. Meanwhile, Bassanio arrives in Belmont with Gratiano and, cautious of being misled by appearances like Portia's previous suitors, correctly chooses the lead casket. Portia gives him a ring as a sign of her love, and he vows to cherish it forever. Gratiano then reveals that Nerissa had promised to marry him if Bassanio won her mistress, and Nerissa presents him with a ring. In the meantime, Jessica and Lorenzo arrive in Belmont with Salerio, who bears a letter from Antonio to Bassanio. In it, the merchant informs his friend that his ships have been lost and that Shylock has demanded payment of his bond. Antonio also asks Bassanio to return to Venice so that he can see him once more before he dies. Bassanio and Gratiano leave immediately after the wedding. Once her husband has departed, Portia sends a message requesting a favor of her kinsman, Doctor Bellario, and announces to Nerissa that they will travel to Venice disguised as men.

Act IV: Once everyone has assembled for Antonio's trial, Shylock expresses his determination to have his bond fulfilled, if only to satisfy his loathing for the merchant. From his newly acquired wealth, Bassanio offers to double the sum owed on the bond, but Shylock insists on taking the pound of flesh, warning that denial of his suit will undermine Venetian law. The Duke of Venice states that he has asked a prominent lawyer, Doctor Bellario, to judge the case. At this point, Nerissa arrives,

dressed as a clerk. She presents a letter from Bellario in which he states that he cannot attend because of illness, but that he has sent a young colleague named Balthazar in his place. Balthazar, who is really Portia in disguise, asks Shylock to moderate his legal claim with mercy, but the moneylender rejects her advice. Portia then asserts that in accordance with Venetian law, Shylock may not cut more than a pound of flesh nor shed a drop of blood while exacting his bond from Antonio. Realizing the impossibility of this feat, Shylock agrees to settle for the money owed him. But Portia points out that the moneylender has, in effect, sought the life of a Venetian citizen and that the penalty for such a crime is forfeiture of estate, half to the city and half to the injured party. The Duke pardons Shylock and reduces the city's portion to a fine, while Antonio decides that he will keep his share in trust for Jessica and Lorenzo if Shylock will convert to Christianity. Shylock, his vengeance turned to despair, can only agree to these terms. After the trial, Antonio and Bassanio profusely thank Balthazar, who insists that the only reward he will accept is Bassanio's ring. At Antonio's urging, Bassanio reluctantly agrees to part with Portia's gift. Gratiano follows suit by forfeiting his ring to Balthazar's clerk.

Act V: Portia and Nerissa return to Belmont, arriving shortly before Bassanio and Gratiano, who are accompanied by Antonio. When the men appear, the wives ask for their rings and chide their husbands when told that the bands were given to the lawyer and his clerk. Portia eventually forgives Bassanio and offers him another ring, which she asks him to keep more faithfully. Bassanio realizes that this ring is the one he gave the lawyer, and the two women reveal their masquerade to their surprised husbands. Portia then announces that she has received word that three of Antonio's ships have returned safely to Venice and that Jessica and Lorenzo will inherit half of Shylock's wealth.

PRINCIPAL TOPICS

Economics is a prime concern in *The Merchant of Venice,* and one major critical perspective treats the play as a clash between emerging mercantile sensibilities and religious traditions. During Shakespeare's time, usury (lending money for interest) became an accepted business practice as profits became increasingly more important than religious principles. The rivalry between Antonio and Shylock is often viewed as an example of two conflicting business ethics. Although Shylock represents usury as a pragmatic and legitimate business practice, Antonio embodies a more idealistic perspective of the profession. Following Christian precepts, the merchant generously lends his money interest-free because his wealth and means allow him to do so. This fundamental economic contention, in addition to the two characters' religious differences, establishes their enmity toward one another and creates a rivalry that reaches its climax in the trial sequence (Act IV, scene i). Bassanio's marriage to Portia demonstrates another economic dimension of the play. Due to rising costs during the Renaissance, aristocrats in many cases had to concern themselves with obtaining more wealth to maintain their expected lifestyle, and a generous dowry was considered a respectable means of achieving this end. Many critics contend that even though Bassanio is virtually penniless because of his extravagant spending, his open desire to marry Portia for her money—in addition to her charm and beauty—should not be construed by modern readers as the shrewd enterprise of an unscrupulous fortune hunter. In fact, they continue, an Elizabethan audience probably would have interpreted Bassanio's suit of love as an ordinary and perfectly acceptable arrangement.

Kinds of love and rivalry in love are other important topics in *The Merchant of Venice*. The suitors who vie for Portia all represent different types of love. Arragon and Morocco—the two unsuccessful petitioners—symbolize a shallow and limited form of love. By selecting the silver casket on the basis of its inscription ("Who chooseth me shall get as much as he deserves" [II. vii. 7]), Arragon reveals that his concept of love is self-serving and vain. Morocco's choice of the gold casket indicates that his notion of love is based on superficiality ("All that glisters is not gold" [II. vii. 65]). However, when Bassanio correctly identifies the lead casket, he demonstrates a superior understanding of love by judging the box on the inner qualities it may possess rather than on its dull appearance. The issue of rivalry in love is evident in the association between Antonio, Portia, and Bassanio. Some critics argue that the relationship between Antonio and Bassanio may be a homosexual one, citing the merchant's unexplained melancholy at the beginning of the play as the result of Portia displacing him as the object of Bassanio's affection. In addition, couples—Bassanio and Portia and Jessica and Lorenzo—represent two antithetical kinds of love in *The Merchant of Venice*. Bassanio and Portia demonstrate a socially acceptable courtship; not only do they obey her father's request that Portia's suitor successfully endure the casket test, but they also uphold the legal provisions of the test as mandated in the father's will. Jessica and Lorenzo's courtship, however, illustrates a romantic love linked to the great lovers of myth, particularly in the illicitness of their elopement. Unlike Portia and Bassanio's union, Jessica and Lorenzo's defies social traditions because their aspiration to get married causes them to step out of the bounds of the accepted rules of society.

Shakespeare's delicate balancing of the worlds of Venice and Belmont is another central issue in *The Merchant of Venice*. Venice represents the realistic, civilized world that is supposedly governed by Christian values. However, the Christians are shown to be hypocritical in their treatment of Shylock. For all his purported charity and virtue, Antonio discriminates against the Jew, ultimately forcing Shylock to renounce Judaism and embrace Christianity. Shylock and the other Jews contribute a mercenary dimension to the affairs of the city, in which lending money for interest is considered a legitimate business practice and breaches of contract are immediately redressed with legal action. Although accepted by the Venetians on an economic level, Shylock remains an outsider in the city. His actions are governed by Judaic law and the Old Testament rather than imposed Christian values. Shylock's quest for revenge against Antonio is therefore a retributive action sanctioned by his faith. This desire for vengeance is due to the fact that Shylock has never received mercy or charity from the Christians, and, not surprisingly, it is another outsider, Portia of Belmont, who attempts to inspire compassion in the Jew during Antonio's trial. Portia's Belmont presents the counterpoint to Venice by embodying the qualities of an idealistic world which markedly contrasts with the hypocrisy, revenge, and commercial exploitation which dominate affairs in the city. In essence, Belmont represents a fairy-tale realm where happiness and love flourish and Christian charity and forgiveness hold sway. These benevolent qualities manifest themselves in Portia, whose confrontation with Shylock can be interpreted as a direct clash between the retributive justice ordained in the Old Testament and the mercy and charity advocated in the New Testament. Shakespeare provides *The Merchant of Venice* with a happy ending by emphasizing the love, joy, and forgiveness that thrives in Belmont; but the reader is nevertheless left with the unsettling impression that hypocrisy and hatred persist in Venice.

CHARACTER STUDIES

The Merchant of Venice is often considered Shylock's play, for the reading of his character generally influences the interpretation of the drama as a whole. If Shylock is perceived as a comic villain, with all the stock characteristics associated with such a role, then he receives his due in the trial scene and the work is truly a comedy. However, if Shylock is seen as the hero of the drama, then his humiliation indicates that the work is a tragedy. Both views can be argued based on the content of the play. Numerous commentators have discussed the extent to which Shakespeare was influenced by the anti-Semitic sentiment of his day. While it is true that the playwright began writing his play with the stereotypical Elizabethan conception of a Jewish usurer in mind, he created in Shylock an ambiguous, yet memorable figure who defies those conventional attributes and who overshadows the rest of the work. By giving Shylock sympathetic human traits—most notably his feelings of persecution at the hands of the Venetians—Shakespeare raised the question of whether Shylock's villainous behavior toward Antonio is purely malicious, or whether his actions reflect the desperate attempts of an outsider to secure justice and revenge against the enemies who have wronged him.

Many commentators assert that Portia is one of Shakespeare's finest dramatic creations. Highly intelligent and resourceful, she is viewed as a paragon of femininity, with much more complexity of character than the fairy-tale princesses found in the literary sources available to the playwright. Some critics view Portia as an initially disruptive force in the play because, as an unmarried and wealthy young woman, she poses a threat to the male-dominated Elizabethan worldview. This dramatic tension is relieved, however, when she conforms to societal conventions through her marriage to Bassanio. On a more symbolic level, Portia represents the influence of Christian mercy and forgiveness. Perhaps the two most notable instances of Portia's benevolence occur when she attempts to persuade Shylock to have compassion on Antonio during the trial scene and when she pardons Bassanio for forfeiting her ring. Shakespeare invented Bassanio by exploiting a popular dramatic convention of the time in which a hero of a play wins the hand of a maiden by solving a perplexing riddle. Due to the significance Bassanio places on Portia's wealth early in the play, his character has been interpreted in two conflicting ways. Some commentators maintain that Bassanio is a scheming opportunist, drawn only to Portia's wealth and position. By contrast, others view the character as a portrait of the ideal Elizabethan lover, arguing that Shakespeare's audience probably considered Bassanio's actions perfectly acceptable.

Critics generally agree that while the title character of the drama, the merchant Antonio, is generally overshadowed by both Shylock and Portia, he nonetheless remains crucial to the interweaving of the Belmont and Venice plots. Commentators note that while Antonio is depicted as the consummate Christian because of his humility and charity, his treatment of Shylock conforms to conventional attitudes toward Jews rather than the unconditional love advocated in the New Testament. In addition, the curious circumstances surrounding Antonio's melancholy at the beginning of the play have generated some debate among critics. Some commentators interpret the merchant's sadness as an indication of his inability to reconcile the accumulation of wealth with his Christian faith; others read Antonio's sorrow as a manifestation of his unconscious homosexual love for Bassanio.

CONCLUSION

The Merchant of Venice is a popular work that allows for a wide variety of interpretations. The complexity of the characters of Portia and Shylock in particular continue to intrigue actors, critics, and readers alike. As S. C. Sen Gupta has stated, "*The Merchant of Venice* introduces us to the middle of Shakespeare's dramatic career" in which "we find not the apprentice of promise but the artist of full genius."

(See also *Shakespearean Criticism*, Vols. 4, 12)

OVERVIEWS

Frank Kermode

[*Kermode presents a concise overview of* The Merchant of Venice, *initially examining Shakespeare's punning of the term "gentle" and discussing the word's various meanings throughout the play. The critic identifies two readings of "gentle" which have a significant bearing on the drama: the sense of "gentleness" as in civility or an improved nature; and the notion of "Gentile," or Christian, which stands in contrast to* **Shylock** *and Judaism. In addition, Kermode asserts that justice is a primary theme of the drama, noting that while the Christians stress mercy, love, and charity,* **Shylock** *advocates the letter (rather than the spirit) of the law, hate, and vengeance.* The Merchant of Venice, *the critic concludes, is about "judgment, redemption, and mercy; the supersession in human history of the grim four thousand years of unalleviated justice by the era of love and mercy."*]

We are not likely, whether or no we share his high opinion of Shakespeare as a comic writer, to fall into Johnson's error when he dismissed the reiteration of the word 'gentle' in [*The Merchant of Venice*] as only another example of Shakespeare's weakness for this 'fatal Cleopatra', the pun. 'Gentleness' in this play means civility in its old full sense, nature improved; but it also means 'Gentile', in the sense of Christian, which amounts, in a way, to the same thing. Here are some of the passages in which it occurs:

> Hie thee, gentle Jew.
> The Hebrew will turn Christian: he grows kind.
>
> [I. iii. 177-78]

> If e'er the Jew her father come to heaven,
> It will be for his gentle daughter's sake.
>
> [II. iv. 33-4]
> (Jessica is also called 'gentle' in l. 19)

Now, by my hood, a Gentile [gentle] and no
Jew
[II. vi. 51]

. . . to leave a rich Jew's service and
become
The follower of so poor a gentleman
[II. ii. 147-48]

The Duke urges Shylock to be merciful; asking
him not only to

loose the forfeiture,
But, touch'd with human gentleness and
love,
Forgive a moiety of the principal. . . .
We all expect a gentle answer, Jew.
[IV. i. 24-33]

Other 'gentle' objects are Antonio's ships, and Portia, many times over; and Portia speaks of mercy as
a 'gentle rain'.

There is a straightforward contrast between gentleness, the 'mind of love', and its opposite, for
which Shylock stands. He lends money at interest,
which is not only unchristian, but an obvious mis-
direction of love; Antonio ventures with his ships,
trusts his wealth to the hand of God (and so they
are 'gentle' ships). It is true that a Jew hath eyes
etc.; this does not reduce the difference between
man and man, when one is gentle and the other
not. To make all this clear, Shakespeare twice in-
serts the kind of passage he later learned to do
without; the kind which tells the audience how to
interpret the action. It is normal to cut these scenes
in acting texts, but only because these plays are so
grossly misunderstood. The first such is the debate
on Genesis, xxxi. 37 ff. (Jacob's device to produce
ringstraked, speckled and spotted lambs) which
occurs when Antonio first asks for the loan [I. iii.
61 ff.]. The correct interpretation of this passage,
as given by Christian commentators on Genesis
(see A. Williams, *The Common Expositor,* 1950), is
that Jacob was making a venture ('A thing not in
his power to bring to pass, / but sway'd and fashion'd by the hand of heaven'; compare *Faerie Queene,* V. iv). But Shylock sees no difference between the breeding of metal and the breeding of
sheep—a constant charge against usurers. . . .
Later, in II. viii, we have a pair of almost Spenserian *exempla* [examples] to make this point clear.
First Solanio describes Shylock's grief at the loss
of daughter and ducats; he cannot distinguish
properly between them, or lament the one more
than the other. Then Solario describes the parting
of Antonio and Bassanio; Antonio urges Bassanio
not even to consider money; the loss of Bassanio is
serious, but he urges him to be merry and not to
think of Shylock's bond. When love is measured
out, confused by the 'spirit of calculation' (R. B.
Heilman's phrase in his discussion of the errors of
Lear [II. ix. 21]), the result is moral chaos.

Bassanio's visit to Belmont is frankly presented as
a venture, like Jason's for the Golden Fleece; and

the theme of gentle venturing is deepened in the
scenes of the choice of caskets. The breeding metals, gold and silver, are to be rejected; the good lead
requires that the chooser should 'give and hazard
all he hath' [II. ix. 21]. Morocco (II. vii) supposes
that Portia cannot be got by any casket save the
golden one, tacitly confusing her living worth with
that of gold, the value of gentleness with that of the
best breeding metal. Arragon (II. ix—the intervening scene contains the lamentation of Shylock over
his daughter-ducats) rejects gold out of pride only,
ironically giving the right reasons for despising the
choice of the 'many', that they are swayed not by
Truth but by Opinion, a mere false appearance of
Truth, not Truth itself. (In this sense the Jews are
enslaved to Opinion.) He chooses silver because he
'assumes desert', another matter from trusting to
the hand of God; and his reward is 'a shadow's
bliss' [II. ix. 67]. After another scene in which Shylock rejoices over Antonio's losses and again laments Jessica's treachery, there follows (III. ii) the
central scene of choice, in which Bassanio comes
to 'hazard' and 'venture' for Portia. The point of the
little song is certainly that in matters of love the eye
is a treacherous agent, and can mistake substance
for shadow. Bassanio, rejecting the barren metals
which appear to breed, avoids the curse of barren-
ness on himself (for that is the punishment of failure); and he finds in the leaden casket Portia's true
image. The scroll speaks of the 'fortune' which has
fallen to him. Portia, in her happiness, speaks of
Bassanio's prize as not rich enough, deploring the
poorness of her 'full sum'; and Gratiano speaks of
the forthcoming marriage as the solemnization of
'the bargain of your faith' [III. ii. 193]. Bassanio the
merchant has 'won the fleece' [III. ii. 241]; but at
the same moment Antonio has lost his. Bassanio
is 'dear bought', as Portia says; but Antonio will
not have him return for any reason save love: 'if
your love do not persuade you to come, let not my
letter' [III. ii. 321-22].

At this point the conflict between gentleness (Antonio's laying down his life for his friend) and a
harsh ungentle legalism becomes the main burden
of the plot. Shylock demands his bond; this is just,
like Angelo's strict application of the law against
fornication in the hard case of Claudio [in *Measure
for Measure*]. It is, in a way, characteristic of
Shakespeare's inspired luck with his themes that
Shylock in the old stories will take flesh for money.
There is no substantial difference: he lacks the
power to distinguish gold, goat's flesh, man's flesh,
and thinks of Antonio's body as carrion. The difference between this and a 'gentle' attitude reflects a
greater difference:

DUKE: How shalt thou hope for mercy, rendering none?
SHYLOCK: What judgement shall I dread,
doing no wrong?
[IV. i. 88-9]

There is no need to sentimentalize this; as Shakespeare is careful to show in *Measure for Measure* the arguments for justice are strong, and in the course of Christian doctrine it is necessarily satisfied before mercy operates. . . . Shylock has legally bought his pound of flesh; if he does not get it 'there is no force in the decrees of Venice' [IV. i. 102]. But as heavenly mercy is never deserved, it is an adornment of human authority to exercise it with the same grace:

> . . . earthly power doth then show likest God's
> When mercy seasons justice. Therefore, Jew,
> Though justice be thy plea, consider this,
> That, in the course of justice, none of us
> Should see salvation.
> [IV. i. 196-200]

But this plea does not work on the stony unregenerate heart; Shylock persists in the demand for justice, and gets it. Like any other human being, he must lose all by such a demand. In offering to meet the demands of strict justice (in accordance with the Old Law) Antonio will pay in blood the price of his friend's happiness; and it cannot be extravagant to argue that he is here a type of the divine Redeemer, as Shylock is of the unredeemed.

Shakespeare's last act, another 'thematic' appendix to the dramatic action, is motivated by the device of the rings. It begins with a most remarkable passage, Lorenzo's famous 'praise of music'. In this are treated 'topics' which, as James Hutton shows in an extremely important study ['Some English Poems in Praise of Music', *English Miscellany* II (1951)], are all evidently the regular parts of a coherent and familiar theme—so familiar indeed, that Shakespeare permits himself to treat it 'in a kind of shorthand'. The implications of this 'theme' are vast; but behind it lies the notion, very explicit in Milton's 'Ode at a Solemn Musick', of the universal harmony impaired by sin and restored by the Redemption. The lovers, in the restored harmony of Belmont, have a debt to Antonio:

> You should in all sense be much bound to him,
> For, as I hear, he was much bound for you.
> [V. i. 136-37]

In such an atmosphere the amorous sufferings of Troilus, Thisbe, Dido and Medea are only shadows of possible disaster [cf. V. i. 1-14], like the mechanicals' play in *A Midsummer Night's Dream;* Antonio on his arrival is allowed, by the *contretemps* [inopportune and embarrassing occurence] of the ring-plot, to affirm once more the nature of his love, standing guarantor for Bassanio in perpetuity, 'my soul upon the forfeit' [V. i. 252]. *The Merchant of Venice,* then, is 'about' judgment, redemption and mercy; the supersession in human history of the grim four thousand years of unalleviated justice by

Solanio, Salerio, and Shylock. Act III, scene i. By Sir John Gilbert.

the era of love and mercy. It begins with usury and corrupt love; it ends with harmony and perfect love. And all the time it tells its audience that this is its subject; only by a determined effort to avoid the obvious can one mistake the theme of *The Merchant of Venice*. (pp. 221-24)

> Frank Kermode, "The Mature Comedies," in Early Shakespeare, *edited by John Russell Brown and Bernard Harris, Edward Arnold (Publishers) Ltd., 1961, pp. 211-27.*

E. F. C. Ludowyk

[*Ludowyk offers a brief synopsis of the main characters in* The Merchant of Venice, *emphasizing the attributes which involve them in situations of trial or test. The critic considers* **Antonio** *a virtuous and generous Christian merchant, who is also "mysteriously and romantically tinged with melancholy."* **Bassanio** *is a romantic hero, Ludowyk asserts, albeit one whose life of extravagance has left him penniless. Shakespeare probably did not intend to depict him as "a mercenary fortune hunter"; rather "he is the ideal man to attempt to win the fairy princess,"* **Portia**. **Shylock** *is the evil outsider, the critic continues, a Jew despised by Christians, and as evil as* **Antonio** *is good.* **Portia** *is the fairy-tale princess of Belmont, Ludowyk maintains, the prize for which the heroes contend. She also embodies divine grace and demonstrates an angelic quality by miraculously appearing in Venice to save* **Antonio** *from* **Shylock's** *bond.*]

The material of [*The Merchant of Venice*] has often been likened to a fairy tale. Enchanting though it may be, . . . the play touches on matters of seriousness, so that there is something to be taken away from it besides the very satisfying impression of romance.

Shakespeare took his story from the Italian. It differs only in its ratio of romance to reality, a reality Elizabethans would understand, from all those stories of love and adventure, which they were eagerly reading in translation—such stories as those of Romeo and Juliet, of Othello, and so on. Whether Shakespeare got his story directly from some Italian source, or from an earlier play, we do not know, nor does it matter greatly. All sorts of fairy-tale material are used in this play, some of it not originally Italian but of very ancient Oriental provenance, as for instance the story of the caskets, and of the pound of flesh. The wealth of story-telling in Eastern, particularly Indian, cultures had given rise to classical Greek, Latin and Islamic analogues, so the story Shakespeare used may have existed in various forms. What is important is the use he made of a well-known tale.

The special stamp Shakespeare gave his material is that of the suggestion of something serious, and real, in addition to the romance or the fairy-tale. We . . . notice throughout *The Merchant of Venice* how everything in the play has a double character: a connection with the externals of romance, and at the same time an allusion to, or some link with, undoubted moral seriousness. In most of his comedies we find a similar tendency—that of evoking through the gaiety, even the light-heartedness, of its situations the suggestion of something more serious and grave.

In the popular theatre there were no strict rules by which plays had to be written, and Shakespeare's form is often a concoction of various materials. Tragedy could be the story of a great man who came to an unhappy end. Comedy could be a story ('historie') with a happy ending, and it could include something other than, or even opposed to, the pleasurable lightness usually associated with comedy today. We . . . see in *Twelfth Night* how the two—the grave and the gay—are blended. There is the same process here. The theatre to Elizabethans was often like the pulpit in the sound morality it preached. And to all people at that time the business of literature and the arts was to teach.

So the romantic story of the extreme situation of Antonio, who is saved from the ogreish Shylock by Portia, the fairy-princess whom Bassanio wins as his bride, and all its other stories have a serious undertone. The impossibility of the 'historie' is based on a moral reality which poses such questions as were the subjects of moral interlude.

The structure of the play depends on a number of situations of trial or test. At various points in the action a character is tested, or a trial takes place. These tests are based on moral criteria such as how should one decide between three offered choices (the casket test), or in the great trial scene which is better: Justice or Mercy? And often everything seems to turn on deciding between appearance and reality. (pp. 118-20)

[By examining] the way in which [the characters] are described and presented we can see how naturally and easily they come to be involved in the situations of trial or test in which they figure.

Antonio. To take Antonio first, the merchant of Venice. He is what the Duke calls a 'royal merchant'. This is Gratiano's description of him too [III. ii. 239]. He is not only wealthy, but also a person of a royal or kingly disposition. As a man of great wealth Antonio is in a prominent position; in most cultures, certainly in Eastern cultures, the possession of wealth would entitle him to respect, for with it went responsibilities and duties. So in the East the man of wealth is often given an honorific title. Not so long ago in India the wealthy Zamindar was often a Rajah; and in Malaya and China there are special terms of respect to designate the rich man. Such men were expected to be generous, to be spenders of their wealth, and not to be miserly but charitable. Antonio is a man of this kind. He gives all, even his life, to help his friend, the poor man Bassanio, with whom he is, in the way of these romances, linked. That Antonio uses his wealth to help others, we know from [III. iii. 21ff.].

He is also mysteriously and romantically tinged with melancholy. It may be that Shakespeare in shaping his materials interposes a hint of what is to follow. He gives Antonio a premonition of his fate. His melancholy would be due, too, to his loss of Bassanio. That he loves Bassanio so devotedly would not make him specially romantic in Elizabethan eyes, for it was a commonplace that two men could be so devoted to each other. In an early play of Shakespeare's [*The Two Gentlemen of Verona*] we have Proteus and Valentine who are sworn brothers, and . . . in *Twelfth Night* . . . the sea-captain, Antonio, risks his life to follow Sebastian only because of his great attachment to him.

But there is something else. Antonio is not only the fabulous merchant, of an interesting melancholic turn of mind. He is a Christian. This is the first remark made of him by his enemy Shylock. In describing him as a Christian Shylock calls him 'fawning publican', which recalls the type of person Christ preferred to the self-righteous Pharisee. Antonio, in the use of his wealth, comes near to the prescription given to the rich young ruler whom Christ advised to sell everything that he had. The rich young ruler did not do as Christ recommended, but Antonio's pledging of all his wealth to help a friend and his generosity should be contrasted with Shylock's miserliness, and be reckoned part of his 'royal', Christian disposition. In Shylock's own words Antonio was wont to lend money 'for Christian courtesy' [III. i. 49]. Of him Salerio says 'a kinder gentleman treads not the earth' [II. viii. 35], where 'kind' would mean not only of a kindly disposition, but also full of what should be natural to human beings—feeling for others. ('Kind' is a word with the two senses of which Shakespeare often played.) To Bassanio he is

> the kindest man
> The best-conditioned and unwearied spir-
>   it
> In doing courtesies.
>
> [III. ii. 292-94]

We shall see in the central scene in the play with what Christian virtue Antonio bears himself.

Round this romantic merchant prince of true Christian virtue are a group of characters of whom we can say little, because the dramatist evidently intends them simply as the train to Antonio. As Morocco is attended by a train, as Bassanio goes on his quest similarly attended, so Antonio is given his Solanios and Salerios. If their number was mistakenly increased and a third by name Salerino invented through confusion between Solanio and Salerio, it all goes to show how unimportant they

are as persons in the play. They have no function but as frame to Antonio—in his glory and in his distress.

Bassanio. Bassanio is another romantic character—the young man without means beloved by the merchant prince. Shakespeare makes him a figure recognizable to the Londoners of his time—the young man who through extravagance (as Bassanio confesses 'somewhat showing a more swelling port Than my faint means would grant continuance' [cf. I. i. 124-25]) has no money. But this weakness of the young should not be held against him, since he shows as much by his attitude as by what is reported of him, that though young and foolish in the past, he is in the play the ideal man to attempt to win the fairy princess. We should not think of him as a mercenary fortune hunter, since social institutions then made the desire of a young man for a wealthy bride perfectly regular. Arranged marriages where the dowry of the girl is an important consideration are well known both in the East and the West. Bassanio, when he first speaks of Portia, describes her as a 'lady richly left' [I. i. 161] (she has inherited wealth from her father), but he goes on to speak of her as 'fair', and

> fairer than that word,
> Of wondrous virtues.
>
> [I. i. 162-63]

He compares her with Brutus's Portia, and then proclaims her the fabulous object of desperate adventure—the golden fleece after which Jason sailed [cf. I. i. 165-72].

Bassanio is, in Nerissa's words which gain Portia's approval, a 'scholar and a soldier . . . of all the men that ever my foolish eyes looked upon, the best deserving a fair lady' [I. ii. 113ff.]. And most important of all, we shall see in the first of the great trials with which this play is concerned, how nobly he bears himself, and how rightly he chooses. To Portia in [III. ii. 60] he recalls the demi-god Hercules who rescued the Trojan maiden. Shakespeare gives Bassanio the character of a man of virtue. We should, remembering the test, judge Bassanio not by the outward show but by what lies within.

He is attended by Gratiano, who is, according to his description in the play and in numerous Italian comedies some of which Shakespeare might have seen in London, a comical figure who always will be talking. In the lists of characters in Italian comedy there is often a Dottore Gratiano, a pompous talker.

Shylock. Shylock is the contrast to the good Antonio. Romance likes to work in black and white, and he is black to Antonio's white. If explanation were needed of his ogreishness, then we should have to say that he is a Jew is reason enough. Christian Europe reviled the Jew, and portrayed him as a hateful monster. If we are inclined to flatter ourselves that we are better in this respect, we need only pause for a moment to consider our own record in this century, when racial hatreds have involved not only Jews but countless others of all races in shameful treatment from people like our own enlightened selves. Shakespeare's reaction to Shylock as a Jew is likely to have been that of his time. We can understand and condemn it, but we need not consider that it detracts seriously from the quality of *The Merchant of Venice,* for in the play Shakespeare is not concerned with teaching his audience, or ourselves, how Jews should be treated. If this had been his object then we could feel that there is something gravely at fault with the play as a manual of ethics. Shylock's vengefulness, not his Jewishness, is the centre of the play, and it is not written by a dramatist who felt Shylock's wrongs or those of his race deeply.

If we read the famous lines Shakespeare gave Shylock in [III. i. 53ff.], we shall see that they do not suggest that a Jew, because he is as much a human being as any Christian, should therefore be treated accordingly. Their intention is to prove that as Jews and Christians are both human beings, it is natural for them both to revenge wrongs done them—a point of view which would seem damnable both to orthodox Christian opinion and Jewish. Shylock is not asking for our tears, he is putting forward the point of view of a detestable ogre.

The desperateness of Shylock's evil intentions would, to the audience of that time, have been adequately accounted for by his religion. The trial and execution of the Jewish physician Roderigo Lopez in 1594 for plotting to assassinate both Queen Elizabeth and the claimant to the Portuguese throne, would have made audiences the more ready to accept the conventional notion that such dastardly conduct came naturally to his co-religionists. We should not forget, too, that Shylock is a 'stranger'—strange in his religion, his dress, his manner of speech probably (certainly his Old Testament allusions give his language a colour of its own). He could quite easily be taken as that figure in the community who by his difference from the rest has to incur hostility. It is easy to remember how strongly emotions could be stirred against shopkeepers of another race who include moneylending as part of their business activities.

Shylock is presented to us by the dramatist not only as Jew, but more importantly and significantly as 'dog', wild beast and devil. There are several references to him which insist on his 'currish' disposition. In this matter, too, Shakespeare would seem to the humanitarians of our time in need of reprimand, for he always associated with the dog traits which were dangerous and contemptible: dogs always fawned and flattered; they were to be seen in great households licking at sweets—a messy and disgusting habit. It was their nature to snarl and bite, which may seem absolutely contradictory to the fawning, but what seems to be clear

is that the image of dog suggested to Shakespeare what was contemptible.

Shylock is time and time again referred to as 'dog'. He himself reports that this is how Antonio had addressed him and treated him. We might ask whether we should think the worse of Antonio on this account. This was the treatment conventionally accorded to Jews, and we shall see, in the most significant scene of the play, how Antonio behaves towards Shylock. His generous attitude to Shylock immediately after he has been saved by Portia is Shakespeare's own invention, and should be taken as characteristic. To the other characters in the play Shylock is 'the villain Jew' [II. viii. 4], 'the dog Jew' [II. viii. 14], an 'impenetrable cur' [III. iii. 18], and Gratiano in execration of him thinks of him as both dog and wolf, with perhaps a reference to Lopez whose name was derived from the Latin *lupus*—wolf. Shylock himself states ironically 'since I am a dog beware my fangs' [III. iii. 7].

As the opponent of the good Antonio, Shylock is thought of as devil. The conflict of the good man with the devil was a simple Christian fable, and the writer without intending to be explicitly moral can give his work a simple moral point of view.

So we can see Shylock as devil, the natural adversary of Antonio. Indeed he is often pictured as such in the play. Antonio himself, in a warning to Bassanio of which he himself fails to take heed, looking at Shylock on the stage lost in his reckonings and mutterings and remembering his reference to the biblical story of Jacob and Laban, says 'The devil can cite Scripture for his purpose' [I. iii. 98]. To Lancelot his master is, 'God bless the mark' [II. ii. 24], as he puts it, because some obscene phrase is to follow, 'a kind of devil' [II. ii. 24]. To Solanio in [III. i] he is throughout the devil. To Bassanio in [IV. i. 287] he is 'this devil'. And the situation facing Portia, as she sees it in [III. iv. 20-1], is that of

> Purchasing the semblance of my soul
> From out the state of hellish cruelty.

This we might take as the substance of the serious side of the play seen in miniature. To the Duke in the trial scene Shylock is an 'inhuman wretch', a term which unites both the suggestions of 'dog' (animal and not human) and 'devil' (wretch being the person expelled and driven out as the devil was from heaven).

Portia. Portia in the romance is the fairy-princess, the rich prize for which the heroes contend. To win her they have to undergo a test or trial, a familiar legend both in the East and West. With Portia are associated all the images of rich treasure and fabulous adventure.

Many critics of the play have contrasted Belmont, where she lives, with the mart of Venice, to which she goes only to rescue Antonio. Her house is associated with music and harmony, while the world outside is 'naughty' or full of wickedness.

In the eulogy pronounced by Morocco in [II. vii. 38ff.] she is the world's wonder. To Portia herself her situation, waiting to be won by the champion, resembles that of Hesione saved from the seamonster by Hercules, the force of classical fable adding its colour to the poet's presentation of her.

On all these scores she is the fairy-princess of romance. The caskets by which she is to be won, the ring she wears and which she presents to the hero who wins her, and what happens to it—all these are its familiar ingredients. Romantic, too, is the mode of her entry into the Duke's court in the disguise of a young lawyer.

But like all the major characters in the play she is associated with things of deeper seriousness. She is not only the princess of romance, she is thought of as divine and a saint. At the very opening of the play Bassanio, in Antonio's words, has sworn 'a secret pilgrimage' to her [I. i. 120]. Her suitors have to swear a solemn oath at a temple or chapel accepting the conditions on which they are permitted to take the test. Morocco thinks of Belmont as a place of pilgrimage where from the four corners of the world the devout come to kiss the shrine of the saint [II. vii. 39-40]. To him Portia is an angel, as he puns on the comparison with the English gold coin, the angel [II. vii. 55ff.]. To Bassanio her portrait is like that of a goddess. When she sets out with Nerissa to the rescue of Antonio, she goes and returns to the accompaniment of suggestions of some religious exercise or retreat in which she is taking part. To Jessica in [III. v. 73ff.] the winning of Portia must be to Bassanio the equivalent of finding the joys of heaven on this earth. And at the very end of the play, to Lorenzo, she is like God who drops manna from heaven on those he pleases to help.

Her role in the main section of the play resembles that of the angel of the Lord who saved Isaac in the nick of time when he was bound on the altar of sacrifice. She comes mysteriously from Belmont to help Antonio, she meets the devil Shylock on his own ground and discomfits him. She departs just as mysteriously, but not without extracting some token by which her miraculous descent into the law-court of Venice is to be made known. Typical of her is the music associated with her home, which she commands at the fateful moment of the test. Music is characteristic of concord, love and the triumph of good over the discordant forces of evil, and it is, on earth, the counterpart of the music of the spheres of which Lorenzo speaks [V. i. 60-5]. This heavenly music, in popular belief, was produced by the motion of the heavenly bodies as they circled round the earth. Human ears could not hear it, but immortal souls . . . could.

Persons such as these could be involved in situa-

tions which are the stock in trade of romantic tale, if we overlooked the serious side in them. The play could be looked at as a series of romantic and impossible tests; it could also be seen to turn on important moral decisions. The latter seems stronger than the former as a mode of approach to the play, for to Elizabethans a comedy which had some moral to enforce would be in a familiar tradition. (pp. 121-28)

> *E. F. C. Ludowyk, "The Merchant of Venice," in his* Understanding Shakespeare, *Cambridge at the University Press, 1962, pp. 118-44.*

USURY

John W. Draper

[*Draper provides historical background on English Jews and the practice of usury (moneylending for interest) as they existed in Shakespeare's time to prove that the chief concern of* The Merchant of Venice *is conflicting economic ideals rather than race or religion. The critic argues that* **Shylock** *hates* **Antonio** *not only because he lends money interest-free, but also because he denigrates Shylock's profession and thwarts his business. According to Draper, Shakespeare is merely representative of his age when he idealistically compares* **Antonio's** *Christian business ethic with* **Shylock's** *more rigid and unforgiving value system. This fundamental distinction, the critic concludes, reflects "the difficult transition from the medieval economic system to modern capitalism" which was occurring in Elizabethan England.*]

The character portrayal of Shakespeare shows the widest human sympathy, but Shylock is an exception. He is an object of loathing and contempt; he is depicted as unprincipled in business and unfeeling in his home. In the end he pays a terrible penalty, even more severe than does his prototype in *Il Pecorone*, the probable source of the play, or indeed in any of the other versions of the old folk tale; and no one, not even the kindly Antonio, says a single word in his favor: the dramatist apparently expected his audience to be even more unsympathetic toward Shylock than toward the notorious Richard III, whose overthrow had brought to the throne the glorious House of Tudor. This unwonted *saeva indignatio* [furious indignation] of Shakespeare is usually attributed to an anti-Semiticism inherited from the Middle Ages and kept alive by the illegal presence of Jews in London and especially aroused at the time by the alleged attempt in 1594 of Lopez, the court physician, to poison the Queen. As a matter of fact, however, the prejudice of the Middle Ages must have been dying out, even in clerical circles, for under Cromwell the Jews were permitted to return; moreover, such few Spaniards of Jewish descent as lived in London had long since been converted to at least outward Catholic conformity, and so were indistinguishable from other Spaniards; and the *cause célèbre* [celebrated case] of Lopez, though perhaps the occasion for one or two anti-Jewish plays, is too far removed both from Shakespeare's character and from his plot to have furnished the chief motive for either. Shylock, the Machiavellian Jew, would seem, indeed, to have been a study not in Elizabethan realism but in Italian local color; for Italy, especially Venice where the Jews were go-betweens in the Turkish trade, had become, since their expulsion from Spain, their chief refuge in Western Europe. Merely as a Jew, therefore, Shylock could hardly call forth the contemptuous abhorrence manifest in the play, for that side of his character was the stuff of exotic romance; and, furthermore, Shakespeare's one appeal to the sympathy of the audience for Shylock is the latter's defense of his race and religion: "Hath not a *Iew* eyes? hath not a *Iew* hands, organs, dementions. . . . ?" [cf. III. i. 59-60].

The conflict between Shylock and Antonio is not so much a matter of religion but rather of mercantile ideals, as Shylock declares in an aside at the entrance of Antonio:

> I hate him for he is a Christian:
> *But more,* for that in low simplicitie
> He lends out money gratis, and brings
> downe
> The rate of vsance here with vs in *Venice.*
>   [I. iii. 42-5]

The audience is amply informed that Shylock hates Antonio because the latter has called him "Usurer," and spat upon him, and "thwarted" his "bargaines"; and Antonio openly glories in having cast such slurs. Upon the Rialto he has railed at Shylock, not for religion, but for usury—as Shylock puts it, "all for vse of that which is mine owne" [I. iii. 113]. In the crucial third act, Shylock twice reiterates this theme; and Antonio himself assures the audience:

> He seeks my life, his reason well I know;
> I oft deliuered from his forfeitures
> Many that haue at times made mone to
> me,
> Therefore he hates me.
>   [III. i. 21-4]

Race and religion, then, are not the main theme of the play; it is rather conflicting economic ideals. In Elizabethan parlance, "usurer" meant anyone who took even the lowest interest on money. Antonio follows the medieval ideal, and, like Chaucer's Merchant [in *The Canterbury Tales*], is supposed "neither to lend nor borrow" [cf. I. iii. 61] at interest; and Shylock, like the modern capitalist, makes interest the very basis of his business.

Again and again, in Shakespeare, this allusion to usury recurs, and commonly with a fling at its un-

Christian ethics and its bitter consequences. It is "forbidden"; and the usurer is a simile of shame; the citizens in *Coriolanus* are outraged that the senators pass "edicts for usury to support usurers" [*Coriolonus,* I. i. 82]; and *Timon* is full of attacks upon the system as undermining the Christian virtues and the state. In other Elizabethan dramatists also the usurer is a common object of hatred shading into contemptuous ridicule. Partly classical, partly medieval in origin, he is often, like Vice in the old Morality plays, both wicked and comic: Shylock is clearly in this tradition, and follows directly upon Marlowe's Barabas [in *The Jew of Malta*] who also combines moneylender and Italianate Jew. The widespread currency of this theme and the intensity of emotion that it aroused suggest that it could not have been purely a dramatic convention, and that it struck closer home to the Elizabethans than a mere medieval tradition or a bit of Venetian local color. Like the *miles gloriosus* [boastful soldier], the Elizabethan usurer owes something to Latin comedy; but, like Falstaff, Shylock is more than a classical survival: if not a characteristic London type, he at least exemplified an immediate and crying problem, the iniquity of English usurers and the interest that they charged; and this theme in *The Merchant of Venice* can hardly be the accidental petrified remains of Shakespeare's "clerical predecessor," the author of the lost play *The Jew;* for it is too prominent both in this and in other plays by Shakespeare.

Indeed, the question of the moral and the legal justification of interest came close home to every Elizabethan, and was crucial in the transition from feudal society to modern capitalism. The hardships of this transition appear in the "misery and squalor" of the age. Gold was pouring into Europe from America; prices were rising, and merchants grew rich, but classes with fixed incomes suffered intensely. The rural aristocracy, whom political life was drawing to London, could no longer live directly off the produce of their estates, but required ample supplies of ready money, which they had to borrow at an interest inflated by competition with the merchants who could afford to pay exorbitant rates. Even miners, weavers, and other classes of artisans worked on small loans often at ruinous interest. The increasing need for large capital, both in industry and in commerce, required similar large-scale organization of finance; and the devolution of the medieval guilds, begun by the exactions of Henry VII and continued during the sixteenth century, put much of this business into the hands of almost unregulated individuals or of new organizations. The players themselves sometimes had reason to be bitter at the demands of [Rose Theatre manager Philip] Henslowe and others who supplied them with buildings and furnishings; and thus both audience and actors had personal motives for hating the usurer. (pp. 37-41)

Shakespeare . . . took the regular attitude of the

1590's. Indeed, most revelatory of the dramatist's point of view are the excuses that Shylock gives for his trade . . . Like the devil, he quotes Scripture to his purpose, though the audience doubtless had by memory more than one text that forbade it. He parodies Aristotle's attack on usury as if it were an argument in favor [cf. I. iii. 76-90]. He declares that he is unjustly hated "all for use of that which is mine owne" [I. iii. 113]; and anyone would have told him that since a usurer's goods were got by a sort of theft, they were not his own. Of course, it was this feeling on the part of the audience that justified the treatment of Shylock at the dénouement. He calls Antonio a "prodigall," though the term is clearly misapplied; for usurers preyed on the youthful heirs of noble families, and so, to the horror of the age, brought ruin on ancient houses. He hates Antonio for reducing the rate of interest "here with us in *Venice*" [I. iii. 45], and so upholds the extortionate charges of the day. With a callous presumption, he publicly demands "justice" for his compounded iniquities; he calls upon his oath in a "heaven" whose law he flouts; and he claims the support of the Venetian commonwealth, whose well-being his practices were supposed to undermine. To the Elizabethans all this was mordant casuistry; and, by making Shylock himself call up almost every argument against his own way of life, Shakespeare, with keen dramatic irony, implies that not one honest word can be said in his favor. For Shylock the Jew, there is no such rationale of bitterness; and so utter and thorough a philippie [tirade] must surely have been intentional.

Not only does *The Merchant of Venice* reflect the Elizabethan attitude toward interest, but the details of the play constantly refer to current business customs. Such a "merry bond," signed under pretense of friendliness, was not without precedent in actual fact. Bassanio, to seal the bargain, follows the usual etiquette of asking the lender to dine; and later Shylock actually goes to a feast, like a true usurer, to help use up the borrowed sum and so insure a forfeiture. . . . Shylock, moreover, carefully avoids the term "usury," is insulted at being called a "usurer," and, with an exquisite delicacy, objects even to having his "well won thrift" [I. iii. 50] described as "interest"—though this euphemism was commonly allowed by contemporary moneylenders. London usurers—perhaps because they had risen from poverty by extreme penuriousness—were supposed to run their households in a stingy, not to say starvling, expenditure; and Shylock and Gobbo mutually complain of each other in this regard. Usurers regularly wished the forfeiture rather than the repayment of the loan; and in [Thomas] Lodge's [*Looking-glasse for London and England*], the young gentleman, like Bassanio, offers much more than the nominated sum; but the moneylender, like Shylock, refuses and demands the forfeiture. Contemporary London, therefore, would seem to have supplied both the commercial decorum and the business trickery of Shake-

speare's Venice; and this suggests that the dramatist intended to bring before his audience with immediate realism his economic theme.

Even the idealized Antonio reflects Elizabethan London. He "was wont to lend out money for a Christian curtsie" [III. i. 49], according to the highest ethics of the age . . . The comparison of Antonio to a "royal Merchant" suggests England as well as Venice; for the London merchants had grown rich, and in their "comely entertainment" were not to be "matched by any foreign opposition." Hunter, on Shylock's word, declared that Antonio condemned interest "through simplicity," and that, as Shylock says, he was a "prodigal" wasting an ample patrimony [in *The Merchant of Venice,* ed. H. H. Furness]; but the dramatist clearly expects us to admire his probity rather than condemn his ignorance and waste. . . . As a matter of fact, Antonio knew well the exactions of usurers, and realized that if he would accommodate his friend, he must accept hard terms. Elsewhere he appears as a skilful merchant who does not risk his "whole estate Upon the fortune of this present yeere" [I. i. 43-4]; and, like a shrewd man of affairs, he does not seem overanxious early in the play to divulge his business secrets. He is, indeed, the ideal merchant, very much as Othello and Henry V are the ideal of army life; and, just as Shakespeare heightened his effect by contrasting Hotspur and Prince Hal with the poltroonery of Falstaff [in *1 Henry IV*], so, in *The Merchant of Venice,* he put Shylock and Antonio side by side as comparative studies in business ethics.

Shylock the Jew was merely exotic local color; Shylock the usurer was a commentary on London life. The moneylender had been hated for centuries; and, in Shakespeare's day, the difficult transition from the medieval economic system to modern capitalism especially subjected both rich and poor to his exactions. Efforts to find realism in Shylock have generally looked to Venice or the Orient—regions of which Shakespeare knew none too much and the groundlings even less: the crux of the play is nearer home; and it reflects the current uses of commercial life and the current attitude toward them. Nevertheless, *The Merchant of Venice* is not strictly a problem play like *All's Well,* or even mainly one as is *Othello,* for it is written *ex parte* [from a one-sided point of view]; to Shakespeare there is but one answer, and so there is no problem; and, moreover, the old stories upon which it is founded dictated a happy ending that forbade the logical conclusion of the theme and kept the play a romantic comedy; but, to the Elizabethans, it had a verve and realism that is lost upon the present reader. Just as the stories of the romances were changed and reinterpreted century by century, so Shakespeare gave timely significance and telling vividness to his borrowed origins; and this intensified reality is perhaps his chief contribution to Elizabethan drama. Usually the matrix from which his play developed was a plot, as in *King Lear;* sometimes both plot and character, as in *Henry V;* and, on this matrix, he built a drama that, almost certainly in details of setting and style and often in motivation and theme, shows the immediate impress of his age. *Julius Caesar* is full of English setting; the background and motives of Desdemona [in *Othello*] are thoroughly Elizabethan; in *Twelfth Night* he transplanted an English household and staff of servants to the confines of Illyria; the character of Falstaff is a realistic foil to the romantic wars of chivalry; and, in *Merry Wives,* even the plot would seem to have been borrowed from common contemporary situations. *The Merchant of Venice* is a romantic comedy built of old folk material, to which has been added a realistic theme and motivation; and this theme, although Shakespeare has not yet learned to make it entirely implicit in his plot, obviously portrays the downfall of hated usury and the triumph of Christian charity in the person of a princely merchant. (pp. 43-7)

> John W. Draper, "Usury in 'The Merchant of Venice'," in Modern Philology, Vol. XXXIII, No. 1, August, 1935, pp. 37-47.

DUALITIES

Marvin Felheim

[*Felheim identifies several dualities in* The Merchant of Venice, *including joy and sadness, Venice and Belmont, Jew versus Christian, and Old Testament justice against New Testament mercy. According to the critic, the play opens with inexplicable sadness, primarily present in the characters of* **Antonio** *and* **Portia.** **Bassanio,** **Salerio,** *and* **Solanio** *interrupt the initial seriousness of the dramatic action with some mirth, Felheim continues, but for the most part a strain of melancholy pervades the play. Perhaps the most concrete example of this duality is embodied in the contrasting worlds of Venice and Belmont. Sadness is the prominent emotion in Venice, the critic notes, where the characters are exposed to usury and legal proceedings; but in Belmont, the "world of candlelight and music," happiness reigns. The oppositions of Jew and Christian as well as of Old Testament and New Testament attitudes are uncovered in the initial rivalry between* **Antonio** *and* **Shylock,** *increase the dramatic tension in the "pound of flesh" episodes, and culminate in the trial scene (Act IV, scene i). Shakespeare develops this opposition between Old Testament and New Testament values in the characters of* **Shylock,** *who represents law and vengeance, and* **Portia,** *who signifies love and mercy. Felheim also examines three significant episodes in* The Merchant of Venice—*the bond plot, the casket plot, and the ring plot—describing their significance to the overall structure of the play.*]

Certainly *The Merchant of Venice* is one of the most challenging of Shakespeare's plays. At first glance, the great court scene with Portia's justly famous speech on mercy and the lovely concluding act, so full of good will and magnificent poetry, seem to give the play its core of meaning: Christian charity and human love will and should triumph; three joyous couples and the merchant of Venice himself are at Belmont to celebrate victory and weddings.

But, on reflection, there are many disturbing elements to upset this all-too-easy view. For one thing, the play opens with inexplicable sadness; for another, the three principal characters—Antonio, Portia and Shylock—are shown more in seriousness than in joy; finally, their seriousness is tinged with a most unsettling kind of melancholy. In the very opening line, Antonio tells us: "In sooth, I know not why I am so sad" [I. i. 1]. He then rejects the suggestions of Salerio and Solanio who offer conventional explanations: worry over his "merchandise," love, and "because you are not merry" [I. i. 48] (a "humourous" explanation). True, Antonio seems to emerge from his melancholy with the appearance of his friend and relative, Bassanio. But we must note that Bassanio confronts him not merely with the face of friendship and kinship but with serious financial problems. So, his change of mood is prompted in large part by the need for his services as financier as much as (more than?) his position as friend and kinsman. Throughout the play, moreover, we never see Antonio in what might be called a merry mood, for almost immediately troubles, in the form of loss of his argosies and the resultant law suit, beset him. And the final moments of triumph are not really his: the saving of his life in Act IV is subordinated, dramatically, to Portia's success as a disguised Doctor of Laws, to the sentencing of Shylock, and to the exchanging of the rings; indeed, at the very moment when his life has been saved, Antonio must turn his attention to thanking Balthazar (Portia) and to persuading Bassanio "to let him have the ring" [IV. i. 449]. Then, in Act V, Antonio is by no means either the central figure or the most joyous. Portia apologizes for her seeming lack of courtesy and hospitality—

> Sir, you are very welcome to our house.
> It must appear in other ways than words,
> Therefore I scant this breathing courtesy—
>
> [V. i. 139-41]

only to become embroiled at once in the question of the rings; again, Antonio must pledge himself for Bassanio, only this time he binds his "soul" rather than his flesh to assure Portia that her husband "Will never more break faith advisedly" [V. i. 253].

Lastly, in the distribution of favors, Portia discloses that she has "better news in store" for him than he expects and she gives him a "letter."

> There you shall find three of your argosies
> Are richly come to harbour suddenly,
> [V. i. 276-77]

but she adds, enigmatically,

> You shall not know by what strange acci-
> dent
> I chanced on this letter,
> [V. i. 278-79]

a curious, somewhat callous attitude which belies the very assertion of friendliness and hospitality she had made earlier. Antonio's reply, less than half a line, is "I am dumb" [V. i. 279]; he even has difficulty in squeezing these three simple words in between Portia's disclosures and Bassanio's and Gratiano's amazement at their wives' virtuosity. To cap his pleasure, Antonio is finally permitted three more lines:

> Sweet lady, you have given me life and liv-
> ing;
> For here I read for certain that my ships
> Are safely come to road.
> [V. i. 286-88]

Thus the role of the merchant of Venice is conclud-ed. One feels that perhaps Salerio was correct in his original diagnosis: that Antonio's sadness was because his "mind is tossing on the ocean" [I. i. 8]. At any event, in this comedy labelled *The Merchant of Venice* one must agree that the merchant him-self has rough sailing, that he opens the play a man wearied and sad, that he endures great tribu-lations and a serious trial in which his life is nearly taken, that his survival is merely a part of more ex-citing goings-on and that his eventual triumph is simply the inexplicable return of his ships. Indeed, he seems doomed, as he states initially:

> But how I caught it [sadness], found it, or
> came by it,
> What stuff 'tis made of, whereof it is born,
> I am to learn.
> [I. i. 3-5]

This notion appears to have had its origin in his (typically Shakespearean) philosophy:

> I hold the world but as the world, Gra-
> tiano,
> A stage where every man must play a part,
> And mine a sad one.
> [I. i. 77-9]

Thus isolated, the merchant appears a pathetic fig-ure. I have not questioned here his goodness, his willingness to help others and his mercy to Shy-lock; presumably these qualities could provide him with a kind of quiet glow. But there is no indication that his initial unexplained sadness is ever miti-gated or that the similarly unexplained return of

his merchandise at the conclusion will do much to make him happy, for as he predicted

> . . .such a want-wit sadness
> makes of me
> That I have much ado to know myself.
> [I. i. 6-7]

Antonio is not alone in proclaiming his sadness, however. Portia's first speech picks up the theme: "By my troth, Nerissa, my little body is aweary of this great world" [I. ii. 1]. As in the case of Antonio, her statement suggests a kind of cosmic condition. And like Salerio and Solanio, Nerissa offers an ex-planation: that Portia has an "abundance" of "good fortunes," that she is simply too rich, sur-feited and bored. But the Lady of Belmont rejects her maid's "good sentences." Her sadness has an-other cause: her father's will which has effectively "curbed" her choice of a husband. It is a mark of Shakespeare's subtle art that he puts these speeches of Portia and Nerissa in prose, just where one would expect poetry, whereas the opening speeches on "A Street. Venice" are in poetry. The purpose is not only to contrast the different types of melancholy in scenes one and two, but to estab-lish, as well, the contrary nature of this play and to suggest that both a mingling of poetry with the business world of Venice and a prose basis for the beauty of Belmont are necessary conditions.

Finally, sadness is also typical of Shylock. The elopement of his daughter with a Christian, the loss of money and the punishments he suffers in court are calamitous episodes in his pathetic life. Clearly, then, a strain of melancholy pervades this comedy and conditions the over-all tone of the play. In this connection I feel that the concluding act, too, despite its apparent joyousness, has overtones of despair, even bitterness. As the last act begins, Jessica and Lorenzo are discussing love and na-ture: "The moon shines bright. In such a night as this" [V. i. 1] lovers have enjoyed . . . what? Well, Troilus "mounted the Troyan walls, / And sigh'd his soul toward the Grecian tents" [V. i. 4-5]; This-by did "fearfully o'ertrip the dew, / And saw the lion's shadow . . ., / And ran dismayed away" [V. i. 7-9]; Dido stood "Upon the wild sea-banks, and waft her love / To come again to Carthage" [V. i. 10-12]; and Medea "gathered the enchanted herbs / That did renew old Aeson" [V. i. 13-14]. Hardly a happy couple among the four. These lines, full of melancholy accounts of tragic loves and lovers, have been much praised, but most critics have failed to note that neither the subject matter nor the love affairs referred to give us a felicitious pic-ture of love; on the contrary, the content of the lines is at odds with the situation itself (although Jessi-ca and Lorenzo include themselves in the list of lov-ers) and casts a disturbing, howbeit lovely, tone over the moonlit scene. This mood, after an inter-lude on the nature of music, gives way to the work-ings-out of the ring plot. And so the act which began with reminiscences about unhappy loves and lovers concludes with the cynical resolution of the ring story.

Counter to all this sadness there is mirth, and there are joyous characters. Bassanio, Salerio and Solanio are consistently optimistic and cheerful, Bassanio particularly so in the face of odds. The course of the love affair between Jessica and Lorenzo runs smoothly, without a hitch. Portia, herself, has periods of intense happiness (in Bassanio's success in choosing the correct casket), of witty triumph (over the unsuccessful suitors) and of joyful satisfaction (both in court and in the final confrontation at Belmont). This beautifully maintained balance is characteristic of *The Merchant of Venice;* indeed, in this play, contrast is the primary dramaturgical method.

The setting provides the most obvious contrast: the Rialto and Belmont, the world of Venice, of usury, of the court, and the world of candlelight and music that is Belmont. We note that certain characteristics of the former place, the Rialto, are present in the latter; there are commercial and material aspects to Belmont, too; the dead, but legal, hand of a wealthy father lies heavily upon this rich world, the prize gem of which is Portia herself, the lady of the "sunny locks" which "Hang on her temples like a golden fleece" [I. i. 170]. Her riches, her beauty and her virtue are, in truth, like the rocks which shipwreck so many Venetian argosies. Even at the moment of Bassanio's triumph over the riddle of the caskets, the speeches of the lovers are replete with commercial terms; he says:

> Fair lady, by your leave;
> I came by *note,* to *give* and to *receive,*
> [III. ii. 139-40]

but he cannot be sure of his success

> Until *confirm'd, sign'd, ratified* by you.
> [III. ii. 148]

She replies, in part,

> That only to *stand high* in your *account*
> I might in virtues, beauties, *livings,* friends
> *Exceed account.* But the full *sum* of me
> Is *sum of something.* . . .
> [III. ii. 156-59]

By introducing into Belmont these symbolic elements from the commercial world of Venice, Shakespeare fuses two aspects of life; they are not separate, the Rialto and Belmont, however much they may be geographically distinct. Bassanio is the "arrow . . . adventuring" from one world into the other; in return, Portia brings wisdom, judgment, and poetry to Venice. The significant linkage of the two in marriage indicates the extent to which the two must be joined in order to exist; each is dependent upon the other and insofar as this is true this comedy presents us with the ultimate in realism: the acknowledgement that these worlds not only coexist but *must* coexist; this is the

human condition, pictured without unnecessary sentimentality, with the romantic elements occupying their proper place, coordinated with the other elements, neither isolated nor superior but equal. The result is what can be called Shakespeare's comic vision, as steady a view of life as is possible, a world of sorrows and joys but essentially human, where even wedded love must wait upon more pressing obligations, where disguise, deception and cynicism can live side by side with sweeter qualities, where contrast and combination are the essential reality.

The delicate balancing of these contrasting elements is Shakespeare's great dramatic skill. And this device pervades the play. For example, there are the human contrasts between parents and children, specifically fathers and children, and between masters and servants. In the later category fit, for instance, Portia and her servants, Nerissa and Balthasar; when Portia disguises herself as a lawyer, to preach the gospel of charity, it seems significant that Shakespeare gives her the name of her servant, Balthazar. Shylock, on the other hand, speaks slightingly of the way Venetians treat some of their servants, those who are "purchas'd slaves," which

> . . . like your asses and your dogs and
>   mules,
> You use in abject and in slavish parts.
> [IV. i. 91-2]

He sets up, as he always does, an absolute of behavior, an Old Testament absolute, against which the action plays. He carries the argument to an extreme: masters become owners, servants slaves. Our sympathies, as usual, are engaged by his characteristic manner. And we realize that he has made a telling point: that he also wants what is his, what he has bought and paid for. But his example also has the effect of setting up the opposite, the ideal, the world beyond Venice (an aspect, perhaps, of Belmont) where there are neither owners nor slaves. What inevitably happens when Shylock talks is that we are confronted with an ideal situation—where there would be no discrimination, no hatred or fear, no cruelty or inhumanity. But such a condition is always predicated in terms of opposites and in almost strictly legal terms, a world, on the one hand, where there is legal usury or, on the other, none at all. Reality—the world of legal usury which must be tempered by human charity—is the world Shylock rejects (or which rejects Shylock). (pp. 94-8)

All these contrasts, whether of physical settings or of human characteristics, have a common basis in the central moral contrast of the play. This contrast is variously embodied, but is nowhere more clear than in the confrontation of Shylock and Portia, specifically in the way in which each suggests one aspect of the Bible, Shylock appropriately the Old Testament and Portia aptly the New. For Shylock the world exists in terms of absolutes, in terms of justice, in terms of Old Testament morality. This approach is most interestingly summarized in his story of Jacob and Laban's sheep: "... thrift is blessing, if men steal it not" [I. iii. 85]. Or, as he tells Jessica, "Fast bind, fast find"—[II. v. 53]. For Shylock there can be no compromise: "all the eanlings which were streak'd and pied / Should fall as Jacob's hire" [I. iii. 79-80]; this is the rule. Human beings are subservient to law, to an absolute code. So he sets up his frame of reference. What makes Antonio evil in Shylock's eyes is that "He was wont to lend money for a Christian courtesy" [III. i. 49]; Antonio was a man who behaved contrary to the customs of the Rialto (could this possibly be the cause of his sadness? his capacity to see the human condition and yet to act independently in terms of friendship and courtesy? is his a cosmic sadness?). And what should be done about him? Shylock, the Jew, the avenging arm of Jehovah, would act: "revenge," both in terms of Old Testament standards and in light of Christian behavior; "The villainy you teach me I will execute" [III. i. 71-2]. Such a philosophy knows no compromise: "I say my daughter is my flesh and my blood" [III. i. 37] asserts Shylock (Jessica has already added the human corollary: "Though I am a daughter to his blood I am not to his manners" [II. iii. 18-19]): further, rather than adjust to the world he insists "I would my daughter were dead at my foot, and the jewels in her ear; would she were hears'd at my foot, and the ducats in her coffin" [III. i. 87-90]. This explains, too, his concern for his money, which, like his daughter, like Jacob's sheep, is his and his alone. He exists only on this level. "I crave the law" [IV. i. 206], he cries; "I am a Jew" [III. i. 58], he states. Could anything be more clear?

As usual, Shakespeare does not stop here. For one thing, he has the advantage of writing at a time when the Jew's place in society was enigmatical, so, in the social sense alone, the role of a Jew cannot be seen simply from a one-dimensional point of view. The Jew, in the Renaissance world, was hedged about with restrictions and superstitions, so that neither his role nor his place in society were clear-cut; Shakespeare has all the advantage of this complex situation. Further, Shylock is, in a dramatic sense, a type character; he is the Old Vice, he is the "humour" character. He evidences this role, for example, in a typically Shakespearean way, in his attitude toward music and gaiety. For, when he learns that there are to be "masques" he warns Jessica against "the drum / And the vile squealing of the wry-neck'd fife" [II. v. 29-30], and orders her

> Let not the sound of shallow fopp'ry enter
> My sober house.
>
> [II. v. 34-5]

His dislike for music marks him as a "villain," had not Salerio and Solanio already used the term to abuse him. But it remains for his new son-in-law, Lorenzo, to put the situation into proper philosophical and poetic terms. As he tells Jessica,

> The man that hath no music in himself,
> Nor is mov'd with concord of sweet sounds,
> Is fit for treasons, stratagems, and spoils.
>
> [V. i. 83-5]

How like Shapespeare to give us both the theory and the reality.

Opposing Shylock is Portia. She stands for Christian charity and mercy—with some human variations (she can, for example, be most caustic about her suitors). Shakespeare shows us her essential character in two significant scenes, one when Bassanio chooses the lead casket and the other in the court in Venice. Like other comic heroines, particularly Rosalind and Viola [in *As You Like It* and *Twelfth Night*], Portia is no demure, passive lady. Forced by the provisions of her father's will to wait for her true lover, she knows in advance whom she wants. In answer to Nerissa's inquiry—"Do you remember, lady, in your father's time, a Venetian, a scholar and a soldier?" [cf. I. ii. 112-13].—she blurts out, "Yes, yes, it was Bassanio" [I. ii. 115], before her maidenly reserve prompts her to add "as I think, so was he call'd" [I. ii. 115-16] And when Bassanio arrives, decked though he may be in borrowed garments, she begs him to "tarry" awhile.

> I could teach you
> How to choose right
>
> [III. ii. 10-11]

she proposes, then withdraws her offer (it would be perjury) only to proclaim:

> One half of me is yours, the other half yours.
>
> [III. ii. 16]

Then, she orders:

> Let music sound while he doth make his choice
>
> [III. ii. 43]

(for Morocco and Arragon there had been only a "Flourish of Cornets"). And when, at last, Bassanio makes the right choice,

> And here choose I. Joy be the consequence!
>
> [III. ii. 107]

her speech rises to the proper pitch, for she is

> Happy in this, she is not yet so old
> But she may learn; happier than this,
> She is not bred so dull but she can learn;
> Happiest of all is that her gentle spirit
> Commits itself to yours to be directed,
> As from her lord, her governor, her king.
>
> [III. ii. 161-66]

Shakespeare preserves the human equilibrium by having her conclude this speech with the giving of the "ring," thereby setting up the somewhat lewd but earthly antithesis to all this lofty eloquence.

But it is in the courtroom that Portia reaches the apex; here, she truly embodies the spirit of Christian charity; for, as she makes clear,

> . . . earthly power doth then show likest God's
> When mercy seasons justice.
> [IV. i. 191-92]

Ironically, it is not she ("He shall have merely justice" [IV. i. 339] she decides) but the Duke and Antonio who practice what she has preached. But, here again, Shakespeare shows his great wisdom, his sense of decorum and reality, which allows the head of the state, the Duke, to be the God-like dispenser of mercy; Portia, having served as the agent of justice, reverts to the clever, somewhat niggling young heroine, concerned about her "ring." It is certainly notable, too, that Shakespeare chooses to present the voice of mercy in disguise. True enough, he had convention (the boy actor) and his source (Ser Giovanni's *Il Pecorone*) as a basis for so doing. But the fact that the words urging divine mercy are uttered in Venice under the cloak of a disguise is still significant. Is Shakespeare saying that mercy cannot come into the real world except it be protected by disguise? One remembers, as well, that Jessica and Lorenzo, two of the symbols of love in this play, cannot live and love in Venice, but must also resort to disguise in order to escape the realities of the city. Apparently only in Belmont can love and mercy exist without false faces, like the candle's beams ("So shines a good deed in a naughty world" [V. i. 91]), but here, too, we recollect, is the lead casket which contains a golden treasure and here, too, are the "rings," symbols of physical love. So the total picture is inevitably complex. And the motto for all might well be the lines spoken by Bassanio as he gazes at the caskets:

> The world is still deceiv'd with ornament.
> In law, what plea so tainted and corrupt
> But, being season'd with a gracious voice,
> Obscures the show of evil? In religion,
> What damned error but some sober brow
> Will bless it, and approve it with a text,
> Hiding the grossness with fair ornament?
> [III. ii. 74-80]

There is another device which serves Shakespeare as a variation to his either/or presentation of comedy, a trinitarian concept. Superimposed upon the basic contrasts or duality, there are innumerable threesomes. There are three young women, two Christians and a Jew; consequently, three pairs of lovers. Antonio and Bassanio have three friends, the pair, Solanio and Salerio, and Gratiano. There are three Jews, Tubal and Chus, in addition to Shylock. Portia has three suitors, the Princes of Morocco and Arragon, who fail, and Bassanio, who succeeds. Further, the whole play is based on three plots: bond, casket, rings. The bond is for three

Sinead Cusack as Portia sits before the three caskets in a 1978 Royal Shakespeare Theatre production of The Merchant of Venice.

thousand ducats for three months. There are three caskets, of gold, silver and lead. Later, Bassanio has three reasons for giving away Portia's ring ("to whom . . . for whom . . . for what . . ."), which arguments Portia parries with three of her own. In addition, in the last act, Portia has three letters which bring knowledge and rewards. But this concept of trinity is most noticeable in the phrasing. Antonio, speaking of his sadness, knows not "how I caught it, found it, or came by it" [I. i. 4]. Solanio and Salerio, as has been pointed out, offer in turn three "causes." Portia, "thrice-fair lady" is, to Bassinio, a trinity: rich, fair, virtuous. Just so, Jessica, according to Lorenzo, is "wise, fair, and true" [II. vi. 56]. Shylock hates Antonio for three reasons, because he is a Christian, because "he lends out money gratis" [I. iii. 44] and because "he hates our sacred nation" [I. iii. 48]. Morocco has a scimitar which slew "a Persian prince / That won three fields," [II. i. 25-6], whereas Arragon enunciates the "three things" he and other suitors are "enjoined by oath to observe" [II. ix. 9]. In a climactic scene Portia "commits" herself to Bassanio, "her lord, her governor, her king" [III. ii. 165]. Bassanio later offers a "forfeit of my hands, my head, my heart" [IV. i. 212] if Shylock will accept his offer to save Antonio. Even Launcelot refers to himself as "your boy that was, your son that is, your child that shall be" [II. ii. 85]. This constant use of triads lends both a consistency and a rhythm to the play. As a result of the playing of triads against a basic pattern of one-for-one contrast a rich and varied counterpoint emerges. (pp. 99-102)

A few final words remain to be said about the over-all plotting, for in this regard, too, *The Merchant of Venice* is an unusual play. For a comedy, the themes of this work are extraordinarily serious and profound; they plumb the depths of human behavior and human character. The enigmatic nature of Shylock, himself, to say nothing of, for example, Jessica or Gratiano, who frequently seems simply a loudmouthed oaf, has troubled many readers. The play's wonderful poetry, some of it among the best Shakespeare ever wrote, sets it apart from other early and middle comedies such as *The Taming of the Shrew* or *Much Ado about Nothing*. Yet after all its superiorities have been enumerated, *The Merchant of Venice* remains in some ways a crude effort. The over-all machinery consists of three obvious, somewhat vulgar plots: the bond plot, the casket plot, the ring plot. All have been much handled and Shakespeare manipulates them rather mechanically.

The bond plot, resulting from Antonio's willingness to help Bassanio but his inability to meet the practical need other than through Shylock, is established first. It can be said to begin in Act I, scene i, and yields precedence only to the theme of sadness. The bond plot is resolved in the court scene, Act IV, scene i, except that one of its by-products (the "deed of gift" [IV. i. 394] for Lorenzo and Jessica) carries over into the final act of the play. This plot concerns mostly Antonio and Shylock; the latter disappears from the action, unwell, at the conclusion of the courtroom scene; Antonio "hangs" around through Act V, not completely cured of his melancholia, a figure of Venice, somewhat out of place in the festive world of Belmont.

The casket plot begins, interestingly, in Act I, scene ii. Although Bassanio has, in scene i, approached Antonio with a request for three thousand ducats to enable him "to hold a rival place" [I. i. 174] among Portia's suitors, he does not mention that his success will hinge upon a "lott'ry," as Nerissa calls it. So not until we meet Portia and Nerissa in scene ii is the casket plot fully set forth. From that point on, until Act III, scene ii, when Bassanio chooses correctly, the scenes developing this story, all set in Belmont, more or less alternate with those connected with the bond plot. In a technical sense, the casket plot could be considered the main plot since it is the one which terminates or is resolved in what is traditionally the climactic act, III. The casket plot has a number of interesting overtones. For one thing, the whole situation vis-à-vis the caskets is based upon the will of Portia's dead father. Certainly she chafes a bit under its restraints: "so is the will of a living daughter curb'd by the will of a dead father" [I. ii. 24-5], she remarks; one may

even conjecture that her sadness is the result of this confinement although Nerissa, probably more correctly, attributes her "sickness" to "surfeit." One wonders, incidentally, why Portia suffers when it would seem reasonable to suggest that her legal acumen should enable her to get around the provisions; at any event, she doesn't suffer long; moreover, she balances whatever unpleasantness does exist with a degree of levity and a certain amount of vituperative cynicism at the expense of the suitors themselves. One particular requirement of the will carries a certain threat with it— that is, the requirement that the suitor if he "choose wrong" must agree

> Never to speak to lady afterward
> In way of marriage.
>
> [II. ii. 41-2]

The casket plot builds mechanically to its conclusion, from the scene when Portia reviews the demerits of the present group of aspirants, through the two unsuccessful attempts of Morocco [II. vii.] and Arragon [II. ix.] to the third trial, the success of Bassanio. To heighten the mechanistic aspects of this plot, Shakespeare uses at least one external device, sound effects. For Morocco and Arragon, there is a "Flourish of Cornets" [II. vii. and II. ix.]; for Bassanio, there is music, the lovely song, "Where is fancy bred?" [III. ii. 63ff.]. Bassanio's character and chances are presumably enhanced by this tribute. At one point, too, during the interview with the Prince of Arragon, the "three things . . . enjoin'd by oath" [cf. II. ix. 9] upon all suitors are enumerated (as a possible parallel with the details of the bond?):

> First, never to unfold to any one
> Which casket 'twas I chose; next, if I fail
> Of the right casket, never in my life
> To woo a maid in way of marriage;
> Lastly,
> If I do fail in fortune of my choice,
> Immediately to leave you and be gone.
>
> [II. ix. 10-16]

These requirements do, indeed, smack of the harsh commercial world of the Rialto; they certainly establish a kind of absolute mood over Belmont and its "golden fleece."

The ring plot takes up exactly where the casket one ends, for with Bassanio's success [III. ii.], Portia not only cedes to him herself and her fortune, but "I give them with this ring" [III. ii. 171] and then she adds three (again magic?) restrictions

> Which when you part from, lose, or give
>   away
> Let it presage the ruin of your love.
>
> [III. ii. 174-75]

The working out of this story is accomplished in two subsequent actions: the first at court and immediately afterwards on "a street" in Venice, and the second at Belmont. The situation is not actually resolved until the final lines of the play itself. If the bond plot sets up the central contrast of the play (justice versus mercy) and if the casket plot establishes the quality of love necessary for a happy marriage, the ring plot certainly undermines some of the ideals of the play. It allows bawdyness, even on the part of Portia; it reduces the marriages and victory at court to a series of double entendres on the nature of chastity in marriage; it puts an extremely realistic, even cynical, conclusion onto a play in which many kinds of problems and many kinds of people have been exposed to searching poetic analysis.

The mechanistic aspect of this plotting suggests that *The Merchant of Venice* might best be analyzed in light of the Bergsonian theory of comedy: the notion of men as puppets, manipulated by a higher power. This idea stresses that comedy results from our perception of the limitations placed upon mankind. Such an awareness seems to underlie Nerissa's couplet:

> The ancient saying is no heresy:
> Hanging and Wiving goes by destiny.
> 　　　　　　　　　　　　　　[II. ix. 82-3]

This concept may also be found in the conclusion of *The Merry Wives of Windsor* where we find Ford's couplet:

> In love, the heavens themselves do guide
> 　　the state;
> Money buys lands, and wives are sold by
> 　　fate.
> 　　　　　　　　　　　　　[V. v. 219-20]

In *The Merchant of Venice* sacred things, such as marriage and justice, are turned into subjects for or causes of merriment, and human beings are seen as the victims of destiny. The mixture here is what, finally, seems to me significant. For the parts all add up to a complex comic vision in which the unifying theme (and method, too, as I've tried to demonstrate) is realism. Hence Shakespeare's willingness to see all the facets of life and to present them with honesty and understanding. The main thrust of the comic elements in these early plays seems to me to be substantially realistic; even the romantic qualities, as I see them, are a part of this larger concept. (pp. 105-07)

Marvin Felheim, "The Merchant of Venice," in Shakespeare Studies: An Annual Gathering of Research, Criticism, and Reviews, *Vol. 4, 1968, pp. 94-108.*

BOND AND CHOICE

William Leigh Godshalk

[*Godshalk discusses the unity of the* The Merchant of Venice *in terms of the Pound of Flesh story and the Story of the Three Caskets, emphasizing in particular the elements of "bond" and "choice." According to the critic, the characters are bound to each other and to different courses of action in many ways. Aspects of bondage in the play include: the legal bond between* **Antonio** *and* **Shylock**; *the provision in* **Portia**'s *father's will that binds her fortune; the suitors' binding oath forsaking marriage if they fail the casket test; the spiritual bondage of* **Portia** *and* **Bassanio**, **Jessica** *and* **Lorenzo**, *and* **Nerissa** *and* **Gratiano** *to the institution of marriage; and the bonds of friendship and society. Godshalk also examines "choice" as an extension of the "bond" issues, noting that even though the characters are bound by legal constructs, religious vows, and social obligations, they are free to determine into which bonds they enter. Such elements of choice in the play include: the option of three caskets;* **Jessica**'s *choosing to elope with* **Lorenzo**; *and* **Shylock**'s *demand for a pound of flesh in the trial scene (Act IV, scene i). The critic maintains that both the Story of the Three Caskets and the Pound of Flesh story begin with a character legally bound and later released through the choice of another. The casket plot represents a suit of love, Godshalk continues, where* **Bassanio**'s *faith in love is rewarded when he chooses the lead casket and wins* **Portia**. *The trial episode is a suit of revenge in which* **Shylock**'s *merciless demand for justice only leads to his downfall. The critic concludes with a discussion of the ring scene (Act V, scene i) in which Shakespeare ironically dramatizes the issues of "choice" and "bond."*]

[Graham Midgley states in his *"The Merchant of Venice: A Reconsideration," Essays in Criticism* X (1960)]: "The problem of *The Merchant of Venice* has always been its unity, and most critical discussions take this as the centre of their argument, asking what is the relative importance of its two plots and how Shakespeare contrives to interweave them into a unity." The two plots are, of course, the Pound of Flesh Story and the Story of the Three Caskets, and the successful critic must account for Shakespeare's success in molding the two divergent stories into one whole. The strategy of the present study will be to examine both plots to ascertain their basic elements—what these two stories at bottom involve—and then to show how these elements interpenetrate the play as a whole.

The Pound of Flesh Story is found in *The Merchant's* Italian source, *Il Pecorone,* and in outline it is the same in both. In the source and the play, an older man is bound to a Jew so that a younger can obtain enough money to seek an heiress. Shakespeare, however, emphasizes two points not found or emphasized in Ser Giovani's tale. First, Shylock and Antonio are known to each other, and their relationship as financial enemies seems to be an old one. Their enmity stems from an ideological conflict over the morality of usury. Shylock, if you will, is a capitalist, Antonio a socialist; and both claim religious sanction for their economic positions. Second, the bond is emphasized. In the first minutes of his negotiations with Shylock, Bassanio says, "Antonio shall be bound" [I. iii. 4-5]. Throughout the scene, "bound" is used three times and "bond" seven. As Shylock prepares to exit, Antonio assures him, "I will seal unto this bond" [I. iii. 171]. Apparently Shakespeare is at pains to underline the concept of the bond here, and the words "bound" and "bond" echo through the play. Thus, it may be suggested that the Pound of Flesh Story as it is presented in *The Merchant* embodies two basic ideas: personal relationship (enemy to enemy as well as friend to friend) and bondage. And further, uniting the two ideas, we may see that the story is, at very bottom, about the binding of one man to another, with a consequent limitation on complete freedom of action. "And Antonio bound."

The Caskets are not found in *Il Pecorone* and may well have been taken from Robinson's translation of the *Gesta Romanorum*. Here the Emperor asks a young maiden to prove herself worthy of marrying his son by choosing among three caskets of gold, silver, and lead. The same procedure is, of course, used in *The Merchant,* where to prove himself worthy of Portia, the lover must make, under the influence of his love, the proper choice. Both in the source story and in the play, 'choice' is the basic idea in the Casket Story. If one would have that which one desires, one must choose, and in so choosing, one reveals something of one's true self.

In the two basic stories out of which the play grows, there are, then, two underlying ideas: bondage and choice. The theme of the bond in various manifestations proliferates throughout the play and even penetrates the Story of the Caskets. For the characters are bound to each other and to different courses of action in many ways. Most apparent in the play is the legal bond, the bond that gives Antonio to Shylock. But if Antonio is legally bound to the evil will of Shylock, Portia is also legally bound, bound by the last will and testament of a perceptive and loving father. She may complain that "the will of a living daughter" is "curb'd by the will of a dead father" [I. ii. 24-5], but Nerissa is quick to remind her that her "father was ever virtuous, and holy men at their death have good inspirations" [I. ii. 27-8]. Later Portia's words, that her father "hedg'd" her "by his wit" [II. i. 18], suggest that she acknowledges the protection implicit in her bondage. She is protected from her own fancy as well as from external coercion to marry.

Portia's suitors are also bound. She tells Morocco that he must

> swear before you choose, if you
> choose wrong
> Never to speak to lady afterward
> In way of marriage.
>
> [II. i. 40-2]

And they go "forward to the temple" [II. i. 44] so that Morocco may take his oath, and later Arragon takes the same oath [II. ix. 2] before he too comes to make his choice of caskets. In the oaths of the suitors, the legal bond modulates into the religious bond. Again the bondage is formal and the terms are clearly set forth [II. ix. 9-16]. And moreover, the oaths of the suitors adumbrate the self-imposed religious oath of Shylock. He tells Antonio: "I have sworn an oath, that I will have my bond" [III. iii. 5]; and in the trial scene, when Portia asks him to accept "thrice thy money" [IV. i. 227], he replies: "An oath, an oath, I have an oath in heaven,— / Shall I lay perjury upon my soul?" [IV. i. 228-29]. The juxtaposition and inversion of values is ironic, and the point is that Shylock has bound himself religiously to a course of irreligious action.

In contrast, the lovers are bound by their religion in the rites and oaths of marriage. Jessica and Lorenzo are presumably married sometime between their elopement [II. vi] and their arrival in Belmont with Salerio [III. ii]. After choosing the right casket, Bassanio marries Portia. Speaking of herself in the third person, she says to Bassanio: "her gentle spirit / Commits itself to yours to be directed, / As from her lord, her governor, her king" [III. ii. 163-65]. "Go with me to church, and call me wife" [III. i. 303], and Gratiano and Nerissa accompany them. The bonds of marriage are symbolized by the rings which the ladies present to their respective spouses and of which we shall hear more later. For the moment, however, we may marvel how many people in the play are bound by law or by religion.

At the same time, it should be realized that the bondage extends in *The Merchant* beyond the formal limits of oath and legal contract. With Cicero, the Renaissance playgoer would have felt that there are "the bonds of human society", a "principle which knits together human society and cements our common interests" [*De Officiis* I. 5, 7; Cicero was a first-century B.C. Roman orator, statesman, and philosopher]. The principle may be called the bond of humanity, and within the play it assumes many forms. On one level, it is the close bond of friendship between Antonio and Bassanio. In our post-Freudian, sexually-oriented era, this friendship becomes latently homosexual—and possibly in many minds, worse. But rather than invoking Sigmund Freud, we may better look at Sir Thomas Elyot, who, in his *Boke Named the Gouernour* discusses "amitie or frendeshyp". Elyot feels that "Sens frendeshyp can not be but in good men, ne may not be without vertue, we may be assured, that therof none euyll may procede, or therwith any euyl thyng may participate". Purity or virtue rather than sexual attraction is the keynote of a Renaissance friendship. . . . It is because of this spiritual bond of friends that Antonio is willing to bind himself legally to his enemy Shylock for the sake of his friend Bassanio. Bondage begets bondage.

Metaphorically, from this bond between Antonio and Bassanio, the social bondage spreads and grows, and is emphasized in the pattern of allusions to eating. When Lorenzo and Gratiano leave Bassanio in the first scene, they promise three times to meet him again at "dinner-time" [I. i. 70, 109, 105]. Trying to gain the financial services of Shylock, Bassanio naturally asks him "to dine with us" [I. iii. 32]. Later, Gratiano promises Bassanio that his friends will be with him "at supper-time" [II. ii. 206]. As Jessica prepares to leave her home, Lorenzo urges her to hurry, for they "are stay'd for at Bassanio's feast" [II. vi. 48]; and while they are the master and mistress of Belmont, they playfully "go to dinner" [III. v. 86]. Having saved Antonio's life at the trial, Portia is entreated by Gratiano to give Bassanio and Antonio the pleasure of her "company at dinner" [IV. ii. 8]. To survive, all men must eat, but the pattern seems to suggest more than common necessity. It points to a stronger bond of love and good fellowship—"for we have friends / That purpose merriment" [II. ii. 202-03]. On the social level, it is equivalent to the Communion Table.

In contrast, Shylock denies the social bond implied in the convivial dinner. . . . Answering Bassanio's request that he eat with the Venetians, Shylock replies:

> Yes, to smell pork, to eat of the habitation which your prophet the Nazarite conjured the devil into: I will buy with you, sell with you, talk with you, walk with you, and so following: but I will not eat with you, drink with you, nor pray with you.
>
> [I. iii. 33-8]

The denial seems absolute, and the linking of eating with praying is perhaps to be taken as an indication of the spiritual separation which Shylock feels. However, his denial is only apparent, for he later tells Jessica:

> I am bid forth to supper Jessica, . . .
> I am not bid for love, they flatter me,
> But yet I'll go in hate, to feed upon
> The prodigal Christian.
>
> [II. v. 11, 13-15]

Thus Shylock subverts the whole idea of social unity implicit in the supper and introduces the rather grotesque element of cannibalism, which again appears in his assurance to Salerio that Antonio's flesh "will feed my revenge" [III. i. 54]. In his outrageous hints at eating human flesh, in his disgust at dining with his neighbors, Shylock demonstrates his lack of the essential feeling of unity which ties one man to another. In effect, he refuses to take part in the communal aspect of the social feast; he does not recognize the social bond. And one may well think back to the denial of humanity underlying the cannibalistic feast which ends *Titus Andronicus*.

Nevertheless, in the same scene in which he prom-ises to feed his revenge with a pound of human flesh, Shylock makes what has been interpreted as a meaningful plea to the Christians for the acknowledgement of his common humanity:

> I am a Jew. Hath not a Jew eyes? hath not a Jew hands, organs, dimensions, senses, affections, passions? fed with the same food . . . as a Christian is? . . . if you poison us do we not die? and if you wrong us shall we not revenge?
>
> [III. i. 58-67]

Shylock appeals to the bodily feelings and appendages which all normal humans have in common; but his final appeal, unfortunately, is not to a universal bond of mercy or justice, but to a universal inhumanity: revenge. His whole plea for inclusion is vitiated by the final, ironic twist. Through his own will and desire, he excludes himself from the general bond of brotherhood which holds society together. (pp. 89-94)

Discussing the bonds of human society, Cicero notes [in Nicholas Grimald's 1596 translation, *Marcvs Tullius Ciceroes Three Bookes of Duties*] that the principle which knits us together has "two parts: Justice is one, in the which is the greatest brightnesse of vertue, whereof good men beare theyr name, and to this is ioyned bountyfulnesse, which same we may tearme eyther gentlenesse, or liberalytye." It may be suggested without straining the point unduly that the bonds in *The Merchant* follow the same dichotomy, though it is restated in basically Christian terms: Justice and Mercy, Law and Charity. The bondage of the play, broadly viewed, falls into these categories. Though the basic intentions are different, the bonds which tie Antonio and Portia to certain agreements are strictly legal. The bonds of marriage and of religious oath seem to form a middle ground in which legality and charity (or, at least, religious emotion) coexist. And finally, there are the extra-legal bonds which hold society together, and these are firmly based on charity. Thus the pattern of bondage embodies the play's chief thematic dichotomy.

Of course, the bonds may be categorized in various ways, and possibly from the most general point of view, they may be seen as the bonds of love and the bonds of hate. Although most of the characters are bound together in what may be called 'love', the initial relationship between Antonio and Shylock must be described in different terms. It becomes immediately apparent that hate, dislike, and repugnance are as binding in their way as charity, though the negative bond is ultimately destructive, and must either be dissolved or replaced. One may compare Portia's initial reaction to her many suitors, or Jessica's reaction to her father's manners. Again, this broad categorization of the bonds fits neatly with what E. K. Chambers feels is central in the play. "The theme of *The Merchant of Venice*", he writes [in his *Shakespeare: A Survey*], " . . . is readily to be formulated as a conflict. It is a conflict in the moral order, between the opposing principles of Love and Hate."

Opposition of principles in the moral world presupposes the element of moral choice; for the concept of moral action is closely related to the idea of free will. To be truly moral, one must have the opportunity of being otherwise. Thus, at this point in our discussion of *The Merchant,* it will be expedient to return to the basic element in the Casket Story: choice. If the characters of the play are bound and their actions are determined by certain legal contracts, religious vows, and social obligations, they are also free, as all moral beings must be, to determine the bonds into which they will enter.

It may be objected, of course, that all drama, to have any dramatic force, must be based on the idea that its protagonists have freedom of action, that choice is essential to drama. Without arguing against this possible objection, I would like to suggest that in *The Merchant* the element of choice is emphasized far beyond the point needed to maintain the requisite tension. It is doubly underlined in the Story of the Caskets.

Portia introduces the idea rather forcefully, "O me the word 'choose'!" [I. ii. 22-3], and goes on to explain, in a passage we have examined before, that her choice has been curbed by her father's will. In turn, Nerissa explains that the suitor "who chooses" her father's meaning and thus the right casket "chooses" Portia also [I. ii. 30-1]. The word echoes throughout the scene. Later, as the several caskets are revealed to Morocco, Portia commands him: "Now make your choice" [II. vii. 3], and he and Portia discuss how he will know if his choice is correct. When Arragon stands facing the caskets, he notes that the word "many" may suggest "the fool multitude that choose by show" [II. ix. 26], and decides that he "will not choose what many men desire" [II. ix. 31]. After Bassanio arrives, Portia tells him that she could teach him "How to choose right" [III. ii. 11]. But to continue with illustrations at this point is a work of supererogation. By the mere repetition of the words "choose" and "choice", Shakespeare forces the idea on the playgoer's consciousness.

Out of this central myth of choosing, the idea of choice radiates through the play. Presented with Shylock's alternatives, either signing the note with a pound of flesh as forfeiture or getting no money, Antonio chooses to "seal unto this bond" [I. iii. 171], even though Bassanio is suspicious. More agonizing is the choice of Jessica:

> Alack, what heinous sin is it in me
> To be ashamed to be my father's child!
> But though I am a daughter to his blood
> I am not to his manners.
>
> [II. iii. 16-19]

To end her inner strife, she chooses to elope with Lorenzo, becoming a Christian. Her situation and choice form an effective contrast to Portia's. Portia, bound by her father's will, freely chooses to abide by its rules. When Nerissa asks her if she will marry the drunken young German should he choose the correct casket, her answer—"I will do anything Nerissa ere I will be married to a sponge" [I. ii. 98-9]—seems to bar the natural solution of refusing to obey her father's will. Later, drawn by her love of Bassanio to show him the proper choice, she decides that she cannot betray her father's trust. Jessica, given a similar choice between father and lover, chooses Lorenzo. (pp. 94-6)

Although we have seen that 'the bond' and 'the choice' are basic elements in *The Merchant,* we must now examine how they fit into the play's larger patterns of action. There is a parallel, we have noted, between Antonio bound to the "will" of Shylock [IV. i. 83] and Portia bound to the will of her father; and from this starting point, we may distinguish two major movements in the play (movements which have some correspondence to the source stories). We may call them the suit of love—Bassanio's winning of Portia—and the suit of revenge—Shylock's pursuit of Antonio. Both suits culminate in a trial centering upon a choice which is, indeed, a test of the moral fiber of the chooser.

The first movement, the suit of love, is the least complex of the two. The audience watches the wrong choice of Morocco, who, making an equation between human worth and physical wealth, takes the golden casket [II. vii. 59-60]. He is followed by Arragon whose choice is governed by his own price: "I will not jump with common spirits" [II. ix. 32], and he picks silver. Thus by the time Bassanio comes to choose, the playgoer is fully aware of the correct choice, and Bassanio, not "deceiv'd with ornament" [III. ii. 74], makes the proper choice of lead, and by hazarding all (as his friend Antonio has done for him), he gains his heart's desire. In the realm of love and personal attachment, to gain everything one must hazard just as much.

The second movement, which we have called the suit of revenge, and which actually runs concurrently with the first, grows out of the suit of love; for Antonio binds himself to Shylock so that Bassanio may have the necessary wealth to court Portia. And in the end, love dominates and destroys revenge, though the victory is not an easy one. Through a series of mishaps, Antonio's several fleets do not arrive in Venice, and the bond is forfeit. Shylock thereupon demands that the pound of human flesh be paid, and a day of trial is set. Shylock, it appears, must have his will of Antonio, just as, in a wholly different context, Bassanio has won Portia.

The trial scene, at first, seems not to offer a direct parallel, since ostensibly the trial is not of the suitor, Shylock, but of Antonio, and therefore cannot mirror Bassanio's trial at the choice of caskets.

However, if we can take advantage of our knowledge of the outcome, we see that the trial of Antonio has, in one way, a foregone conclusion; for Portia is already armed with the quibble that will cause Shylock to break off the suit, and she already knows the forgotten law which will put Shylock in Antonio's place, in danger of his life. It is not then the trial of Antonio; he readily admits that the bond is forfeit; but it is the trial of Shylock, who is presented by Portia with a series of moral choices. First she comments:

> Of a strange nature is the suit you follow,
> Yet in such rule, that the Venetian law
> Cannot impugn you as you do proceed,
> [IV. i. 177-79]

suggesting that Shylock has complete freedom of will to act as he wishes. After finding that Antonio confesses the bond, however, she insists: "Then must the Jew be merciful" [IV. i. 182]. Mistaking the moral imperative for the physical Shylock asks, "On what compulsion must I?" [IV. i. 183], and Portia launches into her eloquent speech on the quality of mercy. Shylock is given the free choice between Justice and Mercy—with a strong incentive in Portia's speech to be merciful—and the choice seems quickly and confidently made: "My deeds upon my head! I crave the law" [IV. i. 206]. Nevertheless, Portia does not give up her testing and shifts her examination to different grounds. The next choice Shylock must make is between "thrice thy money" [IV. i. 227] and the pound of flesh. But even material wealth will not divert his suit of revenge, and his choice suggests the quality of the man. Since his choices are not in accord with the play's scheme of values, he does not gain the object of his desires—which is, rather grotesquely, Antonio's heart. The latter part of the trial scene gives both Antonio and the Duke of Venice a chance to make the proper choice, and they are merciful. Thus both the suit of love and the suit of revenge follow the pattern of 'bond' and 'choice'.

Ironically and comically, both elements are used again at the play's end. The comedy of rings, which are begged from Bassanio and Gratiano by their disguised wives, runs through the end of Act IV and into Act V, recapitulating and mirroring Antonio's bondage to Shylock; for the rings, which the husbands swear so faithfully to wear, are the symbols of the marital bond. The point of the comedy lies beneath Antonio's words to Bassanio:

> My Lord Bassanio, let him [i.e., Portia as
>   Balthazar] have the ring,
> Let his deservings and my love withal
> Be valued 'gainst your wife's commande-
>   ment.
> [IV. i. 449-51]

In different terms, Bassanio is presented with the same choice as Shylock: shall he follow the spirit of charity or the letter of the law? His choice is doubly hard because the ring is the physical symbol of the bond between Portia and himself, but charity wins, and Gratiano is sent after the disguised Portia with Bassanio's ring.

The comedy of Bassanio's aside: "Why I were best to cut my left hand off, / And swear I lost the ring defending it" [V. i. 177-78], at the discovery of his ring's loss sets the tone of the final trial; and the bawdy lightness of the accusation levelled against the recreant husbands by their apparently indignant wives suggests that Portia and Nerissa have interpreted the loss in the proper spirit. The rings are merely physical signs of a bond which is, of necessity, spiritual. Perhaps the suggestion is that all bonds between man and man—or man and woman—are of this nature. But the final binding of the play is Antonio's:

> I once did lend my body for his wealth,
> Which but for him that had your hus-
>   band's ring
> Had quite miscarried. I dare be bound
>   again,
> My soul upon the forfeit, that your lord
> Will never more break faith advisedly.
> [V. i. 249-53]

Portia accepts the new bond and seals her renewed faith by returning Bassanio's ring. The episode ends in laughter—with Gratiano's quip concerning Nerissa's ring—though the words of Antonio fall more seriously on the ear. Once more he binds himself for his friend, with his soul this time, not a pound of flesh, in the balance. The flesh has given way to the spirit, and, though in a higher key, the play ends on the same note upon which it began: 'I dare be bound again' [V. i. 251]. (pp. 97-100)

> *William Leigh Godshalk, "'The Merchant of Venice': Bond or Free?" in his* Patterning in Shakespearean Drama: Essays in Criticism, *Mouton, 1973, pp. 87-100.*

ASPECTS OF LOVE

Lawrence W. Hyman

[*Hyman maintains that the primary action of* The Merchant of Venice *centers on the struggle between* **Portia** *and* **Antonio** *for* **Bassanio's** *affection, or the competition between friendship and marriage. Viewed in this manner, the critic continues,* **Antonio's** *bond with* **Shylock** *represents the merchant's attempt to retain* **Bassanio's** *love. Hyman then discusses the Elizabethan context of* **Antonio** *and* **Bassanio's** *relationship, asserting that it does not necessarily suggest homosexual yearnings on the merchant's part, rather, it reflects a close, platonic association that was quite common in Shakespeare's day. From this issue, the critic contends, Shakespeare creates dramatic ten-*

*sion in the trial scene (Act IV, scene i) not mere-
ly between the adversarial relationship of **Antonio** and **Shylock**, but also through the rival-
rous nature of **Portia** and **Antonio**'s love for
Bassanio. According to Hyman, **Antonio**'s
willingness to submit to **Shylock**'s bond reflects his desperate attempts to maintain his
relationship with his friend, even though he
has already been partially displaced by **Bassanio**'s marriage to **Portia**. The climax of the
play, the critic declares, is also the high point
of **Portia**'s victory over **Antonio**. Not only does
she thwart **Shylock**'s revenge, but by rescuing
Antonio with a legal technicality, she also severs the bond which holds her husband emotionally accountable to the merchant. Even
though **Antonio** loses the contest for **Bassanio**'s affections in the trial scene, Hyman
concludes, he nevertheless makes one final attempt to retain his friend by urging **Bassanio**
to give his ring to the disguised **Portia**. **Portia**
demonstrates her supremacy over **Antonio**,
however, when she presents the forfeited ring
to her husband in the final act and forgives
him for breaking his oath.]*

Aside from the powerful impact which Shylock
makes upon us, the readers and critics of this play
have been most impressed by the remarkable way
in which Shakespeare has woven together the stories of the caskets, the bond, and the ring. And, although interpretations naturally differ, the unity
that the critics have found in the play is usually
based on a contrast between Portia and Shylock,
Belmont and Venice, love and hatred, or mercy and
strict justice. John Russell Brown [in his introduction to *The Merchant of Venice*], for example, although he notices quite clearly the similarity between usury and love (as well as the contrast), still
finds a moral principle coming through at the end:
It is "that giving is the most important part—
giving prodigally, without thought for the taking."

More recently Sigurd Burckhardt [in his "The Merchant of Venice: The Gentle Bond," *ELH* XXIX] has
found greater unity in this play by emphasizing
the interdependence between Venice and Belmont,
particularly between Shylock's insistence on
maintaining the bond and Portia's loosening of
this bond. Burckhardt's initial assumption that
the bond is "the play's controlling metaphor" is an
important advance in unifying this play. But no
critic, as far as I am aware, has seen the full metaphoric meaning of the bond as a link between Antonio and Bassanio, rather than as merely a link
between Antonio and Shylock. The very genius of
Shakespeare, which was able to transform Shylock from a comic dupe into an almost tragic figure, has prevented us from seeing that *in terms of
the structure of the play* Shylock is a minor character. We shall ignore him, for the most part, in
order to focus our attention on Portia, Bassanio,
and Antonio. And once we make this simple step,
we will see that the main action of the play is cen-

tered on the struggle between Portia and Antonio
for Bassanio's love.

To arrive at such an interpretation in which the rivalry over Bassanio is dominant, rather than the
struggle to overcome Shylock, it will be necessary
to see the action more as a metaphor than as a literal rendition of human behavior. Such a reading
will not only allow us to see a greater degree of
unity in the play but also remove the need to justify
the actions of this strange play as being credible in
naturalistic terms. Since the metaphoric nature of
the caskets is made explicit in the play, and the
metaphoric nature of the ring is implicit, we need
go only a little further in order to see that the forfeited bond, with its pound of flesh, is only incidentally a bond between the two merchants. Essentially, that is in terms of Antonio's intention and in relation to the main theme of the play, the bond represents Antonio's attempt to hold on to Bassanio's
love.

To call Antonio a lover of Bassanio is not strange
in Elizabethan language; nor need it be considered
unusual even to a modern audience. Elizabethan
scholars and modern psychologists could be quoted to help define this relationship; but for our purposes, which are strictly literary, and not historical
or psychological, all we need assume is that Antonio feels rejected when he sees that his friend is determined to marry. Some readers might insist that
Antonio has some unconscious sexual feeling for
Bassanio that he would never reveal even to himself. But such an assumption is neither necessary
nor relevant to our understanding of his actions.
All that we need assume is that Antonio knows
that he should be happy in his friend's normal attempt to find a wife and is nevertheless unhappy
at losing him. Because of this ambivalent feeling
he is telling the truth when he opens the play with
his complaint: "I know not why I am so sad" [I. i.
1].

This ambivalence in Antonio's feeling is made
clear when Antonio offers to stretch his credit to
supply the money for Bassanio's suit. Consciously,
Antonio's intentions are genuine; he loves his
friend enough to want Bassanio to win the lady
who is described in such glowing terms. But in offering to put himself into debt for his friend (his
credit will be "racked, even to the uttermost" [I. i.
181]), Antonio is also revealing the depth of his
own feeling for Bassanio.

In a purely literal sense there is no good reason for
Bassanio's wanting a large sum of money to carry
on his suit. It is not the pretense of being rich himself that enables him to win Portia. What is credible and what is essential to the development of the
play is that from the very beginning—even before
the bond literally turns to blood—Antonio's money
is seen as a counterpart to the "golden fleece" that
hangs on the temples of Portia. The emphasis on
Portia's wealth can also be understood in the light

of Antonio's rivalry. Taken literally, Bassanio's insistence on her fortune might jar somewhat the romantic atmosphere which envelops his courtship. But when we realize that Antonio's wealth which he puts at his friend's disposal is a means of holding on to Bassanio's love, we can see that Portia's wealth makes more emphatic her role in displacing Antonio.

All this is made clear in Scene iii when Shylock demands, as security for his loan, "an equal pound / Of . . . fair flesh, to be cut off and taken / In what part of your body pleaseth me" [I. iii. 149-51]. The interconnections between Antonio's love represented by his offer of money, and the love of a woman which, naturally enough, is drawing Bassanio away from Antonio to Portia, is now given dramatic as well as symbolic force. We learn later that the bond, as actually written, calls specifically for the flesh "Nearest his heart" [IV. i. 254].

Although Shylock refers to the forfeit of the pound of flesh as a joke or "sport", Bassanio is shocked at this monstrous proposal. To him the friendship is best represented by a monetary loan which could be easily repaid with the money he would gain by marrying Portia. But to Antonio the link between the money that could be returned and the feeling "nearest his heart" (that unfortunately could not be returned by Bassanio) is not so clearly separated. And without hesitation Antonio consents: "Content, i' faith. I'll seal to such a bond / And say there is much kindness in the Jew" [I. iii. 152-53].

In the light of Shylock's motives the word "kindness" is ironic, and despite Shylock's use of the word "sport", Antonio's reply is barely credible. But in connection with Antonio's feelings at this point, as a rival lover, the eager acceptance of the bond is understandable. Antonio is offering his heart—figuratively but nevertheless with a vivid concreteness—as a means of counteracting the love which he fears Portia will soon offer to Bassanio. The bond legally and literally binds Antonio to Shylock but on a deeper level it binds Antonio to Bassanio. To break *this* bond, the bond between the lover and his friend, we need not only a clever judge, but Portia herself.

The woman who is to receive the love which Antonio is about to lose is introduced to us in a phrase reminiscent of her rival: "By my troth, Nerissa, my little body is aweary of this great world" [I. ii. 1-2]. And like her rival, her sadness is also caused by Bassanio. She, of course, wins Bassanio, and the Casket Scene will be discussed later. But her victory is not complete. Before the marriage can be consummated, we learn of Antonio's losses and the forfeiture of the pound of flesh. The bond which binds Bassanio to his friend now severs his relationship to his wife. Antonio's letter, which "steals the color from Bassanio's cheeks" [cf. III. ii. 244], is described "as the body of my friend / And every word in it a gaping wound, / Issuing life blood" [III.

ii. 264-66]. No dramatist who is also a poet could be expected to give a blunter indication of Antonio's role as a rival lover to Portia.

Shylock's action is brilliantly presented by Shakespeare in such a way that we can be both shocked at his cruelty and moved by the circumstances that provoke his monstrous revenge. But, without reference to the rival lovers, there is still something fantastic, even if it is dramatically effective, about the situation. Could such a bond really be enforced in a court of law which was created to facilitate the commercial life of a great city? Would not the fear of personal revenge combined with his greed serve to make Shylock relent? These questions can be answered negatively; and we are not arguing that the situation is literally impossible. But improbable possibilities are not the best material for great drama. The effectiveness of these scenes can be accounted for and their integral relationship to the rest of the play enhanced by seeing Antonio as a rival lover. The demand for the pound of flesh should be seen as the culmination not only of Shylock's hatred for all Christians (including Jessica), but of Antonio's desperate love for Bassanio.

Antonio's love, at this point, faces death in every sense. And at the Trial Scene [IV. i], his final speech (or what he believes will be his final speech) indicates that he is aware that he will undergo more than one kind of death beneath Shylock's knife:

> Give me your hand, Bassanio, fare you
>   well!
> Grieve not that I am fallen to this for
>   you, ...
> Commend me to your honorable wife.
> Tell her the process of Antonio's end,
> Say how I loved you, speak me fair in
>   death,
> And when the tale is told, bid her be judge
> Whether Bassanio had not once a love.
> Repent but you that you shall lose your
>   friend,
> And he repents not that he pays your debt,
> For if the Jew do cut but deep enough,
> I'll pay it presently with all my heart.
>   [IV. i. 265-81]

The bravery and devotion of Antonio which we feel as we see him submitting to the cruel demands of Shylock are not in question. Virtues are not, or need not be, explained away by rooting them in the needs and desires of men. Antonio's action is no less brave or sympathetic, but simply more understandable and more interesting, when it is seen as a desperate attempt to equal Portia's love for Bassanio. Nor is Portia any different in this respect. For she too tries to counteract her rival. Just as Antonio first tries to win Bassanio with money and later with his heart's blood, so Portia, naturally enough, wins Bassanio first as a woman and later, when she hears of Antonio's plight, with her money. Again her generosity is no more in question than is Antonio's bravery. But, metaphorically, she too is substituting her money for the sexuality which she (for very different reasons of course) cannot offer to Bassanio at this time. The juxtaposition of money and love, blood and gold, daughters and ducats, as many readers have noticed, runs throughout the play.

The climax of the play, Portia's turning the tables on Shylock, is also the high point of Portia's victory over Antonio. She not only saves his life but also prevents him from proving to Bassanio that his love could not be surpassed. The Biblical phrase about the "greater love" would certainly have applied to the man in this context. Nor does Antonio fail to recognize, even if many critics have, that Shylock's defeat is also his. For there now seems to be nothing to prevent Portia from giving her body to her husband in what may be called another kind of death, one that is naturally enough much more welcome to Bassanio. Antonio, however, is not yet ready to give up entirely; and to see his rivalry we must now leave the bond and look at its successor, the ring.

It will be remembered that it is Portia, in her disguise as the clerk, who asks for the ring. And this seemingly perverse action on her part will be explained later when we deal with the caskets. But her entreaty is not sufficient to make Bassanio give up the ring. It is only when Antonio reminds him that this "clerk" saved the life of his friend that Bassanio consents to remove the pledge of his love for Portia. The ring, as Burckhardt has pointed out, is "like the bond . . . of a piece with the flesh. . . ." In this context it represents Antonio's final attempt to separate his friend from Portia. Since we know that the clerk is really Portia, we know in advance that the attempt is futile. Dramatically the play moves to a lower key. Thematically, however, the final joke concerning the ring is a continuation of the rivalry between Antonio and Portia.

To read the final scene merely as a trick which is used to end the play on a light note is quite possible. We are always made aware by Portia's lines that Bassanio is in no danger. But such a reading would imply that Portia is not only very clever but also very cruel. What woman who could display the tenderness that Portia does in Act III, Scene ii, would be so cruel to her husband a few hours after he had witnessed the near death of his best friend? Only, it seems to me, a woman who is still fighting to break the last remaining bond that holds her husband to a former love. That this former love is another man, and is thus not a real rival, allows Portia to fight her battle in the form of a joke. Neither the woman she attributes to Bassanio nor the man she claims as her lover is real. But her jealousy is, and so is the pain suffered by Bassanio in this final scene.

Of course the term jealousy has to be qualified to fit this situation. It is not the jealousy of Othello or

of Cleopatra. As we have mentioned earlier, Antonio never blames his friend for wanting to marry; nor could he in his own conscious thoughts blame Portia for anything that she did. In the same way, Portia could hardly blame Antonio for what is an almost passionate friendship. And in no sense could she blame her husband for responding to the greater love that would lay down life for a friend. What we are concerned with is not a matter of right or wrong conduct, but with the insistent but altogether natural desire of a woman to possess her lover completely coming into conflict with the desire of Antonio to hold on to the love of his friend. We need not concern ourselves with the question as to whether Antonio's desire is equally "natural". For our purposes all we need recognize is that his desire is equally strong.

Portia knows of course that Bassanio really gave the ring to her, and that her accusation is false. But the false appearance in Shakespearian comedy is seldom a mere trick. Just as Viola's disguise [in *Twelfth Night*] and Hero's "seduction" [in *Much Ado About Nothing*] serve not only to conceal but to reveal certain truths, so in this play Portia's pretense that she has been wronged (and that she has in turn betrayed Bassanio) reveals a truth that could not be expressed in any other way. The love between Antonio and Bassanio which caused her ring to be removed was just as strong, and was consequently just as much of a threat to her complete possession of her husband, as a rival mistress. There is an obvious truth in her remark that no man would be "so much unreasonable" [V. i. 203] as to desire the ring, since she was the man. But there is a more significant truth in that phrase insofar as the love of Antonio, which was the real cause of Bassanio's action, is comparable to the love of a woman. That she treats Antonio's feelings for her husband as being equivalent to a woman's is made more explicit a few lines later when she plays with the word ring or "jewel" so as to suggest her own sexuality.

The trick has its effect not only on her husband but more importantly on her rival as well. Antonio, seeing that he is "the unhappy subject of these quarrels" [V. i. 238], finally recognizes that his love for Bassanio is, under the circumstances, too strong, and that the love for a woman must inevitably displace all but the memory of the love between the two friends. Antonio acknowledges that if it were not for Portia he himself would not be alive. And, as if to make explicit in action the complete victory that Portia has won, he himself hands over the ring to Bassanio. Antonio is now, as the play ends, no longer a rival but a willing accomplice in his friend's marriage.

But the placing of Portia's ring on Bassanio's finger is more than the conclusion of the rivalry. The ring was first put on Bassanio's finger in the Casket Scene, and its recurrence should bring to a conclusion not only the story of the bond but also the story of the three caskets. Coming as it does from another source, the choice of a casket is not so explicitly related to the rival lovers as are the bond and the ring. But since the metaphoric meaning of the caskets is explicit, there is no difficulty in reading the whole scene metaphorically, and so relating it to the main action of the play.

The inscriptions on the caskets make clear to us from the beginning that Bassanio's actions are not a matter of chance but a reflection of the nature of love. And Bassanio's love is generous, he would "give and hazard all he hath" [II. vii. 9]. It is interesting to note, however, that this inscription is on the *outside* of the leaden casket, and that when Bassanio opens this casket, some scenes later, the motto reads quite simply: "You that choose not by the view, / Choose as fair, and choose as true!" [III. ii. 132]. A relationship can be established between the two moral maxims. But the first and more significant statement links this scene with the preceding action of Antonio. For it is he, not Bassanio the fortune hunter, who has shown his love by giving all that he has; indeed he has hazarded his fortune to the sea and the wind, while hazarding his heart to his enemy.

Henry Irving as Shylock in an 1879 Lyceum production of The Merchant of Venice.

tune to the sea and the wind, while hazarding his heart to his enemy.

Bassanio, in one sense, has done the opposite. He has looked for and found a "lady richly left" [I. i. 161], and a friend who is willing to put his entire fortune at his disposal. Portia, too, gives herself to him by wishing herself "A thousand times more fair, ten thousand times / More rich . . . " [cf. III. ii. 154] for his sake. So far it is only Antonio and Portia who give and hazard; Bassanio has only taken.

When, immediately after the marriage, we learn that Antonio is about to lose his life for his friend, the irony of the slogan becomes sharper, and as so often in Shakespeare, the action makes a mockery of morality. By giving and hazarding Antonio seems to have lost everything; whereas by taking all that he can get, his friend is on the verge of getting as much beauty, wealth, generosity (and as he soon learns), intelligence, as could be found in any woman. But we must emphasize the words "seems" and "is on the verge of". Shakespeare does not replace moral maxims with cynicism. Bassanio must give up this beautiful wife in order to go to Venice, and is prepared to give up Portia's wealth in order to ransom his friend from imminent death. Conversely, by giving all he has, Antonio has succeeded in displacing Portia, for the moment at least, as the chief interest for Bassanio. Just as Antonio will eventually place Portia's ring on Bassanio's finger in the conclusion, so here his rival must step aside:

> First go with me to church and call me
>   wife,
> And then away to Venice to your friend,
> For never shall you lie by Portia's side
> With an unquiet soul.
>
> [III. iii. 304-06]

The statement on the leaden casket thus becomes more than either a copybook maxim or a cynical reminder that the world does not usually reward generosity. It is a warning to Bassanio that if the leaden casket contained gold, the golden world that he gained can quickly turn again into the harsh world represented by Shylock. But it is the ring, rather than the caskets and the bond, which brings out the true significance of what is implied by giving and hazarding all that one has. We have seen both Antonio and Portia risk all that they have because of their love for Bassanio. It now remains for Bassanio to carry out the maxim.

His opportunity to give and hazard all that he has comes about when his friend and his wife, from different motives, both act to make him give up the ring. It is appropriate that Bassanio, who has so far been accustomed only to taking, has to be urged to part with the symbol of "all that he hath". And it is also appropriate that in giving all, he is really giving nothing, since Portia's ring is received by Portia. But Bassanio does not know this, and the pain which he suffers makes him feel what his friend had experienced earlier in the play—that a moral maxim may be much better as an inscription than it is in practice. For if Antonio's greater love almost results in laying down his life for his friend, Bassanio's "greater love" . . . almost results in his laying down his wife for his friend. The conclusion of the play parallels and develops earlier scenes; yet, as so often in Shakespeare, with no sense of repetition but of continual development in action, character and theme.

A sense of the thematic unity, amidst the bewildering actions, can also help us account for the miraculous return of Antonio's fleet, which Portia announces to him after he has given her ring back to Bassanio. On a literal level this restoration of his ships is both incredible and unnecessary. (Antonio is not concerned with his wealth.) But to Portia the return of the ships is important in removing the last sacrifice that Antonio has suffered for Bassanio. And it brings us back to the Casket Scene in that it fulfills the prophecy implied in the leaden casket, that he who gives and hazards will eventually receive what he desires and perhaps even what he deserves. Or, to use Shakespeare's own images, the lead turns to gold for Antonio as well as for his friend.

But as even Shakespeare and his contemporaries suspected, alchemy is, at least in part, a trick and an illusion. And the happy ending here, as in most of Shakespeare's comedy, depends on our accepting the illusion. Under the surface of the golden world, as Portia's unsuccessful suitors learned, there is often a harsher reality. It is therefore quite in keeping with the ironic current of the play, as well as the tragic undertone, that the conclusion should see Bassanio come so close to the precipice at the very moment when he too gives and hazards all that he has.

Many readers have found a golden world in Belmont in contrast to the cruel business world of Venice. But those critics who have examined the play more closely have usually seen how interdependent the two worlds are. Lorenzo's beautiful description of the harmony of the spheres is interrupted by Jessica's remark that she is never merry when she hears music. Nor should we forget how intimately this love affair is bound up with a more earthy gold than is found in the heavenly spheres. To see the play as a unified action is to realize that there is no clear separation between generous love and selfish love, between those who take and those who give, between the lead and the gold. Bassanio, it is true, is neither a jealous nor a possessive lover, like Antonio and Portia. But then he never has to be. And with all their possessiveness and jealousy, Antonio and Portia can never be accused of refusing to give all for love.

None of the leading characters have to be justified or condemned, only understood. And when we do so we will see not what ought to be by our own standards or by some hypothetical construction of what the "Elizabethan audience" expected, but what human beings actually do when driven by their loves, hates, hopes, and fears. It is not that mercy, generosity, justice, and pity are unreal, or that they are only masks to conceal emotions. On the contrary, the analysis presented here should indicate that these high-sounding virtues are given greater reality when they are grounded in the desires, both conscious and unconscious, of passionate men and women. To see *The Merchant of Venice* as a play about rival lovers is not only to unify the diverse actions but also to give depth and complexity to what is often seen as a clever dramatization of a fairy-tale morality. (pp. 109-16)

> *Lawrence W. Hyman, "The Rival Lovers in 'The Merchant of Venice',"* in Shakespeare Quarterly, *Vol. XXI, No. 2, Spring, 1970, pp. 109-16.*

Helen Purinton Pettigrew

[*Pettigrew argues that Shakespeare portrays* **Bassanio** *as an ideal Elizabethan lover, a character whose "apparent faults were to the Elizabethans mere conventional commonplaces arising from the economic conditions of the age." Marrying for money was not unusual during Shakespeare's time, the critic asserts, and often expected due to the rising cost of living during the Renaissance and the falling fortunes of the aristocracy. Nevertheless, Pettigrew states that the playwright went to great pains to make clear that not only* **Portia's** *wealth, but also her intelligence and beauty attract* **Bassanio.** *Furthermore,* **Portia** *reveals a typical Elizabethan attitude toward marriage in her remarks about suitors and husbands, and once she and* **Bassanio** *are wed, she shows no concern when he immediately assumes the right to use her fortune. Ultimately, the critic determines that based on traditional Elizabethan courtship and marriage practices,* **Bassanio** *is a romantic hero, not a scheming opportunist.*]

In spite of the "absurdities" of its plot, *The Merchant of Venice* is sometimes called the best of Shakespeare's comedies; love is one of its primary themes; and the somewhat ambiguous Bassanio is unquestionably the chief lover. Some commentators give him a qualified praise; and a few, indeed, eulogize him as a "romantic lover," even the "ideal" lover such as [Baldassare] Castiglione celebrated. Many more scholars, on the contrary, form a sort of accusatory chorus against Bassanio: he is, they say, the intellectual inferior of Portia, even "dull in capacity"; he is a peevish, weak spendthrift, both selfish and prodigal—a very "profligate"; he is a mercenary, predatory creature, only the "seeming lover" of Portia, a man "imprudent, impudent and mean"; he is, indeed, a "downright fortune hunter," tolerable to the reader only because, in a romance, we accept a character at the author's evaluation.—And yet Shakespeare clearly intended Bassanio for a hero. If these charges be true, the playwright must have bungled—more, indeed, than some commentators would believe he bungled in the character of Proteus [in *The Two Gentlemen of Verona*]—for to this same Bassanio he gives that pearl of great price, the "radiant" Portia, called by many readers Shakespeare's loveliest woman. In truth, Bassanio's behavior, for a hero, does seem rather odd: though expressing distrust of Shylock, he accepts Antonio's offer to jeopardize himself for friendship's sake; he uses the borrowed money to give a Gargantuan bachelor feast, and to provide himself with a richly appointed *entourage,* so as to arrive impressively in Belmont; he frankly admits that he hopes to retrieve his lost fortunes by a rich marriage: he chooses among the caskets wisely, to be sure, but, in the song, "Tell me where is Fancie bred" [III. ii. 63-72], Portia may have warned him how to choose. When Antonio's difficulties reach a climax, Bassanio hastens back to Venice; but after he has arrived, he does nothing but stand by ineffectually, while Portia rescues his friend. As a husband, Bassanio's only acts are to use Portia's money as freely as his own, and later to break his word to her, and then to lie about the ring. All in all, Bassanio seems to be but a poor thing; and Shakespeare, in his delineation of these two lovers, would appear to have disregarded the cardinal principle of dramatic justice. This is a serious indictment against the world's greatest dramatist, in one of his greatest plays; and surely every effort should be made to examine the indictment. (pp. 296-97)

Not only does Shakespeare's revision of the story from his sources show [a] tendency toward realism, but so also does the detail of the action and dialogue of both Portia and Bassanio, in their miscellaneous social relationships. Portia's pleading of the case before the Duke, according to Lord Campbell [in his *Shakespeare's Legal Acquirements*], shows a considerable realism: her use of legal phrases and her court procedure are Elizabethan. Her relationship with Nerissa, moreover, foreshadowed by that of Julia and Lucetta in *The Two Gentlemen,* and looking forward to that of Olivia and Maria in *Twelfth Night,* reflects a very common status in Elizabethan England,—the friendship between a noblewoman and her lady-in-waiting, who is also of gentle birth. In Portia's dialogue, too, outside the love scenes, occur incidental realistic touches. In discussing with Nerissa her various suitors, she reflects actual customs, opinions, and events of Shakespeare's time: the French Lord, she maintains, "will fence with his own shadow" [I. ii. 61-2], the young Englishman, though lamentably ignorant of foreign languages, incongruously combines in his dress various Continental fashions; the Scotchman has "borrowed a boxe of the ear of the *Englishman* and swore he would pay him

againe when hee was able" [cf. I. ii. 80-1]—a debt for which "the *Frenchman* became his suretie" [cf. I. ii. 82]; and the German nobleman is a drunken sot. She later makes fun of the braggart, a common English type; and she alludes to her coach—an innovation that occasioned much discussion in Elizabethan London. Bassanio's actions also show a realistic coloring: although his indebtedness to Antonio is not Shakespeare's but belongs to the sources, his essential relationship to Antonio, as changed from the originals, illustrates the Renaissance ideal of the excellence of friendship between men: for Bassanio is willing to sacrifice even his new wife, if need be, in discharge of the obligation to his friend. His relationship to Shylock is, again, governed by the sources, but Shakespeare, by making him distrust the Jew at once, gives him a greater realism than in these sources—greater, indeed, than Antonio's. Bassanio's relations with Gratiano and the other young wits is also realistic, for they are typical Elizabethan men-about-town, gay, clever, somewhat cynical, enjoying themselves in the accepted Renaissance way, with a procession accompanied by torch-bearers, a bachelor dinner, and much merriment. Bassanio's long speech in the Casket Scene, furthermore, shows touches of contemporary realism: he comments upon the "many cowards, whose hearts are all as false as stayers of sand" [cf. III. ii. 83-4], who go about wearing "the beards of *Hercules* and frowning *Mars*" [cf. III. ii. 85], but who have "lyuers white as milk" [cf. III. ii. 86]; and he thrusts, in passing, at the Elizabethan fashion of wearing wigs: "So are those crisped snakie locks . . . Vpon supposed fairenesse, often knowne To be the dowrie of a second head" [cf. III. ii. 92-5]. If, then, Shakespeare made Bassanio and Portia realistic in their general social relationships and dialogue, surely in the wooing, which is the main substance of Bassanio's part in the action, one might reasonably expect to find important elements of realism.

Indeed, Bassanio, as Portia's accepted suitor, surely must have been more satisfactory to the Elizabethans than he is to us: perhaps his apparent faults may have their root in the fact that his courtship and marriage exemplify the peculiar creeds and customs of Shakespeare's age, and are therefore, in spite of all they owe to the sources, realistic. Although some readers find Bassanio lacking in friendship toward Antonio, the greater charge against him grows out of his conduct as lover and husband. As a lover, he has suffered in the opinion of critics because he is mercenary, for one of his chief motives in seeking Portia is, indubitably, a desire for a large dowry; and he has suffered further because, as critics declare on the basis of mere inference, he is supposed to have wasted his patrimony in riotous living. An Elizabethan gentleman, however, had to live well: generous spending was a social obligation; and if, as one may suppose, Bassanio's family fortunes had largely diminished with the rising prices of the Renaissance, he might, indeed, have become bankrupt merely through the needful expenditures of a young man of good birth. Elizabethan England, furthermore, did not condemn a mercenary marriage; in fact, a dowry was the chief, if not the only, inducement for a young gentleman to marry. The double standard of morals, regularly accepted in that day, encouraged a young man to delay marriage, economic pressure, on the other hand, operated otherwise. A gentleman, forced to live in the luxury of Elizabeth's court, on a private income or small family allowance, and almost completely debarred from the now overcrowded and rapidly deteriorating professions of serving-man and soldier, usually regarded a marriage for wealth as the only honorable means of recouping his fortunes and of maintaining himself in the social and economic *status quo*. Bassanio's situation seems to be of this unenviable sort:

> *Bas.* Tis not unknowne to you *Anthonio*
> How much I have disabled mine estate,
> By something showing a more swelling
>   port
> Then my faint meanes would grant con-
>   tinuance.
>
> [cf. I. i. 122-25]

Not only in his motives, but in the conduct of the wooing, Bassanio is thoroughly Elizabethan. He suggests to Antonio that, had he "but the meanes to hold a riuall place" [cf. I. i. 174] with the other suitors of the "Lady richly left" [I. i. 161], he "should questionlesse be fortunate" [I. i. 176]. Finally, the betrothal is solemnized in the proper contemporary fashion, by means of a ring, with which, as Portia says, she gives herself and all her goods,—a ring

> Which when you part from, loose, or giue
>   away,
> Let it presage the ruine of your loue,
> And be my vantage to exclaime on you.
>
> [cf. III. ii. 172-74]

Bassanio, too, recognizes the importance of this ring:

> *Bas*   . . . but when this ring
> Parts from this finger, then parts life from
>   hence.
> O then be bold to say *Bassanio's* dead.
>
> [III. ii. 183-85]

The significance of the ring, out of which grows the action of the fifth act, would be instantly plain to an Elizabethan audience, accustomed to the almost invariable exchange of rings in both betrothal and marriage ceremonies. Portia, too, reflects in her attitude the typical Renaissance courtship. She expresses to Nerissa what was doubtless the average Elizabethan gentlewoman's plaint in regard to the prearranged marriage:

> *Portia* . . . O mee, . . . I may neither choose whom I would, nor refuse whom I

dislike, so is the wil of a liuing daughter curb'd by the will of a dead father.

[cf. I. ii. 23-5]

In the Casket Scene, she reiterates the same sentiment, and bemoans "these naughtie times" [cf. III. ii. 18] that "Puts bars betweene the owners and their rights" [cf. III. ii. 19]. She conforms, on the other hand, with Elizabethan theory in her speech to Bassanio on feminine subservience:

> *Por.* Happiest of all, is that her gentle spirit
> Commits it selfe to yours to be directed,
> As from her Lord, her Governour, her
>   King.
>
> [cf. III. ii. 163-65]

She further illustrates an Elizabethan attitude, when she refers to a husband's social responsibility for his wife:

> *Por.* Let me giue light, but let me not be
>   light,
> For a light wife doth make a heauie hus-
>   band.
> And *neuer* be Bassanio so for me.
>
> [cf. V. i. 129-31]

Apparently, then, the courtship of these two lovers contains some definite elements of contemporary realism which might well reconcile Shakespeare's audience to a situation distasteful to the modern reader. The playwright carefully makes clear, moreover, that Portia's money is not her only attraction for Bassanio; for the "faire speechlesse messages" [cf. I. i. 164] exchanged between them before the opening of the play indicate a mutual interest dating from a time perhaps before Bassanio's financial stringency arose, and the reciprocal emotions shown in the Casket Scene should satisfy the devotee of high romance. Bassanio as a lover, thus conforms with Elizabethan conditions and customs, and even with the more practical Elizabethan ideals. As a husband, he has scarcely time to show his mettle, except that he assumes the right, immediately, to use his wife's money. . . . Elizabethans, however, would expect him to do that very thing: indeed, the fortune became automatically his through the act of marriage—perhaps Shakespeare's audience would even assume that, before his frantic departure to Antonio, the marriage was hastily performed chiefly to make that money legally his to offer for his friend. Bassanio's other act as a husband, the giving away of Portia's ring, has never been seriously held against him: the incident, taken almost wholly from Shakespeare's source, is usually regarded as the dramatist's means for lightening and softening the bitterly tragic mood of the Court Scene; and Bassanio's part in it is clearly involuntary and unavoidable, if he is to remain a generous-spirited Renaissance gentleman; for liberality was, perhaps, the prime characteristic which, during the Renaissance, distinguished the nobility. Portia, moreover, seems to represent the marriageable Elizabethan gentlewoman, like Olivia [in *Twelfth Night*], in unusual circumstances, created through the death of her parents. Ordinarily, a young woman of good family was betrothed by her father, although by the reign of Elizabeth, more or less importance had come to be attached to the girl's own preference; in theory, however, it still was thought a shocking thing for a girl to take matters into her own hands and elope: Elizabethan conduct books are full of admonitions to children to obey their parents, and to fathers to provide suitable early marriages for their daughters, who might otherwise grow impatient and marry themselves off. Portia's being an orphan might be supposed to give her more freedom than most Renaissance English girls would enjoy; but her father, like a conscientious Elizabethan gentleman, has left for her protection and guidance, in lieu of himself, a last testament that enjoins her from marrying as she pleases, and attempts to exercise a wise choice among her prospective suitors. No Shakespearean playgoer would consider, as some modern critics do, that Portia was ill-used in her father's will, or that, having educated her highly, he has wronged her by depriving her of free choice in matrimony. As a matter of fact, the present writer finds in the play no evidence that Portia had received an unusual education for an Elizabethan lady of quality. To be sure, when talking to Bassanio in the Casket Scene—and, perhaps, naturally enough, attempting to impress him—she refers to Greek mythological history: but only as any quick-witted, keenly perceptive person might pick up such allusions while listening to the learned: even Chaucer's Partlet could muster up a little classical lore. Indeed, Portia's description of herself to Bassanio as "an vnlessonrd girle, vnschool'd, vnpractiz'd [cf. III. ii. 159], may well be, not a mere exhibition of the humility of love, but the almost literal truth: despite a few notable exceptions, Elizabethan women were not given a liberal education; they were, however, taught practical household management, and Portia's "unusual" education may have been merely an extraordinarily thorough preparation for handling her extensive fortune. Her whole bearing toward Bassanio, moreover, much as it irks some critics in this age of feminism, is typically Elizabethan: her desire to abase and to immolate herself in his interests would seem to Shakespeare's audience only the natural duty of an ideal wife—as various contemporary books on conduct stipulate—to sink her personality in that of her husband; and the very fact that . . . women sometimes disregarded the conduct-books and became unpleasantly independent, would stimulate this preponderantly masculine audience to a greater admiration for the gentle Portia. That lady, foreshadowing a Beatrice, a Viola, and a Rosalind [in *Much Ado About Nothing, Twelfth Night,* and *As You Like It*], is perhaps more sprightly in speech and more resourceful in action than the ideal Elizabethan wife; but her fundamental relationship to Bassanio is, first and last,

an exemplification of the Elizabethan theory of the "weaker vessel." Indeed, the dramatist's departure from his source, in giving the power to choose among the caskets to the man lover rather than to the woman, would seem to bespeak in Shakespeare a belief in the man's greater importance and responsibility in courtship. The poet evidently saw no incongruity in Portia's subservience to the "wastrel" Bassanio; the author, indeed, seems to admire both lovers equally: apparently, therefore, Bassanio's unlovely qualities have been largely read into his character by modern interpreters unfamiliar with the courtship and marriage customs of the time; and a study of these customs would seem to establish Bassanio as a realistic Elizabethan gentleman in love—a high-spirited, noble-hearted gentleman, quite worthy of the incomparable Portia.

On the basis of two, or possibly more, Romantic stories, Shakespeare develops in *The Merchant of Venice* a realism to contemporary economic and social life: Bassanio must have money for his wooing and for his future livelihood, and Portia rejoices to supply his needs. Thus the playwright gives his diverse and disunified originals the significant coherence of great drama. This realism appears in the action and dialogue of the two lovers, not only in their miscellaneous relationships to the other characters, but also most significantly in relation to each other as lovers and as man and wife. Bassanio's apparent faults were to the Elizabethans mere conventional commonplaces arising from the economic conditions of the age. As far as the peculiar circumstances allow, he conducts his courtship according to Elizabethan propriety and custom; thus he is not a mere mercenary wooer but a typical Elizabethan entirely worthy of Portia's hand. Such an interpretation of Bassanio should be significant to an understanding of the play as a whole: the Shylock motif presents one aspect of Elizabethan economics—moneylending: If, then, Bassanio chiefly exemplifies the economics of marriage, *The Merchant of Venice* is, in its entirety, a drama of economic theme—perhaps the first in English literature. This economic problem arises from the social necessity that Bassanio must have ample funds to court with proper circumstance and pomp; and the love-plot, therefore, is the motivating force and is the alpha and omega to the piece. The play would seem to be Shakespeare's first significant and realistic treatment of the theme of love; and one need not wonder that, from his own experience, the economic side of the problem was the first aspect to engage his serious attention. *The Merchant of Venice,* therefore, is not only a great comedy, but also a crucial step in Shakespeare's career as a dramatist; for it is probably the first in which he attempts any serious working-out of those causes and effects, economic, social, and political, that governed contemporary Elizabethan life. (pp. 298-306)

Helen Purinton Pettigrew, "Bassanio, the Elizabethan Lover," in Philological Quarterly, *Vol. XVI, No. 3, July, 1937, pp. 296-306.*

KEY SCENES

John Dover Wilson

[*Wilson examines three key scenes in* The Merchant of Venice: *the casket scene (Act III, scene ii), the trial scene (Act IV, scene i), and the Belmont scene (Act V, scene i). The critic maintains that the casket scene was probably treated as humorous entertainment by Elizabethan audiences, who enjoyed folk tales focusing on the difference between appearance and reality. Wilson then discusses various aspects of the the casket plot, particularly the meaning of the mottoes, the dramatic setting for* **Bassanio's** *choice, and the possible implications of the song that is played while* **Bassanio** *considers his selection. As a result of the trial scene, the critic continues,* **Shylock** *should be regarded as a tragic, not comical, figure. In Wilson's opinion, while* **Shylock** *is "the inevitable product of centuries of racial persecution," Shakespeare did not necessarily mean to present the Jew as a moral example. Although the playwright never takes sides in his dramas, the critic asserts, surely he would advocate the mercy* **Portia** *offers as "the only possible solution of our racial hatreds and enmities." Since the trial scene is unusually serious for a comedy, the critic continues, Shakespeare added the Belmont episode to send his audience home in a happy mood. Wilson concludes that the music and moon offer twin themes of reassuring harmony in* **Portia's** *domain, mediating Elizabethan concerns about the impending dissolution of the universe by reaffirming their world view with the vision of Belmont.*]

> In sooth I know not why I am so sad.
> [I. i. 1]

The very first line of [*The Merchant of Venice*] is ominous—a line uttered by Antonio, a figure of great dignity, much graciousness, and an air quite different from that usually breathed in the world of comedy. So alien is he to that world that when he has to move therein, as he does in the last Act, and not till then, we feel he is quite out of his element. And Shakespeare clearly feels so too, for he keeps him in the background as much as possible and gives him little to say. And in the opening scene he is deliberately contrasted with shallow-pates like Salerio, Solanio, and Gratiano, so that we may have no excuse for doubting his seriousness right from the outset. 'Gratiano', we are told, 'speaks an infinite deal of nothing, more than any man in all Venice. His reasons are as two grains of wheat hid in two bushels of chaff; you shall seek all day ere you find them, and when you have them they are not worth the search' [I. i. 114-18]. Thus Shakespeare dismisses the laughing wit-mongers who had formed the staple of his comedy in *Love's Labour's Lost.*

In *The Merchant* he is going to try a new dramatic experiment—to discover how near he can come to the true note and authentic thrill of tragedy without allowing the tragic wave to break and swamp the comic finale. In 1580 or thereabouts . . . Sir Philip Sidney was condemning 'mungrel tragycomedies'. Some fifteen years later Shakespeare set himself to produce the finest specimen of the kind in our language, perhaps in any language. For *The Merchant of Venice* is a great play, let us make no mistake about that. Alas, that it has been staled and hackneyed for so many readers by the treadmill methods of the class-room where the dull brain of the pedagogue perplexes and retards. (pp. 94-5)

[Let] us glance at the plot of the play and consider in particular the casket-plot, . . . of which Portia is the central figure. For there are . . . two main plots: the casket-plot and the bond-plot. It is known that two stories 'representing the greediness of worldly choosers and the bloody minds of usurers' had already been combined in one play long before Shakespeare handled them. But as this old play is lost, we cannot tell how much Shakespeare invented himself and how much he simply took over from his unknown predecessor. Anyhow, whoever was responsible for it, the master-stroke was the combination of the two plots by means of the device of disguise; and there is no happier or more striking example of the serviceability of this Elizabethan dramatic convention than the impersonation by the Lady of Belmont of the lawyer called in to give judgment between the merchant and the usurer. That impersonation is the pivot of Shakespeare's play; the only occasion on which his two principal characters, Portia and Shylock, confront each other. Moreover, as everyone knows, in addition to these main plots there is a comic underplot, that of an exchange of rings which follows on the trial-scene and is the occasion of much laughter at the end of the play.

From the point of view of plot technique, the *Merchant of Venice* is a masterly production. It is a play, too, of wonderful poetry, most wonderful perhaps in the finale, though reaching greater heights of intensity in the mouth of Shylock. And it contains three magnificent scenes: the casket-scene, the trial-scene, and the last and loveliest of all, at Belmont. (p. 96)

The Casket-Scene

To speak of 'the casket-scene' is to betray a modern standpoint and to wrong Shakespeare; for no less than five scenes are concerned with the caskets and four are almost entirely devoted to them. Spectators are inclined to find the whole business just a little silly, and modern producers cut freely into this part of the play, huddling what remains into a couple of brief episodes introducing the Prince of Morocco and the Prince of Arragon, without which the scene when Bassanio makes his choice becomes hardly intelligible. But the casket theme was of a kind well calculated to suit the Elizabethan palate, and I do not doubt that all five scenes were popular in Shakespeare's day. . . . But the story of the great lady, mistress of much wealth, whom the world sought in marriage; of the strange will devised by her father so as to test the character of successive suitors; the speeches of these suitors, speeches sententious after the true Renaissance fashion; and finally the eloquent discourse of Bassanio himself on the favourite topic of the day, the problem of Judgement by Appearances, and the difference between Seeming and Reality, a topic of which the whole casket-plot is itself an exposition—all this would be very much to men's taste at that period. (p. 97)

We can be sure, too, that the mottoes that stood upon the three caskets, mottoes which seem to pass almost unnoticed by modern readers and commentators, meant much to the proverb-loving Elizabethans. Morocco thus declares them:

> The first, of gold, who this inscription bears,
> 'Who chooseth me shall gain what many men desire'
> The second, silver, which this promise carries,
> 'Who chooseth me shall get as much as he deserves'
> This third, dull lead, with warning all as blunt,
> 'Who chooseth me must give and hazard all he hath'
>
> [II. vii. 4-9]

The meaning of the first motto is patent enough, since it has direct reference to the metal of which the casket is composed, namely what Romeo calls 'saint-seducing gold' [*Romeo and Juliet* I. i. 214] and later speaks of to the apothecary from whom he purchases his poison,

> There is thy gold, worse poison to men's souls
> Doing more murders in this loathsome world
> Than these poor compounds that thou mayst not sell.
> I sell thee poison; thou hast sold me none.
> [*Romeo and Juliet* V. i. 80-3]

As to the second, 'Who chooseth me shall get as much as he deserves', we may go to *Hamlet* for comment. Says the Prince to Polonius: 'Good my lord, will you see the players well bestowed; do you hear, let them be well used,' etc. [*Hamlet* II. ii. 522 ff.]. To which Polonius replies, 'My lord, I will use

them according to their desert', and Hamlet rejoins, 'God's bodkin, man, much better! use every man after his desert, and who shall 'scape whipping?' [II. ii. 528-30].

The third motto brings us to the last of the casket-scenes, in which Bassanio makes his choice. It is a scene still fresh and full of delight for us, both on account of all that happens within it and because of the noble verse in which it is written. Yet I think we miss much that Shakespeare intended us to see there.

What, for example, is the *dramatic* setting for Bassanio's choice? His success, to be effective, must seem at once (*a*) natural, i.e. not just the result of chance, and (*b*) morally satisfying to the audience. Notice, then, the following points: (1) Shakespeare lets us hear the other two suitors argue the matter out, and their arguments reveal some flaw of character or imperfect sense of values which shows them to be undesirable mates for the Lady of Belmont. (2) But when he comes to Bassanio, the scene is arranged differently. We are allowed to hear only the conclusion of his reasoning. The great speech which begins

> So may the outward shows be least themselves—
>
> [III. ii. 73]

tells us that the speaker has already made his choice before he opens his mouth. (3) In place of the reasoning itself we are given a song, sung at Portia's command, 'the whilst Bassanio comments on the caskets to himself' [s.d., III. ii. 62]—as the Quarto, that is Shakespeare's, stage-direction has it. And have you, my reader, ever examined this song closely? If so, you may have noticed some interesting things about it. Here it is:

> Tell me where is Fancy bred,
> Or in the heart, or in the head?
> How begot, how nourished?
> ALL. Reply, reply.
> It is engend'red in the eyes,
> With gazing fed, and Fancy dies
> In the cradle where it lies.
> Let us all ring Fancy's knell . . .
> I'll begin it—Ding, dong, bell.
> ALL. Ding, dong, bell.
>
> [III. ii. 63-72]

Mark the rhymes first of all: *bred, head, nourishéd*—and then medially, *engend'red* and *fed*. Can one think of any apter rhyme than *lead*? And if the rhymes of the first half of the song almost cry out the word *lead*, what about the second half with its talk of Fancy dying 'in the cradle where it lies' and of the tolling of the funeral bell? Would not that, to an Elizabethan, suggest lead also, seeing that in those days corpses were commonly wrapped in lead before interment? Mind you, I am not proposing, as some have done, that in her desire for Bassanio's success Portia is playing a trick upon her dead father and had the song sung in order that her lover might learn the secret before he makes his choice. 'I could teach you', she had said to him,

> How to choose right, but then I am for-
> sworn,
> So will I never be—
>
> [III. ii. 11-12]

and Portia was a woman of her word. To imagine that she *was* forsworn would so detract from her moral stature as seriously to impair the beauty of the play. What then? The song, I take it, though sung at Portia's command (because she is the lady of the house, and all the music therein) is intended to represent, in distillation, so to speak, the thoughts that are passing through Bassanio's mind as he 'comments on the caskets to himself' [s.d., III. ii. 63]. In other words, it is symbolical rather than dramatic, a function which Shakespeare's songs very often perform, as a matter of fact, and perform far more delightfully than the symbolical Dumbshows and Presenters' Expositions with which his rival dramatists commonly sprinkled their plays. And if it be granted that the song gives us the clue to Bassanio's thoughts, the meaning of its words at once becomes plain. The theme is Fancy, by which Shakespeare and his contemporaries understood both what we now call sentimentality and, as the word still signifies, a passing inclination or whim. Originally a contraction of *fantasy,* the meaning of 'illusion', 'error', or 'unreality' yet clung to it, especially when the word was used in connection with Love. . . . Fancy, then, is not true love; it springs from the head, that is, from calculation, not from the heart. It is engendered in the eyes; it feeds upon mere appearances; it has no roots in reality, but dies almost as soon as it is born. And what applies in the sphere of love is equally relevant to inclination and choice in other respects—for example in the choice between the caskets, two of them glittering in gold and silver, the third plain lead with no attractions for the eye whatever but bearing the motto

> Who chooseth me must give and hazard
> all he hath
>
> [II. vii. 9]

Thus Bassanio quite naturally, as if the song had expressed his own thought, continues that thought in the opening words of his speech:

> *So* may the outward shows be least them-
> selves—
> The world is still deceived with orna-
> ment—
>
> [III. ii. 73-4]

and then, after further elaboration of the same topic, unhesitatingly selects the right casket. His choice is guided not by any trick of Portia's, but by the genuineness of his own nature and (which is part of the same thing) by his very real love for Portia, a love ready to give and hazard all, which comes out in the plainness (which moves us more than el-

oquence) of his simple but direct reply to Portia's lovely speech of self-surrender:

> Madam, you have bereft me of all words,
> Only my blood speaks to you in my veins.
>
> [III. ii. 175-76]

Yes, the final casket-scene merits far more attention than it has hitherto received. Its workmanship is more delicate and its implications deeper than most people realize in these crude modern times in which we live; for I have little doubt that 'the judicious' among Shakespeare's own audience took his points readily enough.

But if Bassanio is Portia's true love—the one genuine suitor among the throng of self-seeking egoists who prate of their own worth or claims, as they make their choice at Belmont—which it was surely Shakespeare's business as a popular dramatist to represent him, how does this reading of his character agree with what we learn about him elsewhere in the play? Here we come upon a strange misconception on the part of some critics. Let me quote two of my own masters. To begin with Herbert Grierson [in his *Cross-Currents in English Literature of the XVIIth Century*]:

> Of all the suitors who come to Belmont, Bassanio best deserves the title of a 'worldly chooser'. The others have apparently as much to give as to receive; but Bassanio, like Lord Byron when he proposed to marry Miss Milbanke, was a suitor in order to be able to pay his debts and generally settle himself. . . .

Here he echoes [Arthur] Quiller-Couch, who writes [in his *Shakespeare's Workmanship*]:

> If one thing is more certain than another, it is that a predatory young gentleman like Bassanio would *not* have chosen the leaden casket.

Finally, he quotes from Bassanio's soliloquy the well-known passage:

> The world is still deceived with ornament.
> In law, what plea so tainted and corrupt,
> But, being seasoned with a gracious voice,
> Obscures the show of evil? In religion,
> What damnéd error, but some sober brow
> Will bless it, and approve it with a text?—
>
> [III. ii 74-9]

and is moved to interrupt:

> 'Yes, yes—and what about yourself, my little fellow? What has altered *you,* that you of all men start talking as though you addressed a Young Men's Christian Association?

As Mistress Quickly says to Pistol. 'By my truth, these are very bitter words' [cf. *2 Henry IV,* II. iv. 171] Yet they are quoted by Grierson, who finds 'a strange moral confusion' in *The Merchant of Venice.* In truth, the only confusion in this matter of

Bassanio is a critical one in the mind of his modern interpreters. For what are the grounds upon which they condemn him—or rather condemn Shakespeare for making him so badly? Q's [Quiller-Couch's] exposition of them is too long to meet point by point. But the burden of it is just this: That Bassanio is an extravagant youngster, that he hopes to pay off his debts by marrying Portia, that in order to make the necessary show at Belmont he is forced to borrow still more money from his friend Antonio, and finally that in order to persuade Antonio to put his hand once again into his pocket, he represents his suit to the wealthy Lady of Belmont as more or less of a safe investment, wilfully concealing the fact that his success stood upon the hazard of being lucky enough to choose the right casket.

It is this last point which gives the whole case away. For consider: in order to get his double plot to work at all, Shakespeare has to make Bassanio borrow money from Antonio to pursue his courtship, since that is the reason why Antonio in his turn borrows money from Shylock. And when one man goes to borrow money from another, even his best friend, he likes to be able to offer him *some* hope of repayment. Bassanio therefore speaks of Portia's wealth and of her obvious interest in himself, saying however (as a young man would) less of his own love for her. All this is surely very natural and it would seem even more natural in Elizabethan days, when most matches were what Q calls 'predatory'; i.e. for business reasons. That Bassanio should stress Portia's wealth, then, so far from reflecting on his character, merely shows him to be acting on principles of common caution; and that he should speak of their mutual attraction shows that, unlike most suitors of the age, he intends a love-match. But what about his deception? What excuse has he for concealing the casket-lottery from his friend? One might answer that the deception is not his but Shakespeare's; that the dramatist is careful to tell the audience nothing about the caskets until the second scene of the play. Bassanio's petition to Antonio and the latter's consent provide enough interest for Scene i. To have introduced the casket theme into that conversation would have distracted attention from the main point of the borrowing incident and would have raised an awkward issue—the very issue indeed that Q raises. No spectator would notice its absence; and when it is referred to in Scene ii no spectator would remember that it should have been mentioned by Bassanio in Scene i. As a matter of fact I do not believe that anyone before Q has seen that the story involves a small difficulty here. In short, *dramatically* speaking—and Shakespeare was a dramatist, not a novelist or a historian—the difficulty is not there.

So one could argue and the reply to Q would be valid enough. But no such reply is needed in fact at all, since if one follows the text it becomes clear that Shakespeare intended us to realize that when Bassanio speaks with Antonio in Scene i, he himself knows nothing whatever of the casket lottery or even of the will of Portia's father, for the simple reason that when he last visited Belmont the father was still alive. This is made clear in Scene ii at the first mention of Bassanio. From Portia's complaint that owing to her father's strange will she is allowed no freedom of choice in marriage, from the description of all the suitors who have so far come to Belmont and from the news Nerissa gives that hearing of the caskets they were all packing up to return home unless they can win her 'by some other sort' [I. ii. 102], we gather that Portia's father is only recently deceased, and the contents of his will become known. Thus when Nerissa goes on to ask, 'Do you not remember, Lady, *in your father's time,* a Venetian, a scholar and a soldier, that came hither in company of the Marquis of Montferrat?' [I. ii. 112-14]. Shakespeare leaves no doubt in the mind of those who attend to what he writes that Bassanio had not yet come as a suitor and could have known nothing of the will.

And what is true of this matter holds good also for the whole question of Bassanio's character. Whatever he may seem to modern eyes poring over a book, on the *stage* he is always as he was meant to be, an honest young lover. Shakespeare does not develop him very much; he is in the main a lay figure, whose dramatic function is to choose the right casket and to bring out the more important characters with whom he has to do, namely Antonio and Portia. But the references to him by others leave no doubt of his attractiveness. He is announced at his first entry as 'most noble'; and though sly Nerissa in the second Scene knows of course that praise of him will sound welcome in Portia's ears, when she declares that he 'of all men that ever my foolish eyes looked upon, was the best deserving a fair lady' [I. ii. 117-19], the audience is assuredly expected to accept her words as the truth.

The Trial-Scene

But 'this flaw in characterization' which Q discovers in Bassanio goes, he says [in his introduction to the New Shakespeare edition of the play],

> right down through the workmanship of the play, for the evil opposed against these curious Christians is specific: it is Cruelty; and, yet again specifically, the peculiar cruelty of a Jew. To this cruelty an artist at the top of his art would surely have opposed mansuetude, clemency, charity, and specifically Christian charity. Shakespeare misses more than half the point when he makes the intended victims as a class and by habit just as heartless as Shylock without any of Shylock's passionate excuse.

This passage Sir Herbert Grierson again quotes and endorses, generalizing it in one of his own which begins:

What puzzles one in Shakespeare's plays is that not infrequently while presenting the story and characters so faithfully and vividly that it is difficult for the reader to avoid passing moral judgment on it, Shakespeare himself seems willing not only to omit comment, but to acquiesce in a view that is to us repellent, to accept standards of which his own vivid telling of the story affords the most effective condemnation.

With these statements of the strange case of Shylock and his creator we may turn now to the trial-scene and to the most baffling character-problem, after that of Hamlet, in Shakespeare.

First of all, then, there is no doubt that modern audiences and readers—I stress the word modern—tend to be left at the end of the play with a feeling of frustration or discomfort. The classical expression of this, as will be remembered, is the story told by [Heinrich] Heine [in his *Sämmtliche Werke*], himself a Jew, which runs:

> When I saw this Play at Drury Lane, there stood behind me a pale, fair Briton, who at the end of the Fourth Act, fell to weeping passionately, several times exclaiming, 'The poor man is wronged!'

She was referring, of course, to the judgment of the court. But the wrong, be it noted, comes in reality not from Portia or the Duke; for despite Q's words, Shylock, a would-be murderer, is let off remarkably lightly. And though the compulsory conversion is repugnant to our notions, it would have appeared an enforced benefit to the Elizabethan and medieval mind. Some however have argued that Portia's invalidation of the bond on the grounds that while speaking of a pound of flesh it mentions no blood, is a mere quibble; that she does in fact what Bassanio implores her to do, namely

> Wrest once the law to your authority—
> To do a great right, do a little wrong.
> [IV. i. 215-16]

Yet her conduct of the case, though it may appear strange in the eyes of modern law, is quite in the manner of Elizabethan trials, and in all likelihood excited no comment whatever from an audience which consisted partly at least of law students. For example, the quasi-legal quibbling of the grave-digger in *Hamlet* on the subject of suicide by drowning—'If the man go to this water and drown himself, it is, will he nill he, he goes, mark you that. But if the water come to him, and drown him, he drowns not himself' [V. i. 16-19]—and the rest of it, is an almost exact reproduction of real arguments used at a well-known case of 1554 and probably repeated regularly by counsel on similar occasions later. Portia's law seems reason itself by comparison. No, the wrong to Shylock that we are conscious of is done by Shakespeare and not the court that tries him. The dramatist seems to have

excited our interest in and our sympathy for this Jew to such a degree that we find the levity after his exit intolerable and the happiness of the last Act heartless.

It is the fashion among some critics today to say that this feeling is based upon a misunderstanding; that Shakespeare really intended Shylock as a ridiculous villain; that he was so played up to the end of the eighteenth century; and that first [Edmund] Kean and then [Henry] Irving sentimentalized him; in a word, that our interest and sympathy spring from a humanitarianism which is quite modern and of which Shakespeare himself was totally unconscious.

It is possible, I admit, to sentimentalize Shylock; and I think it has been done. Certainly, if [W. C.] Macready and Irving raised him, in the words of Edmund Booth [quoted in E. E. Stoll's *Shakespeare Studies*], 'out of the darkness of his native element of revengeful selfishness into the light of the venerable Hebrew, the martyr, the avenger' they did something which Shakespeare never intended. But a 'comic Jew'? 'a comical villain'? Is not that label equally misguiding? No doubt he was got up to look grotesque; a typical old Jew would be grotesque to an Elizabethan audience, while Shakespeare makes Gratiano the mouth-piece of the ordinary citizen's attitude.

There are, however, good reasons, I think, why we ought to regard Shylock as a tragic and not a comical figure:

(i) If he is merely comical, the play assuredly loses a great deal dramatically, and it is a sound principle to view with suspicion any critical interpretation which involves dramatic loss—Shakespeare may generally be relied upon to make the greatest possible capital out of his material.

(ii) *The Merchant of Venice* is not the only play of the period containing a detailed study of Jewish character. [Christopher] Marlowe's *Jew of Malta* preceded it, had been (and still was) an exceedingly popular play on the London stage, and belonged to the Admiral's Men, the rival company to Shakespeare's. Shakespeare's Jew would, therefore, inevitably be compared with Marlowe's, and Shakespeare would have striven to the utmost to excel his predecessor. What kind of character, then, was the Barabas of Marlowe? He was, like all Marlowe's heroes, 'conceived of on a gigantic scale . . . a very terrible and powerful alien, endowed with all the resources of wealth and unencumbered by any Christian scruples' [H. S. Bennett in his introduction to *The Jew of Malta*]. Is it likely that Shakespeare would have set up a ludicrous Shylock to outbid this Barabas? Surely he would have desired, especially with [Richard] Burbadge at his elbow also desiring to outdo Edward Alleyn, to create a figure equally terrible, but human and convincing at the same time, which Marlowe's Jew never succeeds in being?

(iii) And my third reason is that a ridiculous villain is unShakespearian. Can you find such a villain in any other of his plays? Is Iago, or Macbeth, or Edmund [in *King Lear*], or even Richard III in this sense comical? But these, it may be said, come from the tragedies, and therefore do not count. Very well, where in the comedies is he to be seen? There are plenty of such villains in Ben Jonson. The Jonsonian comedies are full of them; they are his chief stock-in-trade. Indeed, that is one of the main differences between his conception of comedy and Shakespeare's. Villainy is never comic with Shakespeare; and Shylock is not to be fitted into the formulae of Bergson or George Meredith. He does not belong to what is called 'pure comedy' at all.

Yet, if he is not comical, he is not a mere villain of melodrama like Barabas either. He is a 'tragic' villain, i.e. he is so represented that we feel him to be a man, a terrible and gigantic man enough, but with 'hands, organs, dimensions, senses, affections, passions—fed with the same food, hurt by the same weapons, subject to the same diseases, healed by the same means, warmed and cooled by the same winter and summer, as a Christian is' [III. i. 59-64]. Shylock is a far greater character than Barabas, not because he is less blood-thirsty—his lust for blood is more awful because more convincing—but because he is one of ourselves. And, as he goes out, what we ought to exclaim is not (with Heine's fair Briton), 'The man is wronged', but 'There, but for the grace of God, go I'. . . . (pp. 97-108)

It is, of course, just this common humanity, which Shakespeare brings out and insists upon in stroke after stroke, that the Christians of Venice deny (like the Nazis of modern Germany). And if Shylock is a villain, an awful and appalling human being, who made him such? People like Antonio. Antonio, we are told by one of his friends, is the perfect Christian gentleman,

> The kindest man,
> The best-conditioned and unwearied spir-
>   it
> In doing courtesies;
>
>   [III. ii. 292-94]

yet, when the Jew reminds him

> You call me misbeliever, cut-throat dog,
> And spit upon my Jewish gaberdine . . .
> You that did void your rheum upon my
>   beard,
> And foot me as you spurn a stranger cur.
>   [I. iii. 111-12, 117-18]

he raps out:

> I am as like to call thee so again,
> To spit on thee again, to spurn thee too.
>   [I. iii. 130-31]

But Shakespeare, we are told, shared the prejudices of his age against Jews; he would himself have applauded Antonio's action, might even have imitated it. Shylock excites our modern sympathies because Shakespeare allowed his imagination to run away with him. The humanity of the Jew was an unconscious by-product of his dramatic genius.

For myself, I think we have heard more than enough of the vegetable Shakespeare, of the impersonal, almost witless, imaginative growth, exfoliating plays and poems without premeditation or reflection, as a gourd-vine produces pumpkins. No doubt, as with all the great novelists and poets, once the theme seized upon him, it was liable to take him in charge, so that he could never tell at the beginning exactly how a play might work out. Yet, as he fell under the spell, he must have retained consciousness of his direction, and when all was done, he surely, if he had a mind at all, saw his achievement as a whole and assessed it at its proper worth. Shylock may have taken him to some extent by surprise, but Shylock was the child of *his* imagination and *his* intellect, and it seems to me absurd to suppose that the sympathies of such a father can have been wholly on the side of the spitting Antonio. (pp. 108-10)

The Jew is allowed no defendant in the court to plead for him as a fellow human being and a defenceless alien. There is no one to speak for him except himself. . . . I have no doubt at all that Shylock was intended by Shakespeare to be a comment upon the treatment of Jewry throughout the Christian dispensation.

Why does he not say so? Why did he not even, as Q says he should, oppose to the cruelty of Shylock, clemency, charity, and specifically Christian charity? . . . Would he not depict the ferocious assassin in all his dire ferocity, and yet contrive to *imply*, for those who had ears to hear, that there was another side to the question?

This is no rhetorical flourish. The actual position of Shakespeare when he wrote *The Merchant* was not unlike that I depict in imagination. Shortly before the play was first staged, the London crowds, from whom he drew his audience, had watched in their thousands, and with howls of gleeful execration, a venerable old Hebrew, Dr. Lopez, falsely accused of attempting to poison the Queen, done to death with the hideous ritual of hanging and disembowelling before their blood-lustful eyes. There is even I believe an allusion to the event in the play itself. You remember that strange image which Shakespeare places in the railing mouth of Gratiano:

>   thy currish spirit
> Governed a wolf, who hanged for human
>   slaughter,
> Even from the gallows did his fell soul
>   fleet,

Launcelot, Shylock, and Jessica. Act II, scene v. By H. Hofmann. The Department of Rare Books and Special Collections, The University of Michigan Library.

And whilst thou layest in thy unhallowed
  dam,
Infused itself in thee.

[IV. i. 133-37]

What does it mean? A wolf hanged for human slaughter, who ever heard of such a thing? This wolf was no quadruped, it was a Jewish animal, in other words it was Lopez himself, who is commonly called Lopus or Lupus in the literature of the time.

And there was still more involved. Not only would the groundlings in the audience at the play be inflamed with anti-Semitism at the time, the great ones who might be found among the judicious spectators were in a like mood. Lopez had unhappily incurred the hatred of the all-powerful Earl of Essex, who was the main instrument in bringing him to the gallows; and the earl's bosom friend was another young lord, the Earl of Southampton, Shakespeare's own patron and in all likelihood his intimate.

Such were the perilous circumstances in which

the compassionate Shakespeare was compelled to write his Jew play. I say compelled, for the rival company to his own had revived Marlowe's *Jew of Malta* for the occasion, and were drawing large houses, while his friends at court would doubtless look to him for a Jew-baiting spectacle in the theatre. Well, he gave them what they asked, he gave them an appalling Shylock and the coarse-grained storm-trooper Gratiano to express their sentiments about him; he even represents the best man in the story spurning him like a dog and bespitting him—would not his friends the earls have done the same?

But he did more, by making Shylock a suffering human being, he revealed 'the momtanish inhumanity' of the behaviour of Christians towards the Hebrew race, and in the speech on Mercy, at the very centre and climax of the play, he revealed his own standpoint. Portia's speech, one of the greatest sermons in all literature, an expression of religious thought worthy to set beside St. Paul's hymn in praise of Love, is of course addressed to the Jew. But I find it incredible that Shakespeare intended it for Jews alone. The very fact that it is based throughout upon the Lord's Prayer, which would mean nothing to a Hebrew, suggests that it was composed to knock at Christian hearts.

When Q accuses Shakespeare of not setting up the ideal of 'clemency, charity and specifically Christian charity', to oppose that of Cruelty and Revenge, he strangely forgets 'the quality of Mercy' [IV. i. 184]. And Shylock, as I have said, is let off very lightly. He loses the money he had made by usury—that was only right and proper. He is compelled to become a Christian—that was only an enforced benefit. But he was not hanged, drawn and quartered as Dr. Lopez was—much to Gratiano's disgust.

Shylock is a terrible old man. But he is the inevitable product of centuries of racial persecution. Shakespeare does not draw this moral. He merely exposes the situation. He is neither for nor against Shylock. Shakespeare never takes sides. Yet surely if he were alive today he would see in Mercy, mercy in the widest sense, which embraces understanding and forgiveness, the only possible solution of our racial hatreds and enmities.

Belmont

But the exit of Shylock is not the end of the play. The cloud which had been gathering since the opening scene and looked so black for Antonio, instead of breaking, passes over, leaving him unharmed and even the villain himself with only a light punishment. And so the tension is relaxed for the audience. The trial is followed by an amusing interview between the disguised women and their lovers, together with the surrender of the rings, which promises further fun to come.

Is the incident . . . too trivial, too light to counterbalance the stress of emotion from which we have just emerged? Only if our sympathies have been with Shylock the man, rather than Jewry; and as I said, we misapprehend Shakespeare the dramatist if they are. Certainly, Shakespeare knew that the audience for which he wrote would have no sympathy with Shylock; and it is just because he knew that, that he could afford to exhibit his humanity.

Yet the crisis of the trial scene was unusually serious for a comedy. That he knew also; and realized that all his efforts would be needed to send his spectators home in the mood he wished to leave with them. And so, we have the scene at Belmont—the gayest, happiest, most blessed scene in all Shakespeare. Suddenly we are caught away from Venice, from its scorns, its hatreds and revenges, and transported to a world of magic in which men and women live like gods, without care, without toil, without folly, and without strife—except such folly and strife as lovers use one with another. Belmont is not heaven, because there is much talk of marrying and giving in marriage, and withal a

roguish touch of [Giovanni] Boccaccio now and again. Rather it is Elysium, a Renaissance Elysium, a garden full of music under the soft Italian night, with a gracious and stately mansion in the background.

Shakespeare paints the scene with all his wonderful artistry. Observe, for instance, the part the moon plays in it, how she rides in and out of the shifting clouds as the action goes forward—at one moment it is bright as day, at the next

> The moon sleeps with Endymion
> [V. i. 109]

so that Lorenzo cannot see Portia's face.

Music and the moon are the twin themes of this final movement:

> Sweet soul, let's in, and there expect their
>   coming.
> And yet no matter: why should we go in?
> My friend Stephano, signify, I pray you,
> Within the house, your mistress is at
>   hand,
> And bring your music forth into the
>   air. . . .
> How sweet the moonlight sleeps upon this
>   bank!
> Here will we sit, and let the sounds of
>   music
> Creep in our ears—soft stillness and the
>   night
> Become   the   touches   of   sweet
>   harmony. . . .
> Sit, Jessica. Look how the floor of heaven
> Is thick inlaid with patens of bright gold.
> There's not the smallest orb which thou
>   behold'st
> But in his motion like an angel sings,
> Still quiring to the young-eyed cherubins;
> Such harmony is in immortal souls!
> But while this muddy vesture of decay
> Doth grossly close it in, we cannot hear
>   it. . . .
> [cf. V. i. 49-65]

> The man that hath no music in himself,
> Nor is not moved with concord of sweet
>   sounds,
> Is fit for treasons, stratagems, and spoils,
> The motions of his spirit are dull as night,
> And his affections dark as Erebus:
> Let no such man be trusted. . . . Mark the
>   music.
> [cf. V. i. 83-7]

After Mercy—Harmony!

Grossly closed in by our muddy vesture of decay, it is difficult—perhaps impossible—for us poor mortals to hear it, and missing it we, Jew or Christian, grow 'fit for treasons, stratagems, and spoils', and our 'affections dark as Erebus', the Erebus which Shylock and Jew-baiter alike inherit; but the music is there all the while.

Some day, one blessed day we shall not live to see, perhaps the world may come to Belmont and be moved not with internecine hatred and racial scorn, but 'with concord of sweet sounds'.

And if there be any reader to ask what connexion there can be between music and politics, between our woeful discords and the 'touches of sweet harmony', I do not need to refer him to the *Republic* of Plato, but to a disciple of Plato who had never read his book. I mean Shakespeare himself, who in *Henry V* [I. ii. 180-83] tells us that

> government, though high and
>   low, and lower,
> Put into parts, doth keep in one consent,
> Congreeing in a full and natural close,
> Like music.

Is the world capable of such music? That is *the* political problem of our time and, if we cannot solve it, he prophesies in *Troilus and Cressida,* I. iii. 110-24:

> Hark, what discord follows! . . .
> Force should be right; or rather right and
>   wrong,
> Between whose endless jar justice resides,
> Should lose their names, and so should
>   justice too.
> Thus everything includes itself in power,
> Power into will, will into appetite;
> And appetite, an universal wolf,
> So doubly seconded with will and power,
> Must make perforce an universal prey,
> And last eat up himself

(pp. 112-17)

The prophecy seems nearer fulfilment in 1962 than it did in 1938.

The impending dissolution of the universe . . . was never far from the mind of Shakespeare and his contemporaries; and Prospero supplies a calmer because more contemplative account of it in his famous epilogue after the masque in *The Tempest.* The Prospero however who gave us the vision he called *The Merchant of Venice* had no wish to trouble us at Belmont with thoughts of doomsday or any apocalyptic imaginings. And even our memories of cruel Venice begin to fade when we hear Lancelot winding his mock postman's horn in and out among the trees to announce to Lorenzo and Jessica and to us, the audience, that the travellers are about to return home. And presently, when we return home, or shut our books, the characters themselves begin to fade and melt into thin air, as we realize that Bassanio the young lover, his bosom friend Antonio, Portia the great lady and learned judge, yes, even the fierce Jew himself, rushing with uplifted knife upon his victim—all are spirits, the creatures of dramatic art.

Yet if we are to go home happy, the characters all but Shylock must first of all be given happiness. How was this to be accomplished for Antonio, who though saved from the knife was still a ruined merchant? It was Portia who saved him; it was given

to her to restore his fortune. But mark how she does it.

> Antonio, you are welcome,
> And I have better news in store for you
> Than you expect; unseal this letter soon,
> There you shall find three of your argosies
> Are richly come to harbour suddenly.
> You shall not know by what strange acci-
>   dent
> I chanced on this letter.

[V. i. 273-78]

That three of Antonio's argosies should be 'richly come to harbour suddenly' would be unbelievable if Shakespeare had allowed us a moment to ponder it, yet not more difficult of credence than the 'strange accident' by which Portia chanced upon the letter that told it. It is all a little piece of Shakespearian legerdemain. . . . (pp. 117-18)

And while all this has been passing, the moon has sunk and every thicket around Belmont has begun to thrill and sing of dawn. Portia lifts a hand:

> It is almost morning,
> Let us go in.

[cf. V. i. 295-97]

And so the comedy comes home. 'Pack, clouds away! and welcome, day!' [Thomas Heywood, *Pack, Clouds, Away*]. (p. 118)

> *John Dover Wilson, " 'The Merchant of Venice' in 1937," in his* Shakespeare's Happy Comedies, *Northwestern University Press, 1962, pp. 94-119.*

SHYLOCK

Bernard Grebanier

[Grebanier examines the five scenes in which Shylock *appears in* The Merchant of Venice *in an attempt to determine the nature of his character. In essence, the critic finds* Shylock's *desire for vengeance against* Antonio *motivated by the merchant's lending money interest-free, lessening* Shylock's *customers, and hence, his profits. Further,* Shylock *hates* Antonio *because, according to the Jew, the merchant has repeatedly denigrated his race and religion. Grebanier points out, however, that in keeping with his virtuous character* Antonio *probably did not belittle Judaism, rather* Shylock *himself, an issue the usurer confused with racial discrimination. For further commentary on* Shylock's *character, see the excerpts by Frank Kermode, E. F. C. Ludowyk, John W. Draper, Marvin Felheim, William Leigh Godshalk, John Dover Wilson, Warren D. Smith, and Lawrence Danson.]*

These are the forces at work in *The Merchant of Venice:* the bountiful grace and liberality of Antonio, Bassanio, Portia, and their friends, who are determined that money shall be a prop to those enrichments of life, not the death of them; and the suppression of all grace and liberality on the part of Shylock, who is convinced that money by itself is the only measurement of joy in life. (p. 184)

But Shakespeare could not know that the world would choose, of the two paths open to it, the one in which money became the destroyer of love and friendship. Only Shylock, in his play, prefers that road. Shylock is isolated from love and friendship, and insulated against them, because he has nothing of himself to spare for them. Whatever affections he owns are expended upon the accumulation of money and the making of money from money. He bullies his daughter and starves his servant. Shakespeare, never the creator to put the case weakly, makes this greed for money all the more deplorable in that Shylock is a man of no mediocre qualities. He has dignity, strength, purposefulness, tenacity, courage, an excellent mind, a cuttingly wry sense of humor. It is a great injustice to the man Shakespeare has depicted to imagine him "servile and repulsive," "fawning" or "sneaking and underhanded"—as many commentators and actors have depicted him. It is an equally grave injustice to him to conceive him, as so many others have done, as suffering from racial persecution. He is too strong-minded, too conscious of personal dignity for that. It is he who looks down upon the Christians, not they on him. He stands on too much of an eminence to feel persecuted, and he who does not feel persecuted, is not persecuted. Shakespeare has so presented him that we are bound to feel the great waste that such a man, framed for noble ends, should be debased by his ruling greed. Without the disease of greed, it is easy to imagine Shylock as walking like a king among men. But this one, terrible obsession channels all his best traits into the service of villainy. And for that he comes to grief in the end. The gods are just, Shakespeare always feels, and of our vices make instruments to plague us.

I am aware that to assert so unconventional an interpretation of Shylock entitles me to no more credence than is to be accorded the time-honored views of him as a pathetic, comic, or conventionally villainous Hebrew, without the proof. The proof is in the play.

Shylock appears in but five scenes of *The Merchant of Venice*. Let us trace what Shakespeare shows us of him, step by step, from the beginning. One of the chief causes of confusion concerning his character comes from the failure of commentators to consider Shylock's speeches in the order in which they occur. If I commence by seizing upon the "Many a time and oft" [I. iii. 106] and "Hath not a Jew eyes?" [III. i. 59] passages, I might convincingly enough make out Shylock to be a tragic representative of his race. On the other hand, if I

choose to commence with Gratiano's slurs in the trial scene [IV. i. 364, 379, 398], I might convincingly enough make out Shakespeare's purposes to be anti-Semitic. But if I honestly wish to discover Shakespeare's intentions, I will begin with no preconceptions concerning Shylock's character, and start gauging him from the moment we first meet him in the play. If we are to understand him, we must be patient; we shall be wise to take the advice of the King in *Alice's Adventures in Wonderland:* "Begin at the beginning and go on till you come to the end: then stop."

We first meet Shylock in I. iii. (His name has been said, variously, to be a transliteration of Shalach or Shelach (*Genesis* X, 24), "cormorant," or of Shiloh, the sanctuary of Jehovah. . . .) Bassanio has already broached the subject of the loan. From the very outset we see the moneylender standing firm and as unyielding as solid rock. Bassanio is edgy, Shylock absolutely noncommittal: he may lend the money and then again he may not. In these lines which open the scene, it is Shylock who is in control of the situation:

> SHYLOCK.   Three thousand ducats. Well.
> BASSANIO.   Ay, sir, for three months.
> SHYLOCK.   For three months. Well.
> BASSANIO.   For the which, as I told you, Antonio shall be bound.
> SHYLOCK.   Antonio shall become bound. Well.
> BASSANIO.   May you stead me? Will you pleasure me? Shall I know your answer?
> SHYLOCK.   Three thousand ducats for three months, and Antonio bound.
>
> [I. iii. 1-10]

Shakespeare, as ever, is remarkable in his ability to cause us to hear the very tone in which his characters speak: the calm, deliberately unemotional voice of Shylock, giving not the slightest intimation of his intentions, and the nervous, high-strung anxiety of Bassanio. Nor does Shylock do anything to make Bassanio more comfortable: he is enjoying too much keeping him dangling:

> BASSANIO.   Your answer to that.
> SHYLOCK.   Antonio is a good man.
>
> [I. iii. 11-12]

There is something in his voice so arrogant that Bassanio hotly demands:

> Have you heard any imputation to the contrary?
>
> [I. iii. 13]

To which Shylock rejoins, with the loftiness of an adult quieting a child:

> Ho, no, no, no, no! My meaning in saying he is a good man is to have you understand me that he is sufficient.
>
> [I. iii. 15-17]

And then he begins to enumerate the risks, with

the precision and carefulness of the man who is used to counting every penny—the risks of ships, seas, human fallibility, pirates, winds, rocks; and ends, once more without in any way hinting that he will oblige:

> The man is, notwithstanding, sufficient.
> Three thousand ducats; I think I *may* take his bond.
>
> [I. iii. 25-7]

That he deliberately stresses the "may" to embarrass Bassanio further is proved by the latter's next line:

> Be assured you may.
>
> [I. iii. 28]

Which only calls forth a further piece of haughtiness from Shylock:

> I *will* be assured I may, and that I may be assured, I will bethink me.
>
> [I. iii. 29-30]

In other words, Don't try to rush me; I mean to think this over.

We have progressed only 30 lines from his first appearance, and it is already too late for us ever to expect a cringing, fawning, imposed-upon Shylock. Whatever we hear him say later, we are bound to interpret in terms of the Shylock we already know.

It is now that Bassanio invites him to meet Antonio over dinner, and that he replies haughtily in words that have been so much and so blindly overinterpreted: he will not go to smell pork.

> I will buy with you, sell with you, talk with you, walk with you, and so following; but I will not eat with you, drink with you, nor pray with you.
>
> [I. iii. 35-8]

These certainly sound like the words of a pious Jew. But how seriously are we to take them? Presently we shall learn that he does indeed go to eat and drink with the Christians, and for reasons which do him no credit. Since he has no intention of refusing the invitation, how are we to take his words? In the same spirit as everything else he has thus far said: to make Bassanio uncomfortable.

Antonio now appears, and while Bassanio is greeting him, Shylock has his first soliloquy. (pp. 185-88)

Here Shylock expresses his burning hatred for Antonio for the first time. He would like to pretend to himself that that hatred is based upon lofty, religious grounds. But the truth will out in spite of him:

> I hate him for he is a Christian,
> But *more for that in low simplicity*
> *He lends out money gratis and brings down*
> *The rate of usance here with us in Venice.*
> If I can catch him once upon the hip,

> I will feed fat the ancient grudge I bear him.
>
> [I. iii. 42-7]

(How, after these words, is it possible to construe, as some critics have amiably done, the bond later proposed as really offered in the spirit of friendship?)

> He hates our sacred nation, and he rails
> *Even there where merchants most do congregate,*
> On me, *my bargains, and my well-won thrift,*
> Which he calls interest. Cursed be my tribe
> If I forgive him!
>
> [I. iii. 48-52]

I have italicized the pertinent passages to show that underneath all his pretenses to himself, it is only Antonio's disdain of interest which rankles. Shakespeare is here, as always, fascinating in his psychological presentation. (pp. 188-89)

See how Shylock twists and turns, trying to posture to himself as indignant on grounds purely impersonal and larger. Antonio, according to him, hates the Jews. How does he show it? Not by railing against them but by railing against Shylock. What does he rail against Shylock for? His religion? No. For his taking of exorbitant interest—and, at that, *where other merchants can hear*. All this Shylock chooses to construe as an insult to all the Jews, and on those grounds he vows vengeance. But, for all that, the real basis for his fury has revealed itself. A perfect example of an all-too-human self-justification.

It is part of Shakespeare's profundity that Shylock should not accurately know himself. What miser ever faced the truth about himself, or failed to call his penuriousness by some better-sounding name like thrift or self-restraint? That is why the greed of a Jonsonian miser is not really credible, and Shylock's is. This inability to face what he really is will make itself dramatically vocal when we meet him for the last time, in the trial scene.

Now Shylock forces Bassanio to press him again for an answer, pretends still to be mulling over the loan, and then feigns seeing Antonio for the first time—Ah, how do you do? We were just talking about you. ("Your worship was the last man in our mouths" [I. iii. 60].) Still the condescending Shylock.

Up to this point in the play Antonio, when we have met him, has had nothing to say about Shylock. It is in this scene that we are first given to know how he feels about the moneylender. He speaks to him coldly; this is merely a business matter, and he is quite prepared to pay the interest he disapproves of, since Shylock, of course, will ask for it. His voice is neither friendly nor hostile; Shylock, in responding, lines his words with irony:

ANTONIO. Shylock, albeit I neither lend
nor borrow
By taking nor by giving of excess,
Yet to supply the ripe wants of my
friend,
I'll break a custom. (*to Bass.*) Is he yet
possess'd
How much ye would?
SHYLOCK.   Ay, ay, three thousand
ducats.
ANTONIO. And for three months.
SHYLOCK. I had forgot; three months; you
told me so.

[I. iii. 61-5]

But he still refuses to indicate whether or not he
will lend the money. Moreover, this is too good an
opportunity to miss. I thought, says he, you make
it a practice never to ask or give interest on a loan?
I never do, Antonio replies.

Now that he has Antonio at a disadvantage, Shylock cannot let slip the occasion to justify the taking of interest. By citing the enterprise of Jacob
while serving Laban, he attempts to confute the Aristotelian argument that money, being inanimate,
is put to unnatural uses when it is employed only
to multiply itself. Again Shylock demonstrates the
characteristic precision of his mind: This Jacob
was the third in line from Abraham—let's see,
wasn't he? Yes, he was the third. Antonio, knowing his man, cuts in: Did Jacob take interest? Shylock does not like such a forthright question:

No, not take interest, not, as you would
say,
Directly interest.

[I. iii. 76-7]

But Jacob was not above a little trickery to insure
his own welfare; it was a way to profit, and profit
is a blessing when it isn't stolen. Antonio blasts
through the sophistry: was the Scriptural passage
written to justify the taking of interest,

Or is your gold and silver ewes and rams?
[I. iii. 95]

Shylock answers him and Aristotle wryly:

I cannot tell; I make it breed as fast.
[I. iii. 96]

Antonio seems well aware that Shylock is a religious hypocrite; in disgust he observes that the
Devil knows how to cite Scripture for his purpose:

O, what a goodly outside falsehood hath!
[I. iii. 102]

Unperturbed, Shylock goes back to considering
the loan. No hint from him whether it is to be
granted. No, not yet—let them wait. Thus, Antonio
is compelled to ask again: Will you lend this
money? It is here that Shylock delivers one of his
celebrated speeches. It is odd that despite its fame,
it has never been seen to reveal Shakespeare's psychological cunning.

Shylock has intimated nothing of his intentions
concerning the ducats asked for. First he must
make Antonio—him who condemns interest—
smart, now that he comes asking for a loan. So, for
the hated one's benefit, Shylock cloaks himself in
the dignity of race. But again, in despite of himself,
he reveals that he is not complaining of persecution, only justifying his taking of interest. Many a
time and oft Antonio has berated him on the Rialto
(where merchants most do congregate!)—about
what? His religion? No:

About my moneys and my usances.
[I. iii. 108]

But this Shylock deliberately confuses as though
it were an insult to all Jews:

Still have I borne it with a patient shrug,
For sufferance is the badge of all our tribe.
[cf. I. iii. 109-10]

We may well imagine that Antonio, no fool, is experiencing a queasiness at this smug sanctimonious-
ness. Shylock, thoroughly enjoying himself at the
others' discomfort, now accuses Antonio of having
spat upon his "Jewish" gaberdine. For what? His
religion? No, despite his intention of capitalizing
on the persecution of the Jews, Shylock finds himself saying:

And all for use of that which is mine own.
[I. iii. 113]

It is the need of justifying his greed which rankles
in him. And having a first-rate intelligence and
great powers of expression, he hurls at his enemy
one of the loftiest pieces of sarcasm ever penned:

Well, then, it now appears you need my
help.
Go to, then! You come to me, and you say,
"Shylock, we would have moneys;" you
say so—
You, that did void your rheum upon my
beard
And foot me as you spurn a stranger cur
Over your threshold; moneys is your suit.
What should I say to you? Should I not
say,
"Hath a dog money? Is it possible
A cur can lend three thousand ducats?"
Or
Shall I bend low and in a bondman's key,
With bated breath and whispering hum-
bleness,
Say this:
"Fair sir, you spat on me on Wednesday
last;
You spurn'd me such a day; another time
You call'd me dog; and for these courtesies
I'll lend you thus much moneys"?
[I. iii. 114-29]

The indignation is superb, and it is a callous audience that will fail to be overwhelmed by it. But
coming after what has preceded it, it can have but
one purpose in Shylock's mind. He has been doing

his best to make Bassanio and Antonio squirm. This speech is his crowning effort to humiliate them.

But at this point we have a difficulty. He has charged Antonio with spitting upon him because of his taking interest. Scholars have hastened to ascribe to that contemptuous and contemptible behavior of Antonio the cause of Shylock's hatred. Yet, when we shall presently consider Antonio's character traits, we shall find nothing in his behavior which could possibly be consonant with such conduct. He is at every point a gentle, mild, loving, and modest man. Nowhere up to the very trial scene (Act IV) does he ever say a single thing that is vaguely anti-Semitic about Shylock—not even after he has been taken into custody and his life is in peril. It will not do to say that Antonio's spitting upon Shylock would in that age have been no blot upon his character. That explanation would do very well for a rather vulgar man like Gratiano. Shakespeare proves himself in the play totally alien to bigotry: why should he not have made his hero above it? (pp. 189-93)

Of the world's dramatists, no one believed more firmly than Shakespeare in having characters reveal themselves by what they *do.* For instance, in the scene we have been examining, the salient fact about Shylock is that he has kept Antonio and Bassanio in suspense, has done all he could to aggravate their embarrassment in having to come to him for a loan, and has refused to alleviate their discomfort by even a hint that he might lend the money. This, as far as we have progressed in it, is the basic action of the scene. Now Shylock has *said* that Antonio has spit upon him. But if we were asked to believe that this is the truth, it would be Shakespeare's practice to show us Antonio *conducting himself* elsewhere in the play *in a manner consistent with such an act.* (p. 194)

Now, since we nowhere see Antonio behaving in a way that would make it possible for us to think of him as spitting on anyone, is it not possible that Shylock is making the charge against him—just as Iago makes his charge against Othello—without really believing a word of it, only to erect a false justification for himself, and, most of all, because he gauges that Antonio's pride will not permit the merchant to defend himself?

If, for the sake of argument, we grant that this is indeed the case—if Antonio is aware of what Shylock is up to, trying further to annoy him—should we expect Antonio to deny hotly, "When did I ever spit on you?" If your enemy approached you and accused you of committing incest with your sister, and you were, moreover, an only child, would you be behaving with any dignity to exclaim, outraged, "Why I haven't got a sister!" Would it not be more consonant with manly pride to answer coolly, "With which sister do you mean?"

It is in a similar spirit that I understand Antonio's making response to the charge. At the moment he is revolted at Shylock's attempts to ennoble the taking of interest; he is disgusted at being kept dangling—after all, he and Bassanio have not come to ask a favor but to engage in a distasteful commercial transaction. We may be sure that if this loan were for his own needs, not his friend's, he would have turned on his heel before this. Instead, he masters his ire, and answers coldly and with unconcealed contempt for Shylock's brazen hypocrisy: Very well, I'll do the same things all over again; for we are not talking as friends; we ask for a loan at your usual rates; when did a friend ever ask interest for a loan?

> I am as like to call thee so again,
> To spit on thee again, to spurn thee too.
> If thou wilt lend this money, lend it not
> As to thy friends; for *when did friendship take*
> *A breed for barren metal of his friend?*
> [I. iii. 130-34]

There is no point, Antonio is implying, in your talking to me as though we were meeting as intimates. Your attitude toward taking interest makes this purely a matter of business: let's keep it on that level.

> But lend it rather to thine enemy,
> Who, if he break, thou mayst with better face
> Exact the penalty.
> [I. iii. 135-37]

Shylock is satisfied that he has pushed Antonio to the limits of annoyance, and so his tone swiftly changes: But why do you take on so? I'm perfectly willing to be your friend, lend you the money, and not take a cent of interest. My offer is kind. (Up to this moment he has made no offer!)

Bassanio who, though silent, has necessarily been more upset by the talk than Antonio could be, since he is the cause of it all, with relief cries, "This were kindness" [I. iii. 143].

And now Shakespeare comes to the knottiest problem in the plot. . . . Stipulating for the illusion of flesh-and-blood reality in his plays, how was he to make it credible that Antonio would sign a bond which places his life in jeopardy? His solution was brilliant. Some sort of consideration will be necessary to make the contract legal. Shylock refuses any financial security, since he is acting as a friend. Well then, let us mention as the consideration something absolutely absurd, just to show my complete confidence in your word. Let us make it something as ludicrous as, say, a pound of your flesh. What is important in this speech is that the bond is framed "in a merry sport" [I. iii. 145], as he puts it. (pp. 194-96)

Innocently Antonio accepts the terms as framed in a merry sport, and is ready to believe that Shylock desires to be friendly. He considers the offer very decent of Shylock ("there is much kindness in the Jew" [I. iii. 153]). Naturally, Bassanio, oversensitive because of his role in this affair, expresses alarm. But Antonio reassures him: No need for alarm; my ships come back laden a good month before the money is due. Shylock, gleeful at the success of his ruse, feigns shock at Bassanio's suspicions in a tone which is anything but humble: What creatures these Christians are, who judge others by their own unfeeling ways! Tell me, what should I do with a pound of his flesh, if I seriously hoped to have it? (With mixed insolence and everpresent greed) he says further: a pound of man's flesh

> Is not so estimable, *profitable* neither,
> As flesh of muttons, beefs, or goats.
> [I. iii. 166-67]

I'm willing to act like his friend: let him take the offer or leave it. But in all fairness, don't do me the injustice of ascribing sordid motives to what I am willing to do generously.

Antonio is unworried, and Shylock once more emphasizes that this is to be a "merry bond." Antonio's farewell acknowledges that Shylock's behavior is princely:

> Hie thee, gentle Jew.
> [I. iii. 177]

Before we meet Shylock again, we learn interesting things about him. His household is a joyless one, and he wishes it to be so. Launcelot Gobbo, his poor idiot of a servant, is becoming skin and bones from starvation. This amiable halfwit is the only companion Shylock's daughter is permitted to have; at the prospect of his leaving Shylock's employ she is unhappy:

> I am sorry thou wilt leave my father so.
> *Our house is hell,* and thou, a merry devil,
> Didst rob it of some taste of tediousness.
> [II. iii. 1-3]

That she does not exaggerate will be evident enough in a scene which shortly follows. But apparently the little pleasure she can have in talking to Launcelot must be snatched in secret too. She cuts short their conversation with:

> And so farewell. I would not have my fa-
> ther
> See me in talk with thee.
> [II. iii. 8-9]

In a handful of lines Shakespeare has vividly sketched the gloomy and prisonlike atmosphere of Shylock's home.

Jessica turns out to be something less than an ideal daughter, satisfactory as she is in her devotion to Lorenzo. But there is no reason why she should love her father. It is clear from the outset that she has never known tenderness or love from him. (pp. 196-97)

The next time we meet Shylock [II. v] he is before his house. He assures poor Launcelot, him whose ribs are showing from hunger, that he will not be able to gobble up everything in sight at Bassanio's, as he has done at Shylock's household. (In Shylock's diseased mind every scrap of bread is begrudged his servant.) Shylock is about to go to Bassanio's for dinner. The very invitation shows that Antonio and Bassanio are ready to accept his proffered friendship. And Shylock means to go, despite his earlier high-sounding talk about not eating with Christians. His reason for going? The more he eats of Bassanio's feast, the less Bassanio will have. ("I'll go in hate to feed upon the prodigal Christian" [II. v. 14-15].) How well Shakespeare understood every aberration of human nature! Though extreme, Shylock's point of view is of one piece with his embracing the philosophy of cutthroat competition: the less others have, the richer he himself can feel.

But he has a premonition of something unpleasant in the stars: he dreamt last night of money-bags, and is "right loath to go" [II. v. 16]. Launcelot, appropriating the lofty airs that he feels are owing to his new uniform, says grandly, misusing "reproach" for "approach":

> I beseech you, sir, go. My young master
> doth expect your reproach.
> [II. v. 19-20]

Shylock seizes upon the malapropism, and retorts with concentrated malice masked as wry humor:

> So do I his.
> [II. v. 21]

This quibble is like a sword-thrust: it should be enough to raise goose flesh. It means only one thing: Shylock has every intention of collecting the pound of flesh, and has a plan for making sure he will have it.

Now foolish Launcelot emits what is meant to be a hint to Jessica, but might easily have prevented her intended elopement if Shylock had had any notion of it: there's going to be a masque tonight. At the very mention of purposed merriment, Shylock's hatred of all that is delightful and gay is aroused:

> What, are there masques? Hear you me,
> Jessica.
> Lock up my doors; and when you hear the
> drum
> And the vile squealing of the wry-neck'd
> fife,
> Clamber not you up to the casements
> then,
> Nor thrust your head into the public street
> To gaze on Christian fools with varnish'd
> faces,
> But stop my house's ears, I mean my case-
> ments.
> Let not the sound of shallow foppery enter
> My sober house.
> [II. v. 28-36]

He has no use for music. He does not want even the echo of it to penetrate his house. Obviously Shakespeare will later mean us to take quite seriously Lorenzo's dictum:

> The man that hath no music in himself,
> Nor is not mov'd with concord of sweet
>   sounds,
> Is fit for treasons, stratagems, and
>   spoils. . . .
> Let no such man be trusted.
>
>   [V. i. 83-8]

It certainly applies to Shylock. And luckless Jessica! She is not to dare watch the fun in the streets by looking out the window or even from behind it. Her eyes and ears are to be sealed against the most innocent pleasure. Small wonder that she will leave her father's house without regret.

Launcelot goes off, and Shylock reflects that he is glad to be rid of such a huge feeder (poor, starved Launcelot!); he is, moreover, delighted to think of how he will now help to waste Bassanio's substance. Then, before he himself departs, he threatens Jessica: she had better obey every article of his commands:

> Perhaps I will return immediately.
>   [II. v. 52]

Clearly her life under her father's roof is an endless series of commands and warnings against disobedience—not the sort of existence to evoke love or even duty.

This scene demonstrates how far from the point those stray who insist that it is only Jessica's elopement which turns a benevolent Shylock into a hating one. She has not yet eloped, and we have seen him full of malevolence against Bassanio and Antonio, most of all in that blood-chilling "So do I his." (pp. 199-201)

Before we meet Shylock again . . . , the elopement has taken place. I suspect that neither the dramatist nor his audience understood her taking money and jewels with her to be conduct as heinous as modern interpreters have construed it. Her life with Shylock has been a stunted one; what she has appropriated has not left him impoverished. Even today Europeans generally expect that when a girl of means is married, her father will provide a suitable dowry. It is more than likely that we were intended to feel that Jessica has done little more than take with her the marriage-portion that ought to have been hers. (In the probable source for the Jessica-Lorenzo story . . . the girl in that tale also helps herself to her father's possessions when she elopes.)

After the elopement we hear Salarino and Salanio discussing the effects of it upon Shylock. Their picture of his running through the streets shrieking

> My daughter! O my ducats! O my daugh-
>   ter!
> Fled with a Christian! O my Christian duc-
>   ats!
> Justice! the law! my ducats, and my
>   daughter!
> A sealed bag, two sealed bags of ducats,
> Of double ducats, stolen from me by my
>   daughter!
> And jewels, two stones, two rich and pre-
>   cious stones,
> Stolen by my daughter! Justice! find the
>   girl;
> She hath the stones upon her, and the
>   ducats.
>
>   [II. viii. 15-22]

is deliberately grotesque. But it has some of the ring of truth in it too. The emphasis upon the ducats and the stones sounds like the Shylock we know. Likewise does his wish, not so much to have his daughter back for herself, but to find her so that he can retrieve his ducats and his jewels.

In the scene in which we next meet Shylock [III. i], there is more talk of ships wrecked at sea and the possibility that they could be Antonio's (the talk began in II. viii. 25-32). Shylock comes in, and he is in a terrible rage:

> You knew, none so well, none so well as
> you, of my daughter's flight,
>
>   [III. i. 24-5]

he storms at Salanio and Salarino. The latter tries to moderate Shylock's fury: Shylock must have been aware that Jessica was of an age to think of marriage. But he will not be mollified:

> My own flesh and blood to rebel!
>   [III. i. 34]

Salarino denies that Jessica is a replica of her father, and does so in language that exonerates him from any charge of anti-Semitism:

> There is more difference between thy flesh
> and hers than between jet and ivory; more
> between your bloods than there is be-
> tween red wine and rhenish.
>
>   [III. i. 39-42]

He changes the subject to ask whether Shylock has heard anything of Antonio's ships. The question but adds fuel to Shylock's passion:

> There I have another bad match. A bank-
> rupt, a prodigal, who dare scarce show his
> head on the Rialto; a beggar, that was us'd
> to come so smug upon the mart; let him
> look to his bond. . . . He was wont to lend
> money for a Christian courtesy; let him
> look to his bond.
>
>   [III. i. 44-50]

In wine and in wrath the truth will out. Shylock's list of Antonio's offenses this time significantly omits any reference to spitting on Jewish gaberdines or to insults against the Jews. No, in his fury it does not occur to him to mask the real sources of his fury: Antonio's elegant appearance, Antonio's wasting of money, Antonio's lending money without interest. These are the crimes for which he hates the merchant.

When Salarino asks of what use the forfeiture could be to Shylock, Shylock responds in a way that again is a tribute to Shakespeare's psychological insight. Now that he has been called on to state his grievances, Shylock once more tries to pass off the reasons for his thirst for revenge as better than they are. But, in spite of his tone of injured innocence, he reveals that it is only matters of money which cause his hatred:

> He hath disgrac'd me, and *hind'red me half a million;* laugh'd at *my losses,* mock'd at *my gains,* scorn'd my nation, thwarted *my bargains* . . .
>
> [III. i. 54ff.]

The reference to his "nation" is almost parenthetical—as though he had thought of something that must be slipped in to justify the rest. Again, despite himself, Shylock makes it plain that the only thing Antonio has done to injure him has been to lend out money gratis.

From the indictment he soars into one of the most movingly written orations ever penned:

> And what's his reason? I am a Jew. Hath not a Jew eyes? Hath not a Jew hands, organs, dimensions, senses, affections, passions; fed with the same food, hurt with the same weapons, subject to the same diseases, healed by the same means, warmed and cooled by the same winter and summer, as a Christian is? If you prick us, do we not bleed? If you tickle us, do we not laugh? If you poison us, do we not die? And if you wrong us, shall we not revenge? If we are like you in the rest, we will resemble you in that. If a Jew wrong a Christian, what is his humility? Revenge. If a Christian wrong a Jew, what should his sufferance be by Christian example? Why, revenge. The villainy you teach me, I will execute, and it shall go hard but I will better the instruction.
>
> [III. i. 58-73]

As we have already said, the author who composed these lines must of necessity have stood far above all possibility of nurturing anti-Semitic feelings—else how could he have conceived the passage? It is noble, manly, superbly convincing. But when we have recovered from the power of its appeal (which Shylock fully intended to be powerful) and ask ourselves why Shylock has said all this and why just now, we are forced to realize that it is all an elaborate piece of self-justification for villainy intended. His accusations of injustices visited upon the Jews by Christians in general are meant by implication to apply to Antonio in particular, even though we have not seen Antonio wronging anyone or revenging himself on anyone. By the very force of his elo-

quence Shylock is convincing himself (and has convinced many critics!) that he proposes to take reprisals for the persecutions of his people.

Antonio's friends leave, Tubal comes in, and we are witnesses to a wonderfully written scene. Tubal has just arrived from Genoa; he has often heard of Jessica but did not encounter her. Shakespeare now fortifies our previous knowledge of Shylock's inner drive. Shylock is talking to an intimate (we cannot think of his having a true friend, nor does Tubal behave like one), and he speaks without pretense:

> Why, there, there, there, there! A diamond gone, cost me two thousand ducats in Frankfort! *The curse never fell upon our nation till now. I never felt it till now.*
>
> [III. i. 83-6]

At last the whole truth. Shylock has never felt hurt before. But any wrong to him is a wrong to all Jews. What are the injustices meted out to his co-religionists compared with the loss of two thousand ducats by him? He goes on, and his diseased passion for accumulation vents itself with increasing violence:

> Two thousand ducats in that; and other precious, precious jewels. *I would my daughter were dead at my foot, and the jewels in her ear! Would she were hears'd at my foot, and the ducats in her coffin!*
>
> [III. i. 86-90]

These shocking sentiments are scarcely in harmony with the long-suffering and loving paterfamilias of the sentimental school of critics. They are among the most horrifying sentences in literature. Confronted with them even the critic who finds Shylock *molto simpatico* [very likable] would be compelled to admit that it is not that he loved Jessica less but loves his ducats more. And he continues to lament his losses—though surely the bulk of his vast hoard has remained untouched:

> No news of them? Why so? *And I know not what's spent in the search. Why, thou loss upon loss! the thief gone with so much, and so much to find the thief.* . . .
>
> [III. i. 90ff]

Not a word about missing his beloved daughter, but much on the subject of missing his ducats. And why is it, he cries, that I am the only man to have all this misfortune? Tubal raises his spirits by beginning to say that he has heard in Genoa of Antonio's ill luck. Eagerly Shylock demands to know more. Yes, Tubal says, Antonio is said to have lost a fleet coming from Tripolis. "I thank God, I thank God!" Shylock cries with exaltation. He laughs with delight:

> Good news, good news! Ha, ha! Here in Genoa!
>
> [III. i. 105-07]
>
> (pp. 201-05)

Patrick Stewart as Shylock in a 1978 Royal Shakespeare Theatre production of The Merchant of Venice.

Unless we are willing to conceive that Shylock originally suggested taking a pound of Antonio's flesh purely as a gesture of friendship—an interpretation in violence with his first soliloquy and everything he had been thinking before Jessica ever eloped—we must surely feel that a man of his particular purposefulness would never have stipulated for such terms if he had merely hoped or had left it to chance to bring Antonio within his power. At the time the bond was signed, there was not even a wisp of doubt that Antonio could comfortably repay the money long before it was due. . . . [There] is something terribly ominous about Shylock's turning Launcelot's malapropism, "My young master doth expect your reproach" [II. v. 19-20], with a wry, "So do I his" [II. v. 21]. Nobody ever depended less than Shakespeare upon accident for dramatic effect. His leading characters are always people either of strong will or wilfullness; and his strongest strokes as a storyteller are always closely related to character-traits of the persons involved, not to external, accidental influences. (Even Morocco and Arragon make a choice of the wrong caskets and Bassanio of the right one, because of their own temperaments.) It would be most unlike Shakespearean practice that Shylock, once he has proposed a contract with such terms in it, win power of death over Antonio through the operation of fate.

At the end of the play [V. i. 276-77] it turns out that Antonio's ships have come safely to port richly laden, after all. What has happened to Antonio, then, in the interval between his signing of the bond and Shylock's bringing him to trial?

Obviously, it chanced that nearly all of Antonio's ready money, at the time Bassanio asked for a loan, was invested in his ventures abroad, else there had been no need of borrowing the money from Shylock. What could Shylock do, under these circumstances, to insure his collecting the forfeiture? Only one thing: ruin Antonio's credit. In II. viii, Salarino reported talking with a Frenchman, who had told him of an Italian ship wrecked in the English Channel. Shylock has seized upon this piece of gossip, attributed the loss to Antonio, and broadened it to include the rest of Antonio's ships. . . . I therefore take his exulting cry, "Good news, good news! Ha, ha! Here in Genoa!" to mean, "So at last! These rumors have at last reached Italy, near home!"

To continue with the scene: Tubal, apparently unable to allow Shylock his moment of joy, cuts in with the information that

> Your daughter spent in Genoa, as I heard,
> in one night four-score ducats.
>
> [III. i. 108-09]

The very thought of which brings Shylock back to his misery over his losses:

> *Thou stick'st a dagger in me, I shall never see my gold again. Fourscore ducats at a sitting! Fourscore ducats!*
>
> [III. i. 111-12]

This amusingly inscrutable Tubal continues to play on Shylock as on an instrument: Antonio, he learns from the creditors, is sure to become bankrupt. Once more Shylock rejoices: he is very glad of it; he will plague and torture Antonio. Once more Tubal turns aside Shylock's pleasure:

> One of them showed me a ring that he had
> of your daughter for a monkey.
>
> [III. i. 118-19]

Shakespeare does not deal in monsters, and he here gives Shylock the one softening touch allotted him in the whole play:

> It was my turquoise; I had it of Leah when
> I was a bachelor. I would not have given it
> for a wilderness of monkeys.
>
> [cf. III. i. 121-23]

It is a wonderfully simple human touch, and it reminds us that Shylock, before he gave in to his passion for accumulating money, was once a human being too. Tubal goes back to Antonio's losses, and Shylock eagerly looks forward to his pound of flesh: to be sure of it he arranges a fortnight in advance that an officer arrest Antonio on the day the bond is due.

In the next scene [III. ii] we are in Belmont, and rejoice to watch Bassanio's choosing the right casket. But he and Portia have barely time to revel in the happy fulfillment of their wishes when news comes from Venice that Antonio's ships have been lost and his credit has been ruined. His friends have managed to get together the money owing, but Shylock refuses to accept it, now that the day of repayment is past. Twenty merchants, the Duke of Venice, and leading citizens have pleaded with him in vain; Shylock refuses to accept anything but his pound of flesh. No one can drive him from his malicious stand that he will have only the forfeiture—which he calls demanding justice.

It takes a little time to get a large sum of money together. No one has seriously expected that Shylock would insist upon the terms of the bond. On but one day after the contract's expiration, we are to suppose, Antonio's friends have approached Shy-

lock with the money, and he has refused them on the technicality of the date. No one, naturally, was prepared that he take such a position, particularly when he is notorious for his love of gold. But Jessica tells the others that she has often heard her father say

> That he would rather have Antonio's flesh
> Than twenty times the value of the sum
> That he did owe him.
>
> [III. ii. 286-88]

(We do not like Jessica for saying this. On the other hand, we should like her less if she approved of her father's murderous intentions; she has chosen to be human rather than dutiful.)

In the next scene [III. iii] we are back in a street of Venice. Antonio, in the custody of the Gaoler, and Salarino are pleading with Shylock to be merciful. But he will allow them to speak hardly a syllable. He is absolutely intransigent. Now that he has Antonio completely in his power, now would be the time, if there were any truth in his allegations that he has endured indignities at Antonio's hands, to speak them out. With what crushing force could he now hurl at Antonio that business of spitting upon him and kicking him out of doors—if that had been the truth. But it was not the truth; he seems even to have forgotten his inventions. In his adamantine sense of power he does not try to conceal his motives as other than they are:

> Gaoler, look to him; tell not me of mercy,
> *This is the fool that lent out money gratis!*
>
> [III. iii. 1-2]

After a few words of scornful abuse, he leaves. Antonio is well aware that Shylock hates him only because he has often rescued people who were in debt to Shylock. He is also fairly convinced that the bond is legally unassailable.

We come now to the great scene of the play, the Trial Scene [IV. i], the last in which Shylock appears. Before Shylock's entry, the point is made again that the Duke has done all he could to urge Shylock to accept the sum of money he advanced and renounce the forfeiture, but without success. The Duke now realizes that the moneylender is

> A stony adversary, an inhuman wretch
> Uncapable of pity, void and empty
> From any dram of mercy.
>
> [IV. i. 4-6]

Shylock comes into court, and the Duke goes out of his way to speak gently and without animosity to him, in the hope of softening his cruelty. We all really believe, he says, that you are only pretending to claim the forfeiture so that at the last minute your mercy and pity will appear all the greater; we expect you not only to renounce the stipulation but also to overlook a portion of the sum due you, considering Antonio's losses; surely you will not behave as only Turks and Tartars do; we all expect a civilized answer to what I ask. But the Duke has underestimated his man. Shylock is like rock, and challenges the city to deny its legal processes.

> You'll ask me why I rather choose to have
> A weight of carrion flesh than to receive
> Three thousand ducats.
>
> [IV. i. 40-2]

This sounds like a prologue (an arrogant and insulting one, to be sure) to a rehearsal of wrongs suffered as Antonio's victim. Now is the time, if ever there was time, for him to justify what he wishes to do, to tell the whole world of his injuries and persecutions. What a triumphant moment for him to do himself justice! But he has nothing to say of the old charges of anti-Semitism. He has nothing to say because they were false.

Moreover, no one has asked him why he chooses a pound of flesh rather than accept three thousand ducats. It is his own intelligence which makes him realize the enormity of his choice in the world's eyes. Perhaps this is the first time he has asked himself the question. Well, and what is his explanation? He has none.

> I'll not answer that;
> But say it is my humour. Is it answer'd?
> What if my house be troubled with a rat
> And I be pleas'd to give ten thousand ducats
> To have it ban'd? What, are you answer'd yet?
>
> [IV. i. 42-6]

His insolence to the Duke would be astonishing in anyone other than this proud, strong, powerful man, who has never in his life known what it is to fawn or cringe. There is not even a hint of respect for the Duke's authority in what he says, as he continues: Some men can't stand roasted pig, some can't tolerate cats, some can't listen to the sound of bagpipes without becoming ill,

> *So can I give no reason, nor I will not,*
> More than a lodg'd hate and a certain loathing
> I bear Antonio, that I follow thus
> A losing suit against him. Are you answer'd?
>
> [IV. i. 59-62]

His last line adds sarcasm to his insolence. But again, despite himself, Shylock declares the truth: he can give no reason and therefore will give no reason for wishing to kill Antonio.

Now, it might be asked: If indeed Shylock has so overpowering a greed for money as has been thus far depicted, why has he not accepted the offer of Antonio's friends to pay him a liberal amount in addition to the money he has loaned the merchant? Why will he refuse Portia's offer of thrice the amount of the loan? Why would he rather have, as Jessica has reported, Antonio's flesh than "twenty times" the sum?

The answer to these questions lies in the very na-

ture of hate. The genesis of Shylock's hatred for Antonio was money. But hate is a cancer that grows and feeds on a man until it devours all of him. When hate becomes an obsession, its origin becomes forgotten, and only the hate itself becomes real. (pp. 206-11)

Shylock, eaten up with hate, can really give no reason for desiring Antonio's death. This cancerous hatred, nourished by greed, is all that is left of him.

And here we shall leave Shylock. . . . Presently he, creature of cold hate and greed, bolstering that hate and greed with a demand for the strict letter of the law, will have to confront his great opponent, Portia, the personification of all he despises in life—generosity, warmth, compassion, and love—Portia, with whom mercy is to be preferred far above mere justice.

In Shakespeare's play generosity, compassion, love, and mercy will triumph, as Shakespeare was convinced that they could and should triumph in life.

They could have triumphed, no doubt. Money need not have poisoned the wellsprings of human existence if Christ's teachings had meant anything to Christians.

Alas! in the course of time it is not Portia and Shakespeare, but Shylock who has won out. Nowadays if a man, pillar of his church, synagogue, or mosque, lends his brother a hundred dollars, he will probably expect him to pay him six per cent interest. "Why shouldn't he pay it to me?" he will say in self-justification, "since he will have to pay as much if he goes to a bank? Business is business."

Yes, most of the world has adopted Shylock's philosophy, which is the philosophy of banks. No one expects compassion from a bank. (pp. 212-13)

> *Bernard Grebanier, "Shylock Himself," in his* The Truth about Shylock, *Random House, 1962, pp. 146-213.*

Warren D. Smith

[*Smith considers* **Shylock** *a villain based on his profession as a usurer rather than on his race. He examines Elizabethan beliefs concerning both Jews and usury, maintaining that* **Shylock** *is branded a villain because of two important historical facts: first, as a Jew he is an unbeliever in the Christian faith; second, as a usurer he practices an unpopular vocation. Modern anti-Semitism is not present in* The Merchant of Venice, *Smith continues, and* **Shylock's** *evil is inherent by nature of his humanity rather than by his Jewishness.* **Shylock** *is merely a miserly evildoer, the critic contends, who uses his faith not only as a veil for his nefarious schemes, but also as an expression of his indignation at being discriminated against. Based on this observation, Smith dis-*

*putes the conventional reading of **Shylock's** "Hath not a Jew eyes" speech in Act III, scene i, maintaining that it reflects **Shylock's** "use of religion as a cloak of villainy." For further commentary on **Shylock's** character, see the excerpts by Frank Kermode, E. F. C. Ludowyk, John W. Draper, Marvin Felheim, William Leigh Godshalk, John Dover Wilson, Bernard Grebanier, and Lawrence Danson.]*

The common assumption that Shakespeare's Shylock was created to compete with Marlowe's play, *The Jew of Malta,* in pandering to a wave of anti-Semitism greeting the arraignment and execution for treason in 1594 of Elizabeth's Jewish physician, Roderigo Lopez, becomes untenable upon examination. The evidence seems to indicate that through Shylock Shakespeare is really not satirizing Jews as such but is attempting to depict a usurer, by vocation a villain, who hypocritically conceals his evil designs behind the mask of a religion he himself does not believe in. (p. 193)

Then why did Shakespeare decide to make Shylock a Jew as well as a usurer? Either that the usurer in the source is Jewish or that Shylock as a Jew would be more of a villain is, I believe, only part of the answer. For though [Philip] Stubbes [in his *Anatomy*] and Thomas Wilson [see J. L. Cardozo's *The Contemporary Jew in the Elizabethan Drama*] have the grace to condemn usurers as worse than Jews, early in the Middle Ages the Jew became closely associated with the wicked profession of usury in the public mind. And little wonder since usury for Jews was encouraged by both the Church and the State. According to [Joshua] Trachtenberg [in his *The Devil and the Jews*], in the twelfth century the words *Jew* and *usurer* had become almost synonymous. So that a reappraisal of what Shakespeare was attempting to accomplish in his portrayal of Shylock demands that three historical factors be kept in view: (1) that there were no practising Jews in England to be satirized at the time of the composition of *The Merchant of Venice* and that "New" Christians were as acceptable to Elizabethans as other Christians; (2) that nonetheless a kind of anti-Semitism, purely religious rather than ethnic, based on condemning the Jew as an unbeliever and the slayer of Christ, was an active bias; and (3) that the usurer was by definition a villain in the public mind and the term *Jew* was frequently made equivalent to *usurer.* Most pertinent is what ties all three factors together: the interesting fact that in 1290 the Jews were expelled from England, as some Elizabethans should have recalled, on two counts—as unbelievers and as usurers.

Thus on two historical condemnations, as both an unbeliever and a usurer, Shylock is branded a villain upon his first appearance in the play. The pound of flesh episode is merely a demonstration of the innate evil in the man, or, possibly more important, the trap with which to ensnare the inventor. But anti-Semitism as we know it today, prejudice against personal traits called "Jewishness", is not present in *The Merchant of Venice.* Shylock, in contrast to his daughter (who willingly turns Christian for Lorenzo), is a stubborn infidel; Shylock, again in contrast to his daughter (who on her first appearance gives Launcelot a ducat and is lavish in bestowing her dowry on Lorenzo as well as in giving away a valuable ring for a monkey), is a miser. It is only poetic justice, then, fitting the spirit of comedy, that at the end of his performance the Jew is made to undergo two transformations for the good of his soul: he is converted to Christianity and is forced to give up usury when his wealth is taken from him. Small wonder his name is not mentioned in Act V: since he is no longer a villain, no longer either an unbeliever or a usurer, there is no reason to express animus against him. But it should be emphasized that though the fact that Shylock is a Jew may have been held against him by the Elizabethan audience, throughout the first four acts he is never made the victim of anti-Semitic prejudice by the other major characters in the play. He claims he hates Antonio "for he is a Christian" [I. iii. 42], but his assertion that Antonio mistreats him because "I am a Jew" [III. i. 59] has no foundation in the text. What Shakespeare is really trying to do through Shylock is to depict a character who rationalizes his villainy, as a usurer, by projecting his own ethnic group prejudice onto the shoulders of his innocent opponents. As Romeo and Juliet condemn the stars for what is actually the evil emanating from the family feud, as Hamlet mistakenly blames his difficulties on the fact that "the time is out of joint" [*Hamlet,* I. v. 188], as Lear excuses his own inordinate pride by attacking the pride of Cordelia and Kent, so Shylock, though not so innocently, attempts to excuse his own villainy by emphasizing what the Christians in the play do not emphasize, the fact that he is a Jew.

But being a villain, Shylock is not nearly so blind to reality as are the tragic protagonists. On his first entrance he offers the obtrusively weak rationalization of usury as "well-won thrift" [I. iii. 50], calling on what he must have realized was a completely irrelevant analogy from the Bible of Jacob's behavior towards Laban to defend his own nefarious profession. "The devil can cite Scripture for his purpose" [I. iii. 98] is the appropriate remark of Antonio. But though Antonio and Bassanio reveal their awareness of Shylock's real deficiencies in this scene, there is no indication of anti-Semitism. In addressing Shylock Antonio uses a term of respect, "sir" [I. iii. 91] instead of "sirrah". Bassanio gives Shylock an earnest invitation to supper, which the latter refuses on the spurious ground that he is a devout Jew and therefore will not eat pork. Later he is perfectly willing to "feed upon the prodigal Christian" [II. v. 14-15] despite the ominous dream of money-bags he has experienced the previous night. In the lengthy aside delivered on the entrance of Antonio, Shylock gives the audience what he later refuses to confess to the Duke and Portia in Act IV, the real reasons why he hates Antonio: "for he is a Christian" [I. iii. 42]—"But more for that in low simplicity / He lends out money gratis and brings down / The rate of usance here with us in Venice" [I. iii. 43-5]. In the court scene we hear of neither of these reasons from Shylock. Instead we are treated to a barrage of rationalizations about the pound of flesh which he seeks from the heart of Antonio: it is Shylock's "humour", nothing more than a "lodg'd hate and a certain loathing / I bear Antonio" [IV. i. 60-1]; what if his house is troubled with a rat and he chooses to give ten thousand ducats to have it banned; if the Venetians will not free their slaves and marry them to their heirs, then Shylock cannot be expected to free Antonio; he has taken an oath in "heaven" to have the pound of flesh; and so on. Not a word is spoken about Antonio's being a Christian nor about the merchant's discouraging habit of lending money without interest.

After the Jacob-Laban controversy between Shylock and Antonio, which is an argument purely about usury with no anti-Semitism entering into it, Shylock again uses his religion as a guise for his villainy. He complains that the Christian merchant has often berated him upon the Rialto and "spet upon my Jewish gaberdine" [I. iii. 112], calling him "misbeliever, cutthroat dog" [I. iii. 111], which leads the Jew to ask defiantly, "Hath a dog money? Is it possible / A cur can lend three thousand ducats?" [I. iii. 123]. Antonio's rejoinder—"I am as like to call thee so again, / To spet on thee again, to spurn thee too" [I. iii. 130-31]—has frequently been criticized as jarring in its anti-Semitism. But as a representative hero of the times, who himself lends out money gratis, Antonio would be expected by the audience to mistreat a usurer, whether he was also an unbeliever or not. Again, with the plaintive—"For suff'rance is the badge of all our tribe" [I. iii. 110]—Shylock uses his religion as a mask, for though sufferance may be typical of the oppressed Jewish people as a whole, it is not a characteristic of the speaker, who at the very moment is plotting vengeance against Antonio. That the vengeance is not really against Antonio's alleged expressions of anti-Semitism but his enmity to usury Shylock slips into admitting, when he says that the merchant has berated him "All for use of that which is mine own" [I. iii. 113], the "All" being a dead giveaway. Antonio is fully alive to the real issue because he says, "If thou wilt lend this money, lend it not / As to thy friends—for when did friendship take / A breed for barren metal of his friend?" [I. iii. 131-33] That Antonio's animus against Shylock has all along been based upon his dislike of usury is demonstrated in the merchant's favorable reaction to the Jew's offer of a loan without interest.

The next time we see Shylock we have already been introduced to his daughter. Though in all previous discussions the dramatic function of Jessica has been hurriedly glossed over, to me a reminder of it is necessary to a clear understanding of what the dramatist is attempting to accomplish. Like another Jew in the play, she is very evidently a foil character to her villainous father. As he is covetous, she is generous; as he is anti-Christian, she is pro-Christian; as he blames his suffering on being a Jew, she blames hers, much more honestly, on Shylock's having made their house a hell. No one in the play holds her being a Jewess against Jessica. Yet commentators have taken Jessica severely to task for stealing her father's ducats and jewels (actually the dowry owed to her) and for eloping with a Christian against her father's will. Surely to an audience who had everything against usurers and nothing against New Christians, her giving the ducats and jewels to her future husband would be, in contrast to the behavior of her miserly father, an act of commendable generosity, and her turning Christian for Lorenzo would be a saving grace. The same audience doubtless experienced keen satisfaction later in the play when her father is forced, under penalty of death, himself to give away all his wealth and to turn Christian. The Christians in Venice treat Jessica as an equal, and Portia and Nerissa in Belmont welcome her as a sister. The dramatist gives her a beautiful poetic scene with Lorenzo to open the final act, and she is treated as one of three heroines at the end of the play. Her presence in the play is ample proof that the plot is not aimed at Jews as such (there were none in England to satirize) but rather at a villainous usurer who hides behind what he calls his religion to carry out his nefarious schemes.

For though Shylock is perfectly willing to use the Jewish faith as a cloak, he is not presented by the dramatist as a truly religious Jew. Not only does he willingly go to sup with the Christians after having told Bassanio he would not "smell pork" nor "eat of the habitation which your prophet the Nazarite conjured the devil into" [I. iii. 33-5], but on one or two other occasions he reveals how little he really reveres the Jewish religion. When he learns from Tubal that Antonio has lost all his argosies, Shylock names the synagogue as the place to plot his vengeance on the undone merchant. He tells his compatriot the truth about why he wants the life of Antonio: "I will have the heart of him if he forfeit; for, were he out of Venice, I can make what merchandise I will" [III. i. 127-30]. In short, the synagogue, the place reserved for holy worship, is to be misused as headquarters for a scheme of vengeful murder concocted to eliminate the chief impediment to Shylock's sinful usury. Later, in the court scene, the Jew blasphemes that "by our holy Sabbath" [cf. IV. i. 36] he has sworn to have Antonio's life though he is more than willing to discard the oath made "in heaven" as soon as he realizes he is in danger of losing his property and his life. Finally, after the elopment of Jessica, Shylock has the nerve to cry out to Tubal: "Why, there, there, there, there! A diamond gone cost me two thousand ducats in Frankford! The curse never fell upon our nation till now; I never felt it till now" [III. i. 83-6]. He rates the centuries of suffering by the Jews below the personal loss of two thousand ducats.

Yet much sympathy has been expended on Shylock for the famous "Hath not a Jew eyes" speech which he delivers in the first scene of Act III [III. i. 59ff.]. Though a few unsentimental commentators have declared the passage to be nothing more than an avowal of vengeance, the majority opinion has sentimentalized it to the exalted plane of an impassioned appeal to humanity, an example of magnificent martyrdom, a moment of tragic pathos, a defense of a whole race, a trenchant appeal for tolerance. If the speech had originally been intended to scale such heights, then surely Shakespeare, in accord with his usual custom, would have cast it in poetic verse rather than in prose. Taking all the other evidence into consideration, I think it evident the passage is meant to be a specious piece of rationalizing on the part of the speaker, possibly the most obtrusive example in the play of the use of religion as a cloak for villainy. That Shylock himself is perfectly aware of the real reason for Antonio's hatred is revealed in the wording of his own introduction to the speech: "He hath disgrac'd me, and hind'red me half a million; laugh'd at my losses, mock'd at my gains, . . . thwarted my bargains, . . . " [III. i. 54-7], yet he has the temerity to add, "and what's his reason? I am a Jew" [III. i. 58]. As Shylock proceeds to point out, of course a Jew has eyes, organs, dimensions, senses, affections, passions—but, more pertinent, so does a villainous usurer. Certainly a Jew is fed with the same food, hurt with the same weapons, subject to the same diseases, healed by the same means, warmed and cooled by the same summer and winter as a Christian is—but, again, so is a villainous usurer. The passage is irrelevant to the real issue and specious in essence: it proves nothing beyond the obvious fact that evil men are human. Based on the false premise—"(because) I am a Jew" [cf. III. i. 58]—it must have been greeted with ridicule by the Elizabethan audience for the patent rationalization it really is. For both Shylock and Antonio are vividly aware of the real issue between them throughout the play. In the first scene in which he appears, as we have noted above, the Jew had said, "I hate him . . . more for that in low simplicity / He lends out money gratis and brings down / The rate of usance here with us in Venice" [I. iii. 42-5]. In the same scene he had addressed Antonio with the complaint: "In the Rialto you have rated me / About my moneys and my usances" [I. iii. 107-08]. In the first scene of Act III he says to Solanio and Salerio, after hearing of Antonio's losses, "Let him look to his bond. He was wont to call me usurer. Let him look to his bond. He was wont to lend money for a Christian cursy. Let him look to his bond" [III. i. 47-50]. In the third scene Shylock admonishes

Antonio's jailer with the words: "Jailer, look to him. Tell not me of mercy. / This is the fool that lent out money gratis. / Jailer, look to him" [III. iii. 1-3]. And after the exit of Shylock, Antonio himself reiterates to the jailer the real reason the Jew seeks his life: "I oft deliver'd from his forfeitures / Many that have at times made moan to me. / Therefore he hates me" [III. iii. 21-4].

I think it can safely be concluded that Shakespeare's Shylock is a villain throughout the four acts in which he appears. To the Elizabethan audience, with their traditional religious bias against Jews, his birth may have been enough to arouse suspicion of his motives. But to the dramatist, surely, he was above all a hypocrite who concealed his innate evil behind the mask of a religion he himself did not believe in. (pp. 195-99)

Warren D. Smith, "Shakespeare's Shylock," in Shakespeare Quarterly, *Vol. XV, No. 3, Summer, 1964, pp. 193-99.*

PORTIA

Anne Parten

*[Parten discusses **Portia**'s character in relation to the ring scene (Act V, scene i). According to the critic, the ring episode "acts as a focus for the unresolved—and potentially explosive—issue of the heroine's power." In essence, the ring scene signifies the resolution of **Portia**'s threat to the comic world of The Merchant of Venice. Parten maintains that **Portia** is a discordant element in the comic resolution of the play by virtue of her superiority over all the male characters. Such a situation is unacceptable in Shakespeare's comic world, the critic contends, where the proper hierarchy of men dominating women must be affirmed. Further, Shakespeare uses the cuckoldry theme in the ring episode to initially depict **Portia** as a strong character capable of dominating **Bassanio**, the critic continues, but then eliminates it, thus removing "the prospect of permanent female rule from this comedy of temporary female ascendency." Literally, a "cuckold" is a man whose wife is unfaithful; here, Parten uses the term to represent a social act which symbolizes "women's ultimate weapon and ultimate assertion over men." For further commentary on **Portia**'s character, see the excerpts by Frank Kermode, E. F. C. Ludowyk, William Leigh Godshalk, Lawrence W. Hyman, John Dover Wilson, and Helen Purinton Pettigrew.]*

The ring episode, the last and least of the three interlocking movements of *The Merchant of Venice*, has generally, with some justification, been considered too slight a business to be given the critical attention accorded the earlier phases of the play. The matter of the troth-plight rings and the migrations they make among the various characters is over-shadowed by the actions involving the three caskets and the pound of flesh. The established view seems to be that Portia's gift of a "new" ring in the fifth act restates the theme of mercy set out in the fourth, echoing playfully both the usurer's implacability and the generosity of the triumphant Christians. This is certainly true, as is even the somewhat reductive view that the controversy about the rings is designed merely to provide laughter. . . . The business of the rings, however, has a dramatic function beyond mirroring the main action or providing comic counterpoint. It also serves as an important element of the play in its own right, in that it acts as focus for the unresolved—and potentially explosive—issue of the heroine's power. The ring episode of *The Merchant of Venice* represents Shakespeare's resolution of the threat to the comic world that Portia herself embodies.

In supporting this argument, I will be covering three main points: first, my reasons for seeing Portia as a discordant element in the comic resolution; secondly, the traditional connotations of cuckoldry that account for Shakespeare's choice of it as the central theme of the scenes that deal with achieving that resolution; and finally, the way in which the rings themselves serve as highly significant tokens and emblems in the dramatic commentary on the relationship between the sexes.

It is a donné [known fact] in Shakespearean comedy, and in Elizabethan comedy in general, that the final scenes of the play will present a society to which order and harmony have been restored after a revitalizing interval of saturnalia. The basis for this new and healthy stability is the re-establishment of the ordered social hierarchy: during the earlier stages of the comedy, the normal pattern of relationships between masters and servants, men and women, and parents and children can go wildly askew, but the conclusion of the play sees each figure restored to his or her proper role. If children are not brought back into the position of subordination to their parents that they held at the beginning of the play, it is only in order to allow them the freedom to move on into the properly ordered marriages that will provide the future generations that will in turn endorse and preserve the same social forms.

The triumphant Portia of the courtroom scene . . . is not a piece that can easily be made to fit this conservative pattern, particularly the aspect of it that makes a concluding harmony contingent upon feminine submission. Her conquest of Shylock does eliminate one evil that threatens the comic society, but, from another perspective, she herself is almost as much of a threat to the re-establishment of order. The comic world will remain in its unresolved and inverted state for as long as she stands

in such easy and conspicuous superiority to all the men around her, including her husband.

Portia, after all, represents Shakespeare's first effort to create a comic heroine capable of controlling and directing the action that develops around her, and it is arguable that—at least from the Elizabethan point of view—he overplayed his hand, producing a figure too powerful to be credible as a future wife. In constantly demonstrating her ability to beat men at their own games, Shakespeare allows Portia to emerge as a more potent character than any of her masculine companions. (pp. 146-47)

If one considers the particular focus of the Venetian milieu in which the action of the comedy takes place, the aspect of Portia that is potentially most intimidating is her financial power: she is fabulously wealthy in a society in which wealth is the *summum bonum* [highest good]. Bassanio, on the other hand, comes to her penniless. Though the conventions of the fairy-tale present the pauper-princess alliance in the most positive light, it was not a variety of marriage that the Elizabethans regarded complacently. Contemporary treatises on domestic relations warned constantly against the dangers of financial mésalliances, especially those in which the wife was wealthier than her husband. One such tract, *The Flower of Friendshippe*, phrases that warning in terms that seem especially relevant to the threatened inversion of roles in *The Merchant of Venice*:

> a riche woman, that marieth a poor man, seldome, or never, shake off the pride from hir shoulders. Yea *Menander* sayth, that suche a man hath gotten in steed of a wyfe, a husband, and she of him a wyfe, a straunge alteration, a wonderfull metamorphosis.

Nor is the allusion to metamorphosis in this case necessarily mere rhetoric: influential older literary traditions may have supplied an element of justification for taking such a fear seriously. Ovid's *Metamorphoses*, for example, contains the story of a young woman whose success in passing in disguise as a man is divinely rewarded with true and permanent masculinity [Ovid was a first-century A.D. Roman poet. His *Metamorphoses* was a primary source for Greek and Roman myth and legend.]. The particulars of Portia's case—showing, as they do, her triumph over the masculine world, rather than the mere capacity to be assimilated by it—link her with yet another tradition that dealt with the possibility of the metamorphosis of female into male. Medieval authorities on science and medicine had expressed the opinion that a female's vanquishing her mate could actually lead to somatic change of sex. Vestiges of those beliefs may still have been available to an Elizabethan consciousness, adding to a general underlying anxiety about the problem of reconciling Portia's past actions and accomplishments with her projected assumption of the feminine role of wife.

It is within this context that the function of the ring episode in *The Merchant of Venice* becomes clear. Shakespeare, rather than ignoring that anxiety-provoking element or declaring a happy ending by fiat, creates a dramatic situation in which the imbalance of power between the sexes is exaggerated, and drawn to the audience's conscious attention. For the theme of the last dramatic business before the final harmony of the play is restored, he chooses the social act traditionally seen as women's ultimate weapon and ultimate assertion of power over men: cuckoldry. By making the threat of a breach in the sexual order explicit, and then by dispelling that threat, he eases a dangerous underlying tension in the play.

In order to examine the technique Shakespeare uses to allay anxiety that his competent woman will turn into a dominant wife, it is necessary to review briefly the literary tradition that deals with the domestic horrors that result when women fight their way out of their subordinate position in the marital hierarchy. Alice of Bath [in Chaucer's *Canterbury Tales*], whose use of psychological warfare and physical violence in her struggles for "maistrie" suggests the standard policies of these wives, alleges that she intimidated her fourth husband merely with the suggestion that she was cuckolding him. Other shrews of her sect exhibit no such restraint. The fifteenth-century carol that contains in its refrain the first recorded use of the idiom "to wear the breeches" is part of a genre that celebrates the two principal ways a dominant wife signifies her power over her husband: by beating him, and by making him a cuckold. The literature of the period suggests that the three—domination, husband-beating, and cuckoldry—are intimately related, and that the practice of the one implies the practice of the others.

The frightening prospects that are associated with cuckoldry—loss of one's manhood, one's chattels, and one's place in the familial hierarchy—are capable of arousing very deep-rooted, almost atavistic fears in men. The traditions that treat cuckoldry as comic provide a means by which these fears can be assuaged: the cuckold of the Tudor farce, for example, is made into a grotesque and pitiful figure, one whom an audience of men can reject with its laughter. This laughter at cuckoldry evolves into a social reflex, an automatic and unconscious exorcism of a particularly disturbing specter.

Shakespeare, in his introduction of the theme of cuckoldry into *The Merchant of Venice*, is tapping an established source of both deep anxiety and ready laughter. The laughter, of course, is a boon to any comic author, but Shakespeare is able to make an even more significant use of the fear. Since the idea of cuckoldry is so intimately bound to the idea of feminine ascendancy, Shakespeare is able to adopt that anxiety-provoking image as a compact symbol of all the vicissitudes associated with female domination. By introducing the threat of cuckoldry and then eliminating it, he is able to exorcise the prospect of permanent female rule from this comedy of temporary female ascendancy. Shakespeare's demonstration that Portia will not become a dominant wife is worked out with almost mathematical logic. A mannish, aggressive shrew is a woman who makes her husband a cuckold; briefly, this is precisely what Portia pretends to have done. But when the cuckoldry is shown to be unreal, the other side of the equation loses its force as well. Portia's game is shown to be *only* a game; the episode gives her, in effect, an opportunity to tell the audience explicitly that she would never really cuckold her husband. The rest of the triad follows: she will not beat him, and—more importantly—she will not dominate him.

In order to appreciate the serious side of the final comic clash between the wives and husbands, it is necessary to examine the way in which the emblematic force of the rings is put to use in the play. Portia's ring, in particular, is associated with two separate but constantly interacting issues, her independent power and her sexual identity. The shifting ownership of the ring reflects corresponding shifts in characters' control over these two factors.

The link between the ring and her autonomy is one that Portia herself makes explicit in the speech in which she acknowledges Bassanio as her husband:

> Myself and what is mine to you and yours
> Is now converted. But now I was the lord
> Of this fair mansion, master of my servants,
> Queen o'er myself; and even now, but now,
> This house, these servants, and this same myself
> Are yours, my lord's. I give them with this ring . . .
>
> [III. ii. 166-71]

She specifically makes the ring a token of her submission to her new husband. Above all, it symbolizes her agreement to submerge her identity in Bassanio's, in accordance with the principle that man and wife are one flesh. . . . Portia warns Bassanio that his loss of the ring will occasion her reproach, but in practice the penalty threatens to be far greater. The ring itself is seen almost as the embodiment of the right to control Portia's actions: to forfeit the one is to forfeit the other, and as the gift of jewelry is transferred, so is the gift of self.

It is not necessary to turn to the works of the psychoanalytic commentators on *The Merchant of Venice* to document the association between Portia's and Nerissa's rings and their sexuality. The connection is one that can be established by reference to the bawdy quibble in the final couplet of the play itself. . . . [Any] man who possesses a married woman's ring controls her sexuality. When Bassanio breaks his vow to Portia that he will not part with the ring, it might of course be argued that in delivering the token to his "other self," he has no more broken faith than Portia has in sleeping with the doctor of laws. But ultimately, it is this rather paradoxical matter of variably fusing and separating identities that is at the center of the major statements that the play makes about the relationship between the sexes. In order to understand them it is necessary to explore somewhat more fully the role played by the epicene figure of the young lawyer Balthasar in the action of the comedy as a whole.

Unlike Shakespeare's other disguised heroines, who adopt boys' clothing chiefly as a measure of self-protection, Portia disguises herself as Balthasar for the express purpose of gaining an entree to the man's world. In this world she intends to perform a single, specific action; when the action is complete, one might assume, the masculine character that she has conjured up for the purpose would cease to exist. But Bassanio's failure to keep his word disrupts this pattern. It seems almost as though Bassanio's rejection of the token that makes him one with Portia causes, in addition to the break with her, a secondary fission, enabling the figure of the lawyer to assume a shadowy life of his own.

In returning his wife's ring, Bassanio is in effect surrendering the talisman that Portia's own words have invested with power over her and hers. But the Portia who stands in front of him is a double entity: the disguised woman whom the audience sees co-exists with the capable young man seen by Bassanio. It is to this two-sexed figure that Bassanio yields the token of Portia's independent power and physical love. One could predict the logical result of such a transfer even without reference to the remainder of the play: the woman whose autonomy had been restored would assert her independence, both personal and sexual; the masculine figure who had been given the woman's ring would emerge as a sexual rival to the husband. The events of the fifth act bear this prediction out: Portia browbeats Bassanio, and the doctor of laws "cuckolds" him.

In a very abstract way, Portia's request of the ring from Bassanio represents a comic re-enactment of the casket trial, but this time it is a trial that Bassanio fails: he chooses saving face and preserving his masculine honor over keeping his vow to Portia. In this trial, as in the first, the penalty for failure is enforced celibacy. But where there it was fairy-tale, here it is farce: "By heaven, I will ne'er come in your bed / Until I see the ring!" [V. i. 190-91]. Bassanio, sensing the impending storm of female wrath, murmurs, "Why, I were best to cut my left hand off / And swear I lost the ring defending

it" [V. i. 177-78]. It is a marvelous aside, and it does much to humanize the elegant Bassanio, but it also savors somewhat of incipient cowardice in the face of henpecking. The meaning-charged rings in their possession, women are quick to press their advantage: the declaration of female independence, and independent female sexuality, is brought to a more and more highly menacing pitch. From the promise of withholding their sexual favors, they move to threatening to cuckold their husbands:

> *Portia*　Now by mine honor which is yet mine own
> I'll have that doctor for my bedfellow.
> *Nerissa*　And I his clerk.
>
> [V. i. 232-34]

And from there they go on to present the cuckoldry as a *fait accompli* [accomplished fact]:

> *Portia*　　　　Pardon me, Bassanio.
> For by this ring the doctor lay with me.
> *Nerissa*　And pardon me, my gentle Gratiano,
> For that same scrubbed boy, the doctor's clerk,
> In lieu of this last night did lie with me.
>
> [V. i. 258-62]

It is only for a moment that the men are allowed to taste the full farcical horror of their situation: the return to wifely duty that the new gift of the rings implies lags only an instant behind the actual redelivery. In that moment, however, as Portia and Nerissa lay down their high cards, they stand in absolute mastery of the situation. Bassanio is stunned into silence, but Gratiano yelps in indignation, "What, are we cuckolds e'er we have deserved it?" [V. i. 265]. The word is allowed to resonate with its full set of unpleasant connotations; the prospect of masculine subjugation and female ascendancy is set before the eyes of characters and audience alike.

If, as one critic suggests, bawdiness in Shakespeare is associated with anarchic and dissident impulses, Portia's sudden rejection of the topic in hand is illuminating. She meets Gratiano's outburst with curt propriety: "Speak not so grossly" [V. i. 266]. In the one short phrase she rejects both the bawdy language and the anarchic image of female rebellion that inspired it, her reassertion of womanly modesty signalling her return to unthreatening femininity. She suddenly reveals herself to be not a horn-giving shrew, but rather the embodiment of the Elizabethan ideal virtuous wife. . . . (pp. 147-53)

In summary, I would say that although *The Merchant of Venice* may be the best of Shakespeare's early comedies, it is nonetheless one with a central figure that an Elizabethan audience might have found faintly disturbing. Portia is strong and self-sufficient in both the feminine and masculine roles; she seems neither to need nor, perhaps, to be likely to submit to a husband's guidance. Traditionally, a wife who is stronger than her husband makes him a cuckold; no less traditionally, an outside male who is more clever or more powerful than a husband—again—makes him a cuckold. Portia of the double identity seems more than capable of fulfilling both roles. Unless she is determined to be loyal to the bond of marriage, Bassanio is doomed.

The sharp focus on this potential cuckoldry gives Portia (and behind her, Shakespeare) a chance to demonstrate that the future the comedy points to is in no way threatened by Portia's superhuman and superfeminine gifts. The ring episode at the end of *The Merchant of Venice* is indeed introduced to provoke the audience's laughter, but a context is created in which this can be laughter at the mere thought that such an action as cuckoldry should be performed. Because the threat can be laughed away, it is no longer a threat. One can laugh at danger only from a position of security: laughter at the thought that order could be broken is a sure sign that order has been restored. Bassanio . . . finishes his story with the all-important ring back on his finger. . . . [He] and the audience have Portia's promise and Shakespeare's dramatic proof that that promise will be kept. (pp. 153-54)

> Anne Parten, "Re-establishing Sexual Order: The Ring Episode in 'The Merchant of Venice'," in Women's Studies: An Interdisciplinary Journal, *Vol. 9, No. 2, 1982, pp. 145-55.*

ANTONIO

Lawrence Danson

*[Danson examines **Antonio**'s character and discusses his melancholy. He notes that Shakespeare's audience probably would have attributed **Antonio**'s sadness to his economic activities. The critic also compares the merchant's profession with **Shylock**'s, observing that to Elizabethans, who were generally suspicious of mercantile fortunes, moneylender and merchant were "not entirely separate." **Antonio** is a perfect Christian, the critic argues, in his charitable and unworldly nature, although his treatment of **Shylock** conforms to that of his fellow Christians rather than scripture. Danson also comments on the homosexual interpretation of **Antonio**'s melancholy, noting that while this explanation may account for the character's verisimilitude, it is inconsistent with the structure and thematics of Shakespeare's play. For further commentary on **Antonio**'s character, see the excerpts by Frank*

Kermode, E. F. C. Ludowyk, John W. Draper, Marvin Felheim, William Leigh Godshalk, Lawrence W. Hyman, Bernard Grebanier, and Warren D. Smith.]

The opening dialogue of *The Merchant of Venice* takes us simultaneously inward and outward. In, to a psychologically troubled world ("In sooth I know not why I am so sad" [I. i. 1]), out, to a busy and dangerous world where great trading ships, "Like signiors and rich burghers on the flood," "do overpeer the petty traffickers" [I. i. 10, 12]. The two movements—the inward and psychological, the outward and public—are closely related: "Your mind is tossing on the ocean" [I. i. 8]. By his imagistic joining of the world's ocean with the ocean of the mind, Salerio (whose explanation this is for the merchant Antonio's mysterious sadness) creates at least a provisional reconciliation of opposing principles. And this reconciliation is delicately premonitory of other achieved harmonies with which *The Merchant of Venice* abounds. (p. 19)

The play's opening lines pose something of a riddle. Antonio's sadness, wearisome though he claims it is to all involved, immediately offers an invitation to begin searching for answers:

> In sooth I know not why I am so sad,
> It wearies me, you say it wearies you;

Laurence Olivier as Shylock and Joan Plowright as Portia in the trial scene (Act IV, scene i) in a 1970 National Theatre production of The Merchant of Venice.

But how I caught it, found it, or came by
  it,
What stuff 'tis made of, whereof it is born,
I am to learn:
And such a want-wit sadness makes of
  me,
That I have much ado to know myself.
                              [I. i. 1-7]

What follows, however—the attempt by Salerio and Solanio to solve the apparent riddle—should warn us to proceed with caution. Salerio and Solanio have not fared well at the hands of critics: "the two bland little gentlemen," C. L. Barber calls them [in his *Shakespeare's Festive Comedy*]; and the first item in any bill of indictment ought to be their easy confidence that they can clear up the mystery of Antonio's sadness. (pp. 21-2)

There is one further attempt within the scene to explain away Antonio's sadness: Gratiano's "You have too much respect upon the world" [I. i. 74]. Or perhaps this is not so much a third explanation as a summary of the previous two; both the mercantile and the amorous explanations in effect accuse Antonio of having too much concern for the things of this world. They are the thoughts of "worldly choosers." The reproof sounds especially ironic coming from Gratiano, whose babbling levity, while it places him at an opposite extreme from Antonio, is not the sort of joyful noise unto the Lord commended by the Psalmist. Solanio, Salerio, and Gratiano, with their confident and curiously repetitive explanations for Antonio's sad state, begin to sound like Job's three comforters. Antonio, at any rate, rejects Gratiano's more comprehensive explanation as decisively as he has the previous ones:

  I hold the world but as the world Gratiano,
  A stage, where every man must play a
    part,
  And mine a sad one.
                              [I. i. 77-9]

The terms of Antonio's response here are especially interesting. The idea that all the world's a stage was a poetic commonplace long before Shakespeare began to realize its lively potential. And generally the effect of the trope is to open out fresh imaginative prospects. Here, however, the effect might seem to be the reverse: since Antonio *is* a character in a play, his world indeed merely a stage and his part a sad one, his self-conscious admission of a fictive status appears to rule out any more guessing about his melancholy's motives. His sadness, he seems to be saying, is merely a *donnée* [known fact], and there will be no use searching anywhere for its roots except, perhaps, in the literary and dramatic history of the convention of the Melancholy Man.

Or so it might seem. In fact this commonsensical, literary-historical approach—the sort of approach once used (for instance) by E. E. Stoll to explain away any ambiguities in Shylock's character [in his *Shakespeare Studies*]—is no more valid than the psychologizing guesswork indulged in by the play's own characters, Salerio, Solanio, and Gratiano. The world may be a stage where every man must play a part, but the world of *The Merchant of Venice* is a very special world, governed by laws (dramatic and judicial) as curious as, but not identical with, the laws that govern "the great globe itself" [*The Tempest*, IV. i. 153]. The way to understand the problems raised by Antonio's sadness is to understand the special laws that govern the conditions of dramatic life in *The Merchant of Venice*, and therefore to understand such thoroughly interdependent factors as the play's modes of characterization, the disposition of its fable, and what matters are relevant and what irrelevant to its interpretation.

Of the two explanations offered for Antonio's psychological state, the mercantile would no doubt have seemed to many in Shakespeare's audience an especially plausible one. (Modern audiences have been more attracted to the amorous explanation.) Living at a time when previously unimaginable fortunes were to be made, or suddenly lost, in overseas trade, the Elizabethan audience would easily understand how a man might be sorely weighed down by business worries; and when that man was a *Venetian* merchant—the most splendid embodiment of that boundless wealth available to one who would dare the hazards of such trading—the audience might well be suspicious of his disclaimers. How could such a man, to whom the wealth of the world indeed lay as perilously open as did the golden fleece to the venturesome Jason, *not* be made "sad to think upon his merchandise" [I. i. 40]?

There were further reasons to be suspicious of Antonio. Elizabethan attitudes towards the idea of a "merchant of Venice" were complex, compounded in part of admiration, in part of jealousy, but also in part of moral disapproval. . . . A deep suspicion still attached to these merchants, Italian or English, whose fortunes were made less through the sweat of their brow than through the manipulation of money itself. The ambiguity sometimes felt to reside in Shakespeare's title is no mere undergraduate misunderstanding. The Venetian moneylender and the Venetian merchant were not entirely separate in the Elizabethan mind. (pp. 23-6)

Our first glimpse of Antonio, however, may convince us that he, of all men, is least in danger from the moral precariousness of the mercantile life. We have not only Antonio's own disclaimers; more importantly we are quickly granted an extravagant demonstration of Antonio's unmerchantlike charity or love. (pp. 29-30)

Antonio has said that he counts the world as nothing more than it is, "A stage where every man must play a part, / And mine a sad one" [I. i. 78-9] . . . ; but in his response to Bassanio's need we see Antonio's conception of his role more extensively displayed. His use of the world, and all the things of the world, appears to be all unblameworthy; everything he has or can get (for he must borrow in order to meet Bassanio's needs) is at the service of his friend. And as the action of the play progresses, that original phrase, "My purse, my person, *my extremest means* / Lie all unlock'd to your occasions" [I. i. 138-39], gathers to itself deeper resonance, until the doomed Antonio's plight may bring to mind the words of Christ, "Greater loue then this hathe no man, when any man bestoweth his life for his friends" (John 15:13).

Thus Shakespeare plays with his audience's expectations, giving them a merchant who is (apparently) so far from being guilty of a lack of charity that he comes perilously close to completing literally an *imitation Christi* [imitation of Christ]. But although a man of sorrow, Antonio is in fact no more a "Christ-figure" than is any man who acts with charity. And indeed in this first reversal of ordinary expectations Shakespeare has prepared the way for a further and more subtle reversal. In one extraordinary, vital instance, the imputation of uncharitableness will still come back upon Antonio, but in a way far different from what the comfortable audience would initially have expected. . . . Antonio's un-Christlike but quite merchantlike failure involves his fellow merchant, that insidious doppelganger, Shylock.

Antonio's self-righteously unrepentant answer to Shylock at their first appearance together, that "I am as like to call thee [dog] again, / To spet on thee again, to spurn thee too" [I. iii. 130-31], is shocking to modern ears. No doubt it would have shocked some in Shakespeare's audience; others, familiar with a literature which treated Jews in such a way as to make Shakespeare's creation of Shylock seem remarkably forbearing, might have applauded Antonio's openly expressed hatred. Shakespeare's own judgment on the matter is suggested at the start by Antonio's melancholy and confirmed by the lesson of the trial. Critics who search along a naturalistic bias to find the reason for Antonio's sadness generally condemn Antonio's treatment of Shylock without seeing that the two facts—his sadness and his treatment of Shylock—are intimately related. Antonio's melancholy, I suggest, is his emotional response to a moral failure. Elizabethan ideas about the usury Shylock practices complicate the issue but do not alter the fundamental point: that the Christian is obliged equally to hate the sin but *not* the sinner.

The purposeful ambiguity in the play's title, and the numerous felt similarities between Shylock and Antonio—each one, as the play opens, an odd-man-out—help to make the point. The *malice* with which Antonio has, in the past and now, publicly reproved and humiliated Shylock, convicts him of being, in this instance, himself spiritually a

"Jew." . . . In treating Shylock as he has done, Antonio violates—and has, apparently, repeatedly violated—one of the more difficult spiritual directives given in The Sermon on the Mount: 'Iudge not, that ye be not iudged" (Matt. 7:1). Later in the play, in Portia's curious courtroom—a place as much for moral instruction as for legal judgment—Antonio and the audience will have an opportunity to render another kind of judgment, one which rejects the flesh desired by the inner "Jew" and accepts instead the spiritual circumcision of the heart.

By the end of the fifth act, characters and audience have been granted intimations of that music of the heavenly spheres which is too fine for our crude mortal perception. The idea of musical harmony has by then become a dominant metaphor for the play's actions, and the attitudes of the characters to music has become an important means of knowing them. Jessica, a newcomer to the courtly Belmontese society, is uneasy about her own esthetic response: "I am never merry when I hear sweet music" [V. i. 69], she confesses to her Christian husband. But Lorenzo, more native to the musical place, takes it upon himself to instruct Jessica: "The reason is your spirits are attentive" [V. i. 70]. Far from showing a lack of responsiveness, the fact that Jessica is not "merry" when she hears the music shows that she has an appropriate listening attitude: she is prepared to "mark the music" [V. i. 88], and to hear in it faint echoes of the spiritual music of divine harmony. Jessica's is a norm of appropriate attentiveness against which we can measure the attitudes of other characters—of Bassanio, for instance, who so carefully marks the music when it accompanies his choice of Portia's leaden casket.

At an opposite extreme is the capering Gratiano, whose delight in "mirth and laughter" [I. i. 80] overflows into an ugly sort of joy at Shylock's defeat. And Shylock, of course, is clearly identified as an untrustworthy man who "hath no music in himself, / Nor is not moved with concord of sweet sounds" [V. i. 83-4]. At the trial, Shylock, whose rigid adherence to a literal law rules out the mollifying effects of music, and Gratiano, with his excessive levity, will produce between them a cacophony of lovelessness.

The musical metaphor tells us about Antonio, too. Antonio's melancholy shows that he is out of tune; that despite his spontaneous charity to his beloved Bassanio, his malice towards Shylock—his enemy but therefore, because of his malice, a spiritual kinsman—keeps him from being fully a part of the ideal harmony. But to Portia's challenge at the trial, "What mercy can you render him Antonio" [IV. i. 378], Antonio responds differently than either Gratiano or Shylock. In his response, which goes beyond love of a neighbor to reach as well the love of an enemy, Antonio shows himself to be at last in tune. In his melancholy, Antonio was incapable of fulfilling the Psalmist's injunction to "Sing vnto the Lord a new song" (Ps. 98); but when he extends his love beyond the circle that includes Portia and Bassanio, reaching outwards with charity for Shylock as well, his gesture makes the "new song" of spiritual love. (pp. 30-4)

I want to consider the other explanation beside the mercantile one that has been advanced for Antonio's melancholy. For the opinion that Antonio is in love continues to be widely held, all his "fie, fies" notwithstanding. Not cranks, but some of the play's most eminent interpreters, both academic and theatrical, perceive a homoerotic disturbance as the basis of Antonio's sadness. (p. 34)

For instance, E. M. W. Tillyard writes [in his *Shakespeare's Early Comedies*] that "Antonio suffers from a self-abnegating passion that quenches the springs of vitality in him and makes him the self-chosen outcast from society. . . . Antonio now sees himself as useless. Before Bassanio left him for Portia, his life had some direction; now it has none." . . . [Of] even greater interest is the rhetoric of Tillyard's conclusion: "I do not think Antonio a study of homosexuality; *but* Shakespeare presented him as essentially a lonely figure, strikingly different from all the sociable folk he has to do with, except Shylock." The force of that "but" implies that Antonio's loneliness and his difference from "all the sociable folk" make him like a homosexual, even if he is not "a study in homosexuality." Thus Antonio's homosexual attachment is made to explain his sadness, and his sadness to prove his homosexuality. The logic (by no means uniquely Tillyard's) is as curious as the implication that loneliness and a striking difference from sociable folk are characteristic of homosexuals.

Now this explanation for Antonio's melancholy seems to me quite wrong: its implied consequences (as I will explain shortly) are not coherent with the play's overall shape and tone. And it is important to stress that this reason, rather than any *a priori* [presumptive] theoretical objection, is the basis for rejecting the psychosexual interpretation: for what is at issue here is not only Antonio's sexual preference, but the nature of Shakespearean characterization. The possible extremes are these: that Antonio, as Shakespeare created him, is merely a bundle of personified dramatic conventions—melancholy, generous, unlucky; or (at another extreme) that he is a psychologically "realistic" character in whom it is proper to discover submerged psychosexual motivations. And the difficult fact—the very heart of this Shakespearean matter—is that Antonio is not wholly the one sort of character or the other, but a richly impure mixture (like the play itself) of both dramatic tendencies. We need to give due weight to all that is uniquely Elizabethan and "conventional" in Antonio's characterization—and that means, among other things, recognizing him as a figure capable of standing for

"abstract" ideas, of representing moral qualities. But the necessity to hold on to both sides of Shakespeare's characterizing variousness also makes it important to reaffirm—even in rejecting the idea that Antonio is primarily motivated by a sexual attachment to Bassanio—the character's actual degree of psychological "realism." (pp. 34-6)

The Merchant of Venice is a play in which harmonies are discovered where only discord had seemed possible, and its dominant figure (whether in details of imagery or in the implied shape of the fable as a whole) is the circle, ring, or round. The love of Antonio and Bassanio chimes in that harmonious round, as does the love of Bassanio and Portia. But to suppose a competition between Antonio and Portia introduces a discord more intractable to resolution than that of Shylock, the unmusical man, himself. So it is not the realism nor the humanness, but the consequent introduction of this irreconcilable competition, that leads me to reject the psychosexual explanation for Antonio's sadness. (pp. 38-9)

It is conceivable, I suppose, that one could have a homosexual Antonio without any consequent irreconcilability between Bassanio's two lovers. But then, of course, Antonio's sadness remains inexplicable. And in critical practice, a competition between Portia and Antonio seems the inevitable result of the assumption. According to one account, for instance, friendship is relegated "to a subordinate place" by the end of the play, and Antonio is taught that "there is room for friendship within the house of love, but love holds the upper and controlling hand" [Anne Barton, in her introduction to *The Merchant of Venice* in *The Riverside Shakespeare,* edited by G. Blakemore Evans]. This shrewish love, however, conflicts with all that Portia says about the nature of her relationship to Bassanio when he wins her in the casket test, when "her gentle spirit / Commits itself to [his] to be directed, / As from her lord, her governor, her king" [III. ii. 163-65]. And it conflicts with the actual result of the ring episode, which is (in part) the reaffirmation of Antonio's loving loyalty to both Bassanio and Portia:

> I once did lend my body for his wealth,
> Which but for him that had your husband's ring
> Had quite miscarried. I dare be bound again,
> My soul upon the forfeit, that your lord
> Will never more break faith advisedly.
> 　　　　　　　　　　[V. i. 249-53]

The love of Antonio and Bassanio (whether or not it dares to speak its name) is a textual fact; but a sexual competition between Antonio and Portia is not, and to invent one raises more problems of interpretation than it solves. (pp. 39-40)

Lawrence Danson, in his The Harmonies of "The Merchant of Venice," *Yale University Press,* 1978, 202 p.

SOURCES FOR FURTHER STUDY

LITERARY COMMENTARY:

Barnet, Sylvan, ed. *Twentieth-Century Interpretations of "The Merchant of Venice": A Collection of Critical Essays.* Englewood Cliffs, N. J.: Prentice-Hall, 1970, 122 p.

A collection of essays by prominent critics on various topics concerning *The Merchant of Venice.*

Bentson, Alice N. "Portia, the Law, and the Tripartite Structure of *'The Merchant of Venice'*." *Shakespeare Quarterly* 30, No. 3 (Summer 1979): 367-85.

Argues that Portia is the central character of the play, considering her the drama's protector of law in both the civil sphere of Venice and the natural sphere of Belmont, rather than the embodiment of mercy.

Grebanier, Bernard. *The Truth about Shylock.* New York: Random House, 1962, 369 p.

Reconstructs Elizabethan attitudes toward Jews and the practice of usury, determining how much this climate of opinion affected Shakespeare's writing of *The Merchant of Venice.* Grebanier also offers a critical analysis of the play, which he interprets as an allegorical dramatization of the triumph of love and mercy over justice and hate.

Hapgood, Robert. "Portia and *The Merchant of Venice:* The Gentle Bond." *Modern Language Quarterly* 28, No. 1 (March 1967): 19-32.

Finds in Portia a "large-minded sense of law" which allows her to lessen the harsh effects of the social bonds of marriage, her father's will, and Venetian law by making "enlightened exceptions."

Hill, R. F. "*The Merchant of Venice* and the Pattern of Romantic Comedy." *Shakespeare Survey* 28 (1975): 75-87.

Contends that, unlike Shakespeare's other romantic comedies, *The Merchant of Venice* presents an uncomplicated, idealistic vision of love.

Holmer, Joan Ozark. "Loving Wisely and the Casket Test: Symbolic and Structural Unity in *The Merchant of Venice.*" *Shakespeare Studies* XI (1978): 53-76.

Detailed examination of the manner in which the casket story foreshadows and reinforces themes prevalent throughout the play, especially those related to Shylock and his self-deception concerning wealth, worldly possessions, and the letter of the law.

Krapf, E. E. "Shylock and Antonio: A Psychoanalytic Study of Shakespeare and Antisemitism." *The Psychoanalytic Review* 42, No. 2 (April 1955): 113-30.

Maintains that the central character in *The Merchant of Venice* is Shylock, not Antonio, and that Shakespeare consciously intended this figure to be nothing more than a comic villain. Krapf adds, however, that Shylock evokes our interest and sympathy because Shakespeare himself was uncertain about his feelings towards Jews.

Landa, M. J. *The Shylock Myth.* London: W. H. Allen & Co., 1942, 48 p.

Traces the historical background of Jews and usury in England and uncovers the origins of the bond story.

Murry, John Middleton. "The Significance of Shylock." *The Adelphi* 22, No. 1 (October-December 1945): 1-5.

Presents a view of Shylock as a noble and dignified character, whose actions attempt to address centuries of Christian persecution of the Jews. Murry also compares Shylock and Portia, finding them to be representatives of conflicting orders; Shylock, the old, and Portia, the new. This opposition occurs on many levels, including the social, the religious, and the economic.

Palmer, John. "Shylock." In his *Comic Characters of Shakespeare,* pp. 53-91. London: Macmillan and Co., 1946.

Explores the process by which the comic Shylock that Shakespeare intended becomes the tragic or noble Jew that many critics perceive.

Pettet, E. C. "*The Merchant of Venice* and the Problem of Usury." *Essays and Studies* 31 (1945): 19-33.

Brief examination of English usury and its influence on the plot of the play.

Scott, W. I. D. "Antonio—The Endogenous Depressive." In his *Shakespeare's Melancholics,* pp. 35-46. London: Mills & Boon Limited, 1962.

Maintains that Antonio's sadness is caused by his latent homosexual feelings towards Bassanio.

Shackford, John B. "The Bond of Kindness: Shylock's Humanity." *The University of Kansas City Review* 21, No. 2 (Winter 1954): 85-91.

Analyzes Christian belief and practice as it is presented in the play and argues that Shylock's motive in the pound of flesh bond is vengeance.

Tillyard, E. M. W. "The Trial Scene in 'The Merchant of Venice'." *A Review of English Literature* 2, No. 4 (October 1961): 51-9.

Examines Portia in Act IV, arguing that her role in the play is the reconciliation of mercy and justice.

Tovey, Barbara. "The Golden Casket: An Interpretation of *The Merchant of Venice.*" In *Shakespeare as a Political Thinker,* edited by John Alvis and Thomas G. West, pp. 215-38. Durham, N.C.: Carolina Academic Press, 1981.

Interprets the play symbolically, arguing that Shakespeare criticizes Christianity through his dramatization of Bassanio's relationship with Antonio.

Withington, Robert. "Shakespeare and Race Prejudice." In *Elizabethan Studies and Other Essays in Honor of George F. Reynolds,* edited by E. J. West, pp. 172-84. Boulder: University of Colorado Press, 1945.
    Discusses whether Shakespeare presents a prejudiced depiction of Shylock in *The Merchant of Venice.*

MEDIA ADAPTATIONS:

Merchant of Venice. University of Michigan, 1961.
    Educational video and part of the "Plays of Shakespeare" series. 29 minutes.

Merchant of Venice: Act I, Scene III; Act IV, Scene I. Seabourne Enterprises Ltd., 1971.
    Educational video which allows students to focus on the themes of the play. Distributed by Phoenix/BFA Films. 26 minutes.

The Merchant of Venice. BBC, Time Life TV, 1981.
    Television adaptation of Shakespeare's drama and part of the series "The Shakespeare Plays." Features Warren Mitchell, Gemma Jones, and John Franklyn-Robbins. Distributed by Time-Life Video. 157 minutes.

A MIDSUMMER NIGHT'S DREAM

INTRODUCTION

Widely recognized as a comic masterpiece, *A Midsummer Night's Dream* is one of Shakespeare's most popular works. The play has inspired numerous adaptations, including Felix Mendelssohn's acclaimed musical score for a nineteenth-century production. Written about 1595, *A Midsummer Night's Dream* is considered Shakespeare's first mature comedy. By blending motifs from various classical works, such as the first-century Roman poet Ovid's *Metamorphoses* and the second-century Roman orator Apuleius's *Golden Ass,* the playwright successfully balanced a variety of narrative styles and dramatic procedures to create an unforgettable artistic effect. The plot of *A Midsummer Night's Dream* is Shakespeare's own, however: he did not follow his usual practice of adapting an older story. This account of the tribulations of a love quadrangle during a night of madness imaginatively combines ambiguous allusions, wordplay, sinister hints, fragments of noble poetry, and profound meditations on the nature of art and love. The brilliant characterization, richness of language, and compositional complexity of this play have provided critics and commentators with material for much theorizing. As for the general reader and theater-goer, *A Midsummer Night's Dream* remains a timeless and limitless source of aesthetic pleasure.

PRINCIPAL CHARACTERS
(in order of appearance)

Theseus: The Duke of Athens. He originally supports Egeus's opposition to the marriage of Hermia and Lysander, but later changes his mind.

Hippolyta: Amazon queen. Defeated in battle and captured by Theseus, she is now his betrothed.

Egeus: An Athenian nobleman and Hermia's father. He is intent on forcing her to marry Demetrius, whom she does not love.

Hermia: Egeus's daughter and Helena's friend. She loves Lysander and consequently defies her father's authority, undaunted by the cruel penalties for disobedience.

Demetrius: An Athenian nobleman and Hermia's suitor. His plans to marry Hermia are thwarted by supernatural and earthly circumstances.

Lysander: An Athenian nobleman and Hermia's lover. Affected by misdirected magic, he temporarily renounces his love for Hermia in favor of Helena.

Helena: Hermia's friend. In love with Demetrius, who scorns her, she later finds herself in the awkward situation of being wooed by both Lysander and Demetrius during their bewitchment in the forest.

Quince: A carpenter. He plays the Prologue in "Pyramus and Thisby," the play he organizes as part of Theseus and Hippolyta's wedding festivities.

Bottom: A weaver. He plays Pyramus in the drama performed for Theseus and Hippolyta. Magically transformed by Puck into a person with the head of an ass, he becomes Titania's grotesque paramour. Of all the mortals, only he can see the inhabitants of the fairy-world.

Puck, or *Robin Goodfellow:* An impish sprite. His inexpert handling of a love potion causes Demetrius and Lysander's infatuation with Helena.

Oberon: King of the Fairies. Infuriated by Titania's refusal to hand over a changeling boy to whom he has grown attached, Oberon casts a spell on his wife which causes her to fall in love with the transformed Bottom.

Titania: Queen of the Fairies. She initially resists her husband's will; but after succumbing to the effects of Oberon's magic potion, she suffers humiliation, relents, and regains his favor.

PLOT SYNOPSIS

Act I: In Athens, as Theseus and Hippolyta prepare for their wedding, Egeus approaches the Duke to complain about Hermia's unwillingness to marry Demetrius. Theseus tells Hermia that the punishment for her obstinacy is either death or life imprisonment in a cloister. Undaunted, Hermia decides to seek refuge from Athenian law by escaping with Lysander into the forest. But Helena, in whom Hermia has confided, betrays her friend to Demetrius, hoping to win his favor. Unbeknownst to the aristocratic characters, Bottom and Quince decide to produce a play in honor of Theseus and Hippolyta's wedding.

Act II: Seeking Hermia in the forest, Demetrius instead finds Helena and berates her for following him. In another part of the forest, Hermia and Lysander prepare to spend the night in unfamiliar surroundings. In the fairy-world, Oberon and Titania feud over the queen's favorite attendant, a beautiful boy, whom she refuses to give up, to her husband's chagrin. Seeking revenge, Oberon administers a love potion to Titania. Applied to the sleeping victim's eyes, the potion will make her instantly enamored of the first creature she encounters upon awakening. The malicious Oberon hopes this figure will be some repellent beast. When he overhears Demetrius's angry rejection of Helena, Oberon feels pity for her and orders Puck to use the magic potion on Demetrius as well. However, Puck mistakenly gives it to Lysander, who is sleeping nearby. Lysander sees Helena upon awakening and, to Hermia's horror, immediately professes his undying love for her.

Act III: Bottom and his players assemble in the forest to rehearse their play. As the sleeping Titania awakens she catches sight of Bottom, whose head is transformed by Puck's magic into that of an ass. Titania declares her love for Bottom, and he humorously responds to her expressions of affection. Meanwhile, Oberon discovers Puck's error and rubs Demetrius's eyes with the potion. As a result, however, Demetrius, like Lysander, becomes infatuated with Helena. She is infuriated by Lysander and Demetrius's behavior and lashes out at Hermia, thinking that all three are conspiring to mock her. After a duel between Lysander and Demetrius over Helena has been thwarted by Puck's magic, all four confused lovers fall asleep. Puck then uses the potion to revive Lysander's love for Hermia.

Act IV: As the spellbound Titania willingly gives up the youthful attendant who had sparked Oberon's jealousy, the fairy king decides that she has been humiliated enough and breaks the spell. It is morning, and Theseus and his party are in the forest celebrating the rite of May. They accidentally find the lovers, upon whom Egeus angrily invokes Athenian law, demanding that Lysander be punished for eloping with Hermia. However, Theseus benevolently overrules the law, granting Lysander and Hermia permission to marry. As a result of magic, Demetrius's love for Helena remains firm, and the foursome join the royal couple in joyous anticipation of a triple wedding.

Act V: In Athens, Bottom and his players provide entertainment for the nuptial festivities at the court. Their version of "Pyramus and Thisby," a ludicrous rendition of a pathetic story, concludes the joyful day. Once the performance is finished, Oberon, on behalf of the fairy world, bestows his blessings on the three couples.

PRINCIPAL TOPICS

Focusing on such issues as love, dreams, and reality, *A Midsummer Night's Dream* has been regarded by critics as Shakespeare's first mature comedy, a work which addresses fundamental questions about life. Since love triumphs at the end of the play, dispelling the chaotic magic of the night, the drama seems almost conventional. Thus a traditional reading of the play tends to emphasize the joyful outcome, regarding the supernatural elements as the natural background for a story which celebrates life. However, a rather different interpretation was suggested in 1961 by the eminent Polish scholar Jan Kott, who in his seminal *Szkice o Szekspirze* (*Shakespeare, Our Contemporary*) drew attention to the sinister undercurrents of this seemingly charming and gentle love story. Unlike earlier critics who only touched upon the dark side of *A Midsummer Night's Dream*, Kott dismisses the romantic view of Shakespeare's work, maintaining that the play essentially focuses on brutal eroticism and explores a range of violent sexual fantasies. Furthermore, Kott argues, love is debased by the interchangeability of objects of desire, reaching its lowest ebb in Titania's erotic attraction to a beast.

Kott's reading of the play points to the battle of the sexes as a major topic. As feminist critics have observed, the tensions among the antagonists—such as Hermia and her father—do not stem from a blind urge to inflict pain, but reflect the efforts of a male-dominated society to safeguard its laws and values. Not only are the women in the play debased in love and treated as objects of desire and/or possession, but female bonds—such as the friendship between Hermia and Helena—are undermined by male suspicion, insecurity, and fear of possible exclusion from a world ruled by women such as Hippolyta, the queen of a tribe of women warriors, who was defeated by Theseus and claimed as the spoils of war. Some critics maintain that this male anxiety reflects a dread of sexual powerlessness. As a result, the male characters feel secure only when they are able to divide and conquer their women.

But the ambiguities of love, critics contend, do not exhaust the vast universe of Shakespeare's comedy: *A Midsummer Night's Dream* also attempts to grasp the elusive nature of reality. The boundaries between the real world, represented by the Athenians, and the supernatural world of Oberon and Titania are sometimes fluid, as evidenced by the many instances when a protagonist, such as Bottom, seems caught somewhere between the two levels of existence. According to some critics, Shakespeare, while describing both reality and fantasy as relative, identifies poetry as the lasting, imperishable result of the perilous journey through the fantastic worlds of apparitions, dreams, and nightmares. Based on this understanding of the function of poetry in the drama, some critics contend that it is the playwright himself who directly imparts a sense of wonder to his audience, thus rendering the universe of his play meaningful and inspiring. In fact, Hippolyta acknowledges the audience's aesthetic experience by declaring, "But all the story of the night told over,/ And all their minds transfigur'd so together,/ More witnesseth than fancy's images,/ And grows to something of great constancy/ But howsoever strange and admirable" (V. i. 23-7). Another remarkable feature closely associated to the theme of reality versus illusion in *A Midsummer Night's Dream* is the work's self-consciousness. In other words, the characters not only discuss the nature of drama but also comment indirectly on the play in which they perform. As critics explain, Shakespeare accomplishes this by employing a well-known theatrical device: the play-within-the-play. The performance of "Pyramus and Thisby" can be interpreted as a triple parody: of itself, of *A Midsummer Night's Dream,* and of theater as an aesthetic experience.

The magic wand which conjures up Shakespeare's world is, as critics generally agree, peerless poetic language. Finding the right type of language, metrical framework, allusion, and figure to fit every character and situation, Shakespeare enriches his play with memorable examples of literary virtuosity. For example, a character's psychological changes are illustrated by variations in tone or meter. In addition, there are many moments when the characters' eloquence soars high above the confines of dramatic discourse to the realm of pure poetry. The verbal brilliance of the play was particularly emphasized by Peter Brooke's seminal 1970 Royal Shakespeare Company production, which focused on the text and drastically reduced the visual dimension by staging the dramatic action in a set resembling a white box.

Rich, allusive, melodious, and multi-layered, Shakespeare's dramatic poetry not only fully employs all of the resources of the English language, but also conjures up the power of mythology. Within the complex mythological background of *A Midsummer Night's Dream* one finds interwoven strands of pre-Classical, Classical, Celtic, Anglo-Saxon, and Germanic folklore, particularly in the poet's descriptions of the fairy world. Some of the supernatural figures Shakespeare introduces in the drama represent formidable archetypes which appear in different traditions under various names and form. Such a figure, according to scholars, is Diana, the triple goddess, who performs her celestial role as a moon divinity, lives on earth as the virginal Diana—the hunting deity (called Titania once by Ovid)—and haunts the underworld as the witch-goddess Hecate. The moon, one of the goddess's domains, operates as a potent poetic symbol suggesting possible pathways connecting higher realms and our own world, which the Elizabethans called "sublunar" or "under the moon." In the last act, Theseus mentions "the lunatic, the lover and the poet" (V. i. 7), using the "moon-word" "lunatic" to underline the connections between madness, love, and poetry. Critics who suggest an entirely different genealogy of Shakespeare's fairy-world, however, argue that the Elizabethan

fairies of *A Midsummer Night's Dream* are not characters from folklore, but figures from literary and religious tradition. Tracing the origins of Shakespeare's supernatural world in Arthurian legend and in the Christianized form of Cabala, a Jewish system of reading the Scriptures based on the mystical interpretation of words, these commentators identify the moon goddess as the Virgin Queen, or Elizabeth I. As a result, Shakespeare's references to the lunar divinity could be understood as an homage to the existing cult of Queen Elizabeth.

CHARACTER STUDIES

The characters of *A Midsummer Night's Dream* exist on three different levels: the fairies appear in the supernatural sphere, the lovers wander through the labyrinths of a dream world, and Bottom and his companions belong to everyday reality. Since the lovers, although human, seem vague and undefined, and assume certain qualities of the spectral world, critics have traditionally concentrated on Bottom, praising this earthy, resourceful, and multi-faceted figure as one of Shakespeare's greatest comical creations. Unpredictable, witty, a master ironist, and the only mortal capable of communicating directly with the fairy-world, Bottom embodies the dramatist himself, who introduces his fellow mortals to the rich world of fantasy, using his pen to capture the essence of a dream. In comparison with Bottom, the four protagonists—Lysander, Hermia, Demetrius, and Helena—seem, as critics have remarked, pale and undefined, akin to puppets at the mercy of higher powers. Commenting on what critics have discerned as a certain uniformity of the four lovers, Kott defines them as "exchangeable" and identifies this absence of true individuality as one of the crucial features of the play. As the characters degenerate into faceless objects of desire, thereby relinquishing their individuality, they ultimately cease to exist as characters, and situations become paramount in the play. An alternate view proposes a different interpretation of the four protagonists, however, maintaining that speech clearly identifies each of the principal characters as a distinct person. For example, Helena expresses affection rather tersely, while Hermia uses terms of endearment quite profusely. According to commentators, there are significant similarities between the two royal couples in *A Midsummer Night's Dream*: both Oberon and Theseus rule their women, Titania and Hippolyta, with rigorous authority. Oberon exemplifies the more capricious aspects of power, whereas Theseus symbolizes benign despotism. While submissive to their respective lords, Titania the fairy queen and Hippolyta the Amazon queen retain some of their mythical power. It is particularly Titania, identified by commentators as the moon-goddess, who appears as the guiding spirit that ultimately presides over love's triumph when the four lovers are happily united and reconciled. Despite several convincing arguments brought forth by scholars, characterization in *A Midsummer Night's Dream* seems far from a closed issue, and many ambiguous points and unresolved questions still remain.

CONCLUSION

Scholarly debates concerning the key aspects of *A Midsummer Night's Dream* will doubtless yield new insights and engender new theories of interpretation. But the changing perspectives of scholarship do not seem to affect the enduring popularity of this play, which for many remains emblematic of Shakespeare's comic genius. Appealing to a primordial human desire to cross the boundary between reality and fantasy, *A Midsummer Night's Dream* also brilliantly expresses the profound human uncertainty about love. What makes this work truly immortal, however, is the poetry which enlightens the soul while transforming the entire universe of passions and emotions, ranging from primitive to noble, into a suggestive discourse of extraordinary artistic beauty.

(See also *Shakespearean Criticism,* Vols. 3, 12)

OVERVIEWS

Wolfgang Clemen

[*Clemen provides a general introduction to* A Midsummer Night's Dream, *identifying and analyzing the play's historical background, language, themes, dramatic structure, characterization, and literary significance. Remarking that the transitory nature of love is the principal theme of the play, this critic praises Shakespeare's masterful use of language, particularly images representing the contrast of light and darkness, to suggest the atmosphere of a fantastic dream world. Shakespeare's language, Clemen maintains, is not only remarkably visual but also possesses a certain musical quality, clearly discerned in repetitive patterns of sounds and effects. Not only is* A Midsummer Night's Dream *a great comedy, the critic concludes, but it also offers, using the device of the play-within-the-play, profound insights into the limitations of dramatic art.*]

A study of Shakespeare's development as a dramatic artist shows that one of his supreme achievements during his "middle period" consists in combining heterogeneous elements in a single play. The dramas of Shakespeare's predecessors all exist on a smaller scale, mostly adhering to one particular type and keeping within more limited resources of style and subject matter. However, even in his very first comedies, *The Two Gentlemen of Verona, The Comedy of Errors,* and *Love's Labor's Lost,* we see Shakespeare widening the scope of the dramatic genre to which these plays belong and introducing new elements taken over from other sections of the literary tradition of the past. *A Midsummer Night's Dream,* then, which must have been written about 1595, combines for the first time totally disparate worlds into one unified whole; the sharp contrasts brought together there would have destroyed the play's balance in the hands of any lesser playwright. For, indeed, it required Shakespeare's genius to bring together Bottom and Puck, the crude realism of the artisans and the exquisite delicacy of the fairy world, the stylized and pointed repartee of the Athenian lovers and the dignified manner of Theseus and Hippolyta. What we find are contrasts on many levels, exemplified by diversified means. Yet Shakespeare strikes an equilibrium between these contrasts, reconciling and fusing the discordant factors within the organic body of his comedy. *A Midsummer Night's Dream,* therefore, not only exhibits bold contrasts and divergent elements of plot, atmosphere, and character; it also illustrates the unifying power of the spirit of comedy and the poetic imagination. We further find that the play's unity is reinforced by a subtle technique of counterpoint and juxtaposition, a skillful contrasting of different strands of plot, and the creation of an atmosphere full of illusion, wonder, and strangeness, all of which facilitate the many transitions occurring during the course of the play.

Some facts about its origin and title may help us better to understand the particular nature of the play. *A Midsummer Night's Dream* is clearly related to the practices of midsummer night, the night before June 24, which was the date of St. John the Baptist's festival and hence connected with merrymaking, various superstitions and folk customs, dances, pageants, and revels. More than any other night in the year, midsummer night suggested enchantment and witchcraft, something which Shakespeare has superbly embodied in his fairy world. To an Elizabethan audience, moreover, the play's title would have immediately called to mind the so-called "midsummer madness," which was a state of mind marked by a heightened readiness to believe in the delusions of the imagination that were thought to befall the minds of men after days of great summer heat. Thus, by means of his highly suggestive title, Shakespeare has firmly planted the dreamlike action of his drama in the popular beliefs and customs of his time. Furthermore the title gives theatergoers and readers a clue as to how the work should be understood—namely, as an unrealistic creation of the imagination, a series of dream images containing all the contradictions and inconsistencies that dreams normally possess, but containing too their symbolic content. Indeed, the dreamlike character of what takes place is repeatedly alluded to. In Puck's epilogue, for instance, the audience themselves are explicitly addressed:

> And this weak and idle theme,
> No more yielding but a dream,
> Gentles, do not reprehend . . .
> [V. i. 427–29]

In short, the play's title makes significant allusion to the nature and meaning of the work, though it makes no reference to the period of time during which the events of the drama occur. In fact, the action takes place between April 29 and May 1, the latter date, being that of May Day, demanding of course particular celebrations, and for that reason it is perhaps a suitable day for the marriage of Theseus and Hippolyta.

Now the wedding of the princely pair is not only the destination of the action; it is also the occasion for which the play itself was written. *A Midsummer Night's Dream* was undoubtedly intended as a dramatic epithalamium [a bridal song] to celebrate the marriage of some aristocratic couple. (The attempts made to fix on a definite historical marriage, however, must remain conjectural.) Plays written for such festive occasions addressed themselves to an aristocratic audience. They were mostly performed on private stages rather than in public theaters and revealed an entirely different style of performance from the popular dramas. The relationship of *A Midsummer Night's Dream* to the court masque—something which Act V, Scene i, line 40 draws attention to—also comes in here. The masques formed a central part of the entertainments that were always given at court celebrations, and several noticeable features in *A Midsummer Night's Dream* clearly relate to the genre of the court masque. The music and dances, the appearance of fairylike creatures possessed of supernatural qualities, the employment of motifs involving magic and metamorphosis, and the vigorous stylization and symmetrical structure of some parts do indeed remind one of the court masque. Finally, the scenes with Bottom, Quince, and company may be compared to the antimasque, which formed the burlesque and realistic counterpart performed together with the masque itself.

In referring to the masque, one is only pointing out a single aspect of *A Midsummer Night's Dream*. We must also remember that Shakespeare has similarly taken over stylistic and formal elements from his own early comedies, popular drama, the romantic play, and the mythological dream plays of John Lyly. Shakespeare has tapped many sources, but he has nevertheless been able to create an original and independent form of drama that includes skillful organization of plot—involving the manipulation of three subplots that run parallel to one another—as well as a rich suffusion of the whole by both the atmosphere of nature and that of magic. Between a descriptive and retrospective kind of dramatic method and one that makes us see the process of things in action Shakespeare has struck a perfect sense of balance.

A study of the interrelation of the four plots reveals how their contrasts, juxtapositions, and dovetailing help to disclose the meaning of the drama. The play begins with a scene between Theseus and Hippolyta, who do not appear again until Act IV. In Act V their wedding is celebrated. The plot involving Theseus and Hippolyta can therefore be styled an "enveloping action" that provides the play with a definite framework and a firmly established temporal scaffolding; it stands outside the world of dream, enchantment, and love entanglements, suggesting the sphere of everyday reality out of which the events of the drama first develop and to which they then ultimately return. The section in Scene i with Egeus, Hermia, Lysander, and Demetrius relates the Theseus-Hippolyta plot to that of the lovers, for Theseus himself appears as arbitrator in the love dispute and it will be on his wedding day that the harsh verdict he passes on Hermia is to take effect, should she not have changed her mind by that date. This verdict is the cause of Hermia and Lysander's decision to flee into the wood near Athens, so that with this the events of the second and third acts have already been determined. The comic subplot, moreover, beginning in Scene ii with the gathering of the artisans to prepare themselves for rehearsal, is also announced in Scene i, insofar as we learn of the entertainments to be presented on Theseus' wedding day. Theseus' promise to woo Hippolyta "With pomp, with triumph, and with reveling" [I. i. 19] can also be understood as an allusion to the dramatic entertainments that are to come later. From the very beginning, then, our expectations are raised in connection with the wedding day, which is to bring with it the artisans' play, the decision regarding the love dispute between the Athenian couples, and the festive marriage of Theseus and Hippolyta.

If this were all that Shakespeare had given us, we would have had a comedy little different from his early ones. The plot connected with the fairies, however, with Oberon and Titania at its center, not only brings considerable complications into the course of the above-mentioned matters, but also adds to the whole drama a new feature that Shakespeare had never employed before. For the supernatural, which intervenes in the activities of the characters, turns their intentions upside down, and directs their actions. It is the fairies who are responsible for the confusion, and also for the final reconciliation, thus substituting enchantment and arbitrariness for the lovers' own responsibility and power of will. Yet these influences also have repercussions on the fairies themselves, because Titania thereby falls in love with the ass-headed Bottom.

Thus the world of the fairies is linked with that of the artisans, and we get those incomparably comic situations that are themselves the outcome of the fairies' intervention. Finally, a link between the plots dealing with the fairies and Theseus emerges in the conversation between Oberon and Titania in which the fairy rulers' earlier connections with Theseus and Hippolyta are recalled; and this is a moment that accelerates the pair's mutual jealousy and estrangement.

Since the fairies remain always invisible to the other members of the *dramatis personae* (only Bottom is ironically allowed the privilege of seeing Titania), and their deeds are accomplished without the knowledge of the other characters, Shakespeare has been able to achieve a highly dramatic effect of "double awareness." We as audience are aware of Puck's magic juice and therefore look forward with pleasure to what might develop. We know even more than the usually omniscient Oberon, who does not realize till some time later the confusion that Puck has caused by mistake. This error on Puck's part bears deeper significance, for it shows that even the fairies can err and that the influences they exert as supernatural agents in the play do not in the least answer to anything providential, but rather contain filaments of arbitrariness, self-deception, and folly.

An insight into the peculiar nature of the fairy world in *A Midsummer Night's Dream* helps us to understand the entire play, for although the fairies certainly possess supernatural qualities, they are nevertheless closely linked to the world of mankind and have their share of human frailties. Their origin in the realm of the elemental and their partly instinctive, partly playful nature, together with their capriciousness and irrationality, indicate which forces and qualities Shakespeare wanted us to see as conditioning and influencing human love relationships; for the haphazard and arbitrary game that love plays with the two Athenian couples appears as a projection of the irrationality, irresponsibility, and playfulness characterizing the nature of the fairies themselves. However, the fairies not only make other people behave in a way that corresponds, as it were, to their own fairy natures; they also strengthen and reinforce people's latent tendencies. Previous to the fairies' intervention, we learn from Demetrius that he has loved Helena before bestowing his affections on Hermia [I. i. 106-07, 242-43]; it is not for nothing that he is termed "spotted and inconstant man" [I. i. 110].

Shakespeare has interspersed his text with numerous illuminating hints referring to the fairies' peculiar traits of character and sphere of existence, so that we are able to get a vivid picture of the type of creatures they are. Although the world of the fairies exhibits several characteristics common to popular belief and folklore tradition, it is to a considerable extent a new creation of Shakespeare's

own. This is particularly true when we think of Puck, whose descent from Robin Goodfellow or Hobgoblin, as he is called by one of the fairies when he first appears [II. i. 34, 40], only accounts for one aspect of his being. If one examines the numerous statements that Puck utters about himself and that the other characters utter about him, one immediately realizes that Shakespeare has created a complex dramatic figure to whom is assigned a key position within the fabric of the play. Not only is Puck the comically rough and earth-bound goblin with his mischievous pranks, blunt speech, and intervention in day-to-day affairs; he is also a spirit closely linked with the elements, having command over supernatural powers and capable of moving at incredible speed. As "Oberon's jester" he is close to the fools of Shakespeare's later comedies, enjoying his own jests and possessing the gift of sharp, critical observation. Keeping this last point in mind, we see that Shakespeare has assigned him the role of spectator several times during the course of the play, and as such he comments on the action and aptly characterizes the people taking part. Hence it is he who, in view of the confusion he has caused among the lovers, cries out:

> Shall we their fond pageant see?
> Lord, what fools these mortals be!
> [III. ii. 114-15]

Thus Puck becomes the interpreter of the play's dramatic situations and intermediary between stage and audience as he places himself at a distance from events that have depended on and been influenced by him, and to which in the epilogue, significantly spoken by him, he is able to look back, as from a higher vantage point. Indeed, it is remarkable how many motives determining the play's action derive from Puck, how many invisible wires he holds in his hand. Yet his interventions in the development of the plot are as much the result of a casual mood or mischievous whim as they are the result of premeditated instructions from his master, Oberon. This is shown, for instance, in the case of Bottom's transformation in the first scene of Act III. It is a paradox of the dramatic action that Oberon's well-meaning intention is turned into its opposite through Puck's mistake [Lysander, instead of Demetrius, is anointed with the magic herb], so that the activity of the supernatural forces seems to be largely conditioned by error and coincidence. Still, it is precisely this fickleness and inconstancy of fate that Puck acknowledges in his laconic answer to Oberon when the latter reproves him for the mistake: "Then fate o'errules . . . " [III. ii. 92]. With these words Puck gives utterance to a basic motif in the drama.

It has often been stressed that in *A Midsummer Night's Dream* Shakespeare wanted to portray the irrational nature of love, the shifting and unstable "fancy" that continually falls prey to illusion, regards itself as being playful and short-lived, and is accompanied by a certain irresponsibility; whereas in *Romeo and Juliet,* written during the same period, love appears in quite a different shape, as a fateful and all-consuming force making claims to absolute authority and demanding that the whole of the self be yielded up to it.

But Shakespeare makes clear to us in several ways that the love between the Athenian couples is not rooted in actuality. Puck's magic juice, operating as a supernatural medium, is of course only one of the means by which Shakespeare places the relationships of the four Athenian lovers outside of reality. The love entanglements occur during a night full of dreams and enchantment, of which only an imprecise picture afterward remains in the memory of those concerned. Furthermore, it is undoubtedly the poet's deliberate intention (contrary to his practice in other plays of the same period) that the lovers should be so weakly characterized that it is impossible for us to retain them in our memory as real and differentiated human beings. We may likewise take it for granted that their symmetrical grouping and their appearance in pairs is the result of conscious stylization on Shakespeare's part. And if the style of their dialogues, together with the handling of the verse, often seems to be flat, trite, and frankly silly, this neither signifies Shakespeare's lack of skill nor justifies the contention that passages have been left in from an earlier version of the same play. Rather it gives evidence that Shakespeare intended the four lovers to be just what they are, puppets and not fully realized characters. Even the spectator to those scenes of confusion in the wood soon has no idea where he is or who precisely is in love with whom.

Above all, however, the dreamlike atmosphere of such scenes accentuates our feeling that the four lovers appear to be quite removed from any criteria applicable to reality. "The willing suspension of disbelief" that [Samuel Taylor] Coleridge designated as one of the poet's chief aims Shakespeare achieves by creating a world of illusion that manifests itself from the first scene onward. Dream world and reality merge imperceptibly, so that the persons concerned are not sure themselves in which sphere they move, nor whether what they have experienced has been imagination or truth. The idea that what has happened has been a dream, illusion, or "vision" is often expressed from various standpoints by the characters themselves. "Dream" is a key word in the drama, and the idea that everything is based on imagination is given frequent and subtle variation. The art with which Shakespeare shifts from the dream world to reality is unique. This is evident in the first scene of Act IV, where both the lovers and Bottom are depicted as awaking out of their dreams—a scene in which all four plots are brought together for the first time, whereby the mind of the spectator is made to see the boundaries separating them as being simultaneously nonexistent and yet firmly fixed. Finally, as if in a series of flashbacks, the incidents that

have occurred during the night of dreams are lit up once again from a distance by means of Theseus' famous speech describing "the lunatic, the lover, and the poet" as being "of imagination all compact" [V. i. 7–8]. These words refer once more to that faculty which lies behind not only dreams, but the poet's own creations as well and under whose spell we, as spectators, have been kept during the whole course of the play; for we too have been enchanted, responding eagerly to the call of the poetry and accepting the play as an organism that conforms to its own rules, a world where strange and real things mingle in a curious way.

The illusion of a dream sequence scurrying past is also enhanced by a sense of the forward surge of time. Not only is the passing of night into morning given expression through the shifting movement of light and dark within a series of superb images and subtle allusions: the impatience and longing with which the different characters look forward to the future are perceptible from the very start, thus making time flow in an anticipatory way. Again, the language of the play is rich in images and expressions indicating quick movement, lightness, and transitoriness, thereby contributing to the over-all atmospheric impression. How delicately and accurately the play's particular atmosphere, together with its theme and leitmotifs, is rendered from the very beginning, an examination of the first scene of the play alone would show, although we can permit ourselves only a few observations here.

The very first exchange between Theseus and Hippolyta conveys to us a twofold awareness of time, from the standpoint of which we contemplate a time span that culminates in the wedding day, the date of which is fixed immediately at the outset. This emerges when Hippolyta's "Four days will quickly steep themselves in night; / Four nights will quickly dream away the time" [I. i. 6–8] is contrasted with Theseus' ". . . but, O, methinks, how slow / This old moon wanes!" [I. i. 3–4]. During this initial dialogue Shakespeare skillfully puts us in tune with the moonlit scenes that follow by means of Theseus' comparison of the "old moon" with "a stepdame, or a dowager / Long withering out a young man's revenue" [I. i. 4–6]. In this scene alone "moon" and "night" each occur five times, "dream" three times. The lines just quoted also suggest the aristocratic world of the court, where a part of the action is to take place. A further element is introduced when, immediately following, we read these instructions to Philostrate:

> Stir up the Athenian youth to merriments,
> Awake the pert and nimble spirit of
>   mirth. . . .
>
>   [I. i. 13–14]

Yet the entry of Egeus immediately afterward, leading in his daughter Hermia and, "full of vexation," bringing accusations against Lysander because

Patricia Conolly as Titania, Nicholas Pennell as Oberon, and Diego Matamoros as Puck in a 1984 Stratford, Ontario production of A Midsummer Night's Dream.

the latter "hath bewitched the bosom of (his) child" [cf. I. i. 22-3], ushers in the radically contrasting note of discord, deception, and trickery, something that is never missing in any Shakespearean comedy and is always present as an undercurrent in *A Midsummer Night's Dream;* for the final state of harmony reached at the end of the play both in the world of the fairies and that of the court turns out to be a resolution of previously opposed forces, a reconciliation attained after former estrangement, and "the concord of this discord" [V. i. 60].

The main theme of the drama—namely, the transitoriness and inconstancy of love—is also anticipated in this first scene when Lysander describes love as

> . . . momentary as a sound,
> Swift as a shadow, short as any dream,
> Brief as the lightning in the collied night,
> That, in a spleen, unfolds both heaven and
> earth,
> And ere a man hath power to say "Behold!"
> The jaws of darkness do devour it up:

So quick bright things come to confusion.
[I. i. 143-49]

This passage is illuminating because it shows how Shakespeare not only bodies forth the themes and motifs of his drama in terms of action, but also gives them expression through imagery. In no other play of Shakespeare's middle period do we find so much poetry and verse melody, or indeed nature imagery, with its references to plants, animals, and other natural phenomena; nature itself even enters the drama as a participating agent alongside the characters. *A Midsummer Night's Dream* should therefore be apprehended as poetry and music, and not only be absorbed and endorsed by the eye and intellect as a connected series of actions. For the play's language, by means of its images, its subtle allusions and suggestions, its verbal repetitions and rhythmic patterns, has built up a complex and finely varied tissue of ideas, impressions, and associations that constantly act on our powers of imagination and stimulate them to participate. The great range and delicacy of impact that poetic drama possesses, as opposed to prose drama, can be perfectly witnessed in *A Midsummer Night's Dream.*

The degree to which the language, with its proliferation of allusions, ironies, and ambiguities, creates the over-all dramatic effect is made clear by those prose scenes with the artisans, where the lyrical and poetic are completely lacking. Apart from suggesting a wealth of gestures, the language used by Bottom and company is rich in implications and evokes delightful misunderstandings; it gives expression to the artisans' ludicrous ambition for higher things as well as to their rustic limitations. All this gives rise to that constant incongruity which is the prerequisite for great comedy—the incongruity existing between the basic natures of the characters and their pretensions. The scenes with Bottom, Quince, and company provide a comic and realistic contrast to the poetry of the fairies and the artificial and stylized love scenes of the Athenians. Thus the delicacy, polished bearing, and lightness inherent in all other sections of the play are counterbalanced by the uncouthness, the heavy solidity of everyday life, and a naïve roughness that the artisans bring into the magical fairy world of the moonlit scenes. Puck, the shrewd onlooker, at one stage justly calls them "hempen homespuns." But Shakespeare has made far more out of this antimasque than a merely amusing subplot filled with clownlike figures; during the course of the play one of them has come to be the most unforgettable character in the entire drama. For the lack of vitality and pronounced individuality noticeable in the other personages we are fully recompensed in Bottom, who has justly been described as the greatest comic creation in the dramatist's early work. Abundantly endowed with remarkable qualities, Bottom is continually putting himself in a comic light. There are no features of his character that at one point or another do not lead to some ridiculous situation, some unforgettable moment of contrast or unintentionally provoked comparison. Bottom's supreme satisfaction with himself and his sense of ease remain with him even in his transformed state, while his stage ambitions (he wants to play the part of the lion as well as that of Pyramus, Thisby and the tyrant) parody the profession of acting and yet at the same time form a characteristic trait that fits him remarkably well. That his ambitions are fulfilled even before the Pyramus and Thisby drama takes place, insofar as Bottom has to play the parts of both ass and lover, is significant, just as is the marked irony that Bottom alone, out of all the persons in the play, is permitted to come into contact with the fairies—though this encounter does not impress him in the least or signify for him any unusual experience. In Titania's presence he discards nothing at all of his own personality; the ass's head, which with other people would have resulted in monstrous caricature, in his case is something that illuminates for us his real nature.

If the story of the craftsmen forms a satirical coun-

terbalance to the plot of the lovers, then it is also true to say that the drama of Pyramus and Thisby initiates a twofold, even threefold kind of awareness. For what we get in this parody of the love tragedy is an exaggerated depiction of the four lovers' sentimentality, their highflown protestations of love, and their pseudo-solemnity—a depiction in the form of a flashback that they themselves are now able to contemplate as spectators, serenely calm and reconciled with one another. The lovers' own relationships have likewise been a play that the fairies have found highly amusing, and these entanglements parallel the quarrel between Oberon and Titania, the quarrel from which the confusion among the lovers originated.

"The play within the play," superbly worked out by Shakespeare, makes us particularly aware that the entire drama has indeed been a "play," summoned into life by the dramatist's magic wand and just as easily made to vanish. When Puck refers in the first line of his epilogue ("If we shadows have offended" [V. i. 423]) not merely to the fairies, previously termed "shadows," but also to all the actors who have taken part, we realize that Shakespeare is once more making it clear to us that we have been watching a "magic-lantern show," something where appearance, not reality, is the operative factor.

It is peculiarly ironic that Bottom, Quince, and company perform the tragedy of Pyramus and Thisby as an auspicious offering on behalf of the newly established love union, thereby, one might say, presenting the material of *Romeo and Juliet* in a comic and grotesque manner. Thus an exaggerated form of tragedy is employed so that the preceding scenes may be parodied as comedy. The play of Pyramus and Thisby parodies not only the torments of love, which the Athenian lovers can now look back on with serene calmness, but also the Senecan style of Elizabethan tragedy with its melodrama and ponderous conventions. Shakespeare parodies these conventions here by means of exaggeration or clumsy and grotesque usage—the too explicit prologue, for instance; the verbose self-explanation and commentaries; the stereotyped phrases for expressing grief; and the excessive use of such rhetorical devices as apostrophe, alliteration, hyperbole, and rhetorical question.

Even the elements of comedy and parody in the Pyramus and Thisby performance appear in a twofold light. Though they themselves are being mocked, the lovers smile at these awkward efforts on the part of the craftsmen, and Theseus even adds a highly suggestive commentary.

In the craftsmen's play, Shakespeare is also parodying the whole life of the theater. He calmly takes the shortcomings of all theatrical production and acting, drives them to absurd lengths, and holds them up for inspection. The lantern, which is supposed to represent the moon, makes us conscious of how equally inadequate Pyramus and Thisby are in their roles and suggests that such inadequacy may time and again have made its appearance on the Elizabethan stage. For those Elizabethan playgoers who viewed a play superficially, without using their own powers of imagination, much in Shakespearean drama must have remained completely unintelligible. It is at such narrow-minded theatergoers as these that Shakespeare is indirectly poking fun. And he enables us to see the limitations of his own stage, which had to portray a large world and create atmosphere without the elaborate scenery and technical equipment that we have today.

But the very inadequacy of the artisans' production gives emphasis to the true art of dramatic illusion and magic, as we have witnessed it in the preceding scenes, in which the evocative power of Shakespeare's language, assisted by our imagination, enables us to experience moonlight and nighttime in the woods. Theseus himself makes this point when, in answer to Hippolyta's remark, "This is the silliest stuff that ever I heard," [V. i. 210] he says: "The best in this kind are but shadows; and the worst are no worse, if imagination amend them." [V. i. 211–12]. (pp. xxiii-xxxvii)

> *Wolfgang Clemen, in an introduction to* A Midsummer Night's Dream *by William Shakespeare, edited by Wolfgang Clemen, New American Library, 1987, pp. xxiii-xxxvii.*

Jack A. Vaughn

[*Vaughn outlines the narrative composition of* A Midsummer Night's Dream *and presents a summary of the plot. Characterizing the comedy as an eminently poetic work, this critic discusses Shakespeare's language, with particular attention to eye imagery, such as the blindness of love, which "suggests and reinforces thematic concerns about love, the principal subject of the comedy." He then provides a brief historical overview of memorable productions of Shakespeare's play, focusing on Peter Brook's famous 1970 rendition. According to Vaughn, "through the visual austerity and actor-centered focus of his production, Brook was able to redirect the audience's attention to Shakespeare's text—to its lyricism, its imagery, its fantasy."*]

One could hardly imagine a more unlikely combination of comic plot materials than that of classical Greek mythology, English fairy lore, Italianate love intrigue, and Elizabethan amateur theatricals. Yet that is precisely the mélange that Shakespeare concocted in *A Midsummer Night's Dream*, the play that most critics agree is his first wholly satisfactory comedy.

The virtue of the piece lies partly in Shakespeare's successful blending of disparate plot elements into a unified whole, and partly in the poetic advances that he made here over his four previous comedies. In *A Midsummer Night's Dream* Shakespeare wove the threads of four distinct actions into a tapestry of magical enchantments and courtly festivity, creating a complexity in multiplotting far greater than that of any of his earlier comedies. And in its verse and imagery he achieved a successful union of poetry and drama—a considerable advancement over, for example, the mannered formalism and self-conscious badinage of *Love's Labor's Lost.* (p. 61)

The impending marriage of the Athenian King Theseus to the Amazon Hippolyta constitutes the first thread of plot, one that forms a framing action for the entire play. . . . The opening and closing scenes of *A Midsummer Night's Dream* are dominated by the royal couple. Theseus' first-act decree that Hermia must comply with her father's wishes and marry Demetrius, against her will, causes the lovers' plot of Acts II-IV to come about. It is in order to escape the parental and royal edicts that Hermia and Lysander, followed by Demetrius and Helena, flee to the enchanted wood where they fall under the influence of the "watery moon" and the fairies' spell.

It is generally accepted that Shakespeare wrote this comedy in celebration of some noble marriage, although critics cannot agree on exactly which one. Thus, Theseus and Hippolyta serve as surrogates for the noble couple before whom the work is being played. They stand largely outside the action; the events of the plot happen for them, rather than to them. Therefore, after the opening scene we do not see them again until Act IV. They reappear only after all the confusions, transformations, and love madness have been set aright, and they preside over the play-within-a-play of "Pyramus and Thisbe" in Act V. Because *A Midsummer Night's Dream*, like *Love's Labor's Lost*, was played before a courtly audience, the play-within-a-play is once again a royal-entertainment-within-a-royal-entertainment.

The setting of our play, then, is technically ancient Athens, but this is (as in so many of Shakespeare's "period" plays) of little consequence. Their names notwithstanding, the characters are, throughout, thoroughly English. This is especially true of the fairies, whose actions constitute a second major thread of the plot.

The fairies—principally King Oberon, Queen Titania, and Robin Goodfellow (called Puck)—derive from native English folklore. They control the action of the play once it shifts to the enchanted wood, and their activities serve as the adhesive that binds the four subplots together. This is not to say, however, that they lack direct involvement or are themselves immune from magic. Titania—charmed into loving an ignorant weaver with the head of an ass—is as much a victim of enchantment as Lysander and Demetrius. Still, the fairies, particularly Oberon and Puck, exercise almost complete control over the Athenian lovers.

It is precisely because we know that the fairies are in control that we are able to enjoy the confusions and distress of the four lovers: Lysander, Hermia, Demetrius, and Helena. If a supernatural, external force is causing the entanglements, cannot it also untie them? Puck himself assures us, when the love madness is at its most confusing state, that "Jack shall have Jill, / Nought shall go ill; / The man shall have his mare again, and all shall be well" [III. ii. 461-63].

Puck is the most purely entertaining of the fairy band. His proper name, from traditional English fairy lore, is Robin Goodfellow, "puck" being a generic term for a mischievous sprite. Robin Goodfellow was known as a tricky but essentially harmless household spirit. At his first entrance, another fairy asks him:

> Are you not he
> That frights the maidens of the villagery;
> Skim milk, and sometimes labour in the
> quern
> And bootless make the breathless house-
> wife churn;
> And sometime make the drink to bear no
> barm;
> Mislead night-wanderers, laughing at
> their harm?
>
> [II. i. 34-9]

And Puck replies:

> Thou speak'st aright;
> I am that merry wanderer of the night . . .
> And sometime lurk I in a gossip's bowl,
> In very likeness of a roasted crab,
> And when she drinks, against her lips I
> bob
> And on her wither'd dewlap pour the ale.
> The wisest aunt, telling the saddest tale,
> Sometime for three-foot stool mistaketh
> me;
> Then slip I from her bum, down topples
> she,
> And "tailor" cries, and falls into a cough.
>
> [II. i. 42-54]

Clearly, Robin Goodfellow evolved in fairy lore as a supernatural explanation for the many trivial mishaps and accidents so commonplace in domestic living.

Puck is instrumental in the movement of the plot. It is he who mistakenly administers the love potion intended for Demetrius to Lysander, thinking him the "disdainful youth" Oberon has described. This sets in motion the love chain of cross-wooings that make up the central action of the comedy. It is also Puck who, out of pure mischief, transforms Bottom into an ass.

In addition to his direct involvement in these plot complications, Puck serves as a *raisonneur,* or chorus figure. He observes the love madness of the Athenians as an outsider and comments on their folly, sometimes directly to the audience and sometimes to them through Oberon:

> Captain of our fairy band,
> Helena is here at hand;
> And the youth, mistook by me,
> Pleading for a lover's fee.
> Shall we their fond pageant see?
> Lord, what fools these mortals be!
>
> [III. ii. 110-15]

The fairy king Oberon and his consort Titania, unlike Puck, maintain a certain royal bearing and dignity, the exception being Titania's infatuation with the grotesque Bottom. They do not indulge in mischievous trickery, although their magic is potent. We first see them engaged in a jealous quarrel, exchanging accusations of infidelity. This lovers' altercation and their wrangling over possession of the "little changeling boy" [II. i. 120] precipitate not only the enchantment of the Athenian mortals but also, as Titania states, a "progeny of evils" [II. i. 115] in the natural world:

> Therefore the winds, piping to us in vain,
> As in revenge, have suck'd up from the sea
> Contagious fogs; which falling in the land
> Have every pelting river made so proud
> That they have overborne their conti-
> nents:
> The ox hath therefore stretch'd his yoke in
> vain,
> The ploughman lost his sweat, and the
> green corn
> Hath rotted ere his youth attain'd a beard;
> The fold stands empty in the drowned
> field,
> And crows are fatted with the murrion
> flock; . . .
> And thorough this distemperature we see
> The seasons alter: hoary-headed frosts
> Fall in the fresh lap of the crimson rose,
> And on old Hiems' thin and icy crown
> An odorous chaplet of sweet summer buds
> Is, as in mockery, set: the spring, the sum-
> mer,
> The childing autumn, angry winter,
> change
> Their wonted liveries, and the mazed
> world,
> By their increase, now knows not which is
> which.
>
> [II. i. 88-114]

It is in order to punish and torment Titania that Oberon drops the liquor of the "little western flower" [II. i. 166] on her eyes, effecting the enchantment that causes her to fall in love with the "translated" Bottom. This flower, the same whose juices Puck mistakenly administers to Lysander, is thematically significant. Oberon tells us that it came into being when Cupid once "loosed his love-shaft smartly from his bow" [II. i. 159] at a "fair vestal" but missed his target:

> Yet mark'd I where the bolt of Cupid fell:

It fell upon a little western flower,
Before milk-white, now purple with love's
    wound,
And maidens call it love-in-idleness.
                              [II. i. 165–68]

It is the juice of love-in-idleness, then, that afflicts Lysander, Demetrius, and Titania (and indirectly Hermia, Helena, and Bottom). "Idleness" to the Elizabethans was nearly synonymous with "madness," and it is love madness that dominates the center of this comedy. Sudden passion and overwhelming desire replace rational love, as when Titania dotes on Bottom or Lysander abruptly switches courtship from one lady to another.

The antidote to love-in-idleness is the juice of yet another flower, one that Oberon calls "Dian's bud" (Diana being, of course, the goddess of chastity). When this antidote is applied to the eyes of the enchanted, their love madness is dispelled. The night's "accidents" are remembered by the lovers as but "the fierce vexation of a dream" [IV. i. 69]. Titania, cured of the "hateful imperfection of her eyes" [IV. i. 63], is reconciled to Oberon and the two go with their fairy band to bless the nuptials at the Athenian palace.

The four lovers—and their chaotic night of love in idleness—constitute the third major thread of action in the comedy. As in *The Taming of the Shrew* and *The Two Gentlemen of Verona,* the source of these intrigues is Italianate romance . . . But in *A Midsummer Night's Dream,* Shakespeare gave the material the ultimate in complications, making Lysander's prophetic observation that "the course of true love never did run smooth" [I. i. 134] the understatement of all time.

Quartets of lovers were to become commonplace in Shakespeare's comedies (*Much Ado about Nothing, Twelfth Night,* and *As You Like It,* to name a few), but we never again find the elaborate variations of cross-wooing present here in our Athenian quartet. As the plot develops, we have five distinct states of affairs in the love intrigues:

1. At some point before the play opens, Demetrius was betrothed to Helena, and Lysander and Hermia loved each other.

2. As the play opens, Demetrius has shifted his affections and now loves Hermia, as does Lysander. Helena, still in love with Demetrius, is forsaken.

3. In the wood, Puck mistakenly administers the love potion to the sleeping Lysander who awakes, sees Helena, and falls in love with her. Now Lysander loves Helena and Demetrius loves Hermia—the opposite of the original pairing or norm.

4. Oberon administers the potion to Demetrius who, awaking, sees Helena and falls in love with her. Now both Demetrius and Lysander love Helena, and Hermia is forsaken—the reverse of situation 2.

5. Puck administers the antidote to Lysander, who awakes and once more loves Hermia. Demetrius remains in love with Helena, and the original pairings once again prevail, bringing the plot full circle.

It is somewhat atypical of Shakespeare that most of the plot complication is caused by an external force (the juice of love-in-idleness) and that the four lovers are simply ignorant victims, unaware of the cause of their distresses. But the force is a benevolent one, for although it makes the true lover (Lysander) love falsely it also causes the false lover (Demetrius) to return to true love. Upon finally waking and beholding Helena, Demetrius claims:

To her, my lord,
Was I betroth'd ere I saw Hermia:
But, like in sickness, did I loathe this food;
But, as in health, come to my natural
    taste,
Now I do wish it, love it, long for it,
And will for evermore be true to it.
                              [IV. i. 171–76]

Demetrius and Helena are reunited; Theseus consents (for no apparent reason) to the marriage of Lysander and Hermia; and three weddings are celebrated in the fifth act.

Obviously the three threads of action considered thus far reinforce one another in their "nuptials" themes. In addition, the nuptial celebration extends beyond these three marriages to encompass the reconciliation of Oberon and Titania, a kind of remarriage. It is fitting, then, that our fourth thread of action, that of the "rude mechanicals," as Puck calls them, should deal with a love story: "The Most Lamentable Comedy, and Most Cruel Death of Pyramus and Thisbe" [I. ii. 11–12], enacted by "bully Bottom" and his band.

Shakespeare was undoubtedly well acquainted with the behind-the-scenes activities of amateur theatricals, and his delight in spoofing them is obvious. In the performance by Bottom and the other "hempen homespuns" he gives us a wonderfully entertaining subplot that provides most of the low comedy in *A Midsummer Night's Dream.* So appealing are the mechanicals, in fact, that their plot was (and is, even today) frequently extracted and performed as a playlet in its own right.

An amateur theatrical capped the closing scene of *Love's Labor's Lost,* but with "Pyramus and Thisbe" we enjoy not only the performance [V, i] but also the selection and casting of the script [I, ii] and a rehearsal [III, i], including a hilarious discussion of stage props and settings.

Our amateur Thespians (Bottom the weaver, Quince the carpenter, Snug the joiner, Flute the bellows-mender, Snout the tinker, and Starveling the tailor) choose for their play a love tragedy, a singularly inappropriate choice for a wedding celebration. This "very tragical mirth" [V. i. 57] of the deaths of Pyramus and Thisbe parodies Shakespeare's own *Romeo and Juliet* (written probably a year earlier) and serves as a ludicrous counterpoint to the love entanglements of *A Midsummer Night's Dream*.

Bottom the weaver is one of Shakespeare's finest clowns and a favorite with audiences whenever the play is performed. His portrait had been lightly sketched before in Launce (*The Two Gentlemen of Verona*) and Costard (*Love's Labor's Lost*). He serves, vis à vis the fairy spells and lovers' fantasies, as a touchstone of prosaic reality. So lacking in creative imagination is this simple weaver that he transmutes the imaginative (the theater) into the hopelessly literal—the reverse of *A Midsummer Night's Dream's* world. Bottom is the antidote to the dream.

In preparing the play [III, i], Bottom cannot conceive of an audience's ability willingly to suspend its disbelief. He fears that "the ladies cannot abide" [III. i. 11–12] Pyramus's killing himself and that the appearance of the lion will be "a most dreadful thing" [III. i. 31], the terror of which must be allayed by a prologue:

> Nay, you must name his [the actor's] name, and half his face must be seen through the lion's neck: and he himself must speak through, saying thus, or to the same defect,—"Ladies,"—or "Fair ladies,—I would wish you,"—or "I would request you,"—or "I would entreat you,"—not to fear, not to tremble: my life for yours. . . . " And there indeed let him name his name, and tell them plainly he is Snug the joiner.
>
> [III. i. 36-46]

The play calls for a moon; Bottom wants to know if the moon will shine the night they play. When Quince assures him that it will, the problem is solved:

> Why, then may you leave a casement of the great chamber window, where we play, open, and the moon may shine in at the casement.
>
> [III. i. 56-8]

It is Bottom's immunity to imagination that makes his transformation into an ass and subsequent encounter with the Queen of the Fairies so amusing. He is the only mortal in the play who has converse with the fairy world, and it doesn't faze him in the least. When his fellows run away in terror at his "translated" form, he cannot conceive that *he* has changed; it must be a trick on *their* part:

> Why do they run away? This is a knavery of them to make me afeard. . . . I see their knavery: this is to make an ass of me; to fright me, if they could.
>
> [III. i. 112-13, 120-21]

He is singularly unimpressed with Titania's overtures of love toward him; he might as well be chatting with the village milkmaid. His introduction to her fairy attendants—Peaseblossom, Cobweb, Moth, and Mustardseed—occasions only some feeble jokes upon their names. They are of use to him only for scratching his hairy face and bringing him some hay. Presented with a unique opportunity to commune with the fairy world, he addresses himself to the supernatural as though it were the commonplace, just as he denigrates the fantasy world of the theater with practical considerations and reality.

It is ironic that Bottom is the only one of the enchanted mortals who remembers his transformation. Upon awaking in the morning [IV, i], the four lovers can barely recall how they came to be in the enchanted wood, but Bottom seems to have a distinct, if unsettling, impression of his "dream":

> I have had a most rare vision. I have had a dream, past the wit of man to say what dream it was: man is but an ass, if he go about to expound this dream. Methought I was—there is no man can tell what. Methought I was,—and methought I had,— but man is but a patched fool, if he will offer to say what methought I had.
>
> [IV. i. 204-10]

For Bottom, clearly, the strange is best not tampered with.

The language of *A Midsummer Night's Dream* is richly varied and laden with imagery. The dialogue of its royal personages—Theseus, Hippolyta, Oberon, and Titania—is blank verse, although Oberon speaks in rhyme when discussing magical subjects. Puck's spells are cast in a sing-song verse form, usually trochaic tetrameter. Nearly all of the Athenian lovers' lines are rhymed, occasionally quite artificially so. The effect of this, especially at the height of enchantment and cross-wooing, is to prevent us from taking matters too seriously. The mechanicals speak prose, but their playlet is cast in doggerel and sing-song rhymes that parody medieval romance.

A Midsummer Night's Dream represents Shakespeare's initial achievement, in comedy, in creating and sustaining patterns of poetic imagery that enhance the meaning and mood of the play. Although the subject of imagery here deserves extended treatment, a single example must suffice.

Beginning with the opening scene, an image cluster based upon eyes, looking, and seeing is established. Loving Lysander against her father's will, Hermia protests, "I would my father look'd but with my eyes" [I. i. 56], to which Theseus replies, "Rather your eyes must with his judgement look" [I. i. 57]. Later in the scene, Hermia despairs of her father's preference for Demetrius: "O hell! to choose love by another's eyes" [I. i. 140]. Helena describes Hermia's eyes as "lode-stars." And Hermia tells Lysander that they must "from Athens turn away our eyes" [I. i. 218] and "starve our sight /

From lovers' food till morrow deep midnight" [I. i. 222-23]. This eye imagery continues throughout the play in various forms. According to a count by Ralph Berry [in his *Shakespeare's Comedies*], the word "eye" (including compounds and plurals) occurs sixty-eight times in the play, "see" is used thirty-nine times, and "sight" appears ten times.

The eye imagery suggests and reinforces thematic concerns about love, the principal subject of the comedy. Put most simply, "Love is blind." But on a more complex level, the eyes are treated as the betrayers of judgment and of the rational. Conventionally, of course, love enters through the eyes, but in this comedy it is usually false love—love-in-idleness. Potions and antidotes are squeezed onto the eyes of the sleepers, causing them to see "with parted eye, / When every thing seems double" [IV. i. 189]. Even Titania cannot "see" how ugly Bottom is.

In the first four acts of this comedy, love is a disordered condition of the imagination—a sort of romantic astigmatism. It is so, of course, because the flight to the wood and its fairy world is a retreat from the rational and ordered world of the Athenian court, where parental and societal authority prevails. When morning comes and all the characters return to Athens, order is again restored and each lover returns to the correct beloved. Each lover now "sees" clearly. It is largely through the use of imagery like this that Shakespeare embodied in the language of *A Midsummer Night's Dream* its thematic concerns about love, natural order, rational judgment, and creative fantasy.

Possibly because of its intense appeal to the imagination, *A Midsummer Night's Dream* has been one of Shakespeare's more successful comedies on the stage, particularly in modern times. It was fashionable in the seventeenth and eighteenth centuries to play the work in adapted form. A 1661 version, for example, utilized only the mechanicals' plot, as a "droll" or light entertainment called "The Merry Conceited Humours of Bottom the Weaver." David Garrick turned *A Midsummer Night's Dream* into a full-scale opera in 1755, with some twenty songs and with lavish scenic spectacle.

Shakespeare's original text was more or less restored to the stage by Charles Mathews in his 1840 production, the one that introduced Felix Mendelssohn's famous overture to the play. Other notable nineteenth-century mountings of the comedy were those of Samuel Phelps (who played Bottom) at Sadler's Wells in 1853, of Augustin Daly in New York in 1887, and of F. R. Benson in 1889. All of these productions, typical of their time, emphasized lavish scenic spectacle, pageantry, and music in an attempt to render Shakespeare's extravagant fantasy through concrete, visual opulence of the most literal kind.

In our own century there have been two produc-tions worth noting here for their opposing approaches to the realm of poetic fantasy. Max Reinhardt staged the play a number of times, leading to his 1935 film version for Warner Brothers. Reinhardt, in both the stage and the film versions, took literalism as far as it could go, trusting nothing to the imagination. Dozens of gossamer fairies with glittering wings skipped about on golden moonbeams, through a lush and detailed forest to an Athenian palace rivaling the Parthenon. Unfortunately, much of Shakespeare's text was cut and what poetry remained seemed only to interfere with the visual effects. Reinhardt was as scrupulous in his approach to the magic of *A Midsummer Night's Dream* as Bottom was in rendering the true tragedy of Pyramus and Thisbe.

The other version earned world-wide critical acclaim as a breakthrough in Shakespearean stage production. It was staged by Peter Brook for the Royal Shakespeare Company at Stratford-upon-Avon in 1970 and subsequently toured America. Brook stripped away all preconceived notions about fairies and fantasy, throwing out production tradition accumulated over some three hundred years, and rendered his Athenian world in singularly Spartan terms. His setting was a pure white rectangular room with cushions for the actors to sit upon and ropes and trapezes for them to climb; his lighting was white, bright, and constant; his fairies wore uniforms suggesting jogging suits; and supernatural effects were replaced by full emphasis upon the actors' voices and bodily movements, which included calisthenics and gymnastics.

Through the visual austerity and actor-centered focus of his production, Brook was able to redirect the audience's attention to Shakespeare's text—to its lyricism, its imagery, its fantasy. Therein lay his success. If there is magic in *A Midsummer Night's Dream* (and decidedly there is), it is the magic not of let's-pretend sprites prancing about in gauze-and-glitter fairy suits, but of the English language, raised by the fertile imagination of its greatest poet to full suggestive power. (pp. 62-76)

Jack A. Vaughn, "The Comedies: 'A Midsummer Night's Dream'," in his Shakespeare's Comedies, *Frederick Ungar Publishing Co., 1980, pp. 61-76.*

GENDER AND SEX ROLES

Shirley Nelson Garner

[*Describing* A Midsummer Night's Dream *as similar to a fertility rite, Garner discusses the sexual, psychological, and social implications of Shakespeare's comedy. More than a simple celebration of erotic love, the play, Garner maintains, reflects certain attitudes character-*

Oberon, Puck, Titania, Bottom, and Fairies. Act IV, scene i. By Henry Fuseli.

*istic of male-dominated societies. For example, a woman's entire existence, particularly her sexual and emotional life, is controlled by a powerful male figure, as illustrated by **Egeus's** almost incestuous possessiveness toward his daughter **Hermia.** Further, the extent of a woman's sexual and emotional freedom, Garner argues, is determined by male desire. Thus conventional heterosexual love flourishes only if certain conditions, determined by the male protagonists, are satisfied. For example, a woman must sever all her emotional ties with other women to assuage her husband's fears of possible rejection. As Garner concludes, "the male characters think they can keep their women only if they divide and conquer them. Only then will Jack have Jill; only then will their world flourish."]*

More than any of Shakespeare's comedies, *A Midsummer Night's Dream* resembles a fertility rite, for the sterile world that Titania depicts at the beginning of Act II is transformed and the play concludes with high celebration, ritual blessing, and the promise of regeneration. Though this pattern is easily apparent and has often been observed, the social and sexual implications of the return of the green world have gone unnoticed. What has not been so clearly seen is that the renewal at the end of the play affirms patriarchal order and hierarchy, insisting that the power of women must be circumscribed, and that it recognizes the tenuousness of heterosexuality as well. The movement of the play toward ordering the fairy, human, and natural worlds is also a movement toward satisfying men's psychological needs, as Shakespeare perceived them, but its cost is the disruption of women's bonds with each other. Regeneration finally depends on the amity between Titania and Oberon. As she tells him, their quarrel over possession of an Indian boy has brought chaos, disease, and sterility to the natural world:

> And this same progeny of evils comes
> From our debate, from our dissension;
> We are their parents and original.
>
> [II. i. 115-17]

The story of the "lovely boy" is told from two points of view, Puck's and Titania's. Puck tells a companion fairy that Oberon is "passing fell and wrath" [II. i. 20] because Titania has taken as her attendant "a lovely boy, stolen from an Indian king" [II. i. 23]; he continues:

> She never had so sweet a changeling.
> And jealous Oberon would have the child
> Knight of his train, to trace the forests wild.
> But she perforce withholds the lovéd boy,
> Crowns him with flowers, and makes him all her joy.
> And now they never meet in grove or green,
> By fountain clear, or spangled starlight sheen,
> But they do square, that all the elves for fear
> Creep into acorn cups and hide them there.
>
> [II. i. 23–31]

Shortly afterward, when Oberon tells Titania that it is up to her to amend their quarrel and that he merely begs "a little changeling boy" [II. i. 120] to be his "henchman," she retorts, "Set your heart at rest. / The fairy land buys not the child of me" [II. i. 121-22]. Then she explains the child's origin, arguing her loyalty to the child's mother to be the reason for keeping him:

> His mother was a vot'ress of my order,
> And, in the spicéd Indian air, by night,
> Full often hath she gossiped by my side,
> And sat with me on Neptune's yellow sands,
> Marking th' embarkéd traders on the flood;
> When we have laughed to see the sails conceive
> And grow big-bellied with the wanton wind;
> Which she, with pretty and with swimming gait
> Following—her womb then rich with my young squire—
> Would imitate, and sail upon the land,
> To fetch me trifles, and return again,
> As from a voyage, rich with merchandise.
> But she, being mortal, of that boy did die;
> And for her sake do I rear up her boy,
> And for her sake I will not part with him.
>
> [II. i. 123-37]

Both accounts affirm that the child has become the object of Titania's love, but the shift in emphasis from one point of view to the other is significant. Puck describes the child as "stolen from an Indian king" [II. i. 22], whereas Titania emphasizes the child's link with his mother, her votaress. Puck's perspective, undoubtedly close to Oberon's, ignores or suppresses the connection between Titania and the Indian queen, which, in its exclusion of men and suggestion of love between women, threatens patriarchal and heterosexual values.

Titania's attachment to the boy is clearly erotic. She "crowns him with flowers, and makes him all her joy" [II. i. 27-8], according him the same attentions as those she bestows on Bottom when, under the spell of Oberon's love potion, she falls in love with the rustic-turned-ass. She has "forsworn" Oberon's "bed and company" [II. i. 62]. Whatever the child is to her as a "lovely boy" and a "sweet" changeling, he is ultimately her link with a mortal woman whom she loved. Oberon's passionate determination to have the child for himself suggests that he is both attracted to and jealous of him. He would have not only the boy but also the exclusive love of Titania. He needs to cut her off from the child because she is attracted to him not only as boy and child, but also as his mother's son. Oberon's need to humiliate Titania in attaining the boy suggests that her love for the child poses a severe threat to the fairy king.

Puck's statement that Oberon wants the child to be "knight of his train" [II. i. 25] and Oberon's that he wants him to be his "henchman" have led some critics to argue that the fairy king's desires to have the boy are more appropriate than the fairy queen's. Oberon's wish to have the boy is consistent with the practice of taking boys from the nursery to the father's realm so that they can acquire the character and skills appropriate to manhood. But Puck describes Oberon as "jealous," and his emphasis on the "lovely boy," the "sweet" changeling, and the "lovéd boy" [II. i. 23–7] suggests that Oberon, like Titania, is attracted to the child. There is no suggestion that Oberon wants to groom the child for manhood; he wants him rather "to trace the forests wild" [II. i. 25] with his fairy band. Those critics who attribute moral intentions to Oberon, arguing for his benevolent motives in taking the boy from Titania, overlook that Oberon has no intention of returning him to his father, with whom he, as a human child, might be most properly reared. When we last hear of the boy, Titania's fairy has carried him to Oberon's "bower" [IV. i. 61].

Oberon's winning the boy from Titania is at the center of the play, for his victory is the price of amity between them, which in turn restores the green world. At the beginning, Oberon and Titania would seem to have equal magical powers, but Oberon's power proves the greater. Since he cannot persuade Titania to turn over the boy to him, he humiliates her and torments her until she does so. He uses the love potion not simply to divert her attention from the child, so that he can have him, but to punish her as well. As he squeezes the love flower on Titania's eyes, he speaks a charm—or rather a curse—revealing his intention:

> What thou see'st when thou dost wake,
> Do it for thy truelove take;
> Love and languish for his sake.
> Be it ounce, or cat, or bear,
> Pard, or boar with bristled hair,
> In thy eye that shall appear
> When thou wak'st, it is thy dear.
> Wake when some vile thing is near.
>
> [II. ii. 27-34]

When Puck tells him that Titania is "with a monster in love" [III. ii. 6], he is obviously pleased: "This falls out better than I could devise" [III. ii. 35].

Though the scenes between Titania and Bottom are charming and hilarious, Titania is made ridiculous. Whereas her opening speech is remarkable for its lyric beauty, and her defense of keeping the Indian boy has quiet and dignified emotion power, now she is reduced to admiring Bottom's truisms and his monstrous shape: "Thou art as wise as thou art beautiful" [III. i. 147]. However enjoyable the scenes between her and Bottom, however thematically satisfying in their representation of the marriage of our animal and spiritual natures, Titania, free of the influence of Oberon's love potion, says of Bottom, "O, how mine eyes do loathe his visage now!" [IV. i. 79]. By his own account, Oberon taunts Titania into obedience; he tells Puck:

> See'st thou this sweet sight?
> Her dotage now I do begin to pity:
> For, meeting her of late behind the wood,
> Seeking sweet favors for this hateful fool,
> I did upbraid her, and fall out with her.
> For she his hairy temples then had rounded
> With coronet of fresh and fragrant flowers;
> And that same dew, which sometime on the buds
> Was wont to swell, like round and orient pearls,
> Stood now within the pretty flouriet's eyes,
> Like tears, that did their own disgrace bewail.
> When I had at my pleasure taunted her,
> And she in mild terms begged my patience,
> I then did ask of her her changeling child;
> Which straight she gave me, and her fairy sent
> To bear him to my bower in fairy land.
> And now I have the boy, I will undo
> This hateful imperfection of her eyes.
> [IV. i. 46-63]

Oberon gains the exclusive love of Titania and also possession of the boy to whom he is attracted. But his gain is Titania's loss: she is separated from the boy and, in that separation, further severed from the woman whom she had loved. Oberon can offer ritual blessing at the play's end because he has what he wanted from the beginning: Titania obedient and under his control and the beautiful Indian boy in his bower.

Like the fairy king, the two men in power in the human world, Theseus and Egeus, want to attain the exclusive love of a woman and, also, to accommodate their homoerotic desires. In order to do so, they, like Oberon, attempt to limit women's power, and their success or failure to do so affects their participation in the comic world.

The opening of *A Midsummer Night's Dream* puts Hippolyta's subjugation in bold relief as Theseus reminds his bride-to-be:

> Hippolyta, I wooed thee with my sword,
> And won thy love, doing thee injuries;
> But I will wed thee in another key,
> With pomp, with triumph, and with reveling.
> [I. i. 16-19]

Capturing Hippolyta when he defeated the Amazons, Theseus has abducted her from her Amazon sisters to bring her to Athens and marry her. Though most directors play Hippolyta as a willing bride, I once saw San Francisco's Actors' Workshop, following the cues of Ian Kott, bring her on stage clothed in skins and imprisoned in a cage. The text invites such a rendering, for almost immediately it sets her apart from Theseus by implying that she sides with Hermia and Lysander against Egeus and Theseus, when he sanctions Egeus's authority. After Theseus tells Hermia to prepare to marry Demetrius or "on Diana's altar to protest / For aye austerity and single life" [I. i. 89-90] and then beckons Hippolyta to follow him offstage, he undoubtedly notices her frowning, for he asks, "What cheer, my love?" [I. i. 122]. Shakespeare heightens her isolation by presenting her without any Amazon attendants.

Though Theseus is less severe than Egeus, he is, from the outset, unsympathetic toward women. The first words he speaks, voicing the play's first lines and first image, must be taken as a sign: the moon "lingers" his desires, he tells Hippolyta, "Like a stepdame, or a dowager, / Long withering out a young man's revenue" [I. i. 4-6]. He utterly supports Egeus as patriarch, telling Hermia:

> To you your father should be as a god,
> One that composed your beauties; yea, and one
> To whom you are but as a form in wax
> By him imprinted and within his power
> To leave the figure or disfigure it.
> [I. i. 47-51]

As a ruler, he will enforce the law, which gives Egeus control over Hermia's sexuality and embodies patriarchal order. Though he has heard that Demetrius has won Helena's heart but now scorns her, and has meant to speak to him about it, "My mind did lose it" [I. i. 114]. A lover-and-leaver of women himself, he undoubtedly identifies with Demetrius and forgets his duty toward Helena. He exits inviting Egeus and Demetrius to follow and talk confidentially with him, suggesting his spiritual kinship with them.

Whatever other associations Theseus had for Shakespeare's audience, he was notorious as the first seducer of Helen. As early as Act II, Oberon recalls Theseus's reputation as a deserter of women. When Titania accuses Oberon of infidelity, asking rhetorically why he was in Athens if not to see Hippolyta, "the bouncing Amazon, / Your buskined mistress and your warrior love" [II. i. 70-1], he accuses her of loving Theseus:

> Didst not thou lead him through the glimmering night
> From Perigenia, whom he ravishèd?
> And make him with fair Aegles break his faith,
> With Ariadne and Antiopa?
>
> [II. i. 77–80]

It is significant that the woman whom he at last will marry is not traditionally feminine. She has been a warrior, and in her new role as the fiancée of the Athenian Duke, we see her as a hunter. Nostalgically, she recalls her past experiences:

> I was with Hercules and Cadmus once,
> When in a wood of Crete they bayed the bear
> With hounds of Sparta. Never did I hear
> Such gallant chiding; for, besides the groves,
> The skies, the fountains, every region near
> Seemed all one mutual cry. I never heard
> So musical a discord, such sweet thunder.
>
> [IV. i. 112–18]

Her androgynous character appears to resolve for Theseus the apparent dissociation of his romantic life, the sign of which is his continual desertion of women who love him.

Having found an androgynous woman, Theseus captures her and brings her home to be his wife. By conquering and marrying this extraordinarily powerful woman, he fulfills his need for the exclusive love of a woman while gratifying his homoerotic desires. Unlike Oberon, however, he finds satisfaction for his desires merged in one person. If we imagine Hippolyta played by a male actor who, though cast as a woman, dresses and walks like a man ("buskined mistress," "bouncing Amazon"), Hippolyta and Theseus must have looked more like homosexual than heterosexual lovers. Hippolyta's androgynous appearance is further confirmed by the fact that in Renaissance fiction and drama men were occasionally disguised as Amazons, e.g., lovers, like Sidney's Zelmane, in the *Arcadia*, who wished to be near his lady. Hippolyta, like Viola and Rosalind in disguise [in *Twelfth Night* and *As You Like It*], fulfills a male fantasy, and more happily so since she is not in disguise. Because Theseus's romantic life is fortunately resolved once the young lovers have paired themselves off anew, with Demetrius loving Helena, he can sanction their preferences and ignore Egeus's persistent demand that Hermia marry Demetrius.

By insisting that Hermia marry Demetrius, Egeus hopes to keep his daughter rather than lose her and to have Demetrius near him as well. Shakespeare makes Egeus's motives suspect by creating him foolishly comic, treating him more harshly than he does his other controlling and possessive fathers—Lear, Capulet [in *Romeo and Juliet*], Bra-

bantio [in *Othello*], Shylock [in *The Merchant of Venice*], Prospero [in *The Tempest*]. Unable to make his daughter marry where he wishes, Egeus turns to the law to enforce his will. More outrageous than Brabantio, he turns Lysander's courtship of his daughter into a series of crimes: Lysander has "bewitched the bosom" of Hermia, "stol'n the impression of her fantasy," "filched" her heart [I. i. 27–36]. As Shakespeare depicts the two lovers who compete over Hermia, he is careful to draw them so that Egeus's choice is irrational and not in Hermia's best interests. Lysander states his case before Theseus:

> I am, my lord, as well derived as he (Demetrius),
> As well possessed; my love is more than his;
> My fortunes every way as fairly ranked
> (If not with vantage) as Demetrius';
> And, which is more than all these boasts can be,
> I am beloved of beauteous Hermia.
>
> [I. i. 99–104]

Lysander continues to accuse Demetrius of making love to Helena, who now "dotes in idolatry, / Upon this spotted and inconstant man" [I. i. 109–10]. His accusation is evidently founded, for Theseus confesses that he has "heard so much" [I. i. 111] and Demetrius does not deny it or defend himself. Later, Demetrius admits that he was betrothed to Helena before he saw Hermia [IV. i. 172-73]. Egeus chooses badly for his daughter unless he wishes to keep her for himself, as I think he does. By insisting that she marry a man whom she does not love and one who may be unfaithful to her besides, if his present conduct is a gauge, Egeus assures that she will always love her father; that she will never really leave him.

There are suggestions, as well, that Egeus has a particular affection for Demetrius. Shakespeare does not leave us to assume that Egeus's preference for Demetrius is simply proprietary, i.e., since Hermia is his, he may give her as he chooses; or that it is simply an affirmation of male bonding, like Capulet's demand that Juliet marry Paris, "And you be mine, I'll give you to my friend" [*Romeo and Juliet*, III. v. 191]. Lysander's sarcasm defines Egeus's feeling for Demetrius:

> You have her father's love, Demetrius;
> Let me have Hermia's: do you marry him.
>
> [I. i. 93-4]

And Egeus immediately affirms:

> True, he hath my love,
> And what is mine, my love shall render him.
>
> [I. i. 95-6]

Even after Demetrius has fallen in love with Helena, Egeus continues to pair himself with him. When the lovers are discovered asleep in the forest coupled "right" at last and Lysander begins to explain what Theseus calls their "gentle concord," Egeus urges:

> Enough, enough, my lord; you have enough.
> I beg the law, the law, upon his head.
> They would have stol'n away; they would, Demetrius,
> Thereby to have defeated you and me,
> You of your wife and me of my consent,
> Of my consent that she should be your wife.
>
> [IV. i. 154-59]

Egeus would draw Demetrius back to him, realigning the original *we* against *them.*

Egeus, then, has hoped to have the exclusive love of Hermia and to accommodate his homoerotic feelings by binding Demetrius to him. To give up Hermia and accept that Demetrius loves Helena would defeat him doubly. Consequently, he leaves the stage unreconciled. Had it been left to him to affirm the comic resolution, we would have none.

· · · · ·

Whereas the separation of Hippolyta and Titania from other women is implied or kept in the background, the breaking of women's bonds is central in the plot involving the four young lovers. Demetrius and Lysander are divided at the outset, but the play dramatizes the division of Hermia and Helena. Furthermore, their quarreling is more demeaning than the men's. And once Demetrius and Lysander are no longer in competition for the same woman, their enmity is gone. Hermia and Helena, on the contrary, seem permanently separated and apparently give over their power to the men they will marry. Once their friendship is undermined and their power diminished, they are presumably "ready" for marriage.

Hermia's fond recollection of her long-standing and intimate friendship with Helena calls attention to Helena's disloyalty, occasioned by the latter's desire to win Demetrius's thanks and to be near him. Telling her friend that she intends to run away with Lysander, Hermia recalls:

> And in the wood, where often you and I
> Upon faint primrose beds were wont to lie,
> Emptying our bosoms of their counsel sweet,
> There my Lysander and myself shall meet.
>
> [I. i. 214-17]

Just as Helena breaks her faith with Hermia to ingratiate herself with Demetrius, so later she will believe that Hermia has joined with men against her. Deeply hurt, Helena chastizes Hermia:

> Is all the counsel that we two have shared,
> The sister's vows, the hours that we have spent,
> When we have chid the hasty-footed time
> For parting us—O, is all forgot?

> All school days friendship, childhood innocence?
> We, Hermia, like two artificial gods,
> Have with our needles created both one flower,
> Both on one sampler, sitting on one cushion,
> Both warbling of one song, both in one key;
> As if our hands, our sides, voices, and minds,
> Had been incorporate. So we grew together,
> Like to a double cherry, seeming parted,
> But yet an union in partition,
> Two lovely berries molded on one stem;
> So, with two seeming bodies, but one heart;
> Two of the first, like coats in heraldry,
> Due but to one, and crownèd with one crest.
> And will you rent our ancient love asunder,
> To join with men in scorning your poor friend?
> It is not friendly, 'tis not maidenly.
> Our sex, as well as I, may chide you for it,
> Though I alone do feel the injury.
>
> [III. ii. 198-219]

In a scene that parallels in its central position Titania's wooing of Bottom, the rupture of their friendship becomes final. They accuse and insult each other, with Hermia calling Helena a "juggler," "canker blossom," "thief of love," "painted maypole"; and Helena naming her a "counterfeit" and a "puppet" [III. ii. 282-96]. Their quarrel becomes absurd as it turns on Hermia's obsession, taken up by both Lysander and Helena, that Lysander has come to prefer Helena because she is taller. Though no other women characters in Shakespeare's plays come close to fighting physically, Hermia threatens to scratch out Helena's eyes [III. ii. 297-98]. Her threat is serious enough to make Helena flee [III. ii. 340-43]. Lysander is made equally ridiculous in his abrupt change of heart; yet he and Demetrius·are spared the indignity of a demeaning quarrel and leave the stage to settle their disagreement in a "manly" fashion, with swords. Even though Puck makes a mockery of their combat through his teasing, they are not so thoroughly diminished as Hermia and Helena.

In the course of the play, both Hermia and Helena suffer at the hands of their lovers. Betrothed to Helena, Demetrius deserts her for Hermia. When she pursues him, he tells her that she makes him sick [II. i. 212] and threatens to rape her [II. i. 214–19]. By doggedly following him, she maintains a kind of desperate power over him . . . . Consequently, he cannot sustain the image of the romantic rake, whose women pine and die, commit suicide, or burn themselves on pyres when he leaves them. Disappointed in his love for Hermia, he cannot get loose from Helena. Yet her masochism undercuts her power:

I am your spaniel; and, Demetrius,
The more you beat me, I will fawn on you.
Use me but as your spaniel, spurn me,
    strike me,
Neglect me, lose me; only give me leave,
Unworthy as I am, to follow you.
What worser place can I beg in your love—
And yet a place of high respect with me—
Than to be usèd as you use your dog?
                                    [II. i. 203–10]

When Helena is in a position of positive power with both Lysander and Demetrius in love with her, she cannot take advantage of it because she assumes that she is the butt of a joke. And of course, in a sense, she is right: she is the victim of either Puck's prank or his mistake. Hermia must also bear Lysander's contempt. In the forest, he insists that he "hates" her [III. ii. 270, 281] and calls her outrageous names: "cat," "burr," "vile thing," "tawny Tartar," "loathèd med'cine," "hated potion," "dwarf," "minimus, of hind'ring knotgrass made," "bead," "acorn" [III. ii. 260–64, 328–30]. While both women protest their lovers' treatment of them, neither can play Beatrice to her Benedick [in *Much Ado about Nothing*]. Both more or less bear their lovers' abuses.

After the four lovers sleep and awaken coupled as they will marry, Hermia and Helena do not reconcile. Once they leave the forest, they lose their voices. Neither of them speaks again. Recognizing that it is difficult for an actor to be on stage without any lines, as Helena and Hermia are for almost all of Act V, Shakespeare was undoubtedly aware that he was creating a portentous silence. Since Helena and Hermia are evidently married between Acts IV and V, their silence suggests that in their new roles as wives they will be obedient, allowing their husbands dominance.

. . . . .

The end of *A Midsummer Night's Dream* is as fully joyous as the conclusion of any of Shakespeare's comedies. No longer angry with each other, Oberon and Titania bring blessing to the human world:

Hand in hand, with fairy grace,
Will we sing, and bless this place.
                            [V. i. 399–400]

Though Oberon calls up dark possibilities, he offers a charm against them. The prospect of love, peace, safety, prosperity is as promising as it ever will be. The cost of this harmony, however, is the restoration of patriarchal hierarchy, so threatened at the beginning of the play. This return to the old order depends on the breaking of women's bonds with each other and the submission of women, which the play relentlessly exacts. Puck's verse provides the paradigm:

Jack shall have Jill;
Nought shall go ill;
The man shall have his mare again,
and all shall be well.
                            [III. ii. 461–63]

If we turn to some of Shakespeare's comedies in which women's bonds with each other are unbroken and their power is left intact or even dominates, the tone of the ending is less harmonious or even discordant. In *The Merchant of Venice,* for example, where Portia is in control and she and Nerissa triumph over Gratiano and Bassanio, there is no ritual celebration. Portia directs the scene and carefully circumscribes her marriage with Bassanio to close out Antonio. When she and Nerissa reveal their identities as the doctor and the clerk, they make clear their extraordinary power to outwit and deceive, calling up women's ultimate destructive power in marriage and love—to cuckold. The final moments of the play move toward reconciliation, but not celebration. The last line, a bawdy joke, is spoken by Gratiano, the most hate-filled character in the play, and reminds us of men's fear of women and their need to control them: "While I live I'll fear no other thing / So sore, as keeping safe Nerissa's ring" [V. i. 306-07].

In *Love's Labor's Lost,* where the women remain together and in control, there is no comic ending. Echoing Puck, Berowne makes the point as he speaks to the King of Navarre:

Our wooing doth not end like an old play;
Jack hath not Jill. These ladies' courtesy
Might well have made our sport a comedy.
                            [V. ii. 874-76]

When the King replies, "Come, sir, it wants a twelvemonth and a day, / And then 'twill end," Berowne answers, "That's too long for a play" [V. ii. 872-76]. The refrains of the closing songs call forth images of cuckolding and of "greasy Joan" stirring the pot.

The pattern of these comic endings suggests that heterosexual bonding is tenuous at best. In order to be secure, to enjoy, to love—to participate in the celebration that comedy invites—men need to maintain their ties with other men and to sever women's bonds with each other. The implication is that men fear that if women join with each other, they will not need men, will possibly exclude them or prefer the friendship and love of women. This is precisely the threat of the beautiful scene that Titania describes between herself and her votaress. This fear may be based partially on reality, but it is also partially caused by projection: since men have traditionally had stronger bonds with other men than with women and have excluded women from participation in things about which they cared most, they may assume that women, granted the opportunity, will do the same. Given this possibility or likelihood, Shakespeare's male characters act out of a fear of women's bonding with each other and a feeling of sexual powerlessness. The male characters think they can keep their women only if they divide and conquer them. Only then will Jack have Jill; only then will their world flourish. (pp. 47-61)

Shirley Nelson Garner, " 'A Midsummer Night's Dream': 'Jack Shall Have Jill; / Nought Shall Go Ill',' in Women's Studies: An Interdisciplinary Journal, *Vol. 9, No. 1, 1981, pp. 47-63.*

Jan Kott

[*In Kott's view,* A Midsummer Night's Dream *is the most erotic of Shakespeare's plays. Rejecting the traditional interpretation of the play as a romantic love comedy, Kott focuses on the undercurrents of sexual violence and bestiality which in many ways determine the protagonists' actions. Kott identifies the female characters as the principal victims of sadistic sexual behavior, noting their masochistic tolerance of their lovers' cruelty. The confused lovers in* A Midsummer Night's Dream, *with their brusque shifts from one object of affection to another, resemble exchangeable puppets. According to the critic, the protagonists are not depicted as individuals in Shakespeare's play; rather, they are merely objects defined by their desires. What seemed to be a night of love, Kott concludes, was really a nightmare for the protagonists. "But that night," he adds, "liberated them from themselves. They were their real selves in their dreams."*]

The *Dream* is the most erotic of Shakespeare's plays. In no other tragedy, or comedy, of his, except *Troilus and Cressida,* is the eroticism expressed so brutally. Theatrical tradition is particularly intolerable in the case of the *Dream,* as much in its classicist version, with tunic-clad lovers and marble stairs in the background, as in its other, operatic variation, with flowing transparent muslin and ropedancers. For a long time theatres have been content to present the *Dream* as a Brothers Grimm fable, completely obliterating the pungency of the dialogue and the brutality of the situations.

LYSANDER

Hang off, thou cat, thou burr! Vile thing, let loose,
Or I will shake thee from me like a serpent!

HERMIA

Why are you grown so rude? What change is this,
Sweet love?

LYSANDER

Thy love? Out, tawny Tartar, out!
Out, loathed med'cine! O hated potion, hence!
[III. ii. 260-64]

Commentators have long since noticed that the lovers in this love quartet are scarcely distinguishable from one another. The girls differ only in height and in the colour of their hair. Perhaps only Hermia has one or two individual traits, which let one trace in her an earlier version of Rosaline in *Love's Labour's Lost,* and the later Rosalind in *As You Like It.* The young men differ only in names. All four lack the distinctness and uniqueness of so many other, even earlier Shakespearean characters.

The lovers are exchangeable. Perhaps that was his purpose? The entire action of this hot night . . . is based on the complete exchangeability of love partners. I always have the impression that Shakespeare leaves nothing to chance. Puck wanders round the garden at night and encounters couples who exchange partners with each other. It is Puck who makes the observation:

This is the woman; but not this the man.
[III. ii. 42]

Helena loves Demetrius, Demetrius loves Hermia, Hermia loves Lysander. Helena runs after Demetrius, Demetrius runs after Hermia. Later Lysander runs after Helena. This mechanical reversal of the objects of desire, and the interchangeability of lovers is not just the basis of the plot. The reduction of characters to love partners seems to me to be the most peculiar characteristic of this cruel dream; and perhaps its most modern quality. The partner is now nameless and faceless. He or she just happens to be the nearest. As in some plays by [Jean] Genet, there are no unambiguous characters, there are only situations. Everything has become ambivalent.

HERMIA

. . . Wherefore? O me! what news, my love?
Am not I Hermia? Are not you Lysander?
I am as fair now as I was erewhile.
[III. ii. 272-74]

Hermia is wrong. For in truth there is no Hermia, just as there is no Lysander. Or rather there are two different Hermias and two different Lysanders. The Hermia who sleeps with Lysander and the Hermia with whom Lysander does not want to sleep. The Lysander who sleeps with Hermia and the Lysander who is running away from Hermia. (pp. 218-20)

If *Love's Labour's Lost,* the transparent comedy about young men who determined to do without women, is rightly considered to have been a play with a secret meaning to the initiated, how much more must this be true of the *Dream.* The stage and auditorium [of its first performance] were full of people who knew one another. Every allusion was deciphered at once. Fair ladies laughed behind their fans, men elbowed each other, homosexuals giggled softly.

Give me that boy, and I will go with thee.
[II. i. 143]

Shakespeare does not show the boy whom Titania to spite Oberon has stolen from the Indian king. But he mentions the boy several times and stresses the point. For the plot the boy is quite unnecessary. One could easily invent a hundred other reasons for the conflict between the royal couple. Apparently the introduction of the boy was essential to Shakespeare for other, non-dramatic purposes. It is not only the Eastern page boy who is disturbing. The behaviour of all the characters, not only the commoners but also the royal and princely personages, is promiscuous:

> . . . the bouncing Amazon,
> Your buskin'd mistress and your warrior love, . . .
>
> [II. i. 70-1]

The Greek queen of the Amazons has only recently been the mistress of the king of the fairies, while Theseus has just ended his liaison with Titania. These facts have no bearing on the plot, nothing results from them. They even blur a little the virtuous and somewhat pathetic image of the betrothed couple drawn in Acts I and V. But these details undoubtedly represent allusions to contemporary persons and events.

I do not think it is possible to decipher all the allusions in the *Dream*. Nor is it essential. I do not suppose it matters a great deal whether we discover for whose marriage Shakespeare hastily completed and adapted his *Midsummer Night's Dream*. It is only necessary for the actor, designer, and director to be aware of the fact that the *Dream* was a contemporary play about love. Both "contemporary" and "love" are significant words here. The *Dream* is also a most truthful, brutal, and violent play. (pp. 220-22)

The metaphors of love, eroticism, and sex undergo some essential changes in *A Midsummer Night's Dream*. They are completely traditional to start with: sword and wound; rose and rain; Cupid's bow and golden arrow. The clash of two kinds of imagery occurs in Helena's soliloquy which forms a coda to Act I, scene 1. The soliloquy is about her intellectual capacities and for a while singles her out from the action of the play. It is really the author's monologue, a kind of Brechtian "song" in which, for the first time, the philosophical theme of the *Dream* is stated; the subject being Eros and Tanatos.

> Things base and vile, holding no quantity,
> Love can transpose to form and dignity.
> Love looks not with the eyes, but with the mind;
> And therefore is wing'd Cupid painted blind.
>
> [I. i. 232-35]
>
> (p. 223)

Starting with Helena's soliloquy Shakespeare introduces more and more obtrusively animal erotic symbolism. He does it consistently, stubbornly, al-

most obsessively. The changes in imagery are in this case only an outward expression of a violent departure from the Petrarchian idealization of love.

It is this passing through animality that seems to us the midsummer night's dream, or at least it is this aspect of the *Dream* that is the most modern and revealing. This is the main theme joining together all three separate plots running parallel in the play. Titania and Bottom will pass through animal eroticism in a quite literal, even visual sense. But even the quartet of lovers enter the dark sphere of animal love-making:

HELENA

> . . . I am your spaniel; and, Demetrius,
> The more you beat me, I will fawn on you.
> Use me but as your spaniel—spurn me, strike me, . . .
>
> [II. i. 203-05]

And again:

> What worser place can I beg in your love . . .
> Than to be used as you use your dog?
>
> [II. i. 208-10]

Pointers, kept on short leashes, eager to chase or fawning upon their masters, appear frequently in Flemish tapestries representing hunting scenes. They were a favourite adornment on the walls of royal and princely palaces. But here a girl calls herself a dog fawning on her master. The metaphors are brutal, almost masochistic.

It is worth having a closer look at the "bestiary" evoked by Shakespeare in the *Dream*. As a result of the romantic tradition, unfortunately preserved in the theatre through Mendelssohn's music, the forest in the *Dream* still seems to be another version of Arcadia. But in the actual fact, it is rather a forest inhabited by devils and lamias, in which witches and sorceresses can easily find everything required for their practices.

> You spotted snakes with double tongue,
> Thorny hedgehogs, be not seen;
> Newts and blindworms, do no wrong,
> Come not near our Fairy Queen.
>
> [II. ii. 9-12]

Titania lies down to sleep on a meadow among wild thyme, ox-lips, musk-roses, violets, and eglantine, but the lullaby sung by the fairies in her train seems somewhat frightening. After the creatures just quoted they go on to mention long-legged poisonous spiders, black beetles, worms, and snails. The lullaby does not forecast pleasant dreams.

The bestiary of the *Dream* is not a haphazard one. Dried skin of a viper, pulverized spiders, bats' gristles appear in every medieval or Renaissance prescription book as drugs to cure impotence and women's afflictions of one kind or another. All these are slimy, hairy, sticky creatures, unpleasant to touch and often arousing violent aversion. It is

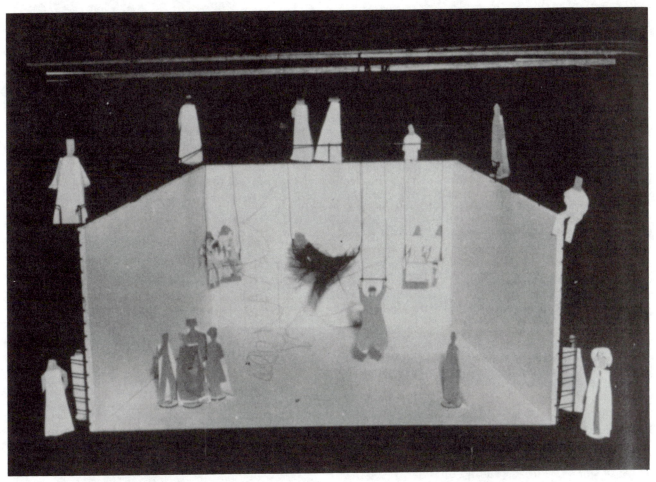

Sally Jacob's set design for Peter Brook's 1970 staging of A Midsummer Night's Dream.

the sort of aversion that is described by psychoanalytic textbooks as a sexual neurosis. Snakes, snails, bats, and spiders also form a favourite bestiary of Freud's theory of dreams. Oberon orders Puck to make the lovers sleep that kind of sleep when he says:

> . . . lead them thus
> Till o'er their brows death-counterfeiting
>   sleep
> With leaden legs and batty wings doth
>   creep.
> [III. ii. 363-65]

Titania's fairies are called: Peaseblossom, Cobweb, Moth, Mustardseed. In the theatre Titania's retinue is almost invariably represented as winged goblins, jumping and soaring in the air, or as a little ballet of German dwarfs. This sort of visual interpretation is so strongly suggestive that even commentators on the text find it difficult to free themselves from it. However, one has only to think on the very selection of these names to realize that they belong to the same love pharmacy of the witches.

I imagine Titania's court as consisting of old men and women, toothless and shaking, their mouths wet with saliva, who sniggering procure a monster for their mistress.

> The next thing then she, waking, looks
>   upon
> (Be it on lion, bear, or wolf, or bull,
> On meddling monkey or on busy ape)
> She shall pursue it with the soul of love.
> [II. i. 179-82]

Oberon openly announces that as a punishment Titania will sleep with a beast. Again the selection of these animals is most characteristic, particularly in the next series of Oberon's threats:

> Be it ounce or cat or bear,
> Pard, or boar with bristled hair . . .
> [II. ii. 30-1]

All these animals represent abundant sexual potency, and some of them play an important part in sexual demonology. Bottom is eventually transformed into an ass. But in this nightmarish summer night, the ass does not symbolize stupidity. From antiquity up to the Renaissance the ass was credited with the strongest sexual potency and among all quadrupeds was supposed to have the longest and hardest phallus. (pp. 224-27)

The scenes between Titania and Bottom transformed into an ass are often played for laughs in the theatre. But I think that if one can see humour in this scene, it is the English kind of humour, *"humeur noire"* ["black comedy"], cruel and scatological, as it often is in [the works of Jonathan] Swift.

The slender, tender, and lyrical Titania longs for animal love. Puck and Oberon call the transformed Bottom a monster. The frail and sweet Titania drags the monster to bed, almost by force. This is the lover she wanted and dreamed of; only she never wanted to admit it, even to herself. The sleep frees her from inhibitions. The monstrous ass is being raped by the poetic Titania, while she still keeps on chattering about flowers:

> TITANIA
>
> The moon, methinks, looks with a wat'ry eye;
> And when she weeps, weeps every little flower,
> Lamenting some enforced chastity.
> Tie up my love's tongue, bring him silently.
>
> [III. i. 198-201]

Of all the characters in the play Titania enters to the fullest extent the dark sphere of sex where there is no more beauty and ugliness; there is only infatuation and liberation. In the coda of the first scene of the *Dream* Helena had already forecast:

> Things base and vile, holding no quantity,
> Love can transpose to form and dignity.
>
> [I. i. 232-33]

The love scenes between Titania and the ass must seem at the same time real and unreal, fascinating and repulsive. They are to rouse rapture and disgust, terror and abhorrence. They should seem at once strange and fearful.

> Come, sit thee down upon this flow'ry bed,
> While I thy amiable cheeks do coy,
> And stick musk-roses in thy sleek smooth head,
> And kiss thy fair large ears, my gentle joy.
>
> [IV. i. 1-4]

Chagall has depicted Titania caressing the ass. In his picture the ass is sad, white, and affectionate. To my mind, Shakespeare's Titania, caressing the monster with the head of an ass, ought to be closer to the fearful visions of Bosch and to the grotesque of the surrealists. (pp. 228-29)

The night is drawing to a close and the dawn is breaking. The lovers have already passed through the dark sphere of animal love. Puck will sing an ironic song at the end of Act III. It is at the same time a coda and a "song" to summarize the night's experiences.

> Jack shall have Jill;
> Naught shall go ill;
> The man shall have his mare again, and all shall be well.
>
> [III. ii. 461-63]

Titania wakes up and sees a boor with an ass's head by her side. She slept with him that night. But now it is daylight. She does not remember ever having desired him. She remembers nothing. She does not want to remember anything.

> TITANIA
>
> My Oberon, what visions have I seen!
> Methought I was enamour'd of an ass.
>
> OBERON
>
> There lies your love.
>
> TITANIA
>
> How came these things to pass?
> O, how mine eyes do loathe his visage now!
>
> [IV. i. 76-9]

All are ashamed in the morning: Demetrius and Hermia, Lysander and Helena. Even Bottom. Even he does not want to admit his dream:

> Methought I was—there is no man can tell what.
> Methought I was, and methought I had—But
> man is but a patch'd fool if he will offer to say
> what methought I had.
>
> [IV. i. 207-11]

In the violent contrast between the erotic madness liberated by the night and the censorship of day which orders everything to be forgotten, Shakespeare seems most ahead of his time. The notion that "life's a dream" has, in this context, nothing of baroque mysticism. Night is the key to day!

> . . . We are such stuff
> As dreams are made on; . . .
> [*The Tempest*, IV. i. 156-57]

Not only is Ariel an abstract Puck with a sad and thoughtful face; the philosophical theme of the *Dream* will be repeated in *The Tempest*, doubtless a more mature play. But the answers given by Shakespeare in *A Midsummer Night's Dream* seem more unambiguous, perhaps one can even say, more materialistic, less bitter.

> The lunatic, the lover, and the poet
> Are of imagination all compact.
>
> [V. i. 7-8]

The madness lasted throughout the June night. The lovers are ashamed of that night and do not want to talk about it, just as one does not want to talk of bad dreams. But that night liberated them from themselves. They were their real selves in their dreams. (pp. 233-35)

Jan Kott, "Titania and the Ass's

Head," in his Shakespeare, Our Con-temporary, *translated by Boleslaw Ta-borski, 1964. Reprint by W. W. Norton & Company, 1974, pp. 213-36.*

BETWEEN FANTASY AND REALITY

George A. Bonnard

[*In his discussion of* A Midsummer Night's Dream, *Bonnard's principal thesis is that the worlds, fantastic and mundane, represented in the play, exist apart from each other, never meeting at any given point. The inhabitants of the fairy world, the critic explains, are indeed ethereal in the sense that they lack true feel-ings and intelligence. But the dream world, Bonnard argues, although beyond the mortals' comprehension, nevertheless strongly influ-ences the entire realm of ordinary life. Al-though separated by a veritable social chasm, the Athenian aristocrats and the common players are all vulnerable to* **Oberon***'s power by the very nature of their humanity. Yet this fairy kingdom is essentially a dream which appears whenever reason goes to sleep. Such illusions and dreams, Bonnard remarks, can be dangerous if they block our perception of re-ality, but there they nevertheless perform an important function in life, as the playwright el-oquently demonstrates.*]

Shakespeare, as we all know, loved to bring togeth-er in the same play a variety of diverse and even in-congruous elements. Of none of his plays is this truer than of *Midsummer-Night's Dream*. It would be difficult to imagine a more fantastic combina-tion of heterogeneous elements drawn from all kinds of sources. Chaucer gave him Theseus and Hippolyta and suggested the festivities that marked their wedding, as well as the idea of con-necting with the story of the Duke of Athens and his fair captive another story of young men who are rivals in love. Ovid provided him with Pyramus and Thisbe. Out of a blend of classical reminis-cences, notions derived from folk-lore, a literary and dramatic tradition he evolved his own fairy-world. To those borrowed elements he freely added others out of his personal experience. But whatev-er he chose to use he altered to suit his purpose. His Theseus is wholly different from Chaucer's. The love story of his young Athenians is a parody of the love story of Palamon and Arcite. Quince's "Pyramus and Thisbe" is a ludicrous caricature of Ovid's touching narrative. Oberon and Titania, elves and fairies, Puck himself are essentially dif-ferent from the King and Queen and inhabitants of any traditional fairy land. And neither had Bottom and his friends exact prototypes in actual life nor was there ever such court performance of a play as theirs. The poet's fancy holds undisputed sway

over all his material. Whatever is, in the world of facts or fiction, is his to do what he likes with. But the originality of *Midsummer-Night's Dream* is not merely due to the manner in which Shakespeare used what he freely borrowed; it also lies in the combination itself of all those elements into a com-edy. For there can be no doubt that he alone was responsible for bringing together the wedding of the Duke of Athens and the Queen of the Amazons, the story of young men in love with the same girl, the staging and acting of a tragedy by humble me-chanics, and a fairy world. And he can hardly have done so merely for the sake of making sure that every one in his audience would be sure to get something to his taste, or simply because it amused him to concoct a successful hotch-potch. He must have had some definite purpose. To find out what that purpose may have been may not add to our enjoyment of the play. It may help us to a ful-ler understanding of it. I propose to try and bring it to light by briefly discussing first each of four main elements and then the structure of the come-dy.

Theseus, the Duke of Athens, and his captive Hip-polyta whom he marries are no longer young peo-ple. As Oberon reminds Titania, Theseus has had a long and varied experience as a lover before con-quering the Queen of the Amazons. And the long war Hippolyta has sustained against Theseus com-pels us to imagine her past her youth. There is something matter of fact about their union. There is no conventional love-making between them, they never even speak of their love. They remind us of Petruchio and Katharina in the latter part of *The Taming of the Shrew*. Not only do they stand for good honest human love shorn of any romantic nonsense, but what does Theseus tell his bride?

> Hippolyta, I wooed thee with my sword,
> And won thy love doing thee injuries.
> [I. i. 16-17]

Could not Petruchio have addressed his wife in the same words? But one thing is certain: their deep happiness, the strong quiet joy they find in each other. Every word of Theseus bespeaks his satis-faction at having found a true mate at last, one that he feels sure will be a good wife to him, a helpful companion through life, one also that will know how to keep her place, as her silence proves when he discusses Hermia's marriage with Egeus and the young lovers. Throughout that scene the Duke acts the sovereign judge of course and Hippolyta knows she has no business to interfere, which is not only tactful but highly sensible of her. And how full of common sense they are when they come upon the lovers asleep in the wood, when they watch the play performed in their honour! In fact, whenever they are present, the air we breathe is light, invigorating, and healthy; the atmosphere is clear, and in it all things appear in their true out-lines and colours, in their due proportions and just relations; a wholly sane view of life seems to prevail. In their eyes, the fairy world does not exist. The King and Queen of the fairies may have come to Athens to bless their wedding: they are totally unaware of it. When they come to the wood with their hounds and huntsmen, their arrival is enough to restore sober reality to that scene of so many delusions, to chase all supernatural beings away. Neither Oberon, nor Titania, nor the fairies, nor Puck can possibly meet them; they all vanish "into thin air"; and at the clear, shrill sound of the hunting-horns the lovers wake up, all their dreams at once dispelled. With Theseus and Hippolyta reality reasserts itself, and triumphs over a world from which reason had fled. But large-minded as he is, full of gentle forbearance for the limitations and absurdities of other people, the Duke is no enemy to imagination. He has no desire to suppress it or curb its activity, for he knows its value. He merely wishes it not to usurp the place of reality. For him there must be no confusion between its creations and the actualities among which we live. His outlook is as broad as can be, and eminently reasonable. Hippolyta's is just as sensible, but narrower. Together they stand for experience, intelligent use of it, good sense and reason.

In full contrast to them, Shakespeare has placed his fairies, with their kingdom in that vague, dream-like East from which legends and myths and impossible stories seem to be for ever coming, with their motion that takes no account of space and time, their love of the moon and her beams, their delight in the dusk and the twilight, that is in the season for dreams, whether one is awake or asleep. For the fairies are essentially the bringers of dreams to mortals, as Mercutio tells Romeo. And . . . Shakespeare has given his fairies a character in harmony with their function. Just as in our dreams we lose all sense of responsibility, all moral impulse, so Oberon, Titania and all their subjects have no morality, no delicate feelings. Puck feels no compunction at the effects of his mischievousness, no sympathy for the affliction of the lovers:

> Shall we their fond pageant see?
> Lord, what fools these mortals be! . . .
> Then will two at once woo one;
> That must needs be sport alone.
> 　　　　　　　　　　　　[III. ii. 14-19]

And again when Lysander and Demetrius, sword in hand, step aside to fight their quarrel out, and the comedy suddenly takes on a sinister aspect, Puck not only proclaims himself blameless but adds

> And so far am I glad it so did sort,
> As this their jangling I esteem a sport.
> 　　　　　　　　　　　　[III. ii. 352-53]

Or take Titania: on awaking from her delusion, she feels no regret, no shame; and there is no scene of reconciliation with her husband: her resentment makes her forsake him, and they make it up in a dance; there is no trace of a real feeling in her. And just as our fairies know no moral impulse, so they never think. They are exquisite, but brainless creatures. The means they use to exert their influence on men are strictly material: changing the lovers' eyes, turning Bottom into an ass-headed monster, counterfeiting voices. Where they reign sense impressions, uncontrolled by reason or common sense, develop unchecked and fancy is allowed free play. No wonder that their life should be all given up to the pleasures of the senses. And because their senses must be for ever delighted, their desire is for all that is most choice, finest and pleasantest; singing and dancing best expresses their unchanging mood of thoughtless happiness. Were it not for that sense of beauty, they would form but an ugly little world, what with their heartlessness, their moral insensitiveness, their thorough materialism, their lack of brains. But their instinctive love of whatever pleases their delicate senses, their natural association with flowers and butterflies, nightingales and glow-worms, their hostility towards all repulsive creatures, spiders and bats, snakes and black-beetles, redeem them in our eyes and lend them a power of enchantment from which there is no escape. Still the atmosphere in which they live and move is, to men in their senses, disquieting, even oppressive. All the laws, moral and material, that govern the world of reality, have no existence in the dream-world of the fairies. In it therefore we no longer know where we are, we have lost our bearings, our sense of being in harmony with our eyes and lend them a power of enchantment from which there is no seem to hover on the brink of lunacy, we feel that at any moment some irresistible delusion, some overpowering image may seize hold on us. Helpless in the grip of lawless fancy, we feel driven here and there . . . until Theseus and Hippolyta, models of human dignity, arrive unexpectedly and, by their mere presence, deliver us of the "nothings" that were tormenting us, and we can exclaim with Demetrius

> These things seem small and undistinguishable
> Like far-off mountains turned into clouds.
> 　　　　　　　　　　　　[IV. i. 187-88]

Dreams, says Mercutio,

> 　　　　are the children of an idle brain,
> Begot of nothing but vain fantasy,
> Which is as thin of substance as the air
> And more inconstant than the wind.
> 　　　　　　[*Romeo and Juliet*, I. iv. 97-100]

The world of Theseus and Hippolyta and the world of Oberon and Titania are exclusive of each other. At no point do they really meet. But the two pairs of lovers and the simple-minded artisans waver between them and fall under the influence now of the one and now of the other. Sound sense and the delusions born of *vain fantasy* struggle for the possession of their souls, and in this they are alike.

But in every other respect how far apart the lovers and the *hardhanded men,* Bottom and his companions, appear to be. The lovers belong to the upper ranks of Athenian society; Hermia's father, Egeus, is admitted to the ducal presence whenever he likes, and addresses Theseus almost like an equal; the young man whom he wishes his daughter to marry is one of those young men whose doings cannot leave the sovereign indifferent; the Duke who had heard of Demetrius' breach of faith with Helena had meant to speak to him about it; and no one thinks of disputing Lysander's claim to be *as well derived, as well possessed* [I. i. 99–100] as his rival; they are courtiers all. After delivering his sentence on Hermia, Theseus bids Egeus and Demetrius come along with him. *I must employ you in some business . . . and confer with you* [I. i. 124-25]. No wonder therefore that Egeus should be in attendance on the Duke when, on the morning of his wedding-day, he goes hunting with his bride, that the two couples, at Theseus' order, should be married in the same temple and at the same time as he and Hippolyta. Peter Quince and his friends stand at the other extremity of the social scale. Weaver, bellows-mender, tailor, tinker, theirs is the humblest class of respectable citizens. Between them and the court circles there is a gulf. Listen to Snug the joiner rushing in to tell the others that the Duke is coming from the temple: *Masters,* he exclaims, *the Duke is coming from the temple, and there is two or three lords and ladies more married* [IV. ii. 15-16]. His excitement is that of one whose only source of information is public rumour. And when they hear their play has been chosen and they must perform it before the Court, they tell one another, in a highly perturbed state of mind in which dismay mixes with elation, not to forget to put on clean linen, and Bottom adds: *And, most dear actors, eat no onions, nor garlic, for we are to utter sweet breath* [IV. ii. 42-3]. Clearly garlic and onions are articles of daily consumption with them, and clean linen an unusual experience. This contrast between the lovers and the artisans as regards their social status is carried out in their speech. Lysander and Demetrius, Hermia and Helena, are always made to use verse and even rhymed verse—they use blank verse when their feelings are roused—; they are fond of conceits and quibbles, of delicate images, many of them exquisite poetry. Their language is the outcome of a refined education. Bottom, on the opposite, uses prose, in spite of his pretensions; for he is fond of big words, of words smacking of books and learning; but he neither knows their true form nor exactly what they mean, and his ridiculous misuse of them is evidence of his illiteracy. And his companions naturally speak good simple English prose.

But however different they may be, our young aristocratic lovers and our poor mechanics all suffer from delusions. Imagination or fantasy makes fools of them all. They all enter the dream-world of the wood where the fairies have them at their mercy. But it is not by mere chance that they fall under their baneful influence. They are partly responsible for their misfortunes. For what is our poor uneducated artisans' ambition to act a play, and act it in the presence of the Duke, but clear evidence that, for the time being, they have lost their common sense? What is Bottom making of himself if not an ass when he confidently proposes to take all the main parts in the tragedy? And as to the lovers, is not love and fancy one and the same thing in their eyes?

What the brief examination of the four main elements of which our comedy is composed is perhaps enough to suggest, namely that the poet did not bring them together without some other purpose than merely to please his audience, an analysis of the structure of the play may bring out more plainly. As its title implies, *Midsummer-Night's Dream* is a dream, such a dream as one might dream on the very night when, according to popular superstition, every one was more or less threatened with lunacy. But it is not altogether a dream. It neither begins nor ends as such. It begins in a world in which people are not only wide awake, but quite normal and it ends in the same matter-of-fact atmosphere. There is a definite entrance into the dream-world, and a no less definite coming out of it. Before we enter it, we are in the everyday world of realities to which the whole of the first act belongs. Still there already one is aware of a deviation from what might be called the straight line of common sense. So long as they are in the presence of Theseus and Hippolyta, how clear-headed, single-minded and sensible Hermia is, how reasonable Lysander, protesting of their right to get married against Egeus' wish. Has not their attitude convinced the Duke that theirs is the kind of love that should not be opposed? What is the "private schooling" he says he has for both Egeus and Demetrius if not some remonstrance by which he means to persuade them to give up their foolish opposition? Does he not, by ordering them to come away with him, leave the lovers together free to plan their escape? But as soon as Hermia and Lysander find themselves alone, imagination reasserts its power over them and they prettily expatiate on the misfortunes that are bound to cross the course of true love, and decide to elope. Our grip on the actual seems to get loose. And this impression is deepened when suddenly Helena appears, complaining of her lover's faithlessness; she it is that, in some of the most significant lines of the play, identifies love with imagination, the power to turn things into what they are not, the power that deprives one of all judgment:

> Things base and vile, holding no quantity
> Love can transpose to form and dignity.
> Love looks not with the eyes, but with the
>   mind:
> And therefore is winged Cupid painted
>   blind.

Nor hath Love's mind of any judgment
    taste . . .

                              [I. i. 232–36]

In the next scene, in Quince's little house where
his friends have all met to receive their parts, we
are still in wholly real surroundings, most realistically suggested. But how strongly does fantasy
sway our amateur players! Of their ability to act as
well as the best professionals they have not the
slightest doubt. Bottom in particular is already living in a world of dreams and delusions. So that,
when the end of the first act is reached, we are
ready to leave the world we know and enter another. And that other world is at once ushered in by
the meeting and the dialogue of Puck and a Fairy.
From this moment and throughout the long night
that follows we remain in that strange unreal
world where everything is different from what we
are used to. We are in a wood, the wood that Lysander and Hermia were to cross on their way to the
old dowager aunt's house, the wood that the Athenian artisans had chosen as a quiet convenient
place for their rehearsal, a real wood therefore, not
far from Athens and the palace of the most reasonable of sovereigns—but the Fairies have taken possession of it and changed it into a haunted wood.
Time within it is no longer what it is outside it: a
few hours of a single night is all that lovers and mechanics seem to be there; but for them, so long as
they are the victims of delusions, time indeed has
stopped and when sanity is restored to them, we
find that for Theseus and Hippolyta four days have
elapsed. Just as the physical law of time is suspended in this dream-world, so has it nothing to do
with measurable space: the wood has become illimitable; for the poor mortals that enter it, there
is no coming out; they wander in it endlessly and
never find an issue; they roam or rush hither and
thither in it, only to lie down in the end, unutter-
ably weary, and lose all consciousness in sleep. For
the 2nd Act, the 3rd and the beginning of the 4th,
that place outside time and space is the sole scene
of the action, and whatever happens in that central
part of the play can only be understood in reference
to its illusory character. When Demetrius, pursued
by Helena, mad, as he himself says, because he has
long and vainly sought for Hermia and Lysander,
wood within this wood [II. i. 192],—is not this
quibble more than a mere pun?—appears at last,
Oberon is present though invisible to them, and we
cannot but connect his presence with their utterly
unreasonable behaviour. Likewise, in the next
scene, Lysander and Hermia seem to labour under
some baneful influence; they have lost their way
and rest they must. On awaking from his sleep, his
eyes anointed by Puck with the juice of *Love-in-
idleness* [II. i. 168], Lysander sees Helena and at
once falls in love with her, forgetting Hermia. And
like many a victim of delusion, he is fully persuaded that he is acting most reasonably:

The will of man is by his reason swayed

And reason says you are the worthier
    maid . . .

Reason becomes the marshal to my will,
And leads me to your eyes . . .

                              [II. ii. 115–21]

When it is the turn of the small band of Athenian
artisans to come under the spell of the enchanted
wood, they bring with them at first a breath of
fresh air from the normal world. Their homely
manners, their naive discussion of the problems of
staging they must solve seem to dispel the distracting atmosphere in which Hermia has just dreamt
her fearful dream and woke up to find it true. For
a while they do not attract the fairies' attention.
The rehearsal begins . . . and Bottom undergoes
his monstrification. The dream-world, in the person of Puck, has suddenly reasserted itself. Frightened out of their wits, the simple-minded artisans
scatter in all directions, while Bottom, alone unconscious of the accident which has turned him
into an ass, wonders at their flight. He is the chief
victim of Puck. And rightly so. For what is he when
he advises Quince to explain in a prologue that
they *will do no harm with their swords,* and that
Pyramus is not killed indeed [III. i. 18-19], when
he shows how easily Snug may prevent the lion he
is to impersonate from frightening the ladies?
What is Bottom the stage-manager who does his
best to destroy all illusion, but an ass? For if it be
foolish to be, like Lysander and Demetrius, the
slaves of mere images, it is no less foolish to reduce
all life to a hard and narrow common sense. But
ass-headed Bottom serves another purpose, too. He
is used to emphasize the idea of the power of love
to lead one astray by making things seem what
they are not, that idea that Helena had expressed
earlier in the play. Here it is the Queen of the
Fairies herself, the mother of illusions, who is
made to serve as an illustration of her own powers
to seduce mortals: Titania, with her instinctive
preference for whatever is most refined, most delicate, in love with the portly weaver, a rude unwashed fellow, the very antithesis of refinement
and delicacy!

And now what with Lysander pursuing Helena,
Demetrius suddenly returning to his former love,
Hermia doubly forsaken, Bottom transformed, Titania doting upon him, distraction reigns supreme
in the haunted wood. How far such distraction can
go is shown in the great scene of the 3rd Act, with
the human passions in it rising to their climax in
the deadly quarrel between the two young men,
when the comedy assumes for a moment, as I said,
almost a tragical aspect. But for a brief moment
only, for Puck parts them, and sleep overcomes all
the actors in that comedy of errors caused by the
dotage of imaginary love. And in that sleep sense
will be restored to them. The effect of *Love-in-
idleness* will be corrected by anointing their eyes
with *Dian's bud,* love born of idle fancy replaced by
love born of the heart, real enduring affection. With

Oberon and Titania reconciled, the long night in the haunted wood comes to an end. The twittering of the morning lark is heard and in the growing light all the Fairies trip away in sober silence. At the sound of hunting-horns, Theseus and Hippolyta arrive and with them the world is fully restored to sanity. The lovers awake and their long errors appear but as idle dreams to them, and they are soon able to appreciate the full absurdity of the fate of Pyramus and Thisbe.

In the first Act, as we have seen, if owing to the Duke and his bride the outlook is generally healthy, normal and sensible, Lysander and Hermia, despite the genuineness of the love that unites them, still preserve romantic notions ultimately derived from the medieval idealisation of love, Demetrius suffers from a worse delusion and the artisans really live already in the dream-world of those who, unaware of their limitations, are guilty of presumptuousness and are likely to make fools of themselves. In the last Act, with Demetrius cured of his sickness—the word is his—and married to Helena, with Lysander and Hermia man and wife, all trace of romantic nonsense has disappeared from the relations of the lovers towards one another. They have become sensible creatures as Theseus and Hippolyta were from the first. Reality has triumphed over unreality, the world of facts over the world of dreams, the right sort of love that leads to its natural consummation in marriage over the delusions of youthful fancy, a clear and firm apprehension of the actualities among which we must live over the vagaries of uncontrolled imagination. But if sense thus celebrates its victory over nonsense, illusions, dreams, fancies of all kinds cannot be suppressed but will sprout again and proliferate on the slightest provocation. Let *cool reason* go to sleep, and there they are again. After our mortals have gone to bed, the Fairies reappear, and in the dark hall of the ducal palace dimly lighted by the glow of the *wasted brands* on the hearth, hold their revels. But they have not come without a definite purpose: they will bless the house and all its inmates. For if illusions and dreams and fancies can be harmful when they stand between man and reality, hindering him from seeing it, they are a blessing too, and Bottom the weaver would be a poor miserable creature if he could never leave his loom and believe himself a wonderful actor, and if they were not a blessing the poet would never have written *Midsummer-Night's Dream* to bring home to us his conviction that they should not be mistaken for reality, to weigh, as it were, the rival claims of imagination and sober vision and decide in favour of the latter while giving the former its due. (pp. 268-79)

> George A. Bonnard, "Shakespeare's Purpose in Midsummer-Night's Dream," in Shakespeare Jahrbuch, Vol. 92, 1956, pp. 268-79.

Allardyce Nicoll

[*A Midsummer Night's Dream, according to Nicoll, clearly reflects the poet's serious preoccupation with dreams and reality. Shakespeare's view of the problem of being and appearance, this critic maintains, is far from superficial, since he does not approach it as a paradox to be overcome. "Appearance and reality interplay in* [A Midsummer Night's Dream] *like two themes in a symphony, rising and falling, changing shape, momentarily coalescing and then, once more separate, producing contrapuntal music." But Shakespeare, Nicoll contends, for all his delight in ambiguities, approaches the puzzling world of fantasy in a level-headed manner. Nicoll concludes that the poet's common sense, which is represented by* Bottom, "embraces the imagination as well as the ordinary real."*]

The lyrical sonnet-like verse of *Romeo and Juliet* becomes more happily allied to content and mood in *A Midsummer Night's Dream*. This, the first of Shakespeare's great comedies, presents itself to us as a kind of amalgam of much that had gone before. The lovers' changing affections give us the situation caused by Proteus' inconstancy [in *The Two Gentlemen of Verona*]; the maze of errors reminds us of the comedy of that name, and even the world of Titania is anticipated there in Dromio's

> O for my heads! I cross me for a sinner.
> This is the fairy land. O spite of spites!
> We talk with goblins, owls and sprites.
> [*The Comedy of Errors*, II. ii. 188–90]

For the idea of the burlesque play-within-the-play Shakespeare turns to the masque of the worthies in *Love's Labour's Lost*, and perhaps even *Romeo and Juliet* inspires the choice of the Pyramus and Thisbe theme. It is all a tissue of earlier material, and all magnificently new spun. Within the framework provided by Theseus and Hippolyta are set the four lovers, the artisans and the fairies, all bound together by the theme of errors. Through the forest the lovers blunder their distracted way, the artisans not only rehearse a playlet of errors but themselves are carried into the maze. Oberon in his wisdom tries to set things right and only succeeds in making confusion worse confounded, while for Puck the creating of error is his spirit food.

Here Shakespeare first clearly introduces another of his potent preoccupations—the concept of dream and reality; and with it he first boldly sets forth the contrast between seeming and being. From both, much of the inner quality of his later dramas, both comic and tragic, was to arise; both were to be the very stuff of his double vision, of his common-sense view of life, of his identification with the force of Nature. Appearance and reality interplay in these dramas like two themes in a symphony, rising and falling, changing shape, momentarily coalescing and then, once more separate, producing contrapuntal music. Nothing in this world of Shakespeare's is so simple as at first glance it may appear. Gently the moonlight falls on us, and we think of the moon beloved of lovers; yet for Shakespeare the gentle loving moon is not all. If we hear Hippolyta, dreaming of her marriage to Theseus, saying

> And then the moon, like to a silver bow
> New-bent in heaven, shall behold the
>   night
> Of our solemnities,
>
>   [I. i. 9–11]

we listen also to Theseus' 'chanting faint hymns to the cold fruitless moon' and to Titania's

> Therefore the moon, the governess of
>   floods,
> Pale in her anger, washes all the air,
> That rheumatic diseases do abound.
>   [II. i. 103–05]

Like the lovers themselves we can but guess and wonder:

> *Demetrius:* These things seem small and
>   indistinguishable,
>   Like far-off mountains turned into
>   clouds.
> *Hermia:* Methinks I see these things with
>   parted eye,
>   When everything seems double. . . .
> *Demetrius:*   Are you sure
>   That we are awake? It seems to me
>   That yet we sleep, we dream.
>   [IV. i. 187–94]

It is almost as though Shakespeare were deliberately invoking in these words the mood with which he wishes to invest us as we listen to his play—and perhaps that is precisely what he is attempting. His epilogue, at least, is consciously designed.

> If we shadows have offended,
> Think but this, and all is mended—
> That you have but slumber'd here,
> While these visions did appear,
> And this weak and idle theme
> No more yielding but a dream.
>   [V. i. 423–28]

Yet the theme is not so idle, after all: looked at carefully it clearly shows the maturing Shakespeare at work. Various critics have pointed out that in Theseus we have, as it were, a level-headed commentator on the action, one who is never likely to mistake a bush for a bear. Beyond this, however, we must certainly go. We have just seen Oberon and Titania, and it is precisely these characters whose very existence Theseus would deny; we have just seen young lyric love, uniting with Nature's force, triumph over man-made law, and it is precisely lyric love that Theseus would reject. Besides Theseus there is another level-headed character—Bottom; but Bottom has a fairy's kisses on his lips. Shakespeare's level-headedness, his sublime common sense, cannot be restricted within the ring of The-

seus' practicality: it embraces the imagination as well as the ordinary real. (pp. 104-06)

> *Allardyce Nicoll, "Man and Society," in his* Shakespeare, *Methuen & Co. Ltd., 1952, pp. 100-32.*

David Richman

[*Richman discusses Shakespeare's effective introduction of wonder into* A Midsummer Night's Dream. *Language, the critic explains, is instrumental in creating wonderment, and the characters from the supernatural world identify themselves by their peculiar rhetorical devices and speech mannerisms. The obviously tragic element in the play, Richman observes, is the powerful, potentially devastating, rage underlying the conflict between* **Oberon** *and* **Titania,** *a dream world confrontation with possibly dire consequences for the denizens of ordinary reality. In Richman's opinion, no director captures the sense of wonder, power, and tragic rage better than Peter Brook, whose 1970 production of* A Midsummer Night's Dream *expanded the feeling of wonder— natural in the dream realm—so it could affect the mortals in the play and even the audience.*]

[The] introduction of wonder into comedy is not original with Shakespeare. Elements of the marvelous can be found as far back as Aristophanes,

Puck. Act II, scene ii. By Sir Joshua Reynolds.

preeminently in *The Birds,* and indeed can be traced even further back to the origins of comedy in ritual. In the relatively recent past of his own country, Shakespeare can find works for the stage that combine the comic with the wondrous, namely the medieval miracle plays and moralities. His immediate forerunners in comedy, [John] Lyly, [George] Peele, [Robert] Greene, and many lesser writers, often mix elements of the supernatural into their comedies. Although none of them evokes the sort of wonder that Shakespeare evokes in *Twelfth Night,* it can be argued that Peele, in *The Old Wives' Tale,* and Greene, in *Friar Bacon and Friar Bungay,* are making serious attempts. (pp. 94-5)

[Shakespeare's] attempts to weave wonder into comedy reach their first complete success in *A Midsummer Night's Dream.* The play is remarkable for many qualities, not the least of which is verse that gives full expression to the marvels the dramatist represents. The king and queen of fairyland astonish the spectators with their language as well as their power. Titania's attendants and even Puck are creatures of a different order from the contending sovereigns of fairyland, and the difference should be made clear in production. In Shakespeare's time Oberon was played by an adult actor, Titania by the star boy, and the other fairies by children of lesser abilities. In a 1978 [Royal Shakespeare Company] production the attendant fairies were puppets, and in Peter Brook's famous production, as well as in several others not so well known, all the fairies, including Oberon, became trapeze artists.

The manner in which the fairies' verse contrasts with the verse of their king and queen suggests differences of degree and kind. The fairies and Puck characteristically speak in tetrameter or pentameter couplets. They exult in and exalt the diminutive. Their verse is full of dewdrops, cowslips, long-legged spinners, and hedgehogs. The mischiefs in which Puck delights are typically farcical pranks—tempting lusty horses, humiliating old ladies, or spoiling the beer. Oberon and Titania speak mostly in blank verse that grows ever more majestic. In describing and enacting their continuing quarrel, the king and queen make clear that their discord is reflected in all sublunary nature. Shakespeare is here varying a rhetorical device that he uses throughout his career. But Titania and Oberon are not mortals like Romeo or Richard II, who imagine all nature to be participating in their grief and rage. Rather these are the very spirits of nature, the originals of natural turbulence. What they describe is not an imagined but an actual result of their anger.

To express this turbulence, the playwright gives Oberon and Titania verse that employs striking rhythmic and figurative resources. The ear encounters inverted iambs and spondees, which force strongly stressed syllables into direct alignment with each other. There is also frequent enjambment and a flexible use of the caesura, which occurs often in the middle of a foot and occasionally in the middle of an inverted foot. The rhythm of a line like "Fall in the fresh lap of the crimson rose" [II. i. 108] has a twofold effect: the juxtaposition of strongly stressed syllables forces the speaker to retard; accented syllables and the caesura, all occurring in surprising places, create an impression of emotional agitation. Moreover, the prosopopoeia [personification] and antonomasia [substitution of an epithet for a proper name] in these speeches invest the unseasonal prodigies with human passion and torment:

> The human mortals want their winter
>   here;
> No night is now with hymn or carol blest;
> Therefore the moon, the governess of
>   floods,
> Pale in her anger, washes all the air,
> That rheumatic diseases do abound.
> And thorough this distemperature we see
> The seasons alter: hoary-headed frosts
> Fall in the fresh lap of the crimson rose;
> And on old Hiems' thin and icy crown
> An odorous chaplet of sweet summer buds
> Is, as in mockery, set. The spring, the sum-
>   mer,
> The childing autumn, angry winter,
>   change
> Their wonted liveries; and the mazed
>   world,
> By their increase, now knows not which is
>   which.
> And this same progeny of evils comes
> From our debate, from our dissension;
> We are their parents and original.
>   [II. i. 101–17]

A key to Titania's speech can be found in a word near its end that Shakespeare typically charges with many meanings. The fairy queen speaks of "the mazed world," calling to mind her earlier reference to "the quaint mazes in the wanton green" [II. i. 99]. The world in its confusion has become literally and figuratively a maze, a labyrinth in which no right path can be found. But the word takes on also its second sense of "amazed," that is, astonished, struck with wonder by the alterations. The speech in performance will stand or fall on the actress's ability to convince the audience of her character's astonishment and shame that she and Oberon are damaging the natural world. To be sure, they are engaged in a farcical love-brawl, but love that is capable of such effects is a great and terrible passion that evokes a Sidneyan admiration. The rage and power of Oberon and Titania stir potentially tragic responses. Peter Brook's recognition and manipulation of these responses may constitute his famous production's greatest achievements.

No Shakespearean comedy offers wider scope to the imagination of directors, designers, and actors, and in no Shakespearean comedy is it more necessary to observe Bruno Walter's admonition to select from among the limitless imaginative possibilities those essential to the play as a whole. Although many of the play's scenes require spectacular visual display and startling or hilarious stage business, the second-act quarrel between Oberon and Titania must guide the audience to focus on language and passion. The director's principal responsibility in this scene is to find actors who possess the talent to speak verse with beauty and power. Having found and worked with such actors, the director must insure that the scenery, lighting, and costumes aid the spectators' response without competing for their attention.

Peter Brook notes that certain of Shakespeare's scenes—most often the prose scenes—can be "enriched by our own invention. The scenes need added external details to assure them of their fullest life." But Brook warns that passages in verse require a different sort of treatment.

> Shakespeare needs verse because he is trying to say more, to compact together more meaning. We are watchful. Behind each visible mark on paper lurks an invisible one that is hard to seize. Technically, we now need less abandon, more focus, less breadth, more intensity.

Surely no director has given the supernatural elements in *A Midsummer Night's Dream* a fuller and more astonishing life than Peter Brook. Yet, true to his own dictum, Brook stilled his acrobatic fairies during Oberon's great speeches, and Alan Howard delivered those speeches unforgettably. I cannot now read or hear "I know a bank where the wild thyme blows" [II. i. 249] without recalling Howard's slow, deliberate cadences.

But Brook did not adhere to his own doctrine in staging Titania's speech. Sarah Kestelman was an intensely sensual Titania. Her crimson feather bed was the only object of color in the stark white brightly lit set. But she gave the impression that she was nothing more than a sexually indulged creature who was somehow responsible for creating the problem that the charming and authoritative Oberon had to solve. In an interview for the *New York Times,* Brook discussed the

> most extraordinary, demonic notion of Oberon having his queen fornicate with a physically repellent object, the ass. And why does Oberon do it? Not out of sadism, anger or revenge, but out of genuine love. It is as though in a modern sense a husband secured the largest truckdriver for his wife to sleep with to smash her illusions about sex and to alleviate the difficulties in their marriage.

This assessment of the couple's marital relations was reflected in Brook's staging of their quarrel. While Titania spoke, Oberon stroked her leg. His action commanded the audience's attention, drawing it away from her words. To the spectators, she seemed to be merely talking about the weather while Oberon generated the scene's true erotic power. The sense of natural turbulence growing out of the fairies' domestic discord was lost. More important, Sarah Kestelman's Titania was diminished into a creature of sensuality without power. The effect was astonishing, but it was astonishment different in kind and quality from the wonder that arises out of Titania's verse. Brook's production was ruled by its Oberon and its Puck, but Titania's scenes were less enriched by a sense of her magnitude than they could have been.

Something of the wonder that Titania's words create remain with her throughout the play. Although she is bewitched into a ridiculous amour, she never fully loses her original stature. Funny as they are, there is a peculiar power in her scenes with Bottom. Much of this power is drawn from her speeches in the second act, and some of it accrues from the astonishing manner in which Oberon introduces the magic herb that will bring about her dotage. Like his consort, he employs striking rhythmic and figurative devices:

> Thou rememb'rest
> Since once I sat upon a promontory,
> And heard a mermaid on a dolphin's back
> Uttering such dulcet and harmonious
>   breath
> That the rude sea grew civil at her song,
> And certain stars shot madly from their
>   spheres
> To hear the sea-maid's music.
>
>   [II. i. 148–54]

Oberon invests the herb with the power of the music he is describing. The playwright diverts attention from the fact that the fairy king is actually playing a rather petty and cruel practical joke on his wife. The diversion by no means mitigates the laughter that the trick will bring about, but it suggests that the device and its accompanying laughter contain elements of wonder. Although what happens to Titania is similar in kind to what happens to the quartet of human lovers, it is raised to a greater order of magnitude.

Even the human lovers, foolish, passionate, and ridiculous in their pain, are not untouched by wonder. When Theseus's huntsman wakes them after they have been released from their enchantments, they are still enraptured by the fading memory of the dream they have shared. "Methinks I see these things with parted eye, / When everything seems double" [IV. i. 188–89]. "And I have found Demetrius like a jewel, / Mine own, and not mine own" [IV. i. 191–92]. Lysander's line to Theseus suggests to directors and actors how all four lovers should speak and act in this scene: "My lord, I shall reply amazedly, / Half sleep, half waking" [IV. i. 146–47]. After the jangling couplets and farcical stage business of their protracted quarrel, the lovers' quiet scene of awakening possesses a startling beauty.

Even Bottom is moved to wonder after his fashion at his night's adventures. Twisting Biblical phrases about the wondrous works of God, he lists the particular incapacities of the various human senses and faculties to conceive or report his vision. The speech is funny, but if the actor plays it quietly and convinces the audience of the character's genuine amazement, wonder will mix with the laughter. Bottom realizes that his dream is good enough to be made into a ballad to grace the end of the tragedy that he and his companions plan to perform at the duke's wedding. What better thing can come at the end of a tragedy than something that moves wonder?

All five of the humans whose lives have been touched by love-in-idleness sense that they have traveled to terrain that lies on the far side of reason. Theseus maps and then dismisses this terrain in his famous speech toward the play's end. But that speech takes on reverberations for the audience that go beyond his conscious intentions because the spectators have seen and dwelt for a time with the fairies, and he has not. Even in Brook's production, in which Theseus dreamed himself into Oberon, Alan Howard's Theseus gave the impression that his conscious mind was tendering a stringent warning to his half-conscious fantasies. The rich counterpoint between Theseus's skepticism and the spectators' memory of the magic can be strengthened in production if, while the actor is talking urbanely about lovers and madmen, his bearing and movement recall those of Oberon and the lighting subtly reminds the audience of the haunted grove.

Albertus Magnus asserts that wonder can be called forth in one who is in suspense as to a cause, the knowledge of which will make him know instead of wonder. It follows from this assertion that reason can dispel wonder. If reason finds out the cause of a seeming miracle, then reactions proper to a miracle are no longer either necessary or possible. As Guildenstern argues in Tom Stoppard's play [Rosencrantz and Guildenstern Are Dead]— which owes more than its plot to Shakespeare— the miraculous unicorn shrinks to a horse with an arrow in its forehead. Now Theseus is using his reason with just such an intent when he ascribes the lovers' wonder to their amorous fancies. But Hippolyta speaks for the audience's larger experience when she raises a caveat that Theseus never answers:

> But all the story of the night told over,
> And all their minds transfigur'd so together,
> More witnesseth than fancy's images,
> And grows to something of great constancy
> But howsoever strange and admirable.
> [V. i. 23-7]

Her last word . . . makes clear that she partakes of the lovers' wonder. The playwright contrives his action and his verse so that the spectators share her response. (pp. 97-102)

> *David Richman, "Introduction: Wonder," in his* Laughter, Pain, and Wonder: Shakespeare's Comedies and the Audience in the Theater, *University of Delaware Press, 1990, pp. 89-120.*

LANGUAGE AND POETRY

Mark Van Doren

[*The immense expanses created by Shakespeare's extraordinary poetic imagination, Van Doren affirms, are vast enough to house the fairy realms and the world of ordinary reality, including all the peculiar manifestations of either place. The critic then examines the dramatist's ability to describe the separate and often quite dissimilar regions of the play's universe by drawing on the rich resources of poetry. Particularly in the supernatural sphere, Shakespeare's descriptions reach a remarkable geographic precision and undeniable suggestiveness. Referring to the playwright's depiction of both worlds, Van Doren further observes that the "poetry of the play is dominated by the words moon and water." As a result of their enormous allusive potential, these images engender an entire network of interlocking symbols which greatly enrich the text. In Van Doren's opinion, this fundamental poetic symbolism affects the entire universe of the play. "Moon," Van Doren concludes, "water, and wet flowers conspire to extend the world of 'A Midsummer Night's Dream' until it is as large as all imaginable life. That is why the play is both so natural and so mysterious."*]

"A Midsummer Night's Dream" shines like "Romeo and Juliet" in darkness, but shines merrily. Lysander, one of the two nonentities who are its heroes, complains at the beginning about the brevity of love's course, and sums up his complaint with a line which would not be out of place in "Romeo and Juliet":

> So quick bright things come to confusion.
> [I. i. 149]

This, however, is at the beginning. Bright things will come to clarity in a playful, sparkling night while fountains gush and spangled starlight betrays the presence in a wood near Athens of magic persons who can girdle the earth in forty minutes and bring any cure for human woe. Nor will the woe to be cured have any power to elicit our anxiety. The four lovers whose situation resembles so closely the situation created in "The Two Gentlemen of Verona" will come nowhere near the seriousness of that predicament; they will remain to the end four automatic creatures whose artificial and pretty fate it is to fall in and out of love like dolls, and like dolls they will go to sleep as soon as they are laid down. There will be no pretense that reason and love keep company, or that because they do not death lurks at the horizon. There is no death in "A Midsummer Night's Dream," and the smiling horizon is immeasurably remote.

Robin Goodfellow ends the extravaganza with an apology to the audience for the "weak and idle theme" [V. i. 427] with which it has been entertained. And Theseus, in honor of whose marriage with Hippolyta the entire action is occurring, dismisses most of it as a fairy toy, or such an airy nothing as some poet might give a local habitation and a name [V. i. 17]. But Robin is wrong about the theme, and Theseus does not describe the kind of poet Shakespeare is. For the world of this play is both veritable and large. It is not the tiny toy-shop that most such spectacles present, with quaint little people scampering on dry little errands, and with small music squeaking somewhere a childish accompaniment. There is room here for mortals no less than for fairies; both classes are at home, both groups move freely in a wide world where indeed they seem sometimes to have exchanged functions with one another. For these fairies do not sleep on flowers. Only Hermia can remember lying upon faint primrose-beds [I. i. 215], and only Bottom in the action as we have it ever dozes on pressed posies [III. i. 162]. The fairies themselves—Puck, Titania, Oberon—are too busy for that, and too hard-minded. The vocabulary of Puck is the most vernacular in the play; he talks of beans and crabs, dew-laps and ale, three-foot stools and sneezes [II. i. 42-57]. And with the king and queen of fairy-land he has immense spaces to travel. The three of them are citizens of all the universe there is, and as we listen to them the farthest portions of this universe stretch out, distant and glittering, like facets on a gem of infinite size. There is a specific geography, and the heavens are cold and high.

> Oberon.   Thou rememb'rest
>
>   Since once I sat upon a promon-
>   tory,
>   And heard a mermaid on a dol-
>   phin's back
>   Uttering such dulcet and harmo-
>   nious breath
>   That the rude sea grew civil at
>   her song,
>   And certain stars shot madly
>   from their spheres,
>   To hear the sea-maid's music?
> Robin.   I remember.
> Oberon. That very time I saw, but thou
>   couldst not,
>   Flying between the cold moon
>   and the earth,
>   Cupid all arm'd. A certain aim he
>   took
>   At a fair vestal throned by the
>   west,

> And loos'd his love-shaft smartly
>   from his bow,
> As it should pierce a hundred
>   thousand hearts;
> But I might see young Cupid's
>   fiery shaft
> Quench'd in the chaste beams of
>   the watery moon,
> And the imperial votaress passed
>   on,
> In maiden meditation, fancy-free.
> Yet mark'd I where the bolt of
>   Cupid fell.
> It fell upon a little western
>   flower. . . .
> Fetch me that flower, the herb I
>   shew'd thee once. . . .
> Fetch me this herb; and be thou
>   here again
> Ere the leviathan can swim a
>   league.
> Robin. I'll put a girdle round about the
>   earth
>   In forty minutes.
>
>   [II. i. 148-76]

The business may be trivial, but the world is as big and as real as any world we know. The promontory long ago; the rude sea that grew—not smooth, not gentle, not anything pretty or poetical, but (the prosaic word is one of Shakespeare's best) civil; the mermaid that is also a sea-maid; the direction west; and the cold watery moon that rides so high above the earth—these are the signs of its bigness, and they are so clear that we shall respect the prowess implied in Robin's speed, nor shall we fail to be impressed by the news that Oberon has just arrived from the farthest steep of India [II. i. 69].

Dr. [Samuel] Johnson and [William] Hazlitt copied [Joseph] Addison in saying that if there could be persons like these they would act like this. Their tribute was to the naturalness of Shakespeare's supernature. [John] Dryden's tribute to its charm:

> But Shakespeare's magic could not copied
>   be;
> Within that circle none durst walk but he

has an identical source: wonder that such things can be at all, and be so genuine. The explanation is the size and the concreteness of Shakespeare's setting. And the key to the structure of that setting is the watery moon to which Oberon so casually referred.

The poetry of the play is dominated by the words moon and water. Theseus and Hippolyta carve the moon in our memory with the strong, fresh strokes of their opening dialogue:

> Theseus.   Now, fair Hippolyta, our nup-
>   tial hour
>   Draws on apace. Four happy
>   days bring in
>   Another moon; but, O, me-
>   thinks, how slow
>   This old moon wanes! She lin-

gers my desires,
Like to a step-dame or a dowager
Long withering out a young
man's revenue.

Hippolyta. Four days will quickly steep
themselves in night;
Four nights will quickly
dream away the time;
And then the moon, like to a
silver bow
New-bent in heaven, shall behold the night
Of our solemnities.

[I. i. 1-11]

This is not the sensuous, softer orb of "Antony and Cleopatra," nor is it the sweet sleeping friend of Lorenzo and Jessica. It is brilliant and brisk, silverdistant, and an occasion for comedy in Theseus's worldly thought. Later on in the same scene he will call it cold and fruitless [l. 73], and Lysander will look forward to

Tomorrow night, when Phoebe doth behold
Her silver visage in the watery glass,
Decking with liquid pearl the bladed
grass.

[I. i. 209-11]

Lysander has connected the image of the moon with the image of cool water on which it shines, and hereafter they will be inseparable. "A Midsummer Night's Dream" is drenched with dew when it is not saturated with rain. A film of water spreads over it, enhances and enlarges it miraculously. The fairy whom Robin hails as the second act opens wanders swifter than the moon's sphere through fire and flood. The moon, says Titania, is governess of floods, and in anger at Oberon's brawls has sucked up from the sea contagious fogs, made every river overflow, drowned the fields and rotted the green corn:

The nine men's morris is fill'd up with
mud,
And the quaint mazes in the wanton green
For lack of tread are undistinguishable.

[II. i. 98-100]

Here in the west there has been a deluge, and every object still drips moisture. But even in the east there are waves and seas. The little changeling boy whom Titania will not surrender to Oberon is the son of a votaress on the other side of the earth:

And, in the spiced Indian air, by night,
Full often hath she gossip'd by my side,
And sat with me on Neptune's yellow
sands,
Marking the embarked traders on the
flood.

[II. i. 124-27]

The jewels she promises Bottom will be fetched "from the deep" [III. i. 161]. And Oberon is addicted to treading seaside groves

Even till the eastern gate, all fiery-red,
Opening on Neptune with fair blessed
beams,
Turns into yellow gold his salt green
streams.

[III. ii. 391-93]

So by a kind of logic the mortals of the play continue to be washed with copious weeping. The roses in Hermia's cheeks fade fast "for want of rain" [I. i. 130], but rain will come. Demetrius "hails" and "showers" oaths on Helena [I. i. 245], whose eyes are bathed with salt tears [II. ii. 92-3]; and Hermia takes comfort in the tempest of her eyes [I. i. 131].

When the moon weeps, says Titania to Bottom, "weeps every little flower" [III. i. 199]. The flowers of "A Midsummer Night's Dream" are not the warm, sweet, dry ones of Perdita's garden, or even the daytime ones with which Fidele's brothers will strew her forest grave [in *The Winter's Tale*]. They are the damp flowers that hide among ferns and drip with dew. A pearl is hung in every cowslip's ear [II. i. 15]; the little western flower which Puck is sent to fetch is rich with juice; and luscious woodbine canopies the bank of wild thyme where Titania sleeps—not on but "in" musk-roses and eglantine. Moon, water, and wet flowers conspire to extend the world of "A Midsummer Night's Dream" until it is as large as all imaginable life. That is why the play is both so natural and so mysterious.

Nor do its regions fail to echo with an ample music. The mermaid on the promontory with her dulcet and harmonious breath sang distantly and long ago, but the world we walk in is filled with present sound.

Theseus. Go, one of you, find out the forester,
For now our observation is
perform'd,
And since we have the vaward
of the day,
My love shall hear the music of
my hounds.
Uncouple in the western val-
ley, let them go.
Dispatch, I say, and find the
forester.
We will, fair queen, up to the
mountain's top
And mark the musical confusion
Of hounds and echo in conjunction.

Hippolyta. I was with Hercules and Cad-
mus once,
When in a wood of Crete they
bay'd the bear
With hounds of Sparta. Never
did I hear
Such gallant chiding; for, besides the groves,
The skies, the fountains, every
region near

Seem'd all one mutual cry. I never heard
So musical a discord, such sweet thunder.

Theseus. My hounds are bred out of the Spartan kind,
So flew'd, so sanded, and their heads are hung
With ears that sweep away the morning dew;
Crook-knee'd, and dew-lapp'd like Thessalian bulls;
Slow in pursuit, but match'd in mouth like bells,
Each under each. A cry more tuneable
Was never holla'd to, nor cheer'd with horn,
In Crete, in Sparta, nor in Thessaly.
Judge when you hear.

[IV. i. 103-27]

Had Shakespeare written nothing else than this he still might be the best of English poets. Most poetry which tries to be music also is less than poetry. This is absolute. The melody which commences with such spirit in Theseus's fifth line has already reached the complexity of counterpoint in his eight and ninth; Hippolyta carries it to a like limit in the line with which she closes; and Theseus, taking it back from her, hugely increases its volume, first by reminding us that the hounds have form and muscle, and then by daring the grand dissonance, the mixed thunder, of bulls and bells. The passage sets a forest ringing, and supplies a play with the music it has deserved.

But Shakespeare is still more a poet because the passage is incidental to his creation. The creation with which he is now busy is not a passage, a single effect; it is a play, and though this one contribution has been mighty there are many others. And none of the others is mightier than bully Bottom's.

Bottom likes music too. "I have a reasonable good ear," he tells Titania. "Let's have the tongs and the bones" [IV. i. 28-9]. So does he take an interest in moonshine, if only among the pages of an almanac. "A calendar, a calendar!" he calls. "Find out moonshine, find out moonshine" [III. i. 53-4]. When they find the moon, those Athenian mechanics of whom he is king, it has in it what the cold fairy moon cannot be conceived as having, the familiar man of folklore. Bottom and his fellows domesticate the moon, as they domesticate every other element of which Shakespeare has made poetry. And the final effect is parody. Bottom's amazed oration concerning his dream follows hard upon the lovers' discourse concerning dreams and delusions; but it is in prose, and the speaker is utterly literal when he pronounces that it will be called Bottom's dream because it hath no bottom [IV. i. 216]. Nor is the story of Pyramus and Thisbe as the mechanics act it anything but a burlesque of "Romeo and Juliet."

O night, which ever art when day is not! . . .
And thou, O wall, O sweet, O lovely wall,
That stand'st between her father's ground and mine!
Thou wall, O wall, O sweet and lovely wall.

[V. i. 171-76]

Shakespeare has come, even this early, to the farthest limit of comedy. The end of comedy is self-parody, and its wisdom is self-understanding. Never again will he work without a full comprehension of the thing he is working at; of the probability that other and contrary things are of equal importance; of the certainty that his being a poet who can do anything he wants to do is not the only thing to be, or the best possible thing; of the axiom that the whole is greater than the part—the part in his instance being one play among many thinkable plays, or one man, himself, among the multitude that populate a world for whose size and variety he with such giant strides is reaching respect. Bully Bottom and his friends have lived three centuries to good purpose, but to no better purpose at any time than the one they first had—namely, in their sublime innocence, their earthbound, idiot openness and charity of soul, to bring it about that their creator should become not only the finest of poets but the one who makes the fewest claims for poetry. (pp. 76-83)

> *Mark Van Doren, "A Midsummer Night's Dream," in his* Shakespeare, *Henry Holt and Company, 1939, pp. 76-83.*

MYTHOLOGICAL BACKGROUND

Northrop Frye

[*Frye traces the literary sources of Shakespeare's play, with particular emphasis on Classical—Greek and Roman—and early Elizabethan comedy. According to Frye, Shakespeare does not follow classical models closely, but relies instead on his English predecessors, especially in the treatment of supernatural elements. The critic then touches upon possible flattering references to Queen Elizabeth I in* A Midsummer Night's Dream, *explaining that the references are purely textual, and that none of the characters can be associated with the monarch. Frye also comments on the title of the play, observing that, as the medieval calendar had only three seasons, the eve of May Day, when the action of the comedy takes place, really is the middle of the summer, since that season starts in March. In his discussion of the fairy world, Frye identifies the poet's sources in Classical, Celtic, Germanic, and Anglo-Saxon folklore and mythology. The dream world of the forest, Frye suggests, "has affinities with what we call the unconscious or* subconscious part of the mind." And only this part of our mind, Frye concludes, holds the key to this wonderful and mysterious play.]

Elizabethan literature began as a provincial development of a Continent-centred literature, and it's full of imitations and translations from French, Italian and Latin. But the dramatists practically had to rediscover drama, as soon as, early in Elizabeth's reign, theatres with regular performances of plays on a thrust stage began to evolve out of temporary constructions in dining halls and courtyards. There was some influence from Italian theatre, and some of the devices in *Twelfth Night* reminded one spectator, who kept a diary, of Italian sources. There was also the influence of the half-improvised *commedia dell'arte* [Italian comedy of the 16th to the 18th centuries improvised from standardized situations and stock characters]. . . . Behind these Italian influences were the Classical plays from which the Italian ones partly derived.

For tragedy there were not many precedents, apart from the Latin plays of Seneca, whose tragedies may not have been actually intended for the stage. Seneca is a powerful influence behind Shakespeare's earliest tragedy, *Titus Andronicus,* and there are many traces of him elsewhere. In comedy, though, there were about two dozen Latin plays available, six by Terence, the rest by Plautus. These had been adapted from the Greek writers of what we call New Comedy, to distinguish it from the Old Comedy of Aristophanes, which was full of personal attacks and allusions to actual people and events. The best known of these Greek New Comedy writers was Menander, whose work, except for one complete play recently discovered, has come down to us only in fragments. Menander was a sententious, aphoristic writer, and one of his aphorisms ("evil communications corrupt good manners") was quoted by Paul in the New Testament. Terence carried on this sententious style, and we find some famous proverbs in him, such as "I am a man, and nothing human is alien to me." When we hear a line like "The course of true love never did run smooth" [I. i. 134] in *A Midsummer Night's Dream,* familiar to many people who don't know the play, we can see that the same tradition is still going strong. And later on, when we hear Bottom mangling references to Paul's epistles, we may feel that we're going around in a circle.

New Comedy, in Plautus and Terence, usually sets up a situation that's the opposite of the one that the audience would recognize as the "right" one. Let's say a young man loves a young woman, and vice versa, but their love is blocked by parents who want suitors or brides with more money. That's the first part. The second part consists of the complications that follow, and in a third and last part the opening situation is turned inside out, usually through some gimmick in the plot, such as the discovery that the heroine was kidnapped in infancy

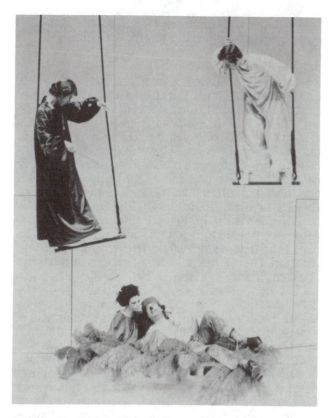

Alan Howard as Oberon, Sara Kestelman as Titania, David Waller as Bottom, and John Kane as Puck. Act IV, scene i. From Peter Brook's 1970 production of A Midsummer Night's Dream.

by pirates, or that she was exposed on a hillside and rescued by a shepherd, but that her social origin is quite respectable enough for her to marry the hero. The typical characters in such a story are the young man (*adulescens*), a heavy father (sometimes called *senex iratus,* because he often goes into terrible rages when he's thwarted), and a "tricky slave" (*dolosus servus*), who helps out the young man with some clever scheme. If you look at the plays of Molière, you'll see these characters over and over again, and the tricky servant is still there in the Figaro operas of Rossini and Mozart. . . . Often the roles of young man and young woman are doubled: in a play of Plautus, adapted by Shakespeare in *The Comedy of Errors,* the young men are twin brothers, and Shakespeare adds a pair of twin servants.

In Shakespeare's comedies we often get two heroines as well: we have Rosalind and Celia in *As You Like It,* Hero and Beatrice in *Much Ado about Nothing,* Olivia and Viola in *Twelfth Night,* Julia and Silvia in *The Two Gentlemen of Verona,* Helena and Hermia in this play. It's a natural inference that there were two boys in Shakespeare's company who were particularly good at female roles. If so, one seems to have been noticeably taller than the other. In *As You Like It* we're not sure which was the taller one—the indications are contradictory—but here they're an almost comic-strip contrast, Helena being long and drizzly and Hermia short and spitty.

Shakespeare's comedies are far more complex than the Roman ones, but the standard New Comedy structure usually forms part of their actions. To use Puck's line, the Jacks generally get their Jills in the end (or the Jills get their Jacks, which in fact happens more often). But he makes certain modifications in the standard plot, and makes them fairly consistently. He doesn't seem to like plots that turn on tricky-servant schemes. He does have smart or cheeky servants often enough, like Lancelot Gobbo in *The Merchant of Venice,* and they make the complacent soliloquies that are common in the role, but they seldom affect the action. Puck and Ariel [in *The Tempest*] come nearest, and we notice that neither is a human being and neither acts on his own. Then again, Shakespeare generally plays down the outwitting and baffling of age by youth: the kind of action suggested by the title of a play of [Thomas] Middleton's, *A Trick to Catch the Old-One,* is rare in Shakespeare. The most prominent example is the ganging up on Shylock in *The Merchant of Venice* that lets his daughter Jessica marry Lorenzo. Even that leaves a rather sour taste in our mouths, and the sour taste is part of the play, not just part of our different feelings about stage Jews. In the late romances, especially *Pericles* and *The Winter's Tale,* the main comic resolution concerns older people, who are united or reconciled after a long separation. Even in this play, while we start out with a standard New Comedy situation in which lovers are forbidden to marry but succeed in doing so all the same, it's the older people, Theseus and Hippolyta, who are at the centre of the action, and we could add to this the reconciling of Oberon and Titania.

In the Roman plays there's a general uniformity of social rank: the characters are usually ordinary middle-class people with their servants. The settings are also uniform and consistent: they're not "realistic," but the action is normally urban, taking place on the street in front of the houses of the main characters, and there certainly isn't much of mystery, romance, fairies, magic or mythology (except for farcical treatments of it like Plautus's *Amphitryon*). . . . [We know that the highbrows in Shakespeare's time] thought that Classical precedents were models to be imitated, and that you weren't writing according to the proper rules if you introduced kings or princes or dukes into comedies, as Shakespeare is constantly doing, or if you introduced the incredible or mysterious, such as fairies or magic. Some of Shakespeare's younger contemporaries, notably Ben Jonson, keep more closely to Classical precedent, and Jonson tells us that he regularly follows nature, and that some other people like Shakespeare don't. Shakespeare never fails to introduce something mysterious or

hard to believe into his comedies, and in doing so he's following the precedents set, not by the Classical writers, but by his immediate predecessors.

These predecessors included in particular three writers of comedy, [George] Peele, [Robert] Greene and [John] Lyly. Peele's *Old Wives' Tale* is full of themes from folk tales; in Greene's *Friar Bacon and Friar Bungay* the central character is a magician, and in his *James IV,* while there's not much about the Scottish king of that name, there's a chorus character called Oberon, the king of the fairies; in Lyly's *Endimion* the main story retells the Classical myth of Endymion, the youth beloved by the goddess of the moon. These are examples of the type of romance-comedy that Shakespeare followed. Shakespeare keeps the three-part structure of the Roman plays, but immensely expands the second part, and makes it a prolonged episode of confused identity. Sometimes the heroine disguises herself as a boy; sometimes the action moves into a charmed area, often a magic wood like the one in this play, where the ordinary laws of nature don't quite apply.

If we ask why this type of early Elizabethan comedy should have been the type Shakespeare used, there are many answers, but one relates to the audience. *A Midsummer Night's Dream* has the general appearance of a play designed for a special festive occasion, when the Queen herself might well be present. In such a play one would expect an occasional flattering allusion to her, and it looks as though we have one when Oberon refers to an "imperial votaress" in a speech to Puck. The Queen was also normally very tolerant about the often bungling attempts to entertain her when she made her progressions through the country, and so the emphasis placed on Theseus's courtesy to the Quince company may also refer to her, even if he is male. But if there were an allusion to her, it would have to be nothing more than that.

Even today novelists have to put statements into their books that no real people are being alluded to, and in Shakespeare's day anything that even looked like such an allusion, beyond the conventional compliments, could be dangerous. Three of Shakespeare's contemporaries did time in jail for putting into a play a couple of sentences that sounded like satire on the Scotsmen coming to England in the train of James I, and worse things, like cutting off ears and noses, could be threatened. I make this point because every so often some director or critic gets the notion that this play is really all about Queen Elizabeth, or that certain characters, such as Titania, refer to her. The consequences to Shakespeare's dramatic career if the Queen had believed that she was being publicly represented as having a love affair with a jackass are something we fortunately don't have to think about.

An upper-class audience is inclined to favour romance and fantasy in its entertainment, because the idealizing element in such romance confirms its own image of itself. And whatever an upper-class audience likes is probably going to be what a middle-class audience will like too. If this play was adapted to, or commissioned for, a special court performance, it would be the kind of thing Theseus is looking for at the very beginning of the play, when he tells his master of revels, Philostrate, to draw up a list of possible entertainments. One gets an impression of sparseness about what Philostrate has collected, even if Theseus doesn't read the whole list; but however that may be, the Peter Quince play has something of the relation to the nuptials of Theseus that Shakespeare's play would have had to whatever occasion it was used for. We notice that the reason for some of the absurdities in the Quince play come from the actors' belief that court ladies are unimaginably fragile and delicate: they will swoon at the sight of Snug the joiner as a lion unless it is carefully explained that he isn't really a lion. The court ladies belong to the Quince players' fairyland: Shakespeare knew far more about court ladies than they did, but he also realized that court ladies and gentlemen had some affinity, as an audience, with fairyland.

This play retains the three parts of a normal comedy that I mentioned earlier: a first part in which an absurd, unpleasant or irrational situation is set up; a second part of confused identity and personal complications; a third part in which the plot gives a shake and twist and everything comes right in the end. In the opening of this play we meet an irrational law, of a type we often do meet at the beginning of a Shakespeare comedy: the law of Athens that decrees death or perpetual imprisonment in a convent for any young woman who marries without her father's consent. Here the young woman is Hermia, who loves Lysander, and the law is invoked by her father, Egeus, who prefers Demetrius. Egeus is a senile old fool who clearly doesn't love his daughter, and is quite reconciled to seeing her executed or imprisoned. What he loves is his own possession of his daughter, which carries the right to bestow her on a man of his choice as a proxy for himself. He makes his priorities clear in a speech later in the play:

> They would have stol'n away, they would, Demetrius,
> Thereby to have defeated you and me:
> You of your wife, and me of my consent,
> Of my consent that she should be your wife.
>
> [IV. i. 156-59]

Nevertheless Theseus admits that the law is what Egeus says it is, and also emphatically says that the law must be enforced, and that he himself has no power to abrogate it. We meet this situation elsewhere in Shakespeare: at the beginning of *The Comedy of Errors,* with its law that in Ephesus all visitors from Syracuse are to be beheaded, and in *The Merchant of Venice,* with the law that upholds Shylock's bond. In all three cases the person in authority declares that he has no power to alter the law, and in all three cases he eventually does. As it turns out that Theseus is a fairly decent sort, we may like to rationalize this scene by assuming that he is probably going to talk privately with Egeus and Demetrius (as in fact he says he is) and work out a more humane solution. But he gives Hermia no loophole: he merely repeats the threats to her life and freedom. Then he adjourns the session:

> Come, my Hippolyta—what cheer, my love?
>
> [I. i. 122]

which seems a clear indication that Hippolyta, portrayed throughout the play as a person of great common sense, doesn't like the set-up at all.

We realize that sooner or later Lysander and Hermia will get out from under this law and be united in spite of Egeus. Demetrius and Helena, who are the doubling figures, are in an unresolved situation: Helena loves Demetrius, but Demetrius has only, in the Victorian phrase, trifled with her affections. In the second part we're in the fairy wood at night, where identities become, as we think, hopelessly confused. At dawn Theseus and Hippolyta, accompanied by Egeus, enter the wood to hunt. By that time the Demetrius-Helena situation has cleared up, and because of that Theseus feels able to overrule Egeus and allow the two marriages to go ahead. At the beginning Lysander remarks to Hermia that the authority of Athenian law doesn't extend as far as the wood, but apparently it does; Theseus is there, in full charge, and it is in the wood that he makes the decision that heads the play toward its happy ending. At the same time the solidifying of the Demetrius-Helena relationship was the work of Oberon. We can hardly avoid the feeling not only that Theseus is overruling Egeus's will, but that his own will has been overruled too, by fairies of whom he knows nothing and in whose existence he doesn't believe.

If we look at the grouping of characters in each of the three parts, this feeling becomes still stronger. In the opening scene we have Theseus, Egeus, and an unwilling Hippolyta in the centre, symbolizing parental authority and the inflexibility of law, with three of the four young people standing before them. Before long we meet the fourth, Helena. In the second part the characters are grouped in different places within the wood, for the most part separated from one another. In one part of the wood are the lovers; in another are the processions of the quarrelling king and queen of the fairies; in still another Peter Quince and his company are rehearsing their play. Finally the remaining group, Theseus, Hippolyta and Egeus, appear with the sunrise. In the first part no one doubts that Theseus is the supreme ruler over the court of Athens;

in the second part no one doubts that Oberon is king of the fairies and directs what goes on in the magic wood.

In the third and final part the characters, no longer separated from one another, are very symmetrically arranged. Peter Quince and his company are in the most unlikely spot, in the middle, and the centre of attention; around them sit Theseus and Hippolyta and the four now reconciled lovers. The play ends; Theseus calls for a retreat to bed, and then the fairies come in for the final blessing of the house, forming a circumference around all the others. They are there for the sake of Theseus and Hippolyta, but their presence suggests that Theseus is not as supremely the ruler of his own world as he seemed to be at first.

A Midsummer Night's Dream seems to be one of the relatively few plays that Shakespeare made up himself, without much help from sources. Two sources he did use were tragic stories that are turned into farce here. One was the story of Pyramus and Thisbe from Ovid, which the Quince company is attempting to tell, and which is used for more than just the Quince play. The other was Chaucer's *Knight's Tale,* from which Shakespeare evidently took the names of Theseus, Hippolyta and Philostrate, and which is a gorgeous but very sombre story of the fatal rivalry of two men over a woman. So far as this theme appears in the play, it is in the floundering of Lysander and Demetrius after first Hermia and then Helena, bemused with darkness and Puck's love drugs. [We know] of the relation of the original Pyramus and Thisbe story to *Romeo and Juliet,* and the theme of the *Knight's Tale* appears vestigially in that play too, in the fatal duel of Romeo and Paris. [We know] also of the role of the oxymoron as a figure of speech in *Romeo and Juliet,* the self-contradictory figure that's appropriate to a tragedy of love and death. That too appears as farce in this play, when Theseus reads the announcement of the Quince play:

> Merry and tragical? Tedious and brief?
> That is hot ice, and wondrous strange snow!
> How shall we find the concord of this discord?

> [V. i. 58-60]

Why is this play called *A Midsummer Night's Dream?* Apparently the main action in the fairy wood takes place on the eve of May Day; at any rate, when Theseus and Hippolyta enter with the rising sun, they discover the four lovers, and Theseus says:

> No doubt they rose up early to observe
> The rite of May.

> [IV. i. 132-33]

We call the time of the summer solstice, in the third week of June, "midsummer," although in our calendars it's the beginning of summer. That's because originally there were only three seasons,

summer, autumn and winter: summer then included spring and began in March. A thirteenth-century song begins "sumer is i-cumen in," generally modernized, to keep the metre, as "summer is a-coming in," but it doesn't mean that: it means "spring is here." The Christian calendar finally established the celebration of the birth of Christ at the winter solstice, and made a summer solstice date (June 24) the feast day of John the Baptist. This arrangement, according to the Fathers, symbolized John's remark in the Gospels on beholding Christ: "He must increase, but I must decrease." Christmas Eve was a beneficent time, when evil spirits had no power; St. John's Eve was perhaps more ambiguous, and there was a common phrase, "midsummer madness," used by Olivia in *Twelfth Night,* a play named after the opposite end of the year. Still, it was a time when spirits of nature, whether benevolent or malignant, might be supposed to be abroad.

There were also two other haunted "eves," of the first of November and of the first of May. These take us back to a still earlier time, when animals were brought in from the pasture at the beginning of winter, with a slaughter of those that couldn't be kept to feed, and when they were let out again at the beginning of spring. The first of these survives in our Hallowe'en, but May Day eve is no longer thought of much as a spooky time, although in Germany, where it was called "Walpurgis night," the tradition that witches held an assembly on a mountain at that time lasted much longer, and comes into Goethe's *Faust.* In *Faust* the scene with the witches is followed by something called "The Golden Wedding of Oberon and Titania," which has nothing to do with Shakespeare's play, but perhaps indicates a connection in Goethe's mind between it and the first of May.

In Shakespeare's time, as Theseus's remark indicates, the main emphasis on the first of May fell on a sunrise service greeting the day with songs. All the emphasis was on hope and cheerfulness. Shakespeare evidently doesn't want to force a specific date on us: it may be May Day eve, but all we can be sure of is that it's later than St. Valentine's Day in mid-February, the day when traditionally the birds start copulating, and we could have guessed that anyway. The general idea is that we have gone through the kind of night when spirits are powerful but not necessarily malevolent. Evil spirits, as we learn from the opening scene of *Hamlet,* are forced to disappear at dawn, and the fact that this is also true of the Ghost of Hamlet's father sows a terrible doubt in Hamlet's mind. Here we have Puck, or more accurately Robin Goodfellow *the* puck. Pucks were a category of spirits who were often sinister, and the Puck of this play is clearly mischievous. But we are expressly told by Oberon that the fairies of whom he's the king are "spirits of another sort" [III. ii. 388], not evil and not restricted to darkness.

So the title of the play simply emphasizes the difference between the two worlds of the action, the waking world of Theseus's court and the fairy world of Oberon. Let's go back to the three parts of the comic action: the opening situation hostile to true love, the middle part of dissolving identities, and the final resolution. The first part contains a threat of possible death to Hermia. Similar threats are found in other Shakespeare comedies: in *The Comedy of Errors* a death sentence hangs over a central character until nearly the end of the play. This comic structure fits inside a pattern of death, disappearance and return that's far wider in scope than theatrical comedy. We find it even in the central story of Christianity, with its Friday of death, Saturday of disappearance and Sunday of return. Scholars who have studied this pattern in religion, mythology and legend think it derives from observing the moon waning, then disappearing, then reappearing as a new moon.

At the opening Theseus and Hippolyta have agreed to hold their wedding at the next new moon, now four days off. They speak of four days, although the rhetorical structure runs in threes: Hippolyta is wooed, won and wed "With pomp, with triumph and with revelling" [I. i. 19]. (This reading depends also on a reasonable, if not certain, emendation: "new" for "now" in the tenth line.) Theseus compares his impatience to the comedy situation of a young man waiting for someone older to die and leave him money. The Quince company discover from an almanac that there will be moonshine on the night that they will be performing, but apparently there is not enough, and so they introduce a character called Moonshine. His appearance touches off a very curious reprise of the opening dialogue. Hippolyta says "I am aweary of this moon: would he would change!" [V. i. 251], and Theseus answers that he seems to be on the wane, "but yet, in courtesy . . . we must stay the time" [V. i. 254-55]. It's as though this ghastly play contains in miniature, and caricature, the themes of separation, postponement, and confusions of reality and fantasy that have organized the play surrounding it.

According to the indications in the text, the night in the wood should be a moonless night, but in fact there are so many references to the moon that it seems to be still there, even though obscured by clouds. It seems that this wood is a fairyland with its own laws of time and space, a world where Oberon has just blown in from India and where Puck can put a girdle round the earth in forty minutes. So it's not hard to accept such a world as an antipodal one, like the world of dreams itself, which, although we make it fit into our waking-time schedules, still keeps to its own quite different rhythms. A curious image of Hermia's involving the moon has echoes of this; she's protesting that she will never believe Lysander unfaithful:

> I'll believe as soon
> This whole earth may be bored, and that the moon
> May through the centre creep, and so displease
> Her brother's noontide with th'Antipodes.
> [III. ii. 52-5]

A modern reader might think of the opening of "The Walrus and the Carpenter." The moon, in any case, seems to have a good deal to do with both worlds. In the opening scene Lysander speaks of Demetrius as "this spotted and inconstant man" [I. i. 110], using two common epithets for the moon, and in the last act Theseus speaks of "the lunatic, the lover and the poet" [V. i. 7], where "lunatic" has its full Elizabethan force of "moonstruck."

The inhabitants of the wood-world are the creatures of legend and folk tale and mythology and abandoned belief. Theseus regards them as projections of the human imagination, and as having a purely subjective existence. The trouble is that we don't know the extent of our own minds, or what's in that mental world that we half create and half perceive . . . The tiny fairies that wait on Bottom—Mustardseed and Peaseblossom and the rest—come from Celtic fairy lore, as does the Queen Mab of Mercutio's speech [in *Romeo and Juliet*], who also had tiny fairies in her train. Robin Goodfellow is more Anglo-Saxon and Teutonic. His propitiatory name, "Goodfellow," indicates that he could be dangerous, and his fairy friend says that one of his amusements is to "Mislead night-wanderers, laughing at their harm" [II. i. 39]. A famous book a little later than Shakespeare, Robert Burton's *Anatomy of Melancholy,* mentions fire spirits who mislead travellers with illusions, and says "We commonly call them pucks." The fairy world clearly would not do as a democracy: there has to be a king in charge like Oberon, who will see that Puck's rather primitive sense of humour doesn't get too far out of line.

The gods and other beings of Classical mythology belong in the same half-subjective, half-autonomous world. I've spoken of the popularity of Ovid's *Metamorphoses* for poets: this, in Ovid's opening words, is a collection of stories of "bodies changed to new forms." Another famous Classical metamorphosis is the story of Apuleius about a man turned into an ass by enchantment, and of course this theme enters the present play when Bottom is, as Quince says, "translated." In Classical mythology one central figure was the goddess that Robert Graves, . . . calls the "white goddess" or the "triple will." This goddess had three forms: one in heaven, where she was the goddess of the moon and was called Phoebe or Cynthia or Luna; one on earth, where she was Diana, the virgin huntress of the forest, called Titania once in Ovid; and one below the earth, where she was the witch-goddess Hecate. Puck speaks of "Hecate's triple team" at the end of the play. References to Diana and Cynthia by the poets of the time usually involved some allusion to the virgin queen Elizabeth (they always ignored Hecate in such contexts). As I said, the Queen seems to be alluded to here, but in a way that kicks her upstairs, so to speak: she's on a level far above all the "lunatic" goings-on below.

Titania in this play is not Diana: Diana and her moon are in Theseus's world, and stand for the sterility that awaits Hermia if she disobeys her father, when she will have to become Diana's nun, "Chanting faint hymns to the cold fruitless moon" [I. i. 73]. The wood of this play is erotic, not virginal: Puck is contemptuous of Lysander's lying so far away from Hermia, not realizing that this was just Hermia being maidenly. According to Oberon, Cupid was an inhabitant of this wood, and had shot his erotic arrow at the "imperial votaress," but it glanced off her and fell on a white flower, turning it red. The parabola taken by this arrow outlines the play's world, so to speak: the action takes place under this red and white arch. One common type of Classical myth deals with a "dying god," as he's called now, a male figure who is killed when still a youth, and whose blood stains a white flower and turns it red or purple. Shakespeare had written the story of one of these gods in his narrative poem *Venus and Adonis,* where he makes a good deal of the stained flower:

> No flower was nigh, no grass, herb, leaf, or
>   weed,
> But stole his blood and seem'd with him to
>   bleed.
>
>   [1055-56]

The story of Pyramus and Thisbe is another such story: Pyramus's blood stains the mulberry and turns it red. In Ovid's account, when Pyramus stabs himself the blood spurts out in an arc on the flower. This may be where Shakespeare got the image that he puts to such very different use.

Early in the play we come upon Oberon and Titania quarrelling over the custody of a human boy, and we are told that because of their quarrel the weather has been unusually foul. The implication is that the fairies are spirits of the elements, and that nature and human life are related in many ways that are hidden from ordinary consciousness. But it seems clear that Titania does not have the authority that she thinks she has: Oberon puts her under the spell of having to fall in love with Bottom with his ass's head, and rescues the boy for his own male entourage. There are other signs that Titania is a possessive and entangling spirit—she says to Bottom:

> Out of this wood do not desire to go;
> Thou shalt remain here, whether thou
>   wilt or no.
>
>   [III. i. 152-53]

The relationship of Oberon and Titania forms a counterpoint with that of Theseus and Hippolyta in the other world. It appears that Titania has been a kind of guardian spirit to Hippolyta and Oberon to Theseus. Theseus gives every sign of settling down into a solidly married man, now that he has subdued the most formidable woman in the world, the Queen of the Amazons. But his record before that was a very bad one, with rapes and desertions in it: even as late as T.S. Eliot we read about his "perjured sails." Oberon blames his waywardness on Titania's influence, and Titania's denial does not sound very convincing. Oberon's ascendancy over Titania, and Theseus's over Hippolyta, seem to symbolize some aspect of the emerging comic resolution.

Each world has a kind of music, or perhaps rather "harmony," that is characteristic of it. That of the fairy wood is represented by the song of the mermaid described by Oberon to Puck. This is a music that commands the elements of the "sublunary" world below the moon; it quiets the sea, but there is a hint of a lurking danger in it, a siren's magic call that draws some of the stars out of their proper spheres in heaven, as witches according to tradition can call down the moon. There is danger everywhere in that world for mortals who stay there too long and listen to too much of its music. When the sun rises and Theseus and Hippolyta enter the wood, they talk about the noise of hounds in this and other huntings. Hippolyta says:

> never did I hear
> Such gallant chiding; for, besides the
>   groves,
> The Skies, the fountains, every region
>   near
> Seem'd all one mutual cry; I never heard
> So musical a discord, such sweet thunder.
>
>   [IV. i. 114-18]

It would not occur to us to describe a cry of hounds as a kind of symphony orchestra, but then we do not have the mystique of a Renaissance prince about hunting. Both forms of music fall far short of the supreme harmony of the spheres described in the fifth act of *The Merchant of Venice:* Oberon might know something about that, but not Puck, who can't see the "imperial votaress." Neither, probably, could Theseus.

So the wood-world has affinities with what we call the unconscious or subconscious part of the mind: a part below the reason's encounter with objective reality, and yet connected with the hidden creative powers of the mind. Left to Puck or even Titania, it's a world of illusion, random desires and shifting identities. With Oberon in charge, it becomes the world in which those profound choices are made that decide the course of life, and also . . . the world from which inspiration comes to the poet. The lovers wake up still dazed with metamorphosis; as Demetrius says:

> These things seem small and undistin-
>   guishable,

Like far-off mountains turned into clouds.
[IV. i. 186-87]

But the comic crystallization has taken place, and for the fifth act we go back to Theseus's court to sort out the various things that have come out of the wood.

Theseus takes a very rational and common-sense view of the lovers' story, but he makes it clear that the world of the wood is the world of the poet as well as the lover and the lunatic. His very remarkable speech uses the words "apprehend" and "comprehend" each twice. In the ordinary world we apprehend with our senses and comprehend with our reason; what the poet apprehends are moods or emotions, like joy, and what he uses for comprehension is some story or character to account for the emotion:

Such tricks hath strong imagination,
That if it would but apprehend some joy,
It comprehends some bringer of that joy
[V. i. 18-20]

Theseus is here using the word "imagination" in its common Elizabethan meaning, which we express by the word "imaginary," something alleged to be that isn't. In spite of himself, though, the word is taking on the more positive sense of our "imaginative," the sense of the creative power developed centuries later by [William] Blake and [Samuel Taylor] Coleridge. So far as I can make out from the *OED* [*Oxford English Dictionary*], this more positive sense of the word in English practically begins here. Hippolyta is shrewder and less defensive than Theseus, and what she says takes us a great deal further:

But all the story of the night, told over,
And all their minds transfigur'd so together,
More witnesseth than fancy's images,
And grows to something of great constancy;
But howsoever, strange and admirable.
[V. i. 23-7]

Theseus doesn't believe their story, but Hippolyta sees that something has happened to them, whatever their story. The word "transfigured" means that there can be metamorphosis upward as well as downward, a creative transforming into a higher consciousness as well as the reduction from the conscious to the unconscious that we read about in Ovid. Besides, the story has a consistency to it that doesn't sound like the disjointed snatches of incoherent minds. If you want disjointing and incoherence, just listen to the play that's coming up. And yet the Quince play is a triumph of sanity in its way: it tells you that the roaring lion is only Snug the joiner, for example. It's practically a parody of Theseus's view of reality, with its "imagination" that takes a bush for a bear in the dark. There's a later exchange when Hippolyta complains that the play is silly, and Theseus says:

The best in this kind are but shadows; and the worst are no worse, if imagination amend them
[V. i. 211-12]

Hippolyta retorts: "It must be your imagination, then, and not theirs." Here "imagination" has definitely swung over to meaning something positive and creative. What Hippolyta says implies that the audience has a creative role in every play; that's one reason why Puck, coming out for the Epilogue when the audience is supposed to applaud, repeats two of Theseus's words:

If we shadows have offended,
Think but this, and all is mended.
[V. i. 423-24]

Theseus's imagination has "amended" the Quince play by accepting it, listening to it, and not making fun of the actors to their faces. Its merit as a play consists in dramatizing his own social position and improving what we'd now call his "image" as a gracious prince. In itself the play has no merit, except in being unintentionally funny. And if it has no merit, it has no authority. A play that did have authority, and depended on a poet's imagination as well, would raise the question that Theseus's remark seems to deny: the question of the difference between plays by Peter Quince and plays by William Shakespeare. Theseus would recognize the difference, of course, but in its social context, as an offering for his attention and applause, a Shakespeare play would be in the same position as the Quince play. That indicates how limited Theseus's world is, in the long run, a fact symbolized by his not knowing how much of his behaviour is guided by Oberon.

Which brings me to Bottom, the only mortal in the play who actually sees any of the fairies. One of the last things Bottom says in the play is rather puzzling: "the wall is down that parted their fathers" [V. i. 351]. Apparently he means the wall separating the hostile families of Pyramus and Thisbe. This wall seems to have attracted attention: after Snout the tinker, taking the part of Wall, leaves the stage, Theseus says, according to the Folio: "Now is the morall downe between the two neighbours" [cf. V. i. 207]. The New Arden editor reads "mural down," and other editors simply change to "wall down." The Quarto, just to be helpful, reads "moon used." Wall and Moonshine between them certainly confuse an already confused play. One wonders if the wall between the two worlds of Theseus and Oberon, the wall that Theseus is so sure is firmly in place, doesn't throw a shadow on these remarks.

Anyway, Bottom wakes up along with the lovers and makes one of the most extraordinary speeches in Shakespeare, which includes a very scrambled but still recognizable echo from the New Testament, and finally says he will get Peter Quince to write a ballad of his dream, and "it shall be called Bottom's Dream, because it hath no bottom" [IV.

i. 215–16]. Like most of what Bottom says, this is absurd; like many absurdities in Shakespeare, it makes a lot of sense. Bottom does not know that he is anticipating by three centuries a remark of Freud: "every dream has a point at which it is unfathomable; a link, as it were, with the unknown." When we come to *King Lear,* we shall suspect that it takes a madman to see into the heart of tragedy, and perhaps it takes a fool or clown, who habitually breathes the atmosphere of absurdity and paradox, to see into the heart of comedy. "Man," says Bottom, "is but an ass, if he go about to expound this dream" [IV. i. 206-07]. But it was Bottom the ass who had the dream, not Bottom the weaver, who is already forgetting it. He will never see his Titania again, nor even remember that she had once loved him, or doted on him, to use Friar Laurence's distinction [in *Romeo and Juliet*]. But he has been closer to the centre of this wonderful and mysterious play than any other of its characters, and it no longer matters that Puck thinks him a fool or that Titania loathes his asinine face. (pp. 34-50)

> Northrop Frye, "A Midsummer Night's Dream," in his Northrop Frye on Shakespeare, *edited by Robert Sandler, Yale University Press, 1986, pp. 34-50.*

Frances A. Yates

> [*Yates discusses the origins of Shakespeare's fairy world, arguing that the "Elizabethan fairies are not . . . manifestations of folk or popular tradition." According to this critic, the characters inhabiting the dream world of Shakespeare's play stem from either Arthurian legend or the Christian variant of Cabala, a Jewish interpretation of the Scriptures based on the mystical value of words. In her further discussion of* A Midsummer Night's Dream *Yates focuses on the "imperial theme," explaining that the poet's references to an "imperial votaress" who resists Cupid's arrows should be viewed in the context of a cult of Queen Elizabeth I. According to Yates, Shakespeare pictures Elizabeth as a Vestal Virgin whose triumph over Cupid affirms her exalted status.*]

Shakespearean fairies are related to the Fairy Queen [in Edmund Spenser's *The Faerie Queen*] through their loyalty and through their fervent defence of chastity. . . . They are defenders of chastity, of a chaste queen and her pure knighthood. They are enjoined to perform a white magic to safeguard her and her order of knighthood from evil influences.

These Elizabethan fairies are not, I believe, manifestations of folk or popular tradition. Their origins are literary and religious, in Arthurian legend and in the white magic of Christian Cabala. The use of fairy imagery in the queen cult was begun in the Accession Day Tilts [jousts], and relates to the chivalric imagery of the Tilts. As taken up by Spenser in *The Faerie Queene,* the fairy imagery was Arthurian and chivalric, and also an expression of pure white magic, a Christian Cabalist magic.

The Shakespearean fairies emanate from a similar atmosphere; they glorify a pure knighthood serving the queen and her imperial reform. To read Shakespeare's fairy scenes without reference to the contemporary build-up of the Virgin Queen as the representative of pure religion is to miss their purpose as an affirmation of adherence to the Spenserian point of view, a very serious purpose disguised in fantasy.

The supreme expression of the Shakespearean fairyland is *A Midsummer Night's Dream.* This play was first printed in 1600; it was probably written for a private performance at a wedding, perhaps in 1595 or thereabouts.

This magical play about enchanted lovers is set in a world of night and moonlight, where fairies serve a fairy king and queen. Into the magic texture is woven a significant portrait of Queen Elizabeth I.

Vivien Leigh as Titania in a 1937 Old Vic Theatre production of A Midsummer Night's Dream.

Oberon, the fairy king, describes how he once saw Cupid, all armed, flying between the cold moon and the earth:

> A certain aim he took
> At a fair vestal, throned by the West
> And loos'd his love shaft smartly from his bow,
> As it should pierce a hundred thousand hearts.
> But I might see young Cupid's fiery shaft
> Quench'd in the chaste beams of the wat'ry moon,
> And the imperial votaress passed on,
> In maiden meditation, fancy free.
>   [II. i. 157-64]

Shakespeare's picture of Elizabeth as a Vestal Virgin, a chaste Moon who defeats the assaults of Cupid, an 'imperial votaress', is a brilliant summing up of the cult of Elizabeth as the representative of imperial reform. A well-known portrait of Elizabeth presents the imagery in visual form. Elizabeth holds a sieve, emblem of the chastity of a Vestal Virgin; behind her rises the column of empire; the globe beside her shows the British Isles surrounded by shipping, alluding to her enthronement 'in the West'. It is a portrait of the Virgin of imperial reform, of which Shakespeare gives a verbal picture in the lines just quoted, using the same imagery. (pp. 148-49)

[Both] the 'Sieve' portrait and Shakespeare's word-picture in the *Dream* are Triumphs of Chastity . . . and the triumph refers both to purity in public life and in private life, to Elizabeth both in her public role as the representative of pure imperial reform, and in her private role as a chaste lady. It is exactly in such a role that Spenser presents Elizabeth, so he tells Raleigh in the letter to him published with *The Faerie Queene*. As Gloriana she is a most royal queen or empress, as Belphoebe she is a most chaste and beautiful lady. Shakespeare's word-picture presents Gloriana-Belphoebe, the Virgin of pure Empire, enthroned by the West, the chaste lady who triumphs over Cupid.

The appearance in the sky of the *Dream* of this Spenserian vision strikes the key-note of the magical-musical moonlight of the play. The moon is Cynthia, the Virgin Queen, and the words 'the chaste beams of the watery moon' might also allude to Walter Raleigh's cult of her as Cynthia. Puns on 'Walter', pronounced 'Water', were usual in referring to Raleigh. Spenser was following Raleigh, so he says, in the 'Luna' book of *The Faerie Queene*. Hence the allusions of the Shakespearean lines would be both to Elizabeth as Spenser's Gloriana-Belphoebe, and also to Raleigh's cult of her as Cynthia, adopted by Spenser.

Thus the complex phenomenon which floats in the night sky of the *Dream* relates the play to the Spenserian dream-world, the Spenserian magical cult of the Imperial Virgin, with its undercurrent of Christian Cabala. (pp. 149-50)

> *Frances A. Yates, "Shakespearean Fairies, Witches, Melancholy: King Lear and the Demons," in her* The Occult Philosophy in the Elizabethan Age, 1979. *Reprint by Ark Paperbacks, 1983, pp. 147-57.*

BOTTOM

J. B. Priestley

[*Priestley identifies* **Bottom** *as "the most substantial figure" in* A Midsummer Night's Dream, *describing him as earthy, quick-witted, and emphasizing his ability to laugh at the inhabitants of the fairy world.* **Bottom**'s *humor, Priestley asserts, is not fully conscious; rather, he symbolizes a peculiarly English variety of a man of the people: ignorant, uncouth, but a brilliantly perceptive and profound humorist, ever ready to castigate the foibles of his fellow human beings, or, for that matter, supernatural creatures.* **Bottom,** *the critic remarks, is also a kind of comical everyman, a character symbolizing the irrepressible comical genius of humankind. Finally, he is also a poet, "wearing the head of an ass (as we all must do at such moments), the beloved of an exquisite immortal . . . coming to an hour's enchantment while the moon climbs a hand's breadth up the sky—and then, all 'stolen hence,' the dream done and the dream left to wonder."* **Bottom**'s *journey through the supernatural realm epitomizes "the destiny of poets, who are themselves also weavers." For further commentary on* **Bottom**'s *character, see the excerpts by Wolfgang Clemen, Jack A. Vaughn, Jan Kott, George A. Bonnard, Mark Van Doren, and Northrop Frye.*]

On any reasonable chronology of Shakespeare's plays, Bottom is the first of his great comic figures. Once we are through the door of Peter Quince's house, when all the company is assembled there, we are at last in the presence of one of the foolish Immortals; we come to celebrate a staggering feat of parturition, for here, newly created, is a droll as big as a hill. Before this, Shakespeare has shown us through a little gallery of amusing figures, but we have seen no one of the stature of "sweet bully Bottom" [IV. ii. 19]. In *The Comedy of Errors*, the two Dromios and the rest are nothing but odd curves in a whimsical design. The comedians of *Love's Labour's Lost* are well enough in their way; the picked and spruce Don Armado, Holofernes with his "golden cadence of poesy" [*Love's Labour's Lost*, IV. ii. 122], Sir Nathaniel and Moth, all capping one another's fantastic phrases; but they are little more than quaint shadows that caper for an hour or so on the sunlit lawns of that park in Navarre and then flit out of mind when the sun goes down. In *The Two Gentlemen of Verona,* Speed and Launce (and the dog) are not so much individual creations as lively examples of an admired formula for comic relief, the Elizabethan equivalents of our crosstalk red-nosed gentry. Bottom is neither a curve nor a shadow nor a formula, but a gigantic individual creation, the first of the really great comic figures. (pp. 1-2)

Bottom is easily the most substantial figure in the piece. This is not saying a great deal, because *A Midsummer Night's Dream* has all the character of a dream; its action is ruled by caprice and moonlit madness; its personages appear to be under the spell of visions or to walk and talk in their sleep; its background is shadowy and shifting, sometimes breaking into absolute loveliness, purple and dark green and heavy with the night scent of flowers, but always something broken, inconsequent, suddenly glimpsed as the moon's radiance frees itself for a little space from cloud and foliage; and the whole play, with its frequent talk of visions, dreams, imagination, antique fables and fairy toys, glides past like some lovely hallucination, a masque of strange shadows and voices heard in the night. The characters are on three different levels. There are first the immortals, who have nothing earthy in their composition and are hardly to be distinguished from the quivering leaves and the mist of hyacinths, tiny creatures spun out of cobwebs and moonshine. Then there are the wandering lovers, all poetry and imagination, driven hither and thither by their passionate moods. Lastly there is Bottom (and with him, of course, his companions), who is neither a flickering elf nor a bewildered passionate lover, but a man of this world, comfortably housed in flesh, a personage of some note among the artisans of Athens and, we have no doubt, in spite of certain unmistakable signs of temperament in him, a worthy dependable householder. We suspect that he has, somewhere in the background, a shrewish wife who spends her time alternately seeing through her husband and being taken in by him, for he is essentially one of those large, heavy-faced, somewhat vain and patronising men, not without either humour or imagination, who always induce in women alternating moods of irritation and adoration. Among his fellow artisans, Bottom is clearly the ladies' man, the gallant. He it is who shows himself sensitive to the delicacy of the sex in the matter of the killing and the lion, and we feel that his insistence upon a prologue, "a device to make all well" [III. i. 16], is only the result of his delicacy and chivalry. Snout and Starveling, who hasten to agree with him, are simply a pair of whimpering poltroons, who have really no stomach for swords and killing and raging melodrama and are afraid of the consequences if they should startle the audience. But Bottom, we feel, has true sensibility and in his own company is the champion of the sex; he

knows that it is a most dreadful thing to bring in the lion, that most fearful wild-fowl, among ladies, and his sketch of the prologue has in it the true note of artful entreaty: *"Ladies,* or, *Fair Ladies,—I would wish you,—*or, *I would request you,—*or, *I would entreat you,—not to fear, not to tremble: my life for yours* [III. i. 39–42]". Such a speech points to both knowledge of the sex and long practice, and given friendly circumstances, the speaker might be a very dangerous man. We should like to see Bottom making love among his own kind; the result would have startled some of his critics. As it is, we only see him, crowned with an ass's head, suddenly transformed into the paramour of the queen of the fairies, and even in a situation so unexpected, so remote from his previous experience, he acquits himself, as we shall see, very creditably. What would happen if one of the gentlemen who call friend Bottom "gross, stupid, and ignorant," let us say the average professor of English literature, suddenly found himself in the arms of a very beautiful and very amorous fairy, even if his head were not discoverable by immediate sight but only by long acquaintance to be that of an ass? He would probably acquit himself no better than would Snout or Starveling in similar circumstances, and Shakespeare took care to wave away his Snouts and Starvelings and called the one man to that strange destiny, that "most rare vision" [IV. i. 205], who was worthy of the occasion. Bottom, as [William] Hazlitt said, is a character that has not had justice done him: he is "the most romantic of mechanics."

Against the background of the whole play, which is only so much gossamer and moonlight, the honest weaver appears anything but romantic, a piece of humorous, bewildered flesh, gross, earthy. He is a trades-unionist among butterflies, a ratepayer in Elfland. Seen thus, he is droll precisely because he is a most prosaic soul called to a most romantic destiny. But if we view him first among his own associates, we shall see that he is the only one of them who was fit to be "translated." Puck, who was responsible for the transformation, described him as "the shallowest thickskin of that barren sort" [III. ii. 13], the biggest fool in a company of fools; but Puck was no judge of character. Bottom, though he may be the biggest fool (and a big fool is no common person), is really the least shallow and thickskinned of his group, in which he shows up as the romantic, the poetical, the imaginative man, who naturally takes command. We admit that he is conceited, but he is, in some measure, an artist, and artists are notoriously conceited. The company of such tailoring and bellows-mending souls would make any man of spirit conceited. Old Quince, who obviously owes his promotion to seniority and to nothing else, is nominally in charge of the revels, but the players have scarcely met together and Quince has scarcely had time to speak a word before it is clear that Bottom, and Bottom alone, is the leader. Quince ("Good Peter Quince"

[I. ii. 8], as Bottom, with easy contempt and patronage, calls him) is nothing but a tool in the hands of the masterful weaver, who directs the whole proceedings, the calling of the roll of players, the description of the piece, the casting of the parts, and so forth, step by step. The other members of the company not having a glimmer of imagination, the artist among them, the man of temperament, takes charge. And he alone shows any enthusiasm for the drama itself, for the others are only concerned with pleasing the Duke; if they do badly, if they should, for example, frighten the ladies, they may be hanged, whereas if they do well, they may receive a little pension. (pp. 2-6)

When the players are first met together and the parts are being given out, it is not just Bottom's conceit that makes him want to play every part himself. Of all those present, he is the only one who shows any passion for the drama itself, the art of acting, the enthralling business of moving and thrilling an audience. The others are only concerned with getting through their several tasks in the easiest and safest manner, with one eye on the hangman and the other on the exchequer. But the creative artist is stirring in the soul of Bottom; his imagination is catching fire; so that no sooner is a part mentioned than he can see himself playing it, and playing it in such a manner as to lift the audience out of their seats. He is set down for the principal part, that of the lover, but no sooner has he accepted it, seeing himself condoling and moving storms ("That will ask some tears in the true performing of it: if I do it, let the audience look to their eyes; I will move storms, I will condole in some measure" [I. ii. 25-8]), than he regrets that he cannot play a tyrant, for he is familiar with Ercles' vein and even shows the company how he would deal with it. Then when Thisbe is mentioned, he sees himself playing her too, speaking in a monstrous little voice. The lion is the next part of any importance, and though it consists of nothing but roaring, Bottom has no doubt that he could make a success of that too, by means of a roar that would do any man's heart good to hear it, or, failing that, if such a full-blooded performance should scare the ladies, a delicately modulated roar that would not shame either a suckling dove or a nightingale. Even when he is finally restricted to one part, that of Pyramus, he alone shows an eagerness to come to grips with the details of the part, particularly in the matter of beards, undertaking as he does "to discharge it in either your straw-colour beard, your orange-tawny beard, your purple-in-grain beard, or your French-crown-colour beard, your perfect yellow" [I. ii. 93-6]. All this shows the eagerness and the soaring imagination of the artist, and if it shows too an unusual vanity, a confidence in one's ability to play any number of parts better than any one else could play them, a confidence so gigantic that it becomes ridiculous, it must be remembered that vanity and a soaring imagination are generally inseparable. It is clear that a man cannot play every

part, cannot be lover, tyrant, lady, and lion at once; but it is equally clear that every man of imagination and spirit ought to want to play every part. It is better to be vain, like Bottom, than to be dead in the spirit, like Snug or Starveling. If it is a weakness to desire to play lover, lady, and lion, it is a weakness of great men, of choice, fiery, and fantastic souls who cannot easily realise or submit to the limitations pressing about our puny mortality. The whole scene, with our friend, flushed and triumphant, the centre of it, is droll, of course, but we really find it droll because we are being allowed to survey it from a height and know that the whole matter is ridiculous and contemptible. These fellows, we can see, should never have left their benches to follow the Muses. But to the gods, the spectacle of Bottom, soaring and magnificent, trying to grasp every part, would be no more ridiculous than the spectacle of Wagner perspiring and gesticulating at Bayreuth: they are both artists, children of vanity and vision, and are both ridiculous and sublime. We can see how droll Bottom is throughout this scene because Shakespeare, having seated us among the gods, has invited us to remark the droll aspects of the situation; but to Flute and Starveling Bottom is a man to be admired and wondered at, and probably to Flute's eldest son (that promising young bellows-mender), to whom he has condescended on one or two occasions, our droll weaver is the greatest man in the world, a hero and an artist, in short, a Wagner. We have but to seat ourselves again among the gods to see that "the best in this kind are but shadows" [V. i. 211], at once droll, heroic, and pitiful, capering for a little space between darkness and darkness.

Once Bottom is metamorphosed, we no longer see him against the background of his fellow artisans but see him firmly set in the lovely moonlit world of the elves and fays, a world so delicate that honey-bags stolen from the bees serve for sweetmeats and the wings of painted butterflies pass for fans, and here among such airy creatures, Bottom, of course, is first glimpsed as something monstrous, gross, earthy. It would be bad enough even if he were there in his own proper person, but he is wearing an ass's head and presents to us the figure of a kind of comic monster. Moreover, he is loved at first sight by the beautiful Titania, who, with the frankness of an immortal, does not scruple to tell him so as soon as her eyes, peering through enchantments, are open. A man may have the best wit and the best person of any handicraftsman in Athens and yet shrink from the wizardries of such a night, being compelled to wear the head of an ass, deserted by his companions, conjured into fairyland, bewilderingly promoted into the paramour of the fairy queen and made the master of such elvish and microscopic attendants as Peas-blossom and Cobweb and Moth. But Bottom, as we have said, rises to the occasion, ass's head and all; not only does he not shrink and turn tail, not only does he accept the situation, he contrives to carry it off with an air; he not only rises to the occasion, he improves it. Now that all the whimsies under the midsummer moon are let loose and wild imagination has life dancing to its tune, this is not the time for the Bottom we have already seen, the imaginative, temperamental man, to come forward and dominate the scene, or else all hold upon reality is lost; that former Bottom must be kept in check, left to wonder and perhaps to play over to himself the lover and the lion; this is the moment for that other, honest Nick Bottom the weaver, the plain man who is something of a humorist, good solid flesh among all such flimsies and whimsies, madness and moonshine. Does the newly awakened lovely creature immediately confess that she is enamoured of him, then he carries it off bravely, with a mingled touch of wit, philosophy, and masculine complacency: "Methinks, mistress, you should have little reason for that: and yet, to say the truth, reason and love keep little company together now-a-days; the more the pity that some honest neighbours will not make them friends. Nay, I can gleek upon occasion" [III. i. 142-46]. And we can see the ass's head tilted towards the overhanging branches, as he gives a guffaw at his "gleeking" and takes a strutting turn or two before this astonishing new mistress.

But nothing takes him by surprise in this sudden advancement. His tone is humorous and condescending, that of a solid complacent male among feminine fripperies. When his strange little servitors are introduced to him, the Duke himself could not carry it off better: "I shall desire you of more acquaintance, good Master Cobweb: if I cut my finger, I shall make bold with you"—then turning regally to the next: "Your name, honest gentleman?" Good Master Mustard-seed is commiserated with because "that same cowardly, giantlike ox-beef hath devoured many a gentleman of your House" [III. i. 182-93]: all are noticed and dispatched with the appropriate word; it is like a parody of an official reception. In the next scene, we discover him even more at his ease than before, lolling magnificently, embraced by his lady and surrounded by his devoted attendants, who are being given their various duties. "Monsieur Cobweb, good monsieur"—and indeed there was probably something very Gallic about this Cobweb—"get your weapons in your hand, and kill me a red-hipp'd humble-bee on the top of a thistle; and, good monsieur, bring me the honey-bag. Do not fret yourself too much in the action, monsieur; and, good monsieur, have a care the honey-bag break not. I would be loth to have you overflown with a honey-bag, signior" [IV. i. 10-16]. Bottom is clearly making himself at home in Elfland; he is beginning to display a certain fastidiousness, making delicate choice of a "red-hipp'd humble-bee on the top of a thistle." And if Puck won the first trick with the love philtre and the ass's head, we are not sure that Bottom is not now winning the second, for every time he addresses one of his attendants he is scoring off Elfland and

is proving himself a very waggish ass indeed. Even his remarks on the subject of music ("I have a reasonable good ear in music: let us have the tongs and the bones" [IV. i. 28-9]) and provender ("I could munch your good dry oats. Methinks I have a great desire to a bottle of hay: good hay, sweet hay, hath no fellow" [IV. i. 31-4]) have to our ears a certain consciously humorous smack, as if the speaker were not quite such an ass as he seems but were enjoying the situation in his own way, carrying the inimitable, if somewhat vulgar, manner of the great Bottom, pride of handicraftsmen, even into the heart of Faerie.

If he shows no surprise, however, and almost contrives to carry off the situation in the grand manner, we must remember that he, like Titania, is only dreaming beneath the moon-coloured honeysuckle and musk roses; the enamoured fairy and all her attendant sprites are to him only phantoms, bright from the playbox of the mind, there to be huddled away when a sudden puff of wind or a falling leaf brings the little drama to an end; and so he acts as we all act in dreams, who may ourselves be "translated" nightly by Puck and sent on the wildest adventures in elfin woods for all we know to the contrary. When Bottom awakes, yawning and stiff in the long grass, his sense of wonder blossoms gigantically, and the artist in him, he who would play the tyrant, the lover, the damsel, and the lion, leaps to life: "I have had a most rare vision. I have had a dream,—past the wit of man to say what dream it was: man is but an ass, if he go about to expound this dream" [IV. i. 204-07]. So fiery and eager is that wonder and poetry in him which all the long hours at Athenian looms have not been able to wither away, as he stands crying in ecstasy in the greenwood, that we cannot be surprised that his style, which he very rightly endeavours to heighten for the occasion, should break down under the stress of it: "The eye of man hath not heard, the ear of man hath not seen, man's hand is not able to taste, his tongue to conceive, nor his heart to report, what my dream was" [IV. i. 211-14]. But no matter; the dramatic enthusiast in him now takes command: Peter Quince (whom we did not suspect of authorship) shall write a ballad of this dream, to be called Bottom's Dream, and it shall be sung, by a newly resurrected Pyramus, at the end of the coming play; and off he goes, his head humming with plans, back to the town to put heart into his lads. There he plays Pyramus as Pyramus was never played before; takes charge of the whole company, does not scruple to answer a frivolous remark of the Duke's, and finally speaks the last word we hear from the handicraftsmen. We learn nothing more of him, but perhaps when the lovers were turning to their beds and the fairies were dancing in the glimmering light, Bottom, masterful, triumphant, was at Peter Quince's with the rest, sitting over a jug or two and setting his fellow players agape with his tale of the rare vision. There was a poet somewhere in this droll weaver and so he came to a poet's destiny, finding himself wearing the head of an ass (as we all must do at such moments), the beloved of an exquisite immortal, the master of Cobwebs and Peas-blossoms, coming to an hour's enchantment while the moon climbs a hand's-breadth up the sky—and then, all "stolen hence," the dream done and the dreamer left to wonder. Such is the destiny of poets, who are themselves also weavers.

It is a critical commonplace that these Athenian clowns are very English, just as the setting that frames them is exquisitely English; and it follows very naturally that the greatest of them is the most English. There is indeed no more insular figure in all Shakespeare's wide gallery than Bottom. A superficial examination of him will reveal all those traits that unfriendly critics of England and Englishmen have remarked for centuries. Thus, he is ignorant, conceited, domineering; he takes himself and his ridiculous concerns seriously and shows no lightness of touch; knowing perhaps the least, he yet talks the most, of all his company; he cannot understand that his strutting figure is the drollest sight under the sky, never for one instant realises that he is nothing but an ignorant buffoon; the soulless vulgarity of his conduct among the fairies smells rank in the nostrils of men of taste and delicacy of mind; in short, he is indeed the "shallowest thickskin of that barren sort" [III. ii. 13], lout-in-chief of a company of louts. But something more than a superficial examination will, as we have partly seen, dispose of much of this criticism, and will lead to the discovery in Bottom of traits that our friendly critics have remarked in us and that we ourselves know to be there. Bottom is very English in this, that he is something of a puzzle and an apparent contradiction. We have already marked the poetry and the artist in him, and we have only to stare at him a little longer to be in doubt about certain characteristics we took for granted. Is he entirely our butt or is he for at least part of the time solemnly taking us in and secretly laughing at us? Which of us has not visited some rural tap-room and found there, wedged in a corner, a large, round-faced, wide-mouthed fellow, the local oracle; and, having listened to some of his pronouncements, have laughed in our sleeves at his ignorance, dogmatism, and conceit; and yet, after staying a little longer and staring at the creature's large, solemn face, a face perilously close to vacuity, have noticed in it certain momentary twinkles and creases that have suddenly left us a little dubious about our hasty conclusions? And then it has dawned upon us that the fellow is, in his own way, which is not ours nor one to which we are accustomed, a humorist, and that somewhere behind that immobile and almost vacuous front, he has been enjoying us, laughing at us, just as we have been enjoying him and laughing at him. It is an experience that should make us pause before we pass judgment upon Bottom, who is the first cousin of all such queer characters, rich and ripe personages who are to be found, chiefly in hostelries but now and then carrying a bag of tools or flourishing a paint-brush, in almost every corner of this England, which is itself brimmed with puzzling contradictions, a strange mixture of the heavy butt and the conscious humorist. Bottom is worlds away from the fully conscious humour of a Falstaff, but we cannot have followed him from Peter Quince's house to the arms of Titania and seen him in Bank Holiday humour with his Cobwebs and Mustard-seeds, without noticing that he is something more than a rustic target. He is English, and he is conceited, ignorant, dogmatic, and asinine, but there stirs within him, as there does within his fellow workmen even now, a poet and humorist, waiting for the midsummer moon. And lastly, he is not dead, he has not left us, for I saw him myself, some years ago, and he had the rank of corporal and was gloriously at ease in a tumbledown estaminet near Amiens [in *As You Like It*], and there he was playing the tyrant, the lover, and the lion all at once, and Sergeant Quince and Privates Snug and Starveling were there with him. They were paying for his beer and I suspect that they were waiting, though obviously waiting in vain, to hear him cry once more: "Enough; hold or cut bow-strings" [I. ii. 111]. (pp. 8-19)

J. B. Priestley, "Bully Bottom," in his The English Comic Characters, 1925. Reprint by Dodd, Mead and Company, 1931, pp. 1-19.

THE LOVERS

Frederick S. Boas

[*Boas considers the various groups of lovers in* A Midsummer Night's Dream, *arguing that Shakespeare's characterization of the couples is more whimsical than serious. The critic first examines* **Theseus** *and* **Hippolyta**'s *relationship, maintaining that although the playwright illustrates* **Theseus** *as a brave soldier who wins* **Hippolyta** *with his sword, the Greek ruler ultimately displays a practicality that exhibits no grasp of aesthetic beauty. In addition, Boas notes that in contrast to the generally serene fortunes of* **Theseus** *and* **Hippolyta,** *the young lovers—* **Lysander, Hermia, Helena,** *and* **Demetrius**—*are "a troubled lot" due to their "purely human failings." The similarity of the characters' shortcomings, the critic continues, reflects an ambiguous interchangeability from one figure to the next that contributes to the confusion of the comic entanglement in the Athenian wood. According to Boas, another pair of lovers—* **Oberon** *and* **Titania**—*add a dimension of rivalry and jealousy to love and relationships in* A Midsummer Night's Dream. *The result of the fairy couples' quarreling, the critic condends, is* **Oberon**'s *"masterpiece of re-*

venge" when he magically transforms **Bottom** *into an ass and makes him the object of* **Titania**'s *affection. The critic also explores the "Pyramus and Thisbe" episode (Act V, scene i), asserting that the play-within-the-play not only parodies love relationships in* A Midsummer Night's Dream, *but also the stage conventions of Shakespeare's day.*]

In its main plot [*A Midsummer Night's Dream*] is akin to *The Comedy of Errors,* for in both cases a humorous entanglement is created out of mistakes. Already, however, Shakespere shows his extraordinary skill in devising variations upon a given theme, for here the mistakes are those of a night and not of a day, and instead of being external to the mind are internal. . . . As in *The Comedy of Errors,* also, the scene is nominally laid amid classical surroundings, but the whole atmosphere of the play is essentially English and Elizabethan.

Thus Theseus, whose marriage with Hippolyta forms the setting of the story, is no Athenian 'duke,' but a great Tudor noble. He is a brave soldier, who has wooed his bride with his sword, and, strenuous even in his pleasures, he is up with the dawn on May-morning, and out in the woods, that his love may hear the music of his hounds, 'matched in mouth like bells' [IV. i. 123], as they are uncoupled for the hunt. He is a true Tudor lord also in his taste for the drama, as shown in his request for masques and dances wherewith to celebrate his marriage. He exhibits the gracious spirit common to all Shakespeare's leaders of men in choosing, against the advice of his Master of the Revels, the entertainment prepared by Bottom and his fellows:

> I will hear that play
> For never anything can be amiss
> When simpleness and duty tender it;
> 　　　　　　　　　[V. i. 81-3]

and though tickled by the absurdities of the performance, he checks more than once the petulant criticisms of Hippolyta, and assures the actors at the close, with a courteous *double-entendre,* that their play has been 'very notably discharged' [V. I. 360-61]. But it has been urged that Theseus shows the limitations of nature which are found in Shakespere's men of action. Though dramatic performances serve to while away the time, even at their best they are to him 'but shadows,' and it is he who dismisses the tale of what the lovers have experienced in the wood as 'fairy toys,' and is thus led on to the famous declaration that

> The lunatic, the lover, and the poet
> Are of imagination all compact.
> 　　　　　　　　　[V. i. 7-8]

Only the practical common-sense Theseus, it has been said, would think of comparing the poet or lover to the lunatic, and Shakespere, by putting such words into his mouth, shows by a side-stroke that the man of action fails to appreciate the idealist nature. But such an inference from the passage is hazardous: there is a sense in which Theseus' statement is true, for the artist and the lover do collide, like the madman, with what 'cool reason' chooses to term the realities of life. The eloquent ring of the words is scarcely suggestive of dramatic irony, while the description of the poet's pen as giving to 'airy nothing a local habitation and a name' [V. i. 16-17], applies with curious exactness to Shakespere's own method in *A Midsummer Night's Dream.*

Contrasted with the serene fortunes of Theseus and Hippolyta is the troubled lot of humbler lovers, due, in its origin, to purely human failings. The fickle Demetrius has shifted his affections from Helena to Hermia, whose father Egeus favours the match, but Hermia is constant to Lysander, while Helena still 'dotes in idolatry' [I. i. 109] upon her inconstant wooer. The Athenian law as expounded by Theseus . . . enforces upon Hermia obedience to her father's wishes on pain of death or perpetual maidenhood. But Lysander suggests escape to a classical 'Gretna Green,' seven leagues from the town, where the sharp Athenian law does not run, and fixes a trysting-place for the following night within the neighbouring wood. That Hermia should reveal the secret to Helena, and that she in her turn should put Demetrius on the fugitive's track, merely to 'have his sight thither and back again' [I. i. 251], is a transparently clumsy device for concentrating the four lovers on a single spot, which betrays the hand of the immature playwright. Within the wood the power of human motive is suspended for that of enchantment, and at a touch of Puck's magic herb, Lysander and Demetrius are 'translated,' and ready to cross swords for the love of the erewhile flouted Helena. Thus all things befall preposterously, and reason holds as little sway over action as in a dream, though it is surely overstrained to find . . . a definitely allegorical significance in the comic entanglement, the more so that the dramatic execution is at this point somewhat crude. Lysander and Demetrius are little more than lay figures, and the only difference between Helena and Hermia is that the latter is shorter of stature, and has a vixenish temper, of which she gives a violent display in the unseemly quarrel scene. But at last, by Oberon's command Dian's bud undoes on the eyes of Lysander the work of Cupid's flower, and the close of the period of enchantment is broadly and effectively marked by the inrush at dawn of exuberant, palpable life in the shape of Theseus' hunting party, whose horns and 'halloes' reawaken the sleepers to everyday realities. But, as in *The Errors,* out of the confusions of the moment is born an abiding result. Demetrius is henceforward true to Helena: the caprice of magic has redressed the caprice of passion, and the lovers return to Athens 'with league whose date till death shall never end' [III. ii. 373].

Deep reflective power and subtle insight into char-

Michael Blakemore as Snout, Julian Glover as Snug, Peter Woodthorpe as Flute, Donald Eccles as Starveling, Charles Laughton as Bottom, and Cyril Luckham as Quince. Act I, scene ii. From a 1959 Shakespeare Memorial Theatre staging of the comedy.

acter came slowly to Shakespere, as to lesser men, but fancy has its flowering season in youth, and never has it shimmered with a more delicate and iridescent bloom than the fairy-world of *A Midsummer Night's Dream*. Through woodland vistas, where the Maymoon struggles with the dusk, elf-land opens into sight, ethereal, impalpable, spun out of gossamer and dew, and yet strangely consistent and credible. For this kingdom of shadows reproduces in miniature the structure of human society. Here, as on earth, there are royal rulers, with courts, ministers, warriors, jesters, and, in fine, all the pomp and circumstance of mortal sovereignty. And what plausibility there is in every detail, worked out with an unfaltering instinct for just and delicate gradation! In this realm of the microscopic an acorn-cup is a place of shelter, and a cast snake-skin, or the leathern wing of a rear-mouse, an ample coat: the night tapers are honey-bags of humble-bees lit at the glow-worm's eyes, and the fairy chorus, to whom the third part of a moment is a measurable portion of time, charm from the side of their sleeping mistress such terrible monsters as blindworms, spiders, and beetles black.

Over these tiny creatures morality has no sway: theirs is a delicious sense life, a revel of epicurean joy in nature's sweets and beauties. To dance 'by paved fountain or by rushy brook' [II. i. 84], to rest on banks canopied with flowers, to feed on apricoks and grapes, and mulberries, to tread the groves till the 'eastern gate all firey red' [III. ii. 391] turns the green sea into gold—such are the delights which make up their round of existence. In Puck, 'the lob of spirits,' this merry temper takes a more roguish form, a gusto in the topsy-turvy, in the things that befall preposterously, and an elfin glee in gulling mortals according to their folly. With his zest for knavish pranks, for mocking practical jokes upon 'gossips' and 'wisest aunts,' this merry wanderer of the night is indeed a spirit different in sort from the ethereal dream fairies, and it is natural that Oberon's vision of Cupid all armed should be hid from his gross sight. Moonlight and woodland have for him no spell of beauty, but they form a congenial sphere in which to play the game of mystification and cross-purposes. Thus his very unlikeness to the other shadows marks him out as the ally and henchman of Oberon in his quarrel with the fairy queen and her court. For the love troubles of mortals have their miniature counterpart in the jealousy of the elfin royal pair, springing in the main, as befits their nature, from an aesthetic rivalry for the possession of a lovely Indian boy, though by an ingenious touch, which unites the natural and supernatural realms, a further incitement is the undue favour with which Oberon regards the 'bouncing Amazon' Hippolyta, balanced by Titania's attachment to Theseus. And as the human wooers are beguiled by the power of Cupid's magic herb, the fairy queen is in like manner victimized. But with correct instinct Shakespere makes her deception far the more extravagant. Fairyland is the world of perennial surprise, and it must be a glaringly fantastic incongruity that arrests attention there. But the most exciting canons of improbability are satisfied when Titania, whose very being is spun out of light and air and dew, fastens her affections upon the unpurged 'mortal grossness' of Bottom, upon humanity with its asinine attributes focussed and gathered to a head. To attack his queen in her essential nature, to make her whose only food is beauty lavish her endearments upon a misshapen monster, is a masterpiece of revenge on Oberon's part. And so persuasive is the art of the dramatist that our pity is challenged for Titania's infatuation, with its pathetically reckless squandering of pearls before swine, and thus we hail with joy her release from her dotage, her reconciliation with Oberon, and the end of jars in fairyland, celebrated with elfin ritual of dance and song.

In designedly aggressive contrast to the dwellers in the shadow world is the crew of hempen homespuns headed by sweet bully Bottom. Among the many forms of genius there is to be reckoned the asinine variety, which wins for a man the cordial recognition of his supremacy among fools, and of this Bottom is a choice type. In the preparation of the Interlude in honour of the Duke's marriage, though Quince is nominally the manager, Bottom, through the force of his commanding personality, is throughout the directing spirit. His brother craftsmen have some doubts about their qualifications for heroic rôles, but this protean actor and critic is ready for any and every part, from lion to lady, and is by universal consent selected as *jeune premier* [lead player] of the company in the character of Pyramus, 'a most lovely gentleman-like man.' Bereft of his services, the comedy, it is admitted on all hands, cannot go forward: 'it is not possible: you have not a man in all Athens able to discharge Pyramus but he' [IV. ii. 7-8]. Fostered by such hero-worship, Bottom's egregious self-complacency develops to the point where his metamorphosis at the hands of Puck seems merely an exquisitely fitting climax to a natural process of evolution. And even when thus 'translated,' he retains his versatile faculty of adapting himself to any part; the amorous advances of Titania in no wise disturb his equanimity, and he is quite at ease with Peaseblossom and Cobweb. A sublime self-satisfaction may triumph in situations where the most delicate tact or the most sympathetic intelligence would be nonplussed.

But Shakespere, in introducing his crew of patches into his fairy drama, had an aim beyond satirizing fussy egotism or securing an effect of broad comic relief. It is a peculiarity of his dramatic method to produce variations upon a single theme in the different portions of a play. *Love's Labour's Lost* is an instance of this, and *A Midsummer Night's Dream* is further illustration, though of a less obvious kind. For in the rehearsal and setting forth of their comedy, Bottom and his friends enter a debateable domain, which, like that of the fairies, hovers round the solid work-a-day world, and yet is not of it. There is a point of view from which life may be regarded as the reality of which art, and in especial dramatic art, is the 'shadow,' the very word used by Theseus in relation to the workmen's play. Thus in their grotesque devices and makeshifts these rude mechanicals are really facing the question of the relation of shadow to substance, the immemorial question of realism in art and on the stage. The classical maxim that 'Medea shall not kill her children in sight of the audience' [Horace, in his *Ars Poetica*] lest the feelings of the spectators should be harrowed beyond endurance, finds a burlesque echo in Bottom's solicitude lest the ladies should be terrified by the drawing of Pyramus' sword, or the entrance of so fearful a wild-fowl as your lion. Hence the necessity for a prologue to say that Pyramus is not killed indeed, and for the apparition of half Snug the joiner's face through the lion's neck, and his announcement that he is not come hither as a lion, but is 'a man as other men are' [III. i. 44]. Scenery presents further difficulties, but here, as there is no risk of wounding delicate susceptibilities, realism is given full rein. The moon herself is pressed into the service, but owing to her capricious nature, she is given an understudy in the person of Starveling carrying a bush of thorns and a lanthorn. It is only the hypercriticism of the Philistine Theseus that finds fault with this arrangement on the score that the man should be put into the lanthorn. 'How is it else the man in the moon?' [V. i. 247-48].

The 'tedious belief scene of young Pyramus and his love Thisbe' [V. i. 56-7], is more elaborated specimen of those plays within plays, of which Shakespere had already given a sketch in *Love's Labour's Lost,* and for which he retained a fondness in all stages of his career. It is a burlesque upon the dramas of the day, in which classical subjects were handled with utter want of dignity, and with incongruous extravagance of style. The jingling metres, the mania for alliteration, the far-fetched and fantastic epithets, the meaningless invocations, the wearisome repetition of emphatic words, are all ridiculed with a boisterous glee, which was an implicit warrant that, when the young dramatist should hereafter turn to tragic or classical themes, his own work would be free from such disfiguring affectations, or, at worst, would take from them only a superficial taint. And, indeed, what potency of future triumphs on the very summits of dramatic art lay already revealed in the genius which out of an incidental entertainment could frame the complex and gorgeous pagentry of *A Midsummer Night's Dream;* and which, when denied, by the necessities of the occasion, an ethical motive, could fall back for inspiration on an enchanting metaphysic, not of the schools but of the stage, whose contrasts of shadow and reality are shot, now in threads of gossamer lightness, now in homelier and coarser fibre, into the web and woof of this unique hymeneal masque. (pp. 184-90)

> *Frederick S. Boas, "Shakespeare's Poems: The Early Period of Comedy," in his* Shakespere and His Predecessors, *1896. Reprint by Charles Scribner's Sons, 1902, pp. 158-96.*

SOURCES FOR FURTHER STUDY

LITERARY COMMENTARY:

Briggs, K. M. "Shakespeare's Fairies." In her *The Anatomy of Puck: An Examination of Fairy Beliefs among Shakespeare's Contemporaries and Successors,* pp. 44-55. London: Routledge and Kegan Paul, 1959.

> Suggests that the diminutive size of the fairies in *A Midsummer Night's Dream* was Shakespeare's invention, but demonstrates that folklore frequently presented these figures as very small.

Bryant, J. A., Jr. "Hippolyta's View." In his *Hyppolyta's View: Some Christian Aspects of Shakespeare's Play,* pp. 1-18. Lexington: University of Kentucky Press, 1961.

> Asserts that Shakespeare's view of poetry in *A Midsummer Night's Dream* is expressed not by Theseus but by Hippolyta, specifically, in her "something of great constancy" speech (V. i. 23-7). Bryant contends that this passage also contains echoes of the playwright's Christian view of life.

Clemen, Wolfgang. "Shakespeare's Art of Preparation. A Preliminary Sketch: A First Scene as an Example, *A Midsummer Night's Dream,* I, i." In his *Shakespeare's Dramatic Art: Collected Essays,* pp. 1-18. London: Methuen & Co., 1972.

> Examines the dialogue, dramatic action, and imagery in the initial scene of *A Midsummer Night's Dream* to demonstrate how Shakespeare prepares the audience "for the kind of love which is to be enacted in the play."

Craig, Hardin. "The Beginnings: *A Midsummer*

Night's Dream." In his *An Interpretation of Shakespeare,* pp. 35-8. Columbia, Mo.: Lucas Brothers, 1948.

> Extols *A Midsummer Night's Dream* as "the best of Shakespeare's early comedies," maintaining that the playwright's management of the multiple plot structure was unequaled by any other Elizabethan dramatists.

Goldstein, Melvin. "Identity Crises in A Midsummer Nightmare: Comedy as Terror in Disguise." *Psychoanalytic Review* 60, No. 2 (Summer 1973): 169-204.

> Maintains that each character in *A Midsummer Night's Dream* struggles to resolve a crisis arising from an incomplete sexual self-definition. Goldstein notes that Helena comes to terms with her sexuality through an acceptance of animality that is a basic element of her nature.

Granville-Barker, Harley. "Preface to *A Midsummer Night's Dream.*" In *More Prefaces to Shakespeare,* by Harley Granville-Barker, edited by Edward M. Moore, pp. 94-134. Princeton, N.J.: Princeton University Press, 1974.

> Asserts that the poetry of *A Midsummer Night's Dream* is the predominant dramatic element in the play.

Green, Roger Lancelyn. "Shakespeare and the Fairies." *Folklore,* No. 73 (Summer 1962): 89-103.

> Affirms that Shakespeare was one of the first authors to depict fairies in a literary work and that his delineation of their diminutive size was not only innovative but widely copied by later dramatists and fiction writers.

Hunter, G. K. *"A Midsummer Night's Dream."* In his *William Shakespeare: The Later Comedies,* pp. 7-20. London: Longmans, Green & Co., 1962.

> Contends that the total structural pattern of *A Midsummer Night's Dream* is more important than any of its individual, constituent elements and that the play "is constructed by contrast rather than interaction."

Kermode, Frank. "The Mature Comedies." In *Early Shakespeare,* edited by John Russell Brown and Bernard Harris, pp. 221-27. London: Edward Arnold, 1961.

> Argues that the principal themes of *A Midsummer Night's Dream* are fantasy and the disorders of fantasy. Kermode contends that Bottom's dream, which offers an interpretation of blind love as a transcendent passion, contradicts the young lovers' belief that their nocturnal adventures have been mere fantasies.

Lewis, Allan. *"A Midsummer Night's Dream*—Fairy Fantasy or Erotic Nightmare?" *Educational Theatre Journal* XXI, No. 3 (October 1969): 251-58.

> Regards *A Midsummer Night's Dream* as "a comedy of sex that is both light and dark." Although Lewis sees bitter elements in the play, he asserts that Jan Kott's interpretation is an overstatement of the sinister aspects of the drama (see excerpt in section on The Battle of the Sexes).

Quiller-Couch, Arthur. *"A Midsummer-Night's*

Dream." In his *Shakespeare's Workmanship,* pp. 77-95. London: T. Fisher Uniwin, 1918.

Speculates on the processes of Shakespeare's imagination as he composed *A Midsummer Night's Dream.* Quiller-Couch asserts that in this play Shakespeare first found the opportunity to give full rein to his natural gifts for poetry and humor.

Schanzer, Ernest. "The Moon and the Fairies in *A Midsummer Night's Dream."* *University of Toronto Quarterly* XXIV, No. 3 (April 1955): 234-46.

Contends that Titania and Oberon are the fairy world's counterparts of Hippolyta and Theseus, and maintains that the quarrel between the fairy king and queen precipitates and reflects the disorder in the natural world.

Stewart, Garrett. "Shakespearean Dreamplay." *English Literary Renaissance* 11, No. 1 (Winter 1981): 44-69.

Discusses the reflexive nature of language in *A Midsummer Night's Dream.* Stewart contends that the non sequiturs, the hesitations between exposition and awe, and the "garbled eloquence" of Bottom's speech emphasize the ambiguous nature of both drama and dreams.

Swinden, Patrick. *"A Midsummer Night's Dream."* In his *An Introduction to Shakespeare's Comedies,* pp. 51-64. London: Macmillan, 1973.

A general treatment of *A Midsummer Night's Dream,* giving particular attention to the way in which structure, discrepancies of time, and the imagery all enhance the play's central concern with the manipulation of the senses.

Vlasopolos, Anca. "The Ritual of Midsummer: A Pattern for *A Midsummer Night's Dream."* *Renaissance Quarterly* XXXI, No. 1 (Spring 1978): 21-9.

An analysis of the Christian and pagan elements in the Midsummer ritual known as St. John's Day. Vlasopolos demonstrates that both the play and the ritual incorporate the rite of fertility in a forest setting and the reemergence of the participants into a renewed, regenerated society that is once more in harmony with nature.

Woodberry, George E. Introduction to *A Midsummer Night's Dream,* by William Shakespeare, edited by Sidney Lee, pp. ix-xxii. *The Complete Works of William Shakespeare,* edited by Sidney Lee, Vol. VI. New York: George D. Sroul, 1907.

Contends that the central theme of the play is illusion and that Shakespeare explores this concern in such forms as illusions of the senses, of the heart, and of art itself.

MEDIA ADAPTATIONS:

A Midsummer Night's Dream. Warner Brothers, 1935.

The classical film version of the play, directed by William Dieterle and Max Reinhardt. Featured stars include James Cagney, Mickey Rooney, Olivia de Havilland, and Dick Powell. Distributed by Key Video. 132 minutes.

A Midsummer Night's Dream. BBC, 1963.

A live television performance, with Mendelssohn's incidental music. This version features Patrick Allen, Eira Heath, Cyril Luckham, and Tony Bateman. Distributed by Video Yesteryear. 111 minutes.

A Midsummer Night's Dream. BBC, London; Time-Life Videos, 1982.

Film version of Shakespeare's comedy, starring Helen Mirren, Peter McEnery, and Brian Clover. Distributed by Key Video and Time-Life Video. 120 minutes.

OTHELLO

INTRODUCTION

Othello is unique among Shakespeare's great tragedies. Unlike *Hamlet, King Lear,* and *Macbeth,* which are set against a backdrop of affairs of state and which reverberate with suggestions of universal human concerns, *Othello* is set in a private world and focuses on the passions and personal lives of its major figures. Indeed, it has often been described as a "tragedy of character"; Othello's swift descent into jealousy and rage and Iago's dazzling display of villainy have long fascinated students and critics of the play. The relationship between these characters is another unusual feature of *Othello.* With two such prominent characters so closely associated, determining which is the central figure in the play and which bears the greater responsibility for the tragedy is difficult. Written in 1604, *Othello* is one of Shakespeare's most highly concentrated, tightly constructed tragedies, with no subplots and little humor to relieve the tension. Although he adapted the plot of his play from the sixteenth-century Italian dramatist and novelist Giraldi Cinthio's *Gli Hecatommithi,* Shakespeare related almost every incident directly to the development of Iago's schemes and Othello's escalating fears. This structure heightens the tragedy's ominous mood and makes the threat to both Desdemona's innocence and the love she and Othello share more terrifying. Although narrow in scope, *Othello,* with its intimate domestic setting, is widely regarded as the most moving of Shakespeare's great tragedies.

PRINCIPAL CHARACTERS
(in order of appearance)

Roderigo: A rejected suitor of Desdemona. He becomes Iago's pawn, wounds and is wounded by Cassio in an unsuccessful attempt to murder the lieutenant, and is killed by Iago.

Iago: Othello's ensign. When Othello promotes Cassio, Iago feels slighted and plots revenge against them both. He manipulates Cassio into discrediting himself and urges Roderigo to slay Cassio. When the plot fails, he kills Roderigo to keep from being exposed. Iago convinces Othello of Desdemona's unfaithfulness and maneuvers him into killing her. He then murders his own wife Emilia and is taken into custody by Cassio at the play's end.

Brabantio: A Venetian senator and Desdemona's father. He charges Othello with bewitching his daughter and dies after Desdemona leaves for Cyprus with Othello and the Venetian forces.

Othello: The Moor, commander of Venice's armed forces, and later governor of Cyprus. He secretly weds Desdemona and provokes Iago's enmity by promoting Cassio. He later relieves Cassio of his rank when he believes that the lieutenant started a drunken brawl. Othello gradually succumbs to Iago's plot, and, believing that Desdemona is unfaithful, smothers her. When he realizes she was innocent of Iago's accusations, he commits suicide.

Cassio: Othello's lieutenant, promoted to that rank over Iago. He is discredited when he participates in a drunken brawl during Othello's wedding celebration. Cassio survives a murder attempt by Roderigo, wounding his attacker, and is appointed deputy governor of Cyprus after Othello is recalled to Venice.

Desdemona: Brabantio's daughter. She elopes with Othello and accompanies him to Cyprus. After Cassio is discredited, she pleads for his reinstatement, an act which her husband interprets as proof of Iago's insinuations that she is unfaithful. She is ultimately murdered by Othello.

Emilia: Iago's wife and Desdemona's attendant. She gives Iago Desdemona's handkerchief, which he had asked her to steal. After Othello murders his wife, Emilia reveals Desdemona's fidelity and is mortally wounded by Iago for exposing the truth.

PLOT SYNOPSIS

Act I: In Venice, Iago and Roderigo discuss their bitterness toward Othello, both for his marriage to Desdemona, whom Roderigo loves, and for his promotion of Cassio instead of Iago to lieutenant. They then arouse Brabantio with the news that his daughter has eloped with Othello. The outraged senator seeks out Othello and accuses him of bewitching his daughter. Since Othello has just received an urgent summons from the Duke of Venice and Brabantio wishes the ruler to hear his grievance against Othello, they agree to meet at the Duke's council chamber. There, senators are discussing reports of a Turkish fleet heading for Cyprus. Othello is immediately appointed governor of the island and charged with defending it from the invasion. Brabantio then presses his charge of witchcraft against Othello, who defends himself by explaining that, while a frequent guest in the senator's home, his tales of adventure had enthralled Brabantio's daughter. When Desdemona herself arrives, she confirms Othello's tale and asks to accompany him to his new post. Iago is assigned to escort Desdemona there. After the others leave, Iago upbraids Roderigo for contemplating drowning himself at the news of Desdemona's marriage. Iago predicts that the marriage of Othello and Desdemona will not last and guarantees that if Roderigo is generous with his money, he too will enjoy her favors. Iago, still brooding over Cassio's promotion and rumors that Emilia has been unfaithful with Othello, resolves to instigate strife in the Moor's marriage by insinuating that Desdemona and Cassio have become intimate.

Act II: In Cyprus, Othello's predecessor as governor, Montano, is informed that a storm has destroyed the Turkish forces and scattered the Venetian fleet. Cassio, Desdemona, Iago, Roderigo, and Emilia reach the island before Othello. Iago reaffirms his desire to arouse Othello's jealousy and enlists Roderigo in the plot to discredit Cassio. Upon arriving in Cyprus, Othello decrees a night of revelry to celebrate his marriage and Cyprus's escape from the Turkish attack. Cassio tells Iago that he becomes easily intoxicated, and Iago uses this information to get the lieutenant drunk and involved in a public brawl with Roderigo and Montano. When Othello arrives and asks who started the melee, Iago, feigning reluctance, names Cassio. Othello punishes the lieutenant by relieving him of his duties.

Act III: Despondent over his demotion, Cassio, at Iago's suggestion, asks Desdemona to intercede for him with Othello. As they are speaking, Othello and Iago enter. Cassio steals away in shame and Desdemona urges her husband to reinstate his friend. Iago uses these events to plant doubts in Othello's mind. Iago expresses surprise to learn that Cassio has long been acquainted with Desdemona and states several times his belief that Cassio is an "honest" man. When pressed by Othello to explain himself, Iago warns him against jealousy. Othello assures Iago that he would not be influenced by mere suspicion; if, however, it were proved that Desdemona were unfaithful, he would disown her. Iago advises him to watch his wife's behavior with Cassio. Subsequently, Othello's bitter musings on marriage and infidelity are cut short by the appearance of Desdemona and Emilia. Desdemona accidently drops her handkerchief, Othello's first gift to her; Emilia picks it up and later gives it to her husband, who had repeatedly asked her to steal it. Othello, tormented now by suspicions, assaults Iago for his insinuations and demands proof of Desdemona's disloyalty. Iago replies that he has heard Cassio talk of her in his sleep and that he has seen him use her handkerchief. Enraged, Othello charges Iago to kill Cassio. Iago agrees, but urges that Desdemona be spared.

Othello, however, plans her death. When Othello later asks Desdemona for the handkerchief, she says she does not have it and attempts to resume her pleas on Cassio's behalf. Her husband becomes enraged and leaves in a fury. Meanwhile, Cassio has found the handkerchief planted by Iago in his quarters and given it to his mistress Bianca.

Act IV: Iago continues to provoke the passions of Othello, who falls into an epileptic trance at his feet. Iago revels in his handiwork. When Othello revives, Iago suggests that he watch while Iago engages Cassio in a discussion about Desdemona. They actually discuss Bianca, but Othello cannot hear what the two men are saying and believes that object of Cassio's laughter is Desdemona. When Bianca appears and returns the handkerchief to Cassio, Othello is shocked by the sight of it. He again vows to kill his wife, and Iago plots to dispose of Cassio. Letters arrive for Othello, commanding him to return to Venice and leave Cassio as his deputy in Cyprus. When Desdemona expresses her hopes that the two can be reconciled, the infuriated Othello strikes her. Later, he openly accuses her of adultery and calls her a whore despite her protests of innocence. Desdemona is distraught and turns to Iago for assistance, but he makes light of her concern. After Desdemona and Emilia leave, Roderigo enters and accuses Iago of doing nothing to bring about the promised liaison with Desdemona; he further threatens to go to Desdemona himself. Iago placates him by saying that Othello will soon be leaving Cyprus without his wife and that if Roderigo kills Cassio, no one will stand between him and Desdemona.

Act V: At Iago's instigation, Roderigo tries to murder Cassio, but is himself wounded. Iago then wounds Cassio from behind and flees. Returning a short while later, he kills Roderigo to prevent his plan from being exposed. Meanwhile, Othello finds Desdemona asleep in their bed. He awakens her with a kiss and tells her to prepare to die. Ignoring her appeals for mercy, he smothers her. Hearing Emilia's calls at the door, he lets her in. Desdemona cries out and when Emilia asks who has done the deed, she replies that it is her own fault. After Desdemona dies, Othello confesses the crime and tells Emilia of Iago's involvement. Initially stunned and disbelieving, Emilia becomes defiant and cries out for help. When Iago, Cassio, Montano, and others appear in response, she confronts her husband and exposes his treachery. Othello lunges at Iago, who fatally wounds Emilia and flees. He is soon captured, however, and Othello stabs him. Cassio then explains how he found the handkerchief, and papers discovered on Roderigo further reveal the extent of Iago's villainy. Othello then stabs himself and dies kissing Desdemona, while Iago is remanded into Cassio's custody.

PRINCIPAL TOPICS

Perhaps the predominant impression created by *Othello* is that of the terrible destructiveness of jealousy. Othello's suspicions regarding Desdemona's fidelity provoke him to rage and violence, and the collapse of his pride and nobility is swift. The speed and intensity of these changes in the hero have led some critics to question whether Iago's insinuations actually cause Othello's doubts or merely unleash his pre-existing fears. Shakespeare's analysis of the nature of jealousy is not limited only to the character of Othello, however. Both Roderigo and Bianca are torn by jealousy: he desires Desdemona and she yearns for Cassio. More importantly, Iago displays numerous symptoms of jealousy. His bitterness at being passed over for promotion and his suspicions that his wife has had an affair with Othello prompt his desire for revenge and give rise to his malicious schemes. Although various forms of jealousy are displayed by these characters, they are all based on unreasonable fears and lead to equally irrational behavior.

Another significant aspect of *Othello,* one related to the jealousy theme, is Shakespeare's manipulation of time in the play. For centuries, readers have noted that the play has a dual time scheme: "short" time, in which the action on stage is an unbroken sequence of events taking place over the course of a very few days; and "long" time, in which characters' statements and other indications suggest that a much greater period of time has passed. Thus, for example, a close reading reveals that all the events from his arrival on Cyprus to Othello's death take place in less than two days. This compression of time heightens the sense of reckless passion and the extreme rapidity of Othello's fall. By contrast, Othello's references to Desdemona's "stolen hours of lust" (III. iii. 338) and to his sleeping well in ignorance of the supposed trysts between his wife and Cassio, as well as Bianca's chastisement of Cassio for keeping "a week away . . . seven days and nights . . . eight score eight hours" (III. iv. 173-74), reflect a longer passage of time. This extension of time may reflect the irrational quality of Othello's and Bianca's jealousy, by which their fears cause them to exaggerate. At the same time, it makes their doubts seem more plausible: if days or weeks have passed, there has indeed been time for repeated trysts between Desdemona and Cassio. Furthermore, in "long time" Othello's decline appears less sudden and absurd, thereby preserving the audience's sympathy with the proud and noble Moor.

Shakespeare's presentation of a black man as the hero of this tragedy has provoked much comment. In Shakespeare's England, blacks were considered exotic rarities. They were commonly feared as dangerous, threatening figures, sexually unrestrained and primitive. On stage, blacks were often stereotyped as villains; Shakespeare himself had employed this figure in Aaron in *Titus Andronicus.* With his presentation of the proud, virtuous soldier Othello, Shakespeare defies many of these stereotypes. In fact, actors and critics for centuries insisted that this noble "Moor" was an Arab rather than an African. However, several characters display racist attitudes and clearly designate Othello as black; this discrimination is most notable in Iago, who not only expresses his own racism but plays on the prejudices of others in his schemes against Othello. Thus, while rejecting stereotypes in his depiction of Othello, Shakespeare also presents characters who attack the hero's color and use his race to isolate and destroy him.

CHARACTER STUDIES

Two primary interpretations of Othello's character have emerged among students and critics of the play: that he is virtuous, strong, and trustful; and that he is guilty of self-idealization and overweening pride. Both views find support in the change in Othello's behavior. Although he is initially presented as a strong, confident character using typical heroic vocabulary, as he succumbs to jealousy and rage he becomes more like Iago and employs the villain's animal and diabolic imagery. According to critics who regard Othello as essentially noble, this change shows the innocent hero falling victim to Iago's schemes and being corrupted by his evil. Others, however, argue that Iago's actions merely cause Othello's noble facade to crumble, releasing his inherent savagery. The first interpretation places most, if not all, the responsibility for Othello's fall on Iago; the second puts much of the burden on the Moor himself.

Regardless of the degree to which Iago is to blame for Othello's downfall, he remains one of Shakespeare's most villainous creations, variously described as a brilliant opportunist taking advantage of the chances presented to him, as a personification of evil, and as a stock "devil" or "vice" figure. Iago's motivation remains a topic of considerable debate. Although he offers numerous motives throughout the play—resentment at being passed over for promotion, suspicions about Othello and Emilia, desire for Desdemona—Iago's plans seem curiously incomplete; he appears to be making up both his schemes and his motives for them as he goes along. The noted nineteenth-century writer and critic Samuel Taylor Coleridge described this process as the "motive-hunting of a motiveless malignity," and for many readers Iago's behavior is simply evil, beyond explanation or understanding. For others, no explanation is necessary. They consider Iago a devil or vice figure, a stock dramatic villain. Many scholars, however, find Iago a more fully fleshed-out character, emotionally and psychologically complex. According to these critics, his pride and desire for power and control, along with his brilliant scheming and his jealousy, make Iago a fascinating, multi-faceted figure.

Desdemona has traditionally been seen as the "good" that contrasts with Iago's "evil." Generally overshadowed by the powerful and enigmatic figures of Othello and Iago, Desdemona has often been judged an uncomplicated character: an idealized goddess or a passive, undeveloped figure. Recently, however, critics have begun to detect a more intricate portrait of Desdemona as a vital, courageous, and sensual woman. Significantly, it is Desdemona rather than Othello who initiates their romance and courtship. In addition, she exhibits a remarkable boldness and independence in marrying Othello in the face of her father's objections. However, she pays a price for her freedom: isolated from her familiar Venetian surroundings, she becomes dependent upon Othello; and when his love turns to violence, she is alone and defenseless.

CONCLUSION

Othello has often been considered the most painful of Shakespeare's tragedies. The fall of a proud, dignified man, the murder of a graceful, loving woman, and the unreasoning hatred of a "motiveless" villain—all have evoked fear and pity in audiences throughout the centuries. If it lacks the cosmic grandeur of *Hamlet* or *King Lear, Othello* nevertheless possesses a power that is perhaps more immediate and strongly felt for operating on the personal, human plane.

(See also *Shakespearean Criticism,* Vols. 4 and 11.)

OVERVIEW

A. C. Bradley

[*Bradley presents an overview of* Othello, *in an attempt to discover what makes this the "most painfully exciting and the most terrible" of Shakespeare's tragedies. He highlights aspects of the play which reinforce its emotional impact: the rapid acceleration of the plot, the intensity of* Othello's *jealousy, the passive suffering of* Desdemona, *and the luck and skill involved in* Iago's *intrigue. According to Bradley, these features combine to produce feelings of "confinement" and "dark fatality" that suggest that the characters cannot escape their destinies. He then discusses three scenes—* Othello's *striking of* Desdemona *in IV. i,* Othel-lo's *treatment of* Desdemona *as a whore in IV. ii, and her death in V. ii.—and maintains that the emotional intensity of these scenes also greatly contributes to the unique, painful quality of* Othello. *He concludes by noting that the play is less symbolic and more limited in scope than Shakespeare's other tragedies, and as a result we are left with the "impression that in* Othello *we are not in contact with the whole of Shakespeare."]*

What is the peculiarity of *Othello?* What is the distinctive impression that it leaves? Of all Shakespeare's tragedies, I would answer, not even excepting *King Lear, Othello* is the most painfully exciting and the most terrible. From the moment when the temptation of the hero begins, the reader's heart and mind are held in a vice, experiencing the extremes of pity and fear, sympathy and repulsion, sickening hope and dreadful expectation. Evil is displayed before him, not indeed with the profusion found in *King Lear,* but forming, as it were, the soul of a single character, and united with an intellectual superiority so great that he watches its advance fascinated and appalled. He sees it, in itself almost irresistible, aided at every step by fortunate accidents and the innocent mistakes of its victims. He seems to breathe an atmosphere as fateful as that of *King Lear,* but more confined and oppressive, the darkness not of night but of a close-shut murderous room. His imagination is excited to intense activity, but it is the activity of concentration rather than dilation. (pp. 176-77)

Othello is not only the most masterly of the tragedies in point of construction, but its method of construction is unusual. And this method, by which the conflict begins late, and advances without appreciable pause and with accelerating speed to the catastrophe, is a main cause of the painful tension just described. To this may be added that, after the conflict has begun, there is very little relief by way of the ridiculous. Henceforward at any rate Iago's humour never raises a smile. The clown is a poor one; we hardly attend to him and quickly forget him; I believe most readers of Shakespeare, if asked whether there is a clown in *Othello,* would answer No.

In the second place, there is no subject more exciting than sexual jealousy rising to the pitch of passion; and there can hardly be any spectacle at once so engrossing and so painful as that of a great nature suffering the torment of this passion, and driven by it to a crime which is also a hideous blunder. Such a passion as ambition, however terrible its results, is not itself ignoble; if we separate it in thought from the conditions which make it guilty, it does not appear despicable; it is not a kind of suffering, its nature is active; and therefore we can watch its course without shrinking. But jealousy, and especially sexual jealousy, brings with it a sense of shame and humiliation. For this reason it is generally hidden; if we perceive it we ourselves are ashamed and turn our eyes away; and when it is not hidden it commonly stirs contempt as well as pity. Nor is this all. Such jealousy as Othello's converts human nature into chaos, and liberates the beast in man; and it does this in relation to one of the most intense and also the most ideal of human feelings. What spectacle can be more painful than that of this feeling turned into a tortured mixture of longing and loathing, the 'golden purity' of passion split by poison into fragments, the animal in man forcing itself into his consciousness in naked grossness, and he writhing before it but powerless to deny it entrance, gasping inarticulate images of pollution, and finding relief only in a bestial thirst for blood? This is what we have to witness in one who was indeed 'great of heart' [V. ii. 361] and no less pure and tender than he was great. And this, with what it leads to, the blow to Desdemona, and the scene where she is treated as the inmate of a brothel, a scene far more painful than the murder scene, is another cause of the special effect of this tragedy.

The mere mention of these scenes will remind us painfully of a third cause; and perhaps it is the most potent of all. I mean the suffering of Desdemona. This is, unless I mistake, the most nearly intolerable spectacle that Shakespeare offers us. For one thing, it is *mere* suffering; and, *ceteris paribus* [other things being equal], that is much worse to witness than suffering that issues in action. Desdemona is helplessly passive. She can do nothing whatever. She cannot retaliate even in speech; no, not even in silent feeling. And the chief reason of her helplessness only makes the sight of her suffering more exquisitely painful. She is helpless because her nature is infinitely sweet and her love absolute. I would not challenge Mr. [Algernon Charles] Swinburne's statement [in his *Study of Shakespeare*] that we *pity* Othello even more than Desdemona; but we watch Desdemona with more unmitigated distress. We are never wholly uninfluenced by the feeling that Othello is a man contending with another man; but Desdemona's suffering is like that of the most loving of dumb creatures tortured without cause by the being he adores.

Turning from the hero and heroine to the third principal character, we observe (what has often been pointed out) that the action and catastrophe of *Othello* depend largely on intrigue. We must not say more than this. We must not call the play a tragedy of intrigue as distinguished from a tragedy of character. Iago's plot is Iago's character in action; and it is built on his knowledge of Othello's character, and could not otherwise have succeeded. Still it remains true that an elaborate plot was necessary to elicit the catastrophe; for Othello was no Leontes [in *The Winter's Tale*], and his was the last nature to engender such jealousy from itself. Accordingly Iago's intrigue occupies a position in the drama for which no parallel can be found in the other tragedies; the only approach, and that a

distant one, being the intrigue of Edmund in the secondary plot of *King Lear*. Now in any novel or play, even if the persons rouse little interest and are never in serious danger, a skilfully worked intrigue will excite eager attention and suspense. And where, as in *Othello,* the persons inspire the keenest sympathy and antipathy, and life and death depend on the intrigue, it becomes the source of a tension in which pain almost overpowers pleasure. Nowhere else in Shakespeare do we hold our breath in such anxiety and for so long a time as in the later Acts of *Othello.*

One result of the prominence of the element of intrigue is that *Othello* is less unlike a story of private life than any other of the great tragedies. And this impression is strengthened in further ways. In the other great tragedies the action is placed in a distant period, so that its general significance is perceived through a thin veil which separates the persons from ourselves and our own world. But *Othello* is a drama of modern life; when it first appeared it was a drama almost of contemporary life, for the date of the Turkish attack on Cyprus is 1570. The characters come close to us, and the application of the drama to ourselves (if the phrase may be pardoned) is more immediate than it can be in *Hamlet* or *Lear*. Besides this, their fortunes affect us as those of private individuals more than is possible in any of the later tragedies with the exception of *Timon*. I have not forgotten the Senate, nor Othello's position, nor his service to the State; but his deed and his death have not that influence on the interests of a nation or an empire which serves to idealise, and to remove far from our own sphere, the stories of Hamlet and Macbeth, of Coriolanus and Antony. Indeed he is already superseded at Cyprus when his fate is consummated, and as we leave him no vision rises on us, as in other tragedies, of peace descending on a distracted land.

The peculiarities so far considered combine with others to produce those feelings of oppression, of confinement to a comparatively narrow world, and of dark fatality, which haunt us in reading *Othello*. In *Macbeth* the fate which works itself out alike in the external conflict and in the hero's soul, is obviously hostile to evil; and the imagination is dilated both by the consciousness of its presence and by the appearance of supernatural agencies. These . . . produce in *Hamlet* a somewhat similar effect, which is increased by the hero's acceptance of the accidents as a providential shaping of his end. *King Lear* is undoubtedly the tragedy which comes nearest to *Othello* in the impression of darkness and fatefulness, and in the absence of direct indications of any guiding power. But in *King Lear* . . . the conflict assumes proportions so vast that the imagination seems, as in [John Milton's] *Paradise Lost,* to traverse spaces wider than the earth. In reading *Othello* the mind is not thus distended. It is more bound down to the spectacle of noble beings caught in toils from which there is no escape; while the prominence of the intrigue diminishes the sense of the dependence of the catastrophe on character, and the part played by accident in this catastrophe accentuates the feeling of fate. This influence of accident is keenly felt in *King Lear* only once, and at the very end of the play. In *Othello,* after the temptation has begun, it is incessant and terrible. The skill of Iago was extraordinary, but so was his good fortune. Again and again a chance word from Desdemona, a chance meeting of Othello and Cassio, a question which starts to our lips and which anyone but Othello would have asked, would have destroyed Iago's plot and ended his life. In their stead, Desdemona drops her handkerchief at the moment most favourable to him, Cassio blunders into the presence of Othello only to find him in a swoon, Bianca arrives precisely when she is wanted to complete Othello's deception and incense his anger into fury. All this and much more seems to us quite natural, so potent is the art of the dramatist; but it confounds us with a feeling, such as we experience in [Sophocles'] *Oedipus Tyrannus,* that for these star-crossed mortals . . . there is no escape from fate, and even with a feeling, absent from that play, that fate has taken sides with villainy. It is not surprising, therefore, that *Othello* should affect us as *Hamlet* and *Macbeth* never do, and as *King Lear* does only in slighter measure. On the contrary, it is marvellous that, before the tragedy is over, Shakespeare should have succeeded in toning down this impression into harmony with others more solemn and serene.

But has he wholly succeeded? Or is there a justification for the fact—a fact it certainly is—that some readers, while acknowledging, of course, the immense power of *Othello,* and even admitting that it is dramatically perhaps Shakespeare's greatest triumph, still regard it with a certain distaste, or, at any rate, hardly allow it a place in their minds beside *Hamlet, King Lear* and *Macbeth?* (pp. 177-83)

To some readers, . . . parts of *Othello* appear shocking or even horrible. They think—if I may formulate their objection—that in these parts Shakespeare has sinned against the canons of art, by representing on the stage a violence or brutality the effect of which is unnecessarily painful and rather sensational than tragic. The passages which thus give offence are probably those already referred to,—that where Othello strikes Desdemona [IV. i. 240], that where he affects to treat her as an inmate of a house of ill-fame [IV. ii. 24-94], and finally the scene of her death.

The issues thus raised ought not to be ignored or impatiently dismissed, but they cannot be decided,

it seems to me, by argument. All we can profitably do is to consider narrowly our experience, and to ask ourselves this question: If we feel these objections, do we feel them when we are reading the play with all our force, or only when we are reading it in a half-hearted manner? For, however matters may stand in the former case, in the latter case evidently the fault is ours and not Shakespeare's. And if we try the question thus, I believe we shall find that on the whole the fault is ours. The first, and least important, of the three passages—that of the blow—seems to me the most doubtful. I confess that, do what I will, I cannot reconcile myself with it. It seems certain that the blow is by no means a tap on the shoulder with a roll of paper, as some actors, feeling the repulsiveness of the passage, have made it. It must occur, too, on the open stage. And there is not, I think, a sufficiently overwhelming tragic feeling in the passage to make it bearable. But in the other two scenes the case is different. There, it seems to me, if we fully imagine the inward tragedy in the souls of the persons as we read, the more obvious and almost physical sensations of pain or horror do not appear in their own likeness, and only serve to intensify the tragic feelings in which they are absorbed. Whether this would be so in the murder-scene if Desdemona had to be imagined as dragged about the open stage (as in some modern performances) may be doubtful; but there is absolutely no warrant in the text for imagining this, and it is also quite clear that the bed where she is stifled was within the curtains, and so, presumably, in part concealed.

Here, then, *Othello* does not appear to be, unless perhaps at one point, open to criticism, though it has more passages than the other three tragedies where, if imagination is not fully exerted, it is shocked or else sensationally excited. If nevertheless we feel it to occupy a place in our minds a little lower than the other three (and I believe this feeling, though not general, is not rare), the reason lies not here but in another characteristic, to which I have already referred,—the comparative confinement of the imaginative atmosphere. *Othello* has not equally with the other three the power of dilating the imagination by vague suggestions of huge universal powers working in the world of individual fate and passion. It is, in a sense, less 'symbolic.' We seem to be aware in it of a certain limitation, a partial suppression of that element in Shakespeare's mind which unites him with the mystical poets and with the great musicians and philosophers. In one or two of his plays, notably in *Troilus and Cressida,* we are almost painfully conscious of this suppression; we feel an intense intellectual activity, but at the same time a certain coldness and hardness, as though some power in his soul, at once the highest and the sweetest, were for a time in abeyance. In other plays, notably in the *Tempest,* we are constantly aware of the presence of this power; and in such cases we seem to be peculiarly near to Shakespeare himself. Now this is so in *Hamlet* and *King Lear,* and, in a slighter degree, in *Macbeth;* but it is much less so in *Othello.* I do not mean that in *Othello* the suppression is marked, or that, as in *Troilus and Cressida,* it strikes us as due to some unpleasant mood; it seems rather to follow simply from the design of a play on a contemporary and wholly mundane subject. Still it makes a difference of the kind I have attempted to indicate, and it leaves an impression that in *Othello* we are not in contact with the whole of Shakespeare. And it is perhaps significant in this respect that the hero himself strikes us as having, probably, less of the poet's personality in him than many characters far inferior both as dramatic creations and as men. (pp. 183-86)

A. C. Bradley, "Othello," in his Shakespearean Tragedy: Lectures on Hamlet, Othello, King Lear, Macbeth, *second edition, Macmillan and Co., Limited, 1905, pp. 175-206.*

JEALOUSY

D. R. Godfrey

[Godfrey examines the portrayal of jealousy in Othello, *determining that it is the cause of evil in the play. The critic exposes the jealousy presented by several characters:* **Othello, Roderigo, Bianca,** *and* **Iago.** *He compares their irrational behavior to that of Leontes, the jealous husband of Hermoine in* The Winter's Tale, *and asserts that each displays a form of sexual jealousy.* **Iago,** *however, exhibits "an all-encompassing jealousy directed not only against sexual love but against love itself in all its manifestations." As a result, envious hatred takes possession of his soul, motivates his actions, and turns him into "the most completely villainous character in all literature."]*

To proclaim Shakespeare's *Othello* as a tragedy of jealousy is but to echo the opinion of every critic who ever wrote about it. The jealousy not only of Othello, but of such lesser figures as Roderigo and even Bianca is surely self-evident enough to be

Paul Robeson as Othello and Peggy Ashcroft as Desdemona in a 1930 Savoy Theatre production of the tragedy.

taken for granted. And yet, though the jealousy of Othello in particular is invariably mentioned and assumed, it cannot be said that any over-riding importance has on the whole been attributed to it. While Othello may deliver judgement on himself as one,

> not easily jealous, but being wrought,
> Perplex'd in the extreme,
>
> [V. ii. 345-46]

critical opinion has hardly gone beyond admitting that jealousy itself has been a contributing factor, of far less importance, for example, than the diabolical "evidence" manufactured by Iago. Until we are left with the conclusion, or at least implication, that had Othello *not* been jealous, the tragedy would still have occurred. This taking for granted or even belittling of the factor of jealousy in *Othello,* is the more surprising in that Shakespeare through Iago and Emilia has taken pains to identify for our benefit the special nature of jealousy, and to call particular attention to the element of irrationality that accompanies it. Jealousy, warns Iago, in order to awaken it in Othello,

> . . . is the green-ey'd monster, which doth mock
> That meat it feeds on.
>
> [III. iii. 166-67]

And the same essence of irrationality is later confirmed by Emilia when, in response to Desdemona's pathetically rational "Alas the day! I never gave him cause" [III. iv. 158], she bluntly retorts:

> But jealous souls will not be answer'd so;
> They are not ever jealous for the cause,
> But jealous for they are jealous: 'tis a monster,
> Begot upon itself, born on itself.
>
> [III. iv. 159-62]

The coincidence of view is remarkable, and presumably intentional, and clearly reflects more than the individual judgement of Emilia or Iago. Moreover the truth of the judgement is demonstrated again and again throughout the play wherever jealousy is manifest. The jealous person, whether Othello, Roderigo, Bianca or, as we shall attempt to show, Iago himself, is revealed as one who, from the moment that jealousy strikes, divorces himself or herself from rationality. Jealousy, once awakened, becomes self-perpetuating, self-intensifying, and where no justifying evidence for it exists, the jealous person under the impulse of an extraordinary perversity will continue to manufacture it, inventing causes, converting airy trifles into "confirmations strong as proofs of holy writ," [III. iii. 323-24]. Any attempt, in other words, to interpret jealousy rationally, to look for logic in the mental processes of a jealous person, will be unavailing. For we will be dealing invariably and in at least some measure with a monster, a form of possession, an insanity. (pp. 207-08)

[In his *Shakespearean Tragedy,* A. C. Bradley argues] that until Iago leaves him alone to the insinuating thoughts he has planted in him [III. iii. 257] Othello is not jealous at all. However, Othello's immediately ensuing soliloquy clearly indicates how deeply his faith in Desdemona has already been undermined, and though at the sight of her he rallies,

> If she be false, O, then heaven mocks itself,
> I'll not believe it,
>
> [III. iii. 278-79]

recovery is momentary, and when he reappears only minutes later, Iago does not need his "Ha, ha, false to me, to me" [III. iii. 333], to recognize the symptoms of a consuming jealousy that all the drowsy syrups of the world can never alleviate. Othello may appear to be resisting insinuation, to recover from the shock of Iago's "Ha, ha, I like not that" [III. iii. 35], and the sight of Cassio stealing away "so guilty-like" [III. iii. 39], but it is soon evident enough that he has not recovered, that the possibility of Desdemona's infidelity has already invaded his mind. And . . . as with Leontes [in *The Winter's Tale*], the passage from initial doubt to the madness of absolute certainty, is incredibly rapid. The action of the whole "Temptation Scene" [III. iii], as it is sometimes called, is continuous, perhaps some twentyfive minutes of stage time, and by the end of it Othello is a man utterly possessed, calling out for blood and vengeance, authorizing Iago to murder Cassio, and resolving "In the due reverence of a sacred vow" [III. iii. 461], himself to do the same for Desdemona:

> Damn her, lewd minx: O, damn her!
> Come, go with me apart, I will withdraw
> To furnish me with some swift means of death.
> For the fair devil.
>
> [III. iii. 476-79]

Already present meanwhile in the initial reactions of Othello is of course that most encompassing of all the characteristics of the jealous man, a consuming irrationality. The presence of Iago with his diabolical insinuations tends somewhat to mask the insanity of Othello, to present him as a man reacting logically in the face of accumulating evidence, indeed of proof. By the end of the Temptation Scene, however, there is still no more than the slenderest of evidence, a handkerchief that Iago *may* have seen Cassio wipe his beard with, and Cassio's alleged, and, as Iago himself admits, inconclusive dream. Leontes, only after a considerable interval of time and after sending to the Oracle for confirmation puts Hermione on trial for her life. Othello, however, with nothing but Iago's word to go on, and without even seeking to confront either Desdemona or Cassio, passes sentence of death. Later, it is true, circumstantial evidences multiply: Desdemona's tactless pleading for Cassio, Iago's statement of Cassio's confession, Bianca's returning of the handkerchief to Cassio before Othello's eyes; but it is strangely apparent that Othello's conviction of Desdemona's guilt is *confirmed* rather than established by such "evidences". In the exchanges between Iago and Othello at the beginning of Act IV it is revealed that the handkerchief had become so incidental to his conviction that he had actually forgotten it [IV. i. 10-22]. In the same way, when at length confrontation comes between himself and Emilia and subsequently with Desdemona, it is apparent that no rational enquiry, no seeking out of evidence is to be undertaken. Emilia's indignant denials are met with:

> She says enough, yet she's a simple bawd
> That cannot say as much.
>
> [IV. ii. 20-1]

And Desdemona, assigned the horrible role of a whore in a brothel, is not to be rationally interrogated but rhetorically denounced, on the assumption, of which there is not the slightest sign, that she is fully aware of her guilt. Perhaps in no other scene is the impregnable insanity of Othello so fully evident.

Nevertheless, the circumstantial evidences are certainly there and must be allowed to provide in some measure a logical justification for Othello's "case" against Desdemona. Against that case however must always be set one unanswerable factor the effect of which is to demolish it utterly, the factor of time. With Desdemona dead, Othello can proclaim calmly and positively,

> 'Tis pitiful, but yet Iago knows
> That she with Cassio hath the act of
>   shame
> A thousand times committed,
>
> [V. ii. 210-12]

Whereas it is obvious to anyone not wholly bereft of reason that the time for one single act of infidelity, let alone a rhetorical thousand, has simply not existed. "What place, what time, what form, what likelihood?" [IV. ii. 138] demands the practical Emilia, and of course the questions are unanswerable.

This very problem of the time factor in *Othello* has been greatly debated. Since Othello and Desdemona left Venice immediately after their marriage, and since Cassio and Desdemona were on different ships, and since but one night had passed on Cyprus, a night that Othello and Desdemona had spent together, when indeed could the thousand adulteries have occurred? And how could the sheer impossibility of Desdemona's multiple infidelities never have presented itself to Othello's mind? Various familiar explanations have been attempted: that the text as it has come down to us is incomplete and that the indication of an interval of time after the arrival on Cyprus has been lost: that Shakespeare in effect is playing a trick on his audience on the valid assumption that they will not notice the time discrepancy anyway: that Shakespeare deliberately adopted a double time scheme, involving a background of "long time" against a foreground of "short time", the latter to accommodate the inconsistencies in Iago's plot against Othello, and his need to bring it to a speedy conclusion.

The respective merits of these various explanations have been copiously debated. Common to all of them is the reluctance of critics to assume that Iago, a supremely clever man, would ever have allowed his whole plot to depend on Othello's unlikely failure to realise the obvious, namely that the infidelities of which Desdemona stands accused could not have happened because there had been no time for them. Iago, it is argued, would never have taken such a risk; and so we, as well as Othello, are being required to assume that in some way or other time for a thousand shameful acts had in fact existed. I would suggest, however, that we cannot so assume, and are indeed not being asked to do so. For Iago knew, and we should realise, that by the time he felt it safe to proceed from hints and insinuations to firm accusations of infidelity, Othello would no longer be himself, but a quite different person possessed by the eclipsing madness of jealousy. Certainly we must agree that there are two time schemes in *Othello,* a long and a short, but equally each must be seen to operate within its own distinct world: on the one hand the long time world of everyday normality, on the other a short time, indeed a timeless universe, in which jealousy, divorced from reality, through distortion, falsification and sheer invention creates a nightmare reality of its own.

It may still be argued, of course that the degree of Othello's irrationality manifest in his blindness to the time factor, is excessive, unrealistic, and that Iago for all his insight and daring would not have taken so great a risk. We must assume however that Shakespeare as always, knew what he was doing and presenting, and that art, the art of the theatre in particular, must concern itself with the archetypal, the universal, with that which is necessarily larger, more extreme than in life. And surely we must take into account that elsewhere in *Othello,* in the case of Bianca, the refusal of the jealous person to be bound by the rationality of time is once again drawn to our attention. Bianca, whose jealousy over Cassio motivates her every word and action, reproaches him on her first appearance with an alleged seven days and nights of neglect:

> What, keep a week away? seven days and
>   nights?
> Eightscore eight hours, and lovers' absent
>   hours,
> More tedious than the dial, eightscore
>   times?
>
> [III. iv. 173-75]

The time here could hardly be more specifically stated, and yet, if we do not postulate the impossibility of an interval of almost a week between scenes three and four of Act III, the alleged duration of Cassio's neglect cannot be accepted. Act II begins with Cassio's arrival on Cyprus, and from this point to the moment of his encounter with Bianca the action on stage is continuous, and no more than a night and two days have elapsed before us. Once again it would seem that the irrationality of jealousy extending even into the reckoning of time is being demonstrated.

No less irrational, and no less typical of extreme jealousy, is the determination of Othello, as of Leontes, to destroy love through the anodyne of a deliberate cultivation of hatred. Here we must recognize that Othello, newly married, overwhelmed with relief to find Desdemona safe on Cyprus, has attained to an intensity of love deeper than that of Leontes for Hermione:

> O my soul's joy,
> . . . If it were now to die,
> 'Twere now to be most happy, for I fear
> My soul hath her content so absolute,
> That not another comfort, like to this
> Succeeds in unknown fate.
> [II. i. 184, 189-93]

Without hesitation, when jealousy strikes, Leontes achieves the transition from love to hate, but for Othello the process will be long drawn out, intermittent, subject to agonizing oscillations. The climax comes following the scene of final "proof", when Bianca has thrown the incriminating handkerchief back at Cassio, before Othello's eyes. The proof is not needed, for Othello's assumption of Desdemona's guilt has long been absolute, unassailable. On the other hand, love, or some remnant of it, still remains, and the moment has come, as Iago realises, for its final obliteration. Again and again, as Othello swings away in the dying agonies of love, Iago savagely recalls him:

> *Othello:* . . . a fine woman, a fair woman, a sweet woman!
>
> *Iago:* Nay, you must forget.
>
> *Othello:* And let her rot, and perish, and be damned to-night, for she shall not live; no, my heart is turn'd to stone; I strike it, and it hurts my hand: O, the world hath not a sweeter creature, she might lie by an emperor's side, and command him tasks.
>
> *Iago:* Nay, that's not your way.
>
> *Othello:* Hang her, I do but say what she is: so delicate with her needle, an admirable musician, O, she will sing the savageness out of a bear; of so high and plenteous wit and invention!
>
> *Iago:* She's the worse for all this.
> [IV. i. 178-91]

Iago, the very voice of jealousy itself, would appear

to succeed. Desdemona is smothered in the bed she had contaminated, and hatred's consummation is achieved. Yet it could be argued in Othello's case, in contrast to that of Leontes, that love is never wholly obliterated. The insane grip of jealousy is such that Othello can no longer doubt his wife's guilt, but he can act against it finally only by assuming the mask of impersonal justice:

> Yet she must die, else she'll betray more men.
> [V. ii. 6]

And we may even wonder whether Othello, still agonizing over the beauty he must destroy, could ever have sustained his assumed and precarious role of just executioner, had not Desdemona's bewilderment and terror, interpreted as prevarication, provoked him to one last paroxysm of rage and hatred.

For a while, beyond the point it had set itself to achieve, jealousy continues to sustain its victim. But the instrument has served its deadly purpose, and can be discarded. As suddenly and totally as Leontes, Othello is abandoned to the hideous and incredulous realisation of what he has done. One moment of explanation, of truth, from Emilia is now enough. The handkerchief—

> She gave it Cassio? no, alas, I found it,
> And did give't my husband.
> [V. ii. 230-31]

Othello, in the full vortex of jealousy, had already heard the truth from Emilia and facilely rejected it, "She's but a simple bawd that could not say as much" [IV. ii. 20-1], but now the vortex is past, the possession ending and truth, with the completeness and instantaneousness that is jealousy's final characteristic, once more assumes control.

While Othello and Leontes, and also Bianca, present jealousy in its most characteristic form, it must be recognized that other forms and manifestations of this most devastating of human emotions are possible. At least two such variations on the play's basic theme of jealousy are to be found in *Othello,* the first of them presented by Roderigo. That Roderigo is jealous first of Othello and then of Cassio cannot be doubted, and Iago, before using him against Cassio, is careful to heighten in him the motivation of jealousy:

> Didst thou not see her paddle with the palm of
> his hand? . . . Lechery,
> by this hand: an index and prologue
> to the history of lust and foul thoughts:
> they met so near with their lips, that their
> breaths embrac'd together.
> [II. i. 253-54, 257-60]

Thus primed and sustained by Iago, Roderigo overcomes his native timidity to the point of provoking the drunken Cassio on guard duty, and later of undertaking his murder. Only the irrationality of a jealous man, we might infer, could explain behaviour so savagely abnormal, could account also for that ludicrous readiness to go on accepting Iago's word, all evidence to the contrary, that Desdemona might still be his. It could perhaps be objected that Roderigo is not so much jealous as simply and deeply in love, as witnessed in particular by his uncritical idealising attitude towards Desdemona, his impregnable devotion. Surely, if jealous, he would have availed himself of the jealous man's most characteristic anodyne, a saving hatred. Need we in fact go any further than Iago in his assessment of Roderigo as one turned wrong side out by love? The answer must undoubtedly be that whatever Roderigo's love may have been at the outset, it has, thanks chiefly to the machinations of Iago, deteriorated, taken on elements of the irrational and ultimately of the diabolical; and to this deterioration jealousy has in large measure contributed. Roderigo, clutching at the straws of hope reached out to him by Iago, to the extent of selling all his land and following the Cyprus wars, has clearly ceased to act and react sanely. And when, quite definitely now under the compulsion of jealousy, he nerves himself to secure Cassio's dismissal and eventually to attempt his murder, he has reached a lower moral level than Othello, who can at least persuade himself that he is the instrument of justice. To the extent, then, of his irrationality and ultimate diabolism Roderigo is at one in jealousy with an Othello or a Leontes. On the other hand his jealousy, unlike theirs, proceeds from a love that has never been requited, and the form of his madness is to persist in hope of an ultimate possession. For him the cuckold's simple anodyne of hatred and vengeance is not available.

The second and final variation on the play's central theme of jealousy is to be found, it is suggested, in Iago. The traditional association of jealousy with sexual passion or possessiveness, must not obscure the fact that other kinds of jealousy, no less virulent in operation, are to be found; although sexual jealousy, his suspicion of the involvement of both Othello and Cassio with his wife, is also a factor in Iago's motivation. Far more, however, than suspicion over a wife he clearly does not love or value very highly, are obviously at work in Iago and must be reckoned with if his extraordinary and diabolical behaviour is to be understood. The problem of Iago's motivation is certainly a major one, no less baffling than the problem of Hamlet's delay. A whole spectrum of explanations has accordingly been attempted, ranging from the famous "motiveless malignity" of [Samuel Taylor] Coleridge, to simplistic assertions that Iago's motives, sexual jealousy and envy at Cassio's appointment, are perfectly adequate to explain him [see his *Shakespearean Criticism*, edited by Thomas Middleton Raysor]. That Iago is indeed a jealous and envious man has of course been generally recognized; such recognition, however, can certainly be taken further, in particular in terms of those

special characteristics of jealousy we have been attempting to establish.

That certain recent events have precipitated a state of jealousy in Iago is revealed to us in the first act of the play; he is jealous of Cassio over the lieutenancy which he considered his due, jealous of Othello whom he suspects of having had a liason with his wife. We can assume that the effect of these experiences, and especially the former, has been devastating, to the point of working a profound and sudden change in Iago, a virtual metamorphosis. That he is indeed villainous becomes clear to us by the end of the first act, but we can hardly believe that he has always been so, and that his universal reputation for honesty has been based over a long period of time on calculation and bluff. That a great change has been involved is further indicated to us by the particular way in which Iago is made to announce his age: "I ha' look'd upon the world for four times seven years" [I. iii. 311-12]—a statement that would reveal, at all events to a Shakespearean audience, that here is a man arrived at one of the great seven year climacterics [critical stages], a time especially liable to crisis and change. A far reaching change, precipitated in particular by Cassio's appointment and to a lesser extent by the apparently malicious evidence presented to him of an affair between Othello and Emilia, can certainly be postulated; and thus a new Iago confronts us, jealous, embittered, vengeful, viciously repudiating the honesty and loyalty that have led him nowhere.

It is clear, however, that the jealousy by which Iago stands possessed, as totally as an Othello or a Leontes, is of a special, a more comprehensive kind. It contains elements of sexual provocation, but it is directed also and even more powerfully against all those whose lives continue to be motivated, as his had once been, by the conventions of love, trust, honesty and goodness, and who continue on such a basis to be happy and successful, where he himself has suffered and failed. Upon them he will proceed to avenge himself, creating out of their now hated and envied love and goodness "the net that shall enmesh 'em all" [II. iii. 362].

Once the fact and comprehensive nature of Iago's jealousy has been established, all his subsequent thoughts and acts become, by reason of their very strangeness and irrationality, intelligible. Many attempts, for example, have been made to explain in rational terms the curious "motive hunting" of Iago displayed in his first two soliloquies. Here he conjures up, or so it would appear, motive after motive for proceeding in his plot against Cassio and Othello: desire to get Cassio's place, suspicion of his wife's infidelity first with Othello and then with Cassio, his own love for Desdemona. Yet there is an element of strangeness in his way of formulating his motives, as though the motive itself rather than the degree of his belief in it were at issue. What could be stranger, for example, than the irrational combination of belief and disbelief contained in his statement on the affair between Emilia and Othello:

> I know not if 't be true . . .
> Yet I, for mere suspicion in that kind,
> Will do, as if for surety.
>
> [I. iii. 388-90]

Also, it is hard for us to suppose that Iago really did suspect Cassio with his "nightcap," or that he was really himself in love with Desdemona. And no less strange is the fact that Iago, having formulated all his motives and proceeded into action, presumably on the strength of them, never once refers to any of them again. The irrational element in the motive hunting is certainly evident, and this, rather than the validity of the motives themselves, is what must concern us. Iago, enumerating his motives and persuading himself to believe them, only to demonstrate their irrelevance by forgetting them later, is certainly not thinking as a rational man; on the other hand, and ironically, he is reacting entirely in accordance with his own remarkable understanding of the nature of jealousy. Jealousy, as he later informs Othello, is that green eyed monster, mocking the food it feeds on. And where there is no such food, what must the jealous man do but persuade himself of its existence, endowing trifles light as air, if need be, with all the certainty of holy writ. The truth or otherwise of the reasons Iago dredges up to justify his jealous hatred of Cassio and Othello is quite irrelevant; they are the food his jealousy needs and that his intellect must provide.

Equally irrational, we must inevitably conclude, is the totality of Iago's behaviour, the way in which, with incredible persistence and ingenuity, he carries out his lunatic plot against Cassio and Othello. By way of rationalization, it is sometimes suggested that Iago starting out with no more than a vague spiteful desire to create mischief, underestimates the passions he is to awaken, and so becomes the unwilling victim of his own machinations. Certainly he is soon caught up in his own web, committed to the lies he has disseminated, unable to retreat; on the other hand he betrays no sign of ever wanting to do so, and views his own successes first against Cassio and then Othello with uninhibited satisfaction. Never once does the intrinsic *insanity* of what he is doing break through to him, the realisation, for example, that *all* the witnesses against him, Cassio, Desdemona, Roderigo, Emilia, Bianca, must somehow be killed if he himself is not sooner or later to be confronted with the awakened wrath of Othello. The truly astounding cleverness of Iago must not be allowed to blind us to the absolute stupidity, indeed the madness, of what he is attempting to do.

Iago, we must conclude, even more so than a Leontes or an Othello, confronts us as the very arche-

type of the jealous man. For here is an all encompassing jealousy directed not only against sexual love but against love itself in all its manifestations. In this connection it is pertinent, by way of conclusion, to consider jealousy as in fact the antithesis of love, as containing within itself the very essence of evil. Iago in the list of actors in the Folio [the first collected edition of Shakespeare's plays] is described as a villain, and in the first act of the play he fully reveals himself as such. However, we have suggested that by reason of his universal reputation for honesty he could not always have been evil but had become so quite suddenly under the impact of jealousy. As a result a consuming, envious hatred of the goodness and love in those who had, as he saw it, betrayed him, takes possession of his soul. Evidences of Iago's hatred of love are everywhere in the play, as for example in his bitter reaction to the outpouring of love between Othello and Desdemona at the moment of their reunion on Cyprus:

> O, you are well tun'd now,
> But I'll set down the pegs that make this music,
> As honest as I am.
>
> [II. i. 199-201]

Or again there is the extremely revealing moment when he recognizes in Cassio the continuation of all those qualities that he himself has irrevocably lost:

> If Cassio do remain,
> He has a daily beauty in his life,
> That makes me ugly.
>
> [V. i. 18-20]

That Iago is a villain, perhaps the most completely villainous character in all literature, is only too evident, and that his villainy originates in, is indeed synonymous with jealousy must also be recognized. By definition the supremely evil man appears as one in whom hatred of love and goodness is carried to the point of containing within itself the desire to reach out and destroy the loving and the good. Not all men of course, fortunately enough, surrender to jealousy with the absoluteness of an Iago, but the implication of *Othello* is that there are such men bearing latent within themselves as a kind of fate a terrible capacity for evil. "God's above all", declares Cassio in a moment of drunken insight; "and there be souls that must be saved, and there be souls must not be saved". To which Iago with tragic irony replies, "It is true, good Lieutenant" [II. iii. 103-05].

That Iago is indeed a damned soul, one predestined by his own intrinsic nature to eventual damnation, is made manifest to us in a number of ways, most frequently by what we might call his conscious diabolism. Iago, in reaction against his former honesty which has failed and betrayed him, dedicates himself in a spirit of jealous revenge to honesty's opposite, evil. Consciously and deliberately he allies himself with the powers of darkness, invoking Hell and night in his first soliloquy and later, after mocking his own "honesty" in advising Cassio to seek Desdemona's help, coming right into the open with devastating explicitness:

> Divinity of hell!
> When devils will their blackest sins put on,
> They do suggest at first with heavenly shows,
> As I do now.
>
> [II. iii. 350-53]

A Shakespearean, witchcraft-conscious audience would have no difficulty in accepting such diabolism as fact, in recognizing Iago as one possessed, glorying in his identification with evil spiritual powers. For them, as he must be for us if we are to understand him, Iago is indeed a "demi-devil", one who can, rhetorically at least, be thought of as possessing the cloven hoof. Equally indicative of diabolism, of the way in which Iago serves and is in turn assisted by the powers of evil, is the disturbing and consistent "run of luck" that he is made to enjoy in carrying out his plans. He causes Roderigo to provoke Cassio on guard, but could not foresee that Cassio in his rage would attack and severely wound Montano. He could advise Cassio to seek the intercession of Desdemona, but could not anticipate her naive importunity or the luckless moments when she should manifest it. Nor could he anticipate that the fatal handkerchief would come into his hands, or that Bianca in a jealous fit would throw it back at Cassio while Othello watched. All this would be sensed in some measure by Shakespeare's audience as indicating the involvement of evil beings, ascendant for the moment, and possessed with a jealous hatred of love and goodness just as their instrument, Iago, is himself possessed.

The close association between evil and jealousy is a dominant issue in *Othello,* almost what the whole play is about; until we are left with the conclusion that there can scarcely be an evil act for which envy or jealousy is not in some degree or wholly responsible. The outcome for love and goodness and innocence in *Othello* is almost unendurably tragic; yet tragedy, as always in Shakespeare, is never allowed the final word. Iago the destroyer is by himself destroyed. Jealousy, self-harming, irrational, demonstrates once again the intrinsic instability of evil, the ultimate impotence of the jealous gods. (pp. 210-19)

> *D. R. Godfrey, "Shakespeare and the Green-Eyed Monster," in* Neophilologus, *Vol. LVI, No. 2, April, 1972, pp. 207-20.*

RACE

Ruth Cowhig

[*Cowhig provides background on blacks in England during Shakespeare's time, stressing the use of racial stereotypes in the dramas of the period. Observing that black people were typically depicted as stock villains, she suggests that Shakespeare's presentation of the noble, dignified* **Othello** *as the hero of a tragedy must have been startling to Elizabethan audiences. Cowhig also examines how several characters in the play, especially* **Iago**, *are racially prejudiced.* **Iago's** *racism is the source of his hatred of* **Othello**, *she claims, and he plays on the prejudices of other characters to turn them against the Moor. Importantly, Cowhig emphasizes that, although Shakespeare consistently challenges stereotypes with his depiction of* **Othello**, *he also demonstrates that, in a white society, the Moor's color isolates him and makes him vulnerable.*]

It is difficult to assess the reactions and attitudes of people in sixteenth-century Britain to the relatively few blacks living amongst them. Their feelings would certainly be very mixed: strangeness and mystery producing a certain fascination and fostering a taste for the exotic: on the other hand prejudice and fear, always easily aroused by people different from ourselves, causing distrust and hostility. This hostility would be encouraged by the widespread belief in the legend that blacks were descendants of Ham in the Genesis story, punished for sexual excess by their blackness. Sexual potency was therefore one of the attributes of the prototype black. Other qualities associated with black people were courage, pride, guilelessness, credulity and easily aroused passions—the list found in John Leo's *The Geographical History of Africa,* a book written in Arabic early in the sixteenth century and translated into English in 1600. Contemporary attitudes may have been more influenced by literary works such as this than by direct experience; but recently the part played by such direct contacts has been rediscovered. The scholarly and original study [*Othello's Countrymen*] by Eldred Jones of these contacts and their effects on Renaissance drama has transformed contemporary attitudes.

Black people were introduced into plays and folk dancing in mediaeval England and later, during the sixteenth century, they often appeared in the more sophisticated court masques. In these, the blackness was at first suggested by a very fine lawn [linen fabric] covering the faces, necks, arms and hands of the actors. Then black stockings, masks and wigs were used; such items are mentioned in surviving lists of properties [theater "props"]. These characters were mainly valued for the exotic aesthetic effects which their contrasting colour provided. The culmination of this tradition can be seen in Ben Jonson's *Masque of Blackness* in 1605, which he produced in answer to Queen Anne's request that the masquers should be 'black-mores at first'. The theme is based upon the longing of the black daughters of Niger to gain whiteness and beauty. This surely contradicts the idea that Elizabethans and Jacobeans were not conscious of colour and had no prejudice: the desirability of whiteness is taken for granted!

Elizabethan drama also used Moorish characters for visual effects and for their association with strange and remote countries. In [Christopher] Marlowe's *Tamburlaine the Great,* for instance, the three Moorish kings play little part in the plot, and have no individual character. Their main contribution to the play is in adding to the impression of power and conquest by emphasising the extent of Tamburlaine's victories. Their blackness also provides a variety of visual effects in the masques. Marlowe's plays reflect the curiosity of his contemporaries about distant countries, and must have whetted the appetites of his audiences for war and conquest; but the black characters are seen from the outside and have no human complexity. (pp. 1-2)

Only as we recognise the familiarity of the figure of the black man as villain in Elizabethan drama can we appreciate what must have been the startling impact on Shakespeare's audience of a black hero of outstanding qualities in his play *Othello.* Inevitably we are forced to ask questions which we cannot satisfactorily answer. Why did Shakespeare choose a black man as the hero of one of his great tragedies? What experience led the dramatist who had portrayed the conventional stereotype in Aaron [in *Titus Andronicus*] in 1590 to break completely with tradition ten years later? Had Shakespeare any direct contact with black people? Why did he select the tale of Othello from the large number of Italian stories available to him?

We cannot answer such questions with certainty, but we may speculate. Until the publication of Eldred Jones' study, *Othello's Countrymen,* in 1965, it was generally assumed that Shakespeare depended only on literary sources for his black characters. Although the presence of black people in England is well documented, it went unrecognised. There are two main sources of information. One is [Richard] Hakluyt's *Principal Navigations,* the huge collection of narratives of Elizabethan sailors and traders which Hakluyt collected and published in twelve volumes. Volumes VI and XI describe voyages during which black men from West Africa were taken aboard, brought back to England, and afterwards used as interpreters on subsequent voyages. Later, between 1562 and 1568, [John] Hawkins had the unhappy distinction of being the first of the English gentleman slave-traders; as well

as bringing 'blackamoores' to England, he sold hundreds of black slaves to Spain.

The other evidence is in the series of royal proclamations and state papers which call attention to the 'great number of Negroes and *blackamoors*' in the realm, 'of which *kinde* of people there are *already here too manye*'. They were regarded by Queen Elizabeth as a threat to her own subjects 'in these hard times of dearth'. Negotiations were carried on between the Queen and Casper van Senden, merchant of Lubeck, to cancel her debt to him for transporting between two and three hundred English prisoners from Spain and Portugal back to England by allowing him to take up a similar number of unwanted black aliens—presumably to sell them as slaves. Although the correspondence shows that the deal never materialised, since the 'owners' of these 'blackamoors' refused to give them up, it is clear that there were several hundreds of black people living in the households of the aristocracy and landed gentry, or working in London taverns. (pp. 4-5)

Thus the sight of black people must have been familiar to Londoners. London was a very busy port, but still a relatively small and overcrowded city, so

Orson Welles as Othello and Michael Mac Liammóir as Iago in Welles's 1952 film adaptation of Othello.

Shakespeare could hardly have avoided seeing them. What thoughts did he have as he watched their faces, men uprooted from their country, their homes and families? I cannot help thinking of Rembrandt's moving study of *The Two Negroes* painted some sixty years later, which expresses their situation poignantly. The encounter with real blacks on the streets of London would have yielded a sense of their common humanity, which would have conflicted with the myths about their cultural, sexual and religious 'otherness' found in the travel books. The play between reality and myth informs *Titus Andronicus:* Shakespeare presents Aaron as a demon, but at the end of the play suddenly shatters the illusion of myth by showing Aaron to be a black *person* with common feelings of compassion and fatherly care for his child. In *Othello* too there is conscious manipulation of reality and myth: Othello is presented initially (through the eyes of Iago and Roderigo) as a dangerous beast, before he reveals himself to be of noble, human status, only to degenerate later to the condition of bloodthirsty and irrational animalism. It is surely not surprising that Shakespeare, the dramatist whose sympathy for the despised alien upsets the balance of the otherwise 'unrealistic' *The Merchant of Venice* should want to create a play about a kind of black man not yet seen on the English stage; a black man whose humanity is eroded by the cunning and racism of whites.

Shakespeare's choice of a black hero for his tragedy must have been deliberate. His direct source was an Italian tale from [Geraldi] Cinthio's *Hecatommithi* (1565); he followed this tale in using the love between a Moor and a young Venetian girl of high birth as the basis of his plot, but in little else. The original story is crude and lacking in subtlety. Cinthio, in accordance with the demands of the time, expresses concern that his tale should have a moral purpose. He gives it as recommending that young people should not marry against the family's wishes, and especially not with someone separated from them by nature, heaven and mode of life. Such a moral has nothing to do with Shakespeare's play, except in so far as he uses it ironically, so his choice of the tale remains obscure. Perhaps he regretted his creation of the cruel and malevolent Aaron, and found himself imagining the feelings of proud men, possibly of royal descent in their own countries, humiliated and degraded as slaves. Whatever his intentions may have been, we have to take seriously the significance of Othello's race in our interpretation of the play. This is all the more important because teachers will find it largely ignored by critical commentaries.

The first effect of Othello's blackness is immediately grasped by the audience, but not always by the reader. It is that he is placed in isolation from the other characters from the very beginning of the play. This isolation is an integral part of Othello's experience constantly operative even if not neces-

sarily at a conscious level; anyone black will readily appreciate that Othello's colour is important for our understanding of his character. Even before his first entry we are forced to focus our attention on his race: the speeches of Iago and Roderigo in the first scene are full of racial antipathy. Othello is 'the thick lips' [I. i. 66], 'an old black ram' [I. i. 88], 'a lascivious Moor' [I. i. 126] and 'a Barbary horse' [I. i. 111-12], and 'he is making the beast with two backs' [cf. I. i. 116-17] with Desdemona. The language is purposely offensive and sexually coarse, and the animal images convey, as they always do, the idea of someone less than human. Iago calculates on arousing in Brabantio all the latent prejudice of Venetian society, and he succeeds. To Brabantio the union is 'a treason of the blood' [I. i. 169], and he feels that its acceptance will reduce Venetian statesmen to 'bondslaves and pagans' [I. ii. 99].

Brabantio occupies a strong position in society. He

> is much beloved
> And hath in his effect a voice potential
> As double as the Duke's
>
> [I. ii. 12-14]

according to Iago. Although he represents a more liberal attitude than Iago's, at least on the surface, his attitude is equally prejudiced. He makes Othello's meetings with Desdemona possible by entertaining him in his own home, but his reaction to the news of the elopement is predictable. He is outraged that this black man should presume so far, and concludes that he must have used charms and witchcraft since otherwise his daughter could never 'fall in love with what she feared to look on' [I. iii. 98]. To him the match is 'against all rules of nature' [I. iii. 101], and when he confronts Othello his abuse is as bitter as Iago's.

But before this confrontation, the audience has seen Othello and we have been impressed by two characteristics. First his pride:

> I fetch my life and being
> From men of royal siege.
>
> [I. ii. 21-2]

and secondly, his confidence in his own achievements and position:

> My services which I have done the Signiory
> Shall out-tongue his complaints.
>
> [I. ii. 18-19]

It is hard to overestimate the reactions of a Renaissance audience to this unfamiliar black man, so noble in bearing and so obviously master of the situation. But however great Othello's confidence, his colour makes his vulnerability plain. If the state had not been in danger, and Othello essential to its defence, Brabantio's expectation of support from the Duke and senate would surely have been realised. He is disappointed; the Duke treats Othello as befits his position as commander-in-chief, addressing him as 'valiant Othello'. The only support Brabantio receives is from the first senator, whose parting words, 'Adieu, brave Moor, Use Desdemona well' [I. iii. 291], while not unfriendly, reveal a superior attitude. Would a senator have so advised a newly married general if he had been white and equal?

Desdemona's stature in the play springs directly from Othello's colour. Beneath a quiet exterior lay the spirited independence which comes out in her defence of her marriage before the Senate. She has resisted the pressures of society to make an approved marriage, shunning 'The wealthy, curled darlings of our nation' [I. ii. 68]. Clearly, Brabantio had exerted no force: he was no Capulet [in *Romeo and Juliet*]. But Desdemona was well aware of the seriousness of her decision to marry Othello: 'my downright violence and storm of fortune' [I. iii. 249] she calls it. Finally she says that she 'saw Othello's visage in his mind' [I. iii. 252]: obviously the audience, conditioned by prejudice, had to make the effort to overcome, with her, the tendency to associate Othello's black face with evil, or at least with inferiority.

It is made clear that the marriage between Othello and Desdemona is fully consummated. Desdemona is as explicit as decorum allows:

> If I be left behind
> A moth of peace, and he go to the war,
> The rites for why I love him are bereft me.
> [I. iii. 255-57]

Othello, on the other hand, disclaims the heat of physical desire when asking that she should go with him to Cyprus:

> I therefore beg it not
> To please the palate of my appetite,
> Nor to comply with heat—the young affects
> In me defunct.
> [I. iii. 261-64]

These speeches relate directly to Othello's colour. Desdemona has to make it clear that his 'sooty bosom' (her father's phrase) is no obstacle to desire; while Othello must defend himself against the unspoken accusations, of the audience as well as of the senators, because of the association of sexual lust with blackness.

In Act III Scene iii, often referred to as the temptation scene, Othello's faith in Desdemona is gradually undermined by Iago's insinuations, and he is eventually reduced by jealousy to an irrational madness. Iago's cynical cunning plays upon Othello's trustfulness:

> The Moor is of a free and open nature
> That thinks men honest that but seem to be so.
> [I. iii. 399-400]

The spectacle of Othello's disintegration is perhaps the most painful in the whole Shakespeare canon: and Iago's destructive cruelty has seemed to many critics to be inadequately motivated. They have spoken of 'motiveless malignity' and 'diabolic intellect', sometimes considering Iago's to be the most interesting character in the play. I think this is an unbalanced view, resulting from the failure to recognise racial issues. Iago's contempt for Othello, despite his grudging recognition of his qualities, his jealousy over Cassio's 'preferment', and the gnawing hatred which drives him on are based upon an arrogant racism. He harps mercilessly upon the unnaturalness of the marriage between Othello and Desdemona:

> Not to affect many proposed matches,
> Of her own clime, complexion and degree,
> Whereto we see in all things nature tends—
> Foh! one may smell in such a will most rank,
> Foul disproportions, thoughts unnatural.
> [III. iii. 229-33]

The exclamation of disgust and the words 'smell' and 'foul' reveal a phobia so obvious that it is strange that it is often passed over. The attack demolishes Othello's defences because this kind of racial contempt exposes his basic insecurity as an alien in a white society. His confidence in Desdemona expressed in 'For she had eyes, and chose me' [I. iii. 189], changes to the misery of

> Haply for I am black
> And have not those soft parts of conversation
> That chamberers have . . .
> [III. iii. 263-65]

This is one of the most moving moments in the play. Given Iago's hatred and astuteness in exploiting other people's weaknesses, which we see in the plot he sets for Cassio, the black Othello is easy game. We are watching the baiting of an alien who cannot fight back on equal terms.

Othello's jealous madness is the more terrifying because of the noble figure he presented in the early scenes, when he is addressed as 'brave Othello' and 'our noble and valiant general' [II. ii. 1], and when proud self-control is his essential quality; he refuses to be roused to anger by Brabantio and Roderigo: 'Keep up your bright swords for the dew will rust them' [I. ii. 58]. After his breakdown we are reminded by Ludovico of his previous moral strengths and self-control: 'Is this the nature / Whom passion could not shake?' [IV. i. 265-66]. Thus the portrait is of a man who totally contradicts the contemporary conception of the black man as one easily swayed by passion. He is the most attractive of all Shakespeare's soldier heroes: one who has achieved high rank entirely on merit. His early history given in Desdemona's account of his wooing is typical of the bitter experience of an African of his times 'Taken by the insolent foe /

And sold to slavery' [I. iii. 137-38]. Othello's military career is everything to him, and the famous 'farewell' speech of Act IV, with its aura of romatic nostalgia, expresses the despair of a man whose achievements have been reduced to nothing: 'Othello's occupation gone' [III. iii. 357]. Spoken by a black Othello, the words 'The big wars / That make ambition virtue' [III. iii. 349-50], have a meaning beyond more rhetoric. Ambition was still reckoned as a sin in Shakespeare's time; but in Othello's case it has been purified by his courage and endurance and by the fact that only ambition could enable him to escape the humiliations of his early life. When he realises that his career is irrevocably over, he looks back at the trappings of war—the 'pride, pomp and circumstance' [III. iii. 354], the 'spirit-stirring drum' [III. iii. 352] and the rest—as a dying man looks back on life.

The sympathies of the audience for Othello are never completely destroyed. The Russian actor, Ostuzhev who set himself to study the character of Othello throughout his career, saw the problem of the final scene as 'acting the part so as to make people love Othello and forget he is a murderer'. When Othello answers Ludovico's rhetorical question 'What shall be said of thee?' [V. ii. 293] with the words, 'An honourable murderer, if you will' [V. ii. 294], we are not outraged by such a statement: instead we see in it a terrible pathos. What we are waiting for is the unmasking of Iago. When this comes, Othello looks down at Iago's feet for the mythical cloven hoofs and demands an explanation from that 'demi-devil', reminding us that blackness of soul in this play belongs to the white villain rather than to his black victim.

The fact that Othello was a baptised Christian had considerable importance for Shakespeare's audience. This is made explicit from the beginning when he quells the drunken broil with the words: 'For Christian shame, put by this barbarous brawl' [II. iii. 172]. In the war he was seen to be leading the forces of Christendom against the Turks. But once Othello becomes subservient to Iago and vows his terrible revenge he seems to revert to superstitious beliefs. How else can we interpret his behaviour over the handkerchief? He seems under the spell of its long history—woven by an old sibyl out of silkworms strangely 'hallowed', given to his mother by an Egyptian with thought-reading powers, and linked with the dire prophecy of loss of love should it be lost. Yet in the final scene it becomes merely, 'An antique token / My father gave my mother' [V. ii. 216-17]. This irrational inconsistency is dramatically credible and suggests that when reason is overthrown, Othello's Christian beliefs give way to the superstitions he has rejected. The Christian veneer is thin. (pp. 7-12)

Shakespeare raises these and other questions about blackness and whiteness without fully resolving them. It rested upon the Elizabethan audience to consider them, this very act of deliberation involving a disturbance of racial complacency. If his purpose was to unsettle or perplex his audience, then he succeeded beyond expectation, for the question of Othello's blackness, and his relation with the white Desdemona, is one that provoked contradictory and heated responses in subsequent centuries. (p. 14)

> *Ruth Cowhig, "Blacks in English Renaissance Drama and the Role of Shakespeare's Othello," in her* The Black Presence in English Literature, *Manchester University Press, 1985, pp. 1-25.*

TIME

Harley Granville-Barker

[Granville-Barker examines the dramatic structure of Othello *and explicates the relation between Shakespeare's manipulation of time and the theme of sexual jealousy. He maintains that time in Act I passes naturally so that the audience can become familiar with the characters. Act II, however, introduces contractions and ambiguities of time that are sustained until Act V, scene ii, when "natural" time resumes, presenting a comprehensive view of the ruined Moor. The critic contends that the precipitous action is both dramatically convincing, since it hurries the audience along, and consistent with the recklessness of* **Iago** *and the pathological sexual jealousy that flaws the character of* **Othello.***]*

[In *Othello*] time is given no unity of treatment at all; it is contracted and expanded like a concertina. For the play's opening and closing the time of the action is the time of its acting; and such an extent of "natural" time (so to call it) is unusual. But minutes stand for hours over the sighting, docking and discharging—with a storm raging, too!—of the three ships which have carried the characters to Cyprus; the entire night of Cassio's undoing passes uninterruptedly in the speaking space of four hundred lines: and we have, of course, Othello murdering Desdemona within twenty-four hours of the consummation of their marriage, when, if Shakespeare let us—or let Othello himself—pause to consider, she plainly *cannot* be guilty of adultery.

Freedom with time is, of course, one of the recognised freedoms of Shakespeare's stage; he is expected only to give his exercise of it the slightest dash of plausibility. But in the maturity of his art he learns how to draw positive dramatic profit from it. For this play's beginning he does not, as we have noted, contract time at all. Moreover, he allows seven hundred lines to the three first scenes when he could well have done their business in half the space or less, could even, as [Samuel] Johnson suggests [in an end-note to *Othello* in his 1765 edition of Shakespeare's plays], have left it to be "occasionally related" afterwards. The profit is made evident when later, by contrast, we find him using contraction of time, and the heightening of tension so facilitated, to disguise the incongruities of the action. For he can do this more easily if he has already familiarised us with the play's characters. And he has done that more easily by presenting them to us in the unconstraint of uncontracted time, asking us for no special effort of make-believe. Accepting what they *are,* we the more readily accept what they *do.* It was well, in particular, to make Iago familiarly lifelike. If his victims are to believe in him, so, in another sense, must we. Hence the profuse self-display to Roderigo. That there is as much lying as truth in it is no matter. A man's lying, once we detect it, is as eloquent of him as the truth.

The contraction of time for the arrival in Cyprus has its dramatic purpose too. Shakespeare could have relegated the business to hearsay. But the spectacular excitement, the suspense, the ecstatic happiness of the reuniting of Othello and Desdemona, give the action fresh stimulus and impetus and compensate for the break in it occasioned by the voyage. Yet there must be no dwelling upon this, which is still only prelude to the capital events to come. For the same reason, the entire night of Cassio's undoing passes with the uninterrupted speaking of four hundred lines. It is no more than a sample of Iago's skill, so it must not be lingered upon either. Amid the distracting variety of its comings and goings we do not remark the contraction. As Iago himself has been let suggest to us:

> Pleasure and action make the hours seem short.

> [II. iii. 379]

Then, upon the entrance of Cassio with his propitiatory aubade and its suggestion of morning, commences the sustained main stretch of the action. This is set to something more complex than a merely contracted, it goes to a sort of ambiguous scheme of time, not only a profitable, but here—for Shakespeare turning story into play—an almost necessary device. After that we have the long last scene set to "natural" time, the play thus ending as it began. The swift-moving, close-packed action, fit product of Iago's ravening will, is over.

> *Enter Othello, and Desdemona in her bed.*

> [s.d., V. ii. 1]

—and, the dreadful deed done, all is done. While the rest come and go about him:

> Here is my journey's end . . .

> [V. ii. 267]

he says, as at a standstill, as in a very void of time.

And as the "natural" time at the play's beginning let us observe the better the man he was, so relaxation to it now lets us mark more fully the wreck that remains.

The three opening scenes move to a scheme of their own, in narrative and in the presentation of character. The first gives us a view of Iago which, if to be proved superficial, is yet a true one (for Shakespeare will never introduce a character misleadingly), and a sample of his double-dealing. Roderigo at the same time paints us a thick-lipped, lascivious Moor, which we discover in the second scene, with a slight, pleasant shock of surprise at the sight of Othello himself, to have been merely a figment of his own jealous chagrin. There also we find quite another Iago: the modest, devoted, disciplined soldier. . . . The third scene takes us to the Senate House, where Brabantio and his griefs, which have shrilly dominated the action so far, find weightier competition in the question of the war, and the State's need of Othello, whose heroic aspect is heightened by this. (pp. 11-14)

The scenic mobility of Shakespeare's stage permits him up to [I. iii] to translate his narrative straightforwardly into action. We pass, that is to say, from Brabantio's house, which Desdemona has just quitted, to the Sagittary, where she and Othello are to be found, and from there to the Senate House, to which he and she (later) and Brabantio are summoned. And the movement itself is given dramatic value by its quickening or slackening or abrupt arrest. We have the feverish impetus of Brabantio's torchlight pursuit; Othello's calm talk to Iago set in sequence and contrast; the encounter with the other current of the servants of the Duke upon their errand; the halt, the averted conflict; then the passing on together of the two parties, in sobered but still hostile detachment, towards the Senate House.

Note also that such narrative as is needed of what has passed before the play begins is mainly postponed to the third of these opening scenes. By then we should be interested in the characters, and the more, therefore, in the narrative itself, which is, besides, given a dramatic value of its own by being framed as a cause pleaded before the Senate. Further, even while we listen to the rebutting of Brabantio's accusation of witchcraft by Othello's "round unvarnished tale" [I. iii. 90], we shall be expecting Desdemona's appearance, the one important figure in this part of the story still to be seen. And this expectancy offsets the risk of the slackening of tension which reminiscent narrative must always involve.

Shakespeare now breaks the continuity of the action: and such a clean break as this is with him unusual. He has to transport his characters to Cyprus. The next scene takes place there. An unmeasured interval of time is suggested, and no scene on shipboard or the like has been provided for a link, nor are any of the events of the voyage recounted. The tempest which drowns the Turks, and rids him of his now superfluous war, and has more thrillingly come near besides to drowning the separated Othello and Desdemona—something of this he does contrive to present to us; and we are plunged into it as we were into the crisis of the play's opening:

> What from the cape can you discern at sea?
>
> Nothing at all. It is a high-wrought flood; I cannot, 'twixt the heaven and the main Descry a sail.
>
> [II. i. 1-4]

—a second start as strenuous as the first. The excitement offsets the breaking of the continuity. And the compression of the events, of the storm and the triple landing, then the resolution of the fears for Othello's safety into the happiness of the reuniting of the two—the bringing of all this within the space of a few minutes' acting raises tension to a high pitch and holds it there. (pp. 14-16)

The proclamation in [II. ii] serves several subsidiary purposes. It helps settle the characters in Cyprus. The chances and excitements of the arrival are over. Othello is in command; but the war is over too, and he only needs bid the people rejoice at peace and his happy marriage. It economically sketches us a background for Cassio's ill-fated carouse. It allows a small breathing space before Iago definitely gets to work. It "neutralises" the action for a moment (a herald is an anonymous voice; he has no individuality), suspends its interest without breaking its continuity. Also it brings its present timelessness to an end; events are given a clock to move by, and with that take on a certain urgency. (pp. 22-3)

[In Act III, scene iii,] the action passes into the ambiguity of time which has troubled so many critics. *Compression* of time, by one means or another, is common form in most drama; we . . . [see] it put to use in the speeding through a single unbroken scene of the whole night of Cassio's betrayal. But now comes—if we are examining the craft of the play—something more complex. When it is acted we notice nothing unusual, and neither story nor characters appear false in retrospect. It is as with the perspective of a picture, painted to be seen from a certain standpoint. Picture and play can be enjoyed and much of their art appreciated with no knowledge of how the effect is gained. But the student needs to know.

We have reached the morrow of the arrival in Cyprus and of the consummation of the marriage. This is plain. It is morning. By the coming midnight or a little later Othello will have murdered Desdemona and killed himself. To that measure of time, plainly demonstrated, the rest of the play's action will move. It comprises no more than seven scenes. From this early hour we pass without interval—the clock no more than customarily speeded—to midday dinner time and past it. Then comes a break in the action (an empty stage; one scene ended, another beginning), which, however, can only allow for a quite inconsiderable interval of time, to judge, early in the following scene, by Desdemona's "Where should I lose that handkerchief, Emilia?" [III. iv. 23]—the handkerchief which we have recently seen Emilia retrieve and pass to Iago. And later in this scene Cassio gives it to Bianca, who begs that she may see him "soon at night" [III. iv. 198]. Then comes another break in the action. But, again, it can involve no long interval of time; since in the scene following Bianca speaks of the handkerchief given her "even now". Later in this scene Lodovico, suddenly come from Venice, is asked by Othello to supper; and between Cassio and Bianca there has been more talk of "tonight" and "supper". Another break in the action; but, again, little or no passing of time can be involved, since midway through the next scene the trumpets sound to supper, and Iago closes it with

> It is now high supper-time and the night grows to waste. . . .
>
> [IV. ii. 242-43]

The following scene opens with Othello, Desdemona and Lodovico coming from supper, with Othello's command to Desdemona:

> Get you to bed on the instant. . . .
>
> [IV. iii. 7]

and ends with her good-night to Emilia. The scene after—of the ambush for Cassio—we have been explicitly told is to be made by Iago to "fall out between twelve and one" [IV. ii. 236-37], and it is, we find, pitch dark, and the town is silent. And from here Othello and Emilia patently go straight to play their parts in the last scene of all, he first, she later, as quickly as she can speed.

These, then, are the events of a single day; and Shakespeare is at unusual pains to make this clear, by the devices of the morning music, dinner-time, supper-time and the midnight dark, and their linking together by the action itself and reference after reference in the dialogue. Nor need we have any doubt of his reasons for this. Only by thus precipitating the action can it be made both effective in the terms of his stage-craft and convincing. If Othello were left time for reflection or the questioning of anyone but Iago, would not the whole flimsy fraud that is practised on him collapse?

But this granted, are they convincing as the events of that particular day, the very morrow of the reunion and of the consummation of the marriage?

Plainly they will not be; and before long Shakespeare has begun to imply that we are weeks or months—or it might be a year or more—away from anything of the sort.

> What sense had I of her stolen hours of
>   lust?
> I saw it not, thought it not; it harmed not
>   me;
> I slept the next night well, was free and
>   merry;
> I found not Cassio's kisses on her
>   lips. . . .
>
>   [III. iii. 338-41]

That is evidence enough, but a variety of other implications go to confirm it; Iago's

> I lay with Cassio lately. . . .
>
>   [III. iii. 413]

Cassio's reference to his "former suit", Bianca's reproach to him

> What, keep a week away? seven days and
>   nights?
> Eight score eight hours. . . . ?
>
>   [III. iv. 173-74]

and more definitely yet, Lodovico's arrival from Venice with the mandate of recall, the war being over—by every assumption of the sort, indeed, Othello and Desdemona and the rest are living the life of [Giraldi] Cinthio's episodic story [in his *Gli Hecatommithi,* from which Shakespeare derived the plot of *Othello*], not at the forced pace of Shakespeare's play. But he wants to make the best of both these calendars; and, in his confident, reckless, dexterous way, he contrives to do so.

Why, however, does he neglect the obvious and simple course of allowing a likely lapse of time between the night of the arrival and of Cassio's disgrace and the priming of Othello to suspect Desdemona and her kindness to him, for which common sense—both our own, and, we might suppose, Iago's—cries out? A sufficient answer is that there has been one such break in the action already, forced on him by the voyage to Cyprus, and he must avoid another.

The bare Elizabethan stage bred a panoramic form of drama; the story straightforwardly unfolded, as many as possible of its more telling incidents presented, narrative supplying the antecedents and filling the gaps. Its only resources of any value are the action itself and the speech; and the whole burden, therefore, of stimulating and sustaining illusion falls on the actor—who, once he has captured his audience, must, like the spellbinding orator he may in method much resemble, be at pains to hold them, or much of his work will continually be to do over again. Our mere acceptance of the fiction, of the story and its peopling, we shall perhaps not withdraw; we came prepared to accept it. Something subtler is involved; the sympathy (in the word's stricter sense) which the art of the actor will have stirred in us. This current interrupted will not be automatically restored. Our emotions, roused and let grow cold, need quick rousing again. And the effects of such forced stoking are apt to stale with repetition.

Hence the help to the Elizabethan actor, with so much dependent on him, of continuity of action. Having once captured his audience, they are the easier to hold. The dramatist finds this too. Shakespeare escapes dealing with minor incidents of the voyage to Cyprus by ignoring them; and he restarts the interrupted action amid the stimulating anxieties of the storm. But such another sustaining device would be hard to find. And were he to allow a likely lapse of time before the attack on Othello's confidence is begun it would but suggest to us when it *is* begun and we watch it proceeding the equal likelihood of an Iago wisely letting enough time pass between assault for the poison's full working. And with that the whole dramatic fabric would begin to crumble. Here would be Cinthio's circumspect Ensign again, and the action left stagnating, the onrush of Othello's passion to be checked and checked again, and he given time to reflect and anyone the opportunity to enlighten him! Give him such respite, and if he then does not, by the single stroke of good sense needed, free himself from the fragile web of lies which is choking him, he will indeed seem to be simply the gull and dolt "as ignorant as dirt" [V. ii. 164] of Emilia's final invective, no tragic hero, certainly.

Shakespeare has to work within the close confines of the dramatic form; and this imposes on him a double economy, a shaping of means to end and end to means, of characters to the action, the action to the characters also. If Othello's ruin is not accomplished without pause or delay, it can hardly be accomplished at all. The circumstances predicate an Iago of swift and reckless decision. These are the very qualities, first, to help him to his barren triumph, then to ensure his downfall. And Othello's precipitate fall from height to depth is tragically appropriate to the man he is—as to the man he is made to be because the fall must be precipitate. Finally, that we may rather feel with Othello in his suffering than despise him for the folly of it, *we* are speeded through time as unwittingly as he is, and left little more chance for reflection.

Most unconscionable treatment of time truly, had time any independent rights! But effect is all. And Shakespeare smooths incongruities away by letting the action follow the shorter, the "hourly" calendar—from dawn and the aubade to midnight and the murder—without more comment than is necessary, while he takes the longer one for granted in a few incidental references. He has only to see that the two do not clash in any overt contradiction.

The change into ambiguity of time is effected in the course of Iago's opening attack upon Othello. This is divided into two, with the summons to dinner and the finding and surrender of the handkerchief for an interlude. In the earlier part—although it is taken for granted—there is no very definite reference to the longer calendar; and Iago, to begin with, deals only in its generalities. Not until the second part do we have the determinate "I lay with Cassio lately . . . " [III. iii. 413], the story of his dream, the matter of the handkerchief, and Othello's own

> I slept the next night well, was free and
>   merry;
> I found not Cassio's kisses on her lips.
>   [III. iii. 340-41]

with the implication that weeks or months may have passed since the morrow of the landing. But why no tribute to likelihood here of some longer interval than that provided merely by the dinner to "the generous islanders" [III. iii. 280], between the sowing of the poison and its fierce, full fruition? There are two answers. From the standpoint of likelihood a suggested interval of days or weeks would largely defeat its own purpose, since the time given the poison to work would seem time given to good sense to intervene too. From the standpoint simply of the play's action, any interruption hereabouts, actual or suggested, must lower its tension and dissipate our interest, at the very juncture, too, when its main business, overlong held back, is fairly under way. Shakespeare will certainly not feel called on to make such a sacrifice to mere likelihood. He does loosen the tension of the inmost theme—all else beside, it would soon become intolerable—upon Othello's departure with Desdemona and by the episode of the handkerchief. But with Iago conducting this our interest will be surely held; and, Emilia left behind, the scene continuing, the continuity of action is kept. And when Othello returns, transformed in the interval from the man merely troubled in mind to a creature incapable of reason, "eaten up with passion . . . " [III. iii. 391], his emotion reflected in us will let *us* also lose count of time, obliterate yesterday in today, confound the weeks with the months in the one intolerable moment.

But the over-riding explanation of this show of Shakespeare's stagecraft is that he is not essentially concerned with time and the calendar at all. These, and other outward circumstances, must be given plausibility. But the play's essential action lies in the processes of thought and feeling by which the characters are moved and the story is forwarded. And the deeper the springs of these the less do time, place, and circumstance affect them. His imagination is concerned with fundamental passions, and its swift working demands uncumbered expression. He may falsify the calendar for his convenience; but we shall find neither trickery nor anomaly in the planning of the battle for Othello's soul. And in the light of the truth of this the rest passes unnoticed. (pp. 30-8)

> *Harley Granville-Barker, in his* Prefaces to Shakespeare: Othello, *fourth series, Sidgwick & Jackson, Ltd., 1945, 223 p.*

Dorothy Tutin as Desdemona and John Gielgud as Othello in Franco Zeffirelli's 1961 Shakespeare Memorial Theatre production of Othello.

OTHELLO

Albert Gerard

[*Gerard examines* **Othello***'s personality, discovering cracks in the "facade" of the generous, confident, self-disciplined husband and general. The critic argues that* **Othello** *believes that his marriage to* **Desdemona** *will transform his life from one of primitive "chaos" to one of civilization and contentment. This naive dream shatters, however, with his increasing jealousy and his growing awareness that his new-found happiness is an illusion. Gerard thus regards* **Othello***'s development as a change from innocence to self-awareness and recognition that he has been looking outside— to* **Desdemona** *and Venetian society—rather than inside himself for his sense of identity. For further commentary on* **Othello***'s character, see the excerpts by A. C. Bradley, D. R. Godfrey, Ruth Cowhig, Wyndham Lewis, and Henry L. Warnken.*]

At the beginning of the play, Othello appears as a noble figure, generous, composed, self-possessed. Besides, he is glamorously happy, both as a general and as a husband. He seems to be a fully integrated man, a great personality at peace with itself. But if we care to scrutinize this impressive and attractive facade, we find that there is a crack in it, which might be described as follows: it is the happiness of a spoilt child, not of a mature mind; it is the brittle wholeness of innocence; it is pre-conscious, pre-rational, pre-moral. Othello has not yet come to grips with the experience of inner crisis. He has had to overcome no moral obstacles. He has not yet left the chamber of maiden-thought, and is still blessedly unaware of the burden of the mystery.

Of course, the life of a general, with its tradition of obedience and authority, is never likely to give rise to acute moral crises—especially at a time when war crimes had not yet been invented. But even Othello's love affair with Desdemona, judging by his own report, seems to have developed smoothly, without painful moral searchings of any kind. Nor is there for him any heart-rending contradiction between his love and his career: Desdemona is even willing to share the austerity of his flinty couch, so that he has every reason to believe that he will be allowed to make the best of both worlds.

Yet, at the core of this monolithic content, there is at least one ominous contradiction which announces the final disintegration of his personality: the contradiction between his obvious openheartedness, honesty and self-approval, and the fact that he does not think it beneath his dignity to court and marry Desdemona secretly. This contradiction is part and parcel of Shakespeare's conscious purpose. As Allardyce Nicoll has observed [in his *Shakespeare*], there is no such secrecy in [Giraldi] Cinthio's tale [the source for Shakespeare's plot of *Othello*], where, instead, the marriage occurs openly, though in the teeth of fierce parental opposition.

Highly significant, too, is the fact that he does not seem to feel any remorse for this most peculiar procedure. When at last he has to face the irate Brabantio, he gives no explanation, offers no apology for his conduct. Everything in his attitude shows that he is completely unaware of infringing the *mores* of Venetian society, the ethical code of Christian behaviour, and the sophisticated conventions of polite morality. Othello quietly thinks of himself as a civilized Christian and a prominent citizen of Venice, certainly not as a barbarian (see II. iii. 170-72). He shares in Desdemona's illusion that his true visage is in his mind.

Beside the deficient understanding of the society into which he has made his way, the motif of the secret marriage then also suggests a definite lack of self-knowledge on Othello's part. His first step towards "perception of sense" about himself occurs in the middle of Act III. While still trying to resist Iago's innuendoes, Othello exclaims:

> Excellent wretch! Perdition catch my soul,
> But I do love thee! and when I love thee
>   not,
> Chaos is come again.
>
> [III. iii. 90-2]

This word, "again", is perhaps the most unexpect-ed word that Shakespeare could have used here. It is one of the most pregnant words in the whole tragedy. It indicates (*a*) Othello's dim sense that his life before he fell in love with Desdemona was in a state of chaos, in spite of the fact that he was at the time quite satisfied with it, and (*b*) his conviction that his love has redeemed him from chaos, has lifted him out of his former barbarousness. Such complacency shows his total obliviousness of the intricacies, the subtleties and the dangers of moral and spiritual growth. In this first anagnorisis [recognition], Othello realizes that he has lived so far in a sphere of spontaneous bravery and natural honesty, but he assumes without any further questionings that his love has gained him easy access to the sphere of moral awareness, of high spiritual existence.

In fact, he assumes that his super-ego has materialised, suddenly and without tears. Hence, of course, the impressive self-assurance of his demeanour in circumstances which would be most embarrassing to any man gifted with more accurate self-knowledge.

This first anagnorisis is soon followed by another one, in which Othello achieves some sort of recognition of what has become of him after his faith in Desdemona has been shattered. The short speech he utters then marks a new step forward in his progress to self-knowledge:

> I had been happy, if the general camp,
> Pioners and all, had tasted her sweet body,
> So I had nothing known. O, now, for ever
> Farewell the tranquil mind! farewell content!
> Farewell the plumed troop, and the big wars,
> That make ambition virtue! O, farewell! . . .
> Farewell! Othello's occupation's gone!
>
> [III. iii. 345-50, 357]

The spontaneous outcry of the first three lines results from Othello's disturbed awareness that the new world he has entered into is one of (to him) unmanageable complexity. He is now facing a new kind of chaos, and he wishes he could take refuge in an ignorance similar to his former condition of moral innocence. The pathetic childishness of this ostrich-like attitude is proportionate in its intensity to the apparent monolithic quality of his previous complacency.

What follows sounds like a *non sequitur*. Instead of this farewell to arms, we might have expected some denunciation of the deceitful aspirations that have led him to this quandary, coupled, maybe, with a resolution to seek oblivion in renewed military activity. But we may surmise that his allusion to "the general camp" [III. iii. 345], reminding him of his "occupation", turns his mind away from his immediate preoccupations. The transition occurs in the line

Farewell the tranquil mind! farewell content!

[III. iii. 348]

which carries ambivalent implications. The content he has now lost is not only the "absolute content" his soul enjoyed as a result of his love for Desdemona: it is also the content he had known previously, at the time when he could rejoice in his "unhoused free condition" [I. ii. 26]. This was the content of innocence and spontaneous adjustment to life. There is no recovering it, for, in this respect, he reached a point of no return when he glimpsed the truly chaotic nature of that state of innocence.

The fact that Othello starts talking about himself in the third person is of considerable significance. G. R. Elliott has noticed [in *Flaming Minister: A Study of Othello*] that the words have "a piercing primitive appeal: he is now simply a name". Besides, in this sudden ejaculation, there is a note of childish self-pity that reminds one of the first lines of the speech. But the main point is that it marks the occurrence of a deep dichotomy in Othello's consciousness of himself. As he had discarded his former self as an emblem of "chaos", so now he discards the super-ego that he thought had emerged into actual existence as a result of his love. It is as if that man known by the name of Othello was different from the one who will be speaking henceforward. The Othello of whom he speaks is the happy husband of Desdemona, the civilized Christian, the worthy Venetian, the illusory super-ego; but he is also the noble-spirited soldier and the natural man who guesses at heaven. That man has now disappeared, and the "I" who speaks of him is truly the savage Othello, the barbarian stripped of his wishful thinking, who gives himself up to jealousy, black magic and cruelty, the man who coarsely announces that he will "chop" his wife "into messes", the man who debases his magnificent oratory by borrowing shamelessly from Iago's lecherous vocabulary.

Thus Othello, whom love had brought from pre-rational, pre-moral satisfaction and adjustment to life to moral awareness and a higher form of "content", is now taken from excessive complacency and illusory happiness to equally excessive despair and nihilism. These are his steps to self-knowledge. That they should drive him to such alternative excesses gives the measure of his lack of judgment.

From the purely psychological point of view of character-analysis, critics have always found it difficult satisfactorily to account for Othello's steep downfall. That it would have been easy, as Robert Bridges wrote [in his essay "The Influence of the Audience on Shakespeare"], for Shakespeare "to have provided a more reasonable ground for Othello's jealousy", is obvious to all reasonable readers. The fact that Othello's destruction occurs through the agency of Iago has induced the critics in the Ro-

mantic tradition to make much of what [Samuel Taylor] Coleridge has called Iago's "superhuman art", which, of course, relieves the Moor of all responsibility and deprives the play of most of its interest on the ethical and psychological level. More searching analyses, however, have shown that Iago is far from being a devil in disguise. And T. S. Eliot [in his essay "Shakespeare and the Stoicism of Seneca"] has exposed the Moor as a case of *bovarysme*, or "the human will to see things as they are not", while Leo Kirschbaum [in the December 1944 *ELH*] has denounced him as "a romantic idealist, who considers human nature superior to what it actually is".

For our examination of *Othello* as a study in the relationships between the intellect and the moral life, it is interesting to note that the ultimate responsibility for the fateful development of the plot rests with a flaw in Othello himself. There is no "reasonable ground" for his jealousy; or, to put it somewhat differently, Shakespeare did not choose to provide any "reasonable" ground for it. The true motive, we may safely deduce, must be unreasonable. Yet, I find it difficult to agree that the Moor "considers human nature superior to what it actually is": this may be true of his opinion of Iago, but Desdemona is really the emblem of purity and trustworthiness that he initially thought her to be. Nor can we justifiably speak of his "*will* to see things as they are not" (though these words might actually fit Desdemona); in his confusion and perplexity there is no opportunity for his will to exert itself in any direction. The basic element that permits Othello's destiny to evolve the way it does is his utter *inability* to grasp the actual. If we want to locate with any accuracy the psychological origin of what F. R. Leavis [in his essay "Diabolic Intellect and the Noble Hero"] has called his "readiness to respond" to Iago's fiendish suggestions, we cannot escape the conclusion that his gullibility makes manifest his lack of rationality, of psychological insight and of mere common sense, and that it is a necessary product of his undeveloped mind.

Othello has to choose between trusting Iago and trusting Desdemona. This is the heart of the matter, put in the simplest possible terms. The question, then, is: why does he rate Iago's honesty higher than Desdemona's? If it is admitted that Iago is not a symbol of devilish skill in evildoing, but a mere fallible villain, the true answer can only be that Othello does not know his own wife.

More than a century of sentimental criticism based on the Romantic view of Othello as the trustful, chivalrous and sublime lover, has blurred our perception of his feeling for Desdemona. The quality of his "love" has recently been gone into with unprecedented thoroughness by G. R. Elliott, who points out that the Moor's speech to the Duke and Senators [I. iii] shows that "his affection for her, though fixed and true, is comparatively superficial". Othello sounds, indeed, curiously detached about Desdemona. His love is clearly subordinated, at that moment, to his soldierly pride. If he asks the Duke to let her go to Cyprus with him, it is because *she* wants it, it is "to be free and bounteous to her mind" [I. iii. 265]. In the juxtaposition of Desdemona's and Othello's speeches about this, there is an uncomfortable suggestion that his love is not at all equal to hers, who "did love the Moor to live with him" [I. iii. 248], and that he is not interested in her as we feel he ought to be. At a later stage the same self-centredness colours his vision of Desdemona as the vital source of his soul's life and happiness: his main concern lies with the "joy" [II. i. 184], the "absolute content" [cf. II. i. 191], the salvation [III. iii. 90-91] of his own soul, not with Desdemona as a woman in love, a human person. It lies with *his* love and the changes his love has wrought in him, rather than with the object of his love. It is not surprising, then, that he should know so little about his wife's inner life as to believe the charges raised by Iago.

On the other hand, his attitude to Desdemona is truly one of idealization, but in a very limited, one might even say philosophical, sense. Coleridge wrote [in his *Lectures and Notes on Shakespeare and Other English Poets*] that "Othello does not kill Desdemona in jealousy, but in the belief that she, his angel, had fallen from the heaven of her native innocence". But Coleridge failed to stress the most important point, which is that this belief is mistaken. Desdemona is *not* "impure and worthless", she has *not* fallen from the heaven of her native innocence. Othello is unable to recognize this, and his failure is thus primarily an intellectual failure.

His attitude to Desdemona is different from that of the "romantic idealist" who endows his girl with qualities which she does not possess. Desdemona does have all the qualities that her husband expects to find in her. What matters to him, however, is not Desdemona as she is, but Desdemona as a symbol, or, in other words, it is his vision of Desdemona.

In his *Essay on Man,* Ernst Cassirer has the following remark about the working of the primitive mind:

> In primitive thought, it is still very difficult to differentiate between the two spheres of being and meaning. They are constantly being confused: a symbol is looked upon as if it were endowed with magical or metaphysical powers.

That is just what has happened to Othello: in Desdemona he has failed to differentiate between the human being and the angelic symbol. Or rather, he has overlooked the woman in his preoccupation with the angel. She is to him merely the emblem of his highest ideal, and their marriage is merely

the ritual of his admission into her native world, into her spiritual sphere of values. Because he is identifying "the two spheres of being and meaning", he is possessed by the feeling that neither these values nor his accession to them have any actual existence outside her: his lack of psychological insight is only matched by his lack of rational power.

The Neo-Platonic conceit that the lover's heart and soul have their dwelling in the person of the beloved is used by Othello in a poignantly literal sense [IV. ii. 57-60]. If she fails him, everything fails him. If she is not pure, then purity does not exist. If she is not true to his ideal, that means that his ideal is an illusion. If it can be established that she does not belong to that world in which he sees her enshrined, that means that there is no such world. She becomes completely and explicitly identified with all higher spiritual values when he says:

> If she be false, O! then heaven mocks itself!
>
> > [III. iii. 278]

Hence the apocalyptic quality of his nihilism and despair.

The fundamental tragic fault in the Moor can therefore be said to lie in the shortcomings of his intellect. His moral balance is without any rational foundation. He is entirely devoid of the capacity for abstraction. He fails to make the right distinction between the sphere of meaning, of the abstract, the ideal, the universal, and the sphere of being, of the concrete, the actual, the singular.

When Othello is finally made to see the truth, he recognizes the utter lack of wisdom [V. ii. 344] which is the mainspring of his tragedy, and, in the final anagnorisis, he sees himself for what he is: a "fool" [V. ii. 323]. The full import of the story is made clear in Othello's last speech, which is so seldom given the attention it merits that it may be well to quote it at some length:

> I pray you, in your letters,
> When you shall these unlucky deeds relate,
> Speak of me as I am; nothing extenuate,
> Nor set down aught in malice: then, must you speak
> Of one that loved not wisely but too well;
> Of one not easily jealous, but being wrought
> Perplex'd in the extreme; of one whose hand,
> Like the base Indian, threw a pearl away
> Richer than all his tribe; of one whose subdued eyes,
> Albeit unused to the melting mood,
> Drop tears as fast as the Arabian trees
> Their medicinal gum. Set you down this;
> And say besides, that in Aleppo once,
> Where a malignant and a turban'd Turk
> Beat a Venetian and traduced the state,
> I took by the throat the circumcised dog,

And smote him, thus.   (*Stabs himself*)

[V. ii. 340-56]

One may find it strange that Shakespeare should
have introduced at the end of Othello's last speech
this apparently irrelevant allusion to a trivial incident in the course of which the Moor killed a Turk
who had insulted Venice. But if we care to investigate the allegorical potentialities of the speech, we
find that it is not a mere fit of oratorical self-
dramatization: it clarifies the meaning of the play
as a whole. There is a link between the pearl, the
Venetian and Desdemona: taken together, they are
an emblem of beauty, moral virtue, spiritual richness and civilized refinement. And there is a link
between the "base Indian", the "malignant Turk"
and Othello himself: all three are barbarians: all
three have shown themselves unaware of the true
value and dignity of what lay within their reach.
Othello has thrown his pearl away, like the Indian.
In so doing, he has insulted, like the Turk, everything that Venice and Desdemona stand for. As the
Turk "traduced the State" [V. ii. 354], so did Othello misrepresent to himself that heaven of which
Desdemona was the sensuous image.

S. L. Bethell [in *Shakespeare Survey* 5 (1952)] has
left us in no doubt that the manner of Othello's
death was intended by Shakespeare as an indication that the hero is doomed to eternal damnation.
Such a view provides us with a suitable climax for
this tragedy. Othello has attained full consciousness of his barbarian nature; yet, even that ultimate flash of awareness does not lift him up above
his true self. He remains a barbarian to the very
end, and condemns his own soul to the everlasting
torments of hell in obeying the same primitive
sense of rough-handed justice that had formerly
prompted him to kill Desdemona. . . . (pp. 100-
06)

> *Albert Gerard, " 'Egregiously an Ass',
> The Dark Side of the Moor: A View of
> Othello's Mind," in* Shakespeare Sur-
> vey: An Annual Survey of Shakespear-
> ian Study and Production, *Vol. 10,
> 1957, pp. 98-106.*

Wyndham Lewis

[*Lewis wrote in a deliberately provocative
style and outside the mainstream of Shakespearean criticism. The majority of his work on
Shakespeare is included in his unusual study*
The Lion and the Fox *(1927). In the following
excerpt from that work, Lewis argues that*
Othello *depicts "the race of men at war with
the race of titans" and that the gods have predetermined that* **Iago,** *the petty Everyman, will
triumph over the grandeur of* **Othello.** *The critic assesses the Moor as the most typical of
Shakespeare's colossi, or giants, "because he
is the simplest" and emphasizes his pure,*
guileless, generous nature and the childlike,
defenseless quality of his soul. Lewis considers **Iago** "no great devil," but instead claims
that he represents an ordinary, average, little
man. For further commentary on **Othello's**
character, see the excerpts by A. C. Bradley,
D. R. Godfrey, Ruth Cowhig, Albert Gerard,
and Henry L. Warnken.*]

Of all the colossi, Othello is the most characteristic,
because he is the simplest, and he is seen in an unequal duel throughout with a perfect specimen of
the appointed enemy of the giant—the representative of the race of men at war with the race of
titans. . . . He is absolutely defenceless: it is as
though he were meeting one of his appointed enemies, disguised of course, as a friend, for the first
time. He seems possessed of no instinct by which
he might scent his antagonist, and so be put on his
guard.

So, at the outset, I will present my version of Othello; and anything that I have subsequently to say
must be read in the light of this interpretation. For
in Othello there is nothing equivocal, I think; and
the black figure of this child-man is one of the
poles of Shakespeare's sensation.

Who that has read Othello's closing speech can
question Shakespeare's intentions here at least?
The overwhelming truth and beauty is the clearest
expression of the favour of Shakespeare's heart
and mind. Nothing that could ever be said would
make us misunderstand what its author meant by
it. Of all his ideal giants this unhappiest, blackest,
most "perplexed" child was the one of Shakespeare's predilection.

The great spectacular "pugnacious" male ideal is
represented perfectly by Othello; who was led out
to the slaughter on the Elizabethan stage just as
the bull is thrust into the spanish bullring. Iago,
the *taurobolus* [bull catcher] of this sacrificial bull,
the little David of this Goliath, or the little feat-
gilded *espada* [matador], is for Shakespeare nothing but Everyman, the Judas of the world, the representative of the crowds around the crucifix, or of
the ferocious crowds at the *corrida* [bull fight], or
of the still more abject roman crowds at the mortuary games. Othello is of the race of Christs, or of the
race of "bulls"; he is the hero with all the magnificent helplessness of the animal, or all the beauty
and ultimate resignation of the god. From the moment he arrives on the scene of his execution, or
when his execution is being prepared, he speaks
with an unmatched grandeur and beauty. To the
troop that is come to look for him, armed and
snarling, he says: "Put up your bright swords or
the dew will rust them!" [I. ii. 59]. And when at last
he has been brought to bay he dies by that significant contrivance of remembering how he had de-
fended the state when it was traduced, and in reviv-
ing this distant blow for his own demise. The great
words roll on in your ears as the curtain falls:

And say besides, that in Aleppo once. . . .
                                [V. ii. 352]

Iago is made to say:

> The Moor, howbeit that I endure him not,
> Is of a constant, loving, noble nature.
>   [II. i. 288-89]

But we do not need this testimony to feel, in all our dealings with this simplest and grandest of his creations, that we are meant to be in the presence of an absolute purity of human guilelessness, a generosity as grand and unaffected, although quick and, "being wrought, Perplexed in the extreme" [V. ii. 345-46], as deep as that of his divine inventor.

There is no utterance in the whole of Shakespeare's plays that reveals the nobleness of his genius and of its intentions in the same way as the speech with which Othello closes:

> Soft you; a word or two before you go.
> I have done the state some service, and
>   they know it.
> No more of that. I pray you, in your letters,
> When you shall these unlucky deeds re-
>   late,
> Speak of me as I am; nothing extenuate,
> Nor set down aught in malice: then, must
>   you speak
> Of one that loved, not wisely, but too well;
> Of one not easily jealous, but, being
>   wrought,
> Perplex'd in the extreme; of one, whose
>   hand,
> Like the base Indian, threw a pearl away,
> Richer than all his tribe; of one, whose
>   subdued eyes, . . .
> Drop tears as fast as the Arabian trees
> Their medicinal gum. Set you down this;
> And say, besides, that in Aleppo once,
> Where a malignant and a turban'd Turk
> Beat a Venetian, and traduced the state,
> I took by the throat the circumcisèd dog,
> And smote him—thus.
>   [V. ii. 338-48, 350-56]

And it is the speech of a military hero, as simple-hearted as Hotspur [in Richard II and 1 Henry IV]. The tremendous and childlike pathos of this simple creature, broken by intrigue so easily and completely, is one of the most significant things for the comprehension of Shakespeare's true thought. For why should so much havoc ensue from the crude "management" of a very ordinary intriguer? It is no great devil that is pitted against him: and so much faultless affection is destroyed with such a mechanical facility. He is a toy in the hands of a person so much less real than himself; in every sense, human and divine, so immeasurably inferior.

> And say besides, that in Aleppo once.

This unhappy child, caught in the fatal machinery of "shakespearian tragedy," just as he might have been by an accident in the well-known world, re-

members, with a measureless pathos, an event in the past to his credit, recalled as an afterthought, and thrown in at the last moment, a poor counter of "honour," to set against the violence to which he has been driven by the whisperings of things that have never existed.

And it is we who are intended to respond to these events, as the Venetian, Lodovico, does, when he apostrophizes Iago, describing him as:

> More fell than anguish, hunger or the sea!
>   [V. ii. 362]

The eloquence of that apostrophe is the measure of the greatness of the heart that we have seen attacked and overcome. We cannot take that as an eloquent outburst only: it was an expression of the author's conviction of the irreparable nature of the offence, because of the purity of the nature that had suffered. The green light of repugnance and judgment is thrown on to the small mechanical villain at the last. (pp. 190-93)

> *Wyndham Lewis, "Othello as the Typical Colossus," in his* The Lion and the Fox: The Role of the Hero in the Plays of Shakespeare, *1927. Reprint by Methuen & Co. Ltd., 1955, pp. 190-98.*

IAGO

A. C. Bradley

[*Bradley closely investigates* **Iago**'s *character by examining his soliloquies. Finding that the motives of hatred and ambition inadequately account for* **Iago**'s *actions, Bradley stresses the importance of the character's sense of superiority and his self-interest in determining his behavior.* **Iago**'s *ego, wounded by the denial of promotion, demands satisfaction, and his schemes and manipulations allow him to reestablish his sense of power and dominance over others. Bradley also finds that* **Iago** *is motivated by a love of excitement and by his perception of himself as an artist. He derives great pleasure from the successful execution of his complex and dangerous intrigues. The critic concludes that* **Iago**'s *evil is comprehensible and therefore human rather than demonic. For further commentary on* **Iago**'s *character, see Bradley's other essay and the excerpts by D. R. Godfrey, Ruth Cowhig, Wyndham Lewis, and Henry L. Warnken.*]

[Let us] consider the rise of Iago's tragedy. Why did he act as we see him acting in the play? What is the answer to that appeal of Othello's:

> Will you, I pray, demand that demi-devil
> Why he hath thus ensnared my soul and
>   body?
>   [V. ii. 301-02]

This question Why? is *the* question about Iago, just as the question Why did Hamlet delay? is *the* question about Hamlet. Iago refused to answer it; but I will venture to say that he *could* not have answered it, any more than Hamlet could tell why he delayed. But Shakespeare knew the answer, and if these characters are great creations and not blunders we ought to be able to find it too.

Is it possible to elicit it from Iago himself against his will? He makes various statements to Roderigo, and he has several soliloquies. From these sources, and especially from the latter, we should learn something. For with Shakespeare soliloquy generally gives information regarding the secret springs as well as the outward course of the plot; and, moreover, it is a curious point of technique with him that the soliloquies of his villains sometimes read almost like explanations offered to the audience. Now, Iago repeatedly offers explanations either to Roderigo or to himself. In the first place, he says more than once that he 'hates' Othello. He gives two reasons for his hatred. Othello has made Cassio lieutenant; and he suspects, and has heard it reported, that Othello has an intrigue with Emilia. Next there is Cassio. He never says he hates Cassio, but he finds in him three causes of offence: Cassio has been preferred to him; he suspects *him* too of an intrigue with Emilia; and, lastly, Cassio has a daily beauty in his life which makes Iago ugly. In addition to these annoyances he wants Cassio's place. As for Roderigo, he calls him a snipe, and who can hate a snipe? But Roderigo knows too much; and he is becoming a nuisance, getting angry, and asking for the gold and jewels he handed to Iago to give to Desdemona. So Iago kills Roderigo. Then for Desdemona: a fig's-end for her virtue! but he has no ill-will to her. In fact he 'loves' her, though he is good enough to explain, varying the word, that his 'lust' is mixed with a desire to pay Othello in his own coin. To be sure she must die, and so must Emilia, and so would Bianca if only the authorities saw things in their true light; but he did not set out with any hostile design against these persons.

Is the account which Iago gives of the causes of his action the true account? The answer of the most popular view will be, 'Yes. Iago was, as he says, chiefly incited by two things, the desire of advancement, and a hatred of Othello due principally to the affair of the lieutenancy. These are perfectly intelligible causes; we have only to add to them unusual ability and cruelty, and all is explained. Why should Coleridge and Hazlitt and Swinburne go further afield?' [see Samuel Taylor Coleridge's *Shakespearean Criticism,* edited by Thomas Middleton Raysor; William Hazlitt's *Characters of Shakespear's Plays;* and Algernon Charles Swinburne's *A Study of Shakespeare*]. To which last question I will at once oppose these: If your view is correct, why should Iago be considered an extraordinary creation; and is it not odd that the people who reject it are the people who elsewhere show an exceptional understanding of Shakespeare?

The difficulty about this popular view is, in the first place, that it attributes to Iago what cannot be found in the Iago of the play. Its Iago is impelled by *passions,* a passion of ambition and a passion of hatred; for no ambition or hatred short of passion could drive a man who is evidently so clear-sighted, and who must hitherto have been so prudent, into a plot so extremely hazardous. Why, then, in the Iago of the play do we find no sign of these passions or of anything approaching to them? Why, if Shakespeare meant that Iago was impelled by them, does he suppress the signs of them? Surely not from want of ability to display them. The poet who painted Macbeth and Shylock [in *The Merchant of Venice*] understood his business. Who ever doubted Macbeth's ambition or Shylock's hate? And what resemblance is there between these passions and any feeling that we can trace in Iago? The resemblance between a volcano in eruption and a flameless fire of coke; the resemblance between a consuming desire to hack and hew your enemy's flesh, and the resentful wish, only too familiar in common life, to inflict pain in return for a slight. Passion, in Shakespeare's plays, is perfectly easy to recognise. What vestige of it, of passion unsatisfied or of passion gratified, is visible in Iago? None: that is the very horror of him. He has *less* passion than an ordinary man, and yet he does these frightful things. The only ground for attributing to him, I do not say a passionate hatred, but anything deserving the name of hatred at all, is his own statement, 'I hate Othello'; and we know what his statements are worth.

But the popular view, beside attributing to Iago what he does not show, ignores what he does show. It selects from his own account of his motives one or two, and drops the rest; and so it makes everything natural. But it fails to perceive how unnatural, how strange and suspicious, his own account is. Certainly he assigns motives enough; the difficulty is that he assigns so many. A man moved by simple passions due to simple causes does not stand fingering his feelings, industriously enumerating their sources, and groping about for new ones. But this is what Iago does. And this is not all. These motives appear and disappear in the most extraordinary manner. Resentment at Cassio's appointment is expressed in the first conversation with Roderigo, and from that moment is never once mentioned again in the whole play. Hatred of Othello is expressed in the First Act alone. Desire to get Cassio's place scarcely appears after the first soliloquy, and when it is gratified Iago does not refer to it by a single word. The suspicion of Cassio's intrigue with Emilia emerges suddenly, as an after-thought, not in the first soliloquy but the second, and then disappears for ever. Iago's 'love' of Desdemona is alluded to in the second soliloquy; there is not the faintest trace of it in word or deed

Othello and Desdemona. Act V, scene ii. By H. Hofman. The Department of Rare Books and Special Collections, The University of Michigan Library.

either before or after. The mention of jealousy of Othello is followed by declarations that Othello is infatuated about Desdemona and is of a constant nature, and during Othello's sufferings Iago never shows a sign of the idea that he is now paying his rival in his own coin. In the second soliloquy he declares that he quite believes Cassio to be in love with Desdemona. It is obvious that he believes no such thing, for he never alludes to the idea again, and within a few hours describes Cassio in soliloquy as an honest fool. His final reason for ill-will to Cassio never appears till the Fifth Act.

What is the meaning of all this? Unless Shakespeare was out of his mind, it must have a meaning. And certainly this meaning is not contained in any of the popular accounts of Iago.

Is it contained then in Coleridge's word 'motive-hunting'? Yes, 'motive-hunting' exactly answers to the impression that Iago's soliloquies produce. He is pondering his design, and unconsciously trying to justify it to himself. He speaks of one or two real feelings, such as resentment against Othello, and

he mentions one or two real causes of these feelings, such as resentment against Othello, and he mentions one or two real causes of these feelings. But these are not enough for him. Along with them, or alone, there come into his head, only to leave it again, ideas and suspicions, the creations of his own baseness or uneasiness, some old, some new, caressed for a moment to feed his purpose and give it a reasonable look, but never really believed in, and never the main forces which are determining his action. In fact, I would venture to describe Iago in these soliloquies as a man setting out on a project which strongly attracts his desire, but at the same time conscious of a resistance to the desire, and unconsciously trying to argue the resistance away by assigning reasons for the project. He is the counterpart of Hamlet, who tries to find reasons for his delay in pursuing a design which excites his aversion. And most of Iago's reasons for action are no more the real ones than Hamlet's reasons for delay were the real ones. Each is moved by forces which he does not understand; and it is probably no accident that these two studies of states psychologically so similar were produced at about the same period.

What then were the real moving forces of Iago's action? Are we to fall back on the idea of a 'motiveless malignity;' that is to say, a disinterested love of evil, or a delight in the pain of others as simple and direct as the delight in one's own pleasure? Surely not. I will not insist that this thing or these things are inconceivable, mere phrases, not ideas; for, even so, it would remain possible that Shakespeare had tried to represent an inconceivability. But there is not the slightest reason to suppose that he did so. Iago's action is intelligible; and indeed the popular view contains enough truth to refute this desperate theory. It greatly exaggerates his desire for advancement, and the ill-will caused by his disappointment, and it ignores other forces more important than these; but it is right in insisting on the presence of this desire and this ill-will, and their presence is enough to destroy Iago's claims to be more than a demi-devil. For love of the evil that advances my interest and hurts a person I dislike, is a very different thing from love of evil simply as evil; and pleasure in the pain of a person disliked or regarded as a competitor is quite distinct from pleasure in the pain of others simply as others. The first is intelligible, and we find it in Iago. The second, even if it were intelligible, we do not find in Iago.

Still, desire of advancement and resentment about the lieutenancy, though factors and indispensable factors in the cause of Iago's action, are neither the principal nor the most characteristic factors. To find these, let us return to our half-completed analysis of the character. Let us remember especially the keen sense of superiority, the contempt of others, the sensitiveness to everything which wounds these feelings, the spite against goodness in men as a thing not only stupid but, both in its nature and by its success, contrary to Iago's nature and irritating to his pride. Let us remember in addition the annoyance of having always to play a part, the consciousness of exceptional but unused ingenuity and address, the enjoyment of action, and the absence of fear. And let us ask what would be the greatest pleasure of such a man, and what the situation which might tempt him to abandon his habitual prudence and pursue this pleasure. Hazlitt and Mr. Swinburne do not put this question, but the answer I proceed to give to it is in principle theirs.

The most delightful thing to such a man would be something that gave an extreme satisfaction to his sense of power and superiority; and if it involved, secondly, the triumphant exertion of his abilities, and, thirdly, the excitement of danger, his delight would be consummated. And the moment most dangerous to such a man would be one when his sense of superiority had met with an affront, so that its habitual craving was reinforced by resent-

ment, while at the same time he saw an opportunity of satisfying it by subjecting to his will the very persons who had affronted it. Now, this is the temptation that comes to Iago. Othello's eminence, Othello's goodness, and his own dependence on Othello, must have been a perpetual annoyance to him. At *any* time he would have enjoyed befooling and tormenting Othello. Under ordinary circumstances he was restrained, chiefly by self-interest, in some slight degree perhaps by the faint pulsations of conscience or humanity. But disappointment at the loss of the lieutenancy supplied the touch of lively resentment that was required to overcome these obstacles; and the prospect of satisfying the sense of power by mastering Othello through an intricate and hazardous intrigue now became irresistible. Iago did not clearly understand what was moving his desire; though he tried to give himself reasons for his action, even those that had some reality made but a small part of the motive force; one may almost say they were no more than the turning of the handle which admits the driving power into the machine. Only once does he appear to see something of the truth. It is when he uses the phrase 'to *plume up my will* in double knavery' [I. iii. 393-94].

To 'plume up the will,' to heighten the sense of power or superiority—this seems to be the unconscious motive of many acts of cruelty which evidently do not spring chiefly from ill-will, and which therefore puzzle and sometimes horrify us most. It is often this that makes a man bully the wife or children of whom he is fond. The boy who torments another boy, as we say, 'for no reason,' or who without any hatred for frogs tortures a frog, is pleased with his victim's pain, not from any disinterested love of evil or pleasure in pain, but mainly because this pain is the unmistakable proof of his own power over his victim. So it is with Iago. His thwarted sense of superiority wants satisfaction. What fuller satisfaction could it find than the consciousness that he is the master of the General who has undervalued him and of the rival who has been preferred to him; that these worthy people, who are so successful and popular and stupid, are mere puppets in his hands, but living puppets, who at the motion of his finger must contort themselves in agony, while all the time they believe that he is their one true friend and comforter? It must have been an ecstasy of bliss to him. And this, granted a most abnormal deadness of human feeling, is, however horrible, perfectly intelligible. There is no mystery in the psychology of Iago; the mystery lies in a further question, which the drama has not to answer, the question why such a being should exist.

Iago's longing to satisfy the sense of power is, I think, the strongest of the forces that drive him on. But there are two others to be noticed. One is the pleasure in an action very difficult and perilous and, therefore, intensely exciting. This action sets all his powers on the strain. He feels the delight of one who executes successfully a feat thoroughly congenial to his special aptitude, and only just within his compass; and, as he is fearless by nature, the fact that a single slip will cost him his life only increases his pleasure. His exhilaration breaks out in the ghastly words with which he greets the sunrise after the night of the drunken tumult which has led to Cassio's disgrace, 'By the mass, 'tis morning. Pleasure and action make the hours seem short' [II. iii. 378-79]. Here, however, the joy in exciting action is quickened by other feelings. It appears more simply elsewhere in such a way as to suggest that nothing but such actions gave him happiness, and that his happiness was greater if the action was destructive as well as exciting. We find it, for instance, in his gleeful cry to Roderigo, who proposes to shout to Brabantio in order to wake him and tell him of his daughter's flight:

> Do, with like timorous accent and dire yell
> As when, by night and negligence, the fire
> Is spied in populous cities.
>
> [I. i. 75-7]

All through that scene; again, in the scene where Cassio is attacked and Roderigo murdered; everywhere where Iago is in physical action, we catch this sound of almost feverish enjoyment. His blood, usually so cold and slow, is racing through his veins.

But Iago, finally, is not simply a man of action; he is an artist. His action is a plot, the intricate plot of a drama, and in the conception and execution of it he experiences the tension and the joy of artistic creation. 'He is,' says Hazlitt, 'an amateur of tragedy in real life; and, instead of employing his invention on imaginary characters or long-forgotten incidents, he takes the bolder and more dangerous course of getting up his plot at home, casts the principal parts among his nearest friends and connections, and rehearses it in downright earnest, with steady nerves and unabated resolution.' Mr. Swinburne lays even greater stress on this aspect of Iago's character, and even declares that 'the very subtlest and strongest component of his complex nature' is 'the instinct of what Mr. [Thomas] Carlyle would call an inarticulate poet.' And those to whom this idea is unfamiliar, and who may suspect it at first sight of being fanciful, will find, if they examine the play in the light of Mr. Swinburne's exposition, that it rests on a true and deep perception, will stand scrutiny, and might easily be illustrated. They may observe, to take only one point, the curious analogy between the early stages of dramatic composition and those soliloquies in which Iago broods over his plot, drawing at first only an outline, puzzled how to fix more than the main idea, and gradually seeing it develop and clarify as he works upon it or lets it work. Here at any rate Shakespeare put a good deal of himself into Iago. But the tragedian in real life was not the

equal of the tragic poet. His psychology, as we shall see, was at fault at a critical point, as Shakespeare's never was. And so his catastrophe came out wrong, and his piece was ruined.

Such, then, seem to be the chief ingredients of the force which, liberated by his resentment at Cassio's promotion, drives Iago from inactivity into action, and sustains him through it. And, to pass to a new point, this force completely possesses him; it is his fate. It is like the passion with which a tragic hero wholly identifies himself, and which bears him on to his doom. It is true that, once embarked on his course, Iago *could* not turn back, even if this passion did abate; and it is also true that he is compelled, by his success in convincing Othello, to advance to conclusions of which at the outset he did not dream. He is thus caught in his own web, and could not liberate himself if he would. But, in fact, he never shows a trace of wishing to do so, not a trace of hesitation, of looking back, or of fear, any more than of remorse; there is no ebb in the tide. As the crisis approaches there passes through his mind a fleeting doubt whether the deaths of Cassio and Roderigo are indispensable; but that uncertainty, which does not concern the main issue, is dismissed, and he goes forward with undiminished zest. Not even in his sleep—as in Richard's before his final battle—does any rebellion of outraged conscience or pity, or any foreboding of despair, force itself into clear consciousness. His fate—which is himself—has completely mastered him: so that, in the later scenes, where the improbability of the entire success of a design built on so many different falsehoods forces itself on the reader, Iago appears for moments not as a consummate schemer, but as a man absolutely infatuated and delivered over to certain destruction.

Iago stands supreme among Shakespeare's evil characters because the greatest intensity and subtlety of imagination have gone to his making, and because he illustrates in the most perfect combination the two facts concerning evil which seem to have impressed Shakespeare most. The first of these is the fact that perfectly sane people exist in whom fellow-feeling of any kind is so weak that an almost absolute egoism becomes possible to them, and with it those hard vices—such as ingratitude and cruelty—which to Shakespeare were far the worst. The second is that such evil is compatible, and even appears to ally itself easily, with exceptional powers of will and intellect. In the latter respect Iago is nearly or quite the equal of Richard, in egoism he is the superior, and his inferiority in passion and massive force only makes him more repulsive. How is it then that we can bear to contemplate him; nay, that, if we really imagine him, we feel admiration and some kind of sympathy? Henry the Fifth tells us:

> There is some soul of goodness in things evil,
> Would men observingly distil it out;
>
> [*Henry V,* IV. i. 4-5]

but here, it may be said, we are shown a thing absolutely evil, and—what is more dreadful still—this absolute evil is united with supreme intellectual power. Why is the representation tolerable, and why do we not accuse its author either of untruth or of a desperate pessimism?

To these questions it might at once be replied: Iago does not stand alone; he is a factor in a whole; and we perceive him there and not in isolation, acted upon as well as acting, destroyed as well as destroying. But, although this is true and important, I pass it by and, continuing to regard him by himself, I would make three remarks in answer to the questions.

In the first place, Iago is not merely negative or evil—far from it. Those very forces that moved him and made his fate—sense of power, delight in performing a difficult and dangerous action, delight in the exercise of artistic skill—are not at all evil things. We sympathise with one or other of them almost every day of our lives. And, accordingly, though in Iago they are combined with something detestable and so contribute to evil, our perception of them is accompanied with sympathy. In the same way, Iago's insight, dexterity, quickness, address, and the like, are in themselves admirable things; the perfect man would possess them. And certainly he would possess also Iago's courage and self-control, and, like Iago, would stand above the impulses of mere feeling, lord of his inner world. All this goes to evil ends in Iago, but in itself it has a great worth; and, although in reading, of course, we do not sift it out and regard it separately, it inevitably affects us and mingles admiration with our hatred or horror.

All this, however, might apparently co-exist with absolute egoism and total want of humanity. But, in the second place, it is not true that in Iago this egoism and this want are absolute, and that in this sense he is a thing of mere evil. They are frightful, but if they were absolute Iago would be a monster, not a man. The fact is, he *tries* to make them absolute and cannot succeed; and the traces of conscience, shame and humanity, though faint, are discernible. If his egoism were absolute he would be perfectly indifferent to the opinion of others; and he clearly is not so. His very irritation at goodness, again, is a sign that his faith in his creed is not entirely firm; and it is not entirely firm because he himself has a perception, however dim, of the goodness of goodness. What is the meaning of the last reason he gives himself for killing Cassio:

> He hath a daily beauty in his life
> That makes me ugly?
>
> 　　　　　　　　　　　　　[V. i. 19-20]

Does he mean that he is ugly to others? Then he is not an absolute egoist. Does he mean that he is ugly to himself? Then he makes an open confession of moral sense. And, once more, if he really possessed no moral sense, we should never have heard those soliloquies which so clearly betray his uneasiness and his unconscious desire to persuade himself that he has some excuse for the villainy he contemplates. These seem to be indubitable proofs that, against his will, Iago is a little better than his creed, and has failed to withdraw himself wholly from the human atmosphere about him. And to these proofs I would add, though with less confidence, two others. Iago's momentary doubt towards the end whether Roderigo and Cassio must be killed has always surprised me. As a mere matter of calculation it is perfectly obvious that they must; and I believe his hesitation is not merely intellectual, it is another symptom of the obscure working of conscience or humanity. Lastly, is it not significant that, when once his plot has begun to develop, Iago never seeks the presence of Desdemona; that he seems to leave her as quickly as he can [III. iv. 138]; and that, when he is fetched by Emilia to see her in her distress [IV. ii. 110], we fail to catch in his words any sign of the pleasure he shows in Othello's misery, and seem rather to perceive a certain discomfort, and, if one dare say it, a faint touch of shame or remorse? This interpretation of the passage, I admit, is not inevitable, but to my mind (quite apart from any theorising about Iago) it seems the natural one. And if it is right, Iago's discomfort is easily understood; for Desdemona is the one person concerned against whom it is impossible for him even to imagine a ground of resentment, and so an excuse for cruelty.

There remains, thirdly, the idea that Iago is a man of supreme intellect who is at the same time supremely wicked. That he is supremely wicked nobody will doubt; and I have claimed for him nothing that will interfere with his right to that title. But to say that his intellectual power is supreme is to make a great mistake. Within certain limits he has indeed extraordinary penetration, quickness, inventiveness, adaptiveness; but the limits are defined with the hardest of lines, and they are narrow limits. It would scarcely be unjust to call him simply astonishingly clever, or simply a consummate master of intrigue. But compare him with one who may perhaps be roughly called a bad man of supreme intellectual power, Napoleon, and you see how small and negative Iago's mind is, incapable of Napoleon's military achievements, and much more incapable of his political constructions. Or, to keep within the Shakespearean world, compare him with Hamlet, and you perceive how miserably close is his intellectual horizon; that such a thing as a thought beyond the reaches of his soul has never come near him; that he is prosaic through and through, deaf and blind to all but a tiny fragment of the meaning of things. Is it not quite absurd, then, to call him a man of supreme intellect?

And observe, lastly, that his failure in perception

is closely connected with his badness. He was destroyed by the power that he attacked, the power of love; and he was destroyed by it because he could not understand it; and he could not understand it because it was not in him. Iago never meant his plot to be so dangerous to himself. He knew that jealousy is painful, but the jealousy of a love like Othello's he could not imagine, and he found himself involved in murders which were no part of his original design. That difficulty he surmounted, and his changed plot still seemed to prosper. Roderigo and Cassio and Desdemona once dead, all will be well. Nay, when he fails to kill Cassio, all may still be well. He will avow that he told Othello of the adultery, and persist that he told the truth, and Cassio will deny it in vain. And then, in a moment, his plot is shattered by a blow from a quarter where he never dreamt of danger. He knows his wife, he thinks. She is not over-scrupulous, she will do anything to please him, and she has learnt obedience. But one thing in her he does not know—that she *loves* her mistress and would face a hundred deaths sooner than see her fair fame darkened. There is genuine astonishment in his outburst 'What! Are you mad?' [V. ii. 194] as it dawns upon him that she means to speak the truth about the handkerchief. But he might well have applied himself the words she flings at Othello,

> O gull! O dolt!
> As ignorant as dirt!
>
> [V. ii. 163-64]

The foulness of his own soul made him so ignorant that he built into the marvellous structure of his plot a piece of crass stupidity.

To the thinking mind the divorce of unusual intellect from goodness is a thing to startle; and Shakespeare clearly felt it so. The combination of unusual intellect with extreme evil is more than startling, it is frightful. It is rare, but it exists; and Shakespeare represented it in Iago. But the alliance of evil like Iago's with *supreme* intellect is an impossible fiction; and Shakespeare's fictions were truth. (pp. 222-37)

> *A. C. Bradley, "Othello," in his* Shakespearean Tragedy: Lectures on Hamlet, Othello, King Lear, Macbeth, *second edition, Macmillan and Co., Limited, 1905, pp. 207-42.*

Henry L. Warnken

[*Warnken examines the relationship between* **Iago** *and* **Othello**, *determining that while* **Iago's** *evil corrupts* **Othello**, *the potential for evil already lurked within the Moor—* **Iago** *merely frees his capacity for evil.* **Iago's** *strengths—his ability to quickly exploit situations, his knowledge of human nature, and his innate cunning—exploit* **Othello's** *weaknesses—sensitivity, pride, insecurity, and short sightedness. The critic finds that* **Othello** *gradually adopts* **Iago's** *speech patterns and world view, and by the play's end* **Iago** *"penetrates* **Othello's** *character, and plays upon its weakenesses, nourishing as he does so, the evil already present within* **Othello.**" *Thus,* **Othello** *ends the play dominated by the emotions over which, in the opening scenes, he had insisted he had control. By succumbing to these emotions, he destroys himself. For further commentary on the character of* **Iago**, *see the excerpts by A. C. Bradley, D. R. Godfrey, Ruth Cowhig, and Wyndham Lewis.*]

Iago is perhaps Shakespeare's greatest villain. He is hate and evil made physical, the most fully developed member of a group of characters that includes Richard III, Edmund [in *King Lear*], and Goneril and Regan [in *King Lear*]. Bernard Spivack, in *Shakespeare and the Allegory of Evil*, has suggested that Iago is the medieval Vice given new life by Shakespeare [the Morality Play character Vice would tempt the protagonist].

Such a judgment is correct; but it would be misleading to conclude that Othello is the embodiment of goodness and trust, and therefore, nothing more than the innocent foil for the other's wickedness. Othello is, in fact, the source of Iago's diabolical inspiration. He contains within himself the potential for evil. Iago could never have succeeded in his designs were it not for Othello's dark suspicions, his predisposition to mistrust and the sense of inferiority it breeds.

Iago repeatedly tries to justify his actions with the same kind of superficial self-righteousness manifested by Othello. He feels and thinks that he has been cheated, betrayed, made a fool of by others—but he has no proof. His arguments for revenge are built on suspicion, feeling, emotion, and impulse. He has no proof, for example, that Othello—or Cassio—has committed adultery with Emilia; he acts merely on suggestion and rationalization. In this he is remarkably similar to Othello, who also has a habit of accepting things at face value, acting on impulse and suspicion rather than on proof. Because he acts and thinks in this manner, Othello—like Iago—comes to accept the notion that mankind is moved only by the most selfish motives. Desdemona herself assumes this aspect in his eyes. Othello comes to see her with the same warped and corrupted imagination displayed by Iago.

Iago is clearly evil; but as the play progresses, Othello appears less good, less innocent than the public image of the opening scenes may lead one to suppose. Iago may manipulate Othello, but Othello is no mere puppet. By the middle of the play, his thoughts and feelings echo Iago's. He is the medium through which Iago works his diabolical plans—but he is a willing medium, responding to Iago's suggestions with the same kind of pseudo-rational justification Iago has insisted on as an excuse for his own actions. Iago thus emerges as a *projection* of Othello, the full embodiment of the weaknesses and limitations of the other. Iago feeds on the errors that result from Othello's self-deception; but he himself is deceived in his vision of the world. For him, mankind is corruptible; love is a mere illusion; women are inferior beings. He acts on these assumptions in the same way that Othello acts on his warped vision of love, trust, and honor. Both act on a false set of premises. The relationship thus established is reflected and magnified, as will be seen, in the imagery and verbal patterns of the play.

One of the most striking of Iago's characteristics is his uncanny ability to take advantage of the situations and opportunities presented to him. His strategy, of course, does not succeed completely: Cassio remains alive, and Iago himself is captured and his plot revealed. On the whole, however, he is unbelievably successful. In his hands, the slightest shred of gossip, hearsay, or overheard conversation becomes a dangerous catalyst, a catalyst that intensifies Othello's reaction to the facts and situations Iago places before him.

Othello is easy prey for Iago because he is extremely sensitive and prone to anger. So long as his confidence remains unshaken, he has complete command of a situation. This is clearly seen when Brabantio, Roderigo, and others, threaten to attack him:

> Keep up your bright swords, for the dew
> will rust them.
> Good signior, you shall more command
> with years
> Than with your weapons.
>
> [I. ii. 59-61]

When moved to anger, however, he tends to ignore reason—as when he comes upon the drunken Cassio, following the street fight engineered by Iago:

> Now, by heaven,
> My blood begins my safer guides to rule,
> And passion, having my best judgment
> collied,
> Assays to lead the way.
>
> [II. iii. 204-07]

Iago has already understood Othello's tendency to react without reason to a situation which touches him personally. He understands well that Othello's emotions feed and wax violent on doubt, that he seems to have a built-in capacity for self-deception, which can be utilized by Iago for his own ends. He works especially on Othello's doubt—planted in him by Brabantio's statements early in the play—that perhaps his marriage to Desdemona is a perversion of nature; he plays on Othello's ignorance of life and people, especially in Venice, and on his inability to distinguish between appearance and reality.

> The Moor is of a free and open nature
> That thinks men honest that but seem to
> be so.
>
> [I. iii. 399-400]

Othello's judgment of Iago is, of course, the best illustration of this. "He holds me well" [I. iii. 390], Iago reminds us, but he himself is a much severer judge:

> . . . little godliness I have . . .
>
> [I. ii. 9]
>
> . . . oft my jealousy
> Shapes faults that are not . . .
>
> [III. iii. 147-48]
>
> I am a very villain. . . .
>
> [IV. i. 125]

The recognition of the contradiction between appearance and reality in his own case gives Iago the confidence he needs to turn fiction into fact and convince Othello that fair is foul. He correctly evaluates Othello's love for Desdemona:

> Our General's wife is now the General . . .
> for . . . he hath devoted and given up himself to the contemplation, mark, and denotement of her parts and graces.
>
> [II. iii. 314-15, 316-18]
>
> His soul is . . . enfetter'd to her love
>
> [II. iii. 345]

—but he has no doubt about his ability to undermine that reality. He succeeds very often with a mere hint—as, for example, the suggestion that Desdemona can not possibly escape the corruption for which the Venetian women (he implies) are notorious:

> In Venice they do let heaven see the
> pranks
> They dare not show their husbands.
>
> [III. iii. 202-03]

In the eyes of others, Iago is understandably "brave," "honest," and "just," for he invariably calls upon the virtues of others to effect their fall. It is the soldier's fearlessness, his impulsive response in critical situations, which he plays upon to bring Othello to ruin. Defending his marriage to Desdemona before the Duke and others in a council chamber, Othello reminds them that

> . . . since these arms of mine had seven
> years' pith
> Till now some nine moons wasted, they
> have us'd
> Their dearest action in the tented field;
> And little of this great world can I speak
> More than pertains to feats of broil and
> battle.
>
> [I. iii. 83-7]

He has known the battlefield and war since early youth. He is a soldier, and therefore accustomed to hardship and cruelty. He himself admits that he can withstand hardship, and may even be stimulated by it:

> I do agnize
> A natural and prompt alacrity
> I find in hardness.
>
> [I. iii. 231-33]

He is also accustomed to acting quickly and making decisions rapidly, concentrating on the present state of affairs, rather than future consequences. In Act II Scene 3, when he puts an end to the drunken brawl going on when he enters, Othello immediately demands the name of the man who started it. The first man he asks is Iago. Iago lies, saying he does not know. Finding no answer here, he turns to Cassio himself. Again, no answer, so he turns to Montano. But he, too, refuses to point a finger, and consequently, Othello learns nothing. He knows what he wants, but he lacks the reason to show him the means to obtain it. It never once enters his mind that he could see each man personally and perhaps in this manner arrive at something reasonably close to the truth. But as the situation stands at that moment, he cannot understand it; his "passion" begins "to lead the way" and his "best judgment" is obscured [II. iii. 206-07]. The whole matter is "monstrous." The proof he finally does accept is Iago's; he makes no real attempt to hear Cassio. Othello's actions here reflect his military manner of thinking. On the field, when danger and uncertainty threaten, one must gather facts as quickly as possible, reach a decision, and implement it. Such a method of handling things may succeed brilliantly when employed on the battleground; but when used in every-day life, when used with respect to one's wife and friends, the results may be disastrous. Physically, Othello is living like a civilian; mentally, like a soldier. When a domestic problem arises he tries to solve it as if he were on the battlefield. Cassio is accused; Othello faces the situation, accepts Iago's "evidence," makes a decision, and Cassio is dismissed. Desdemona is accused; Othello faces the situation, accepts Iago's "evidence," makes a decision, and Desdemona is murdered.

Othello is quick to make decisions and act upon them, and so is Iago. Although Iago makes some attempt to reason out his plans, his reasoning nevertheless comes in flashes; a moment's reason for a moment's advancement. As soon as his plan "is engendr'd," he acts quickly so that he will "Dull not device by coldness and delay" [II. iii. 388]. Later in the play, going to plant Desdemona's handkerchief in Cassio's room, Iago senses that "this may do something" [III. iii. 324]. Like Othello, Iago also knows war. He has served with Othello at Rhodes and Cyprus and has, of course, " . . . in the trade of war . . . slain men" [I. ii. 1]. Although Othello seems to seek understanding rather than destruction, he emerges, in the course of the play, as the image of Iago even in this respect; in his very attempts to understand Desdemona, he will destroy her.

The focal point of the entire play is Act III Scene 3,

and it is here that Othello begins to show most clearly his Iago-like traits, attitudes, and verbal patterns. Watching Cassio leave Desdemona, Iago sets things in motion by exclaiming, "Ha! I like not that" [III. iii. 35]. Iago speaks it but Othello thinks it, for he adds, "Was not that Cassio parted from my wife?" [III. iii. 37]. Iago answers that it could not have been Cassio, for he would never "steal away so guilty-like" [III. iii. 39]. And Othello replies, "I do believe 'twas he" [III. iii. 40], beginning to confirm the doubts he has in his own mind.

Later, defending Cassio (and trying to help him regain Othello's friendship), Desdemona describes him as the one "that came a-wooing with you" [III. iii. 71]. Iago catches this and quickly makes use of it:

> *Iago.* Did Michael Cassio, when you woo'd my lady,
> Know of your love?
>   *Oth.* He did, from first to last. Why dost thou ask?
>   *Iago.* But for a satisfaction of my thought;
> No further harm.
>
> [III. iii. 94-8]

Iago here is the doubt in Othello's own mind. Othello suspects Desdemona and Cassio, and although Iago asks the questions, they are merely "echoes" of Othello's own thoughts. He does not realize how closely Iago's words match his thoughts, but he does recognize that what is in Iago's mind is a "monster," a thing "too hideous to be shown" [III. iii. 108]. Whenever Othello cannot understand something it is "monstrous"; he describes the drunken brawl in Act II Scene 3 in the same way; and later, when Iago tells him of Cassio's supposed dream (in which he makes love to Desdemona) that, too, is "monstrous." Whatever Othello cannot comprehend he sees as some hideous creation; but the creation, in a very real sense, is his own. It is his because in demanding proof, he has already accepted the implications in Iago's veiled accusations. He will accept anything that seems like proof, or rather, anything that "honest" Iago offers him as proof. Interestingly enough, he always demands proof from others: he never seeks it on his own initiative.

Iago is very close to Othello in the sense that he, too, never really obtains proof for the things he fears or believes others have done to him. He lacks proof, for example, that Othello and Cassio have committed adultery with Emilia. And he obviously lacks proof for many of the things he tells Othello about Desdemona. It is perhaps this tendency to accept things blindly, on a kind of perverted faith, that enables Iago to reach Othello so readily with the most far-fetched insinuations and concocted stories.

The more twisted and perverted the information Iago gives to Othello, the more Othello seems to be-

James Earl Jones as Othello and Christopher Plummer as Iago in a 1981 American Shakespeare Festival production of Othello.

lieve it. He still fails to understand Iago: "I know thou'rt full of love and honesty" [III. iii. 118]. Iago, true, honest friend that he is, warns Othello to "beware . . . of jealousy" for it is a "green-ey'd monster" [III. iii. 165-66]. His thoughts are running parallel to Othello's and he uses one of the words Othello originally borrowed from him when he denotes something as monstrous.

Othello, constantly hindered by his limited understanding of others, cannot determine where he stands:

> I think my wife be honest, and think she
> is not;
> I think that thou art just, and think thou
> art not.
> I'll have some proof . . . .
>   Would I were satisfied!
>   [III. iii. 384-86, 390]

And Iago answers:

> I see, sir, you are eaten up with passion.
>   [III. iii. 391]

He has seen Othello like this before, in Act II Scene 3, when he could not comprehend the reasons for the street fight:

> My blood begins my safer guides to rule.
>   [II. iii. 205]

The Moor's passion runs over his reason, and he asks Iago:

> Give me a living reason she's disloyal.
>   [III. iii. 409]

Once again he wants proof, but asks for it, instead of trying to obtain it on his own. Instead of using his own reasoning, he lets Iago do it for him. Iago now goes on to describe how he heard Cassio murmuring in his sleep about his love-making to Desdemona. Othello, still incapable of understanding fully what is happening, utters his old cry "O monstrous! monstrous!" and Iago replies, "Nay, this was but his dream" [III. iii. 427]. But in Othello's mind this dream "denoted a foregone conclusion" [III. iii. 428]. Othello accepts the dream partly because in his aroused emotional state he will believe virtually anything, and partly because Iago, by describing the dream, makes audible the thoughts in Othello's own mind. Though Iago may tell the dream, Othello has already thought it; the dream, in sense, is his own. Iago confirms Othello's own doubts and suspicions.

Iago can easily strengthen such doubts because the two men are so similar. For example, Iago often speaks in a brusque, harsh manner; now Othello speaks in the same way:

> I'll tear her all to pieces.
>
> [III. iii. 431]
>
> I would have him [Cassio] nine years a-killing!
>
> [IV. i. 178]
>
> Ay, let her rot, and perish, and be damn'd tonight; for she shall not live.
>
> [IV. i. 181-82]

Othello can speak this way of Desdemona, because he is ready to "see" that what Iago has been telling him is "true." What Iago tells him merely reinforces his own doubts and fears; proof is not really necessary since Iago's words merely echo Othello's own dark judgments. As the identity between the designs of Iago and the conclusions of the Moor becomes more explicit, Othello comes to sound like Iago more and more. In Act I, Iago had exclaimed:

> I have't! It is engend'red! Hell and night
> Must bring this monstrous birth to the world's light.
>
> [I. iii. 403-04]

And later:

> Divinity of hell!
> When devils will the blackest sins put on.
> [II. iii. 350-51]

Othello soon swears revenge in much the same terms:

> Arise, black vengeance, from the hollow hell!
>
> [III. iii. 447]

Othello, full of "bloody thoughts," now demands "blood, blood, blood" [III. iii. 457, 451], the very word used by Iago on a number of earlier occasions.

Othello's thoughts are now as evil as Iago's, and to think like Iago is to speak like him. Now, in his bewilderment and the confusion brought on by his lack of reason and discrimination, Othello takes evil for good and good for evil. Desdemona has become a "devil" and Iago is now Othello's "lieutenant." And when Iago utters, "I am your own for ever" [III. iii. 479], he echoes the earlier words that Othello spoke to him: "I am bound to thee for ever" [III. iii. 213].

Iago continues to work upon Othello, and in Act IV Scene 1, he plans to have Cassio talk about Bianca, and Othello, hiding and listening, will think that he is speaking about Desdemona. But before Othello goes behind his hiding place, Iago urges him to "mark the fleers, the gibes, and notable scorns that dwell in every region of his [Cassio's] face" [IV. i. 82-3]. Othello accepts Iago's words because they reflect what he has already conceived in his own mind. He agrees with Iago's picture of Cas-

sio because he himself pictures the former officer in the same way. After the conversation between Iago, Cassio, and later, Bianca, Othello emerges from his hiding place completely convinced of Cassio's guilt: "How shall I murther him, Iago?" [IV. i. 170]. His emotions are so intense and his desire for vengeance so strong, that he forgets that Iago has already promised to kill Cassio:

> *Oth.* Within these three days let me hear thee say That Cassio's not alive.
>
> *Iago.* My friend is dead; 'tis done at your request.
>
> [III. iii. 472-74]

He has, for the moment, lost all love for Desdemona, for his "heart is turn'd to stone" [IV. i. 182]. Iago at this point reinforces practically everything Othello says. The two seem in perfect accord. Iago's success is assured; all he does from this time on is to elaborate the evil Othello has come to acknowledge within himself. The following dialogue is, in a sense, the workings of one mind:

> *Oth.*   I will chop her into messes! Cuckold me!
>
> *Iago.*   O, 'tis foul in her.
>
> *Oth.*   With mine officer!
>
> *Iago.*   That's fouler.
>
> *Oth.*   Get me some poison, Iago, this night. I'll not expostulate with her, lest her body and beauty unprovide my mind again. This night, Iago!
>
> *Iago.*   Do it not with poison. Strangle her in her bed, even the bed she hath contaminated.
>
> *Oth.*   Good, good! The justice of it pleases. Very good!
>
> [IV. i. 200-10]

Parallels such as this between Iago and Othello are reinforced by the imagery and verbal echoes found in the play. One of the primary patterns of imagery is that of animals, and more than half of these images are Iago's. The animals which he mentions are usually small and repellent in some way, whether it be for their ugliness, filth, cunning, or some other quality the reader normally associates with them. Iago's use of such images can be seen when he and Roderigo come at night to awake Brabantio in order to tell him that his daughter has eloped with Othello and is by now married to him. Othello's happiness must be destroyed by constant irritation, and he tells Roderigo:

> Plague him with flies.
>
> [I. i. 71]

Animal and sexual images are combined in his conversation with Brabantio:

> Even now, now, very now, an old black ram

Is tupping your white ewe.

[I. i. 88-9]

. . . you'll have your daughter cover'd
with a Barbary horse.

[I. i. 111-12]

. . . your daughter and the Moor are
now making the beast with two backs.

[I. i. 116-17]

With such terms Iago reveals his firm conviction
that all love is lust. By using imagery of this kind
he provides a powerful emotional accompaniment
for his arguments, which are designed to convince
Othello of Desdemona's unfaithfulness. Iago plays
upon Othello's fear that Desdemona might some
day deceive him as she did her father. He manages
to twist Othello's view of his own marriage until it
appears to be nothing more than a perversion of
nature, and corrupts his image of Desdemona,
until she seems to be nothing but a prostitute.

These patterns of animal, sexual and other images
are highly important, because they underline the
close similarities that exist between the two apparently different personalities. It is perhaps even
more significant to note that such patterns of imagery abound in Iago's speech, initially, but are
gradually absorbed and taken over by Othello as
his mind and speech become twisted and corrupted by the evil rising up within him. Throughout
the early part of the play, Iago makes repeated references to animals, most of them possessing cruel
and despicable traits. He mentions the fox, with its
selfish cunning, the ass, with its stupidity, the ba-
boon, the locust, the spider, the wolf, the fly, the
goat, and others. Through images such as these, he
suggests stealth and evil, lechery, disease, and disaster. Such imagery reinforces Iago's view of life
and people as things governed by animal instinct.
Iago's world is similar in this respect to that in
King Lear, where human beings are reduced to
nothing more than a dog-eat-dog relationship.
From Act III Scene 3 onward Othello joins Iago in
the habit of seeing and describing things in terms
of repulsive or dangerous animals. He echoes the
earlier references to the goat, toad, dog, asp, worm,
raven, bear, crocodile, monkey, and fly. . . . The
progression is clear: the images used by Iago are
gradually taken over by Othello. Words such as
monster, monstrous, and *beast,* follow a similar
pattern, as does another group of images which refers to parts of the human body—blood, arms, ear,
heart, lips, brain, legs. In the beginning of the play
it is Iago who uses these images most frequently.
But in the third act, Othello becomes their chief
spokesman, and remains so for the rest of the play.
(pp. 1-12)

Readers of the play cannot help noticing the fact
that Iago very often speaks of things in terms of imagery that contains connotations of, or outright
references to, sex, lust, lechery, and prostitution.
Iago is the first to use terms such as these, but

when Othello begins to see and value things as
Iago does, he, too, begins to use these images and,
when he does, uses them with greater frequency
than does Iago. The frequency and the shift of
these images from one character to the other reinforces the pattern we have already defined . . . In
Shakespeare Survey 5, S. L. Bethell discusses the
shift in the use of diabolical images such as hell,
devil, fiend, and damn, noting that Iago introduces
these references, but Othello takes them over as
evil increases its hold upon him. (pp. 12-13)

All of these patterns of imagery and verbal echoes
elaborate and stress the change in Othello and the
release of the latent evil within him, Iago being the
spark that ignites it. But whereas Iago recognizes
evil for what it is, Othello must regard it as a good
in order to accept it; for him it becomes a means for
obtaining justice and destroying those whom he
considers corrupt—Cassio and Desdemona.

By the end of the play, Othello has become a man
dominated and possessed by the very emotions
which, in the opening scenes, he had insisted he
was not subject to. He thought he had perfect control over his emotions; he felt he could handle any
situation, and often said so with colorful imagery:

Were it my cue to fight, I should have
known it
Without a prompter.

[I. ii. 82-3]

He proclaimed himself free from the heated passions of youth:

—the young affects
In me defunct—

[I. iii. 263-64]

But his actions in the course of the play show that
he does *not* have control over his emotions, and
that he does *not* have the ability to handle any situation. The image he has of himself is as erroneous
as his understanding of others. His ability to weigh
and evaluate character and action is limited; and
when caught in the mire of something he cannot
comprehend, he often asks a series of questions,
begging assistance, and ends with a half-pleading,

Give me answer to't.

[II. iii. 196]

And, of course, Iago is always ready to trigger
Othello's buried passion and evil. Iago, like Othello,
gropes about and makes hasty use of the materials
he finds—gossip, hearsay, rumor—and with these
tries and succeeds in giving direction and assistance to Othello's stumbling thoughts. He is a diabolic crutch, providing the assistance and direction that Othello craves. It is only at the very end
of the play that Othello comes to have some insight
into his own hidden motivations:

[A man] not easily jealous, but, being
wrought,

Perplex'd in the extreme.

[V. ii. 345-46]

By succumbing to the emotions he thought he could control, he destroys himself, of course; by yielding to passion and weak reasoning he murders Desdemona, whose death shatters his "soul's joy." But his realization that he had "lov'd not wisely, but too well" [V. ii. 344] applies to the trusted, "honest" friend, Iago, as well as to Desdemona. His passions aroused, his reason fled and left him "perplex'd in the extreme." When he did try to rationalize, he built his arguments on the trusted words of Iago, which merely reinforced the suspicions and fears which he had already admitted into his own heart. He found true what Iago said about Desdemona because he himself thought it before Iago uttered it. Thus, he took Iago's words as a confirmation of truth. Iago understood this perfectly well, for as he himself explains:

I told him what I thought, and told no
    more
Than what he found himself was apt and
    true.

[V. ii. 176-77]

Iago's powerful hold over Othello is proof of Othello's own potential for evil. Iago penetrates Othello's character, and plays upon its weaknesses, nourishing, as he does so, the evil already present within Othello. As Iago's weakly conceived ideas and convictions are given expression, Othello accepts them as his own, alienating himself more and more from the human and the rational. In his failure to understand himself, Desdemona, and Iago, he paves the way for his own ruin in the same way that Iago comes to destroy himself through his self-absorption. The destruction of one signals, in fact the destruction of the other. Having destroyed Othello, Iago promises that he "never will speak word" [V. ii. 304] of what he has done, much less why it has been done. With Othello dead, the rich field upon which Iago's malice and hate had taken root and flourished now lies wasted and destroyed. The public, dignified, military figure presented to us at the beginning of the play has fallen prey to what it tried most to believe was never there, conquered in large measure by its own weaknesses and delusions. And Iago, the forger of the perfect phrase, the subtle lie, the devastating hint, the man to whom language was both a mirror and a tool of personality, sentences himself to eternal silence. (pp. 13-15)

Henry L. Warnken, "Iago as a Projection of Othello," in Shakespeare Encomium, *edited by Anne Paolucci, The City College, 1964, pp. 1-15.*

DESDEMONA

S. N. Garner

[*Garner elucidates* **Desdemona**'s *character, maintaining that Shakespeare carefully balanced the other characters' accounts of her as goddess or whore to present a complex portrait.* **Othello**'s *sensual view is countered by* **Brabantio**'s *idealized concept in Act I and* **Roderigo** *and* **Cassio**'s *romanticized vision is opposed by* **Iago**'s *coarse innuendo in Act II. Garner then points out that* **Desdemona**'s *liveliness and assertiveness are confirmed by her marriage to* **Othello** *and that these positive traits become a fatal liability. Finally, the critic ends with a discussion of* **Desdemona**'s *powerlessness in the face of her husband's accusations, which leads to her death. For further commentary on the character of* **Desdemona**, *see the excerpts by A. C. Bradley and Albert Gerard.*]

As Desdemona prepares to go to bed with Othello in Act IV, scene iii of Shakespeare's *Othello*, the following conversation occurs between her and Emilia:

Emilia.	Shall I go fetch your night-gown?
Desdemona.	No, unpin me here. This Lodovico is a proper man.
Emilia.	A very handsome man.
Desdemona.	He speaks well.
Emilia.	I know a lady in Venice would have walked barefoot to Palestine for a touch of his nether lip.

[IV. ii. 34-9]

Surely this is startling dialogue coming as it does between the brothel scene and the moment when Desdemona will go to her wedding with death. An actress or director would certainly have to think a great deal about how these lines are to be spoken and what they are to reveal of Desdemona's character. But a reader or critic is not so hard pressed, and he may, if it suits him, simply skip over them. This is precisely what most critics do.

Robert Heilman is representative. In his lengthy book on the play, *Magic in the Web,* he does not discuss the passage. One reason for this omission, of course, is that he, like most critics, is mainly interested in Othello and Iago. Nevertheless, since he uses the New Critics' method of close reading—underscoring images, habits of diction, and grammatical structure—it is peculiar that when he treats Desdemona's character, dealing in two instances with Act IV, scene iii specifically (pp. 189-90, 208-10), he fails to notice these lines. A partial explanation for this failure is that he sustains his interpretation of Othello and Iago and the theme of the play by insisting on Desdemona's relative simplicity and diverges from other critics who make her "overintricate." More significantly, however, the passage is difficult to square with his contention that in the last act Desdemona "becomes . . . the saint," a representation of "the world of spirit." (p. 233)

Many critics and scholars come to Shakespeare's play with the idea that Desdemona ought to be pure and virtuous and, above all, unwavering in her faithfulness and loyalty to Othello. The notion is so tenacious that when Desdemona even appears to threaten it, they cannot contemplate her character with their usual care and imagination.

At what appears to be the other extreme is such a critic as W. H. Auden, one of the few who notices the passage and sees it as a significant revelation of Desdemona's character. Viewing her cynically partly on account of it, he remarks: "It is worth noting that, in the willow-song scene with Emilia, she speaks with admiration of Ludovico [sic] and then turns to the topic of adultery. . . . It is as if she had suddenly realized that she had made a *mésalliance* [marriage with with a person of inferior social rank] and that the sort of man she ought to have married was someone of her own class and colour like Ludovico. Given a few more years of Othello and of Emilia's influence and she might well, one feels, have taken a lover" ["The Alienated City: Reflections on 'Othello'," *Encounter* 17 (1961)]. But isn't Auden finally making the same assumption as the others? Doesn't his cynical and easy dismissal of Desdemona imply that he has expected her to be perfect? If she is not, then she must be corrupt. Isn't this Othello's mistake exactly? Either Desdemona is pure or she is the "cunning whore of Venice" [IV. ii. 88].

The poles of critical opinion are exactly those presented in the play. On the one hand is the view of Desdemona the "good" characters have; on the other is the negative vision of her that Iago persuades Othello to accept. At a time when we have become especially careful about adopting any single perspective of a character as the dramatist's or the "right" perspective, why do many critics now simply accept one extreme view of Desdemona or the other? I can only assume that they share a vision Shakespeare presents as limited.

Desdemona's character is neither simple nor any more easily defined than Iago's or Othello's. Any effort to describe it must take into account all of what she says and does as well as what other characters say about her and how their views are limited by their own personalities and values. Though Shakespeare does not give Desdemona center stage with Othello, as he gives Juliet with Romeo and Cleopatra with Antony, he does not keep her in the wings for most of the play, as he does Cordelia [in *King Lear*] or Hermione [in *The Winter's Tale*]. She is often present so that we must witness her joy, fear, bewilderment, and pain. What happens to her matters because we see how it affects her as well as Othello. The meaning of the tragedy depends, then, on a clear vision of her character and experience as well as those of Othello and Iago.

That Desdemona is neither goddess nor slut Shakespeare makes very clear. He evidently realized that he would have to defend his characterization of her more against the idealization of the essentially good characters than the denigration of the villain. Consequently, though he undermines both extremes, he expends his main efforts in disarming Desdemona's champions rather than her enemy. In her first two appearances, Shakespeare establishes her character and thus holds in balance the diverging views, but he goes out of his way to make her human rather than divine.

He carefully shapes Othello's account of Desdemona to counter Brabantio's initial description of her as "A maiden never bold, / Of spirit so still and quiet that her motion / Blushed at herself" [I. iii. 94-6]. Because Brabantio is unwilling to believe that Desdemona's "perfection so could err" [I. iii. 100] that she would elope with Othello, he accuses him of seducing her by witchcraft or drugs. In Othello's eloquent defense [I. iii. 127-69], he shows not only that Brabantio's accusations are false but also that it was Desdemona who invited his courtship. His description of her coming with "greedy ear" to "devour" his tales of cannibals, anthropophagi, and his own exploits suggests that she is starved for excitement and fascinated by Othello because his life has been filled with adventure. She loved him, he says, for the dangers he had passed. So far is Desdemona from being Brabantio's "maiden never bold" [I. iii. 94] that she gave Othello "a world of kisses" [I. iii. 159] for his pains and clearly indicated that she would welcome his suit:

> She wished
> That heaven had made her such a man.
> She thanked me,
> And bade me, if I had a friend that loved her,
> I should but teach him how to tell my story,
> And that would woo her. Upon this hint I spake.
>
> [I. iii. 162-66]

The scene is carefully managed so as to create sympathy for both Othello and Desdemona. Because Desdemona initiates the courtship, Othello is absolutely exonerated of Brabantio's charge. His cautiousness acknowledges the tenuousness of his position as a black man in Venetian society and is appropriate and even admirable. The Moor cannot be confident of Desdemona's attraction to him, and he undoubtedly knows that marrying him would isolate her from her countrymen. Recognizing Othello's reticence and undoubtedly its causes, Desdemona makes it clear she loves him but, at the same time, maintains a degree of indirection. Shakespeare does not wish to make her seem either shy or overly forward.

When Desdemona finally appears, she strengthens the image Othello has presented. Before the senators, she answers her father's charges forcefully and persuasively, without shyness or reticence. More significantly, it is she, and not Othello, who first raises the possibility of her going to Cyprus. Othello asks only that the senators give his wife "fit disposition" [I. iii. 236], but when the Duke asks her preference, Desdemona pleads:

> If I be left behind,
> A moth of peace, and he go to the war,
> The rites for why I love him are bereft me,
> And I a heavy interim shall support
> By his dear absence. Let me go with him.
> [I. iii. 255-59]

Her wish not to be left behind as a "moth of peace" is a desire not to be treated as someone too fragile to share the intensity of Othello's military life. As though she might have overheard Brabantio tell Othello that she would not have run to his "sooty bosom" [I. ii. 69], she confirms her sexual attraction to him as well as her own sexuality by insisting that she wants the full "rites" of her marriage.

Shakespeare must have wanted to make doubly sure of establishing Desdemona's sensuality, for he underscores it the next time she appears. At the beginning of Act II, while she awaits Othello on the shore of Cyprus, her jesting with Iago displays the kind of sexual playfulness that we might have anticipated from Othello's description of their courtship.

As soon as Desdemona arrives at Cyprus, together with Emilia, Iago, and Roderigo, and is greeted by Cassio, she asks about Othello. Immediately a ship is sighted, and someone goes to the harbor to see whether it is Othello's. Anxious about her husband, Desdemona plays a game with Iago to pass the time; in an aside, she remarks, "I am not merry; but I do beguile / The thing I am by seeming otherwise" [II. i. 121-22]. Their repartee grows out of a debate that Iago begins by accusing Emilia of talking too much. A practiced slanderer of women, he chides both his wife and Desdemona. Although Desdemona rebukes him, "O, fie upon thee, slanderer!" [II. i. 113], she asks him to write her praise. Instead he comments on general types of women:

Iago.	If she be fair and wise: fairness and wit, The one's for use, the other useth it.
Desdemona.	Well praised. How if she be black and witty?
Iago.	If she be black, and thereto have a wit, She'll find a white that shall her blackness fit.
Desdemona.	Worse and worse!
	[II. i. 129-34]

Iago's "praises" commend women for what he might expect Desdemona to regard as faults, and none are without sexual overtones. Though Desdemona remarks that they "are old fond paradoxes to make fools laugh i' th' alehouse" [II. i. 138-39], they do not offend her and serve her well enough as a pastime for fifty-five lines, until Othello arrives.

Critics who take an extreme view of Desdemona see her pleasure in this exchange with Iago as a failure of Shakespeare's art. [M. R.] Ridley, for example, comments [in the Arden edition of *Othello*]: "This is to many readers, and I think rightly, one of the most unsatisfactory passages in Shakespeare. To begin with it is unnatural. Desdemona's natural instinct must surely be to go herself to the harbour, instead of asking parenthetically whether someone has gone. Then, it is distasteful to watch her engaged in a long piece of cheap backchat with Iago, and so adept at it that one wonders how much time on the voyage was spent in the same way. All we gain from it is some further unneeded light on Iago's vulgarity." But this scene is unnatural for Ridley's Desdemona, not Shakespeare's. What the dramatist gives us here is an extension of the spirited and sensual Desdemona that has been revealed in the first act. Her scene with Iago shows her to be the same woman who could initiate Othello's courtship and complain before the senators about the "rites" she would lose in Othello's absence. Her stance is similar to the one she will take later when she tries to coax Othello into reinstating Cassio. That the scene impedes the dramatic movement too long and that its humor is weak are perhaps legitimate criticisms; to suggest that it distorts Desdemona's character is surely to misunderstand her character.

Shakespeare makes a special effort to maintain the balance of the scene. He keeps Desdemona off a pedestal and shows her to have a full range of human feelings and capacities. Yet he is careful not to allow her to fail in feeling or propriety. The point of her aside is to affirm her concern for Othello as well as to show her personal need to contain anxiety and distance pain and fear. As we see how Desdemona acts under stress later in the play, it seems consistent with her character that she should want a distraction to divert her attention in this extremity. Shakespeare brings the exchange between Desdemona and Iago to a brilliant close as Othello enters and greets his "fair warrior." The sensual import of this moment and his address is surely heightened by what we have seen of Desdemona shortly before.

Shakespeare's delicately poised portrayal of Desdemona to this point prepares us for the splendid antithesis between Iago and Cassio in the middle of the second act:

Iago.	Our general cast us thus early for the love of his Desdemona; who

let us not therefore blame. He hath not yet made wanton the night with her, and she is sport for Jove.

Cassio. She's a most exquisite lady.

Iago. And, I'll warrant her, full of game.

Cassio. Indeed, she's a most fresh and delicate creature.

Iago. What an eye she has! Methinks it sounds a parley to provocation.

Cassio. An inviting eye; and yet methinks right modest.

Iago. And when she speaks, is it not an alarum to love?

Cassio. She is indeed perfection.

[II. iii. 14-28]

Such a carefully counterpointed exchange invites us to adjust both views.

Iago distorts Desdemona's character by suppressing the side of it that Cassio insists on and emphasizing her sensuality. His suggestions that she is "full of game" and that her eye "sounds a parley to provocation" call up an image of a flirtatious and inconstant woman. Iago's view is clearly limited by his devious purpose and also by his cynical notions about human nature in general and women in particular.

But Cassio's view is limited as well. He idealizes Desdemona as much as her father did. It is evidently clear to Iago that his efforts to persuade Cassio of his vision will fail when he pronounces Desdemona "perfection," as had Brabantio before him [I. iii. 100]. The extravagance of language Cassio uses earlier in describing Desdemona must also make his view suspect. For example, he tells Montano that Othello

hath achieved a maid
That paragons description and wild fame;
One that excels the quirks of blazoning pens,
And in th' essential vesture of creation
Does tire the ingener.

[II. i. 61-5]

After the safe arrival of Desdemona and her companion in Cyprus, Cassio rhapsodizes:

Tempests themselves, high seas, and howling winds,
The guttered rocks and congregated sands,
Traitors ensteeped to enclog the guiltless keel,
As having sense of beauty, do omit
Their moral natures, letting go safely by
The *divine* Desdemona.

[II. i. 68-73; italics added]

This idealization gives as false a picture of Desdemona as Iago's denigration of her. Cassio's lines in fact comment more on his character than on Desdemona's. To accept his view of Desdemona, as many have done, is as grievous a critical mistake as to accept Iago's.

Desdemona's liveliness, assertiveness, and sensuality are corroborated in her marrying Othello. The crucial fact of her marriage is not that she elopes but that she, a white woman, weds a black man. Though many critics focus on the universality of experience in *Othello,* we cannot forget the play's racial context. Othello's blackness is as important as Shylock's Jewishness [in *The Merchant of Venice*], and indeed the play dwells relentlessly upon it.

It is underscored heavily from the beginning. The first references to Othello, made by Iago to Roderigo, are to "the Moor" [I. i. 39, 57]. Roderigo immediately refers to him as "the thick-lips" [I. i. 66]. He is not called by name until he appears before the senators in scene ii when the Duke of Venice addresses him. He has been referred to as "the Moor" nine times before that moment.

Iago and Roderigo know they may depend on Brabantio's fears of black sexuality and miscegenation. When he appears at his window to answer their summons, Iago immediately cries up to him, "Even now, now, very now, an old black ram / Is tupping your white ewe" [I. i. 88-9] and urges him to arise lest "the devil" make a grandfather of him. The tone intensifies as Iago harps on Othello's bestial sexuality. To the uncomprehending and reticent Brabantio he urges impatiently:

You'll have
your daughter covered with a Barbary horse, you'll
have your nephews neigh to you, you'll have coursers
for cousins, and gennets for germans.

[I. i. 111-14]

Mercilessly, he draws a final image: "Your daughter and the Moor are making the beast with two backs" [I. i. 115-17]. The unimaginative and literal Roderigo adds that Desdemona has gone to the "gross clasps of a lascivious Moor" [I. i. 126]. (pp. 234-40)

Critics speculate about what Othello's marriage to Desdemona means for him but usually fail to consider what it means for her to marry someone so completely an outsider. What are we to make of Desdemona's choosing Othello rather than one of her own countrymen? Brabantio tells Othello that Desdemona has "shunned / The wealthy, curlèd darlings of our nation" [I. ii. 66-7]. It seems incredible to him that, having done so, she should then choose Othello. But Shakespeare intends to suggest that the "curlèd darlings" of Italy leave something to be desired; the image implies preciousness and perhaps effeminacy. He expects us to find her choice understandable and even admirable.

Of all Desdemona's reputed suitors, we see only Roderigo. The easy gull of Iago and mawkishly lovesick, he is obviously not worthy of Desdemona. When Othello and Desdemona leave for Cyprus,

Roderigo tells Iago, "I will incontinently drown my-self" [I. iii. 305], and we cannot help but assent to Iago's estimation of him as a "silly gentleman" [I. iii. 307]. Even Brabantio agrees that he is unsuitable, for he tells him, "My daughter is not for thee" [I. i. 98]. Only by comparing him to Othello does he find him acceptable.

The only other character who might be a suitor for Desdemona is Cassio. But it occurs to neither Cassio nor Desdemona that he should court her. Shakespeare makes him a foil to Othello and characterizes him so as to suggest what Desdemona might have found wanting in her countrymen. He is evidently handsome and sexually attractive. In soliloquy, where he may be trusted, Iago remarks that "Cassio's a proper man" [I. iii. 392] and that "he hath a person and a smooth dispose / To be suspected—framed to make women false" [I. iii. 397-98]. Drawing Cassio as one who is "handsome, young, and hath all those requisites in him that folly and green minds look after" [II. i. 245-47], Iago persuades Roderigo that Cassio is most likely to be second after Othello in Desdemona's affections. In soliloquy again, Iago makes clear that he thinks Cassio loves Desdemona: "That Cassio loves her, I do well believe 't" [II. i. 286].

Though he is handsome and has all the surface graces, Cassio is wanting in manliness. Shakespeare certainly intends Cassio's inability to hold his liquor to undermine his character. He gives this trait mainly to comic figures, such as Sir Toby Belch [in *Twelfth Night*], or villains, like Claudius [in *Hamlet*]. Once drunk, the mild-mannered Cassio is "full of quarrel and offense" [II. iii. 50]. His knowledge of his weakness [II. iii. 39-42] might mitigate it, but even aware of it, he succumbs easily. Though at first he refuses Iago's invitation to drink with the Cypriots, he gives in later with only a little hesitation to Iago's exclamation, "What, man! 'Tis a night of revels, the gallants desire it" [II. iii. 43-4]. His lack of discipline here and his subsequent behavior that disgraces him lend some credence to Iago's objections to Othello's preferring him as lieutenant. (pp. 241-42)

Desdemona's marrying a man different from Roderigo, Cassio, and the other "curlèd darlings" of Italy is to her credit. She must recognize in Othello a dignity, energy, excitement, and power that all around her lack. Since these qualities are attributable to his heritage, she may be said to choose him because he is African, black, an outsider. When she says she saw Othello's visage in his mind, she suggests that she saw beneath the surface to those realities that seemed to offer more promise of life. If the myth of black sexuality (which Othello's character denies at every turn) operates for Desdemona, as it does for some of the other characters, it can only enhance Othello's attractiveness for her as she compares him with the pale men around her.

Desdemona shows courage and a capacity for risk in choosing Othello, for it puts her in an extreme position, cutting her off from her father and countrymen. Brabantio in effect disowns her since he would not have allowed her to live with him after her marriage [I. iii. 240] if she had not been permitted to go with Othello to Cyprus. His last words are not to her, but to Othello, and they cut deep: "Look to her, Moor, if thou hast eyes to see: / She has deceived her father, and may thee" [I. iii. 292-93]. Later we learn that Brabantio died of grief over the marriage [V. ii. 204-06]. We are to disapprove of Desdemona's deception no more than we are to disapprove of Juliet's similar deception of Capulet, or Hermia's of Egeus [in *A Midsummer Night's Dream*]. Shakespeare gives Brabantio's character a comic tinge so that our sympathies do not shift from Desdemona to him.

That her marriage separates her from society is implied because of the attitudes we hear expressed toward Othello, but it is also made explicit. Brabantio does not believe that Desdemona would have married Othello unless she had been charmed partially because of his sense that she will "incur a general mock" [I. ii. 68]. After Othello has insulted Desdemona, Emilia's question of Iago makes clear what lines have been drawn: "Hath she forsook . . . Her father and her country, and her friends, / To be called whore?" [IV. ii. 124-27]. Desdemona does not marry Othello ignorant of the consequences; when she pleads with the Duke to allow her to go to Cyprus, she proclaims:

> That I love the Moor to live with him,
> My downright violence, and storm of for-
>   tunes,
> May trumpet to the world.
>
> [I. i. 248-50]

She knows her action is a "storm of fortunes." Her willingness to risk the censure of her father and society is some measure of her capacity for love, even though her love is not based on complete knowledge. She does not see Othello clearly and cannot anticipate any of the difficulties that must necessarily attend his spirited life. Her elopement is more surely a measure of her determination to have a life that seems to offer the promise of excitement and adventure denied her as a sheltered Venetian senator's daughter.

Because Desdemona cuts herself off from her father and friends and marries someone from a vastly different culture, she is even more alone on Cyprus than she would ordinarily have been in a strange place and as a woman in a military camp besides. These circumstances, as well as her character and experience, account in part for the turn the tragedy takes.

At the beginning she unwittingly plays into Iago's hands by insisting that Othello reinstate Cassio immediately. On the one hand, she cannot know what web of evil Iago is weaving to trap her. On the other, her behavior in this matter is not entirely without fault. It is only natural that Desdemona should wish Cassio reinstated since he is her old friend and, except for Emilia, her only close friend on Cyprus. But her insistence is excessive. She assures Cassio that Othello "shall never rest" [III. iii. 22] until he promises to restore the lieutenant's position, and indeed, she makes sure that he never does. Yet her persistence does not seem necessary, for Emilia has assured Cassio earlier:

> All will sure be well.
> The general and his wife are talking of it,
> And she speaks for you stoutly. The Moor replies
> That he you hurt is of great fame in Cyprus
> And great affinity, and that in wholesome wisdom
> He might not but refuse you. But he protests he loves you,
> And needs no other suitor but his likings
> To bring you in again.
>
> [III. i. 42-50]

Desdemona harps on her single theme playfully, teasingly. Her manner is no different from that which she took when she courted Othello or jested with Iago. Her vision seems not to extend beyond the range that allowed her to manage domestic life in Brabantio's quiet household.

As soon as Othello's jealousy and rage begin to

Laurence Olivier as Othello and Maggie Smith as Desdemona in a 1964 National Theatre production of the tragedy.

manifest themselves, Desdemona's forthrightness and courage start to desert her. She can no longer summon up those resources that might help her. She is not as fragile as Ophelia [in *Hamlet*]; she will not go mad. But neither is she as resilient or as alert to possibilities as Juliet, who was probably younger and no more experienced than she. Before Juliet takes the potion the Friar has prepared to make her appear dead, she considers whether he might have mixed a poison instead, since he would be dishonored if it were known he had married her to Romeo [IV. iii. 24-7]. She confronts the possibility of evil, weighs her own position, and takes the risk she feels she must. There is never such a moment for Desdemona.

Under the pressure of Othello's anger, Desdemona lies to him, by denying she has lost the handkerchief he gave her, and makes herself appear guilty. Her action is perfectly understandable. To begin with, she feels guilty about losing it, for she has told Emilia earlier that if Othello were given to jealousy, "it were enough / To put him to ill thinking" [III. iv. 28-9]. But more important, she lies out of fear, as her initial response to Othello indicates:

> Why do you speak so startingly and rash?
> *Othello.*   Is't lost? Is't gone? Speak, is it out o' th' way?
> *Desdemona.* Heaven bless us!
>
> [III. iv. 79-81]

Then she becomes defensive: "It is not lost. But what an if it were?" [III. iv. 83]. At this point Othello's demeanor must be incredibly frightening. Shortly before this moment he has knelt with Iago to vow vengeance against Desdemona if she proves unfaithful, and moments later, he is so enraged that he "falls in a trance" [IV. i. 43]. In this sudden crisis, latent fears of Othello that are inevitably part of Desdemona's cultural experience must be called into play. Her compounded terror destroys her capacity for addressing him with the courage and dignity that she had summoned in facing her father and the senators when they called her actions in question.

If Desdemona has wanted the heights of passion, she finds its depths instead. That she is simply bewildered and unable to respond more forcefully to Othello's subsequent fury is attributable to several causes. To begin with, his change is sudden and extreme. When Lodovico arrives from Venice and meets the raging Othello, he asks incredulously:

> Is this the noble Moor whom our full Senate
> Call all in all sufficient? Is this the nature
> Whom passion could not shake? whose solid virtue
> The shot of accident nor dart of chance
> Could neither graze nor pierce?
>
> [IV. i. 264-68]

Noble Othello is like the flower that festers and

smells far worse than weeds. Only Iago anticipates the full possibilities of his corruption.

But the most important causes of Desdemona's powerlessness lie within herself. She idealizes Othello and cannot recognize that he is as susceptible to irrationality and evil as other men. She tells Emilia that her "noble Moor / Is true of mind, and made of no such baseness / As jealous creatures are" [III. iv. 26-8]. Evidently surprised, Emilia asks if he is not jealous, and Desdemona replies as though the suggestion were preposterous: "Who? He? I think the sun where he was born / Drew all such humors from him" [III. iv. 29-30]. Though Emilia immediately suspects that Othello is jealous [III. iv. 98], Desdemona does not credit her suspicions since she "never gave him cause" [III. iv. 158]. Emilia tries to explain that jealousy is not rational and does not need a cause:

> But jealous souls will not be answered so;
> They are not ever jealous for the cause,
> But jealous for they're jealous. It is a monster
> Begot upon itself, born on itself.
> [III. iv. 159-62]

Though Iago provokes Othello, his jealousy, as Emilia says, arises out of his own susceptibility. He has romanticized Desdemona, as she has him. Forced to confront the fact that she is human and therefore capable of treachery, he is threatened by his own vulnerability to her. If he cannot keep himself invulnerable by idealizing her, then he will do so by degrading her. His fears are heightened because he thinks his blackness, age, and lack of elegance make him less attractive sexually than Cassio.

Despite the worsening crisis, Desdemona will not be instructed by Emilia, nor will she alter her view of Othello so that she might understand and possibly confront what is happening. Her only defense is to maintain an appalling innocence. The more she must struggle to keep her innocence in the face of the overwhelming events of the last two acts, the more passive and less able to cope she becomes. She must hold on to it for two reasons. First, nothing of her life in the rarefied atmosphere of Brabantio's home and society could have anticipated this moment, and nothing in her being can rise to meet it now. Therefore, she must close it out. Second, if she is deserted by her husband, there is nowhere for her to turn. Rather than suffer the terror and pain of her isolation, she must deny that it exists.

Shakespeare's portrayal of Desdemona from the beginning of Act IV until her death illustrates how finely and clearly he had conceived her character and how well he understood the psychology of a mind under pressure. As Iago's poison works and Othello becomes more convinced of Desdemona's guilt and increasingly madder with rage, Desdemona will become gradually more passive and continually frame means of escape in her imagination.

After the brothel scene, when Othello leaves calling Desdemona the "cunning whore of Venice" [IV. ii. 88] and throwing money to Emilia as to a madam, Desdemona is stunned. Emilia asks, "Alas, what does this gentleman conceive? / How do you, madam? How do you, my good lady?"; Desdemona replies, "Faith, half asleep" [IV. ii. 95-7]. The action is too quick for her to be literally asleep; Othello has just that moment left. Rather, she is dazed; her mind simply cannot take in what it encounters. Almost at once she begins to look for ways out. Directing Emilia to put her wedding sheets on the bed [IV. ii. 105], she hopes to be able to go back in time, to recover the brief happiness and harmony she and Othello shared when they were newly married. Though she will subsequently assert that she approves of Othello's behavior, part of her will not approve and will continue to create fantasies to save herself.

Next, Desdemona begins to anticipate her death, directing Emilia to shroud her in her wedding sheets if she should die [IV. iii. 25-6] and singing the willow song. She not only foreshadows her death but also expresses an unconscious desire for it. Her preface to the song makes her wish clear:

> My mother had a maid called Barbary.
> She was in love; and he she loved proved mad
> And did forsake her. She had a song of "Willow";
> An old thing 'twas, but it expressed her fortune,
> And she died singing it. That song tonight
> Will not go from my mind; I have much to do
> But to go hang my head all at one side
> And sing it like poor Barbary.
> [IV. iii. 26-33]

That the song will not go from her mind and that she has "much to do" to keep from hanging her head and singing it suggest the insistence of a death wish. To express a desire for death here and to plead with Othello later to let her live is not inconsistent. Death wishes are more often hopes of finding peace and escape rather than real wishes to die. The song itself—quiet, soporific—promises calm in contrast to Othello's raging.

Just before Desdemona sings, she starts the conversation about Lodovico quoted at the beginning. That she thinks of Lodovico when she is undressing to go to bed with Othello suggests that she is still trying to find a way around the emergency of the moment. She admires Lodovico as "a proper man"—precisely the phrase Iago used to describe Cassio [I. iii. 392]—and as one who "speaks well," calling up those qualities that Cassio has and Othello lacks. Since the man Desdemona has loved, married, and risked her social position for has turned into a barbarian and a madman, she unconsciously longs for a man like Lodovico—a handsome, white man, with those attributes she recognizes as civilized. In her heart she must feel she has made a mistake.

Desdemona does not know the world, or herself, for that matter. Like Lear, she has been led to believe she is "ague-proof." At the end of Act IV Shakespeare makes it certain, if he has not before, that she is self-deceived and that there is a great discrepancy between what she unconsciously feels and what she consciously acknowledges. When Desdemona asks Emilia whether she would cuckold her husband "for all the world" [IV. iii. 67], Emilia plays with the question, answering, "The world's a huge thing; it is a great price for a small vice" [IV. iii. 68-9]. Desdemona finally says she does not think "there is any such woman" who would [IV. iii. 83]. Her comment underscores her need to close out knowledge that might threaten her. Coming as it does after the passage about Lodovico, her remark can only emphasize her pitiable need to maintain an innocence that must inevitably court ruin.

Like Sleeping Beauty waiting for the prince's kiss, Desdemona is asleep when Othello comes. When he threatens her, the most she can do is plead for her life. Desdemona is not Hermione, who has the wisdom to know that if Leontes doubts her fidelity [in *The Winter's Tale*], she cannot convince him of her chastity by insisting on it. And unlike Hermione, Desdemona merely asserts her innocence rather than reproaches her husband, with whom the final blame must lie. She can only lament that she is "undone" [V. ii. 76] and beg for time. She acts differently from the heroine of *The Winter's Tale* not only because she is more fragile and less wise but also because her accuser is not a white man following at least the forms of justice in a court. Othello is a black man with rolling eyes [V. ii. 38] coming to do "justice" in her bedroom at night.

When Desdemona revives for a moment after Othello has stifled her, she affirms her guiltlessness [V. ii. 122] and to Emilia's asking who has "done this deed," she answers, "Nobody—I myself. Farewell. / Commend me to my kind lord" [V. ii. 123-25]. Her answer is often thought of as an effort to protect Othello. Had Othello stabbed Desdemona, then the notion is plausible that she might pretend to have killed herself to save him. But Desdemona could not have smothered or strangled herself. I think her answer acknowledges instead her full responsibility for her marriage and its consequences. What her implied forgiveness of Othello means is unclear. Her remark of a moment before, "A guiltless death I die" [V. ii. 122], must be rendered with pain or anger, so her forgiveness may merely follow her old pattern of denying what she feels and acknowledging what she must; in other words, it may be unfelt. If her forgiveness is genuinely felt, however, it might suggest that Desdemona has come to see Othello with the prejudices of her countrymen and to regard him as acting according to a barbarian nature that will not allow him to act otherwise. She forgives him, then, as she would a child. Or at its best, her pardoning Othello means that she is finally capable of an ideal love, one that does not alter "when it alteration finds" or bend "with the remover to remove" [Sonnet 116]. But even if we see Desdemona as acting out of pure love, as most critics do, her triumph is undercut because she never confronts the full and unyielding knowledge in the face of which true love and forgiveness must maintain themselves. Furthermore, there is no ritual of reconciliation between Desdemona and Othello. Though Othello is by Desdemona's side when she forgives him, she uses the third person and speaks to Emilia.

Othello learns that he is wrong, that Iago, whom he trusted, has deceived him heartlesstly, monstrously. But he never understands what in himself allowed him to become prey to Iago. The final truth for him is that he has thrown a pearl away. His suicide is a despairing act. He finally sees himself as unblessed and bestial—beyond mercy. Paradoxically, his only redemption must come through self-execution.

Othello is surely one of Shakespeare's bleakest tragedies. Given their characters and experience, both personal and cultural, Desdemona and Othello must fail. They do not know themselves, and they cannot know each other. Further, they never understand the way the world fosters their misperceptions. We must watch as Othello is reduced from a heroic general, with dignity, assurance, and power to a raging, jealous husband and murderer, out of control and duped by Iago. We see Desdemona lose her energy, vitality, and courage for living to become fearful and passive. Both suffer the pains of deception, real or supposed loss of love, final powerlessness, and death. Tragedy never allows its protagonists to escape suffering and death, but it often graces them with the knowledge of life, without which they cannot have lived in the fullest sense. Yet for all their terrible suffering, Desdemona and Othello are finally denied even that knowledge. (pp. 243-50)

S. N. Garner, "Shakespeare's Desdemona," in Shakespeare Studies: An Annual Gathering of Research, Criticism, and Reviews, *Vol. 9, 1976, pp. 233-52.*

SOURCES FOR FURTHER STUDY

LITERARY COMMENTARY:

Adamson, W. D. "Unpinned or Undone? Desdemona's Critics and the Problem of Sexual Innocence." *Shakespeare Studies* XIII (1980): 169-86.

Asserts that Shakespeare has drawn Desdemona as "legally innocent of adultery, morally innocent of idly considering it, and psychologically innocent of even being capable of it."

Auden, W. H. "The Joker in the Pack." In his *The Dyer's Hand and Other Essays,* pp. 246-72. New York: Random House, 1948.

Compares Iago to a practical joker who himself has no personal feelings or values, but contemptuously uses the very real desires of other people to gull and manipulate them. Auden also claims that Othello prizes his marriage to Desdemona not for any great love he holds for her, but rather because it signals to him, mistakenly, that he has fully integrated into Venetian society.

Dash, Irene G. "A Woman Tamed: *Othello.*" In her *Wooing, Wedding, and Power: Women in Shakespeare's Plays,* pp. 103-30. New York: Columbia University Press, 1981.

Contends that *Othello* demonstrates "the cost to husband and wife . . . of attempting to conform to stereotyped ideals of marriage."

Gregson, J. M. *"Othello."* In his *Public and Private Man in Shakespeare,* pp. 156-76. London: Croom Helm, 1983.

Maintains that the characters Othello and Hamlet are opposites, and argues that the true tragedy of *Othello* is the Moor's inability to separate his public conduct as military leader from his private judgments as husband.

Grudin, Robert. "Contrariety as Structure: The Later tragedies." In his *Mighty Opposites: Shakespeare and Renaissance Contrariety,* pp. 119-79. Berkeley: University of California Press, 1979.

Finds that Desdemona's "type of lamblike femininity" is compelling to Othello but not to Shakespeare and thus the dramatist demonstrates that her passive helplessness is implicitly ironic, for it "sharpens the impulse to aggression in others." The ambiguities of her virtue are comparable, Grudin maintains, to the complexities of Iago's wickedness.

Hallstead, R. N. "Idolatrous Love: A New Approach to *Othello.*" *Shakespeare Quarterly* XIX, No. 2 (Spring 1968): 107-24.

Argues that after the consummation of Othello and Desdemona's marriage in Cyprus, the Moor's love for his wife becomes so excessive that it is theologically idolatrous. Asserting that *Othello* is a "morality play in a completely realistic framework," Hallstead contends that the Moor is shown renouncing Christianity when he swears a pagan vow with Iago at the close of Act III, scene iii, but the critic also discovers in the final scene of the drama a clear pattern of Christian penance, concluding that Shakespeare has portrayed the "return of Othello's Christianity."

Hyman, Stanley Edgar. *Iago: Some Approaches to the Illusion of His Motivation.* New York: Atheneum, 1970, 180 p.

Assesses Iago's motives from five different critical perspectives, alternately questioning whether the ensign should be viewed as "a stage villain, or Satan, or an artist, or a latent homosexual, or a Machiavel." A pluralistic approach to this issue, Hyman argues, demonstrates the "tension, paradox, and irony" in Shakespeare's portrayal of Iago, while a single line of inquiry can only produce one perspective that is "inevitably reductive and partial."

Kott, Jan. "The Two Paradoxes of *Othello.*" In his *Shakespeare Our Contemporary,* translated by Boleslaw Taborski, pp. 99-125. New York: W. W. Norton & Co., 1964.

Maintains that the struggle between Othello and Iago is a dramatic representation of a "dispute on the nature of the world" and an enquiry into the purpose of human existence. Kott focuses specifically on two paradoxical events in the play: Iago's own victimization by the evil he himself sets in motion and Desdemona's delight in the erotic aspects of love, which leads Othello to believe her capable of betraying him.

Morris, Harry. "*Othello:* No Amount of Prayer Can Possibly Matter." In his *Last Things in Shakespeare,* pp. 76-114. Tallahassee: Florida State University Press, 1985.

Interprets *Othello* as a Christian allegory about damnation.

Murry, John Middleton. "Desdemona's Handkerchief." In his *Shakespeare,* pp. 311-21. London: Jonathan Cape, 1936.

Argues that Desdemona's loss of the handkerchief symbolizes the perfection of her love for Othello, for she became heedless of it only "when Othello was sick and her concern for the man she loved drove out all concern for the token of their love."

Neely, Carol Thomas. "Women and Men in *Othello:* 'What should such a fool / Do with so good a woman?' " In *The Woman's Part: Feminist Criticism of Shakespeare,* pp. 211-39, edited by Carolyn Ruth Swift Lenz, Gayle Greene, and Carol Thomas Neely. Urbana: University of Illinois Press, 1980.

Analysis of the kinship of the women in *Othello* and the heroines in Shakespeare's comedies which emphasizes their similar capacities to initiate courtship, tolerate men's fancies, and balance romantic idealism with a realistic view of sexuality.

Nelson, T. G. A. and Charles Haines. "Othello's Unconsummated Marriage." *Essays in Criticism* XXXIII, No. 1 (January 1983): 1-18.

Maintains that Othello's anger and passion in Acts III and IV is the result of his frustrated desire.

Rice, Julian C. "Desdemona Unpinned: Universal Guilt in *Othello.*" *Shakespeare Studies* VII (1974): 209-26.

Argues that although Desdemona is apparently the most virtuous of women, she shares with Othello and all the other characters in the drama the frailties, imperfections, and moral vulnerability that are inherent in human nature. Rice maintains that Desdemona is partially responsible for her own murder through her "overconfidence in the power of virtue to triumph."

Rosenberg, Marvin. *The Masks of Othello: The Search for the Identity of Othello, Iago, and Desdemona by Three Centuries of Actors and Critics.* Berkeley: University of California Press, 1961, 313 p.

An overview of the interpretations of the drama's main characters by actors from the Restoration to the mid-twentieth century. Seeking to synthesize the commentary of literary critics with the interpretations offered by leading performers, Rosenberg emphasizes the essential humanity of the play's three central figures.

Sen Gupta, S. C. "Symbolism in *Othello.*" In his *Aspects of Shakespearian Tragedy*, pp. 88-113. Calcutta: Oxford University Press, 1972.

Asserts that Othello and Iago "represent the eternal conflict—both internal and external—between the forces of Love and Hate, of Good and Evil, and the realization that the conflict cannot be resolved is part of the tragedy of human life."

Wain, John, ed. *Shakespeare: Othello.* London: Macmillan, 1971, 244 p.

A collection of essays by prominent critics on various topics concerning *Othello.*

MEDIA ADAPTATIONS:

Otello. National Video Corporation Ltd., 1982.

Performance of Verdi's opera featuring Kiri Te Kanawa, Vladimir Atlantov, and Piero Cappuccilli. Distributed by Home Vision and HBO Home Video. 135 minutes.

Otello. Cannon Films, 1986.

Highly acclaimed film version of Verdi's opera directed by Franco Zeffirelli. Features Placido Domingo, Katia Ricciarelli, and Justino Diaz. In Italian with English subtitles. Distributed by Media Home Entertainment Inc. 123 minutes.

Othello. UFA, 1922.

Silent version of Shakespeare's tragedy featuring Emil Jannings, Lya de Putti, and Werner Krauss. Distributed by Video Yesteryear and Discount Video Tapes Inc. 81 minutes.

Othello. United Artists, 1952.

Film adaptation of Shakespeare's tragedy directed by Orson Welles. The cast featured Welles as Othello, Michael Mac Liammóir as Iago, and Suzanne Cloutier as Desdemona. 91 minutes.

Othello. BBC London, Time-Life Films, 1982.

Television adaptation of Shakespeare's drama featuring Anthony Hopkins, Bob Hoskins, and Penelope Wilton. Distributed by Time-Life Video. 120 minutes.

ROMEO AND JULIET

INTRODUCTION

Romeo and Juliet—one of the most popular romantic tragedies in English literature—has entertained readers and spectators for nearly four hundred years. The play is based on Arthur Brooke's poem *The Tragicall Historye of Romeus and Juliet,* published in 1562, which tells the story of two young lovers thwarted by fate and destroyed by their own reckless passion. Although Brooke's poem is the only direct source for *Romeo and Juliet,* the legend of the unfortunate lovers had become a part of European popular tradition by the time Shakespeare wrote his drama. Perhaps what attracted Shakespeare and his predecessors to the tale was its compelling central theme: the story of ill-fated youthful love opposed by a world of violence and hatred. But whereas earlier authors, such as Brooke, emphasized fate or the lovers' headlong passion, Shakespeare created a more complex tragedy in which not only these elements, but also divine will and Romeo and Juliet's innocence play a role in shaping events. Critics continue to debate the relative effectiveness of the tragic design of *Romeo and Juliet* and have yet to achieve a real consensus. Nevertheless, the combination of such diverse elements in this, one of Shakespeare's earliest tragedies, has intrigued generations of students and scholars alike.

PRINCIPAL CHARACTERS
(in order of appearance)

Chorus: The narrator who appears in the Prologues to Acts I and II.

Balthasar: Romeo's servant. He travels to Mantua to inform Romeo of Juliet's supposed death.

Benvolio: Montague's nephew and Romeo's friend. He attempts in vain to prevent the fight between Mercutio and Tybalt.

Tybalt: Lady Capulet's nephew and Juliet's cousin. After mortally wounding Mercutio in a duel, he is killed by Romeo.

Capulet: The head of the Capulet household and Juliet's father. He arranges Juliet's marriage to Paris and makes peace with Montague after the lovers' deaths.

Lady Capulet: Capulet's wife and Juliet's mother. She favors Juliet's marriage to Paris and, with her husband, rebukes her daughter when she protests the match.

Montague: The head of the Montague household and Romeo's father. He reconciles with Capulet after Romeo's and Juliet's deaths.

Lady Montague: Montague's wife and Romeo's mother. She dies from grief over Romeo's banishment from Verona.

Escalus: The prince of Verona. He attempts to prevent the public brawls between the feuding houses and banishes Romeo from Verona for killing Tybalt in a duel.

Romeo: The son of Montague and Lady Montague. After his secret marriage to Juliet, he is exiled from Verona for killing Tybalt. When he is mistakenly informed that Juliet has died, he visits the Capulet tomb and kills himself with poison.

Paris: A nobleman and Escalus's kinsman. He is engaged to Juliet before her apparent death and is killed by Romeo at the Capulet vault.

Nurse: Juliet's attendant. She helps arrange Juliet's secret marriage to Romeo, but after his banishment advises Juliet to marry Paris.

Juliet: The daughter of Capulet and Lady Capulet. She secretly marries Romeo and, after he is exiled, drinks a potion that produces death-like symptoms to avoid marrying Paris. When she awakes in the Capulet vault to find Romeo dead, she commits suicide by stabbing herself with his dagger.

Mercutio: Romeo's friend and a kinsman of Escalus. He is killed by Tybalt in a duel.

Friar Lawrence: A Franciscan priest. He conducts Romeo and Juliet's secret wedding and devises a scheme to prevent Juliet's marriage to Paris.

Apothecary: A maker of drugs and medicines who sells Romeo the poison with which he kills himself.

Friar John: A Franciscan monk. He is quarantined in Verona because of the plague before he can deliver Friar Lawrence's letter to Romeo.

PLOT SYNOPSIS

Act I: In Verona, servants of the Montague and Capulet households begin a public brawl, which soon involves Benvolio, Tybalt, Montague, and Capulet. Prince Escalus, angered by this latest outbreak between the feuding families, decrees that anyone who participates in future disturbances will be executed. Soon after the fight, Benvolio encounters Romeo, who is in a melancholy state. Romeo tells Benvolio that his recent sadness is caused by his infatuation with Rosaline. Hoping to cure his friend of his lovesickness, Benvolio persuades Romeo to attend the Capulets' ball that night. There, Benvolio asserts, Romeo will discover that Rosaline is not the only beautiful girl in Verona. In another scene, Capulet invites Paris to the ball after granting him permission to marry Juliet. Romeo and his friends, disguised by masks, attend the party, where he and Juliet first see each other; the two fall in love immediately. When the ball is over, they inquire about each other's identities and are shocked to discover that they are members of opposing houses.

Act II: Escaping from the jokes and taunts of Benvolio and Mercutio after the ball, Romeo hides in the Capulet orchard. Juliet appears on her balcony, and Romeo overhears her as she declares her love for him. After he greets Juliet, the two exchange promises of love and make plans to be married the next day. Romeo leaves at daybreak and visits Friar Lawrence. The priest scolds Romeo for his fleeting affections but agrees to marry him to Juliet, hoping the match will bring an end to the feud. Romeo informs Juliet's nurse of the plan for the secret wedding, and the lovers are married that afternoon.

Act III: Tybalt approaches Mercutio and Benvolio, seeking to instigate a fight. When Romeo appears, Tybalt challenges him, but the young Montague, purged of his hatred of the Capulets by his marriage to Juliet, greets his antagonist's insults with kind words. Annoyed by Romeo's apparent cowardice, Mercutio forces Tybalt into a duel. Romeo comes between the two in an attempt to break up the fight, but not before Tybalt fatally stabs his opponent. Mercutio dies, and Romeo, enraged at his friend's death, kills Tybalt. Upon hearing of the incident, Escalus banishes Romeo from Verona. As Juliet grieves over her husband's exile, Romeo laments his situation in Friar Lawrence's cell. The Friar and the Nurse eventually convince him to join Juliet that night to consummate their marriage. The next morning, Romeo reluctantly bids farewell to Juliet and departs for Mantua; immediately after, Juliet learns that her father has arranged for her to marry Paris the following Thursday. She protests, but is harshly rebuked by her parents for her disobedience. Juliet is further upset when the Nurse, too, urges that she marry Paris and forget Romeo.

Act IV: Juliet visits Friar Lawrence and declares that she will kill herself if her marriage to Paris cannot be otherwise prevented. Desperate, the Friar devises an alternate plan; he offers Juliet a potion that will give her the semblance of death for forty-two hours, directing her to drink it the night before the wedding. In the meantime, the Friar tells Juliet, he will send a messenger to Romeo, instructing him to rescue her from the Capulet tomb when she awakes. Juliet returns home and agrees to marry Paris, which prompts Capulet to move the wedding forward one day. That night, Juliet drinks the potion and when she cannot be roused the next morning, the Capulets, the Nurse, and Paris lament her sudden death.

Act V: Unaware of Friar Lawrence's plan, Balthasar hurries to Mantua to inform Romeo that Juliet is dead. Grief-stricken, Romeo buys poison from an apothecary and decides to return to Verona. Meanwhile, Friar Lawrence's messenger, Friar John, reports that he has been unable to travel to Mantua because exposure to the plague has quarantined him in Verona. That night, Romeo goes to the Capulet tomb as Paris is mourning Juliet. Paris suspects that Romeo plans to desecrate the bodies of Juliet and Tybalt, and attempts to stop him from entering the vault. The two fight, and Romeo kills Paris. Romeo then enters the tomb, bids farewell to Juliet, and drinks the poison. After Romeo dies, Friar Lawrence arrives at the vault to rescue Juliet. She awakes, but before he can convince her to leave the tomb, he is frightened by a noise and flees. Juliet then discovers Romeo's body and, not wanting to live without him, stabs herself with his dagger. Summoned by the churchyard watchman, Escalus, Montague, and the Capulets meet at the tomb, where Friar Lawrence recounts the lovers' tragic tale. Capulet and Montague declare peace and vow to erect gold statues in memory of their children.

PRINCIPAL TOPICS

Critics and readers have proposed three main ways to interpret Shakespeare's arrangement of the events and circumstances in *Romeo and Juliet.* (The deliberate construction of the play so that its action seems to lead inevitably to the "catastrophe" of the young lovers' deaths, is known as Shakespeare's "tragic design.") One method is to regard Romeo and Juliet as helpless victims of the arbitrary operation of fate. Numerous tricks of chance in the play support this theory; for example, Romeo's failed attempt to stop the fight between Mercutio and Tybalt and Friar John's inability to leave Verona due to the plague. References to "fortune" and the "stars" throughout the play, particularly the description of Romeo and Juliet in the Prologue to Act I as "star-crossed lovers," also uphold this argument. This emphasis on fortune as a guiding force that determines one's destiny was probably not lost on Elizabethan audiences, who would have been familiar with and likely endorsed this conviction. A second perspective is that *Romeo and Juliet* is a tragedy of Providence or divine will. Proponents of this interpretation maintain that the seemingly coincidental or accidental events in the play are in fact initiated by God to punish, and ultimately reconcile, the feuding families. God finally achieves this reconciliation by using the deaths of the lovers as a moral example for the others. A third reading of Shakespeare's tragic design holds that the lovers' own reckless passion leads to their double suicide. Supporters of this viewpoint sometimes regard Friar Lawrence as a spokesman for Shakespeare himself, for the monk does not completely endorse Romeo and Juliet's impetuous behavior but rather cautions them to "love moderately." These three perspectives of Shakespeare's tragic design are perhaps the most commonly discussed issues in *Romeo and Juliet.* At various times throughout the centuries since the tragedy was written, critics have generally emphasized one or another of these interpretations. Recently, however, commentators have argued that Shakespeare actually presents a balance of all three concepts in the play.

Closely related to the problem of Shakespeare's tragic design is the question of the play's effectiveness as an "authentic" tragedy. In drama, a tragedy traditionally recounts the significant events or actions in a protagonist's life which, taken together, bring about the catastrophe. The ambiguity surrounding the cause of the lovers' deaths has led some critics to regard the play as an apprentice tragedy, one in which Shakespeare had not yet developed his skills as a tragic dramatist. In fact, *Romeo and Juliet* is often considered an experiment in tragedy, in which the playwright attempts to break free of traditional patterns by omitting the necessary cause-and-effect relationship between the lovers' characters and their catastrophe.

Another prominent aspect of *Romeo and Juliet* is Shakespeare's handling of the passage of time to underscore the lovers' hasty action, perhaps most evident in the characters' headlong rush to fulfill their love for each other. Shakespeare most notably emphasizes this haste by compressing the several months' action of Brooke's *Tragical Historye of Romeus and Juliet* to only five days. Further, Shakespeare's masterful use of language as well as his various references to the explicit progression of time combine to establish an atmosphere of hasty action. This technique is evident in Juliet's speech in Act III, scene ii: "Gallop apace, you fiery-footed steeds, / Towards Phoebus' lodging; such a waggoner / As Phaeton would whip you to the west, / And bring in cloudy night immediately. / Spread thy close curtain, love-performing night, / That runaway's eyes may wink, and Romeo / Leap to these arms untalk'd of and unseen!" Subtle patterns of swift imagery and lively dialogue, as well as the Chorus's commentary, create an undercurrent of tension and impulsiveness that is discernible throughout the play. On several occasions,

Shakespeare ironically contrasts the notion of time and haste with a particular character's dialogue. One example of this technique is the contradiction between the play's hurried pace and Friar Lawrence's warning to Romeo: "Wisely and slow, they stumble that run fast" (II. iii. 94). The priest later fails to heed his own advice, however, when, in Act V he is startled and hastens from the tomb, leaving Juliet to her fate. Shakespeare employs all of these devices to create a frantic atmosphere in which the characters behave recklessly.

Examining the nature of Romeo and Juliet's love is also important to achieve an understanding of the play as a whole. In some ways, the lovers' passion reflects the practice of "courtly love." Courtly love is a tradition that defines what love is and establishes a code of behavior for lovers. It flourished in the Middle Ages and had a significant influence on Renaissance literature. In essence, under this system love is illicit and sensual and is accompanied by great emotional suffering. The lover (in literature, usually a knight) falls in love at first sight and agonizes over his situation until his affection is returned. Once he achieves this goal, he is inspired to perform great deeds. Further, the lovers pledge their fidelity to one another and vow to keep their union secret. Romeo and Juliet's affair closely follows this pattern: they fall in love at first sight; their love is strengthened rather than weakened by the feud; they meet at night and vow to conceal their union; and each promptly resolves to commit suicide upon learning of the other's death. Another important feature of Romeo and Juliet's love is its spiritual quality. The couple treats love with great reverence, and it is their faithfulness to it in the face of violence, hatred, and even death which ultimately restores peace and order to Verona.

Many of the central issues in *Romeo and Juliet* are reinforced by Shakespeare's use of opposites and contradictory images, perhaps most notably the contrast between light and darkness. In most cases, the emphasis on light—starlight, moonlight, sunlight, and lightning—expresses Romeo and Juliet's love for one another. Darkness, however, in the form of clouds, rain, and nightfall, reflects the evil of the feud. In addition, star imagery enhances the theme of fate in the play, serving not only as a metaphor for feminine beauty and the lovers' passion, but also for destiny. Another concept fundamental to understanding *Romeo and Juliet* is the struggle between the opposing forces of love and death. Shakespeare developed this theme by constructing images that personify death as Juliet's lover. This overall impression is achieved through the repeated use of oxymora (the pairing of contradictory terms), such as "death-mark'd love," and more subtle word oppositions, like "womb" and "tomb."

CHARACTER STUDIES

While most interpretations of the characters of Romeo and Juliet have focused on the nature of their love, there has recently been a greater tendency to emphasize the manner in which they mature as a result of their passion for each other. This emergence into adulthood is clearly illustrated in the development of their language, which progresses from the forced and artificial rhetoric of their early scenes to a more sincere form of expression later in the play. The lovers can also be interpreted through an explicitly Christian reading of the play. Such a perspective stresses that their maturing love reflects a form of spiritual education in which Romeo and Juliet ultimately accept their destiny as part of God's plan to punish and reconcile the opposing families.

The bawdy, or humorously obscene, language of the Nurse and Mercutio present a stark contrast to the purity of Romeo and Juliet's passion. For this reason, these two characters are often interpreted as comic "foils" to the lovers. (A foil is a character who through strong contrast underscores or enhances the distinctive traits of another character.) The Nurse, a well-conceived, rich, and natural character, is often considered one of Shakespeare's greatest comic creations. Mercutio, too, is renowned for his wit and vitality. He is viewed as an extreme egotist and sensualist, whose open personality and coarse sexual humor reflect his individuality and naturalness. Shakespeare has been particularly praised for his well-defined portraits of these characters. This success is especially significant in Mercutio's case, whom the dramatist created from only a brief reference in Brooke's poem.

Throughout the play, Friar Lawrence serves as a friend and counselor to both Romeo and Juliet. He provides a religious dimension to the play, attempting to restore peace in Verona and dispel the evil of the feud by uniting the young couple in marriage. The Friar is generally viewed as a good man who exercises poor judgment when he hastily marries the lovers. He stands by his actions, however, and tries to prevent Juliet's marriage to Paris by devising the sleeping potion scheme. Ultimately, he acknowledges the intervention of a higher order in determining the lovers' fate when he declares "A greater power than we can contradict / Hath thwarted our intents" (V. iii. 153-54). The play also offers another perspective of the Friar. Numerous references demonstrate that had he, too, acted with less haste, the tragic deaths of Romeo and Juliet may have been prevented. For example, had the priest sent the message concerning Juliet's assumed death to Romeo via Balthasar rather than Friar John, the final catastrophe might have been averted. No matter how one interprets his role in the play, Friar Lawrence is indeed an active agent in bringing about the lovers' tragedy.

CONCLUSION

Each of these characters is an example of the many ways in which Shakespeare skillfully reworked his source. Students and scholars alike have marvelled at his ability to create a lasting work of dramatic art with universal appeal out of the Romeo and Juliet legend. Although there is still no resolution to the debates concerning Shakespeare's tragic design and the relative success of this early experiment in tragedy, there is nearly unanimous agreement that *Romeo and Juliet* is a remarkable and enjoyable play. In attempting to account for the tragedy's enduring popularity, commentators generally point to Shakespeare's moving depiction of the innocence and sincerity of young love. *Romeo and Juliet,* in the words of Robert Metcalf Smith, is "the perfect love poem of the English race and of the world."

(See also *Shakespearean Criticism,* Vols. 5 and 11)

OVERVIEW

Douglas Cole

[*Cole outlines the major elements of* Romeo and Juliet *that have typically generated the most commentary in an attempt to explain both the play's significance and its enduring appeal. The critic discusses the tragedy in relation to Shakespeare's other writings; how the playwright adapted the drama from the sources and traditional dramatic and poetic models available to him; the play's language, structure, and themes; and its adherence to conventional tragic dramaturgy, or theatrical representation. In addition, Cole analyzes three principal thematic readings of* Romeo and Juliet—(1) a tragedy of character in which the lovers are punished for their reckless passion; (2) a tragedy of destiny in which fate is responsible for **Romeo**'s and **Juliet**'s deaths; and (3) a tragedy of divine providence in which God sacrifices the lovers to reconcile the feuding families. The critic then asserts that the play presents a synthesis of all three issues in its emphasis on the idea that tragic disaster is an inescapable consequence of the precarious balance between good and evil in the world.*]

How does one create an enduring literary myth out of a sentimental romance, a love story already rehearsed in prose and verse in several languages? How does one turn a pair of young lovers into figures of such imaginative stature that they will fire the emotions of audiences for centuries to come and even obscure the competing images of lovers from classical mythology and medieval legend? Shakespeare never had to ask such questions of himself when he began to write *Romeo and Juliet,* but the response of the world audience to his play since that time has made them inevitable. No case has to be made for the continuing vitality of *Romeo and Juliet.* Its stage history (outmatched only by *Hamlet's*) reveals a nearly unbroken chain of performances for more than three and a half centuries. It has inspired music, opera, ballet, literature, musical comedy, and film. Modern criticism, taking the play's impact for granted, attempts to elucidate some of the things that made Shakespeare's achievement possible (his source materials, his era's literary and dramatic conventions, and his own earlier writing, for example); to define the qualities of its structure and language; and to explore its relationships to Shakespeare's later tragedies. The results of this critical effort help us understand some of the answers to our opening questions, but not yet all. (p. 1)

Transformation of Sources and Conventions

It was common dramatic practice in Shakespeare's day to draw upon known history, legend, and story for the plot material of plays. Shakespeare did not have to invent the basic story of Romeo and Juliet. Nor did he have to invent a totally new kind of poetic language for handling the theme of love. Such a language lay at hand in contemporary love poetry, with its stock of characteristic metaphors, paradoxes, and conceits derived from Petrarch's famed Italian love poems. Neither was the combination of a lyrically developed love story and dramatic tragedy altogether novel, although it was far more common in the early Elizabethan theater to find love themes treated in comedy. Whatever hints were provided for Shakespeare by all these traditions he was able to refashion into something uniquely superior.

The story of Romeo and Juliet was already an old one when Shakespeare decided to dramatize it for the Elizabethan stage. There were at least half a dozen versions circulating earlier in the century in Italy and France, and two of them had been adapted by English translators. Shakespeare apparently relied chiefly on Arthur Brooke's long poetic version, *The Tragical History of Romeus and Juliet,* first published in 1562 and reissued twenty-five years later. (pp. 2-3)

Many modern readers of Shakespeare may be unaware of the immense difference between the ordinary verse of the Elizabethan age and Shakespearean poetry. They are likely to be even more unfamiliar with the usual quality of dramatic speech written for the developing Elizabethan stage. (pp. 3-4)

The lyricism of Shakespeare's play lifts it far above the stumbling verse of other Elizabethan playwrights, and places it closer to the more literary traditions of love poetry, especially to the flourishing cult of the sonnet. The verse in *Romeo and Juliet* borrows heavily from sonnet conventions of metaphor and feeling, but manages also, as critics never tire of pointing out, to move beyond the conventions to something still more impressive. When Romeo and Juliet at their first encounter share the lines of a sonnet, Shakespeare shows us how a poetic convention can take on entirely new life in a dramatic context.

There is new life as well in Shakespeare's approach to the subject of young love itself. When the Elizabethans wrote tragedies of love, they were likely to emphasize the more lustful and obsessive qualities of passion, aspects which Shakespeare also had taken up in his long poems *Venus and Adonis* (1593) and *The Rape of Lucrece* (1594). The fashion in Italian tragedy, imitated both in France and in England, was to stress the mastery of the god Cupid, who was often portrayed as a malevolent, gloating tyrant. Some of this feeling filters into *Dido, Queen of Carthage,* the love tragedy written by Shakespeare's influential contemporary Christopher Marlowe. In *Dido* the heroine is more a victim than a celebrant of love, and the pattern of action stresses frustration and the pains of love denied or abandoned. The predominant strategy of Elizabethan dramatists was to present characters who were "love-crossed" rather than starcrossed. Their figures lack the sense of mutual dedication and individual purpose that inspires Romeo and Juliet. The love of Shakespeare's characters is conveyed with more compassion and innocence than can be found anywhere else in Renaissance drama.

Although Shakespeare's lovers are more idealized than those found either in Brooke's poem or in Elizabethan love tragedies, and although they speak with a language more lyrical than that of their counterparts in these earlier works, they never become ethereal fantasies. One major reason for this (and another distinguishing element in *Romeo and Juliet*) is the way in which passion and sentiment are modulated with both comic gusto and tragic irony. Mercutio and Juliet's Nurse, for example, are original comic developments of characters mentioned in the source story; in the play they not only become vital and amusing in themselves but also help to link the romance of Romeo and Juliet with an earthy sense of reality. On the tragic side, Shakespeare establishes thematic patterns of greater subtlety and paradox than the usual irony of "destructive passion"; his patterns suggest that even the virtues of loyalty, peace-making, and total personal dedication can unwittingly cooperate to bring about disaster.

Perhaps even more important is the way Shakespeare uses both comedy and tragedy to enhance each other in one play. His earlier *Titus Andronicus* had relied all too heavily on the sensationalistic devices of the neo-Senecan fashion in tragedy: wholesale slaughter, severed hands, rape, children's bodies cut up and served as part of their parents' meal. In *Romeo and Juliet,* thankfully, Shakespeare was trying something new. The tragic pattern he employed was imposed on materials, characters, and moods appropriate to comedy and romance: a comic nurse and clown, obstructing parents, duels of wit and parodic banter, the playful humor of hero and heroine. Shakespeare seems characteristically intent on stretching the range of tone usually assumed in early tragedy. He gives us not a comic play that somehow turns out tragically, but a more complex experience that weaves together intense, lyrically celebrated young love, vivacious and often bawdy wit, and the threatening, obstructive forces of ignorance, ill will, and chance—a combination which expresses the human impulse to affirm what is precious and beautiful in life in the very midst of a more pervasive hostility and baseness in the conditions and circumstances of life itself.

When compared with Shakespeare's later tragedies, the play may reveal a certain lack of profundity, a less far-reaching and momentous drive to open up the disturbing depths of human conduct and capacity. For some critics *Romeo and Juliet* is not yet "mature" tragedy; but we must remember that their norm is based on what Shakespeare himself did afterwards, not on what anyone in the Elizabethan theater had done earlier. It is perhaps fairer to say that the kind of tragic experience *Romeo and Juliet* offers us is different rather than immature, an experience less morally complex than others, but no less valid as an image of deeply moving aspects of our own awareness of life's promises and betrayals.

Poetic and Dramatic Language

If *Romeo and Juliet* marks Shakespeare's first original movement toward serious tragedy, it also marks a movement toward a dramatic language of increasing flexibility and expressiveness. The play shows the poet trying to integrate his skills of verse structure, rhyme, metaphor, and ingenious wordplay with dramatic skills of characterization through style of language and gesture, exposition through action as well as declamation, and imagery patterns that function to blind a diversified scenario into a unified thematic order. Shakespeare's work here displays a texture of marked formality, notable in the abundant rhyme, extended conceits, and above all in a wide range of "set pieces"— among them Mercutio's Queen Mab passage, Friar Lawrence's sermons, Juliet's epithalamion [a song or poem written to celebrate a wedding], Paris's elegy, the sonnet shared by the lovers at their first meeting, and the *aubade* [a song of lovers parting at dawn] at their farewell. In patterning so much of the dialogue on these very literary models, Shakespeare was clearly stretching his medium to

see what it could do. He was writing this play in the period that included the highly elaborated language of *Love's Labour's Lost,* the extended complaints of *Richard II,* the lavishly decorative erotic poems *Venus and Adonis* and *The Rape of Lucrece,* and his own contribution to the sonnet-cycle fashion. In *Romeo and Juliet* we find Shakespeare's virtuosity with formal poetic language extended not only by the demands of dramatic context, but also by an awareness of how easily formality may slip into artificiality. Shakespeare seems to have delighted in trying his hand at many different kinds of verbal play, but always with some tact about crossing the boundaries of what is truly acceptable. More than any other dramatist of the period, he is capable of inserting near-parodies of the conventional themes and devices he is exploiting. By such means he seems to remind his audience, as Juliet reminds Romeo: "Conceit [i.e., true understanding or invention], more rich in matter than in words, / Brags of his substance, not of ornament" "[II. vi. 30-1].

[Samuel Taylor] Coleridge was perhaps right when he claimed that in this play the poet had not yet "entirely blended" with the dramatist, implying that these elements of poetic formality do not always seem to work effectively in dramatic context. Samuel Johnson much earlier had complained that the characters were always left with a conceit [i.e., an elaborate parallel or metaphor] in their misery—"a miserable conceit"; and actors and actresses in every generation have had their problems with the labored lamentations of Juliet and Romeo in Act Three. Critics move from such examples of awkwardness (only awkwardly justified by the Elizabethan taste for that sort of thing), to matters of tired convention or excessively developed imagery, such as we find in Romeo's first speeches on love or Lady Capulet's comparison of Paris to a book. Here there is more room for argument that Shakespeare knew what he was doing in supplying the love-sick pup Romeo with the most familiar catalogue of Petrarchan oxymora [a combination of contradictory terms] ("O brawling love, O loving hate, . . . O heavy lightness, serious vanity, . . . Feather of lead, bright smoke, cold fire, sick health. . . ." [I. i. 176, 178, 180]), or giving Lady Capulet such artificially toned sentiments, or providing such a bathetic chorus of grief in the Capulet household when Juliet's "death" is discovered. One can sense in the kind of language used at such points a corresponding emotional or imaginative immaturity in the character, a weakness which will help define later a strength or intensity somewhere else. In a play that works so well with contrasts in theme and mood, contrasts in language have a fit place.

Most critical skepticism disappears in response to the lyrical language of the balcony scene or of the farewell at dawn. Many playgoers know the purple passages from these scenes by heart, but what is often forgotten is the way Shakespeare has rendered his poetry effective by constructing the scene which contains it so that theatrical dimensions (setting, timing, entrances and exits, interplay between characters, etc.) provide the real foundation for the charm and power of the words. There is a "language" in the scenario itself, and in the sequence of actions and reactions within a given scene, which enables the poetic language to convey its maximum meaning and feeling. (pp. 4-8)

Structure

Critical commonplaces regarding the structure of *Romeo and Juliet* tend to emphasize a handful of its characteristics: the swift pace of the action, which Shakespeare compresses into a few days' duration dramatized in two dozen scenes, many of which center on sudden reversals and the need for quick decisions; the emphatic juxtaposition of comic characters and attitudes with foreboding and destructive situations; the heightening of the young lovers' purity of feeling by contrast both with the lustier attitudes of the Nurse and Mercutio and with Romeo's studied infatuation with Rosaline; the more obvious contrasts between love and hate, youth and age, impetuous action and helpless wisdom; the efficiency and impact of the central reversal scene of Mercutio's death; and finally, for critics with allegiance to Aristotelian tragic formulas, the excessive reliance on sheer accident or chance in order to move the events toward a disaster which seems less inevitable than tragedy demands.

Qualities of pace and contrast are best sensed in performance, where it becomes clear how increasingly masterful Shakespeare's theatrical skill is becoming. He is able to convey more by the pace and proportion of action than he had been even in the violent early history plays. "Proportion" is perhaps a vague term, but it does cover the skill by which Shakespeare shapes his presentation of the lovers' destiny. We are never *directly* aware, for example, that Romeo and Juliet are actually together to share only 330 lines throughout the whole play, about one-ninth of the play's length; but that proportion helps nevertheless to accent the intensity and rarity of feeling embodied in their encounters, as well as to impress upon us the weight and complexity of the outside world's "doings" which obstruct the couple and aid in destroying them. (pp. 10-11)

The comic texture of the play is also kept under a fine control. Roughly one-sixth of the total dialogue can be called comic, and practically all of it is confined to that part of the play before Mercutio's death. It helps to build, even within the more threatening outlines of the family feud, a hearty atmosphere of comradeship, wit, gaiety and high spirits—an atmosphere which seems to hold out a promise for the budding love of Romeo and Juliet, but which turns out to be explosive. Each comic

character or event is made to harbor an ironic counterthrust: the gaiety at the ball is marred by a vengeful Tybalt; the witty Mercutio harbors a fatal itch to fight; the sympathetic Nurse betrays her drastic lack of sensitivity when she urges Juliet to forget Romeo and marry Paris. The unifying symbol for these comic people and events, as well as for the lovers themselves and the bustling world about them, can be found in the Friar's osier cage: those flowers, plants, and weeds—some beautiful, many capable of both healing and destroying, all very natural and part of the mortal earth.

> The earth that's nature's mother is her
>   tomb;
> What is her burying grave, that is her
>   womb;
> And from her womb children of divers
>   kind
> We sucking on her natural bosom find:
> Many for many virtues excellent,
> None but for some, and yet all different.
> O mickle is the powerful grace that lies
> In plants, herbs, stones, and their true
>   qualities;
> For nought so vile that on the earth doth
>   live
> But to the earth some special good doth
>   give;
> Nor aught so good but, strained from that
>   fair use,
> Revolts from true birth, stumbling on
>   abuse.
> Virtue itself turns vice, being misapplied.
> And vice sometime by action dignified.
>   [II. iii. 9-22]

That comedy and tragedy lie down together in this play not only points up the reversal in mood that takes place with the killing of Mercutio and Tybalt, but illustrates again the inner paradox of our mortal nature.

Theme

I take that paradox, as stated by the Friar, to be at the heart of this play, and also a foreshadowing of a theme given further embodiment in Shakespeare's later tragedies. Others have suggested differing central themes for *Romeo and Juliet*, ranging from a literal insistence on the lovers' star-crossed fate, to a Freudian view of their experience as an embodiment of the death-wish; from a neo-orthodox-Elizabethan lesson in the dangers of passion, to a providential triumph of love over hate.

The reasons for such diversity are discoverable in the play, which seems to hold out a number of keys to interpretation. If we look only at the conclusion, with the reconciled parents and the promise of a golden monument, we may be inclined to see the mysterious ways of Providence working toward good. If we listen chiefly to the Friar's moral admonitions, rather than to his reflections on the natural condition cited above, we may agree that haste and lack of wise forethought bring about the disaster. If we catalogue all the tricks played by chance

John Stride as Romeo and Judy Dench as Juliet in a 1960 Old Vic Theatre production of Romeo and Juliet.

(particularly Friar John's undelivered message and the unhappy timing of arrivals and awakenings in the final scene), we may see it all as the workings of a hostile external Fate. Tragic theorists become disheartened at the lack of a more highly developed moral consciousness in the central figures and the corresponding lack of close cause-and-effect integration between such characterization and the destructive outcome. And students of Elizabethan piety (both familial and religious) are inclined to feel more harshly about Romeo and Juliet themselves than even Friar Lawrence does at his most chiding moments. The interpretive problem is a problem involving proportion and balance; a balanced view of the play must rest on an awareness of the delicate balance of its diverse elements. To emphasize one to the exclusion of the rest will not give us a theme worthy of the play's actual structure or the dramatic experience it yields in performance.

It is undeniable that the strategy of the play generates strong sympathy for the lovers, heightens their superiority in richness and purity of feeling,

and awakens our compassion for their plight. It is also undeniable that Romeo in particular is both reckless and desperate at the wrong moments; partly because he is in love, partly because he is young, partly because he is the histrionic Romeo. By the end of the play Shakespeare makes more of a man of him than the miserable boy (of Act III) grovelling in tears on the Friar's floor, but he also gives him a cruel power with that added strength and determination: the slaying of Paris is the dramatic proof. The combination is deliberate: Shakespeare's sources contain neither the heightened sense of the lovers' innocence nor Paris's murder. The play does not prove that Romeo and Juliet should not have yielded to their love for one another, or disobeyed their parents, or been so quick to marry or to kill themselves. It does suggest that the flower of an innocent love, because of the earth in which it was planted, could foster its own destruction. Shakespeare hints at a natural disaster rather than a moral one, but his conclusion urges something beyond disaster: that such a destruction may in turn foster the reconciliation of the elders who do not understand love. The beauty and harmony of the lovers does not die with them. (pp. 11-13)

The envy, ill will, and aggressiveness that characterize the feud do not represent the total threat to the love of the central figures. The feud is always present as a dangerous obstructing condition; it is a reason for keeping things secret which if known would resolve many complications. But it is not of itself a villainous thing that destroys the lovers intentionally. To understand its limitations as an element in the whole balance is to realize that the play cannot be summed up as a conflict between the forces of young love and old hate. Tragic destruction results from a pattern which includes as well the unaccountable element of chance and the more pervading element of unawareness. So many incidents in the play exhibit people who do not know what they are really doing, people who are both agents and victims of an unthinking impetuosity. The spectrum ranges from the vulgar servants of the opening scene through Mercutio's duel, Capulet's marriage-planning, the murder of Paris, to Romeo's suicide and the Friar's fear of being discovered at the tomb. Clearly this kind of unawareness leads to an irony often associated with tragedy (although it is also a standard tool of the comedy writer who builds a complication out of interlocking misunderstandings), but in the context of Shakespeare's play it does more than heighten suspense and trigger an agonized "If only he knew!" audience reaction. It serves to impress upon us a basic condition of human interaction—our unconscious limitations in understanding the motives of others (and of ourselves), our ultimate helplessness in the face of the multiple possibilities of things going awry. Once this quality is fully felt, we cannot be content with condemning either stupidity or "rude will" as the basis of destructive evil. We are led once more to an insight or a perception of the mortal world which is broader than the strictly moral one: tragic destruction, though often the consequence of human decision, is beyond that an irremediable aspect of the natural world and man's limited consciousness. That perception is somewhat muted by Shakespeare's concluding reconciliation, but because it is grounded in the conditions of human interaction in the play, it cannot be an element totally "resolved" by this or any other kind of ending.

Fate and Coincidence

Two final problems related to this quality or insight remain. One is the problem of Fate. The other is the feeling that *Romeo and Juliet* lacks tragic inevitability precisely because so much of the action turns on ignorance that might have been remedied and on sheer mistiming. The prologue, the foreboding dreams and intimations of death, and the futility of the elaborately planned attempts to restore Romeo and Juliet to one another all tend to stress that the destiny of the lovers is fated. Each

move that they make toward each other is matched by some counterthrust; and though there is no villain or human agent behind the opposition, some readers have felt that Fate itself takes on the quality of a destructive agent, moving events and characters in cruel combination to produce the disastrous outcome. Romeo may want to defy the stars, but in that very defiance he is unwittingly cooperating in his own doom. The trouble with this interpretation again lies in what it must leave out or ignore. If we are to judge the reconciling conclusion of the play as inappropriate to the major design of the tragedy, as a last-minute excrescence that does not fit well with earlier motifs, then perhaps we may rest content with the vision of inimical Fate. But if we see the ending as purposeful, and as an evocation of the paradoxical good that can spring from a lamented destruction, the simple view of Fate will not satisfy. Nor can we ignore what Shakespeare characteristically stresses in all his tragic drama: the connections between the character of men and the disaster that may befall them. In this case, we have only to recall the care Shakespeare has taken to show us Romeo in an unheroic and desperate hysteria after he has killed Tybalt: a scene frequently embarrassing to actors but nevertheless integral to the play. It shows us the emotional proclivity in Romeo without which the external misfortunes and mischances would not have culminated in his death. If Shakespeare had wanted to put full strength into the Fate motif, he could also have employed such allegorical devices as had appeared in the contemporary play *Soliman and Perseda* [by Thomas Kidd], in which choral figures called Love, Death, and Fortune debate the relative power of their influence on the human lives in the story. The personification of a hostile Fate or Fortune was a fashionable convention in the neo-Senecan tragedy of the Elizabethans; the theme was equally conventional. In *Romeo and Juliet,* however, Shakespeare was moving in another direction. His developing vision of a tragic universe was not to be defined by hostile fatality, but by a paradoxical and all too precarious balance of good and evil. (pp. 14-16)

Time is the enemy even more than chance; it presses in upon the lovers in countless ways—the dawn brings the threat of discovery; a bare second enables the envious sword of Tybalt to fell Mercutio; the marriage date foreshortened by a capricious Capulet demands swift counterplans and decisions, which bring, in turn, disaster. The fast-paced world that Shakespeare builds up around his characters allows little possibility for adherence to Friar Lawrence's counsel of "Wisely and slow" [II. iii. 94]. In such a world to stumble tragically is surely no less inevitable than it is for Lear to go mad in the face of human ingratitude. In a vivid performance of the play, things happen so swiftly and suddenly that issues of probability hardly arise. Add the fact that the *emotions* behind the catastrophe have been made probable, and we readily see why we do not look upon the death of Romeo and Juliet as merely a terrible accident.

It is possible to step back from the immediate emotional grip of *Romeo and Juliet* and discover that we have somehow been taken in, that the swiftly moving world of sudden love and sudden death has been arbitrarily contrived, that the mechanism of the plot and the ingenious conceits of the language display a rather self-conscious artistry. At this second level of response, we may become aware that, for all its virtues, the play does not exhibit the power, range, and deeply probing qualities of *Hamlet, Othello, Macbeth* or *Lear*. Its reflective, philosophical dimensions are confined rather tightly to a few discourses by Friar Lawrence, where they remain detached from the emotional intensity of the chief characters; in *Hamlet* and *Lear* those who question the dignity of man and the nature of the gods are those who also suffer the greatest torments. *Romeo and Juliet* is surely a more honest expression of human tragedy than the grotesque *Titus Andronicus* or the melodramatic *Richard III*, but it has not yet found the most potent articulation for the paradox of good and evil in the natural world. If we feel finally that the play is not *major* tragedy, it is for such reasons rather than for defects in probability. A moving and compassionate expression of intense and vital passions, it burns with a flame more luminous than searing.

To a certain extent, it cannot do otherwise, granted its subject. As a close-up study of a breath-taking young love, it has little time or place for the probing inner conflicts of Shakespeare's more mature and deeply disillusioned characters. Indeed, one of the marks of the lovers' innocence is that they remain untouched by the experience of disillusionment, the experience that sounds the bass note of tragic anxiety from *Julius Caesar* on and echoes throughout Shakespeare's so-called "problem plays" and later romances as well. Romeo and Juliet are all in all to one another; the radiance of their shared love illumines them with glowing beauty, but casts little light on the world around them. Their experience, and ours as an audience, is thus intense but circumscribed. Shakespeare's structure of contrasts and paradoxes sets off that experience in a rich and colorful design, but he does not choose to emphasize in it the more disturbing deeper shadows that he was soon to explore with such comprehension. Here he was content to temper extremities with extreme sweet, and in view now of the world's reaction to his play who is to say he chose wrongly? (pp. 16-18)

> *Douglas Cole, in an introduction to* Twentieth Century Interpretations of Romeo and Juliet: A Collection of Critical Essays, *edited by Douglas Cole, Prentice-Hall, Inc., 1970, pp. 1-18.*

TRAGIC DESIGN

Franklin M. Dickey

[*Dickey asserts that fate, divine will, and the lovers' passion are inseparably linked in* Romeo and Juliet, *and all of these agents contribute to the catastrophe. According to the critic, the work is "a carefully wrought tragedy which balances hatred against love and which makes fortune the agent of divine justice without absolving anyone from his responsibility for the tragic conclusion." In this sense, Dickey contends,* Romeo and Juliet *reflects the Elizabethan concept of moral responsibility, a tenet which stressed that all sinners must endure the punishment of God, whose will is carried out through the operation of fate.*]

Romeo and Juliet, above everything a play of love, is also a play of hatred and of the mysterious ways of fortune. Although love in the first part of the play amuses us, in the end we pity the unhappy fate of young lovers, a fate which critics find embarrassingly fortuitous or, in the Aristotelian sense, unnecessary, the accident of chance to which all human life is subject. Despite the compelling poetry of the play and Shakespeare's skill at creating the illusion of tragedy, the play is said to succeed "by a trick." Whereas Aristotle demanded a "glimpse into the nature of things" beyond theatrical sensationalism and required of tragedy "an overwhelming sense of inevitability," Romeo and Juliet die, critics often tell us, only as the result of a series of mistakes and misunderstandings. In this light the lovers' death is pathetic rather than really tragic.

Critics are also embarrassed by Shakespeare's paradoxical treatment of the three great themes of the tragedy. On the one hand it can be demonstrated that the catastrophe develops from faults of character: Romeo's impetuous nature leads him to despair and die. On the other hand the text also gives us reason to believe that the love of Romeo and Juliet comes to a terrible end because of the hatred between the two families. And yet a third view makes fate the main cause of the final disaster: Romeo and Juliet had to die because they were "star-cross'd."

The seeming conflict of these themes and the division among critics has given support to the belief that Shakespeare reveals no consistently moral view of the universe in this tragedy but gives us a slice of life without comment, standing apart from the great guiding ethos which dominates both Tudor philosophy and literary criticism. If the play has any final meaning it is to be found in the passionate rhetoric of love with which Shakespeare expresses his own youthful ardor.

Against these prevailing views . . . [I] propose that *Romeo and Juliet* is a true mirror of the Elizabethan concept of a moral universe although Shakespeare does not preach morality. Judged by Elizabethan standards, the play is not merely a gorgeous and entertaining melodrama but a carefully wrought tragedy which balances hatred against love and which makes fortune the agent of divine justice without absolving anyone from his responsibility for the tragic conclusion. Unlike his source Shakespeare attempts a solution to the problem of evil by fitting the power of fortune into the scheme of universal order. Although Shakespeare's viewpoint is not Greek, Romeo . . . is an agent of God's justice but remains responsible for his own doom. (pp. 63-64)

One of the most solid features in the unchanging ground of Shakespeare is the belief in a just Providence. Mysterious as the ways of this Providence are, the pattern remains visible. Although the innocent suffer, the guilty are always punished. Not fate but the corrupt will makes men the agents of their own destruction. . . .

There is no blind fate in Shakespearean tragedy nor in the Elizabethan universe. Behind what looked like chance stood God in control of his creation. Fortune was a figure of speech devised by men to explain the inexplicable operations of the Deity. (p. 91). . . .

[A] belief in individual responsibility forms the philosophical background of mature Elizabethan tragedy. The Renaissance God used fortune as the instrument of his vengeance. In Shakespeare the wayward passions of men subject them to the whims of fate. Thus Hamlet, praising Horatio, equates fortune and the will:

> blest are those
> Whose blood and judgement are so well commingled,
> That they are not a pipe for Fortune's finger
> To sound what stop she please. Give me that man
> That is not passion's slave, and I will wear him
> In my heart's core . . .
>
> [*Hamlet*, III. ii. 68-73]

While viewing drama, especially *Romeo and Juliet*, we often respond passionately as the doomed heroes respond, and this is, as critics have always known, one of the secrets of tragic catharsis. But beneath these passions the ground bass of an unshakable system continues to move, adding harmonies which we who have rejected that ethic no longer hear. Tragic tension results from the contest between human passion and will which work with and against fate in the elaborate Elizabethan harmony.

This *condition humaine* [human condition] helps to explain what otherwise are glaring faults in the progress of *Romeo and Juliet*. Shakespeare has promised us at the very beginning that we are to

see a pair of star-crossed lovers. Romeo himself first dreads the influence of the stars and then curses them for his misfortune. Both he and Juliet have forebodings of the sorrow to come. Again and again the characters gropingly predict the course of the future. Accident and coincidence add to our feeling that blind fate dominates the action.

But to offset this feeling Shakespeare has provided two commentators to remind us that the terrible things we have seen are all the work of divine justice. When Friar Laurence cries,

> A greater power than we can contradict
> Hath thwarted our intents . . .
>
> [V. iii. 153-54]

it seems most natural to suppose that the holy Friar is invoking God rather than blind fate, for he has denied that fate is the cause of Romeo's wretchedness. Earlier he has warned frantic Romeo that his fortune depended upon his own virtue and moderation, that the man who flies in the face of fortune is to blame for his own misery. "Why rail'st thou," he asks Romeo after Tybalt's death,

> Since birth, and heaven, and earth, all three do meet
> In thee at once, which thou at once wouldst lose.
> Fie, fie . . .
> A pack of blessings light upon thy back;
> Happiness courts thee in her best array;
> But, like a misbehav'd and sullen wench,
> Thou pout'st upon thy fortune and thy love.
> Take heed, take heed, for such die miserable.
>
> [III. iii. 119-22, 141-45]

And when he discovers Juliet in the tomb, we learn that he has begged her to come forth

> And bear this work of heaven with patience.
>
> [V. iii. 261]

According to the Friar Romeo's actions must determine his ultimate felicity or doom, and yet at the end he finds Romeo's death to be the "work of heaven." It would seem that . . . the Friar does not dissociate human actions and the power of fortune which represents God's will.

The second commentator Shakespeare gives us to point up the meaning of the tragedy is Prince Escalus, who at the ending of the play and at the point of greatest emphasis, sums up the significance of all that has happened:

> See, what a scourge is laid upon your hate,
> That Heaven finds means to kill your joys with love.
>
> [V. iii. 292-93]

After hearing these words and contemplating the evenhanded justice which has leveled parent with parent, child with child, and friend with friend, would not the audience sensitive to providential fortune and its use in tragedy understand without any tedious explication that fortune has operated here to punish sin and that this avenging fortune is the work of heaven? Such an audience would not have stuck at applying pitiful Rosamond's words to the lovers [in Samuel Daniel's *The Complaint of Rosamond*],

> fate is not prevented, though fore-
> known,
> For that must hap, decreed by heavenly
> powers
> Who work our fall yet make the fault still
> ours.

In *Romeo and Juliet* then fortune may be considered not the prime mover but the agent of a higher power. If fortune is not the independent cause of the catastrophe, then we must look behind fortune for the actions which set it in motion. Friar Laurence warns Romeo that his own folly in love will doom him. Prince Escalus, speaking as chorus, attributes the tragedy to hate. Both are right, for it is the collision of these passions which dooms the lovers.

Of these two forces love overshadows the other dramatically, since it is the passion of the protagonists and since Shakespeare has lavished his most moving poetry upon the love scenes. But the fact remains that this is not a play centered on one passion but a play of carefully opposed passions. The prologue informs us that we are to see a drama of love and hate. Hatred is the first passion to threaten tragedy in the comic opening of the play; hatred brings about the actual climax of the action, Mercutio's death; and hatred is the theme which Shakespeare introduces with love at the end of the play to explain the workings of fate.

The theme of hatred involves more than the opposition of two private families; because of the street brawls, because of the murderous intrigues of the two opposed parties, it involves the whole state. Romeo and Juliet, whose love would unite the two houses, are forced apart by the quarrel which they seek to avoid. Thus the love story in the play, as in *Antony and Cleopatra* and *Troilus and Cressida,* is more than a tale of love, and the problems of the play are not only ethical but in the broadest sense political. (pp. 92-5)

Thus although our main interest is in Shakespeare's handling of love, we must also inquire into Shakespeare's use of the complementary theme of hatred. *Romeo and Juliet* is built about two passions traditionally opposed, and the interweaving of these two themes, like the ambiguous balance between comedy and tragedy, adds to the peculiar irony which pervades the play. (p. 96)

The full power of hatred comes out . . . in Escalus's speech which sums up the meaning of the

action. He calls the miserable fathers from the crowd:

> Capulet! Montague!
> See, what a scourge is laid upon your hate,
> That Heaven finds means to kill your joys
> with love.
> And I for winking at your discords too
> Have lost a brace of kinsmen. All are pun-
> ish'd.
>
> [V. iii. 291-95]

This speech does not make sense unless we take into account the close interaction of fate, hatred, and love in the play.

Escalus's gloomy judgments give us a true criticism of the whole tragedy. The phrase "your joys" must refer to the lovers, the hope of each of the two warring houses. Their death through love is the punishment of heaven, working through fate, upon the families who have carried on the feud. (p. 100)

When we look back over the course of hatred, we see the truth of Escalus's sentence, "All are punish'd." Fate has worked to produce an evenhanded justice. The force of Mercutio's dying imprecation on the houses appears at the end of the tragedy in the mysterious death of Lady Montague on the night of her son's suicide. Her death, Shakespeare's addition to his source as are the deaths of Paris and Mercutio, evens the score between the families. Partisan pays for partisan and kinsman for kinsman. Just as love holds families and nations and indeed the whole universe together, so hatred breaks up families, destroys commonwealths, and, represented by Satan, constantly works to unframe God's whole handiwork. It is precise and ironical justice that quenches the one passion by means of its opposite. *Romeo and Juliet,* no less than Shakespeare's mature tragedies, celebrates the great vision of order by which the English Renaissance still lives. (p. 101)

. . . . .

The play is uniquely constructed in that the same passions which make us tearful or indignant before the action ends, do amuse us with little interruption for almost half the acting time. Even the events leading up to Mercutio's death promise comedy rather than tragedy, and it must have startled the first audience to see laughter so quickly turn to mourning. Yet the play is an exceptionally powerful tragedy, even if it sometimes embarrasses critics. Where the first half delights us with love comedy, the last three short acts explore the tragic potentialities of young love. Fortune and hatred threaten to turn the lovers' bliss to ashes, but the immediate cause of their unhappy deaths is Romeo's headlong fury and blind despair. Thus in both the beginning of the play and at the end Shakespeare's view of love remains sound philosophically and dramatically. (p. 102)

Throughout *Romeo and Juliet* Romeo is precipitate in love. Juliet, who loves as faithfully, is much less subject to the gusts of passion which blind Romeo. Romeo never examines the consequence of his actions, but Juliet fears that their love may be "too rash, too unadvis'd, too sudden" [II. ii. 118]. Romeo never shares Juliet's insight. After they have pledged love at Juliet's window, his only concern is that the love he feels seems too delightful to be true. It is Juliet not Romeo who thinks practically of arranging for marriage and who remembers to ask what time she is to send her messenger in the morning.

On Romeo's inability to control either his passionate love or his passionate grief, his death and Juliet's depend. The boundless love which Romeo felt at the sight of Juliet turns as suddenly to despair, just as any well-versed Renaissance philosopher might have predicted, for the man in the grip of one passion was easily swayed by another. (pp. 105-06)

Romeo therefore is a tragic hero like Othello in that he is responsible for his own chain of passionate actions. When we first see him he is already stricken with love. This first love is comic, but nevertheless it is a real attack of the sickness of love, as his father makes clear when he complains that Romeo's humor will turn "Black and portentous" [I. i.141] unless checked.

Since the man stricken with passion could not readily defend himself against new onslaughts of passion, Romeo's sudden passionate about-face when he sees Juliet would have seemed realistic to an Elizabethan audience. Romeo's transports for Juliet differ from his first melancholy because she returns his affection. For a time he is cured and conducts himself so reasonably that even Mercutio comments on the change in his temper.

But with Mercutio's death Romeo casts aside all reason and begins a chain of passionate action which leads to death. Rejecting the reasonable conduct with which he had first answered his enemy, he attacks and kills Tybalt. It would certainly have spoiled the play for Romeo to have waited for the law to punish Tybalt, but the fact remains that this reasonable action would have turned tragedy into comedy. In this choice between reasonable and passionate action lies one great difference between the genres. Forgiveness produces the happy ending of comedy; revenge produces the catastrophe of tragedy.

Romeo's next passionate mistake is to fall into frantic despair after the Prince sentences him to banishment. When Romeo cries out against his lot, Friar Laurence, the consistent voice of moderation and wisdom, warns him that he is truly unfortunate only in giving way to uncontrolled grief.

The next step in Romeo's march to destruction is his sudden and complete despair when he learns that Juliet is dead. The direct result of Romeo's frenzied desire to kill himself is his killing of Paris, an incident which Shakespeare adds, like the death of Lady Montague and the death of Mercutio, to his source. Thus Brooke's Romeus dies with less on his conscience than does Shakespeare's hero. In Brooke Romeus kills Tybalt only to save his own life, not to revenge a friend, and at the end of the play dies guiltless of any additional blood save his own. In our play, however, Shakespeare is careful to make Romeo guilty of sinful action under the influence of passion, while at the same time making us sympathize with Romeo's agonies of despair. In his encounter with Paris Romeo announces both his own mad desperation and the fact that in bringing the chain of passionate folly to its close, he puts one more sin upon his head.

Romeo's last passion-blinded act is to kill himself just before Juliet awakes, and her suicide may be thought of as the direct result of his. Although Shakespeare does not preach, the Elizabethan audience would have realized that in his fury Romeo has committed the ultimate sin. (pp. 114-16)

[The] tragedy of Romeo and Juliet is a true tragedy, preserving the ambiguous feelings of pity and terror which produce catharsis. Romeo remains a free agent even though he scarce knows what he does. Those who allowed passion to carry reason headlong were guilty of the very fault that Elizabethan ethics were designed to prevent. It is exactly because love could unseat the reason that few men who loved excessively could look forward to a virtuous life and a happy death. (p. 116)

Does this mean that . . . the spectators in [Shakespeare's] day, or that Shakespeare himself, looked upon the play as an edifying lesson in how not to conduct oneself in love? I hardly think so. The pattern of the action, given shape by Friar Laurence's warnings, Mercutio's satiric ebullience, and the Prince's scattered judgments, revolves around two of the most attractive young lovers in all literature. But the patterns of moral responsibility are necessary to give the action its perspective, and it is these patterns of the destructive as well as the creative force of love and the dependence of fate upon the passionate will which most contemporary criticism neglects or denies. We, who have moved so far from Shakespeare's world, need to be reminded of these things. They would have touched his audience far more deeply than they touch us today. (p. 117)

Franklin M. Dickey, in his Not Wisely but Too Well: Shakespeare's Love Tragedies, *The Huntington Library, 1957, 161 p.*

Lorentz Eckhoff

[Eckhoff maintains that **Romeo's** *and* **Juliet's** *tragic deaths result from their own impulsive-*

*ness. The critic then provides several examples
from the play to substantiate this claim.*]

Romeo and Juliet are in a precarious situation, like
two children playing with fire near a barrel of gun-
powder. They should be careful, prudent, mindful
of the future, but they are all too prone to be the
very opposite. They are too strongly infected with
the hectic spirit of Verona, they have the hot blood
and the hot temper of their race. They are like two
flames which merge into one.

Romeo is lyrical, ecstatic, a man who approves of
his emotions and revels in them, goes in search of
them, exaggerates them almost. He is what we
should call one of Love's lovers. He allows his feelings to direct his actions, as he proves, when despite his many forebodings about a premature
death, he sets off for the feast at Capulet's house:

> But he, that hath the steerage of my
>   course,
> Direct my sail! On, lusty gentlemen.
>   [I. iv. 112-13]

At the beginning of the play we hear that he is in
love with Rosaline, but this love affair is not really
to be taken seriously, it is . . . something he has invented, or possibly imagined. At any rate we find it
difficult to believe in it. He speaks in outworn an-
titheses and forced, artificial similes. The truest
word he speaks about it is the very passage which
shows how airy and artificial it is.

> Love is a smoke raised with the fume of
>   sighs. . . .
>   [I. i. 190]

Romeo is the born lover who has not yet found the
real object of his affections, and is wandering
about, conscious or unconscious of the fact, looking for it.

In Juliet's eyes Romeo is not only the lover but the
liberator. She is only fourteen years old, but she
has been waiting for him even before she meets
him. She has yearned to get away from a house
which is no home, merely an uncongenial place of
residence, sometimes almost a prison. She has no
one to love, there is no human being with whom
she has any intimate contact, neither her nurse,
whose broad remarks and stories make no impression on her, nor her subdued mother, nor her hot-
tempered father, jovial, fond of festive occasions
and brutal to boot, a domestic tyrant, who is convinced that it is the child's duty to love and the parent's duty to command; a father who threatens her
with chastisement and expulsion, if she refuses to
obey his orders on the instant.

Juliet has preserved all the tenderness of her feelings, and has learnt to conceal those feelings when
occasion demands. She is beautiful and wise, courageous and quick to act—admirably equipped, in
fact, to play the role which circumstances force her
to adopt.

Romeo and Juliet are made for one another, dearer
to one another than life itself, and instinctively
know this the very moment they meet. They are
carried away by the force of fate, they burn and
glow with a new intensity, every moment they are
tensed and proved to the uttermost of their beings,
and in the course of a few summer days they blossom and develop from callow youth to the maturity
of man and woman, to an all-conquering and all-
besetting passion.

Their very words become music, poetry, fancy. As
scholars are quick to remind us, the first words
they exchange are in the form of a sonnet, and Juliet's soliloquy on the eve of her bridal night is a
nuptial hymn, while their conversation the next
morning is a hymn to dawn, an *aubade.* Their life,
pulsing hotly, beats to a hectic rhythm. Practically
every word Juliet utters in the balcony scene
marks a step forward, an action, a decision. She is
brisk, and anxious at the dizzy whirl of events:

> Dost thou love me? I know thou wilt say
>   "Ay". . . .
> In truth, fair Montague, I am too fond,
> And therefore thou mayst think my
>   haviour light:
> But trust me, gentleman, I'll prove more
>   true
> Than those that have more cunning to be
>   strange. . . .
> Well, do not swear. Although I joy in thee,
> I have no joy of this contract to-night:
> It is too rash, too unadvis'd, too sudden;
> Too like the lightning, which doth cease to
>   be
> Ere one can say "It lightens". Sweet, good-
>   night!
> This bud of love, by summer's ripening
>   breath,
> May prove a beauteous flower when next
>   we meet.
> Good-night, good-night!
>   [II. ii. 90, 98-101, 116-23]

She is impatient when she is waiting for the nurse
to return with an answer from Romeo, and for that
reason a highly comic effect is achieved by the ir-
ritatingly dilatory manner of the nurse, and the
stream of irrelevancies with which she crams her
reply. She is more impatient still before the bridal
night, as she waits for Romeo:

> Gallop apace, you fiery-footed steeds,
> Towards Phœbus' lodging, such a wag-
>   goner
> As Phaeton would whip you to the west,
> And bring in cloudy night immediately.
> Spread thy close curtain, love-performing
>   night!
> That rude day's eyes may wink, and Romeo
> Leap to these arms, untalk'd of and un-
>   seen!
> Lovers can see to do their amorous rites
> By their own beauties; or, if love be blind,
> It best agrees with night. Come, civil night,

Thou sober-suited matron, all in black,
And learn me how to lose a winning
  match,
Play'd for a pair of stainless maidenhoods:
Hood my unman'd blood, bating in my
  cheeks,
With thy black mantle; till strange love,
  grown bold,
Think true love acted simple modesty.
Come, night! come, Romeo! come, thou
  day in night!
For thou wilt lie upon the wings of night,
Whiter than new snow on a raven's back.
Come, gentle night; come, loving, black-
  brow'd night,
Give me my Romeo!

                                          [III. ii. 1-21]

Friar Laurence, who is most likely the poet's
mouthpiece, tries in vain to brake the headlong
speed:

Romeo:
O! let us hence; I stand on sudden haste.

Friar Laurence:
Wisely and slow; they stumble that run
  fast.

                                          [II. iii. 93-4]

Friar Laurence:
These violent delights have violent ends,
And in their triumph die, like fire and
  powder,
Which, as they kiss, consume: the swee-
  test honey
Is loathsome in his own deliciousness
And in the taste confounds the appetite:
Therefore love moderately; long love doth
  so.

                                          [II. vi. 9-14]

Romeo too tries to check his ardour. As we have
seen, he refuses to fight with Tybalt, and when
Mercutio is wounded he is at first calm, and hopes
the wound is slight:

Courage, man; the hurt cannot be much.
                                          [III. i. 95]

But when Benvolio returns, and tells him of Mercutio's death, and Tybalt returns in triumph, there
is an end to Romeo's patience, and his wrath floods
his being, like a river that has broken its banks. It
is worth noticing how he approves his own wrath:

Benvolio:
Here comes the furious Tybalt back
  again.

Romeo:
Alive! in triumph! and Mercutio slain!
Away to heaven, respective lenity,
And fire-ey'd fury be my conduct now!
Now, Tybalt, take the villain back again
That late thou gav'st me; for Mercutio's
  soul
Is but a little way above our heads,
Staying for thine to keep him company:
Either thou, or I, or both, must go with

him.
                                          [III. i. 121-29]

Once again the mood of the moment runs away
with him. When he hears, after Tybalt's death, that
Juliet calls his name and Tybalt's in her despair at
what has occurred, he exclaims to Friar Laurence:

O! tell me, friar, tell me,
In what vile part of this anatomy
Doth my name lodge? tell me, that I may
  sack
The hateful mansion.

                                          [III. iii. 105-08]

And once again he draws his sword; but this time
his impetuosity provokes Friar Laurence's wrath
in the shape of a sharp rebuke.

Hold thy desperate hand:
Art thou a man? thy form cries out thou
  art:
Thy tears are womanish; thy wild acts de-
  note
The unreasonable fury of a beast:
Unseemly woman in a seeming man;
Or ill-beseeming beast in seeming both!
Thou hast amaz'd me. . . .

                                          [III. iii. 108-14]

There is a break of a day and a half between Act III
and Act V, but in the course of those forty odd
hours Romeo has aged many years. Reverie has
gone and given place to grim determination. There
is a crude vigour in his words to the apothecary
who sells him the poison, and even more so in the
last scene by the vault in the graveyard, when he
sends the servant away:

. . . therefore hence, be gone:
But, if thou, jealous, dost return to pry
In what I further shall intend to do,
By heaven, I will tear thee joint by joint,
And strew this hungry churchyard with
  thy limbs.
The time and my intents are savage-wild,
More fierce and more inexorable far
Than empty tigers or the roaring sea.

                                          [V. iii. 32-9]

And again when he opens the tomb, and bids Paris
retire:

I must (die); and therefore came I hither.
Good gentle youth, tempt not a desperate
  man;
Fly hence and leave me: think upon these
  gone;
Let them affright thee. I beseech thee,
  youth,
Put not another sin upon my head
By urging me to fury: O! be gone. . . .

                                          [V. iii. 58-63]

Romeo and Juliet are in a hurry even when it
comes to dying. There is no shadow of doubt in
their souls that they would rather die than live
apart. But had Romeo been in less hurry to die, he
would have found a living Juliet.

We may be sure that Shakespeare loved Romeo and Juliet and their love as much as we do, but it is just as certain that he wished to warn young people in his very discreet way not to follow their example. (pp. 51-6)

> *Lorentz Eckhoff, "Passion," in his* Shakespeare: Spokesman of the Third Estate, *translated by R. I. Christophersen, Akademisk Verlag, 1954, pp. 48-86.*

Irving Ribner

[*Ribner provides a Christian interpretation of* Romeo and Juliet *in which he contends that the lovers' deaths are ordained by God to reconcile the feuding families. The critic notes how Shakespeare altered the play into something more meaningful than both a traditional Senecan tragedy, where arbitrary destiny causes the catastrophe, and a tragedy of character, in which the lovers are punished for their reckless passion (the term Senecan tragedy derives from the Roman statesman and philosopher Seneca, who in the first century A. D. wrote a number of violent, catastrophic dramas that later became models for Renaissance tragedy). According to Ribner,* **Romeo** *and* **Juliet** *mature as they experience evil, ultimately realizing that the world is in fact ruled by a benevolent God. Further, the lovers' suicides reflect their acceptance of death, resulting in the restoration of order and a "rebirth of love" in Verona.*]

Critics have usually regarded Shakespeare's *Romeo and Juliet* as . . . a Senecan tragedy of inexorable fate; some have emphasized the sinfulness of the young lovers. We cannot deny the role of fate and accident in Shakespeare's play; it is established in the prologue and it runs as a constant theme through all five acts. We would not expect this to be otherwise, for this was the formula with which Shakespeare began. But Shakespeare's play is far more than a tragedy of fate. It is, moreover, not at all a story of just deserts visited upon young sinners, although some critics have found it so. The fate that destroys Romeo and Juliet is not an arbitrary, capricious force any more than it is the inexorable agent of nemesis, which in Senecan tragedy executed retribution for sin. Shakespeare's play is cast in a more profoundly Christian context . . . ; the "greater power than we can contradict" [V. iii. 153] is divine providence, guiding the affairs of men in accordance with a plan which is merciful as well as just. Out of the evil of the family feud—a corruption of God's harmonious order—must come a rebirth of love, and the lives of Romeo and Juliet are directed and controlled so that by their deaths the social order will be cleansed and restored to harmony. Shakespeare uses the story of the lovers to explore the operation of divine providence, the meaning of a fate which in the ordinary affairs of life will sometimes frus-trate our most careful plans. . . . It is in Shakespeare's departure from the Senecan tradition he inherited that the particular significance of *Romeo and Juliet* as tragedy lies. Here we see him groping for a tragic design to embody a view of life far more significant and meaningful than what the Senecan stereotypes could afford. (pp. 273-74)

In [the] emphasis upon youth which runs throughout Shakespeare's play, but which is not so evident in his source, we may find a clue to the philosophical pattern Shakespeare imposed upon Senecan tradition. Romeo and Juliet are children born into a world already full of an ancient evil not of their own making. The feud is emphasized in the opening lines of the prologue, and in the opening scene of the play—before either hero or heroine is introduced—the feud is portrayed in all its ramifications, corrupting the social order from the lowliest serving man up to the prince himself, for just as it breeds household rancor, it disturbs also the very government of Verona.

There is a universality in this situation. Romeo and Juliet epitomize the role in life of all men and women, for every being who is born, as the Renaissance saw it, is born into a world in which evil waits to destroy him, and he marches steadily towards an inexorable death. It is a world, moreover, in which his plans, no matter how virtuous, may always be frustrated by accident and by the caprice of a seemingly malignant fate. It is this universality that gives the play its stature as tragedy, for Romeo and Juliet in a sense become prototypes of everyman and everywoman. They attempt to find happiness in a world full of evil, to destroy evil by means of love, for with Friar Lawrence they see their marriage as the termination of the feud, but evil in the world cannot be destroyed; their fate cannot be escaped, and thus, like all men and women, they suffer and die. This is the life journey of all, but Shakespeare's play asserts that man need not despair, for he is a creature of reason with the grace of God to guide him, and through his encounter with evil he may learn the nature of evil and discover what it means to be a man. The ultimate message of Renaissance tragedy is that through suffering man grows and matures until he is able to meet his necessary fate with a calm acceptance of the will of God. The tragic vision and the religious vision spring ultimately out of the same human needs and aspirations.

Shakespeare saw in the legend of Romeo and Juliet a story which illustrated neither retribution for sin nor the working out of a blind inexorable Senecan fatalism. He saw a story that might be used to portray the maturation of youth through suffering and death. *Romeo and Juliet* may thus be called an "education" play, drawing upon the established morality tradition of such plays as *Nice Wanton* and *Lusty Juventus*. Romeo and Juliet learn the fundamental lessons of tragedy; the meaning of human life and death. Their education can culminate only in death and then rebirth in a world in which evil has no place. We can thus see Shakespeare in this play combining a story already cast for him in Senecan mold with a quite alien medieval dramatic tradition, which in its origins was based upon peculiarly Christian assumptions.

Romeo and Juliet are foolish, of course. They are hasty and precipitous and they make many mistakes, but to speak of a "tragic flaw" in either of them is to lead to endless absurdity. The impetuosity, haste, and carelessness of the lovers are the universal attributes of youth. Their shortcomings are what make them the ordinary representatives of humanity that this type of play must have as its tragic protagonists. Their errors, moreover, are all committed with a virtuous end in view, the same end that leads the wise and mature Friar Lawrence to marry them in spite of the dangers he sees both to them and to his own position. Unlike a later Othello or Macbeth, they are guilty of no deliberate choice of evil.

Both Romeo and Juliet mature greatly as the play unfolds, but to demonstrate the particular progress of the human life journey, Shakespeare concentrates upon Romeo. The exigencies of drama required that he concentrate upon one figure, and Romeo, of course, was the natural one. The Renaissance generally held that woman's powers of reason were somewhat less than those of man, and the design of the play called for a free-willed rational acceptance of the Christian stoic view of life to which Romeo comes at the end of the play.

How can a man live in a world in which evil lurks on every side and in which the inevitable end of all man's worldly aspirations must be death, a world in which the cold necessity of Fortune cannot be avoided? The Renaissance had a very simple answer which it carried over from the consolation philosophy of the Middle Ages, itself a Christian adaptation of the classical creed of Stoicism. Good and evil are in the world together, but the entire universe is ruled by a benevolent God whose plan is deliberate, meaningful, and ultimately good. The paradox of the fortunate fall taught that evil itself contributed to this ultimate good. Man, bearing the burden of original sin, had evil within him, but as the chosen creature of God, he had good also. When the evil within him predominated he was ruled by passion, but he had the gift of reason, which by proper exercise could always keep passion under control. Reason, of course, lay in an acceptance of the will of God. This central core of Renaissance belief is perfectly expressed by Friar Lawrence:

> For naught so vile that on the earth doth
>   live
> But to the earth some special good doth
>   give,
> Nor aught so good but, strain'd from that
>   fair use

> Revolts from true birth, stumbling on
>   abuse: . . .
> Two such opposed kings encamp them
>   still
> In man as well as herbs, grace and rude
>   will;
> And where the worser is predominant,
> Full soon the canker death eats up that
>   plant.
>   [II. iii. 17-20, 27-30]

Grace, of course, is reason, and rude will is passion. Man can live happily in the world if he allows his reason to guide his actions, to show him that the plan of the world essentially is good and just and that evil itself is designed to further the ends of a divine providence. With reason thus guiding him, man can become impervious to the blows of Fortune. He will accept his fate, whatever it may be, as contributing to a divine purpose beyond his comprehension but ultimately good and just. Through his encounter with evil Romeo learns to accept his fate in just such a manner.

We first meet Romeo as a lovesick boy assuming the conventional role of the melancholy lover, playing a game of courting a Capulet girl who he knows can never accede to his suit. We may well believe that it is because Rosaline is a Capulet that Romeo pursues her, and that because she knows the basic insincerity of his suit, she spurns him with her supposed vows of chastity. This is the boy Romeo, not yet ready to face the responsibilities of life, unaware of the real sorrows that are the lot of man, but playing with a make-believe sorrow that he enjoys to the fullest. We usually think that at his first sight of Juliet he abandons this childish pose and experiences true love. This may be so, for the dramatist is forced to work rapidly even at the expense of character consistency, but it is not really the sight of Juliet that causes him to change. It is his own precipitous act of leaping out from the dark beneath her window with his

> I take thee at thy word:
> Call me but love, and I'll be new baptized;
> Henceforth I never will be Romeo.
>   [II. ii. 49-51]

With this hasty speech the game of make-believe love becomes no longer possible. The hasty act of impetuous youth is the means to maturity. Romeo must now face the realities of life with all its consequences both for good and evil. There may be a double meaning in that final line. Never again will he be the same Romeo who had pined for Rosaline. Juliet too can no longer be the same once she has poured her heart out into the night. She too must now face the world as it is. Her unpremeditated outpouring of her love parallels the precipitous speech of Romeo.

Like all young people, Romeo and Juliet are uncertain and hasty in their first encounters with the problems of reality. Their plans at best are foolish ones. The force of evil had already intruded into their world immediately following Romeo's first sight of Juliet. His first poetic rapture [I. v. 44-53] had been echoed by the harsh voice of Tybalt:

> This, by his voice, should be a Montague.
> Fetch me my rapier, boy.
>
> [I. v. 54-5]

This is Shakespeare's unique poetic way of showing the ever–present juxtaposition of love and hate, good and evil. Before the marriage may be consummated, Romeo must now face this evil force in the world. He is not yet, however, able to accept it as he should. When Tybalt lies dead at his feet and a full awareness of what he has done comes upon him, Romeo cries out in despair: "O, I am fortune's fool" [III. i. 136]. This is a crucial line and all its implications must be understood. "Fool" had two common meanings in Shakespeare's age. On the one hand it had the connotation of "dupe" or "plaything," and thus the word usually is glossed. On the other hand it was a common word for "child." In three other places in the play it is used with this meaning. When Romeo calls himself the "dupe" or "plaything" of Fortune, he is asserting a capricious, lawless Fortune, and thus he is denying the providence of God, of which in the Christian view Fortune was merely the agent. Romeo here sees the universe as a mindless chaos, without guiding plan; he is proclaiming a philosophy of despair.

With this view of life the secondary meaning of "fool" is in complete accord. As long as man sees Fortune as capricious and the universe as without plan, he must be the slave of Fortune. Romeo is the child of Fortune at this point because he is governed by it as the child is governed by his father. He is constrained to blind obedience. He has not yet learned the way of acceptance by which the control of Fortune may be thrown off. When Romeo's own will is in accord with the universal plan of God, he will no longer be the child of Fortune in this sense. He will be the master of Fortune in that it can never direct him contrary to his own will. In this secondary sense of "child" there is also the implication that Romeo is more fortunate than he himself perceives, that he is protected as the child is by his father. The divine providence whose "fool" he is will lead him, in spite of his present ignorance, to a self-mastery and wisdom, and it will use his present seeming misfortune to restore harmony and order to the world.

From this low point Romeo must make his slow journey to maturity, and Shakespeare shows his progression in three stages. First we find him in the friar's cell, weeping and wailing, beating his head upon the ground and offering to kill himself. This abject surrender to passion is the behavior not of a rational man but of a beast, as the friar declares:

> Hold thy desperate hand:
> Art thou a man? Thy form cries out thou art:

> Thy tears are womanish; thy wild acts denote
> The unreasonable fury of a beast.
>
> [III. iii. 108-11]

Romeo's education now begins at the hands of Friar Lawrence, who in a lengthy speech [III. iii. 108-54] teaches him to make a virtue of necessity, that to rail on Fortune is foolish and fruitless, that careful reason will demonstrate to him that he is indeed far more fortunate than he might have been. When rather than kill himself he stops his weeping and goes to comfort Juliet, he has taken the first step toward maturity.

That his growth is a steady one from that point forward we may perceive from a bare hint as Romeo climbs from Juliet's window to be off for Mantua. "O, think'st thou we shall ever meet again?" [III. v. 51] asks Juliet, and Romeo replies:

> I doubt it not; and all these woes shall serve
> For sweet discourses in our time to come.
>
> [III. v. 52-3]

What is significant here is that Romeo has thrown off despair and can face the future with some degree of hope in an ultimate providence. It is but the barest hint of a change in him, and we see no more of him until the beginning of Act V, where in Mantua we perceive by his first words that he is a new man entirely. All of Act IV had been devoted to Juliet. The dramatist has not had time to show in detail the growth of Romeo. The change must be made clear in Romeo's first speech, and it must be accepted by the audience as an accomplished fact. We immediately sense a new serenity about him as he walks upon the stage at the beginning of Act V:

> My dreams presage some joyful news at hand:
> My bosom's lord sits lightly in his throne;
> And all this day an unaccustom'd spirit
> Lifts me above the ground with cheerful thoughts.
>
> [V. i. 2-5]

He expects joyful tidings, but the news Balthazer brings is the most horrible of which he can conceive. Shakespeare gives his opening speech to Romeo, I believe, so that it may emphasize the shock of the news of Juliet's supposed death coming when happy news is expected, and in the face of this shock to illustrate the manner in which the new Romeo can receive the severest blow of which Fortune is capable. (pp. 274-81)

The design of the tragedy does not call at this point for a Byronic defiance of fate by Romeo, a daring of Fortune to pour its worst upon his head. . . . The design calls for an escape from Fortune's oppression through an acceptance of the order of the universe, and this meaning is implicit in "I denie you Starres" [V. i. 24].

We may ask first what the word "deny" means in

Laurence Olivier as Romeo, Edith Evans as the Nurse, and John Gielgud as Mercutio in a 1935 Oxford University Dramatic Society presentation of Romeo and Juliet.

the context in which Shakespeare here uses it. We do not have far to look, for in the second act we find a significant clue. Here Juliet speaks:

> O Romeo, Romeo! wherefore art thou Romeo?
> Deny thy father and refuse thy name.
> [II. ii. 33-4]

She is asking wistfully that Romeo not be the son of his father, and her wish falls naturally into two parts: that he give up the name of his father and that he break the bond which ties him to his father. To "deny" his father is to negate the natural relationship of son to father, one, as the Renaissance saw it, of subjection and obedience. It is thus, in Shakespeare's sense, to cast off his father's authority, to refuse to be ruled by him. "I denie you starres," the line editors have consistently refused to accept as Shakespeare's, is the very line with which Romeo attains the victory over circumstances which is the sign of the mature stoical man. It is probably the most crucial single line of the play. To deny one's stars is to throw off the control of a hostile fortune, just as a son might throw off the control of his father. To Renaissance man there was only one means by which this might be

accomplished: by an acceptance of the way of the world as the will of God, and by a calm, fearless acceptance of death as the necessary and proper end of man, which releases him from all earthly evil and assures him of a true felicity in heaven. For Romeo this will be reunion with Juliet.

It has been argued, of course, that since the Anglican church taught that the punishment for suicide was damnation, Romeo and Juliet in killing themselves are merely assuring the loss of their souls. We are not dealing here, however, with Shakespeare the theologian illustrating a text, but rather with Shakespeare the dramatist using symbolically a detail inherited from his sources in order to illustrate a greater and more significant truth. The Senecan tradition in which the story came down to Shakespeare endorsed suicide as a means of release from a world full of pain and as a means of expiration for complicity in the death of a loved one. It was in these terms that suicide was so essential a part of the Romeo and Juliet story. There was in the Renaissance, moreover, much respect for the classical notion of suicide as a noble act by which man fulfills his obligations and attains a higher good than life itself, and on the stage suicide was often portrayed in such terms. Only the most insensitive of critics could regard Romeo and Juliet as destined for damnation; their suicide, inherited by Shakespeare as an essential part of the story, must be regarded as a symbolic act of acceptance of inevitable death. Dramatically it is the most effective means by which such acceptance may be portrayed. The results of the act are not damnation, but instead, the destruction of evil by the ending of the feud. Out of the self-inflicted deaths of Romeo and Juliet come a reconciliation and a rebirth of good, a catharsis that would be well-nigh impossible were it bought with the souls as well as the lives of the young lovers.

Shakespeare might easily have written "defy" instead of "deny," for that word might have conveyed a similar meaning. It need not be taken to indicate a Byronic challenge to Fortune. To defy Fortune is to assert one's independence of it, and that is what Romeo does. . . . Shakespeare might have written "defy" had he been a lesser artist, but he wrote "deny" because of the deliberate echo and reminder it might furnish of that earlier and equally crucial line, "O, I am fortune's fool" [III. i. 136]. The fool, or child of Fortune, has now thrown off the authority of Fortune. These two lines mark the two poles of Romeo's development from creature of passion to man of reason. In the meaning of the latter line there is a deliberate echo of the earlier one.

It would, of course, be foolish to measure Romeo's conduct in the final act against a consistent classical ideal of stoicism [a philosophy founded by the Greek thinker Zeno in about 300 B.C. which holds that wise men should be free from passion, unmoved by joy or grief, and submissive to natural law]. A true Stoic would not have committed suicide, but Shakespeare's brand of Christian stoicism was rarely consistent philosophically. The simple point Shakespeare wishes to make is that Romeo has grown to maturity, has learned to accept the order of the universe with all it may entail, that he is ready for death, and that he can accept it bravely and calmly as the necessary means toward the greater good of reunion with Juliet. He will, as he puts it:

> shake the yoke of inauspicious stars
> From this world-wearied flesh.
> [V. iii. 111-12]

When Paris says to him in the graveyard, "for thou must die," it is not merely to Paris that Romeo replies: "I must indeed; and therefore came I hither" [V. iii. 57-8]. In that simple line is a summation of Romeo's development. He has come willingly to embrace the necessary end of life's journey.

The world of *Romeo and Juliet* is a somber, realistic one in which youth is born into evil and must struggle against it ceaselessly until the conflict is ended by inevitable death. But Shakespeare's tragic vision is not one of resignation or despair; it is one of defiance and hope, of pride in those qualities of man that enable him to survive and achieve victory in such a world. It is this tension between pride in man and terror of the world's evil which Clifford Leech [in his *Shakespeare's Tragedies and Other Studies in Seventeenth-Century Drama*] has called the essence of the tragic emotion; and Shakespeare goes far toward achieving this tension in *Romeo and Juliet.* There is a design for tragedy in this early play, a conception of man's position in the universe to which character and event are designed by the artist to conform. There are, of course, inconsistencies in the design; Shakespeare has not yet been able entirely to escape the limitations imposed upon him by his sources, but we can nevertheless perceive, governing and shaping the matter that Shakespeare took from Arthur Brooke, the idea of tragedy as a portrait of man's journey from youth to maturity, encountering the evil in the world, learning to live with it, and achieving victory over it by death. Like the tragedies of Aeschylus, *Romeo and Juliet* proclaims also that man learns through suffering, but even more strongly than in Greek tragedy, there is affirmation in Shakespeare that the ultimate plan of the universe is good, for out of the suffering of individuals the social order is cleansed of evil. The deep-rooted family feud is finally brought to an end. (pp. 283-86)

> *Irving Ribner, "Then I Denie You Starres: A Reading of 'Romeo and Juliet'," in* Studies in the English Renaissance Drama, *Josephine W. Bennett, Oscar Cargill, and Vernon Hall, Jr., eds., New York University Press, 1959, pp. 269-86.*

Harold S. Wilson

[*Wilson regards* Romeo and Juliet *as a tragedy of fate involving "two lovers whose destiny it is to be sacrificed to the healing of their families' strife." Furthermore, the critic claims, the feud is the central concern of the play. Wilson argues that Shakespeare marred this design, however, by making his hero and heroine so attractive that the audience loses interest in the dramatic action once they are dead, thus ignoring the true culmination of the play in the resolution of the feud.*]

The tragic conception of *Romeo and Juliet* is simply stated for us in the opening sonnet-prologue. By thus announcing his theme and describing the central action, Shakespeare prepares us for the method he will follow throughout the play. We are to watch a sequence of events as they move towards the catastrophe in the full knowledge that they are tragic, that the tragic culmination is somehow inevitable. The tragic effect is to be one of anticipation and its realization. The Greek tragedians . . . could count on their audiences' familiarity with the story of the play. Shakespeare

477

uses his opening prologue in *Romeo and Juliet* to establish the same condition.

The action concerns not simply two lovers but two families. An ancient feud breaks forth anew, involving in its course two lovers whose destiny it is to be sacrificed to the healing of their families' strife, "which, but their children's end, naught could remove" [Prologue, 11]. The pathos is that the lovers' sacrifice is inescapable; their love is "death-mark'd"; they are "star-cross'd" [Prologue, 9, 6], fated to die in the fifth act. But the tragic outcome is not quite unrelieved. There is to be a kind of reconciliation at the end, though we are not to expect a "happy" ending. Thus carefully are we prepared to understand and anticipate the ensuing action.

This method of foreshadowing the outcome is carried through the play, in the premonitions and misgivings of the two lovers. "I dreamt a dream tonight" [I. iv. 50], says Romeo, as he goes with Benvolio and Mercutio towards the Capulet party. Mercutio at once takes him up, rallies him, makes his melancholy remark the occasion of his elaborate fancy of Queen Mab. Yet as Benvolio tries to hurry them on: "Supper is done, and we shall come too late!" Romeo reflects,

> I fear, too early; for my mind misgives
> Some consequence, yet hanging in the
>   stars,
> Shall bitterly begin his fearful date
> With this night's revels and expire the
>   term
> Of a despised life, clos'd in my breast,
> By some vile forfeit of untimely death.
> But he that hath the steerage of my course
> Direct my sail! On, lusty gentlemen!
>   [I. iv. 105-13]

As we are later to realize, Romeo's foreboding is all too well justified. Ere another day passes, Romeo will have loved another maiden than the lady Rosaline who now has all his thoughts; he will have married Juliet, anticipating only happiness; but Mercutio will be slain by Tybalt, Tybalt slain by Romeo, Romeo banished from Verona; and the lives of Romeo and Juliet will be eventually sacrificed. (pp. 19-20)

All of these echoes and foreshadowings emphasize and reemphasize a single theme, a single conception: the seemingly inscrutable necessity of the whole action, a necessity imposed by some power greater than men. (p. 22)

The play culminates with the reconciliation of the rival houses, as the prologue states. Old Capulet and Montague, confronted by the terrible results of their hatred in the deaths of their children, are at length brought to recognize their responsibility. The Prince sums it up:

> See what a scourge is laid upon your hate,
> That heaven finds means to kill your joys
>   with love;

> And I, for winking at your discords too,
> Have lost a brace of kinsmen; all are pun-
>   ish'd.
>   [V. iii. 292-95]

The parents are truly penitent, and from this time forth, we are to understand, their hatred was turned to love.

The importance of this ending in Shakespeare's design may be seen by contrasting the culmination of the story in his principal source, Arthur Brooke's poem called *Romeus and Juliet*. In Brooke's version, the various instruments of the outcome—the apothecary who sold Romeo the poison, the Nurse, the Friar—are punished or pardoned, but neither the parents nor the enmity of the two houses is even mentioned in censure. Shakespeare's revision of Brooke's ending and his different emphasis are eloquent of his different conception of the point of the tale.

From another point of view, we may test the importance Shakespeare must have attached to the idea the play is designed to express by observing the very arbitrariness with which he manipulates not merely the plot but the characterizations as well, in the interest of working out his total design. The arbitrary insistence upon ironic coincidence in the successive stages of the action is evident. But equally arbitrary is the lack of coherent motivation in Friar Laurence's crucial role. Granted that Friar Laurence is timid and unworldly, and proud of his herbalist's resources, besides; he is still an odd kind of spiritual adviser, without confidence in his authority with the two families, and, we must surely add, without elementary common sense. In real life, any man of sense in Friar Laurence's position would have reflected that the proposed marriage of Juliet with Paris was impossible. Juliet was already married to Romeo. And he would have used this circumstance to force a reconciliation upon the two families—a motive which he professed in marrying the young people in the first place. It is evident that he could count upon the Prince's support in thus seeking to reconcile the feud, and Romeo's pardon, and his own, would easily follow upon the achieving of this worthy end.

This sort of speculation is obviously not relevant to the play as we have it; for such a solution would have given comedy, and Shakespeare was here intent upon tragedy. We must allow the author such arbitrary means; the tragic idea, and the tragic effect, are more important than any mere question of psychological verisimilitude. In observing the arbitrariness of the contrivance, however, we are able to gauge the more accurately the author's central concern. It is with the idea of the play, and the artificial means are an index of the length he is prepared to go in expressing it. Shakespeare neither blames Friar Laurence for his romantic folly, nor allows the common sense solution of the lovers' difficulties to occur to him or to them; and we must not consider that any such point is worth making in our criticism of the play except in so far as our consideration of it may help us the better to understand what the play is about.

If the cumulatively parallel episodes of *Romeo and Juliet* may be called the warp of the play's structural design, the woof is a series of contrasts. It is a drama of youth pitted against age. . . . Correspondingly, youth stands for love, and age for continuing hate. Most fundamental of all is the contrast, which is not fully revealed until the end, of accident and design.

Arthur Brooke's *Romeus and Juliet* is a translated version of a familiar folk-tale rather clumsily worked up as a popular romance in Pierre Boaistuau's *Histories tragiques;* in Brooke's version, as in Boaistuau's, the ironic succession of reversals is attributed casually to "Fortune"—the customary resource of the romancer intent only upon the turns of his plot. Shakespeare more ambitiously undertook to comprehend the relations of chance and destiny in his tragic design.

Carefully, then, the responsibility of the lovers for their catastrophe, in Shakespeare's play, is minimized, as it is not in Brooke's version. The fact of the feud is emphasized at the outset, and the involvement of Romeo and Juliet is not only innocent but against their will. Even in the catastrophe itself, their self-destruction is hardly more than their assent to compelling circumstance. Romeo, it is true, buys poison to unite himself with Juliet in the grave; but before he reaches the tomb, Paris intervenes to seal with his death the one chance of Romeo's pausing in his resolve. [Harley] Granville Barker oddly remarks that Paris's death "is wanton and serves little purpose." Actually, it is calculated to enhance our sense of the pressure of circumstance upon Romeo. He was distraught before he met Paris at the tomb of Juliet, but not utterly desperate, perhaps. Now, with the blood of Paris upon his hands (again contrary to his will and his anguished protest), he has no remaining ground of hope, no reason to delay his purpose. The death of Paris at Romeo's hands is Shakespeare's own addition to the story and hence an especially significant clue to his conception. It is another irony that prepares us for the most poignant irony of all, as Romeo, in his rapt intentness upon joining Juliet in the grave, fails to interpret aright the signs of returning animation in the sleeping girl. . . . Juliet, as she plunges the knife in her breast, thinks only of joining her lover. Shakespeare, of course, is not excusing their self-destruction; but it is no part of his design to blame them. Their deaths are a *donnée* [known fact] of the story; the point of it lies elsewhere than in their responsibility.

The blame lies with the families, with the elders. But what of the role of chance, of the fate which so evidently has crossed the love of Romeo and Juliet from beginning to end? They fell in love by acci-

dent. Romeo went to the Capulet party expecting to indulge his unrequited passion for Rosaline; Juliet came for the express purpose of seeing and learning to love the County Paris. Amid their later difficulties, if Friar John had been able to deliver Friar Laurence's letter; if Friar Laurence had thought to use Balthazar as his messenger, as he first proposed to do [III. iii. 169-71], or if Balthazar too had been delayed; if Friar Laurence, even had been a little quicker in getting to Juliet's tomb—if anyone of these possibilities had occurred, the outcome might have been very different. We are meant to reflect upon this chain of seeming accidents, for they are prominently displayed.

Here, then, in the play as we have it, is the design—an arbitrary one, to be sure—of "a greater power than we can contradict" [V. iii. 153], that finds means to humble the rival houses "with love." It is a stern conception of Providence, to the working of whose purposes human beings are blind, which fulfils the moral law that the hatred of the elders shall be visited upon the children—"poor sacrifices of our enmity" [V. iii. 304], as Capulet describes them—yet whose power turns hatred in the end to love. The design of the tragedy has been a Christian moral, implicit but still sufficiently manifest to the thoughtful. Herein lies the rationale of the play's structure. The three entrances of the Prince mark the three stages of the action intended to show a chain of seeming accidents issuing in a moral design adumbrated in the sonnet-prologue, implicit from the beginning. The final entrance of the Prince marks the logical climax of a tightly built narrative scheme. This concluding stage of the action reveals, in recapitulation, the significance of the whole design, a design in which the catastrophic deaths of the lovers contribute but a part; the punishment of the elders, and still more their reconciliation, complete the pattern.

But if the logical climax of the play's conception lies in this denouement, the emotional climax comes before, with the deaths of Romeo and Juliet. In this, the world's favourite love story, Shakespeare has endowed his young lovers with all the riches of his earlier lyrical style, with the music of his sonnets which echoes through the play; and he has given them a grace and a purity of motive, in keeping with his larger design, that ensures our complete sympathy from beginning to end. As we follow their story, we cannot help taking sides with them against the elders—against the blind selfishness and perversity of their parents, against the stupid animality, however amusing, of the Nurse, against the absurd ineptitude of Friar Laurence; and as we see them hasten unwittingly to their destruction, we can only pity their youth, their innocence, and their ill luck. They themselves have no awareness of a tragic misstep, of a price justly exacted for human pride or folly, and neither have we: their story is full of pathos, but is has in itself little or nothing of tragic grandeur.

The tragic irony of the story, as Shakespeare tells it, lies in the blindness of the elders to the consequences of their hatred until it is too late, in the reversal brought about by the power greater than they. Yet despite the dramatist's efforts to direct our attention to this larger significance of the action—through the prologue and the structural foreshadowing of his whole scheme; through the chain of unlucky coincidences and arbitrary motives; through the reiteration of the theme of fortune and ill chance and fate—our feelings remain linked with the story of the lovers throughout the play; and audiences and actors alike notoriously feel that with the deaths of Romeo and Juliet the interest of the play is at an end, that the subsequent explanations are prolix and anticlimactic and may well be abridged. This feeling is manifestly contrary to what the dramatist aimed at, but he himself is chiefly responsible for our feeling, in having made his young lovers the centre of our regard.

Thus the play misses its full unity of effect because our sympathies are exhausted before the tragic design is complete. The story of a young and idealistic love thwarted is not enough to make a great tragedy; but Shakespeare, trying to place it within a grander conception, has not been able to achieve a larger unity. There is no failure in any detail of execution, and the conception of the play as a whole is worked out with remarkable regularity and precision. But the love story is not quite harmonious with the larger conception; our sympathies do not culminate in this larger conception; they culminate in pity for the lovers. The awe that we should feel as well is not inherent in their story but is indicated (rather than effected) in what seems to us like an epilogue; it is something explained to us at the end rather than rendered immediately dramatic and compelling as the heart of the design. Shakespeare never made this particular mistake again; and we must surely add that, even though he overreaches himself in his play, he yet enchants us with the beauty of what he holds in his grasp.

Even this judgment, perhaps, is too rigorous. If *Romeo and Juliet* is deficient by the severest standard—by the standard of Shakespeare's own later achievements in tragedy—it yet remains one of the loveliest of all his works. And if we consider it not too closely but as we yield ourselves to its lyrical appeal in the theatre, we may find therein a sufficient argument of its unity. The lines from sonnet CXVI . . . :

> Love's not Time's fool, though rosy lips and cheeks
> Within his bending sickle's compass come;
> Love alters not with his brief hours and weeks,
> But bears it out even to the edge of doom.

commemorate the most lasting impression the play leaves with us, the impression of its imperish-

able beauty. We distinguish between the transitory life and fortunes of Romeo and Juliet and their love, which remains ideal, and, in a sense, beyond the reach of fortune or death. It is not their love that is blighted, after all, but their lives. The tragic episode of their lives may thus be seen as participating in [Dante's] "Divine Comedy"; and, fundamentally, this is what we recognize as we are moved by their story. (pp. 25-31)

> *Harold S. Wilson, "Thesis: 'Romeo and Juliet' and 'Hamlet'," in his* On the Design of Shakespearian Tragedy, *University of Toronto Press, 1957, pp. 19-51.*

ADHERENCE TO THE RULES OF TRAGEDY

G. H. Durrant

[In the following excerpt, three students (A, B, and C), guided by their teacher (Lecturer or Mr. X), debate whether or not Romeo and Juliet *adheres to the guidelines of Aristotelian tragedy; that is, in the instructor's words, "does it show the fall of a good and great man, brought about by a flaw in his own nature, enforced by Destiny or by the law of Nature, and arousing Pity and Terror, and so bringing about a state of tragic purgation?" Students A and B consider the question in light of scholarly essays by H. B. Charlton, A. C. Bradley, Edward Dowden, Thomas Marc Parrott, Muriel C. Bradbrook, and G. B. Harrison, who generally agree that* Romeo and Juliet *is not tragic in the Aristotelian sense of the term because the hero is ordinary and the idea of an all-controlling fate is unconvincing. Student C, however, disagrees with the scholars and offers an impressionistic reading of the play, maintaining that it is solely about love. Student C further argues that the Aristotelian debate is pointless because Shakespeare was not concerned with sustaining an overall tragic design.]*

Lecturer (Mr. X). As I told you, we are today to begin the study of *Romeo and Juliet,* a play that enjoyed a great popularity both in Shakespeare's own day and throughout the following centuries. But since I have frequently impressed upon you the need to consult the best critical opinion before forming your own judgment, perhaps you will tell me now where you have sought for help in reading the play, and what the result of your researches has been.

Student A. Well I've read Professor Charlton [*Shakespearean Tragedy*], and Professor Dowden [*Shakespeare, His Mind and Art*] and Dr. Bradley [*Shakespearean Tragedy*] and Professor Parrott [*William Shakespeare, a Handbook*], and they all speak very highly of the play. Only I'm not quite sure why they like it. . . .

Student B. So do Professor Harrison [*Shakespeare's Tragedies*] and Dr. Bradbrook [*Shakespeare and Elizabethan Poetry*], and the others I've read. But I must admit I'm still somewhat puzzled, too. I suppose that is because I have always taken the play in a very simple-minded way as being a love-story with a sad ending. But now I am beginning to realise that it isn't as easy as all that. You see, *Romeo and Juliet* is a Tragedy—it was called so by Shakespeare. 'An Excellent conceited Tragedie of Romeo and Juliet' and 'The Most Excellent and Lamentable Tragedie of Romeo and Juliet'—that is what it was called in Shakespeare's own day. Now it's all right so long as you simply think that a Tragedy is a story that ends unhappily—I mean *anyone* can understand it then—that is what Dr. Bradbrook calls 'a tragedy in the newspaper sense'. But it seems that, according to the best academic minds, Shakespeare was trying to do something rather different.

Student A. But how can they know what Shakespeare was trying to do? Isn't it all guess-work, after all? I mean, what evidence have they got?

Student B. Well, of course they haven't any direct evidence, but they can *infer* from what they know of Shakespeare's later work. You see, if Shakespeare first of all wrote a Tragedy called *Romeo and Juliet,* and later on wrote some other Tragedies that were very successful and yet quite different in some important respects from *Romeo and Juliet,* doesn't it seem likely that he was really trying to write something like the later tragedies at the time when he actually wrote *Romeo and Juliet*? I mean, isn't it probable that *Romeo and Juliet* was a first shot that didn't quite come off?

Student A. Well, I must say I think that is pretty far-fetched. I can't see why we can't get on and read *Romeo and Juliet* with Mr. X and see what we think of it. After all, Shakespeare has been dead for a long time, and these guesses about what he was trying to do can't help us much.

Student B. Well, I think we ought to ask Mr. X first of all what he thinks of the ideas we found in the critical works. . . .

Lecturer. I'm glad you're coming round to that. It won't do to go off on your own, spinning fancies about the play out of your heads. A little contact with sound scholarship is essential if you are to get to the heart of the matter. But as I want to be sure that you have really read the authorities, I'll ask *you* to tell *me* what they say. Well, B. . . . ? (pp. 23-4)

Student B. . . .[The] worst feature of the play, according to Professor Harrison, is that it 'lacks the qualities of deep tragedy'.

Lecturer. Now at last we are beginning to be really serious. Obviously, we can't simply go ahead and read the play in a hopelessly unscientific spirit. We must begin by considering what Tragedy really is. Then when we have decided that, we can find out whether *Romeo and Juliet* displays the quality of true Tragedy. If it doesn't, then obviously there must be some defect in it.

Student A. Yes, Mr. X, I think that must be right. At any rate, all the best authorities seem to think that the right way to study a play. Look what I've written down in my note-book. I spent Saturday morning in the Library making notes of what the scholars say; and they all seem very doubtful about the play as a tragedy. Here is what Professor Charlton says: First of all, he points out that there are a great many premonitions of disaster in the play. He gives a good many examples of them; and he says that this is Shakespeare's way of giving us the 'sense of an all-controlling Fate' so as to make the play tragic, and not merely a result of the inconstancy of Fortune.

Student B. But Shakespeare does make Romeo say he is 'Fortune's fool' after he has killed Tybalt. And doesn't Juliet cry out on 'fickle' Fortune when Romeo has gone? In the last scene the catastrophe is described as a 'mischance', a 'misadventure', 'some ill unlucky thing' [V. iii. 136]. Would Shakespeare have put those words in if he had been anxious to put the stress on an 'all-controlling Fate' and not on the 'inconstancy of Fortune'?

Student A. I suppose Charlton would say that these were relics of [Arthur] Broke's poem, from which Shakespeare took the story of the play. He says: 'Instead of letting his persons declaim formally, as Broke's do, against the inconstancy of Fortune, he endows them with tragic premonitions.' But, as you say, it isn't quite true. Shakespeare *does* add the 'tragic premonitions'; but he doesn't remove all the references to 'fickle Fortune'.

Lecturer. But you can see what Charlton is getting at. He wants to show how Shakespeare added, or tried to add, a feeling of inevitability to the events of the play, so as to add tragic Terror to the pity you feel for the unlucky lovers of Broke's poem.

Student A. Yes, but Charlton thinks that it wasn't a success. He says that Shakespeare 'gives to the action itself a quality *apt to conjure* the sense of relentless doom'. But he doubts whether 'the sense of an all-controlling Fate is made strong enough to fulfil its tragic purpose'. He shows that the events in the play in themselves provide no real basis for the 'sweep of necessity'. In the end he comes to the conclusion that the play is radically unsound. It won't really bear careful examination, even though we may be carried away by it when we see it on the stage. He says: 'And so, stirred to sympathy by Shakespeare's poetic power, we tolerate, perhaps even approve, the death (of Romeo and Juliet). At least for the moment.' Then he goes on: 'But tragedy lives not only for its own moment, nor by "suspensions of disbelief". Our sentiments were but momentarily gratified. And finally our deeper consciousness protests. Shakespeare has conquered us by a trick: the experiment carries us no nearer to the heart of tragedy.'

Lecturer. Yes, you see judged by the criteria that Aristotle and Bradley lay down for tragedy, the play hardly succeeds. There are too many accidents in it. But what does Dowden say? He was a follower of Bradley, too.

Student A. He says: 'Thus it came about that Shakespeare at nearly forty years was the author of but two or three tragedies. Of these, *Romeo and Juliet* may be looked upon as the work of the author's adolescence, and *Hamlet* as the evidence that he had become adult, and in this supreme department master of his craft.'

Student B. But just a minute; doesn't Dowden give the earliest date for *Romeo and Juliet* as 1591?

Lecturer. Yes, I seem to remember that he does.

Student B. Well then, Shakespeare must have been at least twenty-seven when he wrote the play. Surely Dowden didn't really think Shakespeare was still *adolescent* at that hoary old age?

Student A. Don't be silly—he only means that *Romeo and Juliet* is *immature*. It's *unripe*, compared with the 'true tragedies'. It was written in Shakespeare's salad days, when he was green in judgment.

Lecturer. Don't waste time quibbling. What else does Dowden say?

Student A. He also says that he thinks Shakespeare worked on the play for five or six years—there's the answer to your question about his age—and that in the end 'there still appeared in the play unmistakable marks of immature judgment'.

Student B. What marks?

Student A. Well, I suppose he relied on the good sense of the reader to spot them. . . . He goes on: 'It is not unlikely that even then he considered his powers to be insufficiently matured for the great dealing with human life and passion, which tragedy demands; for, having written *Romeo and Juliet,* Shakespeare returned to the histories, in which, doubtless, he was aware that he was receiving the best possible culture for future tragedy. . . .'

Student B. In other words, Shakespeare wasn't yet equal to the job, and was thoroughly disappointed with the play when he'd finished. It does seem that if he had written it for an examination in Tragedy he wouldn't have been given top marks by the professors. Of course, it's their job to judge by the very highest standards. . . . But didn't people like it when it was produced?

Lecturer. It seems that it was a great success . . . ran into four editions before the First Folio, besides being produced very often. But, of course, mere popular success has nothing to do with the artistic conscience.

Student A. I somehow can't see the Elizabethan audience putting up with the leisurely charm of stilted poetry . . . but we can always suppose that it was cut in Shakespeare's day, can't we?

Lecturer. Yes, that is what some scholars do suppose. It is the scientific method, you see. Go on, A.

Student A. Professor Parrott (he is or was at Princeton) has a book—this green one—on Shakespeare. . . . *William Shakespeare—A Handbook,* he calls it. He seems to agree with the others. Where am I? Oh, here it is:

> *Romeo and Juliet* lacks the depth, the power, the tragic intensity, of the great plays of the third period, and it may well be that Shakespeare, no doubt his own severest critic, felt he was not yet ready to deal competently with great tragic themes. At any rate, in spite of the success of *Romeo and Juliet* on the stage and with all lovers of poetry, he turned his back upon tragedy.

Student B. I see—poor chap—he knew the play was no good. It must have been maddening for him to have everybody praising it when he knew in his heart all the time that future Professors of English would consider it a failure. I wonder he didn't blow his brains out.

Lecturer. That will do, B. We don't want unnecessary facetiousness. The only thing to do now is to go to the fountainhead. What does Bradley say?

Student A. Well, perhaps they all got it from him. It's a bit difficult, because he doesn't deal much with this play in *Shakespearean Tragedy,* which is what I read. But he does make some remarks about it, and they agree with those we've heard so far. He says that *Romeo and Juliet* is a 'pure tragedy', but in some respects, an immature one. As far as I can make out, what he means is that the play is meant to be like *Othello, Hamlet, King Lear* and *Macbeth*—to be a 'pure tragedy', in other words, but that it doesn't succeed because Shakespeare was still too immature for successful 'pure tragedy'. But Bradley talks of Romeo as though he was a tragic hero of the same kind as the heroes of the later tragedies. He says:

> How could men escape, we cry, such vehement propensities as drive Romeo, Antony, Coriolanus to their doom? And why is it that a man's virtues help to destroy him, and that his weakness is so intertwined with everything that is admirable in him that we can hardly separate them even in imagination?

Lecturer. Now we are beginning to see the light. Of course Bradley is considering whether the play is *truly tragic*—does it show the fall of a good and great man, brought about by a flaw in his own nature, enforced by Destiny or by the law of Nature, and arousing Pity and Terror, and so bringing about a state of tragic purgation? That is the real question, and if we can answer that, Bradley realised, we have the answer to the problem of *Romeo and Juliet*.

Student A. But Romeo isn't a great man. He's just an ordinary young chap who falls in love. . . . Oh, now I see . . . that is one reason why the play isn't 'deep tragedy'. The hero isn't a representative figure.

Student B. And there is also this other business about the bad verse. All that tedious stuff about Rosaline, and all those long speeches by Mercutio and the Friar. Most of the writers I've looked at think they can forgive Shakespeare, because after all he was a poet, and poets can't always be businesslike. Professor Harrison, you see, even finds a 'charm' in it, though he thinks it ought to be 'cut' in an acted version. But Dr. Bradbrook—she's a Cambridge don, isn't she?—is very severe. Where are my notes? Here we are: 'Parts of the play are in a manner so rhetorical as to be emptied of all feeling. Romeo like Titus moralises on a fly at the height of his laments.' Incidentally, she thinks that the Elizabethans *knew all the time* that the play wasn't a 'full tragedy'. She says that 'if any Polonius [in *Hamlet*] had essayed its classification' (I wonder why she says that?) he would have decided that the play was 'an amorous tragicomedy'. It seems that, according to Dr. Bradbrook, the play wasn't really an attempt to write Tragedy at all, it was the beginning of Shakespeare's comic style. And Mercutio and the Nurse are to be understood as *comic* characters.

Student A. Now you are getting me thoroughly mixed up. If we don't even know whether to take the play as immature Tragedy or as immature Comedy, we are simply lost.

Lecturer. Well, we had better sum up, and see where we've got to. The general view is that *Romeo and Juliet* is a good play, but that it is immature, and contains bad verse. It isn't truly tragic, because the hero is too ordinary, and because we don't see any *necessity* in the action. It sometimes rings hollow, and Shakespeare was probably disappointed with it. The only problem left is whether it is the beginnings of true Tragedy or the beginnings of true Comedy. There is no reason to feel confused.

(A knock on the door. Enter Miss C.)

[*Lecturer.*] Oh, Miss C., there you are; you are very late.

Miss C. I'm very sorry, I didn't notice the time.

Lecturer. I see. Well, we have just been discussing the views expressed on *Romeo and Juliet* by informed academic critics. Would you like to give us the benefit of your own studies?

Miss C. Oh! I'm very sorry. You see I've not really looked into that very carefully. I mean to say, I've been reading the play again.

Lecturer. And what did you make of it? Can you help us with the problem?

Miss C. The problem? Is there a problem? I'm sorry, I seem to have been so busy this week. . . .

Student A. We have been trying to decide why *Romeo and Juliet* is a comparative failure.

Miss C. But it isn't a failure is it? I mean I think it's simply a wonderful play.

Lecturer. Well, since you have some views after all, Miss C., perhaps you will expand them a little. But try not to be too much carried away by enthusiasm. Impressionistic criticism is never really sound.

Miss C. Well, I expect this sounds very silly, but it seems to me that Shakespeare was writing a play about Love. I think [Samuel Taylor] Coleridge says that he intended it to be a sort of love-poem—he doesn't quite say that, but that is what he obviously means. So Shakespeare shows us two lovers; they have to be young because it is their first love—their first serious love, I mean—and it has to take place very suddenly so that the whole passion can develop to the fullest intensity. And then they must be unlucky and die—not to create Pity and Terror, but simply because their death, and their foreseeing of it, add to the intensity of their love.

Student A. Ah, but you see it all depends too much on bad luck. Juliet's message goes astray by bad luck, and she wakes up just a little too late, and there are lots of other examples. How can that be truly tragic?

Miss C. Well, does it matter whether it is 'truly tragic' or not? The question is: does it work in the play? Surely it does. The lovers are unlucky (though of course they are rash too) and they die. Shakespeare doesn't need to demonstrate that they *had of necessity to die,* because he isn't concerned with the laws of the Universe, and with the tragic terror that these arouse. He only wants to make us realise the *love* as intensely as possible. And the whole play is coloured with the sense of death so as to heighten the ectasy of love. There is no need for tragic necessity. And Romeo isn't meant as a representative tragic hero, who has a 'flaw' and is punished for it by the inexorable hand of Fate. He is a boy who is transformed by love into a man; he is unlucky and he dies. He illustrates the nature of Love, not the nature of the Moral Law. I should have thought that anybody would take the play in that way.

Student A. Ah, but you haven't read the critics. It all seems simple to you. It did to me too, before I read Bradley and Dowden and Harrison and Charlton. But let me ask you one question. Wasn't the play *called* a Tragedy? I mean by Shakespeare, or whoever published the Quarto?

Miss C. Yes, but I don't suppose that the Elizabethans were quite so well up in Aristotle as we are, and of course they hadn't read Bradley or Charlton. It probably seemed quite simple to them, too. I suppose that they regarded almost any story with a sad ending as a Tragedy. Anyway, what's in a name? Though I must say it seems to have brought a great pother on Shakespeare's head. (pp. 24-9)

Student A. It seems to me that your way of looking at it is hopelessly uncritical. (p. 34)

Miss C. No, that isn't quite true. I think there may be weaknesses here and there in the play. . . . But the main thing is that I am convinced that Shakespeare wrote *Romeo and Juliet* at great speed, and with the fullest knowledge of what he was doing. It isn't the sort of play that is written by a struggling adolescent mind. Doesn't the play ring with triumphant poetry, and doesn't it all move with the greatest sureness? I think that the critics who imagine Shakespeare giving up Tragedy in despair after experimenting with *Romeo* have allowed their own ideas to muddle them. They approach the play by way of *King Lear,* and they measure it by *Othello* and by *Macbeth.* It won't fit on that bed of Procrustes, and so they start to cut and bend, stretch and twist it: and when they have finished they blame Shakespeare. They worry fearfully about Shakespeare's *development,* but I don't believe that he himself worried so much. If he didn't write any more plays like *Romeo and Juliet* for a time, it's more likely, to my mind, that he felt he had really done what he wanted to do and could go on to something else.

Student B. Well, its your opinion against theirs.

Miss C. No it isn't. It is common sense and the almost unanimous opinion of readers and play-goers over three hundred years against a few apostles of Bradley's. Everybody knows what *Romeo and Juliet* is about until he has read these books. And I doubt whether we should take the academic critics so seriously if they wrote in plain direct English. It's a kind of fog that gets into the mind of writers and readers. (pp. 34-5)

Lecturer. Well, Miss C., you seem to have very decided opinions. I hope your own essay, which is overdue, will show none of the faults you find in the works of Shakespearean scholars. But you must not allow your distaste for scholarship to make you arrogant. Humility is the best approach to literature. (p. 35)

> *G. H. Durrant, "What's in a Name? A Discussion of 'Romeo and Juliet',"* in Theoria, *Pietermaritzburg, No. 8, 1956, pp. 23-36.*

Clifford Leech

[*Leech discusses* Romeo and Juliet *in terms of what he views as the three principal elements of dramatic tragedy: (1) the events of the plot proceed from no discernible cause; (2) the story focuses on an agonizing situation that cannot be corrected; and (3) at least one of the central characters represents humankind's capacity for evil and the destruction it engenders.* Romeo and Juliet *cannot properly be termed "tragic," the critic argues, because it violates all three of these conditions. Specifically, the drama diverges from tragedy because it fails to fully establish an element of "mystery" in the action, thereby forcing the reader to attribute the progression of events to the operation of fate; the play suggests, through the "moral lesson" at the end, that the lovers' deaths will reconcile the feuding families; and finally, it presents only "ordinary" individuals, none of whom are truly evil.*]

[*Romeo and Juliet* concludes with] a kind of "happy ending." The feud will be ended, the lovers will be remembered. We may be reminded of the commonplace utterance that we have two deaths: the moment of actual ceasing to be, and the moment when the last person who remembers us dies. These lovers have their being enshrined in a famous play. So they are remembered in perpetuity, and their lives, according to the play itself, will be recorded in their statues. Certainly this is a sad affair, like that of Paolo and Francesca in *The Divine Comedy.* But we may ask, is it tragic?

Tragedy seems to demand a figure or figures that represent us in our ultimate recognition of evil. We need to feel that such figures are our kin, privileged to be chosen for the representative role and coming to the destruction that we necessarily anticipate for ourselves. The boy and girl figures in *Romeo and Juliet* are perhaps acceptable as appropriate representatives for humankind: after all, they do grow up. What worries us more, I think, in trying to see this play as fully achieved "tragedy," is the speech of the Duke at the end, which suggests that some atonement will be made through the reconciliation of the Montague and Capulet families. We are bound to ask "Is this enough?" It appears to be offered as such, but we remember that the finest among Verona's people are dead.

Shakespearean tragedy commonly ends with a suggestion of a return to normality, to peace. Fortinbras [in *Hamlet*] will rule in Denmark, Malcolm [in *Macbeth*] in Scotland, Iago [in *Othello*] will be put out of the way. But these later tragedies leave us with a doubt whether the peace is other than a second-best, whether indeed it is in man's power ever to put things right. In *Romeo and Juliet* the ending of the feud is laboriously spelled out.

But there is also the matter of Fate and Chance. Romeo kills Paris: at first glance that was a quite fortuitous happening. Paris was a good man, devoted to Juliet, who unfortunately got in the way of Romeo's approach to Juliet's tomb. At this point Romeo's doom is sealed: he might kill Tybalt and get away with it; he could not get away with killing an innocent Paris, who was moreover the Prince's kinsman. Now it is inevitable that he will die, whatever the moment of Juliet's awakening. There is indeed a "star-cross'd" pattern for the lovers, there is no way out for Romeo once he has come back to Verona. But perhaps Paris's important function in the last scene is not sufficiently brought out: the spectator may feel that there is simple chance operating in Romeo's arrival before Juliet wakes, in his killing himself a moment too early, in the Friar's belated arrival. Later I must return to the matter of the play's references to the "stars": for the moment I merely want to refer to the fact that tragedy can hardly be dependent on "bad luck."

Even so, though simple chance will not do, we may say that tragedy properly exists only when its events defy reason. The Friar thought the marriage of the young lovers might bring the feud to an end, and that was a reasonable assumption. Ironically, it did end the feud but at the expense of Romeo's and Juliet's lives, at the expense too of Mercutio's, Tybalt's, and Lady Montague's lives. The element of *non sequitur* in the train of events common to tragedy—despite the fact that, with one part of our minds, we see the operation of "probability or necessity," as Aristotle has it—is well described by Laurens van der Post in his novel *The Hunter and the Whale:*

> I was too young at the time to realise that tragedy is not tragedy if one finds reason or meaning in it. It becomes then, I was yet to learn, a darker form of this infinitely mysterious matter of luck. It is sheer tragedy only if it is without discernible sense or motivation.

We may balk at "luck," as I have already suggested, but "mysterious" is right indeed (as Bradley splendidly urged on us in the First Lecture of *Shakespearean Tragedy*), for what "sense" or "motivation" does there seem to be in tragedy's gods? The sense of mystery is not, however, firmly posited in *Romeo and Juliet*. Rather, it is laboriously suggested that the Montagues and the Capulets have been taught a lesson in a particularly hard way.

Thus we have several reasons to query the play's achievement in the tragic kind. Do the lovers take on themselves the status of major figures in a celebration of a general human woe? Is the ending, with its promise of reconciliation, appropriate to tragic writing? We have seen that the lovers grow up, and they give us the impression of justifying human life, in their best moments, more than most people do. But the suggestion that their deaths will atone, will bring peace back, seems nugatory: no man's death brings peace, not even Christ's—or the Unknown Soldier's. The play could still end

Romeo and Juliet. Act III, scene v. By Frank Dicksee.

tragically if we were left with the impression that the survivors were merely doing what they could to go on living in an impoverished world: we have that in *Hamlet* and the later tragedies too. Here the laboriousness with which Shakespeare recapitulates all the events known to us, in the Friar's long speech, is surely an indication of an ultimate withdrawal from the tragic: the speech is too much like a preacher's résumé of the events on which a moral lesson will be based. We can accept Edgar's long account of Gloucester's death in *King Lear,* because we need a moment of recession before the tragedy's last phase, where we shall see Lear and Cordelia dead, and because no moral lesson is drawn from Gloucester's death; but at the end of this earlier play, when Romeo and Juliet have already eloquently died, we are with difficulty responsive to the long reiteration of all we have long known through the play's action.

Shakespeare has not here achieved the sense of an ultimate confrontation with evil, or the sense that the tragic figure ultimately and fully recognizes what his situation is. Romeo and Juliet die, more or less content with death as a second best to living together. Montague and Capulet shake hands, and do what is possible to atone. The lovers have the illusion of continuing to be together—an illusion to some extent imposed on the audience. The old men feel a personal guilt, not a realization of a general sickness in man's estate. But perhaps only Lear and Macbeth and Timon came to that realization.

We can understand why Shakespeare abandoned tragedy for some years after this play. It had proved possible for him to touch on the tragic idea in his English histories, making them approach, but only approach, the idea of humanity's representative being given over to destruction, as with the faulty Richard II, the saintly Henry VI, the deeply guilty yet none the less sharply human Richard III. He had given his theater a flawed yet impressive Titus Andronicus and in the same play an Aaron given almost wholly to evil but obstinately alive. But in these plays the main drive is not tragic. The histories rely on the sixteenth-century chronicles, *Titus* on that tradition of grotesque legend that came from both Seneca and Ovid. The past was to be relived and celebrated in the histories; *Titus* was more of a literary exercise in antique horror than a play embodying a direct reference to the general human condition. In *Romeo and Juliet* Shakespeare for the first time essayed tragedy proper—that is, by wanting to bring the play's events into relation to things as they truly are—and he used a tale often told but belonging to recent times and concerned with people whom the spectators were to feel as very much their own kin. He may well have been particularly attracted to the story he found in Brooke's poem for the very reason that its figures and events did not have the authority of history and belonged to the comparatively small world of Verona. No major change in the political order can result from what happens in this play's action. No individual figure presented here is truly given over to evil. Without any precedents to guide him, he aimed at writing about eloquent but otherwise ordinary young people in love and about their equally ordinary friends and families. Only Mercutio has something daemonic in him, in the sense that his quality of life transcends the normal level of being. (pp. 68-71)

[If] Shakespeare had no useful dramatic precedents in this task, he had a manifold heritage of ideas about the nature of love; and many parts of that heritage show themselves in the play. The immoderateness and rashness that the Friar rebukes seem, on the one hand, to lead—in the fashion of a moral play—to the lovers' destruction. On the other hand, not only is our sympathy aroused but we are made to feel that what Romeo and Juliet achieve may be a finer thing than is otherwise to be found in Verona. Both views are strongly conveyed, and either of them might effectively dominate the play. Of course, they could coexist and interpenetrate—as they were to do much later in *Anthony and Cleopatra*—but here they seem to alter-

nate, and to be finally both pushed into the background in the long insistence that the feud will end because of the lovers' deaths. The "moral" is thus finally inverted: the lovers' sequence of errors has culminated in the error of suicide, but now we are made to turn to their parents' error and to the consolation that Romeo and Juliet will be remembered through their golden statues. And it is difficult for us to get interested in these statues, or to take much joy in the feud's ending.

Yet the deepest cause of uneasiness in our response to the play is, I believe, to be found in the relation of the story to the idea of the universe that is posited. We are told in the Prologue of "starcross'd lovers" [l. 6], and there are after that many references to the "stars." So there is a sense of "doom" here, but we are never fully told what is implied. Many coincidences operate: Romeo meets Tybalt just at the wrong moment; the Friar's message to Romeo about Juliet's alledged death goes astray; Romeo arrives at the tomb just before Juliet awakens; the Friar comes too late. I have already drawn attention to Shakespeare's device by which Romeo has to kill Paris, so that, even if he had arrived at the right time, there would have been no way out for him. We may feel that a similar sequence of chances operates in *Hamlet:* if Hamlet had not killed Polonius in a scared moment, if he had not had his father's seal with him on the voyage to England, if he had not managed to escape on the hospitable pirates' ship, if the foils had not been exchanged in the fencing bout with Laertes, if Gertrude had not drunk from the poisoned cup, things might indeed not have been disposed so as to lead him to Claudius's killing at the moment when it actually occurred. Even so, we can feel that, after all, the end would have been much as it is. Hamlet was a man in love with death, far more in love with death than with killing: we may say that only in the moment of death's imminence was he fully alive, freed from inhibition, able to kill Claudius: somehow or other, whatever the chances, this play demanded a final confrontation between the uncle-father and nephew-son. In *Romeo and Juliet,* on the other hand, we could imagine things working out better: the lovers are doomed only by the words of the Prologue, not by anything inherent in their situation. It is not, as it is in Hardy's novels, that we have a sense of a fully adverse "President of the immortals": there is rather an insufficient consideration of what is implied by the "stars." Of course, in *King Lear,* in all later Shakespearean tragedy, there is a sense of an ultimate mystery in the universe: "Is there any cause in nature that makes these hard hearts?" [*King Lear,* III. vi. 77-8], Lear asks in his condition of most extreme distress. Bradley recognized that this mystery was inherent in the idea of tragedy, as is implied too in the passage from Laurens van der Post I have already quoted. But in *Romeo and Juliet* there is no sense of the mystery being confronted: rather it is merely posited in a facile way, so that we have to accept the lovers' deaths as the mere result of the will of the "stars" (the astrological implication is just too easy), and then we are exhorted to see this as leading to a reconciliation between the families.

The final "moral" of the play, as we have seen, is applied only to Old Montague and Old Capulet: they have done evil in allowing the feud to go on, and have paid for it in the deaths of their children and of Lady Montague. But, largely because Romeo and Juliet are never blamed, the children themselves stand outside the framework of moral drama. They have, albeit imperfectly, grown up into the world of tragedy, where the moral law is not a thing of great moment. They have been sacrificed on the altar of man's guilt, have become the victims of our own outrageousness, have given us some relief because they have died and we still for a time continue living. . . . To that extent, *Romeo and Juliet* is "tragic" in a way we can fully recognize. But its long-drawn-out ending, after the lovers are dead, with the pressing home of the moral that their deaths will bring peace, runs contrary to the notion of tragedy. There is a sanguineness about the end of it, a suggestion that after all "All shall be well, and / All manner of thing shall be well," as Eliot quotes from Julian of Norwich in *Little Gidding,* and we can hardly tolerate the complacency of the statement. (pp. 71-3)

[In *Romeo and Juliet* Shakespeare] attempted an amalgam of romantic comedy and the tragic idea, along with the assertion of a moral lesson which is given the final emphasis—although the force of that lesson is switched from the lovers to their parents. But tragedy is necessarily at odds with the moral: it is concerned with a permanent anguishing situation, not with one that can either be put right or be instrumental in teaching the survivors to do better. When Shakespeare wrote "love-tragedy" again, in *Othello* and in *Antony and Cleopatra,* he showed that love may be a positive good but that it was simultaneously destructive and that its dramatic presentation gave no manumission from error to those who contemplated the destruction and continued to live. Nowhere, I think, does he suggest that love is other than a condition for wonder, however much he makes fun of it. But in his mature years he sees it as not only a destructive force but as in no way affording a means of reform. That *Romeo and Juliet* is a "moral tragedy"—which, I have strenuously urged, is a contradiction in terms—is evident enough. It is above all the casualness of the play's cosmology that prevents us from seeing it as tragedy fully achieved: we have seen the need for a fuller appreciation of the mystery. As with *Titus Andronicus,* the nearest play to *Romeo and Juliet* overtly assuming a tragic guise in the chronology of Shakespeare's works, the march toward disaster is too manifestly a literary device. (p. 73)

Clifford Leech, "The Moral Tragedy of 'Romeo and Juliet'," in English Renaissance Drama: Essays in Honor of Madeline Doran & Mark Eccles, *Standish Henning, Robert Kimbrough, and Richard Knowles, eds., Southern Illinois University Press, 1976, pp. 59-75.*

TIME AND HASTE

Tom F. Driver

[*Driver examines* Romeo and Juliet *in terms of the necessity of condensing "real" time into stage time in such a way that the audience will believe the events of the play have actually taken place. The critic points out that Shakespeare compressed the action of* Romeo and Juliet *in two ways: first, he considerably shortened the length of the action as it appeared in his source, Arthur Brooke's* The Tragicall Historye of Romeus and Juliet; *second, he used very brief scenes to account for longer periods of time. This compression, Driver asserts, underscores the theme of haste in the play. The critic also notes how Shakespeare varies the rhythm of the drama, slowing down or speeding up the action to match its meaning.*]

In *Romeo and Juliet* the young Shakespeare learned the craft of creating on stage the illusion of passing time. The Prologue is a kind of author's pledge that we are to see something that really happened. At least, and for technique it amounts to the same thing, it *could* have happened.

> Two households, both alike in dignity,
> In fair Verona, where we lay our scene,
> From ancient grudge break to new mutiny,
> Where civil blood makes civil hands unclean.
>
> [Prologue, 1-4]

The story is further summarized, and the Prologue ends with this couplet:

> The which if you with patient ears attend,
> What here shall miss, our toil shall strive to mend.
>
> [Prologue, 13-14]

Once such a beginning is made, the author is under obligation to be as faithful to the clock as possible. He must show one thing happening after another, according to its proper time, and he must keep the audience informed as to how the clock and the calendar are turning. Shakespeare was well aware of the obligation, *Romeo and Juliet* contains no less than 103 references to the time of the action—that is, 103 references which inform the audience what day things take place, what time of day it is, what time some earlier action happened, when something later will happen, etc. In every case but one Shakespeare was thoroughly consistent.

It is not enough, however, for the dramatist to be consistent. He also must be able to make us believe that in the short time we sit in the theater the whole action he describes can take place. He must compress the action of his story into the length of a theatrical performance.

> The fearful passage of their death-marked
>   love,
> And the continuance of their parents'
>   rage, . . .
> Is now the two-hours' traffic of our stage.
>   [Prologue, 9-10, 12]

Faced with a dramatic necessity, Shakespeare decided to make capital of it. If he has much business to set forth in a short time he will write a play about the shortness of time. In Granville-Barker's words, *Romeo and Juliet* is "a tragedy of precipitate action". No little part of the attraction of the play is due to this frank exploitation of a dramatic necessity.

> Come, Montague; for thou art early up
> To see thy son and heir more early down.
>   [V. iii. 208-09]

In addition to the 103 chronological references noted above, the play contains 51 references to the idea of speed and rapidity of movement.

I shall mention only briefly the two ways by which Shakespeare has achieved the uncommonly tight compression of action in this play. His first stratagem was to shorten the length of the action, as found in his source, from nine months to four or five days. With this he achieved two results: he heightened the sense of "o'er hasty" action considerably, and he enabled himself more easily to appear to account for all the "real" time in the story. He did not, of course, account for every hour, but he came nearer to a correspondence between stage time and "real" time.

His second stratagem was to make very short scenes on the stage account for comparatively long periods of "real" time. This effect, which has been called "double" time, was mastered by Shakespeare in the course of writing *Romeo and Juliet*. The play has two notable scenes in this respect: I. v, the feast at Capulet's house, and V. iii, the final scene. In both, the technique is to focus attention upon a series of small scenes within the major scene, one after another, so that we are forgetful of the clock, and then to tell us at the end that so-and-so-much time has gone by. Because the story has advanced, we are willing to believe the clock did also.

So much for the problem of compressing "real" time into stage time and for Shakespeare's use of the resulting rapidity as a theme in his play. There remains a further complexity owing to the drama's being a performed art. That is the problem of

tempo. The sense of rapidity in the movement of the action must be varied. The play must have a rhythm different from the movement of the clock, however that clock may have been accelerated. There must be a fast and slow, and that fast and slow will account for much of the subtle form which the play assumes under the hand of the dramatist. Here is a major difference between art and life. In life, time is constant. The dull days last as long as the eventful ones, if not longer. In a drama time speeds up or slows down according to the meaning of the action. The excitement of dramatic art lies very largely in the tension thus established between chronological tempo and artistic, or dramatic, tempo.

Roughly speaking, *Romeo and Juliet* has four periods or phases—two fast and two slow. It opens in a slow time. True, there is a street fight to begin with; but that is in the nature of a curtain-raiser skillfully used to set the situation. Basically, the first period is the "Rosaline phase", and it moves as languidly as Romeo's mooning. The second period, of very swift action, begins to accelerate in I. iii. with talk of Paris as a husband. It rushes headlong, with only momentary pauses, through love, courtship, and marriage until Tybalt is impetuously slain. Here there is a pause, while the audience waits with Juliet to see what will happen, and while Friar Laurence cautions Romeo to be patient until he can "find a time" to set matters straight. It is important to notice that this pause accounts for only a very small period of "real" time. The pause is purely psychological—or rather, dramatic. In the midst of it Shakespeare prepares to accelerate the action once more by inserting between two of the lovers' *andante* [moderately slow] scenes the very remarkable *staccato* [abrupt and disjointed] scene iv of Act III, in which Capulet arranges with Paris for Juliet's marriage. In this short scene of 35 lines there are no less than 15 specific references to time and haste. The scene is all about how soon the marriage can take place—counterpoint to the mood of the lovers, who would turn the morning lark into a nightingale. In the final phase of the play, speed takes over again and we rush to the catastrophe.

It is in the last phase that the most interesting relations between dramatic rhythm and chronological clarity may be seen. Two or three days of "real" time are required to pass in order to make sense of the action: Romeo must be exiled, Friar Laurence must put his plan for Juliet's false death into effect, messengers must travel, family must grieve, and a funeral be held. But the drama, once Juliet takes the sleeping potion, requires a swift conclusion. Therefore, after that event, references to exact time, which hitherto have been profuse, almost entirely disappear from the text. There is no way for an audience to know when any of the scenes in Act V begins. There are no clues as to what day it is, let alone what time of day, until line 176 of scene iii, when the Watch informs us that Juliet has been buried two days. The vagueness is deliberate. The "real" time is comparatively long, but the play wants to move swiftly. Therefore the audience is given an *impression* of speed, but specific time references are withheld.

The foregoing remarks should make it clear that in such a play as *Romeo and Juliet,* where the story demands a setting more or less realistic, Shakespeare strings his art between two poles: on one side, accurate imitation of what would really happen; on the other, bold shaping of events into an aesthetic pattern. We may say that the play results from a tension between these two. The actual technique is to move from one to the other. Tension, however, expresses our *feeling* about the play. Imagination and reality seem to be combined in a system of stresses and strains. Time is real, and to imitate action is to imitate time. But there is also in men a capacity for transcending time, which the playwright-artist and his audience know well. Time and its events alone do not produce an action; the imagination, transcending but not escaping time, may do so. (pp. 364-66)

> Tom F. Driver, "The Shakespearian Clock: Time and the Vision of Reality in 'Romeo and Juliet' and 'The Tempest'," in Shakespeare Quarterly, *Vol. XV, No. 4, Autumn, 1964, pp. 363-70.*

Brents Stirling

[*Stirling offers a detailed analysis of numerous elements that contribute to the theme of haste in* Romeo and Juliet. *Concentrating on Acts I, II, and III, the critic shows how Shakespeare underscores the theme through such devices as the characters' dialogue, the chorus's commentary, the effect of sound and movement on stage, and plot development.*]

The unguarded haste of youth as a tragic motive of both Romeo and Juliet appears repeatedly in their lines and in those of characters who describe them. Our common understanding of this needs to be accompanied, however, by an understanding of the haste theme as it marks all aspects of the tragedy. *Romeo and Juliet* is perhaps unique in its clear-cut and consistent expression of theme through character, choric commentary, and action.

The opening scene of the play establishes the pace at which tragic fate will unfold. In little more than a hundred lines the Capulet-Montague feud is introduced with the thumb-biting scene, is extended by infiltration of the gentry, and is dramatically stayed with choric judgment by the Prince of Verona. This quality of events hurrying to a decision is expressed, moreover, by incidental dialogue: in the beginning, Sampson's line, "I strike quickly, being mov'd" [I. i. 6], and Gregory's response, "But thou art not quickly mov'd to strike" [I. i. 7], comically

introduce the theme of impetuous speed, and at the conclusion of the brawl even the interviews decreed by Escalus appear in terms of dispatch: "You, Capulet, shall go along with me; / And, Montague, come you this afternoon" [I. i. 99-100].

Scene ii now presents haste as a theme governing the betrothal: Capulet declares that Juliet "hath not seen the change of fourteen years" and urges Paris to "let two more summers wither in their pride, / Ere we may think her ripe to be a bride" [I. ii. 9-11]. From this is derived the well-worn exposition device of tragic irony which points significantly at a misfortune which will come "too soon."

> *Paris.* Younger than she are happy mothers made.
> *Capulet.* And too soon marr'd are those so early made.
>
> [I. ii. 12-13]

In scene iii the headlong quality continues both in plot movement and thematic dialogue. The question is put to Juliet: "Thus then in brief: / The valiant Paris seeks you for his love. / . . .What say you? Can you love the gentleman? / This night you shall behold him at our feast" [I. iii. 73-4, 79-80]. Twenty lines later, the feast is not only shown as imminent but as characterized by the haste and confusion through which comic characters will express the theme. A servant enters:

> Madam, the guests are come, supper serv'd up, you call'd, my young lady ask'd for, the nurse curs'd in the pantry, and everything in extremity. I must hence to wait; I beseech you, follow straight.
> [I. iii. 100-03]

Scene iv opens with lines which continue the theme ingeniously in terms of a masking. The maskers reject slow and measured "prologue" [I. iv. 7] entries as "prolixity" [I. iv. 3], and propose to give their performance "and be gone" [I. iv. 10]. . . . (pp. 10-11)

Here also is the first entry of Mercutio who both as a character and as a name will point up the quick, the mercurial, mood of the play. And now a scene which began with the maskers as symbols of dispatch ends with a further thematic turn; a feared lateness of arrival at the feast is first made suggestive and then direct in disclosing untimeliness as a tragic theme:

> *Benvolio.* This wind you talk of blows us from ourselves.
> Supper is done, and we shall come too late.
> *Romeo.* I fear, too early; for my mind misgives
> Some consequence, yet hanging in the stars,
> Shall bitterly begin his fearful date
> With this night's revels, and expire the term
> Of a despised life clos'd in my breast,
> By some vile forfeit of untimely death.

But He that hath the steerage of my course
Direct my sail! On, lusty gentlemen!
Benvolio. Strike, drum. *They march
about the stage.*

[I. iv. 104-14]

The theme appears clearly here in exposition
which goes beyond dramatic irony into conscious
prophecy, and becomes a formulation of the tragedy itself: in the "consequence yet hanging in the
stars" the passage echoes the "star-cross'd lovers"
line of the Prologue [l. 6], and it expresses Christian elements of tragedy through Romeo's reference to his "despised life" and his ascription of
"steerage" to God's will. Romeo's lines are thus
plainly designed for choric purposes, and any thematic material in them may be taken seriously. So
it is notable that the passage arises from a quip implying haste (Benvolio's line) and adds earliness,
untimeliness, to the conventional tragic themes of
fate, *contemptus mundi* [contempt of the world],
and divine providence. A concern over exposition
as a "validating" factor should not, however, obscure the art by which Shakespeare supports his
prophetic lines with dramatic action: as Romeo,
sensing untimely death, consigns the steerage of
his course to God, his sudden final words, "On,
lusty gentlemen!" evoke Benvolio's command,
"Strike, drum," and the march about the stage.
Choric comment upon speeding fate is thus succeeded instantly by the peremptory drum and a
quick-time march of maskers which present the
theme in sound and movement.

As scene iv closes with this expression of the haste
theme, the next scene continues it with a comic device already noted in scene iii—servants hastily
preparing for the feast:

> *First Servant.* Where's Potpan, that he
> helps not to take away? He shift a tren-
> cher! He scrape a trencher!
>
> *Second Servant.* When good manners
> shall lie all in one or two men's hands,
> and they unwash'd too, 'tis a foul thing.
>
> *First Servant.* Away with the joint-stools,
> remove the court-cupboard, look to the
> plate. Good thou, save me a piece of
> marchpane; and, as thou loves me, let
> the porter let in Susan Grindstone and
> Nell. Antony and Potpan!
>
> *Second Servant.* Ay, boy, ready.
>
> *First Servant.* You are look'd for and call'd
> for, ask'd for and sought for, in the great
> chamber.
>
> *Third Servant.* We cannot be here and
> there too. Cheerly, boys; be brisk a
> while, and the longer liver take all.
>
> [I. v. 1-15]

In Elizabethan staging this passage would come
immediately after the close of scene iv and hence
would follow Romeo's speech and the lively exit

march begun with Benvolio's "Strike, drum."
Thus, in the sequence, I. iv. 104 ff. through I. v.
1-17, actual, physical pace issues from Romeo's
lines on tragic pace, and this in turn is expanded
into lines and action presenting haste on the comic
plane. It is also interesting, whether Shakespeare
"meant it" or not, that the servant who ends the
passage just quoted comically modifies Romeo's
speech on swift, untimely tragedy: "be brisk a
while, and the longer liver take all."

In the next portion of scene v old Capulet and his
kinsman who are met for the feast immediately
supplement the theme with dialogue on the rush
of time since their last masking; over thirty years
it has been since the nuptial of Lucentio whose
son's age thus points to the unbelievable passage
of a generation. Plot movement then extends this
statement of theme with a quick sequence composed of Romeo's first glimpse of Juliet, Tybalt's
threat of violence which is restrained by his uncle,
and the meeting of the lovers which brings discovery that one is a Montague, the other a Capulet. In
attending to verbal expressions of theme it is easy
to forget that plot structure can thus silently do its
work. In *Macbeth,* for example, the compressed action leading to Duncan's murder parallels the
quality of rash obsession which is so dominant in
the lines. The structure of *Romeo and Juliet* is
similar; from Act I, scene ii onward, audience attention is centered upon a progressively imminent
event, the Capulet feast, which in scene v is suddenly presented for a casting of the tragic die. Here
Romeo and Juliet meet, their fate becomes implicit
in the discovery of their lineage, and prophetic
Death in the person of Tybalt is barely restrained
from a harvest before the seed is planted. The action itself embodies Romeo's choric lines on fated,
fatal dispatch.

The Prologue of Act II continues the theme in its
opening passage,

> Now old Desire doth in his death-bed lie,
> And young Affection gapes to be his heir,
>
> [Prologue II, 1-2]

suggestive lines which are translated into action
by the pursuing of Romeo, who "ran this way, and
leap'd this orchard wall" [II. i. 5]. The balcony
scene now brings a necessary lull or resting point
in the fast pace, but the famous exchange between
the lovers continues the theme of haste. In II. ii Juliet implies it:

> My ears have yet not drunk a hundred
> words
> Of thy tongue's uttering, yet I know the
> sound.
>
> [II. ii. 58-9]

And her lines presently become explicit:

> Although I joy in thee,
> I have no joy of this contract tonight;
> It is too rash, too unadvis'd, too sudden,

Too like the lightning, which doth cease to
    be
Ere one can say it lightens.
                              [II. ii. 116-20]

As before, plot supplements thematic statement;
events become imminent as calls by the Nurse end
the tryst and induce dialogue which expresses
haste compounded with a desire to linger:

> *Juliet.*   What o'clock to-morrow
>   Shall I send to thee?
> *Romeo.*   By the hour of nine.
> *Juliet.* I will not fail; 'tis twenty year till
>   then.
>   I have forgot why I did call thee back.
> *Romeo.* Let me stand here till thou re-
>   member it.
> *Juliet.* I shall forget, to have thee still
>   stand there,
>   Rememb'ring how I love thy company.
> *Romeo.* And I'll still stay, to have thee still
>   forget,
>   Forgetting any other home but this.
> *Juliet.* 'Tis almost morning, I would have
>   thee gone;—
>   And yet no farther than a wanton's
>   bird. . . .
>   [II. ii. 167-77]

If it is to give the illusion of pace, episodic action
must have fluidity, a quality Shakespeare maintains here by beginning II. iii on a note carried over
from II. ii. Romeo and Juliet have closed the later
scene with lines on morning and the haste it
brings. Then, as the next one commences, we hear
Friar Laurence:

> The grey-ey'd morn smiles on the frown-
>   ing night,
> Chequ'ring the eastern clouds with
>   streaks of light,
> And flecked darkness like a drunkard
>   reels
> From forth day's path and Titan's fiery
>   wheels.
> Now, ere the sun advance his burning eye,
> The day to cheer and night's dank dew to
>   dry. . . .
>   [II. iii. 1-6]

It is important to note that this is the first appearance of the Friar and that his role is a distinctly
prophetic one. After the lines just quoted he moralizes aptly on tragic symbolism in the herb which
"strain'd from that fair use, / Revolts from true
birth, stumbling on abuse" [II. iii. 19-20]:

> Virtue itself turns vice, being misapplied;
> And vice sometime's by action dignified.
>   [II. iii. 21-2]

Then as Romeo silently enters, Friar Laurence produces the plant which delights when smelled but
kills when tasted. After thus establishing the
Friar's role as chorus for the tragedy, Shakespeare
then makes him spokesman of the haste theme:
his greeting dwells solely upon Romeo's "earli-

ness" and the "distemp'rature" from which it
arises:

> *Benedicite!*
> What early tongue so sweet saluteth me?
> Young son, it argues a distempered head
> So soon to bid good morrow to thy bed.
> Care keeps his watch in every old man's
>   eye,
> And where care lodges, sleep will never lie;
> But where unbruised youth with uns-
>   tuff'd brain
> Doth couch his limbs, there golden sleep
>   doth reign;
> Therefore thy earliness doth me assure
> Thou art up-rous'd with some dis-
>   temp'rature.
>   [II. iii. 31-40]

Friar Laurence's thematic moralizing now extends
to Rosaline, "so soon forsaken" [II. iii. 67]:

> Lo, here upon thy cheek the stain doth sit
> Of an old tear that is not wash'd off yet.
>   [II. iii. 75-6]

And as scene iii closes, the Friar's admonition by
indirection changes to an outright statement of the
haste theme:

> *Romeo.* O, let us hence; I stand on sudden
>   haste.
> *Friar.* Wisely and slow; they stumble that
>   run fast.
>   [II. iii. 93-4]

The next scene presents dialogue between Romeo,
Benvolio, and Mercutio, in which an accelerated
badinage continues the theme of oppressive haste:
at the end of the exchange, as Mercutio complains
that his "wits faint" [II. iv. 67-8] from the quick
give-and-take, we hear Romeo exclaiming, "Switch
and spurs, switch and spurs, or I'll cry a match" [II.
iv. 69-70], and Mercutio observing, "Nay, if our
wits run the wild goose chase, I am done . . . " [II.
iv. 71-2]. Then, as the scene ends with Romeo's
urging of speed in arranging the lovers' meeting,
we hear the Nurse commanding Peter, "Before and
apace" [II. iv. 217].

Again, as Juliet introduces II. v by reference to the
overdue Nurse, there is a lively "run-on" from the
exit lines of one scene to the entry lines of another.
Juliet's soliloquy and the Nurse's appearance then
combine to assert the haste theme fully and impressively:

> The clock struck nine when I did send the
>   nurse;
> In half an hour she promis'd to return.
> Perchance she cannot meet him; that's not
>   so.
> O, she is lame! Love's heralds should be
>   thoughts,
> Which ten times faster glide than the
>   sun's beams
> Driving back shadows over louring hills;
> Therefore do nimble-pinion'd doves draw
>   Love,

And therefore hath the wind-swift Cupid
   wings.
Now is the sun upon the highmost hill
Of this day's journey, and from nine till
   twelve
Is three long hours, yet she is not come.
Had she affections and warm youthful
   blood,
She would be as swift in motion as a ball;
My words would bandy her to my sweet
   love,
And his to me;
But old folks, marry, feign as they were
   dead,
Unwieldy, slow, heavy and pale as lead.
                               [II. v. 1-17]

The Nurse enters here with comically labored
breathing (a device also of scene iii) which accompanies here exclamation of "Jesu, what haste!" [II.
v. 29] and the scene shifts back to the cell of Friar
Laurence who plays a "slowing" role opposite
Romeo analogous to the Nurse's role with Juliet.
But the lovers meet in the cell and their marriage
is arranged with the dispatch which is now coloring all aspects of the play; Friar Laurence speaks:

Come, come with me, and we will make
   short work;
For, by your leaves, you shall not stay
   alone
Till Holy Church incorporate two in one.
                               [II. vi. 35-7]

Act III, scene i now brings the street fight in which
Mercutio is killed, and speed in the action is again
accompanied by lines which express the haste
theme. Mercutio's challenge comes in such terms:
"Will you pluck your sword out of his pilcher by
the ears? Make haste, lest mine be about your ears
ere it be out" [III. i. 80-2]. And at Mercutio's death
the lament of Romeo points to the rush of events
within a single hour:

This gentleman, the Prince's near ally,
My very friend, hath got this mortal hurt
In my behalf; my reputation stain'd
With Tybalt's slander,—Tybalt, that an
   hour
Hath been my cousin!
                               [III. i. 109-13]

Even the notion of death appears in a metaphor of
souls ascending in quick succession:

Now, Tybalt, take the "villain" back again
That late thou gav'st me; for Mercutio's
   soul
Is but a little way above our heads,
Staying for thine. . . .
                               [III. i. 125-28]

At this point citizens enter in pursuit which results in an episode similar to I.i as the Prince, with
full retinue, quiets the disorder and pronounces
judgment on it. One might expect here a speech
which would slow the movement, but at this stage
of the play all characters, even those rendering ju-

dicial decrees, are given lines which carry the
theme of immediacy and hurry. Escalus closes the
scene:

         And for that offence
Immediately we do exile him hence. . . .
      Let Romeo hence in haste,
Else, when he's found, that hour is his
   last.
Bear hence this body and attend our will.
Mercy but murders, pardoning those that
   kill.
                       [III. i. 186-87, 194-97]

Once more, as a scene is closed with the haste
theme, the next one is begun on the same note. The
transition, moreover, contains irony which has the
sudden quality expressed by the action and the imagery. In III. ii Juliet's opening lines succeed the
Prince's decree which ends III. i. He has banished
Romeo "hence in haste" and Juliet, unaware of
this, calls for Romeo's return with all speed and urgency:

Gallop apace, you fiery-footed steeds,
Towards Phoebus' lodging; such a wag-
   goner
As Phaethon would whip you to the west,
And bring in cloudy night immediately.
Spread thy close curtain, love-performing
   night,
That runaway's eyes may wink, and
   Romeo
Leap to these arms untalk'd of and
   unseen! . . .
Come, night; come, Romeo; come, thou
   day in night;
For thou wilt lie upon the wings of night,
Whiter than new snow on a raven's back.
Come, gentle night, come, loving, black-
   brow'd night. . . .

      So tedious is this day
As is the night before some festival
To an impatient child that hath new robes
And may not wear them.
                       [III. ii. 1-7, 17-20, 28-31]

The Nurse then enters and increases the effect of
haste by maddening the impatient Juliet with confused quibble in reporting Tybalt's death and
Romeo's banishment.

It is unnecessary to discuss the full extent to which
dispatch appears as a theme in *Romeo and Juliet*.
Interpretation need not cover an entire work if it
adequately suggests a way of perceiving it. The last
half of the play [also] shows a wide range of action,
character, and line devoted to the haste theme. . . .
(pp. 12-21)

*Brents Stirling, "'They Stumble that
Run Fast'," in his* Unity in Shakespearian Tragedy: The Interplay of Theme
and Character, *1956. Reprint by Gordi-
an Press, Inc., 1966, pp. 10-25.*

ASPECTS OF LOVE

Leonora Leet Brodwin

[*Brodwin studies* Romeo and Juliet *in relation to the courtly love tradition in Elizabethan romance. Courtly love is a philosophy that was prominent in chivalric times and had a significant influence on Renaissance literature. Though the precise origins of this tradition are not known, the ideas on which it was based were summarized by Andreas Capellanus at the end of the twelfth century in his* The Art of Courtly Love. *Capellanus explained the doctrine of courtly love in thirty-one "rules." In essence, it is illicit and sensual and is accompanied by great emotional suffering. The lover, usually a knight, falls in love at first sight and, until his love is reciprocated, agonizes over his situation. Once his affection is returned, he is inspired to perform great deeds. Moreover, the lovers pledge their fidelity to one another and vow to keep their union a secret. The ideas of courtly love were frequently expressed by the fourteenth-century Italian poet Petrarch in his love sonnets. His exaggerated comparisons and oxymora (the pairing of contradictory terms) describing the suffering of the lover and the beauty of the lady have come to be known as "Petrarchan conceits." In the excerpt below, Brodwin details the aspects of* Romeo and Juliet *that conform to the conventions of courtly love:* Romeo *and* Juliet *fall in love at first sight; their love is intensified by the feud that threatens it; they meet secretly; and, although they marry, they see each other only at night lending an illicit dimension to their love. In addition, they quickly resolve to commit suicide upon learning of each other's death. The critic stresses, however, that* Romeo and Juliet *transcends these stock conventions through its dramatization of the "spiritual mystique" of the hero and heroine's passion. Shakespeare depicts* **Romeo** *and* **Juliet**'s *love as divine, Brodwin asserts, for the protagonists approach death cheerfully, confident that they will at last achieve peace and freedom from the restrictions of mortal existence. Furthermore, their faithfulness in love is virtuous because their deaths bring about an end to the feud.*]

Shakespeare's tragic masterpiece of Courtly Love was written in 1595, when the vogue of courtly sonneteering was at its height. In considering "the fearful passage of their death-mark'd love," critics like E. E. Stoll have been at considerable pains to show that the love of Romeo and Juliet was the normal product of youthful innocence, that "not because there is anything wrong with them do the youth and maiden perish but only because 'love is strong as death,' and fate unfriendly" [see Sources for Further Study]. Granville-Barker has written with greater insight into the specific characteristics [in his *Prefaces to Shakespeare*] of the youth

and maiden which have made their love "strong as death," but he, too, misses the fuller implications of this love. At the opposite extreme is Franklin Dickey who argues, from the vantage point of the Renaissance moralists, that Romeo and Juliet are afflicted with a love disease the evil consequence of which is death: "fortune has operated here to punish sin and . . . this avenging fortune is the work of heaven" [see excerpt in section on Tragic Design]. While Dickey performs a service in stripping the play of its romanticism and showing that the quality of its love leads inevitably to death, he is untrue to the tone of the play. *Romeo and Juliet* is not a tract against Courtly Love, but a supreme expression of its spiritual *mystique*. Of this Paul N. Siegel is clearly aware for, in relating the play to the conventions of a courtly "Religion of Love," he has indicated the literary tradition through which this extraordinary work must be approached and so come closest to an understanding of the precise nature of this love.

The love of Romeo and Juliet, while ever in fatal interaction with the feuding world of Verona, yet exists on a plane of experience totally divorced from its normal expectations. The capsular quality of this love, which can run its complete course without betraying its secret existence, is, in fact, the subject of much of the play's dramatic irony, Romeo's confidants patronizing his love for Rosaline while his true love for Juliet is flowering and Juliet's father bustling about her marriage while still believing that it is an honor that she dreams not of. While this counterpointing of the brawling, bawdy, festive, and practical world with the lovers' poetic night world is meaningful, the vitality of the naturalistic presentation tends to obscure the poetic symbolism. The quasi-comic treatment of much of the play puts readers on their guard against taking the lovers' utterances with too much seriousness, and the lovers' occasional playfulness seems to confirm the impression of youthful impetuousness, singing bird-like of its joy.

But if Shakespeare has endowed romance convention with an unusual naturalism, he, no less than the romancers, is vitally concerned with "the allegory of love." Though his lovers react with greater psychological realism to their dilemmas than do the cardboard lovers of romance, they follow as unquestioningly an implicit code of love and, in their poetic utterances, point to its symbolic implications. Although the psychological and symbolic levels are often interpenetrating, there are moments when the symbolism becomes completely divorced from naturalistic presentation. When, for instance, Romeo refers to Juliet as his "conceal'd lady" [III. iii. 98], the rhetoric of human love has been completely displaced by one appropriate to a mystical religion of love.

The tragedy which is to so transcend the ordinary conventions of romance begins with a caricature of them. Romeo's love for Rosaline has been "rais'd with the fume of sighs" [I. i. 190] and "nourish'd with lovers' tears" [I. i. 192]. He has carefully conformed to all the prescribed rules of Courtly Love, spending the night with tears and making "himself an artificial night" [I. i. 140] with the coming of day. But this stylized behavior is not so different from the convention which allows Romeo and Juliet to fall irrevocably in love at first sight and for Juliet quite naturally to say: "Go ask his name.—If he be married, / My grave is like to be my wedding bed" [I. v. 134-35]. These two loves are not different, then, in kind but in the quality of the poetry in which they are expressed, the earlier a patchwork of conventional Petrarchanisms, the later a profoundly mystical exploration.

Through this conventional behavior, however, suggestions of character do emerge. Romeo is a youth in search of an infinitely thrilling love, a love for which he is prepared to face suffering and even death. Though the indulgence of his feelings for Rosaline causes him to feel slightly ridiculous— "Dost thou not laugh?" [I. i. 183]—he cherishes "the devout religion of mine eye" [I. ii. 88] and longs to put it to the test. Hitherto sinking passively "under love's heavy burthen" [I. iv. 22], he is suddenly jarred from a purely imaginative to an active role by the suggestion that he compare his beloved's beauty with that of others at the Capulet feast.

Although he had only wished to view his love and prove the constancy of his heart, a sudden premonition of the danger of thus venturing into the enemy's camp elicits from him his first profoundly personal utterance:

> . . . my mind misgives
> Some consequence, yet hanging in the
>   stars,
> Shall bitterly begin his fearful date
> With this night's revels and expire the
>   term
> Of a despised life, clos'd in my breast,
> By some vile forfeit of untimely death.
> But he that hath the steerage of my course
> Direct my sail! On, lusty gentlemen!
>   [I. iv. 106-13]

In this speech the character of Romeo emerges from the role of conventional courtly lover to reveal a deeper quality of doom. In terms of the action Romeo rightly fears that in so venturing to see Rosaline he may be forfeiting his life to fate, for it is from Tybalt's recognition of him at the feast that the fatal consequences of his exile are to issue. But however eager he was to nourish his "lover's tears," the prospect of possible death for the love of Rosaline is another thing. Suddenly faced with this prospect, he recognizes that such death would be a "vile forfeit." If he nonetheless continues his fatal voyage, it is no longer the desired sight of Rosaline but the challenge of fate which spurs him on. If fate has marked him out, he will not be "fear-

ful" but hold his "despised life" in as much contempt.

Although it was earlier acknowledged that his immediate love for Juliet was a stock romance convention, this crucial speech, which just precedes his first sight of Juliet, may suggest a motivation for the fatal urgency with which he approaches his love. As he is risking his life in the name of a love which has not inspired him to the point where he can consider his life's loss as more than a "vile forfeit," his need for a truly inspirational love becomes urgent. Having accepted fate's challenge, he is now concerned to transmute this "vile forfeit" into a glorious surrender.

And this inspiration comes to him at the radiant sight of Juliet:

> O, she doth teach the torches to burn
>   bright!
> It seems she hangs upon the cheek of
>   night
> Like a rich jewel in an Ethiop's ear—
> Beauty too rich for use, for earth too dear!
>   [I. v. 44-7]

Where Rosaline's beauty had left him in the utter darkness of an unhappy human love, Juliet's beauty, because it seems to him too precious for the usages of life, can truly illuminate the night. From this first encounter, however, Romeo conceives of his lady not as an ordinary mortal but as a symbol of divine beauty, which, in the "touching," can make him "blessed" [I. v. 51]. His earlier premonition of death has been displaced by this intimation of heavenly blessing; but the close association of these two in "this night's revels" is significant.

From what has just been shown, we can see the way in which Shakespeare invests a stock convention of romance, that of love at first sight, with suggestions of both human motivation and symbolic implication. And what he has done for Romeo he does in lesser measure for Juliet: if Romeo meets Juliet at a fateful moment in his life, the same is true for her. She had just been informed by her mother that she must "think of marriage now" [I. iii. 69]. And, although she had said that "it is an honour that I dream not of" [I. iii. 66], she is forced for the first time to consider marriage as a real and imminent possibility. In doing so, her maiden heart gains a new susceptibility which will cause her to look at men differently this night: "I'll look to like" [I. iii. 97].

As Romeo had come to the feast to behold Rosaline, feeling that in venturing thus into the enemy's camp he was forfeiting his life to fate, so does Juliet come to inspect the man to whom her parents would likewise have her dedicate her fate. Both, however, instead of looking where they had intended, seem compelled to make a last desperate comparison before their fate is irrevocably sealed.

Under a similarly fatal urgency, Romeo finds in Juliet's radiant beauty the inspiration he had been seeking; and Juliet suddenly finds herself inspired by Romeo's passionate prayers. This love at first sight, then, is not simply a submission to fate but a choosing of their fate. When Romeo learns that "my life is my foe's debt" [I. v. 118] and Juliet the same, they can therefore accept their fate with a commitment that redeems it from being a "vile forfeit."

Their love has been born in the heart of obstruction, and if their knowledge of this crucial fact was "muffled still," the passionate need by which they found each other out could "without eyes see pathways to his will" [I. i. 171-72]. For this central obstruction to their love, rather than deterring their passion serves only to intensify it: "Temp'ring extremities with extreme sweet" [II. Pro., 14]. Romeo had chanced such an extremity in coming to the feast and Juliet in choosing another than the one her parents had appointed before they were aware of the true extremity they had embraced, and, when they do become aware of the obstruction to their love, they accept its necessity without question. Though Romeo and Juliet marry, their marriage so approximates the adulterous union of night that it even borrows from the troubadours the traditional verse form of the *aubade* or dawn song, which celebrates the adulterous lovers' hour of parting. "More light and light—more dark and dark our woes" [III. v. 36] is not the language of marriage but of lovers who "steal love's sweet bait from fearful hooks." [II. Pro., 8]. The marriage of Romeo and Juliet . . . in no way changes the obstructed situation which makes the necessity of their partings "such sweet sorrow" [II. ii. 184].

If their meetings can only take place in the night, night has for the lovers a special significance. They do not covet night for itself but because it is only then that the power of love can be truly illuminating. As has been seen, it is Juliet's radiance which first strikes Romeo. Again, as he stands beneath the balcony, she appears to irradiate the night:

> But soft! What light through yonder window breaks?
> It is the East, and Juliet is the sun!
> . . . her eyes in heaven
> Would through the airy region stream so bright
> That birds would sing and think it were not night. . . .
> O, speak again, bright angel! for thou art
> As glorious to this night, being o'er my head,
> As is a winged messenger of heaven . . .
> [II. ii. 2-3, 20-2, 26-8]

Juliet converts the terrors of night to glory. It is for this reason that Romeo can say:

> I have night's cloak to hide me from their sight;

> And but thou love me, let them find me here.
> My life were better ended by their hate
> Than death prorogued, wanting of thy love.
> [II. ii. 75-8]

In a night containing Juliet's love, death need not be dreaded and is far preferable to his otherwise uninspired life. He eagerly ventures into the night since it is only in "the dark night" that Juliet's "true-love passion" [II. ii. 104-06] can be revealed. But if Juliet's love robs death of its terror, it nonetheless is in intimate association with death. As Juliet informs Romeo, in a statement loaded with symbolic as well as practical meaning, the place where she abides is "death, considering who thou art" [II. ii. 64]. Though Romeo faces a practical danger in approaching thus close to her feuding kinsmen, it is also true on the symbolic level that the approach to a Juliet who is heavenly "light" and "bright angel"—that is, to a love object beyond the mortal condition—must ultimately be made by way of death.

Realizing that the way to his "bright angel" is barred by his name, Romeo exclaims:

> Call me but love, and I'll be new baptiz'd;
> Henceforth I never will be Romeo. . . .
> Had I it written, I would tear the world.
> [II. ii. 50-1, 57]

Though Romeo feels that the receipt of Juliet's love would be a rebirth for him, the rebirth in the heavenly love which Juliet represents requires not simply the tearing of his name but of the mortal self which that name identifies. Yet however much it may be symbolic of death, he embraces the night in which the infinitude of Juliet's love has been disclosed as a "blessed, blessed night!" [II. ii. 139].

As Juliet symbolizes a divine love to Romeo, even answering him with a celestial accent, so he assumes a similar role to her. In Juliet's invocation to night, the full implications of this worship of night are revealed:

> Come night; come, Romeo; come, thou day in night;
> For thou wilt lie upon the wings of night
> Whiter than new snow upon a raven's back.
> Come, gentle night; come, loving, black-brow'd night;
> Give me my Romeo; and when he shall die,
> Take him and cut him out in little stars,
> And he will make the face of heaven so fine
> That all the world will be in love with night
> And pay no worship to the garish sun.
> [III. ii. 17-25]

Romeo is a creature of night, and, as such, Juliet coaxes night to loan her Romeo until such time as he shall die and be returned to night, arguing that when such a true lover should be returned by

Romeo's description of the apothecary and his shop. Act V, scene i. By Henry Fuseli. The Department of Rare Books and Special Collections, The University of Michigan Library.

tiz'd" by love. With Mercutio's death on his hands, however, Romeo realizes that he is a Montague still and that, in wishing to deny this fact, he had proved false to himself: "O sweet Juliet / Thy beauty hath made me effeminate / And in my temper soft'ned valour's steel!" [III. i. 113-15] Juliet had called her place "death, considering who thou art," and now Romeo once again has a premonition that, being Romeo, his pursuit of love into the enemy's camp will prove fatal: "This day's black fate on moe days doth depend; / This but begins the woe others must end" [III. i. 119-20]. And again he accepts his fate and challenges Tybalt. Having killed him and understood that the consequences will be disastrous, however, his old fear arises once more and causes him to cry out: "O, I am fortune's fool!" [III. i. 136]. As before he had feared, when accepting fate's challenge, that his "untimely death" would be a "vile forfeit," so, now that fate lowers once again, the prospect of his death seems inglorious. The Prince will immediately ask: "Where are the vile beginners of this fray?" [III. i. 141]. And this is Romeo's fear, that his death will not be a glorious martryrdom for love but the vile execution of a street brawler. Even so, he would prefer vile execution to banishment: "Ha, banishment? Be merciful, say 'death'; / For exile hath more terror in his look, / Much more than death" [III. iii. 12-14].

In his discussion of the implications of banishment, the essential quality of his love is again revealed:

> 'Tis torture, and not mercy. Heaven is
>   here,
> Where Juliet lives. . . . More validity,
> More honourable state, more courtship
>   lives
> In carrion flies than Romeo. They may
>   seize
> On the white wonder of dear Juliet's hand
> And steal immortal blessing from her
>   lips . . .
>
> [III. iii. 29-30, 33-7]

Although viewed from one aspect, the place where Juliet lives is death, from another it is "Heaven," the source of purity and "immortal blessing." In the "courtship" of this "immortal blessing" Romeo sees the only basis for "validity" and "honourable state." "Death, though ne'er so mean" [III. iii. 45], would be preferable to the continuance of a meaningless life, exiled from even the possibility of "immortal blessing," this indeed a fit symbol of hell: " 'banished'? / O friar, the damned use that word in hell; / Howling attends it:" [III. iii. 46-8]. (pp. 53-4)

Exiled from his love, he sees no alternative but to "fall upon the ground, as I do now, / Taking the measure of an unmade grave" [III. iii. 69-70]. Juliet, likewise, does not distinguish between his exile and his death. Thinking he is dead, she says: "Vile earth, to earth resign; end motion here, / And thou and Romeo press one heavy bier!" [III. ii. 59-

death he would impart a special glory to the love of night. Though night and death are here seen to be interrelated and Romeo in their power, it is yet his special virtue to irradiate their darkness. As Juliet had emblazoned the night for Romeo, so he to her is "day in night." While disdaining "the garish sun," that which exhibits all the concreteness and limitations of terrestrial life, it is not the annihilating darkness of night in itself which they worship but the special radiance of the limitless which shines for them in the heart of darkness. If night is symbolic of death, death itself is but the other face of the Infinite. (pp. 44-50)

While Romeo has shown no hesitation in pursuing his love, he soon finds it not such a simple matter to tear his name. However fully his spirit may assent to the aims of his love, his human situation does cause some resistance to it.

This is fully brought out in the duel between Romeo and Tybalt. Romeo first counters Tybalt's overtures in the conviction that he is "new bap-

60]. Learning he is exiled, she nonetheless exclaims: "I'll to my wedding bed; / And death, not Romeo, take my maidenhead!" [III. ii. 136-37]. Rejecting her life as "vile earth," she immediately leaps to the thought of lying with Romeo in death. Like Romeo, she is "wedded to calamity" [III. iii. 3], and in her decision to fulfill her wedding not with Romeo but with death, the meaning of this wedding becomes clear. It becomes yet clearer after the wedding's earthly consummation. Romeo's alternatives, "I must be gone and live, or stay and die" [III. v. 11] exist not only for this dawn but for as long as their love shall last. A premonition of this causes Juliet to see even the departing Romeo "as one dead in the bottom of a tomb" [III. v. 56]. (pp. 54-5)

Upon learning of Juliet's supposed death, Romeo resolves with conventional promptitude upon his own. But it is in his treatment of Romeo's confrontation with death that Shakespeare most fully illuminates the accepted conventions of Courtly Love. Though Romeo is dying in order to be united with Juliet, it is with a Juliet who has at last discarded all earthly vestiges to become pure symbol. And now the supreme symbolic function of Juliet becomes clear; she is the means which permits Romeo to confront his fate as a man with joy. If he has made "a dateless bargain to engrossing death" [V. iii. 115], this steadfast commitment to something beyond all mortal contingency raises him above the normal human condition. Juliet had earlier said of him:

> He was not born to shame.
> Upon his brow shame is asham'd to sit;
> For 'tis a throne where honour may be
> crown'd
> Sole monarch of the universal earth.
>   [III. ii. 91-4]

As in his dream love made him an "emperor" [V. i. 9], so does the honor of his love make him the universal monarch, raise him to godhead. It is through love of a Juliet symbolically raised to divine status that he redeems his own divine birthright from the "shame" of mortality's yoke.

But the paradox of this desire for the Infinite is that it can only be fully embraced in death. . . . Death for him is "love-devouring," "engrossing"; it is a final fact, but a finality irradiated by joy. It is the infinite freedom experienced in the ecstatic instant of self-annihilation. But to this note of ecstasy, Romeo now adds a deeper note of defiance: "Is it e'en so? Then I defy you, stars! . . . Well, Juliet, I will lie with thee to-night" [V. i. 24, 34]. Romeo defies the stars and all mortal contingency by accepting the worst they have to offer, thereby transmuting it into a spiritual triumph.

The love-death as a defiance of fate becomes the dominant note as he approaches the tomb:

> Thou detestable maw, thou womb of
> death,
> Gorg'd with the dearest morsel of the
> earth,
> Thus I enforce thy rotten jaws to open,
> And in despite I'll cram thee with more
> food.
>   [V. iii. 45-8]

Romeo here reveals what is probably his truest attitude toward death. Whereas before he had interpreted every symbolic identification of his love with death as a sign of its infinite glory, betraying no anxiety toward the actual fact of death, he now reveals a deep revulsion toward death. Far from glorious, death here is profoundly felt to be "detestable" and "rotten," and this not in reference to a death vilely brought about through insufficient inspiration or irrelevant accident but chosen by himself under the greatest of inspirations.

Why then, we may well ask, has he been so fatally hasty in choosing his present death? Paradoxical as it may seem, the source of his headlong rush toward death appears to lie not in a love of death but a horror of death so extreme that it has poisoned his life. Unable to accept the anxieties of a contingent mortal existence, he has advanced upon hateful death, daring it to do its worst. Rather than appear fearful of death and give death the victory, he triumphs over death by bringing it upon himself. Not in love of death, but, as he says "in despite I'll cram thee with more food." The ecstasy of self-annihilation at its profoundest level, then, is not due to a feeling of surrender to death but to the triumph of the unconquerable spirit over death, achieving the Infinite in its assertion of ultimate freedom.

It is in this spirit that he views not only his own approaching death but the death of Juliet:

> I'll bury thee in a triumphant grave.
> A grave? O, no, a lanthorn, slaught'red
> youth,
> For here lies Juliet, and her beauty makes
> This vault a feasting presence full of light.
>   [V. iii. 83-6]

Juliet's irradiation of the night has been but a prelude to her radiance in death. When Romeo had earlier said that "her eyes in heaven / Would through the airy region stream so bright / That birds would sing and think it were not night," he did not think that such irradiation made the night less real but that it converted its terrors to glory. So is it now with death. To Romeo, Juliet has not outlived death but she has overwhelmed its horror in radiance. Romeo's exhilaration at the radiance of his love in death produces a "lightning" [V. iii. 90] of his antagonistic mood. In Juliet's triumph over mortality, Romeo sees his own, her excessive beauty in death proving an irresistible goad to his own triumphant conquest of death. (pp. 57-60)

Juliet's death speech has not the poetic grandeur

of Romeo's but, as she was ever "light a foot" [II. vi. 16], so she has that "lighting before death" [V. iii. 90] of which Romeo spoke. Seeing Romeo dead, all previous fears are overcome and she moves to death with cheerful alacrity:

> O churl! drunk all, and left no friendly
>   drop
> To help me after? I will kiss thy lips.
> Haply some poison yet doth hang on them
> To make me die with a restorative. . . .
> Yea, noise? Then I'll be brief. O happy dag-
>   ger!
> This is thy sheath; there rest, and let me
>   die.
>
> [V. iii. 163-70]

Meeting death with a kiss, she dies "with a restorative," the joyous restoration of her initial freedom from constraint and contingency.

The play ends on this final note of the redemptive quality of a death so amorously embraced. Romeo and Juliet had both embraced death as the redemption of their ultimate freedom from mortality's "yoke"; in so doing, their deaths prove to be redemptive as well for the living. In love with the infinite peace they could find only in death, they had spurned the world of strife that gave them being. Now, in the radiant light of their pure sacrifice, the petty futility of that strife is seen. Their deaths not only restore the peace of Verona but confer upon them the special glory of being forever upheld as the city's most shining example of admired virtue. The city immortalizes the "Poor sacrifices of our enmity." [V. iii. 304] who, almost as in a religious ritual, have vicariously atoned for the multiple sins of the populace. The example of their heroic transcendence of the compromises of life and the terrors of death illuminates the more humble path of the ordinary citizen as he attempts to justify, by a more consecrated life, the martyrdom of the gloriously "faithful" [V. iii. 302]. Thus does Shakespeare conclude his great tragedy of a love that has throughout been vehicle and symbol of the "immortal blessing" conferred in the kiss of death. Though the character and reactions of the lovers have been explored in all their earthly reality, they . . . have embarked on a spiritual journey which finds its promised haven only in a death transfigured by their religious devotion to the dictates of Courtly Love. (pp. 61-2)

> *Leonora Leet Brodwin, "The Classic Pattern of Courtly Love Tragedy," in her* Elizabethan Love Tragedy: 1587-1625, *New York University Press, 1971, pp. 39-64.*

Mark Van Doren

[*Van Doren contrasts* **Romeo** *and* **Juliet's** *attitude toward love with that of the other characters. While the hero and heroine view love as holy and solemn, the critic observes,* **Mercutio** *considers it pornographic, the* **Capulets** *prudent, and the* **Nurse** *practical, though, unlike the* **Capulets**, *with a "certain prurient interest." According to Van Doren, the* **Friar** *comes closest to sharing* **Romeo** *and* **Juliet's** *perception of love, though he speaks of it in terms that are foreign to them.*]

One of the reasons for the fame of *Romeo and Juliet* is that it has so completely and clearly isolated the experience of romantic love. It has let such love speak for itself; and not alone in the celebrated wooing scenes, where the hero and heroine express themselves with a piercing directness, but indirectly also, and possibly with still greater power, in the whole play in so far as the whole play is built to be their foil. Their deep interest for us lies in their being alone in a world which does not understand them; and Shakespeare has devoted much attention to that world.

Its inhabitants talk only of love. The play is saturated with the subject. Yet there is always a wide difference between what the protagonists intend by the term and what is intended by others. The beginning dialogue by Sampson and Gregory, servants, is pornographic on the low level of puns about maidenheads, of horse-humor and hiredman wit. Mercutio will be more indecent . . . on the higher level of a gentleman's cynicism. Mercutio does not believe in love, as perhaps the servants clumsily do; he believes only in sex, and his excellent mind has sharpened the distinction to a very dirty point. He drives hard against the sentiment that has softened his friend and rendered him unfit for the society of young men who really know the world. When Romeo with an effort matches one of his witticisms he is delighted:

> Now art thou sociable, now art thou
> Romeo, now art thou
> what thou art, by art as well as by nature.
> [II. iv. 89-91]

He thinks that Romeo has returned to the world of artful wit, by which he means cynical wit; he does not know that Romeo is still "dead" and "fishified" [II. iv. 38], and that he himself wil soon be mortally wounded under the arm of his friend—who, because love has stupefied him, will be capable of speaking the inane lines, "I thought all for the best" [III. i. 10-4]. (pp. 70-1)

The older generation is another matter. Romeo and Juliet . . . will be sadly misunderstood by them. The Capulets hold still another view of love. Their interest is in "good" marriages, in sensible choices. They are match-makers, and believe they know best how their daughter should be put to bed. This also is cynicism, though it be without pornography; at least the young heart of Juliet sees it so. Her father finds her sighs and tears merely ridiculous: "Evermore show'ring?" [III. v. 130]. She is "a wretched puling fool, a whining mammet" [III. v. 183-84], a silly girl who does not know what is good for her. Capulet is Shakespeare's first portrait in a long gallery of fussy, tetchy, stubborn, un-teachable old men: the Duke of York in *Richard II,* Polonius [in *Hamlet*], Lafeu [in *All's Well that Ends Well*], Menenius [in *Coriolanus*]. He is tart-tongued, breathy, wordy, pungent, and speaks with a naturalness unknown in Shakespeare's plays before this, a naturalness consisting in a per-fect harmony between his phrasing and its rhythm:

> How how, how how, chop-logic! What is
>   this?
> "Proud," and "I thank you," and "I thank
>   you not;"
> And yet "not proud." Mistress minion,
>   you,
> Thank me no thankings, nor proud me no
>   prouds,
> But fettle your fine joints 'gainst Thursday
>   next,
> To go with Paris to Saint Peter's Church,
> Or I will drag thee on a hurdle thither.
>   [III. v. 49-55]
>   (pp. 71-2)

The Nurse, a member of the same generation, and in Juliet's crisis as much her enemy as either par-ent is, for she too urges the marriage with Paris [III. v. 212-25], adds to practicality a certain prurient interest in love-business, the details of which she mumbles toothlessly, reminiscently, with the inde-cency of age. Her famous speech concerning Ju-liet's age [I. iii. 12-57], which still exceeds the speeches of Capulet in the virtue of dramatic natu-ralness, runs on so long in spite of Lady Capulet's attempts to stop it because she has become fasci-nated with the memory of her husband's broad jest:

Nurse.   And since that time it is eleven years;
>   For then she could stand high-lone;
>   nay, by the rood,
>   She could have run and waddled all
>   about;
>   For even the day before, she broke her
>   brow;
>   And then my husband—God be with
>   his soul!
>   'A was a merry man—took up the child.
>   "Yea," quoth he, "dost thou fall upon
>   thy face?
>   Thou wilt fall backward when thou
>   hast more wit;
>   Wilt thou not, Jule?" and, by my holi-
>   dame,
>   The pretty wretch left crying and said,
>   "Ay."
>   To see, now, how a jest shall come
>   about!
>   I warrant, an I should live a thousand
>   years,
>   I never should forget it. "Wilt thou not,
>   Jule?" quoth he;
>   And, pretty fool, it stinted and said,
>   "Ay."

Lady Capulet.   Enough of this; I pray thee, hold thy
>   peace.

Nurse.   Yes, madam; yet I cannot choose but
>   laugh,
>   To think it should leave crying and say,
>   "Ay."
>   And yet, I warrant, it had upon it brow
>   A bump as big as a young cockerel's
>   stone;
>   A perilous knock; and it cried bitterly.
>   "Yea," quoth my husband, "fall'st upon
>   thy face?
>   Thou wilt fall backward when thou
>   comest to age;
>   Wilt thou not, Jule?" It stinted and said,
>   "Ay."

The Nurse's delight in the reminiscence is among other things lickerish, which the delight of Romeo and Juliet in their love never is, any more than it is prudent like the Capulets, or pornographic like Mercutio. Their delight is solemn, their behavior holy, and nothing is more natural than that in their first dialogue [I. v. 93-110] there should be talk of palmers, pilgrims, saints, and prayers.

It is of course another kind of holiness than that which appears in Friar Laurence, who neverthe-less takes his own part in the endless conversation which the play weaves about the theme of love. The imagery of his first speech is by no accident erotic:

> I must up-fill this osier cage of ours
> With baleful weeds and precious-juiced
>   flowers.
> The earth, that's nature's mother, is her
>   tomb;
> What is her burying grave, that is her
>   womb;
> And from her womb children of divers
>   kind
> We sucking on her natural bosom find.
>   [II. iii. 7-12]

The Friar is closer to the lovers in sympathy than any other person of the play. Yet this language is as alien to their mood as that of Capulet or the Nurse; or as Romeo's recent agitation over Rosa-line is to his ecstasy with Juliet. The lovers are alone. Their condition is unique. Only by the audi-ence is it understood. (pp. 72-4)

> *Mark Van Doren, "Romeo and Juliet,"*
> *in his* Shakespeare, *Henry Holt and*
> *Company, 1939, pp. 65-75.*

IMAGERY AND LANGUAGE

E. C. Pettet

[*Pettet examines how imagery reinforces two of the central concerns of* Romeo and Juliet: *the role of fate in determining the lovers' tragedy and the feud between the families. The influ-*

*ence of fate, the critic argues, is developed through the use of star imagery, in which stars serve as a metaphor (an implied analogy which imaginatively identifies one object with another) for destiny, and through the "pilot" imagery which is used to describe **Romeo's** maturation and attempts to control his own destiny. Pettet also demonstrates how the paradox (a statement which while seemingly contradictory or absurd may actually be well-founded and true) of **Romeo** and **Juliet's** love arising out of the hatred between the **Montagues** and the **Capulets** is accentuated by the repeated references to opposition and contradiction, particularly the contrasts between love and death and between light and darkness.]*

With so much emphasis on Fate [in *Romeo and Juliet*] there is nothing surprising in the fact that Shakespeare makes frequent use of the time-old symbol of the stars in his imagery. Nor, in such a story of romantic love, is it remarkable to find the star-image employed in a second conventional way—as a metaphor for feminine beauty (especially for the eyes of the Lady) and for the attraction of lovers. What is, however, of interest is the way in which Shakespeare subtly fuses these two sorts of star-image; and perhaps the most striking example of this interpenetration is to be observed in some of the lines spoken by Romeo as he watches Juliet at her balcony:

> Two of the fairest stars in all the heaven,
> Having some business, do entreat her eyes
> To twinkle in their spheres till they return.
> What if her eyes were there, they in her head?
> The brightness of her cheek would shame those stars
> As daylight doth a lamp; her eyes in heaven
> Would through the airy regions stream so bright
> That birds would sing and think it were not night.
> [II. ii. 15-22]

No doubt this passage could be dismissed as yet another typical conceit [an elaborately fanciful idea or metaphor] of the time. But the scene in which the lines occur is singularly free from the extravagant conceits and artificialities of Petrarchan love-poetry, which Shakespeare appropriately reserves for the early Romeo, the youth in love with love; and if we submit our imagination to the full effect of the scene, this sustained star-image transcends the mere conceit to assume a new meaning. Juliet *is* now Romeo's star, his fate; and, as his star, she has the magical power of transforming night into day, of changing his wretchedness into radiant joy and the bitter hatred of their families into love.

There is a similar, though slighter overtone earlier in the play, when old Capulet says to Paris:

> At my poor house look to behold this night
> Earth-treading stars that make dark heaven bright.
> [I. ii. 24-5]

Here, too, it is of course possible to skip the image of 'earth-treading stars' as a familiar cliché for beautiful women; but, taking it in conjunction with the phrase 'dark heaven', we may perhaps catch in it a faint announcement of one of the fundamental themes of the play—of the hardness and misery of human destiny, sweetened, if but for a brief moment, with beauty and love.

In the star-imagery of Juliet's speech when she is waiting vainly, after the killing of Tybalt, for Romeo to come to her—

> And, when he shall die,
> Take him and cut him out in little stars,
> And he will make the face of heaven so fine
> That all the world will be in love with night,
> And pay no worship to the garish sun
> [III. ii. 21-5]

we certainly have, so far as Juliet herself is concerned, a playful, fanciful conceit, for in her passion and fulfilment she cannot really think of her lover as dead. Yet—once more merging into the symbol of the star as fate—how intense this apparent conceit is, with its irony and prophecy. Little as Juliet knows it, heaven and its crossing stars are in reality soon to lay claim to Romeo; and their way will be just that cruel way of violence that she hints, and Romeo will be nothing but a symbol of the lover, a bright, remote star.

Side by side with these delicate combinations of the star-image we should note, as another effect of the Fate motif on the imagery of the play, the triple 'pilot' image, which, emerging at three key-points, illuminates and focuses the development of Romeo.

The first instance of this image is to be found at [I. iv. 112-13]. Though there is something that warns Romeo that it is perilous to accompany Mercutio and Benvolio to the Capulet banquet, he decides at last to follow them:

> But He, that hath the steerage of my course,
> Direct my sail! On, lusty gentlemen.

Here, without experience or thought as yet, and certainly without any religious conviction, Romeo vaguely believes himself to be under the guidance of some exterior force; but he submits to his destiny without resistance, even confidently. Later, when he is assured of Juliet's love and is growing to a rapid maturity, he is bolder and more self-willed, active rather than passive. So, when it occurs for the second time, the pilot-image changes:

> I am no pilot; yet, wert thou as far
> As that vast shore wash'd with the far-
> thest sea,
> I would adventure for such merchandise.
> [II. ii. 82-4]

Once more there is the lack of complete self-possession: he will dare anything, but still with a modest, hesitant doubt of his own powers to shape a course entirely to his own determination—'I am no pilot'. And indeed, in the first rapture of Juliet's avowed love, why should he think of rocks and insidious currents? But, transformed by harsh experience, Romeo continues to grow, and when the pilot-image recurs for the last time, just before his death, the pilot is at last himself: the determining force that challenges and defies his stars is something within:

> Come, bitter conduct, come, unsavoury
> guide!
> Thou desperate pilot, now at once run on
> [V. iii. 116-18]

This image is the exact antithesis of the first version, as Romeo is the antithesis of his old self.

Another salient characteristic of *Romeo and Juliet,* is the simple, single, and all-pervading nature of its conflict. Its basic theme is that of love arising out of family feud, challenging it, momentarily triumphing over it, and ultimately destroyed by it. From beginning to end the play reflects the eternal struggle between Eros (Love and Life) and the forces of Death.

This being so, it is not surprising that the play abounds in images of strife, contrast, contradiction, and paradox. Most of these arise directly and inevitably from the story and its situations, while . . . much of the tedious antithesis and paradox of Romeo's speech in the first Act springs inevitably from Shakespeare's representation of him as a typical lover of contemporary, mainly Petrarchan, love-poetry. But beside these straightforward conflict-images there is another group in which Shakespeare, often subconsciously no doubt, uses the poetry of the play to reinforce and illuminate its themes and motifs.

The most impressive concentration of these strife and contradiction images occurs in Friar Lawrence's speech shortly before the marriage ceremony, which emphasizes, in a resonant Chorus manner, some of the essential implications of the play. To begin with, there is the detached and generalizing, though no less impressive, restatement of the eternal life-death struggle, which is represented as something absolute:

> The earth that's nature's mother is her
> tomb;
> What is her burying grave, that is her
> womb.
> [II. iii. 9-10]

Nor, possibly, is this statement entirely general, for 'womb' suggests love, procreation, perhaps Romeo and Juliet, while 'tomb', once we come to know the play, is a key-word with a charged, peculiar significance: it is the 'detestable maw', the 'rotten jaws' [V. iii. 47], that is soon to swallow Romeo and Juliet, and it is to be noticed that in the last scene 'tomb' is once more associated with 'womb':

> Thou detestable maw, thou womb of
> death. . . .
> [V. iii. 145]

Then, both deepening and extending this theme, follows the Friar's meditation on the contradictory properties of nature's fruits and products, leading, through an inevitable transition, to the contraries and contradictions of human life—the good that may change into evil and the vice that may change into virtue, and the intermingled stuff of man's nature:

> Two such opposed kings encamp them
> still
> In man as well as herbs, grace and rude
> will;
> And where the worser is predominant
> Full soon the canker death eats up that
> plant.

While the words 'canker death' are still ominously echoing in our ears, Romeo enters.

There are several other passages where the incidental imagery serves to illuminate the contradiction or paradox of the situation from which it arises. For instance, the bold conceit struck out by Romeo at the opening of the Balcony scene—

> What light through yonder window
> breaks?
> It is the east, and Juliet is the sun!—
> [II. ii. 1-2]

concentrates the essential meaning of the whole scene. In truth a miracle has taken place: the warm, life-giving sun of love has broken unexpectedly, through the dark night of family hatred and strife. But, next to the Friar's soliloquy, the most striking example of imagery that crystallizes the spirit of conflict and contradiction in the play is the recurrent association of bridal-bed and grave, Death and the lover:

> I'll to my wedding-bed;
> And death, not Romeo, take my maiden-
> head!
> [III . ii. 136-37]

> I would the fool were married to her grave!
> [III. v. 140]

> O son, the night before thy wedding-day

Hath Death lain with thy wife: see, there
   she lies,

Flower as she was, deflowered by him.
Death is my son-in-law, Death is my heir;
My daughter he hath wedded.
                                    [IV. v. 35-9]

      Shall I believe
That unsubstantial Death is amorous,
And that the lean abhorred monster keeps
Thee here in dark to be his paramour.
                                    [V. iii. 102-05]

The tone and the immediate purpose of these passages of course vary considerably; but at the core of them all is the powerful, paradoxical image of the play's basic motif—the passionate, interlocking wrestle of love and death. The 'lean abhorred monster' is the ultimate lover; the final wedding-bed is the grave.

Lastly in this poetic elaboration of the play's fundamental motif we may notice the highly evocative use that Shakespeare makes of light and darkness, though this is as much a matter of setting and stage-properties as of imagery. To suggest the first dramatic movement, of love arising out of and challenging family feud, he creates the illusion of light irradiating and finally shattering darkness. First, faintly and remotely anticipating the Capulet feast and its aftermath, we have old Capulet's

At my poor house look to behold this night
Earth-treading stars that make dark heav-
   en light.
                                    [I. ii. 24-5]

A little later we see Romeo as the torch-bearer and hear old Capulet raising his cries (the more impressive because they are widely separated) for 'More lights' [I. v. 27] and 'More torches' [I. v. 125]. But the effect of such torches as these is slight compared with the light-drenched imagery, the contrasts of brightness and darkness, in Romeo's first entranced vision of Juliet:

O, she doth teach the torches to shine
   bright!
It seems she hangs upon the cheek of
   night
Like a rich jewel in an Ethiop's ear . . .
So shows a snowy dove trooping with
   crows.
                                    [I. v. 44-8]

This brilliant radiance of imagery completely floods the following scene, so that the darkness of night is utterly negated. In this scene, apart from the incidental images of the moon and the lightning, there are the sustained images of Romeo's magnificent opening speeches. First Juliet is the dazzling sun of dawn—then two brilliant stars—then his 'bright angel' [II. ii. 26],

As glorious to this night, being o'er my
   head,
As is a winged messenger of heaven

Unto the white-upturned wondering eyes
Of mortals.
                                    [II. ii. 27-30]

As he leaves, assured of her love, day begins to break, and the image of it is memorably fixed for us by the vivid opening lines of Friar Lawrence's soliloquy:

The grey-eyed morn smiles on the frowning night,
Chequering the eastern clouds with
   streaks of light;
And flecked darkness like a drunkard
   reels
From forth day's path and Titan's fiery
   wheels.
                                    [II. iii. 1-4]

The central image of this passage, of dark-dispersing sunlight, is repeated a little later by Juliet:

Love's   heralds   should   be
   thoughts,
Which ten times faster glide than the
   sun's beams
Driving back shadows over louring hills.
                                    [II. v. 4-6]

The second movement of the play consists of a violent recrudescence of the Capulet-Montague feud, leading to bloodshed, in which the lovers are whirled helplessly apart: 'black fate' suddenly overshadows the bright day of love and sunshine. This development, too, is partly suggested by the imagery, through the invocation of night and darkness, especially in Juliet's soliloquy in the orchard. Here, because of its echoes and lyrical fervour, her speech reminds us of Romeo's rhapsody at the opening of the Balcony scene; but where Romeo's words had been drenched with images of light, Juliet's are, in contrast, sombre and portentous with images of darkness:

      such a waggoner
As Phaethaon would whip you to the west,
And bring in cloudy night immediately.
Spread thy close curtain, love-performing
   night. . . .

      Come, civil night,
Thou   sober-suited   matron,   all   in
   black. . . .

Hood my unmann'd blood, bating in my
   cheeks,
With thy black mantle. . . .

Come, gentle night, come, loving, black-
   browed night.
                        [III. ii. 2-5, 10-11, 14-15, 20]

The wonderful aubade [a song of lovers parting at dawn] of Act III, Scene v, also turns on the lovers' desperate longing for the continuance of the night and darkness, and though in both instances the imagery derives to some extent from the situation since Juliet wants the night to come because it will bring Romeo, and daybreak is feared because it spells separation, the insistence on this wish for darkness, with its reiterated images, has the effect of emphasizing the precariousness, the desperation, and—circumstances being what they are—the unnaturalness of Romeo and Juliet's love. Their love cannot—which is the mark of its doom—exist in the sun, its natural element; and something of this contradiction is brought out by the paradox of Romeo's line

> More light and light; more dark and dark
>   our woes!
>
>   [III. v. 36]

The climax of the play takes place in darkness, the darkness of night, the tomb, and—for we cannot fail to sense his presence—of black, shadow-casting Death. Once again the darkness is challenged and momentarily broken by the small, flickering light of torches; and the torch image instantly recalls the Romeo who first went through the night to Juliet as a torchbearer. But this time darkness is triumphant, and even the dawning day is ominously overcast:

> A glooming peace this morning with it
>   brings;
> The sun, for sorrow, will not show his
>   head.
>
>   [V. iii. 305-06]

Yet light and the love of which it is the symbol are not completely extinguished, even in the catastrophe. A faint radiance lingers. In Juliet's memory there is to be raised a shining statue—'in pure gold' [V. iii. 299]. (pp. 123-26)

> *E. C. Pettet, "The Imagery of 'Romeo and Juliet'," in* English, *Vol. VIII, No. 45, Autumn, 1950, pp. 121-26.*

C. Webster Wheelock

[*Wheelock cites numerous passages in support of his theory that the paradoxical blending of sexual love and death is the central theme in* Romeo and Juliet. *(A paradox is a statement which while seemingly contradictory or absurd may actually be well-founded and true.) Wheelock's essay is written in a humorous vein and is structured as a conversation between himself and Shakespeare in an English tavern in 1598.*]

The figure who filled the doorway of the Mermaid Tavern wasn't the man I'd been expecting. Since I don't teach Ben Jonson's poetry to my high school students, I'd calculated that an evening spent with the dapper, rather acerbic chief of the famous "tribe of Ben" would be social: no business talk, just good wit and good ale. But this fellow now crowding up against my table in the corner snug still carried the surprised look of the countryside on him, something I would not have anticipated for 1598.

He surprised me with the rough edge to his speech, a kind of midlands burr which I won't be able to duplicate in recollecting all he said that night. He broke the awkward silence.

"I came over from the Boar's Head because I heard that one of you teaching types from the far future was around. You the man I'm after?"

I confessed that I must be the one, but that all I'd wanted was a quiet evening of talk, some drinks, no trouble.

"I've just come from a performance of my *Romeo,*" he said, "and what beats me is that nobody up in the galleries seems to understand the thing, or not hardly, at all. I know that I took some chances with it, upset the usual business they're looking for in comedies, but you'd think that all of that grotesque image-making would've smoked out my meaning, wouldn't you?"

"Be plain, good son, and homely in thy drift" [II. iii. 55], I ventured.

"You know the piece? You teach it to young people, too?" he asked. "Then maybe you can help. The young don't turn a deaf ear to what *really* interests them. Mine don't, at any rate; yours, too? Here, let me get you another of those pints. Stay put. You've got some thirsty listening to do, my friend. I don't begrudge a tuppence or two for a pair of good ears."

I sipped appreciatively at the dark-brown, vaguely sweet liquor in the fresh glass before me.

"We both know what the young people are interested in most of all. Well, I thought to give it them in my story from Verona. The trouble is, though, I know their elders wanted a wordplay at least as much as, shall we say, swordplay—if you take my meaning—so I let out all the stops. I did too good a job with all that light and fire imagery, and everybody thinks that all I was after was what you might call the ardor of young love. Damn! Somebody is even supposed to have counted 80 or 90 images of fire or light or astral bodies, all sorts, which adds up to 'the beauty of young love.' Except that nobody seems to have noticed who my main, my triumphant lover really *is* in the play. Maybe it was too grotesque an idea to begin with."

"Look, Will—I may call you Will, mayn't I?—what are you driving at? What is it about *Romeo and Juliet* that disappoints you? Now you've gotten me curious."

"All right. Since you seem to know the play well enough, I'm going to throw a few quotations at you, like an exercise we go through with our prompt books. Let's begin with one of our erotic puns, since that's where my weirdest idea came from anyway. I think you still use, in your time, the old verb, 'to die' to mean the little death, a sexual climax, isn't it so? Well, I started from there, since I was going to be using other bawdy slang to keep the groundlings amused, and I came up with the idea that Death—I mean in person, as a spectral figure—would have to come into my comedy of young lovers and, finally, replace Romeo as the physical lover of darling Juliet. Not on stage, of course, but in the minds of the characters, all of them, young and old. So I started putting in clues in the most incongruous places I could find so that they'd be noticed."

"Wait a minute, Will. You say you made Death the lover of Juliet: actually I *do* remember that, from the final scene in the Capulet tomb. I was a bit shocked at the idea, I'll admit, but that late in the play I didn't really pay too much attention. Let me remember. Romeo says to Juliet,

> Shall I believe
> That unsubstantial Death is amorous
> And that the lean abhorred monster keeps
> Thee here in dark to be his paramour?
> [V. iii. 102-05]

Then he drinks the apothecary's poison."

"Yes, but didn't you notice, before that, all the times I linked death with having sex? And didn't you pick up the *oxymoronic* nature of the young lovers' reality? Why, I brought Romeo onstage for the first time spouting absolute rot as the first clue: 'Feather of lead, bright smoke, cold fire, sick health,' etc. [I. i. 180]. Juliet, too, although she had better reason to be distracted and babbling after hearing Romeo had skewered her cousin Tybalt, she was given her share of oxymoronic nonsense. 'Dove-feathered raven! wolvish-ravening lamb! . . . A Damnèd saint, an honorable villain!' [III. ii. 76, 79]."

"That's right. 'Just opposite to what thou justly seem'st' [III. ii. 78]. She was indicting Romeo for blowing their whole scene, just when it seemed that they might have a chance to get their parents to come around."

"Right, my teacher friend. The oxymoron—the yoking of two contraries, two apparently contradictory ideas—rules my play from almost the start. And the main oxymoron is the linkage of death and sexual love—just as in the pun, remember? I intended to have Juliet stop the whole scene at the end of the Capulet dance, after she's fallen for the masked boy in tights, when she asks her nurse for Romeo's name:

> Go ask his name.—If he is married,
> My grave is like to be my wedding bed.
> [I. v. 134-35]

Maybe you didn't pick that one up because it was so short—and everybody likes the lovers' doing their sonnet together just before that. Well, look again: 'my *grave* my wedding bed.' This from a smitten 13-year old?"

"Okay. I see that better now. And I remember that Romeo had a premonition just before crashing the party: we say that we feel someone walking across our grave—it's a kind of chill. But did you put in any longer hints than Juliet's one-liner?"

"Here, let's fill that up again . . .

"What did you ask? Oh, yes. Do you recollect when Juliet is waiting for her wedding night and doesn't know yet that the two young hotheads have been killed on the streets? Listen to what she says. She goes on for a while with some delicious puns on night/knight and so forth ('Come, gentle night; come, loving, black-browed night' [III. ii. 20]). Hah! And then she switches terms as abruptly as I could make it; really, it's a shocking incongruity if you think about it.

> Give me my Romeo; and, when he shall die,
> Take him and cut him out in little stars,
> And he will make the face of heaven so fine.
> [III. ii. 21-3]

and so forth. Die? Cut him out in little bits? Unless you're buying oranges or something, you've got to be hit by this little bride, dreaming about the bliss of her first night with Romeo, suddenly seeing him dead and scattered about in little pieces. What sort of sense does that make? Unless you go back to my fundamental pun, my oxymoronic double entendre, you're going to have a certain amount of trouble with that one, eh?"

"Yeah, and not long afterwards Juliet does it again, if I remember. She finds out about the killings of Mercutio and Tybalt and that her groom of only hours has been banished, and she says to the nurse (who's too dim to pick it up, anyway), 'come, nurse. I'll to my wedding bed; / And death, not Romeo, take my maidenhead!' [III. ii. 136-37]. Am I right?"

"Good on you. That's right, and the next time I used what I call my love-death theme was something of a con. I put it in the mouth of a character who didn't mean what she was saying, and whom as a consequence you couldn't really believe at the time. Recall that when Lady C., who doesn't know what *you* do—that Juliet *can't* marry him—encounters opposition from her daughter to the proposal that she wed that man of wax, Paris, she turns to her husband in exasperation and seems to curse Juliet grotesquely: 'I would the fool were married to her grave!' [III. v. 140]. Not 'I would the fool were dead,' mind you, but *married* to her death. Note that. Then in the same scene poor Juliet's reply completes the curse:

> Delay this marriage (to Paris) for a month, a week;
> Or if you do not, make the bridal bed
> In that dim monument where Tybalt lies.
> [III. v. 199-201]

Or, as the bewildered bride somewhat later directs, having desperately resolved to dissemble death with the help of Friar Lawrence's drug, 'Or bid me go into a new-made grave / And hide me with a dead man in his shroud' [IV. i. 84-5]. An ugly image for any youngster to dream up and utter, isn't it? I had to take a chance on that grotesqueness because I was setting up my big dress-rehearsal scene for the actual deaths of both youngsters in the Capulets' tomb."

"Which is that, the dress rehearsal?"

"When Juliet is found by her parents, and thought to be dead, I produce a kind of ritual mourning sequence—from father to fiancé to Mom to nurse and round again—which I don't suppose you in your laconic times could be expected to appreciate. It probably even sounds humorous to you, but the thing to look out for is that image of Death returning as Juliet's partner in sex: my grotesque linking of what should be life-producing and exalting with its opposite, in mortuary decay. The foolish old father starts things up (and if you still believe that puns have to be entertaining and amusing, listen in), in such a way that not even the gentility could miss it.

> O son, the night before thy wedding day
> Hath Death lain with thy wife. There she lies,
> Flower as she was, deflowered by him.
> Death is my son-in-law, Death is my heir;
> My daughter he hath wedded."
>
> [IV. v. 35-9]

"Now I see the significance of the speech that old Capulet made just before that. It's sexual again, isn't it? 'Death lies on her like an untimely frost / Upon the sweetest flower of all the field' [IV. v. 28-9]. Poor Juliet. So *this* was the rehearsal for the actual death scene between our lovers, you say?"

"That's so, but don't leave the fake-death quite so fast, good friend. If you listen closely, you'll hear the culminating oxymoron in my whole play, coming from the unlikely source of the old gaffer's mouth":

> All things that we ordained festival
> Turn from their office to black funeral—
> Our instruments to melancholy bells,
> Our wedding cheer to a sad burial feast . . .
> Our bridal flowers serve for a buried corpse;
> And all things change them to the contrary.
>
> [IV. v. 84-7, 89-90]

There you have it: *and all things change them to the contrary.* Can you think of a more succinct description of my play? The flames of sex turn to the ashes of death. My oxymorons would have made my old grammar school instructor in rhetoric proud of me. But I've gone beyond my oxymoronic device to a kind of macabre reality in these two young people's lives, notice. I've given them destinies in which the very seeds of their physical at-traction to each other (and observe that Juliet hasn't even seen Romeo's face clearly until they meet to marry in Lawrence's cell: just his 'gracious self,' in becoming hose) are all along ripening to their blighted, inevitable climax together in that tomb. The big death grows inexorably from out of the little death that we spoke of when I first joined you at this pleasant table. And by now you certainly ought to recognize that not all of my puns are for laughter among the penny-admissions."

"All right, so when Romeo is about to buy the poison and says 'Well, Juliet, I will lie with thee tonight' [V. i. 34], he, too, like her—but unlike her mother and evidently many in your audience—has come to understand the inextricable blending of sex and death in their story."

"Yes, precisely. And you can point out to your classes that there really couldn't be a more appropriate ending to my love-death drama than Juliet's reaching there to kiss the poison she prays remains on Romeo's just-stilled lips. 'Haply some poison yet doth hang on them' she hopes [V. iii. 165], and Death can now take them both—my famous youthful lovers—into his eternal embrace. I've made a special sort of tragedy out of the very materials of comedy, don't you see? They die, and then they die."

"Just think of it! Those kids of yours met at the Sunday dinner-dance and were dead in each other's arms by Thursday midnight. Four brief days in which they hardly had time to be wedded and bedded, much less get to *know* each other—except in the Bible's sense. Not so much 'love in terms of purity and innocence' as sentimental old-sters would like to think [in the Pelican Shakespeare edition of *Romeo and Juliet*], was there, Will? For that matter, both the compactness and the raciness of the action put me in mind a few years back of the limerick, a verse form that we speakers of English invented after your day but which you would've found delightful. Since the first half of your play, up to the sudden death of Mercutio, is like one super limerick, an unending series of bawdy jokes using sexual slang and double entendre, I've encouraged students to write limericks on what's going on, according to their perceptions, in Romeo and Juliet. I find that I get some pretty honest and pretty good ones."

"I'll need an exemplum, since I don't know the form of this limerick as you call it."

"It's hard to remember a limerick verbatim when you've been drinking (unlike everyday dirty jokes, which are almost all content and no form), but I think I can give you the idea with one or two here. Let's see:

> There once were a couple of teens
> Who aspired to commingle their genes
> But, in trying to mate,
> Were the victims of fate

And succumbed in the saddest of scenes.

Some of my students really pick up on the punning side of your poetry, Will, which I figured would please you. They miss being as nimble-witted as Mercutio, of course, but that also means that they truly miss *him* as a character once he's gone from the play—miss his ribald intelligence, which they've been learning how to listen for.

> At the Friar's the kids tie the knot,
> And it puts Juliet on the spot:
> Will the feuders unite,
> Or continue to fight—
> And is Romeo coming, or not?
>
> Because Tybalt, her cousin, was dead
> And her Romeo now banished,
> Juliet could have cried
> That her lover had died,
> But she kept, after losing, her head.

Well, we've been enjoying ourselves, as you can see. And the students turn out to have been right all along about Juliet and her teenage boyfriend, whom she helps to become a man, as they say, overnight. 'Stand, and you be a man. / For Juliet's sake, for her sake, rise and stand!' [III. iii. 88-9], as the nurse so happily puts it. Now, *there's* a woman! Why, when . . .

"Oh, you have to be on your way: no time for another round? That's too bad; I've enjoyed your compa-

Olivia Hussey as Juliet and Leonard Whiting as Romeo in Franco Zeffirelli's 1968 film adaptation of the tragedy. Act V, scene iii.

ny. Well, thanks, and I'll be, uh, hearing you around." (pp. 70-3)

> *C. Webster Wheelock, " 'Not Life, but Love in Death': Oxymoron at the Thematic Heart of 'Romeo and Juliet'," in* English Journal, *Vol. 74, No. 2, February, 1985, pp. 70-3.*

ROMEO AND JULIET

Clifford Leech

[*Leech views* **Romeo** *and* **Juliet's** *love as a maturing experience for the hero and heroine and demonstrates how the development of their language, in particular, marks their entry into adulthood. Although the critic notes several humorous elements in the couple's declarations of love, he points out that they also frequently speak with authority, suggesting the seriousness of their commitment to one another. In Leech's opinion,* **Juliet's** *language displays both her inexperience and her newfound maturity as she struggles to find images to express her love for* **Romeo.** *Her maturation is more pronounced than* **Romeo's,** *the critic asserts:* **Juliet's** *language firmly establishes her adult status in Act III, and it is not until Act V that* **Romeo's** *language approaches hers in terms of maturity. For further commentary on the characters of* **Romeo** *and* **Juliet,** *see the excerpts by Douglas Cole, Lorentz Eckhoff, Harold S. Wilson, Irving Ribner, Franklin M. Dickey, G. H. Durrant, Mark Van Doren, Leonora Leet Brodwin, E. C. Pettet, C. Webster Wheelock, Alice Shalvi, and Martin Stevens.*]

Romeo and Juliet has proved a problem for Shakespeare critics. Franklin M. Dickey [see excerpt in section on Tragic Design] has seen it as exhibiting a simple moral lesson: to be taken up wholly by one's passion for another human being would, he argues, be seen by an Elizabethan as a moral imperfection, as likely to induce a general disregard of the moral law: so Shakespeare's play, despite its sympathy with the lovers, must be seen in relation to the contemporary idea of moral responsibility. But to argue in this way is to take *Romeo and Juliet* as Roy Battenhouse has taken [Christopher] Marlowe's *Tamburlaine* [in his *Marlowe's Tamburlaine: A Study in Renaissance Moral Philosophy*]: Battenhouse tries to disregard the grandeur that goes along with the evil in Marlowe's hero; Dickey misses the sense of an enhanced degree of life which Shakespeare's lovers experience along with the danger they freely encounter. Nicholas Brooke is aware of the problem that faced Shakespeare: he suggests that the love of life Romeo and Juliet is tested against the presentation of the normal current of life, which is indeed strong in the play, and that this love just—and only just—makes itself acceptable as an achieved good [*Shake-speare's Early Tragedies*]. Indeed, when we remember the likely date of Shakespeare's play, we shall not be surprised at this. In *Love's Labour's Lost* he had made fun of the devotion that the King of Navarre and his three lords had manifested to the Princess of France and her three ladies: the men are made to endure a year-long penance, and Berowne's required sojourn in a hospital is, Berowne himself recognizes, almost an impossible demand. Can love outlast the waiting-time? Can it be related to the agony of the sick and the dying? In any event it must, the ending of the play suggests, be put into a total context, not being capable of replacing that context. In *The Two Gentlemen of Verona* love is juxtaposed with the idea of friendship, which, being as it was alleged purely altruistic, had a high standing indeed in the Renaissance, and love was there mocked through the figures of Launce and Speed, who took a more commonplace view of relations between the sexes. At the end it is the sympathetically opportunistic Julia who gets things straightened out. If the heroic lover and friend Valentine had been solely in charge of the play's termination, only disaster would have been possible. In writing a play in which the love of a young man and a young woman was to be considered a proper motive for tragedy, Shakespeare was bound to draw on his earlier treatments of love in comedy, but he would need to make a major departure too.

Certainly there is plenty of comedy here. Were it not for the declaration of the Prologue, with its references to "star-cross'd lovers" [l. 6] and to the ending of the feud through their deaths, we might well take the first two acts as moving toward a fortunate issue for the young people. The atmosphere is here generally one of pleasurable excitement, although Shakespeare has given Juliet a moment of premonition in the first balcony scene:

> Although I joy in thee,
> I have no joy in this contract to-night.
> It is too rash, too unadvis'd, too sudden;
> Too like the lightning, which doth cease to
>   be
> Ere one can say 'It lightens.'
>
> [II. ii. 116-20]

More of such premonitions will be noted later. But, until the moment when Mercutio is killed, the threat is not anywhere heavy. When Romeo and Juliet declare their love, there are moments of pure comedy. Thus Romeo compares himself to a schoolboy, reluctant to go to his books as Romeo is reluctant to leave Juliet: "Love goes toward love as schoolboys from their books; / But love from love, toward school with heavy looks" [II. ii. 156-57]. And there is a touch of absurdity, which we shall applaud when we remember what we all have done in distantly comparable circumstances, when Juliet says she has forgotten why she called him back, and he says he is ready to stay till she remembers:

> *Jul.* I have forgot why I did call thee back.
> *Rom.* Let me stand here till thou remember it.
> *Jul.* I shall forget, to have thee still stand there,
> Rememb'ring how I love thy company.
> *Rom.* And I'll still stay, to have thee still forget,
> Forgetting any other home but this.
>
> [II. ii. 170-75]

We may remember too that Romeo has wished to be the glove on Juliet's hand, a mildly ludicrous idea, and that both lovers would like Romeo to be Juliet's pet bird:

> *Jul.* Tis almost morning. I would have thee gone—
> And yet no farther than a wanton's bird,
> That lets it hop a little from her hand,
> Like a poor prisoner in his twisted gyves.
> And with a silk thread plucks it back again,
> So loving-jealous of his liberty.
> *Rom.* I would I were thy bird.
> *Jul.*   Sweet, so would I.
> Yet I should kill thee with much cherishing.
>
> [II. ii. 176-83]

They will speak differently in the second balcony scene, but even there they will only dimly apprehend the world that threatens them.

Before this, of course, Romeo had been almost totally a figure of fun when he was giving voice to his love for Rosaline, and after meeting Juliet he is in a situation of some embarrassment when he goes to tell the Friar of his new love and of his wish for a secret marriage. When he admits that he has not been in his bed during the night that has just passed, he has to hear the Friar exclaim "God pardon sin! Wast thou with Rosaline?" [II. iii. 44], and there is a particularly ludicrous touch when the Friar claims to see on Romeo's cheek a tear shed for Rosaline's love and not yet washed off. Even so, Shakespeare makes it plain that the new love is a thing of true moment. This is made evident not only in the authority of language that the lovers are sometimes allowed, during their interchange of words at their first meeting in the Capulet house and in the first balcony scene, but also in Romeo's premonition of disaster when he is on his way to the first meeting:

>   my mind misgives
> Some consequences, yet hanging in the stars,
> Shall bitterly begin his fearful date
> With this night's revels and expire the term
> Of a despised life, clos'd in my breast,
> By some vile forfeit of untimely death.
> But he that hath the steerage of my course
> Direct my sail! On, lusty gentlemen!
>
> [I. iv. 106-13]

Because we have hints enough that disaster lies ahead, we cannot see the love merely in terms of comedy.

Moreover, Romeo's behavior when he meets Mercutio and Benvolio again after he has talked with the Friar shows him as a young man ready to cope with danger for his love's sake and also ready, as now an adult lover, to give over affectation and to feel able to parry Mercutio's jests. Then, after the marriage, he has dignity both in his first refusal to fight with Tybalt, his new kinsman, and in his entering into the fray because he has by ill luck been responsible for Mercutio's death. At least, it may at first seem like ill luck, but we are made to see that Romeo's refusal to fight, Mercutio's indignation, and Romeo's revenge for his friend's death all arise, by necessity or at least probability, out of the nature of the characters and their situation in Verona. "O, I am fortune's fool!" [III. i. 136]—Romeo's cry after Tybalt's death—is comment enough on his inability to cope with the situation engendered by the feud, which previously he had been overconfident about. How precarious is his hold on his new adult status is underlined in the scene in the Friar's cell, where his love is expressed again in ludicrous terms:

> More validity,
> More honourable state, more courtship lives
> In carrion flies than Romeo. They may seize
> On the white wonder of dear Juliet's hand
> And steal immortal blessing from her lips,
> Who, even in pure and vestal modesty,
> Still blush, as thinking their own kisses sin;
> But Romeo may not—he is banished.
> This may flies do, when I from this must fly;
> They are free men, but I am banished.
> [III. iii. 33-42]

The poor girl, with those flies on her hand and lips; those lips, so beautifully red because they are kissing each other; that shocking pun of "flies" and "fly": Romeo had uttered no more immature lines when the thought of Rosaline was on him. His extravagance here is similar to that of Valentine in *The Two Gentlemen of Verona,* who was similarly banished from the town where Silvia lived. And the mocker or rebuker is present with both: Launce the clown makes fun of Valentine; Romeo is described by the Friar as "with his own tears made drunk" [III. iii. 83]. He will recover dignity before the play's end, but he has lost hold of it here.

Juliet, on the other hand, has not Romeo's initial disadvantage of a previous, and ludicrous, love-attachment. We see her first as the dutiful daughter, ready to prepare herself to fall in love with Paris, as her parents would like her to. But Romeo is her first true commitment, and if she expresses

herself comically at times in the first balcony scene, that is only a reminder of her extreme youth. And she is much more practical than he is: it is she who suggests how the wedding shall be arranged. Shakespeare has, moreover, given two almost parallel scenes in which she is the central figure: II. v, when she awaits the Nurse's return from her mission to Romeo, and III. ii, when she is looking forward to the coming wedding night. In both instances we have first a soliloquy from Juliet, expressing impatience that time goes for her so slowly, then the Nurse entering and delaying the news she has to give, and finally the Nurse's assurance that things after all will be well. But the differences between the scenes are remarkable. The news that the Nurse withholds is good in the first instance: everything is in order for the secret wedding. In the second instance it is bad news: Tybalt is dead and Romeo banished. The Nurse's delay, moreover, is a matter of teasing in the first scene, the result of incoherent grief in the second. And, although at the end of the second scene the Nurse promises to find Romeo and bring him to comfort Juliet, there is now true darkness here. Act II, scene v ended with Juliet's cry "Hie to high fortune! Honest nurse, farewell" [II. v. 78]. The pun is evidence of pure excitement, and we can imagine Juliet giving the Nurse a quick and affectionate embrace as she goes off to her wedding. The second scene ends also with words from the girl: "O, find him! give this ring to my true knight / And bid him come to take his last farewell" [III. ii. 142-43]. The echo of Courtly Love in "true knight" has something forced and pathetic in it, and "last farewell" will prove to be a fact. Now, too, it is the Nurse who goes. Juliet must wait.

Yet in both scenes Juliet's youth is most poignantly brought out. Her impatience in II. v is of course amusing: for the moment we forget the omens, and know that the Nurse will truly impart her good news. And III. ii opens with one of the most famous speeches in the play, Juliet's soliloquy beginning "Gallop apace, you fiery-footed steeds. / Towards Phoebus' lodging!" [III. ii. 1ff.]. Here we find Juliet trying out image after image to give appropriate expression to her love, her desire to be wholly at one with Romeo. There is an overelaborateness in her invocation of Phoebus and Phaeton, of the "sober-suited matron," "civil night" ("civil" because she gives privacy to her citizens), who will teach Juliet "how to lose a winning match, / Play'd for a pair of stainless maidenhoods"/; there is a playing with the idea of contrast when she sees Romeo as lying "upon the wings of night / Whiter than new snow upon a raven's back"; and she reaches a grotesque extravagance in the famous lines:

> Give me my Romeo; and, when he shall die,
> Take him and cut him out in little stars,
> And he will make the face of heaven so fine

> That all the world will be in love with
>   night
> And pay no worship to the garish sun.
>   [III. ii. 21-5]

The extravagance is, of course, understandable: we do not have to forgive it. Juliet has seen Romeo only at night: she will never see him by daylight, except for the brief moment of their wedding and that half-light of dawn in the second balcony scene. So she can reject the "garish sun" that has never shone on them out of doors. Something more mature immediately follows: "O, I have bought the mansion of a love, / But not possess'd it; and though I am sold, / Not yet enjoy'd" [III. ii. 26-8]. . . . The change of sex is interesting here: Juliet knows that the man is possessed by the woman while he merely penetrates her. Yet we still feel that this inexperienced girl is straining after an appropriate image, trying to be more "grown-up" than she really is. Suddenly the speech ends with an image wholly fitting this character who so recently was herself a child:

> So tedious is this day
> As is the night before some festival
> To an impatient child that hath new robes
> And may not wear them.
>   [III. ii. 28-31]

She is no longer a child, but her childhood memory is here linked with the new experience. Because the memory is now only a memory (yet a vivid one), because Romeo's body will be so startlingly her new clothes (Donne said: "What needst thou have more covering than a man," Elegy XIX), she is using this image from childhood grows suddenly mature as we hear her speak. It will take a good deal longer for Romeo to produce any comparable utterance. Doubtless Shakespeare realized that he had gone further with the girl than with the boy: it was convenient therefore to give the whole of act IV to her concerns, Romeo leaving for Mantua before act III is over and not entering the play again till act V begins. (pp. 61-6)

In act V of *Romeo and Juliet* Romeo at once shows signs of a new status. His response to the false news of Juliet's death has a directness very different from his behavior in the Friar's cell when he was lamenting his banishment: "Is it e'en so? That I defy you stars!" [V. i. 24]. And he at once gives directions to Balthasar on the journey he plans to Verona and Juliet's tomb. Of course, he could have explored the matter more fully. It occurs to him to ask if no letters from the Friar have come with Balthasar, but when he receives a negative answer his "No matter. Get thee gone / And hire those horses" [V. i. 32-3] shows the rashness we have seen in him throughout. Left alone, with the desire for poison in his mind, he turns his attention to the apothecary's shop and to the situation of poor men. This is psychologically true, for in a moment of anguish we naturally tend to take refuge in a thought of something other than a demand that is immediately on us. After that, Romeo's recognition that the gold he gives is a worse poison than the one he buys is largely a Renaissance commonplace, but the eloquence with which he expresses it gives him an authority he has previously lacked:

> There is thy gold—worse poison to men's
>   souls,
> Doing more murther in this loathsome
>   world,
> Than these poor compounds that thou
>   mayst not sell.
> I sell thee poison; thou hast sold me none.
> Farewell. Buy food and get thyself in flesh.
>   [V. i. 80-4]

Earlier Romeo had to face the distinction between "loving" and "doting" [II. iii. 82] that the Friar insisted on: the young man "doted" on Rosaline, which the Friar could not approve, and he must love Juliet "moderately" [II. vi. 14]. Yet of course he did not follow the Friar's advice, though he thought that his love for Juliet was something the Friar could understand. Shakespeare suggests another distinction between love and love: the kind you simply like to maunder over, the kind that ultimately commits you. We do not, as Romeo does, usually kill ourselves for love, but we remember to the end a girl that truly mattered. The utterances from the sympathetic Friar, who thinks the Capulet-Montague feud may come to peace through the marriage, are an echo of the church's view of love in the Middle Ages. The total commitment to another person is, we have seen, in that view a dangerous thing if not kept properly subordinate to one's love of God. Romeo cannot follow the Friar in this: he is so totally committed to Juliet that he will kill himself in her tomb. There is indeed a threefold presentation of love here, not a dichotomy: there is the affected, superficial concern with Rosaline, there is the fatal commitment to Juliet, and there is the "moderation" counseled by the Friar and illustrated in the play's older married couples. Shakespeare gives utterance to the church's counsel, neither endorsing nor rejecting it. If the play's lovers could have lived, some different things would have conditioned their relations to each other perhaps they were lucky to avoid it. (pp. 67-8)

> *Clifford Leech, "The Moral Tragedy of 'Romeo and Juliet'," in* English Renaissance Drama: Essays in Honor of Madeline Doran & Mark Eccles, *Standish Henning, Robert Kimbrough, and Richard Knowles, eds., Southern Illinois University Press, 1976, pp. 59-75.*

Alice Shalvi

[*Shalvi asserts that although* Romeo and Juliet *appears to be a tragedy of fate in which the protagonists are "helpless, innocent victims of arbitrary powers," the play can be more prop-*

erly regarded as a tragedy of character. In the critic's opinion, Shakespeare designed the tragic outcome to be the result of the lovers' "passionate rashness," and particularly Romeo's "passionate nature and his lack of moderation." Noting that Elizabethans considered moderation essential to balancing one's passion and maintaining one's rational senses, Shalvi discusses Romeo's failed attempt to follow this course after his marriage to Juliet. Once he abandons restraint and avenges Mercutio's death by killing Tybalt, the critic observes, he is governed by passionate recklessness throughout the rest of the play. As a result, Romeo's "lack of moderation, the readiness with which he succumbs to all forms of passion, his failure to guide and protect his young wife, bring both of them to their untimely death." Despite Romeo's flawed nature, Shalvi continues, both he and Juliet have our full sympathy, for their experience ultimately conveys the beauty and sincerity of young love. For further commentary on the characters of Romeo and Juliet, see the excerpts by Douglas Cole, Lorentz Eckhoff, Harold S. Wilson, Irving Ribner, Franklin M. Dickey, G. H. Durrant, Mark Van Doren, Leonora Leet Brodwin, E. C. Pettet, C. Webster Wheelock, Clifford Leech, and Martin Stevens.]

[*Romeo and Juliet*] appears to be a tragedy of fate, showing its protagonists as the helpless, innocent victims of arbitrary powers. Several incidents in the play contribute to this impression. The Prologue refers to 'a pair of star-crossed lovers' [Prologue, 6]. Romeo's misgivings, aroused in him by an ominous dream, are not wholly dismissed by his friends' jesting mockery as they urge him on to the feast at the house of Capulet. Intuitively he fears the outcome of the evening's adventures:

> my mind misgives
> Some consequences yet hanging in the stars
> Shall bitterly begin his fearful date
> With this night's revels and expire the term
> Of a despised life closed in my breast
> By some vile forfeit of untimely death.
> But He, that hath the steerage of my course,
> Direct my sail!
>
> [I. iv. 106-13]

Explicitly, Romeo surrenders himself to the guidance of God and the imagery which he employs stresses his view of himself as entirely helpless in determining his own destiny. So, when his awkward attempt to intervene in the fight between Tybalt and Mercutio leads to the fatal wounding of his friend, Romeo despondently asserts 'I thought all for the best' [III. i. 104]; the implication is that man's motives and plans fail to bring about the desired end where Fate decrees otherwise. After he has killed Tybalt, Romeo refers to himself as 'fortune's fool', the helpless victim and plaything of

Fortune, and after killing Paris he speaks of both himself and his victim as being 'writ in sour misfortune's book' [V. iii. 82]. Finally, Romeo refers to suicide as the shaking off of 'the yoke of inauspicious stars' [V. iii. 111].

Indeed, an inimical Fate does seem to guide the lovers' lives. It is by unhappy chance that Romeo happens to meet Tybalt and it is unfortunate that his movement to part the duelists results in Mercutio's being wounded. It is unfortunate that old Capulet decides to move Juliet's marriage to Paris forward by one day, thereby making it necessary for her to take Friar Laurence's potion a day earlier and thus shortening the time allowed for bringing Romeo news of the Friar's plan. It is by chance that the Friar's messenger is delayed by the plague while Romeo's own servant reaches Mantua safely to report the supposed death of Juliet. It is unfortunate that Romeo finds Paris at Juliet's tomb, that Friar Laurence trips over the tombstone and arrives too late to prevent Romeo's suicide by revealing the truth. It is unfortunate that the Friar leaves Juliet alone in the tomb upon her awakening, thus giving here the opportunity to kill herself. Fate or Chance do seem to have a hand in determining what happens to these two young lovers and we may well find ourselves futilely wishing 'If only . . . , if only . . . '

But not only Fate determines the events and outcome of the play. It is noteworthy that in adapting his plot from *The Tragical History of Romeo and Juliet,* a poem by Arthur Brooke published in 1562, the major change that Shakespeare made was drastically to reduce the duration-time of the action from two months to *five days.* Shakespeare takes great care to impress the speed and swiftness of the action upon his audience and he does this in two ways. Firstly, the days of the week are several times mentioned, so that we may never for one moment forget how quickly the lovers fall in love, marry and are forever parted. The play opens on a Sunday and that same evening Romeo, hitherto infatuated by the fair Rosaline, meets Juliet at the Capulets' ball. Their love is instant and mutual and before dawn they are betrothed. The next morning, Monday, the Nurse comes to Romeo at 9 o'clock and by her he sends word to Juliet, bidding her meet him that same afternoon at the cell of Friar Laurence. Here they are secretly married and on his way home from the ceremony Romeo becomes involved in the quarrel with Tybalt. Having killed Juliet's cousin. Romeo flees to his father-confessor, Friar Laurence, and it is at the Friar's cell that the nurse finds him and bids him come to Juliet that night—their wedding night. The next morning, Tuesday, Romeo leaves for Mantua and Juliet's parents tell her that she must marry her suitor Paris on Thursday or else be turned out of their house. She seeks for counsel in her dilemma from the Friar, who gives her a potion that, if taken on Wednesday evening, will enable her to feign death until Friday, by which time he will have sent for Romeo to take her in secret to Mantua, there to await the pardon of the Prince of Verona. Juliet is so much cheered by the Friar's plan that she returns home, blithe and gay, to consent to the proposed marriage with Paris. Her change of mood so overjoys her father that he moves the wedding forward to Wednesday and Juliet therefore has to drink the potion on Tuesday evening, waking up on Thursday. Meanwhile the Friar's messenger to Romeo is delayed and he hurries off to smuggle Juliet away, not knowing that Romeo, believing his wife dead, has himself hastened back to Verona. On Thursday night—four days after their first meeting—the two lovers are united in death.

The swiftness of the action is emphasised by the tremendous mobility facilitated by the open stage of the Elizabethan playhouse, with its several levels permitting incessant movement from one location to another. The action moves from the front of the stage to the curtained recess at the back, from the lower recess to the upper, with such wonderful fluidity and continuity that there need be not a single pause in what the Prologue refers to as 'the two-hours' traffic of our stage' [Prologue, 12].

The whole effect of the play, then—an effect produced both by the plot and by the stagecraft—is of speed, a speed which is itself in accord with the sudden, swift passion that is being enacted before our eyes. What the play describes is a fierce, passionate love that leads the two young lovers to defy the long-standing feud between their houses, a love that leads both of them to death.

Despite the explicit stress on fate, *Romeo and Juliet* is more a tragedy of character than is generally realised. It seems to me that Shakespeare is here showing the tragic outcome to be the consequence of the passionate rashness of the lovers and, particularly, the result of Romeo's passionate nature and his lack of moderation.

At the opening of the play Romeo is deeply in love with Rosaline, but since she has vowed to remain chaste his love is a hopeless one and we find him indulging in the traditional excesses of the forlorn lover: he is melancholy, shuns company, walks in the woods by night and locks himself in his darkened room by day. To cure him of his love his sensible kinsman Benvolio suggests that he attend the Capulet ball in order to see for himself that Rosaline is not the only pretty girl in the world. Romeo accepts the challenge and Benvolio is proved right. No sooner does Romeo see Juliet than he falls in love with her:

> Did my heart love till now? forswear it,
>   sight!
> For I ne'er saw true beauty till this night.
>   [I. v. 52-3]

Overhearing Juliet's soliloquy, as she stands on her balcony after the guests' departure, Romeo learns that his love is requited. It is at this point that the fact of Juliet's youth emerges as so important; she is not yet fourteen and her youth, innocence and naïveté are what emerge most clearly from the famous balcony-scene. Partly because she has no experience of, or desire for, the formal ceremonies of flirtation and courtship, the lovers are contracted even before there has been any wooing. And yet it is the youthful Juliet who has her doubts about the speed of the betrothal:

> I have no joy of this contract to-night:
> It is too rash, too unadvised, too sudden;
> Too like the lightning, which doth cease to
>   be
> Ere one can say 'It lightens.'
>   [II. ii. 117-20]

Romeo, however, seems to have no such fears or presentiments of ill and he hastens off to Friar Laurence to make arrangements for their immediate marriage.

It is now, in Act II, scene iii, that there occurs one of the play's key scenes, a scene which, though it is often excised in modern productions or else performed so as to evoke a response of laughter in the audience, nevertheless affords important clues as to how we are to interpret the play and judge its major protagonists.

Friar Laurence, who has been gathering herbs, comments upon the paradoxical duality of Nature:

> The earth that's nature's mother is her
>   tomb;
> What is her burying grave that is her
>   womb.
>   [II. iii. 9-10]

All the creatures upon the earth are of an equally mixed quality:

> For nought so vile that on the earth doth
>   live
> But to the earth some special good doth
>   give,
> Nor nought so good but strain'd from that
>   fair use
> Revolts from true birth, stumbling on
>   abuse:
>   [II. iii. 17-20]

As an example, he points to one of the flowers in his collection, the scent of which has cordial powers even though to taste of it is fatal. The human parallel is then explicitly stated: grace, the divine power of goodness, and 'rude will', man's natural desire for evil, both exist within man, eternally at war with each other,

> And where the worser is predominant,
> Full soon the canker death eats up that
>   plant.
>   [II. iii. 29-30]

When Romeo bursts in, full of his new tempestuous passion, Friar Laurence's remarks first remind us of the old infatuation for Rosaline, now so startingly and suddenly cast off in favour of a newer love, and then stress the conclusion to be deduced from this change of heart:

> young men's love then lies
> Not truly in their hearts, but in their eyes.
> Jesu Maria, what a deal of brine
> Hath wash'd thy sallow cheeks for Rosaline!
> How much salt water thrown away in waste,
> To season love, that of it doth not taste!
> The sun not yet thy sighs from heaven clears,
> Thy old groans ring yet in my ancient ears;
> Lo, here upon thy cheek the stain doth sit
> Of an old tear that is not wash'd off yet:
> If e'er thou wast thyself and these woes thine,
> Thou and these woes were all for Rosaline:
> And art thou changed? pronounce this sentence then,
> Women may fall, when there's no strength in men.
>
> [II. iii. 67-80]

Nevertheless, aware that an alliance between Romeo and Juliet may bring about a reconciliation between their families, he consents to marry the lovers, only chiding Romeo's 'sudden haste' once more with the warning counsel 'Wisely and slow. They stumble that run fast' [II. iii. 94]. That last line, reminiscent of Juliet's own qualms, should remain in our minds throughout the rest of the play, for the lovers fail to heed the Friar's warning, even though he repeats it in II. vi, where, trying to temper Romeo's almost manic joy, he says:

> These violent delights have violent ends
> And in their triumph die, like fire and powder,
> Which as they kiss consume: the sweetest honey
> Is loathsome in his own deliciousness
> And in the taste confounds the appetite:
> Therefore love moderately; long love doth so;
> Too swift arrives as tardy as too slow.
>
> [II. vi. 9-15]

Moderation is what the wise Friar counsels; moderation, which the Elizabethans considered essential in all of life because it balances the passions and maintains the rule of reason, the rational will which is the divine element in man that distinguishes him from the beasts.

The scene that follows [III. i] stresses the need for moderation in social transactions, switching away from the love of Romeo and Juliet to the family feud which serves as its background. Meeting the quarrelsome Tybalt, Romeo exercises admirable self-control and obstinately refuses to be drawn into a senseless quarrel. But his fiery friend Mercutio, unable to bear such an insult to his friend's honour, challenges Tybalt and is killed. It is then that Romeo decides to dispense with moderation—

and the *decision*, the *choice*, that leads to Romeo's action is explicitly stressed as he says:

> Away to heaven, respective lenity,
> And fire-eyed fury be my conduct now!
>
> [II. i. 123-24]

Romeo explicitly dismisses 'respective levity',— sensible, considerate moderation—and allows himself to be guided by the 'fire and fury' which are associated with Hell. Though it is at this point that he refers to himself as 'fortune's fool', it is precisely here that he has chosen his own course of action, giving way to the angry passion which leads to revenge.

It is by senseless passion that Romeo continues to be ruled. Learning that his sentence is to be banishment rather than death, Romeo is neither grateful nor happy at his prince's mercy. Dismissing 'Adversity's sweet milk, philosophy' [III. iii. 55], he rants and raves in suicidal despair, refusing rationally to consider how his situation may be improved. Again it is the Friar who urges moderation, chiding Romeo's 'womanish' tears and the 'wild acts' which denote the 'unreasonable fury of a beast' [III. iii. 110-11], stressing the grounds for hope and optimism. Though Romeo is temporarily moved to heed the Friar's advice, he remains, essentially, the 'slave of passion', for when he learns of Juliet's supposed death his spontaneous, unreflecting action is to purchase poison and hasten to a romantic death in the arms of his beloved.

The tragic end that befalls the lovers is more the outcome of Romeo's character than the work of a cruel, senseless fate. Romeo's lack of moderation, the readiness with which he succumbs to all forms of passion, his failure to guide and protect his young wife, bring both of them to their untimely death. Just so is it lack of moderation, a senseless pursuit of passion's dictates, that causes the drawn-out family feud, which Shakespeare so brilliantly mocks and satirizes in the opening squabble of the families' servants and in the fiery valour of Tybalt the 'courageous captain of compliments' [II. iv. 20], but the full horror and severe social implication of which he nevertheless brings out in those scenes [I. i; III. ii and V. iii] in which the Prince appears, threatening and reprimanding the culprits. Here, as elsewhere in his plays, Shakespeare sees the lot of the individual in a total social context. To a large extent, the foolish family feud is responsible for the death of the young lovers and the same immoderate passions are responsible both for the feud and for the disastrous outcome of the love-affair. Friar Laurence's hope that the love of Romeo and Juliet will bring peace to their warring parents is fulfilled in all too bitter a manner and 'All are punished' [V. iii. 295].

Despite Romeo's flawed nature, both Romeo and Juliet have our full sympathy. We neither despise nor reject Romeo because of his flaw of passion. It is primarily by conveying the beauty and sincerity of young love that Shakespeare wins over sympathy for the doomed lovers; clearly the lyrical poetry of their exchanges and the intensity of feeling revealed in their final speeches are intended to stress that the love of Romeo and Juliet is not a shallow infatuation like that of Romeo for Rosaline. In fact, it is almost the nature of young love to be as ungoverned by reason as is the love of Romeo and Juliet. But we should not let our sympathy for the lovers blind us to the ultimate moral of the play, to the positive values which Shakespeare here reasserts. And that ultimate moral, here as in others of Shakespeare's plays, is the paramount need for moderation in every aspect of life—the need for man to follow *not* the dictates of his 'rude will' but the dictates of that 'grace', that divine reason, which God has implanted within him. Reason is most easily upset and distracted by love and this is what we see happening in the case of Romeo. It is not the stars that bring about the lovers' death but rather their passion and the passion of their kinsmen—the destructive passions of unreasonable, immoderate, excessive love and equally unreasonable, immoderate and excessive hatred. (pp. 120-26)

Alice Shalvi, "The First Tragedy: 'Romeo and Juliet'," in The World & Art of Shakespeare *by A. A. Mendilow and Alice Shalvi, Israel Universities Press, 1967, pp. 119-26.*

THE NURSE

Harley Granville-Barker

*[Granville-Barker praises the **Nurse** as a well-conceived, rich, and natural character and compares her with Falstaff (in* 1 *and* 2 Henry IV *and* The Merry Wives of Windsor*), one of Shakespeare's greatest comic creations. Remarking on the consistency of the **Nurse's** portrait, the critic notes that all facets of her personality fall into perspective at III. v. 212-17 when she advises **Juliet** to marry **Paris** and forget **Romeo**. For further commentary on the **Nurse's** character, see the excerpts by Mark Van Doren, Martin Stevens, Harold C. Goddard, and Bert Cardullo.]*

The Nurse . . . is a triumphant and complete achievement. She stands four-square, and lives and breathes in her own right from the moment she appears, from that very first

> Now, by my maiden-head at twelve year
>   old,
> I bade her come.
>
>> [I. iii. 2-3]

Shakespeare has had her pent up in his imagination; and out she gushes. He will give us nothing completer till he gives us Falstaff [in *1* and *2* Henry

IV and *The Merry Wives of Windsor*]. We mark his confident, delighted knowledge of her by the prompt digression into which he lets her launch; the story may wait. It is not a set piece of fireworks such as Mercutio will touch off in honour of Queen Mab. The matter of it flows spontaneously into verse, the phrases are hers and hers alone, character unfolds with each phrase. You may, indeed, take any sentence the Nurse speaks throughout the play, and only she could speak it. Moreover, it will have no trace of the convention to which Shakespeare himself is still tied (into which he forces, to some extent, every other character)—none, unless we find her burlesquing it; and then we might fancy that he himself, in half-conscious mischief, is thus forecasting his freedom. But the good Angelica—which we at last discover to be her perfect name—needs no critical expanding, she expounds herself on all occasions; nor explanation, for she is plain as daylight; nor analysis, lest it lead to excuse, and she stays blissfully unregenerate. No one can fail to act her well that can speak her lines. Yet they are so supercharged with life that they will accommodate the larger acting—which is the revelation of a personality in terms of a part—and to the full; and it may be as rich a personality as can be found. She is in everything inevitable; from her

> My fan, Peter,
>
>> [II. iv. 106]

when she means to play the discreet lady with those gay young sparks, to that all unexpected

> Faith, here 'tis; Romeo
> Is banished; and all the world to nothing
> That he dares ne'er come back to challenge you;
> Or if he do, it needs must be by stealth.
> Then, since the case so stands as now it doth,
> I think it best you married with the county.
>
>> [III. v. 212-17]

—horrifyingly unexpected to Juliet; but to us, the moment she has said it, the inevitable thing for her to say.

This last turn, that seems so casually made, is the stroke that completes the character. Till now we have taken her—the 'good, sweet Nurse' [II. v. 21]—just as casually, amused by each comicality as it came; for so we do take the folk that amuse us. But with this everything about her falls into perspective, her funniments, her endearments, her grossness, her good-nature; upon the instant, they all find their places in the finished picture. And for a last enrichment, candidly welling from the lewd soul of her, comes

> O, he's a lovely gentleman;
> Romeo's a dishclout to him; an eagle, Madam,
> Hath not so green, so quick, so fair an eye

As Paris hath. Beshrew my very heart,
I think you are happy in this second
    match,
For it excels your first; or if it did not,
Your first is dead, or 'twere as good he
    were
As living hence and you no use of him.
                                    [III. v. 218-25]

Weigh the effect made upon Juliet, fresh from the
sacrament of love and the bitterness of parting, by
the last fifteen words of that.

> *Juliet.* Speak'st thou from thy heart?
> *Nurse.*   And from my soul too,
>   Or else beshrew them both.
> *Juliet.*   Amen.
>
>   [III. v. 226-28]

It is gathered into the full-fraught Amen. But best
of all, perhaps, is the old bawd's utter unconsciousness of having said anything out of the way.
And when she finds her lamb. Her ladybird, returning from shrift with merry look—too merry!—how
should she suppose she has not given her the
wholesomest advice in the world?

We see her obliviously bustling through the
night's preparations for this new wedding. We
hear her—incredibly!—start to stir Juliet from her
sleep with the same coarse wit that had served to
deepen the girl's blushes for Romeo's coming near.
We leave her blubbering grotesquely over the body
she had been happy to deliver to a baser martyrdom. Shakespeare lets her pass from the play without comment. Is any needed? (pp. 42-4)

> *Harley Granville-Barker, "Romeo and
> Juliet," in his* Prefaces to Shakespeare,
> *second series,* Sidgwick & Jackson,
> Ltd., 1930, pp. 1-66.

Martin Stevens

[*Stevens examines the* **Nurse's** *role as a messenger who acts as a go-between for the young
lovers in* Romeo and Juliet. *Initially focusing
on the humorous aspects of the* **Nurse's** *errands, the critic maintains that her encounter
with* **Mercutio** *in Act II, scene iv provides one
of the comic highlights of the play. The two
characters reflect vastly different comedic
properties—the* **Nurse** *embodies romantic comedy whereas* **Mercutio** *represents satire—and
the meeting sparks a hilarious conflict between
their opposing temperaments. Stevens also
compares the* **Nurse** *to her counterpart in
Shakespeare's source, Arthur Brooke's* Tragicall Historye of Romeus and Juliet, *noting that
the playwright generally expands her function
as messenger by making her the bearer of all
tidings before the lovers' tragic separation. The
critic further traces the* **Nurse's** *role as messenger by closely examining three key passages—
II. v, III. iv, and IV. v. According to Stevens, this
triad of "messenger scenes" reflects the prog-*
ress of love in the play, and the **Nurse** *plays a
central role in this development, for she acts as
love's herald first to arrange the marriage, second to promote its consummation, and third to
lament its expiration. Contrary to many scholars' perceptions, the critic concludes, it is the*
Nurse's *exit in Act IV, not* **Mercutio's** *death in
Act III, which marks the end of romantic comedy and the beginning of tragedy in* Romeo and
Juliet. *For further commentary on the* **Nurse's**
*character, see the excerpts by Mark Van Doren,
Harold C. Goddard, Harley Granville-Barker,
and Bert Cardullo.*]

It is well known that the Nurse in *Romeo and Juliet* has her ancestry in Roman comedy. . . . It is
not to the point to trace this ancestry in its particulars here, but it is important to recognize its presence. Significantly, the Nurse in *Romeo and Juliet*
is a liaison character much like her Roman ances-
tor, and her humor arises from her role as an inarticulate messenger who acts as go-between for the
young lovers.

A close examination of the play will reveal that the
Nurse is on stage or audibly off stage in twelve
scenes. In no less than nine of these [I. v; II. iii, iv,
v; III. ii, iii, v; IV. ii, v] her primary function is to convey information or warning, while in two others
[IV. iii, iv] she lends her presence, uncharacteristi-
cally silent, to the domestic settings inside the Capulet household. The one remaining scene [I. iii] is
primarily concerned with introducing her as Juliet's devoted guardian who is spontaneously given
to effusive and ribald outpourings. Its opening line,
however, spotlights her customary function as
messenger with Lady Capulet's command: "Nurse,
where's my daughter? Call her forth to me." The
Nurse replies with an immodest oath and the verbal blunder we come to expect of her (in this case
on *ladybird* which can mean "a pretty creature"
and "a tart"):

> Now by my maidenhead at twelve year old,
> I bade her come. What lamb! What lady-
>   bird!—
> God forbid!—Where's this girl? What Ju-
>   liet!
>
>   [I. iii. 2-4]

Thereupon Juliet appears and the stage is set. The
Nurse, hereafter, serves as the aged herald to the
impetuous young lovers. Hers is the Dyonesian errand; she is there to assure that Juliet will "grow
by men" [I. iii. 95]. The humor of her role arises in
large part from the contrast between the reality of
her earthbound lameness—she is "unwieldy, slow,
heavy and pale as lead" [II. v. 17]—and the lovers'
fancy of Cupid's wind-swift dispatch. It arises further from the contrast between expectation and
performance: between the demand for the messenger's precise and lucid tidings and the delivery of
an aged gossip's prolix ramblings.

Several scenes in which the Nurse appears as messenger are simply designed to carry forward the progress of the action. In Act I, Scene v, she serves to identify each of the lovers to the other. Later, in the two balcony scenes [II. ii. and III. v.], she is present to protect Juliet from discovery, adding on both occasions a note of urgency to the parting of the lovers. (I shall speak later of Juliet's repudiation of the Nurse at the conclusion of the second scene.) In two other instances, the Nurse serves primarily to bear tidings and hence to advance the action: once when she brings news of Juliet to Romeo at Friar Lawrence's cell [III. iii] and another time when she heralds to Capulet the arrival of Juliet from shrift [IV. ii]. Though most of these scenes give edge to the characterization of the Nurse as love's herald, especially as they reveal her complicity in the consummation, they do not especially focus attention on her comic qualities. These qualities are emphasized in the remaining scenes in which she takes part: the first meeting with Romeo which is also the only meeting with Mercutio [II. iv], the two scenes in the Capulet orchard in which she brings news to Juliet [II. v and III. ii], and her last appearance, the lamentation [IV. v].

The meeting of Mercutio and the Nurse provides one of the comic highlights of the play. As Thomas Marc Parrott has observed [in his *Shakespearean Comedy*], Mercutio is the play's embodiment of "conscious wit" while the Nurse, in striking contrast, is its "unconscious humorist." The scene which brings them together thus sparks the inevitable conflict between the two antithetic comic temperaments, the satiric and the romantic, of which Mercutio and the Nurse, respectively, are the figureheads in the play. Mercutio, from the beginning, is the critic of stale custom: his wit stabs into many conventional respectabilities, from the absurd stance of the bookish melancholic lover to the pretentious pose of the Italianate fencer. He epitomizes the comic spirit which governs Romeo's first and false love, just as clearly as the Nurse personifies the wordly comic spirit which presides over Romeo's second and true love. Like all satire, Mercutio's wit is analytic; and as such it serves to break up, in the words of Northrop Frye, "the lumber of stereotypes, fossilized beliefs . . . oppressive fashions, and all other things that impede the free movement of society" [in "The Nature of Satire," *University of Toronto Quarterly*, XIV (1944)]. In contrast, the Nurse's humor is synthetic; in her province lies the happy union of the lovers with all its traditional life-cycle overtones. It is right, therefore, that Mercutio must perish when Rosaline and Tybalt, the two figureheads of "oppressive fashion," have surrendered their tyranny. So too is it right that the Nurse must be absent when the lovers are brought to their tragic separation. With Mercutio's death, satire comes to an end; with the Nurse's exit, all comedy quits the stage.

The meeting of Mercutio and the Nurse is, consequently, a culminating moment in the play. As

must be the case, high comedy is nourished by the low: Mercutio's wit flashes, but the laughter that it provokes derives more from its object than its source. It is the Nurse's outrage—"What a man are you" [II. iv. 114]—which turns Mercutio's obscenities—"the bawdy hand of the dial is now upon the prick of noon" [II. iv. 12-13]—into sheer hilarity. The Nurse is thus unintentionally "the cause that wit is" in others; in fact, as a loquacious messenger she is consistently the butt of other people's jokes. But where most others will gently amuse themselves at the expense of the Nurse's outer nature—her garrulity, for example—Mercutio cuts deep. He alone is able to goad her into pretentiousness. With his string of obscenities, he bullies her into self-deception; she cannot stand by listening to his "man-talk" without considering her respectability assailed. And so Shakespeare has her resort to that most hilarious verbal device of affectation, the malapropism [a frequently humorous misapplication of a word]. It is testimony to Shakespeare's dramatic skill that he allows the Nurse to utter malapropisms only during the scene in which Mercutio maligns her character.

After Mercutio exits, the Nurse, now provoked to act the *grande dame* [great lady], reprimands her man Peter for failing to come to her defense. Peter lickerishly assures her that his "weapon should quickly have been out" [II. iv. 158] had he seen his mistress used at another's man's pleasure! She is, however, still so angry at Mercutio that she remains ironically oblivious to the similar taunts of her servingman. Mercutio's spirit thus continues to dominate the stage even as the Nurse, quivering with vexation, comes to state her business with Romeo. Here Shakespeare follows Arthur Brooke's account rather closely, though in Shakespeare's version the Nurse is more apprehensive for the honorable treatment of her "gentlewoman" and more concerned for the need of secrecy. In both versions, she takes a liberal tip from Romeo, but in Brooke's she appears more mercenary in accepting it, partly because she is less concerned over her mistress' welfare and partly because she deliberately neglects, in her report to Juliet, to mention "the taking of the golde." The emphasis Shakespeare places on the Nurse's selfless good will thus helps to sustain her role as a catalyst in the consummation of the romance.

At this point, it may be well to compare and contrast other details of characterization and narration in the two versions of the story. Source studies have made clear that Shakespeare is directly indebted to Brooke's poem, which, in fact, is his only known source. One study specifically concerned with Shakespeare's use of Brooke's poem concludes that in almost every scene involving the Nurse, "Shakespeare is merely following the details of Brooke's story" [Robert Adger Law, "On Shakespeare's Changes of his Source Material in Romeo and Juliet," *University of Texas Studies in*

English, No. 9 (1929)]. While, on the surface, most details do indeed derive from Brooke's poem, the total effect that Shakespeare creates with the Nurse's part is in fact quite different from that created by Brooke. Shakespeare sharpens the impact of the messenger function by making the Nurse the bearer of all tidings prior to the lovers' tragic separation. In Brooke's version, not the Nurse but an unnamed person discloses Juliet's identity to Romeo. Later, again, it is not the Nurse but general rumor that informs Juliet of Tybalt's death. The Nurse, moreover, is absent from the first balcony scene. In Shakespeare's play, then, the Nurse's role as messenger and herald is noticeably expanded.

Another change is the reduction of servants and confidants who attend the two lovers. Brooke sends not only the Nurse but also another maid "almost of equal trust" to accompany Juliet on her way to the Friar. He also makes a larger part of Romeus' servant Peter, who becomes Balthasar in the play and who bears no relation to the Nurse's servant. Moreover, Shakespeare quite clearly restricts the intermediaries in the love plot to two:

the Nurse and the Friar. These two characters, however, serve two entirely contrary philosophies. The Nurse is a worldly figure; her interests are immediate and material. Her commitment is to *eros,* and, therefore, toward the physical union of the lovers. She is in the age-old sense queen of misrule and priestess of fertility. The Friar, in contrast, is spiritual father, the bestower of holy matrimony. The love he serves is *agape;* it is "pure" [II. iii. 92], intransitory, pious. It exists outside the limits of Verona's fleeting time and enveloping space. The Nurse and the Friar, therefore, are each necessary confidants of both lovers, and it is thus that Shakespeare depicts them. In contrast, Brooke emphasizes in his portrayals of the Nurse and the Friar their separate, more intimate allegiance to Juliet and to Romeus, respectively. Thus, after Tybalt's death and Romeus' banishment, Brooke's Nurse entreats Juliet and not Romeus—as in Shakespeare's version [III. iii. 88]—to stand up against the force of adversity. The Friar in like manner exhorts Romeus to forbearance, and hence leaves the impression that each of the lovers has his own minister of consolation. In fact, Brooke makes clear this division of roles:

Friar Lawrence, Romeo, Juliet, and Paris. Act V, scene iii. By James Northcote. The Department of Rare Books and Special Collections, The University of Michigan Library.

The old mans woords have fild with joy
  our Romeus brest,
And eke the olde wives talke, hath set our
  Juliets hart at rest.

Later in the poem, moreover, Brooke's Friar makes special reference to his very close bond with Romeus, a bond that implicitly finds its parallel in the affectionate and life-long relationship of the Nurse and Juliet. Before giving Juliet the potion, Brooke's Friar explains:

Even from the holy font thy husband have
  I knowne,
And, since he grew in yeres, have kept his
  counsels as myne owne . . .
And sith thou art his wife, thee am I bound
  to love,
For Romeus frinships sake, and seeke thy
  anguish to remove,

Shakespeare's Friar, in contrast, does not refer to any special bond, nor does he act in Juliet's behalf simply for the sake of friendship with Romeo.

It is well to bear in mind then that Shakespeare changes his source to highlight the intermediary function of the Friar and, even more pointedly, that of the Nurse. Both characters are made to appear less subjective in their relations to the lovers, and both, in consequence, become more effective manipulators of the plot. Though it is risky to make guesses about Shakespeare's reasons for effecting these changes, it does seem clear that the limitations of the stage and the need to hold down the number of supernumerary parts must have been partially responsible for his concentration on the Nurse as the messenger figure in the love plot. (pp. 195-200)

Up to the end of the third act, *Romeo and Juliet* might well be considered a romantic comedy in the medieval sense of the word: namely as a rising action culminating in the good fortune of the principal characters. It is, significantly, at the end of the third act that Juliet repudiates the Nurse with the malediction "Ancient Damnation" and the vow "Thou and my bosom henceforth shall be twain" [III. v. 234-40]. Up to that point, the main action of the play has to do with the bringing together of the lovers, an achievement which owes its success in large part to the labors of the Nurse. As long as she is on stage in her role of intermediary, there is the prospect of "basic harmony," the assertion of which Nevill Coghill finds central to Shakespeare's comic version ["The Basis of Shakespearean Comedy," *Essays and Studies,* New Series, III (1950)]. The rejection of the Nurse thus occurs at the moment when the romantic comedy has come to its fruition and the repudiation serves as prelude to the ensuing tragedy. The Nurse's ultimate disappearance adumbrates the tragic separation and demise of the lovers. (pp. 200-01)

There remains yet a consideration of the Nurse's role in three focal scenes—II. v, III. iv, and IV. v—

which highlight her part as inarticulate messenger. In their related structures, one traces a descent from the high ribald humor of the successful matchmaker to the tragicomic pathos of a rejected confidante. The first of these scenes arises from the frenzy of unspeakable anticipation and the last, from the sobriety of ineffable recollection. It is customary to regard two of these scenes as parallel actions. Much like the two riot scenes [I. i and III. i], those in which the Nurse brings tidings to Juliet [II. v and III. iv] have been called "twin-born scenarios." There is justification, however, to regard the latter set, if not the former, as part of a triad which serves to accentuate the progress of the dramatic action.

In each of the three scenes, apprehension or consternation results from the delivery of a message by the Nurse. In the first of them, it is only the manner of the delivery, not the news itself, which creates disturbance. At the beginning of II. v, Juliet feverishly awaits word from her lover. The Nurse enters, winded and aching from her errand, and there follows an amusing exchange in which the Nurse's prolixity is matched only by Juliet's eagerness to hear the news. This verbal tug of war is prompted by Brooke, but Shakespeare, as he does in many other passages, intensifies it. Notably, Brooke's Nurse, unlike Shakespeare's, is neither out of breath nor weary from her "jaunce"; she simply toys with Juliet for a fleeting moment. In Shakespeare, the situation arises wholly from the Nurse's human limitations in the part of Cupid. Coming as it does, at the height of youthful expectation, the delay of the news simply provokes mirthful anxiety in Juliet. Shakespeare takes the opportunity to let love's aged herald stammer the wedding banns.

The second scene of the triad [III. ii] has much in common with the first. In it, Juliet again opens with a soliloquy revealing her feverish excitement; again the Nurse returns from a "jaunce" with news for Juliet; and again consternation results from the delivery of her tidings. The main difference, of course, is in the news itself, which, in sharp contrast to that of the first scene, is unhappy and ominous in what it forebodes. To sharpen this contrast, Shakespeare provides close verbal parallels as the Nurse appears on stage. In the earlier scene, Juliet greets her with happy exclamation:

Oh, God, she comes! O honey Nurse, what
  news? . . .
Now, good sweet Nurse—Oh, Lord, why
  look'st thou sad?
Though news be sad, yet tell them merrily;
If good, thou shamest the music of sweet
  news
By playing it to me with so sour a face.
                                      [II. v. 18-24]

The second scene echoes the first in the framework of its greeting, though it is stripped of Juliet's commentary, which, ironically, would have been more appropriate here than in the context in which it was uttered. Juliet anxiously inquires:

> Now, Nurse, what news? . . .
> Ay me! What news? Why dost thou wring
> thy hands?
>
> [III. ii. 34; 36]

This time the news is indeed sad, and the Nurse, true to her nature, makes it even sadder by her inept report. Unable to make a forthright statement, she so misleads Juliet that even after thirty lines are spoken, Juliet can still ask "Is Romeo slaughtered, and is Tybalt dead?" [III. ii. 65]. All the time, Shakespeare treads the dim boundary between joy and pain. The news that Juliet eventually hears is indeed dire—Tybalt is dead and Romeo banished—but it is not so dire, she and the audience come to realize, as it might have been. The heavy rhetoric and the elaborate punning ease, from the first, the burden of the sad news. The courier of romance is thus able to bring bitter news without totally destroying the comic tone. Juliet responds to false death with the same ornate and artificial rhetoric with which Romeo had responded to false love earlier in the play. One can see the similarity vividly in the string of oxymorons that each utters in the two scenes: Romeo's "O brawling love! O loving hate" and Juliet's "Beautiful tyrant! Fiend angelical!" [I. i. 176; III. ii. 75].

The last scene in the triad [IV. v] is sometimes known as the "Lamentation." In it, once more, the Nurse bears adverse tidings, though this time to the elder Capulets and not to Juliet. Once more, too, her report misleads its hearer to express heavy grief. But it misleads in a way different from that of her previous report, as indeed that report had differed, too, from its antecedent. In the first scene there was only momentary anxiety prompted by the messenger's blissful though frenzied pursuit of love's tidings. In the second, there was consternation, grief, and anger caused by the inept report of bad news made worse in its hapless iteration. In the last, there is horror and despair occasioned this time not by the messenger's infelicitous report but by the semblance of grief-laden reality. It is, of course, manifest to the audience that Juliet is not dead, just as it was apparent that Romeo was not dead in the earlier scene. One is reminded of that fact by the similarity of the elaborately rhetorical laments in the two scenes:

> Ah, welladay! He's dead, he's dead, he's
> dead.
> We are undone, lady, we are undone.
> Alack the day! He's gone, he's killed, he's
> dead.
>
> [III. ii. 37-9]

> Alas, alas! Help, help! My lady's dead!
> Oh, welladay that ever I was born! . . .
> She's dead, deceased, she's dead, alack the
> day! . . .
>
> [IV. v. 14-15; 23]

The appropriateness of the Nurse's comic lament has often been questioned. Alfred Harbage, for example, feels that the scene "is the least successful in the play" and that it might better have been relegated to a messenger's report [see Sources for Further Study]. There is no denying that the scene contains a difficult dramatic problem: namely, for the actors to play out a comic lamentation. Yet Juliet's false death is a dramatic fact, and, as such, it gains impact from dramatic treatment. With its acknowledgment through the lamentation, the Nurse can be dismissed as a catalyst in the romance plot. In Brooke's poem, where the Nurse is less directly linked with the progress of the romance, her exit can be less effusive (in fact, she is unable, at first, to speak a word, and finally she can only choke out the plain lament: "Dead is my childe").

The triad of "messenger scenes" reflects the progress of the love plot. In each scene, the Nurse plays a central role. She is there as love's herald first to arrange the marriage, then to promote its consummation, and finally to lament its expiration. The humor of her part arises largely from her personal involvement in the affairs which she ought to conduct with detachment, and the result is that she cannot deliver a straightforward, neutral report. In the first instance, her message misleads only momentarily, and she alone is responsible for the sweet anxiety that its delay occasions. In the second, the message misleads more seriously, and she shares with the conspiring events the blame for the resulting misapprehension. In the last, the message misleads egregiously, but only false circumstances—and not the Nurse—are responsible for its effects. The Nurse is thus seen declining as an agent of the dramatic action; gradually she must, along with all others, give way to the ineluctable power of Fortune.

In a recent article, Stephen A. Shapiro observed that "up to Mercutio's death *Romeo and Juliet* is a romantic comedy. After it, it becomes a tragedy" ["*Romeo and Juliet:* Reversals, Contrarieties, Transformations, and Ambivalence," *College English,* XXV (April 1964)]. I believe otherwise. In Mercutio's death, I see the culmination of comedy of manners; it is not until the Nurse makes her exit in Act IV that romantic comedy comes to an end. Her exit thus properly comes at the end of the plot unit which Renaissance commentaries called the epitasis, after which the stage is cleared for the enactment of the catastrophe. It is in this last unit, the catastrophe, that the lovers are left to their own devices and that their worldly fortunes are hopelessly reversed. Tragedy comes with the absence of intermediaries and the failure of messengers, e.g., the unsuccessful mission of Friar John. Harry Levin has said that "tragedy tends to isolate where comedy brings together, to reveal the uniqueness of individuals rather than what they have in common with others" ["Form and Formality in *Romeo* and Juliet," Shakespeare Quarterly, XI (1960)]. It is this uniqueness of individuals, their social isolation, which gives substance to the tragedy of Act V in Romeo and Juliet. With the Nurse silent, and the Friar rendered ineffective, Juliet's earlier words ring as prophecy for the chilling tragic end: "My dismal scene I needs must act alone" [IV. iii. 19]. (pp. 202-06)

Martin Stevens, "Juliet's Nurse: Love's Herald," in Papers on Language & Literature, Vol. 2, No. 3, Summer, 1966, pp. 195-206.

MERCUTIO

Harold C. Goddard

[*Goddard declares that **Mercutio**, like the **Nurse**, is an extreme sensualist and heathen. The critic concentrates primarily on **Mercutio's** crude sexual humor, noting that the character's obscene language underscores the purity of **Romeo's** passion for **Juliet**. Goddard then addresses the issue of **Mercutio's** Queen Mab speech (I. iv. 53-103), which several critics have considered out of character because of the beauty of its language. The critic asserts that the speech is in fact representative of **Mercutio's** style because compared with the imagination and delicacy of the lovers' verse, it appears superficial. According to Goddard, the Queen Mab speech is a device used by Shakespeare to show what constitutes true poetry. For further commentary on **Mercutio's** character, see the excerpts by Mark Van Doren, Martin Stevens, and Harley Granville-Barker.*]

Mercutio and the Nurse are simply youth and old age of the same type. He is aimed at the same goal she has nearly attained. He would have become the same sort of old man that she is old woman, just as she was undoubtedly the same sort of young girl that he is young man. They both think of nothing but sex—except when they are so busy eating or quarreling that they can think of nothing. (I haven't forgotten Queen Mab; I'll come to her presently.) Mercutio cannot so much as look at the clock without a bawdy thought. So permeated is his language with indecency that most of it passes unnoticed not only by the innocent reader but by all not schooled in Elizabethan smut. Even on our own unsqueamish stage an unabridged form of his role in its twentieth-century equivalent would not be tolerated. Why does Shakespeare place the extreme example of this man's soiled fantasies precisely before the balcony scene? Why but to stress the complete freedom from sensuality of Romeo's passion? Place Mercutio's dirtiest words, as Shakespeare does, right beside Romeo's apostrophe to his "bright angel" [II. ii. 26] and all the rest of that scene where the lyricism of young love reaches one

of its loftiest pinnacles in all poetry—and what remains to be said for Mercutio? Nothing—except that he is Mercutio. His youth, the hot weather, the southern temperament, the fashion among Italian gentlemen of the day, are unavailing pleas; not only Romeo, but Benvolio, had those things to contend with also. And they escaped. Mercury is close to the sun. But it was the material sun, Sol, not the god, Helios, that Mercutio was close to. Beyond dispute, this man had vitality, wit, and personal magnetism. But personal magnetism combined with sexuality and pugnacity is one of the most dangerous mixtures that can exist. The unqualified laudation that Mercutio has frequently received, and the suggestion that Shakespeare had to kill him off lest he quite set the play's titular hero in the shade, are the best proof of the truth of that statement. Those who are themselves seduced by Mercutio are not likely to be good judges of him. It may be retorted that Mercutio is nearly always a success on the stage, while Romeo is likely to be insipid. The answer to that is that while Mercutios are relatively common, Romeos are excessively rare. If Romeo proves insipid, he has been wrongly cast or badly acted.

"But how about Queen Mab?" it will be asked. The famous description of her has been widely held to be quite out of character and has been set down as an outburst of poetry from the author put arbitrarily in Mercutio's mouth. But the judgment "out of character" should always be a last resort. Undoubtedly the lines, if properly his, do reveal an unsuspected side of Mercutio. The prankish delicacy of some of them stands out in pleasing contrast with his grosser aspects. The psychology of this is sound. The finer side of a sensualist is suppressed and is bound to come out, if at all, incidentally, in just such a digression as this seems to be. Shakespeare can be trusted not to leave such things out. Few passages in his plays, however, have been more praised for the wrong reasons. The account of Queen Mab is supposed to prove Mercutio's imagination: under his pugnacity there was a poet. It would be nearer the truth, I think, to guess that Shakespeare put it in as an example of what poetry is popularly held to be and is not. The lines on Queen Mab are indeed delightful. But imagination in any proper sense they are not. They are sheer fancy. Moreover, Mercutio's anatomy and philosophy of dreams prove that he knows nothing of their genuine import. He dubs them

the children of an idle brain,
Begot of nothing but vain fantasy.
[I. iv. 97-8]

Perhaps his are—the Queen Mab lines would seem to indicate as much. Romeo, on the other hand, holds that dreamers "dream things true" [I. iv. 52], and gives a definition of them that for combined brevity and beauty would be hard to better. They are "love's shadows" [V. i. 11]. And not only from what we can infer about his untold dream on this occasion, but from all the dreams and premonitions of both Romeo and Juliet throughout the play, they come from a fountain of wisdom somewhere beyond time. Primitives distinguish between "big" and "little" dreams. (Aeschylus makes the same distinction in *Prometheus Bound.*) Mercutio, with his aldermen and gnats and coachmakers and sweetmeats and parsons and drums and ambuscadoes, may tell us a little about the littlest of little dreams. He thinks that dreamers are still in their day world at night. Both Romeo and Juliet know that there are dreams that come from as far below the surface of that world as was that prophetic tomb at the bottom of which she saw him "as one dead" [III. v. 56] at their last parting. Finally, how characteristic of Mercutio that he should make Queen Mab a midwife and blemish his description of her by turning her into a "hag" whose function is to bring an end to maidenhood. Is this another link between Mercutio and the Nurse? Is Shakespeare here preparing the way for his intimation that she would be quite capable of assisting in Juliet's corruption? It might well be. When Shakespeare writes a speech that seems to be out of character, it generally, as in this case, deserves the closest scrutiny.

And there is another justification of the Queen Mab passage. Romeo and Juliet not only utter poetry; they are poetry. The loveliest comment on Juliet I ever heard expressed this to perfection. It was made by a girl only a little older than Juliet herself. When Friar Laurence recommends philosophy to Romeo as comfort in banishment, Romeo replies:

> Hang up philosophy!
> Unless philosophy can make a Juliet . . .
> It helps not, it prevails not. Talk no more.
>   [III. iii. 57-60]

"Philosophy can't," the girl observed, "but poetry can—and it did!" Over against the poetry of Juliet, Shakespeare was bound, by the demands of contrast on which all art rests, to offer in the course of his play examples of poetry in various verbal, counterfeit, or adulterate estates.

> This precious book of love, this unbound
>   lover,
> To beautify him, only lacks a cover.
>   [I. iii. 87-8]

That is Lady Capulet on the prospective bridegroom, Paris. It would have taken the play's booby prize for "poetry" if Capulet himself had not outdone it in his address to the weeping Juliet:

> How now! a conduit, girl? What, still in
>   tears?
> Evermore showering? In one little body
> Thou counterfeit'st a bark, a sea, a wind;
> For still thy eyes, which I may call the sea,
> Do ebb and flow with tears; the bark thy
>   body is,
> Sailing in this salt flood; the winds, thy
>   sighs;

> Who, raging with thy tears, and they with
>   them,
> Without a sudden calm, will overset
> Thy tempest-tossed body.
>   [III. v. 129-37]

It is almost as if Shakespeare were saying in so many words: That is how poetry is not written. Yet, a little later, when the sight of his daughter, dead as all suppose, shakes even this egotist into a second of sincerity, he can say:

> Death lies on her like an untimely frost
> Upon the sweetest flower of all the field.
>   [IV. v. 28-9]

There is poetry, deep down, even in Capulet. But the instant passes and he is again talking about death as his son-in-law—and all the rest. The Nurse's vain repetitions in this scene are further proof that she is a heathen. Her O-lamentable-day's only stress the lack of one syllable of genuine grief or love such as Juliet's father shows. These examples all go to show what Shakespeare is up to in the Queen Mab speech. It shines, and even seems profound, beside the utterances of the Capulets and the Nurse. But it fades, and grows superficial, beside Juliet's and Romeo's. It is one more shade of what passes for poetry but is not. (pp. 122-24)

> *Harold C. Goddard, "Romeo and Juliet," in his* The Meaning of Shakespeare, *The University of Chicago Press, 1951, pp. 117-39.*

Harley Granville-Barker

[*Granville-Barker characterizes* **Mercutio** *as a supreme realist and egoist, commenting on his individuality and freedom from affectation. At many points throughout the following excerpt, the critic refers to* **Mercutio** *as an Elizabethan version of a "young John Bull." The term "John Bull" is derived from a character of the same name in John Arbuthnot's satire* Law Is a Bottomless Pit *(1712); over time the phrase came to represent an individual Englishman who best typifies the favorable qualities of England. For further commentary on* **Mercutio's** *character, see the excerpts by Mark Van Doren, Martin Stevens, and Harold C. Goddard.*]

Mercutio, when Shakespeare finally makes up his mind about him, is in temperament very much the young John Bull of his time; and as different from the stocky, stolid John Bull of our later picturing as Capulet from the conventional heavy father. There can be, of course, no epitomising of a race in any one figure. But the dominant qualities of an age are apt to be set in a pattern, which will last in literature, though out-moded, till another replaces it.

We learn little about Mercutio as he goes racketing to Capulet's supper, except that John Bull is often a poetic sort of fellow, or as he returns, unless it be that a man may like smut and fairy tales too. But he is still in the toils of conventional versifying, and a victim besides, probably, to his author's uncertainty about him. The authentic Mercutio only springs into life with

> Where the devil should this Romeo be?
> Came he not home to-night?
>
> [II. iv. 1-2]

when he springs to life indeed. From now on he abounds in his own sense, and we can put him to the test the Nurse abides by; not a thing that he says could anyone else say. He asks as little exposition, he is what he is with perfect clarity; the more so probably because he is wholly Shakespeare's creation, his namesake in Brooke's poem giving no hint of him. And (as with the Nurse) we could transport this authentic Mercutio into the maturest of the plays and he would fall into place there, nor would he be out of place on any stage, in any fiction.

A wholesome self-sufficiency is his cardinal quality; so he suitably finds place among neither Capulets nor Montagues. Shakespeare endows him . . . with a jolly sensuality for a set off to Romeo's romancings; and, by a later, significant touch, adds to the contrast. When their battle of wits is ending—a breathless bandying of words that is like a sharp set at tennis—suddenly, it would seem, he throws an affectionate arm round the younger man's shoulder.

> Why, is not this better now than groaning
> for love? Now art thou sociable, now art
> thou Romeo, now art thou what thou
> art. . . .
>
> [II. iv. 88-90]

Mercutio's creed in a careless sentence! At all costs be the thing you are. The more his—and the more John Bullish—that we find it dropped casually amid a whirl of chaff and never touched on again! Here is the man. No wistful ideals for him; but life as it comes and death when it comes. A man of soundest common-sense surely; the complete realist, the egoist justified. But by the day's end he has gone to his death in a cause not his own, upon pure impulse and something very like principle. There is no inconsistency in this; such vital natures must range between extremes.

> Rightly to be great
> Is not to stir without great argument,
> But greatly to find quarrel in a straw,
> When honour's at the stake.
>
> [*Hamlet*, IV. iv. 53-6]

That is a later voice, troublously questioning. Mercutio pretends neither to greatness nor philosophy. When the moment comes, it is not even his own honour that is at stake; but such calm, dishonourable, vile submission is more than flesh and blood can bear. That the Mercutios of the world quarrel on principle they would hate to be told. Quarrel with a man for cracking nuts having no other reason but because one has hazel eyes; quarrel, with your life in your hand, for quarreling's sake, since quarrelling and fighting are a part of life, and the appetite for them human nature. Mercutio fights Tybalt because he feels he must, because he cannot stand the fellow's airs a moment longer. He'll put him in his place, if no one else will. He fights without malice, not in anger even, and for no advantage. He fights because he is what he is, to testify to this simple unconscious faith, and goes in with good honest cut and thrust. But "*alla stoccata* carries it away" [III. i. 74]; and he, the perfect realist, the egoist complete, dies for an ideal. Extremes have met.

No regrets though; nor any hypocrisy of resignation for him! He has been beaten by the thing he despised, and is as robustly angry about it as if he had years to live in which to get his own back.

> Zounds, a dog, a rat, a mouse, a cat, to
> scratch a man to death! A braggart, a
> rogue, a villain, that fights by the book of
> arithmetic.
>
> [III. i. 100-02]

He is brutally ingenuous with Romeo:

> Why the devil came you between us? I was
> hurt under your arm.
>
> [III. i. 102-03]

He says no more to him after that, quite ignores the pitifully futile

> I thought all for the best.
>
> [III. i. 104]

He dies with his teeth set, impenitently himself to the last. (pp. 48-51)

> *Harley Granville-Barker, "Romeo and Juliet," in his* Prefaces to Shakespeare, *second series, Sidgwick & Jackson, Ltd., 1930, pp. 1-66.*

FRIAR LAWRENCE

Bert Cardullo

[*Cardullo focuses on* **Friar Lawrence's** *actions to demonstrate that the play's catastrophe results from the rash behavior of several characters. The critic argues that had the priest acted with less haste, the lovers' tragic deaths might have been prevented. Cardullo also contends that* **Friar Lawrence's** *rashness is underscored by the* **Nurse's** *hesitation in informing* **Juliet** *of the arrangements of her secret marriage and of* **Tybalt's** *death. Furthermore, the impulsiveness of* **Romeo, Capulet,** *and the* **Friar** *was bred by the feud, which, according to the critic, accounts for the characters' failure* *to recognize their flaw. For further commentary on **Friar Lawrence's** character, see the excerpts by Lorentz Eckhoff, Harold S. Wilson, Franklin M. Dickey, Mark Van Doren, Clifford Leech, and Martin Stevens.]*

"It has been objected," writes Frank Kermode" [in his introduction to *Romeo and Juliet*, in *The Riverside Shakespeare*, ed. G. Blakemore Evans], "that [*Romeo and Juliet*] lacks tragic necessity—that the story becomes tragic only by a trick. . . . [There is a conviction that] Shakespeare offends against his own criteria for tragedy by allowing mere chance to determine the destiny of the hero and heroine." We learn of the "trick" when Friar John, whom Friar Laurence has sent to Mantua with a letter telling Romeo to come and take Juliet away when she awakens from her long sleep, returns and says:

> Going to find a barefoot brother out,
> One of our order, to associate me,
> Here in this city visiting the sick,
> And finding him, the searchers of the
>   town,
> Suspecting that we both were in a house
> Where the infectious pestilence did reign,
> Seal'd up the doors and would not let us
>   forth
> So that my speed to Mantua there was
>   stay'd. . . .
> I could not send it—here it is again—
> Nor get a messenger to bring it thee,
> So fearful were they of infection.
>   [V. ii. 5-12, 14-16]

The trick, supposedly, is the plague that has afflicted Verona and delayed Friar John, because he just happened to choose for a traveling companion a brother who had been attending the ill. R. G. Moulton is one of those who argue that "the . . . tragedy has all been brought about by [chance, by the] accidental detention of Friar John" [*The Moral System of Shakespeare*]. Brian Gibbons [in the Arden edition of *Romeo and Juliet*] argues similarly of Romeo's discovery that a feast is to take place at Capulet's house: "[Here] Shakespeare emphasizes the element of chance in the action. The servant Capulet has chosen [to deliver invitations] happens to be illiterate, a fact which his master has forgotten. . . . The meeting with Romeo is sheer accident and after the servant turns away, by chance Romeo regrets his off-hand answer and takes the list."

Character, not chance, is at work at this point in the play. Capulet, in his typically rash manner, sends an illiterate servant on an errand that requires reading. The servant's meeting with Romeo may be an accident, but Shakespeare undercuts this aspect of it and emphasizes Romeo's own impulsiveness. He teases the servant, claiming to be able to read "if I know the letters and the language" [I. ii. 61]—the servant interprets this to mean that Romeo cannot read, when it really means that he

can read only the language he knows. When the servant starts on his way to find someone who can read, Romeo suddenly decides to help him and calls him back; he reads the list aloud and learns that the people on it are invited to Capulet's house. Capulet repeats this pattern in Act III, Scene iv: Paris starts to leave and he impulsively calls him back, offering him Juliet's hand. Friar Laurence repeats it again in Act IV, Scene i. After telling Juliet that nothing can postpone her marriage to Paris and hearing her declare that she will kill herself rather than break her vow to Romeo, he says, "Hold, daughter" [l. 68], echoing Romeo's "Stay, fellow" [I. ii. 63] to the servant, and on the spur of the moment offers her, in the sleeping potion, a desperate way out of her dilemma.

Romeo's and Capulet's impulsiveness or rashness has been well documented. Capulet's offer of Juliet in marriage to Paris without first consulting his daughter is followed by the equally impulsive, and ultimately disastrous, action of advancing the wedding from Thursday to Wednesday. The most obvious example of impulsive behavior on Romeo's part occurs when, upon hearing from Balthasar that Juliet is dead, he goes immediately to the Apothecary's to buy poison with which to kill himself at her side, instead of first investigating the circumstances of her "death." Unlike Romeo's and Capulet's, Friar Laurence's rashness has not been explored; it is, however, essential to an understanding of the play as tragic as opposed to pathetic.

Just as the illiterate servant, Paris, and Juliet in the above examples are not offered what they desire by chance, neither is Friar John detained by the plague by chance. The first cause of his delay is Friar Laurence's rashness. He sends John to Mantua alone, when he should remember, as Brian Gibbons points out, that "the rule of the [Franciscan] order forbade [Friar John] to travel without the company of another [Franciscan] friar." John is detained because the companion that he finds has had contact with the sick; as a precaution, both he and the other friar are quarantined to prevent the spread of the disease. Even if it is argued that it was Friar John's responsibility to find a traveling companion, not Friar Laurence's to find one for him, the latter should still have foreseen the improbability of his confrere's choosing a "safe" Franciscan companion in a city beset by the plague (the Franciscans would be ministering to the sick, and would therefore be capable of spreading the infection). He should have gone to the trouble of providing a Franciscan companion for Friar John who had not had contact with the disease, or perhaps he should even have gone with him himself. Surely Friar Laurence knew of the plague's existence in Verona. Had Friar John left the city immediately in the company of a "safe" member of his order, he would never have been delayed and would have been able to deliver the letter to Romeo. (pp. 404-07)

In my view, the flaw of impulsiveness or rashness . . . [explains] the tragedy of *Romeo and Juliet*. Friar Laurence's rashness is responsible for Friar John's detention, not chance. And it is equally responsible for Balthasar's reaching Mantua, undeterred, with news of Juliet's "death." It is the Friar's fault that Balthasar is unaware of her feigned death. In Act III, upon sending Romeo to spend the night with Juliet and then to flee to Mantua, Friar Laurence says to him, "I'll find out your man, / And he shall signify from time to time / Every good hap to you that chances here" [III. iii. 169-71]. We know that, before departing for Mantua, Romeo tells Balthasar of his role as happy go-between, since the latter says to him in Act V, "O pardon me for bringing these ill news, / Since you did leave it for my office, sir" [V. i. 22-3]. It is another mark of Romeo's impulsiveness that he does not question this "*ill* news" from a source whose office it was to "signify from time to time / Every *good* hap to [him] that chances [in Verona]." Romeo asks if Balthasar has been sent by the Friar, but he gets no reply and neglects to ask again. He never inquires what his servant or Friar Laurence knows about the circumstances surrounding the death of one so young as Juliet.

The Friar, of course, never does find Balthasar and apprise him of the plan to get Juliet out of the marriage to Paris so that she can be reunited with Romeo. Had he sent *Balthasar* instead of Friar John to Mantua with the letter, the deaths of Romeo and Juliet would have been prevented. Presumably, Romeo would have returned to Verona at the appointed time to take Juliet away. Just as, in his haste to aid Romeo and Juliet, Friar Laurence forgets about the infectious disease that afflicts Verona and that will ultimately detain Friar John, he forgets to send Balthasar in John's place (as he had told Romeo he would) and even to inform him of the plan to reunite the lovers. Friar Laurence and Balthasar are acting independently to serve Romeo, whereas they should be acting together. Similarly, Friar John is acting "independently" when he leaves Friar Laurence's cell without a Franciscan companion. The image of John and a fellow friar, finally acting together but quarantined for it, and helpless to prevent the tragedy, is the opposite of that of Friar Laurence and Balthasar at the end of the play, finally discovering each other's separate actions but "freed" or pardoned for them by the Prince, and able to join in the two families' reconciliation.

The most obvious example of Friar Laurence's rashness or impulsiveness occurs in Act II, when he decides to honor Romeo's request to marry Juliet. The Friar's intentions are good; he hopes, by joining the lovers in marriage, "to turn [their] households' rancour to pure love" [II. iii. 92]. But

he acts without considering fully the possible consequences of such a secret marriage between members of feuding families. Ironically, he violates his own dictum: "Wisely and slow; they stumble that run fast" [II. iii. 94]. In order to make Friar Laurence's rashness stand out, Shakespeare contrasts it with the hesitation or delay of the Nurse—the only other character (except perhaps Balthasar) with knowledge of Romeo and Juliet's secret union, and one who exhibits her own bit of impulsiveness in switching her preference of husbands for Juliet from Romeo to Paris once the former has been banished from Verona. Like the other characters' impulsiveness, the Nurse's turns out to have tragic consequences: her sudden disparagement of Romeo is the immediate cause of Juliet's decision to ask the Friar how she can remain faithful to him, how she can avoid marriage to Paris.

In Act II, Scene v, the Nurse returns home to give her mistress Romeo's message: Juliet is to ". . . devise / Some means to come to shrift this afternoon, / And there . . . at Friar Laurence's cell / Be shriv'd and married" [II. iv. 179-82]. But, contrary to our expectations, the Nurse does not give her the happy news right away. The scene consists of 78 lines; the Nurse enters on line 17 and does not give her message until lines [68-9]. She claims that she is tired and aching and needs to catch her breath; she is also, of course, teasing the impatient Juliet. But the Nurse's behavior here has an underlying meaning: Shakespeare delays the giving of the message as long as possible, in contrast with his hastening the Friar's agreement to marry Romeo and Juliet two scenes before, in order to suggest that the message is something Juliet should *not* want to hear and abide by. Marriage to Romeo will mean her doom, yet she rushes to it. Throughout Act II, Scene v, she is "hot" to hear what her lover has to say (the Nurse says to her on line 62, "Are you so hot?"; similarly, Lady Capulet tells her husband in Act III, when he is insisting that Juliet marry Paris, "You are too hot" [III. v. 175]).

In Act III, Scene ii, the Nurse hesitates in announcing the sad news of Tybalt's death to Juliet. Although this scene is almost twice as long as Scene v of Act II (143 lines to 78), and the Nurse consequently enters on line 31 instead of 17, she waits only until lines 69-70 to give her message. . . . The Nurse's delay is long enough, however, to provoke this response from Juliet: "What devil art thou that dost torment me thus?" [III. ii. 43]. The Nurse is naturally in shock over the death of Tybalt; she barely acknowledges Juliet upon entering. But, as in Act II, Scene v, her behavior here has an underlying meaning. Shakespeare has her hesitate in giving the news of Tybalt's death, in contrast with his having Friar Laurence rush to get the news of Juliet's seeming death to Romeo four scenes later [IV. i], in order to connect Juliet's own impulsiveness with Romeo's and to prefigure both their deaths at the end of the play. The Nurse's delay brings out a quality in Juliet that the Friar's haste helps to bring out in Romeo. When the Nurse does not immediately reveal who has been slain, Juliet assumes that Romeo is dead and vows to join him: "Vile earth to earth resign, end motion here, / And thou and Romeo press one heavy bier" [III. ii. 59-60].

She does not commit suicide until the last scene of the play, of course; here she is foreshadowing that suicide and Romeo's own. Wrongly believing her dead because Balthasar reached him and Friar John did not, Romeo poisons himself beside her bier; awaking to find him dead, Juliet stabs herself. The Nurse's delay, unlike Friar Laurence's haste, is not itself lethal. She corrects Juliet's erroneous assumption and tells her that "Tybalt is gone and Romeo banished. / Romeo that kill'd him, he is banished" [III. ii. 69-70]. Juliet will live to love Romeo before being parted from him once and for all in Act III, Scene v. Once he receives Balthasar's fateful report, Romeo will not live to love her again.

Character, then—Friar Laurence's, Capulet's, Romeo's—determines the destiny of Romeo and Juliet, not chance. It has often been said that the play is in part about the hastiness of youth. I would say that it is in part about the hastiness of everyone, of the old as well as the young. One of the oddities of this tragedy is that the flaw of impulsiveness or rashness is shared by at least three characters. (Juliet's and the Nurse's impulsive moments are not as numerous and significant as the three men's. Clearly Tybalt and Mercutio are impulsive, though not as central to the action as the trio; the impulsiveness of Capulet extends all the way to his servants, who start the fight with Montague's men in the first scene.)

Another oddity is that neither Capulet, Romeo, nor Friar Laurence ever has any recognition of his flaw. This suggests, less that they are not fully tragic or sufficiently introspective, than that their impulsiveness was bred by the unnatural state in which they lived—by the long-standing feud between the two families, which affected even non-family members like Friar Laurence. This may help to explain Shakespeare's curious mention only one time of the "infectious pestilence" afflicting Verona. The infectious pestilence may be seen as a metaphor for the spiritual one—the feud and its resultant impulsiveness—bedeviling two prominent families in the city and their circles. Friar John is confined so as to prevent the spread of infection and kill the plague. His confinement leads to the deaths of Romeo and Juliet and as a result, paradoxically, to the killing of the spiritual plague afflicting their families.

Once the feud is about to end as a consequence of the deaths of the lovers, impulsiveness in characters like Capulet and Friar Laurence disappears; tranquility rules in its place. Impulsiveness nearly possesses a life of its own in *Romeo and Juliet;* to the extent that no one mentions the original cause of the feud, the flaw that it bred appears almost as one disconnected from character. It comes to Verona, one does not know exactly whence, and it goes. Romeo gives the following speech before going to the feast at Capulet's house:

> I fear too early, for my mind misgives
> Some consequence yet hanging in the
> 　　stars
> Shall bitterly begin his fearful date
> With this night's revels, and expire the
> 　　term
> Of a despised life clos'd in my breast
> By some vile forfeit of untimely death.
> But he that hath the steerage of my course
> Direct my suit. . . .
>
> 　　　　　　　　　　　　　　[I. iv. 106-13]

Perhaps the "despised life" enclosed in Romeo's breast is the very impulsiveness that I have been speaking of. And perhaps the "consequence yet hanging in the stars" is its destruction at its own hands. Impulsiveness has spread among the members of both families, and to their friends, to the point that it must conflict with itself: Romeo and Juliet's marriage, with Capulet's intention to give his daughter to Paris; Friar Laurence's plan to save Juliet from a second union, with Capulet's desire to see her wed even earlier than planned; Juliet's feigned death, with Romeo's suicide.

Impulsiveness is the real villain in this play that has no villains. It finally extinguishes itself, but not before Mercutio, Tybalt, Paris, Romeo, and Juliet are killed by it. Obviously, we do not lament impulsiveness' passing at the end of *Romeo and Juliet.* But we may have been fascinated by its having afflicted almost everyone in the circumscribed world of the drama, instead of isolating itself in a single tragic figure. This may have something to do with the play's origins in comedy. The reconciliation of two feuding houses through marriage is normally a subject of comedy; Shakespeare made it a subject of tragedy. Furthermore, as H. B. Charlton has observed [in his *Shakespearian Tragedy*], unlike the figures of Shakespeare's other tragedies, Romeo and Juliet have "none of the pomp of historic circumstance about them; they [are] socially of the minor aristocracy who . . . stock [the] comedies. . . . To choose such folk as these for tragic heroes was aesthetically wellnigh an anarchist's gesture." To afflict a miniature society with the flaw of impulsiveness, instead of a single tragic hero, was probably aesthetically well-nigh an anarchist's gesture, too. But it had the effect of making the flaw seem endemic to the society and thus of allowing the characters to exhibit it without final awareness, in much the same way that comic characters frequently exhibit foibles without ever being aware of them. Accordingly the thought and the talk at the end of *Romeo and Juliet* are of reconciliation of the Montague and Capulet families, not of full tragic recognition; no one identifies the flaw that led to the catastrophe, or any individual manifestations of it (Friar Laurence admits that he married Romeo and Juliet and gave her the sleeping potion, but he does not connect these actions with impulsiveness or rashness, leaving it to the Prince to decide if he has done anything wrong). Shakespeare has his "comic" ending, arrived at by a tragic route. (pp. 407-13)

> *Bert Cardullo "The Friar's Flaw, the Play's Tragedy: The Experiment of 'Romeo and Juliet',"* in CLA Journal, *Vol. XXVIII, No. 4, June, 1985, pp. 404-14.*

SOURCES FOR FURTHER STUDY

LITERARY COMMENTARY:

Bergeron, David M. "Sickness in *Romeo and Juliet.*" *CLA Journal* XX, No. 1 (March 1977): 356-64.

    A detailed analysis of the imagery of sickness, disease, and remedy in *Romeo and Juliet* and how it contributes to the tragic structure of the play.

Bruce, Brenda. "Nurse in *Romeo and Juliet.*" In *Players of Shakespeare: Essays in Shakespearean Performance by Twelve Players with the Royal Shakespeare Company,* edited by Philip Brockbank, pp. 91-101. Cambridge: Cambridge University Press, 1985.

    Provides a theatrical insight into the Nurse's character, describing how she interpreted the role for a 1981 Royal Shakespeare Company production of *Romeo and Juliet.*

Chapman, Raymond. "Double Time in *Romeo and Juliet.*" *The Modern Language Review* XLIV, No. 3 (July 1949): 372-74.

    Analyzes the methods Shakespeare used to achieve the concept of double time in *Romeo and Juliet,* where action encompasses a longer period of time than is indicated by the repeated references to particular days and hours.

Cole, Douglas, ed. *Twentieth Century Interpretations of "Romeo and Juliet."* Englewood Cliffs, N. J.: Prentice-Hall, 1970, 117 p.

    A collection of scholarly essays on *Romeo and Juliet.*

Craig, Hardin. "The Beginnings." In his *An Interpretation of Shakespeare,* pp. 19-46. New York: Citadel Press, 1948.

    Briefly discusses the play's sources, themes, and language, as well as Shakespeare's characterization of Romeo and Juliet.

Dowden, Edward. *"Romeo and Juliet."* In his *Transcripts and Studies,* pp. 378-430. London: Kegan Paul, Trench, Trubner & Co., 1910.

    Summarizes the plots of various retellings of the

Romeo and Juliet story, then offers a detailed reconstruction of Shakespeare's play, focusing especially on the characters.

Earl, A. J. "*Romeo and Juliet* and the Elizabethan Sonnets." *English* XXVII, Nos. 128 and 129 (Summer-Autumn 1978): 99-119.

    Identifies the dominant qualities of Petrarchan poetry and reviews how the tradition of Petrarch was established in England, and eventually in Shakespeare. Earl then considers certain passages in *Romeo and Juliet* in light of the principal elements of Petrarchan love poetry.

Erskine, John. *"Romeo and Juliet."* In his *The Delight of Great Books,* pp. 99-125. Cleveland: World Publishing Co., 1941.

    Provides an overview of the major themes of *Romeo and Juliet,* focusing on the contrasts between love and hate, youth and age, gentleness and vulgarity, and haste and patience.

Everett, Barbara. "*Romeo and Juliet:* The Nurse's Story." *Critical Quarterly* 14, No. 2 (Summer 1972): 129-39.

    Explores the Nurse's narrative function in *Romeo and Juliet,* focusing on her speech at I. iii. 13-62. Everett asserts that although the Nurse's perspective is crude and not completely trustworthy, her common observations offer the reader a fuller understanding of the lovers.

Gray, J. C. "Renaissance Notions of Love, Time, and Death." *Dalhousie Review* 48, No. 1 (Spring 1968): 58-69.

    Shows how *Romeo and Juliet* exemplifies the ambivalent attitudes toward love, time, and death commonly expressed in Renaissance literature.

Harbage, Alfred. "Mastery Achieved: *Romeo and Juliet.*" In his *William Shakespeare: A Reader's Guide,* pp. 139-61. New York: Farrar, Straus and Giroux, 1966.

    A scene-by-scene plot summary of *Romeo and Juliet* accompanied by critical commentary on various aspects of the play.

Hartley, Lodwick. " 'Mercy but Murders': A Subtheme in *Romeo and Juliet.*" *Papers on English Language & Literature* 1, No. 3 (Summer 1965): 259-64.

    Views Paris's death as thematically crucial to the play because it underscores Escalus's ongoing struggle with the ideas of mercy and justice. In addition, it is structurally important because the deaths of Tybalt and Mercutio foreshadow it.

Smith, Robert Metcalf. "Three Interpretations of *Romeo and Juliet.*" *Shakespeare Association Bulletin* XXIII, No. 2 (April 1948): 60-77.

    Points out flaws in the three leading interpretations of *Romeo and Juliet,* which alternately view the play as a tragedy of character, a tragedy of social justice, and a tragedy of fortune. Smith argues that Shakespeare presents a synthesis of all three readings.

Smith, Warren D. "Romeo's Final Dream." *The Mod-*

ern Language Review 62, No. 4 (October 1967): 577; 580-83.

Considers the lovers' immortality a major theme of *Romeo and Juliet,* arguing that several scenes in the play support the Christian ideal of resurrection after death. According to Smith, this concept is most evident in Romeo's dream in Act V, scene i.

Spurgeon, Caroline F. E. "Leading Motives in the Tragedies." In her *Shakespeare's Imagery and What It Tells Us,* pp. 309-56. 1935. Reprint. Cambridge: Cambridge University Press, 1971.

An important analysis of light and dark imagery in *Romeo and Juliet.* Spurgeon discusses numerous instances where images of light are used to represent love and beauty while images of darkness reflect the misery caused by the feud.

Stoll, Elmer Edgar. "Lecture I. Romeo and Juliet." In his *Shakespeare's Young Lovers,* pp. 1-44. New York: Oxford University Press, Inc., 1937.

Contends that fate brings about the tragedy of the young lovers in *Romeo and Juliet.* The lovers' impulsiveness, Stoll adds, is consistent with Shakespeare's depiction of their falling in love at first sight and, furthermore, heightens the dramatic interest of their story as well as audience identification with them.

Utterback, Raymond. "The Death of Mercutio." *Shakespeare Quarterly* XXIX, No. 2 (Spring 1973): 105-16.

Stresses the significance of Mercutio's death to the structure of *Romeo and Juliet.* Utterback maintains that the pattern of provocation, action, and tragic consequences established in this scene (III. i. 35-108) displays the organizing principle for the rest of the play.

Vickers, Brian. "From Clown to Character." In his *The Artistry of Shakespeare's Prose,* pp. 52-88. London: Metheun & Co., 1968.

Asserts that the bawdy wit of Mercutio and the Nurse plays an excessive role in *Romeo and Juliet.* Vickers notes, however, that Shakespeare created prose styles admirably suited to the characters and situations in the play.

Wells, Stanley. "Juliet's Nurse: The Uses of Inconsequentiality." In *Shakespeare's Styles: Essays in Honour of Kenneth Muir,* edited by Philip Edwards, Inga-Stina Ewbank, and G. K. Hunter, pp. 51-66. Cambridge: Cambridge University Press, 1980.

Examines the content and structure of the Nurse's speech at I. iii. 11-57, noting that its lack of intellectual logic marks a new dramatic style for Shakespeare.

Williamson, Marilyn L. "Romeo and Death." *Shakespeare Studies* 14 (1981): 129-37.

Contends that Romeo's suicide is not motivated by his love for Juliet but rather by a death wish he harbored before he met her. Williamson admits, however, that the feud does play a part in the catastrophe: because of the feud, Romeo not only expects an early death, he desires one to escape the guilt he suffers regarding the conflict.

MEDIA ADAPTATIONS:

Romeo and Juliet. Paramount, 1968.

A film version of the play, directed by Franco Zeffirelli. The movie, which won Academy Awards for costume design and cinematography, features Olivia Hussey, Leonard Whiting, Michael York, and Milo O'Shea. Distributed by Paramount Home Video. 138 minutes.

Romeo and Juliet. BBC, Time Life Television, 1979.

A televised performance of the tragedy, part of the "Shakespeare Plays" series. Distributed by Time Life Videos. 167 minutes.

Index to Major Themes and Characters